Palgrave Studies in the History of Economic Thought

Series Editors
Avi J. Cohen
Department of Economics
York University & University of Toronto
Toronto, ON, Canada

G. C. Harcourt
School of Economics
University of New South Wales
Sydney, NSW, Australia

Peter Kriesler
School of Economics
University of New South Wales
Sydney, NSW, Australia

Jan Toporowski
Economics Department,
SOAS University of London
London, UK

Palgrave Studies in the History of Economic Thought publishes contributions by leading scholars, illuminating key events, theories and individuals that have had a lasting impact on the development of modern-day economics. The topics covered include the development of economies, institutions and theories.

The series aims to highlight the academic importance of the history of economic thought, linking it with wider discussions within economics and society more generally. It contains a broad range of titles that illustrate the breath of discussions – from influential economists and schools of thought, through to historical and modern social trends and challenges – within the discipline.

All books in the series undergo a single-blind peer review at both the proposal and manuscript submission stages.

For further information on the series and to submit a proposal for consideration, please contact the Wyndham Hacket Pain (Economics Editor) wyndham.hacketpain@palgrave.com.

Ashwani Saith

Cambridge Economics in the Post-Keynesian Era

The Eclipse of Heterodox Traditions

Volume I

Ashwani Saith
International Institute of Social Studies
Erasmus University Rotterdam (EUR)
The Hague, The Netherlands

ISSN 2662-6578 ISSN 2662-6586 (electronic)
Palgrave Studies in the History of Economic Thought
ISBN 978-3-030-93018-9 ISBN 978-3-030-93019-6 (eBook)
https://doi.org/10.1007/978-3-030-93019-6

© The Editor(s) (if applicable) and The Author(s), under exclusive licence to Springer Nature Switzerland AG 2022
This work is subject to copyright. All rights are solely and exclusively licensed by the Publisher, whether the whole or part of the material is concerned, specifically the rights of translation, reprinting, reuse of illustrations, recitation, broadcasting, reproduction on microfilms or in any other physical way, and transmission or information storage and retrieval, electronic adaptation, computer software, or by similar or dissimilar methodology now known or hereafter developed.
The use of general descriptive names, registered names, trademarks, service marks, etc. in this publication does not imply, even in the absence of a specific statement, that such names are exempt from the relevant protective laws and regulations and therefore free for general use.
The publisher, the authors and the editors are safe to assume that the advice and information in this book are believed to be true and accurate at the date of publication. Neither the publisher nor the authors or the editors give a warranty, expressed or implied, with respect to the material contained herein or for any errors or omissions that may have been made. The publisher remains neutral with regard to jurisdictional claims in published maps and institutional affiliations.

This Palgrave Macmillan imprint is published by the registered company Springer Nature Switzerland AG.
The registered company address is: Gewerbestrasse 11, 6330 Cham, Switzerland

PREFACE

A SUBALTERN WINDOW

One thing leads to another, and hindsight often makes one wish it hadn't. The project of this book emerged organically from the earlier intellectual biography of Ajit Singh (Saith 2019), in particular from the short narrative there on 'Faculty Wars' in which Ajit was a key figure. That chapter provided an introductory, highly compressed version of the untold story, and the folded leaves of that concertina are opened to full stretch in this book, relying on a much wider range of archival and other inputs.

An effort has been made, as far as reasonably possible, to keep the persona of the author out of the narrative, even though I spent much of the 1970s in Cambridge, the time when the battle lines were being drawn for the purges to come. I had arrived as a doctoral researcher in 1972, the momentous year when Frank Hahn returned triumphantly to a professorship in Cambridge, and so was part of the melee—initially as an observer and then for a couple of years as an occasional protagonist when I joined the Faculty in a lowly academic position reserved for slaves serving the professoriate. As such I had the questionable benefit of being both a marginal participant and a non-participant, observer viewing events unfold through the personal window of my cubby hole in the DAE wing on the top floor of the Faculty building. Life as a PhD scholar was seriously underprivileged but wildly exciting; the temptations and enticements in the ever-changing window displays at Bowes and Bowes—said to have been the oldest bookshop in Britain, now sadly gone—guaranteeing a quick slide into what Amit Bhaduri termed perpetual indebtedness; it was a tough choice: the delights of The Copper Kettle (as was, not as is) on King's Parade, or the odd pint or two at the Hat & Feathers on Barton Road, or treats from the kindly old ladies of Fitzbillies (again, as was, not as is) versus the tactile pleasure of leafing through one's own copies of Mario Nuti's pair of edited volumes of essays of Michal Kalecki, then hot off the press; Kalecki easily won that one, but there were fresh challenges; the following week saw the bespectacled young Gramsci looking one in the eye over the title of *Selections from the*

Prison Notebooks of Antonio Gramsci. Natural empathy and political solidarity with the cause of the striking coal miners was intensified by personal experience, as the OPEC price hikes worked their cost-plus way through to one's shopping basket, quickly halving the real value of the meagre Commonwealth scholarship stipend of GBP 78 per month—much of it earmarked for the Trinity landlady on Grange Road who might well have been charging a locational quasi-rent on account of being next door to the Robinsons—making a luxury even of the weekly 3-pound, 3-minute trunk calls to 'back home' from the red 'Dr Who time-machine' phonebooths. Half-way through, Rekha, my wife, registered for a PhD in Sociology, widening the interface with local intellectual life. The decade of the 1970s saw the arrival of a large cohort of PhD scholars from South Asia, with enough bench strength to kick off its own dedicated seminar and, needless to say, its own cricket team which took the field against a Faculty XI, replete with dodgy umpiring and dubious scorekeeping, usually with a return revenge game. Survival, or at least getting to the jam part of Micawber's equation, depended on the acquisition of college assignments for supervising undergraduate groups, and earnings were generally around GBP 2–3 per session per group of 2–3 students—the tiny payment slips were eagerly awaited and cheque withdrawal amounts at Lloyds on Trinity Street seldom exceeded the luxurious amount of GBP 5/-. As with mountain climbing or village field-work in the Indian summer, these 'character-forming' experiences all seem rather more exciting from the safety of a distant future; on the ground in real time, it was more an episode, with reruns, of hard times. Things eased when I was offered the post of Faculty Assistant in Research (FAR), a position I held for two years, bringing with it the thrill of close continuous contact with DAE and Faculty members otherwise only spotted distantly at Sidgwick Site as they disappeared into their respective sides of the building or encountered in the IBM Computer Room, access to which was through a bizarre route: males and females had to walk through their respective convenience facilities on the lower ground floor under the Marshall Library to re-emerge and be reunited in a dark corridor (stacked with boxes of supplies) in the dungeon on the other side, where there was a research students' workroom with a couple of discarded typewriters waiting their time to enter antique auctions, but also a couple of gleaming devices that were worth getting up early for: a Hermes manual typewriter—IBM golf-ball typewriters were still a long way into the future—and an electronic calculator with a huge footprint and a lurid red display of about a dozen digits, of which any 2 or 3 would have to be guessed as some horizontal or vertical section was always on the blink. Passage through the doors at the far end got you into the small engine room: there were the card punching and reading machines and the IBM computer, and here you waited anxiously for the beast to spit out your results, putting you instantly in a buoyant or foul mood.

As the FAR slave, I was assigned to work with William Brian Reddaway (WBR) and Ajit Singh, mostly to produce the weekly class statistical handouts that Brian was cunningly devising to bamboozle, harangue and then enlighten undergrads in his upcoming lecture.[1] This was a daunting, but hugely rewarding learning exercise; WBR took no hostages, was very demanding, quite brusque though never unfriendly or impolite; and on rare occasions he even managed a smile and a compliment, well measured, lest it might lead to any smidge of complacency. A regular stream of Reddaway-type tasks: This, or that, can't be random; can you do some scatters and check? Why do you have the same number of decimal spaces for all the columns of the table? Somehow, this number (in a publication) doesn't seem right, please go back to the original source and check it is a misprint there; and so on. In between, there were exchanges about real applied economics, what the tables were all about, possible explanations and qualifications, as he would sometimes try out some part in his upcoming lecture using me as a proxy for the class. He was genuinely delighted at my independently acquired facility with the double-quick, rough-and-ready Reddaway-method of deseasonalising time series. The Faculty tea-room was usually to be avoided, not least because there was an existential uncertainty about the nature of the experience lying in wait, ranging from being in the crowds enjoying an entertaining biff-baff between some seniors, to suddenly being biffed and baffed yourself over some stray remark. The Buttery provided the more predictably congenial company of PhD co-workers—a time for frivolity and seriousness in equal measure before everyone disappeared again with furrowed brows to plough their data sets or equations. The market for information, aka gossip, was far from being missing—if anything, there was a high velocity of circulation and a tale heard today was reheard from another source a day or two later enlivened by additional spicing. And of course, there was enough to grin or grumble about, given the fractions and frictions within the deeply divided Faculty; each week brought a fresh tournament of jousting white knights and blackguards. At my personal humble level, this extended sojourn in the 1970s served as a great observation post for keeping track of the daily skirmishes and battles across the divide. In the narrative that follows, I have assiduously attempted to avoid undue reliance on personal experience though inevitably this will have influenced, perhaps subliminally, the gathering and interpretation of 'evidence' and 'facts'.

THE *RASHOMON* SYNDROME

The narrative stretches more than might be usual across time and space, locations and events, and so occupies a panoramic canvas. Assorted materials are used: archival sources for the investigation of some of the key episodes; published personal recollections of various actors and commentators, some long

---

[1] A cherished acquisition then was an acknowledgement in the first footnote on the first page of the first article, 'What has become of Employment Policy?' by Joan Robinson and Frank Wilkinson, in the first issue of the first volume of *Cambridge Journal of Economics*, a lot of self-proclaimed firsts' there, utterly trivial to the wider world, but for a few days I did not need the lift or staircase, I could just float up on a cloud to my top-floor cubicle in the Faculty building—what little it took to lift the spirits of slaves.

lost; and inputs from interviews or communications with several surviving members of the cast, many of whom had direct personal experience of the events. It cannot be said that the characters and actors are all fictional and bear no resemblance to any real person living or dead. That caveat does not apply; as far as possible, the players are named and made to speak for themselves in their own words drawn from archival and secondary sources, often via interviews available in the public domain. It needs to be emphasised that the purpose of the book is to investigate the reorientation of the trajectory of economics as a discipline in Cambridge; while the views and actions of specific individuals or groups are scrutinised and interrogated, this is not to be interpreted as, or conflated in any way, with impugning in any form the character or integrity of the persons concerned; the interpretations and commentaries are strictly intended to be kept at the intellectual level within this extended case study of the sociology of 'knowledge' production and control.

A declaration of interest as an author: no disingenuous pretence is made of being 'neutral', and the story telling is not 'impartial', or 'balanced', say a là BBC *News*, where an artificial superficial equality is notionally projected by granting each side equal media time for making their respective 'party political broadcasts'. It follows, rather, the BBC *Panorama* 'expose' template; it is explicitly an uncompromising narrative from one side of the battle lines and, as with the reporting of a war correspondent, the narrative consciously and admittedly tells one 'truth' as revealed by available evidence while explicitly acknowledging its relativity and mindfully highlighting its perceived contingencies and qualifications. There are very many more tomes by victors on how they won their wars than by losers on how these were lost; the triumphalist history according to the orthodox victors has been told and retold; it has become part of the Cambridge ether; in contrast, stories and memories from the other side have generally tended to lapse into a distressed post-trauma silence—but there are still voices from the scattered periphery or beyond the grave that need to be recorded and archived so that they are not obliterated altogether.

Lawrence Klein (1991: 108) set out his personal retrospective view of the 1944–1947 years at the Cowles Commission, induced by his dissatisfaction at the available 'insider' and 'outsider' accounts of that dynamic formative period. The econometrician suddenly turns anthropological in method: "some of the published accounts are from scholars who were not on hand for the whole period of interest to me, and some are based purely on historical research. Without having been on the scene, historians cannot capture voice inflections, gestures, body language, purely oral commentary (often informal discussion) and other pieces of unrecorded information. There were daily discussions and frequent reliance on oral traditions at the Cowles Commission, then, and the 'outside' accounts sometimes miss relevant points that related to this reliance on oral tradition. Lapses of memory can also affect 'insider' views." In the present case of the Cambridge purges, the acknowledged issues of the methodology of memory recall are compounded by the traumatic nature of the experience that the memory is meant to hold. Often, as a survival mechanism, memories of periods of acute episodic distress are shut down and not easily revived and reached, and this applies both to short-term post-trauma memory loss and to time-distant experiences, indicative perhaps of some form of a generic syndrome-labelled dissociative amnesia. Said one, when asked: "That whole period around 1984–1985 is a bit hazy for me, maybe the sheer unpleasantness of what happened during the period is something that I have expunged from my memory"; said another apologetically: "Sorry my memory is a bit confused. It was a very trying time for many of us and for many years I have done my best to put it behind me"; and said a third: "I feel a bit depressed whenever I think about Cambridge and so I put things off (I am usually a rather cheery person)"; [the respondent referred to the narrative of this book as] "rather depressing even upsetting"; and there were other similar reactions as well. Fortunately, or rather unfortunately, a sufficient number of persons had been cleansed through the purges to enable the construction and validation of what could be appropriately regarded as a collective syncretic memory through rounds of iteration and triangulation, including testing against documentary or archival evidence where available.

The admittedly idiosyncratic writing style takes its inspiration from manner, and manners, of the protagonists in their debates and duels; draining away all that passion in favour of a dismal, dour narration normally associated with the discipline of economics would be disrespectful of the fiery no-holds-barred Cambridge tradition of face-to-face intellectual exchanges in those times, and the reader might encounter a scattering of passages that carry a polemical, pamphleteering or on occasion even a prosecutorial air, and it can only be hoped that this might lighten and brighten the reader's lengthy journey.

While this rendition cannot really escape being partial, in both senses of the word, there is a fair attempt at being fair, though not at the expense of not calling a spade what it really is. I have had the benefit of close consultations with several of those intimately involved in the narratives and they are all wholly absolved of the responsibility for any errors of fact or interpretation that I might have accidentally made. Indeed, following the proverbial pejorative, these 'n' economists might well hold 'n+1' opinions about some of the stories told. As emphasised in the intellectual biography of Ajit Singh, the lead political commissar and Chief Whip of the radical heterodox tribes in these battles, the narrative resonates with Ryunosuke Akutagawa's *Rashomon*, immortalised by Akira Kurosawa, or Lawrence Durrell's *The Alexandria Quartet*—the door remains ajar for readers to enter the open space of oral history with their versions of what happened, whodunnit and howdunnit, and to express their preferences and choices about how it all transpired. At a minimum, what I have attempted is to insert one rendition of the story as seen from the perspectives of the vanquished, firmly into this choice set.

Cigars, Smoke, Mirrors

In stories of cigars, smoke and mirrors, with corpses and smell of cordite but no swaggering gunslingers, an occasional element of speculation is unavoidable in joining the dots, in making judgements from forensic as well as circumstantial evidence. In pursuing the whodunnit mystery, associations, affinities, opportunities, motivations, animosities and grudges, visceral vendettas and poisoned polarities and so on all come into play in constructing plausible scenarios that explain specific events or outcomes. That said, these somewhat amorphous aspects find their credence only in combination with a core of citable archival and personal recollections; in this sense, the speculative dimension, unavoidable as it sometimes is, is held within reasonable limits.

At various turns, the stories offer revelations about the unexpected roles, actions or inactions, of several key players whose linkages to the various purges have generally remained in occluded grey zones of silence, seldom going beyond puzzlement or whispers—reminiscent of the other Cambridge pastime of hunting for the fourth or the fifth man in that infamous spy ring. If nothing else, this adds a flavour of zest and spice to a bubbling brew. What emerges is a spectrum of involvement or culpability: from a direct hands-on hostile action; to strategic and tactical support for one of more purges at specific points in decision-making processes; to oppositions which unwittingly or unintentionally feed the purge campaigns; to wilful, or ostensibly accidental, inaction or passivity and lack of support for the various heterodox groups under threat, despite being regarded as members, friends or fellow travellers; or to careless, wanton actions unmindful of their potentially negative consequences for the heterodox side. It is possible to raise queries of one form or another about several names, some of whom perhaps had a direct, if quiet, hand in the proceedings, while others seemed to be onlookers not raising a hand to help the heterodox cause at critical points along the way. What becomes obvious is that while the central battle lines were clearly between the neoclassical orthodox group against the heterodox tribes, the campaigns of the purges were assisted by the opportunistic, active or passive, support of an intermediate group which, while not answering to the neoclassical label, practised forms of heterodoxy, or had political leanings, or held personalised grudges, that placed them in opposition to the main heterodox groups at specific conjunctures; and similar behaviour of some others was suggestive possibly of the pursuit of individual career agendas over professed political loyalties.

Some cautions are necessary. The closed version of the story, telling as it is, requires that the explanation avoids the risk of seeking a total answer within; the open version demands that in the search for greater completeness, the narrative does not slide into reductionism or determinism, into scripting a short history of the world outside, of everything. Then, there is the usual red herring, the easy allegation of flirting with 'conspiracy theorising'. The explanatory power of coincidence is perhaps oversold, a naïve euphemism for ignorance, or a wilful one for obscuring a cover-up—what enthrals audiences Bollywood audiences might not work equally well in historiography. The forensic art of chasing clues and converting coincidence into explanation often attracts the pejorative of 'conspiracy theorizing', this predictably, from the conspiratorial corner itself. Taking 'conspiracy' out of explanation would often yield a pathetically low R-squared value. Julius Caesar did not accidentally trip and lurch 23 times from dagger to naked dagger, all of which just happened to have bypassed security, held firmly, each pointing in his direction just at that time on that particular day in the Senate. And behind a 'conspiracy' usually lies some uncloaked constellation of hostile interests. That said, not all plots are well planned, not all 'conspiracies' succeed and, of course, not everything answers to the description of a plot; history is not a summation of plots, but that does not rule out their existence or salience of the exercise of coordinated collective agency at specific turning points.

"What If ... ?"

And then, the discerning reader might find the narrative replete with rich opportunities for indulging in that useless game of 'what if ...' counterfactuals—opening up arrays of intriguing simulations for happy-go-lucky modellers. On the one side, these highlight the role of coincidental conjunctures and contexts, accidents, individual idiosyncrasies, follies or percipience; on the other, these turning points beg the question whether, if the 'what if' factor had not occurred, some other constellation of factors might have emerged as a substitute from the deeper material configurations of the time. Even so, the what-if game does raise some teasing and tantalising scenarios. Consider a handful that distracted the author's eye during the labour process.

Take first the interventions of the grim reaper. Bob Rowthorn lamented the early death of Nicky Kaldor; in his view, "the fact that he died relatively young was a great loss; Cambridge economics would have been very different if he had lived another ten years" (Rowthorn 2008). Would it have? By the time of Kaldor's demise in 1986, much of the strategic damage was already done, and further, some of it was attributable to decisions in which Kaldor was himself a culpable party, if not, if accidentally or innocently, a moving spirit. The more, most, obvious 'what-if' surely would be the even more premature death of Keynes in 1946 at the cusp of a critical period for the subject globally and in Cambridge, and in the real world. Or, at a group level, what if the longevity of the neoclassical, neoliberal cohort, with an average age at death around 93 years, was matched by that of the Cambridge heterodox seniors whose average fell, roughly reckoned over small cohorts, well more than 10 years short of that. Another crucial what-if: Lionel Robbins was struck by the influenza bug very many times in his life and happily survived well; but the unfortunate Allyn Young was struck just once and died within a few days, opening the space for Robbins to take over LSE economics and reorient it towards the Austrian and Chicago camps. Given Young's affinity with Cambridge economics (cf. Sraffa's 1926, and Young's 1928 *EJ* papers, and Keynes's letter of condolence to Allyn

Young's wife), LSE and British economics could have taken a distinctly different trajectory, potentially of significance given the sustained antagonistic stance adopted by LSE under the Robbins-Hayek regime. Then, there was an earlier what-if, in the form of the desire of Sidney Webb to appoint Keynes as the Director of LSE in 1919, instead of Beveridge, which again would surely have precluded, or diluted, the entry of Austrian and Walrasian traditions into LSE and the UK. And what if Frank Hahn had not been twice invited to Cambridge, once via Kaldor who might much later have had second thoughts and regrets and then by the likes of Kahn and Reddaway following Kaldor's managed appointment of Robert Neild (over Hahn) to the vacant Joan Robinson chair? And what if Richard Goodwin or Luigi Pasinetti or Geoff Harcourt had been appointed instead; or if, at a potentially game-changing turn, say, Pasinetti, and not Robin Matthews, had been appointed as the new Professor of Political Economy when Brian Reddaway retired in 1980; or perchance, later in the 1980s, the two professorships had gone, again, to someone from that list, or to others from the rising cohort of Francis Cripps or Hashem Pesaran or Ajit Singh? Kaldor had seen Luigi as the lead practitioner of the Cambridge post-Keynesian tradition of 'grand theorizing'; Francis was widely regarded as a potential natural inheritor of the Wynne Godley mantle; and Ajit was a highly accomplished applied economist straddling diverse research specialisations. In such alternative what-if scenarios, could the then ongoing and subsequent purges of heterodoxy have happened or continued with the same gusto and outcomes? Then, David Hendry (2004) recalled that after studies in Aberdeen, "I applied to work with Dick Stone in Cambridge. Unfortunately he declined, so I did an M.Sc in econometrics at LSE with Denis Sargan", becoming one of the stars of the young cohort of 'nephews' in the Hahn-Gorman years there; hindsight induces the speculation whether the tribulations and trajectories of the DAE macroeconomic teams might have gone differently if Stone had said 'yes' and Hendry had settled down instead to a fine career with Stone at the DAE in Cambridge? Then, the professorial vacancy to which Dasgupta was appointed emerged when Robert Neild retired hurt prematurely, six years short of the Cambridge retirement age of 67; what if Robert, with his mild-mannered and persuasive personality, had withstood the heat in the Faculty kitchen till then and fought the decent fight for applied and heterodox economics within the professoriate—later on he came out with trenchant critiques calling mainstream economics "a disgrace in need of a reformation"? So many hypothetical questions, so few firm answers.

Moving to the national stage, what about the committed Labour MP and family doctor, Sir Alfred Broughton, who had insisted even on his death bed to be driven to London to cast his vote in the No-Confidence motion introduced by Margaret Thatcher in 1979; his honourable wish was declined by Callaghan on ethical grounds, and Labour lost the motion 311–310; as Roy Hattersley (2009) recalled later, Labour was in trouble, but getting a few more months— a long time in politics—in government for Labour could well have changed the immediate political climate and discourse, and kept Thatcher out, at least at that time. In turn, this could have kept the umbrella of political protection over the Cambridge left-Keynesian groups for another term and pre-empted the political pressures brought to bear on the SSRC and Michael Posner at the time of the rejection of SSRC funding for the DAE's macroeconomic modelling teams. Or what if Tony Benn, with the Alternative Economic Strategy of the left, had not lost the crucial election to the deputy leadership of the Labour Party, by less than one per cent of the vote, through the combined midnight machinations of the Callaghan, Healey and Kinnock groups which then became a turning point for left labour? All such illicit game-playing in counterfactuals, imagining 'paths not taken' at direction-changing crossroads, is as intriguing as it is futile. Indeed, what if the enraged nationalist 18-year-old student, Gavrilo Princip, had not used his deadly pistol in Sarajevo on 28 June 1914? Or what if …. Oh, the pleasures and pitfalls of idle rumination.

COVID Caveat

Completing large manuscripts is a fraught business anyway, but the overlay of the pandemic made it rather more so. Multiple rounds of unexpected and extended lockdowns in India brought distress, dislocation and delay; travel restrictions to, and in, Europe added to the disruption. More significantly, this affected the possibility of personal access to libraries, of conducting some more personal interviews and made it impossible to consult additional archival materials in London and Cambridge. A year was lost, but then, unlike so very many unfortunate others, one lived to tell the tale; I confess the virus might merely have provided an alibi for an existential reluctance to bid farewell to the manuscript much earlier and consign it irretrievably to the publisher; and, even if disingenuously, one can cite the extended vacant stretches enforced by the pandemic as an alibi for the unusual length of the book.

The Hague, The Netherlands   Ashwani Saith

Cover

St Michael's victory over the devil.
Jacob Epstein, Coventry Cathedral

On 14–15 November 1940, "a bright moonlit cloudless night made navigation simple" for the Luftwaffe operation—fatefully code-named *Moonlight Sonata*—of the blanket bombing of Coventry in which "almost a third of the city was flattened" with its medieval cathedral reduced to rubble. (GCHQ 2021). Wynne Godley was married to Kitty Garman, daughter of Kathleen Garman and the famous sculptor Jacob Epstein, one of whose creations lives on the wall of the cathedral in Coventry evoking the unbroken spirit of the city, with Benjamin Britten composing his *War Requiem* for the consecration of the reconstructed cathedral in 1962. It depicts St Michael—representing the good—slaying the devil. Epstein used a model of his "impossibly handsome" son-in-law, Wynne, to sculpt the head of St Michael. Though Wynne and his research team, along with other celebrated heterodox lineages, lost out proverbially to "the devil" in the Cambridge war of economics, there has subsequently been a defiant phoenix-like revival of the reputation and work of the famous Godley-Cripps Cambridge Economic Policy Group of the 1970s, as well as other renowned radical traditions nurtured since the 1920s in Cambridge, the crucible of heterodox economics. The allegorical symbolism of Sir Jacob Epstein's sculpture resonates with the leitmotif of the book.

Acknowledgements

Much appreciation is due to very many for varied and valuable inputs at different stages of the writing process: from supplying the simple ingredient of encouragement that sustains, facilitating access to sources and materials or to spotting banana skins before I did. The episodes narrated in this book are of a shared lived experience, often traumatic and locked away, of a dynamic cohort of accomplished, radical, socially motivated economists of various heterodox persuasions, of their expulsion or exile from their vibrant intellectual habitat in Cambridge, enforced to different degrees and in variable forms by a sustained onslaught by orthodox economics and its practitioners. This book could not have been written if they had not, to the last woman/man standing, been willing to relive and recount details of those episodes, however personally distressing might have been such exercises of reclaiming and piecing together a lost collective memory of a game-changing turning point in the history of Cambridge economics. In a real sense, I have merely been a scribe, the weaver of this fabric of suppressed untold stories, working the warp and weft to expose patterns formed by knotting together the many individual strings and threads. For generous and unfailing support in reading through, clarifying, correcting and validating various texts, for face-to-face interviews in real or later in virtual space, I am indebted to: Amiya Bagchi, Terry Barker, Bob Blackburn, Vani Borooah, Heinrich Bortis, Jo Bradley, Brendan Burchell, Ha-Joon Chang, Andy Cosh, Ken Coutts, Francis Cripps, Michael Ellman, Valpy FitzGerald, Matthew Frost, Geoff Harcourt, Wendy Harcourt, Alan Hughes, Jane Humphries, Alex Izurieta, Sandeep Kapur, Michael Landesmann, Marc Lavoie, Tony Lawson, Maria Cristina Marcuzzo, Peter Nolan, Jose Gabriel Palma, Prabhat Patnaik, Jill Rubery, Sunanda Sen, Ron Smith, Servaas Storm, John Toye, Brian Van Arkadie, Terry Ward, Frank Wilkinson and Ann Zammit. I hope the final outcome justifies their generosity. They are all hereby absolved of any errors of commission, omission or interpretation that remain.

The editors of the Palgrave series *History of Economic Thought* readily took on this project in its original incarnation and then did not blink as it stretched to three times its initially planned scale; I would like to thank them for their expressed confidence, in particular to Geoff Harcourt—sadly till a week ago, joint senior guru with Luigi Pasinetti, of Cambridge heterodox economics and economists. Geoff encouraged and supported the book from its inception as a chapter in my intellectual biography of Ajit Singh, almost all the way to completion, and it will remain a gnawing sadness that he was taken before he could write a foreword or examine the first copy off the press blocks. Other stalwarts from the times of the tales told here will also be much missed, especially Ajit Singh, John Toye, Mario Nuti and Frank Wilkinson.

I am much in debt to Paula Bownas for her precise and timely editorial preparation of a challenging manuscript for the publishers, though I messed it up again after her work was done; and then to successive teams at Palgrave Macmillan: Rachel Sangster and Joseph Johnson in the commissioning phase, and after that to Wyndham Hacket Pain, to Srishti Gupta, to the production team especially to Dhanalakshmi Muralidharan, Hemalatha Arumugam and Sujatha Mani, and to Palgrave's legal experts, for efficiently and calmly guiding the manuscript through the rest of its sometimes complex journey to publication; and to Srishti and Frido Steinen-Broo for the expeditious processing of my suggestions for the cover design. I would like to express my appreciation to the several anonymous readers of various draft versions for their very valuable feedback during the multiple rounds of reviews. As always, thanks are due to several librarians in Cambridge: to Simon Frost for the efficient and pleasant accommodation at short notice of my requests at the Marshall Library Archives; to Katrina Dean, Jill Whitelock and Michelle Barnes for kindly facilitating quick access to archival materials at the University Library; and to Patricia McGuire, Peter Monteith and Thomas Davies at the King's College Archives.

A collective salaam for the comradely support received from my scattered gang of friends, many of whom also shared the Cambridge journey; and loving familial appreciation for Sanjeev Saith and for the Wazir clan for keeping me in good cheer and high spirits, often literally. The unending, indeed forever extending, canvas of the manuscript exacted its toll of time and life, crowding out both this as well as that—the invisible price paid by someone else for an author's self-indulgence. And so, from the first page to the last, for caring and forbearance beyond calls of anything and everything, an open-arm acknowledgement and salutation for Rekha—gratitude begins at home.

Praise for *Cambridge Economics in the Post-Keynesian Era*

"This book is awesome in both its depth and range. It is avowedly a story of how the Economic Faculty of Cambridge University where not just Keynesian economics but macroeconomics was born and became home not just to Keynesians such as Joan and Austin Robinson, Nicholas Kaldor and Brian Reddaway but also Marxists such as Maurice Dobb, was converted into a fortress of not just neoclassical but neoliberal economics from the 1980s. Saith traces the change in the political atmosphere with the rise to power of Margaret Thatcher and Ronald Reagan. But he also shows how there was a planned attack on heterodox economics and economists by Matthews, Hahn and Dasgupta, who saw to it that only people of their choice were appointed to the Faculty and to all prestigious committees and editorial boards of journals, not only in Cambridge but everywhere else in Britain. They found allies in the LSE and in Chicago and Cambridge, Mass. overseas. The attackers took advantage of dissensions among the leaders of Keynesian economics in Cambridge. Saith also brings in sociology, development and economic history in his intense focus. This book should be required reading for everybody interested in the survival of people-friendly heterodox social sciences, including economics. Readers would realize that very similar tactics have been used by neoliberal economists wherever they have been able to obtain a foothold. That acquisition has been made easier with the omnipresence of the IMF and the World Bank. Saith's book is a notable addition to the history of economic thought and to the history of our times."
—Amiya Bagchi, Emeritus Professor and Emeritus Director, *Institute of Development Studies, Kolkata*; Adjunct Professor, *Monash University, Australia*

"This book explains how Cambridge (and indeed British) preeminence in post-Keynesian economics was undermined in the 1970s. With outstanding forensic scholarship, Saith reveals the institutional and personal networking that replaced a distinctive and empirical tradition in political economy by neoclassical orthodoxy. The book is destined to become the definitive account in the history of economic thought of how neoclassical economists reinforced their hegemony over the academic discipline in the 20th Century."
—Terry Barker, Former Director, *Cambridge Growth Project, Department of Applied Economics, University of Cambridge*; Coordinating Lead Author, *IPCC 1996–2006*; Director, *Cambridge Econometrics Ltd.*

"The Economics Faculty at the University of Cambridge is, arguably, one of the most famous in the world, suffused with the history of great ideas and the remarkable achievements of distinguished men and women. As a history of this Faculty, with particular emphasis on the past 75 years, Ashwani Saith's book is a tour de force. This is a compelling account of the jousts between the heterodox defenders of the Cambridge castle, who eschewed quantitative methods in economics, and their foreign invaders in the form of neoclassical economists who were devoted to the American tradition of using mathematics and statistics. Saith tells a fascinating story of how the seemingly impregnable citadel fell to a combination of enemies within the faculty, aided by the university administration, and with the active assistance of the government of the day in the UK. Was this a Pyrrhic victory, which reduced a once great and independent faculty to an imitation of US economics departments, or was such an overthrow long overdue? And who were the winners and losers? and what became of them? These are all issues addressed by the author in this fascinating analysis of the fall of economics at Cambridge from its glory days."

—Vani Borooah, *Emeritus Professor and Chair of Applied Economics, University of Ulster*; Past President, *Irish Economic Association, and Secretary, Royal Irish Academy*

"The Keynesian-Sraffian double revolution of the *Years of High Theory (1926–1939–1960)* laid the basis for the Keynesian triumph from, broadly, 1945 to 1975—*We are all Keynesians now!*—became a current saying. In his immensely important book Ashwani Saith now pictures in great detail the tragedy linked to the systematic destruction of the Keynesian tradition at Cambridge through the neoclassicals from 1975 onwards. His book represents a substantive contribution to the recent history of economics."

—Heinrich Bortis, *Emeritus Professor of Political Economy, History of Economic Theory and Economic History, Department of Economics, University of Fribourg, Switzerland*

"I came to Cambridge in 1985 to work in the Department of Applied Economics as part of an interdisciplinary project involving Economics, Sociology and Social Psychology, progressing onto a lectureship in Social and Political Sciences (SPS) and finally a Chair and sometime Head of Department in Sociology. This book makes it clear why such a career path is no longer an option and does a lot to make sense to me of the period from the mid 1985s until now. It also explains, in a large part, why the Faculty of Economics has, for a long time now, been seen as an outlier amongst Cambridge institutions, cut off from the other social sciences. Reading this manuscript forced me to reflect deeply on just how things worked out like they did. Perhaps for now the music has stopped, but when (as it invariably will) the music starts playing again, I hope that someone with Ashwani Saith's eye for details and the bigger picture will be around to write the sequel!"

—Brendan Burchell, *Professor in the Social Sciences*; Chair, *Archaeology, Anthropology and Sociology Degree Committee*; President *of Magdalene College, University of Cambridge*

"This book opens up the shadowy world where academic orthodoxy aligns with neoconservative politics and corporate power to block applied research in the Keynesian tradition making the search for solutions to long-standing global problems very, very hard if not impossible. Ashwani Saith digs deep to uncover not only the procedures through which protagonists of the neo-classical paradigm purged researchers whose evidence stood in their way but also the doubts and hesitations of the galaxy of world-famous economists who contributed to the rise and subsequent demise of Keynesian economics at its birthplace in Cambridge. The author describes the step-by-step process of demolition of the Cambridge Department of Applied Economics and purge of heterodox teaching of economics, sociology, development and economic history at a Faculty that had been the birthplace of the twentieth century Keynesian revolution,

attracting graduate students from around the world. People who share concerns about governance in the twenty-first century should read this book and think hard about how damage done in the last quarter of the twentieth century can be repaired and how open and plural research environments demanded by contemporary students can be restored."
—Francis Cripps, Director, *Alphametrics Co., Ltd, Bangkok, Thailand*

"The strange death of Cambridge heterodox economics is a significant development in intellectual history and is well worth the detailed attention it gets in this book. It has an excellent source basis: relevant archival documents, a wide range of publications, and interviews or email exchanges with many of those directly involved. The book covers a wide range of Cambridge issues, from Hahn's self-image as John the Baptist to the critiques of economics by Polly Hill and Michael Postan. However, the book is not confined to internal Cambridge matters but pays attention to national and international developments outside Cambridge that influenced or determined the outcome. These range from the decisions by the SSRC & ESRC to stop funding the major research programmes at the DAE (Department of Applied Economics), to the creation and activities of the Mont Pelerin Society and the vicissitudes of Keynesianism in the USA. This remarkable and well-written book is a mine of information. It is well worth reading and recommending to colleagues and libraries."
—Michael Ellman, Emeritus Professor, *University of Amsterdam, Awarded 1998 Kondratieff Gold Medal*; Co-editor, *Cambridge Journal of Economics*

"I had the great pleasure to read early versions of this meticulously researched history of the rise and demise of Cambridge heterodox economics in the post-Keynesian era. I warmly congratulate Ashwani for his tour de force."
—Geoffrey Harcourt, (27 June 1931–7 December 2021), *Emeritus Professor of Economics, University of Adelaide, Australia; Emeritus Reader in History of Economic Theory, University of Cambridge*

"Ashwani Saith has written a carefully researched and compelling account of the means by which the Cambridge Faculty of Economics and Politics was purged of heterodox applied economic analysis in the last quarter of the twentieth century. It draws on memoirs and interviews with participants in the contest for control, and a detailed archival analysis to reveal the methods by which this was achieved. These methods extended beyond the Faculty into the operations of major research funders. It should be read by anyone with an interest in the ways in which power can be exercised to control the nature of academic discourse and for the implications this may have for the future and relevance of the economics discipline."
—Alan Hughes, *Emeritus Margaret Thatcher Professor of Enterprise Studies and Director*, Emeritus, *Centre for Business Research, Judge Business School, University of Cambridge*; Life Fellow, *Jesus College, Cambridge*

"History is usually written by the victors, but Ashwani Saith speaks for and from the other side of the battlelines of how Cambridge Economics came to expunge its vibrant heterodox traditions, closed its hitherto distinguished applied department, narrowed its methodological approach and rejected

scholarly dissent. It is a voice that should be heard, and a book that must be read, certainly by anyone interested in making economics socially meaningful and fit again for the pursuit of public purpose."
—Jane Humphries, Centennial Professor, *London School of Economics*, Emeritus *Professor of Economic History, University of Oxford*; *Fellow of All Souls College, Oxford*

"When I joined the University of Cambridge in early 2002 and was invited to tutor students of the Faculty of Economics, I was shocked to see that none of those I met ever read Kaldor or Robinson, and the only thing about Keynes they came across was the IS-LM caricature portrayed by Mankiw. Frequent conversations with Ken Coutts, Francis Cripps, John Eatwell, Wynne Godley, Geoff Harcourt, Ajit Singh and others helped uncover important pieces of the puzzle. But this comprehensive and rigorous book offers a full picture. Ashwani's opus excels. Through the painstaking account of events at Cambridge there grows an unmistakable appreciation of the imperative for the economics profession worldwide to become meaningful again."
—Alex Izurieta, Senior Economist, *UNCTAD, Geneva*; Former Senior Researcher, *Judge Business School, University of Cambridge*

"Ashwani Saith's book is monumental, enthralling, beautifully written with its occasional satirical tone, but as we are being warned, depressing. It explains how the Faculty of Economics of the University of Cambridge—the world centre of post-Keynesian economics—was gradually and entirely taken over by neoclassical economics and why the Department of Applied Economics, also at the heart of heterodox economics, eventually came to be dismantled. This was so far an untold story, except for a chapter on 'Faculty wars' in Saith's previous book, the intellectual biography of Ajit Singh. The current book provides 14 chapters of a meticulous detective story, relying mostly on Cambridge archives, but also on testimonies, interviews, emails, and previous articles of participants to these events. The book makes clear that, besides possible strategical mistakes by the incumbent heterodox economists, there were inexorable and ineluctable outside forces that led to this dismal state of affairs, through the Americanization of the economics profession and through the changing political winds that blew out heterodox and left-wing economics nearly everywhere in the world. The last chapter shows that all is not lost, both in Cambridge and elsewhere in the world."
—Marc Lavoie, Professor Emeritus, *University of Ottawa, Canada*; Professor Emeritus, *Université Sorbonne Paris Nord, France*

"This is an important book, and one that makes compelling reading for anyone interested in the developments in economics over the last few decades. It is a fascinating investigation into how ideas are shaped and in turn shape power relations within the academic world, and a passionate defence of the side which was defeated in Cambridge in the feud between heterodox and mainstream economics. Ashwani Saith witnessed the events and, while standing firmly on the side of those who lost the battle, manages to remain fair, balanced and scholarly. Highly recommended."

—Maria Cristina Marcuzzo, Professor, *Accademia dei Lincei, Università di Roma 'La Sapienza'*

"Henry Kissinger once said that "The reason that university politics is so vicious is because stakes are so small". This is often true, but not in the case of the Faculty of Economics at Cambridge in the 1980s. The elections of Thatcher and Reagan and the rise of neo-liberalism made the conflict at Cambridge the exception: the stakes were high because this was part of a much larger conflict. When I started my academic career, Cambridge was the place where to be; but when I got an appointment in 1981, little did I know of what was coming! When I joined, the intellectual life of the Faculty consisted mostly of its own internal controversies between two powerful intellectual groups; those controversies kept everyone on their intellectual toes. But political changes in the outside world gave one group the opportunity to ally themselves with powerful external political interests and with internal bureaucracies always all-too eager to acquiesce to external demands. What this group could not win by the power of ideas they achieved through brute force. Little by little, as it's made clear by the meticulous research in Saith's brilliant book, they squeezed heterodox economics out of the Faculty. When I retired in 2014, a member of the other group told me jokingly: there goes the last of the Mohicans! As a great psychoanalyst discusses in his work, there seems to be an inverse relationship between the expectation of understanding the real, and the tolerance of dissent. As soon as the 1980s began to show the limitation of neo-liberalism as an ideology and neo-classical economics as an economic theory, the dread of having misunderstood the real led to a desperate need for the annihilation of disagreement—as soon as the DAE rightly predicted that Thatcherism will lead to unemployment jumping to 3 million the writing was on the wall. In other words, when expectation of understanding the real is high, difference of opinion is tolerable, but when there is little or no expectation of understanding, the need for agreement is absolute. This brings the destructive instinct into play, turning a belief system into an absolutist one, and this into an engine of ideological genocide. From this perspective Ashwani Saith's book is not just a great contribution to the history of economic thought, but also to the understanding of the intellectual obscurantism of our times."

—Jose Gabriel Palma, Senior Lecturer Emeritus, *Faculty of Economics, University of Cambridge*; Professor of Economics, University of Santiago, Chile; Joint Editor, *Cambridge Journal of Economics*

"The Keynesian Revolution was not just about the vacuity of Say's Law or the correct understanding of the determinants of the interest rate. It revolutionized economics as a whole, by completely opening up the subject, liberating it from the straitjacket of a belief in the desirability of perfect markets, and

bringing in bold, new thinking in many spheres. In development theory for instance it created room for the entry of structuralism; and in development policy it encouraged novel forms of state intervention within the *dirigiste regimes* that came up in the post-decolonization era. The Sraffa Revolution, though of a somewhat esoteric nature, had a similar liberating effect. As both revolutions began in Cambridge, it became a magnet for economists from all over the world. The capture of Cambridge by economic orthodoxy therefore was a major episode in the counter-revolution against the liberation of economics. It occurred not because of the superiority of orthodox ideas, but above all through the use of political and economic power. Ashwani Saith's book is a meticulous and comprehensive discussion of this capture. It is a *tour de force* that throws valuable light on the sociology behind the dominance of ideas. Given the profound significance of this capture, which prepared the intellectual ground for the subsequent ascendancy of neo-liberal thinking, it should be of interest to every economist, not just those who were directly involved; and it is written with remarkable scrupulousness and lucidity. An essential read."
—Prabhat Patnaik, *Emeritus Professor of Economics, Centre for Economic Studies and Planning, Jawaharlal Nehru University, New Delhi*

"This book chronicles the sustained undermining of heterodox economics and the severing of the links between economics and other social sciences in the Cambridge economics faculty from the 1970s onwards. This mattered as Cambridge was the renowned centre for Keynesian and heterodox economics and the suppression of this legacy was important in securing the domination of the neoclassical mainstream. This process was spreading across the world but as Ashwani Saith makes clear, through the most amazingly detailed evidence-based account, it was the specific strategies and practices deployed in Cambridge over decades by a small coterie of powerful academics that led to the evisceration of heterodoxy and cognate disciplines from the Economics Tripos. Painful as it was to relive through this outstanding book the years of intrigue, disrespect and intense job insecurity that I had to experience in a key period of my academic life, for me the saddest consequence is that young people now are denied the inspiring, theoretically diverse and interdisciplinary education that I enjoyed in Cambridge in the early 1970s. After the financial crisis economics students across the world started to ask why the economics curriculum no longer had power to explain or resolve real world problems. Many of the answers are to be found here."
—Jill Rubery, *Emeritus Professor of Comparative Employment Systems, University of Manchester,* Former Director, *Work and Equalities Institute at Alliance Manchester Business School*

"Ashwani Saith has produced a fascinating social anthropology of the warring tribes of Econ at one of their earliest settlements. Drawing on a wealth of original documents and the accounts of a host of participant-observers, he carefully documents the battles for the control of the priesthood, the seminar rituals and

the sacred journals, in the liminal time before the old gods of Cambridge Economics were finally displaced. It is both a revealing account of internecine academic warfare and an entertaining read."
—Ron Smith, *Professor of Applied Economics, Department of Economics, Mathematics and Statistics, Birkbeck, University of London*

"The history of Cambridge Economics in the Post-Keynesian Era is a story that needed to be told—and Ashwani Saith's book does it extremely well. In what reads as a detective story-cum-period-novel-cum-family-drama, Saith offers a persuasive, richly documented and fascinating account of how productive, relevant and innovative heterodox economic traditions were purged from the Faculty of Economics of Cambridge University, for reasons of 'ideology' and in order to align the divided department with an increasingly irrelevant mainstream economics. Saith brilliantly manages to contextualise the local happenings in Cambridge within the global rise of the 'neoliberal thought-collective', highlighting the crucial roles of individual knowledge brokers, networks, thinktanks, politicians and donors. Fundamental theoretical, ideological and methodological disagreements between the major actors in this drama are discussed with impressive clarity and purpose, and with a keen eye for biographical detail and historical setting. In the end, it is the sad story of the better road not taken. Saith's book brings us back to the fork in the road—and forces us to consider and reconsider our earlier decision. Cambridge Economics in the Post-Keynesian Era is an extraordinary piece of research, lovingly told and immensely worthwhile for the new light it sheds on the epoch-making purge of Keynesian thinking right in its original stronghold."
—Servaas Storm, Senior Lecturer, *Faculty of Technology, Policy and Management, Delft University of Technology, The Netherlands*; Joint Editor, *Development and Change*

"This book should be read by anyone with an interest in the freedom of academic study. Ashwani Saith accurately describes the events surrounding the creation of the Cambridge Department of Applied Economic and its development into a successful and prestigious centre for research into economic and social policy, attracting researchers from around the world, and its subsequent dismantling and eventual closure. It is the story of how those who did not subscribe to the dogmas of neoclassical economics, who believed that to start from unrealistic abstract assumptions was not the best way to build models of reality or of understanding behaviour, were driven out of the University, in a number of cases to pursue their research in the private sector. In many cases, they were highly successful in doing so, but to the detriment of economics in Cambridge and to the students who came to study there, attracted by the legacy of Keynes and a desire to understand how economies work and the factors underlying economic and social development. The book is a testament to the investigative skills of the author and his painstaking pursuit of how a shameful episode in Cambridge University history unfolded by uncovering and crawling through countless documents in various archives and interviewing a great many of those that were directly involved. Although it brings back painful personal memories, it is a story that is important to tell, to show how those who have gained academic power can dictate what can be taught, what research questions it is legitimate to try to answer and what methods can be used to do so."

—Terry Ward, Research Director, *Applica srl. Brussels*;
Managing Director, *Alphametrics Ltd. U.K.*

Contents of Volume I

1 **Cambridge, That Was: The Crucible of Heterodox Economics**   1
   1.1   *The Narrative*   1
   1.2   *Evolutions and Revolutions*   4
        1.2.1   *The Great Banyan of Heterodox Traditions*   4
        1.2.2   *Cohorts*   6
        1.2.3   *The Cambridge Habitat*   9
        1.2.4   *Which Cambridge?*   11
   1.3   *Regime Change*   14
        1.3.1   *The World of Cambridge: Stories Within*   20
        1.3.2   *Worlds Beyond Cambridge: Neoliberalism at the Gates*   22
   1.4   *The Dialectic of Competing Paradigms*   26
        1.4.1   *Laissez-Faire: "Receding at last into the distance"*   27
        1.4.2   *The Force of Ideas*   29
        1.4.3   *Opposition Brewing*   32
        1.4.4   *Evolutions and Hegemonic Incorporation*   33
        1.4.5   *Ideological: Not the Techniques but the Purposes of Economics*   36
        1.4.6   *Sociological: Mathematical Whiz-Kids and Ageing Dinosaurs*   38
        1.4.7   *Beyond Kuhnian Reductionism*   39
        1.4.8   *Mankiw's Pendulum*   40
        1.4.9   *Solow's À La Carte Approach*   42
        1.4.10   *Silos and Trenches*   43
        1.4.11   *Joan Versus Hahn—History Versus Equilibrium*   46
   1.5   *Semantics and Pedantics*   56
   References   63

2 The Warring Tribes — 69
- 2.1 A Sanctuary of Sages — 70
  - 2.1.1 Class to Community: The Cement of War — 70
  - 2.1.2 Community to Conflict: Cement to Sand — 76
  - 2.1.3 A Pride of Savage Prima Donnas — 78
- 2.2 Faculty Wars — 95
  - 2.2.1 Paradise Lost — 102
  - 2.2.2 Fault Lines Within — 103
    - Wynne Godley: No Legacy No Synthesis, No Textbooks—The Samuelson Factor — 103
    - Shifting Student Preferences? — 104
    - "Irrelevance" and Irreverence: Joan and K-Theory — 106
    - Inbred Insularity, Complacency — 108
    - Simultaneities in the Demographic Lifecycle — 111
    - Lack of Internal Group Coherence — 115
    - The Heterodox Camp: No Chairs—Sorry, Standing Room Only — 127
    - A Break in Intergenerational Transmission, in the Reproduction of Traditions — 128
- 2.3 Godfathers, Uncles and Nephews: The Gathering Foe — 129
  - 2.3.1 The Trojan Horse: By the Pricking of My Thumbs — 129
  - 2.3.2 Forming the Academy — 132
    - Meanwhile, at the Orthodox Party—A Merry Game of Musical Chairs — 136
  - 2.3.3 The Chess Master — 138
- 2.4 The Campaign: How the War Was Lost and Won — 150
  - 2.4.1 The Orthodox Gambit: Capture the External Commanding Heights — 150
  - 2.4.2 Carrots and Commanders — 153
  - 2.4.3 Modus Operandi: *Masters, Mandarins and Interlocking Committees* — 169
- References — 172

3 Worlds Beyond Cambridge: The Global Web of the 'Neoliberal Thought Collective' — 179
- 3.1 Conjunctures — 181
  - 3.1.1 1930s, The Prelude — 181
    - LSE Versus Cambridge — 181
    - Émigré Economists: The Benefactions of Lenin and Hitler — 185
  - 3.1.2 1940s, The Cascade — 191
  - 3.1.3 Keynesianism: Divergent Receptions — 192
    - Post-war Affinity in the UK — 193
    - Post-New Deal Hostility in the USA — 193

3.2		Spreading the Word: Messiahs, Messages, Methods	195
	3.2.1	Ideas and Ideologies: Manufacturers and Retailers	195
	3.2.2	USA: Early Ideological Entrepreneurs of Libertarianism	202
		Harold Luhnow: The Volker Fund and its Dollars	202
		Foundation for Economic Education (FEE) and its Facilitators	210
	3.2.3	Europe: Friedrich Hayek and the Mont Pelerin Society	212
		Antecedents	212
		Pilgrims Atop a Mountain, Mont Pelerin, Switzerland, April 1947	218
		Financial Sponsors	219
		The First Meeting of Minds	222
		Sarcastic Schumpeter, Sceptical Solow, Scathing Samuelson	227
	3.2.4	UK: Antony Fisher, Global Venture Capitalist of Think Tanks	229
3.3		Branding the Message: The 'Nobel' Prize	234
	3.3.1	The Stockholm Connection: Ideological Entrepreneurs	235
	3.3.2	Some Early Awards: Setting the Direction	240
		Jan Tinbergen—Ragnar Frisch 1969	240
		Samuelson 1970	241
		Gunnar Myrdal—Friedrich von Hayek 1974	242
		Milton Friedman 1976	246
	3.3.3	Mont Pelerin Society and the 'Nobel'—A Golden Embrace	249
	3.3.4	Cambridge Heterodoxy?	250
	3.3.5	'An Ideological Coup'	251
3.4		Reaching Politics: Weaponising the Message	253
	3.4.1	Santiago de Chile: Pinochet the Pioneer	253
		Chicago and its Cowboys	253
		Thatcher: Romancing Pinochet's Chile	257
	3.4.2	The White House: Reagan, a Disciple	262
	3.4.3	10 Downing Street: Thatcher, a Devotee	264
		More than its Weight in Gold—The Market Price of Symbolic Capital	269
	3.4.4	Pulling Together	269
3.5		Besieging Cambridge: The Chicago–MIT–LSE Trinity	271
	3.5.1	A Cross-Atlantic Triangle	271
	3.5.2	Diversity of Practice	271
	3.5.3	Unity of Purpose	275
References			285

4 Camp Skirmishes Over Interstitial Spaces: Journals, Seminars, Textbooks — 295
- 4.1 The Battle of Teruel—The Day before — 296
- 4.2 Journals — 297
  - 4.2.1 EJ Leaves 'Home'—The Loss of a Flagship — 297
  - 4.2.2 CJE Arrives—A Forum of One's Own — 305
  - 4.2.3 Cambridge Economic Policy Review: One Crowded Hour of Glorious Life — 319
- 4.3 Seminars — 322
  - 4.3.1 Cambridge Economic Club—A Marshallian Precursor: 1884–1890, 1896–? — 329
  - 4.3.2 Political Economy Club: From Keynes to Robertson to Kahn—Dazzling to Dour — 330
  - 4.3.3 The Marshall Society: A Socialisation into Economics and Its Purposes — 334
  - 4.3.4 Piero Sraffa's Research Students Seminar: A Precocious Nursery — 339
  - 4.3.5 In Retrospect, Austin Robinson on the Cambridge Circus: The Engine Room of The General Theory — 344
  - 4.3.6 Cambridge–LSE Joint Seminar: Jousting Juniors — 345
  - 4.3.7 Kahn's 'Secret' Seminar at King's: Fires in the Kitchen — 347
  - 4.3.8 The Richard Stone Common Room: Typhoo and Typhoons — 353
  - 4.3.9 Ajit Singh's Political Economy Seminar at Queens': Young Turks — 356
  - 4.3.10 Arestis and Kitson Political Economy Seminar at St. Catherine's College — 360
  - 4.3.11 Hahn's Churchill Seminar: Only Maths and Neoclassicals, Others Beware — 361
  - 4.3.12 Cambridge Growth Project Seminar at DAE — 362
  - 4.3.13 Hahn's 'Quaker' Risk Seminar: The Rising Tide — 363
  - 4.3.14 Matthews's CLARE Group: The Master's Lodge of Moderate Practitioners — 364
  - 4.3.15 Lawson—Realism and Social Ontology: Ways of Seeing and Framing — 367
- 4.4 Textbooks — 369
  - 4.4.1 Distant Thunder: Keynes and McCarthy, Tarshis and Samuelson — 371
  - 4.4.2 Lawrence Klein and the Paradox of The Keynesian Revolution — 377
    - Puzzle — 378
    - Ph.D.—At Samuelson's Feet — 378
    - Cowles Commission—The New Dealers — 379
    - The Keynesian Revolution: The Extra Chapter—Klein, Then a Closet Marxist? — 380

		Beyond Keynes	385
		UMich and McCarthyism	386
		Policy to Forecasting	391
		Resolution	393
	4.4.3	'Death of a Revolutionary Textbook': Robinson and Eatwell	394
	4.4.4	An 'Applied Economics' Textbook That Wasn't: Joan and Young Friends	399
4.5	The Battle of Teruel—The Day After		403
Appendix 4.1: First off the Blocks: Mabel Timlin's Keynesian Economics, 1942			403
References			406

5	**The DAE Trilogy**		415
5.1	Origins and Evolution		415
	5.1.1	Origins	415
	5.1.2	Evolution: Substance and Styles	417
	5.1.3	Foundations of Stone	420
	5.1.4	Reddaway's Method: Eclectic Development	423
	5.1.5	Godley: Turbulent Times	426
5.2	End of the Golden Age: The Decade of Discontent		430
5.3	The Trilogy: Discrete Episodes or a Serial Campaign?		433
Appendix 5.1: DAE—Finding a Good Home			436
References			437

6	**Cambridge Economic Policy Group: Beheading a Turbulent Priest**		439
6.1	Charged Conjuncture		442
	6.1.1	Imbroglios of 1974: Old Versus New Cambridge Versus the Establishment	442
	6.1.2	The Enigma of Kahn	444
	6.1.3	Kaldor: On Radical Policy Implications of New Cambridge, 1976	453
	6.1.4	Cambridge Squabbles: Spillover into Whitehall?	456
	6.1.5	Triggering Crisis: The Pivot of the OPEC Price Hikes	460
	6.1.6	1979: Enter Margaret Thatcher, Right-Wing, Upfront	464
	6.1.7	The Case of the Odd Consensus: The Letter by 364 Economists, 1981	466
	6.1.8	Thatcher in the Garage of the Federal Reserve	470
	6.1.9	1981: Brixton Riots, Toxteth Fires: "A Concentration of Hopelessness"	472
	6.1.10	The CEPG: A Thorn in the Thatcher Hide	474
	6.1.11	The Bogey of Import Controls and the Spectre of Bennism	477

6.2		SSRC and CEPG: Dispensing Instant Injustice	484
	6.2.1	Posner's Parlour	484
	6.2.2	Posner's Process	489
6.3		Epilogue	493
	6.3.1	Vengeance	493
	6.3.2	The Team Scattered	494
	6.3.3	The Model Reincarnated	496
	6.3.4	The Rehabilitation of Wynne	500
	6.3.5	Wynne Godley: 'My Credo' …	502
	6.3.6	The Pacification of the CEPG	505

Appendix 6.1: Old Cambridge, New Cambridge, 1974: and All the King's Men 509

1. Letter WG to RFK 23 May 1974. JVR/vii/228/3/3 509
2. Letter NK to RFK 20 May 1974. JVR/vii/228/3/14-16 509
3. Letter from RFK and MP to NK 24 May 1974. JVR/vii/228/3/17-20 509
4. Letter from RFK and MP to NK 28 May 1974. JVR/vii/228/3/24 510
5. Letter from FC to RFK 29 May 1974. JVR/7/228/3/25 510
6. Reply from RFK to FC 6 June 1974. JVR/7/228/3/24 510
7. In the interim, NK replied to RFK and MP. JVR/7/228/3/26 510
8. Letter from NK to RFK. RFK/12/2/132/3 511

References 511

7 **'Unintended' Collateral Damage? The Cambridge Economic Policy Group and the Joseph-Rothschild-Posner SSRC Enquiry, 1982** 517

7.1	Joseph—Rothschild—Posner—Godley	518
7.2	The Posner-the-Saviour Narrative	520
7.3	Setting Up the Enquiry	533
7.4	Who Proposed Rothschild?	534
7.5	Rothschild Report Writing Process	537
7.6	The Judgement of Rothschild	539
7.7	Between Draft and Release and Response: Handshakes and Cigars	540
7.8	Did Posner Get Away with Just a Change of Name?	543
7.9	CEPG—Collateral Damage? Or, Traded Down the River?	548
7.10	The Rothschild Report: Gleanings on Macroeconomic Modelling	550

	7.11	Lord Kaldor—Off the Record, Off the Cuff, Off the Mark?	551
	7.12	Lord Harris' Vitriol	555
	7.13	Catholicity and Independence	556
	7.14	Rothschild's Last Word	559
	7.15	Joseph's Last Laugh	560
	References		560

8 Cambridge Growth Project: Running the Gauntlet — 563

	8.1	Background and Conjuncture	564
		8.1.1 The Decision	566
	8.2	Substantive Issues	569
		8.2.1 No Innovation?	569
		8.2.2 Catholicity, Turnover and the Value of Disaggregation	569
		8.2.3 Use of Input-Output Tables	572
		8.2.4 CGP Presence in Policy Debates	573
		8.2.5 Insularity	574
		8.2.6 On Exploiting the Cheap Labour of Graduate Students	574
	8.3	Issues of Procedural Probity	576
		8.3.1 Shifting Goalposts Across Evaluations	576
		8.3.2 Unequal Application of Criterion of Commercial Funding	577
		8.3.3 Public Good or Private Resource?	577
		8.3.4 ESRC Ignored CGP Model Performance: Why?	579
		8.3.5 Compromised 'Independent' Evidence	580
	8.4	Other Concerns	582
		8.4.1 'Reds'?	582
		8.4.2 Crowding Out Competitors?	582
		8.4.3 Deadweight Loss of Built-up Intellectual Capital	582
		8.4.4 Gratuitously Offensive: Up Close and Out of Order	584
		8.4.5 The Consortium: 'Revived Talk of Conspiracy Theory'	585
		8.4.6 In Defence, a Lone Voice, Overruled	586
	8.5	Epilogue: CGP—Life After Death?	587
	Appendix 8.1: CGP Staff Members, Timeline 1960–1987		594
	Appendix 8.2: Publications of CGP Staff		595
	References		596

9 The DAE Review 1984–1987: A Four-Year Inquisition — 597

	9.1	The Campaign of Attrition	598
		9.1.1 Occluded Origins	599
		9.1.2 Two Stages, Two Committees	604

9.2	The Orthodox Gambit		607
	9.2.1	The Agenda Revealed	608
	9.2.2	The Game Plan: Four Options	617
		Closure	617
		Separation	618
		Absorption	620
		Capture	623
	9.2.3	External Critiques: Collusion as Consultation?	625
9.3	The Heterodox Defence		631
	9.3.1	Solidarity, Testimonies, Rebuttals	633
	9.3.2	Chinks in the DAE Armour?	643
9.4	On the Rack: Bleeding the DAE		648
	9.4.1	The Secretary General, The Prince and the Chess Master	654
	9.4.2	The Capture	657
	9.4.3	How it Transpired, Perhaps Not Just by Chance	660
	9.4.4	Checkmate: A Constitutional Coup	670
9.5	Epilogue		675

Appendix 9.1: DAE Review Committees: Composition and Terms of Reference 680

    First Advisory Committee. Constituted: Easter Term 1984; Reported: May 1985   680

    Second Advisory Committee: Constituted: Easter Term 1985; Reported April 1987   680

Appendix 9.2: Labour Studies Group: Dispersed, Not Defeated   681

References   687

Contents of Volume II

10 Sociology: The Departure of 'Stray Colleagues in a Vaguely Cognate Discipline'   691
   10.1   Early Years: Hostility, Neglect, Subordination   692
   10.2   Sociology: Growing Up Amongst Economists   716
   10.3   Hostile Public Spaces: SSRC, Rothschild-1982 and Sociology   726
        10.3.1   Entrenched Resistance to the Emergence of SSRC   726
        10.3.2   In the Court of Public Opinion: Open Season on Sociology   728
        10.3.3   The Joseph–Rothschild Assault   730
   10.4   Back in Cambridge, 1984–1986: To Remain Or to Exit, That Was the Question   734
        10.4.1   Sociology in the DAE Review: Crossfire and Crossroads   734
        10.4.2   Cometh the Hour, Cometh ... Tony Giddens   736
   10.5   Archival Insights: Harboured Preferences Revealed   744
        10.5.1   Do Please Stay, Pleaded the Heterodox   744
        10.5.2   Clear Out Now, Growled the Orthodox   746
        10.5.3   Do What Is Best for You, Whispered the Faculty Board   747
        10.5.4   Time to Choose: The Sociologists Speak   748
   10.6   Leaving Home, a Space of Its Own   755
   References   758

11 Development on the Periphery: Exit and Exile   765
   11.1   Cambridge Development Studies: The Heterodox Inheritance   767
        11.1.1   The Capitalist Economy and Its Cambridge Critics   767
        11.1.2   Bridges to Development   769

11.2		Evolution of the Teaching Project: Multiple Identities	777
	11.2.1	Timelines	777
	11.2.2	In University Space: The Professionalisation of 'Development Studies'	779
		The Early Years: Fine-tuning Imperial Instruction, 1926–1969	779
		Turbulence and Transformation: Revising the Mandate, 1969–1982	787
	11.2.3	In Faculty Space: The Disciplining of 'Development Economics'	800
	11.2.4	Against the Mainstream: Subaltern Perspectives	808
11.3		Development Research: Ebbs and Flows	810
	11.3.1	Cambridge–India Highway: Cambridge in India	810
	11.3.2	Cambridge–India Highway: India in Cambridge	818
	11.3.3	Not Just India	821
	11.3.4	Bi-modal Distribution of Development Interest	826
11.4		1996: Divorce and Eviction	828
11.5		A Credible Counterfactual	832
Appendix 11.1: Arguments in Support of Continuation of Development Studies Course in Cambridge			836
References			839

12 From Riches to Rags? Economic History Becomes History at the Faculty of Economics — 845

12.1		Introduction: Economics and Economic History	846
12.2		The Pre-War Period: 1939, Marshallian	847
	12.2.1	At the Faculty of History	847
		Cunningham to Clapham via Marshall	847
		Clapham to Postan via Power	849
	12.2.2	At the Faculty of Economics and Politics	852
		Maurice Dobb, 1900–1976	852
12.3		Post-War Period-I, 1945–1980s: Post-Keynesian	860
	12.3.1	At the Faculty of Economics and Politics	860
		On the DAE Side	861
		On the Faculty Side	875
	12.3.2	At the Faculty of History	881
		'Munia' Postan	881
		The Turn to Business Studies-I, David Joslin 1965–1970	892
		The Turn to Business Studies-II, Donald Coleman 1971–1981	895
12.4		Post-War Period-II, 1980s: Unravelling and Divergence	898
	12.4.1	At the Faculty of History	898
		The Turn to Business Studies-III, Barry Supple 1981–1993	898
		Modern Times: Martin Daunton 1997–2015	899

		12.4.2	At the Faculty of Economics: Turbulence, Transitions and Affinities	902
			Cluster 1: Humphries—Horrell	903
			Cluster 2: Kitson—Solomou—Weale	914
			Cluster 3: Ogilvie—Edwards	918
			Cluster 4: Toke Aidt	924
	12.5	c.2020, Here, to Where?		926
		12.5.1	Economic History at the Faculty of Economics: Full Stop?	926
		12.5.2	At the Faculty of History: New Turnings	931
	Appendix 12.1: Economic History and Accounting at the DAE			934
	Appendix 12.2: Locating Phyllis Deane in National Accounting and Feminist Discourse: A Supplementary Note			938
	References			953
13	Research Assessment Exercises: Exorcising Heterodox Apostasy from 'Economics'			965
	13.1	The Agenda		966
	13.2	The Teaching Body: Unification, Hierarchy, Control		968
	13.3	1986: Swinnerton-Dyer and the Genesis of the RAE		973
	13.4	1986–1989: Frank Hahn and the Orthodox Capture of the RES		976
	13.5	Through the RES: Controlling Panel Selection		983
	13.6	Outcomes		989
	13.7	Consequences and Critiques		991
		13.7.1	Gaming	992
		13.7.2	Competition and Conflict: Managerialism	993
		13.7.3	Individual Stress	995
		13.7.4	Medium Over Message: Diamonds for Ever	997
		13.7.5	Unethical Research Practices and Shaky Quality Proxies	998
		13.7.6	The Atrophy of Collective Research Traditions and Environments	1000
		13.7.7	The Loss of Intrinsic Values	1001
		13.7.8	Undervaluation of Undergraduate Teaching	1002
	13.8	The Suppression of Heterodox Economics and Economists		1003
	13.9	Follow Big Brother: Elimination of Heterodoxy in USA		1007
	13.10	1662, Deja Vu		1012
	References			1014
14	Reincarnations			1019
	14.1	In a Nutshell, à la Joan		1020
	14.2	Purges and Purification		1021
	14.3	Triumphalism		1023
	14.4	A Royal Mess: The Queen's Question		1028

14.5		Students Speak Up	1031
	14.5.1	In Cambridge	1031
	14.5.2	Elsewhere	1032
14.6		Faculty Performance: A Summary Report Card	1033
	14.6.1	Global Ranks	1034
	14.6.2	RAEs, REFs	1034
14.7		Exiles and Reincarnations	1036
	14.7.1	The DAE Flagships: CGP and CEPG	1037
	14.7.2	DAE Industrial Economics: Alan Hughes and the CBR	1038
	14.7.3	Judge Business School	1038
	14.7.4	The Economic Historians	1042
	14.7.5	Sociology: That 'Vaguely Cognate Discipline'	1043
	14.7.6	Development	1043
14.8		Reluctant Regrets	1045
	14.8.1	Robin Matthews	1045
	14.8.2	Frank Hahn	1046
	14.8.3	David Newbery	1047
	14.8.4	Tony Atkinson	1048
	14.8.5	Francois Bourguignon	1052
	14.8.6	Alan Blinder	1053
	14.8.7	Peter Diamond	1054
	14.8.8	Partha Dasgupta via Robert Neild	1054
	14.8.9	Another Snowflake Moment?	1056
14.9		Donors: Leveraging a Reboot?	1057
14.10		The Great Banyan	1068
		Appendix 14.1: Letter of Protest by Graduate Students, 2001	1073
		References	1075

References 1079

Name Index 1147

Subject Index 1175

List of Tables

Table 2.1	Faculty of Economics and Politics—professorships, 1828–2000	80
Table 2.2	Early retirements in the Faculty of Economics, 1981–1985	114
Table 2.3	The CLARE Group of like-minded economists, 1977–2003	147
Table 2.4	Career tracks and the glittering prizes	156
Table 2.5	Cambridge-Oxford-LSE—Musical chairs	160
Table 2.6	Management positions in the Faculty of Economics and DAE	164
Table 2.7	Past Editors of *The Economc Journal*	165
Table 2.8	Past Presidents of Royal Economic Society	166
Table 3.1	Some honours awarded in the tenure of Margaret Thatcher, 1979–1990	266
Table 4.1	Cambridge economics seminars, 1890s–	323
Table 7.1	Timelines of actions and decisions leading up to the closure of the Cambridge Economic Policy Group, DAE Cambridge	521
Table 9.1	Research staff who have left the DAE since July 1984 or who will be leaving by the end of 1986–1987 academic year	651
Table 10.1	Three Decades of Empirical Sociology at the DAE	693
Table 11.1	A century of development teaching—A Cambridge timeline	780
Table 12.1	Economic historians at the Faculty of Economics and Politics, 1924–2021	853
Table 13.1	Presidents and council members of the Royal Economic Society, 1975–2019	980
Table 13.2	RAE panels 1989, 1992, 1996	985
Table 13.3	Journal publications of members of RAE Economics Panels 1989–1996	986
Table 13.4	References in publications of members of Economics Panels, 1989, 1992, 1996	987
Table 13.5	Standing of Cambridge economics in successive RAEs and REFs	990
Table 13.6	Elimination of heterodox economists and economics from 'economics': RAEs 1992, 2001, 2008	1005
Table 14.1	QS global ranks of selected Cambridge units, 2013–2019	1035

CHAPTER 1

Cambridge, That Was: The Crucible of Heterodox Economics

Abstract Cambridge was the crucible of heterodox economics, the habitat of several distinct lineages that took root and evolved there from the 1920s. This opening chapter sketches a frame for the overall narrative of the subsequent purge of these heterodox traditions from Cambridge economics. It offers a discursive review of the intellectual habitat, the waves of cohorts, and the emergence of divergent perspectives, leading up to drawing of new battle lines for the episodes of the elimination of heterodox traditions and lineages from the Faculty of Economics. The chapter critically assesses the notion of paradigm change, and against this backdrop goes on to provide a summary collation of an array of internal explanations of the purges, and then widens and complements these within-Cambridge interpretations with an insertion of the powerful influence and role of external forces emanating directly or indirectly and drawing their authority and power from the neoliberal worlds beyond Cambridge.

1.1 The Narrative

This book recounts an intriguing untold story in the recent evolution of Cambridge economics, adding fresh information, insights and interpretations of the traumatically turbulent period of inflexion when a systematic, serial campaign by the orthodox neoclassical group succeeded in purging virtually all branches of the grand banyan tree of diverse heterodox lineages that had taken root, flourished and matured in the fecund intellectual habitat of Cambridge over half a century since the 1920s. Cambridge was the crucible heterodox traditions in economics; yet, within the narrow time window of just about

© The Author(s), under exclusive license to Springer Nature
Switzerland AG 2022
A. Saith, *Cambridge Economics in the Post-Keynesian Era*, Palgrave
Studies in the History of Economic Thought,
https://doi.org/10.1007/978-3-030-93019-6_1

20 years, approximately 1975–1995, this great banyan was chopped down and uprooted in a succession of purges, with the 1980s forming the key decade of displacement: in quick sequence, the heterodox side lost the *Economic Journal*; saw the termination first, of the radical macroeconomic Cambridge Economic Policy Group of the Department of Applied Economics, and then five years later, of its iconic the structural macroeconomic Cambridge Growth Project; witnessed the exclusion of sociology and sociologists as part of a managed and motivated University review process that facilitated the transfer of the control of the Department of Applied Economics from the heterodox to the mainstream neoclassical group; followed later by the attritional marginalisation and exile of radical development economics and economists from the Faculty; in parallel, a steady atrophy of the long-standing lines of meaningful work on economic history; with the final rites of the virtual end of heterodox economics within the Faculty being performed through the instrumental use of the Research Assessment Exercises and its associated processes, crafted and implemented under the direction of the generals of the orthodox camp that by then controlled all the commanding heights through their legion of carefully nurtured allies, lieutenants and foot soldiers. One day it was all there, the pantheon of the modern greats of Cambridge heterodox traditions; the next, it was virtually all gone. What really happened? What explains the dramatic crash? Whodunnit, and, howdunnit?[1]

The narrative of the book unfolds in three parts.

The first part comprises four chapters. Cambridge was the crucible of heterodox economics, and the opening Chap. 1 sketches a frame for the overall narrative of its subsequent purge of its several distinctive lineages from Cambridge economics. It offers a discursive review of the intellectual habitat, the waves of cohorts, and the emergence of divergent perspectives, leading up

---

[1] Axel Leijonhufvud's teasing self-deprecating satire on his own professional tribe, the *Econ*, written (perhaps only) half in jest half a century ago still tends to ring true of its dominant mainstream lineage:

> The Econ tribe occupies a vast territory in the far North. Their land appears bleak and dismal to the outsider, and travelling through it makes for rough sledding; but the Econ, through a long period of adaptation, have learned to wrest a living of sorts from it. They are not without some genuine and sometimes even fierce attachment to their ancestral grounds, and their young are brought up to feel contempt for the softer living in the warmer lands of their neighbours, such as the Polscis and the Sociogs. Despite a common genetical heritage, relations with these tribes are strained—the distrust and contempt that the average Econ feels for these neighbours being heartily reciprocated by the latter-and social intercourse with them is inhibited by numerous taboos. The extreme clannishness, not to say xenophobia, of the Econ makes life among them difficult and perhaps even somewhat dangerous for the outsider. This probably accounts for the fact that the Econ have so far not been systematically studied. Information about their social structure and ways of life is fragmentary and not well validated. More research on this interesting tribe is badly needed. (Leijonhufvud, 1973)

to drawing of new battle lines for the episodes of the purges of heterodox traditions and lineages from the Faculty of Economics. The chapter critically assesses the notion of paradigm change, and against this backdrop collates an array of internal explanations of the purges, and then complements these within-Cambridge propositions with an insertion of the powerful influence of the neoliberal worlds beyond Cambridge. Chapter 2 deals with the Cambridge arena and provides depictions of the battle field, the opposing camps, profiles their leaders and followers, and examines their strategies and *modus operandi*; Chap. 3 explores the contexts and conjunctures beyond Cambridge and investigates the evolution of the world-wide web and political machine of the 'neoliberal thought collective', and identifies the channels and agencies through which the ideological and political power of this global force impinges on the ostensibly intra-Cambridge battle. And Chap. 4 focuses on developments, inter-camp rivalries and polarisations in interstitial academic spaces, viz., journals, seminar series and textbooks.

The second part, Chaps. 5, 6, 7, 8 and 9, covers the central core, the Department of Applied Economics (DAE) trilogy, focussing in sequence on three major transformative episodes: the closure of the Godley-Cripps Cambridge Economic Policy Group (CEPG) in 1982; the termination of the Stone-Barker Cambridge Growth Project in 1987; and the parallel four-year University Review of the DAE leading, in 1988, to the transfer of effective control of the DAE into the hands of the mainstream orthodox group, thereby giving it dominant power and control over the Faculty. Chapter 5 highlights the hallmarks of the research orientation and work of the DAE in the eras of each of its directors. The CEPG tale is told in the pair of Chaps. 6 and 7: in Chap. 6 an essential contextual account of the politically turbo-charged period of the 1970s and 1980s sets the scene for enactment of the abrupt closure of the Godley-Cripps Cambridge Economic Policy Group (CEPG) at the hands of the Social Science Research Council (SSRC), silencing its politically controversial voice by beheading its turbulent priest; and Chap. 7 offers a speculative circumstantial investigation of the wider background to this decision collating its inter-weaving with the parallel politically motivated Rothschild Enquiry into the SSRC ordered by the Thatcher government through Keith Joseph. Chapter 8 then investigates the second episode of the trilogy, the termination of the iconic, long-running Stone-Barker Cambridge Growth Project (CGP); and Chap. 9 completes the DAE Trilogy with a detailed interrogation of the unorthodox review of the DAE by the University, allegedly instigated by senior members of the orthodox camp in the Faculty, and ending with the installation of one of its core members as the new Director of the DAE.

The final, third part of the book comprises five accounts, covered in Chaps. 10, 11, 12, 13 and 14. Chapter 10 takes up the story of the departure of the sociologists from the DAE as a side-show of the University review, an objective and outcome forcefully pushed by the orthodox group as part of its campaign of purifying economics. The similar experience of the slow expulsion and atrophy of development economics and economists from the Faculty body is investigated in Chap. 11. Both episodes, of sociology and development, are developed against a review of the evolution of these subjects in Cambridge from their respective periods of inception. Chapter 12 investigates the rise, atrophy and eventual demise of the existence of economic history both from the DAE and from the Faculty of Economics. Chapter 13 turns the spotlight on the instrumental use of the new instrument of academic evaluation and control, the Research Assessment Exercises, and reveals the extent of dominance of the orthodox camp over its decision-making procedures, committees, and so its outcomes; the Research Assessment Exercise (RAE) served as the instrument of the cleansing of departments of economics of virtually all vestiges of heterodox apostasy, and the experience of Cambridge was not an exception. Finally, Chap. 14 reviews the spoils, and price, of the orthodox victory, providing some information and offering a reflection on the fates and futures of the heterodox lineages that were expelled from the Faculty of Economics; it finds the purged tribes flourishing as they relocate and revive in their new institutional homes and incarnations; meanwhile, the purified centre now cleansed of diversity, comes to resemble an inferior clone of the parent American body of orthodox mathematical economics. The narration ends with a recognition of some tentative signs of the re-emergence and recovery of some heterodox ground in the Faculty, potentially a bit more than just a sighting of the proverbial single swallow. Paradoxically, this turn is propelled by alumni donors wishing to restore meaning and method into Cambridge economics and make fit for purpose to engage with the real world living outside the confines of orthodoxy.

1.2 Evolutions and Revolutions

1.2.1 *The Great Banyan of Heterodox Traditions*

Alfred Marshall produced his bible of neoclassical economics in 1890 and defined the discipline till the mid-1920s; its eighth edition was published in 1920, the year his pupil and successor, Arthur Cecil Pigou, published his *Economics of Welfare*. Though thoroughly Marshallian and neoclassical, Pigou had brought to the forefront the critical issue of externalities, where private costs and benefits could not be equated with social costs and benefits, raising a profound limitation in the claims of neoclassical doctrine, and thereby opening up one of its fundamental internal critiques; it could be regarded as the first wave of a tide of heterodox interventions that followed. In his iconoclastic proclamation of *The End of Laissez Faire* in 1926, Keynes (1926) expresses his frustration at the stickiness of branded ideas and at the ability of the discipline simply to carry on, taking little notice of the argument which had not escaped Marshall's prior attention. "Some of the most important work of Alfred Marshall—to take one instance—was directed to the elucidation of the leading cases in which private interest and social interest are *not* harmonious. Nevertheless, the guarded and undogmatic attitude of the best economists has not prevailed against the general opinion that an individualistic *laissez-faire* is both what they ought to teach and what in fact they to teach." The second wave crashed on Marshallian neoclassical economics in the form of Piero Sraffa's 1926 *Economic Journal* article which knocked out some of the structural pillars holding up the edifice. Read alongside Allyn Young's piece of 1928, and then with Joan Robinson's *Economics of Imperfect Competition* in 1933, the neoclassical construction was in shambles. The persisting Depression and the hopelessness of that theory to provide any sensible answer set the stage for the third wave, the tsunami of the *General Theory* introducing the post-war era of Keynesian domination of macroeconomic theory and government policy through till the 1970s. Another brainchild of Keynes's fertile mind took off in parallel in 1945 with the DAE and Richard Stone, marking on the one side the start of what Samuelson called the econometric inference revolution and, on the other, the pathbreaking work on national income accounting and the macroeconomic modelling of the process and parameters of structural change in the British economy—work that attracted a 'Nobel' award; econometrics, applied and theoretical developed interactively. As practised at the DAE, this could legitimately be regarded as a fourth category of heterodox applied economics research, though it was not recognised as such by several leaders of Cambridge heterodoxy. This period also witnessed the start of the process of decolonisation; India became independent in 1947, and immediately launched a path of 'socialistic' planned development where the plan models were much inspired by the Harrod-Domar model, but more directly by the Feldman model used in Soviet planning—and several leading Cambridge heterodox economists made fundamental contributions on their visits and attachments to the Indian Planning Commission during the 1950s and 1960s; these included Dick Stone, Nicholas Kaldor, Dick Goodwin, Joan Robinson and Maurice Dobb. These were early days of planned development in the Third World, and this collective effort can be listed as a fifth strand of Cambridge heterodox economics. Back in Cambridge, most of them were deeply engaged in theorising the investment process, to dynamise and convert the Keynesian short-run template into a theory of long-term growth; Joan, Kaldor, Goodwin, Stone and Pasinetti were all deeply involved such exercises, all of them breaking fresh ground, a remarkably compact contribution in this was Goodwin's novel paper on a model of the growth cycle in the Festschrift for Maurice Dobb; these growth theory contributions constitute a sixth wave of work in the heterodox tradition. And all the while in the eaves, Piero Sraffa was beavering away constructing his extraordinary 1960 *Prelude* to his intended critique of political economy; the Sraffa theoretical lineage was unique; also to be recorded in this context is the Sraffa-Dobb 22-year effort on the works of David Ricardo—a seventh wave. Less quietly, Joan was trading sharp blows with the Americans on capital theory, a genre relatively of its own, constituting an eighth branch of the great banyan, the family tree of Cambridge heterodox economics. And finally, not to be overlooked was the work from Maurice Dobb and, separately, from Joan Robinson on the themes of Marxism and socialism, and on economic philosophy, involving much agreement and many disagreements over meanings and methods, though not on the overall mission. Depending on the point of view, other branches, beyond the nine cursorily listed, could well be identified; it was truly a grand banyan, and such was the ecology of Cambridge heterodox economics with its diverse lineages.

1.2.2 Cohorts

E. A. G. 'Austin' Robinson, the tireless institution-builder of the discipline and the keeper of its memory, arrived in Cambridge in 1920, and soon came under Keynes's wing, there to grow till Keynes died in 1946. He was 23, when Alfred Marshall, who still resided in Cambridge, was 77; Marshall's student and successor Arthur Cecil Pigou, 'the Prof' who had taken over Marshall's chair in 1908, was 43 and in that very year, 1920, had published his *Economics of Welfare*. Austin Robinson died in Cambridge 73 years later in 1993, and he had seen and been part of it all: he had started off in sight of Marshall when Cambridge economics was thoroughly neoclassical, and ended his time when that tradition, now in its general equilibrium incarnation, was again seated on the Cambridge throne. The period in between had been spectacular, both in terms of the emergence of a clutch of jostling heterodox traditions all distinct and often in vigorous debate, but all agreed in their rejection of the neoclassical doctrine, whether of Marshallian or the Walrasian stamp, and then also in terms of the remarkably rapid eclipse of these heterodox lineages as the neoclassicals took control of the Faculty from the mid-1980s. Throughout, Austin Robinson was equally a participant, an arbitrator, then an observer; and to the end he retained pride in his band of teachers: "With Pigou, Maynard Keynes, Dennis Robertson, Hubert Henderson, Frederick Lavington, Gerald Shove, Barbara Wootton—the Marshallian generation who taught me in the 1920s—we had what I believe was then the strongest faculty anywhere in the world". So said Austin Robinson in his late years, in 1989.[2]

Half a century later, these greats were all gone, but their mantle had fallen on the many broad shoulders of Austin's own cohort which measured up as well in taking the subject from the high slopes to new heights, horizons and visions. When, in the early 1970s, my cohort of young doctoral researchers found its way to Sidgwick Site, we could be forgiven for feeling that we had been beamed up into what must surely be the heaven of economics, where all those gods whose names and words we knew from our books and teachers seemed rather ethereally to be walking and talking around in our midst—it was, for a while, an awesome and eerie other-worldly feeling. By then, Austin Robinson's band of greats were memories, but we had a pantheon, that was collectively perhaps even more powerful and diverse. Its heterogeneity, its heterodoxy, arose in its acephalous formation—there was no single shining light or guiding spirit holding the scriptures—if there was something resembling this, it was the *legacy* of Keynes, with the praetorian guardians and gatekeepers to

---

[2] Austin Robinson 1989, "Colin Clark", EAGR Papers 5/7/15/1.

the temple of Keynes gaining inherited authority over all comers wanting entry, validation or blessings. But there were more modern gods and goddesses, taking the subject beyond *The General Theory*, as Keynes surely himself might have done had he had more time. The generation of Keynesian apostles boasted the arts and crafts of Austin Robinson, Piero Sraffa, Joan Robinson, Richard Kahn, Nicky Kaldor, David Champernowne, Maurice Dobb, Richard Stone, Brian Reddaway, Richard Goodwin, Phyllis Deane, Robert Neild, Wynne Godley, Robin Matthews, and one should rightly stretch it to include Pierangelo Garegnani, Luigi Pasinetti and Geoff Harcourt, the last two being the youngest in the array of the greats, and now the senior most inheritors and gurus of the Cambridge tradition of grand theorising; the list runs in birth order and spans exactly 30 years, with Austin Robinson born in 1897, and Matthews in 1927, or to 33 years adding the last three. Maurice Dobb died young at 64 in 1976, but apart from that, the full pantheon was in regal authority till the ranks started thinning out from 1983 when Joan died on Piero's birthday, and Piero himself following less than a month later. Of course, retirements had kicked in seriously from the 1970s, so perhaps the mid-1970s till the early 1980s could well be highlighted as being the apogee of the heterodox Cambridge apostles.

The third cohort comprises the radical, general left-oriented young turks, following the heterodox pathways opened by the inheritors of the Keynesian tradition. Typically, this would be the group born approximate in the 1935–1950 period, and formed the backbone of the DAE and the Faculty; there were some very fine economists among them and collectively they formed quite a formidable force and diversified resource.[3] They had different predilections and questions they wanted to pursue, of course; the era of grand theorising was yielding to policy-oriented applied economics, and from individual to team work. Austin Robinson, of the second cohort, compared notes with Luigi Pasinetti of the third cohort, about the standing of the fourth cohort, where they seem to agree that old was indeed gold.[4]

---

[3] The list would include Francis Cripps, Ajit Singh, Bob Rowthorn, John Eatwell, Mario Nuti, Ron Smith, John Wells and Michael Kuczynski, not to mention the battalion of young turks at the DAE, Ken Coutts, Roger Tarling, Hashem Pesaran, Vani Borooah, Angus Deaton, Mervyn King, Michael Ellman, Terence Ward, Frank Wilkinson, Geoff Whittington, Tony Lawson, Terry Barker, Nick von Tunzelmann, John Llewellyn, Martin Weale, Martin Fetherston, Michael Landesmann, Rick van der Ploeg and several others. Many of them, especially those in the two macroeconomic modelling teams of the DAE would have left during the 1980s.

[4] Austin Robinson writes: "I cannot escape from thinking that Cambridge economics of the 1930s had a vigour and contribution that was greater than that of the present generation. But that may merely be that I do not read enough of what they write, and I am not sure that I know what are the questions that they are trying to answer" (*Letter, Austin Robinson to Luigi Pasinetti, Letter 71, dated 4 March 1992*).

Luigi Pasinetti responds: "I tend to agree with you that the Cambridge economists of the 1930s were an extraordinary generation. You have all justification to be proud. The present generation is perhaps better trained, but is a more ordinary one—more similar to what one can find in other universities."

Letter, Luigi Pasinetti to Austin Robinson, Letter 50, dated 11 March 1992.

All these contributions, some sequential and many overlapping, were made over the half century from the 1920s to the 1970s and collectively they showcased Cambridge as the crucible of heterodox economics. The quarter century after the war, till the Organization of the Petroleum Exporting Countries (OPEC) price hike of 1973, have been labelled the golden age of British and west European capitalism; during that window, the pantheon of the Cambridge heterodox lineages was visible in full glory—the period could with justification also be called also the golden age of Cambridge heterodox economics.

Which of these interventions qualifies as repair, or reform, or as a revolution will vary with the assessor. Paul Samuelson (1987, p. 26) recognises four revolutions: "Shortly after 1930 economics burst out into new life. At least four revolutions erupted: the monopolistic competition revolution, the Keynesian macro revolution, the mathematicization revolution, and the econometric inference revolution." He skips over Pigou's welfare economics, and highlights Joan Robinson on imperfect competition, though she herself walked away from it later, famously calling it "a shameful fudge"; nor, in this context does he mention Sraffa's 1926 paper which set off the anti-marginalist trend in Cambridge. Maria Cristina Marcuzzo (2003, p. 545), while recognising imperfect competition and effective demand, cites "capital theory" as the third revolution in which Joan Robinson participated; not surprisingly, Samuelson jumps straight over this storm which in some respects exposed foundational cracks in the neoclassical theoretical edifice. Notably too, Samuelson's first two revolutions address substantive issues in the discipline, where last two concern matters of method and not substance, possibly on his presumption that he had sorted out key matters of substance already. There is no explicit reference to general equilibrium economics on the one side; or to the political text of Hayek's game-changing *The Road to Serfdom* published in 1944 (just short of Samuelson's textbooks) which launched the parallel neoliberal political revolution led by Hayek and Friedman from Chicago; the two establishments, albeit with their variational perspectives, formed a powerful symbiosis in the spread of free-market theory and embedding it globally at the core of neoliberal policy from the 1980s. These, including his own neoclassical synthesis and the Lucasian rational expectations turn, are all subsumed in the 'mathematical revolution'. The Keynesian revolution was losing momentum in the 1970s, just as the neoclassical and neoliberal revolutions were rising to unchecked supremacy, with the 1975–1980 period as the point of inflexion. For the new American mathematical-economics mainstream, the Cambridge Keynesian and other heterodox traditions were now passé, historical relics. In his *The End of Laissez Faire*, Keynes (1926) had cautioned: "A study of the history of opinion is a necessary preliminary to the emancipation of the mind. I do not know which makes a man more conservative—to know nothing but the present, or nothing but the past." Samuelson, with his mathematical revolution, had loaded students with much more homework: "Graduate students need at least 4 hours a night of sleep: that is a universal constant. So something had to give in the economics curriculum. What gave, and gave out, was history of economic thought—followed quickly by attrition of foreign language requirements and of minima for economic history" (Samuelson, 1987, p. 26). Economic theory was being rebooted; the old disc scrubbed clean.

1.2.3   The Cambridge Habitat

Cambridge Economics traditionally had scattered locations: lecturing was done by Faculty staff in university halls, but the really intensive week by week grinding supervisions of undergraduates were conducted by teaching fellows is scattered College studies, under the eye of the college Director of Studies for Economics, only some of whom might hold teaching positions in the Faculty. There was little scope for interaction on common ground, especially for College and Faculty staff, and communications generally took the form of handwritten notes on college pads, conveyed and fetched several times a day by the internal university postal system; even when telephones were installed, many seniors, including Joan Robinson, preferred to keep to their old ways. Interactions were thus by appointment, or in some of the select weekly seminars. A third site of Cambridge economics was conceived in 1939, and delivered after the War in 1945, in the form of a Department of Applied Economics (DAE), a creation of Keynes. Richard Stone was appointed Director, remaining in that position till 1955 when, in a *fait accompli*, he was obliged by the Committee of Management to choose between the posts of Director of the DAE, or the new P. D. Leake Professorship of Finance and Accounting on offer. A displeased Stone opted for the latter, and Brian Reddaway became the Director of the DAE in 1955 for the 15 years till his retirement in 1970. In the interim, Stone's research interests were enshrined and protected in the Cambridge Growth Project (CGP) that was initiated by him and Alan Brown in 1960, and which flourished thereafter, receiving generous support from various external donors, but after 1967 primarily reliant on substantial grants from the SSRC. In 1969, Wynne Godley took over the Directorship in 1970, and in 1971, he added to the DAE spectrum of projects initiated under the open minded and eclectic approach of Reddaway, with his own research initiative in the form of the Cambridge Economic Policy Group (CEPG) of which he was the Director, and Francis Cripps—who came across to the DAE from his Faculty position as his close research partner. The CEPG, like the CGP, was sustained on various external financial grants, again with a significant amount from the SSRC. Godley's term of office, again a maximum of 15 years was to end in 1985. While the CGP dealt with medium- and long-term structural change in the UK economy, and generated forecasts for the future, the CEPG was much more focussed on current macroeconomic policy issues based on its forecasting methods, progressively including modelling, While CGP was the quiet, solid senior project that carried on at its steady pace, CEPG, by its inherent nature, was continually engaged in the cut and thrust and volatility of day-to-day policy issues, which inevitably were embedded in the politics of the times. The two projects, of

Stone and Godley, hardly interacted and had a mutually congenial but independent co-existence in the DAE.

The physical geography of Cambridge economics changed dramatically from 1961 after the completion, at Sidgwick Site, of the Faculty Building, which was rightly named after the quiet builder and, using Geoff Harcourt's words, unsung hero of Cambridge economics, Austin Robinson, on his ninetieth birthday in 1987 (Newbery, 2017, p. 492). The building also had generous housing for the expanding DAE, and for the first time in its history, the larger part of the Cambridge lecturing and research staff came together, sharing the Marshall Library, the Buttery and Staff Common Room, the seminar and lecture halls; corridor and coffee-time meetings now happened far more frequently by chance and serendipity; ideas and ideologies got contested; conflicts generated, resolved, reinvented and regurgitated; if information exchange was a key ingredient in the realisation of externalities and spillover effects, the congregated Faculty provided a good industrial illustration. That was the buzzing and bustling, veritably a beehive environment, that the quiet sustained efforts of Austin Robinson had brought into being.

Since its inception, the DAE had progressively built a formidable national and international reputation: first through the work of the team led by the Stone-Brown partnership centred on the CGP; then enhanced it further through the widening of the scope of research interests under Brian Reddaway who was widely regarded as one of the top applied economists of the country; and finally built on this wider base, including the ongoing CGP (led by Stone till his retirement in 1980, and subsequently by his erstwhile deputy, Terry Barker) through the high-profile CEPG launched by Godley. By the mid-1980s, the DAE team had grown to include nearly 40 researchers, and thus had a size approximately similar to the Faculty across the open foyer. Of these, the two modelling units each had about 10 regulars, and the rest were engaged in a variety of individual and small-group research projects, including those of sociologists based in the DAE.

The open and wide-angled vision of the founding fathers of the DAE foresaw the significance of applied research to complement and interact with the pure theory concerns that had made Cambridge economics famous, and perhaps owed a great deal to the Whitehall work of Keynes and others before and during the war years; and then especially to Keynes who regularly pulled in brilliant young economists from London to Cambridge, including, in the context of the DAE, Richard Stone and James Meade to launch the work on national accounting. But this was not all: for long in the Faculty, and from its origins in the DAE, there was an active presence of sociology and sociologists as researchers, sometimes co-existing, but intended progressively to enter meaningful research partnerships of a multidisciplinary kind. The seniors were aware that economics could not be practised meaningfully or usefully in theory alone, or within its own set disciplinary boundaries. The massive reputation, research and publication record of the Faculty and the DAE bear testimony to the success of the early vision, all the known internal problems of Cambridge economics notwithstanding. It would probably be widely accepted that the apogee of Cambridge economics was in the decade of 1970s when a diverse range of vibrant theoretical and ideological lineages fought it out in the journals, seminars and committees; Cambridge in this period boasted a pantheon of the greats that has perhaps never since been matched and, in the phalanx behind, a rising generation of creative, accomplished and socially engaged theoretical and applied economists of various cohabiting heterodox clans. The most remarkable feature perhaps was that while various theoretical faiths, sects and cults engaged in sharp intellectual contests, they also managed to co-exist as a larger disciplinary, collegiate and collegial body; but underlying this gigantic banyan tree of heterodoxy was a central line of fracture: that between the neoclassicals and the rest, the latter comprising a wide spectrum of core theoretical, and implied ideological, identities rooted in Ricardo, Marx, Keynes, Sraffa or latterly Joan Robinson.

1.2.4 Which Cambridge?

Both Partha Dasgupta and Tony Lawson, from different sides of the Faculty division, had made the journey from LSE to Cambridge—separately, it should be immediately clarified—and their first impressions make an interesting pair.

A viscerally antagonistic perspective is provided with remarkable candour by Partha Dasgupta, brought into the Faculty by Hahn and Matthews in 1985, by which time the radical Cambridge traditions were in steep decline; having been involved with administration from the start and being Chairman of the Faculty (1997–2001), his observations, made from the opposite, orthodox ideological camp, see it all differently. In an extended interview with Alan Macfarlane, Dasgupta says: "When I arrived here I found the Cambridge Economics Faculty to be awful; a number of significant figures from the 1930s, Joan Robinson, Nicky Kaldor, and Richard Kahn had wanted to protect Cambridge economics from the increased post-War use in the US of maths and stats; they conducted a secret economics seminar to which only chosen colleagues were invited; that they used ideology to determine an economic argument was bad enough, but they also mistook technical tools for ideology; they were Keynes's disciples; but the successors had few intellectual credentials, and right through the 1970s they encouraged the appointment of mediocrities so long as they in turn showed a disdain toward modern economics; when I arrived in Cambridge in 1985 I thought I had entered a cesspool; the Faculty of Economics in 1985 was wholly politicized and filled with mediocre people; they didn't lack self-confidence though; they were able to shelter themselves from outside competition by virtue of a lack of central directives from the university; the college system also gave them separate power bases; that's one weakness of the collegiate system; say your college has a Fellow in economics; as he is the only economist in the Fellowship, his is the only voice that's heard in Hall or at Governing Body meetings; so you come to believe what he says about his subject or about others in his department; he tells you there are different methods of doing economics, even different schools of thought, each having equal merit; that convinces you, especially when he breathes the words 'diversity of viewpoints' or 'heterodoxy' in your ear." Dasgupta complains that his favourite professors "were routinely outvoted in Faculty Board deliberations on matters having to do with teaching, research, and appointments; the electoral rules made no sense to me; the Faculty Board was all powerful, but in effect was able to elect itself, because it controlled who could vote in Faculty Board elections". And then some candid remarks: "on the rare occasion I managed to squeeze in the right appointment, I had to take recourse to underhand practice; I hated that, it was corrupting"; but he goes on to say: "I was Chairman for five years and enjoyed that greatly"; "I guess over time I gained the confidence of colleagues in the university", thereby countering the influence of the Faculty Board; and he tells us that "matters changed once the Research Assessment Exercise (RAE) was instituted by the government and the Faculty of Economics scored a 4, which concentrated the minds of the university authorities". The RAE scoring criteria, of course, largely reflected the valuations of external mainstream ideology. This vituperative diatribe effectively sums up the orthodox perspectives and players that the heterodox schools were up against.[5]

Tony Lawson—one of the handful of heterodox survivors of the lost war—entered the same environment that Dasgupta calls "a cesspool"; but though he, like Dasgupta, regarded himself "as a bit of an outsider", critical of many heterodox theoretical positions, his recollections run rather differently.

"The other thing I remember in this early period [1970s and 1980s] was that there existed an environment of critical debate within Cambridge. In contrast to my experience of the LSE, I found in Cambridge that everybody wanted to talk about her or his current views. I appreciated that. At the LSE everyone was so secretive. I still remember a research student telling me that he had an equation that he thought was the answer to everything. I asked him 'What's the equation?' and he replied, 'It's a secret and I'm not going to tell anyone until I've published it'. Cambridge was the opposite. People seemed less bothered about publishing; they were much more concerned with developing insights or ideas and then convincing others who happened to be around" (Dunn, 2009, pp. 482–483). "It was a good environment, even though a lot of the debates were heated and sometimes people fell out with each other. I enjoyed it anyway. After the LSE, which I found to be so boring and so intellectually unsatisfactory, Cambridge was intensely stimulating. There was a lot of creative thinking, and, knowingly or not, it seems that a lot of the foundations for Post Keynesianism were laid here" (ibid., p. 489). "Yes, Cambridge *was* insular. At least this was so for the group of heterodox economists ... if it didn't happen in Cambridge then they were not especially interested. But a lot did happen in Cambridge; there were a lot of arguments, a lot of debate, it was lively, it was open to all willing and able to enter the environment. And it was really sincere, everyone was deeply involved; even the monetarists joined in.

[5] Dasgupta (2010).

Each person or group seemed concerned to win the others over, especially new people. ... Now that's all gone. The concern is more with proving theorems and such like. Students mostly don't like it and lecturers don't really talk to each other about substantive or political matters. I think it's a shame, a real loss. Given the emphasis on modelling at the expense of realisticness worldwide, I would welcome a bit more isolationism in Cambridge if it allowed a return to greater relevance" (ibid., pp. 483–484). These views come not from a card-carrying heterodox insider, but from one who says, "I was a bit of an outsider all round. ... However, I must add that as unpopular or different as my views were, the Cambridge left or heterodoxy were always very positive on a personal level, they were always ready to include me. Intellectual differences did not get in the way of friendships" (ibid., p. 488).

Another classic Cambridge feature, certainly on the heterodox side, was the imperceptible yet ubiquitous phenomenon that is best characterised as collective intellectual osmosis. Writing on Cambridge as a place of economics, Maria Cristina Marcuzzo (2012, pp. 18–19) invokes the wizened Austin Robinson reminding everyone of the Cambridge tradition of the collective, not individual, ownership of ideas: "When a small group is constantly arguing together, arguing with their pupils and arguing with others outside, one seldom knows exactly who was initially response for which elements in the collective thinking, and any one person may be transmitting collective rather than individual ideas". As is well known this norm applied to many of the Cambridge Greats, including many of their Great Works, and the tradition had taken firm root. Geoff Harcourt (Harcourt and King, 1995, p. 41) provides both an elaboration and an exception: speaking of working relationships and the flow of ideas between Joan Robinson, Lorie Tarshis, Kalecki and Kahn, he says: "Joan was a great synthesizer: they claimed that they did economics as a team. It didn't matter who wrote it up. They discussed it and then someone wrote it up. And as Kahn had trouble writing, and Joan didn't, she got into the habit of writing up their ideas, and it wasn't until Nicky came that he told Frank Hahn, 'Don't you dare talk to that woman! She will steal my ideas from you.'" Harcourt (Harcourt and King, 1995, p. 40) refers to "the fight between her and Nicky because each accused the other of having pinched the other's ideas".[6] "So there was this idea, Austin Robinson put it very neatly, that 'Private property in ideas only came with the Ph.D.'" (Harcourt and King, 1995, p. 41). Leaving the Ph.Ds. to their own devices, very many other illustrations could be listed; recently, Francis Cripps, writing about the pathbreaking work at the DAE and in the Faculty on the deindustrialisation of the UK economy during the politically and intellectually tempestuous 1970s, observes: "A lot of things came out of

---

[6] "They were both giant egos. Joan was better at hiding hers than Nicky was. Nicky never thought there was any need to hide his ego at all. But I think he didn't like this notion that anyone could write down his ideas. He said that if he thought them up he ought to publish them. And Nicky thought that he'd thought of every idea in economics anyway! It was one of his endearing qualities, I think" (Harcourt and King, 1995, p. 48).

discussion among a wide group of people and priority was not much of a concern in the Cambridge of those days, at least for the left. What mattered was building positions together (as opposed to traditional academics who worked alone). Ajit Singh was very prescient in understanding the contributions of different people and bringing them together in a way that eventually made the foundation and survival of the *Cambridge Journal of Economics* possible."[7] This chimes with Tony Lawson's experience comparing stifling LSE secretiveness and refreshing Cambridge openness in intellectual exchange. One could be forgiven for wondering if Partha Dasgupta and Tony Lawson alighted at the same railway station.[8]

1.3 REGIME CHANGE

Despite their great history and formidable strength and diversity, Cambridge heterodox traditions and lineages atrophied and virtually evanesced from the Faculty in the period thereafter, as the Faculty, and the DAE, lapsed and collapsed into the control of the neoclassical orthodox camp within the Faculty led initially by Frank Hahn and Robin Matthews, with the 1975–1990 forming the short period of inflexion. How did this remarkable turnaround occur? How could the diverse and productive intellectual ecology that flourished and formed that great banyan tree of Cambridge heterodox traditions mutate so rapidly into a genetically modified single-strain industrial mono-cropping culture? How were intellectual imaginations and curiosities lobotomised? Cambridge economics had not been built in a day, but given the dramatic speed of change, it seemed to have been dismantled in one. The Purges restored orthodoxy giving it comprehensive control over the Faculty viewed as a site of knowledge production.

The habitat of Cambridge economics had forever been a veritable battleground with continual warfare between the orthodox neoclassical camp and the variously and variably combined bands of various co-existing heterodox lineages which, while more than often agreeing disagree amongst themselves, tended always to agree in their shared opposition to the orthodox camp. The continued existence and organic development of the banyan tree of heterodox traditions owed everything to the younger radical economists that consistently and successfully fought to nourish and protect this magically productive, even if introverted, intellectual environment. The story takes the form, then, not

---

[7] Francis Cripps, personal communication, email dated 10 February 2018.

[8] Triangulation comes in the form of recollections of Michael Landesmann who obtained his PhD in Oxford (1975–1978) when economics there was run by Jim Mirrlees and was under the "total control of the Oxbridge neoclassical combine"; Michael described Oxford economics as having a "restrictive atmosphere" that offered "a limiting experience". He recalled being "refreshed" by entering the DAE in Cambridge in 1980—he stayed till 1993; he "enjoyed entering what he called the Cambridge 'zone'—much freer, more open and with many more conversations". This has resonance with Tony Lawson's account of the ethos of practitioners of Cambridge heterodox economics (personal communication, conversations with Michael Landesmann, July 2019.).

just of the fight over and for ideas and theories, but for the material and institutional means underpinning the contending traditions. In turn, this calls for projects of recovery of individual and collective memory of shared experience in this critical phase in the life of Cambridge economics.

It is not enough then, to limit the frame of reference and line of vision simply to the theoretical dimensions of disputes between traditions; no doubt these constituted the heart of the matter. But great 'truths' can be brought down by 'falsehoods' through the exercise of institutional power over definitions and recognition of what constitutes 'useful knowledge' in the first place. Thus, the Cambridge Faculty of economics needs also to be viewed as a site of knowledge production. How is control captured, maintained and utilised, over this production site? This leads to an exploration of the material/institutional roots of ideological power. How did the control over Cambridge knowledge production in economics change hands, shift from the protagonists of one tradition to those of another? This was not through some abstract, pure fight of ideas—you could win that and still not be able to claim the victory in the textbooks, in the setting of curricula or exam questions, in the appointment of new staff or key examiners, in the selection and admission of new inflows of PhD researchers, etc. This was a lesson that Joan would often ruefully verbalise in the context of her feeling she had won the ideas war in the trans-Atlantic capital controversy, and yet lost the wider war for what was taught and by whom in the key process of intellectual reproduction.[9] The narrative here

---

[9] A two-page typescript note, 'The State of Play' written in February 1976 by Joan begins thus: "As the 'mainstream' teachers of economics are unable to defend the logic of their position but go on teaching just the same, I feel that we ought to carry the argument onto a wider front" (Robinson, 1976). She clearly wants to shift the goalposts from the neoclassical trinity of "what, how and for whom to produce" towards structural, institutional and systemic issues of economic organisation within which production and distribution are carried out. The agenda-setting note, written in typical Joan-style, reads like a cryptic aide-memoire and provides a string of bottom lines: "I suppose that we all agree with the following propositions, but they need to be worked out in detail". Joan lists five points. The first declares: "'Capital' is not a 'factor of production'. Capitalism is a particular economic system in which the command of finance permits production to organised by employment labour, supplying other inputs, incurring costs in advance of proceeds and making profits. Profits are related to the finance supplied and not to the 'productivity' of physical inputs." This sets the systemic parameters. She moves to reject the idea of any generic opposition between growth, or GNP, and welfare, a là 'old-fashioned welfare economics': the trade-off reflects the lack of choice under capitalism—"welfare has to be sacrificed to growth, when the two do not coincide, because we have no other way of getting our needs supplied except as a by-product of the pursuit of profit". From this macro observation, she moves to the question of resource allocation; "mainline teaching is rooted in the conception that the market allocates resources between uses"; she flatly rejects this, arguing that at any moment, there is "very little room for choice"—"there is a certain range over which 'market forces' play, but it is very narrow". Investment decisions are controlled and made by governments and "the competitive struggle of big corporations". She proceeds to questioning the role of external investments, loans and 'aid' in the context of the Third World, arguing that their impact is generally overstated and often negative. The final set of observations concern the familiar Cambridge theme of the choice of techniques which she calls 'very complicated'. She again questions 'mainline teaching' where the choice of techniques is discussed "in terms of 'factors of production', 'labour and capital', those costs are

addresses Joan's paradox and deals not with the theoretical dimensions of the conflicts—that is a separate, though not entirely independent enquiry—but sketches the processes and mechanisms through which control over the process of knowledge production was ceded by the heterodox schools and captured, after a sustained multi-site, multi-year campaign by the neoclassical camp. The victories were achieved not through any demonstration of the superiority of their bag of abstractions, ideas, theoretical notions or potions; rather, control was cumulatively and sequentially wrested through the exertion of effective power in a string of decision-making bodies and committees—both inside and outside the University framework—which were influenced and persuaded to reverse their earlier support for the projects of key research groups of the heterodox formation, thus undermining their survival. The focus of the proposed book, therefore, is not on the relative merits of contending theoretical perspectives, but squarely on the Faculty of Economics as an institutional site of knowledge production.

The decline and demise of heterodox traditions was an extended experience of institutional violence that successively attacked or neutralised different parts of the body of heterodox economics. This narrative then takes the form of a string of stories of these sequential purges, constructing and deconstructing each particular episode in this process. The strategists and strategies of the warring sides are first introduced. Then follow investigations of the series of episodes. The decline is presaged by the emigration, or capture by the mainstream, of the *Economic Journal* in 1976. Then follows the dismal DAE trilogy: first, the daylight mugging of the outspoken Godley-Cripps macroeconomic policy and forecasting group CEPG by the SSRC; second, the subjection of the Stone-Barker Growth Project CGP to running and perishing in the SSRC/ESRC (Economic and Social Research Council) gauntlet; and third, the

---

wages and interest. Applying this in the Third World leads to the argument that wages ought to be as low as possible so as to encourage employment and it leads to the paradoxical view that high interest rates are propitious to increasing employment." Here she makes an intriguing allusion that "the Dobb-Sen thesis that developing countries should instal profit maximising techniques because they yield the greatest surplus is an aberration". She sees it differently, and inserts a familiar point of emphasis reflecting her increasing interest in development issues in later years: "China and North Korea have shown how a developing country can organise full employment; countries which cannot follow that path could still make some improvements. *The problem must be approached not as choice of techniques but as the choice of the form of economic organisation.* Alternative 'labour intensive' techniques exist for almost all products but they require an alternative system of organisation. Cooperatives and small-scale family businesses give much more employment per unit of investment that capitalist factories" (emphasis added). Thus, Joan completes the circle, returning to her starting point, emphasising the salience of the specification of the overall economic system within which choices and decisions are to be made about resource use, production and distribution. The note was obviously intended to spark exchanges over how, in her words, "to carry the argument to a wider front". It is notable that she explicitly included 'the Third World' into her sketch. Her analytical imagination and template transcended the narrow perspective and parameters of neoclassicism, and her concerns were far wider than the sometimes abstruse cross-Atlantic controversies where Joan's persistence was unable to overcome American resistance to accepting defeat.

motivated DAE Reviews conducted, seemingly independently and in parallel, by the General Board of Cambridge University, with multiple outcomes—the prime one being the installation of a standard bearer of the Hahn-led neoclassical group as the Director to replace Wynne Godley. Then follows another intrinsically negative outcome of these Reviews in the expedited departure of sociology and sociologists from the DAE, signalling the beginning of the end of the multidisciplinary imagination and project within the economics formation. Economic history quietly dissolves and fades away into history through processes of natural wastage or unnatural neglect.

This story of the return to narrow orthodox disciplinary boundaries has a prolonged sequel within the Faculty and concerns development economics and development studies, which after a period of productive expansion are systematically purged from the Faculty of Economics and banished from the centre to peripheral locations. The attention then turns to the purge of the heterodox economic traditions within the Faculty of Economics itself, facilitated, or manipulated, through the instrumental use of the Research Assessment Exercises (RAEs) and the later Research Excellence Frameworks (REFs) that consolidate the power and hold of the neoclassical mainstream over teaching and research in economics countrywide. At the end of this process, Applied Economics, as an independent Department, ceases to exist and is absorbed into the Faculty in 2004; and in the same year, the Faculty of Economic purifies itself by dropping '& Politics' from its name. The campaign of purges and cleansing, and the rituals of purification are all complete, and the neoclassicals have the place exclusively to themselves, with everyone else out of the subject and the building.

How is this tale to be read? Is it a story of defeat: Troy destroyed after the Trojan horse, in the form of Frank Hahn, is pulled into the city centre of Cambridge economics by the unsuspecting and unlikely duo of Kaldor and Reddaway? Checkmate in three moves by the international chess problematist Robin Matthews? "The truth is this to me and that to thee", and indeed, while the reality of defeat is undoubtedly one painful truth, it is perhaps not the only one to take from this tale. The final part of this book offers a wider reflection, not just on the day, but also on the decades, after these individual battles were lost. Nothing stays won, or lost, forever; the various 'defeated' heterodox bands and brigades reassemble, reform and, phoenix like, rise again in their own 'peripheral' spaces, where defeats get transformed into fresh gains, and those marginalised on the periphery become vibrant new centres. However reassuring and plausible might be such an interpretation of rebuilding victory from the dismantled bricks of defeat, there is nevertheless a core incontrovertible and inescapable truth of the proverbial paradise lost, even if in the form of a counterfactual imaginary, the loss of a flourishing intellectually synergetic, heterodox world of multiple disciplines and traditions that might have been.

How could such a powerhouse, winning most of its battles, wind up losing the war? How was this seemingly impregnable citadel overrun and captured, its inhabitants marginalised or exiled? Not unexpectedly, from the survivors of heterodox camps, there are many answers but no consensus. Perhaps it is time to revisit the battlegrounds, search for new evidence, uncover buried realities, look beyond the walls of the colleges and the City, seek more definitive understandings. This is what the proposed book attempts albeit in a limited way.

This story it narrates could be dismal, if you stand on one side of the barricades, or smugly satisfying if your coordinates place you on the other. If you indeed think of both as imposters, and actually treat both just the same, you could escape both the misery of loss as well as the exhilaration of victory and read it just as another narrative in a hypothesised long-term trajectory of paradigm changes. But for both sides, this is also a cautionary tale, since victories are seldom absolute or permanent. I am not proposing some cyclical theory, only suggesting that both winning and losing have a lot to do with the material and conjunctural circumstances in which either occurs. Perhaps the idiom of cycles is less appropriate than that of continuities and breaks, rather in a Schumpeterian, or a Marxian frame of history. The vicissitudes in the fortunes, or misfortunes, of Cambridge economic traditions offer a context for such ruminations. Long periods of build-up, a revolutionary break which transforms and shifts the frame altogether, then the empire fighting back and restoring its secular supremacy, with those fighting the subaltern corner biding their time for the next propitious moment in the future when material and ideological constellations combine to enable another round of revolutionary change in thinking, Viewed through such a window, the Cambridge era divides into the long Marshallian era; then the build-up of contra revolutionary forces from various quarters of internal disaffection, leading to the installation of a new god, a new scripture, a new way, the Keynesian path—but with the revolutionary victory proving, with the perfect hindsight of the historian, to be an interregnum between the intellectual regime that it overthrew, and itself being overthrown or cast aside by an inexorable process of the restoration of a new incarnation of the ideas propagating the free market with its underlying political philosophy of individualism and the rule of private property. Looking back, there is Luigi's Lament, about "the treasure squandered", where the cumulative gains and achievements of the cohort of the heterodox greats was dismantled and discarded wilfully and vengefully. But, keeping an ear to the ground, there are also whispers and proximate rumblings, growing ever so steadily louder, of signs of life on the periphery, the spotting of green shoots, the construction of new homes and locations, of re-rooting and transplanting to other more congenial, or at least less hostile, intellectual terrains and more open ideological environments.

For three decades immediately after the War, UK economics, unquestionably Keynesian, matured and dominated the university lecture rooms as well as the corridors of official policy making. They were all Keynesians then, albeit with some murmurings of criticism, and variations in the interpretation of the General Theory and its adaptation for the world of policy intervention. The point, or the onset of the period, of inflexion came in second half of the 1970s. While Cambridge economics, whether in its Keynesian form or in of its several other heterodox incarnations, flourished in these decades of its golden age, the processes that would challenge and systematically bring it down had already begun to emerge and take hold, even if in a barely perceptible, scattered manner. By the mid-1970s, as Cambridge economics was at its apogee, the networks and forces of opposition had also grown to full strength and maturity. While this challenge was most characteristically visible and audible in Cambridge in the belligerence and bellicosity in the person and personality of Frank Hahn, a world-wide web of networks of neoclassical and neoliberal adversaries had steadily evolved in the USA, in Europe, and elsewhere in the UK. These geographically dispersed networks were sufficiently interconnected to qualify as a global web constituted of smaller semi-autonomous molecular structures connecting academic, political, advocacy, media and lay constituencies. The chemistry holding these structures together came from their shared zealous, uncompromising adherence to the cause of liberalism, neoliberalism, libertarianism or any other preferred variant in that ideological lineage tracking its proximate intellectual origins back to the Chicago libertarians inspired by Hayek and von Mises on the one side, and to the MIT-Harvard general equilibrium clans of Samuelson and Solow on the other. This global ideological formation has been christened as the Neoliberal Thought Collective by Mirowski and Plehwe (2009), and the last decade has seen a great deal of attention being focussed on the rise, reach and power of this seemingly acephalous ideological force. The eclipse of Cambridge Keynesian and other heterodox traditions from the 1970s was not just an internal phenomenon, a defeat in a local academic or departmental brawl within Cambridge. There was indeed a carefully organised neoclassical assault within Cambridge led by Frank Hahn, Robin Matthews and others; but this campaign drew its strength crucially from direct and indirect support from their counterparts in the external world that was increasingly dominated by this neoliberal thought collective. The evolution of this seemingly amorphous and acephalous, yet well integrated and coordinated world-wide web of neoliberalism can be traced back to a few significant pioneers and launching pads, each with its distinct provenance. This movement evolves from one that is a voice of opposition to state-led Keynesian macroeconomic and socially oriented welfare policies, into a dominant force that overturns the old consensus and replaces it with the universal ideology of the free market at the global level. In Cambridge, just a few years after the launch of his *General Theory*, Keynes had organised a study for Hayek at King's College during the war years; that is where he wrote his *The Road to Serfdom* which quickly became the bible and proselytising tract of the anti-Keynesian and anti-socialist free-market fundamentalists. The battle lines were drawn, resulting eventually in the capture of the Keynesian, heterodox citadel in Cambridge by the two-pronged pincer assault from Chicago and 'the other' Cambridge.

Time, as the aphorism goes, was invented to prevent everything from happening at the same time; and paraphrasing Joan Robinson, space was invented to prevent everything from happening in Cambridge. But, while a world unto itself it might well have been, there *were* worlds beyond Cambridge, and also very much so in economics. Where, when, and how, did these two worlds, of Cambridge and the Rest of the World, interface, articulate, converge or collide? I use this as a device of convenience to narrate two nested stories, the 'closed', and the 'open' versions. This, after a quick traverse across a small selection of commentaries on the 'how' and 'why' of regime, or paradigm, change in Cambridge economics.

1.3.1 The World of Cambridge: Stories Within

Multiple Explanations of the Decline
There is a collection of explanations for paradigm and regime change which focus on factors within Cambridge economics: some would seem off the mark, some which carry weight but are still not sufficient for accounting for the overturn, and then an untold story which, while complete in itself, regards the regime change as essentially a phenomenon that was internal to Cambridge, which started and ended there, where all the battles and the adversaries are located in that space. Some of these are dead ends, some others offer partial leads, and a selective combination can construct a more integrated 'internal' version of an untold story of the purges which nevertheless remains incomplete on account of treating Cambridge as a closed space, analogous to the 'closed economy'.[10]

The first, frequently encountered, 'explanation' points a resentful finger at the inbred insularity, the contented complacency, and smug sense of entitlement ascribed to cocooned Cambridge, almost invariably from quarters not located within it; and so, the seniors remained in a state of benign oblivion. Then, the scene turns mean with direct accusations of the 'irrelevance' of 'dogmatic' and 'doctrinal', 'ideological' passions and obsessions, and the usual suspect cited here is Joan Robinson and the 'capital' controversies—a charge well refuted by Harcourt. A third complaint, voiced from inside, Godley raises the unlikely charge that the modern greats of Cambridge left no legacies, syntheses, textbooks. A fourth factor cites a lack of internal cohesiveness between the diverse heterodox traditions and their proponents, with intellectual differences carrying over into the personal domain, thereby undermining unity of collective purpose. And a fifth, contextual, explanation points to demographics, with an unusually concentrated pattern of near-simultaneous retirements and deaths. All these collectively contribute to an indisputable outcome, viz., a break in the intergenerational transmission of Cambridge theoretical traditions, from the 'second cohort' of the modern greats to the next wave, and that this undermined the process of the

---
[10] A commentary on such 'internal' accounts is offered in Chap. 2.

reproduction of the evolving heterodox lineages within Cambridge. This rupture has complex explanations, some of which point to the role of negative factors beyond Cambridge. Yet, Luigi Pasinetti has a valid argument in saying the greats 'self-harmed' in various ways by not paying sufficient regard to ensuring the position of a class of heirs to their tradition/s. Had they been more attentive and assiduous in meeting this imperative, the heterodox schools might have better withstood the assaults, from within and without, that were to follow from the start of the 1980s.

The Untold Story
Putting together these stray sub-narratives offers insights into the general erosion and weakening of some key elements, loosening of some of the nuts and bolts that maintained the heterodox paradigm, introducing vulnerabilities that could be exploited. However, such partial explanations remain insufficient and only set the stage for a comprehensive rendition of the decline and demise of heterodox traditions within the Faculty of Economics and Politics in Cambridge. This untold story, which forms the core of the narrative of this book, argues that the switch of dominant paradigm was contingent on regime change, which then was the objective and the outcome of a systematic, sustained and serial campaign by the orthodox group to dismantle the heterodox formation piece by piece. The key episodes of these purges are concentrated in the 1980s from which the neoclassical group emerge unquestioned victors. This story has thus far remained occluded in folklore, in whispers, in speculations, but is set down here on more firm ground and in greater detail than hitherto available. However, this tale of The Purges as a campaign can also be told in two versions.

The first rendition is the 'closed' version, where the entire tale is constructed in terms of actors and events that are 'Cambridge', where external forces that influence the episodes of the campaign are all directly connected to the opposing camps, acting, as it were, as their proxies. Here, the heterodox lineages first thrive and flourish as an extended family reaching their apogee in the second half of the 1970s; then the purges set in over the following two decades, and orthodoxy returns triumphant and captures the citadel of Cambridge heterodox economics, suppressing or banishing apostasy in a systematic, sustained campaign to restore economics to its imagined pure sanskritised state. No victory is ever complete, except in the histories written by the victors; and inexorably, new, and some of the old, fault lines begin to re-emerge, as the fig leaf is unable to hide the naked truths of the new emperors, setting the stage, optimistically for a reincarnation of some of the suppressed heterodox traditions. This first story, of the rise and fall, and possible green shoots of recovery of Cambridge heterodox economics can be told as a self-contained, as a 'closed-economy' version, where the action and the agents are all located within 'Cambridge', as a notional space, that is, including both the real physical and institutional forms and the networks of connections closely associated with Cambridge economics, in academe of official policy making circuits. At the end, this closed version of the untold story itself is reflective of the characteristic of Cambridge insularity, where the rise and demise of the heterodox traditions is treated as an exclusive intra-Cambridge phenomenon.

The closed version chronicles how the Cambridge battles were enacted, the strategies and tactics of the opposing warring tribes and their generalissimos and commissars and their allies. This story is revelatory, compelling and credible. But, even as this narrative unfolds, the role of several agents and fields of forces beyond the immediate circles of the intra-Cambridge adversaries can be identified. Likewise, some of the explanations of the outcomes of the wars invoke larger, external phenomena, whether in the form of specific economic and political events, or in the form of the changing *zeitgeist* of the times which undermine Keynesianism and empower neoliberalism. These factors are implicitly treated as being exogenous in character, making the 'closed version' narrative analogous, notionally, to the Keynesian short-period analytical frame.

However, it is unsatisfactory to leave these 'exogenous' factors as 'givens', as fait accompli. Curiosity and completeness call for these exogeneities of the closed-version narrative, to be pursued and traced to their own sources and origins; to be made explicable, as far as reasonably possible, in terms that contribute to a wider 'open version' of the overall story, one which endogenises these factors held as exogenous in the 'closed version'. This brings into play the role of other agents from the worlds beyond Cambridge. Widening the contours of explanation does not eliminate, or endogenise, all the 'givens' or 'exogenous' dimensions of the former, but some significant and proximate 'exogenous' factors now become part of the interconnected explanation. Stretching the canvas has the effect of locating the coordinates of Cambridge story on a much bigger map; the Cambridge episode then becomes not a unique stand-alone occurrence, but one specific manifestation of an intellectual and ideological phenomenon experienced in variational forms by the discipline and practitioners of economics in other locations over the same time frame; this points to the salience of wider and shared material forces across these locations. Inevitably, this induces the question of the specific pathologies of the transmission of the impact of such exogenous or external dimensions on the outcomes and eventual fate of Cambridge heterodox economics.

1.3.2 *Worlds Beyond Cambridge: Neoliberalism at the Gates*

Perhaps reflecting the generally acknowledged attribute of Cambridge insularity, it is not entirely surprising that explanations of the demise of Cambridge heterodox lineages have sought sufficient cause in terms of intra-Cambridge factors and forces, often lapsing exclusively into interpersonal equations between various power figures within Cambridge. There can be little doubt that, in the words of Luigi Pasinetti, Cambridge 'self-harmed' in various ways.[11] However, seeking (even) a (nearly) complete explanation would require following the tracks and trails leading out of the relatively closed contours of Cambridge economics, and doing so would identify the salience of other, external, factors and forces that shaped the larger environment within which the seemingly intra-Cambridge battles were fought by the opposing camps. There did exist planetary systems beyond Earth so even replacing Greenwich as its centre, Cambridge economics was not impervious to the pulls and pushes of external forces.

Two channels of external influence are discernible, the material and the ideational worlds, both beyond the determination of Cambridge, even though not free from having been influenced by Cambridge in the earlier decades of its phenomenal authority and domination of the theoretical and policy discourse.

The source of the first channel is the kaleidoscopic shift in global economic and political realities in the decades immediately preceding as well as following the war. The volatile period is marked by a string of powerful events and interventions: the Marshall Plan; decolonisations and the emergence of the Third World; the Soviet, Chinese and Cuban revolutions; Israel, Suez and Palestine; the Great Depression; Nazi Germany, the holocaust, and the new diaspora of émigré intellectuals moving from Germany and the Soviet Union especially to the US universities; the emergence of multilateral architecture for economic and political cooperation; the rise of the Welfare State in Europe; the New Deal in the USA; all these, within a tectonic shift from the changing of the imperial guard from Britain to America; the USA was defeated in Vietnam, but that engagement been paralleled by other interventions such as in Chile and other parts of Latin America, and indeed the rest of the world.

The second channel comprises the ideological counterpart of these material forces, and is constituted by the challenge from the emergence and rise to prominence of rival intellectual traditions within the discipline taking the forms

---

[11] Narratives of such traumatic events often begin to emerge when time places some distance and takes the edge of the personalised experience. In this category, the main exemplar is the fine volume by the senior most surviving guru of the Keynesian clan, Luigi Pasinetti. It is striking, and understandable, that his candid account of that period of decline, is sometimes still tinged, or singed, with the emotional residues of that loss. Intimately knowledgeable and central as he was in the second generation of inheritors of the Keynesian tradition, he was also a prime sufferer, in that he was one of the potential leaders that was 'purged' from Cambridge—he withdrew to the safe and congenial bastions of heterodox economics in Italy. In his account though, he clearly points the finger at 'self-harm' by the Cambridge Keynesian seniors, Joan, Kahn, Kaldor, in somehow not paying sufficient heed to the need for the reproduction of the school inside the Faculty, and allowing it to dismantle and atrophy, to spill out like sand from their hands. While other factors are indirectly alluded to, this remains the central charge. In turn, this is partially contested by his colleague and friend, the second most senior guru and scribe of the Cambridge tribes, Geoff Harcourt, just a few months junior to Luigi, in his review of the Pasinetti book. Geoff is somewhat gentler in laying the blame primarily or exclusively on the shoulders of the greats. Nevertheless, the story remains a Cambridge story, looking inwards, and ironically displaying that hallmark of Cambridge, its confident insularity.

of competition for intellectual hegemony, academic status, political access, policy influence, as manifest in the rival institutional concentrations, the 'other' Cambridge of MIT-Harvard, or its own counter-punching disputatious partner, Chicago, or the LSE which served both masters. These challenges and hostilities in relation to Cambridge heterodox economics were active and visible generally at both at institutional, but inevitably also interpersonal, levels.

The two channels are interconnected, of course, as politicians in power buy into one policy paradigm or another; in this case, shift from the Keynesian policy template that had dominated Western government economic thinking since the Great Depression, to some variant of monetarism and supply-side economics. This raises the question of the manner and mechanisms through which economics influences politics in real time, and in specific the role of the ideological apparatus of powerful neoliberal think tanks—a vast network inspired by Friedrich Hayek as its unquestioned leader; and the contribution of other networks such as the ideological power group of Swedish economists and bankers behind the so-called 'Nobel' prize in Economics, whose selections provided the vital value-addition of branding the neoclassical and neoliberal messages on the disciplinary and ideological levels.

The channel of external ideational forces influencing the survival of heterodox traditions in Cambridge economics bifurcates, one leading to the other Cambridge, the MIT-Harvard, Samuelson-Solow, combine, and the other to Chicago, and the power of the Hayek-Friedman axis. Much can be made of the distinctions, differences and disputes between these two strands of neoclassical economics at the level of doctrine, but this cannot obscure their fundamental alliance and unity of ideological perspective on the discipline, on the desirability of alternative economic systems, and of the strategies and polices necessary for achieving such shared objectives. For the grand ideological project, it did not really matter if MIT did 'general equilibrium' and denigrated 'monetarism' or if Chicago did the opposite. If MIT and Samuelson worked through textbooks, Chicago wrote the treaties, and more, organised the ground forces of neoclassical and neoliberal dominance. If the former kept its distance from Chile, the latter had its boots deep in the mud. But the underlying agreement on precepts and purpose converted the symbiotic pair into a palpable force on the global stage where Cambridge left-Keynesianism and its several fellow travellers were dealt with as adversaries. And arguably, the local UK agency transmitting this combined ideational force was the Economics Faculty of the London School of Economics, long an ideological and institutional rival of Cambridge Keynesianism. This raises the question about the interfaces, or the docking points of articulation through which the 'external' influences generally impinged on, or were more specifically used instrumentally in the Cambridge campaigns; where were the connections, how and through whom, did they work at both institutional and individual/group levels? These become valid questions to raise, though fully satisfactory answers are more difficult to pin down. The power of the Cambridge orthodox adversaries can arguably be seen to derive not just from intra-Cambridge factors, but crucially in the context of the purges, also if not primarily from centres of authority and power that are located in these 'other' opposing worlds located in Europe and the USA, with the influence working usually through UK-based actors and players that could be regarded as constituent parts of this 'other' external world. The decline and demise of the Cambridge heterodox lineages can then no longer be understood exclusively as an intra-Cambridge matter, it becomes part of a global phenomenon with the Cambridge saga as one location where is it manifested—of course, enacted through the agency of the Cambridge orthodox group that itself drew its strength from the wider extra-Cambridge supportive space and sources. This is the version of 'the untold story' that forms the narrative of the book.

Why and when did Cambridge economics take the neoclassical, and effectively the neoliberal, turn effectively being reduced to an outhouse, a second-hand and second-class clone of its rival, the other, American, Cambridge? Did the diverse heterodox traditions atrophy due to acts of commission or omission within Cambridge? Or were there other 'malevolent' forces that underlay this collapse? The suppressed narratives were perhaps difficult for those caught up in it to narrate: for those on the losing side, the heterodox clans, the defeat was too traumatic to relive; for the victors, such a recounting would likely have had to reveal the unsavoury means and methods employed by them to affect the downfall of the heterodox lineages within Cambridge economics. And so perhaps these accounts of victory and defeat have been fading away, buried deeper, to use Samuelson's infelicitous metaphor, "funeral by funeral".

Of course, there is another spinal story line possible, where the decline would be ascribed to the inherent, intrinsic *intellectual* inferiority of the Cambridge heterodox traditions when compared with the neoclassical mainstream rivals based in Cambridge Massachusetts or Chicago. Such self-serving and self-congratulatory interpretations expectedly form the core of the victors, the far more ideologically homogenous and disciplined mainstream neoclassical group, the stormtroopers of Samuelson's third and fourth revolutions. Living and working as an inbred group guided by a shared thought map and atlas, the new cult speaks in chorus, sings together in the same choir, losing the capacity to admit to imperfection, let alone another way of being.

The chasmic disjuncture between obstinate reality and mainstream theory inevitably generates regular challenges and moments of reckoning, as in periodic financial and other systemic crises, but these tend to fail to puncture the thick skin of hubris. The limping deflecting dissembling mainstream defence induced by 'the Queen's Question' about the last (pre-COVID-19) financial crash of 2007–2008 persuades nobody other than themselves, and perhaps not even all of themselves; rather, it reveals the gross nakedness of mainstream theory, and lays bare the central issue of the intrinsic purpose of economics—the issue that so preoccupied and guided the heterodox schools in Cambridge exemplified, say, by Keynes himself, Joan Robinson, Nicholas Kaldor—and their kindred spirit, Michal Kalecki.

In what follows, there is no regurgitation or chewing of this cud; the narrative here proceeds from the postulate that the heterodox traditions, with all their work-in-progress quality and their diverse and often internally contested positions, together constituted an intellectual formation that was purposeful of economics, drawing its assumptions from reality and aiming to return to it with theoretically endorse policy perspectives, all within a framework where time was defined as history, without demanding that its passage would or should yield some heavenly state of equilibrium. These inter-tradition debates have not lost their edge and have produced a stream of thoughtful literature that seeks to revive the heterodox traditions of Cambridge economics. However, these efforts are visible far more on the heterodox, rather than the mainstream side. Partly, this reflects the fact that the victorious neoclassical mainstream now accounts for the vast proportion of economists, curricula and publications in 'economics' as a whole. Partly it also reflects the withering of any curiosity about the evolution of economics itself. Since the mainstream believes and asserts that it has arrived at the point of the end of ideology, or political economy, etc., delving into the imperfect past is treated as a waste of time. The discipline, or line of enquiry, about the history of economic thought is expunged from the concerns of economics, economists, students and their curricula; what is drilled into their cerebral systems is the present, highest state of the evolution of the subject, without regard to the path to their summit. The wayward thought that there might well be other peaks, even higher, with better perspectives on the land and people below, is not part of the imagination, and this assumed uniqueness of their superior position makes it into the final destination and solution. What use then for the past or for maps of other routes and possible destinations?

1.4 The Dialectic of Competing Paradigms

The narratives of this book could serve as a discursive case study of a significant point of inflexion in the contestations between the paradigms of the 'neoclassical' and the 'Keynesian' traditions in Cambridge. Even though it is neither attempted nor intended to flesh out, or test and validate, some one theory of paradigm change or other, the question cannot be eluded altogether; a broad-brush sketch of the dialectic of what indeed presents as a process of perennially competing paradigms must suffice.

An illuminating starting point is Knut Wicksell's Inaugural Lecture in 1904 where he not only anticipates the basic Kuhnian proposition on paradigms, but succinctly explains why paradigms, in the plural, co-exist in economics: "there is no single doctrine taken to be a scientific truth without the diametrically opposed view being similarly upheld by authors of high repute … in other fields of science these conflicts usually come to an end. … Of course, it is truth that conflicts of opinion take place in other sciences, and indeed to some extent they constitute a real part of scientific life and research; but there is this great difference, that in other fields of science these conflicts usually come to an end, the defenders of the false opinion are defeated and admit themselves beaten; or, as more frequently occurs perhaps, they withdraw from the struggle and no new defenders come forward to take their places" [p. 51]. "It is only in the field of economics that the state of war seems to persist and remain permanent."[12] And there, nearly six decades in advance of Kuhn's intervention, Wicksell provides its essence.

Writing in 1969 in the midst of the 'golden age' of steady growth in advanced industrialised economies alongside low inflation and unemployment rates, Coats (1969) argued that "with the exception of the Keynesian revolution of the 1930s, there have been no phases of paradigm change in economics quite like those in the natural sciences. This is due mainly to the nature of economic paradigms (or 'basic' theories) which are less precise and less liable to falsification. 'Critical anomalies' and 'crucial experiments' do not arise in economics, as in the natural sciences."

Critiques of Kuhn's original exposition abound, and there are further challenges to the weaker exposition in the second edition. Bronfenbrenner (1971) and Blaug (1975) both question the usefulness of Kuhn's framework for economics, with Blaug "arguing that the term 'paradigm' ought to be banished from economic literature, unless surrounded by inverted commas" (ibid., p. 399). In a thoughtful commentary on paradigm change, Kanbur (2015, p. 11), commenting with the benefit of hindsight, supports Martin Bronfenbrenner's (1971) early critique of Kuhn, and tends to concur with "Bronfenbrenner's reasoning was that in political economy, ideas are not displaced permanently, and ideas which were once outmoded reappear". Defending Keynes's focus on the content and limits of the role of the state, he observes: "it is this question which is eternal, and it will have to be answered afresh by every generation of political economists. The balance may move this way and that, depending on the material circumstances and, yes, the ideological map."[13]

1.4.1 *Laissez-Faire: "Receding at last into the distance"*

Jump two decades ahead from one august lecture to another, to 1924 when Keynes, in his *avatar* as persuasive visionary, "strode into the Examination Schools in Oxford"[14] to dramatically pronounce *The End of Laissez Faire*, the eponymous book being published in 1926. Keynes attributes the first relevant (to economics and economists) usage of the phrase "laissez-faire" to Bentham.

---

[12] Wicksell's Inaugural Lecture was delivered at the University of Lund on 16 September 1904 'Ends and Means in Economics', in Lindahl, E. (ed.) 1958, *Selected Papers on Economic Theory*, London: George Allen and Unwin. pp. 51–66); quotation from Snowdon and Vane (1997, p. 452).

[13] For the latest accretions to the many contributions to Keynesianism and paradigm change, see the recent exchange in the *Cambridge Journal of Economics*: Pernecky and Wojick (2019); the comment by Thomas (2020), and the response by Pernecky and Wojick (2019, 2020).

[14] Angus Burgin (2012, p. 1) thus opens his fine book.

"It is not, indeed, until we come to the later works of Bentham ... that we discover the rule of laissez-faire, in the shape in which our grandfathers knew it, adapted into the service of the Utilitarian philosophy. ... 'The general rule is that nothing ought to be done or attempted by government; the motto or watchword of government ... out to be—*Be quiet*'." Keynes argued that by 1850, all doubts about the limits and limitations of laissez-faire had been rubbed out of the popular political script: "In short, the dogma had got hold of the educational machine; it had become a copybook maxim. The political philosophy, which the seventeenth and eighteenth centuries had forged in order to throw down kings and prelates, had been made milk for babes, and literally entered the nursery."[15] Keynes's opening words had heralded the end of that era—somewhat somatic within mainstream economics, though tumultuous in the world outside banging on its doors demanding to be let in. "For more than a hundred years our philosophers ruled us because, by a miracle, they nearly all agreed or seem to agree on this one thing. We do not dance even yet to a new tune. But a change is in the air. We hear but indistinctly what were once the clearest and most distinguishable voices which have ever instructed political mankind. The orchestra of diverse instruments, the chorus of articulate sound, is receding at last into the distance."

Choreographed by Keynes, the world was soon indeed dancing to the new tune in double quick time. Even as Keynes spoke, the Marshallian paradigm was being challenged and overturned on his own patch; and within a decade, the notes of the new strain were being set and fine-tuned by his devoted Cambridge band, or Circus, of young proto-Keynesian revolutionaries chiselling away, sculpting the precise features of the *General Theory* as it began to take shape from the *Treatise* of 1930. *How to Pay for the War* followed in 1940, and by the time of his untimely death in 1946, Keynes would have had the satisfaction of a job done: his new tune was now the fanfare ushering in a dramatically different era of economics both in theory and in policy. The Keynesian revolution—one strand rebutting and escaping from the old Marshallian ideas, the other fashioning the new Keynesian ones—was soon ensconced on the throne of economic theory; it had taken all but 20 years from 1926, to 1936, to 1946 by when, what Aslanbeigui and Oakes (2002) call the "revolutionary consensus" had been established, and thus the dramatic transition to the new paradigm completed. The Keynesian storming of the Marshallian citadel had been an Intense, bruising process with no compromises and no prisoners taken. Aslanbeigui and Oakes (2002) characterise the episode as "a gradual shift rather than a cataclysmic event, a ten-year trend and not ten days that shook the world"—a là Jack Reed on the Russian Revolution—though for totally

---

[15] Keynes elaborates: "Some of the most important work of Alfred Marshall—to take one instance—was directed to the elucidation of the leading cases in which private interest and social interest are *not* harmonious Nevertheless, the guarded and undogmatic attitude of the best economists has not prevailed against the general opinion that an individualistic *laissez-faire* is both what they ought to teach and what in fact they do teach."

dismantling a paradigm "which the seventeenth and eighteenth centuries had forged", a decade might translate to no more than a blink of the eye.

In a highly stylised narrative taking its cue perhaps from Keynes's idiom of warfare, Aslanbeigui and Oakes (2002)[16] construct something akin to a model of the Keynesian revolutionary process[17] in Cambridge based on their analysis of the operational mode of the revolutionary elite, the vanguard, in the form of the "Cambridge Circus". "In a BBC talk in 1934 ... he characterized classical orthodoxy as a heavily fortified citadel. Heterodox economists ... would remain powerless in their assaults on classicism as long as they accepted its basic premises. ... 'I was brought up in the citadel ... and I recognize its power and might' (Keynes, 1935, p. 36, cited by Aslanbeigui & Oakes, 2002). As he argued in his preface to *The General Theory*, the heterodox opponents of classicism could not succeed by attacking the superstructure of the fortress, which was unassailable. The vulnerability of classicism lay in its premises. In order to mount a successful assault on the orthodox position, it was necessary to undermine its foundations" (Aslanbeigui & Oakes, 2002). And the *General Theory* provided the revolutionary vanguard with the necessary weapon to effect this.

1.4.2 The Force of Ideas

Keynes had an unshakeable belief in the power of ideas as the irresistible force to shift 'immovable' vested interests. But there was a lag between the emergence and the adoption of new ideas; in the interim, "practical men, who believe themselves to be quite exempt from any intellectual influences, are usually slaves of some defunct economist", and "madmen in authority, who hear voices in the air, are distilling their frenzy from some academic scribbler of a

---

[16] Military idioms and the terminology of revolutionary warfare are extensively employed, generally to good effect, in their account: "strategy and tactics", "battle plan", "party of the revolution", "revolutionary elite", "vanguard of the party", "*avant garde*", "forging new weapons", "indefensible armed peace", "mount a successful assault", "heavily fortified citadel", "attacking the superstructure of the fortress", "drawn into a battle", "battlegrounds in the wars", "moved to the attack", "a secure base of operations", "the university ... a battleground", "the lecture ... a mode of agitation and propaganda".

[17] "The revolution that Keynes envisioned depended on several conditions:

1. An orthodox hegemony with vulnerable foundations.
2. A belligerent heterodox party armed with new theoretical weapons and the determination to engage orthodoxy in battle.
3. A struggle between orthodoxy and the heterodox party that would convincingly demonstrate the fatal flaws of the orthodox position and the superior strength of the heterodox alternative. In this contest, the new theoretical weapons would be employed to crush orthodoxy by attacking its most vulnerable point: its basic premises.
4. The formation of a revolutionary consensus that would increase the disciplinary power of the heterodox party. Once this final condition was satisfied, the heterodox theory would become the new orthodoxy, and the revolution would be consummated. Classicism would become 'history', a phase in the development of economics that had been superseded and rendered obsolete" (Aslanbeigui & Oakes, 2002).

few years back". In the midst of the "golden age", Dudley Seers (1963, pp. 77–79) offered his own stylisation of the process whereby a powerful new theoretical proposition comes to be accepted in the discourse, distinguishing between three phases in its rise to dominance: the 'Hobson' phase, where the proponent and the proposition are considered deviant and heretical, and therefore ignored or frowned upon; the 'Kahn' phase, where the relevance and meaningfulness of the new theoretical propositions is sufficiently realised to be absorbed into the discourse, to be tested and developed further; and the 'Keynes' phase, where the new ideas stand fully validated and are welcomed as the new universal theoretical currency displacing the original one.[18]

Keynes was not alone in ascribing primacy to ideas over material interests; Paul Samuelson had preferred to write textbooks rather than treaties—though Keynes (nearly) did both—and notwithstanding their many profound and unbridgeable differences, Keynes and Hayek shared a Hegelian perspective on the primacy of ideas as agents of change. They also agreed on the stickiness of old ideas that refused to fade away. In his Inaugural Lecture at LSE in 1933, Hayek observed, very much in Keynesian style,[19] that "the views at present held by the public can clearly be traced to the economists of a generation or so ago. So that the fact is not that the teaching of the economics has no influence at all, on the contrary, it may be very powerful. But it takes a long time to make its influence felt, so that, if there is a change, the new ideas tend to be swamped by the domination of ideas which, in fact, have become obsolete" (Hayek quoted in Birner, 2009). "It may be that we as scholars tend to overestimate the influence owe can exercise on contemporary affairs. But I doubt whether it is possible to overestimate the influence which ideas have in the long run" (Hayek, 1967, p. 194).

Keynes and Hayek agree on the obstinacy of old doctrines to persist beyond their welcome, this despite mounting and incontrovertible evidence of their irrelevance or toxicity. Explanations lie in the inertial force, or rather

---

[18] The question of how a powerful new idea eventually comes to be accepted in the discourse has also induced popular responses. Says Tony Benn (2000): "Progress comes from underneath. And Congress and Parliament are the last place to get the message. My definition of progress is this: As you come out with a progressive idea, it's completely ignored, notably by the media. If you go on, you're absolutely mad. Then if you go on further, you're dangerous. Then there's a pause, and suddenly you can't find anyone who doesn't claim to have thought of it in the first place. That is how progress is made. It begins at the bottom and permeates at the top." Gandhi is generally thought to have said: "First they ignore you, then they laugh at you, then they fight you, then you win". And Dan Evon (2016) puts in an earlier claim for union leader Nicholas Klein in 1914: "And my friends, in this story you have a history of this entire movement. First, they ignore you. Then they ridicule you. And then they attack you and want to burn you. And then they build monuments to you. And that, is what is going to happen to the Amalgamated Clothing Workers of America."

[19] Keynes had made his well-known remark, "the difficulty lies not so much in developing new ideas as in escaping from old ones"; and another that "the ideas which civil servants and politicians and even agitators apply to current events are not likely to be the newest. But, soon or late, it is ideas, not vested interests, which are dangerous for good or evil" (Keynes, quoted in Laidler, 1976, p. 485).

deadweight, of habits of thought, the considerable institutional transaction costs of change, and, of course, the cumulative power of vested interests that come to evolve around and be served by the old doctrines.

Typically, the breakthrough must bide its time and await the emergence of enabling environments, especially of events that serve as trigger points of change, often in the negative form of some crisis, or a positive one of a fresh opportunity. The Depression and war performed those functions for Keynesianism in Britain and Europe; Hayek tried, unsuccessfully, to use the bogey of a slide into 'serfdom' via the rising welfare state, which he characterised as the (not so) thin wedge of socialism, in Europe, though he had far greater success in the receptive material and ideological environment in America; the OPEC oil-price hikes of the 1970s served as opportunities for Thatcherite monetarism in the UK, as well as for the reversal of non-capitalist state-led development in the Third World; and the string of financial crises induced and legitimised a return, albeit a temporary one, to old Keynesianism. Thus seen, changes of paradigms occur not purely through the intellectual demonstration of the analytical and explanatory power of a new theoretical template, but depend critically, for their emergence as well as for the timing of their acceptance on enabling material circumstances and ideological conjunctures; material interests, history and Marx step back into the Hegelian frame.

Keynes's concise commentary on the emergence of the rise of Ricardian and the demise of Malthusian paradigm lucidly confirms his understanding of the factors that gave ideas their force. "Ricardo conquered England as completely as the Holy inquisition conquered Spain. Not only was his theory accepted by the city, by statesmen and by the academic world. But controversy ceased; the other point of view completely disappeared; it ceased to be discussed. The great puzzle of effective demand with which Malthus had wrestled vanished from economic literature. ... The completeness of the Ricardian victory is something of a curiosity and a mystery. It must have been due to a complex of suitabilities in the doctrine to the environment into which it was projected. That it reached conclusions quite different from what the ordinary uninstructed person would expect, added, I suppose, to its intellectual prestige. That its teaching, translated into practice, was austere and often unpalatable, lent it virtue. That it was adapted to carry a vast and consistent logical superstructure, gave it beauty. That it could explain mush social injustice and apparent cruelty as an inevitable incident in the scheme of progress, and the attempt to change such things as likely on the whole to do more harm than good, commended it to authority. That it afforded a measure of justification to the free activities of the individual capitalist, attracted to it the support of the dominant social force behind authority" (Keynes, 1936, chapter 3).

Wayne Parsons (1983, p. 389) defends Keynes against the misinterpretations by his detractors: "As Keynes' comments on Ricardo in the *General Theory* illustrate, he understood that the triumph of an idea could not be divorced from social structures and economic interests. Doctrines were adopted because, as he emphasises, of their 'suitability' to the 'environment' into which they are 'projected'. Revolution in social knowledge and ideas were, as Keynes showed, albeit in a fragmented and piecemeal way, the product of an interplay between a number of influences. Namely, the condition and strength of 'dominant social forces'; the capacity of ruling ideologies to support and legitimize an existing social order; and the effectiveness of the challenge from a competing theoretical community. As may be evidenced by a consideration of the 'monetarist' counter-revolution during the nineteen-seventies, Keynes's insight into the politics of ideas was, perhaps, a more accurate analysis of the impact of ideas on policy-making that his critics would allow, and one for which he is often given little or no credit." Parsons argues that "it was not, therefore, his belief in the power of ideas that was misplaced, over-stated or naïve, but rather a more profound reluctance to realize that ideas—indeed his own ideas—might influence in ways and directions that were not the intention of their originator" (ibid., p. 389).

1.4.3 Opposition Brewing

Even as Keynes and Keynesianism emerged in their pomp, twin opponents were scripting new testaments, gathering their tribes, honing their weapons to bring it down. The first ideological and political attack came from Hayek, writing virtually by Keynes's elbow in the study arranged by Keynes for him at King's College during the war years when LSE relocated to Cambridge. His *The Road to Serfdom*—written during 1940–1943, published with difficulty in 1944, and a raging success instantly thereafter—was a libertarian call to arms raising the alarmist spectre of a slide into socialism, to be read simultaneously as a proxy cautionary tale against a slippage into welfare states in post-war Europe via Keynesianism. Hayek rejected the Walrasian general equilibrium approach, and had his own variations on the laissez-faire doctrine, but in essence, a new variation on free-market fundamentalism had been reborn and was again being dispensed as a substitute for mother's milk through the new international propagandist network with the cross-Atlantic Mont Pelerin Society, formed in 1947 for this purpose, at its core. The second, neoclassical theoretical, challenge came from the Walrasian General Equilibrium corner in the form of Paul Samuelson's interventions: *Foundations of Economic Analysis* in 1947, and then his *Economics* in 1948, reasserting the neoclassical approach and converting economics into one field of application of mathematics; and within a decade, he developed his notion of a 'grand neoclassical synthesis' with the claim that with some adaptations, Keynesian propositions could be absorbed into his holistic neoclassical template.

In the United Kingdom as well as in Continental Europe, Keynesianism, even without its progenitor at its head, withstood both challenges well enough for Hayek to feel marginalised and sink into bouts of depression as Keynesian doctrine dominated economic theory and policy; indeed, for a while in the 1960s he even contemplated winding up the Mont Pelerin Society. In 1947, Hayek had presciently warned his followers of the uphill task and prophesied that their endeavours would take 20 years to bear fruit. And now with a fortuitous turn of events—the hypothesised 'trigger points'—and virtually on cue, the 1970s dramatically transformed the landscape.

The Mont Pelerin Society investment began to pay dividends. The new 'Nobel' prize in economics was launched and the mathematical revolution and neoclassical economics were showcased; Samuelson was awarded in 1970, and in quick succession the neoliberal gurus Hayek and Friedman were anointed in 1974 and 1976; Margaret Thatcher, Hayek's devotee was rising to power and then elected to lead in 1979; and Hayek had found his misplaced mojo. Meanwhile, in 1972 Frank Hahn returned as a professor to launch his local anti-heterodox campaign in Cambridge, appearing as the new self-proclaimed messiah[20]: I have seen the future he pronounced, and it is General Equilibrium with Money, with the new bible written not in literary blah-blah but in the 'scientific' grammar of the new wordless *lingua franca*, mathematics, rather like the Latinisation of church sermons, and the Brahmanical Sanskritisation of Hindu prayer, both devised to empower the priests over the people. The battle lines were drawn.

1.4.4   Evolutions and Hegemonic Incorporation

After its initial gatecrashing into policy, Keynesianism had had a poor reception in the USA; as early the mid-1950s, Paul Samuelson, in the third edition of his *Economics*, was able to say: "In recent years 90 per cent of American Economists have stopped being 'Keynesian economists' or 'anti-Keynesian economists'. Instead they have worked toward a synthesis of whatever is valuable in older economics and in modern theories of income determination. The result might be called neoclassical synthesis and is accepted in its broad outlines by all but about 5 per cent of extreme left wing and right-wing writers" (Samuelson, 1955, p. 212). Years later in his in/famous lecture in 1979, Robert Lucas Jr explicated both Samuelson's position, as well as his own in pronouncing 'the death of Keynesian economics'. "The central message of Keynes was that there existed a middle ground between the extremes of socialism and laissez faire capitalism. … In effect, Samuelson told his colleagues: 'Face it—you live in a world were virtually nobody has any faith in this laissez faire religion of yours. I am offering a substitute ideology which concedes the inability of a competitive economy to take care of itself, but which also offers a management system

---

[20] Meghnad Desai recounted to David Newbery, "a wonderful occasion at the Association of University Teachers of Economics (AUTE) meeting in Aberystwyth in April 1972: 'As we all trooped into a large hall completely packed, Frank came on stage and began 'Although you see a small Hungarian (*sic*) Jew before you, let me tell you that I am John the Baptist. I have come to tell you about what is coming. Having got our attention, he went on to give a memorable lecture about what was passionately occupying him at that time. This was the collective effort by several young theorists and himself to integrate money into Walrasian General Equilibrium theory. … He got us all engaged in what he told us was an absolutely central problem of economics'" (Newbery, 2017, p. 500).

which is, say, 95% consistent with laissez faire.' These were hard times, and this was too good a deal to pass up. We took it. So did society as a whole. What I meant by saying Keynesian economics is dead … is just that this middle ground is dead. … because its intellectual rational has eroded to the point where it is no longer serviceable."[21] A discrete period down the line, Lucas would have ample opportunity to learn a lesson, if he so wished, from the directly observable reality of the 'reality' he saw through his lobotomised models. And so also perhaps would an unsuspecting Alan Blinder, whose hubristic declaration that reality was coming around and behaving as postulated in the generic neoclassical model, was to be ambushed by a real world that wasn't paying attention and had gone off (his) script (Blinder, 2000).

Blinder (1988, pp. 109–110) provides a candid and critical commentary of the ebbs and tides of the 'Keynesian' paradigm in that era as seen from across the ocean. "For a period of roughly 35 years, Keynesian theory provided a central paradigm for macroeconomists, and considerable progress was made on several empirical fronts. It was widely recognized that some of the ingredients of Keynesian economics (e.g. money illusion and/or nominal wage rigidity) rested on slender to non-existent microtheoretic foundations; and there were always dissenters. But, thought of as a collection of empirical regularities that fit together into a coherent whole, the theory worked tolerably well. In the 1970s, however, the Keynesian paradigm was rejected by a great many academic economists, especially in the United States, in favour of what we now call new classical economics. By about 1980, it was hard to find an American academic macroeconomist under the age of 40 who professed to be a Keynesian. That was an astonishing intellectual turnabout in less than a decade, an intellectual revolution for sure. Scientists from another discipline might naturally surmise that the data of the 1970s had delivered a stunning and unequivocal rejection of the Keynesian paradigm. They would look for some decisive observation or experiment that did to Keynes what the orbit of Mercury did to Newton. But they would look in vain. I argue that there was no anomaly, that the ascendancy of new classicism in academia was instead a triumph of *a priori* theorizing over empiricism, of intellectual aesthetics over observation and, in some measure, of conservative ideology over liberalism. It was not, in a word, a Kuhnian scientific revolution. If this is so, it helps explain a phenomenon that a Kuhnian would find puzzling: macroeconomics is already in the midst of another [counter]revolution which amounts to a return to Keynesianism—but with a much more rigorous theoretical flavour."

There is a colouring of sadness in Luigi Pasinetti's appreciation in 1991 for Richard Kahn who had died, an unhappy man, two years earlier. "The disappearance of Kahn marks the end of a historical phase, almost an era, in the recent history of Keynesian economic thought—a historical phase centred in

---

[21] Robert Lucas, quoted in De Vroey, M. and Duarte, P. G. (2012, p. 18). (Lucas Archives Box 22) See also: De Vroey and Duarte (2012, p. 30, Table 1) for a tabular summary of "the evolution of syntheses, visions and consensuses over the history of macroeconomics".

Cambridge" (Pasinetti, 1991, p. 423). It is not difficult to see the reasons for the angst. "Patinkin looks at Keynes's theory as a sort of Walrasian general equilibrium macroeconomic model. By contrast, the Cambridge Keynesian school, and in particular Kahn, always took Marshall's neo-classical economic theory—which was the British version of that stream of economics which on the continent was associated with the names of Walras, Pareto and Menger—as precisely the theory from which the 'Keynesian Revolution' broke away. ... For Kahn, the 'Keynesian Revolution' could not but mean what it literally says—a 'revolution', a sharp break-away from traditional neo-classical economic theory; i.e., to use a fashionable Kuhnian term (Kuhn, 1970), 'a change of paradigm'. In these terms, mainstream economics is in (at least terminological) contradiction. To make all the reinterpretation that is necessary to reabsorb the 'Keynesian Revolution' into the traditional fold is in fact to reduce the 'Keynesian Revolution' to no revolution at all (Pasinetti, 1991, p. 437). ... There remains the more substantial and widely relevant intellectual problem of what it is that the 'Keynesian Revolution' really was (or failed to be). ... Was it really that break-away, that discontinuity with Marshallian (or Walrasian) neo-classical economic theory, which Kahn and the Cambridge group very definitely felt since the beginning, and which they were so excited to work for, in a major effort to reconstruct economic theory on sounder foundations? Or was it in the end (contrary to what they felt) perhaps a sharp or even a violent but *temporary* turmoil, to be reabsorbed into the traditional fold, as the contingent events behind it faded away? No one can honestly claim to be able to answer these questions in a conclusive way, at present" (Pasinetti, 1991, p. 438).

Honestly or not, within a year, Gregory Mankiw (1992/1997), picking up the thread from Blinder (1988), had an uncomfortable answer to Pasinetti's question. Mankiw's ostensible defence of 'Keynesian economics' would have been more appropriate as an obituary, or alternatively as tidings of its 'reincarnation' into a different body. He picks up the thread of Blinder's evolutionary narrative: "Lucas called his article [written in 1980] 'The Death of Keynesian Economics'. From our current perspective [as in 1992], it is clear that this obituary was premature. Today, Keynesian theorizing does not inspire whispers and giggles from the audience. There are many economists under the age of forty who do not take offense when their work is called 'Keynesian', and I count myself as one of them. If Keynesian economics was dead in 1980, then today it has been reincarnated. ... One can say that the new classical challenge has been met: Keynesian economics has been reincarnated into a body with firm microeconomic muscle. I am careful to call this re-emergence of Keynesian economics a 'reincarnation' rather than a 'resurrection'; 'as the rebirth into another body', and that describes well Keynesian economics today. The Keynesian economics of the 1990s shares the spirit of the Keynesian economics of earlier decades. Like their predecessors, new Keynesians question the relevance of the Walrasian paradigm in explaining economy-wide booms and busts. Old and new Keynesians share a skepticism in the invisible hand's ability to maintain full employment. They both see the business cycles as a type of economy-wide market failure. Beyond these broad principles, however, old and new Keynesians differ substantially. In many ways, the Keynesian economics of the 1990s does not look like the Keynesian economics of the 1930s, or even that of the 1960s. To some old Keynesians, new Keynesian economics may be hard to recognize as Keynesian at all.[22] Indeed, new Keynesian economics may appear more similar to the classical economics of David Hume, or even to the monetarist economics of Milton Friedman" (Mankiw, 1992/1997, pp. 445–446).

Mankiw's "new Keynesian economics is far different from old Keynesian economics—so different, in fact, that today the label 'Keynesian' may generate more confusion than understanding. With new Keynesians looking so much like old classicals, perhaps we should conclude that the term 'Keynesian' has out-lived its usefulness. Perhaps we need a new label to describe the school of macroeconomics that accepts the existence of involuntary unemployment, monetary non-neutrality, and sticky wages and prices" (ibid., pp. 450–451). Joan Robinson, typically, did have a rather pejorative new name for the rightward swing of the pendulum; one must wonder how, is she was around, she might have improved on 'bastard Keynesianism'. Seeing this Gramscian process of the incorporation into the body of hegemonic discourse of what at the outset was a radical paradigm would have been sufficient cause for Kahn's disaffection towards the end.

1.4.5 Ideological: Not the Techniques but the Purposes of Economics

Blinder (1988) characterises Keynesianism with a set of six propositions, three 'positive' or technical, and the other three 'normative' in character; the former three are hypothetically resolvable across positions, but the latter three involve policy, politics and ideology and so remain generally irreconcilable. This leads to a permutation of hybrid positions held by economists generally labelled as being monetarist, or neoclassical, or Keynesian of one form or another.

Even in 1926, Keynes's outright rejection of laissez-faire was replete with normative policy positions deriving from differences over premises. "Let us clear from the ground the metaphysical or general principles upon which, from time to time, *laissez-faire* has been founded. It is *not* true that individuals possess a prescriptive 'natural liberty' in their economic activities. There is *no*

---

[22] Mankiw highlights his personal list of six "dubious Keynesian propositions" that in the past were "viewed as basic tenets of [old] Keynesian economics, and that I believe that economists today should discard"; these "show the profound impact that monetarism and new classicism has had on the thinking of my generation of Keynesians". Mankiw's "not entirely idiosyncratic" list involves rejections of: the usefulness of Keynes' *General Theory* as a learning device; the idea that classical economics did not have useful lessons; that deficit spending was good for the economy to avoid excessive saving; that fiscal policy was powerful while monetary policy was not important; that inflation was an acceptable price to pay for low unemployment; and that policy makers should use their discretion instead of adhering to a rigid policy rule (Mankiw, 1997, pp. 446–449). For "old" Keynesians, accepting these six commandments would be tantamount to throwing the proverbial baby (of the social dimensions of economic policy) out with the bathwater (of doctrinal equivocations).

'compact' conferring perpetual rights on those who Have or on those who Acquire. The world is *not* so governed from above that private and social interest always coincide. It is *not* so managed here below that in practice they coincide. It is *not* a correct deduction from the principles of economics that enlightened self-interest always operates in the public interest. Nor is it true that self-interest generally *is* enlightened; more often individuals acting separately to promote their own ends are too ignorant or too weak to attain even these. Experience does *not* show that individuals, when they make up a social unit, are always less clear sighted than when they act separately" (Keynes, 1926, pp. 287–288).[23] By 1936, that initial critique had widened out to embrace the macroeconomic domain; and by 1946, as Kanbur (2015) points out, Keynes had gone global, beyond the Westphalian templates within which the earlier critiques were developed.

It is this positive-normative divide, or chasm, that generically separated the Cambridge Keynesians and post-Keynesians from the neoliberals and the neoclassicals and 'positive' Keynesians of the free-market faith. The attacks on the left-Keynesians and other heterodox groups in Cambridge were almost always justified and disguised in the garb of technicalities hiding the naked fact that underlying such critiques was a fundamental divergence at the policy, political and ideological levels. And in this, the local Cambridge orthodox group could and did muster strategically crucial support from their standards-setting American cousins through the vital 'external', 'independent' testimonies provided by carefully selected 'experts' from the ranks of the American side of the family line to do a hatchet job on the grant applications of the DAE teams' projects. And so those dogs were called bad names and promptly put down. The cases of the closures of both macroeconomic modelling teams of the Department of Applied Economics in the 1980s provide telling illustrations.

Fifty years after Keynes had sensed the new tune, laissez-faire had found a vibrant new life. Blinder recalls the political ethos of the 1970s and 1980s in America when noting the "ideological overtones which played an important role in the neoclassical revival" (Blinder, 1988, p. 120). "The basic neoclassical paradigm is profoundly conservative" and its adherents "tend toward the Panglossian view of private economic transactions and look askance at government intervention. When this world view is transported from microeconomics to macroeconomics, it leads to theoretical models in which business cycles are benign, unimportant, or inevitable—perhaps all three. And it leads, as usual, to *laissez-faire* policy recommendations. … Keynesians do not buy any of this. They argue that the very existence of macroeconomics as a subdiscipline owes to the massive market failures that we observe during recessions but which the neoclassical paradigm rules out. They believe that recessions are important, malign, and ameliorable, and so are ready to support government interventions

---

[23] Keynes, John Maynard. 1926. "The End of Laissez-Faire" in *The Collected Writings of John Maynard Keynes, Volume IX, Essays in Persuasion*, Royal Economic Society, Palgrave Macmillan, 1972.

designed to stabilize aggregate economic activity. ... The relative strengths of conservative and liberal ideology obviously vary both over time and through space. My argument is that new classical theory could have attracted a large following only in a country and at a time when right-wing ideology was on the ascendancy, as was true in the United States in the 1970s and 1980s. Though we academics live in ivory towers, the social winds blow there, too. Many observers have noticed that the new classical revolution was mainly restricted to the United States; it never really caught on in Europe. That was no coincidence, I think, for right-wing ideology has long found more adherents in the US than in Europe. The timing was also no accident; new classicism took root just when the political balance in the US was shifting toward the right. I don't believe such ideas would have sold in American academia during the 1960s."

1.4.6 *Sociological: Mathematical Whiz-Kids and Ageing Dinosaurs*

Alan Blinder, with his welcome literary flair, adds a meaningful 'sociological' insight when he introduces an intergenerational aspect into the explanation of theoretical positions and methods—a dimension that had much traction in the anti-heterodox campaigns in Cambridge. Blinder (1988, pp. 117–118) writes about his contemporary cohorts, but he could as easily have been referring to Britain which in any case was following, even if trailing, their American peers and principals.

"Economics has become a highly technical subject in recent decades, more so in the US than elsewhere. And technicians, of whatever discipline, prize technique; it's how the young cut their teeth. The rational expectations revolution was a godsend for aspiring young technicians. It not only pushed macroeconomic theory in more abstract and mathematical directions, but brought in its wake a new style of econometrics that was far more technically demanding than the old methods it sought to replace. The tools needed to carry out the new brands of theory and econometrics could not be found in the kit bags of the older economists, which gave the young a heavy competitive edge. ... As an extra bonanza, the Lucas critique provided a reason to shun the previously accumulated stock of econometric results as unreliable. Thus freed of any need to absorb the knowledge of the past, newly minted Ph.D. economists could concentrate on developing what they saw as the wave of the future. It was a recipe for generational conflict within the discipline and, sure enough, the young were recruited disproportionately into the new classical ranks while few older economists converted. Traditional Keynesian tools like IS-LM and large-scale macroeconometric models came to be viewed as relics of the past and, in a strange kind of guilt by association. ... By 1980 or so, the adage 'there are no Keynesians under the age of 40' was part of the folklore of the (American) economics profession."

But things were different in the worlds of policy inhabited by business and government economists, and Blinder explains why: "In academia, as in fashion, it is more important to be fresh and creative than to be correct. Cute models, after all, make snappy papers; the real world can be left to less original minds. I have heard it said that the surest route to academic success is to devise a clever proof of an absurd proposition. And dazzling displays of technical fireworks, perhaps accompanied by some impenetrable prose, regularly impress referees and editors of scholarly journals. Incentives are quite different in business or government, where ... methodological innovation and purity count for little, cuteness for nothing, and technical virtuosity is unappreciated. A professional forecaster seeks accuracy, not scholarly kudos. A policy analyst wants to communicate with policy makers, not to dazzle them with technique. That new classical ideas failed to migrate from the academy to the worlds of business and government—as Keynesian ideas had done 40 years earlier—suggests that they failed to meet the non-academic market test: they did not produce useful results." Yet, in Cambridge, they could and did exercise this power in the purge of generally left-oriented macroeconomic modelling teams of the Department of Applied Economics.

Blinder's observations travel well into the Cambridge context where the DAE macroeconomic teams were lectured in no uncertain terms by the new youth of orthodox economics that their models weren't cute enough, even if they were demonstrably more meaningful and accurate for the purposes for which they were intended. The premium placed on technical virtuosity per se was greatly stimulated by the massive wave of émigré economists into American academe from Europe. As Blinder states: "Methodological purity has a seductive attraction to mathematically minded technicians—which helps explain why rational expectations came to be so intimately tied up in the debate.[24] ... Linking rational expectations to new classicism (thus leaving 'irrational' expectations to the Keynesians) helped the new theory win converts in the same way that celebrity endorsements help sell products" (Blinder, 1988, p. 119).

1.4.7 Beyond Kuhnian Reductionism

The narrations of this meandering path of 'Keynesianism', with periodic declarations of its 'rise' and 'fall', raise some critical issues pertaining to the Kuhnian notion of paradigm change. First, 'critical anomalies' do arise in economics periodically, and the global financial crisis, or rather crises, acted as a test for free-market theory and its presumption of self-equilibrating markets, just as the Depression had done earlier. The question is more why, despite spectacular empirical falsification, the paradigm and theory survived and indeed, flourished, again. Answers have to be found in the domains of material interests, institutions and ideology. Conflicting paradigms can and do continue to

---

[24] "Modelling expectations as rational—that is, as optimal subject to informational constraints—is the analogue of modelling consumers as maximizing utility and producers as maximizing profits. Rational expectations was therefore a natural accompaniment—and, indeed, a major impetus—to the 'back to basics' movement. It was no accident, then, that those who favoured frictionless, optimizing, market-clearing models were immediately attracted to rational expectations as a behavioural hypothesis without bothering to look for evidence" (Blinder, 1988, p. 119).

co-exist in parallel. Second, these contending paradigms continue their own, internal, debates and development, strengthening their respective positions vis-à-vis the opposing formulations. Sub-paradigms emerge within competing paradigms; for instance, the wave of positions that evolve out of the original so-called neoclassical synthesis; or internal disagreements, such as between Hayek and Friedman, on monetarism; or various types of liberalism; or different lineages of heterodox economics. It is useful to keep a separation between such intra-paradigm transactions within its different strands, and more existential inter-paradigm conflicts and incompatibilities. Third, the continued overall dominance of the fundamentalist free-market paradigm has little to do with its theoretical legitimacy; its persistence, and its dual relationship with the opposing Keynesian paradigm, has to be understood in material terms, that is, in terms of the range of vested interests that form its social constituencies. Inter-paradigm conflicts in economics are generally to do with the normative, policy dimensions though these are often lost in the charges and countercharges of theoretical and technical weaknesses and flaws. Fourth, the term 'parallel' is questionable in that it implies independent, non-intersecting trajectories for these paradigms; in reality, the contestation, for instance, between the paradigms old Keynesians and the free-marketeers, is such that the two are often seen to dominate in sequential terms: the functioning of free markets under conditions of financial globalisation leads to global financial crises which, subsequently, Keynesian corrective policies—with varying right-wing, populist or 'socialist' optional extras—are used to resolve. In this sense arguably, there is almost a structural and functional symbiosis between the two under conditions of virtually unregulated global capitalism. And fifth, there is a problematic tendency to 'explain' a change of paradigm, or a turn in dominant discourse, exclusively in terms of its internal theoretical weaknesses, leaving aside the societal, structural, material contexts and conjunctures from which these theoretical frameworks arise, and whose dominant interests they tend to serve; eschewing determinism does not legitimise a slide into another reductionism where the evolution and force of ideas is detached from material circumstances; this theme was perhaps the leitmotif of Phyllis Deane's (1978) *The Evolution of Economic Ideas*.

1.4.8 Mankiw's Pendulum

Historical reality becomes the perennial banana skin of mainstream neoclassical economics; notwithstanding the material forces that regularly reinstall it as the default paradigm of capitalism, it comes to grief with each fresh economic crisis generated by the inherent tendencies of capitalism itself. As a new crisis grips the globe, there is much handwringing, consumption of humble pie, of confession and contrition; but as Hyman Minsky, the great student of crises, observed, memories are fickle and ephemeral, material interests return to dominate, and the world lurches on obliviously awaiting the next crisis cycle. Once the state-as-Keynesian-saviour has stepped in and performed the historic task of reflating and refloating the macroeconomy, the 'free' market returns as the vehicle of 'recovery' again legitimising unbridled profit maximisation for 'wealth creation', while picking the pockets of the mass of workers and savers and slashing social provisioning for citizens to restore the 'fiscal balance' after bailing out the bankers, rentiers and sinking corporates—till the next crisis demands handing over the responsibility for saving-capitalism-from-itself once again to "the executive of the modern state, [which] is but a committee for the managing the common affairs of the bourgeoisie" (Marx & Engels, 1967/1888, p. 82); thus, the litany "we are all Keynesian now" is heard in a cycle of repetition in university lecture halls and government committee rooms. While global capitalism in this unregulated form persists, so will such a symbiotic or dialectical dynamic between orthodoxy dominating in an extended 'non-crisis' period, and a turn towards Keynesianism in 'crisis' phase that almost inexorably follows. A sense of *déjà vu* pervades this yo-yo of 'crisis' and 'recovery', and the 'rise' and 'fall' of Keynesianism, which lives on, but not a satisfactory life, locked away in a stifling closet to be let out and aired at times of crisis—and then too within strict limits and on a tight leash.[25]

Mankiw asks if macroeconomics "is destined to oscillate between two irreconcilable extremes". "In some ways, the history of macroeconomic thought seems like a pendulum swinging between two views of the economy. On the right is the view of a well-functioning economy; on the left is the Keynesian view of an economy fraught with market failure. The Great Depression of the 1930s swung the pendulum decisively from the right to the left, and Keynes could plausibly call classical economics 'misleading and disastrous'. The new classical economics of the 1970s swung the pendulum back to the right, and

---

[25] Skidelsky (2009) was not alone in pointing this out in the immediate aftermath of the last, pre-COVID-19 financial meltdown: "We ... have precious little idea about how to stop a succession of such crises bearing down on us in future. To get a handle on these issues we need John Maynard Keynes. ... This is to be expected. For twenty years or so, mainstream economics has taught that markets 'clear' continuously. The big idea was that if wages and prices are completely flexible, resources will be fully employed. Any shock to the system will result in instantaneous adjustment of wages and prices to the new situation. ... This system-wide responsiveness depended on economic agents having perfect information about the future. This is manifestly absurd. ... This so-called 'efficient market theory', should have been blown sky-high by last autumn's financial breakdown. But I doubt that it has been. ... John Maynard Keynes pointed out its fallacy. When shocks to the system occur, agents do not know what will happen next. In the face of this uncertainty, they do not readjust their spending; instead, they refrain from spending until the mists clear, sending the economy into a tailspin. It is the shock, not the adjustments to it, that spreads throughout the system. ... An economy hit by a shock does not maintain its buoyancy; rather, it becomes a leaky balloon. Hence Keynes gave governments two tasks: to pump up the economy with air when it starts to deflate, and to minimize the chances of serious shocks happening in the first place. Today, the first lesson appears to have sunk in: various bailout and stimulus packages have stimulated depressed economies sufficiently to give us a reasonable expectation that the worst of the slump is over. But, judging from recent proposals in the United States, the United Kingdom, and the European Union to reform the financial system, it is far from clear that the second lesson has been learned. A few cosmetic reforms, it now seems to be agreed, are all that is needed. This is to set the scene for the next crisis."

Robert Lucas could plausibly proclaim the 'death of Keynesian economics'. The New Keynesian economics of the 1980s swung the pendulum back toward the left (at least somewhat), and today one can plausibly say that Keynesian economics has been reincarnated" (Mankiw, 1997, p. 450). And that pendulum has kept on swinging, at the risk of running out of new labels and descriptions of the latest 'advances' or 'breakthroughs', though the so-called swings to the 'left' in American economics might leave post-Keynesians in Britain, Australia, Italy, India and other scattered locations, somewhat underwhelmed. If anything, some of the 'left' synthetic turns appear, in Gramscian manner, more as exercises in hegemonic incorporation of Keynesianism into a reformed neoclassical crocodile's belly.

Ideas and concepts emerge from specific historical, societal and ideological contexts, but they tend to outlive them, to mutate, and to be reformed to serve different purposes, agendas and masters. It is not unusual to identify concepts that had radical, transformational motivations at their point of origin becoming themselves transformed and incorporated instrumentally into mainstream hegemonic political and policy agendas.[26]

1.4.9 Solow's À La Carte Approach

To close, a couple of asides from the familiar Samuelson-Solow double act. Little surprise that Bob Solow likes choice, that he reveals his preference for 'à la carte' over a 'fixed menu' or a 'plat du jour' in his personal selection of paradigms. In an interview in 2019, he threw a spanner into the paradigm of 'paradigms' narrative, vehemently rejecting the accuracy or usefulness of labels such as 'Keynesian', 'Centrist' or 'Neoclassical'. "That kind of labelling doesn't make a lot of sense." ... "The plain fact is that I'm a Keynesian in the short run, and a Neoclassical economist in the long run. And I don't think that there is any conflict there ... although it's generally thought that those are two sets with no overlap. ... There is a real intellectual problem about the medium run, about the period which are a little too long for the normal Keynesian assumptions to be right, but maybe a little too short for the normal Neoclassical assumptions to be the right assumptions to make. And how to deal with that medium run is as far as I'm concerned, an unsolved problem by me or by

---

[26] Examples abound: notions of 'democracy' originally meant to empower the excluded masses all too often becoming the political mechanism of keeping them where they were; 'participation', originally intended by Paolo Freire as a force for self-realisation and emancipation of the oppressed, but converted by Robert Chambers, the World Bank and their networks into an instrumental exercise in narrow pre-set project interventions; the work and radical imagination on poverty and deprivation of the likes of Dadabhai Naoroji, Seebohm Rowntree and Peter Townsend, intended as fundamental critiques of inequality and exclusion in society, corralled by the Bretton Woods institutions and governments and converted into lean, 'cost-effective' interventions targeting those in 'absolute poverty' defined by scandalously low poverty lines while leaving inequalities unaddressed. Heterodox, and radical, economics is another domain subject to such processes of Gramscian hegemonic incorporation into mainstream discourse.

anybody else. ... I wish people would talk about particular ideas rather than attaching them to people. ... One of the consequences is that people do not take seriously the work of the other ideology. If you identify with school A, then you don't pay serious attention to what people in school B do, and vice versa. That's too bad" (extracts from Solow, 2019). Solow provides a mix-and-match approach to constructing his own customised grand synthesis.

Paul Samuelson steps into the frame to assuage anxieties: it will be alright in the end. "It is healthy for a discipline like economics to evolve in response to new developments and better understandings of historical reality. ... Funeral by funeral, economics does make progress. Darwinian impact of reality melts away even the prettiest of fanciful theories and the hottest of ideological frenzies. But there are fits and starts on the way" (Samuelson, 1997, p. 159). There is an implication here of an essential underlying linearity of progress in economics, reflective more perhaps of Samuelson's existential optimism than a considered judgement on the recent history of economic ideas. What if the understanding and explanation of historical reality is not admitted into the frame of reference, what if it is abstracted from, as in the neo-neoclassical, or neo-Walrasian, school, not to be used as a criterion for comparative assessment?

1.4.10 Silos and Trenches

Joan Robinson's classic 1974 paper, 'History versus Equilibrium' put down the charge sheet against the timeless, space-free, Walrasian general equilibrium template. In his response on behalf of the broad Walrasian camp, is framed in terms of 'scientific research programmes'—an involuted euphemism for the other problematic term, 'paradigms'. In assessing Joan Robinson's critique of what she called the "neo-neo-classical" framework, E. Roy Weintraub (1985, p. 147) adopts the Lakatosian template of a "scientific research programme" and declares that "by definition, the hard-core propositions are taken to be true and irrefutable by those who adhere to the program. 'Taken to be true' means that the hard-core functions like axioms of a geometry, maintained for the duration of study of that geometry; ... Notice that we do not test the hard-core propositions, as we do not test (with the idea of confirmation or rejection) the inverse square law in Newtonian mechanics, or the fixity of the earth's position with respect to the sun in the Ptolemaic program in astronomy—these hard-core propositions that are maintained by workers in the program." Weintraub (1985, p. 147) defines these propositions pretty much along the lines of Hahn (1984, pp. 1–2); these are unquestionable articles of the faith. "The notion of a 'Walrasian' equilibrium is indeed fundamental to the enterprise that Robinson called 'neo-neoclassical' economics (which roughly corresponds to my term 'the neo-Walrasian program')." But, Weintraub continues: "The equilibrium notion is not testable—it is simply present as an organizing feature of the theories in the protective belts of the program. A monetary theoretic model's 'perfect foresight equilibrium' can neither be corroborated nor falsified. Yet it is not meaningless to work with such equilibria if they lead to propositions that are potentially falsifiable" (Weintraub, 1985, p. 148).

This hard core is surrounded by a 'protective belt' where the further theoretical and empirically falsifiable propositions, based on the hard core, are tested; presumably, if there is such falsification, the prophets and priests of the hard-core faith would need to reskill for another occupation, or switch to an alternative belief system. But things turn out not to be so straightforward. Even as Wicksell (1904, in Lindahl, 1958, p. 51) pointed out in 1904, "in other fields of science these conflicts usually come to an end, the defenders of the false opinion are defeated and admit themselves beaten; or, as more frequently occurs perhaps, they withdraw from the struggle and no new defenders come forward to take their places. ... It is only in the field of economics that the state of war seems to persist and remain permanent." Weintraub (185, p. 148) says much the same if not in the same terms: "The issue of whether, and when, a program (defined by the hard core) is 'rejected' is an issue of the relative progress or degeneration of the program *with respect to a competing research program*. There is no evidence to suggest that economists abandon degenerating programs in the absence of a progressive alternative. We do not, in the face of falsified theories in the belt of a program, abandon that program until there is an alternative program with theories that are themselves corroborated." So, Weintraub, off the shoulder of Lakatos, is effectively pronouncing that the hard core cannot be challenged in itself; and even if its 'protective belt' of subsidiary, derived propositions are falsified, the faith can, and does, carry on regardless—an example of the practice of 'mumpsimus', viz., persistence with something proven to be false, a word that a tickled Joan Robinson had discovered to her delight in the flow of her debates with the neo-neo-classicals, or neo-Walrasians.[27]

Weintraub (1985, p. 148) thus emerges with his conclusion: "All that Robinson's criticisms demonstrate is that she is not used to engaging in neo-Walrasian analysis, something that people perhaps knew already. To repeat, her criticisms of the idea of equilibrium itself, which focus on its presumed lack of realism, only identify Robinson as one who works in a different program." In Weintraub's depiction, the world appears to comprise silos: the neo-Walrasians were in one, and Joan Robinson & Co were in another, viz., the post-Keynesian programme, with very limited possibilities of communication. Ergo, "her criticisms of the neo-Walrasian program must be read as rhetorical set-pieces designed to gather new adherents to her preferred program; that is, her arguments are for the most part exhortations, not exercises in theoretical or empirical logic" (ibid., pp. 148–149). They "cannot withstand close scrutiny"; they are "based on profound misunderstanding"; they "flowed from her flawed understanding"; they are "without merit".

---

[27] David Newbery (2017, p. 486) records that Frank Hahn's father, a chemist but also a considerable literary figure, had founded *Simplicissimus*, a satirical magazine, in 1896; illustrations of mumpsimus could well have found space in those pages.

Weintraub could have found Joan Robinson's reflection on this, written a decade earlier: "Some theorists, even among those who reject general equilibrium as useless, praise its logical elegance and completeness. A system of simultaneous equations need not specify any date nor does its solution involve history. But if any proposition drawn from it is applied to an economy inhabited by human beings, it immediately becomes self-contradictory. Human life does not exist outside history and no one has correct foresight of his own future behaviour, let alone of the behaviour of all the other individuals which will impinge upon his. I do not think that it is right to praise the logical elegance of a system which becomes self-contradictory when it is applied to the question that it was designed to answer" (Robinson, 1974, p. 2). "The lack of a comprehensible treatment of historical time, and failure to specify the rules of the game in the type of economy under discussion, make the theoretical apparatus offered in neo-neoclassical text-books useless for the analysis of contemporary problems, both in the micro and macro spheres" (Robinson, 1974, p. 11).

Joan Robinson is thus reduced, in the eyes of the neo-Walrasian adherent, to the lowly status of a political ideologue, not a serious economist—"a moralist, not an analyst" (Weintraub, 1985, p. 149). He lays the charge that "Robinson has also argued that the neo-Walrasian programme biases the kinds of question that economists can ask, and answer" (ibid.). This charge is entirely valid, of course; and Joan consistently argued that economics had a moral dimension as it could not exclude value judgements. In contrast, the neoclassical Walrasian imagination was blinkered to focus exclusively on "equilibrium" of supply and demand, "how scarce means are allocated between alternative uses in accordance with consumers' tastes" (Robinson, 1979b, p. 92). Consumer sovereignty is the ultimate arbiter of the uses to which scarce resources are put; in turn, consumer sovereignty is conflated by the neoclassicals and neoliberals with individual choice and liberty, the sine qua non and the legitimation of the liberal society. The question of anti-social situations is ruled out by definition. This is what Joan was referring to when she cited "consumers' tastes run to large cars, overheated rooms, and an excessive consumption of meat ... The central doctrine of orthodox economics is the defence of the freedom of anyone who has money to spend, to spend it as he likes" (ibid.). And it can be added that the initial distribution of wealth, income and resources across individuals (and classes, which do not figure in the orthodox lexicon) is taken as a given and not the subject of economics per se. But are poverty and inequality, unsustainable natural resource use, not part of the subject matter of economics? For raising these issues, Joan Robinson and the post-Keynesians are labelled moralists, not economists.

Weintraub (1985, p. 149) goes on: "curiously, preaching *is* one of the few ways that one *can* attack a progressive research program like the neo-Walrasian program. ... The choice which a scientist makes between two competing research programs will be based, using a rational reconstruction of the growth of knowledge, on the relative progressivity of the programs themselves. But such reasoned judgments are, in practice, not often found. The programs may compete for adherents with arguments that transcend reason. Moral suasion may be appropriate to coax a potential convert to the cause, the emergent program. Whether the convert finds the new religion congenial may later depend on the actual progressivity of the program as tested by the theoretical and empirical progress it demonstrates, but in the first instance, converts may be won by emotion, not reason. … The ultimate issue of course is the relative progressivity of the neo-Walrasian and post-Keynesian research programs. What is required to judge the issue is a comparative appraisal of those two competing research programs"; Weintraub frequently refers to the "progressivity" of a programme, without specifying what this attribute embodies—his own neo-Walrasian programme, presumably, would excise all value judgements out of its frame of reference; yet, in so doing, this would be no less ideological a statement than that of the post-Keynesians who would explicitly include value judgements that would be anathema to the neoclassicals. The post-Keynesians (and other Cambridge heterodox groups) challenged the inefficiencies and inequities of the capitalist system; the neo-Walrasians would sweep all that under the carpet of equilibrium and provide a legitimation of the system as was. Cambridge was a perennial, and personal, battleground for this clash between the flag bearers of the diametrically opposed approaches.

1.4.11 Joan Versus Hahn—History Versus Equilibrium

Joan Robinson was Frank Hahn's pet hate—he spoke of a "love-hate" relationship with her, but in all public and academic exchanges, it was the second part of the binary that seemed always to dominate. The exchange over the meaning and salience, or the lack of these, of the notion of equilibrium, especially Walrasian general equilibrium that most engaged Hahn and most enervated Joan offers a specular display of fireworks.

Frank consistently attacked Joan when she was alive and when she was dead: she was 'incoherent', she did not read his papers, she did not understand the first thing about general equilibrium, she set up a false binary between history and equilibrium because she had a wrong understanding of time, like Nicky Kaldor—both, he complained, "let common sense in" into an exercise of pure logic; "where is your model?" he demanded. For Hahn, the problem of fundamental, existential uncertainty was resolved by the assumption "that there is perfect insurance, viz. contingent futures markets" (Hahn, 1974). How happy the world would now be if it had followed his edict and worked out perfect insurance for an inherently imperfect, unstable and unpredictable planet and its people. Hahn complained bitterly of Joan and Nicky: "She was very hostile to equilibrium because in her (just as in Nicky) common sense kept breaking through. They saw the economy in a much more Schumpeterian way, perhaps in a Marxian way, much more historically based" (Hahn, 1989, p. 899). Yes, many would agree that they had their feet in the mud of relevant reality; Hahn had his head in the stratosphere of sterile abstraction. The general-equilibrium-with-money approach was deified by him as his ilk's holy grail, but for all Cambridge heterodox practitioners, it was a trail into a wilderness of vacuous inconsequence. Joan Robinson (1978, p. 108), writing in 1969, observed that "the neo-neoclassicals have succeeded in tying themselves up again in habits of thought from which Keynes had had 'a long struggle to escape'. (However, when it comes to offering advice on questions of national policy many of them propound quite simple-minded Keynesian views.)" Joan had Bob Solow (in his 1964 Wicksell Lectures on *The Nature and Sources of Unemployment in the United States*) in her sights, though she could, later, equally have aimed her slingshot at Frank Hahn who had to take leave of his equilibrium to participate in public debates on Government policy in the 1980s, as for instance in the joint letters with Robert Neild attacking Thatcherite monetarism then practised under the watch of Alan Walters, her economic adviser (Hahn & Neild, 1980, 1981), and by that time "his bête noir" (Newbery, 2017). Solow, in an interview in 2019, declared himself to be a Keynesian in the short term, a neoclassical in the long run, and by default an itinerant wandering soul in search of the truth for the vast real-life space in between. Likewise, Hahn, towards the end, became progressively disenchanted with the usefulness of economic theorising—presumably of the kind he had practised it over his career. Writing three years after Hahn's retirement, Beaud and Dostaler (1995, p. 251) observed that the reconstruction of theory that Hahn wanted, "based on a dynamic theory of general equilibrium that would integrate time, money and growth, [is] a goal that seems remote at this point"; and it slipped further away with the passage of historical time and all that it brought in its wake. Terence Hutchison shared his recollection of the early years of Hahn, Walters and Gorman in Birmingham: "it was a very split Faculty. But these Young Turk types: they varied a lot. ... Alan Walters at least had an interest in the real world. I suppose Hahn and Gorman *thought* they had an interest in the real world, but they didn't realise it *wasn't the real world* up on the blackboard which they were manipulating so magnificently" (quoted in Tribe, 2002, p. 138; emphasis in the original).

A direct fight generates a lot of heat but also sheds light on the roots of their disagreement. In 1972, the year Frank Hahn returned to Cambridge as professor, *Economic Journal* carried Nicky Kaldor's *The Irrelevance of Equilibrium* Economics, his singeing attack on the Walrasian general equilibrium tradition. Two years later, Joan Robinson published her own broadside against the same foe in the form of her *History Versus Equilibrium*. She sent it along to an apoplectic Frank Hahn.

Hahn, of course, accepted the applicability of the 'neoclassical' label to himself (though Joan would have put him in the neo-neoclassical box). "There are three elements in my thinking which may justify it: (1) I am a reductionist in that I attempt to locate explanations in the actions of individual agents; (2) In theorizing about the agent I look for some axioms of rationality; (3) I hold that some notion of equilibrium is required and that the study of equilibrium states is useful" (Hahn, 1984, pp. 1–2). The application of these, and other related postulates, become the basis for Hahn's mission: the "reconstruction … based on a dynamic theory of general equilibrium that would integrate time, money and growth" (Beaud & Dostaler, 1995, p. 251), as prophesied by him in his "I come as John the Baptist" speech to the Association of University Teachers of Economics (AUTE) congregation in the early 1970s.

But here was Joan throwing the kitchen sink at him. "Some theorists, even among those who reject general equilibrium as useless, praise its logical elegance and completeness. A system of simultaneous equations need not specify any date nor does its solution involve history. But if any proposition drawn from it is applied to an economy inhabited by human beings, it immediately becomes self-contradictory. Human life does not exist outside history and no one has correct foresight of his own future behaviour, let alone of the behaviour of all the other individuals which will impinge upon his. I do not think that it is right to praise the logical elegance of a system which becomes self-contradictory when it is applied to the question that it was designed to answer" (Robinson, 1974, p. 2). "The long wrangle about 'measuring capital' has been a great deal of fuss over a secondary question. The real source of trouble is the confusion between comparisons of equilibrium positions and the history of a process of accumulation. … But it is not allowable to flip the stills through a projector to obtain a moving picture of a process of accumulation" (ibid., pp. 9–10). "The lack of a comprehensible treatment of historical time, and failure to specify the rules of the game in the economy under discussion, make the theoretical apparatus in neo-neoclassical text-books useless for the analysis of contemporary problems, both in micro and macro spheres" (ibid., p. 11).

In her critique, Joan enlisted Keynes: "When Keynes summed up what he felt to be the main difference between his theory and that from which he had had 'a long struggle to escape', he pointed to the admission into his argument of the very obvious fact that expectations about the future are necessarily uncertain. The uncertainty that surrounds expectations of the outcome of a plan of investment, of the course of technical progress, of the behaviour of future prices, not to mention the effects of natural and political cataclysms, cannot be reduced to a 'calculated risk' by applying the theorems of mathematical probability. Keynes described equilibrium theory as 'a pretty, polite technique' 'which tries to deal with the present by abstracting from the fact that we know very little about the future'" (Robinson, 1974, p. 1).

Frank Hahn's response comes in a 2-page letter. "Thank you for the copy of 'History Versus Equilibrium'. It is the occasion to break my resolve not to continue with pointless shadow boxing" (Hahn, 1974). "I suppose the basic difference between you and me is that you say 'historical time matters' and assume not only that no has thought of that before, but also throw your hand in. I believe it needs analysis and I claim that on present evidence work is proceeding in a natural way out of this tradition we have. Moreover, this work has produced results for historical models. Where are yours?" (Hahn, 1974, emphasis in original). There is resonance here to Axel Leijonhufvud's (1973, p. 330) entertaining allegorical account of master "modl" makers of the northern tribe of Econ: "While in origin the word 'modl' is simply a term for a concrete implement, looking at it only in these terms will blind the student to key aspects of Econ social structure. 'Modl' has evolved into an abstract concept which dominates the Econ's perception of virtually all social relationships, whether these be relations to other tribes, to other castes or status relations within his caste. Thus, in explaining to a stranger, for example, why he holds the Sociogs or the Polscis in such low regard, the Econ will say that 'they do not make modls' and leave it at that." Joan, disempowered for want of a 'modl', was dismissively relegated by Hahn to the status of Simone de Beauvoir's second sex.[28]

Hahn's harangue continues, becoming more specific: "You really must consider the possibility that Arrow-Debreu, leave alone Arrow-Hahn, knew exactly what they were about. ... You have got the story slightly wrong. It is not true that in Arrow-Debreu the future is known. Indeed they adopt the Ramsey-Savage-Keynes approach of uncertain 'states of the world'. What is supposed is that there is perfect insurance, viz. contingent futures markets. ... I think you are fundamentally mistaken in thinking that uncertainty etc. lead one to have to throw an equilibrium concept out of the window. I made all this crystal clear in my inaugural. Equilibrium is about adaptation and organisms like human beings can certainly adapt to even a stochastic environment" (Hahn, 1974).

In effect, Hahn's device to deny the critique becomes passing on the buck from an assumption of perfect foresight to the substitute assumption of perfect insurance. Not surprisingly, as Jan Kregel (2011) in his piece "Evolution versus Equilibrium", obviously inspired by Joan, points out: "Post Keynesian economists have followed Joan Robinson's criticism of general equilibrium theory as abolishing history by allowing all contracts to be executed today for all future contingencies. This was the justification for the support of financial innovation to provide for the completeness of futures markets. The recent crisis has shown that force of history. Instead, many evolutionary and Keynesian economists have suggested the approach of cumulative causation as an approach that includes history and eschews equilibrium. This approach may provide a way to take history seriously in economic analysis." The sequence of financial crises offers its own judgement in the case of Hahn versus Robinson.

---

[28] The patronising condescension continues: "One of the great sorrows of being in Cambridge is that hardly anybody reads hardly anything. You are welcome to come and browse amongst my odd hundred pre-prints, all directly relevant to what you have to say" (Hahn, 1974, emphasis in original). Elsewhere, ruminating on what he called his "love-hate relationship" with Joan, Hahn persists with his attack: "You know, we all realize there is more to economics than general equilibrium, but the question is: what to do about it? She tried her best, but she never managed ... she never got there" (Hahn, 1989, p. 899). "I had no preconceptions against Joan. From my very early years, Joan was very kind to me. I had no reason to disagree with her other than that she was wrong (ibid., p. 898). ... When I was brought to Cambridge as a young man, I was to become Joan's disciple. It was just impossible! I was very friendly with her. Richard and she were extremely kind to me. But it was often impossible to follow her, she was incoherent, that is all I can say ... I think of economic theory as a way of organizing our minds, so that we do not speak of things that are incoherent" (ibid., p. 904).

It is striking that this exchange takes place in the early 1970s. Kaldor's *Irrelevance of Equilibrium* was in 1972; Joan's *History versus Equilibrium* was in 1974. These sailed past Hahn with no impact; it was at the AUTE Conference in 1972 that he made his dramatic stage pronouncement as "John the Baptist" who had seen general equilibrium with money as the future. But it was precisely in this time frame that there were other—some argue terminal—critiques of the general equilibrium project (Sonnenschein (1972), Mantel (1974), Debreu (1974), followed by Kirman and Koch (1986), Kirman (1989), Saari (1992, 1996)). Ackerman (1999, p. 13) provides a convenient analytical summary of the critiques of general equilibrium project and concludes: "Exactly 100 years after the 1874 publication of Walras' most important work, the Sonnenschein-Mantel-Debreu (SMD) theorem proved that there was no hope of showing that stability is a generic property of market systems. Another quarter-century of additional research has found no way to sneak around this result, no reason to declare instability an improbable event. These negative findings should challenge the foundations of economic theory. They contradict the common belief that there is a rigorous mathematical basis for the 'invisible hand' metaphor; in the original story, the hand did not wobble."

"General equilibrium is still dead after so many years", writes Ackerman who goes on to marvel at the longevity of the notion: "Exactly 100 years after the 1874 publication of Walras' most important work, the SMD theorem proved that there was no hope of showing that stability is a generic property of market systems. Another quarter-century of additional research has found no way to sneak around this result, no reason to declare instability an improbable event. These negative findings should challenge the foundations of economic theory. They contradict the common belief that there is a rigorous mathematical basis for the 'invisible hand' metaphor; in the original story, the hand did not wobble."

Ackerman (1999, p. 13) uses (the invariably apposite) words of Keynes: "how disappointing are the fruits, now that we have them, of the bright idea of reducing Economics to a mathematical application of the hedonistic calculus".[29]

He marvels at the longevity of the notion, notwithstanding all these critiques:

> For years after the Spanish dictator actually died, the mock television newscast on "Saturday Night Live" was periodically interrupted with a "news flash" informing viewers that "General Franco is still dead!" This served both to satirize the breathlessly urgent style of television news reporting, and to suggest that after many decades of taking an absolute ruler for granted, the world needed more than one reminder that he was no longer alive and well. Much the same is true for general equilibrium theory. (Ackerman, 1999, p. 1)

According to Servaas Storm, "It is known that Hahn regarded the Sonnenschein-Mantel-Debreu theorem as a dangerous critique against

---

[29] The quotation is from *Essays in Biography, Collected Writings X, p. 184n.*

mainstream neoclassical economics. ... Hahn was an accomplished general-equilibrium theorist who spent his career on trying to meaningfully introduce money into the Arrow-Debreu (or Walrasian) general equilibrium model. His personal tragedy is that his life project failed; this is the reason that he turned bitter at the end of his life—notwithstanding his successful takeover of the Cambridge ship. One can carry this one step further: not only Hahn's life project failed, it is a fact that around the end of the 1970s, it became clear that the complete general equilibrium research project was a failure. Mathematical economists Hugo Sonnenschein, Ralf Mantel and Gérard Debreu showed in the early 1970s that (perfectly competitive) market processes will not necessarily (leave alone automatically) reach a unique and stable general equilibrium. It is a corollary of Sonnenschein–Mantel–Debreu that a Walrasian auction will not always find a unique and stable equilibrium, even in ideal conditions.

Put differently, general equilibrium was shown to exist under extremely restrictive conditions (including the absence of money), but there was no way in which such a system if and when it is out-of-equilibrium, could return to a stable and unique equilibrium—without the help of an external 'market master' aka social planner. End of story, in other words."

> Hahn. for all his qualities, should have understood that his life project was doomed to fail—as any Keynesian economist (worth the name) could have told him: money is not a commodity but a social institution, the main function of which is to help money owners to deal with fundamental uncertainty. This is the whole rationale of Keynes' liquidity preference, for which there exists no justification in a general equilibrium system with a complete set of contingent (insurance) and future markets. General equilibrium theory can at best deal with risk (in a probabilistic sense), but it cannot by definition deal with fundamental uncertainty à la Knight and Keynes (1921). This means that Hahn's life project was a dead-end street, as it turned out to be and as would have been obvious to anyone who read and understood Keynes.

Partly, no doubt, as a consequence of such a realisation filtering through the neoclassical school, and partly reflecting the very wide spectrum of Hahn's own curiosities and capabilities, the research agenda shifted away from the original unremitting focus on general equilibrium. Partha Dasgupta provides some pertinent details: "With the possible exception of Douglas Gale, none of Hahn's Quakers chose to work on general equilibrium theory. The range covered by that revolving group is extraordinary: Sabourian (member of a later cohort of Hahn's pupils) worked on the theory of repeated games, Hart studied the character of incomplete contracts for understanding the raison d'etre of firms, Heal's PhD thesis was on decentralised planning mechanisms, Atkinson reintroduced the study of income and wealth inequality, Maskin laid the foundations of mechanism design, Stiglitz not only helped to lay the foundations but also applied them to explain features of economic life that can be attributed to asymmetric information among people, Brandenburger's thesis was on the place of beliefs in social engagements, and so on. As for me, I have been all over the place, but never general equilibrium theory. In my obituary notice of Frank

Hahn, I drew attention to Hahn's catholicity of intellectual interests by reporting that at our time we (Quakers) always gave him drafts of our papers to read and that he invariably read and commented on them even though typically they would not have been on general equilibrium theory" (Dasgupta, communication courtesy the publisher).

And Storm takes that narrative towards the present with a quick look at the theoretical predilections of the senior Faculty as currently constituted. "Hahn's coup brought game-theory, microeconomics (industrial organization), micro-econometrics—and mainstream macroeconomics (along WB-IMF lines). One can call this 'Just So' economics: partial, micro story-telling using maths (without the maths, it wouldn't look scientific). Partha Dasgupta has worked mostly on environment/population using Ramsey-growth models; David Newbery worked mostly on microeconomics and micro-econometrics (often using a game-theoretic model). Sanjeev Goyal is a game theorist (and never worked on general equilibrium). The other professors include Leonardo Felli (contract theory), Robert Evans (game theory) and Giancarlo Corsetti (macroeconomics, Corsetti is a former IMF economist)—no general equilibrium theory. Macro-economics turned to rational-expectations models, called Dynamic Stochastic General Equilibrium (DSGE) models, which had nothing to do however with Hahn's general equilibrium theory (notwithstanding the label DSGE); these models, proposed by Lucas and Sargent, are single-eternally-lived representative agent Ramsey-growth models, in which there is no uncertainty (only risk), no money (hence money is neutral), and no distributional problem (because there is only one agent), and no connection with reality whatsoever" (Servaas Storm)

> The death of General Franco was not a panacea for the problems of Spain. Yet it did open many democratic, pluralist options, no longer requiring the whole country to follow one authoritarian leader. Spain after Franco looks a lot more like neighboring countries in the freedom of expression that it offers its citizens, and the diversity of opinions that can be expressed in public debate. The same might yet be true of economics after general equilibrium. (Ackerman, 1999, p. 17)

Mainstream economics has since moved on and reinvented itself along alternative tracks seeking to bypass the key problematic feature of the neoclassical frame, including alternatives to commodity-based models of consumer behaviour; the recognition and analysis of social interactions in influencing behaviour; and at the systemic level, the imperative for some non-market institutional architecture and instruments for countering the innate instability of markets. Colander's (1996) specification of a "post-Walrasian macroeconomics" gives centrality to institutional dimensions.

"General equilibrium is, indeed still dead after all these years. There are two principal causes of the death: the instability of the neoclassical model can be attributed to the inescapable difficulties of the aggregation process; and the highly individual, asocial nature of consumer preferences. These are not recent innovations, but design flaws that have been present since the origins of the theory in the late nineteenth century. ... The guaranteed optimality of market outcomes and laissez-faire policies died with general equilibrium. If economic stability rests on exogenous social and political forces, then it is surely appropriate to debate the desirable extent of intervention in the market ... in order to rescue the market from its own instability" (Ackerman, 1999, p. 16). Along with all the bathwater, out also go all normative claims made for laissez-faire. In a real sense, the agenda of Keynes (1926) gains some renewed salience.

In this context, Leijonhufvud's amusing musing on the symbolic status of the 'modl' as the tribal totem deserves a full reading: "It has become increasingly clear that the Econ associate certain, to them significant, beliefs with every modl, whether or not they also claim that modl to be a 'useful tool'. That taking 'usefulness' as the point of departure in seeking to understand the totemic culture of this people leads us into a blind alley is particularly clear when we consider the Math-Econ caste. The Math-Econ are in many ways the most fascinating, and certainly the most colorful, of Econ castes. There is today considerable uncertainty whether the 'priest' label is really appropriate for this caste, but it is at least easy to understand why the early travellers came to regard them in this way. In addition to the deeply respectful attitude evidenced by the average Econ towards them, the Math-Econ themselves show many cultural patterns that we are wont to associate with religious orders or sects among other peoples. Thus they affect a poverty that is abject even by Econ standards, and it seems clear that this is by choice rather than necessity. It is told that, to harden themselves, they periodically venture stark naked out into the chill winds of abstraction that prevail in those parts. Among the rest of the Econ, who ordinarily perambulate thickly bundled in wooly clothing, they are much admired for this practice. Furthermore, glossolalia—the ability to say the same thing in several different tongues ... (in several Math tongues—the Indo-European languages, for example, do not count) ... is a highly esteemed talent among them. The Math-Econ make exquisite modls finely carved from bones of walras. Specimens made by their best masters are judged unequalled in both workmanship and raw material by a unanimous Econographic opinion. If some of these are 'useful'—and even Econ testimony is divided on this point—it is clear that this is purely coincidental in the motivation for their manufacture. There has been a great deal of debate in recent years over whether certain Econ modls and the associated belief-systems are best to be regarded as religious, folklore and mythology, philosophical and 'scientific' or as sports and games. Each category has its vocal proponents among Econologists of repute but very little headway has been made in the debate. The ceremonial use of modls and the richness of the general Econ culture in rituals has long been taken as evidence for the religious interpretation. But, as one commentator puts it, 'If these beliefs are religious, it is a religion seemingly without faith'. This interpretation seems to have stranded on this contradiction in terms and presently is not much in favor. More interesting are the arguments of those who have come to view certain Econ belief-systems as a form of quasi-scientific cosmological speculation" (Leijonhufvud, 1973, pp. 333–334).

Hahn's quest for his holy grail ended in disappointment. Partha Dasgupta shares insights in his fine obituary: "Frank often said if he had his life all over again he would have chosen to be a cosmologist. ... The beautiful, austere features of general equilibrium of economic systems drew him to their study. ... He couldn't but look astonished at attempts to put general equilibrium models to use in deriving practical policy. The purpose of economic theory was to test the logical coherence of social thinking, or so he often said and occasionally wrote. In that attitude to theoretical musings he resided in Classical Greece and the centuries of the Talmud. When I once remarked to him that his sense of the purpose of theoretical discourse resembled that of logicians in Sanskritic India, he said so much the better for that lost world" (Dasgupta, 2013). Towards the end of an interview by Marcello Basili and Carlo Zappia (2005) on the occasion of his 80th birthday, Hahn suddenly remarks: "By the way, you have not asked me whether I am happy to be an economist. I am not sure that I am. I would have liked to have been a theoretical astronomer, and not because as an astronomer you cannot feel the pressure of reality, but because you can theorize and the reality can catch up with you." Had Hahn, at the end of his career, given up on his early vision—as the self-declared John the Baptist—of general equilibrium being the future of economics? Dasgupta (ibid.) tells us that "over time he saw less and less in the point of economics, even theoretical economics. He read history, biographies, and the New Yorker."[30]

Servaas Storm observes: "There is a sad historical irony that Hahn's hopeless mission failed when he was in exactly the place where the argument had been developed (years before his arrival) why he would fail".

Towards the end, a dejected Joan shared her own sorrows over 'the disintegration of economics', and moved away from her own track of recasting Keynesian economics with a long-term growth framework. Alex Millmow (2003, p. 561) observes: "In her last public comments on the state of economics, Joan Robinson made some extraordinary remarks that conveyed profound pessimism and theoretical nihilism; ... her comment about economic theory disintegrating in her hands was not made casually; it was, rather, an acknowledgement that her project to integrate Keynes with the classical surplus theory had failed. This acknowledgement crystallised into her rejection of the long-period equilibrium interpretation of Keynes's theory of unemployment. At the end of her life Robinson was willing only to embrace the more traditional short-period Keynesian model grounded in uncertainty and expectations." Theory was unable to discipline unruly reality.

"She was very hostile to equilibrium because in her (just as in Nicky) common sense kept breaking through. They saw the economy in a much more Schumpeterian way, perhaps in a Marxian way, much more historically based" (Hahn, 1989, p. 899). Hahn the abstractionist seems to convert history into noise and common sense into a vice not a virtue. The clash of epistemologies

---

[30] David Newbery's (2017) informative and sensitive appreciation of the life and work of Frank Hahn is more guarded in these respects.

and methodologies, of the purposes and questions that defined the discipline, were too chasmic to bridge.

This provides an appropriate backdrop for the reassertion of historical/evolutionary and institutional/sociological dimensions into the frames of analysis. In sharp contrast to Hahn's three-point reductionist distillation of the world according to neoclassicism, his contemporary Robert Neild (2013, pp. 12–13) offers (much later) his preferred three-point condensation of the Cambridge sociologist Garry Runciman's (1989) evolutionary theory of societal change. "[Runciman] argues that:

1. Society is shaped by the pursuit of power, defined as the ability to influence or dictate the behaviour of other people in one's favour.
2. Power comes in three forms: economic power (which Marx dogmatically said was predominant); persuasive power (from the pulpit to modern media); and coercive power (the threat or use of force).
3. As technology and human ideas evolve, these three types of power change in a manner analogous to the genetic evolution of species: new machines, new weapons, new means of communication and new means of organising society keep changing the way each type of power may be exercised and its strength.

What it implies is that you cannot predict how society is going to evolve because new technological ideas and social ideas evolve as unpredictably as new mutations and recombinations of genes in nature. Just as a biologist may be able to explain after the event, but not before, why a new species found a niche and prospered, so we may be able to say after the event why a new species of power was successful in changing a society."

Neild, the eclectic, institutional, practical, short-term Keynesian and long-term Schumpeterian, endorses the approach of Runciman the sociologist: "This theory does not mean that there are no exceptional people who are not driven by a greedy pursuit of power. Nor does it mean that there is no free will or anything like that. Moreover it may be possible to make intelligent short-run predictions when you see that a new species of power is emerging. ... I find this a wonderfully rational, unmoralistic and coherent approach to understanding society."[31] Joan and Nicky might not have yielded as much ground to the ascribed explanatory power of unpredictable evolutionary processes but, with their historically rooted Schumpeterian or Marxian or related approaches, might well have pitched their tents somewhere in this quadrant. Robert Neild (2013) wrote passionately about "Economics in Disgrace", referring to the takeover of the subject by the neoclassical mathematical general equilibrium school à la Hahn, and the consequent huge costs imposed on the world by its adoption in right-wing policy frames in governments and the Bretton Woods

---

[31] See also, Neild (2017) where he develops his case for adopting an evolutionary approach.

institutions. The point to elicit really is that apart from these hard-core neo-neoclassicals, the other groups of Cambridge economists worked within social imaginations and theoretical frameworks which were potentially open to multidisciplinary analysis. Regrettably, and at great cost, that openness was shut down by the cloistered, mono-focal orthodox vision that came to dominate the subject in Cambridge, and beyond. The 'vaguely cognate disciplines' of sociology, history and development studies were systematically exiled or expelled from the reading and staff lists.

1.5 Semantics and Pedantics

There are seriously diminishing returns to obsessing on definitions; too much of it, and the desire will and should surely sicken and die. Yet, the vexed question of identities and labels, of semantics and pedantics cannot be entirely sidestepped. A few rough and sturdy checks could help in establishing fairly firm and usable understandings. On both sides of the orthodox-heterodox line, there is significant internal heterogeneity and theoretical and methodological disagreement; but these 'within' differences do not override the intrinsic 'between' differences which define the hostile polarity characterising the binary.

What and who is 'classical', the point of reference for being 'neoclassical'? What and who is 'orthodox', and likewise, 'heterodox'? What and who is 'radical' or 'dissenting'? And thus, also for conservatives, liberals, neoliberals, ordoliberals, sociological liberals and humanistic liberals (Audier, 2013), libertarians, neocons and so on. A convenient user guide to the 'neoclassicals' is provided by Tony Lawson (2013): "What is this school called neoclassical economics? Does it exist? Should it? Where does the term 'neoclassical economics' come from, and is there any connection between any of the current interpretations of the term and its original meaning? How do we make sense of competing current interpretations? Is there a sustainable formulation? These and related questions are raised and answered in an attempt to bring clarity to ongoing economic discussion and debate."[32] For those of the faith, neoclassicism pervades all nooks and crannies of mental space, and every person and every decision is subjected to individual optimising behaviour—for the believers it could be a form of enlightenment, for the *kafirs* observing the phenomenon, it appears often as a form of delusional lunacy; another leap faith into the promised nirvana of general equilibrium assures the faithful that such individual conformity also produces the best possible outcome for the collectivity; there is no other way. And so, in the face of the technology of amniocentesis being used for sex-selective abortions, the response from the neoclassical state of

---

[32] There are the original neoclassicals, the 'vulgar' economists à la Marx; there is Marshall; across the channel there are the Austrians, then the Walrasians; going across the ocean, there are the contending clans of the purist general equilibrium *wallahs* in MIT and Harvard; Joan Robinson's (1978) "neo-neoclassicals" and the hands-on policy practitioners grouped in Chicago; then starts the sequence of syntheses of various parentage some of them quite dubious; and each category is capable of further subdivisions.

mind would be that such femicide would be self-correcting through market forces: the supply of girls would decline, their price would rise, dowry would come to be replaced by bride price, and parents would no longer indulge in such action. Similarly, why would parents wish to educate their daughters when the returns to education would be reaped after her marriage and for the rest of her life by her husband's family? Such reductionist decision-making algorithms could be extended on a 360-degree basis, from burning down the Amazon, to hunting or fishing species into extinction. That there could be other ways of thinking, acting and living is treated as a deviation from rational choice behaviour as understood by such affected states of mind.[33]

However, in his recent autobiographical work, Sen (2021) expresses unhappiness with the usage of the term 'neoclassical'. In passing, Sen makes references to Joan, Kahn and Kaldor as the "dominant orthodoxy"; "there was a public battle going on between the orthodox and the rebels. Of the latter, Frank was the leader" (2021, p. 369). These binary labels are opposed to those used in the present work where orthodoxy is associated with Frank Hahn and the neoclassical group. Sen stirs the pot: "the contrast between neoclassical and neo-Keynesian economics often figured in these disputes. 'Neoclassical' in the context of economics was not a term I knew before I came to Cambridge, but it was an example of a neologism that had caught on and was widely used in these debates. Any hope that I could guess what it really meant to be 'neoclassical' in economics, by analogy with the more common use of the term in art, sculpture and architecture, proved to be completely hopeless. Recollecting examples of neoclassical art I had seen, such as Jacques-Louis David's masterly painting of the *Oath of Horatii*, or Antonio Canova's sculpture *Psyche Revived by Cupid's Kiss*, offered me no clue." And Thorstein Veblen also comes under the cosh: "A little research revealed that the original use of 'neoclassical' in economics, which was apparently by Thorstein Veblen in 1900, seems to have been intended as a prelude to a criticism of what was thus described and it is still hard to dissociate the term from its original derogatory use. … Veblen was a productive thinker, with much greater clarity on subjects other than his rather messy delineation of neoclassical economics" (Sen, 2021, pp. 288–289). Sen finds it "easier to think of neoclassical simply as mainstream economics, with a cluster of maximizing agents—capitalists, labourers, consumers and so on— who follow mechanical rules of maximization by equating marginal this with marginal that" (Sen, 2021, p. 288). Some, perhaps many, could find this a reduction too far and one that detaches neoclassicism from the ideological and political, and policy premises and positions with which it is inseparably associated. Sen seems to be in agreement here with Dasgupta (2010) who, speaking dismissively of his radical and heterodox colleagues in the Faculty, says, "no doubt Fellows in other disciplines were told by colleagues in my Faculty that Hahn and Matthews were neoclassical economists, a term of abuse among

---

[33] On the first example, see, for instance, Dharma Kumar (1983a, 1983b); for the latter, see the body of literature of the economics of human capital as in the oeuvre of Gary Becker.

progressives at Cambridge in those days; people in other disciplines wouldn't have been expected to know that by the 1970s the term had become meaningless." Curiously though, Hahn himself seems to have little difficulty accepting, using three postulates of neoclassicism that he laid down, that the label neoclassical applied to him.

Then there is the extensive and ever-expanding lexicon spawned by, or rather on, Keynes.[34] First, there was plain old Keynes; the Keynes after being processed by the Circus and kept in shape, and oriented towards long-term analysis, by Joan and Kahn; Keynes à la Harrod, Hicks, Patinkin and others; then come the progeny of dubious synthetic parentage, the shotgun weddings across some clans of neoclassicals and Keynesians—Samuelson's version on his neoclassical synthesiser; the new classicals, the new Keynesians, the new classical synthesis, and so on, and on. And of course, there was (rather) a lot more to Keynes than *The General Theory*, not least his early pronouncement on *The End of Laissez Faire* including the multi-level roles of the state, very distinct from the later macroeconomic agendas within a national as well as a global frame; and then, Keynes was certainly an imperialist, but was he also a socialist?

But is there such a specific species of heterodoxy? What are its attributes? Tony Lawson (2006) expounds: "Heterodoxy serves as an umbrella term to cover the coming together of separate projects or traditions. In answering the question, 'what distinguishes heterodoxy from the orthodoxy?', [Lawson] argues that matters of ontology are central. In answering the question, 'how are the various traditions that make up the modern heterodoxy to be distinguished from each other?', [he] defends criteria other than varying commitments to specific substantive theories, policy measures or techniques (or basic units) of analysis" (Lawson, 2006). Pasinetti's enunciation of the markers of the Cambridge approach also bears clear resonance with the thought-lines being developed by the social ontologists of the Cambridge Realist Workshop (CRW) and the related Cambridge Social Ontology Group (CSOG)—intellectual forums that dug deeper into the foundations of heterodox enquiry giving primacy to a focus on the nature of social reality as a prior level of exploration with links and correspondences to epistemological and methodological

---

[34] Alan Blinder's foray into "what does it mean to be a Keynesian" makes reference to Keynesian theory, models, economics, paradigm, ideas, direction, environment, features, belief, tradition, and world; then uses prefixes such as 'many', 'most', 'thoroughly', 'very'; then separates 'anti-inflation' Keynesians, 'conservative' Keynesians; or 'positive', as against 'normative' Keynesians; 'pre-1970' Keynesians presumably in distinction to later or even earlier species; there are references to 'traditional', 'orthodox' Keynesians; to the Keynesian 'revolution', 'renaissance'; and also to 'super-Keynesian' models; and of course, there are the plain old Keynesians, the post-Keynesians, neo-Keynesians, new Keynesians; to which could be added the 'new Cambridge' as against, implicitly, 'old Cambridge'; and then Skidelsky (2007, p. 5) adds 'hydraulic' and 'fundamental' Keynesians, then dividing the latter into those with theory or methodology preoccupations; and not to be forgotten, Joan Robinson's 'bastard' Keynesians. User guides for negotiating the maze of "who is a Keynesian" and of what type, are available, amongst others, from Blinder and Solow (1978), Blinder (1988), Gerrard (1991), Mankiw (1992), Gordon (2009), Lavoie (2009), Bliss (2010), De Vroey and Duarte (2012) and Skidelsky (2007); however, there is no general guarantee of successfully emerging at the other end.

questions. It might not be far-fetched to speculate that it was the lobotomizations of the orthodox, neoclassical framing of the world of economics that induced the emergence from 1980, and then the sustained evolution, of CRW and CSOG pioneered and led by Tony Lawson from his singular position within the increasingly mainstream Faculty of Economics and Politics (as it was then labelled). Pratten (2014) and Martins (2014) explore different dimensions of the distinct lines of social theory catalyzed substantially by Cambridge traditions of heterodox economics. As with the subsequently widening contours—beyond the Cambridge roots—of the development of post-Keynesian and other heterodox traditions, there is now a flourishing epistemic community around social ontology and social theory for which "Cambridge" has increasingly come to symbolize the original and inspirational source.

Helpfully, Luigi Pasinetti (2007, pp. 219–236) has ventured to pin down what he regards as the foundational premises of the Cambridge school. He stipulates nine attributes which, in his view, could be labelled as key *differentia specifica* of the Cambridge Keynesian and heterodox school ("even at the cost of not always sharing all of them entirely"; he also cautions these are "building blocks" still looking for a systematic integrating theoretical scaffolding in the Cambridge tradition). Here are Pasinetti's nine markers:

- "Reality (and not simply abstract rationality) as the starting point of economic theory";
- "Economic logic with internal consistency (and not only formal rigour)";
- "Malthus and the Classics (not Walras and the Marginalists) as the major inspiring source in the history of economic thought";
- "Non-ergodic" (in place of stationary, timeless) economic systems; "the recognition of the importance of historical time"; "the belief that the economic systems do not have a point of rest, nor do they allow turning back the clock";
- "Causality vs. interdependence"; "economic relations should not all be forced into systems of simultaneous equations";
- "Macroeconomics before microeconomics";
- "Disequilibrium and instability (not equilibrium) as the normal state of the industrial economies";
- "Necessity of finding an appropriate analytical framework for dealing with technical change and economic growth"; and
- "A strong, deeply felt social concern".

Though there could, inevitably, be some intra-'heterodox' quibbling over the list, there is likely to be sufficient consensus for it to serve as a template against which to identify the differences between this, 'Cambridge' approach and that of the neoclassical grouping with all its own internal definitional nuances and jostling—for instance, disagreements over key issues, for example, calculable risk versus Keynesian or Knightian uncertainty; acceptability of the marginal productivity theory of distribution; over market structures and im/

perfect competition; the existence of economies of scale and its implications; assumptions about the historical time and equilibrium; and so on.

Lately, from the same Cambridge quarter, Ha-Joon Chang, someone that most would firmly locate with the 'heterodox' lineages, has expressed concern at such a labelling. "To begin with, 'heterodox' is quite a problematic term. Think about it. If you are a member of the Greek or the Russian Orthodox Churches, the Pope is the heterodox guy in the story, so it is all relative" (in Abdelrahman, 2019, p. 578). This light-hearted dismissal of the term 'heterodox' is perhaps itself a little light; yes, it is all relative, but it is the contextualisation and framing that reveals the lines of separation. Staying within the imagery of religions, perhaps using a binary of Christianity-Islam might have reunited the Pope with the other strands on that side of the line; Ha-Joon's characterisation perhaps reads differences in castes for differences in religions. In the Cambridge tales told here, the orthodox-neoclassical-mainstream campaign against the heterodox groups took the form of the crusades—there was little confusion, apart from a few fence-sitters in no-man's land, about which groups were on which side of the line these confrontations.[35]

Ha-Joon Chang has another grouse about terminology: "At least in development economics, the kind of economics I do now used to be orthodox in the 1960s and the 1970s. Therefore, I try to say 'non-neoclassical' instead of heterodox. By calling ourselves heterodox, we are already conceding the ground" (in Abdelrahman, 2019, p. 578). Are we? There is much to Ha-Joon Chang's complaint, but also much that is problematic. Even, and especially, from the 1950s with the emergence of the Nehru-Mahalanobis planning, five-year plans and Soviet-inspired plan models in India, and the Prebisch-Singer structuralist-historical interventions which laid the parallel basis for State-led import substitution accumulation processes for development; these were both attacks on the rule of the doctrine of comparative advantage. These new approaches quickly became dominant in the post-imperial Third World, but it would be hard work to find any contemporary references to them that labelled them 'orthodox'; if anything, that label applied to the imperial doctrine still, that is, market-led comparative-advantage guided development, as projected, for instance, in the Bhagwati and Desai (1970) critique of Indian planning. Nor did structuralism ever attract the 'orthodox' label. Both approaches, with their dovetailing affinities, were rightly deemed as breakaway initiatives away from imperial economic orthodoxy, and as such could legitimately be regarded as representatives of heterodoxy, as manifest in the Third World development economics. Of course, the state-led, import-substituting accumulation regimes and policies dominated in Third World economics at the time, quickly

---

[35] Tony Lawson (2006) thoughtfully explored "the nature of heterodox economics"; various converging definitions or markers of "heterodoxy" are offered by Frederic Lee (2007, 2009) and in the statements of various journals, sites and blogs using "heterodox" as a descriptor; a very useful mapping of schools of thought is provided by Marc Lavoie (2009, Table 1, pp. 1–24); and Ingrid Kvangraven and Carolina Alves (2019) purposively run through most frequently asked questions pertaining to the utility and usage of the term "heterodox".

inducing the Bhagwati-Desai neoclassical critique.[36] Analogously, Keynesianism emerged as the dominant force in the 1950s and 1960s in UK theorising and policy making, as opposition to the 'orthodox' classical-neoclassical doctrines, till it was itself displaced in Whitehall during the 1970s. A more stable and (even if approximately) usable terminology becomes available if 'orthodox' is variationally applied to the related schools of neoclassicism that emerged and dominated economic theorising, explaining and legitimising the capitalist economy from the late eighteenth century onwards. Likewise, what is deemed 'mainstream' depends on who/what is dominant in discourse and power in that era. In this sense, arguably, the terms orthodox, neoclassical, mainstream sit comfortably together.

The fuzziness of lines of division within and between traditions also takes a different form, where individual economists display multiple or hybrid identities. For instance, Bob Solow seems to adopt an à la carte approach, where he declares himself to be being a Keynesian in the short run, and neoclassical in the long run, and a seeker in the period in between; James Meade was a thoroughbred neoclassical in his trade theory, but he was also a Keynesian, and when it came to policy issues, he was a radical redistributionist though outside the domain of the market—he wanted interventions to significantly equalise the initial, inherited inequalities that characterised British society; and Tony Atkinson was deeply influenced by this policy approach of Meade, and followed a similar radical redistributionist track, while remaining essentially neoclassical in his analytical framework. And recently, Ha-Joon Chang has declared himself to be a pluralist. "I would not call myself a Keynesian, because Keynesianism is mostly about macroeconomics, such as business cycles, unemployment, monetary policy and so forth, which I don't work on. If I did macroeconomics, I would do it the Keynesian way, but I don't do it, so I am not a 'practising' Keynesian. Actually, it is not clear what I am! Even while being extremely critical of neoclassical economics, I use some neoclassical economics, which has some useful and interesting insights. Even though I hate his politics, I have read quite a lot of Friedrich von Hayek and other economists from the Austrian school of economics, who had some profound things to say. I have also been influenced by institutionalism, Marxism and all the early development economists I mentioned above" (ibid., p. 579). "So, I have been influenced by so many different schools—neoclassical, Marxist, Austrian, institutionalist, developmentalist and behaviourist. When I say I am a pluralist, it is not a political ploy. I genuinely believe that all these different schools have useful things to say and people should learn from all of them. I am not carrying the torch for the Cambridge Keynesians, but I guess I am carrying the torch for critical thinking" (ibid., pp. 579–580).

---

[36] For instance, B. R. Shenoy submitted a *Minute of Dissent* in 1955 on the Nehru-Mahalanobis "Soviet-style" Second Five Year Plan document; Shenoy was powerfully influenced by Hayek whose lectures at the LSE in 1931, which developed into his *Prices and Production* book, he had attended; and he was an early member of the Mont Pelerin Society.

Pluralism in pedagogy is surely to be lauded, Frank Hahn wanted two parallel *Principles* courses to be delivered by expositors from opposing traditions; from the other side of the ideological divide, Ajit Singh was famous for ensuring that undergraduates under his charge were properly versed in the neoclassical traditions that he himself critiqued. Indeed, this was the simple demand of the seventeen original signatories of the letter of protest by Cambridge PhD students, endorsed by a list of 797 academics—at the height of the neoclassical, orthodox, control over the Faculty of Economics in 2001. But plurality for its own sake is a slippery slope which would rapidly deposit its practitioners into the embrace of the nihilism of post-modernism, bereft of any operative criteria for selecting one line of theoretical thinking and associated policy messages over any other. It would not do to wander aimlessly admiring the 100 varieties blooming in the field of economics; a criterion for selection would be indispensable if economics and economists were to perform any useful societal function, on either or any side of the line/s. In this sense, pluralism and eclecticism do not conflate; and there is no escape from association with value judgements, inherently 'arbitrary', of one form or another.

One criterion for identification could be whether its use leads to different groups and collectivities; it is quite likely that Ha-Joon would find himself in the same salubrious and intellectually congenial company in the salon named 'non-neoclassical' at one entrance and 'heterodox' at another; and yet other doors to the same salon might be labelled 'dissenters', or 'radicals'. While theoretical conversations could well be as cantankerous, though friendly, as ever, policy discussions might find a far greater degree of convergence, not least because all these differentiated card holders would unanimously reject the 'orthodox'-'neoclassical'-'mainstream'-'neoliberal' perspective on society and policy, viz., one that has individualism and the non-negotiable rule of private property at its heart, conflating human freedom with the 'free market'. And this explains the loose definition used in dictionaries and anthologies 'radical' and 'dissenting' economists as being those that reject and oppose the premises and methods of neoclassical-mainstream-orthodox economics (as, e.g., in Arestis & Sawyer, 1992).

In the words of Joan Robinson: "The movement of the 'thirties was an attempt to bring analysis to bear on actual problems. Discussion of an actual problem cannot avoid the question of what should be done about it; questions of policy involve politics (*laissez-faire* is just as much a policy as any other). Politics involves ideology; there is no such thing as a 'purely economic' problem that can be settled by purely economic logic; political interests and political prejudice are involved in every discussion of actual questions. The participants in every controversy divide into schools—conservative or radical—and ideology is apt to seep into logic" (Robinson, 1977, p. 1318).

REFERENCES

Abdelrahman, M. (2019). A conversation with Ha-Joon Chang. *Development and Change, 50*(2), 573–591.

Ackerman, F. (1999). *Still dead after all these years: Interpreting the failure of general equilibrium theory.* Working Paper No. 00-01, Global Development and Environment Institute, Tufts University. https://sites.tufts.edu/gdae/files/2019/10/00-01Ackerman_StillDead.pdf

Arestis, P., & Sawyer, M. C. (Eds.). (1992). *A biographical dictionary of dissenting economists.* Edward Elgar.

Aslanbeigui, N., & Oakes, G. (2002). The theory arsenal: The Cambridge circus and the origins of the Keynesian revolution. *Journal of the History of Economic Thought, 24*(1), 5–37.

Audier, S. (2013). A German approach to liberalism? Ordoliberalism, sociological liberalism, and social market economy. *L'Economie Politique, 60*(4), 48–76. English translation at: https://www.cairn-int.info/article-E_LECO_060_0048%2D%2Da-german-approach-to-liberalism.htm

Basili, M., & Zappia, C. (2005). An interview with Frank Hahn the occasion of his 80th birthday. *Storia del Pensiero Economico N. S., 2*(2), 13–18.

Beaud, M., & Dostaler, G. (1995). *Economic thought since Keynes: A history and dictionary of major economists.* Routledge.

Benn, T. (2000). Interview. Commanding Heights, Public Broadcasting Service, Interviewed on 26 October 2000. https://www.pbs.org/wl7h/commanding-heights/hi/people/pe_name.html

Bhagwati, J. N., & Desai, P. (1970). *India: Planning for industrialization; industrialization and trade policies since 1951.* Oxford University Press, on behalf of OECD.

Birner, J. (2009). *F. A. Hayek's Monetary Nationalism after seven decades.* Paper Presented at the Storep Annual Conference, Florence. Universiti di Trento and University College, Maastricht.

Blaug, M. (1975). Kuhn versus Lakatos, or paradigms versus research programmes in the history of economics. *History of Political Economy, 7*(4), 399–433.

Blinder, A. S. (1988). The fall and rise of Keynesian economics. *Economic Record, 64*(4, December), 278–294.

Blinder, A. S. (2000). How the economy came to resemble the model. *Business Economics, 35*(1), 16–25.

Blinder, A. S., & Solow, R. M. (1978). What's 'new' and what's 'Keynesian' in the 'New Cambridge' Keynesianism? In K. Brunner & A. H. Meltzer (Eds.), *Carnegie-Rochester conference series on public policy* (Vol. 9, pp. 67–85). North-Holland.

Bliss, C. (2010). The Cambridge Post-Keynesians: An outsider's insider view. *History of Political Economy, 42*(4), 631–652.

Bronfenbrenner, M. (1971). The 'structure of revolutions' in economic thought. *History of Political Economy, 3*(1), 1–11.

Burgin, A. (2012). *The great persuasion: Reinventing free markets since the Depression.* Harvard University Press.

Coats, A. W. (1969). Is there a 'structure of scientific revolutions' in economics? *Kyklos, 22*(2), 289–296.

Colander, D. (Ed.). (1996). *Beyond microfoundations: Post-Walrasian macroeconomics.* Cambridge University Press.

Dasgupta, P. (2010). Interview with Partha Dasgupta 6th April 2010. In S. Harrison & A. Macfarlane, *Encounter with economics*. Interviews filmed by A. Macfarlane and edited by S. Harrison. University of Cambridge. http://sms.cam.ac.uk/collection/1092396

Dasgupta, P. (2013). Obituary: Frank Hahn. *Royal Economic Society Newsletter, 161*(April).

De Vroey, M., & Duarte, P. G. (2012). *In search of lost time: The neoclassical synthesis*. Working Paper No. 2012-07. Department of Economics, FEA-USP. http://www.repec.eae.fea.usp.br/documentos/PedroDuarteN07WP.pdf

Deane, P. (1978). *The evolution of economic ideas*. Cambridge University Press.

Debreu, G. (1974). Excess demand functions. *Journal of Mathematical Economics, 1*(1), 15–21.

Dunn, S. P. (2009). Cambridge economics, heterodoxy and ontology: An interview with Tony Lawson. *Review of Political Economy, 21*(3), 481–496.

Evon, D. (2016). *'First they ignore you, then they laugh at you' quote isn't Gandhi's*. https://www.snopes.com/fact-check/first-they-ignore-you/

Gerrard, B. (1991). Keynes's *General Theory*: Interpreting the interpretations. *Economic Journal, 101*(405), 276–287.

Gordon, R. J. (2009, September 14). Is modern macro or 1978-era macro more relevant to the understanding of the current economic crisis? *Economist's View*. https://economistsview.typepad.com/economistsview/2009/09/is-modern-macro-or-1978era-macro-more-relevant-to-the-understanding-of-the-current-economic-crisis.html

Hahn, F. (1974). *Letter to Joan Robinson*. JVR/vii/182/1-2. In Joan Violet Robinson Papers held at King's College Archives, Cambridge.

Hahn, F. H. (1984). *Equilibrium and macroeconomics*. Basil Blackwell.

Hahn, F. (1989). Robinson–Hahn love–hate relationship. In G. R. Feiwel (Ed.), *Joan Robinson and modern economic theory* (pp. 895–910). Palgrave Macmillan.

Hahn, F., & Neild, R. (1980, February 25). Monetarism: Why Mrs Thatcher should beware. *The Times*.

Hahn, F., & Neild, R. (1981, March 28). Letter signed by 364 economists. *The Times*.

Harcourt, G. C., & King, J. (1995). Talking about Joan Robinson: Geoff Harcourt in conversation with John King. In J. E. King (Ed.), *Conversations with post Keynesians* (pp. 168–186). Palgrave Macmillan. Also in: *Review of Social Economy, 53*(1), 31–64.

von Hayek, F. (1967). *Studies in philosophy, politics and economics*. Routledge & Kegan Paul.

Kanbur, R. (2015). *The end of laissez-faire, the end of history, and the structure of scientific revolutions*. Working Paper No. 2015-04. Charles H. Dyson School of Applied Economics and Management, Cornell University. http://publications.dyson.cornell.edu/research/researchpdf/wp/2015/Cornell-Dyson-wp1504.pdf

Keynes, J. M. (1921). *Treatise on probability*. Macmillan and Co.

Keynes, J. M. (1926). The end of laissez-faire. Hogarth Press (pamphlet). In *The collected writings of John Maynard Keynes* (Essays in Persuasion) (Vol. IX). Royal Economic Society, Palgrave Macmillan, 1972.

Keynes, J. M. (1936). *The general theory of employment, interest and money*. Macmillan.

Kirman, A. (1989). The intrinsic limits of modern economic theory: The emperor has no clothes. *Economic Journal, 99*(395, Supplement Conference Papers), 126–139.

Kirman, A., & Koch, K. J. (1986). Market excess demand in exchange economies with identical preferences and collinear endowments. *Review of Economic Studies, 53*(3), 457–463.

Kregel, J. (2011). Evolution versus equilibrium. *Journal of Economic Issues*, 45(2), 269–275.
Kuhn, T. S. (1970). *The structure of scientific revolutions* (2nd ed.). University of Chicago Press.
Kumar, D. (1983a). Male utopias or nightmares? *Economic and Political Weekly*, 18(3).
Kumar, D. (1983b). Amniocentesis again. *Economic and Political Weekly*, 18(24).
Kvangraven, I., & Alves, C. (2019). *Heterodox economics as a positive project: Revisiting the debate*. ESRC Global Poverty & Inequality Dynamics Research Network Working Paper 19, 24p. https://gpid.univie.ac.at/wp-content/uploads/2019/07/GPID-WP-19.pdf
Laidler, D. (1976). Inflation in Britain: A monetarist perspective. *American Economic Review*, 66(4), 485–500.
Lavoie, M. (2009). *Introduction to post-Keynesian economics*. Palgrave Macmillan.
Lawson, T. (2006). The nature of heterodox economics. *Cambridge Journal of Economics*, 30, 483–505.
Lawson, T. (2013). What is this 'school' called neoclassical economics? *Cambridge Journal of Economics*, 37(5), 947–983.
Lee, F. S. (2007, November 1–3). *Making history by making identity and institutions: The emergence of Post-Keynesian–heterodox economics in Britain, 1974–1996*. Paper presented at the EAPE Conference, Universidade Porto, Porto.
Lee, F. (2009). *A history of heterodox economics: Challenging the mainstream in the twentieth century*. Routledge.
Leijonhufvud, A. (1973). Life among the econ. *Economic Inquiry*, 11(3), 327–337.
Lindahl, E. (Ed.). (1958). *Selected papers on economic theory*. George Allen and Unwin.
Mankiw, N. G. (1992). The reincarnation of Keynesian economics. *European Economic Review*, 36, 559–565. Republished in B. Snowdon & H. R. Vane (Eds.), *A macroeconomics reader* (pp. 445–451). Routledge, 1997.
Mankiw, N. G. (1992/1997). The reincarnation of Keynesian economics. *European Economic Review*, 36, 559–565. Republished in Snowdon, B., & Vane, H. R. (Eds.). *A macroeconomics reader* (pp. 445–451). Routledge, 1997.
Mantel, R. (1974). On the characterization of aggregate excess demand. *Journal of Economic Theory*, 7(3), 348–353.
Marcuzzo, M. C. (2003). Joan Robinson and the three Cambridge revolutions. *Review of Political Economy*, 15(4), 545–560.
Marcuzzo, M. C. (2012). *Fighting market failure: Collected essays in the Cambridge tradition of economics*. Routledge.
Marx, K., & Engels, F. (1967/1888). *The Communist manifesto*, with an Introduction by A.J.P. Taylor. Penguin.
Millmow, A. (2003, October). Joan Robinson's disillusion with economics. *Review of Political Economy*, 15(4), 561–574.
Mirowski, P., & Plehwe, D. (2009). *The road from Mont Pelerin: The making of the neoliberal thought collective*. Harvard University Press.
Neild, R. (2013). *Economics in disgrace: The need for a reformation*. GIDS Discussion Paper No. 01-13. Graduate Institute of Development Studies.
Neild, R. (2017). The future of economics: The case for an evolutionary approach. *Economic and Labour Relations Review*, 28(1), 1–9.
Newbery, D. (2017). Frank Horace Hahn 1925–2013. *Biographical Memoirs of Fellows of the British Academy, XVI*, 485–525. https://www.britac.ac.uk/sites/default/files/23 Hahn 1837 9_11_17.pdf

Parsons, W. (1983). Keynes and the politics of ideas. *History of Political Thought*, 4(2), 367–392.

Pasinetti, L. L. (1991). Richard Ferdinand Kahn, 1905–1989. *Proceedings of the British Academy*, 76, 423–443.

Pasinetti, L. L. (2007). *Keynes and the Cambridge Keynesians. A 'revolution in economics' to be accomplished*. Cambridge University Press.

Pernecky, M., & Wojick, P. (2019). The problematic nature and consequences of the effort to force Keynes into the conceptual cul-de-sac of Walrasian economics. *Cambridge Journal of Economics*, 43(3), 769–783. https://doi.org/10.1093/cje/bey039

Pernecky, M., & Wojick, P. (2020). A response to 'Keynes, Kuhn and the sociology of knowledge: A comment on Pernecky and Wojick'. *Cambridge Journal of Economics*, 44(6), 1425–1428. https://doi.org/10.1093/cje/beaa017

Pratten, S. (ed.) (2014). *Social ontology and modern economics*. London: Routledge.

Robinson, E. A. G. (1989). Colin Clark. In *E. A. G. Robinson Papers* held at the Marshall Library Archives, University of Cambridge, 5/7/15/1.

Robinson, J. (1974, Autumn). History versus equilibrium. *Thames Papers in Political Economy*, 11p. https://docs.gre.ac.uk/__data/assets/pdf_file/0025/122578/TP_PPE_74_3_compressed.pdf

Robinson, J. (1976). *The state of play*. RFK/12/2/81/81-82. 2p. Typed note by Joan Robinson held in the Richard F. Kahn Papers, King's College Archives, University of Cambridge.

Robinson, J. (1977). What are the questions? *Journal of Economic Literature*, 15(4), 1318–1339.

Robinson, J. (1978). *Contributions to modern economics*. Academic Press.

Robinson, J. (1979b). The disintegration of economics. In *Collected economic papers* (Vol. V, pp. 289–297). Basil Blackwell.

Runciman, W. G. (1989). *A treatise on social theory: Volume II, Substantive social theory*. Cambridge University Press.

Saari, D. G. (1992). The aggregated excess demand function and other aggregation procedures. *Economic Theory*, 2(3), 359–388.

Saari, D. G. (1996). The ease of generating chaotic behavior in economics. *Chaos, Solitons & Fractals*, 7(12), 2267–2278.

Samuelson, P. A. (1955). *Economics* (3rd ed.). McGraw Hill.

Samuelson, P. A. (1987). Out of the closet: A program for the Whig history of economic science. *History of Economics Society Bulletin*, 9(1), 51–60. Reprinted in Medema, S. G., & Waterman, A. M. C. (Eds.). (2015). *Paul Samuelson on the history of economic analysis: Selected essays* (pp. 25–36). Cambridge University Press.

Samuelson, P. A. (1997). Credo of a lucky textbook author. *Journal of Economic Perspectives*, 11(2), 153–160.

Seers, D. (1963). The limitations of the special case. *Bulletin of the Oxford Institute of Economics and Statistics*, 25(2), 77–98.

Sen, A. (2021). *Home in the world: A memoir*. Allen Lane and Penguin Random House.

Skidelsky, R. (2007). What is essential about Keynes today? *Annals of the Fondazione Luigi Einaudi*, LI, 5–16.

Skidelsky, R. (2009, September 17). Keynes: The return of the master. *The New York Times*.

Snowdon, B., & Vane, H. (1997). *A macroeconomics reader*. Routledge.

Solow, R. M. (2019). Interview. *Infinite History* (Video). https://infinitehistory.mit.edu/video/robert-m-solow

Sonnenschein, H. (1972). Market excess demand functions. *Econometrica, 40,* 549–563.

Sraffa, P. (1926). The laws of returns under competitive conditions. *Economic Journal, 36*(144), 535–550.

Taylor, L. (1984). Review: Social choice theory and the world in which we live. Review of *Choice, welfare and measurement* by Amartya Sen. *Cambridge Journal of Economics, 8*(2), 189–196.

Thomas, R. (2020). Keynes, Kuhn and the sociology of knowledge: A comment on Pernecky and Wojick. *Cambridge Journal of Economics, 44*(6), 1415–1424. https://doi.org/10.1093/cje/beaa016

Tribe, K. (2002). *Economic careers: Economics and economists in Britain, 1930–1970.* Routledge Taylor & Francis.

Weintraub, E. R. (1985). Joan Robinson's critique of equilibrium: An appraisal. *The American Economic Review, 75*(2), 146–149. http://www.jstor.org/stable/1805586

Wicksell, K. (1904). Ends and means in economics. Inaugural lecture delivered at the University of Lund on 16 September 1904. Reprinted in E. Lindahl (Ed.), *Selected papers on economic theory* (pp. 51–66). George Allen and Unwin, 1958.

CHAPTER 2

The Warring Tribes

Abstract Despite their great history and formidable strength and diversity, the heterodox traditions and lineages of Cambridge economics rapidly atrophied and virtually evanesced from the Faculty from the 1970s as the Faculty, and the DAE, lapsed into the control of the neoclassical orthodox camp within the Faculty through a sustained anti-heterodox campaign led initially by Frank Hahn and Robin Matthews, with 1975–1990 forming the short period of inflexion. How did this remarkable turnaround occur? How could the diverse and productive intellectual ecology that flourished and formed that great banyan tree of organically evolving Cambridge heterodox traditions mutate so rapidly into a seemingly genetically modified single-strain industrial monocropping culture? How were intellectual imaginations and curiosities lobotomised? Cambridge heterodox economics had not been built in a day, but given the dramatic speed of change, it seemed to have been dismantled in one. This chapter reconnoitres the battleground, reviews the opposing formations and reconstructs the strategies and *modus operandi* especially of the antagonists, focussing in particular on the development of Hahn's 'academy' of 'nephews', protégés and fellow travellers and their strategic deployment in gaining control of external and internal commanding heights, that is, decision-making structures, which in turn could be utilised in the campaign against the heterodox groups in the DAE and the Faculty in Cambridge. While some parts of the overall picture are part of folklore of Cambridge warfare, this chapter brings together the many pieces of the jigsaw, and in the process elicits fresh insights into the conduct of the campaign. As such, this has largely been an untold story.

© The Author(s), under exclusive license to Springer Nature
Switzerland AG 2022
A. Saith, *Cambridge Economics in the Post-Keynesian Era*, Palgrave
Studies in the History of Economic Thought,
https://doi.org/10.1007/978-3-030-93019-6_2

2.1 A Sanctuary of Sages

Barring those greats who had passed on—Marshall, Pigou, Robertson and Keynes—the Faculty in the 1960s boasted virtually the full pantheon of Cambridge economics, at once a fabulous treat and a formidable threat to any vyoung recruit.[1] Looming large over all was the triumvirate of Lord Kahn, the anointed disciple of Keynes, the fierce white-haired goddess *Kali*, Joan Robinson and the sage of sages, the venerated muse and recluse Piero Sraffa.

Cambridge was rife with divisions, intellectual and interpersonal. With a few overlaps, Cambridge economics comprised a cluster of uncomfortably co-existing though usually co-respecting tribes: in simplified binaries, there were the abstractionists versus the empiricists; the pure theory *wallahs* versus the applied artisanal group. But there were subdivisions: the numbers people had three strains—the deep statisticians in the form of the DAE working on structural, long-term, foundational dimensions under Richard Stone; the eclectic ready and agile policy practitioners and fixers following the creed of 'Reddaway's Method' and later, in the form of the Cambridge Economic Policy Group (CEPG) under Wynne Godley, those dealing with short and medium period forecasting policy models, simulations and counterfactuals. The abstractionists were also in two broad camps, at first sight, the old and new neoclassicals, both the residual old guard and some fresh Trojan horses, versus The Rest. But the theoreticians of the Rest were a seriously segmented lot comprising several roving heterodox sects each with its venerated gurus, though with followers of shifting or multiple intellectual affinities and loyalties: the neo-Ricardians, the Sraffians, the Marxists, the Keynesians, the neo-Keynesians and other substantial mavericks, like Nicholas Kaldor or Richard Goodwin. These were all rich seams of gold for anyone who could gain entry and negotiate the mazes, tunnels and dead ends. The interfaces and interstices provided creative spaces, and the interplay of ideas and ideologies generated heat and light in equal measure. Keynesianism provided one overarching unifying, if implicit, theoretical and intellectual framework, to argue for, within or against.

2.1.1 Class to Community: The Cement of War

For a while, this assemblage of intellects, as disparate as formidable, shared three powerful unifying bonds of recent collective experiences. The first was their shared loyalty to the memory and perceived precepts of the undisputed

---

[1] Over that period, the Faculty would include, amongst others: Alan Brown, David Champernowne, Phyllis Deane, Maurice Dobb, Charles Feinstein, Pierangelo Garegnani, Richard Goodwin, Frank Hahn, Richard Kahn, Nicky Kaldor, Robin Marris, R. C. O. Matthews, James Meade, Luigi Pasinetti, Brian Reddaway, Austin Robinson, Richard Stone; Robert Neild and Wynne Godley came a little later. Under their watch was a younger cohort including Geoff Harcourt, M. J. Farrell, Francis Cripps, Bob Rowthorn, John Eatwell, Mario Nuti, Ron Smith, John Wells, Michael Kuczynski, not to mention the battalion of young turks at the DAE, Ken Coutts, Roger Tarling, Hashem Pesaran, Vani Borooah, Angus Deaton, Mervyn King, Michael Ellman, Terence Ward, Frank Wilkinson, Geoff Whittington, Tony Lawson, Terry Barker, Nick von Tunzelman, John Llewellyn and several other worthies.

common guru, Keynes, and with it the satisfaction of being part of the Keynesian revolution that had established a new national paradigm for economic policy, one that placed Cambridge at the national and international epicentre of the discipline. The second was the devastating experience of the war in personal and national terms, regardless of having won it. Most seniors had served in some capacity or other, whether as statisticians, economists, researchers, cryptologists or codebreakers: Keynes, Kahn, Austin Robinson, Champernowne, Stone, Kaldor, Meade, Brown, Reddaway, Godley, Neild had all been through those corridors of power as researchers, analysts or policy advisors, coming out with shared, if nuanced, perspectives on the significance of the role of the state, the need for economic management, engaging in strategic policy formulation on the hoof, and with an acute awareness of the paucity of usable statistics oriented towards economic monitoring and policy making. Keynes wrote his *How to Pay for the War* in 1940 as the young Meade and Stone were busy in the back room shoring it up by devising numbers on the national income. The war had been won as much with the bravery of the many and the few, and with sticks and spoons on the beaches, as with intellectual capability, technological advances and industrial might.[2] But there was also a younger cohort that had actually experienced mud and blood, boots and bullets. The palpable feeling of country through this accidental conjuncture of sharing, of belonging within a unitary social fabric, would have been one of the legacies, even if just an ephemeral post-traumatic hangover, of the intoxication of the collective war effort and ensuing victory. The third strand was in the immediate peace time that followed, but no less powerful in initiating another force for social transformation: this was the rise of the welfare state. The National Health Service and an inclusive incomes policy were nurtured in this fertile terrain, underpinning the economic performance of the post-war decades showcased as the so-called golden age, purported to run for a quarter-century from the end of the War. All this was reflected powerfully in Cambridge economics where a deeply imbued sense of the practical was pervasive, even as theglory of pure theory once again reclaimed its traditional throne.

Tony Benn (2000) recalled and conveyed the unusual, even extraordinary, sense of the idealism and the hopes prevalent in Great Britain in 1945 at the end of the war:

> I came back in a troop ship in the summer of 1945. I was a pilot in the RAF, and I was picked as a 19-year-old, to be a Labour candidate for Parliament. And we had all these soldiers that had been fighting in Asia, in Burma. I had been in the Middle East. And of course they all said, "Never again. We're never going back to unemployment, to the means test, to fascism, to rearmament. We want to build a new society." That was the hope, and it was that hope that gave us the welfare state, gave us the National Health Service, gave us full employment, gave us trade union rights. That hope really rebuilt the country from the bottom up. And it was a marvellous system. It was done against a background of terrible

---

[2] On this, see Alec Cairncross's study of the role and assignments of economists during wartime (Cairncross, 1995).

> deprivation. Our houses had been bombed, our factories had been bombed, our railways were bankrupt, our mines were bankrupt. We built it up, and people said, "This is better than allowing a lot of gamblers to run the world, where they're not interested in us, but only in profit".
>
> The war followed the Great Depression. In war you mobilize everything. Governments tore down the railings in Britain and America to make bullets. They rationed food, they conscripted people, and they sent them to die. The state took over. And after the war people said, "If you can plan for war, why can't you plan for peace?" When I was 17, I had a letter from the government saying, "Dear Mr. Benn, will you turn up when you're 17½? We'll give you free food, free clothes, free training, free accommodation, and two shillings, ten pence a day to just kill Germans." People said, well, if you can have full employment to kill people, why in God's name couldn't you have full employment and good schools, good hospitals, good houses? And the answer was that you can't do it if you allow profit to take precedence over people. And that was the basis of the New Deal in America and of the post-war Labour Government in Great Britain.

And there was surely much to talk about among themselves, myriad stories to exchange and share if only to lighten the burden of memories of the inescapable violence of waging war against other human beings; war brought them together, serving as an adhesive, at least for a while, within and between the older and younger cohorts mobilised in the First and Second World Wars. And it is indeed not difficult to imagine that the stocks of recollections would provide an endless flow of conversations papering-over Faculty divisions, among colleagues who might otherwise have been found at war between themselves across theoretical trenches or the trivia of timetables. A small sampler brings this distant past within touching distance.

James 'Alan' Calvert Brown majored in classics, took Part I of the Tripos in 1942, joined the Intelligence Corps where he had the rank of captain and saw service in India and Burma, "his duties there requiring a knowledge of Japanese; he learnt the language in a matter of months; returned to Cambridge and got his degree in 1947; when he came [to the DAE] as a research officer in 1952 he had no idea of switching to an academic career" (Stone, 1985: 191) but he remained till 1965, when he took the Chair of Econometrics at Bristol (a path taken later in 1976 by Angus Deaton).

> During a break for tea [in a conference in Keswick], he talked at length about code breaking during World War II. He mentioned that this staff, working long hours under stress, used to insert numerous obscenities into their own coded messages. However, he refused to tell them to stop the practice, despite an order to do so [as reported by veterans of Bletchley Park, their inclusion in messages makes it easier for others to break the code]. On another occasion, he mentioned a dinner in Merton when he was seated next to a visiting Japanese mathematician. Though he knew it was a silly question, he asked the visitor [presumably in Japanese] what he did in the war: the answer was that he worked out optimal flight paths for suicide pilots. (Creedy, 2008: 11)

A polyglot, apart from Greek and Latin, and Japanese that he learnt in a few months for wartime intelligence duties, and Italian that he picked up by reading local newspapers enough to translate the works of Italian mathematicians, Brown once confided "that he might spend August to learn Persian". Creedy notes that "he also became very keen on the new microcomputers and was developing some econometric software". John Creedy (2008: 3) confesses that Brown's *The Lognormal Distribution,* now a classic, "is the only econometrics book I know that has a perfectly apposite quote from Shakespeare at the head of each chapter"—a proclivity shared with Dennis Robertson who instead favoured products of Charles Dodgson's imagination.[3]

The highly accomplished mathematician, statistician and econometrician David Champernowne's recollections were as vivid in 1972 as they might ever have been, possibly with the accelerated access enabled by the bottle of amontillado that he would pull out from behind the books when diligently attending to his duty as mentor to research scholars assigned to him. In these occasional meetings, after the cursory "Are you alright?", one was regaled with stories, à la *Boy's Own,* of wartime involvements, with how the Enigma codes were cracked and other Bletchley Park folklore. Perhaps these were borrowed from the experience of his fellow King's College mathematician and life-long friend, Alan Turing,[4] with whom he devised, in Oxford, one of the earliest computer chess playing programmes, *TuroChamp*—to test this, he had to teach his wife chess playing so that she could be pitted against the computer programme; losing, as she did, was all in a good cause. Champernowne was a Cambridge man: he went to LSE for a bit, and came back to Cambridge; and later again when, like a homing pigeon, he traded his position of Professor of Statistics in Oxford for a readership in the Faculty of Economics in Cambridge, where apart from his three substantial books, he joined Brian Reddaway and Phyllis Deane to form a celebrated editorial team of the *Economic Journal.*

Robert Neild was 15 years old when the war started. Mary Kaldor (2019) picks up the story:

---

[3] From undergraduate Delhi days, I recall how these quotations from *Alice's Adventures in Wonderland* or *Through the Looking Glass* infected several of my circle, some going round indeed in circles looking for the perfect quotation to put at the top of their essays; the one almost seriously affected by this delightful affliction was Vinod Vyasulu who could not be restrained from giving more thought to digging up a quotation than perhaps to actually writing the essay. Roberston's *Lectures on Economic Principles* was indeed the source of this rogue virus.

[4] He might have felt these 'spy-thriller' cryptology stories more convivial than his experience in the 'S-Branch'—S for statistics—tasked to update Winston Churchill on a daily basis. Here Champernowne fell out with his superior, Viscount Cherwell "who was an excellent physicist but also a strong supporter of eugenics and held the working class, and various minorities, in contempt ... and had proposed saturation bombing of working class areas of German cities; Champernowne showed considerable moral courage to criticise this strategy ... and was moved to the Department of Statistics in the Ministry of Aircraft Production" (O'Connor & Robertson, 2014). Intellectual support for eugenics was quite widespread then, and amongst his colleagues would have been believers was James Meade, who served as Treasurer of the Eugenic Society.

> He was invalided out of the RAF in 1944 and sent to work for operational research. "The beauty of operational research", he later wrote, "was that there was no established discipline; there were just problems to which anyone might contribute. Physicists, biologists and scientists from other disciplines were applying their minds to the problems of war." He set to work collecting information on the sightings of U-boat snorkels with the aim of identifying a pattern of behaviour. He used the knitting needle system, the same system I used in constructing arms trade statistics when I worked for him at SIPRI. Each piece of information was put on an index-card with a row of perforated holes at the top. You punched the top of a specific hole to demarcate a particular characteristic—say, a specific recipient or supplier of a type of weapon. Then if you wanted to sort the data according to that characteristic you put a knitting needle through the relevant hole, and the cards you needed fell out. It is the same principle that underlies the digital databases we use today.

"He was much influenced by his uncle Philip Noel-Baker, a passionate peace activist who won the Nobel Peace Prize" (Kaldor, 2019), and was himself a peacenik, with his concept of 'defensive defence' that obviated the perceived imperative of an arms race; he was the founder-director of the Stockholm International Peace Research Institute (SIPRI); apart of course from winning the Andre Simon food-writing prize for his *The English, the French and the Oyster*, a work which encapsulated his critique of laissez-faire policies, as well has his later turn towards institutional economics.

Then, from John Beath (2015) we have a story on Aubrey Silberston.

> He was called up for army service in 1941 and, after officer training, was gazetted as a second lieutenant in the 8th battalion of the Royal Fusiliers and, after transit via South Africa and India, saw service in the Middle East, North Africa and, eventually, Italy. However, during an engagement following the drive north from the Anzio landings his unit found itself surrounded by German paratroopers and had no option but to surrender. This was in February 1944. As a POW he was moved from camp to camp but eventually ended up near Braunschweig. This was a large camp, filled with hundreds of officers from both British and Canadian regiments and though life was not exactly pleasant, one of the activities was a 'university'. Some of its lectures were on economics (given by David Solomons [1912–1995], who became a major academic figure in accountancy, holding chairs at the Universities of Bristol and Pennsylvania) and on the basis of these and his earlier contact with Joan Robinson, Aubrey decided that he wanted study economics. So he spent much time in the prison library reading relevant books and making copious notes. As an interesting aside, many economists of my generation will be familiar with the famous *Economica* article 'The Economics of a POW Camp' by R. A. Radford, about the network of economic exchanges that emerged in the camp, particularly the currency invention: the 'bullymark'. What few will know is that Radford and Aubrey were contemporaries as POWs in that very camp.

Or, consider the case of the naturally diffident Dennis Robertson, though it would be highly unlikely that he would be freely dispensing this story himself. Dennis Robertson joined the army but, curiously, "was simultaneously a member of the Cambridge University (anti-war) War and Peace Society, and of the Officer Training Corps (OTC)" (Fletcher, 2008: 42–43). His biographer Gordon Fletcher speaks of mules, camels and machine guns. Robertson had been promoted to the rank of captain in the cavalry not as a fighting horseman but as the transport officer for a machine-gun company.

> Machine-guns were being moved up in readiness for an impending battle (the First Battle of Gaza, March 1917) by the usual means of mule-transport. Now, mules had a well-recognised antipathy to camels, which were used for transporting supplies. During the crucial, final night march the customary rule of keeping the mules upwind of the camels was inadvertently broken. The mules scattered into the night, taking the precious machine-guns with them, and all then depended on the skill of the transport officer to ensure that, nevertheless, the guns were delivered in time for the battle. (Fletcher, 2008: 42–43, 45)

It is said that Robertson was always very reticent about the circumstances leading to the decoration; this was easily put down to his naturally shy temperament, though perhaps he might have felt that his story of recovering bolting mules and camels did not stand up to those of the cryptologist codebreakers; but in the end, it was he who was awarded the Military Cross for his acumen and bravery in this action.

There were so many others: Austin Robinson could have exchanged notes, from the First War, on how to pilot flying boats, with Frank Hahn who served as a flight navigator on bombing runs in the Second War. There was the case of Arthur Cecil Pigou, the conscientious objector who was assigned duties as an ambulance driver for the Friends Ambulance Unit in the First World War, who "insisted on taking jobs with particular danger" to assuage his conscience.[5] And then there were others who did no war, but had it done to them: Piero Sraffa, as a national of a hostile power after Italy entered the war, was placed under detention in 1940, and it took Keynes's energetic

---

[5] There is an addendum, or a variation, to this story to be found in the entry for Herbert Somerton Foxwell, one of Marshall's first pupils and early followers, who later fell out with him when Marshall favoured "the younger and more theoretically minded Arthur C. Pigou [as his] heir apparent", and later prevented the funding of a second Cambridge chair for Foxwell by declaring Foxwell unfit. "To this was added insult in 1916, when Pigou petitioned for exemption from military service in World War I, on account that there was 'no one' at Cambridge able to replace him (Foxwell mischievously wrote to the draft council reminding them he was available and ready)." "Herbert Somerton Foxwell, 1849–1936", History of Economic Though Website, Institute of New Economic Thinking. https://www.hetwebsite.net/het/profiles/foxwell.htm.

interventions to get him back to Cambridge.[6] And there was Friedrich Hayek, relocated along with LSE to Cambridge during the war years, being supported and helped by Maynard Keynes in the years that Hayek was busy writing his 1944 game-changing book *The Road to Serfdom* which attacked Keynes and Keynesianism. Hayek's wish to work on official duties was rejected in view of his antecedents; might a favourable dispensation from the government have pre-empted the writing of that fateful book by setting him off on a different track?

2.1.2   Community to Conflict: Cement to Sand

But if the Second World War for national defence and against fascist tyranny united, subsequent post-imperial cathartic adventures of the UK divided. Though it is difficult to gauge how these later experiences filtered through the Faculty, it is apparent that they would induce some discord in contrast to the kind of unity experienced in the earlier waves of national wars. Old habits die hard, as the imperialist invasion by the UK and France of Egypt in the Suez Crisis showed in 1956; Israel was also part of the invasion forces. In Cambridge, the general sentiment had long shifted towards support for decolonisation and assistance for the less developed economies. On the other side, Richard Kahn and others were deeply committed to Israel and had a continuous hands-on involvement with Israeli and Jewish affairs; a decade later, Frank Hahn was to make known that he was ready to go and fight for Israel in the Six-day War.[7] There would be resonance with positions taken with regard to the ensuing crises instigated by the dual oil prices hikes of the 1970s.

The US War on Vietnam had also been bubbling up to a boil, inducing international protest movements, especially from the youth. Cambridge was no exception, and organised and vocal opposition to the imperialist war in Vietnam was led by Ajit Singh, who had already been part of this movement in Berkeley from where he had brought it across to Cambridge when he joined the DAE in 1964. "In those days he was politically somewhat to the left of Chairman

---

[6] Away from Cambridge, but nevertheless revealing of the experience of such arbitrary internment, is Harald Hagemann's (2011: 655–656) reference to the personal account of Paul Streeten who was "born in Vienna in 1917 as Paul Hornig, emigrated to Britain in 1938 after the Anschluss and was among those interned refugees who were transferred from the Isle of Man to Canada under very bad conditions in early July 1940. He later commented (Streeten, 1986, 1989: 83) on the Isle of Man episode: 'Internment was horrid: not so much for the discomfort, meagre and tasteless food rations, often disagreeable company, crowded but mainly for being out of action at a time when one wanted to be in the midst of things. Some authors have recently maintained that the internees were quite happy with their lot and regarded it as an enforced but welcome holiday. This is quite wrong. All of us hated and resented the enforced idleness. And it was humiliating to have been rejected by the Austrians as a Jew, and imprisoned by the English as an Austrian. But Harold Nicolson and Richard Crossman, after a few months, helped to reverse this stupid action.'"

[7] Newbery (2017: 486n1) writes: "I was with Hahn at a conference at Varenna, Lake Como, in June 1967 at the outbreak of the Six-Day War, and Hahn was all for offering his services to Israel—the war was over too soon for this to take effect."

Mao, moderated ever so slightly in later life", so says Ajit's close friend and co-author Geoff Whittington (2016: 302). Whether inside the Faculty or on the street, Ajit quickly became, as one obituary observes, "a diligent tormentor of the established order" (The Times, 2015). The more the war intensified in Vietnam, the stronger anti-war student movements became in the West. Ajit moved along the crest of the wave of protest from Berkeley to Cambridge, and for the next decade, Vietnam dominated his political landscape, not just on the streets but also in the corridors of the Faculty. Geoff Harcourt says that the Faculty at Cambridge and its visitors were, like most other communities then, torn in two between hawks and doves, especially in the early 1960s: for example, in 1963–1964,

> there had been a huge row in the Faculty as Solow was 110% hawk and many of the Faculty were with him. Arrow was a dove; interesting as both were sons of immigrants and these are usually patriots, but Ken thought it an immoral war; people like Hahn and even Meade were inclined to be hawks, partly because Robinson was a raving dove. But by the end of 1966 when I left for Australia there had been a marked increase in the number of doves, including Solow who courageously spoke out for his changed position.[8]

Speaking about himself, Geoff states that he "was appalled by what was happening in Vietnam and was determined to get involved in the anti-war movement" when he went back to Australia at the end of the 1966: "I was meticulously briefed by Ajit and Martin Bernal on the history and the present position of the Vietnam War, which stood me in good stead when I became one of the leaders of the anti-Vietnam War movement in South Australia" (Harcourt, 2008: xv). It is worth noting here that while the UK did not have boots on Vietnamese soil, the Australian government, in its wisdom, had sent soldiers to Vietnam to fight Vietnamese people.

Vietnam politicised and divided the Faculty. This became conflated to a considerable extent with the rise to power of the US neoclassical and neoliberal groups in Cambridge Mass. and in Chicago; and early in the 1970s came the American involvement in Chile, the coup staged via the CIA, defended by Reagan, Thatcher, Hayek and Friedman, and vehemently opposed by all progressive groups, including the large cohort of younger left-Keynesian and other heterodox economists in the Faculty and the DAE. And on its heels came the crises unleashed by the OPEC oil price hikes: the collapse of the incomes policy in the UK, and of the state-accumulation led development strategies in the Third World, with the World Bank and the IMF holding the purse strings and dictating terms—again, leading to sharp divisions of positions amongst economists, including of course in Cambridge.

---

[8] This amalgamated account, in Harcourt's own words, draws on Harcourt (2007, 2012), two of his interviews about his times in Cambridge.

Then to top all this came Margaret Thatcher with her own imperialist foray in the Malvinas-Falklands, a war which deepened Thatcherite unity on the one side, but equally intensified and solidified opposition on the other. Not everyone, especially in Cambridge, bought readily into the Thatcherite bellicosity. Tam Dalyell (1932–2017), 11th Baronet, went into Cambridge a card-carrying Tory, Chairman of the Cambridge University Conservative Association in 1954–1955, came under the influence of the Cambridge left economists, with Joan Robinson encouraging him to take a second degree, in economics, which he did; he came out from Cambridge an independent-minded, incorrigible and intrepid anti-imperialist maverick leftist; he was a Labour Party MP from 1962 to 2005, by which time he had become the 'Father of the House'. (Tam Dalyell and Amartya Sen were contemporaries and became friends in Cambridge, as Sen in his warm recollection writes, "an odd result of being in the Conservative Club of which Tam was then the President" (Sen, 2021, pp. 312–313).) He challenged Mrs Thatcher over the sinking of the Belgrano where he assiduously argued that the ship was pulling away from the war zone when it was sunk. He was no respecter of parliamentary protocol, as evidenced by his "good-character" certificate for Margaret Thatcher in a debate in 1987: "She is a bounder, a liar, a deceiver, a cheat, a crook and a disgrace to the House of Commons" (BBC, 2017), for the pleasure of which utterance he was suspended from the House, neither for the first nor the last time. Wilson (2017): "His charge against the prime minister was that she had ordered the sinking of the Belgrano when it was outside the exclusion zone and heading back to port, posing no threat to British forces. The true purpose of the attack, Tam maintained, was to scupper a peace initiative that Peru was then leading." Using the words of the Argentinian writer Jorge Luis Borges, Tam Dalyell described the Falklands war as "two bald men fighting over a comb" (BBC, 2017). But of course, that comb was not toothless for Margaret Thatcher—she bared her fangs to great domestic and international effect and applause from far-right and neo-imperialist circles, and set the tone of her socially violent policies against miners, minorities and the working classes within the UK. This distant war had a powerful symbolic role in creating the national political environment within which Cambridge heterodox economics was attacked and dismantled during the 1980s.

2.1.3 *A Pride of Savage Prima Donnas*

And so, the glue wore off, the gloves came off, cement became sand, and Keynes, the common bond, had died as the War ended. Cambridge economics was rendered acephalous: common purpose, and old stories by now often repeated, faded into a distant memory; and idiosyncrasies, eccentricities, personalities, egos, individual intellectual passions of wilful prima donnas, resurfaced and took over. It was back to business as usual in the Faculty corridors and College halls. There were internal silos, internecine conflict, trench warfare and guerrilla skirmishes; and the emergence of separations, distinctions, divisions, camps, rivalries, competition and open warfare. And it was there for all to see and, if they had the stamina and stomach, to join (Table 2.1).[9]

The original, main, Chair in Political Economy was established in 1828 with George Pryme as its occupant till 1863, followed by Henry Fawcett (1863–1884), and then Alfred Marshall (1885–1908), the period when the subject really came into its own in Cambridge. This was followed by Arthur Cecil Pigou who held the chair from 1908 till his retirement in 1943. Thus, over the long stretch of 115 years, there were only four holders of the Professorship of Political Economy, a remarkably stable and peaceful era. The post-war period provides a sharp contrast, with most of the succeeding string of Professors of Political Economy, till 2000, holding the position on average for about a decade each: Dennis Robertson 1944–1957; James Meade 1957–1967; Brian Reddaway, 1969–1980[10]; Robin Matthews, 1980–1991; Tony Atkinson, 1991–1994 and finally, Jim Mirrlees, 1995–2003. This shortening of tenure could be regarded both as a cause and as the effect of internal competition and rivalries, not just between aspirants within the same theoretical tradition, but progressively between the divergent disciplinary lineages that had evolved within Cambridge economics from the inter-war period, especially the 1920s, onwards. A part, but far from all, of the internecine strife was allayed by the new practice of creating fixed tenure, ad hominem chairs in the early post-war period. It has sometimes been incorrectly asserted that Robertson was kept out of a professorship by the Keynesians; nothing could be further from reality. Remarkably, Keynes was never a professor in Cambridge, and when he was offered the Chair in Political Economy upon Pigou's retirement, he declined and graciously and unequivocally recommended that the Vice Chancellor offer it to Robertson.

Fixed-period professorships were created for Austin Robinson in 1950, and for Richard Kahn the following year, both chairs being made regular and permanent later; so far, so good. But then entered a period of perpetual turbulence. There was first the case of Richard Stone who had been the for-life Director of the DAE from its inception in 1945; an externally funded chair became a possibility in 1955; and there was then bad blood over him being eased out of the Directorship by being asked to choose one or the other; he chose the

---

[9] In his anthropological caricature of the Econ Tribe residing in the North, Leijonhufvud astutely observes that "for such a primitive people, the social structure is quite complex. The two main dimensions of their social structure are those of caste and status. The basic division of the tribe is seemingly into castes; within each caste, one finds an elaborate network of status relationships. An extremely interesting aspect of status among the Econ … is that status relationships do not seem to form a simple hierarchical 'pecking-order', as one is used to expect. Thus, for example, one may find that A pecks B, B pecks C, and *then C pecks A!* This non-transitivity of status may account for the continual strife among the Econ which makes their social life seem so singularly insufferable to the visitor. Almost all of the travellers' reports that we have comment on the Econ as a 'quarrelsome race' who 'talk ill of their fellow behind his back' and so forth. Social cohesion is apparently maintained chiefly through shared distrust of outsiders. In societies with a transitive pecking-order, on the other hand, we find as a rule that an equilibrium develops in which little actual pecking ever takes place" (Leijonhufvud, 1973: 327–328).

[10] The chair remained vacant in 1968.

Table 2.1 Faculty of Economics and Politics—professorships, 1828–2000

Title	Political Economy	Montague Burton industrial relations	Economics		Stone finance & accounting P. D. Leake	Kaldor personal chair	Champernowne personal chair economics & statistics	Applied Economics (DAE)	Other professorships including various personal chairs
Year established	1828	1930	1949/1964	1950/1970	1955	1966	1970	1980/1988	1981–1999
1828–1863	George Pryme								
1863–1884	Henry Fawcett								
1885–1908	Alfred Marshall								
1908–1943	Arthur C. Pigou								
1931–1942	AP	John Hilton							
1943	AP retires	JH							
1944	Dennis Robertson	Harold Kirkaldy							
1945	DR	HK							
1946	DR	HK							
1947	DR	HK							
1948	DR	HK							
1949	DR	HK							
1950	DR	HK	E. A. G. Robinson						
1951	DR	HK	EAGR	Richard Kahn					
1952	DR	HK	EAGR	RFK					
1953	DR	HK	EAGR	RFK					
1954	DR	HK	EAGR	RFK					
1955	DR	HK	EAGR	RFK	Richard Stone				
1956	DR	HK	EAGR	RFK	RS				

Year						
1957	DR retires; James Meade	HK	EAGR	RFK	RS	
1960	JM	HK	EAGR	RFK	RS	
1961	JM	HK	EAGR	RFK	RS	
1962	JM	HK	EAGR	RFK	RS	
1963	JM	HK resigns	EAGR	RFK	RS	
1964	JM	Herbert Turner	EAGR retires	RFK	RS	
1965	JM	HT	Joan Robinson	RFK	RS	
1966	JM	HT	JVR	RFK	RS	Nicholas Kaldor
1967	JM resigns	HT	JVR	RFK	RS	NK
1968		HT	JVR	RFK	RS	NK
1969	WB Reddaway	HT	JVR	RFK	RS	NK
1970	WBR	HT	JVR retires	RFK	RS	NK David Champernowne
1971	WBR	HT	Robert Neild	RFK	RS	NK DC
1972	WBR	HT	RN	RFK retires; Frank Hahn	RS	NK DC
1973	WBR	HT	RN	FH	RS	NK DC
1974	WBR	HT	RN	FH	RS	NK DC
1975	WBR	HT	RN	FH	RS	NK DC
1976	WBR	HT	RN	FH	RS	NK retires chair lapses
1977	WBR	HT	RN	FH	RS	DC
1978	WBR	HT	RN	FH	RS	DC

Additional notes in column: John Barnes, Professor of Sociology

(*continued*)

Table 2.1 (continued)

Title	Political Economy	Montague Burton industrial relations	Economics	Economics	Stone finance & accounting P. D. Leake	Kaldor personal chair	Champernowne personal chair economics & statistics	Applied Economics (DAE)	Other professorships including various personal chairs
Year established	1828	1930	1949/1964	1950/1970	1955	1966	1970	1980/1988	1981–1999
1979	WBR	HT	RN	FH	RS				
1980	WBR retires; Robin Matthews	HT	RN	FH	RS retires; Chair lapses			Wynne Godley	
1981	RCOM	HT	RN	FH				WG	Phyllis Deane Professor of Economic History PD1
1982	RCOM	HT	RN	FH				WG	PD1 retires JB retires
1983	RCOM	HT retires	RN	FH				WG	
1984	RCOM	—	RN early retirement	FH				WG	
1985	RCOM	William Brown	Partha Dasgupta	FH				WG	Anthony Giddens, Professor of Sociology
1986	RCOM	WB1	PD2	FH				WG	AG
1987	RCOM	WB1	PD2	FH				WG	AG

Year							
1988	RCOM	WB1	PD2	FH	Price Water-house Prof of Financial Accounting; Geoff Whittington	WG & David Newbery	Hashem Pesaran AG HP
1989	RCOM	WB1	PD2	FH	GW	WG & DN	AG HP
1990	RCOM	WB1	PD2	FH	GW	WG & DN	AG HP
1991	RCOM retires; Tony Atkinson	WB1	PD2	FH	GW	WG & DN	Robert Rowthorn AG HP RR
1992	ABA	WB1	PD2	FH	GW	WG & DN	AG HP RR
1993	ABA	WB1	PD2	FH retires	GW	WG & DN WG retires	AG HP RR
1994	ABA resigns	WB1	PD2[a]		GW	DN	Willem Buiter Professor of International Macroeconomics AG HP RR WB2
1995	James Mirrlees	WB1	PD2	C. J. Harris	GW	DN	Ajit Singh AG HP RR WB2 AS
1996	JM	WB1	PD2	CJH	GW	DN	AG HP RR WB2 AS

(*continued*)

Table 2.1 (continued)

Title	Political Economy	Montagne Burton industrial relations	Economics	Stone finance & accounting P. D. Leake	Kaldor personal chair	Champernowne personal chair economics & statistics	Applied Economics (DAE)	Other professorships including various personal chairs
Year established	1828	1930	1949/1964	1950/1970	1955	1966	1970	1980/1988	1981–1999
1997	JM	WB1	PD2	CJH	GW			DN	AG resigns Peter Nolan Sin Yi Professor of Chinese Management[b] HP RR WB2 AS PN
1998	JM	WB1	PD2	CJH	GW			DN	HP RR WB2 AS PN
1999	JM	WB1	PD2	CJH	GW			DN	Alan Hughes Margaret Thatcher Professor of Enterprise Studies[b] HP RR WB2 AS PN AH
2000	JM	WB1	PD2	CJH	GW			DN	HP RR WB2 AS PN AH

[a] Retitled by Grace 13 of 27 April 1994 for the tenure of the present holder and permanently retitled by Grace 1 of 12 January 2011. Cambridge University. (n.d.). *Statutes and ordinances of the University of Cambridge*. University Offices and Grant of Title, Chapter XI. https://www.admin.cam.ac.uk/univ/so/2019/chapter11-section3.html#heading3-15

[b] P. Nolan (in 1997) and A. Hughes (in 1999) shift to Judge Business School

professorship, which he held till 1980. Stone generally kept a peaceful distance from Faculty jousting between the adversarial Keynesian and Robertsonian camps, and further hostilities broke out when James Meade was awarded the Chair in Political Economy when Robertson retired in 1957, over Joan and Nicky who were both aspirants. Folklore has it that James Meade felt sufficiently uncomfortable over time in the Faculty, and therefore resigned his professorship in 1967, though there are variations on this story.[11] Then there are major changes in the mid-1960s. Brian Reddaway, by no means a neoclassical or mathematical general equilibrium type, took over the main Political Economy chair in 1969; Joan had taken over the professorship that her husband Austin had occupied till his retirement in 1964. Nicky Kaldor was apparently quite unhappy about this, and the following year a new fixed-term, non-renewable professorship was created for him, with the position lapsing upon his retirement in 1976.

The next round of disturbances broke out from 1970. There was no problem with the award of a personal chair to David Champernowne in 1970. But after Joan retired the same year, war erupted over her replacement. Kaldor imported and shoehorned his old colleague and friend Robert Neild into the chair, to the chagrin and dismay of Richard Kahn, leading, most significantly, to the installation of Frank Hahn, the field marshal of general equilibrium, in his chair in 1972, when Kahn retired.[12] But Hahn was seriously outnumbered: at the point of Joan's retirement, there were seven professors, including Joan

---

[11] Speaking of the 1950s and 1960s, Amartya Sen observes that "while Meade differed firmly from the Cambridge orthodoxy, he tended at first to be rather quiet and non-combative. This was certainly the case when he and I taught classes together in 1958. With the arrival of Frank Hahn, things began to change. There was a public battle going on between the orthodox and the rebels. Of the latter, Frank was the leader, and he was not reluctant to use his voice to dismiss the alleged centrality of neo-Keynesian ways of looking at the economic world. When I got back from America, I noted a new combativeness in James Meade, directed particularly against the unwillingness of the orthodox to listen to anyone else. He gave the clear impression that he had at last decided that he had had enough—on one occasion raising his voice sky-high to drown out what Joan Robinson was saying after she had treated him similarly. The episode might have been entertaining—as a shouting match between two famous people can sometimes be—but it was also depressing" (Sen, 2021, pp. 369–370).

[12] Robert Neild might not have been without other old friends. Neild had studied at Trinity and held a fellowship there earlier (1956–58); he later wrote about his annoyance at his perception of being corralled or bullied by Kahn over his voting intentions in the Faculty Board meetings; so perhaps there was some history there which had a future when Neild and Kahn were belligerents on opposing, the old and new, sides of the New Cambridge equations. But there is pertinence here to Maria Cristina Marcuzzo's (2008, p. ;) record that "according to Kaldor, Sraffa actually played a decisive role in the election of Neild" to the Trinity fellowship in 1956. When Neild returned to Cambridge in 1972 as professor, it was again with a fellowship in 1971 at Trinity, with Piero Sraffa still very much around, in fine form and flow. That Kaldor and Sraffa were, and remained, close is no secret either. More generally though, any assumption of transitivity in interpersonal attitudes in Cambridge would be a presumption—and so it curiously transpired that a decade down the line in the Faculty, Frank Hahn and Robert Neild were penning joint letters to *The Times*, (Hahn & Neild, 1980, 1981) leading a joint charge against raw Thatcherite monetarism, a topic of course on which almost everyone in Cambridge was at one. But just a few years later in 1984, seven years short of statutory retirement age, Neild opted for early retirement, citing Faculty acrimony as a prime reason, and thereby opened the door for the significant arrival of Partha Dasgupta into Cambridge in 1985; the rest, as the proverb goes, is history.

and H. "Bert" Turner,[13] and none of them could be described as being of neoclassical persuasion, whether Marshallian or Walrasian; and so it remained, apart from Hahn replacing Kahn, till 1975. The period 1970–1975 was perhaps the peak of Keynesian professorial power. Then there was kaleidoscopic change. Keynesian power dwindled, and the balance shifted dramatically in the years to 1980: first, Nicky retired in 1976, and his professorship lapsed; the same happened with David Champernowne in 1979; and likewise for Dick Stone a year later in 1980. Brian Reddaway also retired in 1980. And again, very significantly, his replacement to the Professorship of Political Economy was none other than Frank Hahn's close friend and comrade-in-arms, Robin Matthews, who had quietly resigned the Drummond Chair in Oxford in favour of the Master's sofa at Clare College in Cambridge, making the return five years earlier, in 1975, and positioning himself well. In retrospect, the appointment of Matthews can be seen as a key point of inflexion, marking the subsequent decline in the fortunes of the heterodox lineages, especially its more radical branches. Indeed, the Keynesian ranks were marginally strengthened by the arrival of Wynne Godley in 1980 as the Director of the DAE, taking over the Directorship from Reddaway, and occupying a professorship created for him till his retirement (which would go beyond the fixed 15-year tenure of his DAE Directorship). But now the Hahn-Matthews team was in situ, working in tandem to their agenda to dislodge the Keynesian camp from their perch; and the first serious casualty of this was to be Wynne Godley's Cambridge Economic Policy Group which had its funding terminated in 1982. Then Turner retired in 1983; and Robert Neild, who increasingly found Faculty battles distasteful, took early retirement in 1984. The two vacancies were filled by Willy Brown, and by Hahn's student and disciple, Partha Dasgupta from LSE; both appointments strengthened the Hahn-Matthews camp. Thus, in 1980, the powerful Hahn-Matthews combine faced enfeebled opposition in Robert Neild and Wynne Godley, neither really up for prolonged battles; and by 1985, the transition in power was complete with only five professors in place, with only the

---

[13] Herbert "Bert" Arthur Frederick Turner 1919–1998. As a young left-wing intellectual, Bert Turner had studied with Laski and interacted with the Webbs at LSE, had worked in the research and development department of the TUC, was part of the team that produced the *Interim Report on Post-War* Reconstruction which fed into the Clement Attlee programme, and following academic appointments in Manchester and Leeds and joined Cambridge as the Montagu Burton Chair of Industrial Relations in 1964; he could have continued till the statutory retirement age of 67, but retired well short of it in 1983, when he was replaced in 1985 by William Brown, the son of one of his Leeds colleagues. Brown was a specialist in industrial arbitration. Turner, with his command over economics and statistics in relation to labour markets, led the highly productive labour studies group based in the DAE, and was much travelled, being like several others, for example, Nicky Kaldor and Brian Reddaway, much in demand for government assignments at home and abroad in the era of decolonisation. Brown, while very appreciative of the research of the DAE labour studies group, was not an identifiable member of 'the left' within the Faculty, and apart from reportedly adopting a firm, though losing, position in the context of the appointment to the directorship of the DAE after Godley's term, usually was not on the heterodox side of the line in Faculty battles.

politically ineffective Wynne Godley in theoretical opposition. The orthodox camp further consolidated its stranglehold on the professoriate in 1988 when one of their own, David Newbery, was appointed in Wynne Godley's place as Director of the DAE for the next 15 years and, like Godley, simultaneously as Professor of Applied Economics till retirement. The orthodox, neoclassical takeover of the Faculty of Economics at the professorial level was complete; it had taken all of a decade.

Meanwhile, at ground level, the binaries and matrices of intellectual, ideological and personal affinities and polarities had a life of their own. A startled Australian's view is offered by Wilfred Prest, brother of Alan Prest. He took a sabbatical at St. John's College in 1953 and in his 'Report of the Visit to Britain' notes that he:

> was shocked to find the Faculty there deeply divided on doctrinal, political and, indeed, racial grounds.[14] On the one hand there is the Robertson party comprising, in addition to Sir Dennis himself such diverse characters as Guillebaud, Richard Stone, R.F. Henderson and S.R. Dennison. This group has never quite accepted Keynes without reservation and its members are inclined to be conservative, politically and socially. On the other hand, there is the Kahn party comprising, in addition to Professor Kahn, Sraffa, Kaldor, Dobb, Rostas, Joan Robinson, Ruth Cohen and Harry Johnson [sic]. This group is neo-Keynesian in outlook and is well to the left politically. The conflict between the two is deep and bitter. ... In Faculty meetings I am told that squabbles develop over such things as the appointment of examiners and the arrangement of timetables. Because Dennis Robertson gives a course in interest rates, Kahn must give one too; then the timetable is mangled so that the student hears Kahn's version first![15]

---

[14] Though it is not at all apparent whether this might be a euphemistic reference to the unsavoury aspect of anti-Semitism, some allusions to this could be worth placing on record. Eric Hobsbawm (2002: 121) observed: "Academic Britain in the 1930s was extraordinarily blind to the brilliance of the central European Jewish and anti-fascist refugee intellectuals unless they operated in conventionally recognized fields such as classics and physics. The LSE was probably the only place where they would be given house-room. Even after the war, [Norbert] Elias's academic career in this country was marginal, and the worth of scholars such as Karl Polanyi was not recognized until after they crossed the Atlantic." Then, we have a reference from Adam Kuper the anthropologist: "At our first lunch, when I turned up in King's, a raw colonial, Meyer [Fortes] told me, 'Never forget, they don't like Jews here'" (Kuper, 2016: 137). Kuper came as a student in the 1960s. And in his fine appreciation of Richard Kahn's work, Paul Samuelson remarks: "Kahn was different in being a Jew when Jews were rarer in academic life. More remarkably, he is supposed to have clung to Orthodox practices that teleologically were designed to make assimilation difficult. ... Modern generations, attuned to anti-Semitisms that are less blatant, can hardly realise how customary it was for a Keynes or a Schumpeter or an H. L. Mencken to use language and possess attitudes that would be universally shocking today" (Samuelson, 1994: 60).

[15] Reported in Millmow (2014: 4). Millmow corrects Prest's mistake in placing Harry Johnson in the Kahn group—the error arising possibly from the fact that Johnson was assigned to Maurice Dobb for his studies.

Consider another bizarre glimpse, this time through a contemporary account, backed up with documentation. Michael Posner, presumably then Secretary of the Faculty of Economics & Politics, writes thus to Nicky Kaldor:[16]

> Dear Nicky,
> I have done, with a great deal of personal expenditure of time and effort, the research you demanded.
> From 1956/57 to 1959/60 inclusive you lectured at 11 and Joan for the most part at 12. From 1960/61 until this year you lectured at 12 and Joan sometimes at 10 and sometimes at 12.
> It is clear that the further we go back the more it is true that Joan lectures at 12, and the nearer we come to the present the less this is true. What [right to; these two words crossed through in ink] time preference should we have? I think it is wrong for Joan to say that she has always [underscored in ink] lectured at 12, and I don't see myself that any difficulties would be caused by getting the historians to change the time in their list. To this extent you are quite justified in being difficult.
> But could honour be served (and considerable time saved) by you agreeing, as a free and unconstrained act of gallantry, to lecture at 11 next year on condition that a copy of this letter is sent to Joan and Richard? [This paragraph with double vertical parallel emphasis lines in left margin.]
> I won't send any copies until you give me permission to do so of course.
> I have put down your classes as we agreed and I sent what was meant to be an ironic letter to Luigi. I enclose his reply. [Neither the letter to Luigi Pasinetti, nor his reply are in the file.] I think he is being very [these five words crossed out with a pen] XXXXXXXXXXXXXX [deeply scratched out in ink in the original by some hand].
> If you are doing an applied course in Michaelmas Term I wouldn't mind being asked myself to come and share with you. I would find it great fun. [This last paragraph with a diagonal inked link crossing it out.]
> Yours ever,
> M.V. Posner.

The passage of time morphs the desperate frustration of the writer into amusement for the reader, but the letter does provide a startling peek into interpersonal pique and extreme intransigence even between members of the same 'family' over matters that might indeed appear trivial to the eye of an ordinary mortal academic.

Harry Johnson, in his from-the-gut take on his Cambridge of the 1950s, goes hammer and tongs after Joan Robinson and sets up Dennis Robertson as the harried victim of her persistent attacks; he paints her as something of an ogre.[17]

---

[16] The letter, dated 13 May 1964, is in the papers of Joan Robinson archived at King's College, Cambridge.

[17] "Well, take—on the one hand—Joan Robinson, whose forte in life has been standing up in front of audiences and announcing her political conclusions (with much economic nonsense) without feeling any compunction about it; and—on the other hand—Robertson, who had to write out every lecture in order to give himself the confidence to deliver it. This was certainly no contest; it was a giant challenging a baby to a boxing match. This went on continually" (Johnson, n.d.: 28–39).

He had been prevented from receiving what he (and many others) considered was the final reward of a serious academic career, namely the professorship at Cambridge; for that reason he had gone to the London School of Economics. ... At the end of the War, when it was clear that Keynes was never going to come back to academic life, these people got together and persuaded Robertson to take the chair on the basis of promises by them that they would "stop the persecution", would "live and let live", and so forth. But those promises were very quickly forgotten. The bitter controversy and intellectual guerrilla warfare resumed full sway. (Johnson n.d.; Richard Kahn Papers, King's College Archives, Cambridge, RFK/12/2/57/9)

While cordiality and commensality might indeed have been in short supply between the two camps after Robertson's return, Johnson's allegation that Robertson was "prevented from receiving ... the professorship at Cambridge" seems over-the-top and indefensible: Cambridge economics at the time had but the single chair in Political Economy—the Marshall chair—and that had been occupied by Pigou since 1908, at which point Robertson was 18 years old; he would be 20 when he switched from classics to economics and became a student, amongst others, of Pigou. One wonders then which professorship Johnson refers to, since the next economics professorship to come up was the personal chair for Austin Robinson in 1950; and by then, Robertson had been the Cambridge Professor of Political Economy, having succeeded Pigou a year after his retirement in 1944. At the time Johnson made his charge, he would not have had access to the King's College Archives to read, if he so needed, that the Marshall chair was offered to Keynes, who turned it down and exhorted the Vice Chancellor to offer it to Dennis Robertson and to bring him back to Cambridge. However, Johnson is right in noting the continuation of covert and overt hostilities between the 'left-wing' Keynesians and the 'right-wing' Robertsonians through to the point of Robertson's retirement in 1957. Indeed, the confrontation and hostility carried over to the next incumbent of the chair, James Meade—also deemed to be right of centre—on account of the sense that the professorship should have gone to one of the Keynesians, viz., Joan Robinson or Nicky Kaldor, both awaiting promotion. (Kahn, meanwhile, had also been awarded a personal chair in 1951, a year after Austin Robinson.) Joan, in addition to her other work, had published her *magnum opus* in 1956, *The Accumulation of Capital*; Meade had been a professor of trade at the LSE under Lionel Robbins since 1947.

Then, for the 1960s, there is Robin Naylor's Canadian rendition[18]—drawing on his fellow Canadian Harry Johnson—which expresses equal amazement:

Despite the obvious, continual fluctuations in the composition of the undergraduate population, college life was remarkably stable—in good measure because of the permanent nature of the academic–administrative staff. This stability in turn

---

[18] Robin Naylor was at Cambridge in the 1960s. See his review (Naylor, 1981) of *The Legacy of Keynes* by Elizabeth and Harry Johnson (1978).

explains a great deal about the peculiar viciousness of interpersonal relations among the academic staff (of which Johnson's book itself is a striking affirmation). Once an aspiring academic has survived the initial purges through carefully cultivated deference to whatever faction of the already firmly ensconced was ascendant at the time, it was then assumed that he (the male form is almost inevitably the correct one in this context) would be a fixture of Cambridge life for several decades. Given the normal expectation of dealing with the same small set of colleagues for life, and given the insularity of the context in which one had to deal with them, the fact that academic politics were characterized by a remarkably high development of the arts of petty, personal vindictiveness should be no surprise. Personal conflicts, which throve in such fertile soil, would be turned into artificial differences of intellectual stance on third-rate issues in order to give them a socially respectable basis. These rivalries could even spill over into such matters as the setting of examination questions, with candidates judged by their degree of acceptance or rejection of some rival's doctrines. It was from such a happy institution, where isolation from reality and intellectual narcissism flourished, that Keynesian economics was launched into academic, professional and political respectability. (Naylor, 1981: 219–220)

Perhaps the visceral spite could be partially attributed to the justifiable grudge carried by Canadians in Britain; as Harry Johnson complained, "Canadians often find themselves bitterly resentful at bearing the discrimination which the British love to inflict on ordinary Americans" (Johnson, n.d.: 28).

Turning to another part of the Commonwealth, in 1955–1956, Manmohan Singh, the future Indian prime minister, had entered this crackling intellectual environment as a young Indian student and later recorded his bewildered perspective:

The faculty was a fiercely argumentative group of people with strong professional differences that both drove them apart and drew them together. Some interacted closely, as did Keynes with Kahn, or Kahn with Joan Robinson. They would communicate with each other through handwritten notes sent by post rather than telephone—which they either did not have or preferred not to use. But Kahn and Sraffa, Keynes and Robertson, Joan Robinson and Robertson, or Kaldor and Sraffa, were unlikely to ever consult each other.[19]

Further pairings with opposed polarities could easily be added to Manmohan's list; an Indian sociologist could have had a field day mapping the complex interpersonal and intergroup commensality matrices rife with no-talk, no-meet, no-go cells. The baseline is clear: powerful as the players were, they

---

[19] From the biographical account by his daughter, Daman Singh (2014: 115–116).

could never row together in sync in any agreed direction; except that they were all implacably hostile to the neoclassical theoretical paradigm.[20]

Amartya Sen, who moved from Calcutta to Cambridge in 1953, cautions against simplistic reductionism. He notes that neoclassical economists, including Dennis Robertson, Harry Johnson, Peter Bauer and Michael Farrell, were sceptical of Keynes and what he calls "the new orthodoxy of neo-Keynesianism". On the other side "Richard Kahn was the most bellicose"; Joan Robinson was "totally brilliant but vigorously intolerant"; Kaldor was "much the most tolerant of the neo-Keynesians at Cambridge" (Sen, 1998). "Even though there were a number of fine teachers who did not get very involved in these intense fights between different schools of thought (such as Richard Stone, Brian Reddaway, Robin Matthews, Kenneth Berrill, Aubrey Silberston, Robin Marris), the political lines were, in general very firmly—and rather bizarrely—drawn" (ibid.). "There was no way in which the different economists could be nicely ordered in just one dimension" (ibid.).

Thus, for instance, Kaldor clashed with the 'astute Marxist' Maurice Dobb, who was thought to be soft on neoclassical economics; and Sen observes that "in this desert of constant feuding, my own college, Trinity, was a bit of an oasis". This proved his point, since Trinity hosted "three remarkable economists of *very different* political views" (italics in original); "the Marxist Maurice Dobb and the conservative neo-classicist Dennis Roberson did joint seminars, and Trinity also had Piero Sraffa, a model of scepticism of nearly all the standard schools of thought". Indeed, Robertson had invited Dobb to his fellowship at Trinity. "The peaceful—indeed warm—co-existence of Dobb, Robertson and Sraffa was quite remarkable, given the feuding in the rest of the University." Sen shares a delightful anecdote: on his appointment to the Trinity fellowship, the conscientious Dobb wrote to inform Robertson about his red politics, saying that he would entirely understand if he (Dobb) was deemed inappropriate to instruct Trinity undergraduates; back came the reply from Robertson: "Dear Dobb, so long as you give us a fortnight's notice before blowing up the Chapel, it will be all right" (ibid.).

Geoff Hodgson et al. (2018: n7) make a similar observation and conclude: "ideological divisions within the faculty were complex ... normative or ideological positions did not always correspond one-to-one with theoretical positions", and back this up by citing that "the Marxist Oskar Lange deployed Walrasian general equilibrium theory in his defence of socialism, while Friedrich Hayek criticised the same mainstream theoretical approach in his vindication of

---

[20] And then there is the case of Goodwin and Stone throwing up a puzzle: "friends as we are, we never collaborated. Our aims as economists are the same, our skills complementary, and for over three decades we have lived in the same town"—and I might add shared the same Faculty space, even a common first name. "Together we might have produced some masterly works that would have astonished the world ... but we never got down to it"—so runs Dick Stone's lament (quoted in Pasinetti, 2007: 213). The feeling was mutual and reciprocated; Ron Smith drew my attention to a comment by Dick Goodwin (1995) about how difficult it was for him to be friends with both Stone and Kahn-Robinson (Ron Smith, personal communication, email dated 30 January 2018).

a market economy. The prominent advocacy in Cambridge (and elsewhere) of the term 'left-wing economics' is misleading for these and other reasons." Amartya Sen, similarly, commented that "in these intense fights between different schools of thought ... the political lines were, in general, very firmly—and rather bizarrely—drawn ... there was no way in which the different economists could be nicely ordered in just one dimension. Maurice Dobb, who was an astute Marxist economist, was often thought by Keynesians and neo-Keynesians to be 'quite soft' on 'neo-classical' economics ... when the Marxist Dobb defeated Kaldor in an election to the Faculty Board, Kaldor declared it to be a victory of the perfidious neo-classical economics in disguise ('marginal utility theory has won', Kaldor told Sraffa that evening, in commenting on the electoral success of a Marxist economist!)" (Sen, 1998). And perhaps slips on the same banana skin when he refers to the likes of Robin Matthews, Aubrey Silberston and Kenneth Berrill among those "who did not get very involved in these intense fights between different schools of thought"—that generous observation may well hold for the early years, but is arguably off the mark, and in Matthews's case spectacularly so, for the period of the Hahn-Matthews campaign for control. All that amusement aside, it would be strange to think of Lange or Dobb as anything other than holding socialist convictions, or Hayek anything but the opposite; and that is where the differentiating crunch point generally lay. A broad default classifying criterion is offered by Philip Arestis and Malcolm Sawyer (1992) in deciding whom to include in their anthology of "dissenting" economists: those who were opposed to neoclassical, orthodox, mainstream economics.

In Faculty space, the old Chinese adage, or variations thereof, held sway, "my enemy's enemy is my friend". For instance, upon arriving in Cambridge for his PhD, Geoff Harcourt ran into rough weather with Kaldor, his supervisor; Geoff sought Kaldor's permission to undertake supervisions, usually a standard innocuous request needing but a nod; but here, the offer to Harcourt had come from Henderson who was in the camp of Robertson, whom Kaldor hated. Harcourt's problem with Kaldor was severe enough to cause depression; and Geoff says he "did end up good friends with Kaldor though not for the first ten years of our acquaintance" (Harcourt, 2007: at 25:55:10).[21]

For an insider's view, there is the rueful, if not bitter, very English account by Robert Neild—incidentally, also a Fellow of Trinity College—of his two stints at the Faculty, in the 1950s and the 1970s. Recollecting Faculty life in 1956, Neild writes: "The other dark aspect of life was the political goings-on in the economics faculty" (Neild, 2012: 73). "I found the faculty awful, it was so political and savage and full of prima donnas" (Neild, 2013). Hodgson et al. (2018: 769–770) quote from Neild:

---

[21] Happily, Geoff Harcourt notes elsewhere: "the man who most resembled Keynes in the post-war period—Nicky Kaldor, who was a larger-than-life figure: a completely honest and ultimately lovable man who always said what he thought, who loved and lived life to the full" (Harcourt, 2001: 349).

Neild (2012: 73–74) relates the following illustrative incident. 'Within weeks of my arrival I was approached by Richard Kahn, saying that annual elections to the Faculty Board were coming up and that he thought I should know how "we are voting"'. Neild asked the meaning of 'we' in this statement: 'I didn't mind being told his list, but I would decide for myself how to vote'. Neild voted for a mixed ticket. Later, in the presence of Joan Robinson, 'Kahn led me aside and … said he was sorry to see how I had voted at the faculty election. … I felt I was caught by a mafia and had been subjected to bullying by its capo. My distaste for the ways of the faculty was one reason why I left Cambridge after two years.'

The second stint provided a distinct sense of déjà vu for him, as things had not changed much over the intervening two decades. Writing about the 1970s, Neild observes:

The faculty [in the 1970s] was unpleasant for several connected reasons. Economics was being taken over, with Americans in the lead, by mathematicians. … My earthbound approach was out of fashion. … Politically the faculty was a snake pit in which the rise of the mathematical economists was being resisted by a combination of Keynesians, empiricists and communists. As a Keynesian/empiricist I was in the latter camp. Ruled by the mafia-like methods I had encountered in the 1950s, its members had a majority on the faculty board. (Neild, 2012: 95–96, quoted in Hodgson et al., 2018: 771)

Neild cites Faculty in-fighting as one reason for a second departure from Cambridge—for opting, at 60 in 1984, for early retirement, taking advantage of the golden handshake scheme introduced in response to Thatcher's deep cuts into university budgets.

Each cohort or generation seems to point the finger at some proximate source as the root of this Cambridge malaise: Dasgupta and Newbery, directly or by implication, variously point to the Marxists and Maoists and their fellow travellers in the Faculty and disparage them by characterising them generally as being ideologically motivated 'mediocrities', while this group of left young turks tend to reciprocate the compliment with respect to the orthodox group. A generation up, Robert Neild named Kahn and Joan as the mafiosi and others trace the origin further back and embed it in the long-running conflict between Keynes and Robertson, with their proxies carrying on the battles even after the principals had long gone. Interestingly, Matthews and Supple, both with key instrumental roles in the onslaught against the left Keynesians in the Faculty and the DAE in the 1980s, pick up this pathological thread, and take it further back all the way to Marshall. The context for this assertion is their investigation into Marshall's resistance to economic history.

Matthews and Supple (n.d.: 2) explain Marshall's resistance to offering history too much space in economics which, in Cambridge as also in Oxford, was part of the History or Moral Sciences Tripos; "the issue was whether there was a place for economics as a separate discipline at all, rather than whether economics should be enriched by historical insights", and the Economics Tripos was established in 1903 against stiff opposition. Marshall's endeavours were "an effort to emancipate the study of economics in Cambridge from the study of history ... from the thrall of other subjects", intended to lead to "the professionalisation of academic study" in economics. "They were addressed *urbi*, not *orbi*. The intellectual empyrean was clouded by university politics already in the 1880s."

The focus then shifted to the question of the state of permanent conflict in the Economics Faculty, and they turn to Robertson for an answer where he implicates Marshall.

> Dennis Robertson, at a 70th birthday dinner, related the frictions between himself and Cambridge Keynesians to the professionalisation of the subject, suggesting that Mr Ricardo and Mr Malthus might have conducted their debates with less urbanity if they had been meeting each other continually on Faculty Committees where decisions had to be made (source: RCOM personal recollection). A related conjecture may be interpolated here. It has often been supposed that some virus of proneness to internal strife has existed in the Cambridge Economic Faculty and has tended to outlive particular matters of debate or particular disputants; and it has sometimes been thought that this is to be traced back to the disputes between Keynes and Robertson and to the attempts of the first generation of Keynesians to establish a Keynesian orthodoxy in the 1930s. A reading of the literature about the controversy that surrounds the establishment of the Economics Tripos suggests that the trouble began earlier, with Marshall himself. Marshall was regarded as dogmatic and autocratic not only by Archdeacon Cunningham ... but also by contemporaries of an entirely different turn of mind, such as Neville Keynes and Sidgwick—a feature mentioned in Maynard Keynes's biography, but distinctly played down there (Memorials, p. 57). Marshall ultimately succeeded in his aims, not only about the establishment of the Economics Tripos but also about its content. The result was that in his later life and for a short while after his death Cambridge economics came to consist of a one-man orthodoxy. Hence arose a situation in which change could come about only by revolution and civil war. The revolution began in the 1920s. (Matthews & Supple, n.d.: 21.n4)

The subliminal message is not difficult to divine: the suggestion appears to be that the Marshallian one-man orthodoxy induced revolutionary change (led by the heterodox groups) as the only option; and the subliminal implication is equally clear: that an equivalent revolution (this time by the neoclassicals) was induced and justified by the Keynesian one-man orthodoxy that took over from Marshall. As such, Matthews and Supple appear to be providing a justification for the dismantling of the heterodox lineages from Cambridge economics, by implying that they constituted a hegemonic orthodoxy that had to be smashed by the neoclassical group, viz., Matthews himself, Hahn and their followers and dependants. Such as it is, the hypothesis at least has the advantage of being self-serving. And be it as it may, Ajit Singh, Bob Rowthorn and their band were stepping into well-worn shoes and treading a well-trodden path when they assembled and consolidated the heterodox alliance against the orthodox grouping; they did not invent the battle lines, but they inherited them from the field marshals and generals of yore.

2.2 Faculty Wars

Indeed, any parachutist accidentally dropping in might rightly have felt that Cambridge economics, and economists, were in a state of permanent revolution. It was a fray of intellectual tournaments, of ceaseless gladiatorial jousting. The 20 years that followed could be regarded perhaps as the most volatile decades of Cambridge economics. Apart from the complexities of its own internal interpersonal equations within the heterodox family, the Faculty was engaged in two kinds of wars that were distinct, but not detached, and they both had internal and external fronts.

Attracting the highest merit were the *dharmic* wars: these were celestial, cosmic—the war over who controlled the keyboard to the scriptures, the struggle for the pure abstract heart of economics, a *Brahmanical* enterprise where only erudite and often impenetrable text, equations and diagrams could enter (with the odd exception made for stylised representations of the observable), unsullied by the taint of numbers and empiricism delegated to lower castes of numericists—nobody bearing a statistical table would be given a chair.

The first of these wars was the galactic cross-Atlantic Mahabharata between the very non-identical 'Cambridge' twins: the good *Pandavas* clan of the 'real' Cambridge; and the no-good *Kauravas*, the upstart neoclassical apostates of the 'other' Cambridge that lay on the dark side of the pond, beyond *kala pani*. Lest posterity forgets, Geoff Harcourt has assiduously recorded the day-by-day, skirmish-by-skirmish, blow-by-blow account of this epic encounter; he was, and remains, the learned Vyas, the scribe of the tribe.[22]

The wars were fought simultaneously on two planes: the *dharmic* or *orbi*, and the *karmic*, or *urbi*. The *dharmic* clash was for authority over the scriptures, the *karmic* over control of resources; ideational versus material; one was for the mind and soul, the other over the army and the treasury. One was fought in rude letters, in seminars, in journals, in textbooks, in equations and in diagrams; the other in Faculty meetings, in appointments and promotion boards, in setting curricula and teaching programmes, in examination committees. In the former, there were periodic celestial fireworks lighting up the entire Atlantic passage as opposing *maharathis* or charioteers engaged each other in some specific capital theory or Keynesian controversy; in the latter, there were daily fights, raids and ambushes, and forever blood on the floor; the first seemed a timeless and ethereal battle, the other was always a here-and-now, life-and-death matter; the first was long distance, almost virtual, in cosmic space; the second was local, immediate, proximate and palpable, urban guerrilla warfare

---

[22] See for instance, the definitive account of the famous Cambridge capital controversies by Harcourt (1972), followed up later in 2003 by Harcourt and Cohen (2012).

in Faculty corridors and rooms, in College studies and dining halls. The *Pandava* heterodox schools could be powerful, if they could all fight to an agreed strategy; but they had to both fight their battles across the Atlantic and also take on the *Kaurava* neoclassicals in their own habitat and ranks. It was not easy.

Keeping to the metaphor, the villainous *Kauravas* were led by a pair of generals who combined their complementary skills; one was the master of theory and equations, the other of field strategy and organisation; one addressed the *orbi* world, the other *urbi*; one was Frank Hahn, the other was Robin Matthews; and both had developed schools of apprentices and protégés and camouflaged supporters in key locations. Meanwhile, the virtuous *Pandavas* had a great number of chieftains, each with a few followers, but though they quarrelled and squabbled incessantly amongst themselves, they discovered their common identity and purpose when confronted by the opposing clan. Since the many generals were all preoccupied with their diverse intellectual hobbies and passions, the task of organising these clans was delegated, by default, to the younger generation of scholar warriors. The pantheon of identifiable gurus included Piero Sraffa, Richard Kahn, Joan (and Austin) Robinson, Nicky Kaldor, Maurice Dobb, Dick Goodwin, a.o., with Luigi Pasinetti[23] and Geoff Harcourt[24] at the top of the waiting list for a place; and the younger group comprised the large majority of the research staff of the DAE, and considerable numbers from the Faculty side—they were led in the field by the duo of Ajit Singh and Bob Rowthorn with a phalanx of close colleagues in support. Strategy and action generally revolved around the leftist pair of Ajit Singh and Bob Rowthorn, both initially lecturers who were effectively the opposite numbers to Hahn and Matthews who were both professors from the outset. The battle objective of each side was to capture the key space of the Faculty Board; whoever controlled those heights would be master of all they could survey.

Ajit was not given much to the study of *dharma* for its own sake. His own orientations, combining Kaldorian questions with Reddaway methods, protected him from absorption into the black holes of the pure *dharmic* contestations, be they over standard commodities, transformation problems or capital

---

[23] For a meticulous record and appreciation of the life and greatly significant contributions of Luigi Pasinetti to Cambridge economics, see the intellectual biography by Mauro Baranzini and Amalia Mirante (2018).

[24] Geoff Harcourt, while remaining an unwavering Australian patriot, is quintessentially Cambridge and figures extensively in the narratives of the book as an actor or as a resource. He provides a bare-bone condensation of some of his formal engagements in Cambridge: "I try to bring coherence to the structure of post-Keynesian economics by the pioneers at Cambridge. I was teaching post-Keynesian economics and HET to undergraduates at Cambridge from 1982 to 1998, and that I was in Cambridge from 1982 to 2010. I was on the University Council for 8 years; I was Secretary of the Faculty Board for two periods, being bullied unsuccessfully by Frank Hahn; I always had 8 to 11 PhD students on the go; and I was at various times on important committees or Chairs at university lectureships. I often had up to 12 undergraduate supervisions a week, and with Bob Rowthorn taught Subject 3 in the MPhil which was the economics of Keynes and Kalecki mainly."

controversies and production functions. Ajit ploughed his own fields of theoretical interests. He would have immediately grasped the ideas of Keynes and Kaldor on the accumulation of capital, which was his own prime intellectual interest, but while he was not instinctively attracted by the high abstractions of Joan Robinson's magnum opus of the same name, one would readily agree with Geoff Harcourt when he observes that Ajit "would surely have understood and appreciated Kalecki whose structures were reflected in Joan's volume".[25] Instead, as a practical tactician, the *kshatriya* warrior, he focussed on the second front, the *karmic* war to secure the essential conditions for intellectual reproduction by protecting the production sites, knowledge and knowledge producers of radical economics in the Faculty. And so he brought all his considerable organisational skills to the practitioner's plane of the foundational ideological struggles. The *karmic* battles were essentially motivated by the objective of safeguarding the authority and freedom of the broad-church progressive *dharmic* panoply of Cambridge heterodoxy.

For Ajit, imperialisms had to be countered on multiple battlegrounds. Central to the enterprise was the composition of the all-powerful Faculty Board which functioned like a holding company, making appointments to the various other decision-making committees of the Faculty; membership to the Board was on the basis of elections, and so the success of the leftist slate was of critical importance with all-round externalities. The overall agenda embraced virtually all aspects of decision-making: from appointments, to appointments to appointment committees, to appointments to committees that made appointments to the appointments committee; various sub-committees controlling curricula and examiners, significant visitors, for example, for the Marshall Lecture and lecturer for the Principles course; PhD admissions; promotions and tenure; and so on. Influence on, if not the control of, the Faculty Board was therefore of prime strategic importance.

Ajit had learned battle skills and earned his spurs earlier in Berkeley where he had participated in the multiple ongoing political struggles, the civil rights movement, the Free Speech Movement and the student anti-Vietnam War protests. Upon arriving in 1964, he took to his New Cambridge landscape like a duck to water and was soon the natural *sardar*, leader of the band, the political commissar, the Chief Whip, of the loose left collective, perennially plotting strategies, marshalling the troops, allotting roles, corralling votes. Sheila Rowbotham called his obsession with strategising Machiavellian, and she was right; Chinese chequers simulations; or in military idiom, Ajit's approach could well have been drawn from General Giap's manual or Maharaja Ranjit Singh's tactics of guerrilla warfare in fighting the British in his native Punjab in the colonial era.

As leader of the pack, Ajit was fiercely competitive; all Machiavellian plans and strategies were allowed but all battles, and the hustling corridor politics and politicking for the soul and control of the Faculty, were strictly within the

[25] Personal communication, email dated 16 January 2018.

limits set by the rulebook. A remarkable trait of Ajit's, already noted, was that he always fought the ideas and ideologies, never the person[26]; he could walk away from a bruising committee meeting exchanging a laugh with sworn adversaries regardless of whether his side had won or lost on the day. That there were occasional exceptions to this had more to do with the traits of others than any slippage in Ajit's impeccable personal demeanour and collegial manners. This attribute, supported by his strong personal research credentials, and respected reputation as a principled fighter of socialist causes, greatly added to his effectiveness. He reached parts of the academic body others could not reach. And he was always extremely well prepared for battle, armed with information, plans and options involving permutations of tactical alliances, all with his collective of left radicals.

In a lighter vein, we have the recollection of Vani Borooah, then a Research Officer at DAE, economics Fellow at Queens' College, and a young left loyalist in Ajit's camp:

> I wanted to share here with you my first meeting him. I was in my DAE cubbyhole in the first few days of my arrival in Cambridge, feeling lost and friendless, when there was a knock at my door. Opening it I found you accompanying a tall *sardar* [Sikh] with a flowing beard and piercing eyes. Entirely unknown to me, the Faculty Board elections were around the corner and Ajit had come around to be introduced and to check if I was 'all right'. This was to remain his stock phrase—in a year or so, when I was promoted from foot soldier in his army to sergeant, in charge of mobilising the Growth Project vote, the enquiry (always before Faculty elections) altered slightly from 'Vani, are you all right?' to 'Vani, are we all right?'.[27]

Ajit's co-author Geoff Whittington (2016: 302) tells us how Ajit, at a Faculty cricket game, invoking the guileful reputation of the master Indian spinner Bishen Singh Bedi behind him, clean bowled the batsman with a ball that didn't turn at all, and followed this up with two further wickets using the same stratagem; "this deception gave Ajit as much pleasure as organizing a successful vote on the Faculty Board, which was his main preoccupation during the student revolution of the late 1960s"; apocryphal perhaps, but entirely credible.

And then we have a peep-in from a student's vantage point: "The mid-1970s were a time of intense friction between rival factions of Cambridge

---

[26] Vani Borooah drew a telling comparison: "Frank Hahn attacked the person if he was 'on the other side'; Ajit attacked only the ideas, even if the person was 'on the other side'" (personal communication).

[27] Vani Borooah, personal communication; email dated 23 July 2015. Dr Vani Borooah was a Senior Research Officer in Dick Stone's modelling team at the DAE (1977–1987); Fellow of Queens' College (1979–1987); and then Professor of Applied Economics at the University of Ulster; member of the Royal Irish Academy; President of the Irish Economic Association (1994–1996), and also of the European Public Choice Society; presently Emeritus Professor of Applied Economics at the University of Ulster.

economists, in which Ajit was a major player—we viewed him rather as the party whip for the heterodox economists after overhearing his responses to telephone calls, or interruptions from his co-conspirators, that sometimes gave us breathing room during supervisions" (Earl, 2016: 305).

What is clear is that the orthodox-versus-heterodox battles for the control of the Faculty Board, and hence much Faculty decision-making, had deep roots and a long history; Ajit was stepping into well-worn shoes when taking over the informal charge of keeping the left group mobilised. What would have changed over time were the definitions of 'left' and 'right' and the personages that might identify with either flag, as well as the descriptors used by either camp for the other. Thus, Robert Neild (2012) makes a reference to the presence of "communists"; David Newbery (2017) refers to the Faculty left divided "between Maoists and anti-Maoists". One of the excuses casually heard for launching the highly controversial DAE Review of 1984 was the 'usual suspects', 'reds under the bed' line. In the period under consideration, there were probably no more than two or three active members of the British Communist Party, of which one soon resigned; possibly three or four with intellectual and political sympathies with Maoist China—without being Maoists—and they were possibly in the company of the president of a Cambridge college; and most of them changed their position, using the Keynes dictum, after the Chinese reforms. The extremist labels were used really to mobilise and legitimise university action against these individuals (who played leading roles in Faculty politics) and thereby to weaken the left and bolster right-wing positions. If opposing the war in Vietnam made someone a communist, surely supporting it would make one a stooge or, as the more colourful term goes, a running dog of imperialism. Whichever labels might be used, Ajit was likely to be showcased as a leader of the left subversives. Fortunately, Ajit had tenure, though he had been equally fearless in his very early years in Cambridge when he was effectively on temporary or probationary contracts and appointments.

Many of the accounts of these bickerings between the rival camps portray them simply as personalised incompatibilities and animosities which surface disproportionately over seemingly trivial, apparently non-academic matters. True as this might well have been, there could be more substantive motivations for such disagreements, say over "the appointment of examiners and the arrangement of timetables" (Prest quoted in Millmow, 2014: 4). In the Cambridge Tripos, the lecturers on a course could not act as examiners for that paper; as such, the identity and orientation of the examiner became a highly relevant and charged concern; it would do no good to have a reader from an opposing theoretical lineage. This was also the case for PhD exams, where the supervisor was excluded from the panel of examiners. Likewise, the choice of the Principles lectures was a crucial and highly contested one—that is where the new entrants received their full-scale theoretical introduction to 'economics'; Kahn would obviously have preferred to lay out the thought map for the students in the first round, rather than have to pick his way round and respond to the lines already laid down by Robertson. There were usually substantive issues under the surface, and so, superficially viewed, the conflicts could indeed seem exactly what they were not, that is, superficial. The student protests at the Faculty of Economics of the early 1970s leading up to the famous Sit-in of 1972 had much support from groups of Faculty, most prominently including Ajit and Bob—and were triggered precisely by issues to do with teaching and exam reforms, that is, what could appear to be mundane teaching matters, till their deeper pedagogical and political significance came under the magnifier.

The fulcrum of power and decision-making was the Faculty Board. It is important here to emphasise that in this regard, Cambridge economics stood apart from the economics departments in most other universities where the Head of Department usually exercised considerable, if not dominant, authority over all departmental affairs. In contrast, in Cambridge, the Faculty Board was elected democratically by the Faculty, and it then made all decisions directly or through committees that were elected through it. The rules had been laid down long ago, and had not been devised by one side or the other; rather, the constitutional parity between staff of the Faculty and the DAE was stipulated then as a matter of principle, reflecting the generally held perception that teaching and research staff were the equals of each other. Since this construction goes to the crux of the Faculty wars, it is useful to set down the relevant regulation.

> Although the Department has a separate identity it is closely associated with the rest of the Faculty of Economics and Politics. Holders of University posts on the research staff of the Department are automatically made members of the Faculty, and are eligible for election as members of the Faculty, and are eligible for election as members of the Faculty Board. They may also be appointed by the Faculty to serve as members of the Department's Committee of Management. Teaching officers of the Faculty who are not members of the Department's research staff take an active part in the research activities of the Department. The majority of the research projects being undertaken by the Department in 1964–65 were initiated by teaching officers of the Faculty and were under their immediate direction.[28]

Through the 1970s and well into the 1980s, the Faculty Board had come to be dominated by 'the left', which roughly conflated with those who were not avowedly neoclassical in their disciplinary faith. This had come about not simply because the Faculty teaching staff had overwhelmingly turned left and taken the anti-neoclassical road, though some such tendencies were surely present; rather, it was the result of the electoral participation of the DAE staff, who had a statutory position identical to that of the members of the teaching Faculty; and DAE numbers were almost the same as those of the teaching Faculty. DAE staff could hardly all be labelled 'leftist' or 'radical', or even 'macro' or 'post-Keynesian'; many were microeconomists, or statisticians, or applied economists specialising in particular lines; and there were two large

---

[28] DAE 1965, Fifth Report of the DAE covering the period January 1958–December 1964; p. 5, para 4.

units within the DAE dealing with macroeconomic modelling. What was common though, amongst this staff, was that they were almost all dealing with policy issues to do with the real, actually existing, UK economy, which was in dire straits. While it would be true to say that the applied economists of the DAE might have been unmoved by the passion of the cross-Atlantic capital controversies, as a group dealing with on-the-street policy issues, they would have been generally united in intellectual and professional opposition to the fairy-tale worlds of neoclassical theorising. They also constituted a younger cohort. While the older groups, in general, had their political passions consummated in their collective war effort and in the shared satisfaction of the rise of the welfare state, the younger batch had rather different political imaginations that had been fired by rising American imperialism, the Cold War, Vietnam, class strife and miners' struggles following the OPEC inflations, and the rise of radical youth and democratisation, peace, anti-nuclear and student movements globally, from the USA to Paris to the Cultural Revolution in China (of which Joan Robinson was a prime ambassador).

It would be difficult, on the whole, to get staff groups with varied sympathies in this wide spectrum of left engagements, to side with the policy-vacuous abstractionisms of the free-market general equilibrium 'whateverists', the Cambridge neoclassical gang supported by their American protagonists. And the DAE teams, including the Growth Project and especially the Policy Group, largely comprised younger economists many of whom were socially and politically committed to applying their intellects and creative energies to meaningful policy ends. They combined with the young fiery, and more senior traditional old-guard left on the Faculty to form a grouping that generally controlled the agendas and outcomes of the Faculty Board through the exercise of its democratic decision-making rights. The key to this was effective representation through winning elections to the Faculty Board and then, within it, for its various significant committees that decided on appointments and promotions; curriculum reform and academic matters such as who might deliver the Principles lectures, or the Marshall Lecture; the research degrees committee; funding and infrastructure issues; and above all those controlling appointments, promotions, extensions of contracts and so on. As Dasgupta (2010) later reports: all Hahn could achieve in this configuration was one fresh appointment of his choice in every three made. The battle was over the substance, conduct, directions and indeed the soul of Cambridge economics. It was a loose heterodox formation, with its many constituents loyal to their own chosen versions of the testament; there were Ricardians and neo-Ricardians, Marxists and marxists, Sraffians, post-Keynesian lineages, socially committed Cambridge empiricists or philosophers, economic historians—perhaps all squabbling incessantly with one another, but generally aligned when it came to confronting the threat of a common adversary, the neoclassical tribe led by the crusading Frank Hahn. And it was Ajit Singh, primarily, who was the commissar or Chief Whip of the left, with the charge of converting this ragbag alliance, often wobbly and fraying at the edges, into an effective electoral force that could be mobilised and disciplined, especially at the times of crucial Faculty elections. Such was the configuration in the mid-1970s, the politically tinder-crackling heyday of Cambridge economics.

2.2.1 Paradise Lost

Intriguing and relevant, and ultimately depressing, as these personalised narratives are as explanations of failure, they remain too inward-looking and detached from the wider material contexts and conjunctures within which the Faculty ideological battles were fought and lost or won. In a joint paper, Ajit and his co-researchers (Glyn et al., 1988) had identified the period 1950–1975 as the golden age of modern capitalism, combining steady growth, low inflation and gains in productivity and real wages, all under the framework of macroeconomic management by the state rather than through the uncontrolled functioning of markets.[29] Adding another five years, that would arguably also coincide with the golden age of neo-Keynesian and radical economics in Cambridge.

Yet, despite their great history and formidable strength and diversity, these heterodox traditions and lineages atrophied and virtually evanesced from the Faculty in the period thereafter, as the Faculty, and the DAE, lapsed and collapsed into the control of the neoclassical orthodox camp within the Faculty led initially by Frank Hahn and Robin Matthews, with 1975–1990 forming the short period of inflexion. How did this remarkable turnaround occur? How could the diverse and productive intellectual ecology that flourished and formed that great banyan tree of organically evolving Cambridge heterodox traditions mutate so rapidly into a genetically modified single-strain industrial mono-cropping culture? How were intellectual imaginations and curiosities lobotomised? Cambridge economics had not been built in a day, but given the dramatic speed of change, it seemed to have been dismantled in one.

Any such exploration unavoidably becomes an exercise in collective memory of a shared experience of an especially fraught period of the life of Cambridge economics. At the end of the day, the theoretical dimensions of the deep disputes between traditions, their ideological roots and practical implications constitute the heart of the matter. But great truths can be brought down by falsehoods. The narrative here deals not with the theoretical dimensions of the conflicts—that is a separate, though not entirely independent enquiry—but sketches the processes and mechanisms through which control over the process of knowledge production was ceded by the heterodox schools and captured, after a sustained multi-site, multi-year campaign by the neoclassical camp. The Faculty of Economics is thus treated as a site of knowledge production. You could win the pure fight of ideas, and yet not be able to claim the victory in the textbooks, as in the rueful case of Joan Robinson's cross-Atlantic capital controversies.

---

[29] See, however, Matthews (1968) for an alternative argumentation.

How could such a powerhouse, winning most of its battles, *dharmic* and *karmic*, wind up losing the war? How was this seemingly impregnable citadel overrun and captured, its inhabitants decimated or exiled? Not unexpectedly, from the survivors of heterodox camps, there are many answers but no consensus.

2.2.2 Fault Lines Within

Wynne Godley: No Legacy No Synthesis, No Textbooks—The Samuelson Factor
Some stray superficial positions need clearance, and one somewhat astonishing charge is levied by Wynne Godley, possibly interviewed in a bad mood. Godley registers a damning criticism (were it to be true): "they left no legacy; I knew a lot of Kaldor's ideas but there is no Kaldorian textbook; there is no post-Keynesian synthesis" (Godley, 2008). This last opinion, however, is quite impossible to comprehend or defend; Wynne is surely being more than a touch fretful or forgetful—of course, not everything has to be purveyed in 'textbooks', but even so, Nicky Kaldor had put down much of his testament in his masterly Raffaele Mattioli lectures and also available were several near-definitive post-Keynesian tracts; Cambridge did not work with textbooks per se, though there were some worthy attempts. Whatever the inner theoretical debates on fluid issues, these were never of an order to warrant Godley's sweeping, and untenable, assessment. Perhaps he wanted a simple textbook where it was all laid down—he had confessed he would fail the Tripos Part I—but Cambridge economics was not constructed or conveyed in that style. There could be other faults and flaws, but an absence of legacy would not be one of them. In a personal communication, Geoff Harcourt registers a one-word response to this charge: "Rubbish!".[30]

From Wynne Godley,[31] who, like Luigi Pasinetti, was at King's: "Economists at King's and in Cambridge, powerful people who were 'descendants' of Keynes, were impossible—vain, didn't sponsor other people's work, quarrelsome; found Richard Kahn and Joan Robinson very difficult to talk to and very

---

[30] For a 'legacy' statement from the man himself, see Kaldor (1996) which comprises his series of six Raffaele Mattioli lectures delivered in 1984, two years before he died; see also Geoff Harcourt's review of the book (Harcourt, 1997).

[31] The mild-mannered, professionally accomplished concert-class oboist, and connoisseur of wine and all things fine, Wynne Godley (1926–2010) was also regarded as one of the shrewdest policy and forecasting economists of his day, and for this last quality was lured by Kaldor to Cambridge to lead the DAE, with a Fellowship at King's College. Along with a team of young turks, and prominently seconded by Francis Cripps, he set up the Cambridge Economic Policy Group (CEPG) in 1971 that closely tracked the British economy; its canny forecasts and policy pronouncements were waited upon by researchers and government policy makers alike. CEPG became the second flagship of the empirical facet of Cambridge economics, running in parallel with the more structural Cambridge Growth Project (CGP) pioneered by Alan Brown and Richard Stone, and run subsequently by Stone and Terry Barker. Despite this high esteem and visibility, the troubled Godley was an unhappy man at Cambridge.

opinionated; a tragedy as all gifted" (Godley, 2008). Then, from his vantage point as head of the DAE and the Cambridge Economic Policy Group, he shares his distinctive perspective on the nurturing of the next generation.

> I was invited to Cambridge by Nicky Kaldor ... it was the worst thing I have ever done. I had been used to the Treasury which was entirely hierarchical but absolutely united in purpose; I came supposing as Director that people would do as I told them; I was wrong; all they wanted from me was that I preserve their jobs as none of them had tenure; the appointment committee was also the committee of management; as members of the management committee were also members of the appointment committee and none had tenure, they were very highly motivated to gain tenure; I wrote and complained to the General Board but they did nothing about it; I was very unpopular; I was unhappy and very soon wished I had not come; I very nearly resigned. (ibid.)[32]

That Wynne might have held such a view, questionable as it is, when he first arrived at DAE in 1970 is understandable; that he should retain it decades later seems somewhat thoughtless. He would be right about their foibles, but out of order on the rest. Indeed, they were each ploughing their own furrow, convergence was not a thought and there was no collective project to produce some grand synthesis. There was no composite heterodox doctrine that could easily be set down as a textbook, as was indicated by Joan and John Eatwell's 1973 the unsuccessful attempt. But each stalwart had left their mark in their various signature writings that bore their unmistakable stamp of their approach to constructing a meaningful post-Keynesian, or other independent, theoretical framework for analysing the modern capitalist economy. Godley's critique of 'internal' weakness does not fly. And with the benefit of hindsight, one might legitimately enquire about what legacy was bequeathed by the Cambridge orthodox camp, including prominently Frank Hahn himself.

Shifting Student Preferences?
One demand-side explanation offered for the decline of heterodoxy in economics argues that this reflects the progressive waning of interest in heterodox traditions amongst the student body which, inured of the fiery left politics of earlier years, was primarily motivated by careerism, focussed increasingly on what would be tactically more helpful in the job market in the changed circumstances of neoliberal globalisation; the skills and intellectual orientations demanded by job givers matched those produced in the factories of orthodox

---

[32] Dejected Godley, second son of a Baron, is disdainful of the younger Faculty's lobbying for their jobs; but should this surprise one when young staff have parents, wives and children, and homes and mortgages, and when they like their work, their place of work and their colleagues at work; and it seems they had the quality; in any event all DAE jobs, barring Wynne's own, were on short project-cycle fixed-term funding contracts. Perhaps the problem was that Godley was used to being an executive top-down director in the government bureaucracy, or accustomed to the discipline of an orchestra with everyone on the same page; but that behavioural pattern doesn't travel well into academe, of which he had relatively little prior experience.

economics. Career tracks had shifted away from academe or government policy bodies towards the City, banks, asset management, investment ventures, new financial instruments and markets, and these employers wanted not a Sraffian or a Robinsonian theoretician or a left-Keynesian modeller, but a finite set of immediately usable—whether or not intrinsically useful—skills mostly in the financial sector. Students, facing the prospect of debt incurred in the university years, were drawn to the level of the salary, not to the giddy heights of heterodox thought howsoever intellectually meaningful. Alongside globalisation, the student body was shifting its profile also with significantly increased intakes from East and Southeast Asia, and this strand added to the premium placed on technical, maths and skill-oriented, set-piece learning in economics, since that is where their comparative advantage lay. All this, it is argued, translated into a rising student demand in favour of a curriculum, textbooks, modes of teaching and methods of assessment where students were given unambiguous questions inviting clearly defined 'correct' answers—and this 'market' demand could be readily met by mainstream, orthodox economics with its mathematical toolkits and set-piece puzzles, rather than by heterodox approaches which were inherently open-ended and canned for reflection, argumentation and judgement on the part of the student who had to sift through alternative theoretical perspectives. This trend, it is argued, is self-reinforcing: as the course turns increasingly mathematical, it also leads to self-selection processes where students with more heterodox predilections move away and look elsewhere.

Several qualifications are necessary in hypothesising that a change in students' preferences, in favour of an exclusively orthodox economic curriculum—for its predictability and its marketability later in the job market—was a prime driver in the demise of heterodox economics in Cambridge. First, a Cambridge degree was always marketable; in the period under consideration, it ranked in the top echelon globally, regardless of the orthodox-heterodox balance. Second, the arguments proposed might have applied only to a fraction of the student body. In that period, students in the social sciences—perhaps economics was a more conservative backwater here—were highly politicised and radicalised; and this applied to Cambridge as well where there were some famous movements—including some directly concerning the teaching of economics—that challenged conservative authorities; leftist Cambridge dons, prominently including Ajit Singh, Bob Rowthorn, Ron Smith, amongst many others, were closely involved with various campaigns that involved heavy student backing. As such, the orthodox banking career track cannot be held to have applied to the main student body. The opposite phenomenon is also visible: on the one side, there is a massive boost in the demand for heterodox, radicalised teaching in development studies and economics (though this is eased out from the Faculty); and for another, the research students within the increasingly orthodox curricula of the Faculty take the risky step of mounting a collective challenge to this, demanding 'plurality', a soft euphemism for heterodox alternatives in theory and methods. In parallel, from the onset of the neoliberal globalisation from the early 1980s, the study of development within a global frame was hugely in demand and welcomed in the career tracks leading into international development agencies, international and national non-government organisations and related research establishments within national governments—this, not least because of the problems rapidly unleashed by the mainstream capital-driven strategies promoted by implementation of the orthodox paradigm itself. As such, even to the extent that there was a shift in the preferences of a fraction of students towards orthodox economics teaching, it cannot be read as an original force against heterodox economics—it was derivative in nature and reflected the impact of unfolding globalisation—which, in turn, was driven by the ideological and political muscle of the neoliberal thought machine and the structural material forces of global capitalism. To the extent that such external factors were at play, they reflected the prior victories of neoliberal politics and economics in the global arena.

"Irrelevance" and Irreverence: Joan and K-Theory
Some of the Cambridge greats had been attacked by their 'other' Cambridge numbers for their preoccupation with what were portrayed as abstruse, esoteric theoretical hobby horses; Joan usually was the first one put in this dock for having spent and diverted so much Cambridge energy into the controversies of the measurement of capital.

Matthews (1989: 915) for one, said, "we had reckoned ourselves to be among Joan's admirers, but we became bored by the increasingly theological disputes about the measurement of capital, about the fallacy of the marginal productivity theory, and so on". Such unhappiness, albeit in mild forms, was expressed even within the extended heterodox clans; Ajit Singh was clearly not speaking for himself alone when he wrote that "many younger heterodox economists in Cambridge were as dissatisfied with pure theory of the Cambridge kind (from Joan Robinson and her colleagues) as they were with the abstractions of general equilibrium theory" (Singh, 2008: 21). Samuelson (1988: 328) "On the inadmissibility of a *scalar* aggregate of capital to serve as a productive factor, she was dead right"; and Arrow "praises Joan for having forced the question of the heterogeneity of capital" (Feiwel, 1989: xxxix); half-hearted compliments perhaps since they both go on to disagree on the implications of this agreement. "Cambridge economics was meant to be politically left-wing—a cause to which it was, in some ways, dedicated. However, I found it difficult to believe that the downfall of capitalism, if that were to occur, would be caused by some sophisticated mistake in capital theory rather than because of the nasty way capitalism treats human beings" (Sen, 2021, p. 287). Sen goes on to promote Pigou "who was still alive and living in Cambridge and who tended to be dismissed by neo-Keynesians as an old-fashioned neoclassical economist because he had challenged Keynes on many of his claims" and who in Sen's view "expressed a much better understanding of the real problem" (Sen, 2021, p. 287). Perhaps Sen was responding in equal measure to Joan's rubbishing of his dedication to work on welfare economics and social choice theory that she, amongst others, did not regard as a worthy subject of study. Be that as it may, a neutral referee might ask how precisely axiomatic welfare and choice theorems would further the leftist cause, towards which Sen frequently mentions his "inclination". In his extensive, thoughtful and challenging assessment, Lance Taylor raises a spectrum of critical issues about Sen's field and book, which prompts him to ruefully say, "[W]hat is still lacking is positive advice" (Taylor, 1984, p. 193). Taylor questions Sen's illustrations of relevance: "all these curses [old age, misery, despair] are boiled down to a single number based on the Gini coefficient, with an appropriate axiomatic basis ... but it is fair to say that the poor have not been succoured by the arithmetic ... very few Calcutta nuns or barefoot doctors (or even their superiors' superiors) carry tracts on how to calculate a Gini" (ibid.), and he goes on to list several other criticisms, noting "the lapidary ambiguity of his formal results" and the "Delphic negativism" in which the discourse is embroiled (Taylor, 1984, p. 195). Sen would surely have responded to such a broad challenge, but then so did Joan to Sen's somewhat supercilious trivialising remark with regard to the significance of the controversies in capital theory. Taylor (1984, p. 195) observes that Sen "is reticent about laying his own worldview explicitly on the line"—something Joan, always passionately committed, could seldom if ever be accused of.

Joan had long made plain her view of the significance of the 'capital controversies'. "The long wrangle about 'measuring capital' has been a great deal of fuss over a secondary question. The real source of trouble is the confusion between comparisons of equilibrium positions and the history of a process of accumulation" (Robinson, J., 1974: 9). "The problem of the 'measurement of capital' is a minor element in the criticism of the neo-classical doctrines. The major point is that what they pretend to offer as an alternative or rival to the post-Keynesian theory of accumulation is nothing but an error in methodology—a confusion between comparisons of imagined equilibrium positions and a process of accumulation going on through history" (ibid.: 11).

Avi Cohen and Geoff Harcourt set the record straight from the other side. Looking back at the debates, they ask if it really was what Joan called the outcome of "sloppy habits of thought", or just "a tempest in a teapot of concern now only to the historians of economics". Their answer highlights three key aspects of significance: "the first is the meaning and ... the measurement of the concept of capital in the analysis of industrial capitalist societies; the second is Joan Robinson's complaint that equilibrium was not the outcome of an economic process and therefore an inadequate tool for analysing processes of capital accumulation and growth; the third issue is the role of ideology and vision in fuelling controversy when the results of simple models are not robust" Harcourt and Cohen (2012).

Speaking of the Cambridge heterodox greats, Matthews (1989: 915) says, "But two sides there were, and one was dominant. The dominant side in its turn began to suffer in the 1960s an erosion of its own intellectual coherence. ... So one chapter ended, the later chapters evolved out of it." There are questions about such a reading: the dominant 'side' comprised many of varied heterodox identities, and there is little credible evidence that they were losing ground, or their 'intellectual coherence' in the 1960s: to wit, Joan had recently published her *Accumulation of Capital* followed shortly by her *Economic Philosophy*, Sraffa his *Production of Commodities*, and Kaldor his *Causes of the Slow Rate of Growth*, and Dick Goodwin close the decade with his classic *Elementary Economics from the Higher Standpoint*. Perhaps Matthews, who had teamed up with friend Hahn (who came to Cambridge from Birmingham in 1962) to produce their famous survey of economic growth in 1964, was treating their own rise as definitionally implying the loss of coherence of the heterodox groups they were soon to challenge, possibly a somewhat self-serving interpretation.

Leaving aside these cul-de-sac, unsatisfactory or untenable propositions, there are a few other more credible 'internal' elements that carry more explanatory power.

Inbred Insularity, Complacency

Cocooned Cambridge, and particularly Cambridge economics, might well have had a sense of contented completeness, a world unto itself, the source from which knowledge of economics flowed out; seekers of wisdom came to the fount: had not Champernowne famously given up his Oxford chair to return to Cambridge as reader, had not Robertson returned to Cambridge, difficult as it had been for him, from LSE which had given him a much more congenial intellectual home, and had not Frank Hahn, albeit perhaps with a different long-term agenda, first given up his readership at Birmingham and his valued partnership with Terry Gorman there to come to Cambridge as a lecturer, and then return to it later, giving up his professorship at LSE, as did several others, including Peter Bauer who had also traded a readership in London for a lectureship in Cambridge. And were there not processions of pilgrims, from Australia, from Italy, from India or from Canada, regularly finding their way to this mecca of economics to hear the sermons and carry back the word? Over the decades, Cambridge, insular as it surely was, had become the Greenwich for a world map of economics, and the natural habitat of various genres of heterodox lineages of the discipline, inclusively interpreted.

A smug sense of entitlement was alleged to be the hallmark of these inheritors and guardians of the great traditions, the apostles dispensing and taking them forward, Cambridge was arguably insular often to the point of being oblivious of all else and others; indeed, others were generally 'othered'.[33] Cambridge economics, the unrivalled Mecca of the discipline from the turn of the twentieth century, epitomised this cocooned, elitist state of self-containment

---

[33] Ron Smith, who moved from Cambridge to Birkbeck in 1976, recalls that "Cambridge arrogance and insularity was expressed in the view that the role of external examiners in the Tripos was to raise the standard of economics outside Cambridge. Compared to anywhere else I have been the externals were ignored by all sides in the 1970s when I was there" (personal communication).

and self-contentment. Gossip was legal tender, but only when who said what to whom, where and when, was all "Cambridge-y", using Robertson's term.

For long, the Pigouvian refrain to all and sundry was "it's all in Marshall"; then came the era and gospel of Keynes, which utterly dominated all discourse for a decade before and three decades after the War till it was rudely disturbed by the onslaught of Thatcherism. Indeed, Cambridge economics was insular not just in relation to the world outside Cambridge, it had closed-shop features even within, where gatekeeping and entry restrictions applied to exalted spaces, where admission was only by invitation, for example, the Circus, or the Secret seminar, or even the Political Economy Seminar.

Keynes chaired a Committee of Economists appointed by the Prime Minister Ramsay Macdonald to review the state, and future of the British economy; members were Josiah Stamp, Clay, Henderson, Pigou, Robbins and Robertson. Robbins accepted "with alacrity", and then suggested to Keynes that "our deliberations might be very materially assisted if we could hear the views of three or four foreign economists (a) on the world slump (b) on the British position as it appears to outsiders"; the names mentioned were "Viner for America, Ropke for Germany, Ohlin for Scandinavia and Hayek for Central Europe". Keynes's response is dismissive: "[I] doubt whether outsiders could tell us much to the point which we do not know between us" (Howson, 2011: 180).

From Marcuzzo and Sanfilippo (2008: 89) we have an account of Cambridge insularity as perceived by Robertson, and insider who became, or was made, an outsider. Cambridge was so different that Robertson invented an adjective to describe it: "*Cambridge-y*" (Marcuzzo & Sanfilippo, 2008: 89). Robertson: "More than in a shared theory, the identity of this group is rooted in motivations, values and habits: perhaps it is common lifestyles and work styles that most aptly and tellingly express these aspects. By work styles we mean the importance attached to correspondence and oral discussion in the process of forming ideas and drawing up texts—authoritativeness and authority founded on an internal hierarchy that does not necessarily reflect seniority in terms of age or academic qualification. By lifestyles we mean the importance ascribed to personal relations, affording a framework for scientific intercourse, which explains how so many theoretical divisions left ample safe ground for reciprocal respect and affection" (Marcuzzo & Rosselli, 2005: 15; cited in Marcuzzo & Sanfilippo, 2008: 89).

Robertson's commentary seems to render his notion of "Cambridgeyness" essentially a cultural quality defining interpersonal and collegial relations between the Cambridge economists. But even a cursory reflection would suggest that the LSE crowd could also have been described using the same description, only contextually redefined, that is, relocated to the urban infrastructural and academic context and constraints of LSE and London.

The differences were perhaps far deeper as is apparent from Hicks's, and Austin Robinson's descriptions of the LSE and the Cambridge intellectual environments, respectively, in the crucial formative period of the 1930s. Says

Hicks about the LSE: "We seemed, at the start, to share a common viewpoint, or even a common faith. The faith in question was a belief in the free market, or 'price mechanism' that a competitive system, free of all 'interferences', by government or monopolistic combinations, of capital or of labour, would easily find an 'equilibrium'. ... Hayek, when he joined us, was to introduce into this doctrine an important qualification—that money (somehow) must be kept 'neutral', in order that the mechanism should work smoothly" (Hicks, 1982: 3, cited in Marcuzzo & Sanfilippo, 2008: 74). Marcuzzo and Sanfilippo remark that "by contrast, Austin Robinson's account of the making of the Keynesian revolution brings to light the loss of faith in the market mechanism, neutrality of money, and laissez-faire". They quote Austin: "we learned to distinguish very clearly ... between those propositions that are universally true and those propositions that ore only true in conditions of full employment. ... [What we learned] was really the integration of value theory and monetary theory into what we now call macroeconomics" (Robinson, 1985: 57, cited in Marcuzzo & Sanfilippo, 2008: 74). And, it is worth recalling that Keynes had gloriously declared his position in his The Death of Laissez-faire ten years before the arrival of The General Theory, and two years after the death of Alfred Marshall in 1924.

On this basis, the legendary insularity that was ascribed to Cambridge economics arose not from the cultural "Cambridgeyness" à la Robertson but was a manifestation of a shared intellectual and ideological faith in the Keynesian doctrine then being fashioned. The distance between the two schools needed measure on an ideological scale; it was not merely aloofness or arrogance. As the leading personalities dug in and conveyed their respective 'messages' to their clans, such distances would become greater and attract more vivid description and behaviour. Cambridge, for the 1930s under Keynes would acquire the label of insularity on account of the fact that its message was unique, and sharply distinct from the other tribes and clans, setting it apart as being 'insular'. As Marcuzzo and Sanfilippo (2008: 76) rightly surmise: "the confrontation between the two camps was felt as a threat to either group's identity, which had been built up under the spell of Robbins and Keynes. While Cambridge people, notably Keynes, Kahn, Joan Robinson, and Piero Sraffa, each of them with his or her own agenda, were attacking traditional economic beliefs and customs, the LSE people, Hayek, Robbins, Hicks, Allen and Kaldor were establishing an orthodoxy, based on general equilibrium and intertemporal analysis, highly formalized, and derived from first principles." There is resonance here with the account of the Cambridge Circus by Aslanbeigui and Oakes (2002) whose construction of the episode depicts it as "a revolutionary party".

Things had not changed much two decades later when Angus Maddison sat listening to the Cambridge greats: "The hottest topics were theoretical, and almost entirely concentrated on what Cambridge economists had said. As Dharma Kumar paraphrased Joan Robinson, 'time is a device to prevent everything happening at once, space is a device to prevent it all happening in

Cambridge'. There was not much attention to what people thought in Oxford, or LSE, in Scandinavia or the USA" (Maddison, 1994).[34] Maddison's polite reference to Cambridge insularity takes a rather vituperative expression in Harry Johnson's recounting of Cambridge economics of the 1950s (Johnson, n.d.).

And nor had they changed much another two decades down the timeline when Tony Lawson made his entry into Cambridge economics: "Yes Cambridge *was* insular. At least this was so for the group of heterodox economists ... if it didn't happen in Cambridge then they were not especially interested."

The reality, at least the reputation, persisted. 'Insularity' was one of the sticks used first by the SSRC to beat first the CEPG in 1981–1982; then during 1984–1987, the charge and the stick were shared—the ESRC employed both against the CGP, while the Review Committee of the University used them against the DAE unit as a whole. Wynne Godley confessed to the charge, probably thinking that accepting culpability for such a minor misdemeanour would be harmless, and it came back to bite him and the rest in due course; in contrast, Terry Barker defending the CGP then and later rejected the charge,[35] but to no avail. The Cambridge pedigree had long carried this 'bad' reputation, indeed worn it with pride or distinction, evidence of its closer-to-heaven height in the discipline—and this had long rankled with its rivals, especially the LSE under Beveridge and particularly Robbins. And later in the 1980s it was the LSE/Oxford brigade that were wielding the stick.

Simultaneities in the Demographic Lifecycle

The time pattern of 'natural wastage' took a heavy toll, and in a manner that accentuated the impact of the withdrawal of the greats from the field of battle. The seniors all belonged to a relatively narrow age band. That this was arithmetically reflected in the bunching up of retirements was one an issue. Of course, with exceptions, most of them carried on as before, even if not with the same formal departmental duties (to the extent they had any) so in this sense there was no great perceptible break. But there were two other aspects to this clustering; first, in being able to install appropriate replacements for many of them within, though given the strength of the younger following cohort, they could have been spoilt for choice had they looked and acted in a timely manner in this regard; and second, that many of them fell within a short time frame, leaving great gaps and silences.

Demography and natural wastage played their part in the decline of the neo-Keynesian, heterodox and radical economics at Cambridge. Joan Robinson died in 1983, on Piero Sraffa's 85th birthday, and Piero followed Joan less than

---

[34] Maddison, Angus 1994, "Confessions of a Chiffrephile", *Banca Nazionale del Lavoro Quarterly Review*, No. 189, June. http://www.ggdc.net/maddison/personal/autobiog1994.pdf.

[35] Barker pointed out that the charge of inbred insularity could not be levied against Dick Stone and the CGP: "the techniques developed by the CGP (social accounting, I-O analysis, large-scale econometric time-series analysis in the CGP dynamic models) were focused on international research agendas, indeed leading some of them" (personal communication).

a month thereafter; Nicky Kaldor in 1986,[36] speaking at Richard Kahn's memorial service in 1989 Pasinetti, said his passing "concludes a whole historical phase, an era in the history of modern economic thought".[37] It also created a vacuum in left intellectual leadership.

There is another idiosyncratic and overlooked demographic dimension which could carry some relevance: the longevity of the Cambridge heterodox greats, compared to that for their neoclassical and neoliberal rivals. A casual reading of the age at death is suggestive: all in order on one side are Dobb 76, Kaldor 78, Joan 80, Goodwin 83, Kahn 84, Sraffa 85; then again in order, all on the other side, follow Hahn 88, Hayek 93, Friedman 94, Samuelson 94 and Solow 95 not out. Whether it was all those heavy college high table dinners in shortening prospects on the one side, or an addition of ten years gifted by the award of a 'Nobel' prize, is an open question; but the fact remains that the neoclassical and neoliberal gurus outlived their rivals by a discrete margin, adding to the relative strength of their clans. On the Cambridge side, it is also worth reflecting on the counterfactuals: what if Keynes did not die at 63 in 1946 but lived to 93 to fight his corner till 1976? And what if Allyn Young at LSE but with profound affinities to Cambridge economics did not die at 52 in 1929—short years after Keynes's *The End of Laissez Faire*, and Sraffa's 1926 game-changing article both from 1926—but stayed on for another 40 years, like his other American compatriots, till 1969?

This process of natural wastage, in terms of the timing of statutory retirements, was entirely predictable, and the fact that the seniors did little to preempt it with timely action corroborates the charges made by Pasinetti[38] and Harcourt. The younger cohort had consolidated left power in decision-making in the Faculty for a lengthy stretch, led prominently by Ajit; but the seniors had not converted that opportunity to ensure the continuity of the radical traditions through timely appointments to replace themselves; like the gods they were, perhaps mortality wasn't part of their frame of reference, and then again, gods were generally loners and didn't much collaborate on joint projects, and certainly not ones to replace them; as is their wont, the gods had left loyal mortals in the lurch. On the heterodox side, not only had the old stalwarts retired, but most had passed away without any of the many potential heirs appointed or anointed.

---

[36] Bob Rowthorn (2008) opines "the fact that Kaldor died relatively young was a great loss; Cambridge economics would have been very different if he had lived another ten years"; but Harcourt (2011) tells us that the writing was on the wall when Hahn was installed in Kahn's Chair, and that was due to Kaldor, whose student Hahn had been for a while at LSE. Of course, if wishes were horses, many might have wished Keynes had lived 20 years longer and seen through the consolidation of the new schools of thought.

[37] Address delivered by Luigi Pasinetti at the memorial service for Richard Kahn at King's College Chapel, 21 October 1989.

[38] "The Keynesian group had left no successor in an influential position. In the last few years of his life, Nicholas Kaldor was explicit enough to openly recognize this as a failure. Richard Kahn perhaps felt it even more deeply than Kaldor, but kept it to himself" (Pasinetti, 2007: 85; see also 212–213).

Francis Cripps puts in a kind word for the whimsical forgetful gods:

> The seniors never expected the sudden and effective attack after Thatcher came in. Up to that point and to a large extent thanks to Ajit's organization, the left negotiated appointments in the Faculty of Economics and DAE from a strong position and the neo-classical/orthodox side was in trouble. The manoeuvres that changed the balance started unexpectedly when the General Board of the Faculties (top body of the university) suspended Statutes governing election of the head of the DAE and set up an inquiry into the DAE with hostile referees from elsewhere. This took the Keynesian gods by surprise. Perhaps the question is why gods from other faculties were so motivated as to bypass the normal channels. Was it mainly political (fear of reds and left activism) in an era when the USSR was still seen as a threat or was it the gulf between Cambridge economics of the time and the academic orthodoxy that had invaded universities in Britain and other countries of the Atlantic Alliance? A lot of people in what we used to call 'the Establishment' had been disturbed by the activism of the economics faculty and DAE in the 1970s but couldn't do much about it so long as Labour formed the government. (Personal communication, email dated 10 February 2018)

While the timeline of statutory retirements of professors was known, there was a new destabilising factor which made the actual pattern unpredictable—and the source of this was the savage cuts to university budgets announced upon the arrival of Margaret Thatcher as prime minister; it was left to the universities to decide on the implementation, but cuts on staffing were inevitable.

This unwelcome turn drew Harry Hinsley onto centre stage. "Elected as Master of St. Johns College in 1979, [a position he held till 1989] he also served a two-year stint as Vice-Chancellor of the University in 1981–1983. In both roles, he found himself coping equably with problems that were suddenly thrust upon him, whether it was the admission of women to the college—he had not previously been in favour of this step—or the need to make cuts in the university's budget" Clarke (n.d.: 103). "In the history of the university he will be especially remembered for his promotion of the cause of early retirement" (Linehan, 1998). His performance did not go unrewarded. In 1985, on the day he received his knighthood under the Thatcher government, he was also awarded an honorary doctorate by Wits University in South Africa; the citation included a reference to "the financial cuts in the government's grants to universitates that have become a feature of British academic life under the rule of Margaret Thatcher. It owes much to Hinsley that the cuts were distributed fairly and evenly over all sections and subjects. In the matter of forced (or much-encouraged) early retirement Hinsley's proceedings were tactful and aroused little animosity. His decision to take early retirement as a professor himself was made not because he wanted to but characteristically because he felt he ought to, having to persuade others to do so."[39] Hinsley took early retirement himself, stopping when his term as Vice Chancellor ended in 1983,

---

[39] https://www.wits.ac.za/media/wits-university/alumni/documents/honorary-degree-citations/Harry%20Hinsley%20citation.pdf.

Table 2.2 Early retirements in the Faculty of Economics, 1981–1985

Name	Chair	Year of retirement		Replacement
		Expected	Actual	
John Barnes	Sociology	1985	1982	Tony Giddens (1985)
Phyllis Deane	Economic History	1985	1983	Personal chair—lapsed
Robert Neild	Economics	1991	1984	Partha Dasgupta (1985)
Donald Coleman	Economic History	1987	1981	Barry Supple (1981)
Bert Turner	Industrial Relations	1986	1983	Willy Brown (1985)
Harry Hinsley	*International Relations*	*1983*	*1985*	

simultaneously also vacating his Chair in International Relations two years before the mandatory retirement age of 67. Hinsley was apparently a persuasive operator: "His rasping, sub-Churchillian cadences, were affectionately imitated by his pupils, just as his transparently Machiavellian strategies were indulgently appreciated by his colleagues" (Clarke n.d.: 103). The later highly controversial University Review of the DAE was signalled in a memorandum by A. D. I. Nicol, then Secretary-General of the General Board of the Faculties, and this note written in the tenure of Hinsley as Vice Chancellor was taken over by Nicol's successor K. J. R. Edwards. Ken Edwards was also a fellow of St. John's, and refers to Harry Hinsley as one of heads of colleges that he got to know very well—Edwards (2009) thought it "important to know the movers and shakers, the opinion makers" of the University; Edwards declared himself to be a follower of Machiavelli, so presumably Harry and Ken might have had some interesting conversations about University affairs. Harry Hinsley also had a lateral role in the survival of the Development teaching at a critical turning point (Chap. 1, pp. 26–27).

Whether it was Harry Hinsley's persuasive technique that swayed the balance for very many senior staff to opt for early retirement cannot be proven, but the Thatcher's arrival provided both stick and carrot for many to cross the line (Table 2.2). The extent and impact of this twist has generally gone unnoticed and unremarked; yet, on closer consideration, this demographic dimension was of much potential significance. At the Faculty of Economics, there was a spate of early retirements in the early 1980s, and their clustering could not but have shifted the internal balance of decision-making. Some of seniors might not even have needed any special cajolement from Hinsley: Robert Neild wanted out because the Faculty air had become too noxious to breathe due to the unpleasantness of internal strife; "in 1982 John [Barnes] seized the opportunity for early retirement from Cambridge" (Young, M. Y., 2011: 9); one could also wonder why Phyllis Deane retired early in 1983, two years before the statutory limit, when she had just been (belatedly) appointed professor in 1981. Whether it was the stick of the atmosphere in the Faculty or Hinsley's assortment of carrots, the cumulative result was that there were five early exits from the Faculty of Economics & Politics, opening the space for four fresh entrants to be ushered in and to be seated in the vacated chairs. While opinions would surely vary, it is arguable, when seen from the heterodox side of the Faculty divide, that on balance the change-over further shifted the balance of opinion and power in favour of the orthodox side. Leaving aside Donald Coleman (Professor of Economic History from the Faculty of History), four voices were lost on the heterodox side, and amongst the replacements, only one could firmly be relied upon as favouring heterodox agendas. The significance becomes even more stark when viewed against the other exits and entries in the short window of time: Brian Reddaway retired in 1980 and was replaced by Robin Matthews (then already Master of Clare College since 1975); the formal 15-year tenure of Wynne Godley's directorship of the DAE ended in 1985, but his wings were already clipped by the termination of the Godley-Cripps CEPG; Richard Stone also retired in 1980; and in 1983, the moral authority underwritten by the presence of Joan Robinson and Piero Sraffa was lost, as was the active participation of Nicky Kaldor in 1986. Thus, the short 1980–1986 period witnessed a dramatic upheaval in the configuration in the senior ranks of the Faculty, which in turn translated into a significant shift in the balance of decision-making power between the contending groups.

Lack of Internal Group Coherence
Another 'inside' factor could be the lack of internal cohesiveness between the various heterodox lineages both at the intellectual and personal levels, thereby emphasising divergence over convergence. This would mean missed opportunities of course, but also to a weakening of the totality of the heterodox formation. Many illustrations can be adduced. There was trouble between the three big names: Kaldor had fallen out with Joan and Kahn; they all had good relations with Sraffa, but he kept out of the fray; Maurice Dobb and Joan, both on the left, could not agree on the conceptual language to use for analysing Marx; or again the public and private spats between 'old' and 'new' Cambridge positions represented by Kahn and Kaldor or their seconds; the two Richards, Stone and Goodwin, never got together, at least to the former's expressed regret, to write some joint papers that would make a difference, this on account of concerns on Dick Goodwin's part over how this would go down with Joan and the third Richard, Kahn; Matthews questioned the claim of Keynesian fiscal sources of the post-war boom; on the other side, some raised an eyebrow at Charles Feinstein's use of the Cobb-Douglas production function in processing his historical data; and some were as excited by Joan's Maoist pronouncements as some others were dismayed. Since each (group) of the seniors had a younger set of (overlapping) apprentices or disciples whom they were informally mentoring, these fractions and frictions were accentuated further. And of course, there were more serious divisions between all of the above members of the extended heterodox family and the neoclassicals on the other side; here it was expected that the political or ideological differences would spill over into interpersonal differences, though Amartya Sen tempers this with a delightful

account of the trio of Sraffa, Robertson and Dobb overcoming these barricades with grace and élan in Trinity. Perhaps a unique instance of cross-border collaboration was the joint letter written by Hahn and Neild attacking possibly the one thing they agreed on, Thatcherite monetarism.[40] But less expected, and more damaging, were situations when such interpersonal differences led to breaks in communications between seniors all under the same great banyan. One can rightly view this as evidence of a creative intellectual environment where sparks generate both heat and illumination—and this was always so in these jousts. But to a significant extent they did also undermine the internal cohesiveness and bonds within the group, limit its strategic critical mass and potentially send out confused or least a multiplicity of messages about the state and strength of Cambridge heterodox economics.

On the senior side of the heterodox camp in Cambridge, there were several notables who were also im/perceptibly beginning to walk on two legs, shifting their weight from the left, Labour, leg to some other: Reddaway, Posner, Feinstein, Matthews and Kahn were shifting loyalties, some explicitly, in favour of the SDP following the defeat of Labour in the 1979 election. The big turning point was the defeat of the Tony Benn in his bid for the deputy leadership of the Labour Party in 1981, which incidentally was also the time frame when the Godley-Cripps CEPG was cut down by the SSRC then chaired by Michael Posner, a position to which he had been appointed by Shirley Williams just prior to the formation of the SDP. Thus, the heterodox group comprised many varieties of Keynesianism, socialism and Marxism in their economics, but also a spectrum of political affinities. Even with regard to actions opposing 'the common foe', viz., the neoclassicals, strong unity could not always be taken as read and needed to be mobilised and monitored, ready for the next demand placed on it. Terry Ward recalls that "the non-neoclassicals were such an heterodox group that it was very often difficult to get them to agree about anything—so it was not really true that we held sway over appointments to professorships and the Faculty generally. Potentially yes, but in practice only sometimes" (personal communication; email dated 1 April 2021). And such episodes could lead to self-farm for the heterodox group as a whole; it is possible, though not necessary, to cite cases.

And there were also some counterproductive cracks and splits which could have weakened solidarity. Apart from the problems between the 'old' and the 'new' Cambridge theorists, there were other lines of distance or division. For one, till Kaldor himself broke fully with equilibrium economics, he remained Hahn's friend and supporter in important ways. Both Thirlwall and King record the widely known falling away of Kaldor from Richard Kahn and Joan Robinson in the late 1950s; and Geoff Harcourt had a falling out with Kaldor

---

[40] Ron Smith, in his econometrician avatar, ruefully records another point on which there was agreement: "the main figures on the left and the right, being theorists, were united against econometrics. They both wasted time to ensure no Tripos papers had the title Econometrics—the econometrics paper was called statistical theory" (personal communication).

with the distance taking a decade to be closed again: Kaldor was unhappy with Geoff for having accepted undergraduate supervisions from Henderson who was on Nicky's unwanted list. Then there was the very public and bruising exchange with (the then leftist firebrand) Bob Rowthorn writing against rather than with Nicky Kaldor over Verdoorn's and Kaldor's Laws, enough to make John King, Kaldor's (second) biographer observe: "In Cambridge the most prominent Marxian economist was Robert Rowthorn ('Red Bob', as he was known in 1975, when Kaldor crossed swords with him on the question of Verdoorn's Law). There was never any question of collaboration between them" (King, 2009: 177). Reportedly, there were editorial battles within the CJE where the exchanges were published. King also points to Kaldor's distance from the economics of socialism: and "the Conference of Socialist Economists, an organisation that held absolutely no appeal for Kaldor" (ibid.).[41] Another indication of internal friction was apparent when the group of young radicals, prominently Singh, Rowthorn, Eatwell, Cripps and Ellman, approached Richard Kahn for support in launching a new journal; in response, Kahn rather rudely distanced himself from the leftist orientation of the proposed journal; Kahn involved Neild, who expressed similar reservations quite sharply, and neither took on a role when the *Cambridge Journal of Economics* was formed a couple of years later. Kahn accused the journal of having a propagandist orientation, though Joan remained part of the initiative by the young cohort of left scholars. Such differences, latent as they might have been, could only have weakened communications and solidarity within the broad coalition on the heterodox side.

The 'left' everywhere has come to achieve a general reputation for bouts of internecine discord within its ranks, and this was true also for the older and the younger generations of the heterodox lineages. Distance and difference could and did spill over into disagreement and dispute; sometimes reflecting contending heterodox theoretical positions, sometimes to do with party-political loyalties, and perhaps on occasion also due to latent rivalries over competitive

---

[41] Ron Smith suggests that "Cambridge was also peripheral because it was insular. The main heterodox action was around the Conference of Socialist Economics and *Capital and Class* in the UK, and URPE (Union of Radical Political Economists) in the US. The main heterodox action was in the US which treated Cambridge [UK] as peripheral" (personal communication). This needs qualification. While Cambridge heterodox groups might well have seemed distant on the USA horizon, they occupied a large, if not preeminent, space in UK in that period. For instance, the Conference of Socialist Economists was founded in 1970 and held its first Conference in London in January; of the original 75 participants that attended, as many as 40 Cambridge names were listed as its original "members and fellow travellers" (Lee, 2007: Appendix A1). The list included Maurice Dobb, John Eatwell, Michael Ellman, Charles Feinstein, Jean Gardiner, Richard Goodwin, Donald Harris, Mario Nuti, Suzanne Paine, Luigi Pasinetti, Prabhat Patnaik, Utsa Patnaik, S. K. Rao, Joan Robinson, Bob Rowthorn and Ajit Singh, among others. Hugo Radice, writing in the first issue of the Bulletin of the Conference of Socialist Economists, notes that the second Conference was held in Cambridge with 120 attended: "there were papers and useful discussion on the capital theory debate, on development economics and on the international firm" (Radice, 1971: 5).

promotions. Politically, in terms of party politics, there were several shades of pink to red. At that point, Bob Rowthorn called himself "a classical Marxist" and he held positions which could easily chip the edges of camp solidarity; progressively, he went from red to shades of purple and blue, and eventually took to advising a Tory think tank. In 1974, he, along with Michael Ellman, Ron Smith and Frank Wilkinson had written a pamphlet, published by Ken Coates at the Institute for Workers' Control, laying out a left-labour diagnosis and policy programme which formed the foundation of an Alternative Economic Strategy—the pamphlet to which Richard Kahn was presumably chaffing. Francis Cripps was very closely associated with Tony Benn, and therefore marked as being on the seriously left fringe of Labour politics; there were other CEPG advisers as well, for instance, Terry Ward, part of the same formation.

The cases of three highly regarded members of the younger cohort—all classifiable as 'heterodox' though in quite different ways—serve to illustrate, even if loosely, the shifting complexities of interwoven national politics, individual intellectual and ideological predilections, and career aspirations and tracks.[42]

(Once) "Red" Bob Rowthorn, one legendary stalwart of the Cambridge left economists, was interviewed by Alan Macfarlane in 2008, and the transcript provides glimpses of how far he has evolved away from the leftist identity for which he stood out in Cambridge and beyond; the 'wow' combination of Marxism and mathematics made him especially exotic, and perhaps also attracted the sympathetic attention of seniors in the neoclassical ranks in the Faculty. He identifies some of his 'likes' and 'dislikes'. He thinks Richard Kahn "was a great economist", but "he had very little intellectual influence on me"; "Keynesian economics was a collective enterprise; I think the greatest of that school was D.H. Robertson who was rejected by them and regarded as anti-Keynesian"; Rowthorn is inclined to place Robertson above Keynes on the "greatness" scale saying that Robertson's earlier work on banking had anticipated most of the propositions of *The General Theory*; "this is not an opinion that makes me popular in some circles". He had a "bad relationship" with Joan Robinson, having fought with her over his defence of Hicks's interpretation of Keynes; he calls Joan dogmatic and authoritarian, also one who converted "technical debates into political ones". He progresses further: "An aspect of this period was the ostrich-like approach of the Keynesians here, with one exception, Kaldor; they saw the enemy as the 'neoclassical economists', American Keynesians, and wanted to discredit them; turned to the work of Piero Sraffa to do it; it produced work that I considered to be a complete side track of no real significance at all; I wrote a critical article in 'New Left Review' which marked the break between me and that school of thought; I became much more a classical Marxist; Looking at the Cambridge economics as a whole, there were two strands, the followers (Robinson, Sraffa etc) and others,

---

[42] The cases of several other major heterodox names, for example, Geoff Harcourt, Luigi Pasinetti, Ajit Singh, Francis Cripps, figure elsewhere in the narrative.

Kaldor and to some extent, Pasinetti". ... "I did become too isolated when I broke with the Sraffians and my work suffered then."

Rowthorn then widens his frame and shares thoughts on his political slide to the right. "Looking back on the left, its greatest weakness has been its failure to take responsibility for historical events; an example of that attitude has been Eric Hobsbawm whose book *Interesting Times* showed a failure to recognise that much that has gone wrong in the last 200 years was provoked by the left; not just that it has been defending virtue against the right, it has done many bad things and then produced a reaction from people who were in many cases, desperate to resist them." Remarkably, Rowthorn offers examples from the cases of the Spanish Civil War and Pinochet in Chile, saying that in both cases the authoritarian regimes were induced as reactions to prior provocations or "bad things" done by the utopian leftists. "I think that that kind of utopian left is dying; that is one of the reasons why I would not regard myself as left wing any more as I do not think there is a simple blueprint." Rowthorn now describes his 'socialism' as a concern for the poor—there are too many, and it would be good to do something about that; and a concern over injustice. He acknowledges that he has ended up close the starting point of his parents' dedicated conservative politics, adding that conservatism need not be that of the free-market type—his resembles the collectivist conservative orientation of his parents.

Then he looks ahead: "My interests have shifted though a lot of the people I work with are ex-Marxists; I don't regard myself as left wing any more but as a communitarian, basically think that people have to look after each other but not sure of the structures that can achieve that; no longer have confidence in grand schemes where numbers of people will be killed to achieve it." His research interests have also shifted away from class, socialist or Marxian themes. "In the last fifteen years [since the mid-1990s, soon after his promotion to a personal professorship in Cambridge] a lot of my work has been related to biology and evolution; ... I have got interested in family disintegration and the decline of families; ... north-west Europe and America has had enormous instability of families which I think is a disaster; cause is hedonism caused by decline of the notion of need for binding relationships; the old left was" conservative "on these issues; the lower you go down in the social scale the worse the disintegration; think that family disintegration is a serious issue; public policy has affected this as the welfare state underpins family fragmentation; I was an advisor to the Centre for Social Justice, a Conservative Party think tank." The Santa Fe project in which he was involved "is an attempt to understand the evolution of human beings; ... a well-functioning society rests on the way people interact, the social norms, perceptions of moral responsibilities; reflects economists and biologists moving into sociology and anthropology; Adam Smith's 'Theory of Moral Sentiments' and Darwin's 'Descent of Man' full of things about the evolution of altruism; have done an article on this subject and also work on group selection models which combines genetics and social evolution of human beings."

A few years after this 2008 interview, Rowthorn declared himself on some critical public policy issues. He became a Brexiteer; and he strongly and controversially argued, based on his joint research with David Coleman, that immigration was damaging for the UK, and it "will wreck the dream of a high-wage Britain". Striking is his partnership in this with David Coleman, the Oxford demographer also known for being a founder-advisor to Migration-Watch UK which argues for lower immigration, and for having links to eugenics being a member of The Galton Institute. Their research, published in *Population and Development Review* (Coleman & Rowthorn, 2004), received polarised comment and criticism, but was gleefully welcomed and cited by right-wing organisations in support of their own racist positions on immigration and asylum control.[43] Teresa Hayter (2007), in an article in *The Guardian*, raised a few issues. First, she raises 'the eugenics; question', pointing to "Sir Francis Galton's definition of eugenics as the 'science of improving stock—not only by judicious mating, but whatever tends to give the more suitable races or strains of blood a better chance of prevailing over the less suitable that they otherwise would have had', or to Galton's argument that democracies 'must in self-defence withstand the free introduction of degenerate stock'". She writes, based on her juxtapositions, that "the likelihood is that Coleman's opposition to immigration is driven by a more extreme and conscious desire that is the case with most people to preserve some kind of notional purity of British stock" Against this backdrop, Hayter shifts attention to a conclusion of the joint Coleman-Rowthorn paper: "After 31 pages of statistics and economic argument, they say the 'more important effects' of mass immigration would be 'new and intractable social divisions and a corresponding weakening of national identity and cohesion, with the prospect of an eventual eclipse of the population receiving the migrants and of its culture'". The statistical analysis of their paper concerns the so-called, and so-measured, economic effects of immigration, and provide no basis for this gratuitous conclusion which implicitly alludes to issues of race, colour, ethnicity and culture. Hayter shifts the argument to a political and moral plane: "the problem with migration, if there is one, is that much of it is not free, but forced—by the actions of the rich countries the migrants go to. If the British and other governments genuinely believed that immigration was a problem, there would be things they could do, or not do, which would be more humane and possible less expensive: they could refrain from invading other countries, stop supplying weapons to the participants in civil conflicts, to repressive regimes or anybody else, stop imposing cuts in public spending to raise money to service an unjust foreign debt, and stop stealing other countries' wealth." Teresa Hayter's reaction stands at the other end of the spectrum from organisations such as the British National Party's gleeful reactions to Coleman's alarmism over immigration. In Rowthorn's argument,

---

[43] See also: https://www.civitas.org.uk/research/immigration/ Green (2014), https://www.civitas.org.uk/content/files/econometricmodelsinthreestudiesofthefiscaleffectsofimmigration.pdf Drury (2015).

large-scale immigration would harm the employment and wages of low-skilled British workers who would not be willing to undertake the non-'decent' dull, dirty and dangerous jobs at the wages and with the conditions that immigrant labour would be willing to accept (Drury, 2015); his frame of reference seems to have shifted a long way from the "workers-of-the-world-unite" imaginary as a young radical economist in the Cambridge Faculty, to one which seems to be predicated not upon aspiration of unity but the expediency of national interest and cultural identity. One pertinent aspect which goes unnoticed in Coleman and Rowthorn (2004), and usually in the charged discourse on immigration, is the massive subsidy that many poorer countries—developing or transition economies—provide to the rich north-west economies through the migration of highly educated and skilled migrants that often form the backbone of key services, especially health and education. The host country gets the economic and social benefits of these skills, but does not pay for the resources invested in their training; and these avoided costs need to be reckoned not in the sending country, but the far higher costs that would have been incurred by training a doctor in the rich country. According to a UK Parliament briefing (Baker, 2021), in March 2021, 21.7 per cent of NHS doctors were non-EU nationals, with the most common nationalities here being Indian, Filipino and Nigerian—all countries with strained health systems. It is also worth asking how many of these non-EU doctors might be second-generation children of unskilled immigrants of earlier decades, from poor-end families that sacrificed, saved and educated their children.

Bob Rowthorn, the Engels to Ajit Singh's Marx in the Faculty ideological battles, protests against the Americans in Vietnam, against the Greek colonels, supporter of the Students' Sit-in, and much more, was eventually promoted to Reader (along with Ajit Singh) in 1982, but then outpaced him to the personal professorship, it being awarded in 1991, four years before Ajit; with Geoff Harcourt being denied the promotion all his years in Cambridge, and Luigi Pasinetti confronted with the same bleak predicament, having decided to devote his energies from his home base in Italy where indeed he built up a thriving post-Keynesian capacity.

On all accounts, perhaps barring one, John Eatwell has had a distinguished career in Cambridge as an economist which started in Queens' College under the tutelage of Ajit Singh, followed by a PhD in Harvard, a fellowship back in Cambridge in Trinity College, followed by a dramatic elevation as President of his alma mater, Queens'. Along the way, he served as a top economic advisor to Neil Kinnock, leading on to his elevation into the House of Lords. Under his watch, the College flourished, and was the recipient of a major donation from an alumnus who had himself been a student of Ajit Singh and Andy Cosh. Early in his academic career, he jointly authored *An Introduction to Modern Economics*, the 'Cambridge' textbook that was intended to unseat the reign of Samuelson over undergraduates; he worked closely with Sraffa and was often characterised by his peers as a neo-Ricardian, or Sraffian, but certainly not a Marxist in ideology or a Bennite in politics. Despite being productive in terms of publications, his trajectory through the Faculty was not dissimilar to that of several other rising, or even established, heterodox colleagues who were generally overlooked in promotions. He duly established a base for himself, again as did several other colleagues of the same experience, in the Judge Institute where he became a professor. But a senior rank, or a professorship, in the Faculty remained beyond reach.

While he was closely associated with his mentor Ajit Singh at Queens' College, his political orientation was perhaps more moderate than that of several of his colleagues who had developed a radical alternative economic strategy for Britain at an earlier time, or those argued during the 1970s and the early 1980s by the Cambridge Economic Policy Group led by Wynne Godley and Francis Cripps at the DAE, and also by Nicky Kaldor. The position adopted by John Eatwell in the 1980s, following the arrival of Thatcher (and the closure of the CEPG team at the DAE) was much to the right of the Cambridge left stance. Richard Hill (2001: 209#66) writes, on the basis of an interview, that "Eatwell was encouraged to offer his services to the Labour Party by his Ph.D. student, Roy Green, a member of the Party's Research Department. Hattersley was initially unhappy about Eatwell's appointment." In 1982, Eatwell had published *Whatever Happened to Britain? The Economics of a Decline* and had developed a contrasting market-friendly stance on Labour economic policy that was picked up Neil Kinnock who installed him as his economics supremo.

Heffernan (1997: 118) writes that "the period 1983–1997 is one in which explanations of the changing Labour Party are to be found and understood; taken in the round Labour did not so much change or modernise itself as it was changed by the impact of events: In short, where Thatcherism has led, the Labour Party of Kinnock, Smith and Blair has followed. ... The post-1983 period can only be understood in relation to the pre-1983 period." According to Hefferman and Marqusee (1992: 113–114), "Like many lifelong professional politicians, Kinnock was always ill at ease with economics. From the beginning he knew he would need a specialist adviser he could trust. Originally this was Henry Neuberger, who was appointed in 1983 when his Tribunite leanings and mildly interventionist economics seemed well suited to the Kinnock leadership. Within a few years even this approach came to seem too radical to Kinnock, and Neuberger left Kinnock's staff and went to work for Bryan Gould. He was replaced by John Eatwell, a fellow of Trinity College, Cambridge, described by someone who worked with him on the Policy Review as having 'the deep-seated political instincts of a Tory'. From 1987 onwards Eatwell's was the main voice coaxing Kinnock to endorse the irreplaceable supremacy of the free market. Like Kinnock himself, Eatwell was a late convert to economic orthodoxy. Indeed, as recently as 1985, in a *Tribune* article co-authored with Roy Green [*Tribune* 22 February 1985], he had advanced a sharp critique not only of Thatcherite *laissez-faire* but also of the 'Keynesian compromise', which had been 'fatally flawed by its dependence on traditional neoclassical assumptions concerning the market as a means for the efficient allocation of resources'. It was precisely this 'dependence' which, on Eatwell's advice, was to constrict Labour's economic policy in 1992 to the dreary formula, 'we will not spend what the country cannot afford'. Eatwell's advice was endorsed and fleshed out by others, notably economists Paul Ormerod, director of the Henley Centre for Economic Forecasting and a right-wing activist in the London Labour Party. Another adviser was Gavyn Davies, a leading economist with Wall Street investment banker Goldman Sachs, whose wife, Sue Nye, worked in Kinnock's office. It was rumoured that Davies refused an offer of employment within Kinnock's office on the grounds that he could command a much higher salary in the City. He was often touted as a possible economics supremo in a Kinnock administration in Downing Street."

In Heffernan's (1997: 163) words, "Influenced by his economic adviser, John Eatwell (later ennobled at Kinnock's nomination), Kinnock was persuaded after 1987 to emphasise the argument that Labour could make the existing market economy work better than the Conservatives. As the deregulated marketplace figured larger in Labour's economic plans it marked a shift away from its traditionalist commitment to state intervention to reform the market mechanism in favour of establishing a framework which would complement the workings of the market. Here, 'reform' of the market is replaced by a 'light touch' regulation; the commitment to 'redistribution' over time dramatically overshadowed by the commitment to 'production'."

It is argued by commentators from the left flank that the Kinnock years formed the intermediate stage to the slide into full-blown Blairism which was difficult to firmly distinguish from Thatcherism. Committed to 'enhancing the dynamic of the market, not undermining it', Tony Blair has made it clear that excessive taxing, borrowing and spending were all things of the past as Labour ruled out increasing both personal tax rates and public expenditure in 1995–1997. Building on the 1991 pledge of the Kinnock Shadow Cabinet that a Labour government would not 'spend or promise to spend what the country cannot afford', Labour under Blair firmly accepted the taxation and expenditure projections of the Conservative government in fiscal years 1997–1998 and 1998–1999. So-called tax and spend policies, for so long the identified evils of Mrs Thatcher's political world view in the 1970s and 1980s, came also to be identified as economic problems no longer solutions by Labour's leadership in the 1990s. Labour's transformation reflects a seemingly irreversible shift in the balance of power in favour of right-reformist neoliberal politics at the expense of left-reformist social democratic politics. Its extent is illustrated by the changes wrote in Labour's ideological outlook and evidenced in policy. This long-drawn-out process of change was characterised by piecemeal and gradual policy qualification followed by revision in both the 1983, 1987 and 1992 Parliaments. Labour's policy saw a dramatic alteration in its attitude to the changes brought about by the Thatcher government. Where Martin J Smith defines this transformation as "a post-Keynesian revisionism … for a different era, which has learnt the lessons of the 1970s", Eric Shaw more correctly suggests that the period saw "the abandonment of Keynesian social democracy in favour of pre-Keynesian orthodoxy". "Labour has come to embrace the arms-length regulated market economy it was once pledged to directly manage and control" (Heffernan, 1997: 123–124). In this reading, Kinnock set the stage for Blair's alleged proxy Thatcherism; and John Eatwell was in Kinnock engine room. The left alternative was suppressed, at least till Blairism showed its full hand leading to its revival manifest in the rise of Corbyn's radical alternative with its throwback to the original alternative economic strategy programme of the Labour left in the 1970s—also developed by a group of Cambridge left economists, colleagues of Eatwell in the Faculty; a déjà vu moment for those who could remember.[44]

---

[44] Joe Guinan (2015) provides a 'déjà vu' perspective generally from a radical left-Labour vantage point, written at the "Corbyn crossroads" moment. "The movement for worker's control in the 1970s was among the most promising of the many roads not taken in the forgotten history of the left" (Guinan, 2015: 11). "The recent extraordinary developments in the Labour Party make the recovery of historical memory concerning the 1970s of immediate political relevance. Up until a few months ago, the history of the IWC's failure, together with that of the broader New Left, to gain lasting traction within the Labour Party under far more favourable conditions than those obtaining today, raised searching and somewhat prohibitive questions about the future reformability of Labour and whether the energy needed to create a genuine alternative to the current economic order should once again be absorbed in an attempt to remake British social democracy (Panitch & Leys, 2001: 15). With the surprise election of Jeremy Corbyn as leader of the Labour Party, these propositions will now be tested whether we like it or not" (Guinan, 2015: 31). "Every myth and threadbare cliché about the 'hard left'—of which the IWC was certainly a part—is being dusted off and put to service by a shrieking opposition, inside and outside the Labour Party, unnerved by the prospect of a major breach in the ruling consensus. In fact, the protagonists on left and right at the time took up very different positions vis-à-vis the crisis of the 1970s than they have been afforded in conventional accounts. Clarity on just what was at stake and who had the better answers is once again a matter of current politics" (Guinan, 2015: 32). "Corbyn's leadership could open up space for a much broader political conversation, especially on economics, than has been possible in the UK for many decades. In his first conference speech as Shadow Chancellor, John McDonnell pledged that Labour would 'promote modern alternative public, co-operative, worker controlled and genuinely mutual forms of ownership' (McDonnell, 2015). At precisely the point when it appeared at its weakest historically, the Labour New Left has been granted an unexpected afterlife. It is greatly to be hoped that this does not devolve into a simple reprise of conventional Keynesianism, already tested to its limits in far friendlier conditions and found wanting. Just as dangerous is the bandwagon, already rolling, that seeks to rehabilitate the so-called 'soft left' as a means of managing Corbynism and returning Labour to 'electability'" (Guinan, 2015: 32). "It would be a final grim irony if, granted an unexpected afterlife, the political heirs of the Labour New Left were themselves to snatch defeat from the jaws of victory by either falling back into the arms of the Keynesianism against which they originally defined themselves or succumbing to the same 'soft left' blandishments that previously delivered over the party, bound hand and foot, to its real enemies within" (Guinan, 2015: 33). Events subsequent to time of Guinan's piece clearly seem to have confirmed his apprehensions in the rise of Keir Starmer with his anti-left drive against Corbyn and his supporters with a view, as with Kinnock, to make Labour 'electable' again, even if that meant the jettisoning of some of the foundational principles of the Labour Party. Recently, Richard Hill (who had interviewed John Eatwell earlier) publicly resigned from his positions as Chairman of the Colchester constituency Labour Party and also as a member, with an excoriating letter of resignation attacking Starmer. In this context, it is pertinent to note that Lord Eatwell shifted to the cross benches in the House of Lords after Jeremy Corbyn rose to authority, returning to take up senior Labour Party advisory roles after the takeover by Keir Starmer.

A little further down the timeline, Martin Weale,[45] a future leader in the younger cohort—though not in the 'left' camp—declared his affiliation and helped write the LibDems manifesto. His economics training and subsequent Fellowship at Clare were under the watch of Robin Matthews who was then Master of the College, Charles Feinstein, who was Senior Tutor, and Brian Reddaway, a formidable three-some, significantly all member of the CLARE Group, and all later with LibDem—SDP loyalties. The CLARE Group, through many of its members, had a very significant informal presence in the affairs and governing committees of the NIESR.[46] Along with David Howarth,[47] a Law Fellow also at Clare, and others, he drafted the LibDems' economic policies of the early 1990s (Reyes, 2014) when he was still on the Faculty staff as a Lecturer; shortly after, in 1995, Weale leapfrogged from being a lecturer to being appointed Director of the NIESR, one of the major national centres for policy-oriented applied economics research with close, if indirect, links with Government. The same year, he was also invited to join the CLARE Group. His entry into the Monetary Policy Committee occurred in 2010 with the arrival of the Cameron-Clegg Tory-LibDem alliance. At the time, it was suggested in the media (*The Guardian*) that "The Treasury has appointed leading academic Martin Weale as a member of the Bank of England's monetary policy committee (MPC) in a move widely seen as providing Mervyn King [not left-Keynesian, nor left-Labour, of course, then or earlier] with support for his low interest rate policy". Weale "is fairly relaxed about the government's austerity measures"; his "latest paper for the European Commission argued that Britain's long boom under Labour was based on unsustainable consumption". It is a point of view that brought him into conflict with the Labour hierarchy" (Inman, 2010).[48] And, for those with memories, this position had some resonance with Matthews's 1968 article in the *Economic Journal* which provided a critique of the Cambridge left-Keynesian 'fiscal' interpretations which credited expansionary policies for the post-War boom. Mervyn King is listed as a mem-

---

[45] See also Chap. 12 which refers to Martin Weale's collaborative work with economic historians within the Faculty.

[46] For further comment, see the discussion of the CLARE Group in Chap. 4, pp. 50–52; and Chap. 2, Table 2.3.

[47] David Howarth, Reader in Law, whose "specialism had earned him the nickname 'the god of tort' among some lawyers" became the Liberal-Democrat Member of Parliament for Cambridge city during 2005–2010 (Reyes, 2014).

[48] It is necessary, of course, to cite the official record as well:

> In our Report in November 2010 on the *Appointment of Dr Martin Weale to the Monetary Policy Committee of the Bank of England*, we stated that we would follow previous practice and continue to use the criteria of professional competence and personal independence against which to consider appointees to the MPC. House of Commons, Treasury Committee, Second Report of Session 2010–2012, *Appointment of Dr Martin Weale to the Monetary Policy Committee of the Bank of England*, HC 475-I, para 4 https://publications.parliament.uk/pa/cm201415/cmselect/cmtreasy/205/205.pdf

ber of the CLARE Group till he took up his assignment at the Bank of England. The NIESR and the Monetary Policy Committee had very close links; as many as five members of the Governing Council, presumably the body which appointed the Director of NIESR, had previously been members of the MPC.

The unity of the heterodox clans, and especially of the 'left' groups within it, was therefore a complex phenomenon always somewhat brittle and threatening to implode. While united on the major divides, there was a wide spectrum of shades of red, some of these fading, others startlingly changing colour. Such differences often reflected positions on the national (and international) stage; some shifts were idiosyncratic, and some could be acrimonious. Arguably, national politics also played out on the local Faculty stage in Cambridge and the role of this factor has perhaps gone underemphasised in explanations of the purges—and that possibly because academics might not have generally wished to parade their party-political differences in public. But differences there were, and some were quite entrenched and sharp. While Tory attachments kept generally underground, there were divisions in the middle and left fields, most sharply to do with the fraying and fracture of loyalties within the spectrum of Labour political opinion. In this regard, the period of the 1970s and the 1980s was especially noteworthy—by the 1990s, the orthodox takeover of the Faculty was accomplished, and these political vectors had lost their salience—In Cambridge, these latent tensions manifest themselves in differences and oppositions within individuals and groups which could otherwise be construed as belonging to the broad heterodox church. The arrival of Thatcher was a point of inflexion, though the underlying stresses had been building up under previous Labour governments. The SDP with its middle-of-the-road Oxbridge 'gang-of-four' leadership had made inroads amongst senior economists; Reddaway, Matthews, Posner, Kahn, Feinstein, all carried SDP loyalties and Neild had declared misgivings with left-Labour's position vis-à-vis trade union power.

Unfortunately, even in the good times, the heterodox gurus and seniors of the Faculty had not shown any noticeable propensity towards proactivity. Perhaps four aspects remain noteworthy. First, they did not put into place any viable process of intellectual and organisational reproduction. Second, when opportunities arose, they made idiosyncratic, and to some minds seriously problematic, appointments. Third, they were so Cambridge-centric that they failed to widen the domain of heterodox influence in ways that would create other knowledge sites outside Cambridge, in other universities and centres, where rising, young heterodox economists of the Cambridge tradition could be productively absorbed and placed as professors.[49] Fourth, relatedly, they seemed to lack the lateral vision of taking institutional initiatives within

---

[49] This is not to say in any way that they withheld such support or that they did not support worthy individual cases; Marc Lavoie points out the unsolicited offer of support from Nicky Kaldor when he was facing a potentially difficult tenure committee in Canada (personal communication, email 22 December 2021).

Cambridge to broaden the base of heterodox traditions, say, through the timely creation of affiliated teams or centres, for instance of development studies, business research, economic history and so on, under the overarching umbrella of the Faculty of Economics and Politics. The game was on, but no one on this side was running with the ball; perhaps they were all too preoccupied playing their own games. One implication of this was that there was a severe constraint on the number of professorial positions available for absorbing the rising generation. In sum, the seniors made various errors of commission, and by default, several of omission.

The Heterodox Camp: No Chairs—Sorry, Standing Room Only
In his typical forthright style, Geoff Harcourt points a finger:

> There was one constant characteristic of the Cambridge faculty: they were bantam cocks on a dunghill, fighting for their own position and defining consensus as 'agreeing with what I just said'. Joan Robinson, Nicky Kaldor and Richard Kahn were just hopeless faculty politicians. They did place people in posts, Luigi Pasinetti, me, Ajit Singh, Bob Rowthorn to some extent, and Alan Hughes. But they were hopeless on chairs. That was the reason why Frank Hahn got a major role to play, mainly due to Kaldor's fault who brought Hahn to Cambridge in the 1960s.[50] When Richard Kahn retired, he was replaced by Frank Hahn. And that was the beginning of the end of placing post-Keynesians in chairs. (Harcourt, 2011: 9; see also Harcourt, 2012)

Looking back in 2007, in his reflective and eventually optimistic interpretation in *Keynes and the Cambridge Keynesians*, Luigi Pasinetti is scathing in his assessment of the role played by the senior cohort in the decline:

> they failed completely to follow Keynes, namely in the care in selecting, shaping, preparing and paying attention to the younger generation … they seemed not to care. Worse still, they seemed to compress, or even repress the ambitions of the young. They did almost nothing to prepare their succession … they made no choices, or half choices, or compromise choices, rather than clear ones. This was fatal to the School, which disappeared from Cambridge with them. (Pasinetti, 2007: 40)

"For the 'neoclassical' group, the process of taking over all the key positions was child's play" (ibid.: 217). Pasinetti then turns his fire on "those that formally succeeded them", the neoclassical lot:

> to what they perceived the arrogance of their predecessors, they overreacted by demolishing whatever the Keynesians had left … awfully underestimated the powerful significance of the Keynesian ideas. Worse still they lacked vision. They

---

[50] In his Tribute to Brian Reddaway, however, Ajit Singh writes: "it is not generally known that he [Reddaway] played a key role in the appointment of Frank Hahn, a mathematical economist, to an economics chair in Cambridge" (Singh, 2009: 371).

attached no weight or value to the significance of keeping alive a truly Keynesian (i.e. non-Marxist) alternative to the prevailing orthodox line of economic thought. They failed to realize that such an alternative was a source of theoretical potentialities that represent a treasure, not only for Cambridge but for the world community of economists. Alas, that treasure has been squandered. (ibid.: 40)[51]

Pasinetti certainly does not imply it, but one item in the box of treasures would have to be himself. In December 1975, Luigi Pasinetti decided to resign from his position of reader in the Faculty with effect from 1 October 1976, a decision accepted with 'great sadness' by Kaldor, and other colleagues. Baranzini and Mirante (2018: 95, n1) write:

> It seems that just before moving back to Milan, a senior and much distinguished fellow of Trinity College, Cambridge, had told Pasinetti to stay for few [sic] more years in Cambridge until he would be given a personal professorship. Additionally, in private conversation, three of his former colleagues in Cambridge have confirmed this perspective, had he remained a member of the Cambridge Faculty of Economics.

A couple of years before his death, Kaldor placed on Pasinetti's shoulders the mantle of inheritance of "the tradition of the grand theory which began with Marshall and continued by Dennis Robertson, Pigou, as well as Keynes, and the generation of Joan and myself" (ibid.: 306n3).[52]

A Break in Intergenerational Transmission, in the Reproduction of Traditions
Whichever combination of internal explanations is found to carry traction, and whatever pulling weight is attached to any specific factor, the incontrovertible fact remains that the outcome was a clear rupture in the intergenerational transmission of the lineages of Cambridge heterodox traditions developed from the 1920s. However, culpable the seniors were in one manner or another in allowing this occur whether through acts of commission or lapses of omission, it would be excessive to seek a complete explanation in these internal propositions. The ageing heterodox seniors did not just trip and fall over by accident or frailty. There was another side to it all, a story not within but beyond the backs and walks, the halls and walls of Cambridge.

---

[51] See also Geoff Harcourt's review of Luigi Pasinetti's book (Harcourt, 2009).
[52] Baranzini and Mirante refer to NK/3/30/169/20 in the Kaldor Papers held at King's College Archives, Cambridge.

2.3 Godfathers, Uncles and Nephews: The Gathering Foe

2.3.1 *The Trojan Horse: By the Pricking of My Thumbs*

Such was the self-absorption, inertial complacency and myopia of the greats that they hardly noticed the storm clouds gathering on the horizon. To the contrary, they actually went out and pulled the Trojan horse into their citadel—and out strode Frank Hahn. There was little wrong with his distance vision; and the thoroughbred neoclassical that he was, he was also endowed with perfect foresight. With regard to proactivity in managing placements and promotions for his lieutenants, Hahn was strategic and indefatigable. The contrast between the two camps could not be greater. As the heterodox clan suffered the blows of natural wastage through the cycles of retirements and deaths with few steps taken for replacements and the reproduction of their intellectual lineages, the neoclassicals displayed a diametrically opposite trajectory, riding the wave of the demographic dividend of youth. This did not happen by accident; Hahn, and his fellow seniors, made it happen.

Consider the sequence of arrivals and departures in the Cambridge professorial lounge: Hahn arrived on his high Trojan horse in 1972; Matthews returned to Cambridge as Master of Clare College in 1976 and took over Brian Reddaway's chair in 1980, which was also the year that Richard Stone retired, but his externally funded P. D. Leake Chair lapsed.[53] Of course, Wynne Godley did become a professor in 1980, but then just a year later had the rug pulled unceremoniously from under his CEPG's feet, soon banishing him into a peripatetic nomadic space; Robert Neild sat on the heterodox benches, but he found the kitchen unpleasantly hot and took early retirement in 1984 with the golden handshake introduced after the Thatcherite cuts; Partha Dasgupta was imported back to Cambridge from LSE in 1985, and David Newbery rose rapidly through the promotion ranks from lecturer to reader to professor (as the new Director of the DAE, replacing Wynne Godley) in 1988. Thus, a somewhat disempowered and disorientated Godley faced the triumvirate of Hahn, Matthews and Dasgupta from 1985 through till 1992 when Hahn retired; and from 1988, G3 became G4 with the addition, following the DAE appointment, of Newbery. While the left stalwarts had all passed away, Hahn and Matthews still had years to go to retirement; Faculty power leached away to the mainstream neoclassicals, with Hahn, Matthews, Dasgupta and Newbery at the core from 1985 till Hahn's retirement in 1992, by which time the handover, or rather, takeover, had long been accomplished.

While the heterodox school failed even at guaranteeing any scheme of simple reproduction, the seniors certainly nurtured the next generation and derived (almost) as much strength from them as they imbued in them; yet such nurturing did not evolve into any strategy of promotion and placement in professorships

---

[53] There was another professorship in accountancy later, when Geoff Whittington was appointed the Price Waterhouse Professor of Financial Accounting.

and readerships in a timely manner within the Cambridge hierarch. However, there was another significant dimension to this: it was apparent that the heterodox clans were unable, or insufficiently interested in exploiting the spaces and opportunities opened up in the new universities in the Robbins era of expansion. An aspect of the insularity of the heterodox groups was their relative invisibility in the next rung of universities; but there appeared to be no systematic strategy of expansion, cultivation or proselytisation; and this was perhaps matched by a deep reluctance on the part of the waiting young turks to leave the family home and seek to set up their shops purveying Cambridge heterodox wares in wider markets; the Cambridge home was where their hearts lay and they couldn't drag their feet away, at least not in any numbers to widen the contours of direct heterodox influence and control. In sharp contrast, Frank Hahn and his group moved with alacrity to develop schemes of rapid, extended reproduction using all their interconnected networks in 'the provinces'. He very quickly placed a large cohort of young economists of his tribe into chairs, and these placements paid handsome dividends later in dismantling the heterodox camp.

It remains a minor Cambridge puzzle as to how, given these theoretical predilections—so inimical to the core of contemporary Cambridge theoretical traditions—Hahn was offered the Chair in Economics in Cambridge in 1972. This unexpected event, welcomed by Hahn and the neoclassical group, but viewed with disagreement and apprehension by the heterodox lineages, is attributed by Harcourt to Nicky Kaldor, and with hindsight, is regarded as the point in time from which things began to go askew. Was Kaldor so enamoured of his doctoral student (howsoever briefly) at LSE: was he influenced by Hahn's initial foray into macroeconomic distribution theory? But these had occurred two decades earlier, and Hahn had since evolved into a full-blown neoclassical general equilibrium mathematical theorist. The puzzle remains unsolved. Then, Ajit Singh deepens the puzzle in his obituary for Brian Reddaway— another Cambridge pragmatic applied economist of the highest order. Reddaway "who was certainly no mathematical ignoramus, having obtained a first in Mathematics Part I" and who was not dogmatically opposed to deploying maths, held the view that a variety of interactions between variables in the real world could not be meaningfully captured in a formal system of simultaneous equations, and that "one might fall into the trap of not realizing that the system was under-determined" (quoted in Singh, 2008: 10). Despite this strongly held approach that Reddaway consistently taught, and espoused in all his empirical research, Ajit informs us that "it is not generally known that he played a key role in the appointment of Frank Hahn, a mathematical economist, to an economics chair in Cambridge" (ibid.: 11).[54] A solution to the puzzle is provided by David Newbery: first, with regard to Hahn's appointment as lecturer in the Faculty (and a fellow at Churchill), Newbery (2017: 491) says that "by all accounts Kaldor ... urged Hahn to come to Cambridge

---

[54] Notably, during 1972, the year of Hahn's appointment, Reddaway served as Chairman of the Faculty Board, a position of significant influence—taking over from Richard Stone, and preceding Michael Posner.

[from Birmingham] in 1960 to a lectureship, but it was Richard Kahn, perhaps surprisingly given his suspicion of mathematical economics, who secured Hahn's appointment". Geoff Harcourt[55] writes that Nicky Kaldor and Frank Hahn (and also Donald Winch and Aubrey Silberston) were all visitors at Berkeley in 1959–1960, presumably that led to Kaldor asking Hahn to make the journey from Birmingham to Cambridge. Mirrlees (1996) writes that Hahn "was lured to Cambridge [from Birmingham] by Kaldor" and Sen confirms that "Kaldor had been very impressed by Frank after meeting him at a seminar exactly once, and had subsequently played a leading part both in persuading Cambridge to make a good offer and in persuading Frank to come to Cambridge. I told Nicky I was very pleased that he had taken that initiative", even while teasing Kaldor that it had taken all of one seminar meeting to persuade Kaldor of Hahn's capabilities—something which of course was far from the case since Kaldor had been Hahn's first PhD supervisor (if only for a while) at LSE apart from the interactions at Berkeley. Sen, seems to have been even more impressed than Kaldor and showers almost groupie-esque praise: "Hahn, a great mathematical economist and a hugely effective teacher and communicator, already justifiably famous … Frank rapidly became a close friend, and I came to rely on his and Dorothy's advice on many things." "Frank was a splendid economist and had great leadership qualities …." "I was a strong admirer of Hahn's work, particularly of the way he handled complicated analytical problems." And, in the "public battle going on between the orthodox and the rebels; of the latter, Frank was the leader" (Sen, 2021, p. 369). Hahn duly arrived for an initial five-year stint, and so began the next chapter in the demise of heterodoxy in Cambridge. The story of Hahn's later appointment in 1972 as a professor on the Faculty—this time coming over from LSE—is even more exotic:

> Kaldor manoeuvred the Electoral Board to appoint Robert Neild [in 1971] as Joan Robinson's replacement when she retired from her professorship in order to keep Hahn out … Silberston, [the Faculty Chairman at the time] had a terrific row with Kaldor over Neild's appointment, because by then Kaldor had become anti-mathematical and also anti-Hahn. Apparently, Neild's appointment in preference to Hahn caused so much outrage that when Richard Kahn retired eighteen months later, Hahn was elected to Kahn's chair in economics in 1972, and to a professorial fellowship at Churchill. (Newbery, 2017: 501)

If Hahn was the Trojan horse, he was pulled into Cambridge city centre by no less distinguished a triumvirate than Richard Kahn, Brian Reddaway and Nicholas Kaldor. It might say much for their open-mindedness and generosity, but rather less for their prescience. Be that as it may, 1972, marking Frank Hahn's arrival in Cambridge as a professor, could be regarded as a key date in the history of modern Cambridge economics—for the heterodox clans, things

[55] "The year was a busy one from a social point of view", writes Harcourt.

soon began to wobble and tumble in the face of the sustained personally and institutionally offensive assaults launched by Hahn and his coterie of votaries.

2.3.2 Forming the Academy

Significantly, the young Hahn had started his PhD at LSE under Nicky Kaldor working on the macro theory of distribution, in specific on the share of wages in national income, but Newbery tells us that he moved, after two supervisions in his first term, to Lionel Robbins.

In 1948 Hahn went to Birmingham where a new mathematically oriented Department of Economics was emerging, and "where he met, and found irresistible, Terence Gorman, who had 'by far the best and clearest mind I had yet come across' [Hahn quotation from Szenberg, 1992: 162]; they remained lifelong friends different in manner but equally devoted to the application of mathematics to understanding and illuminating claims in economics" (Newbery, 2017: 489). Hahn gave up his readership at Birmingham to come as a lecturer to Cambridge in 1960,[56] and later, they moved together in 1967 as professors to LSE, Hahn from his lectureship in Cambridge and Gorman from a chair in Oxford, joining Sargan, Harry Johnson and Alan Walters. "He spoke frequently of the influence of Terence Gorman on his thinking. The contrast in their personalities cannot be exaggerated, but the mutual affection and admiration that underlay their banters was evident to all. It was in Birmingham that Hahn became a modern general equilibrium theorist" (Dasgupta, 2013).

Frank Hahn's father, Arnold, was German-speaking, his mother Maria, Czech-speaking; "he would exaggerate his accent—'wee Breeteesh'—[rather like Tommy Balogh in Oxford] and stated most emphatically that 'England made me'. Hahn would delight in reminding one that he was a mittleeuropaisches Jew", but had "toyed with the idea of becoming a Catholic when a student at Oxford"; he served as a flight navigator in the War, and "in June 1967 at the outbreak of the Six-Day War, ... was all for offering his services to

---

[56] Dropping rank to enter Cambridge was not unusual: David Champernowne gave up a professorship at Oxford to a readership in Cambridge; Charles Feinstein, in a variation, moved from a professorship to a readership in Oxford. Of course, Champernowne, Hahn and Feinstein all went on to professorships in their favoured locations. Geoff Harcourt gave up more, and for less: he relinquished a personal Chair at Adelaide to take up a university lectureship in Cambridge in 1982 (personal communication).

Israel"; "he would later hanker for the life of a Trollopian rural dean"[57] (Newbery, 2017: 486). At the AUTE meeting in 1972, he took the stage to announce: "although you see a small Hungarian (sic) Jew before you, let me tell you that I am John the Baptist. I have come to tell you about what is coming" (ibid.: 500), which was general equilibrium economics searching for money; but then Dasgupta (2013) tells us that "Frank often said if he had his life all over again he would have chosen to be a cosmologist. The subject's grandeur was a factor of course, but speculation over possible worlds attracted him ... the beautiful, austere features of general equilibrium of economic systems drew him to their study." But, "over time he saw less and less in the point of economics, even theoretical economics".

Partha Dasgupta (2013) speaks of Hahn as "an intellectually terrifying figure". Newbery knew Hahn equally well, and provides substantiation: "Tony Atkinson, who graduated from Churchill college in economics in 1966, recalls that he first met Hahn as his Director of Studies. His initial greeting was characteristically off-putting: 'are you as stupid as you look?'." Another time: "'Surely', he would say of my essay, 'you can do better than Professor X', the aforementioned X having recently published an article on the topic in a leading journal" (Newbery, 2017: 497–498). Confirmations of Hahn's penchant for in-your-face rudeness[58] come both from friend and from foe. Dasgupta (2013) loyally attempts to dissolve such perceptions and offers a generously euphemistic understanding of Hahn's rudeness: "what appeared to be rudeness was intellectual zest and a love of clarity and depth"; "if he didn't temper his language with niceties, it was because his mind worked many times faster than his

---

[57] Obliquely, a close comrade of Hahn and Matthews in the Faculty wars enters the frame, and possibly explicates Hahn's fascination with Trollope. Robin Matthews, who in Oxford was supervised by John Hicks, supervised the doctorate of Charles Feinstein, who supervised the doctorate of Avner Offer, through whose obituary for Charles emerges a subliminal connection. Offer writes: "during his last few months. ... He was re-reading the novels of Trollope, and we talked about them. It has struck me since that there were affinities between the two men. I think of them both as engineers, each with his own distinctive approach to the same Victorian infrastructure. Trollope, apart from being a novelist, had been a senior official at the post office. He devised the red pillar box and established universal deliveries in Britain. Charles in his turn deconstructed the Victorian economy and reassembled it as a dynamic machine. Trollope's novels convey a sense of stability and order. Underneath the surface narrative, society rolls along in firm grooves of convention, habit, and self-interest. Charles revealed a similar incremental regularity in economic life" (Offer, 2008: 21). Perhaps Trollope, if given another chance, might have wished to be a general equilibrium theorist. W. H. Auden it was who said: "of all novelists in any country, Trollope best understands the role of money".

[58] Frank Hahn was seldom at a loss for words, though I recall an occasion in the mid-1970s when I got lazy going up to my top-floor pigeon coop, and slipped into the tiny Faculty staff lift; Andy Friedman, a Canadian research scholar, was occupying most of it with both arms unsteadily wrapped around too many books to handle, and he was in a dangerously unsteady disequilibrium state; suddenly Hahn entered, took a good look and unexpectedly stretched out his hand towards Andy—"I'm Hahn! Who are you?", he loudly pronounced somewhat unnecessarily, much to the predictable discomfiture of Andy who spilled some tomes in freeing an arm for the handshake— "I'm Friedman", he said. Silence descended till the doors opened and a nonplussed Hahn stepped out, no doubt wondering if he'd been had.

vocal cord [sic] and moved on before the mental error-correcting mechanism that social learning equips us with could be called into operation"; "when on listening to someone he was heard to remark that the person had been educated beyond his natural ability, it would be his way of saying that the person had made a mess of a potentially interesting idea"; "I could never convince him that stupidity isn't a moral failing".

But under all offensive gruffness, he was hugely supportive of and loyal to his chosen, favoured students. Under Hahn's influence, Jim Mirrlees was appointed to the Cambridge Faculty in 1963, and David Newbery says: "I was appointed without even an interview, so powerful was Hahn's influence at that time" (Newbery, 2017: 499); Christopher Bliss was appointed in 1966, and Tony Atkinson in 1967.

Hahn left for LSE in 1967, "at the same time as his close friend, Terence Gorman, making the offer irresistible" (ibid.), where he was reunited with Gorman, alongside Alan Walters and Harry Johnson, all of whom had joined simultaneously (apparently each being told separately that the other three had agreed to come to LSE). And there they set about vigorously restructuring the economics teaching programmes into their new mathematically oriented form.

Partha, a prime recipient of Hahn's avuncular affection and attention,[59] writes that "Hahn persuaded the other professors to call a moratorium on appointments to Lectureships until a suitable cohort had been trained. David Hendry and Stephen Nickell were among the first of the new batch of Lecturers there" (Dasgupta, 2013). He goes on:

> It is the mark of great mentors that those they inspire and influence are able to find their own ways of framing problems. Over the years Hahn's 'academy' (there's no other way to describe it) nurtured as wide a range of economic theorists as Luca Anderlini, Christopher Bliss, Adam Brandenburger, David Canning, Robert Evans, Douglas Gale, Oliver Hart, Geoffrey Heal, Walter Heller Jr., Timothy Kehoe, Mark Machina, Eric Maskin, David Newbery, Joseph Ostroy, Hamid Sabourian, Paul Seabright, Ross Starr, David Starrett, Joseph Stiglitz, and myself, among others. At our time we brought our academic problems to him, we showed him drafts of our writings, and on every occasion he would respond with comments no matter how far removed the work happened to be from his preoccupations or his style of thinking. A frequent refrain would be: 'It's all a lot of nonsense, of course; but what you have done is not bad—although the proof can be tightened. Let Uncle show you how'. (ibid.)

The phenomenal role played by Frank Hahn's powerful personality and driving energy cannot be underestimated. Newbery (2017: 485) observes: "if there is one theme that runs through Hahn's life, it was to attract the right people and move decisively to support them"; "He was hugely supportive of his friends and students"; "he brought outstanding teaching fellows to

---

[59] In his obituary, Dasgupta (2013) refers to his closeness to Hahn; Frank apparently greeted Partha as "dear boy".

Churchill" with these "young and enthusiastic researchers rubbing shoulders with their seniors at Quaker meetings", many of them moving on to "glittering academic careers", jumping the steps from junior research fellowships to full professorships with super acceleration. All this needs to be contrasted with the sadly apposite lament that one finds, say from Luigi Pasinetti or Geoff Harcourt, on the apathy, forgetfulness, or self-centred preoccupations of the heterodox seniors who seemed to be in a state of reverie in the matter of promotions and the reproduction of their outgoing cohort.

In his remarkable obituary of Alfred Marshall, Keynes devotes several pages to the impact, at both individual and institutional levels, of the intellectual intimacy that Marshall created with his pupils; the texture of these master-apprentice relationships is conveyed by some snippets extracted from Keynes's account:

> *Thus in a formal sense Marshall was Founder of the Cambridge School of Economics. Far more so was he its Founder in those informal relations with many generations of pupils, which played so great a part in his life's work and in determining the course of their lives' work.*
>
> *To his colleagues Marshall might sometimes seem tiresome and obstinate; to the outside world he might appear pontifical or unpractical; but to his pupils he was, and remained, a true sage and master, outside criticism, one who was their father in the spirit and who gave them such inspiration and comfort as they drew from no other source. Those eccentricities and individual ways, which might stand between him and the world, became, for them, part of what they loved. They built up sagas round him ... and were not content unless he were, without concession, his own unique self. The youth are not satisfied, unless their Socrates is a little odd.*
>
> *It is difficult to describe on paper the effect he produced or his way of doing it. The pupil would come away with an extraordinary feeling that he was embarked on the most interesting and important voyage in the world. He would walk back along the Madingley Road, labouring under more books, which had been taken from the shelves for him as the interview went on, that he could well carry, convinced that here was a subject worthy of his life's study. ... The subject itself had seemed to grow under the hands of master and pupil, as they had talked. There were endless possibilities, not out of reach. ... 'there was no pretence that economic science was a settled affair—like grammar or algebra—which had to be learnt, not criticised; its was treated as a subject in the course of development'."*
>
> *It must not be supposed that Marshall was undiscriminating towards his pupils. He was highly critical and even sharp-tongued. He managed to be encouraging, whilst at the same time very much the reverse of flattering. Pupils, in after life, would send him their books with much trepidation as to what he would say or think*
>
> *... It is through his pupils, even more than his writings, that Marshall is the father of Economic Science as it exists in England to-day. So long ago as 1888, Professor Foxwell [one of Marshall's first students] was able to write: "Half the economic chairs in the United Kingdom are occupied by his pupils, and the share taken by them in general economic instruction in England is even larger than this". To-day through pupils and the pupils of pupils his dominion is almost complete.* (Keynes, 1924: 365–367)

Allowing for differences between the two eras, Keynes's words about Marshall and his students could be carried across, almost in entirety, to describe Hahn's equation with his youthful 'academy' of 'nephews'. In this regard, perhaps Marshall, Keynes and Hahn, of all the grand pantheon of Cambridge modern greats, stand apart from the rest who, brilliant as they undoubtedly were, did not, or could not, assiduously cultivate and nurture their respective 'schools' to full maturity, though each had loyal followers of their specific offshoot of post-Keynesian, or 'heterodox' economics. As the present narrative confirms, the implications of this contrast for the practice of 'economics' in Cambridge, and indeed in the country, were profound.

Meanwhile, at the Orthodox Party—A Merry Game of Musical Chairs
As the heterodox schools suffered natural wastage, the rival neoclassical team dramatically strengthened through what presently is loosely referred to as the demographic dividend of youth.

Even a cursory comparison between the pathways of the loyal heterodox radicals, who stayed on to defend their haloed Cambridge turf, and the rising young turks of the orthodox/neoclassical side, who left Cambridge to seek fame and fortune elsewhere, is revealing. As a backdrop, recall that Joan Robinson became a professor at the age of 62, when Austin retired; Phyllis Deane at 65; and the bizarre cases of Maurice Dobb, Richard Goodwin and Geoff Harcourt who were kept forever standing in a queue waiting for a chair. Many of that eminent cohort were passed over and turned down; patience worn out, many left to pick up chairs elsewhere: Luigi Pasinetti in Italy, Charles Feinstein at York and then Oxford, Jane Humphries at Oxford, Mario Nuti at Birmingham, Alan Hughes and John Eatwell at the Judge Institute within Cambridge, Ron Smith at Birkbeck, Adrian Wood at Sussex. Those that stayed the longest waited the longest, and generally suffered the most. Of those who did eventually succeed: Bob Rowthorn was 52 when promoted to a professorship, Ajit Singh was 55 and only Hashem Pesaran made the grade in relatively good time, at 42. There is a dramatic contrast with the neoclassical cohort of Cambridge starters, mostly backed by Hahn or other seniors not in the Cambridge heterodox camp: Jim Mirrlees left to a chair in Oxford in 1968 at the age of 32; Angus Deaton went to a professorship in Bristol in 1976 at 31; Dasgupta was a reader at LSE in 1975 and was awarded a personal professorship in 1978 when he was 35; Mervyn King went straight to a professorship in Birmingham at 29, and to a chair at LSE in 1984 at age 36; Stephen Nickell stayed the course at LSE and got a readership in 1977 and a professorship just two years later in 1979 at age 35; Tony Atkinson left to be a professor at Essex in 1971 at 27, and then at 36 to a Chair at LSE; Christopher Bliss was placed in a chair accompanied in Essex in 1971 at age 31; Tony Atkinson joined him there the same year, aged all of 27, and then moved to a Chair at LSE, aged 36; Geoff Heal took up a professorship in Sussex in 1973, age 29, moved to Essex in 1979 and then to a professorship at Columbia Business School in 1983; Oliver Hart, not promoted in Cambridge, went to LSE as a professor in 1981, aged 31; Nicholas Stern was a professor at Warwick in 1978 by age 32, again later to a Chair at LSE; John Flemming would surely have been another, but for his preference to sequence his career differently by joining officialdom as a young high flyer before making a high level return into Oxford academia later; only David Newbery had to wait till the sagely age of 45 to become a professor, but then that was a small premium to pay for a professorship at home in Cambridge (alongside Hashem Pesaran, then 42) in 1988, just 2 years after a promotion to a readership. Clearly these were all, to use a Chinese slang term, helicopter men, with vertical take-off careers. Newbery (2017: 500) ascribes the exodus from Cambridge to "the disputes and disagreements in the faculty [which] were going from bad to worse, hardly providing an attractive place to stay".[60] But other explanations are more credible: there was a long queue for promotions, and very few chairs in Cambridge and it would not take a genius to realise that 20 and 30-somethings would not be climbing and scrambling onto whatever spaces became occasionally available; and so, choosing rationally with good foresight, they opted to move, and all the more with alacrity as Hahn & Co fixed them up straight in professorships all around the country. *Ad Hominem* readerships and professorships had indeed been installed in Cambridge University in 1966, but the procedures were stringent: the case had to be made through the Faculty head, and then the name went into an open University-wide competition across all subjects, and given the few professorships available each round, this route was unpredictable, of low probability, and would inevitably pit one aspiring economist against another. So Newbery, on the orthodox side, and several in the heterodox ranks, had to wait lengthy terms for opportunities to promotion to open up within Cambridge.

Hahn's boys all took short hops (or just occasionally one long jump) to other universities and comfortably landed in chairs; just the odd one had to do the slightly more strenuous hop-step-and-jump. Considering a cohort of 11 leading names of young economists associated with Hahn & Co, it transpires that they were all born in a seven-year period, 1941–1948, and they were all ensconced in chairs, barely a few years after their PhD vivas, at an average age of 32—thus guaranteeing remarkable stretches of 33–35 years in authority and power at the top of the profession.

Meanwhile, in heterodox Cambridge, patience was mutating into frustration, rancour and recrimination, as even after the passage of decades, several brilliant young descendants of varying heterodox lineages had grown

---

[60] Newbery (2017: 501) observes, perhaps forgetting it takes two to tango, that "the factions continued to fight. The Kahn–Robinson axis fought for control of the Faculty Board in order to appoint the Appointments Committee and make nominations to professorial electoral boards, thereby controlling appointments to the Faculty. 1968–1969 saw the students in economics and sociology playing a leading part in their version of the student revolution, and the faculty left was now divided between the Maoists and the anti-Maoists (this was the period in which Joan Robinson was impressed with the Chinese approach to economic development)." Of course, the Vietnam protest movements were picking up steam as well. In all these things 'fractious', the young radicals, prominently Ajit Singh and Bob Rowthorn, occupied leading roles.

middle-aged (and some quite elderly) negotiating the hurdles, pits, jumps and hoops on the marathon obstacle course to promotion; and some of those designing these snares and gauntlets from the late 1980s were none other than some of Hahn's boys, led by a few returnees, one who just stayed on, and other blow-ins, several with LSE links. The old Cambridge firm had been taken over bit-by-bit, bite-by-bite, by the LSE-Oxford, Hahn-Gorman conglomerate.

Thus, by the end of the 1970s, the decade of rapid university expansion, a number of ranking economics departments around the country had a significant presence of these young and ambitious, impatient Cambridge exiters,[61] including LSE, Oxford, Bristol, Essex, Warwick. If Frank was, by self-declaration, John the Baptist,[62] these arguably were the apostles and acolytes, spreading their wings and propelling his gospel at large; or in different parlance, a young flock of birds of a feather, all in their thirties, within an age band of seven years, leaving out Mirrlees who was five years outside the range. Put yet differently, while Ajit and his group were marshalling their cadres and comrades inside Cambridge, the other side was equally busy, assiduously occupying the surrounding territories establishing a young cohort of leaders in positions of rising authority.

2.3.3 The Chess Master

But Frank Hahn wasn't the only uncle[63] leading his 'academy' of nephews, acolytes and battering rams. If Terence Gorman (and Bob Solow even if from a distance) was his soul mate in all things academic and theoretical, Hahn had

---

[61] "The early 1970s were a time of university expansion in Britain, and a great time to be a young economist. In Cambridge, I often played tennis with Mervyn King—currently Governor of the Bank of England and a member of the Wimbledon Lawn Tennis and Croquet Club—and we would relax on the lawn afterwards and work ourselves into a lather over the fact that no one was offering us professorships, professorships that only a few years before, were grudgingly handed out to (sometimes long deserving) aspirants in their late 1950s and early 1960s. (Most British departments then had only one or two professors.) In the event, neither of us had long to wait, and I accepted the Chair of Econometrics at Bristol before my 30th birthday—rather old in those years" (Deaton, n.d.: 5).

[62] The longer quote from David Newbery (2017: 500) provides Hahn's prediction that "This was the collective effort by several young theorists and himself to integrate money into Walrasian General Equilibrium theory. … He got us all engaged in what he told us was an absolutely central problem of economics'." There are two contrasts here: the first with Keynes in 1924 declaring "change is in the air" and pronouncing the end of laissez-faire; and the second, with Joan Robinson, with her Ely Lecture in 1972 and, a few years later in 1977, challenging the discipline and the profession, asking "What Are the Questions?" (Robinson, J., 1977).

[63] In his tribute to Basil Yamey, (now Sir) David Metcalf recalls earlier times: 1968–1975 was a very exciting time to be at LSE. There were new senior people—Frank Hahn, Terence Gorman, Amartya Sen and Alan Walters. And a steady influx of new lecturers such as Richard Layard, David Hendry, Steve Nickell, Chris Pissarides, Mike Bromwich, Christine Whitehead, Brian Griffiths and Ray Richardson—who all went on to great things. … All new lecturers in Economics were allocated a mentor ('uncle')" (Metcalf, 2019). He does not pair uncles and nephews. Did Uncle Frank carry over his practice from Cambridge to LSE, or was it an LSE practice he had experienced in his student days in LSE and taken it over to Cambridge?

in Robin Matthews the perfect strategic partner for all matters institutional and for working the committees in Cambridge and Whitehall. Matthews had started off in Oxford and then was a lecturer in Cambridge for 15 years from 1949 during which period he published his work on the trade cycle (Matthews, 1954a, b); Hahn had returned from Birmingham to Cambridge, also as a lecturer, in 1960, and it was in that period that the two paired up and produced their famous survey of growth theories (Hahn & Matthews, 1964) which propelled Matthews into the Drummond Chair of Political Economy in Oxford taking over the chair from his supervisor, Sir John Hicks; then he published a notable paper challenging the Keynesian 'fiscal' explanation of Britain's economic buoyancy in the immediate post-War years (Matthews, 1968). Meanwhile, in 1967, Hahn left for a Chair at LSE, returning to Cambridge as professor in 1972; Matthews himself returned in 1975 as Master of Clare College. In 1980, Matthews took over the Chair of Political Economy vacated by another Clare colleague, Brian Reddaway on his retirement.

One reliable source holds that Matthews was 'shoe-horned' into the position through the facilitating efforts of Charles Feinstein, his friend at Clare, whose doctoral thesis Matthews had supervised, and who had been the Senior Tutor of the college since 1969; the collaboration intensified over the coming years resulting in a joint study of British economic growth (Matthews et al., 1982), apart from other shared projects and institutional agendas.[64] Feinstein was a significant figure and a deep presence in the Hahn-Matthews campaign against the left-Keynesian and heterodox groups in the Faculty. The career paths of Hahn and Mathews intertwined with their significant prior periods of partnership—and they formed a formidable team, with sustained and loyal support from several peers and protégés, including Feinstein.

Avner Offer was supervised by Charles Feinstein at York, and later came to occupy the same Chichele Chair that his supervisor had earlier held. In his tribute to Feinstein, Offer (2008: 18) writes: "By 1978, when I first met him, Charles had become the image of the superior type of Cambridge don—upright, courteous, well-spoken, well-dressed, and a little aloof. ... Robin Matthews (Master of Clare from 1975) regarded Charles as already fit to be the head of a college, or the vice-chancellor of a university." Offer (2008: 19) records that "Charles gave readily to the wider community, and spent many hours on the councils of the Economic History Society, the Royal Economic Society, as Group Chair and Vice-President of the British Academy, as an advisor to the ESRC and to the University Grants Committee, and on the investment committee at All Souls". Sensitive and informative as it is, Offer's appreciation of Feinstein overlooks his significant involvement in Cambridge, from York or later Oxford, in the Faculty wars in Cambridge as a

---

[64] In Cambridge, the economic historians were all at the History Faculty, and there was only very limited intellectual interaction with them. "More important were in the applied economists who had done some economic history, especially Robin Matthews, who had been my thesis supervisor and who invited me to collaborate with him on the study initiated by Simon Kuznets and Moses Abramovitz that became *British Economic Growth, 1856–1973*" (Feinstein, 2007: 291).

protagonist—sometimes backroom, sometimes up front—of the Hahn-Matthews axis; he was never too far from an engagement with university and institutional politics.[65] It is relevant to note that the politics of the DAE and Faculty young turks, including most (though not all) of the researchers of the DAE teams, especially the CEPG, were (left of) Labour; also, equally pertinent is the fact that Robin Matthews was a supporter of the SDP, as indeed were several others of the CLARE Group, including Brian Reddaway[66]—mentioned by Avner Offer (2008: 10) as "the greatest Cambridge influence on Charles"—and Michael Posner;[67] and Pasinetti, in his appreciation of Richard Kahn writes that in his later years, Kahn had also shifted his loyalties to the SDP. In addition to his string of senior administrative and institutional charges, Charles Feinstein crucially chaired the RAE Economics Panel in 1989, a highly significant year in the middle of the Hahn-Matthews anti-heterodox Cambridge campaign; he was also a member of the ESRC Economic Affairs Committee (1982–1986)[68] which made landmark (negative) decisions of the DAE's Cambridge Growth Project in 1985–1986, the year when he was chairman, in which capacity he also sent in hostile feedback on the DAE ostensibly on behalf of the ESRC to the University DAE Review Committee—again strengthening the Hahn-Matthews agenda on enforcing the changes they wanted at the DAE. It is striking that he kept up these partnerships adding the weight of his contributions to the orthodox campaign against the so-called left radicals in Cambridge economics—both at the Faculty at the DAE—even well after he had left Cambridge. Starting off as something of a Marxist in his early years in South Africa, the conflicted Feinstein had moved significantly to the right; "he actively supported the Social Democratic Party (SDP) when it broke away from Labour in 1981" (Offer, 2008: 18).[69] The conclusion would

---

[65] According to Offer (2008: 17) when Feinstein was in York, "he enjoyed the challenges of university politics in this large and lively department. He did not fare so well with his immediate colleagues, the economic historians. He found some able scholars and appointed some younger ones, but a small number resented Charles and the people he appointed, and thwarted his plans from time to time in group meetings. Such frictions hurt—spite was not so transparent to Charles, perhaps because he had little of it in himself" (Offer, 2008: 17).

[66] It was Brian Reddaway, as Director of the DAE, who asked Charles Feinstein to take over the ongoing work of Karl Maywald on constructing the series on domestic capital formation, which led to his first significant publication (Feinstein, 1965); and later, as fellow Clare members of the CLARE Group, they jointly authored an article on the implications of the OPEC surpluses and the ensuing world economic recession on the UK economy (Feinstein & Reddaway, 1978).

[67] Posner was appointed as Chairman of the SSRC in the final months of the Callaghan government by the Education Secretary, Shirley Williams, who was soon to break with Labour and become one of the key founders of the SDP.

[68] *A Handlist of the Papers of Charles H. Feinstein, 1932–2004*, in the Library of Nuffield College, Oxford, 2006; p. 7.

[69] In his interview with Mark Thomas, Feinstein pronounced that "the root of the problem in the British economy was to do with labour relations and a combination of attitudes on the part of the workforce that were detrimental to productivity, reinforced by employers' refusal to recognize what would have been necessary to overcome those attitudes" (quoted in Offer, 2008: 18). Offer adds his own recollection: "In conversation (and at his lectures), it struck me how strongly he felt about these dilemmas, and what he saw as the mindless unreason of the unions. He actively supported the Social-Democratic-Party (SDP) when it broke away from Labour in 1981" (ibid.).

not be out of place that he gravitated towards, volunteered for or sought positions of administrative and institutional authority and power that could be exercised over his profession and colleagues. He had also been Senior Tutor at Clare College, Cambridge, and "once [in Oxford] volunteered for the time-consuming job of Secretary of the Social Studies Faculty, although his appointment was in History" (Offer, 2008: 19). In the Cambridge years, there were apparently also ricocheting personal and political contradictions between Charles and 'the left' which added further complexities. In his earlier Cambridge years, he observes: "I certainly wasn't an 'Austrian', but I didn't think of myself as a Keynesian either. I don't think I would have said I was a Marxist either, since I had doubts about several aspects, but I was very much on that side of the divide" (Feinstein, 2007: 288).[70] Subsequently, he had himself drifted steadily towards the right; as he observed, "once I got out of the hothouse atmosphere of South Africa and could reflect in the cooler climate of Britain, I remained left wing in my attitudes but came to realize that a lot of what I had believed, particularly about the Soviet Union and about imperialism, was untenable" (Feinstein, 2007: 289).

In the early days, Charles Feinstein was spoken of as a person of left persuasion. He had joined the Communist Party in South Africa in his youth when he took a stand against apartheid—which, of course, does not conflate with being a communist or Marxist. Avner Offer notes that "Charles began to move away from communism in 1956 ... and he left the party in 1960" (Offer, 2008: 8). "Charles was attracted to Cambridge by the presence there of the Marxist economist Maurice Dobb, and the two remained close for years afterwards" (Offer, 2008: 4), even though his youthful left/communist infatuation did not survive for even a few years after arriving in Cambridge, and this despite the link to Maurice Dobb. Charles Feinstein also was my formal, very formal, supervisor in Cambridge in the early 1970s, and it was not easily possible to detect any obvious 'left', let alone 'Marxist' traces in the supervisory exchanges with him; there were no observable residuals of any such proclivity. Indeed, I recall Arvind Vyas—friend and contemporary from student days in Delhi, then doing a PhD on the Russian economy under Bob Davies in Birmingham—and I trying to fathom how Feinstein had come to be the editor of the Festschrift for Maurice Dobb, dyed-in-the-wool Marxist; couldn't they find anyone else

---

[70] Avner Offer (2008: 19) remarks that "in conversations over the years, he surprised me several times with a robust endorsement of an acquisitive and self-interested human nature". Feinstein might then have felt quite comfortable with the philosophical basis and defence of individual utility maximisation in the neoclassical framework that he employed in his own 1982 (joint) work.

with a deeper intellectual and political affinity, we wondered in our innocence.[71] Given his drift away from the left from the mid-1950s, it remains an oddity that he edited the Dobb Festschrift, in which he does not have a piece, nor any reference to his work in the index or the bibliography. He had moved from the DAE to the Faculty, and his first work *Domestic Capital Formation in the United Kingdom* had been published in 1965; the Festschrift appeared in 1967, so he would have been assigned or volunteered for that task before the publication of his own book. Timothy Shenk (2013: 182), the biographer of Maurice Dobb, mentions that "the collection had been in preparation long enough in advance that it even included a piece from Lange [who died in October 1965]. Sraffa, whose perpetual writer's block made submitting an article impossible, helped with the editing." So Feinstein would have been about 32 years old at the time of commissioning of the Festschrift and just moved from the DAE to the Faculty side. In the 93-word editor's preface, he observes, "I have had the invaluable co-operation of the Editorial Board and of Piero Sraffa in the planning of this volume" (Feinstein, 1967: v). Sraffa, of course, would have been the right person for doing the volume, and perhaps that is what he might well have done in the essentials, with delegation to a willing and able young colleague. Be that as it may, this editorship gave Charles a durable proxy 'left' respectability and street-cred which perhaps was less than fully justified—for instance, Offer (2008: 8) writes that at Clare College, where he had become a fellow in 1963, "a few fellows regarded him as a dangerous Marxist"—in error, and perhaps indirectly by association on account of this festschrift for Dobb the legendary Marxist in Cambridge.

The Marxist label could also derive from Feinstein having taught Russian economic history in Cambridge after joining the Faculty in 1963, apropos which, Offer (2008: 8) makes the puzzling remark: "It has since emerged that Charles's lectures had introduced Russian economic history to most of the current British academic specialists in the field". One wonders about Maurice

---

[71] Dobb, much venerated by both Arvind and me, was one of the examiners of his thesis; and he very nearly became my PhD supervisor before I discovered Charles had been assigned by some committee to that role, how and why I still know not. Charles was always dry, polite, correct or putting it differently dull and dour. But beyond that I felt he was light-years away from any of my specific research or wider intellectual concerns. He had visited India in 1972, the year I came to Cambridge, and perhaps that was deemed sufficient cause to assign him as a supervisor for an Indian student. But it did seem that Charles and I had shared a stray experience: both had sought Maurice Dobb as supervisor, but been assigned someone else—Robin Matthews, to his great advantage, in his case; and Charles Feinstein in mine. Interestingly, in his interview with Mark Thomas, Feinstein recounts his encounter, as young research scholar, with Alexander Gerschenkron in the USA. "Gerschenkron himself was very warm as a host. I still have very fond memories of our meetings. The seminar used to be held after dinner, and afterwards he would invite me to his room for a brandy. He always began by wanting to discuss baseball, but with a certain amount of effort, I could bring him around to more interesting topics" (Feinstein, 2007: 292). None of these skills rubbed off on Feinstein who remained dour in his supervisions, not given to any form of levity, diversion, embellishment or small talk, and generally had the gravitas of the chartered accountant (that he had started off as), or an inspector of schools. To my disadvantage, I found no sign of "the Gerschenkron effect" in my encounters, though obviously, Charles was a wonderful supervisor for others perhaps better matched to his personality and interests.

Dobb himself; Alec Nove (*The Soviet Economy: An Introduction*, 1961; *An Economic History of the* USSR, 1969); the massive contributions of Bob Davies, Professor of Soviet Economic Studies in Birmingham in 1965, Director of the Centre for Russian and East European Studies in Birmingham in 1963, *The Development of the Soviet Budgetary System* 1963, *A History of Soviet Russia: Foundations of a Planned Economy* in two volumes with E. H. Carr 1969; apart from a short visit to the USSR and a foray into learning Russian, Feinstein had no manifest qualifications for such a claim to be sustainable, though he did have a two-page review in 1977 in *Economic Journal* of a book on four East European economies. Of course, Cambridge as a university was ever accommodating and indulgent towards the interests of individual staff, and as an appointment in economic history, he would not have met any resistance in deciding to lecture on the history of the Russian economy. The somewhat over-reaching claim is recorded by Offer, not by Feinstein who would surely have done methodical justice to the task. But lecturing on Russia does not equate with being a leftist or Marxist. In 1969–1970, when Jane Humphries took her Finals, the course on Russian economic history was being taught jointly by Charles and Bob Rowthorn, who was indeed at the time a declared Marxist and communist: Charles and Bob, "they made quite a contrasting pair", she recalls. She also reflects, citing his later book on South Africa, that "Charles became more relaxed and returned more to his radical roots as he aged in Oxford".[72]

In their student days, Amartya Sen, Charles Feinstein and Pierangelo Garegnani were all members of the Cambridge University Socialist Club. Sen writes that Feinstein "who came from a communist background to study in Cambridge … remained very much an intellectual activist of the left and I remember on one occasion I was chastised by him for being dismissive of Stalin's writings (I was also criticized for keeping Stalin's books upside down on my shelves). Later on, however, Charles would change his views rather radically and become quite apolitical—without any left-wing inclinations—as one of Britain's leading historians. … He was becoming more apolitical—unrecognizably different from the radical newly arrived from Witwatersrand University in Johannesburg" (Sen, 2021, p. 309).

Leaving aside the untenable ascription as a 'leftist', Feinstein appears more plausibly to be located in the middle, politically and personally conflicted ground, with close long-term partnerships with Robin Matthews, the CLARE group and SDP politics; folklore offers the footnote that, if anything, he had fallen out with the younger local group of left economists who, it goes, had "treated him badly". If anything, the positions that Feinstein was associated with in the course of the campaigns were on the orthodox Hahn-Matthews side, his 'leftism' and apparent affinity with Keynesianism notwithstanding.

Some of the neoclassical methodology adopted in Feinstein's jointly authored book on British Economic Growth (Matthews et al., 1982) would surely have placed the author in theoretical opposition to the heterodox economists in Cambridge; the book "incorporates the Solow neo-classical

[72] Personal communication; 25 August 2021.

production-function growth model as the base of its total factor productivity calculation" (Offer, 2008: 13). The Cambridge critiques had already been sharply enunciated, as for instance in Nuti (1971): neoclassical theory "gives an impersonal and politically neutral solution to what was for Ricardo 'the principal problem in Political Economy'. The state of technology and relative factor supplies determine relative income shares. There are classes but there is no room for, nor point in class struggle in a world where everybody, by implication, is getting his 'fair' share according to his individual contribution to the production process" (Nuti, 1971: 28). Following Marx—and citing "a lucid and learned" critique by Maurice Dobb, Mario Nuti labels "'so-called neoclassical theory' as a species of 'Vulgar Economics'" … "as represented … by the writings of Samuelson and Solow and their British *epigones*" (Nuti, 1971: 27). Stephen Nicolas comments on Cambridge issues with the aggregate production function: "Solow's 1957 seminal article on the geometric productivity index noted that it takes more than the usual 'willing suspension of belief' to talk seriously of the aggregate production function". Twenty years later such a 'willing suspension of belief', due in large part to the Cambridge criticism, is impossible to maintain. However, by continuing to 'suspend belief' cliometric historians failed to state fully the long list of assumptions underlying the productivity model, thus shielding the productivity index from rigorous qualitative and quantitative testing. "The root of the problem lies in the heritage of neoclassical production theory which, at least in the pure form, takes history out of economics" (Nicholas, 1982: 94). Feinstein was acutely aware of the problem[73] but carried on regardless. Avner Offer writes: "Charles took no part in the theoretical debates convulsing Cambridge, on whether capital was a coher-

---

[73] In interviewing Charles Feinstein (in 2002), Mark Thomas pointedly asks a question about this potential conflict (Feinstein, 2007: 291–292).

MT: What was it like writing about capital formation in Cambridge at the height of the capital controversies? Did you perceive any tensions with these new theoretical approaches, which seemed to suggest that trying to measure capital was impossible?

CF: Yes, I did. One couldn't be in Cambridge and not be conscious of the intensity and the fervor with which that debate was conducted. And I obviously had to think it through. The resolution I arrived at quite quickly was that although we were both using the work capital, we were really doing different things. They were saying that there was an inherent circularity which couldn't be overcome: you needed a measure of capital in order to estimate future profits, and you needed to estimate future profits in order to have a measure of capital, and there was no way around that. Whereas I was not trying to estimate the future value of the capital stock in that sense; I was trying to estimate how much money had actually been spent in the pas ton creating the stock of capital.

MT: And was this a point the critics accepted?

CF: I don't think they ever looked beyond the theory. Nothing else mattered.

The trouble remained of course that Feinstein was carrying on using his arithmetical construction for analytical and interpretative purposes which ran afoul of the 'Cambridge' criticism. From the other 'Cambridge', Paul Samuelson—commenting on Joan Robinson—observed: "On the inadmissibility of a scalar aggregate of capital to serve as a productive factor, she was dead right" (Samuelson, 1988: 328).

ent and tractable category. His job, he said, was merely to measure its historical cost. But the acrimony of the debate unsettled him" (Offer, 2008: 16). This was in the 1970s and 1980s, and while Feinstein might have taken no part in the debates, he was a significant presence in the strategic decision-making structures and processes that brought about the downfall of the heterodox camp opposed to his own.

Speaking of the earlier decades, his guru Robin Matthews later remarked:

> Two sides there were, and one was dominant. The dominant side in turn began to suffer in the 1960s an erosion of its own intellectual coherence. We had reckoned ourselves to be among Joan's admirers, but we became bored by the increasingly theological disputes about the measurement of capital, about the fallacy of the marginal productivity theory, and so on. So one chapter ended, the later chapters evolved out of it. (Matthews, 1989: 915)[74]

But it was not to be a bloodless evolution, and Matthews himself was one of the writers of the script of events to come.

Matthews wielded considerable power in university circles on account of his position as Master of Clare College—a long tenure, running from 1975 till 1993, covering the entire period of the DAE–Faculty chess game. He held the Chair in Political Economy in Cambridge from 1980 till 1991 when he retired. Earlier, he had been the Chairman of the SSRC during 1972–1975 in a period when Margaret Thatcher, as Education Secretary in the ill-fated Edward Heath Government, had first wanted to slash it down to size, and he is credited with a fine and effective defence,[75] though his own views on Margaret Thatcher and this episode were apparently rather softer.[76] And he carried on serving on various crucial decision-making committees under the vital Posner Chairmanship period of 1979–1983. He served in Whitehall in senior capacities, and was in the powerful position of authority and patronage of Chair of the Bank of England's Panel of Academic Consultants for an extended period in the 1980s

---

[74] However, Joan's own view of the significance of the "capital controversies" is worth noting: "The problem of the 'measurement of capital' is a minor element in the criticism of the neo-classical doctrines. The major point is that what they pretend to offer as an alternative or rival to the post-Keynesian theory of accumulation is nothing but an error in methodology—a confusion between comparisons of imagined equilibrium positions and a process of accumulation going on through history" (Robinson, J., 1974: 11).

[75] "From a ringside seat in Parliament I can vouch for the fact that it was these skills honed in Cambridge, added to considerable personal charm, which enable Matthews, as its chairman from 1972–1975, to save the Social Sciences Research Council from the extinction with which it was threatened by Edward Heath's Secretary of State for Education and Science, Margaret Thatcher" (McKittrick & Dalyell, 2010).

[76] "Robin Matthews, Chair of the Council from 1971 to 1975 was able to look back on this as a time when the Council enjoyed a period relatively free of political pressures. The then Education Secretary Margaret Thatcher was, he thought, more receptive to the progression of scientific knowledge than many other politicians. Looking back on the period, he reflected: 'it was not too surprising that the years 1971–1975 ... were the last of the SSRC's honeymoon period'" (ESRC, n.d.: 12–13).

and 1990s; he was President of the Royal Economic Society in the period 1984–1986, laying the basis for Frank Hahn stepping in to take it over to huge strategic effect. In Cambridge, he was a participant and presenter at Dennis Robertson's right-of-centre Political Economy Club (McKittrick & Dalyell, 2010). Said to be "a political moderate", he could work both sides; during the early 1980s he served as an advisor to top leadership of the fledgling SDP where his political sympathies lay. And, in 1977 shortly after taking over at Clare College, he (along with Alec Cairncross) formed the CLARE[77] informal group of influential economists, that included: Reddaway, Feinstein (both Clare fellows) and Posner from Cambridge; David Henderson, Tony Atkinson and Aubrey Silberston from London; Alec Cairncross, John Flemming and Peter Oppenheimer from Oxford; Dick Sargent and Marcus Miller from Warwick; and others such as John Kay, Mervyn King, Alan Prest and Brian Tew (Silberston, 2011; Harcourt, 2017: 974). This was an important formation which potentially had the power to use the considerable weight of its network to influence various matters, both in academic affairs but more crucially also behind the scenes in the corridors of power, committee manning and decision-making; and it seems plausible to assume that it was so employed as the Hahn-Matthews game plan unfolded.[78]

Table 2.3 provides some details on the 31 economists who were CLARE Group members at some point over its lifetime. Some features are readily elicited. First, throughout its existence the group displays a remarkably wide age range of members: there is a cohort of seniors, another of upcoming younger economists, and a middle cohort as well; the age distribution is evenly populated. At the start, the oldest, Alec Cairncross, born 1911, is 37 years older than Mervyn King, born 1948; in the final year, 2002, the oldest is Brian Reddaway born 1913, 47 years older than the youngest, Tim Besley at 42. Second, as self-declared, the group is politically moderate and oriented towards middle ground applied and policy matters; theoretically, the backgrounds reflect eclecticism. Third, it is known that several of the prominent members of the CLARE Group were later active SDP supporters, or moved in that direction from a centre-right position in the Labour Party; this would include Robin Matthews himself, Brian Reddaway, Michael Posner, Charles Feinstein and John Flemming, amongst many others. This broad political affinity provided sufficiently strong cohesion to keep the group together; at the same time, it also gave it the flexibility to absorb the inevitable range of differences; thus 'like-mindedness' and 'common purpose' were easier to achieve and maintain. Fourth, it is striking to list, just from Cambridge itself, many who were not part of the Group: Austin Robinson, Joan Robinson, Richard Kahn, Nicholas Kaldor, Dick Goodwin, Dick Stone, Robert Neild, Geoff Harcourt, Ajit Singh, Bob Rowthorn, Francis Cripps and very many other younger left-Keynesian and radical economists (leaving out those like Piero or Mario or Luigi who did

---

[77] CLARE stands for Cambridge, London and the Rest of England.

[78] At its least, the CLARE group published "twice-yearly articles on current economic problems as an antidote to 'extremist' views from either end of the political spectrum" (*The Telegraph*, 2010).

Table 2.3 The CLARE Group of like-minded economists, 1977–2003

			1977	1983	1990	1995	2002	Observations
1	A. Cairncross	1911–1998	*	#				KCMG; FBA; FRSE
2	W. B. Reddaway	1913–2002	#	#	#	#	#	CBE; FBA
3	J. H. B. Tew	1917–?	*	#	#	#		n/a
4	A. Prest	1919–1984	# *					n/a
5	Z. A. Silberston	1922–2015	# *	#	#	#	#	CBE; Sec-Gen, VP of RES
6	M. F.-G. Scott	1924–2009		#	#	#		FBA; Council RES
7	J. R. 'Dick' Sargent	1925–	# *	#	#	#	#	Council RES; Ch. Econ Co ESRC
8	D. Henderson	1927–2018	*	#				CMG, IEA
9	R. C. O. Matthews	1927–2010	# *	#	#	#	#	CBE, FBA Pr. RES
10	M. V. Posner	1931–2006	# *	#	#	#	#	CBE; Ch. SSRC
11	C. H. Feinstein	1932–2004	# *	#	#			SSRC; RAE Ch
12	C. A. E. Goodhart	1936–			#	#	#	CBE; FBA; BoE MPC
13	M. J. Artis	1938–2016		#	#	#	#	FBA; Cons Panel HMT & BoE
14	P. M. Oppenheimer	1938–	# *	#	#	#	#	Ch Econ Shell
15	J. S. Flemming	1941–2003	# *	#		#	#	CBE; FBA; Master, Wadham C Oxf, BoE
16	M. H. Miller	1941	*		#	#	#	n/a
17	D. A. Hay	1944			#			n/a
18	A. B. Atkinson	1944–2017	*	#		#		CBE; FBA; Kt; ++ Warden Nuffield
19	W. A. Brown	1945–2019			#		#	CBE; ESRC; Master Darwin Cambridge
20	A. J. C. Britton	1945@–			#	#	#	Dir NIESR
21	D. Metcalf	1945@–		#				CBE; KT
22	J. A. Kay	1948–	# *	#	#	#	#	CBE; FRSE; FBA; FAcSS
23	M. King	1948–	# *	#			#	Baron; KG; GBE; FBA; Gov BoE
24	C. P. Mayer	1953–					#	FBA
25	M. R. Weale	1955–				#	#	CBE, BoE MPC; Dir NIESR
26	W. J. Carlin	1957–				#	#	CBE
27	P. Seabright	1958–					#	n/a
28	J. S. Vickers	1958–			#		#	Kt; Warden All Souls

(*continued*)

148   A. SAITH

Table 2.3 (continued)

		1977	1983	1990	1995	2002	Observations
29	D. K. Miles	1959–			#	#	BoE MPC
30	S. Wadhwani	1959–		#	#	#	CBE; BoE MPC
31	T. Besley	1960–				#	CBE; FBA; Kt ++

Sources:

1977:

(*) Silberston, Z. A. (2011). Obituary: Robin Matthews. *Royal Economics Society Newsletter*, January, No. 152

(#) Goodhart, C. A. E. (2006). John Stanton Flemming, 1941–2003. *Proceedings of the British Academy, 138*, 71–95

1983:

Matthews, R., & Sargent J. (Eds.). (1983). *Contemporary problems of economic policy: Essays from the CLARE Group*. Methuen

Cover of book lists contributors as: Atkinson, Cairncross, Feinstein, Flemming, Henderson, Kay, King, Matthews, Metcalf, Miller, Oppenheimer, Posner, Reddaway, Sargent, Silberston, Tew. The one additional name (beyond the Silberston (2011) list) is D. Metcalf. This name does not appear in any other source mentioned. https://www.amazon.co.uk/Contemporary-Problems-Economic-Policy-Essays/dp/0416348203/ref=sr_1_fkmr1_2?keywords=Matthews+Sargent+Contemporary+Problems&qid=1566897942&s=books&sr=1-2-fkmr1

1990:

Feinstein, C., & Matthews, R. (1990, August). The growth of output and productivity in the UK: The 1980s as a phase of the post-war period. *National Institute Economic Review, 133*(1), 78–90

1995:

Kay, J., & Silberston, A. (1995, August). Corporate governance. *National Institute Economic Review, 153*(1), 84–107

2002:

Britton, A. (2002, January). Macroeconomics and history. *National Institute Economic Review*, 179

Other:

Harcourt, G. C. 2017:974 in R. Cord (ed.) 2017

The CLARE Group was formed in 1977 and disbanded in 2003

Wendy Carlin was the only female member in the entire period; and she joins the list for only the last eight years (approximately) of the full 1977–2003 period

In 2002, the last year of the CLARE Group, Brian Reddaway was the oldest at 89 years; Tim Besley the youngest at 42 years

@ assumed; n/a not accessible; ++ other similar honours

not express strong political positions locally). By negation, this defines a discrete distance between the CLARE Group and these identifiably more left-wing economists, also with a wide age range. There are no left Keynesians, or New Cambridge, or Marxists of left Labour members in the CLARE list. It is also noticeable that the Group does not include Hahn or any of his Cambridge followers. Fifth, the CLARE, by its very name, has a geographically diverse identity, much wider than the elite groupings of Oxbridge, thereby broadening its catchment and information base, and its reach in diffusion and influence. Sixth, and most importantly, even the sketchy evidence offered in Table 2.3 confirms that the group is powerfully networked; that it is very well represented in the commanding heights of academic and government decision-making committees and bodies; and carries the conventional hallmarks of eminence. The Group could be seriously influential, even if behind the scenes. Of the 31 names on the list, at least 18 share 23 titles and honours among them; at least 6 served on the Monetary Policy Committee of the Bank of England, in addition to King who became the Governor; 19 of the 21 were Fellows of the British Academy (FBAs); there were 4 heads of Oxbridge colleges, and 2 Directors of the NIESR; several who had senior positions in the Royal Economic Society (and the Econometrics Society), including as president, vice-president or council members; others held crucial positions such as the chairman of the SSRC or sat on its important Economics committees making major research awards; and several served in controlling positions in the Research Assessment Exercises, not to mention editorships of important journals. Seventh, the Group needs recognition for its productivity; it wasn't just a talk shop or a dining club; over its lifetime, there was a stream of publications, including some edited volumes of papers written by members of the CLARE Group. And finally, it is pertinent to note that perhaps a dozen or more, including several powerful senior members played noticeable, indeed notable, roles in the demolition of heterodox economics in Cambridge in the two decades from the mid-1970s, the time Matthews returned to Cambridge as Master of Clare College, set up the CLARE Group, served as Chairman of the SSRC, and as Chairman of the Bank of England's Panel of Academic Advisers; a few years later he would add to this list the positions of Professor of Political Economy in Cambridge and President of the Royal Economic Society. Overall, the CLARE Group appears, at least potentially, to be a formidable network which could bring very considerable collective power to bear from several salients on specific points where it might wish to influence policy, or committee decision-making on specific matters of interest to it.

In the context of his long tenure as Master of Clare College, "one shrewd Fellow observed that [Robin] will not be remembered as an impartial Chair", but as one who pondered his responsibilities and high principles, and then "fought his corner with all the expedients he had learned during his stint with the SSRC and ... long term as Master" (quoted in Harcourt, 2017: 972).

Matthews was a wizard at setting chess problems, and in 1957 he won the prestigious Brian Harley Award for an article in the British Chess Magazine; he published a book on chess problems of which one of the co-authors was Michael Lipton, and then in 1995 his big chess book on three-movers, his specialisation; he was named a FIDE International Master of Chess Composition by the World Chess Federation (FIDE) in 1965. Silberston writes that Matthews was regarded by his publisher as "one of the world's leading composers of 3-movers"; and Matthews told Silberston "that he was far more distinguished as a chess problemist than as an economist" (Silberston, 2011). Well, this talent would have stood him in good stead upon his return to Cambridge in 1976 as Master of Clare College, and on taking up the Chair of Political Economy from Brian Reddaway in 1980. Robin Matthews, the composer of chess problems, was now set one himself: how to wrestle control over the Faculty Board.

A crucial feature of the partnership between Frank Hahn and Robin Matthews was the remarkable symbiosis between their areas of institutional and intellectual engagement, networks and powers within the discipline, within the university in Cambridge, and in government circles—they complemented each other, a fine yin-yang combination. While Matthews held sway over officialdom within university and wider governmental circles, Hahn exercised massive influence and power over the practitioners of the discipline; if Matthews worked the (mostly) moderate Keynesian, (mostly) non-mathematical, (mostly) policy-oriented, (mostly) Labour-right and/or SDP, constituencies, Hahn led the vanguard carrying the standard of the American orthodox revolution of the mathematisation and econometrification of economics, reorienting teaching and research across the economics departments in the country. They worked the field in tandem, and the confluence of their authority and power, working both at overt and covert levels, constituted an extraordinary force against their common heterodox foe.

2.4 The Campaign: How the War Was Lost and Won

2.4.1 The Orthodox Gambit: Capture the External Commanding Heights

Of course, cutting through the dense overlay of bureaucratese and obfuscating prose of committee-speak, the core of the problem is easily defined and its locus lay in the Faculty Board. This Board was elected democratically by the Faculty, and it then made all decisions directly or through committees that were elected through it. Whichever side dominated the Faculty Board ipso facto also controlled decision-making influencing the configuration of Cambridge economics; and this power lay with 'the left' groups which, while perennially in theoretical and doctrinal argumentation between themselves, somehow always came together when confronted by their acknowledged common foe, Hahn's neoclassical general equilibrium pilgrims and fellow travellers.

Pondering the deployment of the pieces on the chessboard, it would have been immediately apparent to the chess master that the key obstacle to neoclassical dominance was the joint power exercised by the strategically placed pair of rooks: the radicals of the DAE, and the lefties of the Faculty. How was this power to be dismantled; how were these rooks dominating the board to be neutralised? Since the heterodox camp was generally impervious (with the odd exception) to a volte-face of heart and mind, bench crossings, patronage or persuasion, the only viable strategy was to lay siege to the citadel from external salients and gradients outside its well-defended Faculty boundary. How were the defences of the castled King to be penetrated? How was the Faculty–DAE alliance of heterodox economists—and economics—to be broken?

According to Ken Coutts,[79] Robin Matthews took the view that a change in orientation of the Faculty of Economics could not wait on natural wastage and retirements; even if all new staff thus appointed were of the 'desired' type, there was a stock issue: this change process at the margin would take too long for transforming the balance and orientation of the Faculty as a totality. Hence a more radical approach was necessary for restructuring and reorienting the Faculty profile.

It is possible to recognise three lines of attack. First, there was the classic strategy of cutting off supplies to the besieged—in this case, external funding. Faculty staff were well-ensconced, tenured and with College fellowships, and therefore not to be easily budged or pushed, except by the hand of Nature; but this was not the case with the large DAE cohorts where employment was on fixed-term contracts, usually tied to the funding cycle of the project on which the researcher was hired. For the two big teams of the DAE in the 1970s, viz., the Stone-Barker Cambridge Growth Project (CGP), and the Godley-Cripps Cambridge Economic Policy Group (CEPG), a substantial chunk of this had been rolling in on a regular basis without demur from the SSRC. Choking this flow of funds would also choke the modellers and the models, and undermine the operational viability, indeed the very sustainability of these vaunted units which together employed about 20 staff, and generally punched well above even their considerable weight. Since these groups were also fundamentally non-, if not anti-neoclassical, knocking them out would constitute a double-whammy. But how might this (be made to) happen?

The second line of assault was on the 'governance' front, and was launched from within the University, but at administrative levels outside and above the Faculty Board, viz., at the level of the University's all-powerful General Board of the Faculties, the locus and ultimate arbiter of virtually all decision-making. But how could purchase be achieved on this odd and secretive body, and then brought to bear on the Faculty and the DAE decision-making structures that delivered 'one-staff, one-vote' democratic power to the masses, read 'lefties'?

The third move was a strike at the heart of the matter through a campaign that dissed, denigrated and formally devalued the stature and the quality of the ideas and the worth of the work of the heterodox schools: Joan's inter-Cambridge battles were easily depicted as doctrinal, obsessive and irrelevant and a waste of time; the cosmic Sraffa inhabited the stratosphere, was visible to

[79] Personal communication.

ordinary humanity only rarely on his wayward bike and maintained only divine links to the earthy business of day-to-day economics; others, whether wearing a Sikh turban or a Mao cap, were Marxist bigots; the CEPG soothsayers were unscientific, more polemical than academic, and the CGP was damned with faint praise, "oh, they were very good once"; and so on, and on, and on. But just bad-mouthing could go only thus far and not much further. Loyal friends demonstrated the special relationship with America by providing support in the form of vipers and snipers. But what was needed was an 'objective', 'measurable' and 'conclusive' 'proof' of the poor intellectual quality of the heterodox economists—they had to be shown to research administrators and appointment committees as simply being passé, and not good value for money, and damaging to its reputation as a world-leading centre of economics—ironically, a reputation cumulatively built by the very heterodox lineages now under attack. And how might this be achieved? The strategic weapon here was the new Research Assessment Exercise (RAE) which attempted such measurement and linked it to reputation and more crucially to research funding. The game then was to switch the measuring rods for assessing and rewarding 'quality'. The new measuring rod could then be applied, not sparingly, but vigorously on the heterodox and radical economists in the Faculty. For this weapon to work, it was essential to control, manage and expeditiously orient the RAE process to achieve the desired outcomes. If blocking DAE funding and 'reforming' DAE and Faculty governance could break the leftist vote bank, the RAE would provide a key to controlling appointments, extensions, tenure and promotions, purge the Faculty building of all traces of heterodox impurity or in Dasgupta's less-fragrant lexicon, clean out the "cesspool"[80] he said he had entered in 1985.[81]

So, lo and behold, it had to be a Matthews's special, checkmate in three moves. How was this to be achieved; what was the operational strategy? These three lines of assault had to be coordinated and brought to bear with accuracy on the vulnerable points of the citadel. And to achieve this, it was imperative first to occupy the external commanding heights overlooking the citadel.

---

[80] What goes for the goose does for the gander, and a senior ex-DAE colleague (name withheld) recalls Wynne Godley—following Napoleon's description of his creepy foreign minister Charles-Maurice de Talleyrand-Perigord—famously referring to the holder of the Frank Ramsey Chair in Economics as "shit in a silk stocking" (Buss, 2006). Not much love lost, then; such remarks provide an odious whiff of the noxious interpersonal relations that imbued the Cambridge air. The professor addressed could well respond that Napoleon was irked by Talleyrand conspiring to thwart his autocratic tendencies, and perhaps also that Talleyrand is thought to have had a hand in scripting of the declaration of the rights of man and of the citizen; it must remain doubtful if Wynne Godley would have yielded to such a riposte, and he might have pointed to the Wiki entry which referred to Talleyrand "as a byword for crafty cynical diplomacy"; a contentious draw, then.

[81] The provenance of the term is the interview of Partha Dasgupta by Alan Macfarlane; for the original context of its usage in this interview, see Dasgupta (2010).

2.4.2 Carrots and Commanders

To exploit the commanding heights, it was essential to have loyal commanders ready to take charge at these strategic points, working interactively to the general operational plan. There would be little point in the exercise if you did not have the requisite commanders to install on these heights.

A corollary, even precondition, of this would be systems of incentivisation for the new commanders: they would need to be able to see themselves rising through the ranks to the higher echelons of the profession, through the prospect of bounty and reward in the form of positions and promotions, prizes and honours. Incentivisation came naturally to neoclassicals—it was part of their intellectual creed and professional training.

Uncles had to manage the incentive and reward system, and there were a lot of resources to allocate and distribute amongst the academy of nephews. Their PhDs were long done, they were all seated in comfortable chairs, but there was much else: there were high-status editorships of top journals; appointments to prestigious government posts and panels and strategic decision-making committees in the corridors of power; queuing up patiently for the positions of president, or permanent vice presidents, of the Royal Economic Society and other similar high-status apex professional associations; 'serving' as chairs or members of the economics-and-econometrics subject panel of the sequence of Research Assessment Exercises (and the later Research Excellence Framework) through which the modern Hahn-Gorman US-style mathematical neoclassical economics was mainstreamed into teaching and research nationally; queuing up again for their fellowships of the British Academy; a decent sprinkling of headships of Oxbridge colleges in return for reading Grace before high table dinners; and then various decorations and honours, becoming members, officers, commanders (of a lost empire), knights and barons of the realm (and yes, being economists, they were almost all male). There was certainly enough to go around, also for seconds or even thirds, and much to look forward to. Outside Cambridge, the cohort of nephews gained steadily in authority, power and prestige. On the neoclassical side of the board, the pawns had been steadily advancing, and were all in good places, controlling good spaces; and as much as the pawns, other major pieces were poised at critical spots as well. Matthews the master chess tactician would have been pleased.

Though most of the juniors were quickly seated in chairs, some chairs were more comfortable than others and some were like thrones; and so there was a game of musical chairs ongoing, whereby professors in chairs out in the provinces (such as Warwick, Essex, Bristol or Birmingham), or sometimes London (e.g., UCL) variously switched to others, eventually pitching tent somewhere on the high plateau of LSE, or Oxford, or to the symbolic prize of a chair in the lion's den, the Cambridge Faculty itself. An exemplar is Tony Atkinson, who did a full round: Essex till 1980; then to the LSE as Professor of Economic Science and Statistics (till 1992), no doubt with the approval of Hahn & Co; then in 1992 to Cambridge (when Hahn retired) and finally in 1995 to Oxford (as Master of Nuffield); in many important respects, he stood somewhat apart from, not blatantly visible amongst the rest of the line-up of disciples, and Geoff Harcourt comments that Tony "was the most loved and respected of economists in the UK and internationally" (personal communication), an observation with which very many would wholeheartedly agree.[82] At a more discrete distance was Angus Deaton, an outlier who was never a paid-up member of the neoclassical brigade or of Uncle Frank's academy,[83] notwithstanding the declared affinity with Terence Gorman.

Then, there are the well-behaved queues. The Royal Economic Society provides an illustration. Some of the Cambridge heterodox old guard provided the Presidents of the RES from 1974 till 1982: Nicky Kaldor, followed by Alan Brown (though not then in Cambridge), then Dick Stone, followed by Phyllis Deane just as she retired. But from 1984 when Matthews becomes president, followed by an unbroken string of mainstream economists with the Hahn-Gorman 'academy' as their spiritual *alma mater*: Mirrlees, Hendry, Atkinson, Dasgupta, Nickell, Sutton, Vickers, Blundell … with Nick Stern as the present incumbent. There is high status, but also the authority to influence good-many outcomes for the practice of the profession, not least the choice of other juniors to promote. There is also a strikingly high incidence of LSE, and Cambridge à la Hahn-Matthews in the chain. The concentric contours of influence can be extended outwards to the levels of council members, and to the list of 16 RES Life Vice Presidents[84] which includes Sir Partha Dasgupta, Sir David Hendry, Sir James Mirrlees, Sir Stephen Nickell, Prof Richard Portes, Prof Amartya Sen, Prof John Sutton, Sir John Vickers, Sir Richard Blundell, Sir Charles Bean.

The procession for the Fellowship of the British Academy was also orderly: Mirrlees became an FBA in 1984, and then, between 1988 and 1993, there were FBAs in sequence for Bliss, Dasgupta, Newbery, King, Hendry, Nickell

---

[82] That may well be so, but it does not necessarily distance him from Uncle Frank and his mission: Robert Solow, in his appreciation, writes: "his leadership and encouragement, provided a rallying point for the younger generation who were otherwise disenfranchised. It is a splendid roster, including Anthony Atkinson, Christopher Bliss, Partha Dasgupta, Geoffrey Heal, James Mirrlees, and David Newbery, as well as a number of visitors from elsewhere" (Solow, 2017: 925). Elsewhere, Atkinson (Atkinson and Stern 2017: 7) also explicitly acknowledges the formative and sustained influence of Frank Hahn on his own way of thinking about economics: "the sort of approach I have to economics is very much how Frank thought". Of course, all this did not preclude being a radical neoclassical redistributionist, along the lines, say, of James Meade, whose *Efficiency, Equality and the Ownership of Property* (1964) is highlighted, along with Peter Townsend and Brian Abel-Smith's *The Poor and the Poorest* (1965) as powerful formative intellectual influences (ibid.: 5). Tony Atkinson held a string of strategic committee positions at crucial junctures of the Hahn-Matthews campaign to oust the heterodox and the 'left' from Cambridge economics, including Chair of the Economics Committee of the SSRC during 1979–1981, and member of the important SSRC Sub-committee on Macroeconomic Research; Chair of the RAE Economics Panel in 1992 and a significant external member of the Second DAE Review Committee of the University.

[83] Reminiscing about times in the Faculty tearoom: "Joan Robinson's constant challenges to neoclassical economics have stayed with me, not the detail but the notion that something was (and to me still is) deeply wrong. I learned that economics and politics could not and should not be separated" (Deaton, 2011: 14).

[84] See http://www.res.org.uk/view/council.html.

and Stern—and the list can be extended considerably. And of this list of eight, Newbery brings up the rear with a CBE, King and Stern lead as Barons and the others follow as Knights.

David Newbery, with an insider's perspective, speaks of Frank Hahn "passing on that enthusiasm" to his young students that "prompted many of them to pursue glittering academic careers" (Newbery, 2017: 505). Table 2.4 collates the progress of some of his students to these glittering prizes. The list includes 21 names that span an age range from Jim Mirrlees and Charles Goodhart, both born in 1936, to Tim Besley at the other end, born in 1960. The list is somewhat arbitrary and uses the criterion of affinity with the Hahn-Gorman-Solow mathematical economics neoclassical, general equilibrium paradigm of economic theorising. This is reflected in the identity of their doctoral supervisors. The self-explanatory table then tracks their subsequent progress, checking ages at, and duration between different staging points in the rally that is their career paths. The data can be summarised conveniently, using simple averages, to obtain a notional timeline of a typical career.

This is what emerges.

Age **Stage**

22.1 The BA is done at age 22.1 years, and 15 of the 21 have a Cambridge stamp; only a couple start from outside of Oxbridge or London

27.2 PhD obtained: 7 are from Cambridge; 3 from Oxford; 3 are from London, incl. 2 from LSE; 3 from US Ivy League universities; 1 from Sheffield; 4 bypassed the PhD. For these 17 doctorates, the following supervisors' (or acknowledged mentors') names appear: Hahn, 7x; Gorman, 6x; Mirrlees, 5x; Stone 3x; Meade, Sen 2x each; Solow, 2x; and Buchanan, Patel, Little, Atkinson, Sargan, Feldstein, Arrow, and Nicholson, once. The pattern is sharp and clear.

33.2 First professorial position; obtained by 19 of the 21; Flemming skipped this stage and joined the Bank of England directly; information on Goodhart is not available.
Rate of incidence: 100%

37.5 Chair at major university: Cambridge, Oxford, LSE or UCL. By this age, 19 of the 21 had obtained such positions; of these 12 had already got there in their first professorial appointment; 9 shifted from 'provincial' or second-tier universities to the top level, none of these 9 shifts was into Cambridge. 9 professorships were in London, of which eight were at LSE; 4 at Oxford; 3 in Ivy League universities in USA; and 3 in Cambridge. The lion's den remained the most difficult one to enter.
Rate of incidence: 95%

47.8 FBA: 19 of the 21 become FBAs; others: Heal; Bean (no information).
Rate of incidence: 90%

54.7 President of the Royal Economic Society, and/or Econometric Society. 12 of the starting list of 21 reach these positions; there are 16 instances, 11 cases for the RES and 5 for the ES, with 4 of these 5 also having

Table 2.4 Career tracks and the glittering prizes

Name	Date of birth	University BA univ age yr	University PhD univ age yr	Mentors	1st chair age yr	Chair at Cam/Ox/Lon age yr	FBA age yr	RES President age term	ES President age year	Titles Honours CBE age yr	Titles Honours Kt age yr	Titles Honours Baron age yr	Master/Warden Oxbridge College	Significant positions/remarks
MIRRLEES	36.07.05	Cam 23 1959	Cam 27 1963	Stone[a] Hahn Arrow	Oxf 32 1968	Cam 59 1995	48 1984	53 1989–1992	46 1982		61 1997			Nobel 1996
GOODHART	36.10.23	Cam 24 1960	Harvard 27 1963	n/a		LSE 49 1985	54 1990			64 2000				BoE 1968–1985
BLISS	40.02.17	Cam 22 1962	Cam 26 1966	Frank Hahn[a]	Essex 31 1971	Oxf 52 1992	48 1988							
FLEMMING	41.02.06	Oxf 21 1962	–	Gorman Little	–	–	50 1991			62 2001			Wadham 1993	BoE 1980– 1st Ch Econ EBRD
DASGUPTA	42.11.17	Cam 23 1965	Cam 26 1968	Mirrlees[a] Meade Sen Patel	LSE 35 1978	Cam 43 1985	47 1989	56 1998–2001			60 2002			Fellow of the Royal Society 2004
NEWBERY	43.06.01	Cam 22 1965	Cam 33 1976	Hahn[a]	Cam 45 1988	Cam 45 1988	48 1991			69 2012				
HENDRY	44.03.06	Lon MSc 23 1967	Lon 26 1970	Sargan[a]	LSE 33 1977	Oxf 38 1982	43 1987	48 1992–1995			65 2009			
HEAL	44.04.09	Cam 22 1966	Cam 24 1968	Hahn[a]	Sussex 29 1973									

NICKELL	44.04.25	Cam 21 1965	LSE 26 1970	Hahn-Gorman[a]	LSE 35 1979	Oxf 40 1984	49 1993	57 2001–2004	63 2007	71 2015	Nuffield 2006–2012	BoE; Dir Oxf Instt of Eco/Stat
ATKINSON	44.09.04	Cam 22 1966	n/a	Hahn Meade Solow	Essex 27 1971	LSE 34 1980	40 1984	51 1995–1998	44 1988	56 2000	Nuffield 1994–2005	Cam 1992–1994 Chev. Leg Honn 2001 Lect Essex 1971–1976
HAMMOND	45.05.09	Cam 23 1968	Cam 29 1974	Mirrlees[a] Gorman Heal	Essex 31 1976	Stanford 34 1979	64 2009					
DEATON	45.10.19	Cam 22 1967	Cam 29 1974	Stone[a] Gorman	Bristol 31 1976	Princeton 39 1984	56 2001			71 2016		Nobel 2015
STERN	46.04.22	Cam 21 1967	Oxf 25 1971	Mirrlees[a]	Warwick 32 1978	LSE 40 1986	47 1993	72 2018–2019		58 2004	61 2007	Pres. BA 2013–2017; Chief Econ WB; lect Oxf 1971–1978 Fellow of the Royal Society 2014
KING	48.03.30	Cam 21 1969	n/a	Stone Feldstein	B'ham 29 1977	LSE 34 1984	44 1992			63 2011 GBE	65 2013 66 2014	BoE 1990–; Governor 2003 1966 Order of the Garter
SUTTON	48.08.10	Dub MA 25 1973	Sheffield 30 1978	RJ Nicholson[a]	LSE 32 1980	LSE 32 1980	48 1996	56 2004–2007				Irish

(*continued*)

Table 2.4 (continued)

Name	Date of birth	University BA univ age yr	University PhD univ age yr	Mentors	1st chair age yr	Chair at Cam/Ox/Lon age yr	FBA age yr	RES President age term	ES President age year	Titles Honours CBE age yr	Titles Honours Kt age yr	Titles Honours Baron age yr	Master/Warden Oxbridge College	Significant positions/remarks
HART	48.10.08	Cam 21 1969	Princeton 26 1974	Hahn Atkinson	LSE 34 1982	MIT 36 1984	52 2000							Nobel 2016
BLUNDELL	52.05.01	LSE MA 23 1975	n/a	Gorman	UCL 32 1984	UCL 32 1984	45 1997	58 2010–2013	54 2006	54 2006	62 2014			
BEAN	53.09.16	Cam 22 1975	MIT 28 1981	Solow[a]	LSE 37 1990	LSE 37 1990		60 2013–2015			61 2014			BoE 2000–2014; Dy Gov
MOORE	54.05.07	Cam 22 1976	LSE 30 1984	n/a	LSE 36 1990	LSE 36 1990	45 1999	61 2015–2017	56 2010	63 2017				
VICKERS	58.07.07	Oxf 21 1979	Oxf 27 1985	Mirrlees[a]	Oxf 33 1991	Oxf 33 1991	40 1998	49 2007–2010			47 2005		All Souls 2008–	
BESLEY	60.09.14	Oxf 21 1981	Oxf 24 1984	Gorman[a] Mirrlees Buchanan Sen	LSE 35 1995	LSE 35 1995	41 2001		58 2018	50 2010	58 2018			

[a] PhD supervisor

served as Presidents of the RES, viz., Atkinson, Blundell, Mirrlees and Moore. The ES position is reached, on average, at age 51.6, while the age for RES is 56.5.
Rate of incidence: 55%

60.4 Age at first receipt of Honour, title: CBE, Kt, Baron or other such. 5 have multiple honours: Besley, Blundell, King, Nickell and Stern; (King has three). 16 of the original 21 obtain such an honour, with 22 honours received.
Rate of incidence: 76%

There appears to be just one instance, that of Geoff Heal, where the cells are blank for the last four stages and this could be due to the difficulty in obtaining the relevant information from online sources. Two Nobel awards are registered: for Mirrlees and Deaton. Four of the twenty-one also go on to become heads of Oxford colleges: Atkinson, Flemming, Nickell and Vickers. And, of course, there are very many other distinctions and significant positions of responsibility that members of this list display, for example, honours from foreign countries (Atkinson); serving as Chief Economist of major organisations such as the World Bank (Stern), or the European Bank for Reconstruction and Development (EBRD) (Flemming); or as Governor of the Bank of England (King); and honorary doctorates.

Table 2.4 fully bears out David Newbery's remark about Hahn's boys going on to 'glittering careers'. This table could be extended, both horizontally and vertically, to the next set of contours, and would in all probability reveal a similar, though probably a diluted pattern.

It is pertinent here to explicitly point out that this group pattern of glittering career trajectories should not be read to imply that many or any of these rising stars were intrinsically undeserving of the honours they reaped along their shining paths; they were indeed highly accomplished and qualified economists. What is perhaps relevant here is the contrast between this orthodox cohort and its tableau of rich rewards with the relatively empty display cupboards devoid of silverware and prizes on the heterodox side of the line. In all the categories of recognition in which the younger generation of the orthodox clan could boast of their positions and privileges, medals and gongs, there was barely any representation of the younger aspirants from the heterodox side. No doubt, there were some exceptions, but even here, some could argue that these emerged from walking at least halfway to the other side, whether in the subject, in the Faculty or in the broader realm of government and politics. Equally, this lack of recognition was not because brilliance was in any way lacking on the heterodox side—but who and what was being favoured and rewarded by the new leaders of the discipline was for achievement wearing the uniform, cap and boots of the orthodox movement. On the orthodox side, recognition came quickly, usually frontloaded, often arguably before its time; on the heterodox side, it came, if at all, grudgingly, late and at a cost, generally negating the individual and institutional and purpose of such recognition.

Table 2.5 shifts the focus to another scale, from individual tracks to institutional patterns. The fact that by the age 33, virtually, all starters are installed in

Table 2.5 Cambridge-Oxford-LSE—Musical chairs

Year	Terence Gorman 1923–2003	Frank Hahn 1925–2013	Robin Matthews 1927–2010	James Mirrlees 1936–2018	John Flemming 1941–2003	Partha Dasgupta 1942–	David Newbery 1943–	Stephen Nickell 1944–	David Hendry 1944–	Anthony Atkinson 1944–2017
1948		B'ham								
1949–1960	B'ham	B'ham/Cam	cam							
1961	B'ham to OXF	cam	cam							
1962	OXF	cam	cam							
1963	OXF	cam	cam	cam	Oriel					
1964	OXF	cam	cam	cam	Oriel					
1965	OXF	cam	OXF	cam	Nuffield					
1966	OXF to LSE	cam to LSE	OXF	cam	Nuffield		Churchill			cam
1967	LSE	LSE	OXF	cam	Nuffield		cam			cam
1968	LSE	LSE	OXF	OXF	Nuffield		cam			cam
1969	LSE	LSE	OXF	OXF	Nuffield		cam			cam
1970	LSE	LSE	OXF	OXF	Nuffield		cam		lse	cam
1971	LSE	LSE	OXF	OXF	Nuffield	lse	cam	lse	lse	ESSEX
1972	LSE	LSE to CAM	OXF	OXF	Nuffield	lse	cam	lse	lse	ESSEX
1973	LSE	CAM	OXF	OXF	Nuffield	lse	cam	lse	lse	ESSEX
1974	LSE	CAM	OXF	OXF	Nuffield	lse	cam	lse	lse	ESSEX
1975	LSE	CAM	Master CLARE Cam	OXF	Nuffield	lse	cam	lse	lse	ESSEX
1976	LSE	CAM	CLARE	OXF	Nuffield	lse	cam	lse	lse	ESSEX/UCL
1977	LSE	CAM	CLARE	OXF	Nuffield	lse	cam	lse	LSE	UCL
1978	LSE	CAM	CLARE	OXF	Nuffield	LSE	cam	lse	LSE	UCL
1979	LSE	CAM	CLARE	OXF	Nuffield	LSE	cam	LSE	LSE	UCL
1980	Oxf/Nuff	CAM	CLARE CAM	OXF	Bk of Eng	LSE	cam	LSE	LSE	LSE
1981	Nuffield	CAM	CLARE CAM	OXF	Bk of Eng	LSE	cam	LSE	LSE	LSE
1982	Nuffield	CAM	CLARE CAM	OXF	Bk of Eng	LSE	cam	LSE	OXF	LSE
1983	Nuffield	CAM	CLARE CAM	OXF	Bk of Eng	LSE	cam	LSE	OXF	LSE

1984	Nuffield	CAM	CLARE CAM	OXF	Bk of Eng	LSE	cam	LSE	OXF	LSE
1985	Nuffield	CAM	CLARE CAM	OXF	Bk of Eng	CAM	cam	OXF	LSE
1986	Nuffield	CAM	CLARE CAM	OXF	Bk of Eng	CAM	cam	OXF	LSE
1987	Nuffield	CAM	CLARE CAM	OXF	Bk of Eng	CAM	cam	OXF	LSE
1988	Nuffield	CAM	CLARE CAM	OXF	Bk of Eng	CAM	CAM	OXF	LSE
1989	Nuffield	CAM	CLARE CAM	OXF	Bk of Eng	CAM	CAM	OXF	LSE
1990	Nuffield	CAM	CLARE CAM	OXF	Bk of Eng	CAM	CAM	OXF	LSE
1991		CAM	CLARE CAM	OXF	Bk of Eng	CAM	CAM	OXF	LSE
1992		CAM	CLARE	OXF	Warden	CAM	CAM	OXF	CAM
1993			CLARE	OXF	WADHAM Oxf	CAM	CAM	OXF	CAM
1994				OXF	WADHAM	CAM	CAM	OXF	CAM
1995				CAM	WADHAM	CAM	CAM	OXF	Warden NUFFIELD Oxf
1996				CAM	WADHAM	CAM	CAM	OXF	NUFFIELD
1997				CAM	WADHAM	CAM	CAM	OXF	NUFFIELD
1998				CAM	WADHAM	CAM	CAM	OXF/LSE	NUFFIELD
1999				CAM	WADHAM	CAM	CAM	LSE	NUFFIELD
2000				CAM	WADHAM	CAM	CAM	LSE	NUFFIELD
2001				CAM	WADHAM	CAM	CAM	LSE	NUFFIELD
2002				CAM	WADHAM	CAM	CAM	LSE	NUFFIELD
2003				CAM	WADHAM	CAM	CAM	LSE	NUFFIELD
2004						CAM	CAM	LSE	NUFFIELD
2005						CAM	CAM	LSE	NUFFIELD
2006						CAM	CAM	Warden NUFFIELD Oxf	OXF
2007						CAM	CAM	NUFFIELD	OXF
2008						CAM	CAM	NUFFIELD	OXF
2009						CAM	CAM	NUFFIELD	OXF

(*continued*)

Table 2.5 (continued)

Year	Terence Gorman 1923–2003	Frank Hahn 1925–2013	Robin Matthews 1927–2010	James Mirrlees 1936–2018	John Flemming 1941–2003	Partha Dasgupta 1942–	David Newbery 1943–	Stephen Nickell 1944–	David Hendry 1944–	Anthony Atkinson 1944–2017
2010							CAM	NUFFIELD	OXF	
2011								NUFFIELD	OXF	
2012								NUFFIELD		

Lower case = a non-professorial position
Upper case = professorial position

chairs in Cambridge, Oxford or LSE has profound influence: it implies that these persons enjoy and exercise the authority of professorial power in institutional and academic matters in situ for the next 30 years and more. Since they belong to, and generally function as a connected intellectual group with a fairly well-recognised apex leadership of seniors, this 'collective' constitutes a formidable monopolistic force influencing, indeed governing, the definition and practice of the discipline of economics in the country. Against this background, Table 2.5 provides a confirmation of this stranglehold. It provides information on the academic rank or position, and the location/university of just ten of the main players: three seniors, viz., Gorman, Hahn and Matthews, and seven of their 'nephews', followers or protégés from the next generation. The period covered is 1948 till 2012. Three features stand out. First, virtually all the years in all ten cases are spent in Oxbridge or LSE; apart from the early Birmingham phase for Gorman and Hahn, and Flemming at the Bank of England, and Atkinson. Second, there seems to be a regular circulation of the ten between senior positions in these three universities; only Flemming is Oxford-only; at the other end, Atkinson is the most footloose keeping the movers busy: Cambridge, Essex, UCL, LSE, Cambridge again, finally Oxford. The third feature is the most significant: it shows that over large sections of this time frame, members of this group simultaneously occupied senior, usually controlling, positions at all three major universities. This is most dramatically the case from the late 1970s, when the power of the seniors at the top was hugely extended as their followers began to be placed into chairs in one or other of these top universities. This period extends from the early 1990s, by when the seniors retire, and the next generation take over the reins and the reign for the period through to their own retirement, the last of these being Stephen Nickell from the position of Warden of Nuffield in 2012. Of course, by then, the next cohorts were well launched on their glittering careers. Table 12.1 adds supportive information about leadership positions in the Royal Economic Society, the apex body that the dynamic Frank Hahn revived and then used instrumentally for implementing his agenda on the economics discipline in the UK. Considering the holders of the position of president, it is clear that the start of the takeover by the Hahn-Matthews powerhouse can be dated to the late 1970s when this group starts permeating the Council, with control being achieved from 1984 when Matthews takes over as president with all presidents thereafter, all the way through to 2019, drawn from the Hahn-Matthews root lineage. Some of the younger heterodox economists in Cambridge, watching this full liveried parade from the sidelines might have called it a successful case of planned and sustained extended reproduction (Table 2.6).

Table 2.6 Management positions in the Faculty of Economics and DAE

Faculty Board Chairs
1954–1961	Austin Robinson
1962–1963	Richard Kahn
1964–1967	Austin Robinson
1968–1971	Aubrey Silberston
1971–1972	Richard Stone
1972–1973	Brian Reddaway
1974–1975	Michael Posner
1976–1979	Brian Reddaway
1980–1982	Robert Neild
1983–1988	Alan Hughes
1989–1991	Frank Hahn
1992–1996	Willy Brown
1997–2001	Partha Dasgupta
2002–2003	Bob Rowthorn
2004–2007	Andrew Harvey
2007–2011	Hamid Sabourian
2011–2014	Richard Smith
2014–2018	Sanjeev Goyal
2019–	Leonardo Felli

DAE Directors
1945–1954	Richard Stone
1955–1970	Brian Reddaway
1966–1967	Aubrey Silberston (Acting)
1970–1985	Wynne Godley
1985–1987	Wynne Godley (Ex officio)
1987–1988	Alan Hughes (Acting)
1988–2003	David Newbery

CGP Directors
1960–1980	Richard Stone
1981–1987	Terry Barker

CEPG Directors
1970–1982	Wynne Godley

Table 2.7 Past Editors of *The Economc Journal*

2018–2019	N. Stern
2017–2018	P. Neary
2016–2017	A. Chesher
2015–2016	J. H. Moore
2013–2015	C. Bean
2010–2013	R. Blundell
2007–2010	J. Vickers
2004–2007	J. Sutton
2001–2004	S. Nickell
1998–2001	P. S. Dasgupta
1995–1998	A. B. Atkinson
1992–1995	D. F. Hendry
1989–1992	J. A. Mirrlees
1986–1989	F. H. Hahn
1984–1986	R. C. O. Matthews
1982–1984	G. D. N. Worswick
1980–1982	P. Deane
1978–1980	J. R. N. Stone
1976–1978	A. J. Brown
1974–1976	N. Kaldor
1972–1974	G. D. A. MacDougall
1970–1972	E. H. Phelps-Brown
1968–1970	A. K. Cairncross
1966–1968	S. Caine
1964–1966	J. E. Meade
1962–1964	R. F. Harrod
1960–1962	J. R. Hicks
1958–1960	R. L. Hall
1956–1958	A. M. Carr Saunders
1954–1956	L. C. Robbins
1952–1954	R. H. Brand
1950–1952	H. D. Henderson
1948–1950	D. H. Robertson
1946–1948	R. G. Hawtrey
1945–1946	J. M. Keynes
1940–1945	W. H. Beveridge
1937–1940	A. C. Pigou
1935–1937	W. R. Scott
1932–1934	E. Cannan
1929–1932	H. S. Foxwell
1906–1929	R. B. Haldane
1891	G. J. Goschen

http://www.res.org.uk/view/president.html

Table 2.8 Past Presidents of Royal Economic Society

Date	Name	Role
1891–1925	F. Y. Edgeworth	Editor (1891–1911), Joint Editor (1919–1925)
1896–1905	H. Higgs	Assistant Editor
1912–1944	J. M. Keynes	Editor (1912–1918), Joint Editor (1919–1944)
1926–1934	D. H. Macgregor	Joint Editor
1934–1970	E. A. G. Robinson	Assistant Editor (1934–1944), Joint Editor (1945–1970)
1945–1961	R. F. Harrod	Joint Editor
1951–1970	R. C. O. Matthews	Assistant Editor (1951–1968), Joint Editor (1968–1970)
1961–1970	C. F. Carter	Joint Editor
1968–1975	Phyllis Deane	Joint Editor
1971–1976	D. G. Champernowne	Joint Editor
1971–1976	W. B. Reddaway	Joint Editor
1976–1981	J. Black	Joint Editor
1976–1981	J. S. Flemming	Joint Editor (1976), Managing Editor (1976–1980), Joint Managing Editor (1981)
1976–1981	J. A. Kay	Joint Editor
1976–1977	J. H. Williamson	Joint Editor
1976–1984	D. Winch	Joint Editor
1977–1981	D. F. Hendry	Joint Editor
1977–1996	D. M. Newbery	Joint Editor
1980–2017	D. G. Mayes	Joint Editor (1980–1988), Production Editor (1989–2017)
1980–1986	C. H. Feinstein	Joint Editor (1980), Managing Editor (1981–1986)
1980–1986	J. P. Hutton	Joint Editor (1980–1981), Managing Editor (1981–1986)
1981–1985	W. H. Buiter	Joint Editor
1981–1996	J. P. Neary	Joint Editor
1983–1989	D. A. Collard	Joint Editor
1986–1996	J. D. Hey	Managing Editor
1986–1996	M. J. Artis	Joint Editor (1986–1988), Associate Editor (1988–1996)
1986–1990	M. A. M. Smith	Joint Editor (1986–1988), Associate Editor (1989–1990)
1986–1990	A. J. Oswald	Joint Editor (1986–1988), Surveys and Associate Editor (1989–1990)
1989–1993	P. J. Dolton	Software Review Editor
1989–2000	R. Backhouse	Book Review Editor
1990–1998	D. Greenaway	Policy Forum Editor
1991–1996	L. A. Winters	Associate Editor
1993–2000	G. Judge	Software Review Editor

(*continued*)

Table 2.8 (continued)

Date	Name	Role
1996–1998	H. D. Dixon	Controversies Editor
1996–1998	G. Harcourt	Obituaries Editor
1997–1999	T. Besley	Joint Managing Editor
1997–2004	C. Bliss	Joint Managing Editor
1997–2004	C. Meghir	Joint Managing Editor
1997–2004	M. Wickens	Coordinating Editor
1998–2013	S. Machin	Joint Managing Editor (1998–2004), Joint Editor (2004–2006), Features Editor (2006–2013)
1999–2004	D. De Meza	Joint Managing Editor
2000–2005	J. Dutta	Book Review Editor
2001	G. Van den Berg	Joint Managing Editor
2004–2005	M. Bertrand	Joint Editor
2004–2008	L. Felli	Joint Editor
2004–2011	A. Scott	Managing Editor
2004–2006	J. Ventura	Joint Editor
2005–2012	S. Pischke	Joint Editor (2005–2010), Joint Managing Editor (2010–2012)
2006–2012	H. Daly	Publishing Editor (2006–2008), Publishing Editor (2009–2012)
2007–2012	A. Ciccone	Joint Editor (2007–2010), Joint Managing Editor (2010–2012)
2008–2012	D. Myatt	Joint Editor (2008–2010), Joint Managing Editor (2010–2012)
2008	S. Cheung	Publishing Editor
2012–present	M. Cripps	Joint Managing Editor
2010–2012	W. Den Haan	Joint Managing Editor
2010–present	R. Griffith	Joint Managing Editor
2012–2017	A. Galeotti	Joint Managing Editor
2012–present	K. Salvanes	Joint Managing Editor
2012–2014	S. Seavers	Publishing Editor
2012–present	F. Vermeulen	Joint Managing Editor
2013–present	M. Ravn	Joint Managing Editor
2014–present	B. Rajania	Publishing Editor
2015–present	H. -J. Voth	Joint Managing Editor
2018–present	G. Levy	Joint Managing Editor

http://www.res.org.uk/view/EconomicPastEditors.html

There are some striking features of this network of influence, or 'Uncle' Frank's 'academy' of 'nephews'. They all seem to be birds of a feather; there is a unity of strategic purpose, strong communications through shared forums, and in one permutation or combination or another, they seem to constitute a catenation powered by the proxy authority of their seniors, used to implement shared agendas. Perhaps no great direction from a centralised command might be required when everyone is of a similar mind and looking in the same direction with regard to decisions and recommendations on issues on the table.[85]

As it happens, some of the less visible roles were the more critical ones for the Cambridge game of thrones. These need a special mention by way of an early introduction to the rendition that follows. The first is the link between the office of RES President and the conduct of the periodic Research Assessment Exercise that governs significant outcomes for the profession at both institutional and individual levels. RES has a powerful role in the composition of the subject panel for economics and econometrics. This involves the representation of the profession through an association formed by the RES, the Conference of Heads of University Departments of Economics (CHUDE) which was first formed in the presidency of Frank Hahn. A related body is the Association of University Teachers of Economics (AUTE) of which Hahn was then also president, for good measure. This turns the spotlight on to the selection panels for E&E; these are powerfully influenced by the president, RES in concert with his Council (on which comment has already been made). The panel needs a Chair, who is critical for the orientation of the exercise, and this choice is generally also more under the informal control of the president than the distant university funding body covering all subjects. All RAE and REF panels, from the first major RAE of 1989, were dominated by the Hahn-Gorman-Matthews axis and the chairs were identifiable of this camp. This was another commanding height, securely under mainstream control, from which subsequent attacks were launched on the heterodox groups of economists within the Cambridge Faculty.

Another commanding height of great strategic significance was the SSRC (later the ESRC), the official external body that oversaw the public financing of research; the Department of Applied Economics was heavily dependent on it for underwriting some of its flagship research teams, prominently but not exclusively the CGP and the CEPG teams. The Hahn-Matthews group needed to neutralise the DAE's role in supporting the heterodox camp, and choking SSRC finance was an obvious and powerful line of attack. That is the way things eventually went, and in this context, much relevance attaches to the compositions of

---

[85] Here, a qualification and note of caution is necessary: in a couple of cases, it might be inappropriate to presume that the persons involved followed the disciplinary traditions of Hahn, Gorman, Solow & Co. For instance, Deaton has explicitly distanced himself in this regard, both substantially in terms of his work and through occasional recorded observations; Atkinson's later work does not follow the Hahn-Gorman-Solow track, though he explicitly acknowledged that Hahn was the most powerful intellectual influence on him, and he collaborated closely with him and his group on most institutional matters, even if perhaps as an uncomfortable fellow traveller, possibly unsure or unhappy with the direction of the group's journey.

the decision-making committees involved, and their headmen. There was the overarching powerful Chairman of SSRC; an Economics Committee; and, in the context of DAE, some crucial committees set up by the SSRC Chair to evaluate and judge on grant applications. These committees chose their external experts whose views were used by the committees as they saw fit. All in all, the selection of the members and the experts, especially in a field as contested as economics, virtually determined the outcome. Collating the details of the chairs and memberships of the main and supporting committees involved in the 1980s reveals 'the usual suspects': the Hahn-Matthews group, and allies, dominate the committees, panels, their experts and their chairs; there is virtually zero representation of heterodox economists in these various advisory and decision-making committees. The appointment of the Chair is in the power of the Education Secretary of the Government. Michael Posner was the Chair for 1979–1983, and Douglas Hague, Margaret Thatcher's economics guru, was the Chair for the 1984–1987 period—these together covered the stretch during which the vital damaging decisions were made with respect to DAE.

2.4.3 Modus Operandi: *Masters, Mandarins and Interlocking Committees*

And finally, there are the nearby heights of the administrators of the University of Cambridge under whose purview the Faculty of Economics and the Department of Applied Economics fall. As becomes apparent as the saga unfolds, this was another crucial coordinate that the Hahn-Matthews axis controlled, though in the end, the heterodox groups could put up a resistance using their rights and privileges as members of the University. Yet again, key roles are played by individual experts, referees and advisors whose names variously figure in several of the other Hahn-Matthews attacks on the heterodox camp.

The *modus operandi* of the Hahn-Matthews network was complex in detail, though simple in design. Various stratagems were employed. One was the use of tactical alliances in specific attacks. For instance, while Hahn attacked Thatcherite monetarism—a proxy blast against its chief advocate, and Hahn's adversary, Alan Walters—his group combined with the monetarists in SSRC and ESRC committees to bring down the DAE projects. A second was the continuous barrage disparaging all lineages of Cambridge heterodox economics; and a third was the familiar scaremongering tactic of beating up the spectre of Marxists, Maoists, communists and reds set to take control and ruin the glorious inherited reputation of Cambridge economics.

But at the heart of it was the device of interlocking committees. Each of the sites from where attacks were mounted involved several interrelated committees, the work and decision of one based on that of another, passed on to the next and so on. Given the size and strength of the cohorts of peers and juniors, the Hahn-Matthews axis could strategically influence the composition of virtually every committee that mattered in this chain. Then the negative assessments, conclusions and recommendations of one were fed to the next; so also, the choice of external experts could be influenced. The SSRC and ESRC committees[86] and the RAE panels[87] were stacked with permutations and combinations of the mainstream neoclassical tribe headed by Hahn (and a couple of his peers) as the chief. And further, the device of interlocking could be used to articulate one external site to another. The SSRC/ESRC negative outcomes could be transmitted as inputs into the independent DAE Review by the University of Cambridge. The rate at which the names of a handful of members of the Hahn-Matthews clan appear and reappear on various committees whether as Chairmen, or members, or consultants, challenges any notion that this was by accident, or by virtue of the fact they were the last surviving economists in the country; on the other side, apart from the occasional exception or two that proves the rule, there is virtually no representation on any of these committees from the heterodox schools of economics; so there is no mind or voice within the committees that might interrogate the evidence assembled or offer alternative perspectives. All too often, it is as if there is a heavy prosecuting team, but no defence counsel at all; the final sentence: death by a thousand committees.

The decisions of these various committees eventually accumulate and aggregate to deliver terminal judgements. Each judgement, made by some committee at some location, appears to be independent of the others, and the role of the common underlying network is disguised and occluded. That the various ostensibly independent episodes are actually interconnected and form a concerted, coordinated, if covert, front is a hypothesis that would be difficult to reject altogether. The committees and their networked members provide a display of short passing and teamwork that would have made Barcelona FC envious and reaching for their chequebooks to sign them up.

Ajit Singh was the political commissar, or Chief Whip, of the heterodox left groups; he was an industrial economist specialising in corporate control, and this strategy would have resonated strongly with the devices of the managing agency, and especially of the system of interlocking directorships, used in Indian industry in colonial times but also post-Independence, whereby an occluded family or controlling unit, or 'monopoly house', controlled a vast network of seemingly independent companies through a carefully structured network of interlocking directorships—with the threads eventually leading to the hidden controllers of last resort who often remained in obscurity. The painstaking and pioneering work of the industrial economist, R. K. Hazari in the 1960s, reveals

---

[86] For a quick illustration, easily extendable, the important Economics Committee of the SSRC and ESRC in the 1979–1987 period, when crucial (negative) decisions were made effectively closing down both DAE macroeconomic teams, included, amongst others: Tony Atkinson as chair during 1979–1981, followed by John Flemming as chair during 1981–1984, followed by Charles Feinstein (1984–1986, including the significant 1985–1986 as chair); with David Hendry as a member 1977–1982, also a member of the 1981–1982 Consortium that declined the CEPG application; Stephen Nickell similarly as member during 1984–1987, and David Newbery during 1983–1987; the list can be readily stretched to include other tactical supporters. Much of this was under the watch of Michael Posner as the Chair of SSRC, with the tendency continued in the tenure of his successor, Douglas Hague, an economics mentor of Margaret Thatcher.

[87] On this, see Chap. 12, especially Table 12.2.

these hidden links and makes the case for regarding such networks of companies and their controlling firm as one entity. Doing so also shows that industrial wealth and power were far more concentrated than would appear on the surface of things. The analogy is illuminating.[88]

In contrast, the heterodox formation could be described as a hyper-energetic, undisciplined group of units with multiple internal polarities which could come together variably on specific issues of shared political passions or institutional interests; here too there was an inner circle of young turks and intersecting outer circles of loyalists, followers and fair-weather friends, their composition depending on the specific matter at hand; there was an impressively large number of grandees and prima donnas; and Ajit, as political commissar or Chief Whip, led the inner circle at the core, implicitly entrusted to bring it all together into a voice and a vote when it mattered, a task more easily said than done.

Another crucial difference in the structure and formation of the opposing camps was that while the heterodox group was essentially located within the Faculty, the DAE and the colleges, this was not at all the case with the orthodox camp which had developed extensive and close connections with key decision makers both within Cambridge, more widely in other important bodies in

---

[88] The term at present represents certain particular communities and family names with strong entrepreneurial ability and capacity associated with the process of country's industrialisation. They are the House of Tata, Birla, Mafatlal, Thapar and so on (Indrani, 1990: 106).

Their origins are rooted in traders and moneylenders with narrow religious, regional or caste affiliations and identities

> A large number of companies are found to have registered under each of the [business] houses. All these companies work in close connection with each other. The decision regarding price, output and investment is taken not by the individual company but by the business-group who is supposed to be the sole authority in the system. Annual reports of the companies belonging to the same group shows evidence of coordination with the timings of investment, use of intra-group loans, attempts to restrict the sole selling agency rights to companies within the same group. The companies under the same business house never indulge in competitive spirit among themselves. Rather an atmosphere of mutual understanding and coordination is maintained at inter-house level through the practice of interlocking directorship and inter-corporate investment, and at inter house level through the meeting of Federation of Indian Chamber of Commerce and Industry, and other business associations. (Indrani, 1990: 107)

R. K. Hazari, the pioneer of this field, initiated the concept of the business house and distinguished between its companies that belong to an 'Inner Circle' and an 'Outer Circle', where the business house has sole control or a majority share in the former and a material influence but not the controlling voice in the latter (Indrani, 1990: 438; Hazari, 1958, 1960, 1961, 1966). The device of the 'managing agency', prevalent as a corporate control and management mechanism in British and the early period in independent India, is perhaps also pertinent:

> The managing agents treated all companies within their portfolio as part of a single unity without regard to the separate legal personality and the separate interests of the shareholders of the individually managed companies. The managing agents handled the financial matters commonly across the group as if it were a single entity. ... Such attitudes of the managing agents adversely affected shareholder interest. (Varottil, 2015: 20–21)

the UK, and also internationally, especially with the extended neoclassical families located in the other Cambridge and other US universities, including especially Chicago. These external networks of support were part of the dramatic shifts in the templates of global politics from the 1970s, and these changes, which can be summarised as the emergence and rise to maturity of the global neoliberal thought collective, simultaneously weakened heterodox positions, while greatly extending and augmenting the muscular power of mainstream economics and economists both in Cambridge and beyond.

References

Arestis, P., & Sawyer, M. C. (Eds.). (1992). *A biographical dictionary of dissenting economists*. Edward Elgar.

Aslanbeigui, N., & Oakes, G. (2002). The theory arsenal: The Cambridge circus and the origins of the Keynesian revolution. *Journal of the History of Economic Thought, 24*(1), 5–37.

Atkinson, A. B., & Stern, N. (2017). Tony Atkinson on poverty, inequality, and public policy: The work and life of a great economist. *Annual Review of Economics, 9*, 1–20. https://doi.org/10.1146/annurev-economics-110216-100949

Baker, C. (2021). *National staff from overseas: Statistics*. Research Briefing, UK Parliament, House of Commons Library. https://commonslibrary.parliament.uk/research-briefings/cbp-7783/

Baranzini, M. L., & Mirante, A. (2018). *Luigi L. Pasinetti: An intellectual biography: Leading scholar and system builder of the Cambridge School of Economics*. Palgrave Macmillan.

BBC. (2017, January 26). Obituary: Tam Dalyell. *BBC News*. https://www.bbc.com/news/uk-politics-29367988

Beath, J. (2015). Obituary: Aubrey Silberston (1922–2015). *Royal Economic Society Newsletter, 171*, 17–18.

Benn, T. (2000). Interview. Commanding Heights, Public Broadcasting Service, Interviewed on 26 October 2000. https://www.pbs.org/wl7h/commanding-heights/hi/people/pe_name.html

Buss, R. (2006, November 12). Talleyrand: Napoleon's master by David Lawday. *The Independent*. https://www.independent.co.uk/arts-entertainment/books/reviews/talleyrand-napoleons-master-by-david-lawday-424034.html

Cairncross, A. (1995). Economists in wartime. *Contemporary European History, 4*(1), 19–36.

Clarke, P. (n.d.). *Obituary: Professor Sir Harry Hinsley, 1918–1998*. Obituaries, 1990s – St. John's College, pp. 100–106. https://www.joh.cam.ac.uk/sites/default/files/Eagle/Eagle%20Chapters/Obituaries/Obituaries_1990s.pdf

Coleman, D., & Rowthorn, B. (2004). The economic effects of immigration into the United Kingdom. *Population and Development Review, 30*(4), 579–624.

Creedy, J. (2008). *J. A. C. Brown (1922–1984): An appreciation*. Research Paper No. 1027, Department of Economics, University of Melbourne.

Dasgupta, P. (2010). Interview with Partha Dasgupta 6th April 2010. In S. Harrison & A. Macfarlane, *Encounter with economics*. Interviews filmed by A. Macfarlane and edited by S. Harrison. University of Cambridge. http://sms.cam.ac.uk/collection/1092396

Dasgupta, P. (2013). Obituary: Frank Hahn. *Royal Economic Society Newsletter, 161*(April).

Deaton, A. (2011). My Cambridge in the 60s and 70s. *Cambridge Economics: Cambridge Faculty of Economics Alumni Newsletter, 4*, 3–4. www.econ.cam.ac.uk/alumni/newsletters/Cambridge-Economics-Issue-4-2011.pdf

Deaton, A. (n.d.). *Puzzles and paradoxes: A life in applied economics.* https://wws.princeton.edu/system/files/research/documents/deaton_puzzles_and_paradoxes.pdf. Published subsequently as: Deaton, A. (2014). Puzzles and paradoxes: A life in applied economics. In M. Szenberg & L. Ramrattan (Eds.), *Eminent economists II: Their life and work philosophies* (pp. 84–101). Cambridge University Press.

Drury, I. (2015, December 4). Mass migration 'will wreck the dream of a high-wage Britain': Top economist says large numbers of unskilled workers is 'damaging' for job prospects. *The Daily Mail.* https://www.dailymail.co.uk/news/article-3345332/Mass-migration-wreck-dream-high-wage-Britain-economist-says-large-numbers-unskilled-workers-damaging-job-prospects.html

Earl, P. (2016). Pluralistic teaching: A student's memoir. In G. C. Harcourt, The legacy of Ajit Singh (11 September 1940–23 June 2015): Memories and tributes from former pupils, colleagues and friends. *The Economic and Labour Relations Review, 27*(3), 304–306.

Edwards, K. J. R. (2009, February 5). *Ken Edwards, interviewed by Alan Macfarlane.* Film interview with leading thinkers, University of Cambridge. http://www.alanmacfarlane.com/DO/filmshow/edwardstx.htm

ESRC. (n.d.). *SSRC/ESRC: The first forty years.* ESRC. https://esrc.ukri.org/files/news-events-and-publications/publications/ssrc-and-esrc-the-first-forty-years/

Feinstein, C. H. (1965). *Domestic capital formation in the United Kingdom.* Cambridge University Press.

Feinstein, C. H. (Ed.). (1967). *Socialism, capitalism and economic growth: Essays presented to Maurice Dobb.* Cambridge University Press.

Feinstein, C. H. (2007). Charles H. Feinstein interviewed by Mark Thomas. In J. S. Lyons, L. P. Cain, & S. H. Williamson (Eds.), *Reflections on the cliometric revolution: Conversations with economic historians* (pp. 286–300). Routledge. Interviewed by Mark Thomas on 2 August 2002 at All Souls, Oxford.

Feinstein, C., & Reddaway, W. B. (1978). OPEC surpluses, the world recession and the U.K. economy. *Midland Bank Review,* Spring; reprinted in Matthews and Sargent (1983).

Feiwel, G. R. (Ed.). (1989). *Joan Robinson and modern economic theory.* Palgrave Macmillan.

Fletcher, G. (2008). *Dennis Robertson.* Palgrave Macmillan.

Glyn, A., Hughes, A., Lipietz, A., & Singh, A. (1988). *The rise and fall of the golden age.* UNU-WIDER Working Paper No. 43. UNU-WIDER.

Godley, W. (2008, May 16). Interview with Wynne Godley. In S. Harrison & A. Macfarlane, *Encounter with economics.* Interviews filmed by A. Macfarlane and edited by S. Harrison. University of Cambridge. http://sms.cam.ac.uk/collection/1092396

Goodwin, R. M. (1995). In memory of Sir Richard Stone. In ISTAT (Ed.), *Social statistics, national accounts and economic analysis. International conference in memory of Sir Richard Stone.* ISTAT.

Green, A. (2014, October 24). A divisive peer for a divided time. *The Independent.*https://www.independent.co.uk/news/people/profiles/andrew-green-divisive-peer-divided-time-9817055.html

Guinan, J. (2015). Ownership and control: Bring back the Institute for Workers' Control. *Renewal: A Journal of Social Democracy, 23*(4), 11–36. https://www.academia.edu/20411866/Bring_back_the_Institute_for_Workers_Control

Hagemann, H. (2011). European émigrés and the 'Americanization' of economics. *European Journal of the History of Economic Thought, 18*(5), 643–671.

Hahn, F. H., & Matthews, R. C. O. (1964). Theory of economic growth: A survey. *Economic Journal, 74*(296), 779–902.

Harcourt, G. C. (1972). *Some Cambridge controversies in the theory of capital*. Cambridge University Press.

Harcourt, G. C. (1997). The Kaldor legacy: Reviewing Nicholas Kaldor, *Causes of growth and stagnation in the world economy* (Cambridge University Press, 1996). *Journal of International and Comparative Economics, 5*, 341–357.

Harcourt, G. C. (2001). *Fifty years a Keynesian and other essays*. Palgrave Macmillan.

Harcourt, G. C. (2007). Interview with Geoffrey Harcourt 15th May 2007. In S. Harrison & A. Macfarlane, *Encounter with economics*. Film interviews with leading thinkers, filmed by A. Macfarlane and edited by S. Harrison. University of Cambridge; Created 28 March 2011. http://sms.cam.ac.uk/collection/1092396

Harcourt, G. C. (2008). Preface. In P. Arestis & J. Eatwell (Eds.), *Essays in honour of Ajit Singh. Volume 2: Issues in economic development and globalization* (pp. xiii–xv). Palgrave Macmillan.

Harcourt, G. C. (2009). A revolution yet to be accomplished: Reviewing Luigi Pasinetti, *Keynes and the Cambridge Keynesians*. *History of Economic Ideas, 17*(1), 203–208.

Harcourt, G. C. (2011). The *General Theory* is not a book that you should read in bed! Interviewed by Eckhard Hein and Achim Truger, January 2010. *Intervention, 8*(1), 7–12.

Harcourt, G. C. (2012). Interview with Geoffrey C. Harcourt. In S. Ederer et al. (Eds.), *Interventions: 17 interviews with unconventional economists (2004–2012)* (pp. 83–92). Metropolis Verlag GmbH.

Harcourt, G. C. (2017). Robert Charles Oliver (Robin) Matthews (1927–2010). In R. A. Cord (Ed.), *The Palgrave Companion to Cambridge economics* (pp. 955–978). Palgrave Macmillan.

Harcourt, G. C., & Cohen, A. J. (2012). Whatever happened to the Cambridge capital theory controversies? (Originally published 2003). In G. C. Harcourt (Ed.), *The making of a post-Keynesian economist: Cambridge harvest. Selected essays of G. C. Harcourt* (pp. 112–130). Palgrave Macmillan.

Hayter, T. (2007, March 16). Watching David Coleman. *The Guardian*.https://www.theguardian.com/commentisfree/2007/mar/16/watchingdavidcoleman1

Hazari, R. K. (1958, November 8). Inter-corporate investment: The Birla Group of companies. *Economic Weekly*.

Hazari, R. K. (1960, November 26, December 3, December 10). Ownership and control. *Economic Weekly*.

Hazari, R. K. (1961). *Big business in India: A study in ownership and control*. All India Trade Union Congress.

Hazari, R. K. (1966). *The structure of corporate private control*. Asia Publishing House.

Heffernan, R. (1997). *Exploring political change: Thatcherism and the remaking of the Labour Party 1979–1997*. Ph.D. thesis, London School of Economics and Political Science, University of London. http://etheses.lse.ac.uk/2133/1/U613365.pdf

Heffernan, R., & Marqusee, M. (1992). *Defeat from the jaws of victory: Inside Kinnock's Labour Party*. Verso.

Hill, R. (2001). *The Labour Party's economic strategy, 1979–1997: The long road back*. Palgrave.

Hobsbawm, E. (2002). *Interesting times: A twentieth-century life*. Knopf Doubleday Publishing Group.

Hodgson, G. M., Gagliardi, F., & Gindis, D. (2018). From Cambridge Keynesian to institutional economist: The unnoticed contributions of Robert Neild. *Journal of Institutional Economics, 14*(4), 767–786.

Howson, S. (2011). *Lionel Robbins*. Cambridge University Press.

Indrani, D. E. (1990). *An inter-temporal study of Indian industrial economy with special reference to selected business houses*. PhD dissertation, University of Calcutta.

Inman, P. (2010, July 5). Martin Weale joins Bank of England's monetary policy committee. *The Guardian*. https://www.theguardian.com/business/2010/jul/05/martin-weale-bank-of-england-monetary-policy-committee

Johnson, H. G. (1978). The shadow of Keynes. In E. S. Johnson & H. G. Johnson (Eds.), *The shadow of Keynes: Understanding Keynes, Cambridge and Keynesian economics*. Basil Blackwell.

Johnson, H. G. (n.d.). *Cambridge in the 1950s: Memoirs of an economist*. Men and Ideas, RFK/12/2/57/2-14, pp. 28–39. Richard Kahn Papers, King's College Archives, Cambridge.

Kaldor, N. (1996). *Causes of Growth and Stagnation in the World Economy. The Raffaele Mattioli Lectures delivered in 1984*. Cambridge: Cambridge University Press.

Kaldor, M. (2019, January 8). Robert Neild obituary. *The Guardian*.

Keynes, J. M. (1924). Alfred Marshall, 1842–1924. *The Economic Journal, 34*(135), 311–372.

King, J. E. (2009). *Nicholas Kaldor*. Palgrave Macmillan.

Kuper, A. (2016). Meyer Fortes: The person, the role, the theory. *Cambridge Journal of Anthropology, 34*(2), 127–139.

Lee, F. S. (2007, November 1–3). *Making history by making identity and institutions: The emergence of Post-Keynesian–heterodox economics in Britain, 1974–1996*. Paper presented at the EAPE Conference, Universidade Porto, Porto.

Leijonhufvud, A. (1973). Life among the econ. *Economic Inquiry, 11*(3), 327–337.

Linehan, P. (1998, February 19). Obituary: Professor Sir Harry Hinsley. https://www.independent.co.uk/news/obituaries/obituary-professor-sir-harry-hinsley-1145675.html

Maddison, A. (1994, June). Confessions of a Chiffrephile. *Banca Nazionale del Lavoro Quarterly Review, 189*. http://www.ggdc.net/maddison/personal/autobiog1994.pdf

Marcuzzo, M. C., & Rosselli, A. (Eds.). (2005). *Economists in Cambridge: A study through their correspondence, 1907–1946*. Routledge.

Marcuzzo, M. C., & Sanfilippo, E. (2008). Dear John, Dear Ursula: Eighty-eight letters unearthed. In R. Scazzieri, A. Sen, & S. Zamagni (Eds.), *Markets, money and capital: Hicksian economics for the twenty first century* (pp. 72–91). Cambridge University Press.

Matthews, R. C. O. (1954a). The trade cycle in Britain, 1790–1850. *Oxford Economic Papers, 6*(1), 1–32.

Matthews, R. C. O. (1954b). *A study in trade cycle history: Economic fluctuations in Great Britain 1833–1842*. Cambridge University Press.

Matthews, R. C. O. (1968). Why has Britain had full employment since the war? *Economic Journal, 78*(311), 555–569.

Matthews, R. C. O. (1989). Joan Robinson and Cambridge – A theorist and her milieu: An interview. In G. R. Feiwel (Ed.), *Joan Robinson and modern economic theory* (pp. 911–915). Palgrave Macmillan.

Matthews, R. C. O., & Supple, B. (n.d.). *The ordeal of economic freedom: Marshall on economic history.* Typescript in E.A.G. Robinson Papers, Marshall Library Archives, University of Cambridge, EAGR 6/4/16, 23p. Also published as Matthews, R. C. O., & Supple, B. (1991). The ordeal of economic freedom: Marshall on economic history. *Quaderni di Storia dell'Economia Politica, 9*(2–3), 189–213.

Matthews, R. C. O., Feinstein, C. F., & Odling-Smee, J. (1982). *British economic growth 1856–1973: The post-war period in historical perspective.* Oxford University Press.

McDonnell, J. (2015). *Speech to Labour Party Annual Conference.* http://press.labour.org.uk/post/130055656854/speech-by-john-mcdonnell-to-labour-party-annual

McKittrick, D., & Dalyell, T. (2010, August 10). Robin Matthews: Leading economist and Master of Clare College, Cambridge. *The Independent.* https://www.independent.co.uk/news/obituaries/robin-matthews-leading-economist-and-master-of-clare-college-cambridge-2047930.html

Meade, J. E. (1964). *Efficiency, equality and the ownership of property.* George Allen and Unwin.

Metcalf, D. (2019). *Tribute to Basil Yamey.* http://www.lse.ac.uk/economics/Assets/Documents/basil-yamey/david-metcalf-tribute-to-basil-yamey.pdf

Millmow, A. (2014, July). *The influence of Cambridge upon the professionalisation of postwar Australian economics.* Paper for the 27th HETSA conference, Auckland University, New Zealand. http://docs.business.auckland.ac.nz/Doc/16-Alex-Millmow.pdf

Mirrlees, J. A. (1996). *James A. Mirrlees biographical.* https://www.nobelprize.org/prizes/economic-sciences/1996/mirrlees/facts/

Naylor, R. T. (1981). Johnson on Cambridge and Keynes. *Canadian Journal of Political and Social Theory/Revue Canadienne de Theorie Politique et Sociale, 5*(1–2), 216–229.

Neild, R. (2012). *What next? A memoir.* Privately published.

Neild, R. (2013, December 10). Interview with Robert Neild by R. Gagliardi, D. Gindis and G.M. Hodgson. Cited in Hodgson, G. M., Gagliardi, F., & Gindis, D. (2018).

Newbery, D. (2017). Frank Horace Hahn 1925–2013. *Biographical Memoirs of Fellows of the British Academy, XVI*, 485–525. https://www.britac.ac.uk/sites/default/files/23 Hahn 1837 9_11_17.pdf

Nicholas, S. (1982). Total factor productivity growth and the revision of post-1870 British economic history. *Economic History Review (New Series), 35*(1), 83–98.

Nuti, D. M. (1971). 'Vulgar Economy' in the theory of income distribution. *Science and Society, 35*(1), 27–33.

O'Connor, J. J., & Robertson, E. F. (2014). *David Gawen Champernowne.* http://mathshistory.st-andrews.ac.uk/Biographies/Champernowne.html

Offer, A. (2008). *Charles Feinstein (1932–2004), and British Historical National Accounts.* Discussion papers in Economic and Social History No. 70. University of Oxford.

Pasinetti, L. L. (2007). *Keynes and the Cambridge Keynesians. A 'revolution in economics' to be accomplished.* Cambridge University Press.

Radice, H. (1971). The conference of socialist economics. *Bulletin of the Conference of Socialist Economics, I*(1), 1–5.

Reyes, E. (2014, October 20). Interview: David Howarth. *The Law Society Gazette*. https://www.lawgazette.co.uk/people/interview-david-howarth/5044394.article

Robinson, J. (1974, Autumn). History versus equilibrium. *Thames Papers in Political Economy*, 11p. https://docs.gre.ac.uk/__data/assets/pdf_file/0025/122578/TP_PPE_74_3_compressed.pdf

Robinson, J. (1977). What are the questions? *Journal of Economic Literature*, 15(4), 1318–1339.

Rowthorn, R. (2008). Interview with Bob Rowthorn 13th June 2008. In I. S. Harrison & A. Macfarlane (Eds.), *Encounter with economics*. Interviews filmed by A. Macfarlane and edited by S. Harrison. University of Cambridge. http://sms.cam.ac.uk/collection/1092396

Samuelson, P. A. (1988). The passing of the guard in economics. *Eastern Economic Journal*, 14(4), 319–329.

Samuelson, P. A. (1994). Richard Kahn: His welfare economics and lifetime achievement. *Cambridge Journal of Economics*, 18(1), 55–72.

Sen, A. (1998). *Amartya Sen – Biographical*. https://www.nobelprize.org/prizes/economic-sciences/1998/sen/biographical/

Sen, A. (2021). *Home in the world: A memoir*. Allen Lane and Penguin Random House.

Shenk, T. (2013). *Maurice Dobb: Political economist*. Palgrave Macmillan.

Silberston, A. (2011, January). Robin Matthews. *Royal Economic Society Newsletter*, 152. http://www.res.org.uk/SpringboardWebApp/userfiles/res/file/obituaries/matthews.pdf

Singh, A. (2008). *Better to be rough and relevant than to be precise and irrelevant: Reddaway's legacy to economics*. Working Paper No. 379. Cambridge University Centre for Business Research. www.cbr.cam.ac.uk/fileadmin/user_upload/centre-for-business-research/downloads/working-papers/wp379.pdf

Singh, A. (2009). Better to be rough and relevant than to be precise and irrelevant: Reddaway's legacy to economics. *Cambridge Journal of Economics*, 33(3), 363–379.

Singh, D. (2014). *Strictly personal: Manmohan and Gursharan*. Harper Collins.

Solow, R. M. (2017). Frank Hahn (1925–2013). In R. A. Cord (Ed.), *The Palgrave Companion to Cambridge economics* (pp. 915–927). Palgrave Macmillan.

Stone, R. (1985). James Alan Calvert Brown: An appreciation. *Oxford Bulletin of Economics and Statistics*, 47(3), 191–197.

Streeten, P. P. (1986/1989). Aerial roots. *Banca Nazionale del Lavoro Quarterly Review*, 39(157): 135–159. (Reprinted: [1989]. In J. A. Kregel (Ed.), *Recollections of eminent economists*, Vol. 2. Macmillan, pp. 73–98).

Streeten, P. (1989). Joan Robinson: Utter fearlessness. In G. R. Feiwel (Ed.), *Joan Robinson and modern economic theory* (pp. 861–862). Palgrave Macmillan.

Taylor, L. (1984). Review: Social choice theory and the world in which we live. Review of *Choice, Welfare and Measurement* by Amartya Sen. *Cambridge Journal of Economics*, 8(2), 189–196.

The Telegraph. (2010, July 13). Professor Robin Matthews. *The Telegraph*. https://www.telegraph.co.uk/news/obituaries/finance-obituaries/7888512/Professor-Robin-Matthews.html

The Times. (2015, July 14). Obituary: Ajit Singh. *The Times*.

Varottil, U. (2015). *Corporate law in colonial India: Rise and demise of the managing agency system*. NUS Working Paper No. 2015/016. Department of Law, National University of Singapore. http://law.nus.edu.sg/wps/pdfs/016_2015_Umakanth Varottil.pdf

Whittington, G. (2016). Wit and empirical rigour in pursuing debate. In G. C. Harcourt, The legacy of Ajit Singh (11 September 1940–23 June 2015): Memories and tributes from former pupils, colleagues and friends. *The Economic and Labour Relations Review*, 27(3), 302–303.

Wilson, B. (2017, January 26). Tam Dalyell obituary. *The Guardian*.https://www.theguardian.com/politics/2017/jan/26/tam-dalyell-obituary

Young, M. Y. (2011). John Arundel Barnes (1918–2010). *Cambridge Journal of Anthropology, 29*, 4–12.

CHAPTER 3

Worlds Beyond Cambridge: The Global Web of the 'Neoliberal Thought Collective'

Abstract The battles of Cambridge economics had history, and not just within Cambridge. And there was geography: while Cambridge folklore generally portrays the purge of heterodox economics as an insular intra-Cambridge, even intra-Faculty affair, as the outcome of the organised academic and institutional violence of the local orthodox axis, there were worlds beyond Cambridge exercising deeper and wider influences and networks—academic, political and ideological—that played a crucial role in the transfer of power from the heterodox lineages to their orthodox adversaries. This chapter investigates selected aspects of the processes and strategies that underlay the construction of the powerful global 'neoliberal thought collective', reviewing in turn its core formation, diffusion and operationalisation of its ideational perspectives into wider policy and political domains through a vast network of corporate-funded think tanks; the priceless and well-managed anointing of their ideological doctrine through the global market branding provided by the device of the so-called Nobel Prize in Economic Science through prize committees with affinity and association with the Hayekian Mont Pelerin Society; the subsequent weaponisation of the neoliberal message through its systematic infiltration into the political realm via the agency of political leaderships nurtured by it; and finally, a sketch of how the power of these articulated disciplinary, ideological and political formations came to besiege and displace Cambridge heterodox economics in its own citadel. The chapter complements the internal, insular narrative of the Cambridge purges to provide a more holistic perspective on the process of paradigm and regime change.

The term 'neoliberal thought collective' is part of the book title of Mirowski and Plehwe (2009).

© The Author(s), under exclusive license to Springer Nature Switzerland AG 2022
A. Saith, *Cambridge Economics in the Post-Keynesian Era*, Palgrave Studies in the History of Economic Thought,
https://doi.org/10.1007/978-3-030-93019-6_3

The battles of Cambridge economics had history, and not just within Cambridge. While Cambridge was clearly the locus of the proximate manifestations of the purge of heterodox economics, there were deeper and wider influences and networks—academic, political and ideological—that played a crucial role in the transfer of power from the heterodox lineages to their orthodox adversaries. The preoccupations and focus of the heterodox were essentially Cambridge bound, with extensions into advisory roles mostly in Labour governments where Cambridge Keynesianism was legal tender; and individual forays of a few into the upcoming developing economies. But elsewhere, on the Continent as well as in America, Keynesianism à la Cambridge encountered resistance, in particular to the expanding role that it inevitably prescribed to a state that had to manage the internal and inherent flaws of free-market economies. In the post-war conjuncture, what seemed patently obvious and right to the Keynesians, easily dubbed 'left', was equally questionable and wrong to the rising international intellectual and ideological networks which regarded this as an assault on what they saw as the natural role of the private sector, and on individual liberties which they held to be ethically inviolable; in these battles, the neoclassical schools, whether in their various British Marshallian or Continental Walrasian incarnations, were in an ideological, if not academic, coalition with the politically more fundamentally oriented monetarist clans led by Chicago. The battles were eventually about control over government policy, but their contending positions had deep philosophical and ethical schisms as well: if one side was concerned with outcomes, the focus of the other was on opportunity; if one was motivated by social dimensions, the other concentrated exclusively on individual liberty; if one regarded deep representative democracy as an intrinsically and instrumentally, even if potentially, positive force for the social good, the other side came to view it as a device for bureaucratic and political capture that diminished individual liberty, deemed to be the ultimate criterion of goodness. These were battles of ideas on a grand scale, and though their immediate remit at the time was contained largely within the industrialised capitalist countries, there were profound implications also for what would be regarded as desirable and effective strategies for rapid economic development in the Third World as it rose from centuries of imperialist impositions and extractions. The stakes could not be higher. After a brief commentary on some relevant aspects of pre-battle, and pre-war, conjunctures, this chapter investigates the strategies and processes that underlay the construction of the powerful neoliberal thought collective, reviewing in turn the core formation, diffusion and operationalisation of its ideational perspectives into wider policy and political domains through a vast network of corporate-funded think tanks; the priceless and well-managed anointing of their ideological doctrine through the global market branding provided by the device of the so-called Nobel Prize in Economic Science; and the subsequent weaponisation of the neoliberal message through its systematic infiltration into the political realm via the agency of political leaderships nurtured by it; and finally, a sketch of how the power of these articulated disciplinary, ideological and political formations came to besiege and displace Cambridge heterodox economics in its own citadel. The chapter complements the internal, insular narrative of the Cambridge purges to provide a more holistic perspective on the process of paradigm and regime change.

3.1 Conjunctures

3.1.1 1930s, The Prelude

LSE Versus Cambridge
The London School of Economics figures prominently at strategic points in the story of the demise of heterodox economics in Cambridge. Ever since the inception of the LSE at the turn of the century, closely followed by the establishment of the Economics Tripos in Cambridge in 1903, there was a growing intensity to the natural competition between the two, felt perhaps more immediately at the LSE; this competition was far from perfect, and the rivalry was not always healthy, and indeed often toxic, as was increasingly manifest in the later years with its extreme polarisation between the jostling Cambridge heterodox lineages and the orthodox neoclassicals congregating at the LSE under the banner of Samuelson's third and fourth revolutions. Cambridge exuded complacency within its citadel; LSE expressed covert and overt opposition and antagonism, both in disciplinary and ideological terms, generally in expeditious combination with its allies in the USA in MIT, Harvard or Chicago. LSE was a coveted final destination in the career tracks of orthodox economists; but it also became the staging post for launching the siege of Cambridge heterodox economics; the ultimate prize was being seated in a chair in the lion's den, in the Cambridge Faculty of Economics. Some of 'Uncle' Frank's 'nephews' started their careers doing degrees in Cambridge, later spent time at the LSE and then ended their careers as professors in Cambridge.

The past century of interactions between Cambridge and LSE economics and economists are characterised by ricocheting polarities, suggestive of a double helix. In conventional terms, politically energetic LSE, with the remarkable idealist-activist pair of Sidney and Beatrice Webb, George Bernard Shaw and their Fabian grouping, which regards the university as an agent and site of social transformation, starts off well to the left of ancient Cambridge, with its well-settled liberal Marshallians who, following Marshall, regard the university as a sanctified space for seeking the truth.

But this binary did not hold for LSE economics where Edwin Cannan held the fort; perhaps Dahrendorf (1995) makes too much of the ascribed 'dispute' between the two; Cannan was also called "Marshall's man at the LSE", and little in the exchanges recorded in Marshall's correspondence suggests deep disagreements extending beyond Cannan using the "London phrase, economic theory" in place of the traditional term "general economics" that Marshall was partial to; the terminological 'dispute' causing Marshall, in his words, "to splutter ... puffing, whale like, cold water mingled with a warm breath"; not too serious, then, bearing in mind that Marshall was not inclined to "argue in favour of 'economics' versus 'political economy'". And, if anything, Cannan was most likely Marshall's ally in keeping LSE economics honest and free of political predeterminations in the controlling hands of the Webbs; Marshall also did not like the drift in the LSE economics curriculum towards what would now perhaps be called multidisciplinarity. It has to be recalled that Marshall was trying to distil Cambridge 'economics' of other disciplinary distractions and detours in making the case for the Economics Tripos; in the meanwhile, Seebohm Rowntree had just produced his iconic statistical study providing evidence on the wide incidence and dark depths of squalor, poverty and human degradation in York, standing in for urban Britain at the mature end of the industrial revolution. And, the idealistic Webbs were equally in favour of a proper, scientific approach to policy based on strong economics.

Then came a twist of the double helix. Marshall retired from Cambridge in 1908, with Cannan carrying on at LSE till 1926, a pivotal year in economics, especially in Cambridge. The transformation of the theoretical template of Cambridge economics, from Marshallian to Keynesian, is rooted in the 1920s. Arguably, 1926 was the pivotal year: on the one side, Piero Sraffa, without fanfare, published his iconic, and iconoclastic, piece challenging the foundations of Marshallian economics, a breach significantly widened by Allyn Young then at LSE, with his famous intervention in 1928; on the other, Keynes, in flagrant style, pronounced *The End of Laissez Faire* on other equally powerful grounds that questioned the inherited case for the free market. The central point concerned the role of the state as a corrective and a complement to the market mechanism; economic depression and the problem of effective demand were still around the corner in the future. He argued that "the most important agenda of the State relates not to those activities which private individuals are already fulfilling, but to those functions which fall outside the sphere of the individual, to those decisions which are made by no one if the State does not make them. The important thing for government is not to do things which individuals are doing already, and to do them a little better or a little worse, but to do those things which at present are not done at all" (Keynes, 1926, p. 288); a position that would be anathema to fully paid-up free marketeers.

After Cannan retired in 1926, Jacob Viner was offered the chair by Beveridge, but he possibly used it as leverage in his shift to Chicago, following which the invitation went to Allyn Young, who accepted and arrived at LSE for his fateful short stay. Much earlier, in 1909, he had (in a letter from Stanford University) communicated his great appreciation for Marshall's work by which he had been so influenced; American economics had come to be overly influenced by the Austrian tradition which "had led to a mistaken revolt against the older English political economy". He was "thoroughly convinced that the pendulum is swinging back again; that especially among the younger men there is a strong feeling that an excessive use and development of the marginal utility analysis will not get us very far away from an argument in a circle".[1] His views evolved, and shortly after he arrived at the LSE, he published his foundational 1928 paper with its powerful mutual resonance with Sraffa's 1926 iconoclastic intervention, both in the *Economic Journal*. Clearly, Young had far deeper affinities with traditions of Cambridge economics than with those of the Continent.

Histories are replete with accidental game-changing turns. Susan Howson's (2011) monumental biography of Lionel Robbins has five references to occasions when Robbins was struck by influenza; sturdy Lionel prevailed over the virus each time. Allyn Young was struck but once, and the virus prevailed over him—he died in March 1929 in the space of just a few days. With him also was laid to rest any hypothetical prospect, based on 'what-if' counterfactuals, of LSE economics evolving within a progressive interaction with Cambridge led by Keynes, who held Young in high regard. The LSE chair so vacated fell into the lap of Lionel Robbins, who was in love with Vienna and Austrian economics. He soon had Friedrich Hayek ensconced in the Tooke chair, clearly with the motivation of strengthening the LSE position in its rivalry with Cambridge. 'Robbins against Keynes' is the other dispute highlighted by Ralf Dahrendorf, and it was indeed an intense one, till it dissolved much later when an honestly self-reflective and self-critical Robbins accepted the errors of his earlier ways in relation to Keynes and ways out of the depression. But that was much down the line, and till then Robbins was staunchly a pure neoclassical, having produced his *An Essay on the Nature and Significance of Economic Science* in 1932; Joan Robinson, in her critical review, caustically referred to the unfortunate timing of the book. With the Robbins–Hayek team now in charge, LSE economics swung decisively to the right in theoretical, policy and ideological terms.

LSE and Cambridge crossed paths and positions, as Cambridge entered a radical post-Marshallian, proto-Keynesian era. 1933 provides some significant markers: Joan Robinson's *The Economics of Imperfect Competition*; the deep reorientation of Cambridge economics from the inherited classical to the Keynesian vision then on the anvil of the 'Circus'; and then an open letter from Keynes to Roosevelt. Keynes devised his anti-Depression reflationary scheme in the spring of 1933, and "using cutting-edge technology of the time, promoted his plan in the U.S. in June 1933 via a live transatlantic radio conversation with Walter Lippmann, an eminent American journalist. NBC broadcast the exchange nationally. They agreed on the main policy goals for recovery: cheap money, public works and help for farmers" (Scranton, 2013). Despite some disagreements, Keynes, in an open letter, strongly supported Roosevelt's New Deal, telling him "if you succeed ... we may date the first chapter of a new economic era from your accession to office" (ibid.). It is also the year when

---

[1] Allyn Young to Alfred Marshall, Letter 937, Correspondence, Volume 3, pp. 218–219; dated 3 February 1909, in Whitaker (1996). Young goes on to say: "you ought to know that there is in America a growing appreciation of the fact the *Principles of Economics* represents the highest achievement in economic analysis up to the present, and that it points the way to the most valuable lines for future work, that I have thought it worth while to write this letter".

Friedrich Hayek made his inaugural address at the LSE from his Tooke professorship. And with the launch of Keynes's *General Theory* in 1936, the transition to the new revolutionary theoretical template was in place, laying the basis for three decades of left-oriented Keynesian economics with its powerful hold over economic policy making. LSE was left without any alternative policy response that would address the hot systemic of the day; yet, LSE opposition to Cambridge was well entrenched as Robbins forcefully built a right-oriented school around himself. As Dahrendorf (1995, p. 221) put it in his history of the LSE: "who physically went to Cambridge (in some cases elsewhere) from LSE were more likely to be inclined to left-wing views than those who stayed. However open the LSE department was, Robbins 'could make life rather unhappy' for those who took different views, or so Kaldor remembered; indeed he 'weeded out' people 'who were not ready to echo [his] views'."

After a somewhat wayward interregnum, LSE economics re-established a new identity when, just after the retirement of Lionel Robbins in 1966 (preceded by his resignation in 1961), a group of young turks were recruited simultaneously in 1967 as professors into the department, viz., Terence Gorman, Harry Johnson, Alan Walters and Frank Hahn (from Cambridge)—this was the pivotal point of inflexion when the standard of the American econometrics and mathematical economics revolutions was hoisted high at the LSE. Meanwhile, Cambridge had deepened its entrenchment in left-oriented Keynesian, Sraffian and related traditions, with a rising visible and voluble presence in applied policy-oriented macroeconomics that had little in common, other than well-expressed animosity, with the Walrasian general equilibrium schools of thought that characterised LSE economics.

Cambridge economics had started the century in conservative neoclassical territory, with its young rival LSE (at the level of the school if not of the department) well and disconcertingly to its left; Cambridge shifted steadily to the left until Keynesianism ran into policy sands from the mid-1970s, while LSE reincarnated itself as the aggressive mathematical vanguard of the neoclassical general equilibrium, and monetarist, revolutions—both traditions being flatly opposed by the heterodox left lineages of Cambridge. The twist of the helix now had Cambridge on the left and LSE on the right, having exchanged the positions with which they had started their rivalry. The battle lines for another war were clearly visible, and it is this definitive episode of the decline and demise of the Cambridge heterodox traditions in economics—in the period from the early to mid-1970s (when both Hahn and Matthews returned to chairs in Cambridge) till the mid to late 1980s (when Dasgupta and Newbery were settled in Cambridge professorships)—that is chronicled in this book. The ricocheting relationship between 'Cambridge' and the 'LSE', marked by a competitive doctrinal and ideological, at times visceral, hostility, is spinally embedded in the narrative. In turn, this binary directs attention to the sources of this opposition, and many of these lay in developments in economics in the USA from where the seedlings of the econometrics and mathematical economics revolutions had been imported, transplanted and nurtured within the LSE and other tributary outposts.

Émigré Economists: The Benefactions of Lenin and Hitler
In April 1933 in Vienna, Lionel and Iris Robbins had arranged to have dinner with von Mises; at Hotel Bristol, they ran into Beveridge who was also in the city. Lionel Robbins narrates: "von Mises arrived with an evening paper carrying the shocking news of the first academic dismissals by the Nazis—Bonn, Mannheim, Kantorowicz and others. Was it not possible, he asked, to make some provision in Britain for the relief of such victims, of which the names mentioned were only the beginning of what, he assured us, was obviously to be an extensive persecution. This was one of Beveridge's great moments. ... Slumped in a chair, with his great head characteristically cupped in his fists, thinking aloud, he then and there outlined the basic plan of what became the famous Academic Assistance Council" (Howson, 2011, pp. 236–237). Beveridge becomes the narrator: "As Mises read out the names to our growing indignation, Robbins and I decided that we would take action in the London School of Economics to help scholars in our subjects who should come under Hitler's ban". Affected were those with traces of Jewish ancestry, or with socialist, liberal or pacifist views (ibid., p. 237). On his return, Beveridge got busy with operationalising the scheme, albeit initially on a modest scale, at LSE, but then its scope widened.[2]

Paul Samuelson (1988, p. 319) fulsomely acknowledges the transformational role played by émigré economists in the era of his third and fourth revolutions in economics, viz., mathematical economics and econometrics. Speaking about "the great generation of economists who dominated our science in the 1930–1980 half century", Samuelson lists 23 names. "Some of these named economists have received the Nobel Prize. Most have not. In my judgment every one deserved that award or higher ... most are not American, even the triumphant rise of American economics after 1940 was enormously accelerated by importation of scholars from Hitlerian Europe." Again, in an interview, William Barnett (2004, p. 531) asks him about Harvard in the 1930s: "Hitler (and Lenin) did much for American science. Leontief, Schumpeter, and Haberler brought Harvard to life after a lean period." Barnett (2004, p. 532)

---

[2] It would seem that Beveridge's humanism did not induce camaraderie, let alone loyalty. According to Robert Leeson: "Hayek told Charlotte Cubitt (2006, p. 5) that he and his fellow European émigrés sat in the 'sardonic corner' of the London School of Economics (LSE) Common Room making 'malicious' comments about the competence of their English colleagues. The classically educated Hayek concluded Department of Economics meetings with a call-to-action against the LSE Director: '*Beveridge delendus est*' ('Beveridge should be destroyed'). But, 'it turned out that the LSE economists, and even Lionel Robbins, had not had a classical education. ... I found out that not one of them understood what I was saying. It's a famous phrase, a story from, I believe, Cicero. ... I assumed this to be popular knowledge'" ("Introduction", in Leeson, 2015, p. 13).

adds: "Hitler was responsible for an extraordinary migration of many of Europe's greatest economists to the United States, including Koopmans, Leontief, Schumpeter, Marschak, Haberler, and Kuznets, along with most of the Austrian School of Economics. They in turn helped to attract to this country other major European economists, such as Hurwicz, Debreu, Theil, Bhagwati [*sic*], Coase, and Fischer"; and then asks, "Is America in danger of losing its intellectual comparative advantages for economists to other countries?" Samuelson has a mainstream economist's answer: "I do not discern any trend toward foreign out-competition of U.S. science. Sole reason: our predominant real GDP, and the brain drain *to us* it has induced" (ibid., p. 532, italics in the original).

Hagemann's valuable research on the scale and impact of European émigré economists—based on the earlier record keeping by Blaug and Sturgis (1983) and Frey and Pommerehne (1988)—describes a process of the 'Americanization' of the discipline (Hagemann, 2011). "Whereas the Soviet Union lost 24 of its 36 most outstanding economists and the successor states of the Austro-Hungarian Empire lost 36 of 50, the USA gained a total of 161 through immigration, which accounts for about 30% of those economists born in the USA" (Hagemann, 2011, p. 644). Further, "the substantial contributions made by émigré scholars are even stronger if Russians, Italians and other European economists who moved to the USA during the period of totalitarian regimes were to be included". The list of names is truly spectacular: over a period of about four decades, ten became Presidents of the American Economic Association; and in the twenty years after the AEA established an award of Distinguished Fellow in 1965, "the percentage of émigré scholars selected as Fellows was very high", figuring the names of Marschak, Koopmans, von Mises, Gerschenkron, Georgescu-Roegen, Scitovsky, Morgenstern, Hurwicz, Musgrave, Domar, Hirschman and Rosenstein-Rodan. Using bibliographical data compiled by Hagemann and Krohn on 328 (first- and second-generation) scholars, Hagemann (2011) records that from the German-speaking world, from 1933 when the Nazi government re-established the Civil Service Act which allowed the dismissal of public servants for racial or political reasons, about 3000 scholars were dismissed, 85 per cent for being non-Aryan, and 15 per cent for their political orientation; about 2000 of them emigrated. Within this, up to 1938/1939, 253 economists were dismissed and 221 (first-generation scholars) emigrated. Hagemann reports that after 1945, while 60 per cent of political refugees returned to Germany and Austria, only 4 per cent of all Jewish émigrés did so after the Holocaust (ibid., p. 646 n2). Hagemann points out that the brain-gain by recipient countries did not equal the brain-drain of the source countries of the emigration, in particular due to the public good properties of knowledge which complicated any evaluation of the impact of the intellectual migration (ibid., p. 647). Of the 221 first-generation émigré economists, 131 settled finally in the USA, and thirty-five in the UK (ibid., p. 652).

Émigré economists fleeing Continental Europe, from Russia/the Soviet Union after the Revolution, and from Hitler from the 1930s, made a defining contribution to the subsequent evolution and American domination of the discipline, contributing in major ways to the third and fourth revolutions, à la Samuelson, in the subject, viz., mathematics, and econometrics. In Hagemann's considered assessment:

> The triumphant ascent of American economics after World War II does not only reflect the leading political and economic role of the United States and the pragmatic and technological orientation of Americans, but is also the consequence of a national style of economic research characterized by a high degree of specialization and greater emphasis on technique in applied work. The genesis of highly developed graduate education programmes at research-oriented universities played a decisive role in this process. Harry Johnson (1973, 1977) was the first to suggest that these features of American economics, whereby graduate students gained command of the necessary mathematical and econometric tools, were the decisive reason for its growing significance. With the rise of America's international leadership these features of American economics have established themselves as the decisive characteristics of modern economics, increasingly influencing the development of economics on an international level. The strengthening and extension of the graduate education system at American universities in the first two decades after World War II would hardly have been possible without scientists who had fled the totalitarian dictatorships of Europe. This also holds for economics, where the enormous shift due to emigration from fascist and Stalinist countries contributed significantly to America's predominance. (Hagemann, 2011, p. 644)

This accords with Samuelson's personal assessment. The doctoral advisors for the PhDs of Samuelson, Solow and Friedman happened to be Joseph Schumpeter, Wassily Leontief and Simon Kuznets.

Keith Tribe (2001), in his review of Hagemann and Krohn (1999), points out that "the teaching of economics at the LSE was already, by the later 1920s, heavily stamped by Austrian, Swedish and American work; other major centres, especially Oxford, proved relatively open to an influx of Continental academics. The establishment of the University in Exile (later the Graduate School) as the New School for Social Research in New York provided a custom-built home for refugees" (supporting this was the extensive involvement of the Rockefeller Foundation); "by the 1930s, a distinctively neoclassical American economics was emerging, but the manner in which this favoured a more formal or statistical approach made this 'national' style entirely accessible for younger overseas scholars—this was, therefore one of the ways in which an American national style became an international style" (Tribe, 2001, p. F742). The age cohort of the émigré economists mattered: "the younger generation ... born after 1918, assimilated the style and substance of the economic sciences in the countries to which they emigrated, in many cases bringing with them a more advanced training in mathematics and statistics than was common among young economists in Britain and the United States at that time" (ibid., p. F743).

Hagemann's meticulous research and compilations lead him to a firm conclusion. "On the whole, European totalitarian regimes during the inter-war period made a major contribution to the rapid reversal of Europe's and America's roles in economics as well as in the sciences. After World War II economics, like most other fields, has become a global area of research with English as the lingua franca, very different from what it had been during the 1920s and 1930s. Whereas the Keynesian revolution originated in Great Britain, most later developments such as the 'monetarist counterrevolution' were generated in the USA. The work of the Cowles Commission in the critical period 1943 to 1948 reflects the turning point very well.[3] It also reveals the substantial contributions of European émigrés to the process of the 'Americanization' of economics. This development was enhanced by the Rockefeller Foundation, as Hesse has recently documented for Germany (Hesse (2010) as cited in Hagemann, 2011). In the period between 1945 and 1970 the Rockefeller Foundation financed longer research visits to the USA of 40 economists who all were, or became, university professors. Very often they were hosted at Ivy League universities by former émigrés, who thereby contributed to an international convergence process of economics" (Hagemann, 2011, p. 667); thus, they "transferred modern developments in economics to Europe. Modern economic ideas thereby took the opposite route across the Atlantic than the European émigrés had taken before" (ibid., p. 662).

The remarkable phenomenon of the influx from Europe into America of a vast cohort of highly talented European émigrés was a package with several facets. For one, the sheer numbers, especially when concentrated into a relatively short period of time, greatly amplified its impact on the receiving body.[4] Second, the émigrés were not just individuals seeking a place of refuge under the radar;

---

[3] "The work of the Cowles Commission at Chicago since 1943 was of decisive importance for the mathematisation of economics and the triumphant advance of econometrics after World War II. This international process appeared to many observers as the 'Americanization' of economics, but a closer look quickly reveals that many European-born economists played a substantial role in the econometric revolution" (Hagemann, 2011, pp. 661–662). "The high years of econometrics—that is, the systematic application of mathematical and statistical methods to the study of economic relationships—can be associated with Marschak's tenure as research director at the Cowles Commission, involving a strong Continental European influence. It was during this period that Koopmans (1947) made his famous attack 'Measurement without Theory' on the empirical methods used by Mitchell, Burns, et al. in business cycle research at the National Bureau of Economic Research" (ibid., pp. 663–664). "The contribution to econometrics was by no means the only important one made by émigré economists. Probably the most influential single work was von Neumann and Morgenstern's *Theory of Games and Economic Behavior* (1944), which extended the use of mathematics in economic theory significantly and created the new area of game theory" (ibid., pp. 662–663). Vincent Barnett's (2008) study of the work of three famous émigré economists, Kuznets, Marschak and Leontief, confirms that "in the early post-Soviet period, there was no insurmountable methodological chasm between Russian and Western traditions" and that these cohorts thus made significant contributions to the development of 'mainstream Western economics' in both Europe and America.

[4] Moser et al. (2014), using data on patents, provide parallel evidence and analysis of the scale and impact of the emigration of Jewish émigré scientists from Nazi Germany and their revolutionising impact on the scale and process of innovations in their fields.

rather, they were extremely well qualified, and came in already formed chains and networks with past well-evolved histories of mutual interaction, of cooperation and contestation; this again enhanced their collective empowerment. Third, for a significant strand, the traumatic experience of escape and expulsion, vastly intensified by knowledge of the tragic fate of the millions of the Jewish people who could not flee, could not but have generated a hostility towards a powerful state machine, and made, or confirmed them in their support of, the idea of liberty and freedom, immediately associated by economists, as led then by Hayek & Co, with a free-market economy. Fourth, their inherited intellectual and disciplinary traditions tended to regard economics as a science free of value judgements, and this too connected well with the economics, and especially the politics, of the host country, particularly at that time. In this regard, Hagemann (2011, p. 663) borrows a telling snippet concerning Jacob Marschak, as reported by Craver and Leijonhufvud (1987, pp. 181–182): "[For] the immigrants who had lived through the interwar period in Europe—and some, like Marschak, had fled first Lenin and then Hitler—this hope of building a wertfrei social science, immune to propaganda of every kind, gave motivating force to the econometric movement. One of us (A.L.) remembers standing with Jacob Marschak on the fringes of a UCLA anti-Vietnam demonstration, watching as the police tried none-too-gently to break it up. 'I, too, feel like them that this war is terrible', said Jascha, 'but you know, I still think it is important that we strive always to keep value judgments separate from our work'. We might not be able fully to achieve it, he added, but Wertfreiheit remains an ideal."[5]

Harald Hagemann offers nuanced qualifying insights on these aspects, pointing to the positive role of the 'double education' of the émigré cohorts, and also suggests a possible contrast in this regard between groups that emigrated to America compared to those with Britain as their destination. He takes the case of Hans Singer's intellectual baggage.

> Singer's 'two heroes', Schumpeter (Bonn) and Keynes (Cambridge), point out in an illuminating way the advantages of a double education which made several of the emigres, particularly in the age group between 1910 and 1918 (Austria), to Emigrationsgewinner (emigration profiteers), despite all the hardships caused by expulsion and emigration. This aspect of emigration recently has been highlighted by Richard Musgrave (1996, 1997, as cited in Hagemann, 2011) who was instrumental in the development of modern public finance, in which the best elements

---

[5] At a more general level, Roy Weintraub (2017, p. 571) asks whether mathematics provided safety by camouflaging politics in the McCarthy era. "Historians of the social sciences and historians of economics have come to agree that, in the United States, the 1940s transformation of economics from political economy to economic science was associated with economists' engagements with other disciplines—e.g., mathematics, statistics, operations research, physics, engineering, cybernetics—during and immediately after World War II. More controversially, some historians have also argued that the transformation was accelerated by economists' desires to be safe, to seek the protective coloration of mathematics and statistics, during the McCarthy period. This paper argues that that particular claim (1) is generally accepted, but (2) is unsupported by good evidence, and (3) what evidence there is suggests that the claim is false."

of the German or Continental European tradition of Finanzwissenschaft, having a broader perspective including institutional, historical, sociological and legal aspects, were merged with the Anglo-Saxon tradition of public finance, which had developed as part of pure economics and shared the rigour of its analysis. Singer had the main ideas of Schumpeter's Theory of Economic Development in his emigration baggage, including the emphasis on technological innovation, the role of the entrepreneur, and the importance of credit for financing innovational activities, i.e. a deeper understanding for the necessity of breaking up the traditional circular flow. The high concentration of development economists born between 1910 and 1917 (Arndt, Baran, Hirschman, Hoselitz, Kafka, Singer, Streeten et al.) does not only show that they were benefiting from a double education in economics and a mutual insemination at a time when different national traditions were still important. They themselves were for a greater part instrumental in the internationalisation process of the discipline. In the discussion of the 'Americanisation' of economics in the post-1945 period it is often overlooked that a great part of 'the' American economists were for a greater part colleagues who came from Hitlerian or Stalinist Europe. In interviews with emigrated economists the author of the present paper was often told (by members of the age group born between 1890 and 1910) how deeply they had been influenced by national traditions before, and that emigration had made them feel to become 'citizens of the world' or, in the words of Paul Streeten (1986), adopting 'aerial roots'. It is no accident that a greater number of the younger èmigrè economists, particularly of those who went to the U.K., developed a deep concern for the problems of the developing world and engaged themselves professionally in the improvement of living standards in 'backward areas'". (Hagemann, 2007, pp. 21–22, and sources cited therein)

A fine exemplar of this 'double-education' in the radical tradition was Kurt Martin/Mandelbaum, associated with the Marxist 'Frankfurt School', who came across to Britain to a position during the war in the Oxford Institute of Economics & Statistics, published his seminal *The Industrialisation of Backward Areas* in 1945, then moved in 1950 to Manchester where he had W. Arthur Lewis as a colleague, and after retirement relocated for 17 years to the Institute of Social Studies in The Hague; Hans Singer (1979) refers to Kurt Martin as a root of the core ideas of Arthur Lewis's 'unlimited supplies of labour' thesis. Kurt sourced the study of economic development in classical political economy and Marx (Martin, 1991a, 1991b); he also had an impact in shaping the teaching of development studies in UK (Martin & Knapp, 1967).

This distinction between the American and the British cohorts, hypothetical as it must be given the volatility and the role of chance and accident, as against planned self-selection, in the process of these emigrations especially at the individual level, nevertheless remains important to consider, and arguably carries some explanatory weight in the subsequent ideological separations between the two hosting environments; all generalisations would need qualifications: while there were Singer, Mandelbaum/Martin and Streeten on the one side, there were Hisrchman, Baran and Gerschenkron on the other; and the presence of the neoliberal anti-state and anti-socialist was well represented in the political sphere on both sides, especially in the back rooms of American and British politicians.

3.1.2   1940s, The Cascade

The 1940s was like a cascade even leaving out the actual prosecution of the war itself. Keynes published his *How to Pay for the War* in 1940; the game-changing Beveridge Report on Social Insurance and Allied Services appeared in November 1942 proposing social protection to all from "the cradle to the grave"; James Meade and Richard Stone were engaged in generating the national accounts underwriting the work; 1944 saw the publication of Hayek's *The Road to Serfdom* while LSE was relocated in Cambridge and Hayek was given a study at King's College organised by Keynes. The same year, two other publications appeared, each of which would have given Hayek a serious fright: the first was the appearance of Beveridge's *Full Employment in a Free Society*; and the other, in a land too distant to be on Hayek's intellectual horizon, was the appearance of *The Bombay Plan* which laid out the template of a massive industrialisation campaign for an independent India under the tutelage of a socialistically oriented post-colonial nationalist state. Two further events of major significance occurred that year: the formation of the Bretton Woods institutions, the IMF and the World Bank, where Keynes was heavily involved; and the Butler Education Act in the UK which made secondary education compulsory, universal and free, a major step in the direction of the constitution of a welfare state. In Cambridge, 1945 saw the launching of the Department of Applied Economics (DAE), mooted in 1939 but held over till the Second World War ended with the USA dropping two atomic bombs on Japan; despite victory in the war, Churchill lost the election and a Labour government was installed in the UK hastening the development of the welfare state; and George Orwell published his *Animal Farm*. Fatefully for Cambridge, and economics, 1946 saw the death of Keynes; the enactment of the National Insurance Act; the Yalta conference took place, kick-starting the Cold War; and the Foundation for Economic Education (FEE), which would become a significant player in Team Hayek, was started in the USA. 1947 was another big year: Paul Samuelson published his *Foundations of Economic Analysis*, Lorie Tarshis brought out the first major Keynesian macroeconomics textbook, *Elements of Economics*; William Volker, the retiring American philanthropist-industrialist, died and his nephew Harold Luhnow takes over and reorients the Volker Fund (launched In 1932), using it now for supporting libertarian and conservative movements; significantly, Hayek starts the Mont Pelerin Society (MPS) in Switzerland, with the participation of a large American contingent, including several Chicago economists and FEE officials, funded by Luhnow. And the year sees the start of the McCarthy decade in the USA. The following year, 1948, Samuelson produces the first edition of his *Economics*, with a major impact on the teaching of economics; the Marshall Plan, 1948–1951, is launched in Europe; and Bevan is instrumental in the creation of the National

Health Service in the UK. Stretching the decade a bit, 1950 sees Hayek, following his divorce, giving up his Tooke Professorship in Economics and Statistics at the LSE and becoming Professor of Social and Moral Science at the Committee on Social Thought in the University of Chicago, the high salary he needed again being funded by the Volker Fund under Luhnow. And finally, 1955 sees the launching of what would become an extremely influential right-wing British think tank, the Institute of Economic Affairs pioneered by Antony Fisher, with the support of the American-Chicago institutional and financial 'philanthropic' network; this period also sees the start of the Chicago economics training programme in Chile, initiated by Theodore Schultz and funded by the State Department, thus laying the institutional foundations of the aid connection that produced Friedman's Chicago Boys who gained notoriety in the Pinochet regime. Meanwhile, Cambridge, UK, saw senior staff supporting newly independent India, to develop its socialistically oriented Nehru–Mahalanobis economic plans and planners; Austin Robinson and Richard Kahn become professors in Cambridge in 1950 and 1951 respectively; and in 1956, Joan Robinson published her *Accumulation of Capital*; it was the year also of the Anglo-French neo-imperialist misadventure in the Suez Crisis.

3.1.3 Keynesianism: Divergent Receptions

The conjuncture of the late 1940s is also the cusp, the short and sharp period of inflexion. In Samuelson's depiction of the four revolutions, it marks the switch point denoting the end of the second revolution, viz., of Keynes and effective demand, into the beginning of the third, of the mathematisation of economics, running alongside the fourth revolution in the form of econometrification in the discipline. Paradoxically, while Samuelson's book carried a mathematical treatment of Keynes for the first time in the USA, the first real Keynesian textbook of Tarshis is killed off by American proto-neoliberal opposition. This opposition is home-grown from the ideological opposition from American industrialists and shopkeepers, but crucially also gains its muscularity from the right-wing shift effected by the arrival and assimilation of liberal émigré economists from Russia and Central Europe. A second powerful force that censors and disciplines Keynesianism is the decade of McCarthyism, 1947–1957, the storm rising as the spectre of communism, a fear developed by the state itself, mutating into the Frankenstein of McCarthy's agenda. However, the ebb and flow of Keynesianism is not identical in the UK and the USA. In sharp contrast to the developments in the USA, in the UK Keynesianism actually enters its period of most powerful influence both on economics as a discipline as well as on economic policy; the quarter century from the end of the war is perhaps the crowning period of the Keynesian gospel, though its prophet had fallen in 1946, just as his ideas were spreading their wings into full flight. However, a wide contrast is discernible in the post-war welcome, as opposed to hostility, to Keynesian ideas and policies when considering the UK and the USA.

Post-war Affinity in the UK

The affinity to Keynesianism in the UK in the post-war decades was almost a natural phenomenon. Britain had been physically ravaged by the war; and destroyed infrastructure was to be rebuilt both as a precondition, but also as a mechanism, of economic revival. The burden of war was heavy; there was an immediate need to reabsorb demobbed soldiers on a massive scale; the human costs had been horrendous and between the First and Second World Wars, hardly a family had been left untouched by death or debilitating injury. On the other side, the experience of war, multiplied by victory at its end, had its social and political dimensions. There was an immediate post-war honeymoon period marked by a halo of 'one country', and long-standing and deeply embedded class and status distinctions and related social norms were temporarily shaken and undermined; soldiers and workers had won the war and paid for it with deprivation and death, and post-war Britain was made different by this recognition. Victory, and government performance enabling it, had changed attitudes: as Benn (2000) put it, "if you can plan for war, why can't you plan for peace", and if the government could mobilise vast resources to throw into the war, it could do the same to revive the economy and underwrite full employment, not as soldiers but as workers and citizens. A new social contract and a productive welfare state were as imperative as they were inevitable, and Keynesianism was at the heart of this economic strategy. That all this was well comprehended by the population, and above all the electorate, became patently obvious when the war-winning Churchill was thanked and voted out, and Labour, promising to fight the new economic war in peace, was ushered in 1945.

In a BBC radio broadcast in 1945, no less a person than the eminent historian A. J. P. Taylor, no socialist or Marxist, had said: "Nobody in Europe believes in the American way of life, that is, private enterprise, or rather, those who believe it are a defeated party which seems to have no more future than the Jacobites in England after 1688" (quoted in Appelbaum, 2019, p. 28); Appelbaum adds that "in the early years after World War II, it was also hard to find Americans who believed in that version of the American way of life". Hastened by the Depression, his *General Theory*, and the war, Keynes's prediction of "the end of laissez faire", made in the 1920s, had emerged as a reality in UK and extensive parts of Europe.

Post-New Deal Hostility in the USA

But that was precisely what set the alarm bells ringing for the libertarians in America. A diametrically contrasting prediction was made in 1951 by Friedman: Western countries would soon turn away from collectivism and embrace liberalism with its core hallmarks of free markets and minimal government. "The stage is set for the growth of a new current of opinion to replace the old, to provide the philosophy that will guide the legislators of the next generation. ... Ideas have little chance of making much headway against a strong tide; their opportunity comes when the tide has ceased running strong but has not yet turned. This is, if I am right, such a time" (quoted in Appelbaum, 2019, p. 29).

Several factors go towards explaining this hiatus between the UK and the USA trajectories, and in a popular account, Doris Goodwin (2001) provides an overview of the domestic American experience and impact of the war. She dramatically calls the American response to the war "the most extraordinary mobilization of an idle economy in the history of the world. During the war 17 million new civilian jobs were created, industrial productivity increased by 96 percent, and corporate profits after taxes doubled. The government expenditures helped bring about the business recovery that had eluded the New Deal. War needs directly consumed over one-third of the output of industry, but the expanded productivity ensured a remarkable supply of consumer goods to the people as well. America was the only country that saw an expansion of consumer goods despite wartime rationing. By 1944, as a result of wage increases and overtime pay, real weekly wages before taxes in manufacturing were 50 percent higher than in 1939. The war also created entire new technologies, industries, and associated human skills. The war brought full employment and a fairer distribution of income. Blacks and women entered the workforce for the first time. Wages increased; so did savings. The war brought the consolidation of union strength and far-reaching changes in agricultural life. Housing conditions were better than they had been before. In addition, because the mobilization included the ideological argument that the war was being fought for the interests of common men and women, social solidarity extended far beyond the foxholes. Public opinion held that the veterans should not return jobless to a country without opportunity and education. That led to the GI Bill, which helped lay the foundation for the remarkable postwar expansion that followed. The war also made us more of a middle-class society than we had been before. It is no exaggeration to say that America won the war abroad and the peace at home at the same time. No doubt the historical conditions of America's economic surge during World War II were singular."

Several factors weakened the support for the New Dealers, and then turned the tide against them. America too had fought and won, like Britain, but it suffered no domestic destruction of its productive capacity or infrastructure. Loss of life, military and civilian, was less even in absolute terms for the USA, and as a proportion of the population it was one-third that for the UK. As such it was far more easily absorbed. The economy grew dramatically in the war years, and this greatly facilitated the re-absorption of demobbed soldiers into the economy, especially through the GI Bill; Samuelson rushed to write his textbook to supply, or absorb the demand, of this booming market. The position of corporations was much strengthened in the economic expansion of the war years, and a new consensus was being manufactured to push back the New Deal type agenda, to roll back social claims and to claw back profits; any expansion of the role of the state was vilified; one bogey raised was the spectre of runaway inflation, as in Germany; another was the spectre of the communist ogre, constructed by McCarthyism and deployed as its blunt bludgeoning instrument. Toxic or not, the environment created a highly fertile political ethos for the diffusion and absorption of the Hayek–Friedman, or Chicago–Mont Pelerin, libertarian agenda.

Thus, America and Britain went in somewhat different directions, with the corporations as the key drivers in the former and state-led expenditures and investments in the latter. For Britain, the period of 1950–1972, dubbed 'the golden age' of sustained growth alongside low inflation and low unemployment rates, was to last till the OPEC oil-price hikes of 1973, and then 1979, pulled the rug from under the social contract that defined the welfare state. The ensuing inflation, as stagflation, revived the old debates about the limits of Keynesianism, the Kaleckian depictions of inflation as a form of class conflict, and the role of trade unions.[6]

Within a few short years James Callaghan was out, defeated by Margaret Thatcher who lost no time in attacking the miners. Almost in step, Ronald Reagan in America launched an assault on the air traffic controllers' strike. Both leaders had been to the same school and sat at the feet of the same gurus; Keynesianism went out, and monetarism strode in. But behind these 'successes' of neoliberalism lay a generation of sustained multi-level strategic advocacy efforts of an extensive international organisational network of social sector, academic and media organisations and think tanks whose activities were underwritten by corporations and philanthropists straddling the two continents.

3.2 Spreading the Word: Messiahs, Messages, Methods

3.2.1 Ideas and Ideologies: Manufacturers and Retailers

Messiahs of all creeds believe in the power of their word and message, but successful mass conversions depend on the efficacy of their delivery systems, the bands of apostles to purvey the scriptures with their promises and

---

[6] At the Labour Party Conference, James Callaghan, then prime minister, sounded a warning which was quoted with relish by Milton Friedman in his 'Nobel' Prize Lecture in 1976: "We used to think that you could just spend your way out of a recession and increase employment by cutting taxes and boosting Government spending. I tell you, in all candour, that that option no longer exists, and that insofar as it ever did exist, it only worked by injecting a bigger dose of inflation into the economy followed by higher levels of unemployment as the next step. This is the history of the past 20 years" (Friedman, 1976). Friedman's quotation is accurate, but was Callaghan's statement? Glyn et al. (1988, p. 107, Table 6) provide data on comparative economic performance for the 1952–1973 period and it is interesting to contrast the fortunes of rueful Callaghan's UK, and the gleeful Friedman's USA: average unemployment ranged between 4.5 and 5.0 per cent for the USA, and 2.5–3.2 per cent for UK; consumer prices rose at 2.7 per cent for the US and 4.6 per cent for the UK, slightly higher but hardly runaway inflation, especially when considering that some of the impact of the OPEC oil-price hike would have kicked in for 1973, the end year, with UK exposure greater that than of the USA; real GDP grew at 2.2 per cent for the USA and at 2.5 per cent for UK. This pattern questions Callaghan's sweeping judgement on "the history of the past twenty years"; more likely it should have been the past two years; and perhaps Friedman might have paid closer attention to the statistics than to the loose statement flung out by Callaghan at a party political meeting where he was under severe pressure to justify a change of course.

commandments; persuading and proselytising the masses is a multi-stakeholder exercise. Systems and styles vary. Keynes, the great persuader, had first to produce and demonstrate the power of his message, which enabled him to diffuse it to those in authority and power, in academe and in the corridors of politicians and policy makers in government. Some messiahs, like Hayek, concentrated their efforts in educating the base of the pyramid, changing the modes of thinking of the masses and opinion makers, not starting with policy makers and politicians who would be converted, in due course, by the sea change in popular opinion initiated from the base (though, not wanting to leave it to chance, Hayek frequently offered advice, in public or in private, to the Thatcher government and indeed directly to Thatcher herself). Others, like Friedman with his own monetarist interpretation of the free-market gospel, preferred to cut to the chase, to go straight for the policy jugular, working the message directly through the constituencies of power and politics. In contrast, Samuelson chose to espouse his revolutionary message through the medium of his new testament, famously preferring to write textbooks rather than treaties (though this did not stand in the way of serving as a presidential economic adviser). But some others, even following the same faith, did not believe in the fixity of commandments written in stone or the rigidity of textbooks. Thus, Hahn, of the same tribe as Samuelson, and who had styled himself as John the Baptist spreading the general-equilibrium-with-money gospel of Samuelson's mathematical neoclassical revolution, had his own idiosyncratic means for reaching the shared ends; he preferred a more Socratic approach to put his flock through its paces exploring zones of ambiguities and through it, bringing them home to a stronger faith.[7] But all free-market messiahs pulled in the same libertarian direction, each with their set of product-differentiating qualifications which set the boundaries of their tribe's identity, with well-aired doctrinal differences camouflaging the naked reality of a shared god. At the core was the strategic primacy they all placed on the force of ideas; but ideas needed to initiate and inspire movements which had then to translate into political action. While Keynesianism and the welfare state ideology associated with it had risen into dominance in the UK in the 1950s and 1960s, across the Channel on the Continent, the foundations of neoliberal ideology were being laid by Hayek, with powerful support from across the Atlantic from the Friedman-Stigler-Director Chicago libertarians backed by the financial power of big corporate

---

[7] "In Cambridge I am one of the strongest advocates of having, for instance, two principles courses taught by people of different persuasions. The main thing I want to avoid is textbook-style economics. That makes people believe that they are doing 'science'. I think of economic theory as a way of organizing our minds, so that we do not speak of things that are incoherent. I do not mean that we are stating the 'truth'" (Hahn, 1989, p. 904). "The fact is ... that the textbooks in America are mainly written as 'science' and stop recognition of the ambiguities of the subject. The macro is worse, but even the micro theory is pretty awful." And then, in rare 'love' moment of his 'love-hate' relationship with Joan Robinson: "If one takes what Joan said just to stop all this nonsense, she would deserve our applause" (Hahn, 1989, p. 898).

donors and the organisational drive of ideological entrepreneurs with their influence stretching into government circles. The societal imaginaries and economic policy frameworks of the two tracks were entirely different and, in head and heart, neither group would have countenanced much of the other.

Speaking for the Chicago school in 1995, a satisfied Milton Friedman observed: "I think the libertarian movement is doing fine. ... It takes many kinds of people to make a movement. And one of the most important things are publications. In any activity you have manufacturers, wholesalers, and retailers; and all three are essential and necessary. There are only a relatively small number of manufacturers of ideas. But there can be a very large number of wholesalers and retailers" (Doherty, 1995).

The other big manufacturer of ideas was Paul Samuelson, no less satisfied with the progress of his approach which focussed on the writing of textbooks, purveying mathematical neoclassical economics built around general equilibrium, a notion that generally had attracted the enthusiasm neither of Friedman nor of Hayek in Chicago, not to mention the Keynesians in the old Cambridge. There were stresses in the ideational frames of Chicago and MIT. As Friedman put it: "The fundamental difference between Chicago at that time and let's say Harvard, was that at Chicago economics was serious subject to be used in discussing real problems, and you could get some knowledge and some answers from it. For Harvard, economics was an intellectual discipline on a par with mathematics, which was fascinating to explore, but you mustn't draw any conclusions from it. It wasn't going to enable you to solve any problems, and I think that's always been a fundamental difference between Chicago and other places. MIT more recently has been a better exemplar than Harvard" (Friedman in Hammond, 1988, p. 17). And both schools had their apostles and taught and proselytised on a grand scale through their teaching and especially the research degree programmes which reproduced the doctrine and discipline through the development of interconnected and mutually supporting networks of scholars all on the same page, or model.[8]

---

[8] The ongoing Mathematics Genealogy Project of the North Dakota State University attempts to create a data base of all mathematicians, with 'mathematics' understood in a very inclusive sense. In so doing, it lists the name of the supervisors/advisors of the mathematician, as well as the person's own students, and then also the number and names of 'descendants' of the mathematician, defined as "all mathematicians reachable by following links from an advisor to a student, regardless of whether the advisor is Advisor 1 or Advisor 2, as descendants. We're doing this by creating an adjacency matrix for the directed genealogy graph and then performing a breadth first search from each person until no new nodes are reached, which eliminates the problem of double counting." https://www.genealogy.math.ndsu.nodak.edu/id.php?id=137085

A quick exercise yields some indicative findings: Paul Samuelson had 24 direct students and 277 descendants; Bob Solow: 73, 1406; Milton Friedman: 12, 318; Kenneth Arrow: 41, 984; Robert Lucas: 27, 215; Frank Hahn: 5, 173; Terence Gorman: 4, 471; Lionel Robbins: 7, 532; Nicholas Kaldor: 2, 176; Allyn Young 5, 1317. Most of the Cambridge, UK, economists of the era are not visible probably because they do not qualify on the definitions used, or simply for lack of information. The quick check tends to confirm the massive network of the US economists which dwarfs that of the UK in terms of absolute scale. The MGP is a live, regularly updated project.

Chicago, of the time, did hands-on policy in the real world as was; MIT did theory and models of the imaginary world of general equilibrium. But in terms of ideology, the publicly aired spats between them notwithstanding, they pulled in the same ideological direction: they were both free marketeers in heart and head; they were the unidentical twins, the yin and the yang of the free-markets paradigm that underwrote the rising neoliberal order in economics and politics and national and global levels; of course, with some significant qualifications for product differentiation. If Samuelson and Co. wrote difficult mathematical textbooks and articles, and managed the gate-keeping into the profession to keep all youngsters thinking and pointing in the same direction, Friedman extended the brief with writing for the lay public to directly influence the orientation of public discourse, in the prescribed Hayekian style à la *The Road to Serfdom*. In this, Hayek and Friedman were alike with Keynes's penchant for public policy engagement with intelligent lay opinion which could not be reached or influenced by erudite articles in academic journals. As Austin Robinson (1978) put it: "If you have something in economics that you think it is extraordinarily important to persuade the rest of the world about, do you do it by writing an article which everybody is going read and pass over in the *Economic Journal*? Do you leave the people concerned to see how they might conceivably modify their current models of thinking? Or do you go bald-headed at them and try to emphasise the differences? I believe Keynes was right to emphasise the differences rather than the minor progressions."

Hayek was the most explicit in strategising the role and power of ideas, perhaps best expressed by a practicing lieutenant of his movement, Ralph Harris: "The whole of the direction of policy in the end depended upon a battle of ideas in a stratospheric bank of high intellectuals, refining their concepts and engaging in argument, and the fallout of all that is among the voters and the politicians and journalists who will be guided by the outcome. He argued that the great strength of the socialists is that they had the courage to be idealistic, to have a theory, to have a project and a vision, and to go on working towards that, through thick and thin, and not to deviate, whereas the non-socialists, Conservatives and so on, were pragmatic people who were always involve in bits of compromise and what was practical and how to accommodate the existing opinion. Ignore existing opinion, Hayek said, because in the long run it's ideas" (ibid., p. 11). But fresh new ideas ran into rigid old habits of thought, hence his exhortation: "Don't look for immediate successes, but keep on driving towards this vision of a free society, of individual responsibility, self-help as a foundation of an individual fulfilment, and then of wealth creation, innovation, investment, and all the great things that follow from it. ... So this notion [was] that we were the high command, the military terms of high command and high strategy" (Harris, 2000, p. 11). Blundell (1990) another Hayekian disciple had employed the same idiom referring to the "waging the war of ideas, there are no shortcuts".

But like Keynes, Hayek and Friedman also recognised the stickiness of old ideas and the lengthy time lags in the acceptance of new ones. Keynes cautioned: "the ideas which civil servants and politicians and even agitators apply to current events are not likely to be the newest. But, soon or late, it is ideas, not vested interests, which are dangerous for good or evil" (quoted in Laidler, 1976, p. 485). In remarkably similar vein, Hayek, in his Inaugural Lecture at the LSE in 1933, warned: "The views at present held by the public can clearly be traced to the economists of a generation or so ago. So that the fact is, not that the teaching of the economist has no influence at all; on the contrary, it may be very powerful. But it takes a long time to make its influence felt, so that, if there is change, the new ideas tend to be swamped by the domination of ideas which, in fact, have become obsolete" (quoted in: Birner, 2009). Both recognised the necessity to wait for enabling conjunctures and trigger points which would usher in the new vision; for this to happen, and till then, the imperative was to diffuse, to persuade, to prepare and to intervene in academic and public domains arguing and pushing their corner. The neoclassical and neoliberal groups found these turning points in the 1970s which threw up the circumstances, as well as the political leaders, that could force the change.

While there would be considerable agreement about the grammar of the process of change, there was virtually none with regard to the substantive content of the programmes. Keynesianism as practised in Cambridge, UK, stood far apart from Chicago monetarism, or MIT general equilibriumism; there was scarcely any meeting ground in the policy domain. If one was involved in setting up a welfare state, the other was set upon pulling it down. Hayek and Friedman would have found no common grounds at all in Keynes's pronouncement on the limitations of the free market and the necessary agenda of the State in his *The End of Laissez Faire*—and that even before the issue of Keynesian macroeconomics was brought into the frame. Hayekians and Neoclassicals would find the Keynesian pronouncements anathema: if some activities were not being done by individuals, it was because they had been deemed by them to be not worth doing; as and when it came to be felt that they were indeed worth doing, a new market—for a good or a service—would be induced and these things would start getting done. If the State jumped in, it would not only do them worse for reasons of inherent weakness—lack of information, regulatory capture and so on—but would also crowd out individual effort and private entrepreneurship. The gospels were dramatically different in their essential intent and purpose.

Even prior to the formation of the MPS, but strongly after, a vast network of think tanks and ideological organisations had evolved, mostly centred around the core formed by the Volker Fund, Foundation for Economic Education and a few others; these were the unceasing engines for the generation of intellectual inputs into the libertarian cause and the diffusion of its philosophy into the public domain. This Hayekian long-term campaign sought to clear the ground of all roots and remnants of 'collectivism' and then to sow the seeds and nurture the growth of his libertarian movement, with the chain of 'persuasion' eventually entering the national policy domain. Friedman was a master of this craft, and the case of, or rather, his case against the draft illustrates this in full measure. Appelbaum (2019, p. 29) provides relevant details of the speech delivered by Friedman, "the star attraction at a summer camp for young economics professors staged by the William Volker Fund, where he launched an assault on 'fourteen misguided public policies, including national parks, the postal service, and public housing', arguing that through such interventions, the government was 'interfering with the freedom of men to shape their lives'. Friedman made a frontal assault on the idea of the draft, likening it to slave, or forced labour that built the Pharaoh's pyramids and argued the case for a military job be become like any other, entered into by any young person voluntarily at a rate of remuneration that the person was willing to accept." This powerful attack was directly addressed to the younger generation, making the case for "positive freedoms to" as denoted by Isiah Berlin.

That speech, and some others, formed gist and grist of his famous 'popular' book, *Capitalism and Freedom*, processed by his wife Rose and published in 1962. The book made a massive impact, augmented no doubt by the widening contours of the catchment area, the target audience, that had been developed by the prior efforts of the network of think tanks. "Ronald Reagan numbered amongst its fans". The royalties paid for the Friedmans' summer house, named 'Capitaf', drew the attention of Barry Goldwater who endorsed the book and boosted its sales. Friedman went on to become an advisor to the Goldwater campaign, including lectures such as 'The Goldwater View of Economics' (for the *New York Times Magazine*) (Appelbaum, 2019, pp. 29–30). The argument against the draft was won, and an unquestioned and seemingly unquestionable policy that had long been part of the furniture went up in smoke, greatly enhancing Friedman's reputation as a vanguard fighter for individual liberty and the free market.

It is significant that the abrogation of the draft came in a period where the Red Scare and the Cold War were shifting frontstage on the national and international scene. As part of this larger-than-life characterisation of the spectre of communism, USA, under Eisenhower, was increasingly intervening covertly or openly militarily, on a global scale. Alongside, the USA was also deploying soft power to influence the direction of political change through a range of educational and cultural programmes in a wide range of developing countries. From the US side, these programmes saw many academics in leadership positions, as for instance: Gustav Papanek in Pakistan and Indonesia; Harberger, John Lewis, Theodore Schultz, Simon Kuznets, a.o. supported through an organisational division of labour between the Ford Foundation, Rockefeller Foundation, USAID, MIT, Harvard, Michigan, a.o. If one arm carried a gun, the other carried a university degree and a bag of greenbacks and the promise of an academic career or a professional one in government or within the growing neoliberal policy-oriented institutional network—as in the case of Chile from the 1950s. Friedman had a leading role in overthrowing the draft at that point; but he was as fundamentalist when pushing the soft and hard power interventionist neoliberal agendas globally.

Eisenhower's presidency witnessed, or rather executed, more than a short list of covert or direct interventions in developing countries in Latin and Central America, Africa and Asia—all to spread free markets and democracy, the latter defined as installing a regime amenable to the former, friendly with the USA, and hostile to USSR. But even as Eisenhower was spreading 'freedom' abroad, he was concerned about the threat to democracy within—and by this he did not have in mind the trade unions, or any commies that had survived the McCarthy cull, or the New Dealers that Hayekians and Friedmanites disparaged. In terminology now commonplace but at that time startling, he used the term "military-industrial-complex", which despite its alien leftist resonance was entirely home-grown. The threat to American democracy would come from within, from the disproportionate influence that the corporates exercised on the Government, as well as on the university and scientific establishments. This position resonates with that of C. Wright Mills, the radical sociologist at Columbia University, where Eisenhower relocated after completing his term, and much later with the variation on this theme from Jagdish Bhagwati, also a Columbia professor; the left and the right eye seemed to be coordinating well in pinning down the big joker in the democratic pack, and it was not the trade unions, but the super capitalists. Such a possibility had been alluded to by Alexis de Tocqueville over a century earlier Marx, of course, referred not just to the hand-in-glove symbiotic relationship between the capitalists and the state, but also theorised on the historical tendency towards the centralisation of capital through a process of monopolisation. Indeed, the early Chicago liberals, under whose wing Friedman, Stigler, Harberger and Co had matured, were strongly anti-monopoly and belonged to the regulation school involving government oversight and intervention in order to prevent the known downsides of monopoly. But the Chicago young turks were more pragmatic than purist: Friedman, Stigler and later Buchanan (of the 'Virginia' school, but closely associated with Chicago and the Mont Pelerin Society brands of libertarianism) all questioned the emphasis on anti-trust regulation, arguing that the cure was worse than the disease; that regulation led to 'capture', to 'rent seeking' and to inefficiencies; that the known devil, monopoly, was less of an evil, than the unknown one, political and bureaucratic capture which led to greater inefficiencies. And so, the spectre to which Eisenhower was pointing was ignored and evolved into the plutocratic reality that dominates American economy, policy and polity. As with Hayek's rejection of the Walrasian position that made the efficiency outcomes of free markets contingent on the assumption of perfect competition, this Chicago group defended capitalist realities as intrinsically superior regardless of the absence of perfect competition; their prime focus was on making things better, in neoclassical terms, from what they were, whatever they were; perfect competition was not relied on in theory, not expected in reality and not an objective in policy practice. In contradistinction, the MIT-Harvard economics complex—with some empiricist exceptions—seemed to be in an addictive trance, living in its own world, dancing to its own tune, serving as the vanguard of Samuelson's third and fourth revolutions in economics. But viewed within a wider frame, the two made a yin-yang pair: the mathematical abstractionists sought perfection in their models—without looking out of the window—and sold imaginary dummies of the 'free markets' paradigm which underwrote the real neoliberal agenda; the pragmatic practitioners crudely defended and legitimised the reality of markets, unsavoury as they might be, on the grounds that any alternative would be worse. The former made it their business, literally and profitably, to send out textbooks; the latter made it their enterprise, no less profitable, to send out hands-on advisors and fixers. They formed a formidable pair, even if not a collaborative team.

There was a long journey from dreaming dreams to changing ground realities: there were the difficult textbooks and easy bibles, but they needed modes of diffusion, whether through professional descendants, the cadre of students and researchers but also crucially in the public domain through supportive think tanks; then, there was the huge premium of branding when marketing the message, and awards and prizes, above all the so-called Nobel Prize, performed this function admirably; global diffusion and infiltration of the political establishment were equally essential, and this needed not just corporate finance but also the usually covert and unkind facilitation of government agencies, including the CIA in some spectacular exemplar cases; and then there was the critical need for nurturing charismatic, iconoclastic far right political leaders who could force the change through the last mile. It was a long chain that needed much effort and time on the anvil, and then its opportune moment.

3.2.2 USA: Early Ideological Entrepreneurs of Libertarianism

Harold Luhnow: The Volker Fund and its Dollars
The Volker Fund, set up in 1932 as a conservative mid-West philanthropic organisation by William Volker, a rich Kansas businessman, was instrumental in Friedrich Hayek coming to the University of Chicago; and it also supported other classical liberal intellectuals, including Ludwig von Mises[9] and Aaron Director to occupy positions in US universities. It funded the publication and diffusion of the writings of such scholars by setting up publication and distribution outlets for their ideas; and significantly, it provided the financial support for the participation of a considerable sized American contingent at the inaugural conference of the Mont Pelerin Society in Switzerland in 1947.

---

[9] "Ludwig von Mises started teaching at NYU in February 1945, his salary wholly financed by outside funds. Though the exact sources of funding are obscure, at least part of it appears to have been paid by the Volker Fund. By 1946 Mises was speaking so frequently at FEE that they were required to list him as an employee. Mises was an ideal academic spokesman for their views" (Caldwell, 2020, p. 23n19).

In the 1920s and 1930s, Harold Luhnow worked for his uncle William Volker in Volker's Kansas City-based wholesale firm.[3] In 1932, Volker had established the William Volker Fund and upon his death in 1947, he was succeeded by Harold Luhnow, his nephew, as the Fund's president.[10] Under William Volker, the Volker Fund made extensive donations for the development of Kansas City, many of these anonymously made, such that Volker acquired the nickname 'Mr Anonymous'. "Luhnow had already been exposed to liberal thought through Loren Miller … who incidentally was intimately acquainted with such important business intellectuals as Jasper Crane of DuPont, B. E. Hutchinson of Chrysler, Henry Weaver of GE, Pierre Goodrich, the Indianapolis businessman and creator in 1960 of Liberty Fund, and Richard Earhart, founder of the Earhart Foundation" (Blundell, 1990).

The interactions between American libertarian think tanks (such as the Volker Fund and the FEE), Hayek and the MPS reveal the close intertwining of roots and connections, including those between Chicago and the LSE. The story can be picked up from the point when Hayek, was in Cambridge where LSE was located in the war years. In Ralph Harris's colourful terms: "In 1945, he made a speech in Cambridge and talked about the need for an international academy. And he then suddenly—this is an academic in Cambridge; this is Hayek during the war—he said, 'What I think we probably need is something like $500,000 in order to establish [such an institution]'. Well, $500,000 in those days multiplied by 30, it's $15 million. Fifteen million—he hadn't got a bean, anything, and [he] didn't know any businessmen. 'Just $15 million, then we can have an academy with people around the world who research.' It's crazy. The thing would have come to a halt if he tried to run the battle on the ground" (Harris, 2000, p. 16). Caldwell (2020, p. 2) notes that Hayek made this proposal in a lecture in Cambridge, chaired by Sir John Clapham, in February, a month *before* the first publication of *The Road to Serfdom* by Routledge in UK.

Stephen Stigler (2005, p. 307) notes that "Aaron [Director] played a pivotal role in getting the University of Chicago Press to publish Hayek's *The Road to Serfdom*". The two had known each other from 1937 when Director spent a year at the London School of Economics—Caldwell (2020, p. 17) notes that "Director had attended Hayek's seminar when he visited LSE in 1938". Bruce Caldwell, writing on the 75th anniversary of the publication of *The Road to Serfdom*, writes: "In August 1942 [Hayek] wrote to Machlup to ask if he would help him find a publisher for an American edition. Over the course of a year, Machlup tried three different presses, but all of them turned the manuscript down. By then Machlup was doing war work in Washington alongside Aaron Director at the Office of Alien Property Custodian, and Director, who had been at LSE in the late 1930s and attended Hayek's seminar there, offered to send it to his contacts at the University of Chicago Press. It received a

---

[10] The Fund closed shop with the death of Harold Luhnow in 1965.

lukewarmly positive report from Frank Knight (who agreed with Hayek's overall point of view) and an effusive one from Jacob Marschak (who disagreed but thought it would start the right conversation), and they agreed to publish it. The British edition of Road came out in March 1944, and the American in September" (Caldwell, 2019, p. 27). The Routledge edition was reprinted five times in fifteen months; and Caldwell (2019, p. 39) writes that "within ten days of its publication the University of Chicago Press had ordered a second and a third printing, bringing the total to 17,000". One of these copies was sent from the Press to Max Eastman a 'roving editor' for the *Reader's Digest*. Caldwell writes: "In his youth Eastman had been radicalized, traveling to the Soviet Union for nearly two years in the early 1920s to study the Russian experiment. He married a Russian woman and befriended Trotsky, but after Lenin's death he became increasingly critical of Stalin and his policies. By 1940 he was writing that Stalinism was worse than fascism, providing lines that Hayek could not help but quote in Road (Hayek, [1944] 2007, p. 79). ... Eastman loved the book, [declaring that] *The Road to Serfdom* is, in my opinion, the most important political book of this epoch" (ibid., p. 39). Soon following the subsequent publication of the American edition, and then the *Reader's Digest* condensation in spring 1945, Hayek made a promotional lecture tour to the USA in the course of which his path fatefully crossed that of Loren Miller. "The most intriguing character among the foundation [FEE] men was Loren 'Red' Miller. One of the many hats that Luhnow wore was that of Chairman of the Board for the Civic Research Institute in Kansas City. Miller worked there, and soon after they met Miller began to influence Luhnow to turn the focus of the Volker Charitable Fund away from local projects and towards the support of free market causes" (Caldwell, 2020, p. 22). Even after changing jobs, Miller "continued to be a key adviser for Luhnow; it seems he had his hand in everything. Thus Miller had been in the audience when Hayek, on his *Road to Serfdom* tour, spoke before the Economic Club of Detroit. Impressed by Hayek's talk, he set up the initial meeting between Luhnow and Hayek." Hayek was pursuing his grandiose plan, and Luhnow asked for a concrete proposal; when it came briefly titled "Memorandum on the Proposed Foundation of an International Academy for Political Philosophy Tentatively Called 'The Acton-Tocqueville Society'", the price tag, as big as the title, was half-a-million dollars; it was declined inside a month (ibid., p. 3); and "it was Miller who sent Hayek an encouraging letter of rejection" [in November 1945] (ibid., p. 23). Later, on reading *The Road to Serfdom*, Luhnow became a thoroughgoing classical liberal and, as head of the William Volker Fund, was able to contribute financially to the cause of liberalism. In 1945, he met Hayek and was soon instrumental in bringing him to the University of Chicago" (Blundell, 1990). And subsequently, Luhnow provided funding from the Volker Fund to sponsor the large American delegation to the inaugural and subsequent meetings of the Mont Pelerin Society, not to mention underwriting Hayek's expensive professorship in Chicago from 1950 to 1962. It was the success of *The Road to Serfdom* that got Luhnow to fund the American delegation to the inaugural Mont Pelerin Society meeting, and the news of the success of that venture, brought back by Miller and Director to Luhnow, that moved Luhnow to fund Hayek's move to Chicago.

A word is necessary about the elusive figure of Aaron Director, who set the presses rolling, and it is best provided by his peers. George Stigler (1982) wrote about him in his Nobel Biographical: "It was in the 1960s that I began the detailed study of public regulation. My interests were aroused, and my faith in the cliches of the subject destroyed, as so often with other subjects, by the discussions with my friend, Aaron Director. This wonderful man is that rarest of scholars: a clear-headed, imaginative, erudite man who enjoys the task of constructing luminous and original theories but does not even write them down!" Stephen Stigler writes further that his father, George, "likened him to Socrates" (Stigler, 2005, p. 308). He refers to his influence as a teacher: "Paul Samuelson recalls that it was a course of Aaron's that introduced him to economics when he was a college student here and that course first excited his interest in the subject"[11] (Stigler, 2005, p. 310). He was at the heart of the setting up of the discipline of Law and Economics at Chicago University. Stephen Stigler writes about the paradox of the power of his influence and virtually non-existent publishing record. "The faculty of the University of Chicago Law School is, and has been for some time, an extraordinary group. Aaron Director was unusual even within this group. In a group where the average annual number of publications per single faculty member exceeds that of the whole of many law schools, Aaron published next to nothing—a co-authored book and a pamphlet on unemployment in 1932 before he hit his stride and little more than a few book reviews after that. In a group decorated by all manner of academic honors (even a Nobel Prize), Aaron did not even have a Ph.D. In a group of forceful and dynamic intellects, Aaron never raised his voice, and casual observers might well have overlooked him, unless they noticed his colleagues lowering their own voices to hear what Aaron had to say" (Stigler, 2005, p. 307). Aaron Director also happened to be Milton Friedman's brother-in-law. And it was Aaron Director who had the critical hand in the publication of Hayek's *The Road to Serfdom* through linking and expediting its acceptance by the University of Chicago Press when several others had rejected the manuscript. And Aaron Director was Harold Luhnow's eyes and ears at the first meeting of the Mont Pelerin Society, reporting back on promising candidates to be encouraged and funded in the future, Hayek being prominent in this regard. Milton Friedman and George Stigler were there too, of course. The trip to Mont Pelerin was Friedman's first travel outside America; Stephen

---

[11] "My very first teacher, Aaron Director (now [in 2003] around 100), I liked as an iconoclastic teacher. ... Long without Chicago tenure, his bibliography was epsilon. ... Director's published works are nearly nil. ... But without any database, [with] his stubborn iconoclasm he was a primary creator both of the second Chicago School—of Friedman, Stigler, Coase and Becker after Knight, Viner, Douglas, Schultz, Nef, and Simons—and present-day antitrust inactivism" (Samuelson, 2004; Barnett, 2004, pp. 528–529; text combined).

Stigler writes that his father, George, and Aaron "first became closely acquainted in 1947 when were invited (with Milton Friedman, already by then Aaron's brother-in-law) to the first meeting in Switzerland of the Mont Pelerin Society. In pictures from that time they look like three mischievous East German spies" (Stigler, 2005, p. 307). They were all thick as thieves.

Hayek's move in 1950 to America and Chicago had everything to do with his wish to obtain a quick divorce following his wife Hella's adamant refusal to grant one; it was possible in some states in America, and Ebenstein (2018, p. 305) reports that the source of this idea was Helene, his wife to be. This was an expensive affair, and Harold Luhnow and The Volker Fund underwrote the finances necessary for his appointment. The Volker Fund apparently stood in good favour with Robert Maynard Hutchins, the chancellor of Chicago University. "In a 9 May 1948, letter from Hayek to Volker Fund director Harold Luhnow, Hayek was very clear that he required a large salary in order to finance his personal circumstances (citing Hoover, 2003, pp. 190–191). The figure he mentioned was $15,000 per year, which would have been a top academic salary at the time" (Ebenstein, 2018, p. 305, also for original archival source). A sizable fraction of this was to be used for various financial obligations in the subsequent divorce settlement with Hella. The Volker Fund sponsored Hayek's appointment in Chicago at the Committee on Social Thought from 1950 to 1962.

Murray Rothbard (1926–1995) was a leading intellectual of the American libertarian movement, an anarcho-libertarian fundamentalist well to the right of Milton Friedman, and later a critic of the Foundation for Economic Education (FEE) for watering down the movement's message. Brian Doherty (in Rothbard & Gordon, 2010, p. ix) says: "When it comes to modern American libertarianism, Rothbard was the Man".[12] In his hitherto confidential internal memos in the 1950s and 1960s to the principals of the Volker Fund, he has advice on "What is to be Done". Rothbard takes the question explicitly from Lenin and sketches his "theory of revolutionary strategy" for the libertarian movement; his investigation provides some rare insights into the vicissitudes of the movement.

> I am here using the shock term 'revolution' not in the sense of violent, or even nonviolent revolution against the State. I mean by 'revolution' the effecting of an ideological revolution in the framework of ideas held by the bulk of our fellow men. We are, in this sense, revolutionaries—for we are offering the public a radical change in their doctrinal views and we are offering it from a firm and consistent

---

[12] "Institutionally, he helped form or worked closely with every significant libertarian group or organization from the 1940s to the 1990s, from the Foundation for Economic Education to the Volker Fund, to the Institute for Humane Studies, to the Libertarian Party, to the Center for Libertarian Studies, to the Cato Institute to the Ludwig von Mises Institute. Every other significant libertarian thinker was personally influenced by him or felt obligated to grapple with him where they disagreed, from Leonard Read to Robert Nozick" (Doherty in Rothbard & Gordon, 2010, p. ix).

base of principle that we are trying to spread among the public. (Largely, this comprehensive system is 'libertarian', i.e., the pure libertarian system, or, as a step to that, the *laissez-faire* system. But it also encompasses other aspects of 'individualist' thought.) Here we stand, then, a 'hard core' of libertarian-individualist 'revolutionaries', anxious not only to develop our own understanding of this wonderful system of thought, but also anxious to spread its principles—and its policies—to the rest of society. How do we go about it?. (Rothbard & Gordon, 2010, p. 8)

Rothbard wrote this in 1961, a time when Keynesianism was still in its steeply rising phase, enough to send Hayek falling equally steeply into depression leading to his return to Europe in 1962. Rothbard's 'revolution' would appear to be approximately equivalent to the Kuhnian notion of 'paradigm change'.

Rothbard is willing to learn from the enemy: "I think here we can learn a great deal from Lenin and the Leninists … particularly the idea that the Leninist party is the main, or indeed only, moral principle". "In the course of [his] work, the hardcore libertarian should try to advance the knowledge of both the masses and his fellow [movement] members, toward fuller libertarian ideals, … to 'push' his colleagues and others toward the direction of hardcore libertarian thought itself. (In Communist-Leninist terms, this is called 'recruiting for the Party'.) … The hardcore man is working for his idea on two levels: in a 'popular' or 'united' front for limited libertarian goals, and to try to influence his colleagues as well as the masses in the direction of the total system. (This is the essence of the much-misunderstood Leninist theory of 'infiltration'.)" "One of the reasons behind the idea of 'infiltration' is that we can never hope to have everyone an intellectual. Since the hard core will always be relatively small, its influence must be maximized by giving it 'leverage' through allied, less libertarian 'united fronts' with less libertarian thinkers and doers."

Phase I, being the period of Second World War, was the nadir of libertarian thought in America. "There was no movement; there was no open center for a libertarian to go to … to find congenial and like-minded thinkers. … The dominant fact of this era was isolation for the libertarian. Here and there, in the catacombs, unbeknownst to us struggling neophytes, were little, separated groups of people; … this was Phase I of the libertarian movement in this era: 'in the depths'. Ludwig von Mises, unhonoured and unsung, was eking out a pittance at the NYU School of Business." Rothbard cites scattered pockets of activity, involving a.o., Leonard Read, Orval Watts, R. C. Hoiles, F. A. Harper and some others, but they collectively were the exception to the general state of isolation of libertarians.

Phase II began: "with the formation of the FEE in 1946—the libertarian movement turned a corner and began its post-war renaissance". FEE "can be proud [that] it gathered together the many isolated and loose strands of the libertarians, and created that crucial *open center* for a libertarian movement. It not only disseminated libertarian literature; it provided a gateway, a welcoming place, for all hitherto isolated and neophyte libertarians. It launched a movement. ... Not only did this open center provide a channel and gateway for people to enter the libertarian ranks; not only did its agitation convert some and find others; it also, by providing an atmosphere and a 'center' for likeminded students of liberty, provided the atmospheric spark for rapid advance from old-fashioned *laissez-faire* to 100 percent liberty on the part of much of its staff and friends. In short, FEE, by its very existence, exerted an enormous multiple leverage in creating and advancing and weaving together the strands and people in the libertarian cause. For this may it always be honored!" "Leonard Reed it was, of course, who performed this feat, and he drew together at or near FEE the various strands of the movement: Harper and his students from Cornell" amongst many others. "FEE from the very beginning, devoted itself to the task not only of spreading its ideas, but also of finding and developing hardcore ... libertarians. I believe it safe to say that virtually every libertarian in the country found his way into the ranks through FEE, and that almost every leading libertarian was, at one time or another, connected with FEE staff." It was this Volker Fund, and the FEE, that underwrote the formation meeting of the Mont Pelerin Society in 1947 in distant Switzerland; and Leonard Read and 'Baldy' Harper were both part of the 'hardcore' within the original gang of 36 founding members.

Phase III is marked by the emergence of "the Volker Fund Concept" originated by Harold Luhnow and Herbert Cornuelle, and then Richard Cornuelle and Ken Templeton. The focus now was on grants to individual libertarian and right-wing scholars to further their work, to draw them into seminars and conferences, and to "permeate them with libertarian ideas". In addition, it sponsored intellectuals and professors such as Mises at NYU and Hayek at Chicago, giving fellowships to scholars to study with them. In this, the Fund could claim success: Rothbard notes: "virtually every libertarian or even economist in the country has been a student or either Ludwig von Mises, Frank Knight, or F.A. Harper".[13]

This weakness of a 'hardcore' is then identified by Rothbard as the strategic weakness in Phase III (in the 1960s). While lauding 'the magnificent achievements' of the Volker Fund, Rothbard complains about the direction taken by libertarian foundations and think tanks: "the outstanding weakness ... is that, while a broad base of 'right-wing' intellectuals has been developed and nourished, it has been done to the neglect of the vital task of building up the hard

---

[13] "The Volker Fund list consists largely of individual scholars who are vaguely sympathetic with libertarian or 'conservative' aims, with others scattered through who more and more approach the hard core. There is little more that can be accomplished through *widening* the list; the time has come for a *deepening* of that list." "For successful infiltration, there must be a strong hard core which functions as a nucleus, a center from which the infiltration emanates. There is not, and has not been, such a hard core. Without a strong hardcore center, the 'infiltration' process inevitably leads *not* to the 'revolutionary' road of exerting leverage on less-advanced persons, *not* to drawing new members into the hard core, *but to the weakening and dissolving of the hard core itself*, ... they *begin to lose their own hardcore libertarian principles*; this is bound to happen when the hard core is not nurtured and made strong, and *it has happened increasingly* over recent years."

core. There can be no successful 'infiltration' or 'permeation' unless there is a flourishing hardcore nucleus that does the infiltrating."

> In World War II, ... the danger and despair of the individual hardcore libertarian was his isolation. Now, in 1961, with the libertarian and right-wing movements seemingly flourishing and growing apace, on scholarly and more popular levels, he is, once again, increasingly in danger of being *isolated*. Except this time, the danger is less apparent and more insidious. For it is the danger of the hardcore libertarian being swamped by a growing mass of 'conservative' and right-wing thinkers.

"Although libertarians, under first FEE and then Volker aegis, grew in number and influence, a reversal has begun to set in, caused by a confusion of everyone of the Right, a growing erasure of the important lines that separate the hardcore libertarian from the 'conservative'. The result of exclusive emphasis on popular-front work has meant that build-up of the 'Right' in general has diluted the hard core, made the public, and the Right itself, increasingly unaware of the crucial *differences* between a hardcore libertarian and a plain conservative. The hardcore libertarian movement—the essence and the glory of what the struggle is all about—is in danger of dying on the vine."

"Thus, any given Volker Fund seminar will have only one or two hardcore men to a dozen 'confused' conservatives. This is inevitable, given the numerical weakness of the hardcore. But, if there is no hardcore centre, no firm, well-nourished nucleus, the hardcore men will have little influence on the conservatives who heavily outnumber them; hardcore strength itself will be diluted and vanish; and the whole purpose will be lost." And funding isolated libertarian professors in situ is also ineffective: "outnumbered by the faculty colleagues, he will be held up to ridicule by faculty and students alike as an isolated 'crackpot'. He will, then, generate no influence, as he will be isolated and cut off from productive interchange with fellow hardcore men ... and he will therefore eventually lose his libertarian drive, if not his libertarian principles themselves."

> The chief trouble now with the theory of the 'popular front' is that this 'front' has been largely infected with enemies of, rather than friends of, liberty. Fortunately, the Volker Fund's own program suffers much less than other from this problem because the fund's concentration has been on economists, who, in their capacity as economists (Chicago School, etc.) have been, at least on balance, proponents of liberty.

Rothbard's recommendation is for concentrating effort on the development of the hardcore libertarian. He ends with a handful of concrete suggestions, all geared to deepen the libertarian movement, and to give it greater traction and leverage in spreading the word. First, a high-profile, scholarly libertarian institute at the postgraduate level, a counterpart to the Institute for Advanced Study; second, a counterpart of the Social Science Research Council with its own libertarian mandate and agenda to channel grants, stimulate seminars and conferences; third, to increase the number of high-profile Volker-funded professors, along with fellowship to students to study with them, as being done in the case of Von Mises and Hayek; fourth, a libertarian counterpart of the Mont Pelerin Society with annual papers, read, a scholarly journal. It is evident that Rothbard's scheme mirrors parts of the mainstream academic institutional architecture, except that this parallel structure is exclusively and purposively oriented to furthering the hardcore libertarian movement in all its forms. Rothbard's comment on the MPS is curious, though, since the MPS could already be regarded as being a hardcore libertarian enterprise—an initiative incubated by the Volker Fund and FEE through the agency of some of Rothbard's highly regarded original libertarians. Perhaps, writing in 1961, Rothbard was unduly pessimistic about the future prospects of the anarcho-capitalist, fundamentalist libertarian movement he worked for: had he lived another couple of years, he would surely have been a star guru in the 50th Anniversary Conference of the MPS in 1997 in its original location; the 36 pioneer members, of whom only 3 then survived, would have been remembered by over 100 participants; the membership of the MPS then exceeding 500.

Foundation for Economic Education (FEE) and its Facilitators
The Foundation for Economic Education (FEE) which claims to be "the first free-market organization in the United States, was founded in New York in March 1946 by Leonard E. Read to study and advance the freedom philosophy". In its first year, prior to the first MPS meeting in 1947—FEE had published the influential tract 'Roofs or Ceilings?', calling for the removal of rent controls, authored by Milton Friedman and George Stigler; FEE has also published Ayn Rand's novella *Anthem*; published by FEE founder Leonard E. Read's Pamphleteers, Inc. "Our mission since 1946 has been to inspire, educate, and connect future leaders with the economic, ethical, and legal principles of a free society. We captivate and inspire tomorrow's leaders with sound economic principles and the entrepreneurial spirit." Hayek raised the bar further: "The Foundation for Economic Freedom is committed to nothing more nor less than the defense of our civilization against intellectual error".[14]

Others intimately involved with the setting up and running of the FEE were Baldy Harper and Orval Watts. Floyd Arthur 'Baldy' Harper (1905–1973) was a Cornell University Professor of Economics, who had helped to start the FEE, had co-directed the William Volker Fund and founded the Institute for Humane Studies in 1961. He was the chief economist and theoretician of the FEE; Rothbard (1973) called him "the heart and soul and nerve center of the libertarian cause. ... Baldy and I came to anarchocapitalism from laissez-faire at about the same time in 1949–1950." Belying his nickname, "Baldy" apparently "had a full head of hair" (Caldwell, 2020, p. 22n18). Orval Watts was one of the founders of the FEE in 1946 and served as its editorial director. "An early critic of the New Deal, Watts maintained a lifelong commitment to

---

[14] https://fee.org/about/#history

laissez-faire principles, opposing government intervention in the economy and most social welfare programs" (OAC, Online Archive of California, 2015).

Blundell (1990) provides some rare personal detail: "F. A. 'Baldy' Harper was a professor of economics at Cornell University when he, too, like Luhnow and Read, read *The Road to Serfdom*. He promptly began using it in his classroom teaching at Cornell. I vividly remember talking with his widow, Peg Harper, in the summer of 1983, about the reaction to Baldy's use of *The Road to Serfdom*. She described how one night a trustee of Cornell, who was a friend of Baldy's, came to visit them at their home and asked that Baldy discontinue using *The Road to Serfdom* in the classroom. In the view of the trustees, its message was more than contentious and, after all, Cornell, like so many private universities, received and looked forward to receiving a great deal of government funding. From that moment on, Baldy no longer considered himself in any way tied to Cornell. He very quickly went to join Leonard Read on the staff of FEE and by the mid-fifties had moved to California to join the senior staff of the William Volker Fund. In 1961, with the Volker Fund due to expire, he made his third move, namely to set up his own shop, to found the Institute for Humane Studies. In this endeavor, he was joined by people formerly associated with Volker such as Leonard P. Liggio, George Reach, Kenneth S. Templeton, Jr., and Dr. Neil McLeod; and among his earliest business supporters were R. C. Hoiles, J. Howard Pew, Howard Buffet, William L. Law, and Pierre Goodrich. Initially, the Institute for Humane Studies continued many of Volker's programs and was involved in conferences, publishing, and talent-scouting. IHS inherited Volker's staff, approach, and the strategy of Loren Miller and Herb Cornuelle."

The field of American libertarian think tanks was densely inhabited and they tended to be interconnected and overlapping, but while they were variously differentiated in philosophical tenets or operational strategies, these were often cosmetic and stylistic—they generally tended all to point in a similar direction in terms of domestic and foreign affairs, though the issue of faith and religion could evoke clear disagreements. Illustrations are provided, amongst others, by the aggressively neoconservative Heritage Foundation set up by Edwin Feulner, the American Enterprise Institute,[15] the Institute for Humane Studies set up by Baldy Harper in 1961 as an offshoot from the FEE and the Cato Institute[16] involving Charles Koch.

---

[15] Established by Lewis Brown, a New York businessman, the American Enterprise Institute set up in 1938 and is perhaps the premier American neoconservative think tank, with associations with Gerald Ford, George W. Bush, Dick Cheney, John R. Bolton, Paul Wolfowitz, Milton Friedman, Ronald Coase, Arthur F. Burns, Martin Feldstein, Newt Gingrich, Richard Perle and Irving Kristol, amongst many others.

[16] The Cato Institute is a top-ranking American libertarian think tank founded originally in 1974 as the Charles Koch Foundation by the anarcho-libertarian Murray Rothbard, Ed Crane and Charles Koch, the Koch Industries boss; in July 1976, it was renamed the Cato Institute. Its mission is "to originate, disseminate, and increase understanding of public policies based on the principles of individual liberty, limited government, free markets, and peace ... to create free, open, and civil societies founded on libertarian principles". https://www.cato.org/mission

3.2.3 Europe: Friedrich Hayek and the Mont Pelerin Society

The Mont Pelerin Society[17] was the primary vehicle for the international transmission of Hayek's ideas, and has served as the spearhead of the movement ever since. Starting from a group of 36 in 1947, it grew into a global organisation which included in its list of members presidents, prime ministers, senior politicians, corporate honchos, financiers and bankers, media chiefs, think tank heads and hands and a wide range of established intellectuals.

Antecedents

The Mont Pelerin Society had its antecedents in a string of independent meetings in Europe. Conferences in 1935 and 1937 were organised by the Institut Universitaire des Hautes Etudes Internationales (IUHEI) which was established in Geneva through funding by the Rockefeller Foundation; "these conferences were different from standard scholarly meetings in the sense that they had a public relations objective as revealed by the number of invited journalists" (Roehner, 2007).

Paris

Then followed an initiative sparked by the angst of liberal intellectuals about the threatening political developments in continental Europe; this was labelled the Colloque Lippmann, organised by the French political philosopher Louis Rougier, and held in Paris during 26–30 August 1938. The immediate stimulus was the publication of the celebrated American liberal journalist, Walter Lippmann's *An Enquiry into the Principles of the Good Society* in 1937, critiquing the New Deal. Rougier assembled 26 prominent liberal intellectuals to debate and develop a shared vision of the significance and future of liberalism; CIERL (Comite Internationale d'etude pour le Renouveau du Liberalisme) was set up to consider what might be done to promote the cause. Unsurprisingly, however, this assembly of political thinkers was divided in opinion and so the discussions proved inconclusive. (For a treatment of the nineteenth century antecedents of French liberal thought as evolved in the Paris School of Liberal Political Economy, see David Hart (2019)).

Colloque Lippmann had little direct impact, partly because of internal ideological differences within the participants where Hayek and Co took a more purist position and rejected the socially oriented versions of liberalism that were accommodative of specific forms of state regulation and intervention à la

---

[17] "There were also discussions ... most entertainingly, [about] its name. Suggestions ran the gamut from individuals (Acton-Tocqueville of course; Director suggested 'the Adam Smith-Tocqueville Society') to descriptive (Morley came up with the rather laborious 'International Society for the Study of Freedom in Society') to the classically heroic (Robbins offered 'the Protagonist Society' and Popper 'the Periclean Society'). When Karl Brandt proposed 'the Mont Pèlerin Society' Popper responded, 'That is meaningless'. Whether it was meaningless or not might be debated, but it was sufficiently inoffensive that the group ultimately adopted it" (Caldwell, 2020, p. 43).

Keynes, as espoused by Raymond Aron; and then, due to the War. But the initiative made its mark by inspiring Hayek. In 1939, he set up the *Society for the Renovation of Liberalism* in London; and after the war to the momentous meeting and creation of the Mont Pelerin Society in 1947. Several participants of the Colloque Lippmann were part of the MPS 1947 meeting[18]; Louis Rougier was an MPS member, introduced by Hayek himself, though he was absent from the inaugural meeting on account of his involvement with the Vichy Regime and his subsequent defence of it. Virtually all participants, apart from Lippmann, were German or French, unlike the first MPS meeting which had a strong presence of Americans, British and some other nationalities, including of course Lionel Robbins (for the inaugural meeting) from LSE and Stanley Dennison (as a regular) from Cambridge.

Vienna

In his tribute to Ludwig von Mises on his 80th birthday in 1961, Haberler reminisced about the inter-war period in Vienna where, despite "one calamity following another" at the national level, "intellectual life especially in the realm of science was exciting and stimulating in Vienna until the rise of Nazism in the middle 1930s. There existed several internationally famous centers with numerous connections between them ... psycho-analysis, pure theory of law, ... logical positivism ...; and last but by no means least, a group of economists, sociologists and philosophers which had their center in the famous 'Privatseminar' of Professor Ludwig von Mises. ... Most original members of these various groups left Vienna before 1933." Regular participants included several who would later become key figures of the Mont Pelerin Society, Hayek, Machlup, Alfred Schutz, John V. Van Sickle and several others—philosophers, mathematicians, economists, musicians. Ragnar Nurkse was a member of the seminar, as was Oskar Morgenstern, and Alfred Stonier who went later to University College London. Mises himself took up W. E. Rappard's offer and joined the Institut Universitaire de Haute Etudes Internationales in Geneva in 1935, emigrating to America in 1940; meanwhile Hayek had shifted to the London School of Economics at the invitation of Beveridge prompted by Lionel Robbins who had also been one of several distinguished international visitors to the Mises seminar. Rappard was also to be a significant founder member of the MPS in 1947. Haberler laments: "those who remained in Vienna until the night fell in 1938, felt lonely and forlorn ... Mises' departure and the disappearance of the other schools ... left a big void in the intellectual life of Vienna which has never been filled again, not even after the spectacular economic and political revival of Austria after World War II" (Haberler, 1961).

---

[18] These included: Ludwig von Mises, Friedrich Hayek, Michael Polanyi—neoliberal brother of socialist Karl; Wilhelm Ropke; Louis Rougier was absent for reasons discussed, and Walter Eucken was invited but could not attend as he was denied permission to leave Germany.

The Mises seminar[19] met every Friday (according to Haberler (1961), every two weeks, according to Quinn Slobodian [2018, p. 48]) in Mises' office in the Chamber of Commerce, with its fine library—"Mises boasted that it contained material that even the University of Vienna did not have" (ibid.) located on the Stubenring. Haberler and Slobodian evoke the style and ethos of the times: "every two weeks at 7:00 p.m., a flock of young intellectuals in their twenties and thirties would pass under the leaded glass of the entrance and up the stairs past the art nouveau caryatids to Mises's office" (Slobodian, 2018, p. 48). Haberler (1961) recounts:

> Mises sat at his desk and the members of the group [of up to twenty-five] around him. The meeting would be introduced by a paper by Mises himself or by another member on some problem of economic theory, methodology of the social sciences or economic policy. Sociology, especially the 'Verstehende Soziologie' of Max Weber and related problems were favorite topics. The always lively discussion lasted until 10 p.m. when the group walked over to the nearby Italian Restaurant 'Ancora Verde'—'Der grune Anker' in Kaufmann's song—where dinner was served. There the discussion continued on finer points of theory and later usually took on lighter tones. At eleven thirty or so those members who were not yet exhausted went to the Cafe Kunstler, opposite the University, the favorite meeting place of economists in Vienna in those days. Mises was always among the hardy ones who went to the Kunstler Cafe and was the last one to leave for home, never before 1 a.m. Next morning, fresh as a daisy, he was at his office at 9 a.m. At eighty he still keeps to his habit of working late and rising early. (Haberler, 1961)

There was camaraderie: Haberler writes that Kauffman was moved to write a song about the experience—"I'm going tonight to Mises, because that's where I love to be, there's nowhere so nice in Vienna, to talk about economy, truth and society" (Slobodian, 2018, p. 49)—the literary worth of the ditty would no doubt have been better in the original German.

The libertarian revolutionary and devotee of Ludwig von Mises, Murray Rothbard, wrote an informative and evocative appreciation of his mentor, described as "scholar, creator, hero". Rothbard documents and examines why Mises, despite his prominent contributions to economic theory, never held a paid formal university appointment, apart from the lack of support from the powerful Bohm-Bawerk, whose illustrious student he was. In the context of the charged, foetid atmosphere in Vienna, with the dual spectres of Russian communism and German national socialism, Rothbard relies on Earlene Craver's diagnosis of why "Mises was not appointed to a professorial chair because he had three strikes against him: (1) he was an unreconstructed laissez-faire liberal

---

[19] There was a precursor to the Ludwig von Mises's Privatseminar in Vienna in the form of the seminar conducted by Eugene von Bohm-Bawerk's after he returned to the University of Vienna in 1904, and amongst the participants were some of his students, including Ludwig von Mises, Joseph Schumpeter, Henryk Grossman and Marxist scholars such as Rudolf Hilferding. Bohm-Bawerk was an ardent follower of Carl Menger, and his critiques of Marxism carried over to his student Ludwig von Mises.

in a world of opinion that was rapidly being captured by socialism of either the Marxian left or of the corporatist-fascist right; (2) he was Jewish, in a country that was becoming increasingly anti-Semitic; (3) he was personally intransigent and unwilling ever to compromise his principles." Mises's former students F. A. Hayek and Fritz Machlup concluded that "Mises's accomplishments were such that two of these defects might have been overlooked—but never three". The degree of exclusion seems to have been extreme, with implications for students as well. The university authorities "made it very difficult for those doctoral candidates in the social sciences who wanted to write their theses with me; and those who sought to qualify for a university lectureship had to be careful not to be known as my students" (Mises, quoted in Rothbard n.d.). "Students who registered for Mises's seminar without registering for the seminar of one of his rivals, were not allowed to use the economics department library; but Mises triumphantly notes that his own library at the Chamber of Commerce was 'incomparably better' than that of the economics department, so this restriction, at least, caused his students no hardship" (ibid.).

Rothbard's narration of the ethos, functioning and transactions of Mises's Privatseminar—held in his office in the Chamber of Commerce where he had a position, and not in the University—is culled from the first-hand accounts of several participants and of Mises himself, and provides context and detail, and testifies to the wide range and intensity of its impact on the young participants.

"Mises's enormous influence, as teacher and mentor, arose instead from the private seminar that he founded in his office at the Chamber of Commerce. From 1920 until he left for Geneva in 1934, Mises held the seminar every other Friday from seven to approximately ten o'clock (accounts of participants differ slightly), after which they repaired the Italian restaurant Anchora Verde for supper, and then, around midnight, the seminar stalwarts, invariably including Mises, went on to the Cafe Künstler, the Favourite Vienna coffeehouse for economists, until one in the morning or after. The Mises seminar gave no grades, and had no official function of any kind, either at the University or at the Chamber of Commerce. And yet such were Mises's remarkable qualities as scholar and teacher that, very quickly, his *Privatseminar* became the outstanding seminar and forum in all of Europe for discussion and research in economics and the social sciences. An invitation to attend and participate was considered a great honour, and the seminar soon became an informal but crucially important centre for post-doctoral studies. The list of later-to-be eminent names of *Miseskreis* participants, from England and the USA as well as from Austria, is truly staggering."

"Despite Mises's reputation as an intransigent fighter for his beliefs, all participants testify that he conducted his private seminar as a discussion forum, with great respect for everyone's views, and without trying to bludgeon the members into his own position. Thus, Dr. Paul N. Rosenstein-Rodan, a student of Hans Mayer and later to be an economist at the United Nations, wrote in reminiscence of Mises's seminar: 'I was an enthusiastic admirer of Mises' theory of money and very skeptical of his extreme [laissez-faire] liberalism. It was a proof of how elastic and tolerant (in spite of a contrary general opinion)

Mises was that we maintained a very good relation in spite of my being 'pink' or rather having a very Fabian outlook on life, which I did not change.'

Mises himself wrote movingly of the seminar and the way he conducted it: "My main teaching effort was focused on my *Privatseminar*. ... In these meetings we informally discussed all important problems of economics, social philosophy, sociology, logic, and the epistemology of the sciences of human action. In this circle the younger [post-Böhm-Bawerk] Austrian School of Economics lived on, in this circle the Viennese culture produced one of its last blossoms. Here I was neither teacher nor director of seminar, I was merely *primus inter pares* [first among peers] who himself benefited more than he gave.

All who belonged to this circle came voluntarily, guided only by their thirst for knowledge. They came as pupils, but over the years became my friends. ... We formed neither school, congregation, nor sect. We helped each other more through contradiction than agreement. But we agreed and were united on one endeavor: to further the sciences of human action. Each one went his own way, guided by his own law. ... We never thought to publish a journal or a collection of essays. Each one worked by himself, as befits a thinker. And yet each one of us labored for the circle, seeking no compensation other than simple recognition, not the applause of his friends. There was greatness in this unpretentious exchange of ideas; in it we all found happiness and satisfaction."

> The result of Mises's method was that many of the seminar members became full Misesians, while the others were stamped, one way or the other, with at least a touch of Mises's greatness. Even those Mises followers who later shifted to Keynesian and other anti-Misesian doctrines still retained a visible thread of Misesianism. Hence, for example, the Keynesianism of Machlup or Haberler was never quite as unrestrained as in other, more unalloyed disciples. Gerhard Tintner, a Mises seminar member, went on to become an eminent econometrician at Iowa State, but the first chapter of Tintner's *Econometrics* took Mises-type reservations about econometrics far more seriously than did his colleagues in the econometric profession. Mises made a mark on all of his students[20] that proved to be indelible. (Rothbard, n.d., and sources cited therein)

[20] "A partial list of Mises private seminar members, followed by their later affiliations and accomplishments, will serve to illustrate both the enormous distinction achieved by his students, and the Misesian stamp placed upon all of them:

Friedrich A. Hayek; Fritz Machlup; Gottfried von Haberler; Oskar Morgenstern; Paul N. Rosenstein-Rodan; Felix Kaufmann (author of *The Methodology of the Social Sciences*); Alfred Schütz (sociologist, New School for Social Research); Karl Bode (methodologist, Stanford University); Alfred Stonier (methodologist, University College, London); Erich Voegelin (political scientist, historian, Louisiana State University); Karl Schlesinger; Richard von Strigl; Karl Menger (mathematician, son of founder of Austrian School, Carl Menger, University of Chicago); Walter Fröhlich (Marquette University); Gerhard Tintner (Iowa State University); Ewald Schams; Erich Schiff; Herbert von Fürth; and Rudolf Klein.

Members and participants from England and the United States included:

John V. Van Sickle (Rockefeller Foundation, later Wabash College); Howard S. Ellis (Berkeley, author of *German Monetary Theory*); Lionel Robbins (London School of Economics); and Hugh Gaitskell (British Labour Party). Other participants who, it must be conceded, showed little influence of Mises in later life were the Swedish Keynesian Ragnar Nurkse (Columbia University) and Albert Gailord Hart (Columbia University)" (Rothbard, n.d., and sources cited therein).

Murray Rothbard then proceeds to share the experience of his personal exposure to Mises and his seminar at New York University, where again, he did not have a formal professorship, but one financially underwritten by Harold Luhnow and his corporate think tank. "For the present writer, who was privileged to join the Mises seminar in its first session in 1949, the experience at the seminar was inspiring and exhilarating. The same was true of fellow students who were not registered at NYU, but audited the seminar regularly for years, and consisted of libertarian and free-market scholars and businessmen in the New York area. Due to the special arrangements of the seminar, the university agreed to allow Misesians to audit the course. But even though Mises had a small number of excellent graduate students who did their doctorates under him—notably Israel M. Kirzner, still teaching at NYU—the bulk of the regular students were uncomprehending business students, who took the course for an easy A. The proportion of libertarians and budding Austrians to the class total ranged, I would estimate, from about one-third to one-half.

Mises did his best to replicate the conditions of his great Vienna *Privatseminar* including repairing after the end of the formal session at 9:30 p.m. to Childs' Restaurant to continue informal and animated discussions. Mises was infinitely patient and kind with even the most dim-witted of us. ... However wonderful the seminar experience for knowledgeable students, I found it heartbreaking that Mises should be reduced to these frowzy circumstances. Poor Mises: there was scarcely a Hayek or a Machlup or a Schütz among these accounting and finance majors, and Childs' Restaurant was no Viennese café" (Rothbard n.d.).

The significance of this early seminar is highlighted through its subsequent impact through the work of its participants in various countries and international organisations, in universities and in think tanks. The cohort includes some of the key actors in the formation of the second Chicago school; of the influence on the ideological and disciplinary orientation of the economics transacted at the London School of Economics; in the formation and subsequent development of the Mont Pelerin Society (also accounting for the earlier Parisian initiative of Louis Rougier); in the setting up of a spectrum of libertarian, neoconservative, neoliberal or neoclassically oriented corporate donors and think tanks in the USA and UK—many of these waves of influence being propelled by Friedrich Hayek. The hostile interface with the Cambridge Keynesian economic tradition arguably had significant roots in Ludwig von Mises's Privatseminar in Vienna.

Geneva

Slobodian follows the episode into the next stage of its evolution. "The stage shifted from Vienna to Geneva as liberals fled the coming fascist wave"; as Mises left to take up his professorship, "members of his seminar saw their master off with the wish that 'his strong spirit will show the League of Nations the way'". Slobodian writes: "the core cohort of the neoliberal intellectual movement that had coalesced in Vienna had found their closest partners in the Businessman's International of the ICC and the League of Nations" (2018, p. 54).

Cooperation flourished; Slobodian points to the support from Arthur Salter, then head of the League of Nations economics section, and later a member of the MPS; Mises and Hayek founded a research institute on business cycles in Vienna in 1927 with the support of the ICC; Hayek linked up with the centre for global economic research in Geneva; the League of Nations hired Gottfried Haberler in 1934 to work on the world economy, work which followed on from that of Bert Ohlin (also a prominent member later of MPS); in 1937, Wilhelm Röpke, a key neoliberal figure and core member later of the MPS, moved to Geneva. Gathering the scattered evidence, Quinn Slobodian rightly points out that "the core group of the future neoliberal movement either relocated to Geneva or passed through the Swiss city in the 1930s. ... Historians refer to the famous 1938 Lippmann Colloquium in Paris as the 'birthplace of neoliberalism'. They rarely note, though, that it was only one episode in a decade of overlapping projects devoted to studying the conditions of 'the Great Society', not at the national but at the scale of the globe; ... In the 1920s and 1930s, Geneva was confronting not only the problems of the world as individual concerns, but the problem of the world itself—how to manage the globe as a whole. ... The city seemed like the only candidate for the capital of the world policy that H.G. Wells called Cosmopolis" (ibid., p. 57).

Slobodian (2018, p. 58) highlights a second hallmark of 'the Geneva School of neoliberals', one that was subsequently ensconced at the centre of future strategy: this was rooted in "Hayek's conclusion in that decade, building on an earlier skepticism about statistics cultivated in Viennese debates, that comprehensive knowledge itself would always, and must always, elude the economist because of its necessary dispersal among all members of society". By the end of the 1930s the Geneva School neoliberals agreed that the most important pillars of integration could not be represented or understood through graphs, charts, tables, maps, or formulas". "They redirected their attention to cultural and social bonds ... the framework of tradition and the rule of law ... to the search for state and legal forms ... at the level of the nation but also, more importantly, at the level of the world". One can see here, simultaneously, Hayek's subsequent critical emphasis on the power of ideas for desired change; and simultaneously the basis of his views on information exchange and knowledge building through social interaction, leading to, and deriving from, his theoretical objections to the Walrasian tatonnement-type general equilibrium framework.

Pilgrims Atop a Mountain, Mont Pelerin, Switzerland, April 1947
April 1947, in Pelerin Palace, aka Hotel du Parc, a belle époque-style luxury hotel built in 1906 in the mountain village of Mont Pelerin soon after a funicular rail link was established in 1900 with Vevey on Lac Leman, between Montreaux and Lausanne, Switzerland. The hotel had "a breath-taking panoramic view", "a quiet semi-rural setting conducive not only for reflection, but for hiking as well" "many of the original Pelerinians, including Hayek, were accomplished hikers and mountaineers", so they could well have huffed and

puffed up and down the mountain without the rail. However, the hotel was not up to the standards desired for the 50th anniversary conference of the MPS, which met in April 1997 at the nearby Hotel Le Mirador, though there were only three left standing of the original 36 who could have made any comparison with the venue of the inaugural 1947 meeting, viz., Friedman, Director and Allais (Kaza, 1997, with reference to the year 1996).

Financial Sponsors
Ever from its birth, the Mont Pelerin Society was promoted by finance, banks and corporates.

"In April 1947 Albert Hunold, a senior Credit Suisse official, brought together thirty-six scholars at the pretty Swiss resort of Mont Pelerin near Geneva to plan for a revival of liberalism ... the foundation of the global intellectual fightback against Keynes." "From the start the Mont Pelerin Society was funded by the three biggest Swiss banks and two largest insurance companies, not to mention the Swiss central bank" (Shaxson, 2011, p. 83). Switzerland was at the time "the world's pre-eminent tax haven".

This is how Hunold, writing in 1958, recalls it: "It was November 1945 that Professor Hayek who has become world famous through his book, *The Road to Serfdom*, was on a lecture tour through America and Europe. In the course of this tour, he addressed the students of the University of Zurich and as afterwards invited to a reception given by a group of distinguished Swiss industrialists and representatives of the banking and insurance business. After dinner they discussed the possibilities of regenerating the ideas of classical liberalism in order to refute the growing danger of socialism in the period following the Second World War. ... Only one year later [I] was able to raise sufficient money from Swiss businessmen to pay free board for about fifty people for ten days in a Swiss hotel. Professor Hayek, then staying Chicago, succeeded in raising the necessary funds for the travelling expenses of a dozen Americans to Switzerland and we both agree to send out invitations to about one hundred economist, sociologists, historians, journalists and social philosophers, mainly first rate scholars at American and European universities" (Hunold, 1958, p. 1). Other reports refer to fifty invitations being sent out in December 1946, with 39 eventually participating in the opening conference. With Hayek in the lead, Hunold was at the heart of the MPS, raising and running its finances, editing a journal he started, amongst other activities, till he fell out with other seniors of the MPS, in particular Fritz Machlup, leading to an unseemly public airing of critiques with Hayek himself; he resigned from the MPS in 1962.

The MPS deliberately raised funds from a diversity of sources in order to maintain its independence as a core think tank, and kept clear of direct donations from political parties, though its funders could well also have been supporting political parties and organisations of the MPS ilk. Burgin notes that "the 1954 Venice meeting was financed by the Banca d'Italia, industrial organizations based in Rome and Milan and a Venetian foundation; the 1957 St Moritz meeting was financed by 23 firms throughout Switzerland; and the

1960 Kassel meeting was financed by six enterprises from five German cities. The organization of each meeting required its own capital campaign and the cultivation of new regional sources of support."

In the early years, from 1947 till 1958, the Volker Fund made a vital contribution through underwriting the substantial travel costs of the large American delegations; these were subsequently picked up by the Earhart and Reim foundations (Burgin, 2012 see Butler/Hartwell). This support covered academics but also representatives from the Volker Fund and the FEE who could monitor and assess the event from the point of view of future donations and take a proactive role in setting up new activities and connecting with promising individuals. In the first meeting, this group included Baldy Harper, Leonard Read, Orval Watts and Loren 'Red' Miller.

> Miller had multiple reasons to attend the first meeting. Luhnow could not attend, so he was there to represent him and to see whether the Volker Fund's monies had been well-spent. Aaron Director would be in attendance, so he could also inquire into how the (Volker-funded) Free Market Study was coming along. He also wanted to identify who among the various people in attendance were 'sound', the sort who might be worthy of further support. Friedrich Hayek would be among those who passed the test. In a year's time Miller would use the connections he had made with Director to start the ball rolling to bring Hayek to the University of Chicago. (Caldwell, 2020, p. 23)

> From the start, the Mont Pelerin Society had strong links to the City of London, via Sir Alfred Suenson-Taylor, later Lord Grantchester, chairman of a major insurance company in the city of London and brother of a British member of parliament. Suenson-Taylor not only provided a welcome link to a network or wealthy anti-government City financiers, but he also helped unlock Bank of England funds to support British delegations to the Mont Pelerin Society meetings. To actively support an overtly anti-government movement is a curious role for a central bank. (Shaxson, 2011, p. 84)

Since its inception, the Bank of England was a law unto itself and beyond the control of government, its workings were enveloped in secrecy; "it was only in 1946, during Keynesianism's brief dominance after the horrors of war and the Great Depression, that the politicians had the political strength to nationalise it" (ibid.) though this did little to make it any more susceptible to political control. "The Bank of England has also remained a powerful lobbyist within the British state, a sort of praetorian guard protecting the City of London and its libertarian world view—and by extension of the global offshore system." It was called "the single most powerful repository for liberal thought in Britain" (Gary Burn, cited by Shaxson, 2011, p. 85).

Hayek had also discussed his plans most closely with Sir John Clapham,[21] who died a year before the inaugural MPS meeting in 1946; Clapham, who in

1944 had completed a two-volume history of the Bank of England, was also instrumental in securing financial support from the Bank for the MPS. Clapham studied under Marshall at Cambridge, alongside Pigou and JM Keynes his colleagues at King's, but notwithstanding their theoretical positions and great influence on the discipline, he practised differently; Peter Mathias (2008) observes that "Clapham was widely admired by the economists at the London School of Economics, agreeing with their advocacy of economic liberalism in current policy". The liberal tradition matured at LSE after the appointment of Lionel Robbins after the death of Allyn Young in 1929; and Clapham's contact with the LSE group, including especially Hayek—though perhaps not Robbins who was on official government duties—would have greatly increased during the war years when LSE shifted its operational base to Cambridge. Keynes and Clapham both died within the space of a month in 1946. At the Mont Pelerin meeting, Hayek expressed his regret that "two men with whom I had most fully discussed the plan for this meeting both have not lived to see its realisation"[22]; these were Henry Simons at Chicago and John Clapham at Cambridge.

Despite its growing size and international spread, the MPS never seemed to be short on funds for its meetings. Referring to the meeting of the MPS in Brussels (1974): "As is customary, the Mt. Pelerin meetings were held in one of the most expensive hotels in the city as befitted the fact that almost all attendees were either think-tank executives travelling on expense accounts, South American latifundia owners, for whom hundred-dollar bills were small change, or the officers of the Society itself, a self-perpetuating oligarchy who, thanks to its members' dues, travelled around the world in first-class accommodations" (Ronald Hamowy quoted in Leeson, 2015, p. 10). This description comes not from some external critic but from one of their own; Ronald Hamowy, a Canadian libertarian political scientist, was in the inner circle of the Chicago group's activities and himself a long-standing member of the MPS; he obtained his PhD on social thought working under Hayek in Chicago, and went on to compile a heavy encyclopaedia of libertarian thought (Hamowy, 2008).

British intellectual life at the time had a distinctly different orientation, with the proximate, palpable experience of war shortages, rationing and planning in a centralised, economic system; planning was not a bad word, nor was state regulation, and indeed, nor was socialism (of some unspecified kind). The Continentals, in contrast, were "these chaps [who] took themselves too seriously in coming together and discussing the routes and origins and prospects for freedom. But the whole world was shadowed by the Iron Curtain, the Russian threat, by the failure to establish democracies in the Eastern European countries, and by the prevalence everywhere intellectually of these ideas of

---

[21] Sir John Clapham chaired a talk given by Hayek to the Political Society at King's College, Cambridge, in February 1944 (Caldwell, 2020, p. 1).
[22] Wiki, "Mont Pelerin Society", https://en.wikipedia.org/wiki/Mont_Pelerin_Society

collectivism arising from the war" (Harris, 2000, p. 2). This deeply embedded anti-state, anti-collectivist, anti-socialist sentiment was generally shared by this group of radical libertarians who believed that only an entirely free market, individualism and a system based on private property could deliver its ideal. This was the message of Hayek's *The Road to Serfdom*, the bible of this intercontinental movement; Ralph Harris states: "the road to serfdom he took as generally as being a descent into the Dark Ages" (ibid., p. 6). He referred to it as "a life-and-death struggle"; "there was something of a religious war about it" (Harris, 2000, p. 7).

The First Meeting of Minds

These pilgrims and apostles came together, quite appropriately at Mont Pelerin, viz., Mount Pilgrim, and their high priests and oracles were the two characters who dominated the Society from the beginning, Hayek and Friedman. "The participants at the Society's first meeting were a diverse group, a mix of American libertarian economists mostly from Chicago, and European free-market moderates.[23] Disagreements were apparent during the session. One was between Chicago School monetarists and adherents of the Austrian School, another between theists and agnostics." But there was a lot between these markers of disagreements, and "the original Pelerinians could agree on everything save the subjects of God and gold".[24] Strong disagreements emerged between the continental gold-standard proponents and the Chicago monetarist school, the former led by Ludwig von Mises—an extreme outlier on the classical liberal policy scale—who, as Lionel Robbins wrote in a letter to his wife, hurled accusations against others accusing them of being socialists.

---

[23] The participants at the first meeting of the Mont Pelerin Society were: Friedrich Hayek; Ludwig von Mises, Austrian School; Wilhelm Ropke (key figure in the 1948 German currency reform, with Walter Eucken); Walter Eucken; Maurice Allais, French economist; Karl Popper; John Davenport, American journalist; Henry Hazlitt, American journalist; Lionel Robbins; Leonard E. Read, from Foundation for Economic Education (FEE) newly established in 1946; F. A. Baldy Harper, from FEE; Vernon Orval Watts, from FEE; Milton Friedman, Chicago school; Aaron Director (Milton Friedman's brother-in-law) Chicago School; Frank H. Knight, Chicago School; George J. Stigler, Chicago school; Carlo Antoni, Rome; Hans Barth, Zurich; Karl Brandt, Stanford Cal; Stanley R Dennison, Cambridge; Erick Eyck, Oxford; H. D. Gideonse, Brooklyn, N.Y.; F. D. Graham, Princeton, N.J.; T. J. B Hoff, Oslo; Albert Hunold, Zurich; Bertrand de Jouvenal, Cexbres, Vaud; Carl Iversen, Copenhagen; John Jewkes, Manchester; Fritz Machlup, Buffalo, N.Y.; L. B. Miller, Detroit; Felix Morley, Washington DC; Michael Polanyi, Manchester; William E. Rappard, Geneva; Herbert Tingsten, Stockholm; Francois Trevoux, Lyon; Miss C. V. Wedgwood, London.

"The Oxford-trained historian and sole female participant Cecily Veronica Wedgwood was an editor at the British weekly *Time and Tide*, which had been an outlet for a number of contributions by Hayek: in 1945 alone he published seven pieces there" (Caldwell, 2020, p. 21). Miss Wedgwood was not the only female in the gathering it would seem as, according to Frank Hahn, Dorothy Salter, his contemporary at LSE and his future wife, attended the inaugural meeting; she was working as an assistant to Hayek at the LSE at that time. However, there is no reference or record to hand of Frank Hahn ever having joined the MPS.

[24] Kaza (1997); comment attributed to Davenport in the MPS meeting in Cambridge in 1984.

(Elsewhere, Samuelson [2009] recalled that Ludwig von Mises had accused Gottfried Haberler of being a communist.) And there were other contrasts between Mises (a refugee from Nazi totalitarianism) with those of the Chicago School, and with those of the Freiburg School. Given the inherent tendency of intellectuals to argue and bicker and fall apart, Ralph Harris (2000, p. 3) asks: "how did this thing keep on the road, and what kept it together?" The answer lay in the bond between the two gurus: "these two were always ... absolutely together, no rivalry, no fractions, committed to understanding and extending the free economy" (ibid., p. 3). "The strength of the MPS was that you combined Hayek and Friedman as you have two feet to walk—you had both the political economist in Hayek and you had the scientific positive economist in Friedman" (ibid., p. 25). "Some of us would be Hayekian in the mornings and Friedmanite in the evenings. ... It was a marvellous combination, a very powerful combination" (ibid., p. 25).[25]

Harris was too young to be part of the cast of 36 economists, historians, journalists and other libertarian intellectuals at the start of Hayek's 'great dream'—the creation, in 1947, of the Mont Pelerin Society at "this idyllic spot, this marvellous congenial hotel". Harris says "Hayek wouldn't have had any idea how to run a conference. ... I can't imagine Hayek running a picnic" (ibid., p. 15). The moving organising force behind this original act was a German-Swiss, Renault, "who treated Hayek as a god". There was a handful of entities from England, Lionel Robbins from London, John Jewkes then at Manchester and later at Oxford, Stanley Dennison (Dennis Robertson's close associate) from Cambridge. The event and the Society were overwhelmingly dominated by Americans, "who had the great commitment to constitutional freedom, and also had cash to travel around a bit more easily". And so, "here they were in this rather traditional old-fashioned hotel, comfortable sofas and all that, just holding discussions entirely among themselves, almost as a secret society, in a manner of speaking" (Harris, 2000, pp. 1–2).

A sense of the gathering is provided by Ola Innset (2017) in his doctoral dissertation a good part of which is devoted to the Mont Pelerin Society.[26]

---

[25] There might also have been powerful undercurrents of deeper differences. "The [editorial introduction to the] files [of Hayek's correspondence held by the MTF Archives] show Hayek in one vital respect at odds with the new Conservatism: he was not a monetarist in the manner, say, of Milton Friedman. Indeed Hayek's distance from Friedman and from modern economics as a whole is one of the most striking features of the correspondence, set out for example in a letter he wrote to Arthur Seldon in May 1985: 'I do indeed regard the abandonment of the whole macroeconomics nonsense as very important, but it is for me a very delicate matter and I have for some time avoided stating my views too bluntly and would not have time to state them adequately. The source of the difficulty is the constant danger that the Mont Pelerin society might split into a Friedmanite and a Hayekian wing. I have long regretted my failure to take time to criticise Friedman's *Positive Economics* almost as much as my failure to return to the critique of Keynes *General Theory* after I had dealt with his *Treatiese. [sic]*'" https://www.margaretthatcher.org/archive/Hayek.asp

Innset offers several insights. On ethnicity, he points out that the group was 100 per cent white (ibid., p. 163); the group comprised all "middle-aged, suit-clad men" and in the room, "the rich smell of pipe smoke lies heavily in the air" (ibid., p. 134). A striking observation pertains to life expectancy of the attendees: while the average life expectancy in UK and Germany in 1900 was 45.6 years, the average lifetime of the thirty-six participants turned out to be 84 years! (ibid., p. 159). He comments: "life expectancy is closely linked to social class, where those in comfortable material circumstances, on average and for a multitude of different reasons, live much longer than those with less financial freedom. It could possibly be argued that the early neoliberals wanted to extend that fabled 'freedom in economic affairs' to more people than themselves, but arguments pointing in a different direction could also easily be posed. It is certainly beyond discussion that the early neoliberals' own position within the social order they wanted to save was one of great privilege" (ibid., pp. 159–160). The point is driven further home: Almost without exception, the attendees of the first Mont Pelerin Conference were white men with PhDs,[27] and with materially comfortable lives hailing from materially comfortable backgrounds. This is not to detract from the value or logical consistency of their arguments, but when contextualising their intellectual efforts, it is worth noting at the very outset of this narrative what a homogenous group the attendees of the first Mont Pèlerin meeting really were, especially since they were discussing matters pertaining to all of human kind and the way in which modern society was to be organised. Their view was one located in a very specific social stratum. Their view of the growth of state power and government expenditure was thus that of a privileged elite, something which is highly visible for instance in Wilhelm Röpke's 1947 text "International crusade against luxuries", which was circulated to all members of the society just after the meeting. In the midst of what we will later read was a starvation crisis of catastrophic proportions, Röpke found it opportune to write a long article complaining about the difficulty of obtaining luxury goods, like fine leather satchels, and he blamed this horrid state of affairs on taxation and illiberal government intervention (Innset, 2017, pp. 157–158). Innset refers to the exercise as the formation of "a neoliberal

---

[26] Not entirely unsurprisingly, Caldwell (2020, p. 1n2), himself both a scribe and a vocal member of the Mont Pelerin Society seems not to approve of Ola Insett's work on the MPS. He cites Hartwell (1995) and Burgin (2012) as "good books"; but "sadly a recent dissertation, Innset (2017), half of which focuses on the 1947 meeting, is rather a disappointment. The author knows little economics, has a presentist bias, and though he claims to offer a corrective to more ideologically driven accounts he consistently represents liberalism as the ideology of an upper class elite worried principally about redistribution and loss of power." Another critical work on the MPS is Mirowski and Plehwe (2009), not acknowledged in Caldwell's footnote. George Stigler (1985) also devotes pages to the first meeting of the MPS in his *Memoirs*, and Hunold (1958) has provided an insider's view of the setting up and the early years of the MPS in his personal note presented at the 9th meeting of the MPS.

[27] The possible exceptions Innset mentions are: "the American journalists Felix Morley and Henry Hazlitt and libertarian activists Loren Miller and Leonard Read" (ibid., p. 157n1).

cadre", calling the group "an army of fighters for freedom". A glimpse of a global perspective is constructed by Innset by citing Rappard's stereotypical caricature of 'the lazy and idle' Arabs in Algeria, allegedly indifferent to improvement through work, an ascription casually extended in conversation at the conference also to be applicable to Welsh miners (ibid., pp. 161–162); and then Innset jumps to the MPS meeting in St. Moritz a decade later, where there was a discussion on the theme of the liberation of colonies, and where, in the account of the historian Kim Priemel, the "main thrust was an embarrassingly simplistic and brazenly racist justification of European imperialism, indicating that the plight of the world's people of colour was not a very pressing issue for the society's members" (Innset, 2017, pp. 161–162).

In contrast, Harris provides an insider's reassuring perspective: "they were extremely peaceful chaps. They weren't all militant. You couldn't imagine them rousing up crowds of people. They were very thoughtful, serious people" (ibid., p. 4). And Hayek receives a completely clean chit: "he was quite a cuddly man … an extremely attractive and vulnerable and gentle and shy figure, shrinking sometimes from too much attention.[28] You couldn't imagine him as a dictator. And yet that's how some people saw him, as a Hitlerian, counter-Hitler authoritarian figure. It's absurd. Actually, it's the reverse of his nature, his argument, and his message" (ibid., p. 8). This portrayal is both beguiling and somewhat disingenuous, and certainly over-sanitised: indeed, while Hayek was the source of the vision and the ideas, the programme of implementation was outsourced to ruthless politicians, such as Thatcher, Reagan or Pinochet.

Friedman attended the inaugural meeting of the MPS, but then kept away for the next decade; after he returned, he was fully engaged. Apparently, Hayek had mooted winding up the MPS after 10 years when it was in difficult times. At Mont Pelerin, Hayek had spoken of the life-and-death struggle they were embarking on and said would take 20 or more years to win. But politics and society took the road Hayek and his followers were warning against: UK was in the middle of its 'golden age' of capitalism, and Harris tells us that Hayek "went through a stage of intense depression"; from being one who "had led an active, vigorous and contentious existence, [he] began to show signs of disorientation and lack of concentration and disinterest in the 1960's", became "more broody [with] less spring in his step" (ibid., p. 8). On top of this, "Hayek went through a period in the '50s and '60s [when] he was hated, execrated. Academics on the left, who were by no means unpleasant individuals, would not meet him. … It was deep hatred" (ibid., p. 6). He concludes

---

[28] Innset (2017, p. 249) also ploughs through the archives, counts the lines of the minutes of all speeches and converts it—admittedly rather approximately and imperfectly—into an index of the 'total speaking time' of each participant; even bearing in mind the necessary qualifications, the bottom line speaks for itself: Hayek alone accounted for 42 per cent of the speaking time, and the next on the list was Rappard with 6.9 per cent—though with Friedman and von Mises in the room, such a distribution might seem incredible!

that the "hatred for Hayek or Friedman was a tribute to their effectiveness" (ibid., p. 7).

Separately, Friedman, as MPS President in 1970, had suggested that MPS close shop in 1972, after a "grand 25th anniversary meeting ... and then disbanding ... in a blaze of glory; ... Organizations have a tendency to persist after they have outlived their function. Unlike old soldiers, they generally do not ever fade away" (Friedman, quoted in Leeson, ed. Collaborative Biography Part 1:29). These impulses are explicable in terms of the continuing hold of Keynesian ideas and prescriptions over intellectuals and policy makers over this entire period; enough to make on wonder which 'blaze of glory' Friedman might have been referring to. It is quite obvious, with the benefit of looking back in time, that closure would have been a disastrous move not least for Hayek and Friedman, in terms of the imminent favourable turn of events that not just propped up and imparted massive credibility and intellectual status to Hayek, Friedman and MPS, but also made the MPS-centred networks infinitely more powerful than before; this halo and afterglow effect of the 1974 and 1976 'Nobel' Prizes to Hayek and Friedman respectively lasting well into the future. By 1977, a delighted Hayek pronounced that "the main purpose [of the MPS] had been wholly achieved" (ibid., p. 29). Deepak Lal (2009, p. 2), as President of the Mont Pelerin Society, in his lecture at a specially convened meeting of the Society, noted that it was the "seeming intellectual 'victory' of classical liberal ideas [in the 1980s and 1990s] which led some distinguished members to argue for the winding up of the society (in 1975 and again in 1991). Current events show this would have been premature." The global financial crisis had shifted the goalposts of economic discourse. Classical liberal ideas, as Deepak Lal (2009) put it, had ruled the 1980s and 1990s "but, the current crisis requires us to assess whether our views and the policy conclusions we had derived from them were misguided. For all ideas need to be continually re-examined to test their continuing relevance and validity."[29]

---

[29] As the late member of this society Gottfried Haberler (a close friend and member of Hayek's Austrian circle) noted in his astute appraisal of Hayek's business cycle theory: "Keynes, Robbins, and many others were correct: if a cyclical decline has been allowed to degenerate into a severe slump with mass unemployment, falling prices, and deflationary expectations, government deficit spending to inject money directly into the income stream is necessary. Moreover, Hayek himself has changed his mind on this point" (Haberler, 1986, p. 422). (However, neither Austin Robinson (1978), nor Robert Skidelsky (2020, p. 8n.ii) found grounds to believe that Hayek had ever changed his mind or position on this.) So also, according to Lal, had the former Chairman of President Reagan's Council of Economic Advisors, the distinguished fiscal conservative Martin Feldstein who argued for a fiscal stimulus "because the current recession is much deeper than and different from previous downturns. Even with successful countercyclical policy, this recession is likely to last longer and be more damaging than any since the depression of the 1930s" (Feldstein [2009], quoted in Lal, 2009, p. 2).

Sarcastic Schumpeter, Sceptical Solow, Scathing Samuelson

Joseph Schumpeter came eventually and permanently to Harvard in 1932 from Austria, via England, Egypt and Germany. Days before he died in 1950, he delivered a lecture to the American Economic Association in New York. He asserted that liberalism had had its day and was no longer a force in public life and policy; sarcastically, he referred allegorically to the Mont Pelerin Society as a meeting of liberal economists "on the top of a Swiss mountain of which I have forgotten the name" (Hunold, 1958, p. 2). In reporting this, Hunold, who was the organisational catalyser enabling that first MPS meeting, asks: "Was Schumpeter right in his prophecies, and would he have said the same if he had been invited to join the group meeting above the Lake of Geneva?" Was it just a case of sour grapes? Hunold suggests Schumpeter might have had a different, more positive, assessment of the impact of the MPS had he lived to see "the enormous change, both in the ideological field and in policy-making which has since taken place in the Western World" (ibid.).

If Schumpeter did not take the MPS seriously at the point of inception, Solow is casually dismissive of its significance or achievements 60 years later. The MPS began "the work of transforming nineteenth-century liberalism and converting it into a force in the world", but Solow (2012) questions Burgin's recent account of the MPS on the grounds that "it tends to endow the MPS with more significance that it ever really had, whether within the economics profession or in the world at large". However, Solow's dismissal is somewhat too condescending and quick, perhaps because his focus and questions are too narrow. Solow would be quite right in terms of the direct impact of the MPS on the economics profession, but arguably quite wrong in terms of the impact on "the world at large". Of course, it has to be kept in mind that Chicago and Cambridge (USA), despite both being in the broad right-wing economics camp, were rivals and adversaries when it came to styles of theory and policy advocacy; and MPS was utterly 'Chicago', Solow was very 'MIT' and Schumpeter, 'Harvard'.

While acknowledging the worth of Hayek's work on markets, information and knowledge, Samuelson (2009) is scathingly dismissive of the rest of his economics, and especially the politics of *The Road to Serfdom*, including caustic asides to the Mont Pelerin Society.

> Two-thirds of a century after the book got written, hindsight confirms how inaccurate its innuendo about the future turned out to be. Consider only Sweden's fig-leaf middle way. As I write in 2007, Sweden and other Scandinavian places have somewhat lowered the fraction of GDP they use to devote through government. But still they are the most 'socialistic' by Hayek's crude definition. Where are their horror camps? Have the vilest elements risen there to absolute power? When reports are compiled on 'measurable unhappiness', do places like Sweden, Denmark, Finland and Norway best epitomize serfdoms? No. Of course not. American conservatives ... confronted by such counter evidence would say to me up to his last years: 'Paul, just you wait'. I never tired of waiting. Actually, let the

contents-analyst anthropologist go on to put her microscope on the many forewords to *The Road to Serfdom* quoted in forewords by the late Milton Friedman (see Hayek, 1994). She will conclude that the 'serfdoms' believed to have occurred in accordance with Hayek's 1940 crystal ball are not at all the Nazi-Burma-Mao-Castro totalitarian catastrophes. Instead they are the mixed economies that have flourished almost everywhere in the post-1945 years!

And bypassing the recent greening and reinventing of Hayek, à la Caldwell amongst others, as a moderate liberal,[30] Samuelson weighs into Hayek's stance on key social issues: "The Hayek I met on various occasions—at the LSE, at the University of Chicago, in Stockholm (1945), at Lake Constance-Lindau Nobel summer conferences—definitely bemoaned progressive income taxation, state-provided medical care and retirement pensions, fiat currencies remote from gold and subject to discretionary policy decisions by central bank and treasury agents. Not only is this what constitutes his predicted serfdoms, do notice that when the same anthropologist scans Milton Friedman's various admiring forewords, her verdict will be that Hayek and Friedman were in essential agreement on what their singular verbal definitions are connoting" (ibid.). Hayek's economics, apart from the one strand cited above, fares even worse: Hayek's *Prices and Production*, "mumbo-jumbo … grossly misdiagnosed macroeconomics"; he refers to Sraffa—"Keynes's bulldog" Sraffa's annihilation of it, and to Kahn's "Hayek is a nut" aside; *The Pure Theory of Capital* "was a pebble thrown into a pool of economic science that seemingly left nary a ripple"; "so you might say Hayek as an economist fell into what physicists call a black hole". Samuelson regards Friedman being far more effective than Hayek in reaching economists with their message, with the converse holding true in influencing the lay public. Together, they made a formidable team.

So did the MPS convert its dream into reality? Harris: "the answer is yes. If, in 1947, some super-intelligence had asked what to do to change the dominant economic ideas of this age, they could not have done better than what happened spontaneously through Hayek. … A journalist described the Mont Pelerin Society as comparable to the Communist Third International … and actually, these 36 men meeting for ten days in Switzerland did lay the foundation to a development throughout the world. It was based … on networking … a system of informal contacts between scholars who met rarely, but were in touch with their writings. That has been a powerful way of spreading this gospel" (ibid., pp. 27–28).

The faith in the power of capital and capitalism has maintained its hold and has withstood the recessions and depressions, and the global congregation was

---

[30] A prominent strand of this is to cite Keynes' appreciative comments on *The Road to Serfdom*; another is to argue that Hayek was really in favour of various kinds of social redistribution; yet another is to challenge Hayek and Friedman's involvement with or expressed support for fascist and totalitarian regimes. For a partial rebuttal focussing on the exchange with Keynes, see Skidelsky (2020).

on full display at the celebratory conference at the Hoover Institution, Stanford, to mark the 40th anniversary of the first MPS meeting that was held at Stanford in 1980. (https://www.mpshoover.org/)

3.2.4 UK: Antony Fisher, Global Venture Capitalist of Think Tanks

> Hayek advises Fisher; Fisher recruits Harris; Harris meets Seldon. In nine words, that is the start of the IEA. (Blundell, iea.org.uk)

Antony Fisher was born into "a family of mine owners, members of parliament, migrants and military men" (Blundell, 2004, p. 16). Eton was followed by Trinity College, Cambridge, and then the war intervened, interrupting a life of extravagance and luxury. His father was killed by a Turkish sniper in 1917. His brother Basil and he were fighter pilots in the war where Basil was shot down and killed, as were other close friends. A devastated Antony was grounded, and turned to developing the Fisher trainer, a machine to train pilots to shoot better. Blundell reports that Fisher "was also an avid reader of *Reader's Digest*. Every copy was devoured, read aloud to his family, heavily underlined and kept in order in his study. His first child Mark, recalls a wall of Antony's study lined with row upon row of years—decades even—of copies of *Reader's Digest*" (ibid., pp. 16–17). Blundell carefully assembles the subsequent timeline of how Fisher had his first encounter with Friedrich Hayek—a meeting that was personally life-changing, as well as landmark event for subsequent political developments. *The Road to Serfdom* was published by Routledge in UK in March 1944, and ran into five reprints in 15 months, the wartime shortage of paper notwithstanding. The University of Chicago published the American edition in September, and given its popularity, it was published in a condensed form in *Reader's Digest* in April 1945—and so landed on the desk of 'Fisher, the *Digest* junkie' (ibid., p. 19). Blundell tentatively reconstructed the story, with the help of conversations with the Fisher, Hayek and their respective sons, Mark and Laurence. After the war, both LSE and Hayek were back in London; Fisher was a squadron leader working at the War Office in Central London, "just a ten-minute walk from the LSE". Fisher read the cover story, noted that the author was at nearby LSE, made a phone call to confirm that the LSE was back in situ in London, and one lunchtime or late one afternoon, Fisher makes the short walk from his office to the LSE and knocks on Hayek's door. Fisher also recalled the physical setting of Hayek's office in minute and accurate detail including its proximity to that of the dreaded Harold Laski. Fisher claimed that after small talk (which neither excelled at) the conversation went like this:

Fisher: I share all your worries and concerns as expressed in *The Road to Serfdom* and I'm going to go into politics and put it all right.
Hayek: No you're not! Society's course will be changed only by a change in ideas. First you must reach the intellectuals, the teachers and writers,

with reasoned argument. It will be their influence on society which will prevail, and the politicians will follow. (ibid., p. 20)[31]

For close to ten years, the inspiration and idea were put on hold, as Fisher pondered Hayek's advice and searched for a viable approach. Meanwhile, he was systematically developing his farming business. In the late 1940s (or in 1952 according to Denham & Garnett, 1998) he travelled to the USA and visited the Foundation for Economic Education where he learned from Baldy Harper of a new agricultural breakthrough, the factory farming of chickens, and, armed with an introduction from Baldy, he travelled to the outskirts of Cornell and "met my first chicken farmer" (Blundell, 1990). "During the trip, he was shown a new farming method at Ithaca, New York. Fisher, [was] impressed by both the revolutionary method of broiler chick-farming and the work of the FEE." FEE put him in touch with Cornell specialists on chicken farming, which made him his millions to start IEA (Denham & Garnett, 1998, p. 66). Fisher returned primed both with the financial and institutional strategy to further the libertarian cause. "So the entrepreneur turned fighter pilot turned gunnery trainer turned stockbroker turned dairy farmer turned chicken pioneer turned turtle saviour became the Johnny Appleseed of the free-market movement, going all over the world and setting up new IEA-type operations" (Blundell, 2004, p. 24).[32]

"The IEA was formally set up in November 1955 with three founding trustees, Fisher, Smedley and Harding; and Advisory Council included, in addition, Lord Grantchester (formerly Sir Arnold Suenson-Taylor who had facilitated the financial support of the Bank of England for the first meeting of the Mont Pelerin Society in 1947), Sir Oscar Hobson, Professor Eric Nash and three LSE economists, George Schwartz, Graham Hutton and Colin Clark" (Denham & Garnett, 1998, p. 68). Ralph Harris was appointed the first Director of IEA in July 1956, and he was joined the following year by Arthur Seldon who had been a student of Lionel Robbins, Arnold Plant and Friedrich Hayek at the LSE from where he had graduated with a First in economics. It was he that decoded complex and difficult-to-read economic papers into readily comprehensible de-jargonised popular tracts for the engaged lay readers who were the carriers of 'public opinion' and who, in the Hayekian, strategy, were the targets

---

[31] "On this issue, let me quote Fisher's own words of 3 July 1985 when he spoke at a party at the IEA to celebrate its 30th [sic, should be 70th] birthday." At that party in July 1985 Fisher said: "It was quite a day for me when Friedrich Hayek gave me some advice which must be 40 years ago almost to the day and which completely changed my life. Friedrich got me started ... and two of the things he said way back are the things which have kept the IEA on course. One is to keep out of politics and the other is to make an intellectual case. ... If you can stick to these rules you keep out of a lot of trouble and apparently do a lot of good" (Blundell, 2004, pp. 20–21).

[32] To this chain could be added: owning a successful car rental firm; then a successful plane rental firm; and as a venture capitalist supporting the design and manufacture of a cheap sports car called Deroy which was under-powered and hence a failure (Blundell, 2004, p. 16).

of the strategies and instruments of libertarian persuasion. "The party's ideas originated in 'heavy tomes, then they get popularised and put in more digestible form by an IEA pamphlet, and then a *Daily Telegraph* article, chat, etc. And it permeates in that way': (Whitehead, 1985, p. 334). This is almost exactly the method which Hayek had laid down after the war" (ibid., p. 77). So from being "regarded as a bit of a joke by most economic writers", (Ronald Butt quoted in Cockett, 1994, p. 196) in its first decade, IEA's pamphlets and messages had "taken on a new relevance" by the mid-1970s. IEA publications addressed, unlike those say of the NIESR, to the politically engaged intelligentsia.

Ralph Harris describes the IEA as "the direct result of the Mont Pelerin Society, of *The Road to Serfdom*, of Hayek's meeting with my friend Antony Fisher. Its purpose was to bring together likeminded individuals to explore alternative policies, and that depended upon analysis and theory before prescription and policy" (Harris, p. 16); the IEA "became the vehicle for Hayek and Friedman and all of these great economists and philosophers; ... he wouldn't have been capable of assembling this gathering at Mont Pelerin" (ibid.).

While the CPS was a narrowly focussed task-driven political unit, the IEA steadily grew in its catchment and reach in the Thatcher reign in the establishment of which it had played an instrumental role over two decades. Over the period, it developed its clientele, recruited its protagonists and influencers in politics, in the media and in the academic world.

Through till 2009, IEA was associated with as many as 13 winners of the 'Nobel' economics prize through their publications: John Hicks, Friedrich Hayek, Milton Friedman, James Meade, George Stigler, James Buchanan, Ronald Coase, Gary Becker, Douglas North, Vernon Smith, Edmund Phelps, Oliver Williamson and Elinor Ostrom. It had published hundreds of books, pamphlets, articles, briefs; organised a vast number of public lectures; launched the *Journal of Economic Affairs*; been instrumental in opening the privately run University of Buckingham; received any number of honours, awards and recognitions from friendly governments and bodies, including an honorary fellowship for the Arthur Seldon at the LSE, and also the first ever honorary fellowship of the MPS; taken various leading positions in the Mont Pelerin Society; organised the MPS Oxford meeting and the bicentennial conference of Adam Smith; established other research and advocacy centres and units.[33]

Think tanks 'educate' and manipulate the lay public on one side of the equation, and prepare and support political leaders on the other. The IEA, and its offshoot, the CPS, virtually tutored the political education of Margaret Thatcher and Keith Joseph. Thatcher was an assiduous student; she read up and digested her readings, did her homework, was well prepared, and therefore usually well prepared to use her handbag in any argument; it helped that she

[33] For a detailed time line, see https://iea.org.uk/wp-content/uploads/2016/08/Chronology.pdf

could choose her battlefields. Yet, she was no blind follower of her gurus; they might know the principles, but she knew the lie of the land where they had to be enacted. Charles Moore (2013) in his authorised biography provides some glimpses into her style and sources. The process of the preparation of a speech ["The will-o-the-wisp of the classless society" in 1977] is typical of her style of preparation. "She heavily underlines articles from current newspapers and magazines by Shirley Robin Letwin, P.T. Bauer, Milton Friedman, Samuel Brittan, Robert Skidelsky, Hayek, Alan Walters and Paul Johnson" (Moore, 2013). When she met Alan Walters in September 1977, she had already read his *Money in Boom and Slump*; and Douglas Hague, her informal economics proxy tutor, found her "good on finance, very good on law, not very good on economics", but she had "the best memory I've ever met in anybody" (ibid.).[34]

Moore says "Mrs Thatcher was the most clamorous customer in the ideological market-place. As a result, she was able to stimulate a good supply, and buy up more than any rivals" (ibid.). The supply side of libertarian analysis and ideology was already reasonably well developed before she entered the fray, through the prior network of think tanks and thought organisations encouraged and catalysed by the impact of Hayek, combining the organisational and financial acumen, and entrepreneurial drive of pioneers such as Antony Fisher, Ralph Harris, Harold Luhnow, Leonard Read, Murray Rothbard and Baldy Harper in UK and USA; these, indeed, had served as the agents of economic, political and ideological instruction, nurturing potential leaders for future roles, including Keith Joseph, Margaret Thatcher and, to the extent possible, Ronald Reagan. The period after she and Ronald Reagan came to power witnessed a phenomenal expansion of the reach, voice and power of such right-wing libertarian think tanks and networks, such as the Institute of Economic Affairs, Centre for Policy Studies and the Adam Smith Institute in the UK.

Keith Joseph was virtually tutored by IEA policy pamphlets in the 1960s; then in 1974 set up the Centre for Policy Studies (CPS) of which he and Margaret Thatcher were the first directors, with Alfred Sherman running the show, and writing many of the speeches for Keith Joseph. Harris (2000) refers to Sherman as "a rough character"; others describe him a little less generously. Alfred Sherman, the political "adviser who preached Thatcherism before the term was invented"; a fundamentalist free marketeer whose "crude expressions, particularly about immigrants and non-whites, could give plain speaking a bad name"—overlooking the Russian origins of his own parents—speech

---

[34] But others felt differently; Paul Johnson, "although a strong Thatcherite, ... looked down on Mrs Thatcher somewhat. He described her as 'the most ignorant politician of her level that I'd come across until I met Tony Blair', but she was touchingly aware of her ignorance, being 'the eternal scholarship girl'" (Moore, 2013). She "had an innate distrust of the Bank of England for what she saw as its Keynesian approach, and she was particularly suspicious of Gordon Richardson, the Governor", describing him at one time as "a peacock of a man" (Moore, 2013); another time, "I must put someone there I can rely on". Moore gratuitously observes that "he was also a handsome man, but one who did not treat her as if she were an attractive woman—a fatal combination in her eyes: 'He was feline; she was canine'", according to one contemporary diagnosis (ibid.).

writer, from the Centre for Policy Studies, for Keith Joseph and Margaret Thatcher; "I articulated her instincts", he said; gave up on both for being too soft; invited Jean-Marie Le Pen to speak at a fringe meeting of the 1987 Conservative conference; an adviser to and defender of Radovan Karadzic; "as for the lumpenproletariat, coloured people and the Irish, let's face it, the only way to hold them in check is to have enough well-armed and properly trained police" (Kavanagh, 2006). He started on the extreme left as a youth fighting in the Spanish Civil War, but within a few years began his slide to the extreme and racist right. Thatcher rewarded him in 1983 with a knighthood; some years later he said of her: "Lady Thatcher is great theatre as long as someone else is writing her lines; she hasn't got a clue."[35]

Ralph Harris, who was made a baron, provides a corrective to Sherman's wild hubris with a reminder of Thatcher's instinct and exercise of raw power as unequivocally expressed in the 1970s and 1980s when "The hottest potato in the kitchen was depriving trade unions of privileges they had enjoyed for the previous 70 years. Since 1906, trade unions have been untouchable, specialized, privileged institutions that could impose damage on others without any charge against themselves, could cause strikes at a drop of a hat, not notice given. That she set up the trade union legislation was the influence of a lady totally, ruthlessly determined to go for the jugular, to attack the enemy in its heartland, the trade union movement. It was amazing that she should have done that. I can't think of any other politician who would have. Keith Joseph would not have had the spunk to do that and persevere with that. She was very determined and utterly blinkered once she'd got this thing, rather like the Falklands War, with all the people around saying you can't send this army, you can't service them, the ships will be shot to pieces. If it works, it's magnificent, and it worked" (ibid., p. 22).

Meanwhile, Antony Fisher had shifted gears and moved ahead to his next, this time global, horizon. By the time Margaret Thatcher and Ronald Reagan came to power, Fisher and his networks were deeply embedded in public policy and media establishments in the USA, UK and globally. In 1979, he set down his vision for what would become the Atlas Network: "I'm hoping to establish another 25 IEA-type institutes in some 24 countries, ultimately producing 250–350 new books per annum in some 17 languages".[36] He was already running the International Center for Economic Policy Studies ICEPS, and his board of advisors included the extreme libertarian James Buchanan (future chairman of the MPS and 'Nobel' Prize winner), Alan Peacock and Alan Walters (both with LSE provenance, with Walters being the economic adviser to Thatcher); the President was Edwin J. Feulner Jr (creator of the Heritage Foundation, and future chair of the MPS), and William J. 'Bill' Casey, future director of the CIA under Reagan, was the chairman. By 1984, there were 18

---

[35] Wikipedia: "Alfred Sherman".
[36] http://www.chafuen.com/atlas-economic-research-foundation-early-history

institutes in 11 countries[37]; by 1988, there were already 35 think tanks (Butler, 2015); three decades later in 2019, Atlas Network connects 502 think tanks across 99 countries.

Oliver Letwin,[38] Conservative MP till 2019, summarised Antony Fisher's contribution with the following equation[39]: "Without Fisher, no IEA; without the IEA and its clones, no Thatcher and quite possibly no Reagan; without Reagan no Star Wars, no economic collapse of the Soviet Union; quite a chain of consequences for a chicken farmer."[40]

3.3 Branding the Message: The 'Nobel' Prize

Reason: You certainly have a respectability and presence that most people and organizations labelled libertarian don't have ....
Friedman: That's because of one thing only; I won the Nobel Prize.[41]

Delighted as I am with the award, I must confess that the past eight weeks have impressed on me that not only is there no free lunch, there is no free prize. It is a tribute to the worldwide repute of the Nobel awards that the announcement of an award converts its recipient into an instant expert on all and sundry, and unleashes hordes of ravenous newsmen and photographers from journals and TV stations around the world. I myself have been asked my opinion on everything from a cure for the common cold to the market value of a letter signed by John F. Kennedy. Needless to say, the attention is flattering but also corrupting. Somehow, we badly need an antidote for both the inflated attention granted a Nobel Laureate in areas outside his competence and the inflated ego each of us is

---

[37] https://medium.com/@K_Gallowglaich/sir-antony-fisher-the-whetstones-thatcher-cameron-579084295c70

[38] Oliver Letwin is the son of William Letwin and Shirley Robin Letwin, both from families of Jewish immigrants from Ukraine; they met in Chicago where Shirley was a student of Hayek; both settled in London where William retired as a professor at the London School of Economics; Shirley taught at LSE and at Peterhouse, Cambridge, and worked at the Centre of Policy Studies; she met Margaret Thatcher through her friend Keith Joseph and then worked for her; their home in Regent's Park hosted the big names of the libertarian movement, including Hayek and Friedman. She shared an interest with Frank Hahn and Charles Feinstein: she wrote a book about Trollope in his centenary year, and in his review, Noel Annan (1983) writes "her book is not only about Trollope. It is a subversive book about England—subversive, that is to say, of those who until very recently brought about a consensus between the center and the left of the Conservative Party and the center and right of the Labour Party." Young Oliver was sent as a trouble-shooter by Keith Joseph to the SSRC to rummage through its archives to sniff out material Joseph could deploy in connection with the negotiations around the Rothschild Review of the SSRC in 1982.

[39] Oliver Letwin in *The Times*, 26 May 1994.

[40] 'James' has a comment on Eamonn Butler's (2015) eulogy to Fisher on the blog on the Adam Smith Institute website: "You forgot to mention the part about his battery chicken business being set up with the state compensation he received when his cattle herd contracted foot and mouth".

[41] Doherty (1995).

in so much danger of acquiring. (Milton Friedman, December 1976, quoted in Lebaron, 2006, citing Puttaswamaiah, 1995)

The Nobel prize tends to personalize science by concentrating symbolic capital in a small number of producers: this process is consistent with classical observations about the concentration of productivity and prestige in science. The Nobel prize is a central bank of symbolic capital which distributes this resource to exemplary figures, distinguished by the possession of this rare title. Laureates are crowned for a particularly innovative aspect of their work ... however, in the multiplication of discourses which follows the prize award, a person is constituted as a model: as the incarnation of a scientific life and even a life philosophy. (Lebaron, 2006)

3.3.1 The Stockholm Connection: Ideological Entrepreneurs

Two questions arise: first, how could a small country such as Sweden claim a central global initiative such as the new prize in economics? Sweden did have a respected tradition in economics, but it was still relatively small in scale. And second, why would Swedish decision makers want to make such an intervention?

There could be several responses to the first question: perhaps it was precisely because Sweden stood on the sidelines as a small yet respected player that it had the necessary potential credibility; a position of relative international neutrality was perhaps a relevant consideration; but maybe crucially, there was already a massive stock of accumulated credibility through the Nobel Prizes awarded in the five disciplines since 1895; the new prize could simply take a free ride and acquire respectability and acceptance purely on that stock of symbolic capital associated with the names of Nobel and Sweden. Seeking an answer to the second question uncovers the role played by sharp ideological entrepreneurs who recognised this massive potential of a new economics prize, and who intended to use it systematically for leveraging a shift in the national narratives of economic policy, away from social democracy, towards free-market liberalism favoured by big industrialists and their bankers.

Offer and Soderberg (2016, p. 102), in their fine study, sketch the context. "The post-war Social Democratic 'golden age' of economic growth, low unemployment, and expanding welfare states, then at its very height, was widely attributed to Keynesian demand management. It was easy to regard economists as technocratic facilitators. Economics education was on the brink of expanding in Sweden, but the discipline had not yet penetrated deeply into policy. Gunnar Myrdal, the leading Social Democratic economist, had described economists just a year before as the 'cavalry of the social sciences'. Tage Erlander, the prime minister, who had read some economics at university, believed that the Keynesian/Stockholm School synthesis was consistent with, and indeed supportive of Social Democracy, and could eliminate harmful slumps. His favourite economist was John Kenneth Galbraith, whose book *The Affluent Society* he quoted, a book which he regarded as a cornerstone of a renewed Social Democratic movement, one more sensitive to individual needs and their public provision." Sweden's model, or path, of steady growth, low inequality and high productivity seemed to be working. This pulls in that old aphorism:

"if it ain't broke, don't fix it". Of course, to the right-wing neoliberal economists who were the ideological agents of the proposal, social democracy was a philosophy at odds with their belief system and accompanying template of free market, minimum government, economic policy; and most of these economists, bankers, corporate chiefs formed the natural constituency of the Mont Pelerin Society, of which several had been members for many years by that time. Also, the prize potentially had a massive payoff: the cost to the Swedish Riksbank was minuscule, the reward for the individual was of course massive; but there were huge externalities in the form of the symbolic capital it generated in favour of the type of economics that the prize would favour. Thus, control over the prize-awarding committee was critically important; and this was fully achieved. The ideological entrepreneurs, from their vantage point, had pulled off a brilliant coup.

Erik Lundberg, and his supervisee and close associate Assar Lindbeck, effectively ran the 'Nobel' economics prize committee for its first twenty-five years. But the economics prize was the brainchild of Per Asbrink, the dynamic governor of the Swedish Riksbank from 1955 to 1973; he proposed it in the context of the 300th jubilee of the Bank. "In 1964, on Asbrink's request, Lindbeck began to advise him by means of late-night telephone calls a few times every month" (Offer & Soderberg, 2016, p. 99); then Asbrink, "a man of wayward brilliance and impulsive coups" (ibid.) got the idea to launch a new Nobel Prize for Economics; he bounced it off Lindbeck who consulted and got support from some important economist members of the Royal Swedish Academy of Sciences, viz., Myrdal, Ohlin, Lundberg and Svennilson. "The Nobel Foundation was dominated by businessmen. Lindbeck acted as the go-between" (ibid.). The proposition was developed largely without the benefit of feedback from the relevant regulatory decision-making bodies who were eventually confronted with either a Hobson's Choice or a fait accompli virtually on the eve of the formal announcement. It was a rich award, and 65 per cent of the value would be added on as an annual fee to cover processing overheads for the Nobel Foundation; alongside, it was thought that the Riksbank offered further financial incentives, pertaining to the Foundation's tax-free status, or the types of investments permitted—generosity which apparently somewhat leavened the passage. Although, on the requirement of the Nobel family, it would be named differently, in all other respects it would be administered on the same basis as the other Nobel Prizes.

As far as branding goes, the Riksbank Prize for Economic Sciences in Memory of Alfred Nobel is "an unparalleled example of successful trademark infringement" (see Buzaglo, 2010). A fascinating, if depressing, tale of near intrigue was told by Peter Nobel, a lawyer and descendent of Alfred Nobel, in a public statement on 11 October 2010, with a translated version provided in Buzaglo (2010).[42] The statement criticises the Economics Prize both because

---

[42] The original source is the Swedish (public service) television blog: http://svtdebatt.se/2010/10/vi-i-nobelfamiljen-tar-avstand-fran-ekonomipriset/

it is biased and because "it is a deceptive utilisation of the institution of the Nobel Prize and what it represents". Economics was not one of the original prizes: perhaps the first generation of Swedish economists (Cassel, Wicksell) were still too young to be famous enough to attract his attention in 1895, though the subject was already on firm and mature ground on the Continent, with Walras, Menger, Pareto well into their good years and works; or more simply, perhaps, as Peter Nobel suggests, Alfred Nobel apparently "disliked economists". When approached by the Nobel Foundation to obtain their assent, the Nobel family, like their forefather, wasn't keen either and made it clear that "it should not become like a sixth Nobel Prize" but should be kept discretely independent and at a distance from the regular prizes. Peter Nobel reports that the Rector of the Karolinska Institute "opposed the idea", and the Norwegian Parliament which makes the Nobel Peace Prize had "expressed serious misgivings"; to this can be added other evidence that Swedish physicists in the Academy also opposed the plan. Nevertheless, the family came under pressure to provide a rapid approval; Peter Nobel asks, "Why? Riksbanken's chief Per Asbrink had close contacts within the government, and for the Nobel Foundation it was vitally important to conserve its tax privileges". The burden fell especially on 87-year Martha Nobel the eldest, "with severely impaired hearing but intellectually in good form"; she was paid a visit by von Euler, the President of the Nobel Foundation; a written approval was obtained "under given conditions" that the new award would be kept separate; she told her nephew that "the whole thing was prearranged and impossible to oppose, so that one could only hope that they would keep their pledge that no confusion with the real Nobel prize should occur". Peter Nobel notes that "there was no approval from the Nobel family as a whole. We were informed only much later"; fait accompli by the Nobel Foundation, in similar style to the fait accompli practised by Asbrink and Lindbeck to finesse the official levels of the Bank and Parliament through an expeditiously short-circuited procedure. A pained Peter Nobel concludes: "What has happened is an unparalleled example of successful trademark infringement. However, nobody in the world can prevent journalists, economists and the general public from talking about the 'Nobel prize in economics', with all its connotations. That is why, in the name of decency and in order to honour Alfred Nobel's memory, this bank prize in his memory should be given on a different occasion than the Nobel day (a day of ceremonies headed by the King)." The outcome is known: the name indeed was "Sverige Riksbank Prize in Economic Science in memory of Alfred Nobel"; but for the rest, it was the PR bonanza that the right-wing economists and bankers had intended and anticipated, one that would revalue and dramatically enhance the reputation and street cred of the kind of mainstream economics that would underwrite and 'independently' validate their visceral ideological and material opposition to contemporary Swedish Social Democracy, which at the time was at full strength.

The proposal for a prize for economics had been opposed, amongst others, by the science lobby: in his wide-ranging interview with Assar Lindbeck, Gylfason points to the frequent criticism from natural scientists that "economics is too soft, too subjective, and too imprecise to merit such a prestigious prize"; one set of learned critics claimed that "the economics prize reduces the value of all other Nobel prizes" (Gylfason, 2005, p. 14). Lindbeck defends the award, pointing to the "enormous expansion of social science research, not least in economics" since the inception of the original Nobel Prizes; indeed, there had been suggestions to make the prize one for the social sciences in general rather than just for economics. But this was not feasible: "it is easier to agree about a prize in economics than in social sciences in general, which would have been a very heterogeneous area to reward. Moreover, the donor of the prize, Bank of Sweden, happened to be interested just in a prize in economics."

The editors of *Monthly Review* put it bluntly: "The reasons for the funding of the economics prize were purely political. In 1968, neoclassical or 'marginalist' economics was threatened as never before. The Swedish Social Democratic Party was at its height. Meanwhile, rebellions were breaking out everywhere against orthodox economics. The Union of Radical Political Economics (URPE) was formed in the USA that year. The Riksbank, advised by a young Swedish Social Democrat turned conservative economist, Assar Lindbeck, opted to establish the prize as a device to enhance the prestige of neoclassical economics—giving it a monopoly over 'economic science'—in its war against Swedish Social Democrats and radical economists. The original selection committee for the Riksbank Prize included two leading members of the Mont Pelerin Society (associated with arch-conservative economists Friedrich Hayek and Milton Friedman), but its driving force then and for the next quarter century was Lindbeck. In 1971, he published his most popular book, *The Political Economy of the New Left* (with a foreword by Paul Samuelson, who had received the prize the year before). Lindbeck's book was directed against URPE, and focussed its attacks on Paul Baran and Paul Sweezy's *Monopoly Capital* and the radical economics of *Monthly Review*."

In the original committee of six, Lundberg and Lindbeck (his doctoral students) would have needed the support of just a couple of other members to carry a decision; the committee, as seen, was quite like-minded, mainstream, right-wing and mathematically oriented, and as such, this pair would, in effect, have the award more or less under their control, essentially theirs to give. The committee composition remained remarkably stable.[43]

---

[43] The composition of the 14 committees during 1969–1982 can be summarised as below:

Ragnar Bentzel	14
Assar Lindbeck	13
Herman Wold	13
Erik Lundberg	12
Bertil Ohlin	1st 6
Ingvar Svennilson	1st 3
Sune Carlson	9

"Ingemar Stahl joined the Nobel Committee in succession to Lundberg in 1980 and also the Mont Pelerin Society in the same year" (Offer & Soderberg, 2016, p. 105).

Whereas the links with the Mont Pelerin Society were very strong, "the links with business were tighter" (Offer & Soderberg, 2016, p. 105), involving Lundberg, Lindbeck, Wold, Svennilson and Bentzel. "Four out of the six of the original Nobel Committee members were thus strong market advocates and had links with the IUI (Industrial Institute for Economic and Social Research)", set up by Swedish businessmen to challenge the government institute (ibid.). "Throughout the entire period after 1955, Lundberg also served as advisor to one of Sweden's largest banks. During the period 1973–1976 he was President of the Royal Swedish Academy of Sciences and he served as chairman of the Nobel Prize Committee for Economics from 1975–1980" (Baumol, 1990, p. 3). "The prize was defined as 'scientific', which in practice meant academic, and the committee was thus protected from left-wing interlopers ... no left-leaner would penetrate the circle of Nobel selection until the 1990s" (Offer & Soderberg, 2016, p. 106); Lundberg and then Lindbeck had kept the gates firmly shut over the 25 years they held the keys; and even subsequently, no change of criteria or direction has been discernible in the pattern of the economics awards.

Between 1969 and 1994, Lundberg and Lindbeck—in varying capacities as chairman, secretary or member—were key, perhaps dominant, parts of the Committees which made a remarkable seven awards to members of the Mont Pelerin Society, viz., Hayek, Friedman, Stigler, Buchanan, Allais, Coase and Becker. Offer and Soderberg (2016, p. 187) point out that Bertil Ohlin was also a member of the Committee for the prize to Hayek; he was part of the inaugural 1947 meeting of the MPS, "but did not join the society due to a prior commitment to a competing organization". Lundberg and Lindbeck were both members during 1969–1974; Lundberg became the chairman for 1975–1979, with his supervisee Lindbeck continuing as a member before taking over the chair for 1980–1994.

An exchange on Keynes is revelatory of Lindbeck's own *modus operandi*. In interviewing Lindbeck, Gylfason asks: "if you want to wield influence as an economist, what, in your view, is the way to do it?". Gylfason draws a comparison: Keynes was not a career politician; "yet Keynes probably had more influence on the political climate in Britain than most politicians in his day. The comparison is pertinent here, I think, because you have probably had more influence on the way Swedish politicians think about economic policy and organization than any other individual, and you have managed this without direct political involvement." Lindbeck agrees: "although Keynes probably had considerable direct influence on policies by being an advisor to governments, there is no question that his main influence came about indirectly via his influence on our minds—largely via textbooks for several generations of students and newspaper articles by many economists and others who had been influenced by his ideas. My own experience of policy advice and participation in public debate point in the same direction. To convince a politician in private about policy reforms is like writing in the sand on a beach. The writing will be washed out by the next storm" (ibid., pp. 10–11). The parallel with the

Hayekian strategy of building influence by shaping the political climate, the zeitgeist, is almost explicit.

Offer and Soderberg (2016, p. 187) reveal that in Sweden in the post-war decade, Erik Lundberg had been part of an attack on central planning and nationalisation, equated with the slide into serfdom à la Hayek. He published 'an influential book' on the subject, financed by the same business house that had funded the translation of Hayek's *Road to Serfdom* which had catalysed the attack on social democracy. Offer and Soderberg also report that Lindbeck opposed plans for carving a share from profits for a workers' fund to be managed by trade unions; and it is noteworthy that the Wallenbergs, a dominant force in Swedish financial and corporate sectors, provided financial support for Lindbeck's Stockholm Institution; and the Bonnier media empire owned the publisher of Lindbeck's memoirs (Offer & Soderberg, 2016, p. 190 n66).

Lindbeck elaborates: "Ohlin's and Lundberg's main imprint on Swedish society, I believe, is that they helped to dampen the political enthusiasm for central planning and nationalization during the first decade after World War II. They were also important advocates of free trade. Lundberg, moreover, convinced many Swedish economists about the limits, indeed dangers, of attempts to 'fine tune' macroeconomic policies. He also helped Swedish economists to appreciate the advantages of well-functioning markets, although the work that clarified this point most effectively for me was Hayek's little article 'The Use of Knowledge in Society', in the *American Economic Review* in 1945—an article also highly appreciated by Lundberg" (Gylfason, 2005, p. 9).

3.3.2 Some Early Awards: Setting the Direction

Jan Tinbergen—Ragnar Frisch 1969
Erik Lundberg delivered the opening speech at the presentation of the first prize shared by Ragnar Frisch and Jan Tinbergen, and these momentous words provide a clear indication of the criteria for the recognition of quality in 'economic science':

> In the past forty years, economic science has developed increasingly in the direction of a mathematical specification and statistical quantification of economic contexts. Scientific analysis along these lines is used to explain such complicated economic processes as economic growth, cyclical fluctuations, and reallocation of economic resources for different purposes. In economic life there is an elusive mixture of relatively systematic inter-relations, for which one can find a more or less regular repetitive pattern, and historically unique events and disruptions. To the layman, it may seem somewhat reckless to seek, without support from experiment, for laws of development within these extremely complicated processes of economic change, and to apply for this purpose the techniques of mathematical and statistical analysis. However, the attempts of economists to construct mathematical models relating to strategic economic relations, and then to specify these quantitatively with the help of statistical analysis of time series, have in fact proved

successful. It is precisely this line of economic research, mathematical economics and econometrics, that has characterised the development of this discipline in recent decades. It is therefore only natural that when the Bank of Sweden's prize in economic science, dedicated to the memory of Alfred Nobel, is awarded for the first time, it should be to the two pioneers in this field of research. (Lundberg, 1969, p. 3)

The first award clearly reveals the motivations and orientation of the Committee: away from 'vague' and 'literary' styles, unambiguously to mathematics and econometrics, that is, in the domain of Samuelson's third and fourth revolutions in modern economics. This has been one continuous leitmotif that unifies the award over time; but there has been a second running thread as well: the theme of individualism, free markets, property and the push back against regulation and the state, a theme purporting to demonstrate the viability and efficiency of free-market arrangements.

If the first running theme deals with the purist world of abstractions, the second thread is concerned with the hands-on world of policy design; if the first group is epitomised by MIT and Harvard, the second is embodied in Chicago. These two themes and groups, including their satellite spin-offs, have accounted for the large majority of the awards. In the first fifty years of the prize, seventy-eight awards were made; of these, fifty-six were from the USA, confirming the Americanisation of economics, and as many as thirty went to economists linked to MIT, Harvard and Chicago. Ten awards are marked against the UK, though these include Hart, Coase, Sen and Deaton who spent much of their professional careers in the USA, with Hayek arguably in the same category. While five prizes are listed against Cambridge (UK), this does not in any manner conflate with recognition of Cambridge's heterodox or deep Keynesian traditions: Meade and Mirrlees were thoroughly neoclassical; Sen received his for his contributions to axiomatic welfare economics à la Harvard and Arrow. Of the ten, only Stone, and his doctoral supervisee Deaton, could be classified as working in the tradition of Frisch, Tinbergen and Kuznets. And of the others, Hicks was recognised for his neoclassical contributions to general equilibrium theory, leaving only W. Arthur Lewis to be the sole representative of the 'other': of the colonies, of colour *and* of classical thinking.

Samuelson 1970
Lindbeck, in his Introduction Speech for the award to Paul Samuelsson, picks up the thread from Lundberg's introduction for the first award shared by Ragnar Frisch and Jan Tinbergen. Lindbeck also clearly locates Samuelson's prize within the criteria of the Prize Committee: "One of the salient features of the development of economics during the last decades is the increased degree of formalization of the analytical techniques brought about partly with the aid of mathematical methods. We can perhaps distinguish two different branches of this development. One branch is econometrics, designed for immediate statistical estimation and empirical application; ... the second branch is orientated

more toward basic theoretical research, without any immediate aims of statistical, empirical confrontation" (Lindbeck, 1970). He goes on to highlight the merit of Samuelson's work: "Samuelson's basic achievement during recent decades is that more than anyone else he has helped raise the general analytical and methodological level of central economic theory. In fact, Samuelson himself has rewritten considerable parts of central economic theory. He has also shown the fundamental unity of both the problems and analytical techniques in economics, partly by a systematic application of the methodology of maximization for a broad set of problems. This means that Samuelson's contributions range over a large number of different fields"[44] (ibid.). The next year, Samuelson wrote "an admiring introduction" to Lindbeck's polemical book attacking the Union of Radical Political Economists movement and critiquing the New Left (Lindbeck, 1971; Samuelson, 1971), which he later referred to as "a valuable account of what turned out to be a nondurable movement" (Samuelson, 1997, p. 159), but skipping the sharp critiques of it by Paul Sweezy and others in *Monthly Review*. The admiration seemingly was mutual.

Gunnar Myrdal—Friedrich von Hayek 1974
Hayek returned from Chicago to Freiburg in 1962 but then experienced a period where he became seriously depressive, enough to keep him from productive work. "This was the era when faith in the power of government was at its highest and support for free markets was at its lowest"; Friedman told Cassidy (2000) that "he was depressed, I think mostly because he saw the condition of the world as depressing, and he felt he wasn't receiving the kind of recognition he hoped for". This was indeed the era of high Keynesianism and the rise of the welfare states in Europe, both anathema in Hayek's scheme of things. This was the 25-year post-war stretch, dubbed in Cambridge as the golden age of capitalism, where high growth was combined with low rates of unemployment and inflation. Keynes was dead yet omnipresent; Hayek alive but invisible. This marginalisation of Hayek's ideas on the grand stage was to last another decade. In 1967, he was called "a prophet in the wilderness" by Eric Hobsbawm, and "a magnificent dinosaur" by the philosopher Anthony

---

[44] In contrast, Robin Matthews, far from being an unqualified supporter of Joan Robinson's work, highlighted what, in his view, was an important insight to be found in her *Accumulation of Capital*: "One characteristic of the book is the sharply different roles and motivations attributed to different types of economic agents (wage earners, entrepreneurs, rentiers). Joan was hostile to the now more fashionable notion of an undifferentiated utility maximizing economic agent. She held that economic conduct was culturally conditioned. ... This was a fruitful area for exploration, though, as Joan admitted, her own treatment was rudimentary. 'Economic analysis requires to be supplemented by a kind of comparative historical anthropology which is still in its infancy as a scientific study' (Joan Robinson, 1956, p. 56)" (Matthews, 1989, pp. 913–914). Joan's position is epistemologically open to insights from other social sciences, including sociology, anthropology, psychology; her position is antithetical to the basic neoclassical premise of universal utility maximisation and stands at a discrete distance from the one-size-fits-all optimisation template demonstrated by Samuelson in his *Foundations of Economic Analysis*.

Quinton (Cassidy, 2000) and, another time, "a mad professor" by Michael Foot. In 1972, Hayek expressed morosely that his had been "an externally rather uneventful life" (Leeson, 2013, p. 3); he was "in the middle of the second of three major depressive episodes". But then, just two years later, fortunes changed dramatically, storm clouds lifted and life became lively again: Hayek was almost magically rejuvenated by the surprise award of the Nobel Prize in 1974; "suddenly, he found the energy and inspiration to think, write and travel again" (Cassidy, 2000). Apparently, the award had come as a complete surprise as it was quite contrary to the intellectual flow of the times, and Hayek was no longer thought of as a top echelon practising professional economist.

So, where did that prize come from—how did it drop virtually unannounced into Hayek's lap? How was Hayek's name pulled out of the blue, how did he come to be recommended? Lindbeck enlightens us that what is important is "not how many suggestions each candidate has received but rather *who* the proponents of the various candidates are. Thus, very competent nominators, whose judgment the committee ranks highly, may have strong influence on the committee, particularly if their supporting arguments are convincing" (quoted in Turner, 1989, p. 214). So in its generosity, the Nobel Selection Committee asked Fritz Machlup to make the case for Hayek, a task he completed in September 1971, having spent the earlier part of the month with Hayek and other MPS members planning their 1972 silver anniversary meeting; Machlup was a founding member of MPS, and a close friend of Hayek (Leeson, 2013, p. 29). Hayek had close prior links with at least half of the members of the Selection Committee: Lundberg, who became an MPS member in 1958; Ohlin (the chairman), whom Hayek had invited to become a founding member which conflicted with his role in a parallel Liberal International (LI) organisation (where Hayek had declined membership of their executive committee due to the LI's association with the agenda of Beveridge, someone Hayek regarded as an enemy); subsequently LI and MPS coordinated their meetings (ibid., p. 28); and Lindbeck, who later took over from Lundberg as chairman. And to boot, on the sidelines beyond the Committee, there was Herbert Tingsten, political science professor at the University of Stockholm, and editor-in-chief of Sweden's largest daily newspaper, *Dagens Nyheter* from 1946 to 1959. Tingsten was a founding member of the MPS, a very handy partner to have close to the heart, or head, or hands, of Swedish decision-making on such matters as the 'Nobel' Prize[45]; Tingsten died in December 1973.

---

[45] Mikael Nilsson (2011, p. 147) describes Tingsten as "perhaps Sweden's most influential publicist during the Cold War"; he was closely connected with the CIA-sponsored organisation Congress for Cultural Freedom (CCF) and its Swedish chapter, SKfKF (Svenska kommittén för kulturens frihet). "Tingsten was the foremost propagator for the 'end of ideology' thesis in Sweden and the article argues that this campaign was inspired by the CCF's advancement of this idea in the 1950s and 1960s. Tingsten was personally acquainted with several CCF intellectuals ... visited several of the CCF's conferences, helped the CCF and the SKfKF's causes and furthered their agendas in a number of ways during his time as editor-in-chief of *DN*. CCF network of intellectuals influenced opinion making in non-aligned Sweden" (ibid.).

Blundell (2004, p. 23): "Hayek had moved from Chicago back to Europe, and in December 1974 received the Nobel Prize. He was 75 and his health had not been good. He was also depressed. However, the prize (and the big cheque) cheered him up no end." Offer and Soderberg (2016, p. 187) write: "Awarding the Prize to Hayek was a gesture that moved Lindbeck personally: 'He'd been in a very deep depression he told me. It was terribly satisfying to indicate his greatness'. The prize had a more positive effect on Hayek's visibility and reputation than on any other recipient."

Surprisingly, the award was a joint one to two persons standing at different ends of the political spectrum—Hayek and Myrdal. Myrdal had been in the reckoning even before the first award; now it came as what he regarded perhaps as a form of gratuitous insult. There was history, not chemistry, between Hayek and Myrdal, and it could be traced back to the 1930s; both were annoyed at the Nobel pairing; Leeson quotes Myrdal's daughter, Sissela Bok, who speculated whether the joint award was a "condescending joke on the part of the members of the Swedish economics establishment" (Leeson, 2013, p. 30). Both Robert Leeson and David Laidler[46] report conversations, in 1995 and 1973 respectively, with members of the Selection Committee and confirm that while there was pressure for an early award to Myrdal, his position on the investigation on US War Crimes in Indo-China got in the way; "he was allegedly personally and politically disliked by the members of the Committee; a compromise was apparently reached: he was given the Prize jointly with the right-wing Hayek, someone he despised" (ibid.). It appears that Myrdal was given the prize on sufferance.

Hayek responded to Myrdal's attack on the Nobel economics prize, and on its conferment on Hayek (along with Myrdal himself) in 1974, calling it "a rather extreme case ... with an intellectual arrogance that, even among economists, is rare. Myrdal has been in opposition on these issues even before Keynes came out. His book on monetary doctrines and values and so on dates from the late 1920s. He has his own peculiar view on this subject which I think is wrong. His book couldn't even be reproduced now. I don't think he has ever been a good economist" (Lebaron, 2006, p. 91).

In the same vein, Lindbeck also offers a nuanced, two-sided, critically quizzical view of Gunnar Myrdal. "He was very fast not only in identifying new

---

[46] Laidler (in Leeson, 2013) offers his recollections, "firstly of his relationship with Hayek's work as an undergraduate and in his early career, and secondly of a conversation about Hayek's Nobel that occurred between Herbert Giersch and Erik Lundberg, the latter of whom had been on the 1974 Nobel awarding panel. The conversation occurred following a paper Laidler delivered at the Kieler Vortrage series in 1973. Laidler recalls that Myrdal's name was being strongly touted for the award, but that Lundberg confided to Giersch his worries that this would be received badly in some quarters, to which Giersch replied that the politics of the situation would be easier if there was a joint award with Hayek as the other recipient. Whether Hayek was already in the running Laidler cannot comment upon and indeed he qualifies his recollection by saying that the conversation was an exchange 'that I think I recall'" (Irving, 2014). This quoted paragraph is from Sean Irving's (2014) review of Leeson (2013).

problems, but also in expressing personal views on them, although often without giving up his previous opinions on the same issues. Over time, his views therefore looked more and more like 'archeological layers' of positions that he had taken during different phases of his life—each of them usually quite profound. It was, however, not always easy to know which of the layers you were confronted with when you talked to him—for instance, Myrdal the central planner, or Myrdal the anarchist" (Gylfason, 2005, p. 9).

Myrdal went public later, regretting his acceptance of the award alongside Hayek, especially after the award to Milton Friedman in the midst of his support to Pinochet following the overthrow of the elected Allende government in Chile. Meanwhile, the right-wing Selection Committee, with its close links to the Mont Pelerin Society and its precepts, had achieved its purpose: Hayek was again a name, his work was now revalued, his voice was heard with new respect, even if by proxy.[47]

Samuelson (2009) thought that "his was a worthy choice", if only on account of his work on markets, information and knowledge. But the award did not persuade everyone, and this is what a later prize winner, Paul Krugman, had to say: "Friedrich Hayek is not an important figure in the history of macroeconomics. These days, you constantly see articles that make it seem as if there was a great debate in the 1930s between Keynes and Hayek, and that this debate has continued through the generations.... Nothing like this happened. Hayek essentially made a fool of himself early in the Great Depression, and his ideas vanished from the professional discussion. So why is his name invoked so much now? Because *The Road to Serfdom* struck a *political* chord with the American right, which adopted Hayek as a sort of mascot—and retroactively

---

[47] Hiroyuki Okon has argued that "without Hayek's 1974 Nobel Prize combined with funding from the Institute for Humane Studies, Austrian Economics may never have been revived" (Okon, 2018, p. 213). "It was much more difficult to communicate ideas and establish networks before the Internet, www, e-mail, and PC. In orthodox academic circles, published journals and formal conferences played a major role in the communication and exchange of ideas—and were even more important for the development of 'unorthodox' schools of economics. In the 1970s, Austrian economics experienced a resurgence in the English-speaking world, especially in America—the *Austrian Economics Newsletter* played an important role of communicating, diffusing, and developing Austrian ideas. The first ten *AEN* issues reveal *how* the Austrian revival took place; and what its *infrastructure and personalities* were. They also illustrate the *ideas and problems* that came to characterize the resurgence in Austrian economics: dynamics, process, expectation, time, entrepreneurship, (Knightian) uncertainty, knowledge, discovery, learning, equilibration and disequilibration, spontaneous order, subjectivism, Austrian methodology and praxeology, criticism of general equilibrium, price system as a conveyor of information, monetary policy, etc." While the 'Nobel' Prize provided the branding, the Institute of Humane Studies ensured the funding. It needs to be recalled though that the original impulse in this regard came from Lionel Robbins at the London School of Economics in the early 1930s; Robbins, whom Skidelsky (2020, p. 8n.ii) calls "the British cheer-leader of the Austrian school", had long been deep into the Austrian economics tradition, was in love with Vienna and entirely taken with Friedrich Hayek whom he brought over from Austria to be his intellectual partner in challenging Keynes and Cambridge Keynesianism. Okon's contention, of course, is about a later period, the UK roots of which lay at the LSE of the 1930s.

inflated his role as an economic thinker. ... The Hayek thing is almost entirely about politics rather than economics. Without *The Road to Serfdom*—and the way that book was used by vested interests to oppose the welfare state—nobody would be talking about his business cycle ideas" (Krugman, 2011). The only marginal qualifications to be made perhaps are: first, that Hayek was more than a 'mascot'—he was the icon projected on to the global stage, a brand that could sell the neoliberal idea anywhere anytime; and second, that while his book was undoubtedly used by vested interests to roll back the welfare state, Hayek was leading this charging pack in this assault; and third, Hayek was adopted as the messianic leader of the cause not just by the American right, but also in the UK, in Chile and other Latin American countries, and much more widely globally, including by the Swedish right.

Milton Friedman 1976
At the Award Ceremony, held with strict security in view of the local protests against the anointment of Friedman, the introductory oration was delivered by Erik Lundberg, the chair of the Prize Committee, who also happened to be a fellow member of the Mont Pelerin Society. Friedman's work is praised, but the laudation is sprinkled with some carefully nuanced qualifying words or phrases; even for his fellow traveller, it was professionally difficult to come down unequivocally on the Friedman side of the line in the debates over money, monetarism and macroeconomics; it might have been even more unacceptable to acknowledge that Friedman's roles in overtly political policy processes also played a role in the choice.

Notwithstanding his position as a former prize winner, Bob Solow had no such constraints of politeness in pronouncing on Friedman's (un)fitness for receiving the award on academic grounds. In pooh-poohing the Nobel Award to Friedman, Bob Solow (2012) says "it is absurd ... [to believe, as the Friedman-faithful seem to do] that Friedman's Nobel Prize was delayed by elite hostility to his public role as a champion of free markets"; and one could readily agree with Solow. But then he carries on: "the Nobel Prize in economics is not about advocacy. It is intended to reward important contributions to the discipline of economics." Solow goes on: "a more plausible case might be made that Friedman's prominence on the public stage led to some overestimation of his professional achievement"; his permanent-income measure was "an important and useful idea", but had been anticipated, albeit in a weaker form, by James Duesenberry, and in a "more satisfactory theory at almost the same time" by Franco Modigliani (at MIT); furthermore "monetarism ... has not proved to be tenable analytically or empirically"; and his work on US monetary history (jointly with Anna Schwarz) "while highly interesting, is not a towering intellectual achievement". Why then did the august Nobel Committee make the award? Solow suggests they overestimated his intellectual contributions to the discipline, and one might well agree with him; but the alternative explanation remains that the Committee used different criteria from the superficial, ostensible one that Solow takes for granted, viz., contribution to the subject, and consciously made awards that would bring notice, lend respectability and confer public legitimacy on certain traditions of economics that the Committee, as constituted, had reason to favour and prioritise at the time of the award; or, in other words, that 'public advocacy' overtook 'disciplinary contributions' as the motivation underlying the award; the Committee wanted to support Friedman and all that he stood for, and the Chilean episode would certainly have been in the decision-making frame of reference.

It is striking that in his Nobel Prize 'biographical' write-up, Friedman (1976) makes absolutely no reference to Friedrich Hayek, or to the Mont Pelerin Society, or to Chile and his Chicago Boys. Could it be because "demonstrations took place against awarding him a Nobel Prize" (Illarionov, 2008, p. 6)? The award was made when Friedman was a proxy mentor, and in significant respects an indirect CEO, of the Pinochet regime's economic reforms—managed directly by Friedman's students—reforms which were accompanied by a pogrom of killings, torture and disappearances. It is remarkable indeed that such an award should have been made at all, let alone at that point in time. Of course, the Prize Committee might have said disingenuously that they kept economics and politics apart; Friedman didn't. Friedman was flying high at the time; his own mentor, Friedrich Hayek, had been awarded the Nobel Prize in 1974, setting off a series of awards for economists of the libertarian tradition that was then rising into domination, assisted no doubt by the symbolic ideological capital bestowed by the series of Nobel awards. The instrumental influence of the powerful and secretive MPS network in this phenomenon, and in Friedman's rise to prominence, is incontrovertible; but all this is airbrushed out by Friedman; Illarionov (2008, p. 7) tells us that Friedman "maintained clarity of thought and continued to work until two weeks before his death" at the age of 94; so the omission cannot be ascribed to an early bout of selective amnesia.

It is arguable that Lindbeck's position was seriously compromised—he was in rapid transition away from the precepts of social democracy: "by the end of 1976, Lindbeck had transferred his loyalty from labour to capital"; he "abandoned them [the Social Democrats] in a sequence of public gestures"; Offer and Soderberg employ the word 'treachery' to convey the perception. He had spent time at the Hoover Institution, a super-conservative think tank from which Reagan drew many of his economic advisors in his election campaign; and apparently "he found that Olof Palme, a long-time confidant, neighbour, and friend of the family, would no longer speak to him" (Offer & Soderberg, 2016, p. 195). "In 1977, the trade union economist Villy Bergstrom cast the history of economics in Sweden as one long legacy of hostility to Social Democracy, motivated by class animosity", running in a line from Heckscher and Cassel, now down to Lindbeck, a position that Erik Lundberg apparently conceded, but which Lindbeck explosively rejected with the standard defence of the claimed value-free objectivity of positive economics, and its self-professed separation from politics. This was also the time "the academy flew Lindbeck home from Yale to meet ... a group of students [who] had published a protest against the award" of the economics prize to Milton Friedman, deeply implicated as he was in the eyes of many in the violent and bitter aftermath of the CIA–Pinochet Chilean coup against the democratically elected Allende government (ibid., p. 194). Myrdal, in retrospect, went public "criticizing the secretive procedure by which the economics committee presented the academy with a fait accompli. He thought the award to Friedman had fatally discredited the prize, and regretted accepting the prize himself two years before" (ibid., p. 194). One can legitimately regard the award, as well as the subsequent whitewashing of it by the academy, as disgraceful; but its significance was much greater, in view of the globally visibly public legitimation that it provided to the Hayek–Friedman Chicago camp and to the US government's neo-imperialist intervention in Chile specifically, and to a variety of unsavoury totalitarian regimes globally, not least the war in Vietnam, from where the US military had to ignominiously withdraw in 1975. It is worth recalling that, paradoxically, it was the Swedish embassy that was the liaison with the Vietnam socialist government after the US forces were defeated, a position of trust on the side of the Vietnamese leaders; while in Stockholm, the most august academy of Swedish intelligentsia and society was conferring one of its top recognitions on a vociferous super-right-wing economist whose involvement with the Chilean dictatorship could not simply be air-brushed away.

Much later, it could be speculated that the Academy of Letters, perhaps in a gesture to make amends for the embarrassment caused by the economics committee, awarded the 1982 Literature prize to Gabriel Garcia Marquez who, in his prize acceptance speech,[48] passionately reminded the attendees at the prize ceremony of the past; of "the unearthly tidings of Latin America, that boundless realm of haunted men and historic women [who] have not had a moment's rest. A promethean president, entrenched in his burning palace, died fighting an entire army, alone; and two suspicious airplane accidents, yet to be explained, cut short the life of another great-hearted president and that of a democratic soldier who had revived the dignity of his people. There have been five wars and seventeen military coups; there emerged a diabolic dictator who is carrying out, in God's name, the first Latin American ethnocide of our time. In the meantime, twenty million Latin American children died before the age of one, more than have been born in Europe since 1970. ... Numerous women arrested while pregnant have given birth in Argentine prisons, yet nobody knows the whereabouts and identity of their children who were furtively adopted or sent to an orphanage by order of the military authorities. Because they tried to change this state of things, nearly two hundred thousand men and women have died throughout the continent. ... If this had happened in the United States, the corresponding figure would be that of one million six hundred thousand violent deaths in four years. One million people have fled Chile, a country with a tradition of hospitality—that is, ten per cent of its population. The country

---

[48] https://www.nobelprize.org/prizes/literature/1982/marquez/lecture/

that could be formed of all the exiles and forced emigrants of Latin America would have a population larger than that of Norway. I dare to think that it is this outsized reality, and not just its literary expression, that has deserved the attention of the Swedish Academy of Letters. A reality not of paper, but one that lives within us and determines each instant of our countless daily deaths, and that nourishes a source of insatiable creativity, full of sorrow and beauty, of which this roving and nostalgic Colombian is but one cipher more, singled out by fortune." Neither Friedman, before Marquez, nor Buchanan after Marquez, would answer to Marquez's self-characterisation as "one cipher more, singled out by fortune"; they both had the deep support of the MPS political machine, and both dipped their pens and hands deep in the blue and red of the CIA's and Chicago's Chilean unsavoury saga. The previous Latin American winner of the Literature prize had been the great Pablo Neruda in 1971; ironically, the next, in 2010, would be Mario Vargas Llosa, who had started on the left, became increasingly right, joined the Mont Pelerin Society and was advertised as a notable member on its website.

3.3.3 Mont Pelerin Society and the 'Nobel'—A Golden Embrace

Even given the open secret of the agenda, and the composition, of the Prize Committees, it is astonishing to note the domination of the Chicago–MPS alliance in the awards. Up to 2010, as many as nine MPS members are on the list, of which the first eight received their awards, in the 1974–1992 period; it is almost bizarre to note that five of these went on to win the prize within a few years after their term as President of the Mont Pelerin Society; and these eight awards were made in the overlapping tenures of Lundberg and Lindbeck, mostly with one or the other in the chair of the Prize Committee. Bertil Ohlin, intimately associated with the MPS from the start, could also be listed as a proxy member in the headcount of the 'Nobel' Prize winners; in a different way, Theodore Schultz, the Chicago stalwart who started the academic collaboration with Chile that later bred the Chicago Boys, could also be counted, even if not formally, as a member of the tribe, as also could Robert Lucas Jr.

Name	MPS president	Nobel Prize
F. Hayek	1947–1961	1974
M. Friedman	1970–1972	1976
G. Stigler	1976–1978	1982
J. Buchanan	1984–1986	1986
G. Becker	1990–1992	1992

Just as the Mont Pelerin Society boasts its Nobel Prize winners on its website, its UK sister organisation and a pioneer, vanguard institution of the 'neoliberal-thought-collective', the Institute of Economic Affairs (IEA), proudly lists the IEA publications authored by Nobel Prize winners associated with it: the list (up to 2009) names: Hicks, Hayek, Friedman, Meade, Stigler, Buchanan, Coase, Becker, North, Smith, Phelps, Williamson and Ostrom; there is an overlap of seven names with the MPS list.

3.3.4 Cambridge Heterodoxy?

So, what of the Cambridge heterodox economists, what about Joan Robinson, and Nicky Kaldor? Both were alive and active for far more than the first decade of the awards.

One of Joan's biographers, Marjorie Turner (1989, p. 220), quotes Lindbeck: "It is also clear that the prize awarding authority has tried to favour 'constructive' contributions rather than contributions that are 'destructive' in the sense of mainly launching criticism that does not lead anywhere. To provide 'shoulders' on which other scholars can stand, and thus climb higher, has been favoured over attempts to show that 'everybody else' is wrong, or that the world is so complex that simple and coherent analytical structures are useless. Skilful polemics that do not seem to push research forward have not been regarded as worthy of being honoured."

In sharp contrast, Joan had famously pronounced that most of economics was 'negative knowledge', and that it was essential to prevent economists from bamboozling people. And with regard to the mainstream tradition, she had typically and acerbically remarked (in the context of Bagicha Minhas's CES—aka SMAC, Solow–Minhas–Arrow–Chenery—production function): "it was like looking in a dark room for a cat which isn't there". Lindbeck would clearly not have appreciated such 'destructive' ideas; rather, one must think he would have preferred looking for a Swedish matchbox to peer into the dark and continue looking 'constructively' for the 'assumed' cat. So Joan was regularly nominated, was on the short list at least once when she was one of the 'hot names'; but nothing came of it (Turner, 1989, p. 214). Would she have accepted it? Turner records Eichner as saying, "It would be my fervent hope that she would never accept it", and apparently she told Sol Adler, "I would rather have a grievance" (Turner, 1989, p. 221).

After a considered airing of such anecdotal and indirect clues as fly in the wind, Marjorie Turner provides the following summary:

> Reading the record, one can infer Robinson's sins before the committee: she disowned the method in her early contributory work, *Imperfect Competition*; she worked diligently to undermine the hegemony of the central core of general equilibrium theory in all of her later work; she proposed another path in *Accumulation* but this path led nowhere as far as *mainstream* research programs were concerned (because it did not employ general equilibrium models); she engaged in the capital controversy which was also destructive of the central core of general equilibrium analysis, its complacency, and its methodology; she failed to use the latest mathematical techniques. Being a leftist, or what members of the Mont Pelerin Society are fond of calling "a Marxo-Keynesian", did not help.

Being an unconventional woman did not ingratiate her. Perhaps Schor was right in saying that most men were a little afraid of Joan Robinson and her sharp tongue. The Nobel committee for choosing an economist is all male; ... that Joan Robinson never won the Nobel Prize is mainly a reflection of the kind of economics which has been dominant in the profession and within the selection committee since the prize was initiated in 1968. (ibid.)

Of course, the Committee would surely have been terrified by the thought, not entirely unrealistic, that had she been awarded, Joan would have used the Nobel speech as the occasion to broadcast her critique of mainstream economics to the world, a radical message that would surely have gone viral and global, effectively denting the legitimacy and credibility of the tradition that the prize wanted to enhance. And the same would probably hold also for irreverent Nicky Kaldor with his sustained assaults on monetarism and his tirade on "the irrelevance of equilibrium economics" in 1972, sandwiched between the awards to Samuelson on the one side and Hayek on the other, not to mention Friedman following shortly thereafter. "Leijonhufvud doubted whether there was anyone in Sweden to argue for a Cambridge Keynesian, and as the record shows, no Cambridge Keynesian has been awarded a Nobel Prize" (ibid., p. 221).

Speaking of "the passing of the guard ... the great generation of economists who dominated our science in the 1930–1980 half century", Samuelson lists twenty-three names. "Some of these named economists have received the Nobel Prize. Most have not. In my judgment every one deserved that award or higher. Each time when a Kalecki died, or a Harrod or Robinson, or Blankety-Blank, it made my blood boil that the Committee in Stockholm had missed doing its duty" (Samuelson, 1988, p. 319).

3.3.5 *'An Ideological Coup'*

Year by year, prize by prize, the Committee has bolstered and added to the brand value of MIT–Harvard neoclassicism and Chicago neoliberalism. There have surely been exceptions: some of the surviving venerable greats provided the initial respectability; the award to Tinbergen and Frisch, and later to Kuznets, implicitly gave the impression that empirical methods and policy applications were a significant part of the criteria, though such a deduction was to be systematically dispelled. Periodically, some names surprised, pleasantly: Myrdal (but he was home grown and widely respected even if in social democratic circles); Arthur Lewis (which gave a dash of colour and 'otherness', valuable political assets in broadening the market reach and value of the brand); Sen (signalling another contributory stream into modern economics, though he was cited for his generally do-no-harm work in axiomatic welfare economics and not for the potentially disruptive interventions on famines); Elinor Ostrom (some day, a woman had to be let in; it also gave a green tinge to the prize, and memories of the scandalous exclusion of Joan Robinson, and Joan herself, were long buried and gone). But these periodic image-corrective exceptions aside, the lineage of the prize has kept steadfastly loyal to the original criteria indicated by Erik Lundberg in his introductory remarks at the time of the first award in 1969, or as the editors of *Monthly Review* (2016) put it, loyal "to scholars who represented economics for the 1 percent".

Lindbeck's reference to a criterion of making contributions to 'central economic theory' begs the question as to what defines this 'centrality'. The answer can be derived inductively from the revealed preferences of the Committee over the years, especially from two of the key gatekeepers of the award, Lundberg and Lindbeck. Lundberg lauds moving away from the vagueness of literary styles of writing and conflates precision with mathematics; this would immediately rule out the likes of Joan Robinson with her famous aphorism "I did not know maths so I had to think instead"; it would also slide over Paul Samuelson's assessment of the rigorous and precise theoretical thinking of Joan and Nicky Kaldor, and the role of intuition and creative openness (Samuelson, 1988, p. 320). Lindbeck follows up with his critique of the value of critiques—making marginal contributions to 'central' economic theory is deemed invaluable; making a critique of the central tenets of 'central' economic theory is thought to be subversive, polemical, vague and literary, and passé, of the lapsed ancient order, old debris that needs to be swept aside by the new brooms of the third and fourth revolutions of mathematisation and econometrification of the discipline. The use of such 'criteria' clearly explains very many of the choices for the award of the prize, for example, Samuelson, Arrow, Solow, Debreu, Lucas and others.

The second string of awards comes from the school of Chicago neoliberalism intimately linked in their provenance both to their prominent positions in the Mont Pelerin Society and to a number of members of the Prize Committees. In some of these cases, it is credibly arguable that the driving criterion for selection could more likely have been the attraction felt by the Prize Committee to the neoliberal ideological orientation of their work, enough to overlook the unsavoury associations of several of their chosen winners with questionable right-wing politics at home and abroad.

That said, it is remarkable that a small cabal should exercise such strong influence over such a lengthy stretch of time—perhaps its authority and power come precisely from the fact that it stood on the sidelines of the main centres of political economy, and as such could be projected as being outside them, ostensibly interest free, claiming to be 'scientific', impartial and unbiased. And paradoxically, it can draw strength from the other developed hallmark of Scandinavia as a self-professed home of high social values, internationally being ethically minded—the contradiction between reality and projection is somewhat bizarre, since the origin of the award lies arguably in its instrumentality as a device against radical social democracy within the country. The prize was the tail wagging the dog, with Lundberg and then Lindbeck as ringmasters for the first twenty-five years of the show.

As the editors of *Monthly Review* remarked: "the Riksbank Prize was embraced by the mainstream media and academia as a genuine Nobel Prize, carrying the same prestige as all the others. It paid off: the Riksbank and the conservative economists associated with it achieved their objectives to an extent that must have exceeded their wildest dreams. The prize has been enormously successful in narrowing the conception of what constitutes economics—a field that was previously much wider. The ideology of an economics serving the 1 percent has become entrenched in academic, policy, and media discourse, with all other approaches downgraded as eccentric and 'non-scientific'. Winners of the Riksbank Prize form a kind of 'Nobility' in economics that has elevated some approaches while practically extinguishing others" (*Monthly Review* Editors, 2016). By stealth and design, the Swedish conservative economists, and the bankers that stood behind them, had managed to affect a spectacular ideological coup within the discipline.

3.4 Reaching Politics: Weaponising the Message

3.4.1 Santiago de Chile: Pinochet the Pioneer

Chicago and its Cowboys
Valdes (1995) conducts a meticulous examination of US government records of the 'Chile Project', the technical cooperation agreement signed in "March 1956 by Chile's Catholic University, the University of Chicago, and the International Cooperation Administration, the precursor to the Agency for International Development in the US State Department. The 1956 agreement permitted von Hayek's Chicago, 'Austrian School' economics, led by the chairman of the Economics Department, Theodore Schultz, to set up Catholic University's economics department, achieving complete control over it by 1964; and by 1970, one hundred economists had been trained in the Austrian School of Economics' theories" (ibid.). Valdes reports that "Arnold Harberger, regarded as the 'father' of the Chile Project, emphasized that it was necessary to 'de-Latin Americanize' the Chilean students" (ibid.). Free markets and comparative advantage, not state interventions and import-substitution à la Prebisch—that was the formula. By 1972, they had worked out a full economic programme for a post-Allende scenario.

Larry Sjaastad, described as the last 'Old' Chicagoan by Clements (2004)—representing the old Chicago tradition where policy relevance was the object of theory—supervised 139 PhD dissertations over forty-two years, on average 3.3 completions per year; about 20 per cent of all doctorates in economics awarded from Chicago (Clements, 2004, p. 5). "Larry has had strong ties with Latin America in the form of research, teaching and students from the region of Chicago. Together with Al Harberger, Larry organised the highly productive Latin American Workshop at Chicago; ... such is his knowledge of, and influence in, Latin America that he is treated almost as a god when he visits, certainly a guru" (Clements, 2004, p. 4). Allan Meltzer refers to the "long struggle to break with the Prebisch tradition" and notes "that your contributions had a major impact on making that tradition possible". Robert Mundell, another Chicago Nobel Prize winner, cites his close association with the Chicago Boys (who "became known for their evangelical spread of the wisdom of free markets, laissez-faire and economic stability"); Mundell: "the 'Chicago Boys' were sometimes associated with Milton Friedman. However, I once heard our friend Al Harberger complain: 'The Chicago boys are *my* boys!' He was right! But without Larry Sjaastad, who was, at the beginning at least, Al's lieutenant, Chicago's impact on Latin America would have been much less" (Meltzer, and Mundell, quoted in Clements, 2004, p. 4).

Harberger elaborates. "I've taught something like 300 or more Latin American students in American universities, plus many more in the shorter courses that I've given down there. In any case, I am very proud of what they have accomplished. I think my number of ministers is now crossing 25, and I know my number of central bank presidents has already crossed a dozen. Right now the central bank presidents of Chile, Argentina and Israel were my students, and the immediate former central bank presidents in Argentina, Chile and Costa Rica were also my students. So that's at one level. ... In the international agencies they have also built an enviable record. There was one moment in time when four regional chief economists at the World Bank had been my students in Chicago. One of them, Marcelo Selowsky, went off to be the chief economist for the newly minted ex-Soviet empire area, which is the biggest such job in the whole bank. And guess what? He was replaced by yet another former student, Sebastian Edwards. ... And I think the reason why these Chicago products of the 1960s and 1970s rose like corks in the international agencies and in other policy arenas came from the fact that, on so many different occasions in countless boardroom and brainstorming sessions, they seemed to see problems more clearly; diagnose them more accurately, and to draw more direct policy implications from their analyses than most of their competitors. And to build these attributes, I believe their fundamentals-based, real-world-oriented training was the key" (Levy, 1999).

Harberger is somewhat dissembling in trying to qualify his involvement with what he calls "my Chilean adventure". "I don't know how people ever got the idea that I somehow was acting as the conductor of Chile's economic policy orchestra. It was nothing like that. When people see 'my hand' in the package of policies actually put in place in Chile, the source of that 'hand' was more than 90 percent likely to be my lectures and seminars in Chicago, and the interminable bull sessions that I and my Chilean students had been having ever since the late 1950s." So his 'hand' was rather invisible. The dissembling continues: "Moreover, at the same time I was troubled by some of the things that were happening on the political scene during and after the military coup—[when, as Harberger (2000) says, 'Allende was put out of office']. As a consequence there were five years at least, in which I absolutely refused to be a 'consultant' to the Chilean government in the same way as I worked in other countries. The closest I got was writing a couple of papers for a private think tank, the Center for Policy Studies, in Chile." How invisible was his 'hand'? Harberger continues: "But at the same time I took every opportunity I could get to go to Chile, to see what was going on and to talk to my former students who were ministers, vice ministers or president or vice president of the central bank. We would meet at lunch and talk about problems. I don't know if I did anything except express my enthusiasm for the positive things I saw being done, and maybe every now and then emphasize the need for them to approach their policy problems in a mature and measured way, weighing benefits against costs, and trying to find policy designs that would strengthen support for and lessen the opposition to their programs" (Levy, 1999).

Harberger then complains that his Chicago boys of the Pinochet dictatorship era did not receive the adulation they deserved: "I think that they had, at great personal sacrifice, [worn] themselves out, so to speak, in order to implement the economic reform and bring about these major changes that we've seen in these economies, and not only the ones at the top, but I feel that the man in the street does not appreciate enough the amount of sacrifice that serious economists and other public servants do when they're engaged in these battles to change some reality that has at least outlived its usefulness. The struggles are enormous, and the strain on the individuals is tremendous, the amount of time that they devote—70, 80 hours a week, and this for years on end. They really deserve the appreciation at least of their fellow citizens" (Harberger, 2000).

As Harberger (2000) points out with pride, the Chilean programme was transplanted in Argentina from the 1960s, and "we had a continuing flow of Argentines, and by this time Mexicans, Brazilians and so on were mingling in so that Chicago, in its heyday, had 40 to 50 Latin American graduate students out of a total stock of, say, 150–180 ... that is what gave Chicago such importance in the Latin American scene. ... it's partly the result of our admissions policy." In parallel to this spreading of Chicago economics and Friedmanite policy across a range of Latin American countries, there was a different, covert form of internationalisation ongoing, Operation Condor. "During the 1970s and 80s, eight US-backed military dictatorships jointly plotted the cross-border kidnap, torture, rape and murder of hundreds of their political opponents" Tremlett (2020); US and European governments knew much about it, and did not care much.[49]

---

[49] Operation Condor, "called after the broad-winged vulture that soars above the Andes, ... joined eight South American military dictatorships—Argentine, Chile, Uruguay, Bolivia, Paraguay, Brazil, Peru and Ecuador—into a single network that covered four-fifths of the continent.... Condor was formally created in November 1975, when Pinochet's spy chief, Manuel Contreras, invited 50 intelligence officers form Chile, Uruguay, Argentina, Paraguay, Bolivia and Brazil to the Army War Academy on La Alameda, Santiago's central avenue. Pinochet welcomed them in person" (Tremlett, 2020). "many of the men who carried out Operation Condor were alumni of the US Army's School of the Americas—a training camp in Panama for military from allied regimes across the continent". Western intelligence agencies knew well what was going on. "A Swiss company had, for decades, supplied cryptography machines to military, police and spy agencies around the world. The company, the Washington Post revealed, had been secretly owned by the CIA and West Germany's BND intelligence service. Any messages sent via its cryptography machines could, unbeknownst to the users, be read by the US and West Germany. Among the company's clients were the regimes in Argentina, Brazil, Chile, Peru and Uruguay. As the Washington Post put it, the CIA 'was in effect, supplying rigged communications gear to some of South America's most brutal regimes and, as a result, in [a] unique positions to know the extent of their atrocities'" (ibid.).

The close involvement of Friedrich Hayek, Milton Friedman and James Buchanan in devising and guiding Chile under Pinochet are also well known and established. The reactions to this have been polarised: on the one side is intense global opprobrium attached to their despicable support for a violent dictator; on the other side are varying defences, ranging from nuanced rewritings, or selective airbrushing and pulling their reputations out of this fire,[50] to the branding provided by the highly provocative 'Nobel' Prize awards to each of them, and each after the rise of Pinochet. "He [Friedman] advised Goldwater, Nixon, Reagan, but always as an outsider, never (since that War experience) as a paid employee in the style of the Council of Economic Advisors" (McCloskey, 2003). Such a defence is again entirely specious; rewards come in many forms, not from receiving a consultant's salary.

There are other advocates defending the indefensible. Recently, Birsen Filip (2018b) has interrogated the soft gloss placed on Hayek's visits to Chile by Caldwell and Montes (2015) in their detailed study in which Hayek is presented "almost as a naïve and saintly figure—in the face of persuasive evidence to the contrary". She argues that "In spite of his reputation as a defender of freedom, Hayek did *not* value human rights, claiming it to be a relatively recent concept derived from combining 'the old civil rights' with rights derived from

---

[50] An illustration of the nuanced airbrushing is provided by McCloskey (2003) who raises an internal Chicagoan family defence in her appropriately hagiographic laudation for Milton Friedman on his 90th birthday. "Chicago had of course a connection to Chile, but Milton was not it: Al Harberger and Larry Sjaastad and Gregg Lewis were; not Milton. I, Deirdre McCloskey, probably taught more future Chilean economists associated with torturing and murdering citizens in soccer stadiums than Milton did, as did many of us, to our regret. (Yet it needs to be realized that the connection was formed originally with a free country, before Pinochet, just as Harvard had a connection with a free government in Venezuela, say, or with Pakistan before the generals, and a little after. And the economic advice that Chicago economists gave to Chile was very, very good: witness Chile now)" (McCloskey, 2003). "Let me tell you a story about Milton's actual, revealed-preference attitude towards authoritarian governments. Sometime shortly before 1977, when Milton left Chicago for the Hoover Institution, a proposal was made to the Department of Economics to form with Iran one of those educational connections, such as we already had with (free) Brazil and (free) Chile: admit a few excellent students (in the Latin American cases from non-state universities, by the way: more detachment from government) and train a set of professors to raise Iranian education in economics to international standards. Understand, this was the Iran of the Shah (whose rule ended in 1979), and a great deal of money was to come with the deal. A professorship at Chicago might be supported, for example. The negotiations were far advanced. The central administration had signed off on the proposal. Everyone thought it was a grand idea. I did, for example, because Gale Johnson and other people I admired spoke as though it was good for the Department and the world. The proposed connection was about to be adopted by the faculty of the Department assembled on an afternoon in Social Science 105. Then Milton spoke, from one of those classroom seats with writing arms, over on the right in the front row, to this effect: 'Wait a minute. We can't do this. Iran under the Shah is a *dictatorship*. It is not a democracy. This Department and University shouldn't get mixed up with thugs like these.' End of discussion. The proposal died, because we all suddenly realized that Milton was right" (McCloskey, 2003). Indeed, Milton might have been right, but then how would McCloskey, and Friedman, classify the Pinochet military dictatorship?

Marxism. His conception of freedom is a minimal form of freedom, which serves as a very useful tool in promoting the superiority of the 'free' market economy. His concept of freedom includes economic freedom in the 'free' market (with negative freedom as components) while, at the same time, excluding positive freedom and ignoring ethical and moral values. It should, therefore, come as no surprise that Hayek accepted the invitation to visit Chile during General Pinochet's dictatorship—or that he claimed 'personal freedom was much greater under Pinochet than it had been under Allende'" (ibid.).[51] All contemporary sentiments notwithstanding, the regional MPS meeting of 1981 was held in Vina del Mar in Chile.

Filip (2018a) takes up the case of Hayek's visit to Argentina under General Jorge Rafael Videla during the Dirty War and, relying on Hayek's views expressed in a contemporary interview conducted during his visit, argues: "By defending the practice of relying on dictatorial regimes to achieve the conditions of a 'free' market economy, Hayek contradicted his own concept of freedom, which he defined as 'absence of coercion.'" In the course of the visit, Hayek received an honorary doctorate from the Universidad Francisco Marroquin; it was touted as a great honour, shared by two other 'Nobel' Prize winners, viz., Milton Friedman and James Buchanan, and also by Ludwig von Mises, the father figure after whom the library was named and of whom there was a bust on the campus, and whose birthday is celebrated with a Viennese party—the other bust on the campus is that of Hayek himself; the library also houses the private collections and papers of Gordon Tullock and Alan Walters. The private university was launched with the support of the IEA, MPS and Atlas Network ideological entrepreneur, Antony Fisher.[52]

Thatcher: Romancing Pinochet's Chile
Chile under Pinochet provided the original template for the neoliberal economic programme; this was in 1975, well before Thatcherism in the UK, but tracked and lauded by the conservative camps in the UK and USA. A folklore was fabricated around what Milton Friedman dubbed the Chilean 'economic miracle'; its 'success' and 'lessons' were spun into a global development

---

[51] Filip (2018b) actually goes much further: "In their efforts to preserve Hayek's reputation by providing justifications for his decision, Bruce Caldwell and Leonidas Montes resort to providing incomplete information and concealing certain facts, while misrepresenting others. Furthermore, the discrepancies between the English and Spanish language versions of 'Friedrich Hayek and His Visits to Chile' (in terms of the information included and omitted) appear to have been strategic decisions based on the audiences being targeted—which suggests a deliberate and concerted effort to mislead their readers." Several other similar critiques are available: see for instance, Felipe Moreno (2008) and Andre Gunder Frank (1976).

[52] For further studies on the broader dimension of transnationalisation across regimes, see Leeson (2018), Teacher (2018a, 2018b) and Ravelli and Bull (2018) who report on the persistence of transnational relations between the Pinochet regime and the Italian neo-fascists, noting the safe haven provided to them by countries such as Argentina and Chile at that time in order to avoid judicial prosecution in Italy.

narrative, and fed into the Bretton Woods policy package, or the Washington Consensus as it evolved, resembling the original contours of the Chilean 'experiment'. Moreno (2008, p. 95) quotes Alvaro Bardon, a Chicago boy who was President of the Chilean central bank in the Pinochet regime: "after the 1970s came a new fashion of liberal economics that has increasingly become the economic rule. But we started it here much before Margaret Thatcher."

Alan Walters was the Thatcher Boy in Chile. He was a disciple of Friedman, having converted to monetarism by the 1960s; and then and later was actively involved in the IEA and the Centre for Policy Studies (CPS) to embed monetarist doctrine in the Conservative Party's and the Thatcher government's thinking and policy template. "He and his wife Paddie were regulars at Mont Pelerin Society meetings" (Blundell, 2010).

The US government set up a scholarship scheme for Chilean students from the conservative Catholic University in Santiago, to study at Chicago; the Chicago Boys. "With American money, its campus was moved to the foothills of the Andes, east of the city, the habitual preserve of the Santiago rich, where the smog and the bustle of the slightly shabby capital would not disturb the student's ambitious thoughts" (Beckett, 2002, p. 172). "As Allende struggled against this opposition in public, the Chicago Boys met privately with the military and the other groups who were turning in favour of a coup, and drew up a plan for a new Chile, to be implemented when the gun-smoke had cleared" (ibid.).

Walters went to Chile for the first time in 1975 when working with the World Bank, and liked the Chileans; "the civil servants were very good, very honest", though "I can't say I positively liked Pinochet at that time. Later I came to like him" (quoted in Beckett, 2002, p. 170). During the 1980s in Britain, "even a decade after the coup, Walters felt 'Everyone Hated Chile—except Margaret' (ibid., p. 177). [Pinochet] had been having tea with her in London for years. He had sent her flowers and chocolates. In return, she sent Alan Walters, her chief economic advisor, to Chile to draw lessons from their privatisations and slashing of social welfare programmes (ibid.)". Walters visited Chile frequently in the 1980s. "It was very exciting. I was an honorary Chicago Boy ... which I quite enjoyed. It was the great experiment in liberal economics. The reform of the social security ... that was a pure Chicago leap! A great thing" (Walters quoted in Beckett, 2002, p. 177).

When being interviewed by Andy Beckett, Alan Walters casually brushed aside the brutalities of Pinochet's regime. "I knew that with revolutions of that kind you are going to get causalities. Obviously, nasty things went on." Every time Walters visited Chile during the 1980s, he would alert Thatcher to his plans. She would whisper: "Keep quiet about it. Don't advertise it" (reported in Marriott, 2002). "Come the Falklands War, the relationship [between Thatcher/Britain and Pinochet/Chile] was so robust that Chile gave support to Britain in the form of communications, information and refuge for its armed forces, a fact publicly acknowledged by Thatcher during Pinochet's arrest" (ibid.). "Most bizarrely, senior figures in the Tory opposition chose to speak out so volubly in his [Pinochet's] defence." Speaking later in a Conservative Party Conference, Thatcher declared: "President Pinochet was this country's staunch, true friend in our time of need when Argentina seized the Falkland Island" (Thatcher, 1999), and she went on to expand on this theme at length with fulsome praise for the dictator and railing against the Spanish magistrate who had wanted Pinochet to be extradited to stand trial in a Spanish court. Mat Youkee (1999) writes, on the basis of Charles Moore's biography of Thatcher, that "while he was under house arrest in Surrey in 1999, the former Chilean military dictator Augusto Pinochet received a fine malt from an old friend. 'Scotch is one British institution that will never let you down', read the accompanying note from its sender: the former British prime minister Margaret Thatcher." Apparently, "Pinochet's taste in tipples was for years kept under wraps by US secret services"; an uncensored profile released under pressure later noted: "drinks scotch and piso sours; smokes cigarettes; likes parties" (ibid.).

"When our esteemed outgoing President, Professor Deepak Lal, asked Alan 'what was your key role at Number 10?'—Alan replied, 'to pour her a whisky at 10 p.m. and to stiffen her spine!' And she knew his advice was common sense based on a solid foundation" (Blundell, 2010). Within days of coming into power, the Thatcher government machine swung into action on a step-by-step restoration of diplomatic, economic and military relations with Pinochet's Chile. There was heavy two-way traffic: while British politicians were welcomed into Chile with great public fanfare, Chilean ministers were feted, wined and dined by banks, corporates, politicians, ministers and their advisors across the range of portfolios, with commercial and military interests dominant. Praise was showered on the Chileans for having saved democracy and for their package of economic policies following extreme free-market recipes including assaults on the trade unions and workers' organisation, rights and conditions. The Thatcherites expressed envy of Pinochet's Chile; Pinochet's 'Chicago Boys' strutted and soaked it all up, claiming they had been the original Thatcherites before Thatcher. As relations were fully 'normalised', British exports to Chile, especially arms sales, shot up—making it all worthwhile for a government fronting for banks, corporates and shopkeepers; Livingstone (2018, p. 100) observes: "the wining and dining paid off: British foreign direct investment in Chile rose sharply after Margaret Thatcher came to power, from GBP 28m in 1978 to GBP 114 in 1984" with British exports following a similar trend. Thatcher's handpicked chief economic advisor, Alan Walters, had been a closest Chilean supporter and admirer well before he practised his advocacy on a willing Thatcher. International law, human rights and electoral democracy went by the wayside as an illegal, brutal, totalitarian regime was whitewashed by Thatcher & Co.—à la Hayek, Friedman and Reagan—as a device for the restoration of democracy, when it was a democratically elected government itself that had been overthrown by Pinochet supported by the CIA in a systematically planned premeditated coup. Nicholas Ridley "frequently compared Chile favourably to Eastern Bloc countries, commenting, for example when he met the widow of Salvador Allende: 'Left-wing governments seemed not to condemn abuses of human rights in left-wing countries'" (Livingstone, 2018, p. 101).

Many of the gang of Chicago Boys came in and out of ministers' offices, bank and corporate receptions and meetings with heads of top think tanks, including especially the top super right-wing Conservative ones—the IEA, the CPS and the Adam Smith Institute. Grace Livingstone's account of these intimacies catches the cosiness of it all: the MP Eldon Griffiths struck up a friendship with the Chilean ambassador, enough to invite him to spend a week in his home in Suffolk; the ambassador wished for senior members of the Pinochet regime to be received by government ministers, and suggested the name of Jose Pinera, who was the Chilean minister of mines, and had earlier been the minister who had privatised the pensions and health systems of Chile—to great international right-wing acclaim. He "was consequently invited later that year and met trade minister Peter Rees, as well as the editor of *The Economist*, senior representatives of BP, Consolidated Goldfields, RTZ and other mining companies. He lunched with directors of Rothschild, Lloyds of London, Standard Chartered Bank and Baring Brothers and was a guest speaker at the London Metal Exchange. He also met the head of two Thatcherite think tanks, the Centre for Policy Studies and the Institute of Economic Affairs. Pinera was delighted at his reception; he told the British ambassador that he really valued his discussions with public and the private sectors and he predicted 'some envy when he wears his Adam Smith tie at the next meeting of the Chilean cabinet!' A month later, Miguel Kast, the Chilean labour minister responsible for anti-trade union legislation, was invited to London, where he met foreign office minister Richard Luce and trade minister Peter Rees. He had a private meal with Margaret Thatcher's advisor Alan Walters, and was a guest at a dinner hosted by the heads of leading banks, including Lloyds, Morgan Grenfell, Samuel Montague and Charter Consolidated" (Livingstone, 2018, p. 100). Other recipients of such hospitable hugs included Sergio de la Cuadro, another ranking Chicago Boy of General Pinochet.

Margaret Thatcher and Pinochet met only in 1994, but their cosy long-distance relationship had been flourishing since the early 1970s, when "Thatcher admired Pinochet for putting Allende out of office", to use Alan Walters' dark euphemism for assassination. She had proclaimed, in *Statecraft*, that "I was and am convinced that General Pinochet by his actions turned Chile into the free and prosperous country we see today" (quoted in Livingstone, 2018, p. 86). Thatcher's closest advisors were extreme supporters of Pinochet. One of these was Robin Harris, the Director of the Conservative Research Department and part of her policy advisory group. He wrote that Pinochet had first saved and then fully restored democracy to Chile, bringing it "order, stability, legality and prosperity". And apropos the violence of the coup: "you can't make an omelette without breaking eggs ... some eggs—too many, probably—were also broken under Pinochet, but surely Latin America never saw a larger omelette"; his piece drew praise from Thatcher who called it 'excellent' (quoted in Livingstone, 2018, p. 87). Another was Robert Moss whose book which justified the coup had 10,000 copies bought by the Chilean government for distribution overseas. Livingstone (2018, p. 87) writes that "Thatcher hired Moss as a speech writer, and he wrote her famous anti-Soviet 'Iron Lady' speech ... in 1976. She warmly praised Moss in her autobiography. She had met Moss at NAFF (National Association for Freedom), the anti-trade union lobby group that she and he supported." Another was Brian Crozier who was the Director of the Institute for the Study of Conflict "which specialized in studying trade union 'subversion' in Britain. Crozer had written a book warning against 'the bombardment of our minds with subversive poisons' in

1970 and, in a speech to military officers in Harrogate in the late 1970s, had called for an army takeover in Britain. Crozier became a confidante of Pinochet, helping him draft a constitution" (Livingstone, 2018, p. 87).[53]

The hospitality of Thatcher's regime would have made the UK feel like a holiday home to the Chicago Boys and Santiago gunmen of the Pinochet regime.

[53] James Buchanan, another MPS President and the 1986 'Nobel' economics prize winner, and the third member of the senior triumvirate of the MPS–Nobel assisting Pinochet in Chile, had the mission to protect capitalism from unbridled democracy, ideas that he took to Chile. "In 1980, he was able to put the programme into action. He was invited to Chile, where he helped the Pinochet dictatorship write a new constitution, which, partly through the clever devices Buchanan proposed, has proved impossible to reverse entirely" (Monbiot, 2017). See also Tanenhaus (2017). Relying on the serendipitous discovery of James Buchanan's office archive of office papers, including extensive correspondence between him and Charles Koch, Nancy Maclean (2017), who describes herself as "a historian of American social movements and their impact on public policy", and self-deprecatingly as "an academic archive rat like me", has written an extraordinary revelatory expose of "the attempt by the billionaire-backed radical right to undo democratic governance" … "a stealth bid to reverse-engineer all of America, at both the state and the national levels", uncovering the nexus between the stealth and libertarian billions of Charles Koch – "ordinary electoral politics would never get Koch what he wanted" … "an unrealized dream of liberty, or a capitalism all but free of governmental interference" – and the revolutionary libertarian ideas and strategies of James Buchanan. For Buchanan, the focus had to shift from relying on a particular party or candidate to "figure out how to put legal – indeed, constitutional – shackles on public officials, shackles so powerful that no matter how sympathetic these officials might be to the will of majorities, no matter how concerned there were with their own re-elections, they would no longer have the ability to respond to those who used their numbers to get government to do their bidding." And Maclean writes, that "a second, more diabolical aspect" of Buchanan's proposal was that "once these shackles were put in place, they had to be binding and permanent". "By the late 1990s, Charles Koch realized that the thinker he was looking for, the one who understood how government became so powerful in the first place and how to take it down in order to free up capitalism – the one who grasped the need for stealth because only piecemeal, yet mutually reinforcing, assaults on the system would survive the prying eyes of the media – was James Buchanan." And "Charles Koch and his inner circle turn[ed] the ideas into a revolutionary plan of action with frightening speed and success." For running the next lap, the libertarian baton had passed from Luhnow-Hayek to Koch-Buchanan. Within the Chilean context, Jose Gabriel Palma (2020), in Cambridge, poses the question: "how is that the rich stay rich, no matter what! – confirming the iron law of oligarchies … how oligarchies are able to landscape new scenarios to continue achieving their fairly immutable rent-seeking goals". He offers an answer: "When in democracy, they have used three main channels for this: they have enforced 'Buchanan'-style constitutional and legal straitjackets to restrict the scope of change and to debilitate the State; they have been able to reengineer their distributional strategies to suit the new scenarios; and they have cleverly absorbed elements of opposing ideologies (such as now accepting the need for 'social protection') to maintain their hegemony. The trump cards are ruthlessness in the first channel, and … fancy footwork in the other two". This cocktail of threats and subterfuges has obvious worked quite well for the Chilean far right; less than three months before the national plebiscite on acceptance or rejection of the dramatically reforming new constitution drafted by the 155-member Constitutional Convention, opinion polls indicate a steadily declining voting intention for "accept", and a rise well into the mid-50s of the percentage of those polled who say they would "reject" the proposed new Constitution and thereby prefer to stay with the Pinochet constitution with its inherent perpetuating stabilizing legal devices carefully crafted by Buchanan. In his Nobel Prize Lecture, Buchanan (1986) says about his work: "my purpose was ultimately normative rather than antiseptically scientific. I sought to make economic sense out of the relationship between the individual and the state before proceeding to advance policy nostrums." In fact, through his work on the constitution, Buchanan was designing the relationship between the Pinochet regime and the people of Chile.

But they would have had to tear themselves away from the social largesse and graces of the "ambassadors and embassy staff in Chile [and Argentina] [who] socialised in a ... tightly knit social milieu, comprising the British business community, many of whom were virulently right wing and in favour of military rule, along with upper-class Argentines and Chileans, including military officers. Embassy functions drinks funded by private companies, polo matches, dinner parties, as well as the more formal tasks of hosting trade missions or meeting Argentine or Chilean government officials were all part of the British diplomat's life in South America. ... [there was a] convergence of view between the Foreign Office and Britain's financial and commercial elites. Certainly, the Foreign Office, as an institution, articulated a conception of the 'national interest' which reflected the interest of the dominant industrial, financial, professional and landed groups of post-war Britain" (Livingstone, 2018, p. 10).

In this fine study, Livingstone (2018, p. 85) summarises Britain's change of course on Chile: "The Conservative Government of Margaret Thatcher dramatically changed policy towards Chile. An ambassador was reinstated, the arms embargo was lifted, and export credit guarantees were restored. The special programme for welcoming Chilean refugees was closed and funding for Chilean exiles to study in the UK was stopped—although the government did later fund a programme for exiles to return to Chile. The policy of ostracizing the regime was abandoned; four months after coming to office, Foreign Secretary Lord Carrington met the Chilean foreign minister in London, the first time a member of the cabinet had received a Chilean minister since the coup. Trade minister Cecil Parkinson visited Santiago a year later. A British defence attaché to Chile was appointed in 1981 to encourage arms sales. After Chile helped Britain in the Falklands war, Britain further loosened restrictions on weapons sales and helped to undermine United Nations' efforts to investigate human rights in Chile."

3.4.2 *The White House: Reagan, a Disciple*

Of Reagan's 76 economic advisors, 22 were members of the Mont Pelerin Society. Thatcher's chief economic advisor, as well as many other economists close to her, were members of the MPS, too. Since then, members of the MPS have actively promoted their extreme free-market ideology throughout the world. They include several past heads of state (Germany, Italy, Czech Republic, Sri Lanka); ministers of finance economics, and trade (U.K., U.S., Belgium, Hong Kong); ex-heads of U.S. Federal Reserve; members of the U.S. Supreme Court; officials from the Bank of England; a U.S. Secretary of State; and nine Nobel laureates in economics. The fact that so many have won a Nobel Prize is no surprise, however. The MPS helped create what is officially called the Nobel Memorial Prize in Economic Sciences specifically to legitimize free-market economic thinking. Mont Pelerin's members are also responsible for the establishment of a large number of right-leaning and very prominent think tanks that spread free-market economic thinking around the world. Many of these also produce the reports on climate change that deny the scale of the problem or cast doubts about the evidence. Many prominent journalists are also members of the MPS, including several Pulitzer Prize winners. The society has worked across the world to reform the teaching of economics in universities and to help ensure that the articles published in academic journals support its ideas. In many university departments, the free-market model has become the only one that is taught. (Maxton & Randers, 2016, pp. 76–77)

"By the early 1980s, 'Chicago' itself had become more dispersed. Friedman retired from teaching and, along with others, shifted his base to the Hoover Institution at Stanford, which afforded direct connection to Ronald Reagan and his advisors" (Yergin & Stanislaw, 1988, p. cxcviii). "By then it became clear that the Chicago School had carried out a devastatingly successful 'neo-classical counterattack' in economics and in its applications. Macroeconomics management did not work, while tinkering with the money supply only increased uncertainty and discouraged investment. And the Chicago School also showed that regulation would inevitably drift away from the ideal of promoting an impersonal public good; instead, it would be captured by special interests. On top of everything else, government had failed to prove itself a forecaster. Faith in 'big government' fell under the attack" (ibid.).

The Hoover Institution, the conservative think tank set up by Herbert Hoover in 1919, was attached to Stanford University, Hoover's alma mater. In 1975, Ronald Reagan, then Governor of California, was appointed as its first honorary fellow; and in 1977 Milton Friedman joined him there after he retired from Chicago. At least thirteen Hoover-linked scholars were advisors to Reagan for his election campaign in 1980, and the number went up to over thirty after he won the election in 1981. Hoover Fellows have included George Shultz, Condoleezza Rice, Generals John Abizaid and James Mattis who served as Defense Secretary under President Trump ('Hoover Institution', 26.09.2019). Friedman's *Free to Choose* ten-part TV programme (broadcast by the Public Broadcasting Service) was developed during 1977–1980 when he was at Hoover; he advised Reagan informally during his 1980 campaign, and then served on Reagan's Economic Policy Advisory Board during the Reagan administration years. Friedman had earlier been economic advisor to Barry Goldwater during his 1964 presidential campaign. During 1968–1978, he and Paul Samuelson participated in a bi-weekly economics debate programme. Friedman wrote a weekly column for *Newsweek* during 1966–1984. In 1988, Reagan awarded him the Presidential Medal of Freedom; three years later George H. W. Bush made the same award to Friedman's guru, Friedrich Hayek; the sequence was reversed—Hayek was awarded the Nobel economics prize in 1974, with Friedman following in 1976.

The Heritage Foundation provides another, one of many possible, illustrations of the reach and influence of libertarian think tanks, all fundamentally loyal to the message of Hayek and Friedman, into US government circles. The Heritage Foundation, founded in 1973 by a group including Edwin Feulner, is regarded as one of the most influential conservative think tanks in America; it came into prominence through the leading role it played in the Reagan era, espousing neoconservatism, anti-communism and the Christian right. Its libertarian report of 1981, *Mandate for Leadership*, listed over two thousand recommendations of which the Reagan administration took up about 60 per cent in its first year in office; it helped fashion the aggressive Reagan Doctrine, argued for the Star Wars policy and supported US military involvements in

Afghanistan, Angola, Cambodia and Nicaragua, and then in the George H. W. Bush presidency it was a leading advocate of the American invasion of Iraq; and the Heritage Foundation has been a keen supporter of the Trump presidency in which "at least 66 foundation employees and alumni were given positions in the administration", and "several hundred people from the Heritage database [of about 3000 trustworthy conservatives] ultimately received jobs in government agencies".[54] Feulner was a member and President of the Mont Pelerin Society; and he, along with John Blundell, had introduced a later *Reader's Digest* condensed version of Hayek's *The Road to Serfdom*.

In the 1950s, the Chicago group was "a small beleaguered minority regarded as eccentrics by our fellow intellectuals", but by the 1980s, the same ideas were "at least respectable in the intellectual community and very likely almost conventional among the broader public"; and by the 1990s, Krugman was to say that Friedman's "long campaign against the ideas of Keynesian economics" had made him into "the world's best-known economist". As Gary Becker explained: "It was a result of what was going on in the economics profession and what was going on in the world. They came together" (Yergin & Stanislaw, 1988, p. cxcix).

3.4.3   10 Downing Street: Thatcher, a Devotee

The adoration of Hayek by Keith Joseph, Thatcher's mentor, is so obvious as to be touching, as snippets from the Margaret Thatcher Archives reveal. In August 1974, he writes from the House of Commons to Ralph Harris, confessing, "I'm steeping myself in Hayek—and am ashamed not to have read the great *The Constitution of Liberty* long ago";[55] a couple of months later, in October, after his speech in Preston highlighting the monetarist position on inflation, he writes, again from the House of Commons, directly to Hayek in Salzburg: "I am most grateful for your blessing on what I said at Preston";[56] in July 1975 he writes again to Hayek in Salzburg: "I am touched that so outstanding a man as you should take the time to write to me so encouragingly on reading the report of the Free Enterprise luncheon"[57]; and in March 1977, writing from the Centre for Policy Studies, Joseph comes clean and tells Hayek that "you are in a class of your own".[58]

Hayek had been in a psychological trough, but then things changed dramatically from the 1970s: he got the Nobel Prize in 1974 and that "was the making of him", and then with "the coming of Thatcher, there's no doubt that really smartened him up. He was really uplifted by seeing this movement in the stuffy old Conservative Party in a radical redirection of policy along the lines that he had charted" (Harris, 2000, p. 10).

[54] Wikipedia, "The Heritage Foundation", accessed 1 September 2020.
[55] Keith Joseph to Ralph Harris, Letter dated 8 August 1974. https://www.margaretthatcher.org/document/114767
[56] Keith Joseph to Friedrich Hayek, Letter dated 28 October 1974. https://www.margaretthatcher.org/document/114605
[57] Keith Joseph to Friedrich Hayek, Letter dated 11 July 1975. https://www.margaretthatcher.org/document/114607
[58] Keith Joseph to Friedrich Hayek, Letter dated 14 March 1977. https://c59574e9047e61130f13-3f71d0fe2b653c4f00f32175760e96e7.ssl.cf1.rackcdn.com/37A7B82277C144099B5EB0CBD570445A.pdf

Harris records how he made the first introduction between the guru and the believer. Hayek left LSE around 1950 and moved to Chicago, and then returned to Germany in the 1960s from where he regularly made a couple of visits a year to England; Harris managed his diary and served as his "networker with all his press and policymakers who wanted to see Hayek". Harris narrates: "one time when he was with us for the day Thatcher's office came on and said, 'When is the great man about?' Could she come and drop in to see him? And so she called by, and sat down at the desk, and the unkind quip I make is that there was a period of unaccustomed silence from Margaret Thatcher as she sat there, intense, attending to the master's words, not her usual dominating conversation. And he actually thought she was beautiful" (ibid., p. 10). Michael Foot put it slightly differently, calling Hayek "a mad professor" who had Margaret Thatcher "in his clutches".

Later, he congratulated her on her victory at the General Election of 1979, and she wrote back: "I was very touched by your kind telegram. It has given me great pleasure and I am very proud to have learnt so much from you over the past few years. I hope that some of those ideas will be put into practice by my Government in the next few months. As one of your keenest supporters, I am determined that we should succeed. If we do so, your contribution to our ultimate victory will have been immense."[59] In 1984, Hayek was on Thatcher's Honours list, elevated to Companion of Honour; Sir Karl Popper, a mate from old LSE days, had got his CH a couple of years earlier also from Thatcher, and both joined another LSE friend, Lord Robbins, who became CH in 1968.

An introductory comment in the Margaret Thatcher Archives states: "After the 1979 general election the figure of Milton Friedman bulks larger in the story, as monetarism came to define the political battleground. ... If by this stage Hayek was the benign philosopher king, Friedman was the frenetic man of business, jetting from lecture theatre to presidential suite, all but omnipresent on the op-ed pages and the tv screen. His ten-part television series making the case for capitalism, *Free To Choose*, was broadcast in Britain in early 1980s and the government approached his arrival pre-screening almost as a state visit. Where MT met Hayek one-to-one for quiet chats, a deputation of ministers was arranged for Friedman and his wife Rose."[60]

Hayek and Friedman were lavishly feted and honoured by Reagan and Thatcher in their own ways. Of course, they were not alone in being thanked and honoured for services rendered to the cause. A quick gleaning of the honours bestowed by Thatcher during her tenure produces an extensive list of the ranking neoliberals in that period highlighting the influence of Hayekian doctrine (Table 3.1).

---

[59] Margaret Thatcher to Friedrich Hayek, Letter dated 18 May 1979. https://www.margaretthatcher.org/document/112178
[60] https://www.margaretthatcher.org/archive/Hayek.asp

266   A. SAITH

Table 3.1 Some honours awarded in the tenure of Margaret Thatcher, 1979–1990

Name	Lifespan	Title	Year	Institution/services
Ralph Harris	1924–2006	Baron	1979	IEA/MPS Conservative ideologue/political educator/privatisation promoter
Max Beloff	1913–1999	Kt Baron	1980 1981	Thatcherite trouble shooter, adviser; House of Lords; Oxford, later principal, Univ College, Buckingham, now Univ of Buckingham
Hugh Thomas	1931–2017	Baron	1981	Historian, adviser, chairman CPS 1979–1990 (?)
Douglas Hague	1926–2015	Kt	1982	One of MT's economic gurus; served in policy unit; Chair ESRC 1983–1987
Robin Ibbs	1926–2014	Kt KCB	1982 1988	Head, CPRS 1980–1982; the 'Next Steps' report 1988
John Hoskyns	1927–2014	Kt	1982	DG Institute of Directors 'Stepping Stones' Report for Conservative Party 1977
Karl Popper	1902–1994	CH	1982	LSE; senior ideological guru; Hayek friend
Alan Walters	1926–2009	Kt	1983	LSE; Chief Econ adviser; link to Friedman; liaison with Chile-Pinochet
Arthur Seldon	1916–2005	CBE	1983	Founder, President IEA; VP, MPS; Hayek Society. LSE, under Hayek, Plant, Robbins; "intellectual begetter of the private University of Buckingham" (Obituary; Daily Telegraph)
Alfred Sherman	1919–2006	Kt	1983	CPS; super-right ideological bulldog and political strategist of Conservative Party
Peter Bauer	1915–2002	Baron	1983	LSE; Mont Pelerin associate of Hayek; anti-foreign aid; "charmed Mrs Thatcher" (DT)
Friedrich Hayek	1899–1992	CH	1984	Libertarian ideological supremo-godfather
David Young	1932–	Baron	1984	Director CPS from 1979; then overseeing the privatisation agenda
Nigel Vinson	1931–	Baron	1985	Co-founder of CPS; trustee, Civitas; donor for conservative causes, incl. Univ of Buckingham; anti same-sex marriage, investment in renewable energy sources, and UK in EU
Antony Fisher	1915–1988	Kt	1988	Originator and financier of libertarian Conservative think tanks; MPS-Hayekian; IEA founder; Atlas network, also, CPS, ASI role
Michael Richardson	1925–2003	Kt	1990	'Mr Privatisation'; investment banker; MD of NM Rothschild & Sons; informal advisor to Thatcher and HMT; business career ended in disgrace with loss of licence to trade
Brian Griffiths	1941–	Baron	1990	City University Business School Chief Policy Advisor from 1986; Chairman CPS 1991–2001; "taxpayers should tolerate the inequality for the common good" (2009), two years after financial meltdown); facing criminal charges by Malaysian Government for fraud in the 1 MDB case
Denis Thatcher	1915–2003	Hereditary Baronetcy	1990	Husband

Notes: The significance of the influence of the Central European cohort of Hayekian neoliberalism is apparent. The roles of Hayek (moved to Britain from Vienna in 1931), Beloff (parents moved to Britain from Russia in 1903) and Popper (moved from Vienna in 1937 to New Zealand, then to Britain in 1946), for instance, are well established, as are those from the British side, such as Antony Fisher, Ralph Harris, Anthony Seldon, Alan Walters and Patrick Minford, among others. Additional notes are limited, arbitrarily, to four snapshots by way of illustration of the substantial impact Thatcher's advisers made even if usually shielded from direct public gaze.

Peter Thomas Bauer (1915–2002)

Born into a Jewish family in Budapest, Peter Bauer moved to Britain in 1934; Cambridge BA econ 1937; LSE; Mont Pelerin Society; Hayek's friend; Thatcher was a friend and admirer; winner of the first Friedman Prize for Advancing Liberty awarded by The Cato Institute—a libertarian think tank with roots in the Hayekian tradition and network. He died a week before receiving the prize worth $500,000, awarded by a selection panel that included Margaret Thatcher and Vaclav Klaus the former Czech prime minister, both great admirers and followers of Hayek and Friedman; Klaus was also an active member of the MPS, as was Bauer, alongside Hayek and Friedman, both founder members and friends; Rose Friedman was also amongst the panel members. Klaus: "I am glad to say I didn't hesitate one second and from the suggested list of candidates I immediately picked up Peter Bauer. Margaret Thatcher told me later that she did the same" (Klaus, 2018, 'Notes for Peter Bauer's Speech in Budapest', 27 March). https://www.klaus.cz/clanky/4254

Hugh Thomas, Baron Thomas of Swynnerton (1931–2017)

Hugh Thomas, one time leftist, author of the classic *The Spanish Civil War*, but then changed colours and became a follower, and adviser, of Thatcher, running the CPS after Keith Joseph in 1979. Thomas made a couple of attempts to stand for a Labour ticket to stand in the election, "but was thwarted by members of the Militant Tendency on the selection committee" (Preston, 2017). "Thereafter, if not in consequence, he publicly declared his abandonment of the Labour party and his embrace of Thatcherite free-market economics. He became one of Margaret Thatcher's unofficial advisers and was made chairman of her thinktank, the Centre for Policy Studies, in succession to Keith Joseph" (ibid.). He read history at Queens' College Cambridge, "not very assiduously, but did attain prominence as a swashbuckling Tory president of the Union. After graduating, he led a champagne-fuelled life as a man-about-London." Thatcher wrote the foreword to one of his pamphlets in 1979; and he was made a life peer by Thatcher in 1981. In 1997, he resigned the Tory whip and crossed over to the Liberal Democrat benches in the House of Lords; thus, well-travelled, been everywhere, done everything, in one way or another. His home hosted glittering literary parties, with famous names, including Maria Llosa Vargas (who incidentally was a member of Hayek's Mont Pelerin Society), and sometimes, Margaret Thatcher, for whom apparently it was a convenient neutral space to meet with Enoch Powell.

Preston, Paul 2017, "Lord Thomas of Swynnerton: Obituary", *The Guardian*, 9 May. https://www.theguardian.com/books/2017/may/09/lord-thomas-of-swynnerton-obituary

Sir Alfred Sherman (1919–2006)

If Hugh Thomas, the ex-leftist-turned-Thatcherite had written about the Spanish Civil War, Alfred Sherman had actually fought in it on the Republican side. Sherman was born in Hackney, London, to Jewish parents who were immigrants from Russia. He was at LSE where in 1948, he was the president of the student branch of the CP which he had joined in 1937 as a 17-year-old. But then he changed sides and swung over to the extreme right, becoming one of a band of Joseph-Thatcher 'political entrepreneurs' who mounted a sustained frontal attack on the political consensus of the times. The others included Ralph Harris and Arthur Seldon at the IEA, and Madsen Pirie and the ASI. Kavanagh says, "there was never to be any middle ground in Sherman's life; he believed in absolutes, revelled in conflict and detested the consensual complacency of the middle way." Joseph and Thatcher had set up and headed the CPS in 1974; Sherman ran it; promoted and tutored Keith Joseph as he became the heir apparent for the post-Heath Tory leadership, wrote his speeches and promulgated key salient elements of the new Tory free-market and monetarist agenda, "preaching Thatcherism before the term was invented". The CPS drew in other 'talent', including John Hoskyns and David Young. After the Tory election victory in 1979, he was writing speeches for Margaret Thatcher, but then it all began to fray as the undisciplined Sherman over-exerted and over-asserted himself. Sherman felt that "I articulated her instincts"; he certainly pushed the Tory agenda further towards the right edge. Like Thatcher, "he aroused strong feelings; he could be arrogant and offensive to those (the

(*continued*)

Table 3.1 (continued)

great majority) whom he regarded as 'second-rate'; his crude expressions, particularly about immigrants and non-whites, could give plain speaking a bad name." He is said to have prompted Thatcher into adding 'swamping' into the Tory political lexicon; he invited Jean-Marie Le Pen to a fringe meeting at the 1987 Conservative conference, subsequently aborted in the face of the uproar it induced; later he became an adviser and apologist of Radovan Karadzic. "He seemed to despise most politicians and civil servants whose goodwill he depended on. His lack of tact combined with his quest for recognition made it difficult for Whitehall to know what to do with him." So Hugh Thomas, the CPS chairman, cut him loose and the original iconoclast meandered into an undisciplined wilderness; and in 1983, Thatcher—who confessed to retaining "an exasperated affection" for him—knighted him.

Kavanagh, Dennis 2006, "Sir Alfred Sherman: Adviser who preached Thatcherism before the term was invented", *The Guardian*, 29 August. https://www.theguardian.com/news/2006/aug/29/guardianobituaries.conservatives

Sir Douglas Chalmers Hague (1926–2015)

In 1967, Michael Spicer (then a young staffer in the Conservative Research Office, later Lord Spicer) introduced the rising Margaret Thatcher and her mentor Keith Joseph to Douglas Hague, the co-author (with Alfred Stonier, who was a student of Ludwig von Mises and a member of his Privatseminar in Vienna) of the undergraduate textbook on economic theory; "a copy of the textbook was duly presented; … the relationship flourished; Hague sent regular notes on issues to which he felt she should attend, and helped her to understand the theories of Milton Friedman and others who were challenging the Keynesian consensus; … [even when in the Heath government] she insisted that they lunch occasionally (at the Epicure restaurant in Soho) because 'the Department is full of communists and I need to check on issues … with someone whose views are like mine'." Later, he served in her policy unit, and also wrote several of her speeches; "after the election was won, an early paper in her Downing Street in-tray was from Hague urging the abolition of exchange controls—which was done within a year". (*The Telegraph* 2015, "Sir Douglas Hague, economist—obituary", 2 March) https://www.telegraph.co.uk/news/obituaries/11444810/Sir-Douglas-Hague-economist-obituary.html

More than its Weight in Gold—The Market Price of Symbolic Capital

A dejected Hayek had wanted to wrap up the MPS after its 10th meeting in 1957, a time when Keynesianism was at its zenith; Friedman had wanted the 25th anniversary in 1972, when Keynesianism still ruled the day, to become the valedictory, final meeting. This might well have been a serious plan: at the 25th anniversary meeting, Friedrich Hayek was presented with a 200-gramme pure gold ingot; this was auctioned by Sotheby's on 19 March 2019; it carried an estimate of GBP 5000–7000; it sold, as it happened, for GBP 27,500. The gold price that day was $1306 per ounce, thus valuing the ingot at $9213; at GBP 1.0 = USD 1.3262, this comes to GBP 6947. For a lark, this divides the hammer price into a gold value of GBP 6947, with the remaining GBP 20,553 or 74.7 per cent, as the value of the symbolic capital embedded in the metal ingot.

Eight years earlier, in June 2011, Margaret Thatcher's in/famous Asprey handbag, the one she had on her arm standing with her political soulmate Ronald Reagan in 1985, sold at Jeffrey Archer's charity auction for GBP 25,000. Says Edwina Curry, one of her cabinet ministers: "it wasn't a shield, it was a weapon. It said, 'I am Margaret Thatcher, I'm the boss, I'm in charge. I have all this power and I have control. That was why the handbag was always so neat and tidy and black and shiny and dominant. It would go on the Cabinet table. She used it as her filing cabinet. ... As an additional hard drive if you like" (BBC, 2011). From the Margaret Thatcher Foundation, "there is a story ... beloved of biographers and documentary makers and perhaps a little too perfect to be actually true, that as Leader of the Opposition MT once cut short a presentation by a leftish member of the Conservative Research Department by fetching out a copy of [Hayek's] *The Constitution of Liberty* from her bag and slamming it down on the table, declaring '*this* is what we believe'" (Margaret Thatcher Foundation, n.d.). But this Mont Pelerin Society pure gold ingot paled into insignificance against the glitter of Hayek's Nobel Prize Medal, of the same 200-gramme weight (though of 23 not 24-carat gold), awarded to Hayek in 1974, two years after the gift of the ingot. The Prize medal, being auctioned—in the same sale on 19 March 2019—by Sotheby's in honour of the 75th anniversary of the publication of *The Road to Serfdom*, carried a pure-gold value of approximately $12,000 when the Sotheby's hammer went down on it at $1.53 million (Foundation for Economic Education, 2019, 27 March).

3.4.4 Pulling Together

A frank interview given by Paul Volcker[61] in 2000 provides insights into the parallel tracks with distinct points of comparison between the US experience in the Reagan years and the UK when Thatcher was in power. One of these was

---

[61] "The appointment of Paul Volcker as Chairman of the Federal Reserve in that year [1979] symbolised the triumph of monetarist policies and ushered in a period of deliberate heavy deflation, widely-imitated abroad, especially in the UK. This effectively put paid to any prospect of overcoming the second oil price hike by conventional demand management. It finally ended attempts to breathe life back into the Golden Age economic regime" (Glyn et al., 1988, p. 2).

the relationship between labour and government in the time of inflation. Volker says "one of the major factors turning the tide on the inflationary situation was the [air traffic] controllers strike [of 1981] about wages [and] working conditions. But the controllers were government employees, and the government didn't back down. And he [Reagan] stood there and said, 'If you're going to go on strike, you're going to lose your job, and we'll make out without you'. That had a profound effect on the aggressiveness of labor at the time, in the midst of this inflationary problem and other economic problems. That was something of a watershed" (Volcker, 2000, p. 14). Reagan fired 11,345 striking air traffic controllers and banned them for life from federal employment, and decertified their union. The comparison with the miners' strike in the UK, and Thatcher's direct assault on trade unions, is immediate.

"There was a Reagan revolution in terms of the cutting edge of this moving back from this feeling that [if] you've got a problem, the government would answer it. Here's a big brother here to help you, as Mr. Reagan used to mock. ... He did it with some vigor ... in a way that helped restore the confidence of America in America, which had been lost, or at least greatly eroded, during the 1970s" (ibid.). America had been humiliated in Vietnam; Reagan's bellicose stance and his Star Wars dramatics reinjected American nationalism into the political bloodstream. Thatcher did the same with the Falklands war.

"In some ways what we were doing was paralleling what she was trying to do, and even in some ways on the inflation side it was very close. She admired tough monetary policies. We got along pretty well. ... I was a great admirer of hers. She was taking a tough stand, trying to change the direction of Britain. They had had a lot of problems that we had in the 1970s, so I had enormous respect for what she was trying to do. I thought she was much tougher, ... much more driven that I was" (ibid., pp. 14–15). Thatcher would drop in to see Volker when she was in the USA, and he would reciprocate when in London. "She always came to see me, which was always slightly embarrassing that the prime minister of the UK was driving into the Federal Reserve garage instead of the other way around."

"Inflation is related to monetary policy. It's related to the issue of money. The issue of money is a governmental responsibility predominantly, and to use that authority in a way that leads to inflation is a system that fools a lot of people, and to keep fooling them you have to do it more and more; [that] is a moral issue. I put myself in that camp. ... It corrodes trust, particularly trust in government. It is a governmental responsibility to maintain the value of the currency that they issue. And when they fail to do that, it is something that undermines an essential trust in government" (ibid., p. 12). Here, Volcker's position is virtually identical to that adopted by Friedman and Hayek, Joseph and Thatcher, though the second pair could be regarded as derivatives of the first.

Volcker regards the parallel movements in the USA and UK against inflation, alongside the privatisations in the UK and the deregulation drive in the USA, as marking the beginning of a world movement with the so-called retreat of government from the economy: "what happened in the United States, similar to what happened in Britain, had a big influence on others". One might add, with respect to the developing economies, that this influence was often exerted through the structural coercion by multilateral agencies which were under the control primarily of the OECD group, as demonstrated in the global roll out of the Washington Agenda of structural adjustment and stabilisation in the developing economies after the debt crisis following the oil price hikes of the 1970s.

3.5 Besieging Cambridge: The Chicago–MIT–LSE Trinity

3.5.1 A Cross-Atlantic Triangle

Conceivably, there was a cross-Atlantic triangle defined by the coordinates of MIT/Harvard, Chicago and LSE, and it was a space bristling with hostility towards the Cambridge heterodox groups, in particular the left-Keynesians be they pure theoreticians, policy advisors or macro-modellers. Pitched battles were fought, and insults regularly hurled across the waters in both directions; the codes of warfare allowed representatives of the opposing camps to visit one another, to assess the other's strength and to demonstrate their own, in seminars and lectures; though, on the day, these sometimes degenerated into gladiatorial fight-to-the-death performances, say, in the Colosseum of the secret seminar at King's College. The strength of The Triangle lay significantly in the fact that while the three often squabbled and disagreed with each other, and quite rudely, these were all really squabbles within the family which remained steadfastly united in confronting their common Cambridge Keynesian foe. In this, The Triangle had the great strategic advantage in already having significant internal support within the Cambridge camp. This took two forms: first, the neoclassicals that remained within the Faculty—contrasting with the enforced extinction of the genuine Keynesian (say, à la Joan and Kahn) and other heterodox species within their triangle through a tight control over the grant of appointments and tenures; and second, the arrival, in a Trojan horse, of senior gladiators such as Hahn, who could then nurture and strengthen the neoclassical line within the old Cambridge. In this strategy, the outpost of the LSE, in combination with the neoclassical column within Cambridge, was greatly supported, in different ways—in men, morale and materials—by the other two points of The Triangle, which provided vital 'strategic depth' to the anti-heterodox campaign in Cambridge at pivotal points.

3.5.2 Diversity of Practice

Paradoxically, there were chasmic doctrinal and policy divisions between the two American points of the Triangle, sprinkled liberally with the spice of personality clashes between their titans. Paul Samuelson was perennially in disagreement with 'his friend' Milton Friedman, on television, in lecture rooms or on paper. And this was probably carried over into the next life: "Samuelson, at 93, gave an interview where he declared that the ongoing crisis validated his own economic views—and invalidated those of his long-time rival, the late free-market economist Milton Friedman. 'Today we see how utterly mistaken was the Milton Friedman notion that a market system can regulate itself', Samuelson said. 'Everyone understands now, on the contrary, that there can be no solution without government. The Keynesian idea is once again accepted that fiscal policy and deficit spending has a major role to play in guiding a market economy. I wish Friedman were still alive so he could witness how his extremism led to the defeat of his own ideas'" (Peter Robinson, 2009). It can be safely presumed that Friedman would have risen to the challenge and responded. More generally, Friedman had said much earlier, that "the fundamental difference between Chicago at that time and let's say Harvard, was that at Chicago economics was a serious subject to be used in discussing real problems, and you could get some knowledge and some answers from it. For Harvard, economics was an intellectual discipline on a par with mathematics, which was fascinating to explore, but you mustn't draw any conclusions from it" (Friedman quoted in Hammond, 1992). This would apply with equal or greater force to MIT economics.

Meanwhile, the younger Paul (Krugman) penned some seriously hostile remarks about Hayek, as did Bob Solow, though Solow distinguished between a 'good Hayek' working on knowledge and the market, and a 'bad Hayek' characterised by his Mont Pelerin Society and its agenda. Hayek himself, as also Friedman, had no time for the Samuelson–Arrow type of mathematical GEEQ approach propped up by extreme assumptions.[62]

---

[62] In recent work, Bowles et al. (2017a, 2017b) have returned a qualified positive assessment of Hayek's analysis of markets with the emphasis on the process of information exchange as distinct from the Walrasian general equilibrium tradition. They "find considerable lasting value in Hayek's economic analysis [of markets] while nonetheless questioning the connection of this analysis to his political philosophy", concluding that "fortunately, Hayek's economics and his political philosophy do not have to be taken as a package—one can appreciate his insights into the functioning of market economies without idealising the system itself" (Bowles et al., 2017b).

Hayek did not require markets to be perfectly competitive; rather market competition was a procedure or process of information exchange and discovery that guided individual economic behaviour; no assumption was imperative that this system evolved to any equilibrium, or that it maximised welfare as was claimed in the case of general equilibrium analysis. Hayek's main thrust was to attack the displacement of the market, and the freedoms held to be virtually synonymous with it, by socialist planning devices for economic decision-making and the allocation of resources. He distanced himself explicitly from the Walrasian general equilibrium approach; he saw markets bringing coherence and stability, without claiming equilibrium and profit or welfare optimisation.

Offer and Soderberg (2016, p. 188) provide their elaboration on these differences. "Hayek's famous article of 1945 was at odds with the North American neo-classical market-clearing equilibrium approach of Samuelson and Arrow. For their mathematical models to work, the person making

Not that Hayek and Friedman agreed between themselves. Even at the inaugural meeting of the Mont Pelerin Society there were disagreements between the Austrian and the Chicago monetarist lines of thought. And much later, in 1980, their views had still not converged. Disagreements between the two on monetary and related policies had been simmering for a while and were aired in 1980 in the UK in Hayek's publicly expressed criticism of Friedman's position on the cures for inflation in the British economy, and on how to deal with the trade unions. On one of his visits to the UK, Hayek announced that "my hopes of Britain saving herself have shrunk a little. I'm not hopeless, but I'm becoming apprehensive". He revealed the cause of this anxiety: "I'm afraid Mrs Thatcher is following the advice of Milton Friedman. He is a dear friend of mine and we agree on almost everything except monetary policy. He thinks in terms of statistics, aggregates and the average price level and does not really see that inflation leads to unemployment because of the distortion of the structure of relative prices" (Bradley, 1980). But he has another grouse. Ian Bradley (1980) reports that Hayek "also sees Professor Friedman's influence as a major factor in the Government's failure to curb the power of trade unions, which he regards as an essential precursor to monetary reform". Hayek had written directly to Thatcher earlier from Freiburg about "the crucial problem of trade union policy"; he asks: "is it not one of such decisive importance as to justify the now (*sic*) constitutional resort to a referendum?"[63] Hayek was urging rapid and drastic action on deflation and also on trade unions, again in contrast to Friedman's apparently more moderate position. Hayek pronounced: "As a result of a mistake of legislation in the past, [the trade unions] have Britain by the throat and cannot understand they are killing the goose which lays the golden eggs ... this is killing enterprise after enterprise and causing a continuous dissipation of capital ... an economic recovery would be impossible unless the unions were stripped of their coercive powers ... so long as they possess them, even the wisest union

an economic choice had to know all the options available. This bland requirement implied the more far-fetched one of complete information about all commodities and services and their prices relative to each other, not only in the present but for all time. In contrast, Hayek assumed (more realistically) that every individual in the economy could know only a small part of the whole, conveyed to him by prices. Markets co-ordinated this multitude of individual choices and gave rise to the 'spontaneous order' of the liberal society. This order was assumed, not proven with any rigour."

> Hayek's imaginary world may have been ordered, but was not necessarily benign. It was not an invisible hand utopia, and indeed had some authoritarian undertones. But it was superior to central planning as practised in the Soviet Union, and although it fell short of the imaginary best, Hayek regarded it as the best available. The imaginary auctioneer of general equilibrium, who brought prices into agreement for all time, was suspiciously similar to the socialist central planner, an affinity exploited by some socialist equilibrium economists. Walras ... had been a socialist. Hayek expressed his disdain for such models in his Nobel speech, stating ... that their certainty was not science, but 'scientism'. (ibid.)

[63] Hayek to Thatcher, Letter dated 28 August 1979. Margaret Thatcher Archives, Churchill College, Cambridge. https://c59574e9047e61130f13-3f71d0fe2b653c4f00f32175760e96e7. ssl.cf1.rackcdn.com/C26CCF21BE974C549D249A9E815E64D1.pdf

leaders can, as we see every day, be forced by little groups to exercise them"; citing intimidatory picketing, demarcation rules and the closed shop, Hayek exhorted Thatcher that "the only hope is that an appeal to a large number of workers over the heads of their present leaders will lead to the demand for a reduction in their powers".[64] Hayek's recommendation was to go for the jugular with a bang-bang deflationary intervention: "You can cure inflation suddenly or gradually. Politically, it is impossible to do it gradually. To put it crudely, I would say that it is possible to cause 20 per cent unemployment for six months if you can hold out a hope that things will be better after that. You cannot have 10 per cent unemployment for three years. Yet that is what the Government's present course asks for and I don't think it can hold out."[65] His cure was "bigger and better bankruptcies". He had no time for "what are officially called the wets, and what I call the descendants of the muddle of the middle, [who] are the obstacle to her doing what she would like to do" (Bradley, 1980).[66]

He had been urging this for a while, and indeed had earlier received a response from Thatcher: "Although I understand your view that it might have been easier politically to have reduced our borrowing and monetary expansion more rapidly, I think this would have caused too much social and economic disruption in the short run for it to have been feasible" (Bradley, 1980). Incidentally, Hayek's meetings with and frequent missives to Thatcher offering advice, and his regular public utterances on the course of her monetarist policies, give the lie to the notion that he kept away from politics and politicians: that may well have been what he preached but not what he practised, whether in the UK, or in the Chilean contexts. It is perhaps pertinent that this closeness of Hayek and Friedman, with their avowed hostility to the Cambridge left-Keynesians, was fully manifest and operational precisely in the period when the anti-heterodox campaign within Cambridge took a turn that came to involve decision-making in bodies outside the Cambridge Faculty, whether within the university structure, or in grant-making bodies in London.

But, even if as the proverbial exception, there were also stories of mutual admiration. Hahn visited MIT in 1956, and Bob Solow remembers it thus: "I cannot remember whether it was literally love at first sight. By the end of the that year, however, a lifelong friendship had come into being" (Newbery, 2017, pp. 485–486). Subroto Roy was Hahn's student in Cambridge in the 1970s, and recalls: "once a week, with one other student, I met with him in his rooms in Churchill College where he critiqued our weekly essay" and these were brusque enough to become memorable; but one of his "unerasable memories of these meetings was … the two blue airmail letters always on his desk,

---

[64] Source: *The Times*, 1 December 1980; digital version in Margaret Thatcher Archives, https://www.margaretthatcher.org/document/114512

[65] https://www.margaretthatcher.org/document/114510

[66] Ironically, in Chile, it was Friedman who was pushing Pinochet for a more precipitate big bang deflation, though Hayek surely agreed. Again, Thatcher is on record saying that such extreme measures would not be politically feasible in the UK.

one addressed to Professor Paul Samuelson, and the other to Professor Robert Solow; I don't know if he wrote to them every day or every week on the day of my tutorial" (Roy, 2013).

3.5.3 Unity of Purpose

There were internal differences over scriptures and rituals between Chicago and Cambridge (Massachusetts), but all this surface warfare notwithstanding, both were engaged but united in their shared mission of evangelical proselytisation using their contrasting means and methods; Samuelson went via textbooks, and strict gatekeeping to discipline; Friedman went straight over all that to directly address the politicians and the people with his simple, simplistic remedies, Mrs Beecham's powders for all their ailments. Binyamin Appelbaum provides the bottom line:

> American economists are sometimes divided into two camps, one of which is said to be headquartered in Chicago and to favour markets in everything, while the other is said to be headquartered in Cambridge, Massachusetts, and to favour the heavy hand of government. These camps are sometimes referred to as 'freshwater' and 'saltwater'. Far too much is made of such distinctions; the leading members of both groups ... shared a confidence that economies tend toward equilibrium. They agreed the primary goal of economic policy was to increase the dollar value of the nation's economic output. They had little patience for efforts to address inequality. A 1979 survey of the members of the American Economic Association found 98 percent opposed rent controls, 97 percent opposed tariffs, 95 percent favoured floating exchange rates, and 90 percent opposed minimum wage laws.[67] Their differences were matters of degree, and while these differences are consequential ... the degree of consensus was consequential, too. Critiques of capitalism that remained a staple of mainstream debate in Europe were seldom heard in the United States. The difference is nicely summarised by the political scientist Jonathan Schlefer (2012, p. 189): 'Cambridge, England, saw capitalism as inherently troubled; Cambridge, Massachusetts, came to see capitalism as merely in need of 'fine-tuning'. In time, the American consensus shifted the boundaries of debate in other countries, too. (Appelbaum, 2019, p. 16)

Milton Friedman reflected on all this from a higher plane; the market for their joint services was vast enough to permit, indeed require, a division of labour. "I think the libertarian movement is doing fine. ... It takes many kinds of people to make a movement. And one of the most important things are publications. In any activity you have manufacturers, wholesalers, and retailers; and all three are essential and necessary. There are only a relatively small number of manufacturers of ideas. But there can be a very large number of wholesalers and retailers" (reported in Doherty, 1995).

---

[67] The survey is reported in Kearl et al. (1979).

How, then, does this panoramic external environment—disciplinary, ideological, political—interface the trajectory of Cambridge heterodox economics? What could be the points of articulation through which these external influences could have contributed to its demise? Several channels of transmission suggest themselves, some fairly specific and direct, others more indirect but perhaps no less potent.

For Hayek, the key objective was to prevail in the battle of ideas, and Keynesianism, especially in its Cambridge 'left' manifestation, was the prime target. Socialism was anathema of course, but it was the prospect of a slide towards 'serfdom' in the Western civilisation that kept him (and Friedman) awake at night and going in the day.[68] However, neither Friedman nor Hayek (after his initial bruising exchanges with Cambridge in the 1930s and his far more productive wartime stay there) had much direct contact with Cambridge economists. Monetarism found general opposition in Cambridge both from the various heterodox lineages but also vehemently from the neoclassicals led by Frank Hahn, as unequivocally expressed in the famous '364' letter jointly written by him and Robert Neild against the practice of monetarism in UK policy. Further, neither Friedman nor Hayek were believers in the mathematical general equilibrium passions that motivated Hahn and his followers in Cambridge, UK, or their like numbers in Cambridge, USA. And the redistributive tendencies of James Meade, even though he was a thorough neoclassical in most of his work, would hardly have found favour with any wing of the Chicago–Virginia neoliberal camps. As such, there wasn't much common ground to operate in tandem on the Hahn–Matthews campaign against the heterodox camps in Cambridge, though surely both Friedman and Hayek might have been quite pleased and supportive of such an agenda. This lack of virtually any *direct* connection between Cambridge and the Hayek–Friedman axis is also reflected in the Mont Pelerin Society. Stanley Dennison, close friend and in the circle of the 'anti-Keynesian' Dennis Robertson, was indeed one of the original thirty-six founding members of the MPS, but his was perhaps the sole name from Cambridge during that era. The only other Cambridge-connection person was Frank Hahn's wife, Dorothy, who, as Hayek's research assistant at the LSE, was the rapporteur and took minutes, in shorthand, for most of the sessions of the inaugural meeting at Hotel du Parc on Mont Pelerin in April 1947. Frank Hahn had some incidental communication with James Buchanan, but it was about a research supervision for one of his doctoral students, Subroto Roy. Some of the money for the inaugural meeting of the MPS was facilitated by the Cambridge and King's College economic historian Sir

---

[68] "The threat to a free society that we envisaged at the founding meeting of the Mont Pelerin society was very different from the threat to a free society that has developed over the intervening period. Our initial fear was of central planning and extensive nationalization. The developing threat has been via the welfare state and redistribution. Unfortunately, the threat did not disappear but simply changed its character" (Friedman, in a letter to a friend in 1985; Offer & Soderberg, 2016, quoted in Warsh, 2016).

John Clapham through his close links with the Bank of England, but he died in March 1946, before the inaugural meeting. The MPS held one of its annual meetings, in 1980, in Cambridge; but these all remain straws in the wind, and there is little serious evidence of any immediate involvement of local Cambridge economists in the proceedings whether from the neoclassical or, needless to say, from the heterodox sides.

It is also striking that there is no participation from the Samuelson–Solow–Arrow MIT or Harvard neoclassical, mathematical general equilibrium groups in the Chicago-driven, Hayek/Friedman-led Mont Pelerin Society; the reason, credibly, is to be found in Hayek's rejection of the Walrasian approach. The rejection would have been mutual, since the Cambridge-USA groups would not be willing to settle for the 'weak' defence of the free-market system as expounded by Hayek and Friedman, viz., that though it might not yield the optimum claimed by the Walrasians, it would provide outcomes superior to allocation systems run, or interfered with, by the state. And Friedman worried much more about policy interventions and outcomes in an imperfect real world and had a simplified reductionist toolkit for the purpose; he was not particularly bothered by the mathematical games played in virtual 'reality' by MIT and Harvard, and said so quite plainly. And more substantively, there were some major differences in the policy domain: Hayek–Friedman were fundamentalist in their free-market, minimum-government doctrine; the Samuelson–Solow position of fervent scriptural GEEQ became conditionally Keynesian in the short run, also accepting, indeed advocating, a moderate role for state intervention to save the free-market system from itself. As such, they might not have wished to be members of the MPS, even if they had received invitations, which they didn't. In fact, Solow was rather dismissive of the significance and impact of the Mont Pelerin Society—a judgement possibly based more on ignorance than evidence about that organisation.

Also remarkable is the fact that in this panoramic narrative, Cambridge heterodox perspectives are virtually invisible—except as strawmen to be demolished. This could be ascribed by Cambridge critics to their alleged insularity, or to the 'irrelevance' of the Cambridge dialogues; but more pertinently it points to the high degree of intellectual and disciplinary polarisations that had occurred across locations hosting contrasting and conflicting ideologies underlying their visible 'theoretical' differences.

At the level of the discipline, the external attacks on Cambridge heterodox economics came from two distinct sources and through different channels. The first assault was from the general equilibrium brigade, directed from MIT and Harvard, and led locally by Frank Hahn and his battlegroups straddling Cambridge and LSE and its outposts. This took various forms: direct theoretical challenges which led, in a Gramscian manner, to the capture and recasting of definition/s of 'Keynesianism', thus shifting the locus of the origin from one Cambridge to the other; the enforced exclusion and consequent extinction of original versions of Keynesianism, and other Cambridge heterodox traditions, from curricula and journals under their tutelage; extreme gatekeeping into the discipline by controlling the criteria, procedures and compositions of committees making appointments or promotions, which was greatly strengthened by gaining command over the discipline-wide research assessment and evaluation exercises which allowed them to define the 'quality' of economists and the work, and indeed to pronounce whether it was 'economics' at all. And when tactically necessary in local battles in Cambridge, cross-Atlantic support was forthcoming in the form of experts and consultants invited to act as referees on the quality of various applications made by members of the heterodox side—whether to do with external grants, or internal promotions. The baseline was that the American GEEQ groups greatly added to the decibel power of the Cambridge neoclassicals in disparaging and undermining the relevance and quality of the work of their local opponents at the Faculty or the DAE. This influence was significant within the discipline domain and given the widening professional control over the practice of economics, it was quite effective in the assassination of reputations, even of senior figures; but it remained relatively weak in government and official circles, not least because general equilibrium mind games did not much amuse policy makers of any creed.

The second source from which challenges emanated were the monetarists, both gurus and followers, Hayek and Friedman, but then also Walters, Minford, Laidler and others of various degrees of faith in the doctrine. The heterodox groups easily beat back these charges and monetarism per se remained a dead religion in Cambridge, for both neoclassicals under Hahn, as well as the post-Keynesians, Sraffians and Marxists. Thus, their impact on Cambridge economics was negligible in strict academic terms. In contrast, they exercised a good deal of influence against the left-Keynesians through the informal power they wielded by virtue of the fact that the monetarist gurus, read Hayek and Friedman, had a god-like status in the eyes of the political leaders of the time (Thatcher, Joseph, Howe and many others). Both monetarist mentors and their minions could be expected to lend a shoulder or a shout, or worse, in contests involving Cambridge Keynesians in various academic or financial decision-making committees and processes; at ground level, theirs was a proxy power, derived from the fact that the political leaders were the followers of their shared monetarist gurus. This monetarist power structure had been developed over the previous two decades by the libertarian ideological entrepreneurs who had had the foresight, deep dedication and matching pockets, to set up an extensive soft infrastructure for shifting the public narrative and the terms of policy discourse in the country, with the Institute of Economic Affairs and its other creations in the lead. In turn, this formation was closely integrated with its American and global counterparts which could jointly exercise phenomenal outreach. At the heart of this was the Mont Pelerin Society, though many of its satellites had evolved and matured into strong organisations in their own right.

An interesting point of distinction with regard to the LSE was the sustained co-existence of representatives of both the monetarist lineage, with their loyalties mainly to Chicago, as well as the general equilibrium group, which had powerful local leaders who were strongly integrated with their counterparts in the larger American networks, with MIT and Harvard as their parental homes. The two groups could seemingly practice forms of co-respective commensality in the LSE outhouse that were generally not visible in America; perhaps it was more challenging to profess and practise the more extreme forms of monetarism in the British context steeped in Keynesianism of one sort or another, though the Friedmanite following gained voice and muscle as Thatcher rose to power, leading to breakdowns.

Three into two won't go, and the triangle of doctrines—Keynesianisms, Walrasian, Friedmanite—was always unstable and tended to induce tactical alliances of expediency, temporary marriages of convenience, made feasible by often blurred or fuzzy boundaries, and several 'Keynesians' or 'monetarists' with plural identities operating, following personal conviction or pursuing personal advantage, in the grey zones between the camps. An illustration of this was the famous joint letter written by Frank Hahn and Robert Neild and signed by 364 economists from universities ranged across the country, against Thatcherite monetarism. Within Cambridge economics, Hahn and Neild stood at two ends of the doctrinal spectrum, but found it useful to join forces against monetarist fundamentalism; since Hahn had written the letter, all his neoclassical followers and protégés also signed—even if some did so with less than full willingness, as came to be revealed later. Cambridge Keynesians had always been on the other side of the line from Thatcherism, but for the neoclassicals, this public demonstration provided some brownie points and a welcome veneer of relevance in the raging debate on public policy; and possibly for Frank Hahn, it was an opportunity to gloat over Thatcher's monetarist chief economic advisor Alan Walters, who had been Hahn's colleague at the LSE, but was now his bête noire (Newbery, 2017, p. 489). But even while the ink was drying on this joint letter, the Hahn–Matthews camp was deep in its campaign against the left-Keynesians in Cambridge, especially targeting the macroeconomic modelling teams of the DAE. And in this campaign, where much of the action took place outside the Faculty, Hahn & Co. found tactical support from some of the monetarists for whom this was a welcome opportunity to displace the old Cambridge firm and usurp its long-standing position when the Social Science Research Council (SSRC) committees decided to deny the Cambridge teams further funding and effectively closed them down; these decision makers came from the Hahn–Matthews grouping, some from the monetarist camp, and some, arguably, from those strictly professing the old Keynesian gospel. Hahn's group and campaign wound up on the winning side on both occasions. Going further afield from the SSRC/ESRC episodes, a similar tactical alliance was at work within the economics unit of successive research assessment exercises for which the direction and template had been prescribed by Frank Hahn in his tenure as President of the Royal Economic Society. It is striking that in the course of time, several leading younger members of the Hahn anti-heterodox campaign in Cambridge wound up with their names on lists of supporters, advisors or authors at the Institute of Economic Affairs, the Thatcherite propagandist think tank that was the engine room for changing the goal posts of public debate away from Keynesianism towards monetarist and supply-side free-market capitalism as practised by Thatcher and Reagan and as preached by their gurus, Hayek and Friedman. Another strategic cluster was the CLARE (Cambridge, London and the Rest of England) group of economists led by Robin Matthews, and after his retirement by John Flemming; not many general equilibrium types were to be found in these ranks which were replete with 'moderates', disgruntled Keynesians, monetarists who had not taken their vows, right-wing Labour, proto-SDP or closet-Tory economists, many of whom were embedded in government circles; this CLARE grouping was productive and proactive, and under Matthews, who was a long-running Chair of the Bank of England's Panel of Economic Consultants, the views of the CLARE group found visibility and a hearing at times in Thatcher's government in Downing Street and at Chequers. John Flemming was in the CLARE group from start to finish, and was simultaneously its chairman and also a member of the academic advisory council of the Institute of Economic Affairs. The influence of the Hahn–Matthews group extended through diverse means and channels into a range of decision-making structures, and many of these platforms were used strategically in undermining the economics and economists of the various heterodox lineages of Cambridge. In this mission, they drew credibility and strength from the hostility of British and American neoliberalism towards Cambridge left-wing Keynesianism and non- and anti-neoclassicals, be they Marxists, structuralists, Robinsonians, Sraffians, Kaldorians, Kaleckians, multi-disciplinarians or just good free-thinking eclectic, applied economists who, like Pigou, thought that the purpose of economics was to improve the well-being of people. These traditions were duly eliminated in the purges; but it was not just a ring-fenced local battle—the victorious Hahn–Matthews campaign was the local manifestation of the power of the rapidly evolving phenomenon of global neoliberalism of which it was a vanguard grouping, galvanised by its mission to storm the old heterodox citadel.

Of late, the Hayek academic brand appears to be undergoing something of an orchestrated revival beyond its extended home turf, including, somewhat ironically in Cambridge itself, in the Keynesian lair where his economic theories and his political ideology were perhaps most rebuffed. Unless mistaken, there have been sightings of the Hayek pennant fluttering over King's College, the home of his prime adversary Keynes, who organised his study space there during the war years, facilitating the writing of *The Road to Serfdom*, the tract that became the popular bible of the neoliberal right alliance. On the 60th anniversary of its publication, in 2004, an international conference was held at King's College, organised by its Joint Centre for History and Economics headed by Emma Rothschild; the conference provided a fresh assessment of the current significance of Hayek's work, with an introductory paper by Bruce Caldwell, a Hayekian specialist and member of the Mont Pelerin Society, with Amartya Sen and Meghnad Desai amongst the participants. Two years later Cambridge University Press produced its *Cambridge Companion to Hayek*, edited by

Edward Feser (2006), a libertarian philosopher whose subsequent books include *Five Proofs of the Existence of God* (2017) and *By Man Shall His Blood be Shed: A Catholic Defense of Capital Punishment*. The 2006 *Companion* includes a paper by Robert Skidelsky 'Hayek versus Keynes: The Road to Reconciliation' which "charts the path to their reconciliation". In the meantime, Bruce Caldwell (2019) wrote another reflection on Hayek's significance, this time on the 75th anniversary of the publication of *The Road to Serfdom*; this year, 2020, the Hoover Institution held a big celebratory 40th anniversary conference of the first meeting of the MPS at Stanford, providing another occasion for a fresh round of burnishing the Hayek brand.

The flip side of the favourable reconstruction of the 'Hayek' brand is the melting down and recasting of 'Keynes'. This recent phenomenon displays a bizarre characteristic: on the one side, there are the steady efforts of some Hayekians and Pelerinistas to seek a 'reconciliation' between the two icons, citing both as being deeply committed to liberal values and politics. Bruce Caldwell leads this effort from the Hayekian camp, repeatedly arguing that the distance between Hayek and Keynes was not really so great as to be unbridgeable; and from the Keynesian side, Robert Skidelsky has provided qualified support for this proposition in pointing out strong areas of agreement, while also listing 'four buts', where the distance between the two remained significant. In 2006, Skidelsky pronounced that "in political economy and political philosophy Hayek is the greater and deeper thinker"; … "Hayek, with his wider intellectual range, left a more general message than did Keynes" (Skidelsky, 2006, p. 107). But "death removed the possibility of what would have been one of the most thrilling, and necessary, intellectual encounters of the twentieth century" (ibid., p. 108). In 2020, at the Hayekian gala event of the 40th anniversary of the previous conference of the Mont Pelerin Society at the Hoover Institution, Skidelsky, presumably a willing invitee and not a gatecrasher, brushed up his 2006 notes, and expanded on the theme of a reconciliation: "In the end, you can't prove either Hayek or Keynes to have been right" (ibid., p. 7); "the two old fogies might have found more common ground in deploring the decay of capitalist civilization than they managed in 1944" (Skidelsky, 2020, p. 8). Barring some open ends, there appears to be convergence between Caldwell, a Hayekian revivalist and MPS member, and Skidelsky, as proxies arguing the corners of their respective subjects.

Paradoxically, while Caldwell and Skidelsky highlight the shared commitment to liberalism, thus making Hayek more palatable and acceptable in polite liberal circles, there is a second parallel debate, another strand which runs in the opposite direction, emphasising not the political or economic closeness, but rather the distance between Hayek and Keynes—with the former retaining his liberal badge, but Keynes being depicted as a socialist placed at the other end of the political spectrum. That Keynes was of socialist belief had been argued earlier by Rod O'Donnell (1999) and recently by James Crotty (2019) who uses the term 'liberal socialist'. Alongside, from the libertarian side, Edward Fuller has strongly argued in a series of articles—almost all published in journals closely associated with libertarianism à la Mises and Austrian economics à la Hayek—that Keynes was a 'non-Marxist socialist'—unbridgeably distancing him from Hayek's liberalism. Mongiovi (2020) points out that "Keynes's biographers, Roy Harrod, Robert Skidelsky, and Donald Moggridge, position him as a liberal with progressive sensibilities; Skidelsky in particular is skittish about identifying him as a socialist". Skidelsky (2020, p. 8) writes that "Keynes had earlier given liberalism an economic agenda to fight back against socialism and communism, by demonstrating that societies didn't need 'serfdom' to secure full employment". But Fuller (2019) takes issue with this and argues that "Skidelsky has misinterpreted Keynes's political philosophy". In a recent paper,[69] Fuller "presents unexplored evidence that shows Keynes was a non-Marxist socialist from 1907 until his death in 1946"; he aligned himself with the socialist cause, advocated socialist policy and engaged in socialist political and journalistic activities. This follows a stream of earlier papers by Fuller picking on some part or other of Keynes's life, economics and political thought: Fuller (2013a) argues that "Keynes's ethical theory is flawed because it is based on his defective logical theory of probability ... consequently, Keynes's ethical theory is not a viable ethical justification for socialism"; Fuller (2013b) is a broadside attack on Keynes's concept of the "marginal efficiency of capital"; in Fuller (2017) "the central thesis ... is that Keynes invented the IS-LM model to justify non-Marxist socialism". Fuller and Whitten (2017) then launched a full-sale attack on Keynes's role in the First World War, challenging "the traditional view [that] Keynes heroically resigned from the British delegation at the Paris Peace Conference of 1919 to write his book in protest of the harsh reparations clauses of the Treaty of Versailles", and arguing instead "that Britain's war-debt problem, not German reparations, led Keynes to resign from the British delegation and write *The Economic Consequences of the Peace*" (Fuller & Whitten, 2017, p. 2). The authors have much to say on and against 'the traditional view' of Keynes. "Keynes saw the war as an opportunity to advance his career. While. Many British men were enlisting in the army, Keynes wanted to fulfill his lifelong dream of working in the British Treasury" (Fuller & Whitten, 2017, p. 4) "Keynes was desperate for a job connected with the war" (ibid., p. 5). "Keynes was the chief architect of Britain's war-debt problem, and he was aware that the system of war loans he developed and applied would create significant problems for postwar Britain. But to his mind, this system of war debt was the only way to save the British Empire from defeat. Keynes deserves much

---

[69] Ironically, the Fuller's latest piece, arguing that Keynes was a non-Marxist socialist, was carried by the left-leaning, heterodox *Cambridge Journal of Economics* which cites Keynes, along with Marx, Kalecki, Joan Robinson and Kaldor, as those whose traditions it follows and is inspired by; if anything, this demonstrates the intellectual openness of the journal—perhaps both the extreme right and the Cambridge left were happy to see Keynes being proven to be of socialist convictions, thus distancing him from 'liberalism', an outcome perhaps equally desirable to the Hayekian right and the Cambridge left. The journal has recently published another piece (Sousa, 2020) which excavates and brings to light 'the lesser known affinities' between Keynes and Hayek.

responsibility for creating Europe's war-debt problem and shifting the balance of financial power from Britain to the United States. The Paris Peace Conference of 1919 marked the beginning of his failed lifelong struggle to win back Britain's economic and financial hegemony from the United States" (Fuller & Whitten, 2017, p. 6). Keynes was a fervent imperialist, but at the same time he was a key member of the Bloomsbury group. This clique of eccentric writers and artists passionately opposed the war. Following his Bloomsbury friends, he applied for exemption from conscription as a conscientious objector in February 1916. His friends did not approve of his work in the Treasury, and they demanded that he resign. While he loved his work organising war loans, his friends accused him of being a hypocrite. To them it was "impossible to reconcile his avowed sympathy for conscientious objectors with the job of demonstrating how to kill Germans as cheaply as possible" (Holroyd, 1995, p. 343). "He had spent the war financing the slaughter of 10 million combatants, and saw the peace conference as an opportunity to sanitize his conscience and repair his reputation within the Bloomsbury group" (Fuller & Whitten, 2017, p. 9, citing Skidelsky, 1983, p. 353). "Keynes's lifelong fight for British imperialism was counterproductive and self-defeating. While each of his wartime efforts was aimed at preserving British imperialism, the system of allied war loans he developed and applied destroyed the financial foundation of the empire. The war-debt problem masterminded by Keynes contributed to the trade and currency wars of the interwar period that played an important but neglected role in causing the Second World War. ... By creating the war-debt problem and then advising the government to default, Keynes destroyed the financial basis of Britain's imperial power and handed the American government the lend-lease weapon it used to tear it apart. Although he fought vigorously throughout his life for the British Empire, Keynes actually deserves much credit for its demise" (Fuller & Whitten, 2017, p. 24).

Then, the persistent Fuller (2018) takes the campaign to a different level of personality and mentality, where he argues that Keynes was "a tragic victim of the fatal conceit"; he provides "an overview of Keynes's personality and character, with an emphasis on his intellectual arrogance and his sense of omniscience" before moving on to "Keynes's supremacism as reflected in his sexism, eugenicism, racism, and imperialism. Finally, the paper shows that Keynes was a non-Marxist socialist, and his non-Marxist socialism was an intellectual error resulting from intellectual pride." Meanwhile, libertarian historian Ralph Raico (2008, pp. 176–177), a close associate of the likes of Ayn Rand, Murray Rothbard and Ronald Hamowy, and a follower of von Mises, Stigler, Friedman and Hayek who was his PhD supervisor, summed it up: "How can someone who expressed a wistful sympathy for the 'experiments' of the Nazis, Fascists, and Stalinist Communists, and whose threadbare Bloomsbury mockery was reserved for the freely functioning society of laissez-fair be considered a clear-cut example of a liberal or any liberal at all?"

Mongiovi (2020) sounds a caution over the provenance of those making the judgements whether Keynes was a socialist, and of which strain. "This terrain has been explored before. Rod O'Donnell [1999] has already made a persuasive case that Keynes was a socialist in his philosophical outlook, his political orientation and his economics. A favourite pastime of some libertarian intellectuals is to tar Keynes with the socialist label and then feather him with misleading insinuations that he approved of Stalinism, National Socialism, and Italian Fascism."

The new mantra, however, is 'liberty': in the assessment of Melissa Lane (2013, p. 56), "liberty rather than efficiency becomes the leitmotif of Hayek's defence of capitalism". She goes on to approvingly observe that "an economist as different from Hayek as Amartya Sen would later herald Hayek for his insistence on the importance of freedom as a human value" (ibid., p. 57).[70] Melissa Lane was the co-organiser, and Amartya Sen a participant, at the conference at King's College, Cambridge, in 2004. An indirect clarification is provided by Sen himself. In writing about Janos Kornai recently, Amartya Sen recalls how he tried to dissuade him from using the title of his book, Kornai (1990), *The Road to Free Economy*. "I had wondered whether his chosen title—with freedom linked to an economy rather than to the persons in a society—might make the reader expect some kind of a deeply conservative institutional structure—in the way that Friedrich Hayek proposed in his similarly named book, *the Road to Serfdom*" (Sen, 2020, emphasis in the original). It is clear from comment that Sen places himself at a discrete distance from Hayek's notion of freedom which was predicated and causally linked to the achievement of a 'free' market economy, and it might therefore be questionable to interpret Sen's consistent arguments for freedom and liberty as he enunciates these, as equating to or supporting the notions of freedom and liberty as defined in Hayek's lexicon.

And Skidelsky (2020, p. 7), speaking about Keynes and Hayek, equates the two on the 'liberty' scale: "Both were lovers and defenders of freedom", says Skidelsky (2020, p. 7). However, seen from the other side of the power equation, the credentials of both would need some skilful qualification and

---

[70] Since the original source of the position attributed to Amartya Sen is not cited, it is not possible to appreciate the full basis of Sen's heralding of Hayek and the qualifications and limits that he might have placed on it. That said, it does remain difficult to reconcile the importance that Hayek, in theory, attached to his notion of liberty, and the coercive and violent dictatorial regimes that he was willing to romance in practice—on the specious grounds that the means, a fascist dictatorship, sometimes justified the end, his version of 'liberty'. The libertarian industry has been busy with its cosmetics, airbrushing away the warts and polishing the images of Hayek, Friedman and Buchanan in this regard. Again, writing about much earlier times in Cambridge, Amartya Sen records his frustration at not being able to pursue his passion for social choice theory in the 1950s, and his fascination over Buchanan's "two extremely interesting papers" (1954a, 1954b) and his "wonderfully foundational question" that challenged Arrow's impossibility theorem. The "very agreeable but rather conservative" Buchanan's work receives close attention without any reference from Sen, writing in 2021, to Buchanan's subsequent role and position in the pantheon of libertarian politics (Sen 2021, p. 376–378). Of course, both count as profound believers in the ideal of "liberty", though the word might have carried rather different meanings for either. Be that as it may, Buchanan received the "Nobel" economics prize in 1986, and Sen, in some senses an antidote, followed in 1988..

airbrushing: Hayek for his links with ruthless and bloody dictators, or for his conditional support for Italian fascism, both disingenuously justified in the name of creating the preconditions for the liberty of the free-market system; and Keynes, for his staunch defence of British imperialism, with the subjugation of the 'subject peoples' justified in the name of bringing them to the door of civilisation—à la Marx.

At the end of the saga, when all the academic and public battles over words, ideas and models are done, there is scarcely need to belabour the global transformative force—for good or otherwise remains an open question of choice—of the power of the neoliberal Reagan–Thatcher double act. All the caveats notwithstanding, this power was used unremittingly in the cause of a global capitalism led by big corporations, finance capital, the mission marketed by their surrogate and proxy think tanks and where necessary by military bullying, and it was exercised remorselessly against all that stood in its way, whether abroad or at home, be it in Chilean economy and society, or in the Welsh mines, or American flight controllers, or left-leaning Cambridge Keynesians and heterodox economists. Behind the fights over ideas lay the irresistible force of material interests of capital in its multiple manifestations. Servaas Storm rightly observes that "the demise of old Cambridge itself is proof of the importance of material interests, rather than ideas. What happened in the Cambridge Faculty of Economics was so strongly driven from the outside that a counterfactual—the heterodox tribe winning the battle—is a bit like the small indomitable tribe of Asterix the Gaul winning the battle against Caesar's Romans, it is almost unthinkable." Helpfully, he adds: "After all, Asterix and Obelix had a magic potion which gave them superhuman strength, which the Cambridge tribe did not have".[71] The experience of the purges of the heterodox schools in Cambridge was replicated almost universally in the departments of economics elsewhere. The Cambridge story has to be placed in this wider context.

REFERENCES

Annan, N. (1983, February 3). How should a gent behave? *New York Review of Books*. https://www.nybooks.com/articles/1983/02/03/how-should-a-gent-behave/?pagination=false

Appelbaum, B. (2019). *The economists' hour: False prophets, free markets, and the fracture of society*. Little, Brown and Company.

Barnett, W. A. (2004). An interview with Paul A. Samuelson, December 23, 2003. *Macroeconomic Dynamics, 8*, 519–542. Republished in Working Paper Series in Theoretical and Applied Economics, University of Kansas.

Barnett, V. (2008). Russian émigré economics in the USA. In J. Zweynert (Ed.), *Economics in Russia: Studies in intellectual history* (pp. 107–122). Ashgate Publishing.

---

[71] Personal communication.

Baumol, W. J. (1990). Erik Lundberg, 1907–1987. *The Scandinavian Journal of Economics, 92*(1), 1–9.

BBC. (2011, June 27). *Margaret Thatcher Asprey handbag raises 'just' GBP 25,000.* https://www.bbc.com/news/uk-england-lincolnshire-13932845

Beckett, A. (2002). *Pinochet in Piccadilly: Britain and Chile's hidden history.* Faber & Faber.

Benn, T. (2000). Interview. Commanding Heights, Public Broadcasting Service, Interviewed on 26 October 2000. https://www.pbs.org/wl7h/commanding-heights/hi/people/pe_name.html

Birner, J. (2009). *F. A. Hayek's Monetary Nationalism after seven decades.* Paper Presented at the Storep Annual Conference, Florence. Universiti di Trento and University College, Maastricht.

Blaug, M., & Sturgis, P. (Eds.). (1983). *Who's who in economics.* MIT Press.

Blundell, J. (1990). *Waging the war of ideas: Why there are no shortcuts.* Presentation given at the Heritage Foundation, Atlas Economic Research Foundation, January. https://web.archive.org/web/20050419113153/http://www.atlasusa.org/toolkit/waging_war.php

Blundell, J. (2004). *Introduction to the IEA condensed version of the Reader's Digest Road to serfdom.* Institute of Economic Affairs.

Blundell, J. (2010, October 15). *Obituary – Professor Sir Alan Walters.* Institute of Economic Affairs. https://iea.org.uk/blog/obituary-%E2%80%93-professor-sir-alan-walters

Bowles, S., Kirman, A., & Sethi, R. (2017a). Retrospectives: Friedrich Hayek and the market algorithm. *Journal of Economic Perspectives, 31*(5), 215–230.

Bowles, S., Kirman, A., & Sethi, R. (2017b). *The market algorithm and the scope of government: Reflections on Hayek.* VOX CEPR Policy Portal, December 8. https://voxeu.org/article/reflections-hayek

Bradley, I. (1980, November 12). The Hayek cure: Bigger and better bankruptcies. *The Times.* Digitalised version available in the Margaret Thatcher Foundation Archives. Retrieved August 14, 2020, from https://www.margaretthatcher.org/document/114510

Buchanan, J. M. (1954a). Social choice, democracy and free markets. *Journal of Political Economy, 62*(2), 114–123.

Buchanan, J. M. (1954b). Individual choice in voting and the market. *Journal of Political Economy, 62*(3), 334–343.

Burgin, A. (2012). *The great persuasion: Reinventing free markets since the Depression.* Harvard University Press.

Butler, E. (2015). *Antony Fisher, Herald of Freedom.* Adam Smith Institute. https://www.adamsmith.org/blog/miscellaneous/antony-fisher-herald-of-freedom

Buzaglo, J. (2010, October 22). *The Nobel family dissociates itself from the economics prize.* Real-world Economics Review Blog. https://rwer.wordpress.com/2010/10/22/the-nobel-family-dissociates-itself-from-the-economics-prize/

Caldwell, B. (2019). *The Road to Serfdom after 75 years.* CHOPE Working Paper No. 2019-13, Center for the History of Political Economy at Duke University, 60p.

Caldwell, B. (2020). Mont Pelerin 1947. Paper presented at the Conference commemorating the 40 Anniversary of the Mont Pelerin Society meeting of 1980 at Stanford University, Hoover Institution – Stanford University, January 15–17, 58p.

Caldwell, B., & Montes, L. (2015). Friedrich Hayek and his visits to Chile. *Review of Austrian Economics, 28*(3), 261–309. https://doi.org/10.1007/s11138-014-0290-8

Cassidy, J. (2000, June 30). The Hayek century. *Hoover Digest, 3*. https://www.hoover.org/research/hayek-century

Clements, K. W. (2004). *Larry Sjaastad, the last Chicagoan*. http://www.library.uwa.edu.au/__data/assets/pdf_file/0009/99873/05_02_Clements.pdf

Cockett, R. (1994). *Thinking the unthinkable: Think-tanks and the economic counter-revolution, 1931–1983*. Harper-Collins.

Craver, E., & Leijonhufvud, A. (1987). Economics in America: The continental influence. *History of Political Economy, 19*(2), 173–182.

Crotty, J. (2019). *Keynes against capitalism: His economic case for liberal socialism*. Routledge.

Cubitt, C. E. (2006). *A life of Friedrich August von Hayek*. Authors OnLine.

Dahrendorf, R. (1995). *A history of the London School of Economics and Political Science, 1895–1995*. Oxford University Press.

Denham, A. (2005). *British think-tanks and the climate of opinion*. Routledge.

Denham, A., & Garnett, M. (1998). *British think-tanks and the climate of opinion*. UCL Press Ltd.

Doherty, B. (1995, June). Best of both worlds: An interview with Milton Friedman. *Reason*. https://reason.com/1995/06/01/best-of-both-worlds/

Ebenstein, L. (2018). Hayek's divorce and move to Chicago. *Econ Journal Watch, 15*(3), 301–321. https://econjwatch.org/articles/hayeks-divorce-and-move-to-chicago

Feldstein, M. (2009, January). *The case for fiscal stimulus*. Reprinted by Project Syndicate. www.aei.org

Feser, E. (Ed.). (2006). *The Cambridge companion to Hayek*. Cambridge University Press.

Filip, B. (2018a). Hayek on limited democracy, dictatorships, and the 'free' market: An interview in Argentina, 1977. In R. Leeson (Ed.), *Hayek: A collaborative biography. Part XIII: 'Fascism' and liberalism in the (Austrian) classical tradition* (pp. 395–421). Palgrave Macmillan.

Filip, B. (2018b). Friedrich Hayek and his visits to Chile: Some Austrian misrepresentations. In R. Leeson (Ed.), *Hayek: A collaborative biography. Part XIII: 'Fascism' and liberalism in the (Austrian) classical tradition* (pp. 423–462). Palgrave Macmillan.

Foundation for Economic Education. (2019, March 27). *Hayek Nobel Prize fetches $1.5 million at auction*. https://fee.org/articles/hayek-nobel-prize-fetches-15-million-at-auction/

Frank, A. G. (1976). Economic genocide in Chile: Open letter to Milton Friedman and Arnold Harberger. *Economic and Political Weekly, 11*(24), 880–888. https://www.jstor.org/stable/4364704?seq=1#page_scan_tab_contents

Frey, B. S., & Pommerehne, W. W. (1988). The American domination among eminent economists. *Scientometrics, 14*(1–2), 97–110.

Friedman, M. (1976). *Milton Friedman: biographical*. https://www.nobelprize.org/prizes/economic-sciences/1976/friedman/biographical/

Fuller, E. W. (2013a). Keynes and the ethics of socialism. *Quarterly Journal of Austrian Economics, 22*(2), 139–180.

Fuller, E. W. (2013b). The marginal efficiency of capital. *Quarterly Journal of Austrian Economics, 16*(4), 379–400.

Fuller, E. W. (2017). Keynes's politics and economics. *Procesos de Mercado: Revista Europea de Economia Politica, 14*(1), 41–88. http://www.procesosdemercado.com/wp-content/uploads/2017/07/41-88-170705-Visual-Procesos-de-Mercado-COMPLETO-n%C3%BAmero-27-Vol.-XIV-n.-1-3.pdf

Fuller, E. W. (2018). Keynes's fatal conceit. *Procesos de Mercado: Revista Europea de Economia Politica*, 15(2), 13–65. https://search.proquest.com/openview/a1a638fd68c12766b7878865efc4f8f3/1?pq-origsite=gscholar&cbl=686495

Fuller, E. (2019). Was Keynes a socialist? *Cambridge Journal of Economics*, 43(6), 1653–1682.

Fuller, E. W. & Whitten, R. C. (2017). Keynes and the first world war. *Libertarian Papers*, 9(1), 1–37.

Glyn, A., Hughes, A., Lipietz, A., & Singh, A. (1988). *The rise and fall of the golden age*. UNU-WIDER Working Paper No. 43. UNU-WIDER.

Goodwin, D. (2001, December 19). The way we won: America's economic breakthrough during World War II. High growth needn't require a war. *The American Prospect*. https://prospect.org/health/way-won-america-s-economic-breakthrough-world-war-ii/

Gylfason, T. (2005). *Interview with Assar Lindbeck*. CESIFO Working Paper No. 1408.

Haberler, G. (1961, October 15). *Mises's private seminar: Reminiscences by Gottfried Haberler*. Mises Institute; Reprinted from *The Mont Pelerin Quarterly*, III(3). https://mises.org/library/misess-private-seminar-reminiscences-gottfried-haberler

Haberler, G. (1986). Reflections on Hayek's business cycle theory. *The Cato Journal*, 6(2).

Hagemann, H. (2007). German-speaking economists in British exile, 1933–1945. *BNL Quarterly Review*, 60(242), 323–363.

Hagemann, H. (2011). European émigrés and the 'Americanization' of economics. *European Journal of the History of Economic Thought*, 18(5), 643–671.

Hagemann, H., & Krohn, C. D. (Eds.). (1999). *Biographical guide to the emigration of German-speaking economists after 1933*. K. G. Sauer.

Hahn, F. (1989). Robinson–Hahn love–hate relationship. In G. R. Feiwel (Ed.), *Joan Robinson and modern economic theory* (pp. 895–910). Palgrave Macmillan.

Hammond, J. D. (1988, May 24). *An interview with Milton Friedman on methodology*. Hoover Institution, Stanford University. https://miltonfriedman.hoover.org/friedman_images/Collections/2016c21/Stanford_05_24_1988.pdf

Hammond, J. D. (1988, May 4). An interview with Milton Friedman on methodology. Stanford, CA: Hoover Institution, Stanford University. https://miltonfriedman.hoover.org/friedman_images/Collections/2016c21/Stanford_05_24_1988.pdf. Reprinted as Hammond, J. D. (1992). An interview with Milton Friedman on methodology. In W. J. Samuels & J. Biddle (Eds.), *Research in the history of economic thought and methodology*. Greenwich, CT: JAI Press.

Hamowy, R. (2008). *The encyclopedia of libertarianism*. Sage.

Harris, R. (2000, July 17). Interview. *Commanding Heights*. 28p. https://www.pbs.org/wgbh/commandingheights/hi/people/pe_name.html

Hart, D. M. (2019). The Paris School of Liberal Political Economy. In: M. Moriarty and J. Jennings (Eds.), *The Cambridge History of French Thought*. Cambridge University Press, 301–312.

Hartwell, R. M. (1995). *A history of the Mont Pelerin Society*. Liberty Fund.

Hayek, F. A. (1944). *The road to serfdom*. Routledge.

von Hayek, F. (1974). *The pretence of knowledge. Lecture to the memory of Alfred Nobel, December 11*. Sveriges Riksbank Prize in Economic Sciences in Memory of Alfred Nobel, 1974. https://www.nobelprize.org/prizes/economic-sciences/1974/hayek/lecture/

Harberger, A. (2000, March 10). Interview with Arnold "Al" Harberger. *Commanding Heights*. PBS. https://www.pbs.org/wgbh/commandingheights/shared/minitext/int_alharberger.html

Holroyd, M. (1995). *Lytton Strachey*. London: Vintage.
Howson, S. (2011). *Lionel Robbins*. Cambridge University Press.
Hunold, A. (1958, September 8–15). *The story of the Mont Pelerin Society*. Paper for the 9th Meeting of the Mont Pelerin Society, Princeton, New Jersey.
Illarionov, A. (2008). Friedman and Russia. *Cato Journal, 28*(1), 1–10. https://object.cato.org/sites/cato.org/files/serials/files/cato-journal/2008/1/cj28n1-1.pdf
Innset, O. (2017). *Reinventing liberalism: Early neoliberalism in context, 1920–1947*. Thesis submitted for the degree of Doctor of History and Civilization of the European University Institute, Florence.
Irving, S. (2014). R. Leeson (Ed.), *Hayek: A collaborative biography. Part I: Influences, from Mises to Bartley*. Oeconomia [Online], 4–3, 451–458.
Johnson, H. G. (1973). National styles in economic research: The United States, United Kingdom, Canada, and various European countries. *Daedalus, 102*(2), 65–74.
Johnson, H. G. (1977). Cambridge as an academic environment in the early 1930s: A reconstruction from the late 1940s. In D. Patinkin & J. C. Leith (Eds.), *Keynes, Cambridge and the general theory*. Palgrave Macmillan.
Kavanagh, D. (2006, August 29). Sir Alfred Sherman: Adviser who preached Thatcherism before the term was invented. *The Guardian*. https://www.theguardian.com/news/2006/aug/29/guardianobituaries.conservatives
Kaza, G. (1997, June 1). *The Mont Pelerin Society's 50th anniversary: The society helps keep alight the lamp of classical liberalism*. Foundation for Economic Education. https://fee.org/articles/the-mont-pelerin-societys-50th-anniversary/
Kearl, J. R., et al. (1979). A confusion of economists? *American Economic Review, 69*(2), 28–37.
Keynes, J. M. (1926). The end of laissez-faire. Hogarth Press (pamphlet). In *The collected writings of John Maynard Keynes* (Essays in Persuasion) (Vol. IX). Royal Economic Society, Palgrave Macmillan, 1972.
Klaus, V. (2018, March 27). *Notes for Peter Bauer's speech in Budapest*. https://www.klaus.cz/clanky/4254
Koopmans, T. (1947). Measurement without theory. *Review of Economics and Statistics, 29*(3), 161–172.
Kornai, J. (1990). *The road to a free economy: Shifting from a socialist system. The example of Hungary*. W.W. Norton & Company.
Krugman, P. (2011, December 5). The conscience of a Liberal: Things that never happened in the history of macroeconomics. *The New York Times*.
Laidler, D. (1976). Inflation in Britain: A monetarist perspective. *American Economic Review, 66*(4), 485–500.
Lal, D. (2009, March 5). *The Mont Pelerin Society: A mandate renewed*. Presidential address, Mont Pelerin Society. http://www.econ.ucla.edu/lal/MPS%20Presidential%20Address%203.5.09.pdf
Lane, M. (2013). The genesis and reception of *The Road to Serfdom*. In R. Leeson (Ed.), *Hayek: A collaborative biography. Part I: Influences, from Mises to Bartley*. Palgrave Macmillan.
Lebaron, F. (2006). 'Nobel' economists as public intellectuals: The circulation of symbolic capital. *International Journal of Contemporary Sociology, 43*(1), 88–101.
Leeson, R. (Ed.). (2013). *Hayek: A collaborative biography. Part I: Influences, from Mises to Bartley*. Palgrave Macmillan.
Leeson, R. (Ed.). (2015). *Hayek: A collaborative biography. Part VI: Good dictators, sovereign producers and Hayek's 'ruthless consistency'*. Palgrave Macmillan.

Leeson, R. (2018). Introduction: 'How we developed a consistent doctrine and some international circles of communication'. In R. Leeson (Ed.), *Hayek: A collaborative biography. Part XIII: Fascism and liberalism in the (Austrian) classical tradition* (pp. 3–78). Palgrave Macmillan.

Levy, D. (1999, March 1). Interview with Arnold Harberger: An interview with the dean of the "Chicago Boys". *The Region*. Federal Reserve Bank of Minneapolis.

Lindbeck, A. (1970). *Speech at the presentation of the prize for economic science in memory of Alfred Nobel to Paul A. Samuelson.*

Lindbeck, A. (1971). *Political economy of the New Left: An outsider's view.* Harper and Row.

Livingstone, G. (2018). *Britain and the dictatorships of Argentina and Chile, 1973–82: Foreign policy, corporations and social movements.* Palgrave Macmillan.

Lundberg, E. (1969). Speech at the presentation of the prize for economic science in memory of Alfred Nobel to Ragnar Frisch and Jan Tinbergen. In A. Lindbeck (Ed.), *Economic sciences 1969–1980: Nobel lectures including presentation speeches and laureates' biographies* (pp. 3–5). World Scientific Publishing Co. and the Nobel Foundation.

MacLean, N. (2017). *Democracy in chains: The deep history of the radical right's stealth plan for America.* New York: Viking, Penguin Random House.

Margaret Thatcher Foundation. (n.d.). *Thatcher, Hayek & Friedman.* https://www.margaretthatcher.org/archive/Hayek.asp

Marriott, E. (2002, June 10). In bed with Chile's torturers. *Evening Standard.* https://www.standard.co.uk/showbiz/in-bed-with-chiles-torturers-6319873.html

Martin, K. (Ed.). (1991a). *Strategies of economic development: Readings in the political economy of industrialization.* Palgrave Macmillan.

Martin, K. (1991b). Modern development theory. In K. Martin (Ed.), *Strategies of economic development: Readings in the political economy of industrialization* (pp. 27–73). Palgrave Macmillan.

Martin, K., & Knapp, J. (Eds.). (1967). *The teaching of development economics. Its position in the present state of knowledge. The proceedings of the Manchester Conference on teaching economic development, April 1964.* Routledge.

Mathias, P. (2008). Clapham, John Harold. In *International encyclopedia of the social sciences.* Thomson Gale. https://www.encyclopedia.com/social-sciences/applied-and-social-sciences-magazines/clapham-john-harold

Matthews, R. C. O. (1989). Joan Robinson and Cambridge – A theorist and her milieu: An interview. In G. R. Feiwel (Ed.), *Joan Robinson and modern economic theory* (pp. 911–915). Palgrave Macmillan.

Maxton, G., & Randers, J. (2016). *Reinventing prosperity: Managing economic growth to reduce unemployment, inequality and climate change. A report to the Club of Rome.* Greystone Books.

McCloskey, D. (2003). Milton. *Eastern Economic Journal, 29*(1), 143–146. http://www.deirdremccloskey.com/editorials/milton.php

Mirowski, P., & Plehwe, D. (2009). *The road from Mont Pelerin: The making of the neoliberal thought collective.* Harvard University Press.

Mirrlees, J. A. (1996). *James A. Mirrlees biographical.* https://www.nobelprize.org/prizes/economic-sciences/1996/mirrlees/facts/

Monbiot, G. (2017, July 19). A despot in disguise: One man's mission to rip up democracy. *The Guardian.* https://www.theguardian.com/commentisfree/2017/jul/19/despot-disguise-democracy-james-mcgill-buchanan-totalitarian-capitalism

Mongiovi, G. (2020). Was Keynes a Socialist. *Catalyst*, *3*(4). https://catalyst-journal.com/vol3/no4/was-keynes-a-socialist

Monthly Review Editors. (2016). Notes by the editors. *Monthly Review*, *68*(7).

Moore, C. (2013). *Margaret Thatcher: The authorized biography. Volume one: Not for turning*. Penguin Books.

Moreno, F. (2008). Silent revolution: An early export from Pinochet's Chile. *Globalization, Competitiveness & Governability*, *2*(2), 90–99. https://www.google.com/url?sa=t&rct=j&q=&esrc=s&source=web&cd=10&ved=2ahUKEwjypdCnq7TkAhUPPVAKHeplCk0QFjAJegQIARAC&url=https%3A%2F%2Fgcg.universia.net%2Farticle%2Fdownload%2F339%2F465&usg=AOvVaw24IyK-3m_XXS2rNJVtqaZ6

Moser, P., Voena, A., & Waldinger, F. (2014). German Jewish emigres and US invention. *American Economic Review*, *104*(10), 3222–3255.

Newbery, D. (2017). Frank Horace Hahn 1925–2013. *Biographical Memoirs of Fellows of the British Academy*, *XVI*, 485–525. https://www.britac.ac.uk/sites/default/files/23 Hahn 1837 9_11_17.pdf

Nilsson, M. (2011). The editor and the CIA. Herbert Tingsten and the Congress for Cultural Freedom: A symbiotic relationship. *European Review of History/Revue Europeeanne d'histoire*, *18*(2), 147–174.

OAC (Online Archive of California). (2015). *Register of the Vervon Orval Watts papers*. https://oac.cdlib.org/findaid/ark:/13030/kt7c60394c/entire_text/

O'Donnell, R. (1999). Keynes's Socialism: Conception, Strategy and Espousal. In P. Kriesler & C. Sardoni (Eds.), *Keynes, Post-Keynesianism and political economy: Essays in honour of Geoff Harcourt*, Vol. 3, 149–175. London: Routledge.

Offer, A., & Soderberg, G. (2016). *The Nobel factor: The prize in economics, social democracy, and the market turn*. Princeton University Press.

Okon, H. (2018). The Austrian revival. In R. Leeson (Ed.), *Hayek: A collaborative biography. Part XIII: Fascism and liberalism in the (Austrian) classical tradition* (pp. 213–244). Palgrave Macmillan.

Preston, P. (2017, May 9). Lord Thomas of Swynnerton: Obituary. *The Guardian*. https://www.theguardian.com/books/2017/may/09/lord-thomas-of-swynnerton-obituary

Puttaswamaiah, K. (1995). *Nobel economists: Lives and contributions* (3 Vols.). Indus Publishing Company.

Ravelli, G., & Bull, A. C. (2018). The Pinochet regime and the trans-nationalization of Italian neo-fascism. In R. Leeson (Ed.), *Hayek: A collaborative biography. Part XIII: Fascism and liberalism in the (Austrian) classical tradition* (pp. 361–393). Palgrave Macmillan.

Robinson, E. A. G. (1978). Comment on Brian Corry's presentation at the Third Keynes Seminar, "Keynes and Laissez Faire", held at the University of Kent, Canterbury in 1976. In A. P. Thirlwall (Ed.), *Keynes and Laissez Faire: The Third Keynes Seminar held at the University of Kent, Canterbury 1976*. London: Palgrave Macmillan.

Robinson, J. (1956). *The accumulation of capital*. Macmillan.

Robinson, P. (2009, February 20). Paul Samuelson vs. Milton Friedman (a debate). *Forbes*. http://www.freerepublic.com/focus/news/2190904/posts

Roehner, B. M. (2007). *Driving forces in physical, biological and socio-economic phenomena: A network science investigation of social bonds and interactions*. Cambridge University Press.

Rothbard, M. N. (1973, August 17). *Floyd Arthur 'Baldy' Harper, RIP*. Mises Daily Articles, Mises Institute. https://mises.org/library/floyd-arthur-baldy-harper-rip

Rothbard, M. N., & Gordon, D. (2010). *Strictly confidential: The private Volker fund – Memos of Murray N. Rothbard*, edited by D. Gordon. Ludwig von Mises Institute.

Roy, S. (2013, January 30). Frank Hahn has passed away. *Marginal Revolution*, blog. https://marginalrevolution.com/marginalrevolution/2013/01/frank-hahn-has-passed-away.html

Samuelson, P. (1971). Introduction. In A. Lindbeck (Ed.), *Political economy of the New Left: An outsider's view*. Harper and Row.

Samuelson, P. A. (1988). The passing of the guard in economics. *Eastern Economic Journal, 14*(4), 319–329.

Samuelson, P. A. (1997). Credo of a lucky textbook author. *Journal of Economic Perspectives, 11*(2), 153–160.

Samuelson, P. A. (2004). William A. Barnett: An interview with Paul A. Samuelson, December 23, 2003. *Macroeconomic Dynamics, 8*, 519–542. Republished in Working Paper Series in Theoretical and Applied Economics, University of Kansas.

Samuelson, P. A. (2009). A few remembrances of Friedrich von Hayek. *Journal of Economic Behavior and Organization, 69*(1), 1–4.

Schlefer, J. (2012). *The assumptions economists make*. Harvard University Press.

Scranton, P. (2013, July 9). Why John Maynard Keynes supported the New Deal. *Bloomberg Opinion*. https://webcache.googleusercontent.com/search?q=cache:ITadeOyjZKsJ:https://www.bloomberg.com/opinion/articles/2013-07-08/why-john-maynard-keynes-supported-the-new-deal+&cd=21&hl=en&ct=clnk&gl=nl&client=safari

Sen, A. (2020). Marx after Kornai. *Public Choice*. https://doi.org/10.1007/s11127-020-00838-x

Shaxson, N. (2011). *Treasure islands: Tax havens and the men who stole the world*. Penguin Random House.

Singer, H. (1979). A generation later: Kurt Mandelbaum's *The Industrialisation of Backward Areas* revisited. *Development and Change, 10*(4), 577–584.

Skidelsky, R. (2006). Hayek versus Keynes: The road to reconciliation. In E. Feser (Ed.), *The Cambridge companion to Hayek* (pp. 82–110). Cambridge University Press.

Skidelsky, R. (2020, January 15–17). *Keynes v Hayek: The Four Buts*. Paper presented at the Conference commemorating the 40 Anniversary of the Mont Pelerin Society meeting of 1980 at Stanford University, Hoover Institution – Stanford University, pp. 160–167.

Slobodian, Q. (2018). *Globalists: The end of empire and the birth of neoliberalism*. Harvard University Press.

Solow, R. M. (2012, November 16). Hayek, Friedman, and the illusions of conservative economics. *The New Republic*.

Sousa, Filomena de (2020, October 7). Keynes: The object of Hayek's passion? *Cambridge Journal of Economics*, beaa043, https://doi.org/10.1093/cje/beaa043

Sraffa, P. (1926). The laws of returns under competitive conditions. *Economic Journal, 36*(144), 535–550.

Stigler, G. (1982). *Nobel prize biographical*. https://www.nobelprize.org/prizes/economic-sciences/1982/stigler/biographical/

Stigler, G. J. (1985). *Memoirs of an unregulated economist*. University of Chicago Press.

Stigler, S. M. (2005). Aaron Director remembered. *Journal of Law and Economics*, 48(2), 307–311. https://www.jstor.org/stable/10.1086/498417?seq=1#page_scan_tab_contents

Streeten, P. P. (1986/1989). Aerial roots. *Banca Nazionale del Lavoro Quarterly Review*, 39(157): 135–159. (Reprinted: [1989]. In J. A. Kregel (Ed.), *Recollections of eminent economists*, Vol. 2. Macmillan, pp. 73–98).

Tanenhaus, S. (2017). The architect of the radical right: How the Nobel Prize-winning economist James M. Buchanan shaped today's antigovernment politics. *The Atlantic*, July-August.

Teacher, D. (2018a). 'Neutral academic data' and the international right. In R. Leeson (Ed.), *Hayek: A collaborative biography. Part XIII: Fascism and liberalism in the (Austrian) classical tradition* (pp. 245–320). Palgrave Macmillan.

Teacher, D. (2018b). Private club and secret service Armageddon. In R. Leeson (Ed.), *Hayek: A collaborative biography. Part XIII: Fascism and liberalism in the (Austrian) classical tradition* (pp. 321–360). Palgrave Macmillan.

Thatcher, M. (1999, October 6). Pinochet was this country's staunch, true friend. Full text of Margaret Thatcher's speech to the Blackpool fringe. *The Guardian*.

Tremlett, G. (2020, September 3). Operation Condor: The cold war conspiracy that terrorised South America. *The Guardian*.

Tribe, K. (2001). German émigré economists and the internationalisation of economics. Book Review of Harald Hagemann and Claus-Dieter Krohn (eds.), 1999, *Biographical guide to the emigration of German-speaking economists after 1933*, Munich: K. G. Sauer. *Economic Journal*, 111, F740–F746.

Turner, M. S. (1989). *Joan Robinson and the Americans*. M.E. Sharpe.

Valdes, J. G. (1995). *Pinochet's economists: The Chicago School in Chile*. Cambridge University Press.

Volcker, P. (2000). *Interview. Commanding heights, public broadcasting service*. Interviewed on 26 September, 2000. https://www.pbs.org/wgbh/commandingheights/hi/people/pe_name.html

Von Neumann, J. & Morgenstern, O. (1944). *Theory of games and economic behaviour*. Princeton: Princeton University Press.

Warsh, D. (2016, December 4). Presentiments of Nobel future. *Economic Principals – A Weekly Column about Economics and Politics*.http://www.economicprincipals.com/issues/2016.12.04/1950.html

Weintraub, E. R. (2017). McCarthyism and the mathematization of economics. *Journal of the History of Economic Thought*, 39(4), 571–597.

Whitaker, J. K. (Ed.). (1996). *The correspondence of Alfred Marshall, economist* (Towards the close, 1903–1924) (Vol. 3). Royal Economic Society Publication. Cambridge University Press.

Whitehead, P. (1985). *The writing on the wall: Britain in the 1970s*. London: Michael Joseph.

Yergin, D., & Stanislaw, J. (1988). *The commanding heights*. Simon and Schuster.

Youkee, M. (1999, October 4). Thatcher sent Pinochet finest scotch during former dictator's UK house arrest. *The Guardian*.

CHAPTER 4

Camp Skirmishes Over Interstitial Spaces: Journals, Seminars, Textbooks

Abstract This chapter explores heterodox-versus-orthodox camp rivalries over interstitial spaces that are all too often sidelined, namely journals, seminars and textbooks. In particular, it deals with the loss of the flagship of economics, *Economic Journal* (EJ), relocated from its de facto long-term home in Cambridge into orthodox neoclassical space in Oxford in 1976; it delves into the formation of the new *Cambridge Journal of Economics* launched in 1977 by the younger left-oriented Cambridge economists in anticipation of the loss of the EJ and access, as authors, to its pages in the future; and attention is also drawn to the short-lived life of the *Economic Policy Review*, the carrier of the often provocative macroeconomic policy-oriented research by the Godley-Cripps Cambridge Economic Policy Group. The second interstitial space reviewed comprises the sprawling tree of seminar series stretching over decades. Over time, there was diversification and polarisation in this doctrinally, politically and personally charged space, with rival camps running competitive series for their adversarial constituencies. There was also the lodge-like country-wide CLARE Group of like-minded moderate Keynesians—run by Robin Matthews from Clare College—that could also operate as a lobby on specific issues, and which served as a resource pool of influence brought to bear generally against the positions of the radical left-Keynesian and heterodox groups; and then there was the crucible, or colosseum, of gladiatorial jousting, the Faculty Common Room. Textbooks constitute the third domain. The diversity of Cambridge views on the f/utility of textbook writing stands in contrast to the commitment of Paul Samuelson and his neoclassical followers in the other Cambridge, as well as to the high premium attached by Friedman and Hayek and their neoliberal devotees in Chicago to the popular diffusion of their doctrines. Samuelson succeeded; Chicago did not really compete; and heterodox Cambridge, in the form of Joan Robinson's short-lived alternative textbook,

© The Author(s), under exclusive license to Springer Nature Switzerland AG 2022
A. Saith, *Cambridge Economics in the Post-Keynesian Era*, Palgrave Studies in the History of Economic Thought, https://doi.org/10.1007/978-3-030-93019-6_4

on the whole fell short in a hostile publishing and university environment dominated by neoclassicals. The contrasting parallel cases of the spectacular success of the Samuelson textbook, the scandalous suppression of the preceding textbook by Lorie Tarshis and the curious survival of Klein's radical work on the Keynesian revolution provide a case study of the stifling impact of McCarthyism. Put together, the investigations of the wide range of transactions in these interstitial spaces inject texture, nuance and zest into the narratives of the life of Cambridge economics in the period of the purges.

4.1 The Battle of Teruel—The Day before

This chapter explores camp rivalries over interstitial spaces that are usually sidelined, in the domains of journals, seminars and textbooks. In particular, it deals with the loss of the flagship of economics, *Economic Journal* (EJ) from Cambridge in 1976, as it was relocated into orthodox neoclassical space in Oxford, and it delves into the formation of the new *Cambridge Journal of Economics* (CJE) that was launched by the younger left-oriented Cambridge economists in anticipation of the loss of the EJ and the expectation that their kind of research work would generally be denied access to its pages into the future; attention is also drawn to the short-lived *Economic Policy Review* that was the carrier of the often sharp and provocative applied macroeconomic policy-oriented research by the Cambridge Economic Policy Group (CEPG). If EJ was lost, CJE was gained, and for the heterodox group, this might have seemed to have limited the damage; indeed, CJE might never have come into existence but for the loss of EJ; that is a counterfactual worth considering. The second interstitial space reviewed is the diverse collection of the seminar series that ran over the years. Over time, there was diversification and polarisation in this often charged contested space, and rival camps ran competitive series for their adversarial constituencies; there was also the lodge-like CLARE Group of like-minded moderate Keynesians who could also operate as a lobby on specific issues and was not entirely independent of the competitive polarisation between the left-Keynesian and the neoclassical camps; and then there was the crucible of jousting, the Faculty Common Room. Textbooks constitute the third domain. The multiple Cambridge views on textbook writing stand in contrast to others, originating from Paul Samuelson and his neoclassical followers in the other Cambridge, or from Friedman and Hayek and their neoliberal devotees in Chicago; Samuelson succeeded; Chicago did not really compete; heterodox Cambridge, whether through Lorie Tarshis earlier in the USA, or Joan Robinson later in Cambridge, on the whole fell short. These spaces and activities, the outcomes and the protagonists, together provide texture and nuanced insights into the progress and result of the disciplinary and ideological wars between the long-running heterodox lineages and the rising orthodox mainstream in Cambridge. As such, these investigations could add to the intellectual history of the period of the purges in Cambridge economics.

The 1970s marked the turning point in the evolution of Cambridge economics, and this would be reflected in tussles over journals, clashes in seminars and competing through textbook writing. But these reflections look somewhat different reviewing this period in hindsight, compared to viewing it in real time as it unfolded. There are perceptible indications that despite the loss of the EJ, the mood in the heterodox camps was upbeat and optimistic about their place in the Cambridge and the national scheme of things; there was tremendous intellectual energy within the various heterodox groups and between them collectively and the neoclassicals. New lines of research, for example, deindustrialisation, were emerging; the Godley-Cripps CEPG was at the centre of crucial national policy debates; the position of the students and the Faculty Board had been vindicated by Lord Devlin looking into the Students' Sit-in; US troops had left ignominiously from Vietnam; it even appeared the capital controversies might have been settled in favour of Joan of the Cam. It was a scene out of Andre Malraux's *Days of Hope*, when optimism ruled the day on the eve of the fateful Battle of Teruel which marked the turning of the tide, thereafter running against the republican forces in the Spanish Civil War.

4.2 Journals

The precursor to the campaign of orthodox assaults was the loss, in 1976, of the flagship *Economic Journal*, the editorship of which was whisked away from Cambridge and taken over mainly by the Oxford branch of the neoclassical camp. The heterodox formation withstood this initial attack and possibly even came out of it stronger in some respects with the creation of the *Cambridge Journal of Economics*; nevertheless, the departure of *Economic Journal* signalled the appearance of storm clouds on the horizon, and then the storms duly arrived.

4.2.1 *EJ Leaves 'Home'—The Loss of a Flagship*

The first commanding height to fall, in 1976, was the standard bearer of British economics, the *Economic Journal*, the editorship of which comes under the purview of the Royal Economic Society (RES).[1] The identity of the editors, and consequently of the journal and its orientation, changed dramatically when it was moved to Oxford, and for the first time since its inception, under Edgeworth in 1891, Cambridge economics had no representation on the editorial board. A team of Oxford neoclassical votaries of the Hahn-Gorman camp replaced what Geoff Harcourt regards as perhaps the best editorial team ever of *Economic Journal*: Brian Reddaway, David Champernowne and Phyllis

---

[1] Puzzlingly, during 1974–1976—the span of years when this change would have been affected—the President of the Royal Economic Society, which oversees the selection of editors, was none other than the redoubtable Nicky Kaldor. Perhaps the editorship was surreptitiously whisked away when Nicky was in one of his gentle slumbers in some committee meeting and not roused in time; more likely, it was the outcome of a well-prepared challenge mounted despite Kaldor's watch.

Deane.[2] Ajit Singh, in his appreciation of Reddaway's legacy, remarks: "He and his colleagues did influence the academic economic profession, not only in the UK but also in the US and elsewhere, in the sense that unnecessary mathematics in articles was discouraged and papers were selected on their economic merit rather than because of the sophistication of the techniques used. Authors were encouraged to present their critical assumptions and their main result in plain English. However, after he and his co-editors left the journal, the academic profession went back to its traditional ways" (Singh, 2008, p. 14).

On the first page of the first issue of the journal in 1891, Edgeworth had declared its key intended attribute: tolerance. "It will be open to writers of different schools. The most opposite doctrines may meet here as on a fair field. Thus, the difficulties of Socialism will be considered in the first number, the difficulties of Individualism in the second. Opposing theories of currency will be represented with equal impartiality. Nor will it be attempted to prescribe the method, any more than the result, of scientific investigation." Clearly, Edgeworth's idealism knows no bounds: "is it extravagant", he asks, "to hope that this toleration of the difference between the votaries of economic science may tend to produce agreement between them? 'A little generous prudence, a little forbearance for one another, ... might win all these diligences to join and unite into one general and brotherly search for truth.' What Milton hoped for theology in the seventeenth century may prove true of political economy in the nineteenth." And meanwhile down on earth, "it will be the task of the Editor and his coadjutors, unbiased by their personal convictions, to select the ablest representative of each important interest" (Edgeworth, 1891, p. 1).

On the opening page of the 8th Volume of EJ in March 1898, the Council of the British Economic Association provides its view of the state of the journal, saying that "it may speak more freely here of the Journal than can be done by the Editors", and declares:

> a mere glance at the Contents of the seven volumes will be enough to show that the spirit of the Journal has been the spirit of the founders of the Association. As was said on the first page of the first number, both Association and Journal are 'open to all schools and parties'. This toleration has been a discipline for the authors as well as for the Editors, and (it may be hoped) for the readers. The effect has been not to accentuate, but gradually to tone down, the acrimony of partisanship. Writers have become aware that they are addressing not only their own friends, but friendly, and even unfriendly, critics, as well as a number of readers to whom their opinions are entirely novel and incredible. On the whole there have been few pitched battles. Economic instruction has proceeded in the safer though less exciting way of constructive essay, not of course uncritical or uncriticized. The writers have been numerous; the Journal has welcomed the counsels of the young men as well as of the old. (*Economic Journal*, 1898, p. 1)

---

[2] "In my view these were some of the greatest years of the *Journal*. That the *Journal* no longer contains either reviews ... or book notes, or even obituaries, is a sad reflection on it not being what it used to be" (Harcourt, 2012a).

4 CAMP SKIRMISHES OVER INTERSTITIAL SPACES: JOURNALS, SEMINARS... 299

And so it had effectively remained over the generations. The journal was nourished for the next eight decades under the watch of just a handful of lead editors (assisted variously by a few worthies): by Edgeworth for the first 21 years till 1911, by Keynes for the following 33 years till 1944, then by Austin Robinson for the 26 years till 1970, when Brian Reddaway took over the reins for the short period till the journal was shifted away in 1976. After that point, the editor's hat seemed to have been passed around faster than the ball at Barcelona.

1891–1970	8 editors in 80 years—1 name per 10 years
1891–1976	11 editors in 86 years—1 name per 7.8 years
1976–2018	52 editors[3] in 43 years—1 name per 10 months

The velocity of editorial circulation drops from one name change every ten years for the first eight decades, to every ten months (approximately) in the last four decades. Behind these unusual numbers is an even more dramatic regime change in editorial roles and practices: from the editorship being a long-term commitment undertaken as a service to the profession, at a high personal cost, by seniors who were not in need of promotions, to a new scenario where the editors' hats became a-year-a-dozen, passed around selectively by the new leaders as a discretionary perk amongst a large cohort of rising aspirants, adding 'Editor, *Economic Journal*' to their competing CVs.[4] At EJ, it was a case of 'all change'—all travellers were off-loaded, new ones came on board, with a new set of drivers, directions and destinations. The ideological, theoretical and methodological frame of the journal was transformed with alacrity as it became the British instrument of Samuelson's so-called third and fourth revolutions, purveying the mantras of the cross-Atlantic neoclassical general equilibrium axis; alongside, its medium of communication atrophied from English to math-

---

[3] Under various editorial hats.
[4] *Economic Journal* editors, 1891–1996. For a detailed list, see Table 2.6

1891–1911	Francis Ysidro Edgeworth
1912–1944	J.M. Keynes is Editor
	1918–1925, F.Y. Edgeworth is Joint Editor
	1926–1944, D.H. Macgregor is Joint Editor
	1934–1944, E.A.G. Robinson is Assistant Editor
1944–1970	E.A.G. Robinson is Joint Editor
	1945–1961, R.F. Harrod is Joint Editor
1951–1970	R.C.O. Matthews is Joint Editor
1961–1970	C.F. Carter is Joint Editor
1968–1976	Phyllis Deane is Joint Editor
1971–1976	W.B. Reddaway, D.G. Champernowne are Joint Editors
1976–	New Editorial teams, comprising variously: J.S. Flemming 1976–1981; J.A. Kay 1976–1981; J.H. Williamson 1976–1977; D. Winch 1976–1984; D.F. Hendry 1977–1981; M.J. Artis 1986–1996; D.M.G. Newbery 1977–1996.

ematics. For the 20 years following the move away from Cambridge, David Newbery provided a link of continuity, serving as an editor over the following two decades, from 1977 till 1996.

A few years down the line, Austin Robinson writes ruefully about the evolution of the *Economic Journal* to Kenneth Berrill, both old school Cambridge: "At the R.E.S. [Royal Economic Society] I was conscious of your agreement with me that the E.J. has now become irrelevant and unreadable. It makes me realise what Maynard did for the Journal in making it face up to the realities of the current economic problems and to filling up gaps in theory when a major problem was hitting the country and we did not really know what we ought to be doing." ... "In some degree what you have been doing at the Institute (NIESR) slightly compensated for the badness of the E.J. But I hope that you will go on kicking the officers of the R.E.S. into sanity." ... "I thought for a time that I was suffering from senility. But I find that my views on this correspond with the views of the brighter people in the faculty here and in the D.A.E."[5] Four months later, Austin writes to Gus Ranis: "Your interests in economics seem to me to correspond with my own. I had been brought up by Pigou to think that economics was about people and the welfare of people. Both then and now I was convinced that good economics was about people and not about curves and mathematics. I am very depressed by the trends of the *Economic Journal*, which seems to me to publish very little that would be worth reading if I had the capacity to read it (which I do not). None of my friends in Cambridge are any better at reading it than I am. I read the reviews and nothing else. I am amused [sic; assured?] that this is not wholly the consequence of senility. Most of the younger generation in Cambridge write English and contribute to the Cambridge Journal and disregard the contributions of the mathematicians."[6] Austin was certainly not senile, but equally certainly he was not impartial in this case, and at the Faculty and the Department of Applied Economics (DAE), he might well have been taking soundings from the heterodox clan; after all, David Newbery had taken over as Director of DAE and changed its orientation towards technical econometrics-based work on applied microeconomics within a neoclassical frame; and significantly, he had been an editor of the EJ since 1977, just a year after it left Cambridge for its new address in the Oxford neoclassical camp; it would not have been David Newbery who confirmed Austin Robinson's negative views of the recent direction taken by the journal.

As an aside, A.W. Coats's *contretemps* with the journal provides an insight into the editorial practices of EJ in the Keynes-Robison years comes through an exchange between Austin Robinson and an author denied publication.

---

[5] Austin Robinson to Kenneth Berrill, dated 9 December 1990. Strikingly, this view is expressed in 1990, the year of publication of John Hey and Donald Winch's laudatory review, *A Century of Economics: 100 Years of the Royal Economic Society and the Economic Journal*; of course, these authors, having been editors of the journal, were as much 'interested parties' as Austin Robinson.

[6] Austin Robinson to Gus Ranis, dated 17 April 1991. EAGR Archives, Marshall Library, University of Cambridge.

A.W. 'Bob' Coats had submitted an article titled "Productivity and Prestige in British Economics: A Statistical Study of Contributions to the *Economic Journal* and *Economica*, 1920–1969" to EJ in the early 1970s, during the tenure of the final Cambridge editorial trio of Brian Reddaway, David Champernowne and Phyllis Deane. It was considered and rejected; the author was sufficiently moved to engage laterally with Austin Robinson, instead of directly with the decision-making editors themselves, seeking explanation. Austin Robinson had retired from his long-held editorial responsibilities in 1970. The exchange between the ex-editor and the rejected author is interesting on several counts. First, there is a serious charge of editorial bias being laid at the door of the *Economic Journal*; in Austin Robinson's words: "His article is very largely concerned with the proposition that the E.J. devoted a 'disproportionate' amount of its space to Oxbridge economists" (Austin Robinson to Reddaway, Letter dated 19 October 1973, E.A.G. Robinson Papers); no such allegation of editorial partiality could be taken lightly. Coats seemed to be fighting the corner of the subalterns and the provinces against the elite Oxbridge citadels[7]; though really the alleged bias would reside in Cambridge alone, all three members of the journal's editorial board being there. Second, Coats's article purports to make a direct comparison between the flagship journals of Cambridge and London School of Economics (LSE), respectively, over a period marked by intense rivalry. Coats's use of 'statistics' over such a lengthy time frame lays an implicit claim to his being a 'scientific' investigation, based on 'empirical evidence', thereby raising the stakes. Coincidentally, the allegation of bias effectively against the Cambridge-based editorial board arrives a short period before the journal is shifted away from Cambridge. And fourth, the paper makes a case of bias against the editors in the earlier periods—dominated by Keynes and Austin Robinson—but when the paper is rejected, he pursues and 'pesters' Austin Robinson directly for a response; the implication could conceivably be that the rejection was itself motivated, and Coats was looking for EAG to justify it, in the process possibly providing feedback that would serve as ammunition for Coats to have another go at the editors, questioning their rejection, this time potentially with benefit of EAG's feedback.[8]

Coats held strong views on the culture of Cambridge economics: "Keynes' career exemplifies, albeit in a heightened form, certain enduring features of British academic life as epitomized in Cambridge economics, which has recently been penetratingly, even ruthlessly, exposed by the late Harry Johnson. In the cosy, complacent, deferential, and highly personalized British academic

[7] A few years earlier, Coats had engaged in a detailed empirical investigation of the origins of the Royal Economic Society, profiling the occupational and social origins of members of the economics profession and of the RES in the early years, presumably pursuing his curiosity about whether some degree of elitism, or some selectivity bias, was embedded in the genetic structure of the institution from its nascence. Coats draws a blank, not finding any reliable evidence of a pattern; "it would be unwise to attempt too precise an identification of the beginnings of the economics profession" (see Coats & Coats, 1970, p. 79).

[8] A.W. Coats to E.A.G. Robinson, Letter dated 5 July 1973; E.A.G. Robinson to A.W. Coats, Letter dated 1 November 1973; in E.A.G. Robinson Papers, Marshall Library Archives, Cambridge.

environment, prestige readily filtered down from an acknowledged great man to his disciples. ... It was implicitly assumed that informal networks of communication would suffice because everyone in a given field already knew everyone else worth knowing This personalization is evident (not only in economics) in the management of journals and scholarly societies and in the crucial process of making academic appointments" (Coats, 1993, p. 75).[9] With this article, he seemed to be on his mission to subjective opinion into an objective "fact".[10]

EAG sought feedback and advice from Roy Harrod (who did not respond), Brian Reddaway (who said "I have '0' to say on this beyond, I agree"[11]; and Donald Winch, then Dean of the Social Sciences at the University of Sussex), who did, and rather freely, though these comments are more on Coats, with whose works Winch was familiar, rather than on having seen the paper in question, which he had not.[12] "My personal opinion ... is that Coats likes to see himself as a gad-fly to economists. In fact, he frequently retails 'gossip' as a way of enlivening perhaps some pretty boring statistics. You can call it sociology if you like, but my tolerance for such exercises is strained when the gossip is not accompanied by much evidence of interest in the substantive concerns of economists, past or present. This evidence is lacking in Coats." Winch then proceeds to caution Austin Robinson: "Coats should be very grateful to you for going to so much trouble. Indeed, I would not be surprised if he did not try to incorporate bits of your note as 'evidence'. You ought perhaps to make clear your attitude to such usage. If the article is published elsewhere

---

[9] The quotation comes from the text of an address by Coats at the History of Economics Conference at Urbana, Illinois, in May 1979 (Coats, 1993, p. 78n). It is apparent that the interaction with Austin Robinson over Oxbridge and London economics and over the editorial practices of *Economic Journal* had not made much of an impression on Coats—not enough to prevent him from expressing the same visceral hostility against what he perceived the culture of Cambridge economics to be, significantly including the 'management of journals'.

[10] For what it might be worth, Coats—the 'gadfly' in Winch's terms—uncritically refers to Harry Johnson's diatribe against Cambridge and its Keynesians; he also had Fritz Machlup—Hayekian and a founder-member of the Mont Pelerin Society—as his PhD supervisor and mentor at Johns Hopkins when Coats was studying in the USA, and Machlup was not kindly inclined towards 'Cambridge' either; as such, it could be conjectured that, sociologically and ideologically, Coats's predilections might not have run in favour of Cambridge, as he perceived it as a self-ascribed 'outsider'.

[11] Letter dated 19 October 1973; Austin Robinson Papers, Marshall Library Archives, Cambridge; Letters, p. 75.

[12] Writing to Brian Reddaway, Robinson observes, "my difficulty in commenting has been that I regard him as barking up the wrong tree and looking for political bias where all that existed was honest preference for good articles rather than bad articles. I either had to do something fairly serious or nothing at all"; as it turns out, he does the former. Donald Winch is quite correct in saying to Austin Robinson that "you have gone to considerable trouble to answer what I take to be Coats's main contention. In this case, for reason you have indicated, I would have thought that the statistical evidence alone would not warrant conclusions about disproportionality." Austin Robinson writes: "I have done a certain amount of digging in the Keynes papers and through the actual volumes of the E.J. which he was analyzing statistically." It is remarkable that a loosely constructed allegation should draw such a heavy response—this says more perhaps about the kind of man that Austin Robinson was than the quality of the paper by Coats.

you may find it necessary to reply along similar lines to your present note."[13] He notes: "Speaking as someone who is entirely non-Oxbridge", Winch says that "the statistical evidence alone would not warrant conclusions about disproportionality".[14]

And so, Austin Robinson writes back to Coats. "In recent years, as a matter of principle, no article has ever been accepted or rejected by an editor on his own responsibility if it came from someone in his own university. ... You will find that I am rather critical of some of your conclusions. Frankly I do not think that when one goes below the surface the facts support your hypothesis and I would urge you to look again at some of your arguments before you publish the article" (Robinson to Coats, Letter dated 1 November 1973). Attached to his letter to Coats is a dense six-page rebuttal,[15] virtually an article in itself, containing two summary tables of his statistical investigations over the reference period testing the hypothesis.[16]

At the end of a comprehensive dismissal, Austin Robinson asks: "May I come back to the original question was there or was there not a bias towards 'Oxbridge' so that a 'disproportionate' share of space was given to Oxbridge authors. May I make the simplest of simple points? An editor with an issue to fill can only choose between articles that exist, are available to him, and ready to be printed? Did the articles that we ought to have been printing, and which it would have been better for the development of economics if we had printed, really exist outside your imagination? Were they printed in other journals? ... Were there a great number of rejected, but really publishable articles languishing in the drawers of scholars? I do not believe it. ... I think you are barking up the wrong tree."

And then, perhaps adding Oxbridge injury to Redbrick insult, Robinson concludes his letter by arguing that it would be normal for the journal to have a relatively greater share of articles with Oxbridge provenance: "Oxbridge in the early years had fringe benefits that kept the theorists and gave greater opportunities for specialization in teaching. It was Macgregor and Clapham, the applied economists, and not Pigou, the theorist, who went off to Leeds. Most of the Redbrick chairs were help by applied economists who taught, and sometimes wrote books, but very seldom wrote articles (I have been surprised how many Heads of Redbrick Departments never wrote an article). There were

---

[13] A quick search did not locate this paper, or any other paper with a similar title, in the usual databases, though its argument and evidence, in some mutated form, could have found their way into some other writings of Coats.

[14] David Winch to E.A.G. Robinson, Letter dated 23 October 1973; Austin Robinson Papers, Marshall Library Archives, Cambridge; Letters, pp. 98–99.

[15] E.A.G. Robinson, "A Note for Professor Coats on *Economic Journal* Editorial Policy", E.A.G. Robinson Papers, Marshall Library Archives, Cambridge, 6p.

[16] One table investigates the profile of those counted broadly in the profession of economics, including their geographical location, who had actually published an article on economics, comparing 1915, 1925 and 1935; the second investigated the processing of a set of the first 272 manuscripts received by Keynes between 1911 and 1915.

exceptions—Shield Nicholson for example. But it does not surprise me that a journal that was sincerely trying to publish the best professional economics should find a large proportion of its articles coming in the 1920s and 1930s from Oxbridge. Indeed anything else would have been a sad reflection on the industry of Oxbridge scholars." And so ended the dusting off of Coats; in the process Austin Robinson offers a keyhole to peep into the editorial ethos and practices of the journal over an extended period.[17]

Since the orthodox takeover in the mid-1970s, the Journal has lost rank and reputation, and regularly features in various ranking lists and bibliometrics—measures generated, supported and used instrumentally by the orthodox mainstream—in the second, or lower, echelons; it is never listed, for instance, in the top five, or even ten. In this, it has settled on the relative scale in a range that is roughly similar to the position of Cambridge economics in global university/subject ranks. Alongside this, the Journal, like Cambridge economics, has lost its unique selling point, its 'comparative advantage', its *differentia specifica*, whichever term is found preferable—its open, heterodox, eclectic character which prioritised substance and argument over unnecessary displays of mathematical virtuosity pursuing questions often detached from observable reality, also with diminishing policy relevance; perhaps not much disciplinary value-deduction would occur if it were to merge with some other mainstream journal or submerge altogether.

If Austin Robinson, even while rejecting the hypothesis of Oxbridge bias, suggests that a degree of overrepresentation of Oxbridge articles and authors in Economic Journal could reasonably be expected in view of Oxbridge

---

[17] Robinson is right in saying that scholars who had qualified for the privileges and resources bestowed by Oxbridge could and should be expected to show higher productivity and high-quality publications—for the question at hand, in the *Economic Journal*. Coats's motivation, however, was to sniff out social privilege being converted into academic 'merit' as measured by publication in EJ or similar journals. The connecting question was: did those with prior social privilege disproportionately enter Oxbridge? If Austin had pursued this question, he might have confirmed that Coats was actually barking up the right tree. Twenty years later, Austin Robinson, in a letter to Geoff Harcourt, somewhat ruefully observes:

> It surprised me to find the distinction between the great economists of this country and those of the United States and the rest of the world. Maynard and Dennis came from Eton; Pigou came from Harrow; most of our great economists have come from snob schools. Very many of the great economists of the rest of the world have had to fight their way up from impecunious and difficult backgrounds and have succeeded in making themselves great. I hope that in this country also we have not reached the point where our economists come from similar backgrounds and have had to face similar difficulties while climbing their profession. (E.A.G. Robinson to G. Harcourt, Letter dated 7 April 1992; Folder: Letters. E.A.G. Robinson Papers, Marshall Library Archives, Cambridge.)

Coats was probably wishing to highlight the dimension of education in the well-entrenched cumulative processes of the reproduction of privilege and inequality, something to which James Meade had drawn attention in his classic 1964 study *Efficiency, Equality and the Ownership of Property*.

pre-eminence of academia, Keith Tribe (1992), in his assessment of the interface between British economics and EJ in the journal's first five decades, also rejects the hypothesis of Cambridge domination, though on different grounds: "Despite the pre-eminence of Marshall's Cambridge as an early centre of academic economics in Britain, little evidence can be detected in the pages of the journal of direct influence from Cambridge economics and Cambridge economists during its first decades—even when, from 1912 onward, it was edited from Cambridge by Keynes. Contrary to the image of British economics given shape by the diffusion of a Cambridge-centred economic orthodoxy associated with Marshall's *Principles*, the pages of the *EJ* during its first 50 years resist, in their sheer diversity and heterogeneity, such an interpretation of the course of British economics to mid-century" (Tribe, 1992, p. 33).

4.2.2 *CJE Arrives—A Forum of One's Own*

Would Edgeworth's tolerance that "no person is excluded because of his opinions" survive when the orthodox mainstream took over the reins? In 1975, four young radical economists, with prescience, thought otherwise, and so the *Cambridge Journal of Economics* was launched in March 1977.[18]

Frederic Lee (2007, p. 8) records it thus: "Responding to the pending move of the *Economic Journal* from Cambridge to Oxford (which took place at the end of 1976) and the consequence that the new editors would be more likely to reject papers critical of mainstream economics, the younger heterodox socialist economists—John Eatwell, Ajit Singh, and Bob Rowthorn—began thinking in late 1974 about establishing their own journal. ... To ensure that the prospective journal remained under their control, a cooperative was formed in 1976, the Cambridge Political Economy Society (CPES), which would own and produce it."[19]

Eatwell (2016, p. 365) provides an account from the horse's mouth: "In late 1975 Ajit Singh, Bob Rowthorn, Frank Wilkinson and John Eatwell held

---

[18] In fact, there is a disproportionately large fall in the share of Cambridge authors in *Economic Journal* when comparing 1980 to 1970 (Backhouse, 1996, p. 55). Several combinations of names are listed in different exchanges: Francis Cripps, John Eatwell, Michael Ellman, Bob Rowthorn, Ajit Singh, and Frank Wilkinson.

[19] Lee (2007, pp. 8–9) writes further: "The CPES was intended as an intellectual, organizational, and institutional focal point at Cambridge for the ongoing engagement in heterodox economics. In particular, it was ... founded to provide a focus for theoretical and applied work, with strong emphasis on realism of analysis, the provision and use of empirical evidence, and the formulation of economic policies. This initiative springs from the belief that the economic approach rooted in the traditions of Marx, Kalecki and Keynes has much to contribute to the understanding and treatment of current economic and social issues: unemployment, inflation, the organization of production, the distribution of social product, class conflict, uneven development and instability in the world economy, the underdevelopment of the third world and economic and social change in socialist countries" (*Cambridge Journal of Economics*, Vol. 1.1 [March, 1977]). In his brief account of the lead up to the formation of the journal, Frederic Lee says that "further discussions took place with Cambridge and non-Cambridge heterodox economists, including Geoff Hodgson, Ian Steedman, Darid Purdy, and Barbara MacLennan from Manchester" (Ibid.).

a number of dinner meetings at a restaurant called *La Garçonne* in Mill Road, Cambridge"; on their menu was the challenge of founding a new journal to inhabit the space that would be vacated by the departure of *Economic Journal* from Cambridge; "for the first time since 1912 it would not have a Cambridge editor and it was feared that the scope of the journal would narrow, particularly with respect to the publication of less orthodox material." Francis Cripps notes that "we knew the EJ was moving in another direction and Kaldor and Reddaway couldn't do much about that. This was what motivated the concept of a CJE whose founders would have lifetime membership and would therefore not lose control" (personal communication, email dated 25 August 2019).

The CJE started in 1977, though plans to launch such a journal had apparently been incubating and maturing over the previous decade. The first formal move towards starting a new journal would seem to be a letter, dated 1 August 1975, from John Eatwell at Trinity, writing on behalf of a group of colleagues (the others named are Jo Bradley, Francis Cripps and Ajit Singh), to Richard Kahn at King's; this covering letter carried a four-page attachment that was the proposal for launching a *Cambridge Journal of Political Economy*.[20]

There were two specific and immediate considerations that motivated this initiative. First, the group points out: "The EJ is due to leave Cambridge for Nuffield College, Oxford, at the end of 1976. This means that not only will Cambridge no longer have a journal 'in house', but also it is probable that the character and tone of the EJ will change in an unfortunate direction." This apprehension was well founded, and the prediction turned out to be true in quick time. Second, the group observes: "The world economic situation has reached a stage at which the presentation of concrete analysis from a progressive viewpoint is more important than at any time since the war." Hence, a journal which fills this first gap, and meets the second need, both "matters of immediate concern".

> We would like Joan, Nicky, Maurice Dobb, Piero and yourself to be patrons of the project and wish to obtain your aid and advice in overcoming the financial and organisational difficulties involved in getting the Journal going. If we may, we would like to come to see you next week, on either Tuesday or Friday, to discuss the matter. Up to now all our discussions have been confined to the four persons named in the first paragraph, plus Mario Nuti (on the telephone to Italy) and Bob Rowthorn. (John Eatwell to Richard Kahn, Letter dated 1 August 1976; RFK/12/2/47/2)

The proposal begins: "The idea of starting a new economics journal in Cambridge—in particular, a journal with a 'left' orientation—has been mooted for the last ten years or so. Over most of this period the motivation behind the idea derived from the desire to promote 'Cambridge' theory, in the form both of the critique of neoclassical theory and of the development of alternative

---

[20] Records in the Richard Kahn Papers held at the King's College Archives in Cambridge shed more detailed light on the initial stages of the formation of the CJE.

theories and empirical knowledge to promote a better practical understanding of economic realities. The need to pursue the former task has undoubtedly receded, and such work as remains to be done can probably find adequate space in current journals. The second task remains, and its encouragement would be the main aim of a new journal." The proposal also makes clear that "whilst the journal must adopt a proper academic standard it should be written in a manner which can win a readership amongst economists working outside academic circles, e.g. those in the government, the research departments of trade unions, companies and so on."

Three points are striking. First, that the initiative had been developing over the past 'ten years or so'; this dates it to around 1965. It is notable that Ajit Singh had joined DAE in 1964 and the Faculty, and Queens' as a Fellow, in 1965; Bob Rowthorn had come across from Oxford first to Churchill in 1964–1965, switched to King's a year later and joined the Faculty as Assistant Lecturer in 1966; Francis Cripps had completed his BA at Cambridge with a top first in 1964 and begun his career with a stint of three years as a Junior Lecturer in the Faculty before forfeiting a claim to a tenured position in favour of joining Wynne Godley as Senior Research Officer to set up the famous Cambridge Economic Policy Group with the DAE in 1971; Mario Nuti had also become a Fellow of King's in 1965, got his Cambridge PhD in 1970 and became lecturer in the faculty, having put together two volumes of Kalecki's essays in 1972, and was co-editor with Alec Nove of *Socialist Economics*; the same year, Frank Wilkinson, at DAE, had co-authored *Do Trade Unions Cause Inflation* on the eve of the first OPEC oil price spike of 1973; John Eatwell, the youngest in the group, had himself been one of Ajit Singh's star undergraduate pupils at Queens' in the mid-1960s before taking a PhD from Harvard and returning to Queens' as a research fellow till 1970, when he took up a fellowship at Trinity. Jo Bradley had been at Oxford where Bob Rowthorn (then doing maths there) drew her attention to that other, better, place, and so she came over to Cambridge University Press also in 1964, to edit and handle the DAE-CUP (Cambridge University Press) stream of publications from both sides, in the process of editing Ajit's two books. This was a powerful and rising cohort of young turks, all academically highly accomplished; they had all 'arrived' in Cambridge at the same time and had soon begun to form the nucleus of a cohesive and committed group, even as they pursued their particular academic paths and projects in their Cambridge posts and locations. So the group dinners at *La Garconne* that John Eatwell speaks of had some history behind them; and the informal collective that formulated and propelled the CJE initiative included several others who might not have been at table for these group dinners. For instance, when asked, Francis Cripps, much at the heart of the initiative, recalled: "I wasn't at the dinners because I didn't have dinner with people—in 1974–1975 I was often on the train to/from London or staying the night in London and when I was home, spent the evening with my wife and her friends (not university people). The plotters brought me in and I was glad to join" (personal communication, email dated 25 August

2019). In an earlier communication, Francis noted that "Ajit was the key organizer of the progressive electorate (DAE as well as Faculty staff could vote in elections to the Faculty Board). He was also an effective strategist / negotiator in the set up of appointment committees and with Bob Rowthorn convinced us all to support establishment of the *Cambridge Journal of Economics*" (personal communication, email dated 19 May 2018).

Second, the proposal makes it explicit that the journal was intended to be 'left-oriented'. This would have been plainly obvious given the known intellectual and political predilections of the team members. While each one was distinct, they shared a deep commitment to some socialist perspective as individually defined and pursued. In particular, but not only, Ajit Singh and Bob Rowthorn had acquired a reputation as high-profile, dynamic leaders of left politics within the Faculty, the University, the city and in wider circles through their activist involvement variously in the anti-Vietnam War and CND (Campaign for Nuclear Disarmament) movements, with trade union politics, with Labour Party or British Communist Party; Francis Cripps was deeply embedded in left-Labour policy work, including with Tony Benn; Frank Wilkinson was deep in trade union engagements; and Mario Nuti was connected with various socialist fronts especially but not exclusively oriented towards East Europe. And it should be added that while these young and energetic economists might have been a thorn in many a right-wing flank, they had come to earn respect and a following with the DAE, the Faculty and more widely on account of their demonstrable academic merit and principled politics. The extensive and vibrant associations at the time of the various strands of the Cambridge heterodox economists with various lines of the political left was well established, and this applied with special force to the younger cohort, and all the more to most of the group now taking the initiative with regard to the formation of the new journal.[21]

Third, there is an intriguing, almost casual, statement—as if it was already obvious to all—that "the need to pursue the ... task [of the critique of

---

[21] Frederic Lee's account provides a summary overview: "Cambridge in the 1960s and into the 1970s had many economists—staff, post-graduate students, and visitors—that were skeptical and/or identified their theoretical orientation as Marxist, Keynesian, Kaleckian, Sraffian, and perhaps Post Keynesian—see Appendix A.1.13. As a whole, they were conscious that their intellectual engagement, scholarship, and theoretical and applied research were creating a 'new economic analysis'. These activities were supported outside of Cambridge by the CSE of which many engaged with and within Cambridge through seminars, workshops, and study groups. One example of a seminar was the 1969–1970 Marxism seminar (which was still running a decade later). Its aim was to stimulate Marxist discussion of political issues within the Cambridge Socialist Society. There were a total of 19 seminars covering the Marxist socio-economic critique of capitalism, Marxist social philosophy, classless society, and the historical development of Marxism. In addition, in 1971 there was a seminar on the corporation in monopoly capitalism, a workshop on 'British Capitalism Today,' and a study group reading Capital. Finally, there was the Cambridge Political Economy Group which was established in the early 1970s to analyse the problems of the British economy from a Marxist perspective" (Lee, 2007, pp. 7–8). Lee's account is informative, but perhaps also a little approximate in some respects; for instance, radical as the CEPG was in its policy stance, it could not be labelled 'Marxist'.

neoclassical theory] has undoubtedly receded, and such work as remains to be done can probably find adequate space in current journals." This is striking: was the group expressing a view that was at that conjuncture generally taking shape on the Cambridge left-Keynesian-heterodox side, viz., that the business of critiquing neoclassical economics was done and dusted by 1975? Supporting this perception is an item in the Richard Kahn Papers held at the King's College Archives: in a letter concerning the organising of a Seminar on the Development of Economic Theory in Cambridge, John Eatwell writes to Richard Kahn on 19 November 1975, that is a couple of months after the exchange with Kahn about the creation of the CJE, saying: "Joan, Schefold, Garegnani and Dick Goodwin will all be talking on different aspects of the development of economic theory, now that the capital theory business is finally settled" (RFK/11/2/81/2). At this seminar, held on 21 and 22 February 1976, Joan presented a note, "The State of Play", where she also wants to move on: "As the 'mainstream' teachers of economics are unable to defend the logic of their position but go on teaching just the same, I feel that we ought to carry the argument onto a wider front" (Robinson, 1976).[22]

Was this premature hubris? With the help of that great resource, hindsight, it would certainly appear to have been so. Of course, Joan's *Accumulation of Capital* had appeared in 1956, Piero Sraffa's *Production of Commodities* in 1960, Dick Goodwin's *Elementary Economics from the Higher Standpoint* appeared a decade later in 1970, Piero Sraffa and Maurice Dobb has only just, in 1973, put the final 11th volume of the magnificent *The Works and Correspondence of David Ricardo* to bed, thereby freeing Dobb to release his final intervention *Welfare Economics and the Economics of Socialism* on which the ink had barely dried in April 1975, just four months prior to the proposal. Geoff Harcourt had followed up on his 1969 article and produced his *Some Cambridge Controversies in the Theory of Capital* in 1972. Luigi Pasinetti's *Growth and Distribution* essay collection was released by CUP in 1974. And, had Nicky Kaldor's swingeing *The Irrelevance of Equilibrium Economics*, published in *Economic Journal* also in 1972, been the last straw that had broken the neoclassical camel's back? Meanwhile, this younger group of Ajit, Bob, Francis, Frank and Mario had themselves entered the fray and made significant contributions in diverse academic forms and forums in the immediately preceding years: prominently, Ajit's applied work on the modern corporation had empirically refuted neoclassical tenets; Francis, with Wynne and the CEPG team, was deep in applied macroeconomics that raised radical left-progressive challenges to government policy on the crucial issue of employment; Frank (with Dudley Jackson and H. Turner) had come out with a repudiation of the allegation that trade unions cause inflation; Bob, apart from his squabbles with Nicky, was arguing, following Kalecki, that the rampant inflation in the UK was a manifestation of

---

[22] The substance of this note is discussed in Chapter 1, p. 13n9. At the weekend seminar, there were presentations, as indicated by Eatwell, not only by Bertram Schefold and Pierangelo Garegnani but also by Luigi Pasinetti, Ian Steedman, Luigi Spaventa and Richard Kahn, though Dick Goodwin is not listed for a presentation (RFK/12/2/81/99).

class struggle; and collective research was becoming visible on the progressive, or more appropriately, regressive, deindustrialisation of the UK economy.

As the benefit of hindsight enlightens us, rumours of the demise of neoclassicism were indeed greatly exaggerated. American imperialism might have lost its war in Vietnam, but that did not much change things for the Samuelson-Solow or Hayek-Friedman duos, with both pairs flying high. The premature hubris of Cambridge UK was confronted by the combination of soft power and raw arrogance of Chicago and Cambridge, USA, backed by their massive world-wide web of ideological think tanks peddling market fundamentalism and political libertarianism.

The group's proposal about the journal, sent to Richard Kahn on Friday, 1 August, induced an instant reaction from Kahn, and a meeting was held on Monday, 4 August in Joan's garden. Kahn clearly put some thought into the proposal and his scrawled—not always easily deciphered—notes pertaining to the proposal put down quite a few markers as an aide memoire, apparently in preparation for the upcoming meeting.

"Patrons—why only retired?????"[23] *"Why stress 'left oriented'?" "Why stress critique of neo-classical theory?" "What does 'progressive point of view' mean?" "Alternative theories—K not mentioned."*

There are further scribbles on finances,[24] launch dates and other practical matters; and the use of the term 'Cambridge Political Economy Group' is

---

[23] Kahn has a list of names: David Champernowne, Brian Reddaway, Phyllis Deane (these were the three incumbent Cambridge editors at the time); Charles Feinstein; David Goodwin; Robert Neild (with a cross and a scribble saying 'No hostile'); Adrian Wood (with a cross and a scribble saying 'besides, do not get on with him'); Wynne Godley (with a scribble 'quite keen'); Susan Howson (with a question mark); James Meade. It needs mentioning that Kahn's handwritten scribbles are not always readily readable. Coincidentally, Pasinetti (1991, p. 431) makes a reference to Kahn's handwriting as being "almost illegible". Paul Samuelson takes the matter of Kahn's handwriting to a deeper level of the subconscious: "Michael Postan once rationalized for me Richard's perfectionism as a writer, saying that he had a crabbed handwriting; never having mastered the use of typewriter or short-hand typist [sic]—this conversation antedates of course the advent of the word processor—Richard found it a chore to set his thoughts down on paper and one tends to avoid chores, until with time the avoidance becomes chronic. Kahn's several letters I did find not always easy to decipher ... Freud had names for those who retain and those who emit ..." (Samuelson, 1994, p. 62). Postan hypothesises further that the longer the writing delayed, the greater become the expectations of the piece of writing, which further raises the stakes and the force of the writers' block.

[24] According to Frederic Lee, writing without citing any specific source: "For the start-up financing of the journal, Eatwell and colleagues intended to ask Joan Robinson, Nicholas Kaldor, Maurice Dobb, Piero Sraffa, and Richard Kahn for contributions. However, when approached, Kahn suggested that Academic Press would be interested in such a project. The Press was and agreed to provide the start-up financing" (2007, p. 30n14). Kahn's scribbles notes also cover finance, with a mention of an amount of GBP 7000–10,000, with mentions of OEP (Oxford Economic Papers) and several names (though their specific relevance is not mentioned) including Asa Briggs, Kennedy, G.B. Richardson and A.J. Brown. This allows for the possibility that Kahn might have had some role on the financial role at these early stages, but the records in the Kahn Papers do not offer further information on this. Separately, in the context of the troubles which Joan Robinson and John Eatwell were having with McGraw-Hill over the treatment of their *An Introduction to Modern Economics*, Kahn had been critical of their choice of publisher in the first place and offered some suggestions though the matter was effectively closed by that time.

highlighted, the reasons for which become clear subsequently when Kahn writes back, on 15 August, to the members of the group (other than Mario Nuti who was in Italy), with a copy to Joan Robinson for information, later also copied to Robert (Neild) and Nicky (Kaldor). The letter is a good example of Kahnian belligerence and is unambiguously negative in tone.[25]

Kahn: "The document sent to me by John in 1st August suggests that the Journal would be the property of a Society to be called the Cambridge Political Economy Group. This was a grossly misleading statement. The Cambridge Political Economy Group already exists, and it was under its auspices that Bob Rowthorn and others recently published their Left-Wing pamphlet.[26] It now appears that the real intention is to publish a regular Left-Wing Propagandist Journal of Economic Policy. I suggest that this be made clear to anybody asked to have his name used in connection with it. So far as I am concerned, I must withdraw my name." And then he unsettles matters further: "I still think there probably will be a need for a decent Journal of Economics in Cambridge, and this is a matter which I intend to discuss with various people."

Kahn's letter of 15 August is presumably sent on soon after to Robert and to Nicky. On file is a reply from Robert Neild, dated 21 August 1975. Neild says: "I agree … that a new journal of left bias is no answer to the neo-classical bias of other journals. I will not touch it, if it is like that."[27]

In the meantime, on 20 August, the group responded to Kahn's trenchant letter, correcting his 'misunderstanding' and offering reassurance that there was no such intention—of producing a leftist-propagandist journal—as Kahn had alleged. The group clarified that the body establishing the journal "would be entirely distinct from the Cambridge Political Economy Group which published the pamphlet to which you refer"; the misunderstanding arose from "a mistake on our part to use the same name in the proposal to start a new journal"; this seems straightforward. The group then addresses Kahn's objection: "The suspicion expressed in your letter that our proposal was to publish a 'Left-Wing propagandist Journal of Economic Policy' is quite unfounded. Our

---

[25] Richard Kahn to Jo Bradley et al., Letter dated 15 August 1975; RFK/12/2/47/10.

[26] The authors of this pamphlet were Michael Ellman, Bob Rowthorn, Ron Smith and Frank Wilkinson. "This pamphlet is offered as a discussion document in a hope that it will stimulate debate within the labour movement on alternative socialist strategies for the British economy." The Authors' Preface opens with the statement: "The Cambridge Political Economy Group consists of a number of academic economists at Cambridge University who are engaged in analysing the problems of the British economy from a Marxist perspective. This project was started to combat the reactionary doctrines being preached by many of our colleagues at the present time" (Cambridge Political Economy Group, 1974). An online version is available in the Digital Archives maintained by the Cambridge Political Economy Society as Michael Ellman et al., "Britain's Economic Crisis" *CPES Online Archive*, accessed October 12, 2019, http://cpes.org.uk/om/items/show/168. This pamphlet was published independently by Ken Coates, founder of the Institute for Workers' Control from Nottingham (Ellman et al., 1974); the pamphlet was a significant precursor to the Alternative Economic Strategy (AES) as formulated and developed by the left wing of the Labour Party, with close Bennite affinities (which Kahn did not possess).

[27] Robert Neild to Richard Kahn, Letter dated 21 August 1975; RFK/12/2/47/12.

intention is precisely to start a 'decent' journal with the highest academic standards, and we have no wish to exclude anyone who would make a serious contribution to this, whether their views are 'left-wing' or not."[28] This does appear to be either a retraction, or distraction, since the original intent was indeed to establish a journal with 'left-wing orientation'.

The inaugural issue in 1977 of CJE announced that it was

> founded to provide a focus for theoretical and applied work, with strong emphasis on realism of analysis, the provision and use of empirical evidence, and the formulation of economic policies. This initiatives springs from the belief that the economic approach rooted in the traditions of Marx, Kalecki and Keynes has much to contribute to the understanding and treatment of current economic and social issues: unemployment, inflation, the organization of production, the distribution of social produce, class conflict, uneven development and instability in the world economy, the underdevelopment of the third world and economic and social change in socialist countries.

Did Richard Kahn and Robert Neild (if at all he was invited) find even this statement too propagandist, perhaps by the reference to Marx, and to 'class conflict'? The statement does, however, break from the original editorial aspirations proclaimed by the *Economic Journal* in its own inaugural issue where it had welcomed contributions from "the most opposite doctrines [which] may meet here as in a fair field ... with the Editor and his co-adjutors unbiased by their personal convictions". Howsoever open, this was a declaration of a broad disciplinary, intellectual and ideological identity.

The group's original proposal had included a list of 'persons so far suggested as editors'; these were Francis Cripps, John Eatwell, Mario Nuti, with Jo Bradley serving as the Managing Editor. Fifteen names were listed as suggestions for the wider Editorial Board: Mahmoud Abdel-Fadil, Ken Coutts, Michael Ellman, Alan Hughes, Barry Moore, Suzy Paine, Luigi Pasinetti, Bill Peterson, Bob Rowthorn, Ajit Singh, Roger Tarling, John Wells, Frank Wilkinson, Alan Winters and Vivian Woodward. The Faculty and the DAE seem to be represented in roughly equal and proportionate number. Unlike the EJ, which was essentially housed in the Faculty, the CJE was camped midway between the Faculty and the DAE; in demographic terms, there was also clearly a generational jump from the EJ to the CJE; and while EJ was referred to as 'in house', its editors were appointed by, and accountable to, the Royal Economic Society; while, in contrast, CJE was run from inside the Cambridge heterodox group as represented in the society owning it (RFK/12/2/47/1–14).

Arguably, the formation of the CJE can be regarded as a defensive reaction, but in fact, it was simultaneously a tremendous proactive initiative. There were five positive effects: first, it not only created a sense of community but provided a flagpole for the assembly of the community of heterodox economists in

---

[28] John Eatwell et al. to Richard Kahn, Letter dated 20 August 1975, RFY/12/2/47/11.

Cambridge. Second, it strengthened this community by explicitly linking the older and the younger generations in a real sense; the seniors were supporters, patrons and protectors. Third, as intended, it provided the outlet for heterodox research. Fourth, it provided a focal point to articulate Cambridge heterodox economists with the wider international community that had been evolving around, and independently of, the Cambridge core. And finally, the very existence of the journal—an intellectual space regularly to be filled—developed and disseminated, and arguably induced, research and publication, giving a creative fillip to the community of economists now committed to making the CJE a success. It could be added that there was also a reputational impact, in that the remarkable array of heterodox thought and concerns, ranging from deep aspects of the history of ideas to the contemporary red-hot policy preoccupations of the day, could all get high international visibility in the same issue. The journal, now in its 45th year, constitutes a highly valuable cumulative resource on the evolution of the Cambridge heterodox traditions in economics; apart from Keynes and a small handful who had fallen by the mid-1970s, CJE has had personal support and contributions from virtually the entire galaxy of heterodox traditions, and as such can rightfully be regarded as the proud inheritor, representative and perpetuator of those traditions—a worthy, and perhaps even more focussed replacement of the parent *Economic Journal*. The creation of the CJE was nothing less than a stroke of genius, prescience, a case of 'perfect foresight'.

Volume 1, Issue 1 of the *Cambridge Journal of Economics* duly appeared in March 1977, and it proudly displayed all the hallmarks of high Cambridge heterodoxy. The issue carried eight titles, the first of which sadly was an obituary by John Eatwell paying homage to one of the Cambridge greats: Maurice Dobb had died before seeing the inaugural issue of the journal of which he was to be a patron; the first regular article was by Joan Robinson and Frank Wilkinson, asking in true Joan style, 'What has become of employment policy?'. Then followed a landmark paper by Amartya Sen where he introduces his general approach to starvation and exchange entitlement and applies it to the Great Bengal Famine of 1943; given its provenance, the acknowledgements run to no fewer than 32 names. Ron Smith, who had just been eased out of Cambridge by the local neoclassical group a year before, provides a Marxist analysis of the workings of military expenditure in capitalism, a topic of profound significance generally understudied even in the Keynesian-Schumpeterian traditions, though it connected closely with the peacenik concerns of Robert Neild who had recently returned to Cambridge as professor, prior to and supposedly inducing the award of a Cambridge chair to Hahn the following year. The issue also introduced its format of the Review Article, the first of these being a reflection by Gareth Stedman Jones on Eric Hobsbawm's *The Age of Capital*. And finally, Francis Cripps joined battle against the monetarists in all guises in his article 'The Money Supply, Wages and Inflation'. The first issue set and raised the standard aloft—Cambridge heterodox economics had a space of its own.

The nuanced nature of the relationship between the senior heterodox gurus and the cohort of young turks is also reflected in the formative years of CJE. Consider the issue of identity: the initial proposal circulated by the younger group named Joan Robinson, Nicky Kaldor, Maurice Dobb, Piero Sraffa and Richard Kahn as the slate that the group wished to declare as the patrons of CJE. Luigi Pasinetti (2005, p. 839) writes: "The young Editors asked senior members to support their initiative, but in a way that would not entail interference with their choices, thought of course welcoming suggestions and criticisms. In this spirit, they invited those whom they judged to be significant members of the Cambridge School to become Patrons of the Journal." But of the slate of five desired Patrons named in the opening proposal—Joan Robinson, Nicky Kaldor, Maurice Dobb, Piero Sraffa and Richard Kahn—only Joan wound up on as a Patron in the colophon of CJE's first issue of the first volume. Maurice Dobb died in 1976, so the opening issue carries his obituary which refers to him as "one of this Journal's distinguished Patrons" (Eatwell, 1977, p. 1); it would be a fair presumption that before his death Dobb had agreed to serve as Patron. But what of the other three gurus whose names did not appear in the inaugural issue? Clearly, other senior colleagues were approached, as is obvious from Luigi Pasinetti's account. So clearly much happened between that first proposal and the first issue of the journal; Kaldor, Sraffa and Kahn were not inclined to become Patrons then, and the editors then would have looked further. In Pasinetti's account, "At the very beginning [sic], only Richard Goodwin, Luigi Pasinetti and Joan Robinson accepted the invitation. Two-and-a-half years later, Kaldor and Sraffa were also persuaded to join. Kahn decided to remain aloof but, during those years, he did contribute papers [sic] to the new Journal" (see Kahn, 1977).[29]

After all the internal discussions, the new journal boasted three inestimable, quintessentially Cambridge patrons: Richard Goodwin, Luigi Pasinetti and Joan Robinson, and announced a panel of 11 editors based in Cambridge, and another seven associate editors overseas; together, they formed the backbone of the rising cohort of Cambridge heterodox economists of distinct though contiguous and compatible intellectual, ideological and theoretical affinities. A striking feature is the youthfulness of the editors: apart, perhaps, for a couple of associate editors that scored over 40, all others were still in their 30s.[30]

As a person is proverbially known by the company s/he keeps, so a journal by the names it selects to associate with itself. Apart from the patrons, the names

---

[29] In fact, this is the only paper contributed by Kahn, and it was a review article of Malinvaud's 1977 book. It would be more accurate to say that Kahn kept "aloof" of CJE whether as an editor or as an author.

[30] In 1977, the original panel of "Editors" was drawn from Cambridge and comprised: Mahmoud Abdel-Fadil, Jo Bradley (Managing Editor), Francis Cripps, John Eatwell, Mario Nuti, Suzy Paine, Bob Rowthorn, Ajit Singh, Roger Tarling, John Wells and Frank Wilkinson. The extended slate named seven 'Associate Editors', economists of deep affinity with the identity of the Journal: Geoff Harcourt (Australia), Amiya Bagchi (India), Ron Smith and Ian Steedman (UK outside Cambridge), David Gordon and Anwar Shaikh (USA), and Michael Ellman (The Netherlands).

of the greats explicitly declared as inspirations were, originally, Marx, Keynes and Kalecki, later expanded when Joan and Nicky transitioned from being patrons in this world to becoming inspirations from the next. Notably, neither Sraffa[31] nor Kahn entered any CJE list of inspirationals. Interestingly, Pasinetti (2005, p. 838) observes: "I remember Dick Goodwin regretting that Joseph Schumpeter was not included among the economists mentioned for inspiration", but that disappointment did not interfere with his support for CJE.[32]

The 1979 colophon indicated a couple of noticeable changes: first, the panel of patrons gained another august pair, in Nicky Kaldor and Piero Sraffa; and second, Bob Rowthorn left the panel of editors. Between 1979 and 1980, the editorial panel was further extended and strengthened through the inclusion of another seven colleagues. The year 1984 was the next point where significant

---

[31] Perhaps it is worth noting at face value, that in *Contributions to Political Economy*—the annually published parallel Cambridge journal from the same CPES stable—set up in 1982 by a group (including Murray Milgate and Giancarlo de Vivo) led by John Eatwell, with the objective of publishing "articles on the theory and history of political economy within the critical traditions in economic through associated with the work of the classical political economists, Marx, Keynes and Sraffa" (*Contributions to Political Economy, Volume 1, 1982*)—the inclusion of Sraffa perhaps reflecting Eatwell's deep intellectual association; Kalecki, Joan, Kaldor, Goodwin or Pasinetti are not visible.

[32] It is not difficult to appreciate Goodwin's position on Schumpeter. The intellectual, and indeed personal, affinity between Schumpeter, born in 1883, and Goodwin, born in 1913, travels back to their shared years (early 1930s–1950) in Harvard where Schumpeter tried hard but unsuccessfully for a tenured position in the faculty for the young Goodwin, thus setting in chain the events that brought Goodwin to Cambridge UK. Massimo Di Matteo and Serena Sordi (2009, p. 4n1) provide some personalised texture: "In his intervention at the Celebration of RMG's 75th birthday, held in Siena on 25 March 1988, Samuelson reconstructed the event as follows: 'Ten days before Joseph Schumpeter died, he and I met, naturally, in the bar of the hotel where the American Economic Association was having its meeting [...] What we discussed in our final moments was this. Schumpeter said to me: "Paul, what are we going to do about Dick Goodwin?". I said: "What do you mean, what are we going to do about Dick Goodwin?" And he said: "Dick Goodwin, *quite without regard to merits*, has not been offered a tenured position at Harvard"' (Di Matteo, 1990, p. 18; emphasis added)." Intellectually, the affinity is reflected profoundly in the search for integrated dynamic mechanisms in the mature capitalist economy that simultaneously generate both growth and cycles—though Schumpeter's literary style contrasted in the extreme with Goodwin's mathematical methods. Hardy Hanappi (2015, n. 8) writes: "Sill an assistant professor at Harvard, Richard Goodwin in private lessons tried to teach Schumpeter some mathematics. Though Schumpeter was extremely fond of mathematics Richard Goodwin once told me that he was a very untalented pupil!" As an undergraduate in Harvard, "he wrote a thesis on Marx, *A Critique of Marxism*. He also met Joseph Schumpeter as a seminar—Schumpeter was to become one of Goodwin's heroes and, towards the end of Schumpeter's life, a close friend. Schumpeter, who had been in Bohm-Bawerk's seminar in Vienna, knew Marx's work thoroughly, provided a learned and intelligent critique which caused the young Goodwin to take a great dislike to Schumpeter because he could not bear to have Marx, his newfound hero, criticized!" (Harcourt, 1985, pp. 413–414). Theoretical investigations of the relationship between the approaches of Schumpeter, (Keynes) and Goodwin are provided by Harcourt (1985, 2015), Velupillai (2015a), Hanappi (2015) and Goodwin (1991) himself; for crossing over into issues of economic development, see Prabhat Patnaik (2015b) and Velupillai (2015b); and for a full appreciation of his work, see the special issue in his honour in the *Cambridge Journal of Economics* (2015, 39(6)). It is not difficult to fathom why Goodwin would have regarded Schumpeter as a legitimate name for the panel of the greats whose work and perspectives on the dynamics of capitalism were held as inspirations for the new journal.

changes occur: sadly, Joan and Piero are missing, both having died in 1983, while Hashem Pesaran and Jane Humphries join the editorial panel. Volume 9 in 1985 sees a revamping: on the panel of patrons, Dick Goodwin, Nicky Kaldor and Luigi Pasinetti are joined by Sukhamoy Chakravarty and Brian Reddaway; the editorial panel keeps its strength at 16, with the exit of John Eatwell, and the entry of Michael Landesmann, with Ann Newton taking over from the founding Managing Editor, Jo Bradley. Noticeably, two of the original group of founders, Bob Rowthorn and John Eatwell, had dropped off the editorial board of the journal.[33] The following year, 1986, Volume 10, was marked by the loss of Nicky Kaldor. At the end of the first decade of its life, CJE could justifiably be said to have matured rapidly to occupy a prime position as the lead heterodox journal, widely respected and read, a position it retains to this day.

Two additional observations are appropriate. The first concerns the entry of Brian Reddaway into the panel of patrons, which calls for comment from both the demand and the supply sides, so to speak. Ajit Singh sets the matter straight. In his appreciation for his mentor Brian Reddaway, Ajit refers to a paradox, viz., why this group of young left-wing economists chose to ask Reddaway to be the patron of the new journal. The answer lay in their intellectual affinity with Reddaway's approach: "scepticism about economic theory"; "emphasis on empirical and policy analysis"; "distrust of the over-use of mathematical and econometric techniques" and lack of concern with ideology, while Reddaway saw "that these people were doing economics in much the same way as he was doing it himself" (Singh, 2008, p. 19); and then Brian Reddaway was a man of impeccable intellectual and personal integrity.[34] It should be mentioned here

---

[33] In Eatwell's case, this could perhaps be related to the fact that he, along with Murray Milgate and Giancarlo de Vivo had, in 1982, launched a new annual journal in Cambridge, *Contributions to Political Economy* with the objective, declared in its inaugural issue, of publishing "articles on the theory and history of political economy within the critical traditions in economic thought associated with the work of the classical political economists, Marx, Keynes and Sraffa".

[34] From Maria Cristina Marcuzzo's fascinating rendition of her extensive interviews and conversations with Richard Kahn in the mid-1980s, we have a most apposite anecdote narrated by Richard Kahn. During the war, the Board of Trade initiated a scheme for rationing clothes, initially planned to take the form of "each year one pair of shoes, two shirts and so on, and perhaps a new suit every three years". Kahn pointed out the obvious, "that different people had different requirements", and strongly advocated a points system along the lines employed by the Germans. But how would this pattern of consumption match the available production resources? "We called in to our help my Cambridge colleague, Brian Reddaway", who duly resolved the problem. Richard Kahn goes on to offer a remarkable insight into Reddaway's character. "For help on women's clothing Reddaway could not consult his wife, as it would have involved betraying the prospect of clothes rationing, which it was most important to keep secret. He consulted an elderly woman from the Bank of England who was covered by the Official Secrets Act. The result was most successful. Brian Reddaway was and still is a highly conscientious man. Because he had been involved in the preparation of the clothes rationing scheme, he thought it wrong for him to benefit from it. Each year he solemnly burnt his ration book, but I am glad to say that he did not enforce this imposition on his beautiful wife. In the later stages of the War his clothing was in a dreadful condition. 'Those Brits certainly practice what they preach' was the remark of an American who was visiting this country" (Kahn & Marcuzzo, 2020, pp. 14–15).

that for many years, Brian and Ajit jointly delivered the course on Applied Statistics, and Ajit was clearly a prime mover in associating Reddaway with the journal; it also bears testimony to the intellectual openness and the self-imposed demand for methodological rigour that characterised the founding group of the journal, attributes that subsequently stood the journal in good stead. With resonance to Brian Reddaway's approach, Ken Coutts (2021, p. 31) points out that "As a general peer-reviewed journal, it has a policy on the use of mathematics which limits papers that are essentially technical and cannot be understood without the mathematical argument. But if papers are pre- sented with the technical material in appendices and give an explanation of the arguments in the main text that is clear to the non-mathematical reader, the Journal will be pleased to accept submissions for review." Clearly, Reddaway had left an indelible stamp on the journal.

In similar vein, Luigi Pasinetti (2005, pp. 840–844) draws pointed attention to the striking congruence between what he regards as eight "building blocks provided by the Cambridge School of Keynesian Economics" and "the Notes to Contributors that the CJE displays on its cover" which guide potential authors about features to which the Journal attaches intrinsic value. These eight blocks are elaborated again in *Keynes and the Cambridge Keynesians* (Pasinetti, 2007).

The second comment pertains to the puzzling absence of Richard Kahn, of the top echelon of Cambridge heterodox economists, from the list of patrons of the journal throughout the overlapping periods of his and the journal's life. Of course, not all Cambridge professors, or Nobel Prize winners, made it to the list, but the case of Kahn immediately stands out as anomalous. Nor, apart from one review article on Edmond Malinvaud's *The Theory of Unemployment Reconsidered* (Kahn, 1977) in the first year of the CJE, is there any other item carrying his name as an author. Other left-Keynesians are fully represented; hence, this curious absence can only be explained by equally curious idiosyncrasies. Kahn had drifted away from Labour to the right and supported the Social Democratic Party (SDP); he had had very public disagreements with Kaldor and the DAE left group over Old and New Cambridge; and, significantly, at the very outset when he was the very first 'great' to be approached by the pioneering group for advice and to be a patron, he had attacked the idea and the group on account of its declared leftist predilection; this matter had ostensibly, but obviously not really, been cleared, and some combination of some or all of the above considerations would go into explaining this very 'Cambridge' oddity.[35]

---

[35] Luigi Pasinetti's comment on the CJE, on the passing of Dick Goodwin, adds another possibility. Luigi writes: "The CJE loses with him the second of its three *original* Patrons (since Joan Robinson died in 1983). I may briefly remind the reader of what being a 'Patron' meant at the beginning. The group of non-conformist young economists who started this Journal (in 1977) asked senior colleagues for support, *without* interference, though of course welcoming suggestions and criticisms ..." (quoted in Baranzini & Mirante, 2018, p. 42, italics in the original). Perhaps Kahn did not wish to be a hostage to fortune and be associated with the journal's contents and politics by default; there is ample room for speculation (Pasinetti, 1996).

Time has taken its toll, and in relatively quick succession, Ajit Singh, Frank Wilkinson and Mario Nuti have passed on. With Frank's demise, the list of CJE patrons is down to two: Luigi Pasinetti who has been one from the start, and Amartya Sen who has been welcomed in with this high status from over the past decade. It is no secret that Sen, while in many senses quintessentially 'Cambridge', was not a card-carrying member of the Cambridge heterodox macroeconomic school in its heyday in any of its uniforms; visiting M.I.T. in 1960–1961, he "found it a great relief to get away from the rather sterile debates that the contending armies were fighting in Cambridge" (Sen, 1998). He ploughed his own individual and, generally individualist, furrow with resonances to Adam Smith, John Stuart Mill, Pigou and Dobb (in his incarnation as a welfare economist), rather than to Marx, Sraffa, Kalecki, Joan or Kaldor and their diverse brands of macroeconomic theoretical and contemporary policy concerns. It is moot whether this convergence in the form of Sen's formal patronage denotes the proverbial return of the prodigal son through the doors back into the Cambridge fold, or if the location of the doors has itself shifted in the interim—perhaps some movement on both sides of the equation?

The *Cambridge Journal of Economics* celebrated its 40th Anniversary with a Conference held on 12–13 July 2016 at St. Catherine's College, Cambridge.[36] Between the plenary meetings, three parallel sessions ran on both days with 49 papers presented covering a full spectrum of themes and topics reflecting the concerns of the broad church of post-Keynesian and heterodox economics; on a loose count, only a fifth of the speakers were 'of Cambridge', testifying to the international vibrancy of the mushrooming intellectual constituency; the Conference was launched, most appropriately, with an Address by the senior post-Keynesian maestro Luigi Pasinetti, and the proceedings continually enriched by the contributions, interactions and the infinitely elastic supply of anecdotes from the omnipresent other senior guru, Geoff Harcourt; included in the plenaries were defining talks by Tony Lawson and Simon Deakin on ontology; a session and a round table on pedagogical aspects—curriculum (non-)reform, the (re-)teaching of economics and on the future of economics teaching—Joan would have been delighted; and another striking one on developing a career in heterodox economics. It was indeed a landmark event, a full-feathered display of the intellectual energy of the field and the central role of the CJE in serving as a cementing core. It was an impressive assembly of the great and good, and the rising and aspiring of the growing clans; poignantly, Gabriel Palma presented his paper as 'a tribute to Ajit Singh', one of the pioneers of the CJE and stalwarts of the clans, who had sadly passed away in the previous year. CJE has on occasion commissioned special issues on some of the modern greats of Cambridge economics, including Joan Robinson and Nicky Kaldor. Worthy of special mention in this context is the conference, fittingly titled "Economics for the Future", organised in 2003 by the Cambridge

---

[36] The Conference programme can be accessed at:
http://www.cpes.org.uk/dev/wp-content/uploads/2016/07/40CJE_Programme.pdf.

Political Economy Society (CPES) to mark the centenary of the creation of the Cambridge Tripos in 1903 through Marshall's efforts. A selection of the conference papers was then published in the CJE. In his introduction to the special issue, Michael Kitson (2005, p. 829) notes: "Cambridge Economics was originally grounded in moral philosophy, its *raison d'etre* was traditionally to understand why societies malfunction, and the devising of policies to offset the impact of malfunctioning and, especially, to protect those most vulnerable to their impact. The purpose of the conference was to build on this tradition by encouraging open dialogue amongst social scientists concerned about the future prospects for economics."

CJE has steadily remained at the top of the list of journals of heterodox economics, and heterodox journals open to economics submissions. EJ, meanwhile, has dropped rank significantly and, while included in the Diamond list, is only in the second category of the ABS (Association of Business Scholars) list of economics journals, the top category of five journals being all from the USA.

4.2.3 Cambridge Economic Policy Review: *One Crowded Hour of Glorious Life*

In the context of the exit of EJ and the entry of CJE, worthy of an honourable mention is the annual *Cambridge Economic Policy Review* produced by the Cambridge Economic Policy Group that carried the latest workings and predictions from their model, engaging always in a provocative but analytically rigorous manner with the burning macroeconomic policy issues at the time. The Review had quickly earned a high reputation, attracted a wide readership within Cambridge, in government policy circles and beyond, and was a hot item with the media; the reason was that its empirical analysis was thorough, its policy discussion bold, its critiques outspoken and its recommendations unambiguous. It rode on the high wave of interest—to some extent created by the CEPG itself through the very frequent media interventions by various members of the CEPG team, which provided a critical parallel commentary of the state of economic affairs. The Review paired extremely well with the CJE which itself carried a substantial interest in the highly charged macroeconomic challenges confronting the UK economy in the 1970s and 1980s. Unfortunately, this publication, valuable as it was, was also short-lived and permanently silenced when the Social Science Research Council (SSRC), in 1982, summarily terminated its funding for the CEPG's regular macro-modelling work which formed the basis for the group's policy analysis carried in its Review. It was a case of Hello-Goodbye for the new kid on the block.

In the Introduction to Volume 3: "[In the *Review*] each year the Group has published assessments of medium-term problems confronting the UK as they appear at the time. The result has been not only a running series of analyses of specific problems and prospects, but also the development of a detailed model of the main aspects of the UK economy, as well as the formulation of more general theoretical propositions and principles for economic policy."[37] The Reviews variously covered aspects of the UK regional and national economies, but also analyses of the European and the world economies, drawing out implications for UK economic performance and policy.

The research publication was called the *Policy Review* for the first four years between 1971 and 1974. It then became the more formal *Economic Policy Review*, of which Volumes 1–5 were annual numbers, released (early in the year) between 1975 and 1979; from 1979, the title changed to *Cambridge Economic Policy Review* (CEPR); Volume 6, in 1980, expanded to three separate numbers; Volumes 7 and 8 each had two numbers. Volume 8 Number 2 in December 1982 was the final publication of the series. Leaving aside the first four Reviews (1971–1974), these 12 issues carried 74 papers, including frequent valuable statistical compilations on various themes, ranging from historical data to trends in the national and world economies, to regional accounts.[38]

In 1976, Volume 2 of the *Economic Policy Review* lists the members of the CEPG: Paul Atkinson, Kenneth Coutts, Francis Cripps, Martin Fetherston, Wynne Godley, Barry Moore, John Rhodes, Roger Tarling, Terry Ward and Frank Wilkinson. In 1982, Volume 8 has three additional names: Michael Anyadike-Danes, Iain Begg and Graham Gudgin; two of the earlier names drop out, being Paul Atkinson and Martin Fetherston. Five of the eight survivors of the original ten members of the CEPG team—Ken Coutts, Francis Cripps, Martin Fetherston, Terry Ward and Frank Wilkinson—also serve on the CJE as editors, associate editors or on the panel of patrons. Of the founding members, Ajit Singh passed away in 2015, and two others, John Eatwell and Bob Rowthorn, are not formally linked in any editorial capacity with the journal at present.

It is worth noting that the CEPG's *Policy Review* was not just an in-house publication, nor was it a promotional public relations glossy for government departments and banks. In a different context—when the decision-making Consortium of the Social Science Research Council rejects CEPG's grant application, citing CEPG's limited interaction within the academic profession as a reason—Godley makes a pertinent observation in his response to the Consortium's letter of rejection: "I do not accept that by comparison with the other existing UK modelling teams we have in any sense a poor record in the quantity and manner of our interaction with the academic profession. All modelling groups produce their main output in the form of in-house publications because the need for rapid publication and the quantity of material involved precludes the use of academic journals for this purpose. Our main publication, the Policy Review, has a considerable *academic* [emphasis in the original] circulation, going to some 100–150 universities overseas and 150–200 academic

---

[37] *Economic Policy Review*, Volume 3, March 1977, 'Introduction and Table of Contents', *CPES Online Archive*: http://cpes.org.uk/om/items/show/52 (accessed 12 October 2019).

[38] The Cambridge Political Economy Society maintains a digital archive that holds the full series of the publication from 1971 till April 1982. See http://cpes.org.uk/om/cepr.

institutions in the UK (precise figures are not available because many academic orders come through agents)."[39]

The cessation of the CEPG's much anticipated *Review* was a prime illustration of the significant collateral damage inflicted by the SSRC's peremptory termination of the grant; of course, the heaviest loss was in the dispersal of the accomplished team that produced the research that underlay the *Review*. For researchers focussing in any depth on that volatile period of recent UK economic history, or on some of 'new Cambridge' innovations, howsoever contested, of the theoretical basis of macroeconomic policy, the cumulative stock of CEPG research remains a unique and incisive resource.

It is significant to note that the majority of the founding editors of the CJE were either DAE researchers or Faculty staff who had conducted substantial research projects based at the DAE with the research output published under DAE auspices. With the exception of John Eatwell, all the others who were collectively involved in the launch of the CJE were from this list, viz., Ajit Singh, Bob Rowthorn, Francis Cripps, Michael Ellman, Ron Smith, Frank Wilkinson and Jo Bradley (who was the Managing Editor). This confirms the close intellectual affinity and camaraderie across the two sides of the building. In 2020, Gennaro Zezza and Dimitri Papadimitriou edited a special issue of the *Journal of Post Keynesian Economics* to mark to celebrate the career, achievements and approach of Wynne Godley—it was the tenth anniversary of his death. It went unremarked, but it was also exactly the fiftieth anniversary of the arrival of Wynne Godley in Cambridge as Director of DAE, replacing Brian Reddaway. The collection was marked by a diverse set of assessments, some by the old guard and some by the rising generation.

In his personal tribute, Ken Coutts observes: "Wynne lived long enough to appreciate that young researchers were beginning to take up his approach and to elaborate and develop the ideas in the [Godley-Lavoie] book. In the ten years since his death, there has been an explosion in the number of research papers taking a SFC approach to Post-Keynesian macroeconomics." Ken especially cites the survey by Michalis Nikiforos and Gennaro Zezza (2017). Of particular significance is his conclusion: "I would like to finish by giving a plug for the *Cambridge Journal of Economics*, which has supported this work, including papers by Wynne and by Wynne and Marc. Alan Shipman, in his introduction to a virtual special issue of November 2018, Stock flow consistent macroeconomics—the foundations, summarizes work in this area published in the *CJE* and papers that were antecedents to the approach. The *CJE* continues to support this work" (Coutts, 2021, p. 31). The point to elicit is that though ideological adversaries had managed to bring down the Cambridge Economic Policy Group at the beginning of the 1980s along with its own house journal *Economic Policy Review* which predated the CJE and ran parallel to it till its termination, the CJE, to a notable extent, effectively became the forum and

---

[39] Wynne Godley, 'Response to the Consortium's Provisional Conclusion on the Cambridge Economic Policy Group's Application', 5 April 1982; #5.

outlet for the lines of research that the CEPG had been engaging in. The CEPG and its *CEPR* had been suppressed, but not its ideas.

4.3 Seminars

After acknowledging the presence of a Marshallian precursor in the late nineteenth century, the lineage of economics seminars in Cambridge[40] is picked up from the famous Political Economy Club (PEC) started by Keynes in the 1920s where he was the multi-tasking busker, playing king-philosopher-teacher-entertainer-economist, and follows the main trails down, taking shortcuts, till the 2010s. The coverage is selective, roughly chronological and unapologetically idiosyncratic; the intention is to convey a sense of the changing character and ethos of the times contemporary to the various series and to tentatively elicit some identifiable tendencies over time, or between different, often competing, series.

Some series have primarily pedagogical objectives, others are more peer-group conversations around research, and yet others combine the two. Each series is associated with one or two initiators and moderators whose personal style stamps it carries, and addresses a catchment or constituency that is self-defining, depending on the disciplinary and ideological orientation of the seminar; each series develops path dependence with the emergence of distinct

---

[40] *Kushti*, Indian freestyle wrestling, is an ancient Indian sport, imbued with history and folklore, distinct from the Greco-Roman and other styles. The locus is the *akhara*, the ring or the wrestling sandpit where wrestlers, those retired with legendary reputations to young aspirants, and everyone in between, regularly assemble to teach and to learn, to practise their arts, under the gaze of their *ustads*, the gurus, the senior *pahalwans*, concentrating on preparing their upcoming *shagirds*, loyal apprentices, for being pitted in open competition with their opposite numbers from rival *akharas*, each under the watchful, frowning eye of his resident senior *pahalwan*. Performance in such tourneys determines the reputation not just of the junior wrestler, but of his *ustad*, and then, importantly, of the collective comprising the *akhara*. It is serious business, war not a sport, and much depends on it; fine performances are rewarded with promotions and favoured access to the seniors; failures lead to de-recognition, even polite or impolite invitations to leave for a lesser *akhara*. Each *akhara* has a distinctive style that defines it, reflecting that of the senior *pahalwan* whose name it often carries; these styles have their own grammar of moves and countermoves, offensive and defensive, rules and protocols of fair and unfair play, extending even to prescribed dietary regimes; honour and loyalty, skill and success are the common currencies. On special occasions, inter-*akhara* or district or even national competitions are staged, where there is great suspense and aficionados and amateurs assemble in large numbers to shout out appreciation for their own, and/or hurl sometimes rude verbals at the opponents; spiced descriptions of legendary bouts are passed down from grandfather, who saw Gama wrestle Imam Bux, to father, who saw Dara Singh grapple King Kong, to son, who saw Dara Singh floor Tiger Joginder Singh, or now to granddaughter, who saw not a bout but a film about the sisters Geeta and Babita, India's world-class female wrestlers raised and trained by their wrestler father all within a patriarchal society. And so reputations are continually forged, regurgitated and refashioned, the store of folklore augmented with fresh tales of in/famous victories and defeats, of cunning new moves; and so the *akharas* and their clans reproduce their communities and their craft in a timeless flow, often oblivious to the incidental goings on in the lives and worlds outside the *akhara*. There, one has a fair description of Cambridge economics seminars, as patriarchal and macho as the sport.

Table 4.1 Cambridge economics seminars, 1890s–

Year	Economic Club	Keynes/ Robertson/ Kahn Political Economy Club	The Marshall Society	Sraffa Research Students Seminar	Cambridge Circus-I and Circus-II at King's	Cambridge-LSE Joint Seminar	Hayek's Informal economics at home in Cambridge	Kahn 'Secret' Seminar
1	2	3	4	5	6	7	8	9
1884	Economic Club starts							
1896	Last reference to Club							
1909		Keynes starts Political Economy Club						
1920s			Marshall Society formed; 1st meeting in 1927					
1930–1931				Sraffa Seminar starts y=? Seminar active	Circus-I: Closed group on Keynes's Treatise run by Kahn			
1931–1939					Circus-II: Circus Extended to include selected Faculty; run by Kahn			
1933–1935						Also separate half-way meetings for young staff Till when?		
1940–1944		War; seminar stops			War; Circus ends			
1945		Robertson takes over Pol Econ Seminar; JMK 1st guest (?)					Hayek Cambridge meetings for LSE eco dept.	Kahn's 'Secret' Seminar Starts, as new incarnation of Circus

(*continued*)

Table 4.1 (continued)

Year	Economic Club	Keynes/ Robertson/ Kahn Political Economy Club	The Marshall Society	Sraffa Research Students Seminar	Cambridge Circus-I and Circus-II at King's	Cambridge- LSE Joint Seminar	Hayek's Informal economics at home in Cambridge	Kahn 'Secret' Seminar
1957		PES stops as Robertson retires 1957 Kahn takes over the Political Economy Club						
1961								
1960s				Seminar stops In 1965? as Sraffa retires				
1969		Kahn ends Political Economy Club; closure could have been a few years earlier or later till 1972						
1970								
1975								Secret Seminar closed
1976								
1987								
1990								
1991								
1995			Still running					
2003								
2007								
2020								Kahn: 'some of us' thinking of re-starting King's Secret Seminar. But did not happen

Year	Faculty Tea-Room opens at EAGR Building	Ajit Singh Queens' Seminar	Arestis and Kitson St. Catherine's Seminar	Hahn Churchill Seminar	DAE Cambridge Growth Project (CGP) Seminar	Hahn Quaker/Risk Seminar	CLARE Group Seminar; Matthews-Cairncross	Lawson's Realism & Social Ontology Groups
1	10	11	12	13	14	15	16	17
1884								
1896								
1909								
1920s								
1930–1931								
1931–1939								
1933–1935								
1940–1944								
1945								
1957								
1961	Staff Common Room (later Stone Tea-Room) opens							
1960s			Seminar starts in 2nd half of 1960s		Seminar Starts some time in 1967–1969			
1969								

(*continued*)

Table 4.1 (continued)

Year	Faculty Tea-Room opens at EAGR Building	Ajit Singh' Queens' Seminar	Arestis and Kitson St. Catherine's Seminar	Hahn Churchill Seminar	DAE Cambridge Growth Project (CGP) Seminar	Hahn Quaker/Risk Seminar	CLARE Group Seminar; Matthews-Cairncross	Lawson's Realism & Social Ontology Groups
1970					CGP Internal Seminar starts in DAE			
1975								
1976						Hahn's Risk 'Quaker' Seminar begins; 15-year Economic and Social Research Council (ESRC) project	CLARE Group formed; meetings at Clare begin	
1987					CGP seminar ends with closure of CGP			
1990								Tony Lawson's Cambridge Realist Workshop (CRW) starts
1991						Hahn's Risk Quaker Seminar ends; one year before Hahn retires		
1995							John Flemming takes over Chair from Matthews	

2002			Tony Lawson's Cambridge Social Ontology Group (CSOG) starts
		CLARE Group ends	
2003	Ajit Singh retires; Queens' Seminar ends	Queens' Seminar shifts to St. Catherine's with Philip Arestis	
2007			
2020		Still running	

identities and even silo mentalities; clients and participants develop loyalties, and usually sign up to a particular series generally ignoring the others; each series evolves its own culture and credo, which tends to cement affinities within, while making entry a little daunting, akin to gatecrashing. While all these features are common, there are some distinguishing tendencies that can be detected even if tentatively.

At the origin is Keynes's Political Economy Club, which served staff and selected students, with the elementary proviso that they be male, since initially women were not allowed into the Tripos. As the size of the market expanded, so did the division of labour and the degree of functional specialisation, with the emergence of the research students' seminar run by Piero Sraffa on the one side, and later the Circus around Keynes's writing of the *Treatise* and then the *General Theory*. Such divisions as they were amongst the Faculty would then have an airing in the common, shared space of the PEC, of course under the tutelage and indulgence of Keynes. Things change immediately after the war, with the appointment of Denis Robertson as Professor of Political Economy, and with his taking over of the PEC at Trinity. Meanwhile, Richard Kahn, Joan and Co. start the so-called Secret Seminar at King's. Two tracks emerge, the right-wing and the left-wing; Robertson, Denison, Henderson, Farrell and perhaps a few others on the anti-Keynesian side remain uninvited to the Secret Seminar, reflecting the distance and hostile polarity between the camps; yet, faculty, including Keynes, go and make presentations at Robertson's PEC, and some staff attend both. Robertson retired in 1957, and with him the PEC.

The Secret Seminar, left-oriented and zealously and jealously Keynesian, does include various orthodox economists, especially Frank Hahn after he arrives in Cambridge from Birmingham in 1962; neoclassical icons from the USA, Samuelson, Arrow, Solow, amongst others, put in appearances, adding to the combative zest of proceedings. However, such deep differences, and the principle of selective participation, become sufficiently unsustainable or disagreeable for a new pattern to emerge. There is sharp separation from the neoclassicals as Frank Hahn sets up his competitive Churchill Mathematical Seminar on the same day as the Secret Seminar. On the other, home front, the exclusion of many younger heterodox staff and researchers from the Secret Seminar leads to the launching of Ajit Singh's Political Economy Seminar at Queens' which, while welcoming of the heterodox participants of the Secret Seminar, also tends to exclude neoclassical 'extremists'. These developments from the mid-1960s lead, in 1969, to the closure of Kahn's Secret Seminar altogether. That leaves the two major seminars: the heterodox at Queens' and the orthodox at Churchill, both running on the same day, both mutually exclusive, and both mutually hostile in disciplinary and ideological terms. The overall timeline of the seminar series thus mirrors the internal polarisations that emerge within the Faculty of Economics; perhaps the only common, shared space that remains is the Faculty tea-room which, after the building at Sidgwick Site comes up in 1961, becomes the colosseum for the gladiatorial challenges and fights between the rival camps. The tribes display high degrees of internal solidarity, loyalty and like-mindedness, though this cohesion is more pronounced in the unitary orthodox school with its single ruler, Hahn, than in the heterodox tribe, where such solidarity is frequently challenged and chipped by internal doctrinal differences between the various strands of the family of heterodox schools. In general, there is breakdown of commensality, civil society turning uncivil.

4.3.1 Cambridge Economic Club—A Marshallian Precursor: 1884–1890, 1896–?

Three references may be cited regarding the formation of an 'economic club' in Cambridge in the late nineteenth century. The first of these comes from the Archives of the Marshall Library which holds "two slim volumes of papers read to the Cambridge Economic Club; … no written record remains as to the circumstances of their deposit in the Marshall Library, but the first bears the name of John Ellis McTaggart of Trinity College and the list of contents of the second was written by Joseph Robson Tanner of St. John's, the first known President of the Club. They provide the only evidence that the 'Economic Society' was meeting as early as May 1884. The latest paper in these volumes is from 1890, after which it may have ceased to function." The archival introduction then cites the second reference below, with the implication that there was a break between 1890 and 1896 (Econclub 1, Cambridge Economic Club Papers, Marshall Library, Cambridge). The two volumes list of 22 papers on diverse themes, including two on "Socialism: Doctrines and Schemes" and "The Alternative to Socialism in England"; two on Karl Marx including "Comments on the Use of The Blue Books made by Karl Marx in Chapter XV of "Le Capital""; on "Co-operation"; one on "Factory Legislation"; one on "Some Problems of Popular Government"; two on "The Emancipation of Labour"; a couple on education and "The Economic Advantage of Introducing Manual Work into Schools" following the Swedish example; one on "Sir William Petty as an Economist"; another on "Poverty"; one on "The Logic of Statistical Method"; three on aspects of economic theory, including on the rate of interest, laws of distribution and on aspects of demand; one on "Trade and the Flag"; and one from a Japanese author comparing Japanese village communities with those described by Sir Henry Maine (whose influential writings had dealt with Indian villages). The first page of the first volume records "three points submitted for investigation to the 'Economic Society': possible evils resulting from employment of married women, health and life expectancy of factory workers, [and] women's wages" (Econclub 1/1 and 1/2, Marshall LBB 6, Marshall Library Archives).

The second reference to the existence of an Economic Club[41] in Cambridge is buried in a letter from Alfred Marshall to Frank William Taussig in 1896.[42]

---

[41] Whittaker (1996, p. 171n1) notes that "no records of the 'Economic Club' appear to have survived".

[42] Marshall to Taussig, Letter dated 14 October 1896, Letter 506. In Whittaker (1996, pp. 170–171).

Taussig had sought any chapter from Marshall's Vol II to publish in the *Quarterly Journal of Economics*. Marshall says, "The search has not succeeded, so now I have decided to offer you something else": a paper which Marshall was soon to deliver as "the opening address to an Economic club that is just being founded among the Junior Students here. Foxwell is Vice President, & I am President for this year". Marshall warns Taussig: "It is a slight & fragmentary thing ... quite inadequate ... not elaborated with any care or finish; I should have no hesitation in deciding it to be unworthy of your journal, if I had to be judge. But you said you wished English people wd write more for. You as an expression of sentiment: & if you happen to have a number, wh wants its specific gravity lowered by the admixture of a little miscellaneous jabber (about 6000, or 7000 words), perhaps you may like to have it *on approval*. ... I shan't be in the least surprised or offended if you 'regret that it is not suitable' &c." The paper appeared as "the Old Generation of Economists and the New" (Marshall, 1897). Keynes (1924, pp. 364–365) uses an extract from it in his obituary of Marshall. Keynes writes of his teacher as "the first who devoted his life to building up the subject as a separate science, standing on its own foundations, with as high standards of scientific accuracy as the physical or the biological sciences. It was Marshall who finally saw to it that never again will a Mrs. Trimmer, a Mrs. Marcet, or a Miss Martineau earn a goodly reputation by throwing economic principles into the form of a catechism or of simple tales, by aid of which any intelligent governess might make clear to the children nestling around her where lies economic truth" (Marshall, 1897). "But—much more than this, after his time Economics could never be again one of a number of subjects which a Moral Philosopher would take in his stride, one Moral Science out of several, as Mill, Jevons, and Sidgwick took it. He was the first to take up this professional, scientific attitude to the subject, as something above and outside current controversy, as far from politics as physiology from the general practitioner." The words and sentiments of Marshall and Keynes convey the orientation of the newly formed Economic Club.

The third is a fleeting allusion, in the webpage for Herbert Somerton Foxwell in the *History of Economic Thought* website, which mentions that Foxwell was the *first* President of the Cambridge Economic Club in 1897; this could be reconciled with Marshall's letter if the Foxwell entry is amended to give him the slightly reduced honour of being not the first but the *second* President of the Economic Club in 1897.

4.3.2 *Political Economy Club: From Keynes to Robertson to Kahn— Dazzling to Dour*

The Political Economy Club was primarily oriented towards high-performing undergraduates, and as such had a character distinct from the other series of seminars in the Faculty. Unlike the open entry to the Marshall Society (which started much later in 1927), "the Political Economy Club was a markedly elitist reserve where students could exercise their intelligence to the full"

(Marcuzzo et al., 2012, p. 18). Founded in 1909, it met on a fortnightly basis in Keynes's rooms, and "admission was solely by invitation, extended after careful selection" (ibid.) and, according to some, students would have to have gained a First in Part 1 of the Tripos to be included in the list of invitees. Austin Robinson provides a list of the members of the Political Economy Club for 1923/1924, which includes 32 names, drawn from 11 colleges, of which about 10 are faculty members. King's leads the list, with Keynes, Pigou and Shove the first three names; other faculty names include Robertson, E.A.G. Robinson, Ramsey and Dobb (EAGR/5/6/3–9, Marshall Library Archives).

Eric Hobsbawm (1967, p. 3) writes how Maurice Dobb, who got a first in Part 1 of the Tripos in 1921 and a first again in Part 2 in 1922, recalled Keynes's "support against bitter attacks by other undergraduates at one of the meetings of the Political Economy Club, though the older man had little contact with the younger, and certainly neither sympathy with nor understanding of Marx".

Keynes the originator was never found short on substance or style. In Cambridge, Lorie Tarshis who got a First in the distinguished cohort of 1934 recalls his experience of Keynes's political economy seminar, 'Keynes's club': "Sometimes—I guess usually—the paper and the discussion that followed it were merely the springboard from which after gentle criticism and encouragement for the students who had participated, he jumped into any or many related topics—with a wit, a grace and an imagination that were a joy to experience" (quoted with original source [Patinkin & Leith, 1977, pp. 50–51], in Marcuzzo & Sanfilippo, 2008, p. 74). Elsewhere, Tarshis[43] adds another reflection: "Keynes was exciting because he was Keynes—brilliant and frighteningly quick" (Tarshis, 1989, p. 918).

Dennis Robertson became the Professor of Political Economy, taking over the Chair vacated by Pigou on his retirement. The Vice Chancellor had offered the post to Keynes, who declined, citing his deteriorating health, his constraints on time and availability and his clearly expressed wish that in this regard no exceptions to the established norms be made. The Vice Chancellor then wrote to Robertson on 1 February 1944 (RFK/12/2/57). And so Robertson returned to Cambridge, also taking over the Political Economy Seminar which, with the changeover from Keynes, went from dazzling to dour.

Harry Johnson shares his experience of Keynes, Robertson and the Political Economy Club in the 1940s. How did this seminar work?

> They had in Cambridge a 'Political Economy Club' (it had been founded by Keynes) which had a set of rules based on the society of the 'Cambridge Apostles'. ... One of the rules was that somebody would read a paper, and before the paper was read those present would draw numbers from a hat. The numbers would run from 1 to 6, and this would determine the order in which you spoke. If there were more people present that six then there were blanks in the hat, and

---

[43] Tarshis wrote up his ideas in his PhD dissertation in 1939 and then carried these theoretical perspectives, experiences and enthusiasms back to America; they were the ingredients of his pioneering, but ill-fated, Keynesian textbook, *The Elements of Economics* in 1947.

if you drew one at the PEC you could heave a sigh of relief and devote yourself to getting close enough to Robertson's coal fire to keep you warm, Robertson was pretty much of a miser, and the coal fire was always lit but it never generated too much warmth. So that if you arrived a little later for the meeting you found yourself frozen, and you had to follow the lecture carefully as you shifted from foot to foot, or else you spent so much of your effort combating the cold that you could not follow what was going on. It made a great difference whether you had a number or not. If you had a number *and* came late, you were really in trouble. ... The membership included only those students who were *2–1's* or *firsts*.... Faculty members had the right to get up at any time, having interspersed themselves amongst the students. (Johnson, n.d., pp. 30–31; RFK/12/2/57/6–7)

Harry Johnson was 'eventually invited' by Robertson to join the Political Economy Club, and recalls his first and only encounter with Keynes when he was the guest speaker (just weeks before he died), and Johnson had picked the #1 chit to have the awesome task of commenting on Keynes's argument.[44] "Keynes was a brilliant phenomenon", but what struck Johnson the student was his style of participation.

One of the secrets of his charm was that when it was a student, he would go out of his way to make something flattering out of what the young man had said. If the student had made an absolute ass of himself, Keynes would still find something in it which he would transform into a good point. It might well be the very opposite of what the student had said; but the student was so relieved to find that he was not being cut to pieces that he was really impressed by the brilliance of what he was told he *had* said. On the other hand, when a faculty member got up ... he simply cut their heads off. No matter how ingenious what they said was, he would make nonsense of it. And that, again, flattered the students, because they had been told that they were really incisive and then somebody they knew was really clever was being reduced to rubble before their eyes. That was a doubly flattering thing. (ibid.)

And then, we have a glimpse from Robert Neild who attended the same (and final) talk given by Keynes at the Political Economy Seminar in early 1946: "[Although he] looked tired and weak ... he came to life in an extraordinary way. It was not what he said but how he said it. He had a gift with words I have never seen equalled. ... I liken him to Mozart: one could pluck musical

---

[44] Don Moggridge writes of Harry Johnson: "He met Keynes once, as a member of the Cambridge Political Economy Club in February 1946, when Keynes spoke on 'The balance of payments of the United States'. Harry took full notes of the speech (which Harrod used in his biography; Harrod, 1951, p. 622n)" (Moggridge, 2019, p. 506). Lloyd (2006) provides a summary of the Keynes's address, accompanied by an introduction from the Editors of the *Cambridge Journal of Economics* (2006); the talk was delivered on 2 February, and Keynes died on 21 April 1946.

notes from the air with magical effect, the other, words"[45] (Hodgson et al., 2018, p. 769).

Angus Maddison (1994) provides another student's snippet: "I was a member of the Political Economy Club set up by Keynes, and continued by Robertson, who selected the membership of about 20. It was the only seminar where students gave papers which were subject to discussion. I gave a paper on Anglo-American differences in industrial productivity, basing myself largely on Laszlo Rostas's new book which came out in 1948. This was the topic on which I wanted to do my graduate work, so I was grateful for Robertson's hospitality."

Maddison the student might have welcomed his cup of tea at the meeting, but from Robbins, coming up from London, we have a grumble about Robertson's abstemious hospitality: "In Trinity College, Robertson had inherited a desirable 'set' of rooms overlooking Great Court and situated between the Master's Lodging and the Chapel … In these rooms he entertained his guests and his pupils (supervisees) and held the meetings of the Political Economy Club which he took over from Keynes and organised very efficiently. Vaizey recalls 'frugal' teas being served and if this was due at least in part to the food rationing prevalent in the early days after the war, Robertson was never … 'lavish' with his hospitality. In fact he seemed to relish discomfort. He had nursed a life-long fear of poverty"—also having suffered significant personal financial losses in the Great Crash; "even so, suffering seems to have been taken to inordinate lengths." Robbins, in judging Robertson's life to have been 'lonely and often depressed', noted that "… even in regard to his physical environment he had an almost unique capacity for self-torture—he made his rooms at Trinity, splendidly placed looking over the great court, as uncomfortable and chilling to the spirit as it is easy to conceive" (Robbins, quoted and cited in Fletcher, 2008, pp. 232–233).

Robertson retired in 1957. With it ended his stewardship of what Tam Dalyell referred to as "the somewhat right-wing Political Economy Club".[46] And, so also, with it died the Political Economy Club; or did it? Intriguingly, in an exchange of letters with Ajit Singh over the latter's Queens' College seminar series that he started in the mid-1960s, Richard Kahn writes: "I have a clear memory that at a time when I was running the P.E. Club, I was able on more than one occasion to attend both the Mathematical Seminar and your Seminar." Hahn's Mathematical Seminar also began in the early to mid-1960s. This suggests that Kahn had taken over the running of the Keynes-Robertson Political

---

[45] Quotation cited in an interview of Robert Neild (2013b) by Hodgson et al. (2018); Neild's words are originally from a letter to Simon Keynes, dated 19 February 2007.

[46] Tam Dalyell recalled, in his obituary of Robin Matthews: "I shall never forget the calm composure with which he withstood an onslaught from the formidable left-winger Mrs. Joan Robinson on the one hand, and his contributions to Sir Dennis Robertson's somewhat right-wing Political Economy Club, on the other" (Mckittrick & Dalyell, 2010); this would date it to 1956/1957 when Dalyell was up at Cambridge.

Economy Club; and also that Kahn was running this, as well as his Monday 'secret' seminar at King's simultaneously; the latter series was stopped by Kahn in 1969—but what about the PEC? Cambridge seniors, such as Geoff Harcourt, cannot explicitly recall Kahn running the PEC alongside his King's seminar. But clarification is provided by Richard Kahn himself, as reported in Cristina Marcuzzo's extensive document recording her interviews with Kahn in the mid–late 1980s. Included prominently in the diverse and heavy responsibilities that Richard Kahn had on his shoulders in the post-war period, and particularly after the death of Keynes, is the Political Economy Club. "I took over from Keynes and Dennis Robertson the Political Economy Club. The members were the best undergraduates studying economics, some graduate students and a number of University teachers. An undergraduate read a paper; it was then discussed by a number of undergraduates followed by some of the University teachers. The Club served as a breeding ground for the leading undergraduates. With the growth of College Economic Seminars, the Club has now[47] lapsed. Since its establishment by Keynes in 1910 its record was remarkable" (Kahn & Marcuzzo, 2020, p. 26).

4.3.3 *The Marshall Society: A Socialisation into Economics and Its Purposes*

The Marshall Society held its inaugural meeting on 9 February 1927; the minutes[48] state its purpose was "to bring together members of the university and of the women's colleges who were interested in social questions; to increase an interest in such questions in the University and women's colleges; and to study these questions unbiased by Political or Religious prejudices. ... The Society initially met in The Marshall Library and had 119 members by the Easter Term 1927. It had two main interest groups: economics and industrial welfare and education. These later changed" (Marsoc1; Marshall Society Papers). The orientation founding members—who included Philip

---

[47] Kahn does not specify to which year 'now' applies. He retired in 1972, so the PEC would have stopped then, or by then; further, Kahn pulled down the shutters on his King's 'secret seminar' in 1969, and it may be speculated that it is unlikely that he would have wished still to carry on with an undergraduate seminar after that closure. Ajit Singh joined Queens' College in 1965 and set up his economics seminar there prior to 1969—it is known that his seminar ran in parallel with the 'secret seminar'. Kahn explicitly observes that he had been able to attend the PEC and Ajit's Queens' Seminar in those years, so the PEC was still running in the second half of the 1960s. Ron Smith confirms: "I gave a paper to the PEC in 1967–1968 as a third-year undergraduate. I was not a regular and was only invited the once. I had submitted an econometric paper for the Adam Smith Prize and that prompted the invitation" (Personal communication). Without an explicit date, the stoppage could most likely have been either in 1969, when he stopped the secret seminar, or in 1972, when he retired. A reviewer of this manuscript observed that the PEC was still running (sponsored by Kahn) in the late 1960s. Not much hangs on whether the PEC stopped after functioning for, say, 59 years or 62 years.

[48] The records of the Marshall Society are available as Marshall Society Papers, Marshall Library of Economics, University of Cambridge.

Sargent Florence[49] as President, Maurice Dobb as Treasurer, and Pat Sloan[50] and David Archer[51] as Joint Secretaries—is indicative of the ideological impulse of the Society at the point of origin in favour of left-humanist positions. Honorary Vice Presidents included, among others, John Maynard Keynes, Mary Paley Marshall, Goldsworthy Lowes-Dickinson[52] and A.C. Pigou.

With regard to the minutes of the first meeting of the MS for 9 February 1927, Matthew Chambers (2020)[53] quotes the text of some promotional material: "Have you ever thought of taking an interest in the lives of other people? In all of us as a community? Of the boons of some and of the sorrows and difficulties of others? Oh, no, not a political society; nor a religious society—but

[49] Philip Sargent Florence, an American, was an 'indirect', or second rung Marshallian, that is "indirectly, because as students after Marshall's retirement, they were trained by his 'pupils'" (Groenewegen, 2007, p. 2); he was then a lecturer in Cambridge, later a professor in Birmingham. He was an active 'design enthusiast', part of the 'Birmingham Group' connected with the Bloomsbury set. He had a grand residence, "with plenty of land, including a lake, [on which] it was proposed to build a single block of twenty-four flats" (MacCarthy, 2019); the [Louis] MacNeices lived in the coach house of his "sumptuous house [which] was open to all with something to contribute to the discussions" on the "shared interest in realistic depictions of working-class life ..." (Stray, 2019, p. 13).

[50] Pat Sloane, a member of the Communist Party of Great Britain (CPGB), was variously described as a "Party stalwart", "a commissar of Party orthodoxy" or "Pat Sloan, the Communist, Left Book Club author and Stalinising Russophile" (Smith 2005–2008, p. 364); she later edited *John Cornford: A Memoir*, Jonathan Cape 1938. Cornford, born to privilege and a great-grandson of Charles Darwin, was an internationalist and communist, and was at Trinity College, Cambridge, before he fought and fell in the Spanish Civil War in 1936, aged 21.

[51] "David [Archer] went up to Cambridge in 1925, examining (sic) in economics and psychology with a special subject in the British novel, earning his BA in 1928. Most formatively, during his time at Cambridge, he co-founded the Marshall Society. During the time of Archer's involvement ... the minutes show David to be an active member: ... volunteering to coordinate the Industrial Welfare and Educational Group, joining the Arts Committee to help produce ads, putting his name to an unrealized plan to start a journal ...." Later after Cambridge, "David Archer's bookshop at 4 Parton Street, became most famous for publishing Dylan Thomas's first book; ... for a time, the street gave its name to a community of poets, artists, and activists moved by W.H. Auden, Dylan Thomas, surrealism, the Communist Party of Great Britain (CPGB), and the Spanish Civil War; [David Archer's bookshop] ... brought all those individuals and interests together" (Chambers, 2020; some text rearranged).

[52] Dickinson (1862–1932), a free-thinking radical humanist with diverse academic and political interests and "possessing considerable poetic and musical skill", was fellow of King's College; lectured on political science in Cambridge and also at the LSE; "at the invitation of Professor Marshall, in 1903, helped to establish the Economics Tripos"; served as "first secretary of the Economics Board"; a convinced pacifist, he was also, from 1915, the progenitor of the idea of a League of Nations, which, a few years later, came to pass; joined the Labour Party in the 1920s and was closely associated with the Bloomsbury group; as a youth, he worked at a co-operative farm as part of "an experiment in simple living; he was proud of his hoeing, digging, and ploughing". en.wikipedia.org/wiki/Goldsworthy_Lowes_Dickinson; other details are drawn from the Cambridge University Alumni Database at:

http://venn.lib.cam.ac.uk/cgibin/search018.pl?sur=&suro=w&fir=&firo=c&cit=&cito=c&c=all&z=all&tex=DKN881GL&sye=&eye=&col=all&maxcount=50).

[53] Chambers cites the source of this quotation as: "T.E.B. Howarth, *Cambridge between the Wars*, London: William Collins Sons & Co., 1978, pp. 150–1."

a society unmoved by such prejudices." From the start till May 1928, "the society hosted talks with a strong social welfare emphasis, took field trips to local villages and the social settlement Toynbee Hall in London, and there was apparently an unrealized plan to start a journal" (ibid.). Later, a regular magazine, *The Cambridge Economist* was launched and ran under that name till 2013.

From Alec Cairncross's fine biography of Austin Robinson, we have a good glimpse of the early life and times of the Marshall Society. "Before the war contacts with staffs of other universities were very limited. Almost the only economists from elsewhere whom on ever saw in Cambridge were Keynes's guests or invited speakers at his Monday night Political Economy Club. When Philip Sargant Florence helped to create the Marshall Society in the 1920s for the benefit of undergraduates, few dons attended its meetings and the speakers were nearly all business men or politicians, not theoretical economists. At the time when took his Tripos, Austin knew hardly any economists from outside Cambridge except Hawtrey, whom he had encountered over lunch with Keynes. Later, when he was doing research for a short time, he met Ohlin and a daughter of Cassel where were then the only other postgraduate students in Cambridge. Once he succeeded Florence in 1929 as President of the Marshall Society,[54] he met many speakers from outside Cambridge, but, as before, few were economists. He came to know more economists as an external examiner and (by correspondence at least) when he had to find reviewers for the *Economic Journal* from 1934. But it was not until the war years that he encountered in person a wide circle of economists outside Cambridge. This was a not uncommon experience at any British university in those days. There were no economic conferences, either in Britain or abroad, no international organizations in need of staff, no spells in government, no research teams drawn together to work on a common project Economists worked almost whole-time as teachers and very much on their own, preparing an occasional article or making slow progress with a piece of research in such spare time as they had. Within Cambridge the opportunities for discussion were limited ... All faculty members were heavily engaged in university lecturing and college supervision and, as Harry Johnson emphasized in a paper on 'Cambridge as an Academic Environment in the early 1930s', the economists were scattered around the colleges and had few occasions to come together" (Cairncross, 1993, pp. 38–40).

The intellectually stimulating and catalytic role played by the early seminar series, viz., the Marshall Society and the Political Economy Seminar, have to be appreciated against this backdrop of isolation in which regard Cambridge, as Cairncross points out, was not exceptional or different from the experience of other universities. Intellectual exchanges and transactions with 'the outside world' changed dramatically after the war, but in Cambridge even during the war years as LSE relocated to Cambridge.

---

[54] Austin continued "to look after the Marshall Society", at least till 1939 (Cairncross, 1993, p. 38).

Cairncross's recollection that speakers were mostly businessmen and that dons were mostly missing might have applied to the first decade, but from the 1930s, the Marshall Society was the forum for an early airing or interrogation of many significant theoretical and policy interventions that were then dominating contemporary discourse or that were still on the anvil and emerged a little later in their fully fleshed-out form; as such it was much more than simply an undergraduate extracurricular activity in the timetable. The vigorous spirit and ethos of the transactions is richly evoked by Maria Cristina Marcuzzo. As Marcuzzo et al. (2012, p. 17) point out with regard to the attitude to teaching, "it was necessary to win over the hearts and minds of the students" … "ultimately, a great deal was seen to be at stake, which accounts for both the fierceness of the clashes and the spirit of proselytism that characterized the work of, say, Kahn, or Joan Robinson". According to A.M.C. Waterman, a pupil supervised by Joan in the 1950s: "She expected that we would immediately see the point and become her allies in the godly crusade against the dragon of neoclassical orthodoxy—which she saw as ideological tear-gas, blinding us to all the worst feature of a capitalism she hated with the enthusiastic zeal of a true believer" (Waterman, 2003, pp. 593–594, quoted in Marcuzzo et al., ibid.).

The Marshall Society, which was open to all comers, undergraduates, staff and guests, convened weekly in a room above the Marshall Library. Presentations often came in for 'scathing criticism', as in the case of the hapless Mr. Coates who obviously came in for a tongue-lashing, as Maria Cristina Marcuzzo (2012, p. 18) records: "Joan Robinson, a great debater, attended the Marshall Society assiduously in the 1930s," and as might be expected when she was in full flow, the seminar would shed light while emitting even more heat. In Joan's own words in a subsequent letter to Kahn: "Mr Coates turns out to be even nastier than he is stupid and stupider that you could believe. I baited him scandalously to the unconcealed delight of the Marshall Society. Towards the end there were shouts of No, and loud laughter at everything he said" (Kahn Papers, 13/90/1/168–169; quoted by Marcuzzo).

An intriguing sampler from the first three decades—regrettably all before the possibility of video recording—includes: John Maynard Keynes on "The Causes of the Slump" in 1931, and on "The Economic Outlook 1932" in 1932; Maurice Dobb on "The Marxian Theory of Imperialism" in 1934; John Maynard Keynes on "War Potential and War Finance" in 1939, and on "Bretton Woods" in 1945; Nicholas Kaldor on "Inflation and Stabilisation in Hungary" in 1946; Richard Kahn on "The Civil Service as seen by an Economist" in 1946; Evsey Domar on "The Problem of Economic Growth" in 1953; Milton Friedman on "The Case for Flexible Exchange Rates" in 1953; Joan Robinson on "Problems of Indian Growth" in 1955; James Meade on "The Common Market" in 1957; Dennis Robertson on "The Reflections of an Ex Magus" in 1959; Roy Harrod on "The Radcliffe Report" in 1959.

On the suggestion of Hubert Henderson, in 1927 Keynes had commissioned Roy Harrod to write a book on International Economics for the *Cambridge Economic Handbooks* series. The completion of the book, which was originally intended to serve as a general introduction, was much delayed, but "went much further and introduced a key concept in international trade, the foreign trade multiplier" (Caldentey (2019, p. 46). Marcuzzo and Rosselli (2005) report that in March 1932, Roy Harrod presented his paper, "The Theory of Balance of Foreign Payments" at the Marshall Society, "which stimulated some correspondence with Kahn in which Harrod apparently expounded the first version of his foreign trade multiplier".

However, not every customer was happy, and a less sanguine view comes from John Barnes, who took his B.A. in 1939, and was later to be the first Chair holder of Sociology, had contemplated doing an Economics Tripos, till he found the subject and prospect too dull and boring. "I joined the Marshall Society, the university economics club, but found its meetings dull compared with those of the university English club where I listened to talks by T. S. Eliot and other literary giants. I gradually forgot about switching to economics ..." (Barnes, 2007, pp. 46–47).

Times change, and 90 years is a good and long stretch: the Marshall Society is still up and running, even if not perhaps in any radical iconoclastic direction, having realigned its compass from the original left-humanist societal idealism or hard politics towards a city-corporate-career seeking orientation. Its proudly announced list of financial sponsors includes: Citadel ("leading investors in the world's financial markets"; Cornerstone Research ("an economic consulting firm providing financial analysis and expert testimony in all phases of commercial litigation and regulatory proceedings"); FTI Consulting ("a global business advisory firm"; NERA Economic Consulting ("a global firm of experts dedicated to applying economic, finance and quantitative principles to complex business and legal challenges ... dedicated to methodically applying microeconomic theory to litigation and regulatory matters"); RBB Economics ("provides expert economic advice on all aspects of competition law, including mergers, restrictive agreements etc"; and Oxford Economics ("is a leader in global forecasting and quantitative analysis with the world's only fully integrated economic model and 250 full-time economists"). Earlier, there was apparently a distinction between 'premier sponsors', such as Deloitte and Deutsche Bank, and 'ordinary corporate sponsors', such as UBS, Merrill Lynch and PricewaterhouseCoopers. One current mission statement announces that "we offer academic and speaker events on contemporary economic issues, career events for those interested in areas such as banking and consulting, and social events including a Winter Ball and Garden Party that continuously sell out" (https://ec.linkedin.com/company/the-marshall-society). In 2013, *The Cambridge Economist* was renamed *The Dismal Economist* "in an attempt to breach the confines of Cambridge and broaden the horizon for ideas"—a long jump to a recognition that Cambridge as a place no longer had a distinctive status or intellectual pulling power in the discipline that it once boasted.

4.3.4 Piero Sraffa's Research Students Seminar: A Precocious Nursery

Piero's Seminar was up and running by the early 1930s—possibly as early as 1931–1932 as indirectly indicated by Austin Robinson—though Geoff Harcourt (1995a, p. 40) mentions that at the time of Lorie Tarshis, "there were very few Ph.D students around Cambridge in the 1930s. There was Tew[55] and there was Tarshis, but the graduate school, as we now call it, was non-existent. There'd be just one or two people working for a Ph.D."; Tarshis's PhD was from 1939.

Maria Cristina Marcuzzo's archival dig excavates some interesting snippets on Sraffa in relation to the research seminar and related matters. On his appointment in May 1927, Sraffa was advised by Keynes that "Sraffa should not accept too many students but limit himself to five or at the most ten 'specially selected men, possibly research students'" (Marcuzzo, 2008, p. 52). Sraffa resigned from his lectureship in 1931 and from 1935, became the Assistant Director of Research (ADR), overcoming his reluctance to relinquish his post as librarian of the Marshall Library and the 'time' freedoms that it bestowed; "he was ... ill-disposed to have a set timetable to receive students" (ibid., p. 58). Sraffa's held the position of ADR—which was "equalized with the role of lecturer"—till 1965, *en route* being made a reader in 1963. This time sequence suggests that the Sraffa seminar for research students might have begun its 30-year life around 1935. In parallel, he was appointed secretary of the Degree Committee, holding the position till 1965, dealing with the admission of research students to various research degrees, and the choice of their thesis topics and their supervisors. Marcuzzo tells us that "Sraffa was a very assiduous member of the committee, hardly ever absent in the thirty years he spent on it" (ibid., p. 60).

Maria Cristina Marcuzzo provides a fascinating account of a couple of interactions between Keynes, Sraffa and his research student seminar, which simultaneously shed light on Keynes's mode of working, as well on the exciting nature of the seminar itself. In October 1937, Keynes asked Sraffa "to submit a problem to the students, namely, how to account for the fact that the quota of wages and salaries in the income of the United States remained fairly steady, at around 66%, between 1919 and 1935, although prices and wages had undergone huge fluctuations; moreover, how was it that a very similar percentage

---

[55] Hsu was also a graduate student at the time, in 1938. Marcuzzo (2008, p. 63), in writing on the unfortunate exchange between a committee comprising Austin Robinson, Sraffa and Champernowne on the one side and Kalecki on the other over the latter's report on his case studies on the economics of specific industries, mentions, "the collaboration of two research students Hsu and Tew, who were attending Sraffa's seminar"; in the face of this committee's criticism, "Kalecki responded by resigning from his post, turning his back on Cambridge once and for all to leave for Oxford at the end of the summer of 1939 probably with the help of Sraffa." Cord (2013, p. 36) cites the letter where Sraffa, a little mischievously, reports to Joan Robinson about Kalecki who had "settled down to work quite happily, with his two research students (Tew and Hsu, of whom only one is a Chinese): he certainly is a great success with them, and they are very devoted to him)".

emerged from the statistics on other countries, too? Keynes asked Sraffa to get his students to 'rack their brains' to see if the data were in fact credible, and what the explanation was. ... Sraffa responded immediately and enthusiastically ..." (Marcuzzo, 2008, pp. 58–59). Incidentally, answers came from Kalecki, "who followed Sraffa's seminar while he was at Cambridge" (ibid.), with a paper by him being published by him in 1938 on this; a second response came from another seminar participant, J.T. Dunlop, and yet another from Lorie Tarshis; Keynes apparently published both in the *Economic Journal* in 1938 and 1939, respectively (ibid., p. 60). A week after the first, Keynes sent a second query for Sraffa to process in his seminar: "whether it was 'historically correct' to say ... that the traditional theory 'never held that Saving and Investment could not be unequal', but only that 'their inequality [...] was inconsistent with equilibrium" (ibid., p. 60). Marcuzzo observes that "unfortunately, no evidence has survived of the students showing any reaction ..." These instances testify to the highly accomplished level of interactions within the Sraffa seminar which seemed to have this characteristic of becoming, on call, a collective thinking unit. But Marcuzzo perceptively observes that these episodes "show just how Keynes counted on him [Sraffa] to nurture and train the research of the budding economists at Cambridge. At the same time they show how Keynes himself worked, thriving on the criticism, suggestion and prompts that he sought to draw from colleagues, pupils and students. Unlike Sraffa, Keynes needed a scientific community to refer to, interacting with in and acting within it" (Marcuzzo, 2008, p. 59).

These illustrations might encourage a conclusion that Sraffa was a hands-on, one-to-one, research supervisor, but any such generalisation could well be unwarranted. "Sraffa accepted supervision of a very limited number of students, and a large proportion of those initially assigned to Sraffa would find themselves under another supervisor after one term, or a year at most. The total number of students who came under Sraffa's supervision is somewhere in the region of fifteen, of which one alone appears to have completed his thesis under his supervision" (ibid., p. 61).[56] But Cristina Marcuzzo registers a very appropriate caution in this regard. "Sraffa's modest 'official' showing may prove misleading; actually, he exerted great influence over the directions taken in research by a great many students who were attracted to Cambridge to a large extent, possibly even above all, by his presence there, especially in the final years and even when he had retired" (ibid., p. 61).

A second insightful window into the functioning of Sraffa's Research Students Seminar opens into the 1950s; glimpses are provided, even if in

---

[56] A qualification is appropriate here. Baranzini and Mirante (2018, p. 50), having "carefully checked the *Cambridge University Reporter*" [for the 1950s], found that research students were usually promoted to PhD candidate status at the earliest after six terms, and often after 6, 9 or even 12 terms; "supervisors were in general quite severe in their reports to the Degree Committee. ... We know of research students who simply dropped out, or who submitted their thesis after 18, 21 or even 24 terms, in a limited number of cases with success" (ibid., p. 51). Sraffa's score sheet thus might appear to be worse than it really might have been in this overall scenario.

passing, by Geoff Harcourt and Luigi Pasinetti, who started off as Cambridge contemporaries, both in the Sraffa seminar, and are now the two senior most gurus and reservoirs of knowledge on Cambridge economics. The Seminar was clearly in full flow in the post-war years. Geoff Harcourt (1999a, pp. 39–40) confirms that he served as the research student in charge of the Seminar in 1955–1956; speaking of the 1955–1958 cohort, he observes: "These were exceptional vintage years, with Tom Asimakopoulos, Charles Feinstein, Piero Garegnani, Geoff Harcourt, Luigi Pasinetti, Amartya Sen, and a bunch of others"; elsewhere, Geoff also mentions Aubrey Silberston and "Hugh Hudson, who by common consent was the brightest of us all 'adopted' by Robinson and Kahn and won the Stephenson Prize" (Harcourt, 2007); and elsewhere, he lists also "a whole host of bright Australians"—Allan Barton, Keith Frearson, John Harper, Hugh Hudson, Duncan Ironmonger and John McCarthy (Harcourt 1999a, p. 63n). He recalls that Robin Marris invited him to give a paper at Sraffa's Seminar and that was when he met Joan Robinson for the first time; subsequently he gave two papers to the graduate Seminar on Joan's *Accumulation of Capital* (published in 1956). Geoff recalls that "when I came to Cambridge in the Michaelmas Term of 1955 to do a PhD, Piero was the mentor, together with Robin Marris, of the research students. They presided over the main research students' seminar which was held each Thursday afternoon of Full Term in the old Marshall Library in Downing Street, and which was noted for the provision of tea and chocolate biscuits. We all admired Piero, but were very much in awe of him" (Harcourt 2016a, p. 258). From personal experience, Geoff Harcourt notes that "Sraffa could be a disconcerting chair of the seminar, for his comments and questions were often as unexpected as they were unnerving". Geoff remembers that "at that time [Piero] was rather reserved, partly because, though the Ricardo volumes … had been published … he had not yet delivered his *magnum* opus, *Production of Commodities by Means of Commodities* [1960]. Moreover, he was still recovering from the serious injuries he incurred when he had a bad fall while climbing. He fractured his skull and temporarily lost his memory"; but later, "when I returned to Cambridge in 1963, … he was a changed person, at ease with himself and fulfilled" (Harcourt 2016a, p. 259).

There were some stellar performances: "Amartya Sen impressed us all by having the paper he read to the class published in the *Economic Journal*.[57] It certainly provided inspiration" (Harcourt 1999a, pp. 39–40); and Luigi Pasinetti apparently stunned the seminar with a mathematical exposition of the Wicksell Effect, something none of the students or some of the staff such as Robin Marris were aware or in control of, this impressive presentation being

---

[57] Presumably, Sen, Amartya Kumar, "A Note on Tinbergen on the Optimum Rate on Saving", *Economic Journal*, Volume 67, Issue 268, December 1957, pp. 745–748. Incidentally, Sen published four papers in *Economic Weekly* in 1956 and another two in 1957: one on the choice of capital intensity in development planning in the *Quarterly Journal of Economics* and the other in *Economic Weekly*, apart from any others that might have escaped attention.

the basis for Luigi to be exceptionally admitted to the formal status of a PhD candidate after just two terms, a most unusual, if not unique feat at the time. Pasinetti recounts: "On the instruction of my supervisor Richard Goodwin I was probably the only research student what had read Wicksell, and in this way I was able to explain in rigorous terms the Wicksell effect to my fellow research students and even to dons, like Robin Marris" (quoted in Baranzini & Mirante, 2018, p. 51n34). Elsewhere, Geoff recalls his own seminar performance where his presentation ran into Piero in a querulous mood!

There was still a decade between this famous cohort of the 1950s and Piero Sraffa's retirement in 1965, but it is striking what little, if any at all, mention is made of the Sraffa Seminar for the rest of the period till Sraffa's retirement, and the Seminar's end, in 1965. Notably, the early 1960s were also the years when Frank Hahn was assiduously sowing the seeds of his nursery, or his 'academy' as some called it. Unsurprisingly, he, and his campaign partner Robin Matthews, held rather baleful views on their intellectual adversaries. Thus, Robin Matthews, in his comments on the 'secret seminar' in an interview (1989, pp. 914–915), is rather disdainful of Sraffa's influence in the 1950s: "Sraffa came hardly ever. Nor did he ever lecture. It is a myth of later creation that Sraffa was an intellectually influential figure in Cambridge at this time. Any influence he may have had, except perhaps within Trinity, was mediated mainly through private conversations with Joan and Richard." That was the somewhat disparaging manner in which Matthews, looking back from the 1980s, referred to Sraffa; the grudging, if not negative, attitude perhaps also permeates the treatment in the Hahn-Matthews 1964 survey of the theory of economic growth, where "Sraffa's model [*Production of Commodities*, 1960] is somewhat dismissively treated on a par with similar 'Leontief-Samuelson-Sraffa' multi-sector models" (Newbery, 2017, p. 518).

Hahn was imported from Birmingham in 1960: "Look, when I was brought to Cambridge as a young man, I was to become Joan's disciple. It was just impossible! I was very friendly with her and Richard and she were extremely kind to me. But it was often impossible to follow her; she was incoherent, that is all I can say" (Hahn, 1989a, p. 904). Hahn, of course, took the other road. Joe Stiglitz came to Cambridge for 1965–1966 and testifies to the rising star of 'Uncle Frank' and his 'nephews'. Joe had been assigned Joan Robinson as his tutor and had fallen out with her after "a tumultuous relationship" (as had Frank Hahn earlier). "She wasn't used to the kind of questioning stance of a brash American student ... and after one term, I switched to Frank Hahn. He was flamboyant, and always intellectually provocative. Cambridge was in ferment. The quality of the students and the young lecturers matched that of the gray eminces (*sic*): Jim Mirrlees ..., Partha Dasgupta, Tony Atkinson, Geoff Heal, David Newbery and a host of others. There was a sense of excitement ..." (Stiglitz, 2002). The 1960s witnessed the spectacular spread and ascent of this cohort, managed brilliantly by Hahn: they acquired their PhDs and were immediately seated in chairs in various (new and traditional) universities.[58] Also in the early 1960s, Frank Hahn strode out from the wings, threw his hat into the ring and set up his Churchill 'Mathematical' Seminar consciously intended as direct competition to Kahn's secret seminar. And it would appear that while the fortunes of H seminar rose, those of the K seminar dwindled till Kahn terminated it in 1969; and incidentally, Kahn recalls attending the Hahn Mathematical Seminar on occasion.

Thus, the 1960s saw a full-scale change in the configuration of seminars in and around the Faculty: Sraffa's research students seminar brought its shutters down in 1965, and Kahn did the same for his secret seminar in 1969; thus, the two long-running seminars on the heterodox side fell into silence; in this space, Ajit Singh had set up his stall at Queens' College with his Political Economy Seminar in the mid-1960s, also overlapping with the secret seminar for a few years. On the other side, following the 1957 closure of the (Keynes) Robertson Political Economy Club/Seminar, Hahn opened up his Churchill Seminar in the early sixties. New generations of rivals had stepped into the old vacated spaces. In Hirschman terminology, the young heterodox economists (such as Ajit Singh, Bob Rowthorn et al) were loyal to the cause, but were not given 'voice', being largely excluded from the Kahn enterprise, so there was a semi-enforced 'exit' and they set up their own seminar at Queens'; the Hahn group exhibited an absence of 'loyalty' to the Kahn seminar, experienced a lack of 'voice' there, and also staged an 'exit', also setting up a seminar space of their own. Both new constituencies, at Queens' with Ajit Singh and at Churchill with Frank Hahn, displayed strong intra-group loyalty, enjoyed freedoms of voice. From rivalry within shared seminar spaces, the new configuration was marked by differentiation, polarisation and generally mutual exclusion.

However, it would appear that, for a while, nothing systematic replaced the Sraffa seminar for research students after 1965. Neither this Seminar nor any descendent was in regular operation in 1972, when I came as a doctoral student, though I recall that a small dedicated band of (mostly) Italian visiting academics and research students did frequently seek Piero's wisdom.[59] The absence of a regular graduate seminar was keenly felt and induced the spontaneous formation of an informal South Asia Economics Seminar which held frequent meetings in the 1970s where research scholars (mostly) from the region put up various drafts of chapters or articles for scrutiny by the unusually large regional cohort that had joined Cambridge economics in the early 1970s

---

[58] The progression of this cohort through the early stages of their careers, under Hahn's tutelage, is elaborated upon in Chapter 2. Mirrlees (working with Stone) obtained his PhD in 1963; Bliss in 1966; Dasgupta and Heal both in 1968; Newbery did not get his PhD till 1976 but was at Cambridge through the period.

[59] Alfredo Medio, Ricardo Parboni, Paolo Garonna, Heinrich Bortis and also the Canadian John Burbidge who had studied under Tom Asimakopoulos were all around and active; contrary to popular imagination, though, not all Italian research scholars were working on Sraffian economics!

following the formation of Bangladesh.[60] Ken Coutts, who joined in 1971 and became the Assistant Director of Research (ADR) in the Faculty in 1988, refers to "an informal series run by research students" for some years; "later the graduate research seminar became formal and was incorporated into the research training programme where students gave presentations of their first-year work and also gave job seminars" (personal communication).

4.3.5 In Retrospect, Austin Robinson on the Cambridge Circus: The Engine Room of The General Theory

Much is known about the famed Cambridge Circus of the 1930s and this makes it unnecessary to dig and dwell further on this theme. That said, a couple of reflections, coming straight from (one of the) horse's mouth, might be worth an airing.[61]

In a letter dated 19 September 1989 to Austin Robinson, Paul Samuelson asks two questions. First "My correspondent claimed that Sraffa had *started* the Circus for Keynes—what truth can there be in this? (emphasis in the original)". The second question concerned the role of "the Oxford contingent, Roy and James"—did they have "more peripheral involvement than the rest ... [or were] they quite important in their own right"?

Austin Robinson's reply, dated 29 September 1989, starts: "What very difficult questions you ask. Let me do my best." After bringing Samuelson up to speed on his confusion about Sraffa's role,[62] he explains the sequence of two stages of the Circus:

> One has to think of the Circus in two separate parts. First came what I regard as the creative part of the Circus, when five of us sat round and argued. That went on through part of the October term of 1930 and the Lent term of 1931. ..... The Circus was extremely informal at this first stage. It grew out of the worry of Joan and myself over the problems of teaching our pupils. The second stage grew out of ideas that were thrown up in the process of these early discussions. By the end of that [first stage] we had reached a point where we had something that might be communicated to others and the second part, which was much more formal,

---

[60] The list of South Asian doctoral research scholars during the first half of the 1970s included: Iqbal Ahmed, Rashid Amjad, Monojit Chatterji, Abu Haroon Wahiduddin Mahmud Chaudhury, Naeemuddin Chowdhury, Ajit Ghose, Mahabub Hossain, Satish Mishra, Ghazi Mujahid, Muhammed Muqtada, Sikander Rahim, Atiqur Rahman, Ashwani Saith, Sam Samarasinghe, Abhijit Sen, Vela Velupillai and Piyasiri Wickramasekhara (Saith, 2019, p. 166). Nine of seventeen had Bengali as their mother tongue; and predictably, the designated chair at the seminar quite often had a hard time keeping English as the lingua franca at the presentations, especially when the discussion got animated, which was more than quite often.

[61] Source: EAGR/5/6/3–9, Marshall Library Archives.

[62] "I can say categorically that it was not Piero Sraffa who started it. He was not that sort of person. If there was anything that it was his duty to do, he did it. He never went round trying to think of things which might be done and starting them up. But when it was his duty to do something, he was extremely conscientious."

began. We held in effect, a faculty seminar. Admission to it was by selection of first class people by Piero Sraffa and myself, I was secretary of the faculty and could act in that capacity. Piero Sraffa was responsible for graduate students and knew them and he was the right person to select from them. But that was Piero's only formal relationship to the Circus. Piero had a very remarkable capacity for silence. When he had something to say he said it. When he had nothing to say, he sat in silence.

James Meade was invited "because he was interested"; Piero Sraffa was invited "because he was a close friend with an interest".

Luigi Pasinetti provides a brief description: "It was in 1930, that Kahn started chairing and conducting the so-called 'Cambridge Circus', a group (or rather a closed club) of young Cambridge economists (which included Joan and Austin Robinson, Piero Sraffa and James Meade, besides Kahn) that was originally set up to discuss Keynes' *Treatise on Money*, but then went on regularly to discuss, criticize and propose changes to subsequent drafts of what was to become Keynes's *General Theory*" (Pasinetti, 1991, p. 428).

And Geoff Harcourt rounds it off typically with a fascinating anecdotal insight which conveys the sense and texture of these animated discussions. "It was Margaret Meade, James' wife, who described the nature of the Circus. It was like a Greek play in which the principal character was never seen, Kahn was the messenger from the gods who took the findings of the Circus to tell Keynes what their criticisms were. Keynes would tell him why they were wrong or why he agreed with them. Kahn would then return and give then the messages from the god, a very vivid scene, I think, but quite in keeping with Margaret Meade, as I remember her" (Harcourt, 2012b, p. 16).[63]

4.3.6 Cambridge–LSE Joint Seminar: Jousting Juniors

There was never a cross-country traffic jam of economists between Cambridge and Oxford; London was served always as the interconnecting hub.

Marcuzzo and Sanfilippo (2008) refer to the plethora of seminar series involving Cambridge and London: the London Political Economy Club founded in 1822; the Economic Club, founded in 1891, drawing economists from LSE, Cambridge and the rest of London generally and which shifted base from University College London to LSE under Beveridge in 1923; and three others: the 'Joint Seminar', started in November 1935, involving mainly research students but also some seniors, from LSE and Cambridge; Piero Sraffa's Seminar for Cambridge Graduate Students; and an equivalent one at

---

[63] Aslanbeigui and Oakes (2002, p. 13) have a variation on this theme as reported by James Meade, presumably Margaret's source: "From the point of view of a humble mortal like myself Keynes seemed to plan the role of God in a morality play; he dominated the play but rarely appeared himself on the stage. Kahn was the Messenger Angel who brought messages and problems from Keynes to the 'circus' and who went back to Heaven with the results of our deliberations." The source for both would be Moggridge (1973).

LSE, the Hayek Seminar especially for his students. No doubt others could be added, for instance, the Tuesday Club patronised, amongst others, by Keynes in the 1920s. "In November 1922, [Dennis Robertson] was elected under Keynes's patronage into membership of the Tuesday Club, a private dining club whose members—academics, bankers, civil servants and journalists—met for uninhibited discussion of economic and financial questions at the Café Royal in London" (Fletcher, 2008, p. 87). And there are references to the Tuesday Club much later in the Austin Robinson papers, concerning the (successful) nomination of Robert Neild to the membership of the Club.

Drawing on a set of 88 letters—that serendipitously became available to them recently—between John Hicks and Ursula Webb exchanged during the three months before their marriage in December 1935, Marcuzzo and Sanfilippo sketch some insightful and delightful images of the intellectual and personal transactions between some of the leading lights of Cambridge and LSE in an era where their rivalry and animosities were becoming explosive. Yet even in this intellectual strife, there are institutionalised spaces for intellectual jousting and challenges to be fought out face to face in a series of seminars, whether every Monday over tea at the LSE in London under Robbins, or every other Monday over tea and fruit cake at King's College in Cambridge under Keynes. The styles of the seminars followed the personalities of the gurus and were quite distinct. "Robbins's seminar was more cosmopolitan, attracting mostly Continental scholars and visitors passing through London, while Keynes's seminar was much more imbued with the clubby atmosphere that permeated Cambridge societies and colleges. Moreover, the two theoretical approaches favoured at the LSE and Cambridge could not be farther apart" (Marcuzzo & Sanfilippo, 2008, p. 74). A.K. Dasgupta—father of Partha Dasgupta (of Cambridge, LSE and Cambridge) who did his PhD under Robbins—refers to "Robbins in the Socratic role".

Marcuzzo and Sanfilippo (2008, p. 76) quote Joan Robinson's delightful account of a meeting between "the younger generations from Cambridge and the LSE" seeking, in Joan's words, "a meeting ground to get behind the backs of their embattled seniors". LSE launched *The Review of Economic Studies* in 1933, referred to in Cambridge as 'the children's magazine'; and they organised joint sessions of the younger groups. One such took place in 1933:

> A weekend meeting was arranged at an inn half-way between London and Cambridge. Cambridge was represented by Kahn, Austin Robinson and myself, and James Meade who had been back in Oxford for a year ... Abba Lerner brought three contemporaries (none of whom remained in the profession). It was agreed that there should be no appeal to authority; every point must be argued on its merits. At the first session, James explained the multiplier; Kahn, who came later, went over it again. Then it was the turn of London. They said that before they could discuss employment, they must analyse what would happen if everybody confidently expected that the world was coming to an end in six months; time ... the point was to distinguish what capital goods could be consumed in six

months, by ceasing replacements from what would have to be left. ... Next day, Abba was asked to go over the multiplier argument. With some help, he repeated it correctly and seemed to be convinced. His companions were quite shocked and were seen afterwards walking him up and down the lawn, trying to restore his faith. (Robinson, 1979, p. xv, quoted in Marcuzzo & Sanfilippo, 2008, p. 76)

Perhaps one can time Abba Lerner's conversion, and defection from the Robbins-Hayek LSE tribe to the Keynesian camp, to this fateful meeting in an inn located in neutral, no-man's land half-way between the two warring camps.

4.3.7 Kahn's 'Secret' Seminar at King's: Fires in the Kitchen

"The 'Secret Seminar' (also known as the Tuesday Group, though it met on Mondays) was a post-war version of the early 'Cambridge Circus'. It was held in Kahn's rooms in Webb's Court. There it was that the major contributions generated by the Cambridge Keynesian school of economics took shape. The secrecy of the initiative was a joke, but it was very characteristic of the atmosphere created by its convener and leader, Richard Kahn. Unsympathetic outsiders gave it all sorts of mysterious, even hidden meanings. But the essence of it was very simple: it was a way to keep the meetings closed to a small group" (Pasinetti, 1991, p. 431). Perhaps this reflected Kahn's personality and preference. "Kahn's character never brought him to extrovert expressions or to easy communication. He was a clumsy lecturer, as soon as the size of the audience became moderately large. Very rarely did he go to conferences or to public meetings; never to large congresses. When decisive stands had to be taken, he let others come out on the battle forefront. He preferred to stay behind the scenes. But in private conversations or in small groups he was unequalled: persistent, punctilious, relentless" (ibid.).

Asked about the 'secret' seminar, Harcourt (1995b, p. 172) says, "I saw it peaking and dying." "The nucleus of it was that Kahn always hosted the speaker, and Joan, Nicky and a sort of revolving group of people would eat and drink far too much at the Arts Theatre Restaurant beforehand. Then you went off at 8.30 to King's for the seminar. Someone would read a paper, and there'd be comments on it."

Matthews speaks of the years up to 1965 when he left Cambridge for Oxford:

> It was an exciting time, especially at the beginning. At the now famous 'secret seminar' topics connected with growth and accumulation were at the core of the agenda ... The seminar was 'secret', i.e., exclusive, because Joan and Richard Kahn thought that discussion between economists of totally uncongenial views was unprofitable. The topics were central, they were discussed in a real world context, and they were sufficiently non-technical to avoid scholastic segmentation. It would not be true to say that Joan did all the talking, but she and Richard largely determined the agenda. Nicky Kaldor's arrival in the early 1950s added another star with similar interests. Others included: Harry Johnson, Frank Hahn, Robin Marris, Amartya Sen, Aubrey Silberston, Kenneth Berrill, Jan Graaff, and

> Luigi Pasinetti—quite a list and, while never a school, sufficiently like-minded to form a coherent group. Among the seniors, Dobb never attended, nor did Austin Robinson or Dick Stone, whose influence in Cambridge was exercised through a different channel, the Department of Applied Economics (DAE). Dennis Robertson, of course, was not invited. Sraffa hardly ever came. … One of the reasons why the secret seminar was important to some of us was that there was throughout the 1950s no Faculty building where staff had rooms (apart from members of the DAE). People worked in their colleges and had to make special arrangements to foregather. With the construction of the Sidgwick Avenue building in the early 1960s, contacts became easier. At the same time, the secret seminar had begun to deteriorate. The disputes became more disputatious and more repetitive. Bob Solow's participation, when on a visit, though vastly enlightening to most of us, was an irritant to Joan; and there were other personality clashes. At the end, the management were right to call it a day. (Matthews, 1989, pp. 914–915)

And, of course, there were clashes and fireworks galore, the stuff of anecdotes. Just a few are necessary, and sufficient, to convey a sense of the tone and buzz at these live congregations.

> Then there was my famous confrontation with Nicky. I'd published this paper criticising him, and he asked me to come along to his King's research students' seminar to read it, and we could argue it out. Luigi Pasinetti came along to see fair play, but Nicky behaved disgracefully. … Every time I got him on a weak point he would either shout me down or change the assumptions, and then he'd smirk at the research students and they'd go greasing around Nicky. I remember going up to one person who'd also behaved disgracefully; I picked him up by the lapels and said, 'Look, son, if you want to grease around Kaldor and curry his favour at my expense, at least do your bloody homework beforehand!' And I plonked him down, white at the gills! But, thanks to Luigi, at least I had my say, and then he summed up very judiciously. After that Nicky and I became friends, as a matter of fact. We'd both got it out of our systems … (Harcourt, 1995b, p. 173)

Kaldor had prior history, or form, with Harcourt, who says, in his interview with Alan Macfarlane (Harcourt, 2007), that he got "a rough reception" from Kaldor, his assigned supervisor when he arrived in Cambridge, because Geoff had accepted some supervision work from Henderson, a Robertsonian and therefore an anti-Keynesian, whom Kaldor hated, and that "problems with Kaldor caused depression", and that it took ten years before they struck up a friendship. It appears that the seminar at King's was where things came to a boil but then led happily to recovering what became a lifelong friendship. As Kahn put it: "Discussion on occasion became somewhat heated but we remained close friends" (Kahn & Marcuzzo, 2020, p. 26).

Amartya Sen offers his recollections, somewhat more detached than Geoff Harcourt's. "The fights seemed to go on endlessly. There was a weekly seminar for a small number of strictly chosen economists who formed a 'secret' club called the Tuesday Club, though it met on Monday evenings (or perhaps it was the Monday Club and met on Tuesdays)." "The discussions there were occasionally interesting", but he "invariably relished the pre-meeting dinner at the restaurant above the Arts Theatre to which Richard Kahn and Joan Robinson use to take us (Kahn was one of the most generous hosts I have known)" (Sen, 2021, p. 370). It would appear that, for Sen, "thought for food" was winning over "food for thought".

Robin Matthews (1989, p. 914) recalls the hapless plight of Leontief, the fixed-coefficients man ironically caught out assuming flexibilities: "Wassily Leontief, on a visit to Cambridge around 1950, opened a paper to the secret seminar by some such words as, 'I shall assume there is full employment, brought about by wage-flexibility.' He got no further—the rest of the evening was spent challenging that."

Then, the case of Paul Samuelson, with Dick Goodwin and I.G. Patel offering contrasting accounts, possibly of different occasions, which combine to make an amusing pair showing Joan in her (rare) *Durga* and (regular) *Kali* incarnations.

Goodwin, on Joan as *Kali*:

> I remember Paul Samuelson giving a talk to a small group in which he made some sort of allusion to the role of profit. Joan interrupted to demand what determined the rate of profit. He began a rather conventional explanation, at which she interrupted again with the same statement, and she continued to do so through the remainder of his presentation. (Goodwin, 1989, p. 916) This was Joan as *Kali*, her default form!

I.G. Patel on Joan as *Durga*:

> It was only a year or so after being at King's when I was invited to seminars where Mrs. Robinson used to be present that I began to appreciate what a warm heart lay behind that stern exterior. I would not have thought that her sense of fairness—of taking the side of those pilloried or just misunderstood—would make her defend on occasion views not her own or person not particularly to her liking. I remember an occasion soon after the war when Samuelson came to Cambridge and gave a lecture where he annoyed everyone by the arrogant and messianic tone in which he tried to tell us what exciting advances in economic theory were being made in the other Cambridge, when British economists were merely going round and round in meaningless controversies. It was decided to invite him to address a small gathering next day in the Marshall Library where several academics, notably Sraffa were ready to take him on and to bring his ego down a few notches.[64] But when the fun began and everyone was almost shouting at

---

[64] The question about Samuelson's ego is best resolved by Samuelson pronouncing on his favourite topic, himself. "My talent happened to be such that praise and reputation came early and in full measure, so that in advancing age I carry no unfulfilled desires for achievement or recognition—and this despite the fact that I was born with no deficient quota of ambition and vanity" (Samuelson, 1989).

Samuelson, Mrs. Robinson said in a loud voice drowning everyone else's, that surely what Samuelson meant was something else and went on to outline it as if she had known it all along and agreed with it, which was certainly not the case. But the point was made, Samuelson grabbed at the lifeline offered and everyone was well behaved thereafter. (Patel, 1989, pp. 863–864)

Some charges that needs recording, and resolution, concern treatment of James Meade and, in particular, his alleged wilful exclusion from the 'secret' seminar. There are variations on this theme by Dasgupta (2010), Arrow (2010), alluded to also in Newbery (2017).

When I arrived here I found the Cambridge Economics Faculty to be awful; a number of significant figures from the 1930s, Joan Robinson, Nicky Kaldor, and Richard Kahn had wanted to protect Cambridge economics from the increased post-War use in the US of maths and stats; they conducted a secret economics seminar to which only chosen colleagues were invited; that they used ideology to determine an economic argument was bad enough, but they also mistook technical tools for ideology, for which the university paid a heavy price for a long while; they were Keynes's disciples, and when I say disciples I mean DISCIPLES; as far as I can tell these renowned economists established an intellectual tone that not only led to James Meade's resignation from his professorship in political economy six years before he was due to retire. (Dasgupta, 2010)

In a similar vein, David Newbery writes more explicitly: "Joan Robinson made his life a misery, to the point that he took early retirement to continue writing his books" (Newbery, 2017, p. 492).

Dasgupta's comments regarding his father-in-law James Meade are made in 2010; in the same year, Ken Arrow was a visitor at the Faculty and seemed to echo similar sentiments. "Differences had come to something of a head with the appointment of James Meade to a Chair in Political Economy. Meade was, with Kahn and Robinson, one of the original disciples of Keynes, but his interests were broader than simply discussion of unemployment. For some reasons not entirely clear to me, his appointment was resented. A 'secret seminar' was created to discuss issues, to prevent his attendance. It seemed to me that Meade felt keenly his exclusion and was very hurt" (Arrow, 2010).

And years later, in the obituary of Frank Hahn, Newbery returns to reiterate a variation of the charge, this time involving other economists, including an aside regarding the non-participation of James Meade. "One measure of the pettiness and vindictiveness of Kahn and Robinson is that when Kahn took over Keynes's Monday seminar, known as the 'secret' seminar, Farrell, with some other prominent faculty like Malcolm Fisher and Ron Henderson, supporters of Robertson, were excluded. Meade and Hahn were invited to the 'secret' seminar, although Meade then withdrew" (Newbery, 2017, p. 493).

It takes an old hand to set matters straight, and the resolution comes from Aubrey Silberston, hardly one of 'the leftist gang'.

Ken Arrow is quite right that James Meade's election was not universally popular, especially among the Keynesians, who had hoped that Nicky Kaldor or Joan Robinson would be elected. Ken Arrow is, however, wrong about the secret seminar. This took place weekly on Mondays during term in Richard Kahn's rooms in King's. It had been going for several years before James came to Cambridge. The supporters of Richard and Joan were there, together with several others—at different times, Nicky Kaldor, Richard Goodwin, Brian Reddaway, David Champernowne, Harry Johnson, Jan Graaf …, Robin Matthews, Luigi Pasinetti, Ruth Cohen, Michael Posner, Kenneth Berrill, myself and others. Piero Sraffa was invited but very rarely came. He confined himself to Sunday walks with Richard and Joan. Distinguished visitors to Cambridge were often invited, including, on at least one occasion, Paul Samuelson. James Meade was invited to attend the secret seminar, and did so initially. He felt however that the atmosphere was not friendly to him, and after a time he withdrew, and started a lunch time seminar for all Faculty members. This was not a great success, and eventually James returned to the secret seminar, which could certainly be a very stimulating group. (Silberston, 2011b, p. 4)

William Peterson, in the obituary of James Meade carried in the Alumni website of Christ's College,[65] provides another balanced assessment: "The move to Cambridge [in 1957] also brought James into the acrimonious politics of the Economics Faculty, a change which he did not enjoy. Looking back, it is clear that the debates reflected not only the combative personality of some of the key participants, but also deep intellectual differences about the ways in which Keynes's original insights should be developed. For James, economics was about moderate and carefully designed reforms which would make a market economy fairer and more efficient, and which would allow growth with stable prices and full employment. But for others, who saw themselves as the guardians of the 'Cambridge' tradition, Keynes's key contribution had been to show that, since financial markets could not allocate capital efficiently (either within a single country, or across international borders), most forms of investment should be the outcome of a government-led planning process. Conflicts within the Economics Faculty, and the wish to focus on his research and writing, led James to resign his Chair in 1968, and to take up a Senior Research Fellowship at Christ's."

Dasgupta seems peeved by the exclusionary nature of the 'secret' seminar of the senior Keynesians held in Richard Kahn's rooms at King's, but appears to see no contradiction here with his membership of the ultra-elite secret society, the Cambridge Apostles, which was historically characterised by streaks of dynastic nepotism, and often (though not always) tended to work virtually as a lodge easing pathways for one another (see Vervaecke, 2011). Dasgupta, who was appointed to a Cambridge professorship in 1985 over the likes of Luigi Pasinetti, would have been in the company, amongst others, of his great mentors Frank Hahn and compatriot Amartya Sen (who, while in India, was a

---

[65] https://alumni.christs.cam.ac.uk/james-meade

supervisee of his father, A.K. Dasgupta), their friend Harry Johnson[66] (later all colleagues at LSE), as well as his own PhD supervisor, James Mirrlees.

More considered and pertinent, though, is the insider's assessment of Luigi Pasinetti (2007, p. 201), who notes that the 'secret' seminar "played a major role in the development of new concepts and ideas," but he also refers to the "unwise behaviour" (ibid., p. 203) of the senior group which "should have become conscious of the collateral damage that such a peculiar arrangement inevitably would generate" (ibid., p. 202); it "irritated many participants (especially the young)" and "generated a kind of blockage to potential contributors, who otherwise might have helped the strongly sought 'revolution' to explode" (ibid.). So the secrecy scored many theoretical successes, but also damaging own goals undermining longer-term strength and sustainability. The Queens' Seminar organised by Ajit and colleagues was open in principle and included doctoral researchers, though it was ignored by the neoclassicals who grouped around their own Churchill Seminar run by Hahn; there was little overlap or love lost between the two, so issues of 'closure' across the two groups practising mutual disdain are to some extent merely notional.

There are several points that can be briefly elicited from the narratives of the so-called secret seminar. The most basic point is that the Kahn Monday seminar at King's was the prime arena of exchange, a clearing house, where Cambridge Keynesian and heterodox economics ideas were put up, put through the mill to survive, evolve or perish. Its contributory power diminished after the Austin Robinson building came up, and alongside, as some of the cohort of the greats aged and retired. The 'secrecy' ascription was hugely overdone and misunderstood. Of course, those with consistently and sharply opposed views would find the seminar a waste of time and self-exclude, or not be invited, to avoid counterproductive argumentation. But leaving aside the fake allegations of specific exclusions, for example, James Meade, there were other externalities that surfaced. On the one side, Frank Hahn eventually withdrew to set up, defying good utilitarian ethics, his own seminar directly intended to conflict in timing with the pre-existing Monday seminar, resembling an act of visceral hostility. On the other side, it has been pointed out perceptively by Luigi Pasinetti that excluding, that is, not inviting, many of the younger heterodox, radical rising cohort to participate in the seminar was an act of self-harm; it discouraged and disheartened these younger colleagues and became a potential source for generating negative feelings of difference, hierarchy and disunity. Paradoxically, from this negative externality emerged a positive initiative: the younger cohort, still followers of the seniors by virtue of the simple fact that they were all in Cambridge rather than any other university environment, set up a complementary seminar that did not exercise such selectivity and exclusivity—this was the Queens' Economics Seminar the prime mover of which was

---

[66] "When Harry returned to Cambridge in January 1949 ... he was still an outsider. However, he soon became an insider in the holy of holies—a fellow of King's College and an Apostle" (Moggridge, 2001, p. 655).

Ajit Singh, the radical political commissar of the left and heterodox lineages of Cambridge economics. The Queens' Seminar began proceedings in the mid- to late-1960s and was well established and flourishing at the point, in 1969, when the 'senior' Kahn's Monday 'secret' seminar finally called time.

There remains a twist in the tale: in the mid-1970s, it appears that Richard Kahn was moved to resume his Monday seminar. But it doesn't come to pass, for reasons as unknown as those for which he might have wished to restart it.

4.3.8 The Richard Stone Common Room: Typhoo and Typhoons

Box 38 of the Austin Robinson Papers held at the Marshall Library Archives, c.1960–1961, has a description which runs: "Unlabelled folder, Site plan, elevations of lecture block, leaflets and correspondence re furniture for Economics common room" (3/2/8).

The construction of the Faculty Building was a legacy of the untiring labour of Austin Robinson, and it predictably transformed the life of Cambridge economists, especially their eccentric, perhaps anachronistic, modes of communication. The dispersed seminars in college rooms continued, but now Faculty members had the shared luxury of a common space. Hustling and hassling in corridors apart, there was now the prospect of encounters in the tea-room, even if it generated exchanges more acrimonious than the proverbial storms in teacups. Several staff members avoided being drawn into the slinging matches; some generally withdrew from the Common Room; and there was the usual separation between academic and non-academic staff.

While some loved and looked forward to the mid-morning show, it was not everyone's cup of tea: strong brew, often bitter, sometimes toxic. But it remained, perhaps, the only regular forum where different, opposing tribes shared a physical space, with predictable fireworks, but also on rare occasions, quite unexpected agreements and collaborations, for example, the Hahn-Neild letter signed by 364 economists. Often calm, sometimes theatre, if not a theatre of war.[67]

Visitors were quite taken by it, even if they were not fully socialised into local protocol. Arrow shares an experience: "A senior economist of considerable weight in the history of economic thought who was present at Cambridge then was the rather mysterious (at least to me) Piero Sraffa. … At coffee (a daily ritual at the Faculty), I met him and challenged some of his assumptions. Suddenly the room grew very quiet, an effect rather more than I had intended" (Arrow, 2010). No, Mr. Arrow, even you do not go about challenging Piero Sraffa on his assumptions; no, not in the Faculty Common Room!

"Like so many, his [Peter Diamond's] main experience of the Economic Faculty was in the Coffee Room. There he saw the giants of the time, Nicholas Kaldor and Joan Robinson in particular. He did try to engage with Mrs

---

[67] A perplexed Ron Smith raises a serious question: "There is an issue as to why economics seminars are so unpleasant relative to other disciplines. This seems to be true whateverdox they are."

Robinson. After an exchange of notes about the marginal productivity of capital, he stopped responding. When challenged about that at coffee, he explained that 'there was nothing to respond do', which led to a face-to-face discussion" (Cockerill, 2012).

Depending on the mood and the topic of contention afloat, singles matches could pitch contestants from the same team against one another, or a junior against a senior. Ajit Singh recounted his first encounter with Brian Reddaway, subsequently a mentor and long-term friend.

> There was a tempestuous start to my association with Reddaway when I started work on the project. One afternoon in the DAE common room we embarked on a serious and noisy disagreement about econometrics and time series analysis. Reddaway was scathing about the regression analysis of economic time series, as it led to spurious correlations, for reasons which are much better understood today than they were then. I provided what I thought was a spirited defence of the textbook model of doing such regressions, which at Berkeley I had been taught was an adequate approach to the problem. Reddaway was not at all convinced, but never held my wrong-headedness against me, regarding it as an honest difference of opinion. What was remarkable about this exchange was that it took place between a graduate student and a highly distinguished economist for whom academic hierarchy seemed to have no relevance. Indeed, one of Reddaway's characteristic traits throughout his professional life was that he was interested only in the validity or otherwise of the argument being made, rather than the formal status of the person making it. This did not always endear him to his senior colleagues, whose sometimes feeble arguments might be summarily rejected in public. Brian Reddaway was a blunt person and habitually called a spade a spade, though neither with malice nor with any intention of point scoring. (Singh, 2008, p. 3)

On the other hand, sometimes a doubles-team paired players from opposing sides, with the duo displaying uncharacteristic tactical cooperation and strategic understanding. A prime case of this was the joint 'anti-monetarist' letter written by Frank Hahn and Robert Neild, who would probably not be easily found rubbing shoulders. Newbery (2017) recounts the episode in his obituary for Hahn.

> The 1970s were turbulent times politically, with the high inflation following the oil shocks of 1973, strikes and labour unrest culminating in the 'winter of discontent' of 1978–1979. In 1979 the country elected Margaret Thatcher's Conservative Government to replace a failing Labour Government. Hahn was much incensed by the monetarist advice his former colleague, Alan Walters, had been providing the Government. In the view of Milton Friedman, much lauded by Sir Keith Joseph and other Conservatives, high inflation was simply due to an excessive expansion of the money supply. This is where the great value of the Cambridge faculty coffee room showed its worth. The faculty (and the DAE) met for coffee every day in term time and argued vigorously not just over theory (these were disputatious academics, after all) but also about policy (many of the faculty were active policy advisors and commentators).

Perhaps surprisingly, given their prior history, Hahn and Neild (whose appointment to a professorship had pre-empted Hahn's earlier return) criticised monetarist doctrine in an article in *The Times* (25 February 1980) 'Monetarism: why Mrs Thatcher should beware'. Friedman responded aggressively, claiming that reducing monetary growth 'may increase unemployment temporarily, to be rewarded by a much sharper reduction in unemployment later' (*The Times*, 3 March 1980). Unemployment had risen from 7 per cent in 1980 to 10 per cent in 1981. Geoffrey Howe, Chancellor of the Exchequer, delivered the Budget on 10 March 1981, after which Hahn and Neild sat down in the coffee room and drew up a response, circulated it and secured the signatures of 364 economist academics (including themselves) to a letter published in *The Times* on 29 March 1981. (Newbery, 2017, pp. 501–503)

Was this out-of-character collaboration the exception that established the rule?

But there are other recollections of Frank Hahn's persona and performance in the theatre of the tea-room. In his feedback on a draft of the intellectual biography of Ajit Singh, his ex-colleague and fellow Fellow of Queens', Vani Borooah chided me for trying hard to be "non-controversial". "You skated over the viciousness of the Cambridge Faculty and the attacks on Ajit. You skated over the satanic figure of Frank Hahn who made academic disagreements into a blood sport which was then continued by his acolytes."[68] Vani was extremely critical of Frank Hahn, in particular, and his *chelas*, or acolytes as he calls them. He amplified this by citing an incident in the Staff Common Room where Hahn was holding forth to a group around him. There was some reference to Ajit and Parkinsons in the conversation. Hahn apparently remarked: "Well, that's one way to get rid of one's opponents." Another colleague present (name withheld) was sufficiently offended to demand an apology from Hahn. Vani's view is that this summed up the aggressive and brazen hostility and hubris that Hahn emitted towards his academic and professional opponents. Partha Dasgupta, who Vani refers to as Hahn's 'acolyte', mentions in his piece on Hahn that he was greeted as "dear boy" when he visited the ailing Hahn in his retirement. In contrast to Hahn, Ajit was rock solid and consistent in extending courtesy and politeness to all opponents in the Faculty—even to the proverbial 'running dogs of imperialism' in the case of Vietnam. Frank Hahn attacked the person if he was 'on the other side'; Ajit Singh attacked the ideas, even if the person was 'on the other side'.

One can safely gather that Vani Borooah was not a great fan or follower of Frank Hahn; but Bob Solow was indeed a great pal and old buddy, and strikingly he ends an obituary saying Frank Hahn's "was a career of honor and dignity especially for an economist whose personal style was usually critical and anything but dignified" (Solow in Cord, 2017, p. 916).

Angus Deaton's memories call time on the tea break.

[68] Vani Borooah email of 9 October 2017, and telephone conversation.

And then there was the tea-room where, in my time, Nicky Kaldor and Joan Robinson were king and queen, each surrounded by a group of courtiers, but with comments thrown from group to group. ... When Frank Hahn came back to Cambridge in 1972, there was a third court, and there were many other individuals I remember ... Although much of the discussion flew over my head, I picked up a lot, including just how much there was to know. One notable lesson was the breadth of economics, many different positions were held in that room, often well-thought through and eloquently defended in what could be a cacophonous and even bitter debate. Joan Robinson's constant challenges to neoclassical economics have stayed with me, not the detail but the notion that something was (and to me still is) deeply wrong. I learned that economics and politics could not and should not be separated. Nicky Kaldor's intelligence, wit, eloquence and deep knowledge of economics shone brilliantly in a group where none of these qualities were in short supply. He was the best debater I have ever heard, but his dismissals and arguments could wound, no less so for their wittiness and the merriment that they provoked. The tea-room atmosphere did not favour those with a limited taste for this sort of thing, and James Meade and Richard Stone were rarely present. That the tea-room is now the Stone room marks a welcome recognition that would not have been forthcoming 35 years ago, although it is also hard to escape the irony. (Deaton, 2011, p. 4)

Richard Stone, a mild-mannered gent, would have been quite unsuited to the jousting and blood-drawing cut-and-thrust of the inter-tribal verbals and felt out of place in the tea-room bearing his name.

4.3.9 Ajit Singh's Political Economy Seminar at Queens': Young Turks

The Queens' Political Economy Seminar set up by Ajit Singh was partially induced by the selective inclusion of the next generation in the by-invitation Kahn Seminar at King's. This Seminar set up shop in the second part of the 1960s and in principle was open, also to doctoral researchers, though it seems that 'the known extremists', viz., Frank Hahn, David Newbery and Gordon Hughes were kept off the list of invitees.

Ajit's Queens' Seminar assembled the disparate strands and sometimes belligerent personages of the heterodox schools into one lively, contested but congenial debating chamber on a sustained basis. Even on this side of the no-man's land dividing the warring factions at the Faculty, unity of purpose or intellectual connectedness was fairly elusive, and it was not often that all the big guns pointed in the same direction. Ajit saw the vacated space, a clearinghouse for a regular exchange of ideas.[69] Vani Borooah, Fellow in Economics at

---

[69] In this connection, see also Prabhat Patnaik's recollection: "Besides participating in demonstrations and meetings, he also played a crucial role in starting or reviving intellectual forums where left-wing dons could meet and discuss" (Patnaik 2015a, p. 32). Prabhat mentions in particular the Tawney Group, and the meetings usually in Lord Kahn's room at King's College. And from the mid-1970s, there was the Matthews-Cairncross CLARE (Cambridge, London, and the Rest of England) Group of economists that met on a frequent basis at Clare College (Silberston, 2011a).

Queens' and a member of Ajit's band, picks up the story: "He was the moving spirit behind the Queens' Economics Seminars[70] which were held every Thursday in term time at 8 pm in either the Munro Room or in the adjoining Old Combination Room (Ajit was very particular that only these rooms provided the appropriate venue). The Queens' Seminars were an institution in Cambridge. Although they pre-dated the rival Churchill college seminars, in later years they were intended to showcase an alternative perspective to the dreary exercises in mathematical economics at Churchill" (Vani Borooah, personal communication). Vani continues: "That they began at 8 pm was to accommodate Cambridge luminaries like Joan Robinson and Richard Kahn who would stroll over after dinner at High Table. Ajit was a generous host and alcohol was served at these seminars but, being a lifelong teetotaller, he had no idea what to serve: by a process of divine intuition he settled upon Newcastle Brown Ale. This was to be served, by Ajit's deputy, only after the main talk was over and before the Q&A began. Discussions were lively, though outside speakers were often bemused when the snores of the more elderly participants rose, like some heavenly choir, above their words. On one memorable occasion, in the days of Thatcherite pomp, Lord Kahn, woken from his slumbers by hearing Bob Rowthorn utter the word 'monetarism' promptly walked out because, in his words, 'he hadn't come to listen to this rubbish'.[71] Occasionally, when the discussion flagged, Ajit would go into undergraduate supervisor mode and ask: 'So, what are the policy implications?' To this query there were either a volley of answers or else people took it as a signal that they should now

---

[70] The Faculty Seminar in Political Economy at Queens' was sponsored by the Cambridge Political Economy Society Trust.

[71] An independent rendition of what must be the same seminar at Queens' comes from an interview with Tony Lawson (Dunn, 2009, p. 483):

"In the mid-1970s Cambridge was a very lively place and the battles were fought everywhere, not least in the coffee room of the top floor of the Economics Faculty. The debates covered policy and economic understanding. I remember, too, the fortnightly Queens Seminar (which still goes on, although less regularly) where there were lots of arguments going on .... I remember [a] seminar when Bob Rowthorn said you can't just take account of the demand side of the economy; the supply side matters too. I distinctly remember Richard Kahn asking slowly 'Did I hear you say that the supply side matters too?'. Bob Rowthorn said 'Yes' and I remember Richard Kahn just putting his papers together very slowly, putting them in his briefcase, standing up and walking out of the room. It was that kind of environment". Lawson goes on to provide another snippet from this lively seminar room: "I remember, too, a first time when the idea of rational expectations was talked about at the Queens Seminar. Probably it was the only time. I forget the name of the non-local speaker. But I do remember Kaldor being in the audience, because after the speaker had defined rational expectations, Kaldor stuck his hand up and said something like 'Did I understand you to be saying the following ...' and repeated the definition of rational expectations. The speaker replied 'Yes' and then Kaldor just started laughing. And you know what Kaldor looked like? Massive. His whole frame was shaking and he was giggling and it was so infectious the whole audience fell about laughing too. And this was happening at a time when much of the rest of the economics profession was already well on its way to being taken over by this really quite daft idea".

go home."[72] Ajit retired in 2007, and so effectively did the Queens' Economics Seminar, shifting its base to St Catherine's College.

The Queens' Seminar seems to have its roots, curiously, in the Kahn 'secret' seminar at King's. The latter, it is well known, was invitation based, with specific participants invited apart from a set of regulars, led by Richard Kahn and Joan Robinson. There were various entries and exits, including some luminaries, such as James Meade, amongst others; and visiting economists graced, or suffered, the seminar, depending on their experience on the day. Such personalities included Paul Samuelson, Kenneth Arrow and Bob Solow, setting up some memorable exchanges with belligerent and sometimes hostile opposition prominently from Joan. While the neoclassical camp—as for instance Dasgupta (2013) and Newbery (2017)—have generally written dismissively about the 'secret' nature of the seminar, this exclusionary approach to attendance applied also to many of the large band of younger heterodox economists that were making their mark in that period. Pasinetti has observed that the exercise of such selectivity in admission to the inner circle could not but have had a discouraging and negative impact on this rising group of economists who shared the intellectual predilections and orientations of the seniors. It was perhaps through a desire to overcome such exclusion, and to have a more inclusive space for all members of the extended family of Cambridge heterodox economists, that the parallel Queens' Seminar emerged. While most of the participants of the Queens' Seminar might have been of intermediate or junior rank within the Faculty, the seniors were very supportive and made it a point to attend—this applied especially to Joan Robinson and to Richard Kahn who were frequent, if not regular, participants. Equally, those presenting papers were also diverse, including both junior researchers and often seniors from the top rung.

Additional insights may be gleaned from a taut exchange of letters between Richard Kahn and Ajit Singh in 1975—at a point when the young Singh-Queens' Seminar had established itself as an entity, but a few years after the venerable old Kahn-King's Seminar had decided to pull down the shutters in 1969. Richard Kahn retired from his professorship in 1972, and his chair had been occupied by Frank Hahn.

The exchange begins with an undated notice from Ajit Singh and Andy Cosh, handwritten by the former, announcing the next Faculty Seminar at Queens' on 24 November 1975, at 8:30 pm in Singh's rooms in Queens', when Professor Champernowne would read his paper on the Gini measure of inequality in income distribution (RFK/12/2/38/3).

Kahn writes to Ajit Singh on 12 November 1975, with a request "to be given or lent a copy of the invitation list of your Monday Seminar. I may be wrong, but I have a feeling that the composition of the group has considerably altered. I am of course all in favour of people like the majority of those who attended last Monday being given a Seminar in addition to the Joint Faculty-D.A.E. Seminar and the Research Students' Seminar." But after this

---

[72] Vani Borooah, personal communication, 10 August 2015.

4 CAMP SKIRMISHES OVER INTERSTITIAL SPACES: JOURNALS, SEMINARS... 359

endorsement, Kahn goes on to share his concern at this rather open, all-comers approach to participation: "at the same time, some of us are rather anxious that there should once again be a Seminar more on the lines of the one which I used to conduct."[73]

This is striking: in 1975, Kahn (and 'some of us') is desirous of reviving the old concern, the King's 'secret' seminar! Such a wish would not have arisen from nostalgia; even a cursory scan would reveal that the intellectual and political scene in 1975 was turbo charged, with Cambridge having several irons in various raging fires, both external and internal. The UK economy was in the throes of a perpetual crisis through the 1970s raising deep structural questions, as well as immediate issues of macroeconomic management; there was striking research emanating from the DAE on the deindustrialisation of the UK economy; there were running battles over soft monetarism creeping into official policy; and above all, there was the emergence of the theoretical phenomenon 'new Cambridge' espoused by Kaldor, Godley, Cripps, Neild, et al., and resisted and critiqued by the 'old' Keynesians led by Kahn himself with Posner as his second. Internationally too, Kahn closely monitored the volatile situation in the Middle East, including the economic implications of the OPEC price hikes—topics very close to Kahn's political interests. Clearly, the energy was such as to induce Richard Kahn, having first given up his Seminar three years *prior* to his retirement in 1972, to consider restarting the Seminar three years *after* having retired; he might have wished to escape the frustration of being a bystander and to jump into the fray of the raging debates using the familiar platform of his weekly seminar. And, of course, one might wonder who those "some of us" were who were "rather anxious" to restart the Monday seminar at King's.

Then, to the matter of timing, in specific, the clash with the Churchill Seminar also held on Mondays. "Does it [Ajit's Queens' Seminar] really have to meet on Monday? I have a clear memory that at a time when I was running the P.E. Club, I was able on more than one occasion to attend both the Mathematical Seminar and your Seminar. If all three met on Mondays, this would not have been possible. ... I would have thought that dovetailing this with the P.E. Club should not have presented much difficulty" (RFK/12/2/28/2).

And Kahn goes on to note that the costs of the refreshments served at the Seminar, all those Brown Ale bottles, appears to fall on Ajit personally, and suggests that these be shared with Seminar regulars imbibing these refreshments, at the least.

Ajit's reply, on 18 November, makes intriguing reading: "The only people excluded from our seminar are those known extremists in the Faculty such as Frank Hahn, David Newbery and Gordon Hughes. If you wish some others to be added to this exclusion list, please let me have their names and I shall inform them of your objections" (RFK/12/2/38/4).

---

[73] It can be presumed here that Kahn is referring to his 'secret' seminar held in his rooms at King's College, till he terminated it in 1969.

This induces an irritated reaction from Kahn on 24 November, the date of Champernowne's announced seminar. Kahn complains: "You deal neither with the financial question which I raised, nor with the question of the clash with the Churchill Seminar. You go out of your way to disregard the wording of the rest of my letter. I was not suggesting that people should be excluded from the Seminar. What was worrying me—and still does worry me—is whether people are being excluded other than the 'non-extremists' [*sic*; Kahn says he is dictating this letter, and obviously he is referring to 'known extremists', the term used by Ajit in his earlier letter]. I wonder how many of them there are. You mention three, but your use of the phrase 'such as' indicates that you want to maintain the whole thing as a mystery." Kahn goes on to question in some detail, the criteria for the issuance of invitations, and concludes: "It does seem to me that something is very wrong somewhere ... I shall be interested to see what the position is tonight." He asks why, generally, Bob (Rowthorn) and John (Eatwell) are not present. He closes by suggesting that Susan Howson be added to the list (of invitees) if not already included in the list (RFK/12/2/38/5). And there the exchange rests, and some questions arise.

First, it is obvious that Kahn wishes to restart the Political Economy Club under his tutelage, again on Mondays, presumably—otherwise there would be no hassle about the Queens' Seminar clashing with the Churchill on Mondays; he is obviously concerned about the overlap with Ajit's Queens' Seminar and not with Hahn's Churchill Mathematical Seminar—this because the Kahn and Ajit Seminars would be addressing largely the same constituency, with minimal overlap with the Hahn Seminar.

What also emerges, perhaps accidentally, from the exchange is that the usual neoclassical suspects, 'the known extremists', are consciously excluded from the invitation list for the Queens' Seminar; and interestingly, Ajit Singh asks Kahn if wishes to extend the 'exclusion' list to others; perhaps this harks back to the practice of Kahn's 'secret' seminar, where exclusions again were not explicit, just effected via invitations not being issued to certain people deemed undesirable for the purpose of the seminar. Further, the two existing seminars, Ajit's at Queens' and Hahn's at Churchill, seem to consciously practise mutually assured exclusion by sticking to the Monday timing for their respective meetings. Here, it is worth noting that according to Newbery, Hahn (in the 1960s) had tactically slated his Churchill Mathematical Seminar explicitly to clash with Kahn's Monday 'secret' seminar.

4.3.10 *Arestis and Kitson Political Economy Seminar at St. Catherine's College*

The Ajit-Queens' Seminar was in business till 2007, when Ajit retired, wheelchaired, and the baton was passed on to one of its regulars, Philip Arestis, with the Seminar relocating to his college, St. Catherine's. Ken Coutts, close to both, informs that "the Queens' seminar became the St Caths seminar. After the financial crisis, there was a series of seminars organised by Philip Arestis and

Michael Kitson (both at St Catharine's College) to discuss the crisis and its aftermath, including many on austerity in the UK. It has replaced the Queens' seminar as the outlet for non-mainstream economics and is financially supported by the CJE" (Ken Coutts, email of 25 Oct 2018). In combination with the Ajit Singh Seminar at Queens', which started in the 1960s, this Political Economy Seminar can lay fair claim to being the longest continuously running seminar series in Cambridge economics. Usefully, the complete programme speakers and titles of seminar presentations at the Arestis-Kitson series from 2009 to date can be found on the Seminar's webpage,[74] and it provides a very useful profile of the range and vibrancy of the heterodox lineage in Cambridge over the period.

4.3.11 Hahn's Churchill Seminar: Only Maths and Neoclassicals, Others Beware

The Mathematical Seminar, aka the Churchill Seminar, was started in the late 1960s and purposely set up to clash with the ongoing Kahn 'secret' seminar on Mondays at King's College. "In the early 1960s the [Kahn's pre-existing] 'secret seminar' was still in full swing, with Hahn very much in attendance"; ... "but then Hahn and the growing number of young Turks that he attracted were to set up the Churchill seminar as a direct rival to the 'secret seminar', which they outcompeted in attracting attendees, until Kahn dissolved the seminar in 1969" (Newbery, 2017, pp. 496, 499). The Kahn Seminar at King's had always been on Mondays, and clearly Hahn set up his Churchill Seminar also on Mondays as an act of direct competition, if not confrontation; he was forcing colleagues to choose one or the other, obviously an intrinsically sub-optimal way to go. Newbery, however, quotes Christopher Bliss: "the arrival of Frank Hahn into this fetid atmosphere was like a breath of fresh air" (ibid., p. 496), but then most fragrances, at high levels of concentration, can be foul. Hostility was clearly a two-way street.

Ron Smith, then multi-tasking as an econometrician, political activist and a Marxist, noted: "I seem to remember that the Churchill and Queens' Seminars were on the same day,[75] so that you had to sign up to one side or the other. I went to the Churchill seminar for the econometrics and Frank and David were

---

[74] https://www.politicaleconomy.group.cam.ac.uk/events/past-events

[75] Ron Smith here is referring to the 1970s, by which time Kahn's 'secret' Monday seminar had shut down (in 1969); presumably at some point after that, the Queens' Seminar shifted also to Mondays so that the earlier clash between the Kahn and Hahn seminars now mutated into one between the Singh and Hahn seminars. The experience of one avid seminar participant in the 1970s suggests that it was possible to attend both the Queens', Ajit Singh seminar and also Hahn's Churchill Seminar, but at the cost of having to skip supper! Ron Smith, however, managed to have his seminars and his supper too: "My memory is that the Churchill seminar started at 6 pm on Mondays, then there was a buffet supper after it, while the Queens' started later, so it was just possible to attend both. But my memory may be wrong." The matter awaits a casting vote for a resolution.

very unhappy to discover that the Marxist troublemaker came from the Churchill seminar not the Queens'" (personal communication, email dated 30 January 2018). Leftists were not welcome, was Ron's perception. Given the theoretical and methodological distances between the mathematical neoclassicals and the heterodox groups, it is probable that only a small number from either group might have wished to attend the seminar of the 'other', had there been no timetabling clash. Even so, this was a good illustration of the belligerent hostility generally displayed by Hahn towards those not in his camp.

The Churchill Seminar illustrates some distinctive Hahn traits. He was brought over from Birmingham to Cambridge by Kaldor, his position in Cambridge was apparently due to Kahn, Hahn says himself that he was brought over to become Joan's disciple; yet, within just a few years of arriving, he set up the rival Churchill Seminar in blatant opposition, with the insult of holding it on the same weekday as the Kahn Seminar. A second trait runs in the opposite direction, loyalty to his followers and the massive sustained input to establish his 'academy' and imbue an identity in them distinct from the rest of Cambridge economics. Hahn dropped from a readership in Birmingham to a lectureship in Cambridge in 1960 and then left for LSE to become professor there in 1967, returning to Cambridge triumphant as a professor in 1972. In the first stay, he had set up the Churchill Seminar; in his absence while at LSE, he nurtured it from LSE, from Churchill where he kept his fellowship, and from his home where he entertained his followers; and he picked up the leadership again of a viable group shaped in his image when he returned to Cambridge in 1972. David Newbery provides some detail: "[when Hahn left for a chair at LSE in 1966] he continued to live (in … the house in Adams Road that he purchased from Matthews when he moved to Oxford)" … was elected to an Extraordinary Fellowship at Churchill, "and continued to engage with the young Turks in the faculty, at the rival Monday seminar held in Churchill College and at his house, where he hospitably entertained with Dorothy" (Newbery, 2017, p. 499). In the interim, the Kahn Seminar had terminated in 1969, leaving the field to the Ajit Singh Queens' Seminar. Had Hahn not been proactive, neoclassical mathematical economics might not have had the strong institutional platform that he systematically developed for it; and the Churchill Seminar was the core for the period till the mid-1970s, when he started his parallel Risk Project seminars that continued for another 15 years virtually till his retirement.

4.3.12 *Cambridge Growth Project Seminar at DAE*

The archived papers of the Cambridge Growth Project of DAE, held in the Marshall Library Archives, Cambridge, include a file, CGP/48/1, which contains all CGP Seminar Notices for the period 1970–1984, including correspondence relating to the Seminars, lists of discussion topics and proposed papers. Terry Barker provides information on this CGP Seminar:

The seminars were weekly on Thursday afternoons during term time and were an informal requirement for CGP staff. They were internal to the project research, and included presentations by outsiders, both visiting academics and other Faculty, when relevant. There was a limit of about 15 participants given the size of the room. It was held in the room of the CGP Director. This was the time that the project's work was agreed and coordinated. The atmosphere was informal, friendly and helpful. It was always supportive and constructive. These seminars went on until the project finished in 1997. (Personal communication; Terry Barker email dated 14 July 2021)

4.3.13 Hahn's 'Quaker' Risk Seminar: The Rising Tide

Hahn's Risk Seminar—the Quaker Seminar—ran for the duration of the 15-year Risk Project from 1976 till 1991, till a year before Hahn retired.[76] The Risk Project was funded by SSRC/ESRC; the unusual rather open-ended grant to Hahn was made when Robin Matthews, his close colleague, friend and comrade-in-arms in Faculty politics, was the Chairman of the SSRC between 1971 and 1975.[77] This Seminar is best described in the words of two of Hahn's juniors, David Newbery and Partha Dasgupta, both participants over different periods in the seminar.

Dasgupta:

> Hahn made a move that displayed ... his gifts as an academic visionary and administrator. He obtained, what would be impossible today, a loosely specified research grant for studying risk and incentives from the then Economic and Social Research Council. Over a period of fifteen years (the project ended in 1991, a year before his retirement) Hahn used the project's grant to attract from outside Cambridge Ken Binmore, David Easley, John Geanakoplos, Sanford Grossman, David Kreps, Mark Machina, Louis Makowski, Eric Maskin, and Herakles Polemarchakis, among others. The group's weekly seminar was conducted in the manner presumed of those gathered in Friends' Meeting Houses; and so, inevitably, the group came to be known as the 'Quakers'. To commemorate the Quakers Hahn (1989b) edited a selection of their articles in 1989. (Dasgupta, 2013)

David Newbery picks up the refrain:

> Hahn's intellectual energy knew no bounds and he used this remarkably successful research programme to redress some of the shortcomings of General Equilibrium theory—its lack of a theory of unemployment, money and market adjustments. The so-call *Risk Project* attracted an amazingly impressive group of young researchers such as Eric Maskin, David Kreps, Oliver Hart, Mark Machina,

---

[76] Hahn's 'Risk' Project was based at the Department of Applied Economics. The first reference to the 'Risk' Seminar is in the DAE's Annual Report for activities during 1968–1969.

[77] Towards the end of the period, Matthews initiated a restructuring of SSRC funding procedures between different categories of expenditure which opened the space for fresh creative initiatives through panels leading innovative conferences and seminars (ESRC, n.d., pp. 14–15).

> Lou Makowski, Douglas Gale, Ben Lockwood, Jonathan Thomas, Paolo Gottardi, David Canning, Bob Evans, Paul Seabright, Luca Anderlini, Costas Gatsios and David Kelsey, as well as many members of the Faculty, such as myself. Most of the researchers funded under this project went on to distinguished academic careers, many in the United States; Paul Seabright moved from Churchill College to Toulouse in France. Some fortunately stayed in Britain (where those who left Cambridge all became professors). Hahn's weekly internal *Risk* seminars were typical of his idiosyncratic but effective research style. They became known as 'Quaker' meetings, as they had no formal agenda but let the spirit move participants to speak—if they were quick enough to seize the chalk. Newly minted post-docs could hold forth before visiting Nobel laureates, rapidly gaining insights, experience and confidence that stood them in good stead later on. These Quakers were intensely productive, producing a steady stream of green discussion papers that in those pre-pdf times were posted around the world, signalling the vigour of the Hahn enterprise. ... He believed passionately in the merits of the Cambridge supervision system and the Socratic Method—which his Quaker seminars and the Churchill seminars exemplified. (Newbery, 2017, pp. 502, 505)

The Hahn Risk Project, in which these Quaker Seminars were embedded, was based in the 'hostile' Keynesian territory of the Department of Applied Economics, though these coordinates generally tend not to be mentioned by its protagonists.

4.3.14 Matthews's CLARE Group: The Master's Lodge of Moderate Practitioners

The 1970s were a turbo-charged period in UK politics, and this reflected sharply in Cambridge since Cambridge economists were very closely involved with the formulation and/or the critiques of official policies under successive governments. The political spectrum of involvement varied considerably, though arguably the most prominent and vociferous critiques came from the left-Keynesian quadrant, the vanguard of which was in the DAE macroeconomic teams. But there were other voices and opinions as well from the more 'moderate middle' or 'right of centre' fields.

Aubrey Silberston, who was a good friend of Robin Matthews (and of Frank Hahn) remarks:

> Soon after he became Master [of Clare College, Cambridge, in 1975], Robin together with Alec Cairncross, decided that there was room for an informal group of economists who could tackle conflicting views of the problems of the British economy in as objective and clear manner as possible. Thus was born the CLARE Group,[78] which was in existence from 1976 to 2002. Its members were economists from some dozen different institutions. Among its members from Cambridge were Brian Reddaway, Charles Feinstein, and Michael Posner, from

---

[78] The CLARE Group is discussed also in Chap. 2, and extended details of its membership over the years are provided there in Table 2.2.

London David Henderson, Tony Atkinson and myself, from Oxford Alec Cairncross, John Flemming and Peter Oppenheimer, and from Warwick Dick Sargent (later chief economist of the Midland Bank) and Marcus Miller. Other members included John Kay, Mervyn King, Alan Prest, and also Brian Tew from Nottingham. Members of the CLARE group produced over 50 articles in total, published initially in the *Midland Bank Review* and then in the *National Institute Economic Review*.[79] (Silberston, 2011a)

Charles Goodhart (2006, p. 78), in his appreciation of John Flemming, writes that the CLARE Group emerged "out of concern that political economy in Britain was becoming polarised between a left-wing, often interventionist Labour government and a right-wing, neo-liberal and monetarist Conservative opposition. The idea was to show that there remained a sensible, Keynesian middle ground." It was this space that Robin Matthews mobilised into a powerfully networked group of senior economists who collectively wielded considerable influence in government, Treasury and Bank of England circles. This was the CLARE Group. Though it met at the eponymous Clare College under the Master, Robin Matthews's hospitality, the acronym stood for Cambridge, London and the Rest of England, from where the members of the group were drawn. Membership was by invitation, and their meetings were not open seminars. The CLARE Group was chaired by Matthews from the start till a year after he retired as Master in 1993, with chair passing to John Flemming, who had been a member from the start, till 2003, when the group wound up "because it had served its purpose (no one any longer much disagreed with its main positions), and its founders had grown old" (ibid.).

Matthews was in several positions of significant authority and wielded huge influence: he was Chairman of the SSRC during 1972–1975 when he had to contend with the hostility of Margaret Thatcher, then Secretary of State in the Heath Government, against social scientists and social sciences in general; he served as Chairman of the Bank of England Panel of Economic Consultants over a 16-year stretch (1977–1993); he held sway as Master of Clare College Cambridge over an 18-year period (1975–1993); he occupied the original

---

[79] R.C.O. (Robin) Matthews and J.R. (Dick) Sargent edited a volume of the earlier papers of the group—*Contemporary Problems of Economic Policy*—in 1983; subsequent publications were carried in the *Midland Bank Review*, explained by the fact that Dick Sargent was the Chief Economist of Midland Bank, and then in the *National Institute Economic Review*, explained by the significant overlap between the members of the CLARE Group and the advisors of the National Institute. There was a regular arrangement between the two for CLARE publications. An example is provided by Charles Feinstein and Robin Matthews (1990), 'The Growth of Output and Productivity in the UK: The 1980s as a Phase of the Post-War Period', *National Institute Economic Review*, 133(1), 78–90. Articles were cited thus:

"The Review is pleased to give hospitality to the deliberations of the CLARE Group but is not necessarily in agreement with the views expressed. Members of the CLARE Group are: M.J. Artis, A.J.C. Britton, W.A. Brown, C.H. Feinstein, C.A.E. Goodhart, D.A. Hay, J.A. Kay, R.C.O. Matthews, M.H. Miller, P.M, Oppenheimer, M.V. Posner, W.B. Reddaway, J.R. Sargent, M. F-G. Scott, Z.A., Silberston, J.H.B. Tew, J.S. Vickers, S. Wadhwani."

Cambridge chair, Professor of Political Economy, from 1980 when Brian Reddaway (also incidentally of Clare College and the CLARE Group) retired, till his own retirement in 1991; and he occupied the Presidency at the Royal Economic Society over 1984–1986, handing over the seat to his Cambridge friend and proverbial 'partner in crime', Frank Hahn, for the following three eventful years. These were all surely positions of high responsibility, but they were also conveyors of considerable privilege, power and patronage. In this context, the CLARE Group, running over the nearly three decades, clearly constituted a network not just for the exchange of information and ideas but also for influencing decision makers and decision-making in key committees and arenas through a collaborative approach. Silberston (2011a) reports that Matthews himself felt "that he was far more distinguished as a chess problematist than as an economist". His publisher called him one of the world's leading composers of three-movers, his specialisation. To this one might add, unsurprisingly, that he was a shrewd strategist in the politics of Cambridge economics.

Over the 27 years of its existence, the membership of the group took on younger cohorts as older ones thinned out.[80] Table 2.2 (in Chap. 2) provides membership lists for specific years and testifies to the spread and strength of the network.[81]

Matthews's CLARE Group occupies a place of indirect significance in the overall narrative of the Cambridge heterodox traditions, and in particular with respect to the dismantling of the DAE's two macroeconomic modelling teams, the Godley-Cripps Cambridge Economic Policy Group and the Stone-Barker Cambridge Growth Project, and arguably, even for the outcome of the Review of the DAE conducted by the General Board of the University, widely believed to be at the instigation of none other than Professors Hahn and Matthews. Coincidentally, several crucial members and experts on committees making the (unfriendly) decisions in all three episodes happened to be members of the CLARE Group and close associates of Matthews, including, amongst others, Michael Posner, Charles Feinstein, John Flemming and Tony Atkinson with cameo roles in those set piece dramas. The CLARE network easily reached the SSRC, the Treasury, Whitehall and the Bank of England, all key decision-making platforms. All this paired well with the purely academic networks of neoclassically oriented economists that were mobilised and nurtured by Frank

---

[80] It appears there could have been some uncertainty about the group late in 1987: Willy Brown in a letter to Robin Matthews remarks: "We shall be meeting at the Midland Bank to consider the future of the Clare Group—I do hope it has one …" It did. (Willy Brown to Robin Matthews, Letter dated 29 December 1987, p. 3)

[81] It is noteworthy that Richard Kahn is never listed as being involved with the CLARE Group—this despite the close association with Michael Posner (from the New vs Old Cambridge controversies in the mid-1970s)—and also in view of the strong presence in the CLARE Group of Cambridge economists (such as Robin Matthew, Charles Feinstein, Brian Reddaway and Michael Posner) displaying affinity with the Social Democratic Party towards which Kahn himself clearly drifted over the years. Richard Kahn was thought to be not generally comfortable in public participation or in seminars except on his own turf.

Hahn, as for example, through the Mathematical Seminar at Churchill, or the long-running Quaker/Risk Seminars, funded by the SSRC when Matthews was its Chairman. Of course, those members of the CLARE Group who had a position in the decision-making chains that led to the demise of the two DAE macroeconomic teams would have been acting in their individual professional capacities, as the CLARE Group was an informal assemblage. Given the broad academic (moderate or right-wing Keynesians) and political affinities (sympathetic orientation towards the SDP), and quite close intra-group interactions (in seminars, publications and committees), it could be a fair speculation that their roles in such decision-making chains would not have been particularly sympathetic to the left-wing Keynesians that were associated with the policy positions of these teams within the DAE and generally in charged public discourse of the time.

4.3.15 Lawson—Realism and Social Ontology: Ways of Seeing and Framing

Tony Lawson had done serious time in the DAE as an applied macroeconomist in Richard Stone's Cambridge Growth Project, from 1977 for a decade till the CGP was rudely terminated. He shifted base then to the Faculty side of the building. From the 1980s, he developed his initiative on social ontology in what would have appeared as quite a reincarnation; many colleagues might have been encouraging, some would have grasped its essence, but few might have turned up. He stood out "like someone standing alone at a party" (Pratten, 2013, citing Edward Fullbrook). But he stuck it out and walked his talk, a la Tagore,[82] or perhaps Majrooh.[83] A group of research students gathered around him in the late 1980s, and the Cambridge Realist Workshop (CRW) came into formal existence in October 1990. In the introduction to his book on social ontology and economics, Stephen Pratten (2014) shares an extract from Lawson's open letter, dated 15 October 1990, to his Faculty colleagues, providing what must have been a necessary aide to their understanding:

> Although it is anticipated that the workshop will entail some philosophical (as well as History of Thought) orientation the concern is centrally with the doing of substantive economics. All that is presupposed is a commitment to the view that there exists a knowable (under some description) social reality and that economics should primarily address such matters as identifying and understanding real world economic structures, mechanisms, processes and events, etc. This commitment though minimal, does entail acknowledging that the nature of economic

---

[82] Rabindrnath Tagore's Ekla Chalo Re was a Bengali protest song written in 1905. "If they answer not thy call, walk alone .... open thy mind and speak out alone ...". Or,)
[83] Majrooh Sultanpuri, in *Urdu: Main akela hi chala tha jaanib-e-manzil, magar log saath aate gae, karvan banta gaya* .... "I began walking alone towards my goal, people kept joining me, a caravan formed ...")

reality bears upon both the types of theories we can legitimately entertain as well as the methods of theory assessment that can be rationally supported. In philosophical jargon it is a presupposition of the realist program that questions of ontology are in some sense prior to, and bear upon, questions of epistemology and methodology as well as substantive economic research.

Pratten records that the CRW "quickly obtained a relatively prominent profile" and drew large numbers of participants. This, alongside the departure of some of the originals to other employments, meant that "the nature of the Workshop began to change". So, while the CRW, which continues to the present, became a "general forum for philosophically inclined economists" pulling in famous speakers and many participants from diverse social science constituencies, "it was felt that something was by now missing. The sense [of] organic evolution of the early days had inevitably declined with change in the size and the composition of the Workshop". And this led to the formation of the Cambridge Social Ontology Group (CSOG) in October 2002, a smaller and more focussed forum focussing on ontological discussions; CSOG has also run through to the present. Pratten (2014) and Martins (2014) have pulled together and assessed the significance and impact of this turn to social ontology in Cambridge. There is something then to be said for the dictums of Tagore and Majrooh.

The throwback to the inspiration from Keynes's reflections on probability is clear, but there are other productive interfaces and debates with different heterodox traditions prominent in Cambridge, and of course critical rejections of the reductionist neoclassical paradigm that surrounded Tony Lawson and the CRW and CSOG groups in Cambridge as the orthodox gang gained near-total dominance over the Faculty of Economics. In a real sense, that the intellectual project survived at all, much less flourished, is a testimony both to its originator, but also a confirmation of the rising intellectual dissatisfaction and dissent building up with respect to ways of modern mainstream economics and its local practitioners. The existence and operation of these groups has to be viewed in conjunction with the earlier emergence of the other major radical heterodox economics forum, the *Cambridge Journal of Economics*. So, even as the local orthodox group could control appointments and promotions, research programmes and teaching curricula, they could not entirely suppress the radical heterodox voice, as is confirmed by the sustained success of the *CJE*, and of the CRW and CSOG groups, alongside the Singh-Arestis-Kitson political economy seminar series in turn at Queens' and St. Catherine's, and the relocation of meaningful applied economics research at the Judge Business School. These were the meeting grounds where the heterodox clans assembled, regrouped, and continued to reassert their critiques of orthodoxy and continue with the development of progressive alternative approaches. In a real sense, these social ontology workshops return to the original agenda of exploring the potential social meaningfulness of the discipline focussing on how to make modern economics fit for social purpose.

4.4 Textbooks

Textbooks define a discipline; as one evolves so does the other. In this sense, the doctrinal stability of the orthodox mainstream has enabled ready codification into texts, many of which have taken on a scriptural status, with occasional amendments and revisions to suit modern times and to serve as the 'bible' on which entrants to the faith swear allegiance. Samuelson, the high priest, has written some of these texts in stone having famously declared that he did not care who wrote the nation's treaties so long as he could write its textbooks, and so he did, with *The Foundations of Economic Analysis* in 1947, followed up by *Economics*, the entry textbook, in 1948.

But there was a general problem for the student: 'economics' as in these textbooks bore little resemblance to the economies to which they were meant to be applied; there was a chasm between scriptural knowledge and texts, and practical manuals for addressing real-world problems—a problem well recognised within the branches of the family of orthodox economics, prompting the practically minded Milton Friedman to observe: "The fundamental difference between Chicago at that time and let's say Harvard, was that at Chicago economics was a serious subject to be used in discussing real problems, and you could get some knowledge and some answers from it. For Harvard, economics was an intellectual discipline on a par with mathematics, which was fascinating to explore, but you mustn't draw any conclusions from it. It wasn't going to enable you to solve any problems, and I think that's always been a fundamental difference between Chicago and other places. MIT more recently has been a better exemplar than Harvard" (Friedman in Hammond, 1988, p. 17). Friedman preferred the common sense of his hands-on policy tools based on the premise that the market, such as it was, was the best thing for everything; and this needed practical lessons in policy making. But criticism also came from the other end of orthodox persuasion. Frank Hahn was a pure theory man, had little time for policy per se. He did not like textbooks either: "The main thing I want to avoid is textbook-style economics. That makes people believe that they are doing 'science'. I think of economic theory as a way of organizing our minds, so that we do not speak of things that are incoherent. I do not mean that we are stating the 'truth'" (Hahn, 1989a, p. 904). "The fact is … that the textbooks in America are mainly written as 'science' and stop recognition of the ambiguities of the subject. The macro is worse, but even the micro theory is pretty awful. If one takes what Joan said just to stop all this nonsense, she would deserve our applause" (ibid., p. 898). He added: "In Cambridge I am one of the strongest advocates of having, for instance, two principles courses taught by people of different persuasions" (ibid.).

Back in the real Cambridge, there had been a deep tradition of textbook writing, with the craft taken to its best levels with Marshall and Pigou. But there the chain broke, with Keynes and the general attack on the Marshall-Pigou neoclassical construction of economic theory. The heterodox traditions unleashed in Cambridge were too fast moving and diverse, looking, challenging, reformulating, replacing, in multiple directions to have the stability to set down an agreed doctrine, beyond a generally shared perspective, that could be codified into a textbook readily intelligible to undergraduates. Compounding this would be the question of who the scribe would be, with little prospect of any consensus in the pride of prima donnas that Cambridge heterodox economics boasted. The paradox is that ideas were shared and forged on shared anvils, with many hands and hammers shaping any particular concept, proposition or theoretical construct. So while individual authorship was not necessarily the key issue, there would be enough nit-picking over fine-tuning to scuttle such an effort. Several individual forays can be identified: Joan Robinson (1956), Maurice Dobb on Marxist discourses, Nicky Kaldor[84] (1966), Dick Goodwin (1970), amongst others, but these could not really be called viable textbooks carrying the general Cambridge message. Kahn wrote little. And, of course, Sraffa's monastically frugal classic was but a 'prelude' to a systematic critique that never came. Effectively Cambridge had abdicated the space on conventional textbooks, and that was a great pedagogical gap hugely felt at the level of undergraduate (and post-graduate) teaching, where fresh young entrants had to depend on the classroom interpretations of teachers (few of whom might be fully enabled and empowered to introduce them into the complexities of Cambridge economics) and having to go to the journals for specific pieces by the greats (which would generally prove to be too difficult to absorb and imbibe effectively on their own). Third, these diverse bands of Cambridge economists of the post-war period were too preoccupied in the *doing* of economics to find the days in the year or hours in the day, or an inclination to withdraw to Corfu, Skye or Bellagio to slave over a textbook that all their colleagues would surely pick at, and one that might soon be overtaken by fast-moving theories and their contending interpretations.

Three episodes are addressed. The first concerns the faraway story, both in time and in space, of the successful writing of a significant Keynesian textbook and its immediate suppression by the right-wing, clearing the space for the triumphant global entry of Samuelson's *Economics*. The second takes the form

---

[84] Wynne Godley (2008) complains about Nicky Kaldor: "They left no legacy; I knew a lot of Kaldor's ideas but there is no Kaldorian textbook; there is no post-Keynesian synthesis"; he believes "that Marc Lavoie and I had made a statement on macroeconomics which is enough for other people to build on". He is out of order here, and this drew a one-word riposte ("Rubbish!") from Geoff Harcourt. Kaldor did set down his thoughts, but not in conventional textbooks, though Kaldor (1966) and especially his Raffaele Mattioli Lectures in 1984, posthumously published, unfortunately more than a decade later (Kaldor 1996), stand out as more or less complete statements of his evolved views, as they stood at those points in time. Probably Wynne was too preoccupied with his book with Marc Lavoie in 2007 to notice the publication of a significant assessment of Cambridge Keynesians and Keynesianism the same year (Pasinetti, 2007); and Geoff might have been all the more peeved for Wynne to have overlooked his *The Structure of Post-Keynesian Economics: The Core Contributions of the Pioneers*, published the previous year (Harcourt, 2006); also not to be overlooked should have been his co-researcher Marc Lavoie's contribution (Lavoie, 2007), *An Introduction to Post-Keynesian Economics*, or the earlier work of Jan Kregel (1973) (see also: Chapter 2, pp. 26, 26n26.).

of a reminder of the Robinson-Eatwell effort at producing a rival 'Cambridge' introduction to modern economics, which sadly died, or was suffocated, in its infancy. The third is an example, representative of so many others at Cambridge, of an aborted collective effort at the production of a comprehensive textbook of applied economics in the Cambridge tradition. The three cases that follow bear testimony to the unfortunate fact that Cambridge never really got its act together in the crucial arena of textbooks; Samuelson did have a point, and cashed in, financially of course, and ideologically; he and his followers won by default, by a walk-over; the other Cambridge team didn't show up.

4.4.1 Distant Thunder: Keynes and McCarthy, Tarshis and Samuelson

The conjuncture of the late 1940s is also the cusp, the short and sharp period of inflexion. In Samuelson's depiction of the four revolutions, it marks the switch point denoting the end of second revolution, viz., of Keynes, and effective demand, and the beginning of the third, of the mathematisation of economics. Paradoxical that Samuelson's book also carries a mathematical treatment of Keynes for the first time in the USA and that the real Keynesian textbook of Tarshis is killed off by American proto-neoliberal opposition. This opposition is both home-grown through the ideological opposition from American industrialists and shopkeepers, but, crucially, also gains its muscularity from the right-wing shift effected by the arrival and assimilation of liberal émigré economists from Russia and Central Europe. A second powerful force that censors and disciplines Keynesianism is the decade of McCarthyism, 1947–1957, the storm rising as the spectre of communism, a fear developed by the state itself, mutates into the Frankenstein of McCarthy's agenda. However, the ebb and flow of Keynesianism is not identical in the UK and the USA. In sharp contrast to the developments in the USA, in the UK Keynesianism actually enters its period of most powerful influence both on economics as a discipline and on economic policy; the quarter century from the end of the war is perhaps the crowning period of the Keynesian gospel, though its prophet had fallen in 1946 just as his ideas were spreading their wings into full flight. Thus, a wide contrast is discernible in the post-war welcome, as opposed to hostility, to Keynesian ideas and policies when considering the UK, parts of Europe and the USA.

Dick Goodwin clarifies the link between McCarthyism and his move from the USA to Cambridge UK:

> It was the height of the McCarthy period and so there was a witch-hunt against those who had been or were still members of the Communist Party. I was no longer a member, but this did not protect me from the committee because they forced us to appear before it demanding the names of the others who had been communists. At that point, the choice was between responding or the risk of being sent to prison. It was a very grave situation and the atmosphere was getting

worse. In reality they had not yet summoned me to appear before McCarthy's committee, so it is not true that I left America as a political refugee as was subsequently suggested. It was however a fact that those on the left—like me—were very vulnerable. It was very difficult to find employment and hang onto it: the situation was therefore very unpleasant. This is probably the real reason why I did not want to stay in America.[85]

In contrast, he liked Britain "where one could be left and not left out",[86] and Cambridge "where he could teach what he wanted".[87] Worth noting here is Geoff Harcourt's view of the Harvard decision not to offer Goodwin an appointment: "Goodwin charitably attributes the decision as a mistaken one made purely on academic grounds but I, less charitably, suggest the McCarthyite funk was a factor influencing some of the decision-makers" (quoted in Baranzini and Mirante (2018, p. 43n23).

The case of the McCarthyite suppression of Lorie Tarshis's pioneering 699-page Keynesian textbook, *The Elements of Economics*, published in 1947 is especially significant as it bears directly on the question of why Keynesianism met an unreceptive, indeed hostile, reception in the USA in the immediate post-war years. Attention has been drawn to this shabby episode by several authors, prominently including Geoff Harcourt (1982, 1993, 1995a), Colander and Landreth (n.d., 1996). Lorie's nasty story is interconnected, and contrasts dramatically, with the spectacular success of Paul Samuelson's *Economics*, the first edition of which, also carrying a treatment of Keynesian macroeconomics, was released the following year in 1948; and the unfortunate pairing of the suppression of Tarshis's highly regarded book, and the quick rise to dominance of Samuelson's formulaic textbook induced a rather rueful explanatory lament from Samuelson half a century later (Samuelson, 1997); it is perhaps noteworthy that Samuelson's recollections are registered a year after the appearance of David Colander and Harry Landreth's 1996 book on the entry of Keynesianism into America, where the Tarshis textbook episode is extensively discussed.

Samuelson (1997, p. 153) notes "the 1920s and 1930s were a fallow period in textbook writing"; the mid-1940s "was a time of singular opportunity. The colleges were crowded with returning veterans. For those who had lived through the 1929–1935 Great Depression, the best of the existing texts were almost comical in their *macroeconomics*. The word had not yet been invented."[88]

So when he returned to MIT after the war, with 800 juniors taking a year of compulsory economics and no suitable textbook, Ralph Freeman, his department head, came with a proposition: "Paul, will you go on half time for a semester or two? Write a text the students will like …" So Paul set aside the finalisation of *Foundations*, and after "night and summer slaving" came up with

---

[85] Richard Goodwin, in an interview he gave to Maura Palazzi in 1982, as reported in Di Matteo and Sordi (2009, pp. 16–17).
[86] As conveyed in a letter to Velupillai, see Di Matteo and Sordi (2009, p. 17).
[87] As conveyed in his tribute by Pasinetti, see Di Matteo and Sordi (2009, p. 17).
[88] Samuelson notes the attribution of the first usage of the term to Lindahl in 1939.

Economics 1948, stepping into "the window of opportunity", and "I did cash in on bringing simple Keynes to the elementary classroom" (ibid., p. 157); "My 1948 first edition's macro concentrated on the early General Theory paradigm" (ibid., p. 156). Lorie Tarshis was "a neighbour and a good personal friend, but I first heard of his book when as a 1947 MIT teacher I was given a promotional copy. It was a good book; a very good book. Maybe in 1945 I would have stuck to my mathematical-economics knitting if the Tarshis text had then been available; … my book would have inevitably become a competitor, but of course the beginners' market is gigantic in scope, big enough for several worthy competitors" (ibid., pp. 156–157). Samuelson would surely have known of *An Economic Program for American Democracy*, the 1938 book jointly authored by Tarshis and six other Harvard and Tufts economists (Gilbert et al. 1938)[89]; Colander and Landreth (n.d., p. 1) note "that book received significant attention and, in academic circles, it closely associated Tarshis with liberal and Keynesian ideas".

Tarshis's book was killed by the McCarthyite right-wing. Samuelson recalls, "never could I understand the variety and virulence of the attackers; … Tarshis was not notorious as a leftist, … was a low-keyed teacher and researcher. The attackers, I recall, included names then considered extremely on the right: a Colonel Namm who owned a Brooklyn department store; also someone named Zoll, for a small fascist-leaning group on the right; … a Philip Cortney who headed the Cody cosmetic company and lectured at Harvard," also Rose Wilder Lane, the author and daughter of the famous author Laura Ingalls Wilder, and the leader of the pack was William Buckley, the right-wing libertarian journalist. Samuelson's preliminary classroom version of the first edition was challenged for a short while, but escaped unscathed because "fortunately for me, I had considered it good business to articulate carefully just when and why an unorthodox paradigm might make sense under certain conditions, whereas at other times orthodox paradigms would commend themselves. Interested in maximizing not PQ book revenues but rather Q influence, I could only gain from being eclectic and centrist. Critics from both right and left began to complain that I wrote carefully (as if a lawyer were at my elbow)" (Samuelson, 1997, pp. 158–159).[90]

Giraud (2020, p. 177) in his examination of the manner in which Samuelson and his publishers managed the market for his *Economics* textbook in the politically charged climate during 1967–1973 when radical economics emerged as a

---

[89] The seven economists were Richard V. Gilbert, George H. Hildebrand jr., Arthur W. Stuart, Maxine Yaple Sweezy, Paul M. Sweezy, Lorie Tarshis and John D. Wilson.

[90] This might have been a long-term tendency. An observant reader in 2015 of the 50th Anniversary reissue of the "original" unchanged 1948 edition of *Economics* writes: "A sentence … from the first edition read: 'John D. Rockefeller's dog may receive the milk that a poor child needs to avoid rickets.' The current edition reads: 'A rich man's cat may drink the milk that a poor boy needs to remain healthy'."

https://www.amazon.com/Economics-Original-1948-Paul-Samuelson/dp/0070747415?ref_=nav_ya_signin&.

critical force against mainstream economics of the Samuelson type "show[s] how Samuelson, helped by his editorial team at McGraw-Hill, attempted to take into account these changes in order to ensure the continuing success of subsequent editions of his textbook in an increasingly competitive market". Giraud "emphasizes Samuelson's ambiguous attitude toward his contenders, revealing, on the one hand, his apparent openness to discussion and outsider's suggestions, and, on the other hand, his firm attachment to mildly liberal politics and aversion to Marxism, unchanged through revisions."

If Samuelson had an imagined lawyer at his elbow, Tarshis had the spectre of McCarthyism in his face. The 1938 Keynesian policy book "was not altogether positive for me" says Tarshis. "The president of Tufts [where Tarshis was] thought it was awful. He kept sending me reminders of donors who were going to give money to Tufts but who had decided not to, because of the book. In fact, I was regarded as an absolute Red" (Colander & Landreth, 1996, p. 64). So after the war, in 1946, Tarshis adopted a conventional tactic to write a textbook. He was "an excellent writer and expositer", and quick too, as he finished the 699-page book in 1947. Colander and Landreth (n.d.) observe that "perhaps the biggest difference between Tarshis's book and earlier books was in policy sensibility. Most earlier books had espoused classical political economy interpreting laissez-faire precepts in a general way, with little or no discussion of current problems. ... The message conveyed to students ... was that unimpeded markets were the best way to organize an economy. Any statements to the contrary were heresy." And in this sense, Tarshis was wildly 'heretical': his book "conveyed a quite different policy perspective. Tarshis saw the government as an agency through which people acted collectively for the common good ... combined with the belief that the market needed government assistance to assure full employment" (ibid.). It is worth viewing the scene, as it subsequently unfolded, through Lorie Tarshis's eyes.

> When the book came out ... I kept getting glowing telegrams from the publisher. I thought, 'Oh, my God, this is just beyond belief.' I would get letters from my publisher saying Brown has adopted it, maybe Middlebury adopted it, Yale has adopted it—one place after another had adopted it. Every time I got a letter like this that indicated ten or twenty more adoptions, I thought, 'Boy, that bank account will be picking up'. (Tarshis quoted in Colander & Landreth, n.d.)

But that was as good as it got. Suddenly, there as an organised campaign against the book: in Tarshis's words: "Merwin K. Hart organized a thing called 'The National Economic Committee'; he got Rose Wilder Lane to write a newsletter for it and he sent copies of this newsletter to all the members of every Board of Trustees of every university anywhere, including politicians, Republican universities and so on", demanding it be taken off the lists; "removing the Tarshis book from economics classes became a cause celebre of conservative organizations" (Colander & Landreth, n.d.). "In August 1947, the National Economic Council (sic) published an essay saying that *The Elements of*

Economics 'plays upon fear, shame, pity, greed, idealism, hope. ... This is not an economics text at all; it is a pagan-religious and political tract'."[91] Tarshis says, "It was villainous stuff. They were after Paul Baran, who was a Marxist; they were after Ed Shaw, who was a monetarist, and me. They thought Stanford should get rid of all of us," but Stanford stood its ground. "But sales, instead of staying at that beautiful peak, went down just like that ... the book ... really died in 1948 or 1949" (ibid.); Tarshis was not to be a millionaire book author.[92]

Prominent in the attack on Tarshis was William F. Buckley Jr., the libertarian conservative (author of *God and Man at Yale* in 1951, which explains the title of the Colander and Landreth paper) who "laid the groundwork for the rightward shift in the Republican Party exemplified by Barry Goldwater and Ronald Reagan", served as a CIA operative during 1951–1953, including a year in Mexico City working under E. Howard Hunt who was later convicted for his role in the Watergate affair[93]; as a committed Catholic, co-authored *McCarthy and his Enemies* in 1954, the book which provided a strong defence of McCarthy—who was also deeply and politically Catholic—portraying him as a patriotic crusader against communism. Buckley supported Pinochet, attacked Allende as a supporter of Fidel Castro and mobilised support—as did Milton Friedman—for Barry Goldwater's presidential campaign. He was a member of Hayek's Mont Pelerin Society and long-serving editor of the influential conservative publication *National Review*.[94]

Buckley wielded a McCarthyite hatchet. According to Tarshis: "That bastard Buckley—I get so angry when I think of him, because, you know he's *still* parading his objectivity and concern for 'moral values', and so on. The amount of distortion is enormous. He would pick a phrase and tack it onto a phrase two pages later, another page later, another four pages earlier, and make a sentence that I couldn't recognize as anything I'd written ... and make it seem as though I was no supporter of market capitalism, which I felt I always was" (quoted in Colander & Landreth, n.d.).

And then: "Buckley asks, where does Tarshis examine the views of Hayek and Mises?" (Colander & Landreth, n.d.), telling us how quickly and powerfully the Hayekian *Road to Serfdom* attack on Keynesianism had filtered into the libertarian discourse and been adopted as a measuring rod for what ideas were acceptable, right down to classroom textbooks.

---

[91] Stanford University News Service, "Author of First U.S. College Textbook on Keynesian Economics Dies", 'News Release', 10/11/93.

[92] Samuelson (1997, p. 159), when recounting the (comparatively limited) attack on his book by one businessman in 1948, and its defence by the MIT President, observes, "Later, when my book was accorded bestseller status, this particular businessman critic even developed some grudging admiration for it. Money talks. Lorie Tarshis was never so lucky with any of his opponents." No, he wasn't, perhaps because he argued a more politically straightforward case for Keynesianism and the New Deal, without that 'lawyer at the elbow' à la Samuelson.

[93] Wikipedia, "William F. Buckley Jr.", accessed on 10 April 2020.

[94] Reagan: "I'd be lost without *National Review*" (quoted in Fuelner, 2018). Fuelner was the founder and former President of The Heritage Foundation, "the bastion of the American conservative movement since our founding in 1973".

For a substantive view on Tarshis's textbook, and the loss entailed by its suppression in the USA, we can do little better than turn to Geoff Harcourt, one of the two long-serving gurus, with Luigi Pasinetti, of the Cambridge 'grand theory' vision. The exceptional academic merit of Tarshis's exposition has been highlighted by Geoff and is worth citing in extenso:

"He went to the lectures which became Keynes's General Theory; ... he obtained a First in an exceptional year (1934) and stayed on to do one of the earliest PhDs in the Faculty of Economics and Politics .... His dissertation 'The Determinants of Labour Income' was a pioneering work which, disgracefully, was never published. Tarshis used the insights of the theory of imperfect competition in Richard Kahn's lectures on 'The Economics of the Short Period' and Joan Robinson's *Economics of Imperfect Competition* (1933) explicitly to establish realistic microeconomic foundations for the macroeconomic system of The General Theory .... Tarshis thus discovered, independently, the macro theories of distribution, now principally associated with Michal Kalecki and Nicholas Kaldor—a discovery which brought Tarshis and Kalecki close together when they met in Cambridge in the late 1930s. Tarshis also played a vital role in converting Abba Lerner from his LSE-Hayekian stance to Keynesianism." Speaking about Tarshis's pioneering Keynesian textbook, Harcourt says, "It was deeply and intelligently true to Keynes's vision. There are still many people who say that Tarshis's exposition of the Keynesian system is the best they have ever read." With regard to the suppression of the textbook, Harcourt regrets the loss of a superior understanding of the Keynesian system at that time: "It would also have limited the damage ... that has been done because of the different way in which Keynesian thinking came through the textbooks into the profession, especially in the United States. ... Paul Samuelson's introductory textbook with its less satisfactory way of expositing Keynes's theory thus became the dominant textbook when it was published the next year" (Harcourt, 1993). And there we have the view of it all as seen from the Cambridge of Keynes.

Tarshis had received Keynesian wisdom through lectures at the fount, sitting at the feet of the original greats. Lorie Tarshis and his friend Bob Bryce were "enthusiastic students of J.M. Keynes" in Cambridge in 1936, and upon return "they started introducing Keynesian economics to Harvard, Cambridge, and to the United States. ... Bryce began spreading the gospel among the heathen; Schumpeter, as reported by John Kenneth Galbraith, called Keynes Allah and Bryce his Prophet" (Colander & Landreth, 1996, p. 137).

Colander and Landreth probe the question: why Tarshis and not Samuelson, and suggest various reasons, of which two are notable. First, that Tarshis had history, in that the earlier 1938 Keynesian policy book had marked him out as a New Deal protagonist, anathema to the libertarian right, from liberals to McCarthyites. In contrast, "Samuelson's reputation was as a scientist and he only played a tangential role in the spreading of Keynesian policy views prior to the publication of his introductory textbook. Tarshis's perception of Samuelson was that in the 1930s 'Paul Samuelson was not in the Keynesian group. He was busy working on his own thing. That he became a Keynesian was laughable'" (ibid.). Second: "The Tarshis book talked more about policy issues than did the other books, and it came to more conclusions. The Samuelson book presented the analysis with more detachment, more mathematically, than did Tarshis. Tarshis put heart into the policy discussion ... his was a book of passion as well as of analysis. Samuelson's work appeared to be a book of dispassionate analysis" (ibid.). "The result of this episode was to sanitize economics textbooks from much of the controversy that makes economics teaching exciting. It helped create a technalization of what we teach students, and in doing so has influenced the direction of economics away from the true policy debates which necessarily involve clashes of ideology, and toward a discussion of make-believe policy fights centred around technical aspects of models—debates that do not arouse the passions that the real-world ideological debates arouse" (ibid.). No doubt, Samuelson would agree, but at the same time also defend the sanitisation of the subject of any vestiges of contestation of alternative political values and policy positions. Paraphrasing his words about his tribe of economists, we are highly trained athletes who do not run races.

Half a century after his classic effectively disappeared from American courses, a memorial volume pays "tribute to a most faithful, true Keynesian, who read, thought, dreamt and promoted Keynes" (Hamouda & Price, 1998). Too late; the gap had been filled, the damage done.

4.4.2 Lawrence Klein and the Paradox of The Keynesian Revolution

Born in 1920, Lawrence Klein, winner of the Sveriges Riksbank Prize in Economic Sciences in Memory of Alfred Nobel in 1980, began his illustrious career in economics with a Ph.D. at MIT in 1944; then moved to the Cowles Commission during 1944–1947; published his left-inclined book *The Keynesian Revolution* in 1947; spent a year in Norway, visiting Frisch and Haavelmo, *en route* having built a model for the Canadian economy in the summer of 1947; and met up with Richard Stone and his team at the DAE in Cambridge in 1948[95]; then followed a brief stay at NBER (National Bureau of Economic Research) in New York; and then a fateful stint at the University of Michigan

---

[95] The 'List of Distinguished Visitors' noted in the DAE's Annual Report (1946–1948, pp. 20, # 54):

"*July* 1948. Dr. L. Klein of the Cowles Commission, University of Chicago, spent a month at the Department as part of a tour of European countries which was undertaken to study problems of economic planning and econometric research. *October* 1948. Professor Paul A. Samuelson of the Massachusetts Institute of Technology spent a fortnight at the Department." The previous year, Klein had published *The Keynesian Revolution*, and Samuelson his *Foundations* followed in 1948 by the first edition of his *Economics* textbook. These 'distinguished visitors' were, respectively, 28 and 33 years old.

during 1949–1954, after which, pushed by McCarthyism, he shifted to Institute of Statistics in Oxford 1954–1958[96]; and subsequently returned permanently to University of Pennsylvania.

Puzzle

A puzzle suggests itself. Lorie Tarshis demonstrably ran afoul of the McCarthyites for his espousal of radical Keynesianism as the theoretical scaffolding for the New Deal, both projects being anathema to the red-hunters, and his Keynesian textbook was torpedoed and sank. Samuelson, as he said, wrote apolitically with care, as if with a lawyer scanning his words as he wrote, so he survived the heat. Klein, in contrast, had identified communist associations around that time and, significantly, added a chapter, "Keynes and Social Reform", to his thesis before it was published, where he elaborated on his radical leftist, near-Marxist, interpretations on the critical policy issues of the day. The books by Tarshis and Klein both appeared in 1947, but while the former was suppressed, no flash of McCarthyite lightning struck the latter which ran into several editions and came to be regarded by some with fair justification, as a Marxist-influenced take on Keynesianism; although supervised by Paul Samuelson at MIT, it had rather a Cambridge-UK character.

Klein's text frequently has a perceptible Marxist resonance in language, with reference to classes of capitalists and workers, to owners of the means of production, to Marxist and bourgeois economists, "economic laws of motion of capitalism", and much else in that vein; hardly surprising, since Lawrence Klein, in the period of writing his doctoral dissertation in 1944 and converting it into a book in 1947, was also a member of the Communist Party and engaged in imparting instruction in economics to workers and cadres. The book's leftist policy stance, which "apparently Dr. Klein favors", was recognised in contemporary reviews (Wright, 1948, p. 145).

Ph.D.—At Samuelson's Feet

Klein states that the suggestion that he should write his thesis on the Keynesian system came from Samuelson (cited in De Vroey and Malgrange (2012, p. 115). "A chance to study at M.I.T. under the rising star of the period—Paul A. Samuelson—was an unforgettable experience. I successfully vied for his time

---

[96] Kalecki, rendered peripatetic by the war and related circumstances, had spent the war years at the OIS (1940–1945), writing some of his classic papers while there. It was a wartime refuge. But it came at a cost, or a cross, which Kalecki was unwilling to bear; he felt discriminated against on account of being dealt with as an immigrant, and left, and eventually—after stints in Paris, Warsaw and Montreal—joined the UN in New York in 1946 as Deputy Director of the Department of Economic Affairs. He stayed there till 1955, then hounded out by McCarthyism, the same year that Klein tendered his resignation at the University of Michigan, ironically, for the safe and free haven of Oxford Institute of Statistics, which Kalecki had left with a sense of exclusion a decade earlier. George Feiwel wrote of Michal Kalecki: "Most significant[ly], he simply would not compromise his principles. Looking back over his troubled years, Kalecki once made the sad but true observation that the story of his life could be compressed into a series of resignations in protest against tyranny, prejudice, and oppression" (Feiwel, 1975, p. 455).

and attention which were instrumental in giving me a good grasp of economics and mathematical ways of dealing with significant problems of the subject" (Klein, 1980). In the acknowledgements recorded in his dissertation, Klein's records an exceptional tribute to Samuelson "at whose feet I have sat for two years; ... for those arguments which represent real contributions, Professor Samuelson deserves much of the credit. Oftentimes I feel that I have in many cases done nothing more than paraphrase what I have learned in classes and innumerable discussions with Professor Samuelson" (Klein, 1944, p. i). Klein received his Ph.D. from MIT in 1944. "He was the first Ph.D. in economics from that institution and Paul Samuelson's first doctoral student" (Bodkin & Kanta, 1997, p. 361). Samuelson was just five years older than Klein.

His work with Samuelson at MIT "was intended to gain acceptance for mathematical methods and for Keynesian thinking and to establish its relevance to macroeconomic realities. ... It might surprise modern-day critics of macroeconomics to learn that, in this article ['Macroeconomics and the Theory of Rational Behavior', 1946], Klein addressed the problem of microfoundations of macroeconomics, though what Samuelson has termed 'envelope aggregation'" (Bodkin & Kanta, 1997, p. 362).

Cowles Commission—The New Dealers

From MIT and Paul Samuelson, the young Klein moved to the Cowles Commission and Jan Marschak. Klein (1991) provides an account of his years at Cowles with unambiguous reference to the political divide in Chicago at the time.

"There were two worlds of economics at Chicago then, 'us' and 'them', the former were the Cowles group, who were overwhelmingly New Deal democrats"; he recalls how "we were all struck with grief" when news arrived in the midst of a seminar that Roosevelt had died. "The latter were the stalwarts to the Chicago School, and we nearly always took polarized positions at general economics seminars on campus. Our intellectual opponents were Frank Knight, Henry Simons, Lloyd Mints, and at the end of this period, Milton Friedman. ... There were fights over method; Jacob Viner's main quarrel with us was on the issue of mathematical methodology. In general, members of the Chicago School, particularly Milton Friedman, were sympathetic with the non-mathematical approaches to quantitative economics pursued by the National Bureau of Economic Research under the leadership of Wesley Mitchell and Arthur Burns. When Tjalling Koopmans reviewed their massive work on *Measuring Business Cycles* under the heading 'Measurement without Theory', bitterness reached even a higher pitch. ... I could sense the tension in the dispute over methodology with the Cowles Commission. ... It was not purely methodology, however. A central issue was that we members of the Cowles Commission were seeking an objective that would permit state intervention and guidance for economic policy, and this approach was eschewed by both the National Bureau and the Chicago School" (Klein, 1991, p. 112). "The ideological split in Chicago played some role in the move to Yale but it also brought the Cowles name back to the alma mater of Alfred Cowles. His views of economics were probably more compatible with our opponents at the University of Chicago, but Mr. Cowles was attached to the mathematical methodology, and gave free rein in the present sense of academic freedom to our research activities. Jacob Marschak once told me that he was originally dubious about accepting the directorship of the Cowles Commission because he found the anti-Roosevelt (anti New Deal) attitudes of Mr. Cowles and his close associates to be intolerable, but a *modus vivendi* was finally worked out between them" (Klein, 1991, p. 113).

Additionally, in 1944, as Klein was completing his dissertation applauding Keynesian economics and its template for the role for some state management of the capitalist economy, Hayek was completing his *Road to Serfdom* polemic against all that; and during the following three years while Klein was part of the Marschak team of New Dealers at the Cowles Commission, Klein wrote up his new Chapter VII, "Keynes and Social Reform" to include in his thesis before it was published in 1947 as *The Keynesian Revolution*—meanwhile, Hayek and his ideological camp were busy frantically spreading its message, significantly also marking the birth of the Mont Pelerin Society in that year. Klein would have had the opportunity to address Hayek's assault on Keynesianism, egalitarian or social-democratic social policy, the drift to a welfare state on economic planning in capitalist economies, but he chose not to—Hayek's political project is entirely absent from Klein's, 1947 book. It is not difficult to see that Hayek would have had sufficient reasons not to support Klein's contract on ostensibly 'academic' or 'professional' grounds. Coincidentally, Kalecki's essay "Three Ways to Full Employment" also appeared in 1944 (in Burchardt et al., 1944, pp. 39–58), and there is much resonance to this in Klein's new Chapter VII, though there is no reference to this work in his book.

The Keynesian Revolution: *The Extra Chapter—Klein, Then a Closet Marxist?*

"In the past few years there has grown up a large group of younger economists who have accepted the theoretical doctrines of the Keynesian Revolution and who have come into national prominence through their support of an economic policy of full employment" (Klein, 1947, p. 165). This can fairly be presumed to be an indirect reference to the Harvard-Tufts 1938 book that gained high visibility in public discourse and in policy circles at the time. There are no other references or allusions to this significant intervention in the rest of the book though the thesis was completed in 1944.

It might be admissible to speculate that Klein's additional chapter could have been inspired in its message, method and structure, by Kalecki's "Three Ways to Full Employment" published in 1944. In its method and lines of argument, it runs nearly on a parallel track where the messages of Kalecki's article resonate with Klein's analysis directed at American realities. Curiously, there is no reference to Kalecki's article or to his earlier famous article in 1943 on "Political Aspects of Full Employment"; his 1938 piece in *Econometrica* on the Determinants of the Distribution of Income is listed in the references of the thesis but does not figure in the book—though Klein does make a favourable reference to the imperative of the Beveridge Report of 1942 (on which also Kalecki wrote in 1943). Notwithstanding the formal invisibility Kalecki, Klein's chapter leaves the reader in little doubt about the extent to which his analysis and prescriptions are Kaleckian in nature.[97]

Having reaffirmed the Keynesian imperative of full employment, Klein takes the Kaleckian road, comparing the three systemic alternatives of fascism, socialism or reformed capitalism. Fascism is quickly addressed and dismissed. "Fascism ... represents the worst stage of capitalism. It is the form that our capitalist society will acquire unless we are successful in bringing about Keynesian reforms or a socialist economy. If we let nature take its course, the economic law of motion of capitalism will take us down the same road that Germany followed so recently" (Klein, 1947, p. 167); here there is a resonance with the analysis of Kurt Mandelbaum (1944) included the *Six Studies* of the Oxford Institute of Statistics, and Keynes's view of full employment as an imperative for peace is acknowledged.[98]

"Do the policy measures advocated by the Keynesians lead to socialism, or do they endeavour to preserve capitalism?" In the opening paragraph of his Foreword, Klein poses this as one of the questions pursued in the book. Midway, Klein develops analytical dialogues between Keynes and various precursors, including an incisive and sympathetic treatment of the Marxian theoretical schema (pp. 130–134). However, there is no systematic treatment of options under socialism, though frequent contextual comparisons are provided by Klein with respect to various policy variations and constraints, and it is

---

[97] Kalecki was a towering intellectual figure for Klein. Significantly, in the course of his appreciation of Keynes, he broke off to register his high esteem for Kalecki: "Recently, after having re-examined Kalecki's theory of the business cycle, I have decided that he actually created a system that contains everything of importance in the Keynesian system, in addition to other contributions. Kalecki does not deal at all with liquidity preference and the interest rate; yet I believe that he has a theory of employment that is the equal of Keynes's. .... Some respects in which Kalecki's model is superior are that it is explicitly dynamic; it takes income distribution as well as level into account; and it makes the important distinction between investment orders and investment outlays ..." (Klein, 1951, pp. 447–448).

[98] The potential link between large-scale unemployment and the appeal of fascism was not too imaginary. James Meade, in his 'Nobel' Bio, alludes to it thus: "My interest in economics had the following roots. Like many in my generation I considered the heavy unemployment in the United Kingdom in the inter-war period as both stupid and wicked. Moreover, I knew the cure for the evil, because I had become. A disciple of the monetary crank, Major C.H. Douglas, to those works I had been introduced by a much loved but somewhat eccentric maiden aunt. But my shift to the serious study of economics gradually weakened my belief in Major Douglas's A+B theorem, which was replaced in my through by the expression $MV=PT$" (Meade, 1977). In his book, Lawrence Klein is more forthright, referring to Douglas as "the colorful crank [who] has done much to lower the scientific achievement of this [underconsumptionist] school. ... one of the best examples of an amateur economist supporting a reasonable economic policy on the basis of a nonsensical theory. ... His movement is filled with political dynamite. It was one of those pre-war movements with all the trappings of green-shirted legions, anti-labor propaganda, and anti-Semitism"; and then Klein proceeds to demolish the Douglas A+B proposition (Klein, 1947, pp. 140–142).

noticeable that 'socialism' always comes out the winner over options deemed available under contemporary capitalism; Paul Sweezy receives a laudation as the best of contemporary Marxists, though his joint authorship, with Tarshis and others, of the 1938 Tufts-Harvard intervention is not cited.

Klein's central focus is firmly on the conditions for constructing 'true economic democracy' under capitalism, using Keynesian tools, but augmented with other interventions beyond its scope, or outside Keynes's political preferences. At the core is a strategy of full employment "which seems to be such a desirable economic policy that we may well be led to wonder why there must be any opposition to it". He identifies three opposing arguments from 'conservative economists': "(1) it takes away individual freedom. (2) It leads to inflation. (3) It increases the public debt" (Klein, 1947, p. 179).

He rejects the first out of hand, citing Kalecki's "very elegantly [expressed] remark in an informal talk that the regimentation of unemployment and poverty is infinitely more severe than the regimentation of economic planning".[99] On the second, he is equally trenchant. "Conservatives who fear 'a revolution of the bondholders in our society ... oppose the full employment because they believe it may lead to excesses, to inflation. There does exist the possibility that the plans will be carried to excess, but if the alternative is the misery of the unemployed, then, by all means, let us have a little inflation" (ibid., pp. 179–180). He adds that "in the Keynesian spirit we may always prefer inflation to deflation if the choice must be made ... but we should like, even better, to have neither. There is no reason why intelligent economic planning cannot be of just the correct amount, that amount which gives permanent full employment and stable prices. There are several administrative methods of gaining full employment without inducing inflation" (ibid., p. 180). On the third objection, viz. the public debt, he is no less uncompromising: "The building up of the public debt to counteract unemployment is inevitable in our society where the means of production (the steel, machinery, tractors, concrete) are privately owned" (ibid., p. 182). But, Klein rhetorically asks, "Is public debt an evil? The funds raised by the public debt are used to put otherwise idle men to work, constructing homes, bridges, roads, and schools that make us richer in real terms; this kind of debt cannot possibly be an evil. The debt can become cumbersome, but it need not be evil" (ibid., p. 182).

Under full employment equilibrium finds a Kaleckian explanation through "the superior bargaining power of the employer over the employee" (Ibid., p. 87); and "the present writer must remain unconvinced by the arguments that wage cuts cure depressions" (ibid., p. 110). He also questions the salience of the rate of interest in influencing the rate of investment, marking one of his differences with Keynes. The answer for him lies in government investment, and the young leftist Klein (ibid., p. 170) shares his vision: "The level of investment can be stimulated most directly by outright government investment.

---

[99] This can be dated to the period 1945 till mid 1946 when "Michal Kalecki was at the International Labour Office, then located in Montreal, and came to the Cowles Commission to lecture on his macrodynamic models" (Klein, 1991, pp. 110–111).

There are many socially useful projects which need to be undertaken from the point of view of the economic welfare of the entire community but which will not be undertaken by private entrepreneurs operating according to the profit motive in a capitalist society. For example, the slums in every metropolitan district of the United States should be cleared away and replaced with modern low-cost dwelling units. Cities should be redesigned to diminish the nuisance of smoke, provide better traffic arteries, allocate space more rationally between dwelling areas and recreation areas, etc. these investment projects have not been and are not being undertaken, yet they are certainly desirable. They are not carried out by private entrepreneurs because they are risky—if we use a money profit criterion. These projects, if they are to be socially useful projects, must be carried out for the masses of the people who cannot pay high rents. But low-rent housing will pay for itself slowly, more slowly than private capitalists require in the world of today. Useful investment schemes like these must be undertaken by the sole agency which can afford to take the risk of slow or zero return, the government. It is well known that the magnitude of all such building programs that are socially desirable could insure full employment in the United States for several years, at least. Here is an obvious method for stimulating the level of investment: the government directly invests in socially desirable projects which will supplement private investment so that full employment can be maintained"—an early statement of public investment 'crowding in' private investment, and he is not in favour of business subsidies or lower corporate taxes as they could not achieve the required result.

Apart from the central plank of government infrastructural investment, Klein's main emphasis is on how to lift the 'consumption schedule' and, alongside, how to lower the 'saving schedule'. His answers are unequivocal. On stimulating effective demand through private consumption, Klein opposes cutting taxes for the rich, rejecting the measure legitimised by Classical doctrine; he goes the opposite way, asking for the redistribution of income in favour of the poor, since this would reduce the overall propensity to save. But he cautions that "this procedure will not, in itself, be sufficient to insure full employment. There is tendency to regard income redistribution as a panacea, but this tendency is misleading"; this could be but one, essential, element in the policy package (Ibid., p. 177). A raft of other measures is proposed: labour-saving technology in agriculture to enable migration into higher productivity and earning jobs in the cities, thereby raising consumption; education, "which serves to teach people to enjoy the fruits of life. We earn to use complex labor-saving devices int the form of durable consumer goods that increase the propensity to consume or decrease the propensity to save ... with a small income augmented by the use of consumer credit, whereby borrowed funds as well as current and past income can be used to purchase these goods" (ibid., p. 175). Advertising is given a role in stimulating consumption, but then gets a lashing: "The advertising industry has certainly had a bad influence on many aspects of our lives. ... Consumers were propagandized by advertisements that the 'American Way of Life' called for certain expenditures (two cars in every garage e.g.). It has been grossly untruthful; it has caused waste; it has served to support wealthy vested interests ... it is not the best way to get to a high-consumption, low-savings economy, but it is *a* way (emphasis in the original)" (ibid., p. 175).

But what about the other side of the equation, savings? Here, "we can attempt to tinker ... but we can also attempt more fundamental reforms". Klein asks, "How are savings habits formed? What are the causes of savings?" He expounds: "In our modern industrial society built on individualistic principles ... they save for the rainy day when they will be unemployed, sick, disabled, or too old to work. They will attempt to provide for future outlays to set up a home during married life, to educate their children, to cover the expenses of maternity, to cover funeral expense, etc." He draws a leaf from the embryonic British welfare state then being fashioned by the year. "These", he observes, "are some of the primary causes of need listed in the famous *Beveridge Report* of 1942. The obvious way to diminish savings on account of these primary causes of need is to have the state provide for these needs at the cheapest possible cost." What about private insurance? His answer is negative: private insurance companies cannot always "find profitable and safe investment outlets for these funds", and the "private insurance industry has not been able to make low-cost policies available to the people so that they can cover adequately these primary causes of need"—a gap which has only grown chasmic over the decades since. And then we have Klein's flagship intervention, effectively a universal social security programme: "We need a non-profit institution like the government, which can provide a comprehensive, minimum program of social security in order to reduce the propensity to save. This program must cover the entire population, and it must cover all those contingencies which cause people to save on a large scale for the future. A program like that embodied in the *Beveridge Plan* or the Wagner-Murray-Dingell Bill in this country is necessary ..." (ibid., pp. 176–177). For good measure, he adds: "If we diminish the fear of the unknown future on the part of consumers, they can enjoy the fruits of our economic activity in their youth when it can best be appreciated"— clearly his high rate of discounting future consumption reflects his own youthfulness, he was all of 27 years and was recently married.

What the USA has experienced since has certainly followed the exhortation to increase consumption and reduce savings, but this, through regressive policies and interventions that in real senses are diametrically opposite of those proposed by Klein, be it on the issue of military expenditure, or tax cuts for the rich, or social insurance, or redistribution, or the nature of advertising; the only shared dimension is the theme of stimulating private household expenditures financed by credit, but in the absence of the other elements of Klein's integrated policy package, this has led to the even more problematic outcome of burgeoning indebtedness of households, especially the poorer ones, at unsustainable levels, causing traumatic upheavals in their lives.

Klein argues that "a high-level-consumption economy is really the long-run hope for capitalism". What about the future? "Suppose we rebuild our cities and roads, what peaceful investment project should come next that could be large enough to insure full employment? Maybe there will be something available, maybe not. This question cannot be answered definitely in advance. But if we have reached a position of high consumption, the population will be better off from any welfare criterion and the unemployment problem will be at a minimum" (ibid., p. 177). Notable here is the use of the adjective 'peaceful' in seeking new areas of investment; Klein is perhaps putting in a prescient warning against investment being diverted into military expenditure.[100]

But is such a radical programme of saving-capitalism-from-itself possible? Klein seems obviously to take a cue from Kalecki (1943) (though this is not explicitly cited). "Keynes, it has been stressed, is not a radical. He wanted to reform capitalism in order to make it work better and to preserve it. How is it possible that nay capitalist could object to a policy of the preservation of capitalism? The answer is that many capitalists are unaware of the precarious state of the system during a period of serious depression, and do not see the proper relationship between their own position and that of the system as a whole. It is inevitable that most of the effective measures listed in the full employment legislation above will be strongly opposed by some group of the capitalist population" (ibid., p. 184); he cites the 'huge obstacles' set up by special-interest lobby groups, like the medical societies. "The Marxists will argue that our society is permeated with groups which will act toward other parts of the program just as the insurance trusts and medical societies have acted toward social security" (ibid., p. 185). "Unless entrepreneurs can be brought to look upon the entire system and their social responsibility toward it, the Marxists will be correct in contending that the Keynesian policies are not politically feasible" (ibid., p. 185). Without explicitly endorsing it, Klein comes as close as can be implied in observing that for the Marxists, "the only smooth-working long-run solution for them is socialism" (ibid., p. 186).

Beyond Keynes
At the end, Klein makes an exhortation to go beyond the solution to unemployment offered by Keynesianism; he identifies two further bridges to cross.

"Our program of social reform must continue even after we have solved the problem of unemployment. ... Fair employment as well as full employment must become part of our reform slogan. It is true that fuller employment makes for fairer employment, but we cannot relax our efforts to advance the economic position of minority groups with the achievement of a full employment economy. If full employment, with the Negroes in menial jobs, means a national income of $180 billion per year, then our goal should be a national income greater than $200 billion per year, which can be produced in a society where Negroes have exactly the same economic opportunities as everybody else. Just as the existence of unemployment causes disease in our economic system, preparing the way for disaster, so does the existence of unfair employment create an equally serious disease. A complete economic theory must tell us how to get both fair and full employment. We may accept the Keynesian theory as a step

---

[100] Lawrence Klein was a lifelong peacenik: later, he was a founding trustee of the UN accredited and registered *Economists for Peace and Security* organisation; see also, for instance, his writings on the theme of turning guns into ploughshares.

toward the formulation of the comprehensive doctrines for which we are now groping" (p. 186).

Second: "Keynes has shown us a way to get higher levels of income, but he has not assured us that this income will be distributed in an equitable manner. Many of the Keynesian policies [at least of the progressive kinds that Klein endorses in the course of his book] will serve to benefit the poor more than the rich. For example, social-security benefits which require a large employer contribution will represent a shift of resources from the capitalist to the working class. But such redistributive schemes are not adequate, in themselves, to prevent the existence of great social injustices. A successful program of full-employment policies in a capitalist environment will still leave us with a highly skewed income distribution. This is another type of economic injustice, like the injustice of unfair employment, which eventually must pass away if we are to have true economic democracy" (p. 187).

Klein is very critical of Keynes's critique of the Soviet system in saying that "if Communism achieves a certain success, it will achieve it, not as an improved economic technique, but as a religion". Klein reacts: "This statement shows a complete lack of understanding of the political, technological and economic basis of the Soviet system. Keynes, glorifier of the bourgeois life, little knew that the arguments why the Russian economy has been and will continue to be on of uninterrupted full employment under socialism follow directly from his own simple model" (Klein, 1947, pp. 77–78).[101] Klein's animosity might have been somewhat assuaged had he patiently worked through the last paragraph of Keynes's commentary on Russia, when he concludes:

"So, now the deeds are done and there is no going back, I should like to give Russia her chance; to help and not to hinder. For how much rather, even after allowing for everything, if I were a Russian, would I contribute my quota of activity to Soviet Russia than to Tsarist Russia!" (Keynes, 1925).

UMich and McCarthyism

Riding a wave of early stardom, Klein arrived at the University of Michigan and ran into the storm of McCarthyism. The period of his stay there, 1949–1954, was when the witch-hunt for 'communists' and their sympathisers was at its peak, led by McCarthy, who had become Chairman of the Senate Permanent Sub-committee on Investigations in January 1953 and used his position for furthering his anti-communist campaign. The purges had actually begun before and continued after McCarthy; and even during the height of McCarthy's crusade, his was not the only committee at national or lower levels that was actively

---

[101] Klein was treading a fine line. At UMich, "an FBI agent once visited [Vice President] Niehuss's home and listed for him the Michigan faculty whom the FBI would 'pick up tomorrow if war with the Russians broke out'. On the list was Dean Dayward Kenniston When Niehuss pointed to the absurdity of this, the FBI agent explained that Kenniston had once agreed to speak before a society devoted to American-Soviet friendship." (Hollinger, n.d. "Academic Culture at Michigan, 1938–1988: The Apotheosis of Pluralism". Fn45)
https://www.rackham.umich.edu/downloads/Hollinger.pdf

pursuing the same agenda of political purification. The House Un-American Activities Committee (HUAC) became a permanent House committee in 1946 and did not involve McCarthy.

In the early 1950s, at the height of the McCarthyite frenzy, three junior members of the University of Michigan (UMich) came under HUAC's hostile scrutiny: Chandler Davis, Clement Markert and Mark Nickerson. James Tobin (n.d.) picks up the narrative: "But there was another thread to this story, one far less well known that the public ordeals of the three men. Behind closed doors, a fourth member of the faculty went through a parallel ordeal. He escaped the spotlight of scandal." This was Lawrence Klein, who had joined UMich as a research fellow at the Survey Research Center in 1949 after a dazzling period at MIT and then at the Cowles Commission; the following year he also became a lecturer in the economics "where he was promised swift promotion. ... Members of Economics Department knew they had an academic superstar on their hands. Early in 1953, Professor Leo Sharfman, the long-time chair, told Klein that in one more year, the Department would leapfrog him from lecturer to full professor with tenure, a rare and prestigious sign of confidence."

Then, in 1953, HUAC informed UMich that Klein was on a list of 15 academics and students suspected of being secret members of the Communist Party. Klein had indeed been a member for a short while. Like a swathe of idealistic and frustrated youth of the times, he was attracted to leftist causes; around 1944–1945 he went to Party meetings and "taught some adult classes on Keynesian economics offered a Party-run schools in Boston and Chicago". Tobin observes that Klein broke the link in 1947 "after he married ... and began to raise a family. He remained a leftist. He defined himself as a democratic socialist in favor of national economic planning on the Scandinavian model."

UMich assured the HUAC of its full cooperation and negotiated to whittle down the list of 15 to a shorter list naming 2 students and 5 staff, including Davis, Markert, Nickerson and Klein. The cases took different courses. Davis, Markert and Nickerson refused to testify to the HUAC invoking the First and/or the Fifth Amendment and were promptly suspended by the university. Markert and Nickerson acknowledged their earlier communist ties and announced that they were no longer members; the former was censured, but the latter was fired. Chandler Davis refused to answer, saying in effect that his views were none of their business. Chandler was then fired, spent years in court and six months in jail for contempt of Congress.[102] In 1952, he had financed

---

[102] Whitfield (1987) in his review of Ellen Schrecker's remarkable study *No Ivory Tower: McCarthyism and the Universities* picks out the case of Davis: "Here is how Chandler Davis, a mathematician at the University of Michigan, argued to no avail before his colleagues: 'If you suspect, for instance, that Communists must be detected because they promote violence, and if you convince yourselves that I do not promote violence, then you must believe, either that I am not a Communist, or that your reason for insistence on detecting Communists was invalid' (Schrecker, 1986, pp. 225–26). This logic was so impeccable that the president conjectured that Davis must have been lying. So the mathematician was fired and, convicted of contempt of Congress, was sent to Danbury Federal Penitentiary" (Whitfield, 1987, p. 482).

the printing of a pamphlet against the HUAC and McCarthy campaigns. "I've never been able to get normal employment in the U.S. since then"; he moved to Canada in 1962, becoming a professor of mathematics at the University of Toronto (Daubenmier (1990). Markert's recollection was that "they didn't want testimony. They wanted us to prostrate ourselves, to humiliate us in public"; he was linked to the Communist Party during the Depression and in 1938 he had enlisted in a communist brigade to fight against the fascists in the Spanish Civil War (ibid.), not very different from George Orwell.[103] Nickerson told Daubenmier that "the only reason they wanted to talk to you was to get other people's names"; he had refused to cooperate—"there are some things you can do and some things you can't. You don't put somebody else in jeopardy to save your own job." He too moved to Canada and took a job at half his earlier salary, serving later as the Chairman of the medical school at McGill University in Montreal (ibid.).

Following the powerful expose by Schrecker (1986), Lionel Lewis (1988) in his book *Cold War on Campus* investigated the experience of 126 individuals on 58 university campuses. Apparently, the targets were disproportionately from the physical sciences and not the social sciences.[104] "Lewis notes that investigative committees did not seem to be concerned about what was taught in the classroom. The salient questions of the investigators were over and over again: Are you a member of the Communist party? Were you a member of the Communist party? Did you belong to a Communist-front organization? Will you name other professors who are or were Communists? In short, the picture

---

[103] Ellen Schrecker (1986, p. 61) puts up a fair defence for American communists of that era: "Neither dupes nor conspirators, the academics who passed through the American Communist Party during the 1930s and 1940s were a group of serious men and women who sincerely hoped to create a better world. They opposed Hitler, supported the Spanish republicans, and struggled, as best they could, to build a movement for social change within the United States." Something equivalent could be said in the British context of those turbulent decades.

[104] McDonagh (1989, p. 315), in reviewing Lewis's book, expresses surprise at this fact which appears to him to be counterintuitive, on the presumption that "the social sciences [was] where the teaching of controversial subjects is pervasive"; he complains that "Lewis does not speculate on possible reasons for these differences ..." However, the focus on scientists was hardly surprising, given their lead role, on both sides of the war that was ended (in the eastern theatre) by the atomic bombs developed by this community under extreme secretive conditions and under the acute surveillance and continual scrutiny of the security and intelligence services sniffing for any leads to the enemy side, now quickly declared to be the Soviet Union; the long-drawn-out saga of J. Oppenheimer who, from 1942, was the director of the Los Alamos Laboratory and was but the visible tip of this iceberg. Oppenheimer was known to have had extensive communist contacts; in 1954 his security clearances were withdrawn after a month of public hearings; later, he had to testify before the HUAC made 'to name names' most of whom suffered the consequences. This was also the time when international cooperation between scientists developed, leading in 1955 to the celebrated Russell-Einstein Manifesto which had 11 signatories all of whom, apart from Bertrand Russell, were leading scientists from different countries; this was the precursor to the formation of the Pugwash Conference and its first meeting in 1957. It was not surprising that the focus of the HUAC investigations was prominently on scientists.
https://web.archive.org/web/20190214145114/http://www.spokesmanbooks.com/Spokesman/PDF/85russein.pdf

emerges that it was not the professor's campus teaching behavior that matter but his or her current or past off-campus radical political behavior" (McDonagh, 1989, p. 315).

Those picked up by the McCarthyite searchlight had few options to save themselves: taking the Fifth Amendment would provide protection from having to lie under oath and risk perjury if the lie was found out or contradicted in any way by information from some informant; "but the refuge of the Fifth Amendment was commonly assumed to be a sign of concealing something reprehensible, and therefore was itself proof of unfitness to teach" (Whitfield, 1987, p. 483, citing Schrecker), and there were cases where those pleading the Fifth were fired anyway, sometimes, because the bosses did not think that "a man with that kind of background should be teaching in the University". So, "probably the only reliable way for professors to prove that they were not—or no longer—Communists would be, as others subpoenaed to appear before HUAC realized, to become informants. Schrecker estimates that about 20–25 percent did so, and named names—an act ordinarily so repugnant that committing it became the proof of one's patriotism and loyalty. But even that might not be enough"—and there were case of informants being fired as well. Based on Schrecker, Whitfield (1987, p. 482) write of Lawrence Klein as someone "who cooperated with HUAC in 1954 but was not promoted by the University of Michigan". Hollinger (n.d.) observes "that Dean Odegaard in communicating support for Klein's appointment to Niehuss, was careful to cover the 'integrity' ground ... and to contrast Klein favourably in this respect to the three who had refused to answer the questions of the HUAC subcommittee" (ibid.: fn58); "Klein had repudiated communism in a private HUAC hearing, and thus passed the 'integrity test' in spades" (ibid.).

Lawrence Klein's experience, as reported by Tobin (and himself), was rather different. Tobin (n.d.) describes thus: "Klein did exactly what the University asked of him. With the HUAC hearing looming, he went to his chair, Professor Sharfman, and Vice President Niehuss. He told them frankly about his earlier association with the Communist Party—why he had joined and why he had quit. Next he met with HUAC investigators and did the same. HUAC gave him a clean bill of health and said he would not be called to testify in public. A few friends and colleagues knew what had happened, but Klein's name never surfaced in press reports." Tobin continues: "Congressional red-hunters normally demanded a price for the absolution that HUAC had given Klein—the person under suspicion must 'name names'. That is, he must inform on other Communists to prove he had renounced the Party. Whether Klein did so in his private meetings with HUAC is not known." And there is no confirmation available on this score from Klein himself, then or later. Tobin says: "He quietly went on with his work."

Tobin writes that while Sharfman, the Department Chair, "was buying time until the HUAC storm had passed ... Klein himself asked for a postponement." In autumn 1954, while the Faculty was conducting its hearings with Davis, Markert and Nickerson, he took a leave without pay and went to the Institute of Statistics in Oxford as a senior researcher, leaving Garner Ackley, the new Chair, to pick up and push the case for Klein's promotion, which he did forcefully, obtaining an overwhelmingly favourable 18–2 verdict in the Department. But there was trouble at the next level in the form of an assault on Klein by Professor William Paton of the business school, "a man so conservative he thought Social Security 'was a curse on our society', as an admirer once put it … he revered free enterprise, hated Franklin Roosevelt and assaulted the safety-net thinking of New Deal economists; … Paton declared war" (Tobin (ibid.). Ackley sent up the recommendation to Dean Odegaard for a shared appointment at the Economics Department and the Survey Research Centre, with lifetime tenure. But the proposal was diluted at higher level, and in June 1955, the President recommended to the University Regents that Klein be appointed professor, but without tenure for the time being. From Oxford, Klein overcame his resistance "in recognition of the sincere efforts made on my behalf by friends and colleagues, and decided to accept the professorship even without the tenure. But then in the fall of 1955, Paton got into the act; his view had been that Klein 'was a postwar member of the Communist Party, and remains a "dedicated" supporter of the Norwegian type of socialism, generally conceded to be the nearest thing to the totalitarian brand to be found outside the Iron Curtain'" (Tobin, ibid. (Chapter 10). There are also allusions that other influences and undercurrents might have played some role.[105]

Meanwhile, Klein, in Oxford, received "a very nasty letter telling me not to come to [UMich] and all the dire things that would happen if I did come" (Klein, quoted in Tobin, ibid.). "Members of the Department told Klein later that Paton had written it" (ibid.). Klein wrote to Vice President Niehuss for a clarification and received only a guarded and tepid response, informing Klein

---

[105] Leeson (2017, p. 116) indicates the possibility of Hayek being involved in making negative decisions on Klein's contract, with an implication that anti-Semitism might have had a role to play. Anti-Semitism, unfortunately, was not uncommon; Modigliani, for instance, referred to anti-Semitism influencing decisions at Harvard, a reason why he kept away from there (see Barnett, 2004, p. 156). That anti-Semitic prejudice also had an independent role in the sordid saga of Klein at UMich seems undeniable going on reports from some of those involved in the episode. In the later interview by Marjorie Cahn Brazer in 1979, Gardner Ackley states that "There were two reasons he [William Paton] opposed it [Klein's professorship]. One was the former Communism. The other—I'm sorry to have to say this but I think it might as well get into this record …—was pure anti-Semitism … One day … [Paton] came over to explain to me that this was all a plot by Sharfman and Haber and [Richard] Musgrave and [Wolfgang] Stolper … all the Jews he could think of in the Department … to solidify the Jewish control of the Department. And I ought to understand that and to recognize it for what it was, and that the Klein appointment was just part of that." Ackley told Brazer that he had all but thrown Paton out of his office and never spoken to him again (Tobin, n.d.: Chapter 11). With regard to the allusion specifically to Hayek's opposition to Klein's contract, there could be an alternative explanation arising from the manner in which Klein had dismissively dealt with Hayek's work in his book. There are several engagements with the "theory of Hayek's in the light of the Keynesian Revolution, for the central notions of the Hayek school are directly opposite to those which have made the Keynesian theory so important" (Klein, 1947, p. 52); Hayek always comes away the loser: "Hayek's description of the economic process just does not fit the facts" (ibid.). Friedrich von Hayek might have needed no look for no further reason to register a thumbs-down on such an illiterate writer.

that at the end of the year, he would recommend an extension for another year, but still without tenure, on which Regents would have to take a decision. Shortly before Christmas 1955, Klein resigned from Michigan, despite earnest pleas from Ackley, and accepted Oxford's "magnificent offer, with long tenure ... this and other British universities have given me such a strong sense of freedom of thought that I feel I cannot refuse this offer at Oxford" (Klein, quoted in Tobin, ibid.). Earlier in the process, he had sent a telegram, *Badly Want Tenure*; now he wrote: "I don't put much value in tenure as such; I simply don't like the reasons for which it is withheld ..." (ibid.)

"In the McCarthy era, I left Michigan for the peace and academic freedom in Oxford."[106] Klein's words and sentiments resonate with those of Richard Goodwin, who had come across in the same period to Cambridge "where he could teach what he wanted" and "where one could be left and not left out" (p. 52). Klein had gone to the Institute of Statistics in Oxford; Goodwin had first gone to the Department of Applied Economics in Cambridge, before entering the Faculty of Economics there.[107]

Policy to Forecasting
The rest is, indeed, history. Lawrence Klein's star career progressed smoothly, picking up recognition and honours, including of course the 'Nobel' prize in 1980, and significantly, an honorary doctorate from the University of Michigan in 1977, perhaps an overdue act of institutional contrition, "though with no public acknowledgement of how he had left the faculty in the 1950s" (Tobin n.d. Chapter 12). He was sought in high Presidential company and felt sufficiently empowered to decline a chair at the kitchen table: "Klein was chief economic advisor to Jimmy Carter during his successful 1976 presidential campaign, then returned to academia rather than take a position in the new administration. In declining an appointment, he avoided controversy over his brief membership, in the 1940s, in the Communist Party."[108] And he was hugely successful, in academic and commercial terms, in his professional forecasting career, aided by the tailwind of technological change; looking back, Klein (1991) reflects that not in their "wildest dreams" could they imagine the explosion of computer power that took place from the 1970s and 1980s, and that took Klein into his orbit of his massive forecasting modelling enterprises; his

---

[106] Cited in "Klein, Lawrence R. 1920", in: Durlauf, S. and Blume, L. (ed.) (2008). *The New Palgrave Dictionary of Economics*. London: Palgrave Macmillan, 2008.

[107] "The Department has welcomed a number of distinguished economists and statisticians from abroad for varying lengths of time and several have given papers at the Department's seminars. In particular, Mr. R. M. Goodwin of Harvard University was invited to spend the year 1951–1952 at the Department as a Fulbright Fellow and was provided with working space at the Department from October 1951 until taking up an appointment as University Lecturer in Economics in October 1952" (DAE Annual Report, 1951–1953, p. 16, #106).

[108] Bloomberg News, 2013, October 21. Lawrence Klein dies at 93; won Nobel Prize for his econometric models.
https://www.latimes.com/local/obituaries/la-me-lawrence-klein-20131022-story.html

business became making forecasting models, and policy choices were his client's job.

In his 'Nobel' biographical piece, Klein shares his credo. "It is my firm belief that the only satisfactory test of economics is the ability to predict, and in crucial predictive situations such as reconversion after World War II, the settlement of the Korean War, the settlement of the Vietnam War, the abrupt economic policy switch of the Nixon Administration in August 1972, the oil shock of 1973 (forecast of a world-wide succession by LINK), the recession of 1990. In these crucial periods, econometric models outperformed other approaches, yet there is considerable room for improvement, and that is precisely what is being examined in development of high-frequency models that aim to forecast the economy, every week, every fortnight, or every month, depending on the degree of fineness of the information flow. My present research deals directly with weekly forecasting for the United States, fortnightly forecasting for China, and monthly forecasting for Russia" (Klein, 2005).

A comparative reflection on the Lawrence Klein and Wynne Godley styles of modelling may be pertinent. In the course of his criticism of Paul Krugman for wrongly equating Wynne Godley's approach to "the old hydraulic Keynesianism, i.e., Neoclassical Synthesis", Matias Vernengo (2013) draws a comparison between the modelling approaches of Klein and Godley: "Conventional hydraulic models, including the sort of Cowles models like the Klein-Goldberger model of the US economy, put great emphasis on the estimation of parameters based on certain simplistic macro behavior. Wynne took a very different approach to modeling than Klein-Goldberger. He was more concerned with what he referred to as 'model architecture' than with parameter estimation. The architecture, which was careful about stock-flow consistency, showing that everything came from somewhere and went somewhere so to speak, also imposed a clear causality structure, which determined most of the results. In fact, Wynne believed that significant variations of the parameters might not greatly influence the end result of the model, which was used for simulations and scenarios that helped to understand how the economy functioned, rather than for strictly forecasting purposes."

As it happens, Klein, writing in 1991, seems to agree with the imperative 'to understand the economy'. "There are many contributing factors to successful macro-econometric model analysis. Contributions from economics, mathematics, and statistics which formed the basis for early enthusiasm at the Cowles Commission were obviously important, but I feel that my colleagues wanted results that were quite robust, in small confidence areas, and very discriminating among competing hypotheses. Quantitative economics is not like that. It is inelegant, very tedious, very repetitive, and capable of forward movement in small increments. I admired the elegant theorems that my associates produced, but it seemed to me that their assumptions had to be very strong and not very realistic in order to get their beautiful results. I felt that if one paid unusual attention to data—very much in the painstaking tradition of Simon Kuznets—replicated analyses regularly, looked at more detail for the economy, learned as much as possible about realistic economic reaction, and stayed in touch with the economic situation on a daily basis that it would be possible to use econometric models for guidance, both in the fields of policy application and it the pure *understanding*, of the economy" (italics in the original).

Resolution
One resolution of the puzzle lies in Colander and Landreth's (1996, p. 137) explanations for why the Tarshis textbook was suppressed, but not Samuelson's. They offer two: first, that the earlier (collaborative) book by Tarshis (Gilbert et al. 1938) identified him as keen supporter of the New Deal; and second, that Tarshis was not coy about addressing policy issues directly, while Samuelson's analysis, couched in mathematics, carried the air of technical objectivity. Would this reasoning hold if these two textbooks were to be compared with Lawrence Klein's contemporary book on Keynesian economics? A mathematical interpretation of the Keynesian system was, indeed, also the unique distinguishing feature of Klein's thesis and book which carried a 25-page, 76-equation technical appendix including a mathematical model of the Treatise, a mathematical derivation of the system of the General Theory, mathematical models dealing Keynesian and Classical Economics, and a treatment of the Long-Run Equilibrium. But perhaps more prominent might have been the additional final chapter in the book where Klein is far from being shy about his radical value judgements and policy positions which call for interventions going beyond the conventional Keynesian template. In this, he was far closer to Kalecki and implicitly to Tinbergen's notions of functional socialism where the countervailing power of deep democracy controls and redirects the innate profit-seeking tendencies of a capitalist system in order to reorient it towards meeting desirable and democratically adopted social objectives; this is clearly indicated in Klein's consistent espousal of the Norwegian/Scandinavian type of national economic planning. But such radicalism, all there to see in the additional chapter, seems not to have got in the way and the book surviving, indeed, thriving. An answer could be that the McCarthyites were less interested in what you wrote rather than in what you did, and in your political affiliations, and Klein had, on available accounts, renounced these to the HUAC, so that a satisfied committee could have felt that it had achieved its agenda with respect to Klein; another could be that he left the country for several years; and yet another could be that after his radical sermon from the pulpit, the position of the additional chapter, Klein withdrew from the active domain of public policy engagement into the safe, backroom, space of the methods and techniques of forecasting modelling. In his Addendum to his 'Nobel' Biographical (Klein, 2005), Klein cites various non-profit initiatives that "have been intellectually rewarding—well worth the efforts"; he ends by singling out "one particular for-profit board", W. P. Carey & Co, and investment banking company with a parallel philanthropic non-profit foundation; he ends, noting that "I gained a great deal of knowledge about providing useful economic advice in business decision making" ... "I have earned and learned." Lawrence Klein, an avowed

Marxist in his youth, then politically silenced by McCarthyism, an econometric forecaster and consultant through his professional career, peacenik and believer in good causes, had perhaps found his "middle path".[109]

4.4.3 'Death of a Revolutionary Textbook':[110] Robinson and Eatwell

Many of the most celebrated battles in which Joan Robinson and her Cambridge colleagues participated in challenging neoclassical orthodoxy were around the core and roots of the economic theory appropriate for analysing a mature capitalist economy. The Keynesian Revolution—in which Joan, still only a lecturer, was one of Keynes's brilliant seconds, before adopting a more radical Kaleckian approach and growing into the roles of exponent, defender, mentor, muse and sage—developed not just an alternative theoretical perspective involving dramatically different policy perspectives, but also generated an alternative set of tools that were intended to empower a social democratic state in meeting the objective of full employment.

According to Cambridge Keynesians prominently led by Joan, the progressive potentialities and intentions of the Keynesian theoretical revolution mutated later, in the hands of her perennial American opponents, into what she termed 'bastard Keynesianism', involving a synthesis of a distorted version of Keynesianism with orthodox neoclassical microeconomic theory. In parallel, it became increasingly apparent that the new tool kit would not be used as much for social democratic agendas where economic expansion favoured expenditure on social service provision and welfare enhancement, as for justifying tax cuts for the rich and the heavy diversion of state spending towards militarism and armaments. Taking the fight to the lion's den, Joan launched a fierce attack on the regressive trends in theory in her celebrated Richard T. Ely Lecture on 'The Second Crisis of Economic Theory' in 1971 to the American Economic Association under the invitation of its President, J.K. Galbraith, a kindred spirit (Robinson, 1972). But the sun quickly set on this Indian summer of optimism, prompting a distressed Joan Robinson (1977) famously to ask of her discipline and peers: 'What are the Questions?' What was full employment for? Her earlier hard-won theoretical victories in cross-Atlantic battles with the other Cambridge in 'the capital theory controversy' turned out to be pyrrhic in nature, as the mainstream development of neoclassical economics sidetracked, and virtually ignored, the implications of the radical Cambridge schools.

She had bravely attempted, with John Eatwell in 1973, to launch a new textbook that could challenge, if not displace, the hegemony of Paul Samuelson's *Economics*. The 'Cambridge' textbook *An Introduction to Modern Economics* by Joan Robinson and John Eatwell appeared in 1973; the intervention was 'revolutionary', providing a radical and inevitably eclectic entry into the

---

[109] See also, Chapter 6, p. 59; 59n42.

[110] This is the title of the excellent piece by John King and Alex Millmow (2003) on the unfortunate trajectory of *An Introduction to Modern Economics*, co-authored by Joan Robinson and John Eatwell in 1973.

discipline for young minds and one that might inoculate them from neoclassical doctrine, with antecedents in her earlier pedagogically oriented Exercises in Economic Analysis (Robinson, 1961). At the time of its birth, it served as a clarion call, a challenge to mainstream orthodoxy now led by Frank Hahn who had entered the Faculty with much fanfare just the year before. Appropriate as it might have been, its reception was mixed, and its life was to be unfortunately short.

As it turned out, it could not penetrate the incumbent's market ascendancy. Paul Samuelson's *Economics* was in its ninth edition in 1973, the year of publication of Joan Robinson and John Eatwell's 'alternative', refreshingly heterodox, textbook. Its sales had peaked at 441,941 in 1964 and stood at 303,705 in 1973, but had resisted the competition and risen to 317,188 in 1976 (Skousen, 1997). The story of "the death of a revolutionary textbook" is well told by John King and Alex Millmow (2003), and by Geoff Harcourt and Prue Kerr (2009). King and Millmow report that sales for 1974's second edition of Robinson and Eatwell in the USA "were approaching death" and that "a thousand copies of the second edition would be pulped unless the [McGraw-Hill] UK branch could find some use for them" (ibid., p. 125). The project was laid to rest separately, and for different considerations, by the publishers as well as by the authors. Robinson and Eatwell (1973) "was designed to revolutionize the teaching of elementary economics and to displace the influence of mainstream texts like those of Paul Samuelson and Richard Lipsey. Its lack of success marked something of a turning point in the history of economics, since it symbolized the collapse of the radical attempt to challenge orthodox theory at the pedagogical level," write King and Millmow (2003, p. 105) in their excellent analysis of this unfortunate episode. It might be useful to add a few related observations. After Marshall and Pigou, none of the Cambridge economists seemed to place any great premium on writing textbooks; rather, they wrote books and articles which illuminated parts of the subject they were absorbed in, with a varying balance between the two formats; and some, of course, chose to write only when the muse took them. Given the diversity of the traditions within the heterodox grouping, it was therefore unlikely that any one book or set of articles would constitute lingua franca across the board, let alone be acceptable on either side across the orthodox-heterodox divide. Heterodox doctrines, as fashioned by the several practicing masters, were never congruent enough to be thought of as a stable set of propositions to convey to students as the bottom lines of the discipline. It was more of a maze, with competing route maps being handed out to often non-plussed students entering economics. In Cambridge, the heart of the teaching was in the flagship Principles course, and that was handed around from time to time across the senior faculty, and students had to relate its contents to other contending expositions—with the added challenge that the persons who set, and market, the exam would very likely belong to different sub-traditions. This contrasted with the neoclassical side. Though Frank Hahn was famously opposed to writing and teaching from textbooks, again for the reason that the subject was still on the anvil and not a finished product, the neoclassical camp, and pedagogical traditions, in the USA ran on textbooks, with a huge premium, including potentially massive financial rewards, for getting your textbook into the university curricula. This was not so in the world of non-mainstream economics in Cambridge where its pedagogical idiosyncrasies left little space for getting rich and famous through this route. Anyone breaking ranks in that world of prima donnas would need first to do a careful assessment of the transaction costs of such ambition. The case of the missing textbook is thus not overly difficult to solve. The closest attempts at surrogate textbook material took the form of the prized thematic surveys which attempted the impossible and sometimes succeeded fairly well, such as there were rare and startling exceptions: obviously Piero Sraffa's (1960) *Production of* Commodities; Joan's own 1960 *The Accumulation of Capital*; then, Richard Goodwin's (1970) classic *Elementary Economics from the Higher Standpoint*, which only a brave tutor would recommend to an undergraduate as a go-to textbook, and so it soon acquired the status of a prized underused rarity to be marvelled at. The complexity of some of the debates—through which some strands of Cambridge economics itself evolved—opened up a strategic space for intellectual interlocutors, the prime example of which must remain Geoff Harcourt's (1972) *Some Cambridge Controversies in the Theory of Capital*, not a textbook in itself, but mandatory reading for all serious students. And then there was Joan Robinson as missionary, passionately involved with the issues of 'what is economics': with what questions the beginner was to enter the maze, with which thought-map as a guide, and with what bottom lines to leave; Robinson and Eatwell (1973) was such an entirely laudable attempt. That said, however, as a stand-alone reading experience or learning device for undergraduates, it remained quite idiosyncratic and intractable, and could not compare pedagogically with the streamlined, carefully constructed, learning manual that Samuelson's *Economics* was designed to be. If King and Millmow describe it as "the death of a revolutionary textbook", Harcourt and Kerr call it 'a light that failed", and ask "why did it fail as an alternative textbook?" Even after a re-reading, Harcourt and Kerr "continue to admire both its aims and execution". Yet, it failed, primarily, because, as they say, "Joan Robinson was no strategist", not configured in the Samuelsonian style of textbook management. "It was less the substantial theoretical approach presented in the book that the manner of presentation, its pedagogical style, that caused it to fail" (Harcourt & Kerr, 2009, p. 186). Joan "felt that having a co-author who was very much at the coal face, lecturing and supervising, was absolutely necessary for the tone and content of the proposed book" (Harcourt & Kerr, 2009, p. 165). In the context of Joan's *Economic Heresies* published just a couple of years earlier in 1971, they observe, a touch ruefully, that "more and more of what she presented to readers were by the tips of icebergs, with the submerged portions of which she was only too familiar but which were increasingly to baffle others, especially new readers" (ibid., p. 119); indeed, "which often troubled even experienced readers who were familiar with her work" (Harcourt & Kerr, 2009, p. 166). This issue of communication, of course, would have been what was intended to be resolved by the 'coalface worker', namely John Eatwell. King and Millmow (2003) surveyed the reviews of the book, and Harcourt and Kerr (2009, p. 186) summarise their findings: "the book, aimed at beginners, was consistently judged as too difficult for this audience, that there were no exercises to test understanding, no chapter summaries or summaries of new concepts, that the lack of statistical material and of discussion of contemporary economic institutions meant the abstract theory was more difficult to grasp". Harcourt and Kerr (2009, p. 166) take this further: "A far as the pure mechanics of presentation are concerned, especially the level of presentation, it has to be conceded that both authors were only used to teaching very bright undergraduates so that they vastly overestimated the absorption capabilities of more average students. Had Joan Robinson collaborated with, say, either Tom Asimakopulos or Keith Frearson, both superb teachers of the less gifted as well as the gifted, mainly in Canada and Australia, this limitation may have been overcome … whether that would have ensured the success of the book is still problematic". They allude to the hostile political stance in America in relation to Joan who was vociferous as ever on Vietnam. But as has been argued here earlier, writing an introductory textbook for beginners was a far easier exercise when dealing with the simplistic reductionisms of neoclassicism convertible into mechanical mathematical form—that was a far cry from the ambition to meaningfully, and in simple fashion, introduce new comers into the complexities in which Cambridge heterodox economics was embroiled at the time. As Harcourt and Kerr (2009, p. 165) observe with respect to the wizened Joan the elder, 70, and the energetic John the young, all of 28: "on most issues, she and Eatwell were then at one, though increasingly they were to part company on the application of the long-period method in economic theory championed by, especially, Garegnani's interpretation of Piero Sraffa." Try explaining that in simple layman's terms to a fresher; there you have perhaps the key road sign towards finding an answer; Cambridge heterodox economics was something of a multi-level maze out of Escher's book and sketching a simple map for new entrants was more easily said than done.

Richard Kahn sharply pointed out that they had gone to the wrong publisher, also McGraw-Hill—which suggests that he had not been too closely involved with the enterprise in its earlier phases, but by this time the die had been cast. McGraw-Hill had been Samuelson's original publisher, and *Economics* was one of their 'immortal' trophy items. How far would they go to promote a product that explicitly sought to challenge, intellectually and commercially, the 1970 'Nobel' Prize winner's virtually monopoly control over the American textbook market and policy-making domain? King and Millmow (2003) confirm that in the end, the publishers pulled the plug on the British challenger and remaindered and pulped unsold stocks. In 1997, McGraw-Hill was "proud to make available this meticulously detailed reproduction of the watershed economics textbook. In *Economics: The Original 1948 Edition* in which every word, idea, phrase, even the typestyle remain unchanged from the original"; "the timeless wisdom and applicability of his words still ring true in today's turbulent world." Samuelson concurs and purrs: "It has been a pleasant surprise to discover how much of the original verve and relevance is still there. That is the only kind of immortality that an author could have or want."[111] Then, of course, there was the elephant in the room—Joan's strident advocacy of the anti-imperialist cause in Vietnam where American aggression was peaking, and of the path of Chinese socialism including Mao's Cultural Revolution, then also in full swing; this was not an ideological stance that was likely to induce its adoption as a basic textbook on a mass scale in American university courses. And so it sank without trace, even as Samuelson chugged along from edition to edition, pulling in its wake a motley collection of assorted texts vying for some, even minor shares in a massive global market. Given the scale differences between the American and the British markets, any economics textbook that would not be welcomed in the American market would hardly have two legs to run on, let alone fly high, commercially. It is striking that even the early or later textbooks on Keynesianism did not originate from Keynes's Cambridge, but from a variety of followers on the Continent or in America many of whom the Cambridge guardians of Keynes's 'true' legacy were reluctant to endorse.

Thus, the standard medium for the intergenerational transmission of accumulated knowledge within (branches of) heterodox traditions was not a conventional textbook but a confusing total immersion in the landmarks of live debates between the different sub-traditions, and above all with the shared opposition, the neoclassicals. The student had to rely on their absorptive capacity and their dedication; supervisors were (not always) there to guide; there were no ready-to-hand manuals which converted economics into finite series of solvable mathematical exercises as in the neoclassical textbooks of Samuelson or Lipsey's, 1963 *Positive Economics*, or in Joan's pithy aphorism, "I didn't do maths, so I had to think instead." It was a very Cambridge recipe.[112]

In her last decade, Joan Robinson became deeply disillusioned with the state of the discipline,[113] and her attention was focussed significantly on international peace (Robinson, 1981), the subject of her Tanner Lectures. There seems to be a sad parallel between the political subversion of the progressive social potentialities of Keynesianism into providing a perverse legitimation of government expenditure on what Eisenhower, with some prescience in 1961, had called the military-industrial complex, and the experience of the progressive atomic and nuclear scientists who thought their project enhanced human capacities for social purposes, only to be confronted by the reality of Hiroshima. Joan had won all her battles but lost the war.

---

[111] https://www.amazon.com/Economics-Original-1948-Paul-Samuelson/dp/0070747415

[112] Joan was unusual, also in this regard; most senior economists of Cambridge had done mathematics in conjunction with economics, though many of them preferred not to use it unless essential, for example, Marshall, Keynes, Reddaway and Kahn.

[113] King and Millmow (2003) provide a sensitive and informative account although, as with the large body of contributions on Joan Robinson's work, the treatment ignores her engagement with Third-World development.

4.4.4 An 'Applied Economics' Textbook That Wasn't: Joan and Young Friends

In the DAE 50th Anniversary collection of essays, John Llewellyn, in 1970 a dandy young dasher in the DAE, took advantage of his opportunity to rush Joan to catch her train—as he says "in the pride of my life, my open top, wire-wheeled, British racing-green MGB"; emboldened by Joan's tossing of her mane of white hair and her observation that "This takes me back to when I was a girl", John blurted his million-dollar question, a come-down after his build-up: "Joan, if you were a young girl today, starting out in economics, what would you elect to be, a theorist or an applied economist?" There was a cult of theory about "something that the younger neoclassicals, and particularly Frank Hahn, were clearly keen to perpetuate … it was almost received wisdom within the DAE at the time that the Faculty view was that really bright people did theory, the less bright did applied work. … I thought this silly." But having just done his PhD on the 'applied' side of the line, John wondered, "So had we chosen wrong, were we missing the boat? Would we come to regret our decision? Hence the question to Joan. Imagine therefore my surprise when, without a moment's hesitation, almost as if she had been reflecting upon that very subject herself and had been waiting only for me to put the question, she replied 'Oh, an applied economist, no doubt about that.' She explained. I can remember the words almost perfectly to this day. 'When I was a young girl', she said, 'there were not many theories about how the economy worked, and those that there were absolutely dotty. So we had to come up with theories that made sense.' 'But today', she continued, 'there are lots and lots of theories. Too many in fact. What we really need today is to find out which ones are right'" (Llewellyn, 1998, pp. 247–248).

Joan was right: in those years, amongst the heterodox clans, there was perhaps a rising sense that the inter-Cambridge capital theory battle was settled and won; attention was shifting to the hot policy debates in which the DAE took a lead, with Faculty theoreticians joining DAE teams in developing new hypotheses to be tested for practical application; deindustrialisation and stagflation dominated the stage in UK; debt and IMF-World Bank structural adjustment programmes in developing economies. It is not surprising then that in the early 1970s, just after the Robinson-Eatwell introductory theory textbook had been done and dusted, that Joan's energies were turning fully towards the applied side of things.

What perhaps is not known is that in the same year, there was also a concrete plan to follow up on the new elementary economics textbook with another independent volume, this one to be a textbook on applied economics, a collective enterprise of a group of policy-oriented Cambridge rising stars each deeply immersed in different aspects of public policy. The group comprised Terry Barker, Francis Cripps, Michael Posner and Ajit Singh, with the venerable Joan Robinson playing mother, godmother or Mother Goddess. Discussions were sufficiently serious and formal to be minuted (by Michael), and initial plans for the structure, contents and design of the textbook were put to paper and circulated for the meetings. The first meeting took place on 1 November 1973, and another meeting was planned in about two weeks and was held on 5 December. Everyone was asked "to produce their own ideas on either sections or the whole of the present proposals—if possible in writing, and very desirably before our next meeting". And intriguingly, the minutes state that "meanwhile Posner was asked to circulate a note (being largely a transcript of Cripps lecture [sic]) for subsequent discussion".[114]

The book was to focus on "the advanced capitalist and mixed economies—broadly the OECD group". The initial plan had four parts: the theory of production, distribution and factors of production, trade and payments, and public policy. By the time of the second meeting on 5 December, these had become six sections: households, labour market, production, corporations, trade and public policy. 'Production' had the initials FC against it; 'Corporations', AS; 'Trade', TB; and 'Public Policy', MP, with 'Labour', and 'Households' carrying question marks instead of initials—though at a later point, "perhaps Atkinson" is to be found against "Households, distribution of property". Two of the (four) editors—Joan did not have a specific task at this point—had duly sent in their outlines: Terry Barker on Trade, and Michael Posner on Public Policy. Both outlines provided a clear and comprehensive structure of the contents of these sections of the textbook. On a Cambridge time scale, this was pretty sharp progress, and the enterprise seemed well launched with a fair expectation that the final product would roll out in 1974.[115]

Thought had also been given to organisational and practical parameters of their internal labour process of this 'inner editorial group'. The textbook would take the shape of an integrated compendium of papers "by friends and acquaintances" which, in each section, would address key questions formulated by the editors in general and in specific by the editor in charge of each section. "We should *not* solicit articles on individual 'subjects', and we should always seek to work out with contributors very carefully the questions to which they were addressing themselves." Also generally agreed was "that we would need to work out a fairly full table of contents before we talked to other people".

Was this a collective of joint editors or of joint authors—or should they follow Francis who "put forward the notion that the individual authors of individual chapters or sections should not be identified, but that the book should genuinely be a co-operative effort. This seemed to at least one of the group to raise some difficulties (the willingness of young men [sic] to participate in this sort of exercise is often thought to depend on the attraction of seeing their

---

[114] Archival materials for this section are from The Papers of Joan Violet Robinson, King's College Archives, Cambridge, JVR/7/353.

[115] The Cambridge applied economics textbook would have stood alongside *The UK Economy: A Manual of Applied Economics* by A.R. Prest and D.J. Coppock which was first published in 1966, and has then seen new editions roughly every second year, sometimes with an additional editor.

name in print"; this issue would have to be settled before "we go to the market to find potential authors".

Then: the role of the "editorial chairman" would require "further elucidation". "In a 'normal' exercise, the editorial chairman would do a considerable amount of work, and would have considerable powers to argue with individual contributors." But, Michael writes, "in the scheme roughly outlined to the group so far, it might well be that the 'editorial chairman' would serve mainly to protect individual contributors from the over-enthusiastic collaboration of others!" Very 'Cambridge' indeed.

Each designated person would take delegated, if not exclusive, responsibility for the construction of his/her respective sections. "The next stage … is for each of us to write a fairly extensive 15,000 [sic; it should almost definitely be 1,500] word summary of the section for which we are primarily responsible. This would be a very early draft of the sort of 'summary introduction' which might appear at the beginning of each section of the book itself"; this piece, along with a re-draft of the note on the contents of each section, was to be circulated early in February 1974. It was also agreed that by early spring, "each of us should try to write a 'chapter' at rather greater length [of 3,000 words] so as to have a specimen so show to other potential authors". Authors were to be recruited and the book organised by summer 1974; and Michael, ever in practical mode, suggests "that we do not try to be too ambitious either about the length or our draft 'chapters' or about the beauty of our prose style". This constitutes the last observation recorded in Posner's circulated notes for the meeting of 5 December. And there the recorded story ends, and the project sinks without trace into the great repository of good intentions.

Arguably, this aborted project potentially constituted a significant loss and missed opportunity. The conjuncture, in the discipline and in Cambridge, was ripe for such an intervention. Within Cambridge, Frank Hahn had just arrived and begun organising the neoclassical camp, while Joan had recently returned from her famously provocative Ely Lecture in 1972 in the USA and followed up the next year by challenging the supremacy of Samuelson's *Economics* with her own alternative textbook with John Eatwell. Wynne Godley had launched the Cambridge Economic Policy Group with Francis Cripps and others, leading Cambridge economics more prominently than ever into hot and high-profile public policy debate in academic circles and prominently in national media. It was in 1973 that OPEC had catapulted the world into galloping oil-price-hike-driven inflation catalysing Kaleckian class struggles and conflict—with spectacular face-offs between the government and trade unions, especially the miners, about to trigger the collapse of the Heath Government; DAE had just published its topical occasional paper *Do Trade Unions Cause Inflation* (Jackson et al., 1972); Kalecki, whose essays (in English translation) were edited by Mario Nuti in 1972, had pithily and classically summarised inflation as class conflict; the realisation of the end of the golden age and realities of the slide into British deindustrialisation were writ large; and Whitehall corridors were echoing with the contested arguments and advice of a band of outspoken Cambridge economic advisers over devaluations and import tariffs; and relatedly, Cambridge Keynesians, 'old' and 'new', were about to begin what Francis Cripps referred to as 'theological' squabbling in public, significantly and directly involving at least two of the five editors of the proposed textbook. The stage could hardly have been set better for the dramatic entry of a heavy textbook that encapsulated and explicated the application of the Cambridge heterodox thinking to contemporary policy issues by a band of committed, if not passionate, Cambridge economists.

Perhaps it was the power of this politically charged conjuncture that brought the team together in the first instance: Francis of CEPG (with its short-term policy-oriented forecasting and simulations) and Terry of CGP (the Cambridge Growth Project, with its longer-term structural growth projections and analysis) were both stalwarts of the DAE, but of distinct, though not incompatible, orientations, while arguably Francis and Michael stood at diametrically distant positions in the spectrum of Labour politics, with Ajit, in 1973 just back red-hotfoot from China in the throes of the Cultural Revolution, perhaps rubbing shoulders with Joan. It was striking that Michael Posner was the editor responsible for the section on public policy, and therefore perhaps unsurprising that the minutes, recorded by Posner, note: "The last section of the book (on public policy and so on) may involve problems, particularly in the mind of Cripps; Posner was fairly firm that such a section could be composed and needed to be composed ... Posner agreed to think about this section of the book more closely before the next meeting."

Why did the proposed textbook not find its way into bookshops and on to bookshelves? Speculatively, there could be various explanations. Could it be that there were too many cooks in the kitchen, each with a 'best' recipe? Was the concept too ambitious? Just Posner's section, one of the four planned, was weighing in at 50,000 words; and if a healthy list of authors were to be commissioned to write on various sections, the product would need to be a multivolume series, not one compact and integrated textbook. Or perhaps it was too demanding in terms of the time and effort required from the editors, each of whom had multiple irons in many fires. They were all perhaps too busy *doing* policy and therefore with too little time left for *writing* about it. Both survivors of the group, Terry and Francis, seem to recall that they were just busy doing it all and so had little time to write a book about the doing of it (personal communications).

Or was it the issue of collective authorship, a laudable and idealistic call beyond the grasp of authors with an eye on individual CVs? Or even within the idealists, an unwillingness to being co-opted willy-nilly on to the policy stance political position of the book as a whole? Or, very credibly, the fact that the first meeting of the inner editorial group was planned for February 1974, a few weeks after 'old' versus 'new' Cambridge warfare surfaced in national newspapers, with mutually traded innuendo, invective and insults between Kahn and Posner, the 'old' team, and the 'new' gang of Kaldor, Godley, Neild and Cripps, an exchange that simmered and continued in irate letters between the parties within Cambridge, indeed mostly within King's? All, or none of the above, explanations might be valid of course; Cambridge after all. It is worth noting though that if harm was done, it was self-harm; the Keynesians did it to themselves all by themselves; neoclassicals were nowhere in sight; at least not in this case of the missing textbook. Spare a thought, though, for Joan: her theoretical textbook, born in 1973, saw but a brief life, died in its infancy; her applied textbook was conceived and aborted that same year, did not live to see the day.[116] Meanwhile, Samuelson's *Economics* went into yet another edition, gaining strength by the million from year to year, from country to country, from language to language.

4.5 THE BATTLE OF TERUEL—THE DAY AFTER

Seen on the eve of the fateful battle, it was arguable—and indeed so it was widely then perceived—that heterodox forces were on the ascendant. Most of the 'greats' were still walking the corridors at the end of the 1960s, and even those that had retired from positions had not retired from the calling. The loss of the *Economic Journal* was significant—but only when taken in isolation. However, when the scene is viewed from 'the day after', it is possible with perfect hindsight to identify the early markers of the emergence of the orthodox campaign. The 1970s ushered in powerful opposition both within Cambridge and beyond. Outside, the defensive political shield that Labour governments provided, even if passively, to the left-Keynesians began to break down bringing in Thatcher and Thatcherism, aided by the think tanks and political machinery inspired by Hayek, Friedman and their corporate and ideological devotees. At Sidgwick Site, looking back, it is possible to imagine a bizarre sight: an unlikely trio comprising Kahn, Reddaway and Kaldor pulling in the Trojan Horse, bearing Frank Hahn, into the heart of Cambridge economics. Cambridge heterodox economics stood at its peak, ready to be pushed down on the other side.

APPENDIX 4.1: FIRST OFF THE BLOCKS: MABEL TIMLIN'S *KEYNESIAN ECONOMICS*, 1942

As it happens, it was none of Klein, Tarshis or Samuelson who were the quickest to publish a book on Keynesian economics in North America; first off the block was the remarkable Mabel Timlin who is credited to have been the one—after due acknowledgement to Bob Bryce—to have brought Keynes to Canada.

Born in Wisconsin, Mabel Timlin (1891–1976) moved to Saskatchewan after both parents died in 1916, taught typing and shorthand till 1921, then became a secretary at the university there for nine years, while working part-time to earn a bachelor's degree during that period. Her father, a stationmaster, whetted her appetite for economics; he "was given to lecturing his children

---

[116] Adding to the despair was the rather indifferent or critical reception to her foray, in the last productive year/s of her life, into issues of development, a theme forever close to her heart. Her book, *Aspects of Development and Underdevelopment*, was published in 1979; it was the outcome of an ILO project though the ILO failed to publish it, and it has since faded and fallen away from discourses on development. See Chapter 11 for further discussion; also see Saith (2008).

on such matters as bimetallism and comparative advantage" (Spafford, 1977, p. 279). She didn't care for the economics courses at the university, took up English, reflecting later that "nothing was lost to my development as an economist, for through systematic reading I did much better myself" (ibid.). She became director of the university's extramural correspondence course in economics in 1929, then registered formally as a doctoral candidate at the University of Washington in 1932, completed her residential requirements by 1935, and then, at the age of 43, she finally entered her first regular academic appointment as instructor in economics.[117] She wrote her thesis in 1939–1940, Spafford observes "working largely on her own", though Dimand (2008, p. 58) writes that her *Keynesian Economics* (1942) "was based on a dissertation begun before the publication of Keynes's *The General Theory* in 1936"; for this, Dimand (2019, p. 456) records her debt "to Benjamin Higgins coming to Saskatoon with a copy of Robert Bryce's London School of Economics seminar paper on Keynes, based on Bryce's notes of three years of Keynes's Cambridge lectures". Timlin's thesis was accepted in July 1940 and, after revisions, was published by the University of Toronto in 1942—her thesis was completed four years before Lawrence Klein completed his, and published five years before Klein's was published in 1947 where, incidentally, there is no mention of Timlin. One reason, speculatively, could be the kinds of issues raised by Goodwin—then at Harvard—in his rather critical review,[118] which could possibly have been seen by Klein—then at MIT. A positive allusion comes from fellow Canadian Harry Johnson who described Mabel Timlin's *Keynesian Economics* as "a remarkable personal achievement which extended the Keynesian model by replacing the long-term interest rate by an analysis of the structure of

[117] Spafford writes of "her mission to seek out the brightest students and win from them a commitment to making a vocation of the teaching or application of economics", of "her exacting standards", and of her nurturing and mentoring of her students, to whom she was 'Timmie'. "Her honours seminars were held in her lodgings, away from the university classroom whose atmosphere, she believed, encouraged flaccidity of thought. Her comments on seminar papers, written between the lines and up and down the margins, ran sometimes to a thousand words: one handed in an essay and got back two" (Spafford, 1977, pp. 280–281).

[118] "It is not Keynes for kiddies, yet it does make easier reading than the General Theory ... useful introduction to the Keynesian system for able students." After appreciative remarks about her attempt "to dispense with the inadmissible simplification of using 'the' interest rate; ... one might question whether the result is entirely a happy one. In order to use a simple graphical technique, she also is forced to employ one rate (the ultra short-term rate) and to relegate the complex of rates, or expected rates. To verbal qualifications." Again, he approves of her exposition of the marginal propensity to consume and the multiplier—"should be welcomed by teachers as good material for an introduction to the subject"—but questions her, and Oskar Lange's route that she follows, "in making net new investment depend on consumption, as well as on the rate of interest. Would it not be nearer the truth to say that the stock of capital (the time integral of new investment) are late to consumption or income? ... This is not a question of details since it entirely changes the character of the system (from static to dynamic) making it much more difficult to use." Finally, he cautions against "the ease with which [Lange's formulation] can be represented graphically. Yet there are grounds for doubt in the advisability of using this formulation ..."; "her results are merely the result of the particular curves she happened to draw; they do not follow from her assumptions about the slopes of the various curves. ... The only way around the impasse would be to determine empirically the actual functions at any one time and place, a task which is rather utopian for the present" (Goodwin, 1944, p. 162).

interest rates and its role in the general equilibrium of the system" (Johnson 1968a, p. 131).[119] Timlin's dissertation and book are quite distinct from those of Klein, and so seem to be their Cambridge connections, as suggested by the strikingly different acknowledgements they register.[120]

More recently, Dimand (2019, p. 456) points positively to Timlin's "innovative diagrammatic treatment of shifting equilibrium", something that has actually drawn earlier comment. Venkatachalam, Velupillai and Zambelli (2012, p. 13) in their revivalist homage to Hugh Hudson's near-forgotten classic article "A Non-linear Model of the Trade Cycle", 1957, remark favourably on his geometric, diagrammatic expository technique, a predilection exhibited generously also by Richard Goodwin, whom they refer to as a "geometer in the classic Coxeter class". They add: "Incidentally, one of the most elegant—yet also as neglected as Hudson's classic—Keynesian exposition, and also one of the earliest, Mabel Timlin's *Keynesian Economics* (1942) was richly, elegantly and appropriately illustrated with diagrams of unparalleled precision by H.S.M. Coxeter—easily the pre-eminent geometer of the twentieth century." This was indeed acknowledged by Timlin (1942) in her Preface, "Professor H.S.M. Coxeter of the Department of Mathematics of the University of Toronto redrew my charts and his fine draughtsmanship has added greatly to the appearance of the book." But her reviewers disagreed: Wilson (1943) complains of "an overelaborate method of treatment with too many diagrams"; more telling are the comments from Richard Goodwin himself in his review of the book (in *Review of Economic and Statistics* 1944) where he highlights the pitfalls of making the graphical method of exposition live beyond its means.

---

[119] In his survey of Canadian contributions to economics since 1945, Harry Johnson (1967)'s criterion was if "a piece of work of general interest to the international profession of economists, one that can be said to have contributed something to the general advance of our subject", and the only woman who then qualifies is Mabel Timlin (Alexander, 1995, p. 206). Alexander challenges Johnson's exclusion of Timlin from the list of those who had ever served as President of the Canadian Economic Association, pointing out that she had been President of the earlier Canadian Political Science Association in 1959–1960 and that the erstwhile Canadian Journal of Economics and Political Science which "later lives on in the two daughter journals, the Canadian Journal of Economics and the Canadian Journal of Political Science" (ibid., p. 207). Alexander also notes that "the first and only obituary I could find was that for Mabel Timlin" (ibid., p. 211). Again, highlighting the gendered nature of the discipline and the impact of this on the undervaluing of female contributions and roles, Alexander observes that "the 'rules of the game' in academic economics were established at a time when this was a male profession. The only woman who was outstanding then under those rules was Mabel Timlin" (ibid., p. 213).

[120] Timlin singles out the influence of Oskar Lange; also acknowledged are D.H. Robertson, J.R. Hicks, A.P. Lerner, Bertil Ohlin and P.N. Rosenstein-Rodan (Timlin, 1942, p. vii). Absent is the recognition of influence or intellectual debt to any of the Cambridge Circus. Klein names, amongst others, Oskar Lange, J. Marschak and Don Patinkin, though the influence of some of them might have been more on the preparation of the book during his years at Cowles rather than the dissertation, for which his supervisor Paul Samuelson is praised in the highest terms. In contrast to Timlin, Klein's dissertation gives frequent visibility to the Cambridge group of Kahn, Joan Robinson, Kaldor, Meade and Reddaway, also to Kalecki, and then to Hicks and Robertson; he also jousts frequently with the Hayek, Knight and Hawtrey amongst others, often in a group along with Ropke, Mises, Machlup and others similar.

References

Alexander, J. A. (1995). Our ancestors in their successive generation. *Canadian Journal of Economics, 28*(1), 205–224.

Arrow, K. J. (2010). Recollections on Cambridge economics. *Cambridge Economics: Cambridge Faculty of Economics Alumni Newsletter, 3,* 5. www.econ.cam.ac.uk/alumni/newsletters/Cambridge-Economics-Issue-3-2010.pdf

Aslanbeigui, N., & Oakes, G. (2002). The theory arsenal: The Cambridge circus and the origins of the Keynesian revolution. *Journal of the History of Economic Thought, 24*(1), 5–37.

Backhouse, R. E. (1996). The changing character of British economics. In A. W. Coats (Ed.), *The post-1945 internationalization of economics,* Annual Supplement to volume 28, *History of political economy* (pp. 33–60). Duke University Press.

Baranzini, M. L., & Mirante, A. (2018). *Luigi L. Pasinetti: An intellectual biography: Leading scholar and system builder of the Cambridge School of Economics.* Palgrave Macmillan.

Barnes, J. A. (2007). *Humping my drum: A memoir.* https://www.amazon.com/Humping-my-drum-J-Barnes/dp/1409204006

Barnett, W. A. (2004). An interview with Paul A. Samuelson, December 23, 2003. *Macroeconomic Dynamics, 8,* 519–542. Republished in Working Paper Series in Theoretical and Applied Economics, University of Kansas.

Bloomberg News. (2013, October 21). *Lawrence Klein dies at 93; won Nobel Prize for his econometric models.* https://www.latimes.com/local/obituaries/la-me-lawrence-klein-20131022-story.html

Bodkin, R. G., & Kanta, M. (1997). Klein, Lawrence Robert. In D. Glasner (Ed.), *Business cycles and depressions: An encyclopedia* (pp. 361–363). Garland Publishing Inc.

Burchardt, F., et al. (1944). *The economics of full employment.* Blackwell for the Oxford Institute of Economics and Statistics.

Cairncross, A. (1993). *The life of an economic adviser.* Palgrave Macmillan.

Caldentey, E. P. (2019). *Roy Harrod.* Palgrave Macmillan.

Cambridge Journal of Economics Editors. (2006). Keynes's last time at the Political Economy Club: Editorial introduction. *Cambridge Journal of Economics, 30*(1), 1. https://doi.org/10.1093/cje/bei091

Cambridge Political Economy Group. (1974). Britain's economic crisis. Spokesman pamphlet No. 44. Bertrand Russell Peace Foundation, for *The Spokesman.*

Chambers, M. (2020). *London and the modernist bookshop.* Cambridge University Press.

Coats, A. W. (1993). *The sociology and professionalization of economics: British and American economic essays, volume II.* Routledge.

Coats, A. W., & Coats, S. E. (1970). The social composition of the Royal Economic Society and the beginnings of the British economics 'profession', 1890–1915. *British Journal of Sociology, 21,* 75–85.

Cockerill, T. (2012). The Marshall lectures. *Cambridge Economics: Cambridge Faculty of Economics Alumni Newsletter, 5,* 5–6. http://www.econ.cam.ac.uk/alumni/newsletters/Cambridge-Economics-Issue-5-2012.pdf

Colander, D., & Landreth, H. (1996). *The coming of Keynesianism to America.* Edward Elgar.

Colander, D., & Landreth, H. (n.d.). *Political influence on the textbook Keynesian revolution: God, man, and Laurie (sic) Tarshis at Yale.* http://community.middlebury.edu/~colander/articles/Political%20Influence%20on%20the%20Textbook%20Keynesian%20Revolution.pdf

Cord, R. (2013). *Reinterpreting the Keynesian revolution*. Routledge.
Cord, R. A. (Ed.). (2017). *The Palgrave companion to Cambridge economics*. Palgrave Macmillan.
Coutts, K. (2021). The legacy of Wynne Godley: Notes for a talk on the legacy of Wynne Godley, Wednesday 12 May 2020. *Journal of Post Keynesian Economics, 44*(1), 27–31.
Dasgupta, P. (2010). Interview with Partha Dasgupta 6th April 2010. In S. Harrison & A. Macfarlane, *Encounter with economics*. Interviews filmed by A. Macfarlane and edited by S. Harrison. University of Cambridge. http://sms.cam.ac.uk/collection/1092396
Dasgupta, P. (2013). Obituary: Frank Hahn. *Royal Economic Society Newsletter, 161*(April).
Daubenmier, J. (1990, February 25). Professors recall hard lessons of McCarthyism: Free speech: Some want the University of Michigan to apologize to three professors who were branded as potential subversives because of their former communist sympathies. *Los Angeles Times*. https://www.latimes.com/archives/la-xpm-1990-02-25-mn-1928-story.html
De Vroey, M., & Malgrange, P. (2012). From the *Keynesian Revolution* to the Klein-Goldberger Model: Klein and the dynamization of Keynesian theory. *History of Economic Ideas, 20*(2), 113–135.
Deaton, A. (2011). My Cambridge in the 60s and 70s. *Cambridge Economics: Cambridge Faculty of Economics Alumni Newsletter, 4*, 3–4. www.econ.cam.ac.uk/alumni/newsletters/Cambridge-Economics-Issue-4-2011.pdf
Di Matteo, M. (Ed.). (1990). *Celebrating R. M. Goodwin's 75th Birthday Quaderni del Dipartimento di Economia Politica No. 100*. University of Siena.
Di Matteo, M., & Sordi, S. (2009). *Richard M. Goodwin: A pioneer in the field of economic dynamics between the two Cambridges*. DEPFID Working Paper No. 7/2009. Dipartimento di Politica Economica, Finanza e Sviluppo, University di Siena.
Dimand, R. W. (2008). How Keynes came to Canada: Mabel Timlin and Keynesian economics. In M. Forstater & L. R. Wray (Eds.), *Keynes for the twenty-first century* (pp. 57–79). Palgrave Macmillan. https://doi.org/10.1057/9780230611139_4
Dimand, R. W. (2019). Mabel Timlin. In R. Dimand & H. Hagemann (Eds.), *The Elgar Companion to John Maynard Keynes* (pp. 456–461). Edward Elgar.
Dunn, S. P. (2009). Cambridge economics, heterodoxy and ontology: An interview with Tony Lawson. *Review of Political Economy, 21*(3), 481–496.
Eatwell, J. (1977). Maurice Dobb. *Cambridge Journal of Economics, 1*(1), 1–3.
Eatwell, J. (2016). Tribute to Ajit Singh. *Cambridge Journal of Economics, 40*(2), 365–372.
Economic Journal. (1898). After seven years. *Economic Journal, 8*(29), 1–2.
Edgeworth, F. W. (1891). The British Economic Association. *Economic Journal, 1*(1), 1–14.
Ellman, M., Rowthorn, B., Smith, R., & Wilkinson, F. (1974). *Britain's economic crisis*. Spokesman Books.
ESRC. (n.d.). *SSRC/ESRC: The first forty years*. ESRC. https://esrc.ukri.org/files/news-events-and-publications/publications/ssrc-and-esrc-the-first-forty-years/
Feinstein, C., & Matthews, R. (1990). The growth of output and productivity in the UK: The 1980s as a phase of the post-war period. *National Institute Economic Review, 133*(1), 78–90.

Feiwel, G. R. (1975). *The intellectual capital of Michal Kalecki: A study in economic theory and policy*. University of Tennessee Press.

Fletcher, G. (2008). *Dennis Robertson*. Palgrave Macmillan.

Fuelner, E. J. (2018, February 28). *The legacy of William F. Buckley Jr*. The Heritage Foundation. https://www.heritage.org/conservatism/commentary/the-legacy-william-f-buckley-jr

Gilbert, R. V., Hildebrand, G. H., Stuart, A. W., Sweezy, M. Y., Sweezy, P., Tarshis, L., & Wilson, J. D. (1938). *An economic program for American democracy by seven Harvard and Tufts economists*. Vanguard Press.

Giraud, Y. (2020). Addressing the audience: Paul Samuelson, radical economics, and textbook making, 1967–1973. *Journal of the History of Economic Thought*, 42(2), 177–198.

Godley, W. (2008, May 16). Interview with Wynne Godley. In S. Harrison & A. Macfarlane, *Encounter with economics*. Interviews filmed by A. Macfarlane and edited by S. Harrison. University of Cambridge. http://sms.cam.ac.uk/collection/1092396

Goodhart, C. A. E. (2006). John Stanton Flemming, 1941–2003. *Proceedings of the British Academy*, 138, 71–95.

Goodwin, R. M. (1944). Review of *Keynesian economics* by Mabel Timlin. *Review of Economic Statistics*, 26(3), 162.

Goodwin, R. M. (1970). *Elementary economics from the higher standpoint*. Cambridge University Press.

Goodwin, R. M. (1989). Joan Robinson – Passionate seeker after truth. In G. R. Feiwel (Ed.), *Joan Robinson and modern economic theory* (pp. 916–917). Palgrave Macmillan.

Goodwin, R. M. (1991). Schumpeter, Keynes and the theory of evolution. *Journal of Evolutionary Economics*, 1, 29–47.

Groenewegen, P. D. (2007). *Alfred Marshall: Economist 1842–1924*. Palgrave Macmillan.

Hahn, F. (Ed.). (1989a). *The economics of missing markets, information, and games*. Clarendon Press.

Hahn, F. (1989b). Robinson–Hahn love–hate relationship. In G. R. Feiwel (Ed.), *Joan Robinson and modern economic theory* (pp. 895–910). Palgrave Macmillan.

Hammond, J. D. (1988, May 24). *An interview with Milton Friedman on methodology*. Hoover Institution, Stanford University. https://miltonfriedman.hoover.org/friedman_images/Collections/2016c21/Stanford_05_24_1988.pdf

Hamouda, O. F., & Price, B. B. (Eds.). (1998). *Keynesianism and the Keynesian revolution in America: A memorial volume in honour of Lorie Tarshis*. Edward Elgar.

Hanappi, H. (2015). Schumpeter and Goodwin. *Journal of Evolutionary Economics*, 25(1). https://www.researchgate.net/publication/271732427_Schumpeter_and_Goodwin

Harcourt, G. C. (1972). *Some Cambridge controversies in the theory of capital*. Cambridge University Press.

Harcourt, G. C. (1982). An early post Keynesian: Lorie Tarshis. *Journal of Post Keynesian Economics*, 4(4), 609–619.

Harcourt, G. C. (1985). A twentieth-century eclectic: Richard Goodwin. *Journal of Post-Keynesian Economics*, 7(3), 410–421.

Harcourt, G. C. (1993, October 9). Obituary: Professor Lorie Tarshis. *The Independent*.

Harcourt, G. C. (1995a). Lorie Tarshis, 1911–1993: In appreciation. *Economic Journal*, 105(432), 1244–1255.

Harcourt, G. C. (1995b). Interview with G. C. Harcourt. In J. E. King (Ed.), *Conversations with post Keynesians* (pp. 168–186). Palgrave Macmillan.

Harcourt, G. C. (1999a). Horses for courses: The making of a post-Keynesian economist. In A. Heertje (Ed.), *The makers of modern economics* (Vol. IV, pp. 32–69). Edward Elgar.

Harcourt, G. C. (2006). *The structure of post-Keynesian economics: The core contributions of the pioneers*. Cambridge University Press.

Harcourt, G. C. (2007). Interview with Geoffrey Harcourt 15th May 2007. In S. Harrison & A. Macfarlane, *Encounter with economics*. Film interviews with leading thinkers, filmed by A. Macfarlane and edited by S. Harrison. University of Cambridge; Created 28 March 2011. http://sms.cam.ac.uk/collection/1092396

Harcourt, G. C. (2012a, October). Phyllis Deane. *Royal Economic Society Newsletter, 159*.

Harcourt, G. C. (2012b). Keynes and his Cambridge pupils and colleagues. *Meiji Journal of Political Science and Economics, 1*, 12–25.

Harcourt, G. C. (2015). Fusing indissolubly the cycle and the trend: Richard Goodwin's profound insight. *Cambridge Journal of Economics, 39*(6), 1569–1578.

Harcourt, G. C. (2016a). Piero Sraffa: A tribute. In J. Halevi, G. C. Harcourt, P. Kriesler, & J. W. Neville (Eds.), *Post-Keynesian essays from down under* (Essays on ethics, social justice and economics – Theory and policy in an historical context) (Vol. III, pp. 258–261). Palgrave Macmillan.

Harcourt, G. C., & Kerr, P. (2009). *Joan Robinson*. Palgrave Macmillan.

Harrod, R. F. (1951). *The life of John Maynard Keynes*. Harcourt, Brace and Company.

Hobsbawm, E. (1967). Maurice Dobb. In C. H. Feinstein (Ed.), *Socialism, capitalism and economic growth: Essays presented to Maurice Dobb* (pp. 1–12). Cambridge University Press.

Hodgson, G. M., Gagliardi, F., & Gindis, D. (2018). From Cambridge Keynesian to institutional economist: The unnoticed contributions of Robert Neild. *Journal of Institutional Economics, 14*(4). https://doi.org/10.1017/S1744137417000534

Hollinger, D. A. (n.d.). *Academic culture at Michigan, 1938–1988: The apotheosis of pluralism*. https://www.rackham.umich.edu/downloads/Hollinger.pdf

Jackson, D., Turner, H. A., & Wilkinson, F. (1972). *Do trade unions cause inflation?* Occasional Paper No. 36. Cambridge University Department of Applied Economics.

Johnson, H. G. (1968a). Canadian contributions to the discipline of economics since 1945. *Canadian Journal of Economics, 1*(1), 129–146.

Johnson, H. G. (n.d.). *Cambridge in the 1950s: Memoirs of an economist*. Men and Ideas, RFK/12/2/57/2-14, pp. 28–39. Richard Kahn Papers, King's College Archives, Cambridge.

Kahn, R. (1977). Malinvaud on Keynes. Reviewing: Edmond Malinvaud, *The theory of unemployment reconsidered*, Basil Blackwell, Oxford, 1977; Three lectures delivered for the Yrjo Jahnsson Foundation, Helsinki. *Cambridge Journal of Economics, 1*(4), 375–388.

Kahn, R., & Marcuzzo, M. C. (2020). Richard Kahn: A disciple of Keynes. *History of Economics Review*, 57p. https://doi.org/10.1080/10370196.2020.1767930

Kaldor, N. (1966). *Causes of the slow rate of economic growth of the United Kingdom*. Cambridge University Press.

Kaldor, N. (1996). *Causes of Growth and Stagnation in the World Economy. The Raffaele Mattioli Lectures delivered in 1984*. Cambridge: Cambridge University Press.

Kalecki, M. (1943). Political aspects of full employment. *Political Quarterly, 14*(4), 322–330.

Keynes, J. M. (1924). Alfred Marshall, 1842–1924. *The Economic Journal*, *34*(135), 311–372.

Keynes, J. M. (1925). A short view of Russia. In J. M. Keynes (Ed.), *Essays in Persuasion. The collected writings of John Maynard Keynes* (Essays in Persuasion) (Vol. IX). Royal Economic Society, Palgrave Macmillan, 1972.

King, J. E., & Millmow, A. (2003). Death of a revolutionary textbook. *History of Political Economy*, *35*(1), 105–134.

Kitson, M. (2005). Economics for the future. *Cambridge Journal of Economics*, *29*, 827–835.

Klein, L. R. (1944). *The Keynesian revolution*. Ph.D. thesis, Massachusetts Institute of Technology, Department of Economics. https://dspace.mit.edu/handle/1721.1/11300

Klein, L. R. (1947). *The Keynesian revolution*. Macmillan & Co.

Klein, L. (1951). The life of John Maynard Keynes. *Journal of Political Economy*, *59*, 443–451.

Klein, L. (1980). *Lawrence R. Klein: Biographical. The Sveriges Riksbank prize in economic sciences in memory of Alfred Nobel*. https://www.nobelprize.org/prizes/economic-sciences/1980/klein/biographical/

Klein, L. R. (1991). Econometric contributions of the Cowles Commission, 1944–47: A retrospective view. *BNL Quarterly Review*, *177*(June), 107–117.

Klein, L. (2005). *Lawrence R. Klein: Biographical: Addendum. The Sveriges Riksbank prize in economic sciences in memory of Alfred Nobel, 1980*. https://www.nobelprize.org/prizes/economic-sciences/1980/klein/biographical/

Kregel, J. (1973). *The reconstruction of political economy: An introduction to post-Keynesian economics*. Macmillan.

Lavoie, M. (2007). *Introduction to post-Keynesian economics*. Palgrave Macmillan.

Lee, F. S. (2007, November 1–3). *Making history by making identity and institutions: The emergence of Post-Keynesian–heterodox economics in Britain, 1974–1996*. Paper presented at the EAPE Conference, Universidade Porto, Porto.

Leeson, R. (Ed.). (2017). *Hayek: A collaborative biography. Part X: Eugenics, cultural evolution and the fatal conceit*. Palgrave Macmillan.

Lewis, L. S. (1988). *Cold war on campus: A study of politics of organizational control*. Transaction Books.

Lipsey, R. (1963). *Positive economics*. Weidenfeld & Nicolson.

Llewellyn, J. (1998). Empirical analysis as an underpinning to policy. In I. Begg & S. G. B. Henry (Eds.), *Applied economics and public policy* (pp. 247–257). Cambridge University Press.

Lloyd, I. (2006). Summary of an address by Lord Keynes to the Political Economy Club, Trinity College, Cambridge on the 2nd February 1946. *Cambridge Journal of Economics*, *30*(1), 2–6. https://doi.org/10.1093/cje/bei096

MacCarthy, F. (2019). *Walter Gropius: Visionary founder of the Bauhaus*. Faber and Faber.

Maddison, A. (1994, June). Confessions of a Chiffrephile. *Banca Nazionale del Lavoro Quarterly Review*, *189*. http://www.ggdc.net/maddison/personal/autobiog1994.pdf

Mandelbaum, K. (1944). An experiment in full employment: Controls in the German economy, 1933–1938. In F. A. Burchardt (Ed.), *The economics of full employment: Six studies in applied economics prepared at the Oxford University Institute of Statistics* (pp. 181–203). Basil Blackwell.

Marcuzzo, M. C. (2008). Piero Sraffa at the University of Cambridge. In H. D. Kurz, L. Pasinetti, & N. Salvadori (Eds.), *Piero Sraffa: The man and the scholar. Exploring his unpublished papers* (pp. 51–77). Routledge.

Marcuzzo, M. C. (2012). *Fighting market failure: Collected essays in the Cambridge tradition of economics.* Routledge.

Marcuzzo, M. C., & Rosselli, A. (Eds.). (2005). *Economists in Cambridge: A study through their correspondence, 1907–1946.* Routledge.

Marcuzzo, M. C., & Sanfilippo, E. (2008). Dear John, Dear Ursula: Eighty-eight letters unearthed. In R. Scazzieri, A. Sen, & S. Zamagni (Eds.), *Markets, money and capital: Hicksian economics for the twenty first century* (pp. 72–91). Cambridge University Press.

Marshall, A. (1897, January). The old generation of economists and the new. *Quarterly Journal of Economics*, No. 11, 115–135.

Matthews, R. C. O. (1989). Joan Robinson and Cambridge – A theorist and her milieu: An interview. In G. R. Feiwel (Ed.), *Joan Robinson and modern economic theory* (pp. 911–915). Palgrave Macmillan.

McDonagh, E. C. (1989). Book review: *Cold war on campus: A study of politics of organizational control. Lionel S. Lewis. American Journal of Education, 97*(3), 315–318.

McKittrick, D., & Dalyell, T. (2010, August 10). Robin Matthews: Leading economist and Master of Clare College, Cambridge. *The Independent.* https://www.independent.co.uk/news/obituaries/robin-matthews-leading-economist-and-master-of-clare-college-cambridge-2047930.html

Meade, J. E. (1977). *James E. Meade: Biographical.* https://www.nobelprize.org/prizes/economic-sciences/1977/meade/biographical/

Millmow, A. (2003, October). Joan Robinson's disillusion with economics. *Review of Political Economy, 15*(4), 561–574.

Moggridge, D. (1973). *Collected writings of John Maynard Keynes, volume XIII.* Macmillan.

Moggridge, D. E. (2001). H. G. J. as a biographer's subject: Some autobiographical writings. *American Journal of Economics and Sociology, 60*(3), 651–666.

Moggridge, D. E. (2019). Harry Gordon Johnson. In R. Dimand & H. Hagemann (Eds.), *The Elgar companion to John Maynard Keynes* (pp. 506–509). Edward Elgar.

Newbery, D. (2017). Frank Horace Hahn 1925–2013. *Biographical Memoirs of Fellows of the British Academy, XVI,* 485–525. https://www.britac.ac.uk/sites/default/files/23 Hahn 1837 9_11_17.pdf

Neild, R. (2013b, December 10). Interview with Robert Neild by F. Gagliardi, D. Gindis and G. M. Hodgson. Cited in Hodgson, Gagliardi and Gindis (2018).

Nikiforos, M., & Zezza, G. (2017). Stock-flow consistent macroeconomic models: A survey. *Journal of Economic Surveys, 31*(5), 1204–1239.

Pasinetti, L. L. (1991). Richard Ferdinand Kahn, 1905–1989. *Proceedings of the British Academy, 76,* 423–443.

Pasinetti, L. L. (1996). Richard Murphey Goodwin (1913–1996): A pupil's tribute to a great teacher. *Cambridge Journal of Economics, 20*(6), 645–649.

Pasinetti, L. L. (2005). The Cambridge School of Keynesian economics. *Cambridge Journal of Economics, 29*(6), 837–848.

Pasinetti, L. L. (2007). *Keynes and the Cambridge Keynesians. A 'revolution in economics' to be accomplished.* Cambridge University Press.

Patel, I. G. (1989). Images of Joan. In G. R. Feiwel (Ed.), *Joan Robinson and modern economic theory* (pp. 863–865). Palgrave Macmillan.

Patnaik, P. (2015a). Ajit Singh (1940–2015): A formidable economist. *Economic & Political Weekly, 50*(30), 32–34.

Patnaik, P. (2015b). Goodwin on the optimal growth path for a developing economy. *Cambridge Journal of Economics, 39*(6), 1579–1586.

Patinkin, D., & Leith, J. C. (Eds.). (1977). *Keynes, Cambridge and the general theory*. Macmillan.

Robinson, J. (1956). *The accumulation of capital*. Macmillan.

Robinson, J. (1961). *Exercises in economic analysis*. Macmillan.

Robinson, J. (1972). The second crisis of economic theory. *American Economic Review, 62*(1–2), 1–10. Richard T. Ely Lecture delivered in New Orleans in 1971.

Robinson, J. (1976). *The state of play*. RFK/12/2/81/81-82. 2p. Typed note by Joan Robinson held in the Richard F. Kahn Papers, King's College Archives, University of Cambridge.

Robinson, J. (1977). What are the questions? *Journal of Economic Literature, 15*(4), 1318–1339.

Robinson, J. (1979). *Aspects of development and underdevelopment*. Cambridge University Press.

Robinson, J. (1981, April 14 and 16). *The arms race. The Tanner lectures on human values delivered at the University of Utah*. https://tannerlectures.utah.edu/_documents/a-to-z/r/robinson82.pdf

Robinson, J., & Eatwell, J. (1973). *An introduction to modern economics*. McGraw Hill.

Saith, A. (2008). Joan Robinson and Indian planning: An awkward relationship. *Development and Change, 39*(6), 1115–1134.

Saith, A. (2019). *Ajit Singh of Cambridge and Chandigarh: An intellectual biography of the radical Sikh economist*. Palgrave Macmillan.

Samuelson, P. A. (1989, September 19). *Letter from Paul A. Samuelson to Austin Robinson*. EAGR Archives, Marshall Library, Cambridge; #389.

Samuelson, P. A. (1994). Richard Kahn: His welfare economics and lifetime achievement. *Cambridge Journal of Economics, 18*(1), 55–72.

Samuelson, P. A. (1997). Credo of a lucky textbook author. *Journal of Economic Perspectives, 11*(2), 153–160.

Schrecker, E. W. (1986). *No Ivory Tower: McCarthyism and the universities*. Johns Hopkins University Press.

Sen, A. (1998). *Amartya Sen – Biographical*. https://www.nobelprize.org/prizes/economic-sciences/1998/sen/biographical/

Sen, A. (2021). *Home in the world: A memoir*. Allen Lane and Penguin Random House.

Silberston, A. (2011a, January). Robin Matthews. *Royal Economic Society Newsletter, 152*. http://www.res.org.uk/SpringboardWebApp/userfiles/res/file/obituaries/matthews.pdf

Silberston, A. (2011b). Ken Arrow, James Meade and the secret seminar. *Cambridge Economics: Cambridge Faculty of Economics Alumni Newsletter, 4*, 4. www.econ.cam.ac.uk/alumni/newsletters/Cambridge-Economics-Issue-4-2011.pdf

Singh, A. (2008). *Better to be rough and relevant than to be precise and irrelevant: Reddaway's legacy to economics*. Working Paper No. 379. Cambridge University Centre for Business Research. www.cbr.cam.ac.uk/fileadmin/user_upload/centre-for-business-research/downloads/working-papers/wp379.pdf

Skousen, M. (1997). The perseverance of Paul Samuelson's *economics*. *Journal of Economic Perspectives, 11*(2), 137–152.

Smith, S. (2008). 'Hard as the metal of my gun': John Cornford's Spain. *Journal of English Studies, 5*, 357–373.

Spafford, D. (1977). In memoriam: Mabel Timlin. *Canadian Journal of Economics, 10*(2), 279–281.

Sraffa, P. (1960). *Production of commodities by means of commodities: Prelude to a critique of economic theory.* Cambridge University Press.

Stiglitz, J. E. (2002). Biographical. https://www.nobelprize.org/prizes/economic-sciences/2001/stiglitz/biographical/

Stray, C. (2019). An Irishman abroad. In C. Stray, C. Pelling, & S. Harrison (Eds.), *Rediscovering E. R. Dodds: Scholarship, education, poetry and the paranormal* (pp. 10–35). Oxford University Press.

Tarshis, L. (1989). Remembering Joan Robinson. In G. R. Feiwel (Ed.), *Joan Robinson and modern economic theory* (pp. 918–920). Palgrave Macmillan.

Timlin, M. F. (1942). *Keynesian economics.* University Press.

Tobin, J. (n.d.). Lost star. *Heritage Project.* University of Michigan. https://heritage.umich.edu/stories/lost-star/

Tribe, K. (1992). The *Economic Journal* and British economics, 1891–1940. *History of the Human Sciences, 5*(4), 33–58.

Velupillai, K. V. (2015a). Richard Goodwin: The Indian connection. *Economic and Political Weekly, 50*(15), 80–84.

Velupillai, K. V. (2015b). Perspectives on the contributions of Richard Goodwin. *Cambridge Journal of Economics, 39*(6). Special Issue: *Perspectives on the contributions of Richard Goodwin,* 1485–1496.

Venkatachalam, R., Velupillai, K. V., & Zambelli, S. (2012). *A non-linear model of the trade cycle: Mathematical reflections on Hugh Hudson's classic.* https://econpapers.repec.org/paper/trnutwpas/1215.htm. Also in: *Australian Economic Papers, 52*(2), 115–125.

Vernengo, M. (2013, September 14). Hydraulic Krugman on Wynne Godley. *Naked Keynesianism: Hemlock for Economics Students.*http://nakedkeynesianism.blogspot.com/2013/09/hydraulic-krugman-on-wynne-godley.html

Vervaecke, P. (2011). Review of William C. Lubenow, *The Cambridge Apostles, 1820–1914: Liberalism, imagination and friendship in British intellectual and professional life,* Cambridge University Press, 1998. *Cercles, Revue Pluridisciplinaire du Monde Anglophone.* http://www.cercles.com/review/r47/Lubenow.html

Waterman, A. M. C. (2003). Joan Robinson as a teacher. *Review of Political Economy, 15*(4), 589–596.

Whitaker, J. K. (Ed.). (1996). *The correspondence of Alfred Marshall, economist* (Climbing, 1681–1890) (Vol. 1). Royal Economic Society Publication. Cambridge University Press.

Whitfield, S. J. (1987). Review of Ellen W. Schrecker, *No ivory tower: McCarthyism and the universities. Reviews in American History, 15*(3), 480–485.

Wilson, T. (1943). Review of Mabel F. Timlin, *Keynesian Economics,* Toronto: University Press, 1942. *Economic Journal, 53*(210/211), 224–226. https://doi.org/10.2307/2226324

Wright, D. M. (1948, March). Review: The Keynesian revolution by Lawrence R. Klein. *American Economic Review, 38*(1), 145–152.

CHAPTER 5

The DAE Trilogy

Abstract Over its lifetime of fifty eight years, the DAE ship had just four captains at the wheel: Dick Stone from 1945 till 1955, followed by the three 15-year terms of Brian Reddaway (1955–1970), Wynne Godley (1970–1985), and David Newbery (1988–2003). The DAE journey is best traced through the course followed during each period, the route strongly influenced by the respective helmsmen. In orientation and substance, the work of the DAE was shaped by their research predilections, intellectual imaginations and idiosyncrasies, by their styles of institutional leadership, and by their ideological stance both in terms of national politics as well as the disciplinary framing of economics. Each period is thus stamped by a distinctive character, with significant shifts in direction, balance, and flavour at each switch point. The purposive commentary in this chapter provides the necessary backdrop for the subsequent unfolding of the traumatic episodes comprising the DAE Trilogy: first, the closure of the Cambridge Economic Policy Group; then, the termination of the Cambridge Growth Project; and, finally, the unusual and unorthodox University Review of the DAE.

5.1 Origins and Evolution

5.1.1 Origins

The Department of Applied Economics (DAE) was a glint in the Cambridge eye in the 1930s, conceived in 1939 and born, when the war was ending, in 1945.

A Report of the General Board of the University dated 1 November 1939 (Cambridge University Reporter, 1939/1940, p. 241) includes a Report by a

© The Author(s), under exclusive license to Springer Nature Switzerland AG 2022
A. Saith, *Cambridge Economics in the Post-Keynesian Era*, Palgrave Studies in the History of Economic Thought,
https://doi.org/10.1007/978-3-030-93019-6_5

committee chaired by Professor Pigou and which comprised Keynes (as well as Professor Austin Robinson, Kahn and Champernowne) as members. The opening two paragraphs summarise the raison d'etre for the formation of a new Department of Applied Economics (DAE):

> In a considerable number of British Universities, economic research, particularly in the descriptive and statistical fields, is being fostered with the aid of grants which are not available from certain outside bodies. The Board are of the opinion that it would be of advantage to the stud and teaching of economic in the University if similar provision were made in Cambridge. They consider, however, that the Faculty Board is not a suitable body either for administering such grants or for exercising any supervision that may be desirable, both because of its size and because its responsibilities and membership cover so wide a field. They have considered the various arrangements which might be made for these purposes and have reached the conclusion that the need could best be met by setting up of a Department in the Faculty of Economics and Politics under the general control of a Committee of Management.
>
> Besides assisting research in the narrower sense, a Department of this kind might render useful service to the teaching activities of the Faculty by helping University Teaching Officers in the Faculty to obtain first-hand information about current economic conditions, a matter in which Cambridge is at some disadvantage as compared with the Universities in industrial centres.

In a Note, c.1944, E.A.G. Robinson reaffirms these pre-war formative intentions of the DAE and adds:

> After the outbreak of the war, the University passed the necessary Grace for the creation of the Department, but it was decided to suspend for the time being its actual establishment. A large number of those members of the Faculty of Economics who would have been most closely associated with its work had been called into government service, and it was the general view that it was not desirable to start the Department in circumstances that would necessarily have involved the acceptance of standards of work lower than those which should ordinarily be set.

It is the wish of the Committee (and the Faculty Board of Economics and Politics concurs) to make full provision for bringing the Department into effective action at the earlier possible moment after the war. In this, it has two main motives. Firstly, the economic problems of transition from war to peace and of the reorientation of international commercial relations are certain to be of the very greatest importance, and it is most desirable that study of them, in the field as well as by statistical methods, should be begun at the earliest possible moment. Secondly, a large number of the economists who are best fitted to serve on the staff of such a Department will be considering their future plans and making arrangements to leave government service. It will be most important to be able to make quite definite offers at the earliest opportunity to those whom it is desired to secure.[1]

---

[1] Extracted from EAGR Note "The Cambridge Department of Applied Economics". EAGR/3/1/2/1–4.

It is apparent that the foundational orientation of the DAE was very broad in its remit, embracing a wide range of emerging policy concerns, while simultaneously building up an institutional capacity in applied economics both in the DAE and amongst the staff in the Faculty with such interests. From its inception, the DAE was a national project with an international vision.

Following this, in 1944, the Faculty Board constituted a Committee of Management, chaired by Keynes, which included David Champernowne, Dennis Robertson, E.A.G. Robinson, G.F. Shove, Joan Robinson and Piero Sraffa. Sraffa was the pen holder for the minutes. The Committee appointed Dick Stone, then all of 32, as the DAE Director for life, effectively for the next 35 years till retirement, and the offer was conveyed to a 'surprised and delighted' Dick Stone by Piero in November 1944; the University approved the appointment on 15 May 1945, and Stone was appointed from 1 July 1945 (Pesaran & Harcourt, 2000, F149). The DAE lived for almost 60 years, till its life was ended in 2004 through a wilful merger with the parent body of the Faculty of Economics from which it had sprung; the Faculty had been creative and responsible for bringing the DAE to life; in the end it was also responsible for leading it to its enforced end. In the interim, the DAE enjoyed a remarkable, chequered existence, full of intellectual creativity, incorrigible curiosity and adventurous academic exuberance, all addressed with high academic merit—attributes that made it the first amongst its peers in the field of applied economics. After rapid early growth, its body of staff stabilised at a scale which roughly matched that of the Faculty, though it was still well below the size of the National Institute of Economic and Social Research (NIESR). But size notwithstanding, whether in the national or international arena, the DAE consistently punched well above its weight—aided no doubt by the possibility that it could, and did regularly, draw on the very considerable strength of its reserve bench, the Faculty itself.

5.1.2   Evolution: Substance and Styles

In his appreciation on the death of Colin Clark in 1989, the venerable Austin Robinson, then 92 himself, conjured up the ethos, and chaos, at the point of inception, and evokes the pioneering spirit of the times, and of Keynes and his band. His words demand a full airing.

> "Colin Clark has [a] strong claim to be regarded as the progenitor of our Department of Applied Economics here in Cambridge". He was brought to Cambridge as a lecturer in economic statistics in 1931 and stayed till 1937 when he went to Australia. "During those six years, almost single-handed he permanently changed the character of Cambridge economics. Colin Clark ... was not at that time, or indeed at any time, an economist of the kind that we all were before he arrived. We were old-fashioned logical non-quantitative model makers with little evidence other than guesswork of the size or importance of the things we were talking about. ... [W]e had what I believe was then the strongest faculty anywhere in the world. But we were, as I say, non-quantitative. Colin, considerably, but not wholeheartedly encouraged by Keynes (remember his review of Tinbergen), set out to make us quantitative.

His unique advantage was that when he arrived among us in Cambridge, he knew no formal economics. He did not know what we had regarded as beyond our capacity to measure. We were all bubbling with excitement at that time just after the publication of Keynes's Treatise and on our way to the General Theory. We were worrying about savings and investment and gaps and their elimination. Colin started off to measure all these things.[2] ... Meanwhile, Colin was doing two things. He was teaching and infecting a first generation of keen and active Cambridge economic statisticians. He was writing two large and very important books.[3] Those whom as his pupils he infected with his contagious enthusiasms included Dick Stone, ... and V.K.R.V. Rao, later to produce the first national income of India and to create the Delhi School of Economics.

"My earliest memories of him are of an uncouth, untidy ill-dressed youngster, completely uninterested in any college life, who was to be found at the top of a rickety Elizabethan staircase opposite the east window of Benet Church." When the Marshall Library moved to Downing Street, "we made a space for him and what had become his little group of enthusiasts in the attics above the library. I cannot remember that we provided him with any equipment."

It gradually penetrated our non-quantitative heads, however, that his sort of research needed research assistants and equipment to make any real success of it. ... Keynes made some unsuccessful explorations in this country. He and I then tried much more successfully the Rockefeller Foundation. We had arrangements all sown up just before the war broke out. ... We put the whole scheme to bed for the duration of the war. We did not forget it however. ... When Keynes and I were both in Washington in the autumn of 1944 ... we saw our friends in the Rockefeller Foundation and confirmed with them our plans and their willingness to start the D.A.E. as soon as possible after the war.

Meanwhile we had lost Colin. He had gone off to Australia in 1937. This meant that he was out of England ... when the D.A.E. was ... inaugurated after the war in the shed on the lawn in Downing Street ... It was obvious that the first Director should be Dick Stone, one of Colin Clark's early pupils. With Keynes now dead, I, infected by Colin, had the privilege of being the first chairman[4] of its Committee."[5]

---

[2] Austin Robinson might have had in mind here, apart from several other contributions, Colin Clark's article in the *Economic Journal* (Clark, 1938) on the determination of the multiplier from national income statistics. Austin was working on the journal, with Keynes as Editor. Skidelsky (1992, pp. 690–691) later writes: Colin Clark "helped Richard Kahn with the first sketch of the multiplier theory ... JMK thought him 'a bit of a genius—almost the only economic statistician I have ever met who seems to me quite first-class.'"

[3] *The National Income 1924–31*, published in 1932, and *The Conditions of Economic Progress* (1940), described by Robinson as "a book of remarkable originality at that time".

[4] The Minutes of the 12 Meeting of the Committee of Management of the DAE, held on Sunday, 5th May 1946, begin thus: "While no formal record can justly express all that is lost to Cambridge by the death of Maynard Keynes, his friends and colleagues forming the Committee of this Department desired to have recorded in these minutes their sense of the great loss the Department has suffered in the death of its first Chairman. He had its foundations and future always at heart and no more severe blow could have befallen it." After Keynes's death, Austin Robinson—the unstinting indefatigable institutional workhorse of Cambridge economics—continued as Chair of the DAE Committee of Management till December 1967.

[5] Extracted from E.A.G. Robinson Papers, Marshall Library Archives, University of Cambridge; EAGR/5/7/15/1–3; c. September 1989.

Geoff Harcourt and Michael Kitson (Harcourt & Kitson, 1993, p. 435) observe that "Cambridge economics has always been a broad church and it could be even argued that the Directors of the DAE have been patriarchs drawn from different denominations". Over its near six-decade lifetime, the DAE ship[6] had just four captains at the wheel: Dick Stone from 1945 till 1955, followed by the three 15-year terms of Brian Reddaway (1955–1970),[7] Wynne Godley (1970–1985) and David Newbery (1988–2003).[8] The DAE journey is best traced through the course followed during each period, the route strongly influenced by the respective helmsmen. Both in substance and style, the work and orientation of the DAE was shaped by the idiosyncrasies of their research predilections, intellectual imaginations and styles of institutional leadership, and by their ideological stance in terms of both national politics and their disciplinary framing of economics. Each period is thus stamped by a distinctive character, with significant shifts in direction, balance and flavour at each switch point. A brief purposive commentary must suffice to provide the necessary backdrop for the enactment of the episodes of the DAE Trilogy.

Stone remained in the post of Director of DAE for the first decade till 1955, when he became the P.D. Leake Professor of Finance and Accountancy and relinquished the position (under controversial circumstances). Brian Reddaway took over for what became a stipulated 15-year term, till 1970. It was in this period, in 1960, that Alan Brown and Dick Stone set up the Cambridge Growth Project (CGP), which Stone ran as a de facto autonomous unit within the DAE till he retired in 1980. Wynne Godley took over from Brian Reddaway in 1970 and immediately set up the high-profile policy-oriented Cambridge Economic Policy Group (CEPG) along with Francis Cripps—who gave up his Faculty position to move across to the DAE—as his illustrious research partner. On the surface, the DAE went full steam ahead till 1982, with both macroeconomic modelling teams moving in fast-forward mode, till the Godley-Cripps

---

[6] What constituted this DAE ship—who counted as crew, which as passengers, etc.—is itself as simple or complex a question as defining the population of an Indian village. Ron Smith (1998, p. 89) perceptively cautions: "the standard questions: Who? When? What? Why? become quite sensitive. *Who* should be counted in the DAE can be a matter of fine judgement because there was a constant movement of personnel to and from other institutions, in particular the Faculty, and because there was a constant flow of distinguished visitors who worked for a time in the DAE. This often raises questions of attribution about what really was DAE work, and some may differ with my judgements."

[7] "Professor W. B. Reddaway's tenure as Director, which began in 1955, came to an end on 30 September 1969, but he is continuing as Acting-Director for a year, until his successor is available. The Hon. W. A. H. Godley has been elected into the Directorship for a period of ten years from 1 October 1970" (DAE Annual Report 1968–1969, p. 15). Subsequent Annual Reports make no mention an extension of another five years, so this would have been communicated recorded in the minutes of the meetings of the Committee of Management.

[8] Wynne Godley stayed on for a while as the head awaiting the appointment of the new director who was to succeed him, but then left on a sabbatical; Alan Hughes, then ending his term as Chair of the Faculty Board, took on the role of Acting Director of DAE for the year (under the eye of R.C.O. Matthews as Acting Chairman of the DAE's Committee of Management) leading up to the installation of David Newbery as the Director in 1988.

adventure, and also the DAE as a whole, ran into a submerged reef of opposition. The following five years mark the period of inflexion, where the DAE as it had been suffered repeated assaults—externally at the hands of the Social Science Research Council (SSRC) and Economic and Social Research Council (ESRC) funders, and internally through a hostile campaign initiated and coordinated by the Hahn-Matthews axis.

This short period saw the demise of the CEPG, then the CGP, and then the capture of power over the DAE by the Hahn-Matthews orthodox group, denoting a sea change in the course of the DAE for the 15-year term (1988–2003) of the incoming David Newbery, a period ending with the demise of the DAE as a distinct institutional entity in October 2004 after the end of his tenure as Director. Indeed, it was generally understood in local informal circles that some key powerholders within the orthodox group on the Faculty side of the building would have wished to enforce an earlier closure apparently to capture and absorb DAE resources, for instance, precious space and funds, into the Faculty; even within the orthodox group there had been divisions and disagreements, including some over the value of the kind of applied work done on the DAE side, before and after David Newbery took over, but this challenge to his shop was warded off successfully by Newbery, a committed applied microeconomist, till the point of his retirement.

The DAE Trilogy focusses on the eventful period of inflexion, 1982–1987, though it is impossible to assess these episodes without due reference to the earlier and later periods. This was a traumatic quinquennium of enforced, irreversible change which might be characterised by some as creative destruction, but by others, to borrow Barry Supple's phrase from the context of the Thatcher-Joseph assault on the SSRC, as intellectual vandalism. It has to be emphasised that the objective here is not to provide an academic assessment of the merits of the contending approaches to the discipline, but rather to investigate the processes and devices through which one tradition of the discipline, the connected group of heterodox lineages, was displaced by another, of the orthodox neoclassical faith.

5.1.3 Foundations of Stone

There are several commentaries on Richard Stone and his lead role in the early pioneering years of the DAE: Stone (1984) has written about it himself in his autobiographical notes on the occasion of the Nobel Prize; one of his (two Nobel) prize doctoral students, Angus Deaton (1987, 1993, 2008, 2014) has registered his thoughts, and so have Ron Smith (1998, 2014) from his years Cambridge till he was eased out by the orthodox brigade and left for Birkbeck in the 1970s; Hashem Pesaran (1991; Pesaran & Harcourt, 2000) who worked closely with him over the years; and Terry Barker (2017) who was Stone's long-standing deputy in the Cambridge Growth Project and took over as its Director when Stone retired in 1980 and valiantly saw it through to its enforced termination in 1987.

The label 'the Stone Age' is actually not at all inappropriate, since the early iconic achievements of the DAE under Dick Stone really are writ in stone in every narration of the DAE of that time. Deaton rightly calls him "the inheritor of the British empiricist tradition in economics that saw its first flowering among the 'political arithmeticians' of the English Restoration, men such as William Petty, Gregory King and Charles Davenant" (Deaton, 2008, pp. 1–2)— perhaps Colin Clark might have deserved an honourable mention for setting the ball rolling in Cambridge. The first decade saw the laying of the technical foundations, with work on the development of the systems of national accounts (SNA), methodologies and tools of inference, and related advances, signalling the systematic development and introduction of econometrics into economics.[9] There was a stream of significant advances involving, amongst others, three partnerships: Cochrane and Orcutt, Durbin and Watson, and of course Stone and Brown. Then in 1960, Stone and Brown set up the CGP; in 1962, the team developed the Social Accounting Matrix (SAM) that became standard fare soon after through the efforts at the World Bank of Graham Pyatt, one of the DAE team. With justification, Deaton remarks: "To a large extent [Stone] abstained from providing short-term policy advice, preferring to concentrate on the advancement of his science. But his contributions have had an incalculable effect on economic policy and his career provides eloquent testimony to the long-run social value of scientific scholarship in economics" (ibid., p. 2). It is important to recognise that, subsequent to the early period of the development of inference methodologies, Stone was progressively involved over time with the development and application of the Cambridge Growth Model as an instrument to track, analyse and project processes and pathways of structural change at the macroeconomic level; this was the essence of the Cambridge Growth Project that he ran for 20 years up to his retirement. Indeed, setting up systems of accounts, as epitomised in the SNA, had forever been one of his intellectual passions from the earliest years of the DAE. Despite his contributions in this regard, Stone was by no means a pure theoretical econometrician dealing exclusively, or even mainly, with developing tests of inference or pure tool kits; his theoretical work was driven by an imperative to develop methods and instruments designed to be directly applied to illuminate policy issues, even if in a medium- to long-term structural time frame; it would be difficult to overemphasise the value of such work in the post-war context of reconstruction and transition. And Geoff Harcourt rightly puts down a further reminder: "I should especially mention the seminal work on economic history, using a Keynesian framework, associated with Max Cole, Phyllis Deane, Charles Feinstein, Robin Matthews and Brian Mitchell, which commenced under

---

[9] Samuelson speaks of mathematisation and econometrification as the third and fourth revolutions in economics. If mathematisation can be dated from Samuelson's *Foundations of Economic Analysis* in 1947, econometrification can be sourced, in good measure, in the DAE of the 1940s and 1950s, not forgetting the earlier contributions of Jan Tinbergen and Ragnar Frisch in continental Europe.

Stone's benign leadership and encouragement. In a sense this filled an essential gap associated with Marshall's inability to complete his original project" (Harcourt, 2001, p. 349). Subsequently, the prime protagonists moved away from Cambridge, as Charles Feinstein did when shifting base to York in 1978, or retired, as, in 1982, with the retirement of Phyllis Deane who had long served as an interlocutor in the intersecting space of Stone's national income accounting work, economic history and (gendered) development studies. The vicissitudes in the trajectory of economic history, leading up to this virtual evanescence at present, are chronicled later in Chap. 12.

There have been constant allusions to, and much—perhaps too much?—has been made of, the friction between the Cambridge 'Keynesians' and Richard Stone, himself a Keynesian, indeed a Keynes protégé. Was it that Dick Stone, "a gentle soul" as Ron Smith describes him, did not have the stomach for the cut-and-thrust of the intergroup battles in the Faculty corridors? Was it that his political leanings were perhaps not as far to the left, say, as those of the Robinson-Kahn group? Or was it that he suffered from the collateral damage of the inherent hostility of the Cambridge Keynesians to econometrics, following on from Keynes's assault on Tinbergen—even though Keynes's own attitude did greatly mellow over time? Probably, there is some truth all of the above. Be it as it may, Richard Stone, who had been appointed for life as Director of DAE, "was manoeuvred out of the directorship by the Cambridge 'Keynesians' in the mid-1950s" (Deaton, 2008, p. 2); Ron Smith adds: "In 1955 Stone obtained the P.D. Leake Chair of Finance and Accounting and the University rules for the chair were written so it could not be held in conjunction with the Directorship of the DAE. Kahn was a consummate University politician, and many believed that he had ensured that the rules for the Chair were written in this way" (Smith, 2014, p. 4). There is little doubt that something like this is what actually happened; Stone was given the harsh choice to opt for the Chair and out of the Directorship of the DAE, or continue as Director, but not as Professor. And thus, Brian Reddaway came into DAE as its new Director in 1955, with the proviso that Stone would continue as Professor in the DAE running his own CGP team autonomously, though under the overall watch of the Committee of Management, to which Reddaway, as the Director, reported. In his personal recollections of his career as "a lucky economist", Reddaway himself records his appointment as the Director of DAE in 1955 as "my next important piece of good luck". He writes: "In the ordinary way he [J. R. N. Stone the first Director] would have continued to hold the post (for which he was admirably qualified) for many years. But an outside donor (P. D. Leake) gave the University funds with which to found a new 'Professorship of Finance and Accounting'; Stone was appointed to this, and I succeeded him as Director of the DAE" (Reddaway, 1995, p. 10). There is no hint of controversy or intrigue in Reddaway's allusion to this seemingly serendipitous event.

Several rebalancing caveats might be in order. First, the original sin perhaps was to appoint a 32-year-old, even if he was Richard Stone, Director for life of a new unit such as the DAE. The 15-year term used later on seems a good length of tenure; perhaps if it had been applied from the start, the awkward situation might not have arisen. Second, the DAE was a brand-new unit, set up by the initiative and effort of Keynes and Austin Robinson. The plans for the DAE were actually quite a lot more wide-ranging than Dick Stone's interests and specialisations. There was a good deal of support necessary, and received, from the Committee of Management, for instance, in terms of housing, financing, projects. As was inevitable at the time, the Committee comprised 'Keynesians', with the Keynesian-in-Chief, viz., Keynes himself, in the chair till he died in the middle of 1946. The gap between Stone's interests and the foundational framing of the DAE was bound to become noticeable, if not to widen, irrespective of the Keynesians' hostility towards econometrics. Third, it can be speculated that when the possibility of the Chair arose, the Committee saw that as an opportunity to change the terms of engagement, knowing or expecting that Stone would opt for the Chair in preference to the Directorship. Fourth, while many have commented justifiably on the pioneering econometric work at the DAE under Stone's eye, no one has said much about his capacities and penchant as an administrator; as Hashem Pesaran and Geoff Harcourt (Pesaran & Harcourt, 2000, F157) have observed, "giving up the Directorship of the Department had very little effect on his research, and if anything it freed him from administrative duties"; arguably, he was liberated from managerial responsibilities and so could devote all his energies to his and the DAE's scientific endeavours. Fifth, Deaton (2008, p. 6) points out that on the side of econometrics and statistics, "there is no doubt that the best years were at the beginning, in the late 1940s and early 1950s"[10], but it is worth noting that many key developments in the Stone-Brown stable took place in the period after 1955: for instance, CGP was set up successfully in 1960; Stone and Brown released their first SAM (social accounting matrix) work in 1962. And finally, looking at it with hindsight, one might well wonder if the range of research activities and projects that were initiated under Brian Reddaway could have been stimulated, or have flourished, in the Stone framework which was strongly focussed on the narrower-range themes of theoretical and applied econometrics and macroeconomic modelling. Stone and his work do not seem to have been harmed by his stepping away from Directorship, while the DAE diversified into a range of productive research themes, including, for instance, sociological research from 1960. In the end, then, the controversy over the Director versus Chair choice could be archived under the category, "storm in a teacup".

5.1.4 Reddaway's Method: Eclectic Development

Brian Reddaway was a formidable economist, and most unusual in his ways. Instinctively and immediately brilliant as he was, unnecessary abstractions and theorising were impatiently dismissed as 'talky talk', quick back-of-the-envelope

---

[10] About these early years, Deaton (2008, p. 6) writes: "Not only did all of this work owe much to Stone's presence and to the existence of the Department of Applied Economics, but the joint output of all of these people represents an explosion of econometric and economic knowledge that has never been exceeded in the history of the subject and has perhaps only been equaled by the work of the Cowles Commission."

calculations and novel short-cut methods replaced dependence on computers; there was both extreme respect and extreme suspicion of numbers and data which had to be personally assembled and interrogated in violation of the Geneva Convention before they were let loose for use in his ready-made exercises of policy application to illuminate some particular issue. He was par excellence and literally a hands-on applied economist; upon request, he obliged by producing a weekly cyclostyled sheet tracking a portfolio of investments that he had sniffed out—and he regularly beat the market and its professionals. A practical liberal Keynesian, he shared with Keynes, his teacher, a scepticism, if not an antipathy, towards fancy econometrics—where he had deep methodological misgivings—and misplaced precision. Single-handedly, he came to be the creator of a new genre of applied economics, fondly and proudly labelled 'Reddaway-type economics' which was legal tender in Cambridge, an approach which, through his students, percolated with acknowledged effect into Whitehall, the City and policy research organisations. Reminiscing at the 50th anniversary of the founding of the DAE, John Llewellyn (1998, p. 248) recalled: "Frank Hahn once told me, in tones almost of the confessional, that the economist he most admired was—guess—Brian Reddaway."

Ajit Singh's account of Reddaway's DAE is both concentrated and comprehensive. Ajit had entered the DAE from Berkeley in 1964, with his PhD still to complete but with a fine reputation, to work on Robin Marris's and then his own research on the modern corporation; Reddaway became a lifelong mentor. It is pertinent to recount Ajit's testimony in full measure:

> Reddaway's assumption of the directorship of the DAE in 1955, on Stone's appointment to his chair, led to a decisive change in the department's research agenda. Under Stone's leadership the DAE had built up an international reputation as an outstanding centre for research in econometric theory. Stone's was a hard act to follow, but Reddaway did so with great energy and total conviction. He changed the direction of the department's research towards applied economics and economic policy. Under his leadership in the 1960s the DAE was a vibrant and exciting place, which was generally regarded as one of the world's leading institutions for applied economic research. Reddaway, as many observers have noted, was in his element as the Director. He was a liberal academic in the best sense of the term and let a hundred flowers bloom. The DAE hosted projects on a wide range of subjects, including notably economic history, corporate finance, labour markets, regional economies and economic sociology, to each of which he himself made significant contributions. Reddaway provided autonomy to the investigators, but they had to perform to his high intellectual and critical standards. He was unstinting in his help when a project, for whatever reason, got into difficulties or an investigator sought assistance. In my view, one reason why the Department was so successful at this time was that it had under the same roof economists with effectively two different approaches to applied economics—that of Reddaway himself, as outlined above, and that of Stone, who continued to have a large research group in the Department even after he resigned the Directorship. However, by then, Stone's interest had shifted from theoretical to applied econometrics, and his

new group worked mainly on the latter issues (Smith, 1998). The Cambridge Growth Project, which he and Alan Brown co-directed at the DAE, was concerned with a real-world question of applied economics and policy analysis—to formulate a comprehensive indicative plan for the UK economy. However, its methods differed from those of Reddaway and his collaborators, in that it made extensive use of applied econometrics. I believe it was the unexpected synergy between the economists working on the growth project and those working in the non-econometric Reddaway paradigm which made the Department *the* place to do applied economic research. The diversity of its research output was widely appreciated. The institution had a vigorous research culture and enormous self-confidence. Instead of being the research wing of the Faculty, it acquired its own intellectual autonomy and became as well if not better known than the Faculty, which still included among its teaching officers, legendary figures like Richard Kahn, Joan Robinson, Nicholas Kaldor, James Meade, David Champernowne and Richard Goodwin. (Singh, 2008, pp. 13–14; italics in the original)

A few additional observations are relevant. First, in contrast to Dick Stone, Brian Reddaway did not enter the DAE importing and pursuing a personal research project; he was happy to do his own work in his time while supporting the new ecology of diversity in widening DAE research. He was also particular in inducing staff from the Faculty side to conceptualise projects to bring across to the DAE. Second, Brian's relations with the Committee of Management, chaired through the period by Austin Robinson, were friction free. Third, he knew the Faculty and also the University system backwards and could fight and win his DAE battles with the bureaucracy. Fourth, Reddaway was a committed democrat in Faculty, student and University affairs. And finally, it is worth noting that while Stone's tenure covering the immediate post-war era was one of the reconstruction of the UK economy, with Brian Reddaway, Britain had entered the 25-year period labelled the golden age; growth was steady, research budgets were easier, national politics relatively calm and policy discourse overwhelmingly Keynesian, creating a congenial enabling macro-environment for the DAE to spread its wings and flourish. Perhaps there was more than a touch of hubris in the ascription of the label, golden age, and there was a clear recognition that the sustained period of growth was beset with serious structural problems on a medium-term fuse.

It is pertinent here to insert an apposite reflection from Francis Cripps: "Although the 1960s were a good period for W Europe and Japan this wasn't perceived as a golden age in Britain at that time and the US was running into its own serious problems (race, Vietnam, the international financial system). The UK was losing export markets, could not keep up with productivity growth in Germany, Italy and Japan or catch up with productivity levels in the US, teetered on the edge of sterling crises and had slowly-increasing inflation, all of which made maintenance of the postwar social contract increasingly difficult. Kaldor's *Causes of the Slow Growth of the United Kingdom* was a response to a widespread perception that Keynesian management (+ mid-1960s planning) was not working. At the time, in the Faculty and DAE, I don't think we thought the UK was enjoying a golden age. The best one could say is that things got a whole lot worse in the 1970s as consensus in Britain broke down, big companies went broke, the stock market collapsed etc." (personal communication, email dated 16 January 2020).

The stage was set for the entry of the Godley-Cripps Cambridge Economic Policy Group and its introduction of the policy-oriented macroeconomic modelling agenda into the DAE.

5.1.5   Godley: Turbulent Times

Wynne Godley was brought over from the Treasury into the DAE by Nicky Kaldor, and the contrast between him and Brian Reddaway was as great as the one earlier between Reddaway and Stone. Like Stone, Wynne did not really participate much in Faculty life, did not engage in economics teaching; unlike Stone and especially Reddaway though, he disliked his times in Cambridge (and King's), and in the early years even in the DAE: "I was unhappy and very soon wished I had not come; I very nearly resigned" (Godley, 2008). For one, as he said himself: "I was not properly trained as an economist and would not have been able to pass Part I as I only had my Treasury experience" (ibid.). But what he had was very considerable—a masterful capacity for short-term diagnostics of the macro economy that relied on a deep understanding of the data and of government fiscal decision-making on the one side, and an instinctive capability for short-term forecasting on the other—qualities that Kaldor would have greatly valued in the context of his own research in Cambridge and advisory work in Whitehall. Unlike Reddaway, but rather as in the case of Stone, Godley was attracted to DAE by the possibility of pursuing his own research agenda on a full-time basis: "I … knew that the economy was very badly covered in public discussion and knew more than any of the journalists at that time," and so he "decided to do my Treasury work in the Department of Applied Economics" (ibid.). Indeed, that is what he did with the immediate setting up of the Godley-Cripps Cambridge Economic Policy Group in 1971. Godley's influence was to be seen dramatically, though perhaps exclusively, in the work of the CEPG: active policy engagement and a regular and distinctive voice, fearlessly courting controversy in national debates, became the hallmarks of the Godley period; when it came to public policy discourse, Godley put the DAE willy-nilly into fast-forward mode, partly induced by his own predilections and partly induced by the charged macroeconomic and political environment which made such involvement in public policy an intellectual, ethical and political imperative. He now had his own accomplished team with him.

Therein lay a problem, and another point of contrast with the earlier Directors, in particular with Reddaway. Somewhat ruefully, Godley complains: "I had been used to the Treasury which was entirely hierarchical but absolutely united in purpose; I came to Cambridge supposing as Director that people would do as I told them; I was wrong" (ibid.)—by a long mile, and in the early period he "was very unpopular" (ibid.) at the DAE round table. There was also the question of an active (and sometimes constraining) Committee of

Management that he had to work through, not always successfully. Godley was sufficiently moved to complain formally to the General Board of the Faculties of the University, a move that much later was to be used as one device by the orthodox camp to attack the DAE structure and staff. Clearly, Wynne was a political novice and, though honourably motivated, did neither himself nor the DAE any great favours in this regard.

A special feature of the Godley years is the co-existence in parallel of two similar sized, heavyweight, research teams working on macroeconomic modelling, though in quite different and independent ways. Though Godley, much later, wished to see his oeuvre in the lineage of Keynes and Stone, there is no serious evidence of contemporaneous interaction between the two teams or their respective leaders. An insight can be elicited from the draft record, with visible corrections, of a CGP meeting with the SSRC:

> On the [CGP] team's relations with Wyne (*sic*) Godley, Terry Barker said that they have completely different outfits without any [word inserted: 'formal'] interaction. [Sentence crossed out: 'They might as well be in two different institutions.'] The two teams are [word deleted: 'diametrically'] different in terms of dimensions; Wyne's (*sic*) team is a fairly close group and has moved towards the EEC regional development approach.[11]

There are no grounds for any presumption of hostility between the two teams; relations were entirely amicable between staff, but they ploughed their own, separate fields: CEPG operated primarily on the short (and medium) term; CGP on the medium and long term. But, as Terry Barker points out, while both models were evolving into more open dynamic versions at regional and global levels, "there was never any notion of bringing the two models together. They originated from different traditions in Keynesian thinking: the CEPG worked on macroeconomic aggregates, emphasising financial stocks and flows; whilst the CGP worked on the structure of consumption, production and trade, with the macroeconomic aggregates built up from the detail. The CEPG developed their own econometric approach; the CGP developed input-output analysis, then formal stochastic econometric estimation of dynamic behavioural equations at a sectoral level."[12]

The paradox is that Wynne Godley, replete with eccentricities and idiosyncrasies, also carried the air of a lost soul and often behaved as one; his brutal honesty, especially about himself, could more readily embarrass others than himself (as exemplified in a searingly personal piece of writing, Godley, 2001). Never unapproachable, but then not always quite there either. A one-time concert-class oboist, his personality is perhaps fleetingly captured in a

---

[11] Notes of a Meeting between Dr. Terry Barker and William Peterson from the CGP and Michael Posner of the SSRC Committee on Macroeconomic Research; Christina Hadjimatheou attending; 21 July 1980. Seeing the extensive amendments to the draft, and also the misspelling, twice, of Wynne's name, it can be surmised that the draft was written not by Terry Barker but by Christina Hadjimatheou, Secretary of the SSRC committee, with amendments by Terry Barker.

[12] Personal communication; email dated 18 January 2021.

photograph—shared in Alan Shipman's (2019) biography—which has Wynne playing the oboe with a blackboard full of equations in the background; and indeed, musical notes often floated across and down from the DAE floor in the Austin Robinson, then Faculty, building. Wynne's personality was perhaps a trifle more unique than most others. The always elegantly turbaned Ajit Singh recalled that for a period after Wynne arrived at the DAE, he would greet and address Ajit in French, much to the latter's puzzlement and amusement; when broached, Wynne's explanation was that in Paris his neighbour, the Indian ambassador to France, was also bearded and wore the same headgear as Ajit and spoke fluent French—so direct observation led to a cunning deduction about the linguistic preferences of turbaned Sikhs (Saith, 2019, pp. 58–59n6).

Ken Coutts writes of his early encounter: "I had the most peculiar interview by Wynne for the lowly post of Junior Research Officer at the Department of Applied Economics when I was 21 years old and recently graduated from the Cambridge Economics Tripos. During the interview, Wynne took off the shelf a copy of the UK Official National Accounts, published by the statistical authority and commonly known among UK economists as the Blue Book. At that time, the Economics Tripos gave students a good grounding in national accounts. We had, after all, been taught by Brian Reddaway and Ajit Singh. Today's students have little comprehension of the national accounts of a country as a detailed measurement system of economic activity. Wynne started explaining obscure items such as inventory revaluation. He emphasized how boring the work would be in extraction and manipulation of such data. Despite this discouraging foretaste of things to come, I was pleased when I was offered the job. Although I thought I understood national income accounting, it was Wynne who really taught me to understand it thoroughly. I worked with Wynne for the next twenty years" (Coutts, 2021, p. 27). And Graham Gudgin provides additional coordinates for a triangulation: "Like Ken, my own interview to join the Policy Group in 1978 was unusual. Wynne stumbled down the corridor to personally take me to the interview room, and my first sight was of aa striking figure with elegant manners. But this view was somewhat undermined by his baggy trousers and the holes at the elbows of his ancient cardigan. Halfway down the corridor he appeared to have fight with a fire door, which on reflection indicated that he was much more nervous in interviewing a young new recruit than I was in being interviewed by the great man. ... From the start it was impossible not to warm to Wynne's genial eccentricity and his quiet good humor" (Gudgin, 2021, p. 32). Ken, like others, highlights Wynne's "playfulness and humour" (Coutts, 2021, p. 27). He seemed often to be oblivious of time, in the sense of the ticking clock—his time zone was often not shared by others burdened with the more mundane urgencies of life. With affectionate ruefulness, Ken Coutts writes "that I could expect a phone call at home from Wynne at any time when he was worrying away at a problem and these could be quite long calls when for me domestic duties of childcare were uppermost" (Coutts, 2021, p. 30); and I recall Alex Izurieta—Wynne's later computing go-to Man Friday in Cambridge and at the Levy Institute—(almost) complaining with a sense of bewilderment about how Wynne just carried on working and expecting him to carry on working alongside too, losing all sense of the time of night or day, late night calls about computer malfunctions included. And Jill Rubery adds: "The evening before I was to be interviewed for promotion to SRO, he rang me at 10.30pm the night before to ask me what on earth I did so he wouldn't be embarrassed before the committee"; in her opinion, Wynne, with all his other sterling qualities, was "a completely negligent manager".[13] Later, Graham Gudgin, also resident in Northern Ireland, "saw him frequently, in visits which were always enjoyable and indeed productive, since Wynne always wanted to discuss macroeconomics, even up to his final week, when I saw him last" (Ibid.).[14] Ken and Graham were both pallbearers at Wynne's funeral.

A brilliantly intuitive mind was coupled occasionally with a startling degree of innocence, naiveté, gullibility and extreme candour. While he enjoyed his public role in the adversarial cut-and-thrust of the bloody economics and politics of the time, as Director, he was not equally equipped to defend the DAE and its constituent units against the assaults from the orthodox camps, both internal and external.[15] In these personal respects, Wynne Godley stood at a discrete distance from the savvy nous of the cut-and-dried, almost brusque manner of Brian Reddaway and his ability to deal with university bureaucracy. And Wynne was to prove no match for the well-prepared strategies and games of Frank Hahn and Robin Matthews in their DAE campaign.

---

[13] Personal communication, email dated 29 November 2021.

[14] Alex Izurieta's recollection runs in parallel: "This [the stability of Stock/Flow ratios] is something about which Wynne insisted a lot, including last time I saw him, when he was talking to me from his bed, weak already, as if he was depositing on me his most precious intellectual insights" (Personal communication: Alex Izurieta, email dated 22 December 2021).

[15] Geoff Harcourt, in his various writings, shares his bottom lines on the successive Directors of the DAE. "Richard Stone used mathematics in order to express theory rigorously and precisely and in a form in which it could be tested by quantitative methods, many of which he and his colleagues developed, just as they did the theory itself. Stone started from Keynes's work in macroeconomic theory and, of course, was pioneer in developing the Keynesian framework of national accounts. His microeconomic theory had Marshallian roots, but he very quickly put his own unique stamp on the development with which he was associated. This view permeated not only his own work but also the work of the officers of the DAE while he was Director" (Harcourt, 2001, p. 220). "The tradition which Stone started has been continued, with different emphases, by the various Directors. Brian Reddaway took over from Stone in 1955; Reddaway undertook himself (and encouraged many others to do likewise) applied projects characterised by the 'Reddaway Method'— thorough knowledge of data and its limitations, careful statistical analysis of t and of what it can be used to show, and what it cannot. ... Wynne Godley, as Director, carried on both the Keynes and the Marshall stories, because he was very interested, first of all, in the role of forecasting in economic policy and, secondly, at a theoretical level, in showing how in the short term and in the long term the real and the monetary aspect of the economy may be combined together in a consistent set of stock and flow accounts. He was then succeeded in 1988 by David Newbery, about whom I may only say that I used to beat him at squash (I think!)" (Harcourt, 2001, p. 349). Separately, he does provide an elaboration: "In the Newbery era, there has been great interest in the problems of restructuring in Eastern Europe and Russia as well as work on the environment, privatisation and various microeconomic problems" (Harcourt, 2001, p. 221).

5.2 End of the Golden Age: The Decade of Discontent

In any reflection on the Godley period of the DAE, it is crucial not to overlook the shift in the tectonic templates of national politics and associated macroeconomic policy making. The Stone era had been one of national reconstruction and transition to, or a search for, a new normal; the Reddaway years had benefited from the relatively benign macroeconomic environment of the new, upward though structurally compromised growth path of 1950–1973, somewhat optimistically labelled the 'Golden Age', with a desirable combination of economic expansion, low inflation and low unemployment; but soon after Godley stepped into the DAE, the national and international economies were thrown into turmoil. A deeper structural economic malaise might well have been building up in the previous decade, but it was the first OPEC oil price hike of 1973 that dealt the decisive blow bringing the 25 years of the 'Golden Age' to an abrupt and disruptive end; the decade ended in greater turmoil with the second price hike. Glyn et al. (1988) establish that "the period of explicit erosion of the Golden Age" [is] "the inter oil shock period 1974–79" (Glyn et al., 1988, p. 61); then, "the second oil shock thus hit the system at a critical period and led to the final unhinging of the coordinating and rules upon which the Golden Age had been based" (Glyn et al., 1988, pp. 62–63).

Already by the start of 1974, barely months after the first oil price hike, the moderate Liberal MP John Pardoe spoke of "an epidemic of national misery", sounding the alarm that

> we are about to become submerged in a mood ... of doom, gloom and national despondency best described perhaps by Samuel Brittan the other day in the *Financial Times* with the words 'sado-masochistic doom-mongering'. ... There is doom and gloom by the bucketful—in the national Press, in this House, on television and elsewhere. ... There are calls for cuts in public expenditure and more cuts on top of these we have already had, calls for increases in taxations ... There are calls for every conceivable form of foul-tasting economic medicine.[16]

Pardoe is clearly a Keynesian at heart; he goes on: "At present everyone is obsessed with the problem of inflation ... but on the horizon already is the spectre of world deflation." At this point he cites, favourably, the fiscal expansionary suggestions of Wynne Godley.[17] Then he closes with his solution:

> I nail my colours to the mast immediately by saying that the long-term problem of the British economy, at least over the 25 years, the problem of debilitating low

---

[16] House of Commons Debate on Public Expenditure, 29 January 1974, vol 868 cc 307–310.

[17] Pardoe refers to Godley thus: "Mr. Godley can hardly be called the 'voice of reckless expansion', yet he wrote in the London and Cambridge Economic Bulletin in *The Times* [sic] ... that if not measures are taken now to expand demand, the likelihood is for a rapid adjustment [downwards] and recession" (ibid.).

level of investment and its consequent low productivity, has been brought about by lack of effective demand for the goods that such investment will produce. That is the base of all our problems today.[18]

A couple of years later, still in the era of doom and gloom—even before Thatcher had arrived—Michael English, a Labour MP and Chairman of the House of Commons Expenditure Committee,[19] turns funny when commenting on the White Paper on Public Expenditure:

> I do not quite agree with the remark of the right hon. Member for Down, South that the forecast for the next five years is not worth the paper it is printed on. If he thinks about it, he will realise that that remark contains a fallacy. I think that the forecast is just about worth the paper it is printed on and the cost of the labour which went into printing it. But I gravely doubt the future of these forecasts of—as he called them—the Tottenham parabolas or ballistic curves of these White Papers.

John Nott, a member of the same Committee, carries on:

> It [the White Paper] certainly provided an endless source of intellectual debate in virtually incomprehensible language—one moment it is in factor cost, the next survey prices and the next current prices, with the years continually changing—for the economic establishment. It is a sort of endless dialogue between, on the one hand, 20 Wynne Godleys and, on the other, 20 civil servants with first-class honours in classics.[20]

Wynne Godley who had earlier been at the Treasury, years before he shifted base in 1970 to the Cambridge DAE, had figured at intervals in the debates on such matters, though was not always taken as seriously as Pardoe did.

The golden age had been quietly and steadily going leaden, before being torpedoed and sunk without a trace after the 1973 oil price hike took the lid of Britain's long-festering structural problems; no easy solution seemed to be in sight; the left felt the Labour government was dithering as much as the Heath Government had before it, but another opinion was that the Labour Party was providing the best Tory government that was possible; and things were yet to get worse with the second oil price hike of 1979. The foregoing and ensuing crises heralded the arrival of Margaret Thatcher and the rise of full-blown monetarism in national policy and, significantly, the folding up of the protective umbrella, and the concomitant loss of access to authority and power in

---

[18] (ibid.). Pardoe also observes that "Professor Neild has recently suggested a commission to investigate how we manage our demand and what we can do to improve it".

[19] Terry Ward, of the CEPG, served as Special Advisor to the Committee, having taken over the role from Wynne Godley around 1975.

[20] Both comments in the Debate on Public Expenditure, HC Deb March 1976, Vol 907, cc430–574, Hansard. Terry Ward recalls: "I had endless fun pointing out the continuously changing price bases and their implications" (Personal communication).

policy-making circles in Whitehall, that the Labour governments had provided to the Cambridge Keynesian economists, especially those of left persuasion. What could be, and had been, taken for granted was now sorely missed; and admiration, however grudging, was replaced by hostility, often overt. To this cocktail could be added a strong dose of another ingredient, rivalry, as the macroeconomic modelling domain, earlier dominated by select incumbents, was populated by various new start-ups, including some from the politically in-fashion monetarist camp; there were now lots of elbows and toes round the table, and not enough cake to go around.

Within the realms of the politically possible, the DAE would surely have received strong support during this critical period from its two eminent past Directors, Richard Stone and Brian Reddaway. Reddaway was savvy and skilful at working the University system and was almost always successful in his exchanges with various University committees and boards.[21] However, the demographics of Faculty and DAE seniors, that is, retirements and recruitments, arrivals, departures and deaths, coincidentally denied the DAE any prospect of protection from these quarters. Both Stone and Reddaway were born in 1913, both reached the Cambridge mandatory retirement age of 67 in 1980 and were thus no longer part of the fray. Joan Robinson, Richard Kahn and Nicky Kaldor, though still in full flow in the intellectual transactions of Cambridge economics, had already retired from Faculty Chairs in 1970, 1972 and 1975, thereby losing influence over operational decision-making; there were other proximate retirements (and departures) of stalwarts: Richard Goodwin also in 1980; David Champernowne in 1979; Charles Feinstein, thwarted at Cambridge, left to a Chair at York in 1978; Phyllis Deane, given the parting gift of a Chair as late as 1981, retired in 1983; Robert Neild retired hurt with an early golden handshake in 1984; and there were significant deaths, of Joan Robinson and Piero Sraffa both in 1983 within a month of each other, with Joan going first on Piero's 85th birthday; and Nicky Kaldor was lost round the corner in 1986, with Richard Kahn yielding in 1989, denoting what a lamenting Luigi Pasinetti rightly called the end of the era of greatness in Cambridge economics. In a decade, the ranks of heterodox leaders had seriously thinned out. Yes, Wynne Godley got a professorship in 1980, but then the assembling orthodox gang was already getting a good hold on the rug about to be pulled from under his, and his research group's feet a year later. On the other side, there were significant arrivals, as Robin Matthews took over Reddaway's Chair in 1980, and Partha Dasgupta voluntarily, for the

---

[21] "Reddaway's academic legacy includes his commitment ... to the teaching and welfare of students. He also believed in extending to them the democratic governance of the university. In the 1970s as Faculty Board chairman, he sided with the students and the majority in the Faculty, in conflict with the central authorities over students' demands for representation and for changed methods of assessment. He was in the forefront of these struggles with all his formidable debating skills. Thus, student participation in the university governance was another important aspect of Reddaway's legacy as a Cambridge academic" (Ajit Singh, 2008, pp. 17–18). Ajit also records other similar aspects on which Reddaway clashed, and often won, against the central University authorities.

sake of Rome, returned from the fragrant London School of Economics (LSE) to what he termed the flagrant 'cesspool' of Cambridge economics as Professor in 1985, joining his mentor, and thereby completing the new triumvirate of Hahn-Matthews-Dasgupta, with honourable support at hand from Barry Supple (a long-standing associate of Matthews, appointed in 1981 to a Chair in Economic History located within the Faculty of History) and Willy Brown appointed to the long-standing Montagu Burton Chair in Industrial Relations in 1985, located in the Faculty of Economics; the orthodox professors firmly opposed to the left-Keynesian group, thus enjoyed overwhelming strength within the professoriate that dominated committee decisions within the Faculty and the University on crucial matters concerning both the Faculty and the DAE.

On the heterodox, and DAE, side, the band of radical young turks were strong both numerically and intellectually, but while this strength was effective in mounting political campaigns relating to initiatives such as the setting up of the *Cambridge Journal of Economics*, students' rights, Tripos reforms, CND, anti-Vietnam War activism and protest action against the Greek colonels, it had less effective traction in, say, Faculty appointments and promotions or in influencing University or external decision-making concerning the DAE. Earlier, this broad left-oriented younger cohort found ready support amongst the Cambridge seniors, but with demographic change, the rising radical heterodox generation was generally confronted by an orthodox professoriate, dominated by Frank Hahn and Robin Matthews.

At the same time, the left 'post-Keynesian' groups, whether senior or junior, were also coming under fire from the right-wing Thatcher government and its supporters in the media, in its think tanks and in official policy-making circles. Simultaneously, Cambridge economics, whether Keynesian or Robinsonian, was coming under sustained attack from the standard bearers of the mathematisation and econometrification revolutions headquartered in Cambridge Mass., from the hands-on free-market fundamentalists of Chicago, as well as from Hayek and his followers. The constituent elements of the emerging 'neoliberal thought collective' were maturing and beginning to articulate economic research and teaching with the new political power pyramids of libertarianism: Reagan-Thatcher power was getting functionally dovetailed with the Hayek-Friedman-Samuelson axes. Cambridge heterodox economics and economists were under siege in the universities, in government, in the media and in the world of public opinion. The stage, thus, was set for the curtain to be raised on the DAE Trilogy, a tragedy enacted in three parts.

5.3 The Trilogy: Discrete Episodes or a Serial Campaign?

The trilogy unfolds in three woeful episodes. The first is the short, and deceptively simple, tale of the abrupt, arbitrary and arrogant closure of the Godley-Cripps Cambridge Economic Policy Group in 1982 at the hands of the SSRC under the watch of its Chairman Michael Posner, effectively silencing a fearless collective voice that critically engaged, through models and the media, in the full visibility of public space, with contemporary government policies. The CEPG modelling and policy work stops, and its team disperses. Then, over the 1984–1987 years, the two other episodes unfold on parallel tracks: one again external, at the ESRC, where the Stone-Barker CGP, the surviving macroeconomic modelling team, is put through another questionable (de-) funding process, leading to its demise; the other internal, through the General Board of the Faculties of the University of Cambridge which, out of the blue, sets up an unusual departmental Review of the DAE itself, leading to some life-changing outcomes for the DAE as a whole. As earlier with the CEPG, most CGP team members also receive their P45 forms[22] and scatter.[23] And through the University Review, the DAE management structure is overhauled to make it subservient to the new Director who turns out to be a card-carrying member of the Hahn-Matthews orthodoxy. The year 1987 thus marks the year of its pacification, the end of the DAE 'as we knew it' from the time of its creation.

Sliced with a different knife, the history of the DAE separates into three phases. The first covers the long run of organic evolution, where two major modelling teams emerge as a central core in the midst of an eclectic array of applied projects ranging from the Labour Group, Industrial Economics, National Accounts, Social Accounting Matrices and accounting systems, economic history and historical statistics, empirical research by the Sociology Group, Regional Economy, and other more idiosyncratic and exotic research themes such as car parks, psephological research, the study of political ideology, to which we can add a wide range of research projects on development both within the framework of underdeveloped economy and at the international level; and such special ventures as the Frank Hahn Risk project which was institutionally housed in the DAE. Over the period spanning the three directorships from 1945 till 1982, the two macroeconomic modelling teams account for approximately one half of the staff strength of the DAE. When entering the DAE environment as a graduate student, the intellectual buzz was almost palpable.

Then follows the quinquennium of convulsions, 1982–1987, as narrated here, when both macroeconomic teams, strongly of Keynesian and post-Keynesian character, are dismantled, and when the central axis of DAE research is reoriented towards applied microeconomics practised within an orthodox

---

[22] In UK, a metonym for termination of employment, equivalent in usage to the 'pink slip' in the USA. P45 forms provide details of an employee leaving work.

[23] Since these teams were all on project-linked funding, only a few of the staff could be absorbed into Faculty positions, so they effectively left the DAE when their terms ended to build distinguished careers elsewhere, whether in Cambridge or outside.

neoclassical theoretical frame.[24] Alongside this, management authority and power are transferred—through the device of the University Review of the DAE—from the loose formation of the heterodox, post-Keynesian clans to the rising, tightly knit and controlled neoclassical group led by Frank Hahn and Robin Matthews, supported by others, prominently including Partha Dasgupta, recruited from the LSE in 1985. This short period constitutes a critical point of inflexion in the evolution of Cambridge economics.

The last phase, 1988–2003, is co-terminus with the tenure of the last director, David Newbery; there could surely have been a joint valedictory send-off for him and the DAE. There is a twist in the tail, and tale, here: on received accounts, as he retired, David Newbery, strongly committed to applied policy work, fought for the continuation of the DAE, but apparently lost the battle against an intransigent Faculty Board which decided otherwise; and ironically, it was the one-time Marxist Bob Rowthorn who was then the Chairman; perhaps, as one ex-CEPG exile puts it in defence of Bob: "There was arguably little point in continuing the DAE in its emaciated state with the focus wholly on applied microeconomics; maybe it was best to put it out of its misery".[25] Of course, Newbery might have demurred with such an assessment.

A plain narration could record the sequence of Cambridge closures, purges and expulsions, aka 're-structuring', as independent occurrences that just so happened, one by one, so to speak. This would be an erroneous reading. At a formal level, each episode seemingly has its own idiosyncratic and discrete history: there are separate organisational units, different groups of staff, specific

---

[24] Geoff Harcourt (2007, p. 232) regards David Newbery "very much as a sophisticated Marshallian interested in applied microeconomic problems and also in developing economies, and, now, the problems of transition economies"; Begg and Henry (1998, pp. 3–4) in their Introduction to the DAE's 50th Anniversary volume state: "Since David Newbery became Director, the balance has shifted towards applied microeconomics, but there has also been a renewed focus on state-of-the-art econometrics. The DAE has contributed extensively to the debate on privatization and how to regulate privately-owned utilities with dominant market positions. The econometric work has ranged from the establishment of a large-scale model designed to monitor income distribution to more theoretical work on disaggregation techniques for handling complex cross-sectional data. Influential new work over the last few years, on the methodology of modelling structural time-series models with applications to macroeconomic models, returns to earlier DAE interests in macro-modelling and macro-policy advice. A major Economic and Social Science (ESRC)-funded project on small businesses paved the way for the recently established ESRC Centre for Business Research which has taken up the DAE tradition of research on industrial and company performance, and linked it with complementary work in law, engineering, geography and management studies." This informative description could be extended to mention that the new macroeconomic work actually does *not* 'return' in any significant manner to the substantive modelling or policy interests and orientations of the CEPG (especially) or the CGP (except through the continuation, by Terry Barker, of his projects within the DAE); and that the new CBR centre and its subsequent work was soon relocated in the Judge Institute of Management, as was research on finance; while it is right to point to some of the continuities within the sea change in orientation, it is necessary to acknowledge that perhaps the biggest points of change were the disappearance of the two macroeconomic modelling teams—though this happened before Newbery took over as Director. The new Directorship was not unconnected with the earlier episodes of the Hahn-Matthews campaign for control over the nature and direction of DAE and Cambridge economics.

[25] Personal communication.

external committees each with its own structure, independent mandates and terms of reference, empowered to make decisions about the fate of the various Cambridge units in question. That is indeed as it looks—but perhaps also intended so to look. One would not need to possess the nose or *nous* of a Reddaway to sniff something unpleasantly suspicious about any null hypothesis asserting the independence of this sequence of episodes. Taking a magnifier up close reveals the complex occluded interconnections in the molecular structure where key atoms of one molecule could act as message transmitters and form bonding and binding agents with another molecule, resulting in the end in a networked molecular chain which arguably has an overall internal coherence, and could be regarded as a single organism with a core cerebral centre directing operations interactively in favour of a long-term shared vision and more immediate strategic objectives. The stories come together at the end, like pieces of a jigsaw, to reveal a story behind the stories. But first, a narration of the episodes as they occurred, each within its proximate context and conjuncture.

APPENDIX 5.1: DAE—FINDING A GOOD HOME

...the D.A.E. was ... inaugurated after the war in the shed on the lawn in Downing Street...[26]

Until the latter part of 1947 the Department was accommodated on the top floor of the Marshall Library. A temporary brick building was erected by the University in one of the courts on the Downing Site, close to the Marshall Library, and the Department moved in on 19 September 1947. The new building is excellently equipped and provides eight research rooms, a small library and meeting room, offices and a computing room, but it is already proving too small for all the requirements of the Department.[27]

The growth of the Department meant that by the middle of 1949 the temporary building on the Downing Site, excellently equipped though it was, was quite inadequate for the Department's needs. Unfortunately the Regent House decided against a proposal to add another wing to the existing building, and it has been necessary to seek accommodation elsewhere. After a period towards the end of 1950 when members of the research staff had again been accommodated on the top floor of the Marshall Library, the University made available, in January 1951, the house in Lensfield Road which had just been vacated by the Appointments Board. This, together with the building on the Downing Site, provides ample accommodation for the Department's present needs; but it is only a very temporary solution since the house must soon be pulled down to make way for new chemical laboratories. In addition there are marked disadvantages in having the Department housed in two buildings some distance apart. Although care has been taken to make the two parts as self-contained as possible, the library and computing facilities have necessarily to be retained on the Downing Site, and it is a considerable inconvenience to the research staff in Lensfield Road to be separated

---

[26] Extracted from Austin Robinson's note on Colin Clark. E.A.G. Robinson Papers, Marshall Library Archives, University of Cambridge; EAGR/5/7/15/1-3; c. September 1989.

[27] DAE Annual Report 1946–1948, # 63, p.24.

from these ancillary services. It is earnestly hoped that it will soon be possible for the University to house the whole Department in a single permanent building.[28]

The period of over five years during which the Department was accommodated in two separate buildings, some distance apart, was brought to an end in March 1957 when the entire staff of the Department was housed at 7 West Road. The premises consist of a large nineteenth-century house adapted for office use, onto which a single-storey extension has been built. In addition to a library and a meeting room, the building contains thirty offices, eight of which accommodate computers and clerical and secretarial staff. Most of the remaining research rooms are capable, when necessary, of accommodating two persons. Four rooms are at present used by visiting economists and members of the Faculty who are not on the Department staff.[29]

In January 1962 the Department moved to a new building on the University's Sidgwick Avenue Site. This building was designed by Sir Hugh Casson and Partners. In addition to accommodation for the Department it contains the offices of the Faculty, rooms for Faculty teaching officers, a joint common room, a lecture-room and two seminar rooms, the Marshall Library of Economics, an African Studies Centre, and the offices of the Royal Economic Society. Some forty rooms on the third and fourth floors of the building are occupied by the Department, including the P.D. Leake Professor and his staff. Ten of these offices are occupied by computing, statistical, and secretarial staff. Most of the remaining research rooms are capable, when necessary, of accommodating two persons and are at present being used in this way. Storage space and accommodation for the counter-sorter, which is used jointly by the Faculty and the Department, have been provided in the basement of the building. Thanks to a grant from the University Grants Committee for initial furniture and equipment, and a generous subvention from the Mary Marshall Fund, it was possible to refurnish the Department on moving into the new building.[30]

References

Barker, T. (2017). Richard Stone (1913–1991). In R. A. Cord (Ed.), *The Palgrave companion to Cambridge economics* (pp. 835–855). Palgrave Macmillan.

Begg, I., & Henry, S. G. B. (Eds.). (1998). *Applied economics and public policy*. Cambridge University Press.

Cambridge University Reporter. (various years). University of Cambridge.

Clark, C. (1938). Determination of the multiplier from national income statistics. *Economic Journal, 48*(191), 435–448.

Coutts, K. (2021). The legacy of Wynne Godley: Notes for a talk on the legacy of Wynne Godley, Wednesday 12 May 2020. *Journal of Post Keynesian Economics, 44*(1), 27–31.

Deaton, A. S. (1987). Stone, John Richard Nicholas. In J. Eatwell, M. Milgate, & P. Newman (Eds.), *The new Palgrave dictionary of economics* (Vol. IV, pp. 509–512). Macmillan.

Deaton, A. S. (1993). John Richard Nicholas Stone 1913–1991. *Proceedings of the British Academy, 82,* 475–492.

---

[28] DAE Annual Report 1948–1951, # 97, 98, pp. 31–32.
[29] DAE Annual Report, 1954–1957, # 89, p. 17.
[30] DAE Annual Report, 1958–1964, # 119, 120, p. 29.

Deaton, A. (2008). Stone, John Richard Nicholas (1913–1991). In S. N. Durlauf & L. E. Blume (Eds.), *The new Palgrave dictionary of economics* (2nd ed.). Palgrave Macmillan. https://www.princeton.edu/~deaton/downloads/Deaton_STONE_JOHN_RICHARD.pdf

Deaton, A. (2014). Puzzles and paradoxes: A life in applied economics. In M. Szenberg & L. Ramrattan (Eds.), *Eminent economists II: Their life and work philosophies* (pp. 84–101). Cambridge University Press. https://wws.princeton.edu/system/files/research/documents/deaton_puzzles_and_paradoxes.pdf

Department of Applied Economics. (various years). DAE Annual Reports, 1946–48 to 1986–87. Cambridge: Department of Applied Economics, Marshall Library Archives, digitalized.

Glyn, A., Hughes, A., Lipietz, A., & Singh, A. (1988). *The rise and fall of the golden age*. UNU-WIDER Working Paper No. 43. UNU-WIDER.

Godley, W. (2001). Saving Masud Khan. *London Review of Books*, 23(4), 3–7.

Godley, W. (2008, May 16). Interview with Wynne Godley. In S. Harrison & A. Macfarlane, *Encounter with economics*. Interviews filmed by A. Macfarlane and edited by S. Harrison. University of Cambridge. http://sms.cam.ac.uk/collection/1092396

Gudgin, G. (2021). The legacy of Wynne Godley: Notes from Graham Gudgin. *Journal of Post Keynesian Economics*, 44(1), 32–37.

Harcourt, G. C. (2001). *Fifty years a Keynesian and other essays*. Palgrave Macmillan.

Harcourt, G. C. (2007). *What is the Cambridge approach to economics?* Republished in G. C. Harcourt, *On Skidelsky's Keynes and other essays: Selected essays of G. C. Harcourt* (pp. 219–240). Palgrave Macmillan, 2012.

Harcourt, G. C., & Kitson, M. (1993). Fifty years of measurement: A Cambridge view. *Review of Income and Wealth*, 39(4), 435–447.

Llewellyn, J. (1998). Empirical analysis as an underpinning to policy. In I. Begg & S. G. B. Henry (Eds.), *Applied economics and public policy* (pp. 247–257). Cambridge University Press.

Pesaran, M. H. (1991). The ET interview: Professor Sir Richard Stone. *Econometric Theory*, 7(1), 85–123.

Pesaran, M. H., & Harcourt, G. C. (2000). Life and work of John Richard Nicholas Stone 1913–1991. *The Economic Journal*, 110, F146–F165.

Reddaway, W. B. (1995). Recollections of a lucky economist. *BNL Quarterly Review*, 192, 3–16.

Saith, A. (2019). *Ajit Singh of Cambridge and Chandigarh: An intellectual biography of the radical Sikh economist*. Palgrave Macmillan.

Shipman, A. (2019). *Wynne Godley: A biography*. Palgrave Macmillan.

Singh, A. (2008). *Better to be rough and relevant than to be precise and irrelevant: Reddaway's legacy to economics*. Working Paper No. 379. Cambridge University Centre for Business Research. www.cbr.cam.ac.uk/fileadmin/user_upload/centre-for-business-research/downloads/working-papers/wp379.pdf

Skidelsky, R. (1992). *John Maynard Keynes: The economist as saviour, 1920–1937*. Macmillan.

Smith, R. P. (1998). The development of econometric methods at the DAE. In I. Begg & S. G. B. Henry (Eds.), *Applied economics and public policy* (pp. 88–103). Cambridge University Press.

Smith, R. P. (2014). Richard Stone. Published later as Smith, R. P. (2019). In R. Dimand & H. Hagemann (Ed.), *The Elgar Companion to John Maynard Keynes* (pp. 419–423). Edward Elgar.

Stone, J. R. N. (1984). Richard Stone: Biographical. *The Nobel Prize*. https://www.nobelprize.org/prizes/economics/1984/stone/auto-biography/

CHAPTER 6

Cambridge Economic Policy Group: Beheading a Turbulent Priest

Abstract The Godley-Cripps Cambridge Economic Policy Group (CEPG) of the Department of Applied Economics (DAE) was effectively terminated by the abrupt and unexpected refusal by the Social Science Research Council (SSRC) to continue to fund its policy-oriented macroeconomic modelling research. The closure of the CEPG cannot be treated as just some wayward project application turned down—it was a landmark intervention that epitomised the turn to Thatcherism, dovetailing with the agendas of several other stakeholders, be they professional rivals to the CEPG outside Cambridge, but then also with the hostile strategies of the Hahn-Matthews orthodox axis with its own axe to grind and ambitions of dominance to pursue within the Faculty of Economics in Cambridge. This chapter unravels the occluded and complex story of an ostensibly simple event. The first part of the narration highlights some relevant features of the wider national context and political conjuncture that form the backdrop against which the specific episode occurs. The spotlight then shifts to the SSRC, the scene of action. Here, the quick decision of the SSRC to terminate CEPG funding is dissected forensically to investigate its antecedents; the post-mortem reveals that behind the hostile SSRC decision lay a lengthy trail leading to a complex network of multiple stakeholders whose combined interests came to be well served through the coup de grace delivered by the SSRC then under the direction of Michael Posner, himself a Cambridge economist. Pulling together the many floating pieces of the puzzle confirms that, as with an iceberg, what is directly visible is but a minor fraction of the whole story. As such, this rendition, albeit speculative in parts about the shape of the submerged sections of the iceberg, also serves as a necessary corrective to the received internal narratives on the fall of the Cambridge heterodox traditions which have tended to focus, almost exclusively, on methodological and

© The Author(s), under exclusive license to Springer Nature Switzerland AG 2022
A. Saith, *Cambridge Economics in the Post-Keynesian Era*, Palgrave Studies in the History of Economic Thought,
https://doi.org/10.1007/978-3-030-93019-6_6

technical issues of CEPG's research ignoring deeper political and ideological dimensions that might account for the hostility towards the CEPG team and its high-profile radical policy-oriented research.

In 1995, on the occasion of the 50th Anniversary of the formation of the Department of Applied Economics (DAE), Wynne Godley recalls: "Soon after Mrs. Thatcher came to power, the Cambridge Economic Policy Group forecast that the policies of her government would cause the worst slump of the post-war period; simultaneously, Patrick Minford forecast that they would cause a boom. Angus Deaton (privately) made a 'semi-serious' forecast that, whatever else happened, we should all still be in business two years later" (Godley, 1998, p. 258). There is more than a tinge of dark humour in this, for within that time frame, Godley's Cambridge Economic Policy Group (CEPG) had in fact been scythed down, out of business. Frederic Lee, scribe of the evolution of the heterodox tradition and lineages, observed: "The activities of the Cambridge Policy Group, which existed in the 1970s, also contributed to the development of Post Keynesian-heterodox economics at Cambridge, but its history, hence contributions, have not been written up. In general, the social and organizational history of economics at Cambridge is undeveloped, especially for the post-1945 years. Consequently, while the eventual demise of Post Keynesian-heterodox economics at Cambridge was seen as early as 1974, the actual process by which it occurred has not yet been told" (Lee, 2007, pp. 30–31n17). The rapid development, and then the arbitrary and ruthless cutting short, of the Godley-Cripps Cambridge Economic Policy Group (CEPG) over the decade of the 1970s marked the first major episode of the trilogy of attacks on key heterodox and radical research groups within the DAE.

Wynne Godley had risen rapidly through the ranks in the Treasury to senior positions and become a key go-to person for anything to do with public expenditure; he was also a savvy forecaster and had a hand in the production of the white papers and other materials for the relevant committees and politicians; his name cropped up quite regularly in parliamentary debates. Hemmed in by the constraints of his position, he was enticed by Nicky Kaldor—a collaborator in policy affairs at Whitehall—to trade salary for freedom and takeover. Godley wanted very much to continue his Treasury work through Cambridge, now pursuing his own questions and agendas and free to speak and write and engage in public debate, freedoms that he enjoyed and effectively exercised in full measure in the years ahead. Promptly, he set up his engine room, the new Cambridge Economic Policy Group (CEPG) in 1971 in partnership with Francis Cripps who gave up a much sought-after position in the Faculty to come across to the DAE to launch the exciting enterprise. From the very next year, the CEPG team, growing in numbers to approximately ten, began to issue their economic reviews, involving short- to medium-term forecasts with variational analysis of alternative policy configurations. These Economic Policy Reviews, incorrigibly free thinking and (therefore) controversial, opened new salients in policy and theory and were awaited with anticipation or apprehension—depending on one's position. The CEPG, along with others in the Faculty, such as Nicky Kaldor, Robert Neild and other young turks, came to be associated with strong policy positions, including the tariff protection to revive manufacturing, as well as with new departures in Cambridge, that is, Keynesian theory, as with the development of the 'New Cambridge' genre. Cambridge Keynesians, and the CEPG, were staunchly anti-monetarist and, not surprisingly, fed a continuous stream of criticism into the national press, undoubtedly annoying and antagonising the Thatcherite clans.

CEPG was a public good plus—in the sense that it was free of the official restriction placed on the formal 'public good' as represented by the modellers in the Treasury, Bank of England (BoE) or its out-sourced contractors. But its work was funded not by the University but by the Social Science Research Council (SSRC), which in turn received its funds from the Department of Education. There were regular cycles of SSRC project funding supporting the work of the CEPG from the outset; then, after Posner was appointed the Chairman of the SSRC (in the last months of the Callaghan Labour government), and Thatcher took over the government a few months later in 1979, CEPG made its regular periodic application to the SSRC—and in a shock outcome was abruptly denied any further funding for its macro-modelling team. The CEPG unit shut down in 1982.

How was the CEPG ship sunk? Was it a badly engineered model, hull full of holes, or was it torpedoed? Whodunnit? Why? And therein lies (many) a tale, perhaps one for each teller of the story. But before getting to the exchange of blows, it is useful to set the scene.

The closure of the CEPG cannot be treated as just some project application turned down—it was something of a landmark intervention that epitomised the turn to Thatcherism, dovetailing with the agendas of several other stakeholders, including professional rivals to the CEPG outside Cambridge, but then also with the hostile strategies of the Hahn-Matthews orthodox axis with its own axe to grind within the Faculty in Cambridge. Any card-carrying Indian astrologer might have pointed skywards to a unique synchronicity of hostile planetary formations in different quadrants of the cosmos. It becomes necessary to unravel the occluded complex story of an ostensibly simple event.

The first part of the narration maps the wider context and the conjuncture and introduces various relevant features of the backdrop against which the specific episode occurs, and probes academic, official and political domains within a national and international frame. The focus then shifts to the SSRC, the scene of action. Here, the simple decision of the SSRC to terminate CEPG funding is dissected forensically to investigate its antecedents; the post-mortem suggests that behind the final SSRC decision lay a lengthy pathological trail involving a complex network of multiple stakeholders whose combined interests came to be served through the coup de grace delivered by Michael Posner at the SSRC.

Slotting the many pieces of the jigsaw into place confirms that, as with an iceberg, what is directly visible is but a seventh of the whole story. As such, this analysis, surely speculative in parts about the shape of the submerged parts of the iceberg, also serves as a necessary corrective to the received internal narratives on the fall of the Cambridge heterodox traditions which tend to almost exclusively focus on intra-Cambridge factors.

6.1 Charged Conjuncture

6.1.1 Imbroglios of 1974: Old Versus New Cambridge Versus the Establishment

The year 1974 was a landmark year due to the bursting on to centre stage of the New Cambridge 'School', aka 'Model', or 'Hypothesis' or just 'equation', associated with Nicky Kaldor, Wynne Godley, Francis Cripps (all Labour government advisors from 1974) and Robert Neild, the implications of which openly challenged and undermined prevailing policy tenets and internal positions. But this fresh Cambridge theory and policy advice rocked the boat and was not much appreciated. John Maloney (2012), in his careful study based on files released after the 30-year embargo ended, reports that "there was opposition to all the Cambridge advice from Sir Kenneth Berrill, the government's Chief Economic Adviser" (ibid., p. 1002). And the Treasury, in its submission to the Public Expenditure Committee, is condescendingly dismissive of New Cambridge, referring to it as "a doctrine that has been presented primarily to the daily press and not in any reputable academic journals ... a prolonged attempt to elucidate and cope with the implications of the unorthodox and rapidly changing Cambridge doctrine may be felt by some of us to be a misdirection of endeavour" (cited in Maloney, 2012, p. 1004). There was a full-scale Treasury "attack on Wynne Godley" and Maloney observes that "all these charges were levelled before Cripps, Godley and Martin Fetherston had actually appeared before the Committee, and some of them bore little relation to what they went on to say" (ibid., p. 1005). Godley and Fetherston provided explanations and qualifications,

> but none of these concessions [they] argued, provided one iota of rehabilitation for the short term discretionary fiscal policy to which the Treasury remained wedded. The Committee's report agreed with them: demand management over the past 20 years had been 'extremely poor', a view contested only by the Treasury and the Bank of England, 'and they could hardly be expected to [agree]'. (*Report of the Public Expenditure Committee 1974, House of Commons*, cited by Maloney, 2012, p. 1005)

There were other slashing and swingeing bouts in which Kaldor and Cambridge took on the relative inefficacy of devaluation and the contingent necessity and potential advantages of selective import controls, positions that were vehemently opposed by the Treasury establishment and the monetarist camp. Kaldor was adamant that the structural root of the problem was that "we are not capable of producing up-to-date products with the design and quality required"; that industrial modernisation was essential and dependent on "large imports of machinery of a kind we are not at present able to produce at home".[1] For these reasons the heavy decline of sterling had had little positive impact on exports. This need for essential industrial imports strengthened the case for import controls on non-essential consumer goods. Here was the Kaldorian strategic policy template for late industrialisation in a follower economy, reminiscent of Meiji Japan in some ways. And it is worth recording that it is at this juncture that the group of radical Cambridge economists, including Ajit Singh, Bob Rowthorn, Francis Cripps, John Wells, was working on the thesis of the deindustrialisation of the UK economy, leading to some path-breaking papers on this theme from 1977. The process of deindustrialisation was accelerated by the Thatcher government allowing the sterling exchange rate to appreciate as the exploitation of North Sea oil and gas discoveries increased over the 1980s.[2]

Also worth noting is the fact that strong opposition to New Cambridge came not just from the trenches of the Treasury and the Bank; there was also a flank ambush in 1974 from within Cambridge. In response to an editorial on the budget in *The Times*, Robert Neild, of his own pen, wrote a letter to the editor expounding the New Cambridge view, which induced a bruising critique in the form of two articles from Lord Kahn and Michael Posner: "Challenging the 'elegant and striking' paradoxes of the New School", followed the next day by "Theory Dogged by Its Assumptions" (Mata, 2012).[3] Godley was unhappy and suggested private contact in Cambridge rather than "a confused debate in public"; this happened, up to a point, but through a 'heated' and 'ill tempered' exchange of letters between Kaldor, Kahn and Posner ending with Kaldor withdrawing and with Francis Cripps persuading Kahn that "little is to be gained by a 'theological' debate with attendant dangers of misrepresentation and misunderstanding" and that it would be better to wait for the results of significant empirical analysis being done by the DAE on the issues of contention (Mata, 2012, p. 18). Mata notes that Godley and Cripps preferred to refer to their position not as a New Cambridge 'school' but as a 'hypothesis' or 'equation'. "The semantic difference defused any claim to a challenge to Cambridge's Keynesian heritage, and made their work evidence of Cambridge's vitality" (ibid., p. 20). That would have been a good damage-limiting spin to put on the squabbles, but it would not hide the deeper

---

[1] Kaldor quoted in Maloney (2012, p. 1012).

[2] Terry Barker argued at the time for a North Sea Investment Fund to stabilise the exchange rate and provide for the time the oil ran out (Personal Communication; email dated 22 January 2021).

[3] In his perceptive and informative piece, Mata provides some details of these exchanges between the stalwarts of Old Cambridge and the rising young turks of New Cambridge. The editorial of *The Times* was carried on 26 January 1974; Neild's Letter to the Editor appeared on 31 January; and the two Kahn-Posner articles followed on 17 and 18 April. For references to some of the ensuing private correspondence, see Mata (2012, pp. 16–20).

divisions. It is worth noting that Michael Posner served as Chairman of the Faculty Board during 1973–1975, the critical period of the internal jousting between 'old' and 'new' Keynesians, and in this capacity was also the Chairman of the important Committee of Management that oversaw the running and progress of the DAE, with the Director, Wynne Godley, reporting to it in its meetings; Posner was in a position of privilege with regard to all aspects of the internal affairs of the DAE.

It is striking that in this seemingly private internal Cambridge debate, the correspondence was being circulated, even as the ink dried on the irate notes and letters, amongst the Cambridge group, but also to an external list which notably included Douglas Wass, then Permanent Secretary to the Treasury, and Kenneth Berrill, then Chief Economic Advisor at the Treasury. Thirlwall (1987a, p. 252) notes that inside the Treasury, "in 1976 there were sharp exchanges of views between Kaldor on the one hand, and Posner and Britton on the other". There were also tensions between Kaldor and Berrill when the latter was Chief Economic Adviser, and Thirlwall (1987a, p. 250) observes that "there was no love lost between him and Kaldor". Both were King's men, though Berrill, in sharp contrast to Kaldor, was close to Kahn. This could not but have inflicted significant collateral damage on the CEPG New Cambridge group which was thereby shown as having serious internal theoretical challenges *within* Cambridge itself. Berrill and Posner had shared long years in the Cambridge Faculty of Economics prior to their professional association in London; on the other side, Berrill and Kaldor were well known not to be overly fond of each other. Thus, one story would have it, with good reason, that the game was lost partly because of own goals, since Cambridge United was actually Cambridge Disunited; on the day of the big game, there was too much internal rivalry and bickering on the pitch, and no coach or manager (read, Maynard) on call to bang heads together and make them point in the same direction and face the common opponent.

6.1.2 The Enigma of Kahn

In the wings is the shadowy enigma of Richard Kahn. Richard Kahn retired in 1972, the year that he ensured that his 'K' was replaced by Frank's 'H' in the professorship he had held. Kahn was apparently instrumental in the decision to induct Frank Hahn into the Cambridge professoriate, taking umbrage at Kaldor having managed to have Hahn sidelined and Robert Neild appointed to the professorship that came free when Joan had retired the previous year. During 1972–1974, Harry Johnson, then at London School of Economics (LSE), helped Richard Kahn to arrange a lecture tour of American universities, which took place in 1974. The letters suggest a close personal equation. Robin Matthews (1989, p. 914) says that Johnson's "later virulence against Cambridge economics was *never* manifested so long as he was there; was it tact, or did his attitudes change?" (emphasis in the original). Johnson joined Hahn, Gorman and Walters at LSE in 1966, a group not known for being particularly Cambridge-friendly; Hahn returned to Cambridge to launch his campaign in 1972; in February 1973, Johnson read his savagely anti-Cambridge and anti-Joan paper at Amherst (Johnson, 1973) and a printed version of the article is filed in the Kahn Papers at King's; and between 1972 and 1974, Kahn and Johnson exchange friendly letters ("My dear Harry ...") where the former solicits the latter's help in arranging his desired lecture tour in the USA; this, following some of Kahn's own approaches being rejected earlier. Johnson readily obliges; he had approached Rosovsky earlier at Harvard, and Kahn received a tentative opening; and then Harry writes to Richard: "I am writing to various people on your behalf, as I think that is better than your writing for yourself" (Johnson to Kahn, Letter dated 25 January 1974, Papers of Richard Ferdinand Kahn, King's College Archives, Cambridge; RFK/12/2/80/9). Notwithstanding Johnson's visceral attacks on Cambridge economics and economists, including especially on Joan Robinson, the famously prickly Kahn appears to continue to have remarkably good dealings with him.

Prima facie, there could be a certain residue of puzzlement over Kahn's position/s in the local wars and, hypothetically and speculatively, about his role at some key turning points. Why should he have been so virulently against the appointment of Robert Neild to the chair Joan vacated on her retirement to have Frank Hahn shoe-horned into the next Cambridge professorship in 1972? What virtue might he have imagined in that game-changing move? Were two negatives to make a positive? What lay behind his sharply expressed hostility to the nascent idea of establishing (what became) the *Cambridge Journal of Economics*? He is explicit in not wishing to be associated with what he uncharitably and somewhat condescendingly calls a leftist propagandist journal. Upon his retirement, he solicits the assistance of Harry Johnson for his desired lecture tour of US ivy league universities; sleeping with the enemy? He has close relations with Posner, with whom he jointly publicly attacks the leftist 'new Cambridge' group's writings, and clearly there is no love lost there. He had very close dealings with Ken Berrill, who, as much as Kahn, were not great admirers of Kaldor; and Berrill had supported Posner's position in the context of the Rothschild Enquiry into the SSRC when Posner was its Chairman. Berrill was also a key member of DAE Review Committee-II that pushed the Hahn-Matthews agenda in reforming the DAE and bringing it under their control. Kahn is quite tetchy with Ajit Singh in his exchange over the latter's Political Economy Seminar at Queens' and indicates a wish, well after his retirement, to possibly relaunch 'his' seminar at King's—could this be viewed as anything but a vote of dissatisfaction, if not hostility, towards the rising younger heterodox group? He was made a Life Peer by Harold Wilson, "himself a convinced Keynesian [and] and admirer of Kahn's academic work, but Kahn was never part of the group of Labour Party counsellors; he always kept a detached attitude. In the House of Lords, he sat on the cross benches" (Pasinetti, 1991, p. 430); and Pasinetti (ibid., p. 432) informs us later that "he became dissatisfied with both major political parties, and in fact became a supporter of the Social Democratic Party",[4] as indeed were Michael Posner and others of the Matthews CLARE

[4] Philpot (2017) writes that "Labour's lurch to the left in the early 1980s might have provided an opening for the newly formed SDP to woo left-leaning Jews. Certainly, the SDP managed to attract a number of prominent Jewish Labour defectors, including the MPs David Ginsburg, Edward Lyons (who sat on the new party's National Committee) and Neville Sanderson, as well as the publisher George Weidenfeld, former Cabinet ministers John Diamond and Edmund Dell, and Cambridge economist Richard Kahn ... Within four months of the party's launch, an SDP Friends of Israel had been formed with Weidenfeld as its chair and one of the 'Gang of Four'—Bill Rodgers—as its president. Another of the quartet, the former Labour Foreign Secretary, David Owen, promised that the SDP would be 'zealous in the preservation of the State of Israel'." Arguably, the Labour Party was clearly too 'left-wing' for Kahn's political comfort on the Palestine-Israel issue; but, for others, like Tony Benn, the Labour Party position was too 'right-wing'; "In protest against Israel's position on the question of Palestinian statehood and its involvement in Lebanon, Eric Heffer and Tony Benn resigned from LFI [Labour Friends of Israel] in 1982" (Edmunds, 1997, p. 124). And the 'left-Keynesian' groups of the DAE and the Faculty were associated with the left-wingers of the Labour Party; indeed, Francis Cripps had worked directly with Tony Benn as his adviser, an equation established by Nicky Kaldor. Kahn had deep affinities with Israel from its early days, through to the end.

"Richard Ferdinand Kahn came from a Jewish family of strict religious observance ..."; both parents were German. "The Kahn family was described as a 'comfortable, cultured family which had a commitment to communal service and combined punctilious and decorous orthodoxy with a thirst for education and culture ... [following] ... a form of Judaism associated with a very distinguished Jewish thinker, Rabbi Samson Raphael Hirsch who, in the middle of the nineteenth century ... [advocated] strict observance of the laws of the Torah, combined with openness to secular learning' (Tabor, 1989). Richard remained strictly faithful to his religious upbringing well beyond his adolescence. It is said that, as Bursar of King's, he would not sign cheques on the Sabbath day. But later in life he abandoned orthodoxy. He was encouraged to eat meat on account of his health, and became less and less active in religious practice. 'Only on the rare occasions could one see him a Synagogue ... observance, ritual and the religious tradition no longer touched him ... [yet] ... he retained his identity as a Jew with pride and took a positive—if sometimes somewhat critical—attitude to Israel ... In his last years there was some turning back' [to the Jewish religion] (Tabor, 1989)" (Pasinetti, 1991, pp. 425–426). "An important aspect of his life was his strong Jewish identity, even when he gave up religious practice, as testified by the fact that he wanted to be buried in the Jewish part of the Cambridge cemetery" (Marcuzzo & Rosselli, 2019, p. 80).

Schiffman (2013, p. 1) provides a listing of "Jewish economists from the Diaspora [who] have played an active role in Israeli economics, on both the academic and policymaking fronts" since the establishment of the State of Israel in 1948. The list is impressive and includes Richard Kahn's 1957 and 1962 visits apart from those of many other famous economists. (See, for further details: Chap. 11, p. 5, n3.) Schiffman concludes however that "Ultimately, Israeli policymakers ignored Kahn's advice ... Kahn was unsuccessful as an advisor, but he was probably successful in the more limited sense of helping government officials attain a greater clarity on economic issues" (ibid.). "What motivated Kahn to visit Israel?" Schiffman cites four reasons: family—two of his three living sisters resided in Israel; religion—"Kahn was raised as an Orthodox Jew ... continued to support Orthodox Jewish causes. Indeed, the notations in his 1962 and 1973 travel diaries reflect a traditional (but nonpracticing) Judaism"; academics, in particular through his "close friend and collaborator Don Patinkin"; and, business: "Kahn was a director of the Anglo-Israeli Bank (AIB) which was the UK subsidiary of Israel's Bank Leumi" (ibid., pp. 12–13). The SDP's policy on Israel could thus have been an additional factor drawing Kahn in its favour.

(Cambridge, London and the Rest of England) Group, prominently including Charles Feinstein who was a significant player and activist in the Hahn-Matthews axis. Pasinetti also observes that "in the last decade of his life, Richard Kahn became more and more withdrawn. Most of all, he was saddened by the turn that mainstream economics had taken. In his last few years he was a very deeply disappointed man. At times he appeared grumpy. Yet he never made much apparent fuss about it, though never hiding his disapproval, if explicitly asked." As Luigi delicately puts it: "He suffered in the depth of his conscience, but preferred the sombre dignity of silence to any form of what might have appeared old-age hysterical complaint" (ibid., p. 432). Such silence seems as remarkable as puzzling—and possibly costly to the Cambridge left-Keynesian and heterodox cause—in the face of the all-out mainstream assault on heterodox economics and economists within the Faculty in the last decade of his life.

Maria Cristina Marcuzzo (Kahn & Marcuzzo, 2020) has recently provided a remarkably rich resource into Kahn's thinking, analysis and aspirations based on her extended interviews and conversations with him in the mid-1980s. Kahn speaks his own words; Marcuzzo introduces the context in hers. This joint narration covers roughly the same period during which the Hahn-Matthews campaigns against the Cambridge heterodox lineages were in full swing, and as such there are valuable insights to be gleaned from this Marcuzzo's account of these interviews.

Kahn speaks of "the tragic influence of the mystique of monetarism" (ibid., p. 27), of "the curse of monetarism" which he likens to "a savage, defeatist belief" (ibid., p. 52). In his interviews, c. 1986–1987, he strikingly asserts, and reconfirms, his sense of optimism about the near future, both in economics as a discipline and with regard to the direction national economic policy.

"While in universities in many countries monetarism is on the decline and there is a renaissance of Keynesian thought, this movement has not proceeded sufficiently fast to provide a basis for an influential international group of leading Keynesian economists to be formed as a means of exercising successful influence on governments and central banks" (ibid., p. 52). But, speaking in the mid-1980s, Richard Kahn appears unexpectedly sanguine about future prospects: "By nature I am an optimist. I strongly believe that in the course of a few years reason must prevail. Sadly I have to admit that the battle, even though courageously conducted, will be won only in the course of a few, though not many, years. My own guess is about five years" (ibid., p. 52).

This is a remarkable comment, given its mid-1980s timing, especially when considering Cambridge. By then, the Hahn-Matthews anti-heterodox campaign was in full swing; the Godley-Cripps project that had so annoyed Kahn had been shut down; the University authorities had been sufficiently coaxed, cajoled and compromised to launch a motivated inquiry into the DAE; Joan,

Piero and Nicky had recently passed away; and in 1985, the orthodox camp, presumably with some tactical support from some key fence-sitting members of the selection committee, had contrived to import one of Frank Hahn's 'nephews', Partha Dasgupta, into Cambridge to occupy the Austin Robinson-Joan Robinson professorship vacated by its incumbent Robert Neild who had become sufficiently disenchanted with the goings on at the Faculty to take the unusual step of voluntary early retirement; the main candidate of the 'left' for the professorship was Francis Cripps, with Luigi Pasinetti as another possibility. Clearly, within heterodox Cambridge, these should have been strong reasons for alarm and dismay, not for optimism.

Perhaps Kahn's gaze was fixed on the national political horizon and the rise of the Social Democratic Party (SDP), which he thought opened up space for political arbitrage and bargaining that could tilt the balance in favour of his desired approach to trade unions and employment, on the one side, and to the public sector budgetary requirement and investment, on the other. "My main concern has been the possibility of reconciling a high level of employment with a low rate of increase of prices" (ibid., p. 28); "Ideally, money wages should rise at a rate no higher than the rate of increase in productivity, about 3% per annum, a very satisfactory rate" (ibid., p. 32). Productivity increases depended on investment, which needed to be profitable, which required the money wage increases to be less than that of productivity. Investment, then, was the capitalist goose that would lay the golden egg for the workers.

"I [was] especially concerned with our unduly low rate of investment and the extent to which the productive resources of the country were devoted to consumption rather than investment. In many speeches I pointed out that the level of real wages was higher than the productivity of labour justified, and that the low rate of growth of productivity was attributable to our low rate of investment" (ibid., pp. 37–38).

"I was also of course very much concerned with the behaviour of money wages and during the period of Labour Government, while strongly supporting their attempts to curb the rate of increase of money wages, I expressed fairly strong criticisms of failure due to establishing targets which quite obviously could not be achieved, thus discrediting the whole policy. As I said earlier, many post-War Keynesians out-Keynesed Keynes. They advocated over a period of years, with unfortunate success, a higher level of employment than Keynes or even Beveridge thought safe" (ibid., pp. 37–38).

"I was a strong supporter of the Labour Government's attempts at achieving success by an incomes policy, mainly based on legislation"; failure due to chasing unachievable targets was disappointing. "While there was close collaboration between the Government the Trades Unions Congress, the TUC could exercise no control over the individual Trades Union leaders" (ibid., p. 29).[5]

This leads Kahn to introduce the mechanism of the wage-wage spiral. The wage-cost-price inflationary spiral was standard fare; in addition, Kahn was the Chairman of an OEEC Group of Experts which, in 1959, "introduced the concept of the wage-wage spiral as contrasted with the wage-price spiral". The mechanism is inherently sociological in nature and highlights the sequential aspects of instability arising from dynamic interactions between micro agents all motivated by their individual targets. Each individual union, with its own leadership, fought and bargained not just for on overall increase in money wages, but crucially also to obtain an increase that would maintain, if not improve their position in the relative pattern of wages across trades and trades unions. He quotes from this report: "We believe that the wage-wage spiral has been one of the main causes of excessive wage increases. Each Trades Union

[5] While zealously wanting to discipline the rise of money wages within a warranted band, Kahn provides amusing anecdotal evidence of his empathy with the lot and lives of mining communities: "I was tremendously impressed by the spirit of the miners and their courage. In many pits which I visited conditions at the 'face' were far from pleasant; quite often it was necessary to stoop, and it was hot and damp ... I was also tremendously impressed by the spirit of spontaneous gaiety which prevailed in the north of England—very unlike the gaiety in the South of England, which, far from being spontaneous, had to be stimulated by heavy consumption of alcohol. Though I cannot entirely deny, in exhibiting their spontaneous gaiety, the miners of the north of England consumed large quantities of beer. I took part in the New Year festivities of the Durham miners. It was an experience which I shall always cherish and never forget. As I had to return that night in a sleeping car, I had to keep a careful check on the number of pints of beer which I consumed. There was very slippery ice on the path leading from the miners' club to the car, and it seemed to me extremely important that I should leave the miners just before the New Year in an upright rather than in a horizontal position. I can clearly recall that I limited my consumption of the strong miners' beer, brewed at their own brewery in Newcastle, to seven pints" (Kahn & Marcuzzo, 2020, pp. 24–25).

While seven pints is indeed impressive, it might have been but a drop in an ocean on a scale measuring Tony Benn's lifelong affinity, close association and deep commitment to the miners' political struggles; Arthur Scargill, the firebrand leader of the miners, had worked with Benn from the NUM since the 1970s and "admired him and came to cherish him as a friend". In 1984, around the time of the Kahn-Marcuzzo interview, and just prior to the miners' strike of 1984–1985, Tony Benn returned to the House of Commons. Said Scargill in 2014, paying tribute to Benn when he died in 2014: "to that historic struggle he gave unstinting support ... Tony campaigned with ... me against the Tories' pit closure programme all over Britain. Our Union did not forget this solidarity and in 1985, Tony became the NUM's first honorary member" (ITV News, 2014). Earlier, Tony Benn had been MP for Bristol South East for 20 years, 1963–1983, having 'inherited' this, his first, parliamentary seat from Sir Stafford Cripps, grandfather of Francis Cripps who served him as his economic adviser when he was Energy Secretary in the Wilson-Callaghan Labour Government in the fiery 1970s, at the height of the New versus Old Cambridge controversies. Francis, placed with Tony Benn by Nicky Kaldor, was very closely associated with Benn, and he and Kahn were, of course, on opposing sides in that very public scrap between the old and new Cambridge gladiators. Through the 1970s, most of the Godley-Cripps CEPG team at the DAE stood well to the left of Kahn and Posner.

leader feels that he has to justify his salary to his members. His object is to secure wage increases which keep pace with the wage increases secured by other unions. The position is one of unstable equilibrium. The rate of increase of money wages is liable to escalate as it did some years ago. This tragic failure is largely a matter of lack of economic education. It is not realised that an all-round increase in money wages does not result in any increase in real wages" (OEEC, 1961; Fellner et al., 1961) (Kahn & Marcuzzo, 2020, p. 30).

Speaking in 1986–1987—or very nearly thereabouts—he cautions: "The defeat of {James} Callaghan's [Labour] Government in the General Election of 1979 is attributable to failure to curb the high rate of increase of money wages.[6] Success for the present policy of the Labour Party and of the Social Democratic Party in my country for reducing unemployment depends on education. My own hope is that the leaders and members of the Trades Unions by now realise that if their response to a substantial reduction in unemployment is a more than very modest rate of increase in money wages, a defeat of the Conservative Government will force the new Government to fall back on the Conservative Government's method of keeping the rate of increase of wages under control: massive unemployment" (ibid., p. 31).

Labour's 'reluctant monetarism' had yielded abjectly to Thatcher's raw, full-blooded monetarist assault, understood as "adopting a simplistic Friedmanite definition implying adherence to strictly non-discretionary quantitative rules for the conduct of macroeconomic policy" also involving publicly stated growth rate targets for money supply. Smith identifies 1979–1982 as the high tide of Thatcherite monetarism in the UK and marks Geoffrey Howe's budget of March 1982 as its end, signalled by a retreat from a rigid rule governed monetarism to a more pragmatic and less straitjacketed monetary discipline. David Smith (1987, p. 123) declares that by January 1985, "Britain's monetary experiment had been consigned to the dustbin of history and Conservative politicians were already amending the records … the January 1985 sterling crisis marked the changeover point from pragmatic monetarism to pragmatism" (Smith, 1987, p. 121). Going further, Kahn—while observing that "Smith presents a slightly exaggerated picture"—"strongly sympathises" with Smith's statement that "now that even Conservatives have safely consigned monetarism to the scrap-heap of history, the search is on for ways of undoing the damage done in its name" (Kahn & Marcuzzo, 2020, p. 44). But as Phyllis Deane (1988b, p. 486) remarked, "the rise of monetarism was a well-attested international event. Its *fall* is a debatable matter, depending, of course, on how one chooses to define the term" (emphasis in original). Smith's chosen definition was an extreme one, and Kahn himself notes that the news of the death of monetarism was "exaggerated"; according to Kahn, it needed another five years for the tide to turn.

A switch in political allegiance, in terms of parties though not in his beliefs, could have provided the basis for his declared optimism and sense of

---

[6] For a detailed analysis of the breakdown of 'the social contract' in this period, see Tarling and Wilkinson (1977).

expectation of imminent change in the landscape of politics and policy. The arrival of the SDP on the scene, in his view, opened up political space and possibilities for alternative routes to 'educating' trades unions through progressive dialogue rather than disciplining them through the monetarist punishment of unemployment.

"I left the Labour Party and joined this [the Social Democratic] Party because I saw little hope that a Labour Government would have much success with the leaders of the Trades Union Congress and the Trades Union leaders" (Kahn & Marcuzzo, 2020, p. 43). "Monetarists reject direct measures of controlling the behaviour of money wages. They rely simply on the pressure of unemployment, secured by monetary restrictions: a savage, defeatist belief" (ibid., p. 52); "Keynesians strongly believe in a number of methods" (ibid., p. 43).

The British Social Democratic Party—"of which I am proud to be a member" (ibid., p. 52)—"believe in at least three methods" (ibid., p. 52). Kahn

lists these. First, "a tax imposed on companies (and other employers) which between one year and the next raise wages by more than the norm fixed by the government (Layard, 1982); this tax is a tax on the excess of the wages over the norm; such a tax would discourage companies from paying more than the norm" (ibid., pp. 52–53). Second: "compulsory arbitration ... it is essential that some supreme overall body should coordinate the decisions of the individual bodies" (ibid., p. 53). Third: "trades union and employer negotiations would prove less damaging if they were synchronised, with representatives of the government serving as mediators and coordinators" (ibid.). And Kahn adds a fourth, essentially corporatist, mechanism due to James Meade: "a scheme devised by James Meade involving a central wage-guidance institution consisting of representatives of employers, employees and the government. It would fix a 'norm'—a non-inflationary rate of increase of money wages. It would be empowered by the government not only to monitor the behaviour of the various pay packets, but also to impose sufficient penalties on those who leave the norm" (ibid.).

He then explicitly sketches the political scenarios that could provide a route out of the British impasse. "I am not of course so foolish as to foresee any possibility of my country in the near future being governed by the Social Democratic Party with a majority in Parliament. But I do see the possibility of a Labour Government—or possibly even a Conservative Government—without an absolute majority in the House of Commons, being dependent on the Social Democratic and Liberal Parties for a majority. So that the Social Democratic Party would make it a condition of cooperation, and possibly of participation in a coalition government, to enforce acceptance of their policies for securing wage restraint. I am forced to make the sad confession that in my opinion the only practical solution involves close cooperation between the government and the leaders of the Trades Union Congress—and far more influence by those leaders over the leaders of individual Trades Unions. Incidentally, a simplification of our Trades Unions structure would be helpful. The lesson to be taught is the one which I have been emphasising: that the level and the behaviour through time of real wages does not depend on that of money wages. The leaders and members of Trades Unions have got to accept the simple fact that until they have learnt their lesson there is no alternative method to Mrs Thatcher's of keeping down to an acceptable level the rate of increase of the price level: a high level of unemployment" (ibid., pp. 53–54).

But then at the close, a tinge of doubt manages to creep in: "I fear that I am being unduly optimistic in expressing the hopeful view that a government which regarded the Trades Unions, neither as its foe, like our Conservative Government, nor as its main support, like a British Labour government, but as its ally, like a government which depended on the support of the Social Democratic Party, which believed in friendly cooperation with the Trades Union movement, would pretty rapidly achieve success in teaching the lesson. What is at stake is not only the relief of human misery and degradation but national prosperity; not just greater output and employment but a higher rate of growth of productivity, and hence of real wages, resulting from a higher rate of investment, resulting from higher profitability, embodying the new techniques" (ibid., pp. 53–54).

In February 1987, just months before the General Election, "the [Liberal-SDP] Alliance had cut Labour's lead over it to single figures and had also score a notable victory over Labour in the Greenwich by-election"; Richard Kahn's optimism index would have spiked at the prospect of a hung parliament with the Alliance becoming king makers, dictating terms and choosing their partner in government. As often, political reality went its own way. "The biggest area of doubt was over which of the main two parties would be preferable allies in a hung Parliament. Dr Owen discounted the chances of the Alliance jointing with Labour, while Mr Steel made similar comments regarding the Conservatives" (BBC, 1997); and of course, there was no operational tactical alliance to avoid splitting the non-Conservative vote on the day. The election results unambiguously confirmed this Achilles' heel. The Conservatives coasted home with a majority of 102; they polled 42.3 per cent of the votes cast, but converted these into 57.8 per cent of the seats won; Labour had 30.8 per cent of the votes for 35.2 per cent of the seats; and the Alliance got 22.5 per cent of the votes, but an abysmal 3.4 per cent of the seats. The popular vote of Labour and Alliance together was a quarter more than that of the Conservatives, but converted into a third fewer seats.

It would be patently wrong to rigidly conflate monetarism with neoliberalism. The monetarists, à la Friedman, Chicago and British followers, were both; but any watering down of dogmatic monetarist policy by injecting some eclectic pragmatism did not automatically imply any softening of the neoliberal political stance or strategy. Indeed, if monetarist contraction was the device for disciplining the trades unions through (the threat and/or reality of) mass unemployment, Thatcher had more direct instruments in her arsenal, as her suppression of the 1984–1985 miners' strike clearly demonstrated; in this specific tactical sense, monetarist contraction as a political instrument was to a considerable extent rendered redundant. Further, moderating monetarism in no way translated into left-Keynesianism in wider socio-economic terms or in terms of the role of the state. And on the wider stage, Thatcher had revealed her hand, or fangs, with the wanton sinking of *Admiral Belgrano*, not to mention her political romancing of Pinochet at the height, or depths, of his violent dictatorship in Chile. The basis of Kahn's optimism thus remains something of a puzzle; it seems to have been little more than that single swallow promising a summer. The high hopes he had invested in the SDP perhaps might have had an equally high fall.

Be it as it may, in the crucial decade in the decline and fall of the Cambridge heterodox lineages, the Kahn episode provides an indication that all was not well amongst those groups. Kahn's travails and tribulations with the Labour Party, and especially perhaps its left flank, occupy the same period over which Cambridge Keynesian economics is decimated by the orthodox camp in the Faculty. It would not be out of order to imagine that, at that time, Kahn might have felt only measured affinity with the left-Keynesian and radical groups of young turks in the Faculty and the DAE, and not overly exercised about their fate and future. If indeed there was a personal lament at the 'tragedy' that had befallen Cambridge economics—and as Pasinetti (1991, p. 438) points out "it is precisely this that saddened him so deeply in the last few years of his life", it came too late to rectify anything, well after the dust had settled on the lost war. A hard, unflinching interrogation might credibly attach some culpability, beyond just forgetful carelessness or casual complacency, in this regard.

6.1.3 Kaldor: On Radical Policy Implications of New Cambridge, 1976

In his 11-page typescript Note sent to Sir Bryan Hopkin on 7 January 1976, Nicky Kaldor provides a clear statement of 'the New Cambridge Approach' and starts by chiding Hopkin for having argued that "the theory so far lacks theoretical underpinning. It may 'work' but if it does, we are not at all clear how and why it does." Kaldor opens his lengthy exposition thus:

> As a considerable part of my work on economic theory for the past 35 years was concerned with the question of providing such a 'theoretical underpinning' I hope you will forgive me if I inflict on you a rather lengthy statement of the underlying theory—an exposition which is distinct from, but also prior to, the discussion of the merits of the particular equation by Godley and Cripps for short term forecasting or other purposes. Such an attempt is called for because I find that in the recent papers on New Cambridge (such as the evidence given by Godley and Cripps to the Select Committee or the account of last summer's seminar given in the Stamler-Miller paper) the theoretical hypotheses underlying the New Cambridge equation are not discussed at all—as if Godley and Cripps followed the precepts of the 'positive economics' of the Chicago School, which holds that there is no point in hypothesising as to why and how a particular relationship works, provided it predicts well. I know for a fact that this is not either Godley's or Cripps's view, and though I have not 'cleared' this paper with either of them, I should be surprised if they disagreed with my statement of the theory

in any important aspect. (Richard Kahn Papers, King's College Archives, University of Cambridge; RFK/12/2/132/9)

The 'New Cambridge School', (a term invented by Posner and Kahn) amounts, as far as I am concerned, to no more than a reversal of this [the traditional Keynesian] emphasis. I would certainly not wish to say that an insufficient level of effective demand cannot be caused by over-saving (or, rather, by under-investment in fixed capital or stocks in relation to the normal flow of savings) and Keynes was undoubtedly right in emphasising the 'collapse of the marginal efficiency of capital' as the main cause of the world-wide recession of the 1930s. But I gradually came to the conclusion (as a result of our post-war experience) that for countries like the UK it is the export/import relationship (or expressed more precisely, the relationship of the propensity to import to the propensity to export, the latter defined as export demand expressed as a percentage of potential output) which poses a far more serious (or far less tractable) obstacle to the pursuit of full employment growth policies than the tendency of a capitalist economy to save in excess of profitable opportunities for investment. (This need not, or not necessarily apply to other countries, such as the US.) (RFK/12/2/132/14)

You find that the origins of the 'New Cambridge theory' go back to the so-called 'generalised theory of the multiplier' which forms the core of my paper on 'Speculation and Economic Stability', published in the *Review of Economic Studies* of October 1939 (and reprinted as the first essay in my Essays on Growth and Stability, published in 1960). A further statement, more directly related to the working of the British economy was contained in my Presidential Address to the British Association in Durham in September 1970 and printed in the *Economic Journal* of March 1971.[7] Finally my latest exposition (though written on a level of generality which may not make its relevance immediately obvious) is contained in an article in the August 1975 issue of the *Quarterly Journal of Economics* (of which I enclose an offprint). (RFK/12/2/132/9)

Looking back from much later in the mid-1980s, in an extensive analytical recounting of theoretical positions, political contexts and policy controversies, Kahn trawls the Old versus New Cambridge controversy of the 1970s, forcefully restating the Kahn-Posner critique of Kaldor-Neild-Godley-Cripps, and challenging their assumed causalities between the budget and the exchange rate on the policy-instruments side, and the level of employment and the foreign balance on the policy-objectives side. "As expressions of causation these [their] statements were strongly repudiated by Michael Posner and me. ... The validity of the theory of the New Cambridge view depended on the implicit

---

[7] "Preceding this there were a number of minutes written by myself, Francis Cripps (who was then my assistant) and Wynne Godley in the Treasury during March–April 1967 in connection with the 1967 Budget. This discussion started (if I remember correctly) with my minute to Sir William Armstrong on 'The Budgetary Outlook in a Longer-Term Setting' of 17 March 1967 in which I asserted the existence of a strong negative correlation between the fiscal deficit and the current balance of payments. This was supported by some simple regression equations produced by Cripps on quarterly data extending to the previous ten years, and these in turn were criticized by Godley who was then an adherent of the 'old Cambridge' view. (These papers must still exist somewhere in the Treasury's files.)."

assumption that in Britain the surpluses of the personal and corporate sectors and the balance of payments on the current account are roughly constant from year to year. The complete falseness of this assumption was easily demonstrated in a statistical table which we published in our articles" (Kahn & Marcuzzo, 2020, pp. 49–50); unsurprisingly, New Cambridge had responses to this repudiation.

Back in real time, in a follow-up incremental four-page Note dated 15 January 1976, Kaldor concludes:

> I am ready to admit that I am more sceptical than I have been in the matter of the stability of the relationship of the fiscal deficit in the current balance of payments. But one thing that does seem to emerge from all this is the purely negative conclusion that we are not in a position to formulate a reliable system of forecasting except for very short periods. In contrast to Mr Posner I do not believe that the fact that New Cambridge does not provide an alternative model for forecasting entrenches the position of any existing forecasting system. (RFK/12/2/132/8)[8]

The core thesis of the Cambridge view, as evolving through the CEPG, inspired, espoused and argued by the Cambridge left-Keynesians with Kaldor as an apostle, was that the problems of the British economy were structural, not amenable to quick fiscal fixes and short-term patchwork policies. The loss of industrial competitiveness was not just the problem of price competition, but something rather more structural: significant sections of British industry had got left behind, lost their technological edge and could not produce the kinds of products demanded by potential buyers, and supplied by competitors, in overseas markets. In such a situation, more structural and deeper, longer-term policies were essential: import tariffs; well-designed policies for supporting industry; appropriate labour market policies, education, science, research and development. It is worth emphasising that in Cambridge, this structural, longer-term perspective was at the core of the proposition that Britain was in the throes of a spiral of premature deindustrialisation. But all this was well outside the professionally blinkered, short focal-length approach of the Treasury and Bank bureaucrats; and of economists, most of whom belonged to schools of thought, whether neoclassical or monetarist, that did not accept the legitimacy of policies addressing structural issues of industry and growth, and to whom talk of protection might have been totally out of order; nor did this message sit well with the functionally adapted templates of received Keynesian wisdom geared to the immediate fiscal and inflation concerns of bureaucrats and politicians lurching from one 'short term' to another, from budget to

---

[8] In these Notes, Kaldor uses, or refers to, variously "New Cambridge"; "New Cambridge Approach"; "New Cambridge School" (though this phrase is ascribed to Kahn and Posner); "New Cambridge equation""; "New Cambridge Theory"; "Old Cambridge view"; "New Cambridge model". These Notes are addressed to Sir Bryan Hopkin and copied to Posner, Liesner, (Miss) Brown, Cassell, Shepherd, Stamler, Todd, Hibberd, Miller, Britton, Sedgwick, Carr, Riley, Mortimer.

budget. New Cambridge economics, à la Kaldor, shifted the focus from managing short-term trade and fiscal imbalances to the longer-term development issue of generating effective demand through a revived productive investment process in the languishing manufacturing sector leading to export-led growth; this called for a different raft of policies, including protection much along the lines of the traditional infant industries rationale. But a move away from unrestricted free trade was a place too far in the academics, policy establishment and politicians of the time. Inevitably, sparks flew in all directions, and some singed the CEPG itself.[9]

6.1.4 Cambridge Squabbles: Spillover into Whitehall?

So, Old Cambridge could be set against New Cambridge, while the establishment could applaud from the galleries, firmly holding on to their traditional inherited views and practices, ignoring, if not misrepresenting, the pertinent policy messages that were at the heart of the Old–New disagreements. A credible indication of this is offered by J. Christopher Dow, then Chief Economist of the Bank of England in his *Memoirs*.

> Economists, like theologians, are trained to detect misstatements and, equally important, misleading half-statements of the truth; but they are very far from infallible. The practical conclusion of New Cambridge is to reverse Keynesian orthodoxy. It emerged, I suppose, from the conjunction of three heads put together in Cambridge; those of Nicky Kaldor, Wynne Godley and Robert Neild, of whom I would suppose that the two first were predominant. If I and others like me are right, they are exceptionally wrong-headed. How can such intelligent, indeed brilliant, men be brought to think like this? (Dow et al., 2013, pp. 39–40)

> If one pushes rational distrust of reason too far it becomes irrationalism. Wynne—once the government's chief forecaster—now denies the possibility of forecasting, and consequently, the kind of policy that tries to keep the economy on keel by reacting to forecasts.[10] ... There is another strand in both Nicky's and Wynne's thinking: that foreign trade is not greatly sensitive to price changes, so that the correction of the present external deficit will require import controls—for which there has long been pressure from Wedgwood Benn and the Tribunites. New Cambridge can thus also be said to have gone along with the irrationalism of the Left. (ibid.)

---

[9] For a contemporary analytical account on the treatment of issues of demand management in the 'New School', see Ron Smith (1976).

[10] This provides an example of facile misrepresentation. Tiago Mata, writing about Godley's position in 1980, says, "the government seemed to make policy choices on the grounds of doctrinal conviction alone, without presenting clear forecasts of policy scenarios. [Godley] asserted that 'unless a government is merely capricious, its policy is essentially based on a forecast, otherwise it can have no grounds for doing one set of things rather than another.' Godley was depressed that forecasters, those that imagined economic futures, had been removed from the policy debate" (Mata, 2012, p. 25).

New Cambridge and CEPG were being caricatured and stereotyped—the first stage of an attack in the making. Economists disagree, but they also fight, their egos bruise easily and they nurse grudges—proof, and many ordinary citizens do need it, that they are human after all. The CEPG group had more than their fair share of aggro and animosities, whether overt or covert, amongst Whitehall mandarins, especially those of rank. Christopher Dow shares his thoughts, publicly, on Wynne:

> Though he looks detached and unworldly, Wynne in his way has a liking for publicity, and various characteristics that ensure that he gets it. He always feels he is right, and right in a good cause: this makes him simple, persuasive and with the ring of conviction in what he says or writes. He quite likes, too, to be shocking or controversial. When he had attacked Treasury control of spending (in 1975), his phrases were not designed to be most acceptable to his former colleagues. Nor were they: he probably never thought how much they were resented. Wynne has continued to propagate his views. (ibid., p. 40)

But what Christopher Dow regarded as a penchant for personal publicity was perhaps viewed very differently by Wynne Godley, as the responsibility of a public intellectual; here is what Wynne says years later about all this: "I also knew that the economy was very badly covered in public discussion and knew more than any of the journalists at that time; decided to do my Treasury work in the Department of Applied Economics; that was very successful, at least in the sense that we got a lot of cover in the newspapers" (Godley, 2008).

Then Dow takes aim at Nicky Kaldor, another irritant:

> Kaldor was incorporated into the Treasury from 1974, and could argue only inside—as he did, indefatigably, and, so I have always been told, to the great disruption of public business. There is a story told of Nicky just after the war, that when he called on Pigou in his base in the Lake District at tea-time, without knowing as he did it, or realizing afterwards, he ate Pigou's week's butter ration. He is like that: never seeing any damage he does and with the kindest of feelings to everyone. (Dow et al., 2013, p. 40)

Sprinkled (un)generously in various accounts of the times are anecdotes poking seemingly harmless fun at intellectual opponents; and Nicky and Wynne, like Nicky and Tommy (Balogh), (*aka* Buda and Pest) with their gregarious, forthright and unfiltered personalities, made easy targets, ignoring the hard core of their powerful intellects and convictions. Francis Cripps, then a young advisor to Tony Benn, recalls, "Kaldor told me that the problem with Britain is that people will say anything required if instructed from above, using his experience with [a senior Oxford economist] when they were young as an example. His point was that I must never be like them and must tell the truth as I saw it"[11] (personal communication, 11 February 2018). Wynne, perhaps forever, and despite his very extensive talents, was a troubled soul, but he was never to be found short of his truth—he spoke his mind without fear or favour, notably also concerning his personal trials and tribulations as can be immediately fathomed from his remarkable and painfully honest personal accounts which embrace, rather than deny or disguise, realisations of fallibility, whether intellectual, professional or personal.[12] Dow might be right in that Wynne could have seriously antagonised his ex-establishment colleagues by his style—but they could have been wrong in ascribing this to arrogance or ulterior designs.

Nevertheless, Wynne Godley is dismissed as an egotistical publicity seeker and Nicky Kaldor as an unstoppable butter eater. All this petulance would be of little consequence, but for the fact that quite a few of these petulants, including Christopher Dow amongst others, occupied seats in committees making or influencing decisions on the CEPG.

Nicky Kaldor evoked mixed reactions. On the one side, as John King (2009, p. 108) writes, was Richard Crossman who "was prepared to forgive him anything, including his tendency to fall asleep—on the sofa at home while talking to Crossman and even at High Table in the middle of a King's College Feast", and according to whom Nicky was popular with civil servants and advisers to politicians, including the Treasury and Inland Revenue. But this feeling was far from universal, as evidenced in the notes of Christopher Dow at the Bank of England, or indeed some of his fellow advisers and ex-colleagues, or even the bemused senior ministers he advised. Wilson and Jenkins were not enthused, and Denis Healey, despite regarding Nicky "as the most brilliant economist of his generation in Europe", expressed his frustration, "government was not his metier" (as reported in King ibid.) and in the end Healey was happy to let Kaldor return to academe. Significantly, "Kaldor also clashed with academics-turned-mandarins like Alec Cairncross and Kenneth Berrill. Cairncross found him long-winded and excessively reliant on logic, without any firm grasp of human behaviour (Cairncross cited in King [2009, p. 109]), while he got on so badly with Berrill that the latter had to be moved from the Treasury by an exasperated Chancellor. '*Odium academicum* is quite as virulent a disease as *odium theologicum*' Healey concluded; 'political rivalries pale in comparison'" (King, 2009, p. 109). Kenneth Berrill was close to Richard Kahn, and Alec Cairncross was one of the founder members of the influential CLARE Group of politically middle-of-the-road economists with Robin Matthews at Clare

---

[11] Tony Benn, Industry Secretary, had been a strong advocate of import controls in the 1970s; in this he reflected the views of Kaldor, and Francis Cripps who served as his special adviser; Maloney (2012, p. 1015), after due confirmation from both Benn and Cripps, writes: "as both men confirm, Benn's views can be taken as a reliable indicator of those of Francis Cripps". Godley and Cripps had argued for import controls since January 1973 (Godley & Cripps, 1973; see Shipman, 2019, pp. 108–110).

[12] See the remarkable autobiographical essay by Wynne Godley in the *London Review of Books* (Godley, 2001).

College Cambridge. King (2009, p. 178) writes that Kaldor "had by the early 1960s fallen out" with Richard Kahn and Joan Robinson, but also refers to "his break with Joan Robinson and Richard Kahn in the late 1950s" (ibid., p. 180).

A word should be put in also for the Buda-Pest twins, usually acting in tandem whether upfront or backstage. Jon Davis quotes Sir Donald MacDougall as saying that "Balogh didn't trust the Treasury or the Bank of England one little bit and wanted a department to keep an eye on the wicked things the Treasury wanted to do" (Davis, 2007, p. 26). Davis points out that this attitude was vigorously shared by Bevan and that

> this was a deeply held belief across a wide swathe of the Labour Party, not just its left wing; it was also widely shared throughout intellectual circles sympathetic to labour and Wilson himself disliked the Treasury all his life; Balogh was convinced that sustained British economic success could never be achieved without the humbling of the myopic Treasury and the installation of a more pro-growth bias at the heart of government. (ibid., pp. 26–27)

Though Kaldor was on the inside, he surely shared these concerns. The Buda-Pest twins made a forceful, garrulous and usually very entertaining pair—but they also aroused animosities and were not necessarily welcomed even by their professional peers or juniors.[13]

Clearly, there was potentially serious damage caused by the public airing, in the press and other forums, of 'internal' Cambridge differences, such as the

---

[13] An insider clue about how welcome the Buda-Pest twins were with the Whitehall lads comes from Wilfred Beckerman, reminiscing about the late 1960s in an interview by Keith Tribe. "Most of the economists in Whitehall were members of the Reform Club. Tommy was a member. Nicky was a member. Christopher Dow was a member, everybody. Donald MacDougall was a member. John Jukes was a member. It was known as the Treasury Cafeteria. So one could meet and discuss things. And one did so all the time without having to meet officially ... There was no point in having an official organisation. There was a dining club set up by me, actually, with Ralph Turvey—who was also a member of the Reform Club—soon after I joined the Board of Trade. It was a dining club just for senior economists in the government service"; others who were in included Ken Berrill, Wynne Godley, Michael Posner, Fred Atkinson, Alan Williams, Leonard Nicholson and Kit MacMahon; "so that was one a month. It was a dining club, but every month somebody would have to introduce a topic and then after the food, we would seriously discuss the topic." "The top economic advisors in the relevant departments used to meet once a week and we arranged this informally. We became known as the Council of Economic Advisors, copying the American system." "There was a little club within it [The Reform Club] called the Political Economy Club ... I only went along to a couple of meetings. There would be two or three good people there, but there would also be a lot of members of the Reform Club who thought they were economists and weren't ... they would talk an awful lot and I just got bored." And in this narration of the gangs and ganging up of the boys from different parts of Whitehall, Beckerman says: "it was a dining club just for senior economists in the government service. We didn't want to have the top boys in. We didn't have Nicky in, because Nicky would have dominated the conversation, you wouldn't have got a word edgeways in. Or Tommy, the two of them together would have been just arguing, haggling all the time" (Beckerman, in Tribe, 1997, p. 175). These economists' lunches at the Reform Club also provoked a vitriolic assault on the lot, including especially Nicky Kaldor; see Chapter 12, section 12.3.2 for Postan's attack on Kaldor and Colin Clark.

clashes between different 'Keynesian' camps over the 'new' Cambridge equation or model, with Godley, Neild, Cripps and others on one side, and Richard Kahn and Michael Posner on the other (see Mata, 2012; Smith, 2016). By the end of the 1970s, Posner was to take over the Chairmanship of the SSRC. Mata (2012), Smith (2016) and Maloney (2012) all comment on the theoretical and (what Francis Cripps referred to as) the 'theological' doctrinal aspects of the differences between the different Keynesian camps in Cambridge; what tends to go unnoticed is that it was under Michael Posner's watch, precisely in this tense period of negotiation, that the SSRC withdrew its funding from Wynne Godley's high-profile, high-decibel CEPG that had become a thorn in the Thatcher side, leading summarily to its silencing.

6.1.5 *Triggering Crisis: The Pivot of the OPEC Price Hikes*

From the 1950s, Chicago economics had spread its reach wide into Latin American countries through education and training programmes, with a steady and expanding inflow of students; a new cadre of Chicago 'policy economists' was being nurtured and embedded into national and international systems. While all this evolved apace, things were not going as well for Chicago's other, Hayekian, arm of 'social thought'; Hayek had returned to the continent, but Keynesianism was at its peak, diminishing the voice and visibility of the Hayekian creed, and its central cerebral organ, the Mont Pelerin Society (MPS), to a point where Hayek went into a bout of depression and contemplated bringing the shutters down on the MPS shop, notwithstanding his earlier prophecy, prescient as it was to turn out, that making an impact would take two to three decades. Milton Friedman was also of the view that the liberal movement had to wait for enabling trigger points that would project their political philosophy and policy economics to the national and global centre stage; till then, the movement would sharpen its toolkit and await (im)patiently for such a conjuncture.

Arnold Harberger, the godfather who spawned the Chicago boys, elaborated on the role of crises as turning points in policy making. "The maturation of economic ideas in the cauldron of academic life is a continuing process; goes on forever. But I think that for making major policy changes in a country, the element of crisis is critical. Most major economic policy changes come in moments either of actual crisis or perceived crisis … societies that are comfortable rarely want to change their comfort level even though sensible reforms promise to improve things; … they may be willing to make 'little' sacrifices but not big ones in the hope of promised improvements; … major changes have nearly always come at moments when people were reacting to a crisis situation—where in some sense they had 'had it up to here' and were willing to risk taking daring new trails; … it is typical of crises that people really don't know what to do; … the authorities are often just as perplexed as everybody else; … it creates opportunity and that opportunity may fall into the lap of somebody who just doesn't know what to do or does it badly; … they too often have turned to the wrong people for advice, people who prescribed medicine that was altogether wrong and that drove the country's economy to the wall; ... but with luck the reins of policy will be given to people who really know what to do and how to do it"[14] (Harberger in Levy, 1999).

OPEC's dramatic price hikes of 1973 and 1979 were the catalysts of such crises, opening up sweeping opportunities and threats, imperatives for changes in economic strategies and policy regimes, with kaleidoscopic impacts at national and global levels, starting a veritable game of snakes-and-ladders, where national fortunes were determined by ownership of oil, and the capacity to insert national financial institutions into the gargantuan recycling of finance and new debt that emerged from the tectonic shifts in the volume and the locus of global oil revenues. For the oil-importing developing economies, the price hike spelled a disastrous slide into debt and the clutches of international moneylending agencies, by then stacked with 'Chicago' policy economists. But even for UK, which anticipated cushion of its North Sea oil once it came on tap, the price hikes unleashed high waves of economic and political destabilisation. The domino effect consumed the Labour government in 1979 and ushered in Thatcher and her 'isms'.

"The winter of 1973–1974, ... was a 'silly season' for news reporting; when consulted today [in 1975], the journalistic representations of the 'crisis' reveal a remarkable lack of interest in how the situation had come about and an equal lack of prescience about how it might evolve" (Daedalus, 1975, p. v). Writing at the time, Raymond Vernon (1975, p. 245) asks, "Whether the strength displayed by the oil exporters in the October 1973 crisis represented a solid new fact in the international distribution of power or an aberrant condition that would soon disappear." Vernon notes that "the reply of the rich industrialized countries has been muted and equivocal. So far [in mid 1975] there has been neither a credible threat of gunboat diplomacy, nor a significant effort at economic sanctions, nor any other of the traditional responses of seemingly powerful nations" (Vernon, 1975, p. 245).

In contrast, Norman Girvan (1975, p. 145) rightly says: "The OPEC offensive of 1970–1973 was long in the making"; and Edith Penrose (1975, p. 39) identifies three historical developments, each evolving independently but moving synchronically to a combined crisis. "First, the rising bargaining power of the governments of the oil-exporting countries of the Middle East vis-à-vis the international companies that had discovered, developed, and long controlled Middle Eastern oil; secondly, the growing dependence of the United States on

---

[14] Harberger's "bad examples", unsurprisingly, are "Indonesia in the time of Sukarno, Chile in the time of Allende, Nicaragua under the Sandinistas, Argentina under Isabelita Perón, Peru under Alan Garcia". Equally predictably: "and then there are those wonderful occasions where people who really know what to do, and who embody good economics, are given their head, so to speak. Having such people in the right place at the right time can really propel an important revolution. I think the Indonesian miracle of 1968 and onward, the Brazilian miracle of 1965 and onward, Chile's performance since 1973 and Argentina's since 1990 all have that characteristic" (Harberger in Levy, 1999).

Middle Eastern, and specifically Arab, oil; and thirdly, the establishment and expansion of Israel in Palestine against the bitter opposition of the Arab countries, but with the strong support of the United States."

Girvan frames the crisis in different terms: "Ultimately it was a direct response to the structure of unequal power relations that existed—and continues to exist—in the contemporary world capitalist system. It formed the most concrete and dramatic manifestation of a more general phenomenon in contemporary international relations, that of Third World economic nationalism. It represents ... the vanguard of a movement by which states in the Third World—or more precisely, the classes that control these states—are seeking to redefine their role in the world economic system and, in particular, to gain a more nearly equally role in their relations with the centers of power. ... What was unusual about the OPEC action," asks Girvan; not the cartel-like behaviour, which was well known to modern capitalism; not the use of a trade embargo as a political weapon, "as every Cuban knows"; yes, oil quadrupled in price, but so had grain prices after the poor harvest of 1972–1973. Girvan's answers his own question: "The OPEC action was unusual and unprecedented because it was taken by a group of Third World countries, primary-produce exporting countries. For the first time in modern history, some non-industrialized countries had succeeded in securing market power in world trade in their export commodity, and they had used this market power to impose a substantial improvement in their terms of trade with the industrialized West. This rudely disrupted the established pattern of center-periphery power relations that had governed the economic relationships between the developed countries and the Third World" (Girvan, 1975, p. 145).

Girvan's contemporary interpretation, in 1975, is powerful, even if a little influenced by the Latin dependency school framework in aggregating 'the Third World' into a collective political entity or analytical category. The same oil crisis was the proximate and primary cause of the oil-importing developing countries sliding inexorably into a vortex of indebtedness to meet its bill for oil imports. Having, or not having, oil became a fundamental divider within 'the Third World'. In turn, this indebtedness—against the background of tectonic economic shifts in the socialist bloc of countries—ushered in the IMF and the World Bank as the moneylenders, of course with their lengthy list of conditionalities, including the reversal of strategies and aspirations for the project of industrialisation in the lagging developing economies. At a stroke, the OPEC oil strike provided a spectacular, if not generalisable, contra-example to the Prebisch-Singer thesis on the long-term decline of the terms of trade for the primary exports from developing economies; simultaneously, it sounded the death knell for the state-led model of import-substitution industrialisation in developing countries and returned the development narrative to market-led, comparative advantage (i.e. primary exports) driven economic strategies for these countries. So while Girvan is surely correct in hailing this as a historic case of Third World standing up to the West, in reality the consequences were terminally damaging for the prospects for autonomous industrialisation in the non-OPEC 'third world' countries; the Bretton-Woods package of conditions, stabilisation, structural adjustment, reforms, etc., put paid to that. The 'development' project entered its new non-aspirational open-market globalisation phase.

The Western oil multinationals, at the heart of the dissatisfaction of 'third world' oil producers, hardly suffered as they simply passed on the higher prices to the oil buyers. But there were severe all-round implications downstream. The massive explosion in OPEC oil revenues created its own consequences. For one, there was a veritable tsunami of fresh liquidity in the OPEC economies. Raymond Vernon (1975, p. 1) points out that "by the midyear of 1974, the concern over the price had been converted into a concern over the international monetary mechanism as a whole; considerable doubt arose over whether institutions existed or could be created that would be capable of handling the massive shifts in financial resources that were developing." Of course, these worries were but temporary. The vast quasi-rents captured by the OPEC countries were quite quickly, easily and cunningly redirected back into Western banks, property and financial markets. Another heavy tranche went back into the infrastructural modernisation of the OPEC countries, mostly limited to the capital cities and tourist tracts; a huge return flow came into the cavernous pockets of arms exporters of the West, as Arab countries were (all too easily) persuaded they needed to invest in expensive guns and planes from the West; a never-ending bonanza for the armament producing and exporting companies and countries, but an ongoing nightmare for countries and peoples on which these came subsequently to be used. A very minor fraction of this liquidity eventually went to the poor oil-importing countries through multilateral agencies as loans, described by Frances Stewart as "irresponsibly given and irresponsibly taken", leading in due course to the curious finding that the private capital outflows from these poor countries exceeded the inflows.

The rich oil-importers had to absorb huge inflationary pressures. For the UK, despite having got some its own North Sea oil from the mid-1970s, the catapulting inflation had dire consequences. Kalecki called inflation a form of class conflict, as workers organised and struggled to seek higher money wages in response to higher prices. And in the early 1970s, the prices of food stuffs had also experienced a spike on account of a string of bad harvests in various countries, leading to a sudden increase in international demand. North Sea oil provided limited protection, but inflation also entered the British economy through imports other than oil. The miners' strikes led to a three-day week, with inflation well into double digits; trade unions demanded compensatory wage increases which repeated the cycle of inflation; UK's manufacturing sector suffered a serious decline; the conservative Heath Government fell in 1974, but that simply passed on the problems to the labour Wilson Government which fared little better, with a tumultuous period ending with the collapse of the labour Callaghan government in 1979, as the second oil price spike—following the Iranian Revolution and the fall of the Shah of Iran—again fuelled sharp inflationary pressures and attendant labour struggles and conflicts, intensifying the attritional decline of the UK manufacturing base. If open unemployment had been the hallmark of the Great Depression, stagflation was the defining characteristic of the crises of the 1970s and 1980s. If the problem then had been how to generate employment, the issue now was how to control inflation without damaging impacts on labour, industry and the wider economy.

There were reverberations in Cambridge too. Just the year before the first price hike, in the midst of the turmoil of strikes, Jackson et al. (1972) produced their DAE study, *Do Trade Unions Cause Inflation?* As the national and global economy restructured around the impact of the price hikes superimposed on underlying economic issues, debates intensified around deindustrialisation and stagflation. In their celebrated paper on *The Golden Age of Capitalism*, Glyn et al. (1988) marked 1973, the year of the first oil price hike, as the turning point but emphasised that this served as a catalyst for laying bare the deeper structural problems of the UK economy. Charles Feinstein and Brian Reddaway (1978), collaborating from the CLARE Group, analysed the impacts of the price hike, especially considering the impact on world demand and growth prospects for the UK economy; and Richard Kahn closely tracked the routes taken by the mushrooming oil revenues of the Arab OPEC countries back into the financial systems of Western economies through OECD banks and real estate and other investments. And writing later about the period, Cunningham (2006) bestowed the power of clairvoyance on Michael Posner (under whom she had worked at the SSRC) in claiming that he "with Rothschild ... predicted by six months the first significant rise in oil prices" which, if valid, would have been a lottery-winning ticket.[15]

6.1.6   1979: Enter Margaret Thatcher, Right-Wing, Upfront

Jim Callaghan's in the 1970s was a minority Labour government, often living by the session, if not the day. The general sentiment in the Labour Party was that it "would have won if the election had been called in October 1978" (before things turned really bad), and that there would be "hope of winning in October 1979"; as Roy Hattersley remarked, "if a week is a long time in politics, six months is an eternity. By the autumn, memories of 'the winter of discontent'—public sector workers on strike, rubbish piling up in the streets and hospital porters turning away patients—might have faded. We had recovered

---

[15] Rothschild indeed was closely involved in tracking and shaping UK oil policy in that fraught period, and Posner, who had an interest in energy policy, had worked under him. However, the uncorroborated claim is possibly somewhat generous, understandable in the context of an obituary. It was the canny and hugely connected Rothschild who would have been on the inside track. That there would be a break in the oil regime was hardly a secret, and multi-level interactions and negotiations had been ongoing for years with a perennial apprehension, at every stage, of the old neo-imperial arrangements imminently breaking down and oil prices breaking out. Most likely no single player in the game could have credibly had made any reliable prediction for what might happen six months down the line. For a contemporary narrative of an insider, see Levy, W.R. (1971, 1982); for a later in-depth analysis of the period, see Kuiken (2013, 2014).

from the IMF crisis" (Hattersley, 2009). But the no-confidence motion called by Margaret Thatcher was to be voted on 28 March 1979; Labour's prospects for survival teetered on a knife-edge, dependent on working out the usual political bargains and bribes with various 'odds and sods' and fringe groups whose loyalty could be swayed temporarily on the day, if not bought on a more secure basis.

Callaghan did not want to sully his hands with a handshake with Enoch Powell who could have saved the vote had his demand (for a pipeline to provide cheap energy to Ulster) been accommodated, presumably by Tony Benn, then Energy Secretary, but Hattersley recalls that Callaghan "dismissed the idea out of hand; his government was not up for auction". There were other possibilities: "Could Clement Freud have been persuaded to abstain by the promise of an easy passage for his Freedom of Information Bill? Was it true that a Tory—Alan Glynn—would have accepted an instant peerage?" (Hattersley, 2009). A couple of Unionist MPs had complained of Northern Ireland suffering from relatively higher rates of inflation and wanted something done about this; Hattersley offered them a separate price index for Northern Ireland which would justify special assistance; "I was already considering a separate index for pensioners and the ever-demanding Scots. So it was not a difficult promise to make" (ibid.); the ploy worked.

On the day, it was a 311–310 result that ushered in the Thatcher revolution, just one additional vote would have achieved a tie and the survival of the Labour government since the Speaker of the House would be bound to abstain, and hence the no-confidence motion would have been denied a majority. This fixes the spotlight poignantly on the single Labour abstention of the day—that of the mortally ill, retired family doctor, Sir Alfred Broughton, who had earlier wished to give up his seat, with Labour preferring him to stay on, even if in bed, instead of having to defend his thin majority, of 8248, in electorally bad times. "In the little group that the chief whip called together to fight the rearguard action, there was deep disagreement about whether or not a dying man should be brought 200 miles to the House and left in the ambulance in Speaker's Court while he was 'nodded through' the division lobby by a whip—a procedure which was only acceptable if an invalid was 'in the precincts' of the House of Commons when the division was called" (Hattersley, 2009). "Once he had arrived safely in Speaker's Court, his vote was secure", but "what would happen if he was dead on arrival". The 'Doc' "himself was prepared, indeed determined, to do what he regarded as his duty, even though he had been warned that he might not survive the journey"; "the Broughton Family was besieged by journalists who were more interested in the life expectancy of the government than the health of the local MP"; "on the morning of the vote, Lady Broughton telephoned to say that her husband was determined to come to the aid of the party, but it would be madness for him to do so" (ibid.).

Walter Harrison "the unsung hero of a dozen votes in which Jim Callaghan's minority government had scraped home" had to take the decision. And so "at 1:20 on the afternoon of Wednesday 28 March 1979, he decided that it would be morally wrong to expose Broughton to the perils of the journey"; "not all of us, who scrambled for votes that day, agreed with him", but Jim Callaghan wrote to him to say he "did the right thing". A week later, Sir Alfred Broughton was dead—one can only wonder what kind of regret he might have carried with him; would his vote have delayed, even if not turned, the tide of Thatcherism? History records the result, 311–310, a one-vote win in 621 votes cast; a general election ensued, and in romped Margaret Thatcher in her pomp, opening the floodgates to the neoliberal tsunami that followed. What price counterfactuals, the ifs and buts of history.

The tale is not without a final twist of irony: in the dying months of his government, Callaghan, or rather Shirley Williams, the Secretary of State for Education, made an appointment of some consequence (as it later turned out, though it would hardly have been apparent at the time) for the fortunes of Cambridge heterodox economics: Michael Vivian Posner, with all his baggage of Whitehall and Cambridge rivalries and scuffles, was appointed Chairman of the Social Science Research Council, the body on which the two powerful DAE projects depended for their grants and thereby their institutional sustenance, indeed their existence. The appointment was for a four-year period that proved, in direct or indirect ways, to be a fateful, if not fatal, one for DAE macroeconomics. And, of course, alongside Margaret Thatcher, in strode Keith Joseph as the new Secretary of State for Education, clutching his baggage of grudges against leftist academics, social science generally and sociologists in particular, the vociferous trouble-making Cambridge Keynesians, and the SSRC itself that had supported these various nefarious types.

6.1.7 The Case of the Odd Consensus: The Letter by 364 Economists, 1981

Margaret Thatcher came into power in 1979 and immediately started setting up her monetarism stall. There were internal theoretical and doctrinal divisions and separations galore within Cambridge economics, but none of them involved monetarists, simply because the species could not survive that hostile habitat. And so, in 1980, Robert Neild and Frank Hahn wrote a joint letter to *The Times*, frontally challenging the Thatcherite turn to monetarism; this was followed a year later with the now-famous statement, making much the same arguments, which was signed by 364 economists across the country, including several of neoclassical orientation.

Prior questions arise: How was it that Hahn and Neild, from opposite sides of the Cambridge spectrum, with the latter brought in by Kaldor allegedly as a foil to Hahn, collaborated in this high-profile venture? And, why did Hahn, not given to media flourishes, wish to write the letter in the first place?

To answer the first, Newbery (2017, p. 489) cites the collaboration as an illustration of the power of conversation in the coffee room of the Cambridge Faculty building, regular and unregulated exchanges that Newbery himself, though not all others, enjoyed. The answer to the second lies perhaps in Hahn taking the opportunity to express himself in relation to Alan Walters, a monetarist and economic advisor to Thatcher; Hahn had Walters (perhaps then not converted to the monetarist faith) as a departmental colleague when he joined Birmingham in 1948 and became "later Hahn's bête noire" (ibid.). Hahn and Walters both joined LSE as professors in 1967. For Hahn, the letter served also as a direct challenge to Walters.

Harcourt points to a more intellectual basis when he refers, elsewhere, to Hahn's "courageous attacks on the Monetarists and New Classical macroeconomics", which "seem to suggest that he recognises aspects of Keynes's method" (Harcourt, 2012b, p. 233). Was Hahn now jumping into bed with the Keynesian policy camp? Not necessarily, as Lewis Allan rightly points out: "while the letter was explicitly anti-monetarist ... it was not explicitly pro-Keynesian ... [it] teasingly mentioned 'alternative policies' rather than a Keynesian alternative, and this phrasing allowed economists ... such as Steve Nickell to sign" (Allan, 2008, p. 36). This silence, or implicit ambivalence, with regard to alternative policies is exploited by the government in its response to the 364 signatories. After flatly rejecting the assertions of the letter, the government's reply pointedly notes: "It is conspicuous that although the 364 economists assert that there are alternative policies, they are unable to specify any such agreed alternatives" (Booth, 2006b, p. 133). The agreement of the 364 was limited to a rejection of the monetarist policy agenda; beyond that, proverbial wisdom would hold sway, with 'n' economists holding at least '$n+1$' opinions, with little prospect of a shared view when $n = 364$.

The statement went out on 13 March to one member of each university, and the published letter was dated 28 March; the set of signatures would be an autograph collector's delight, not least for the reason that you find people signing the same statement even though they might not agree with each other on the time of day. Robert Neild provides the likely explanation: "The statement was circulated as university terms were ending. The rates of response have therefore been influenced by when term ended, by how dispersed is the community of university teachers in the vacation, as well as by the climate of opinion in each university" (Neild, 2012).

Apropos the letter, Maurice Peston, the Labour peer, said, "There would have been hundreds more queuing up to sign it if it had not been sent over Easter" (Booth, 2006a). Robert Neild notes that the letter was sent out in a hurry and rather haphazardly and that this and especially its timing and short-time window for responding would have meant that many who would have liked to sign it could not do so. This would explain, for instance, why the Cambridge list of signatories incredibly does not include the names of Ajit Singh, Bob Rowthorn, Suzy Paine and Alan Hughes; and also of Frank Hahn's friend Robin Matthews,[16] among several others.

---

[16] Matthews might have refrained from signing the letter more because he was then Chairman of the Bank of England's Panel of Academic Consultants.

Cambridge stood out as the epicentre of the anti-monetarist protest. The 364 signatories were from 42 units across the country. Cambridge alone posts 54 signatures, as many as six London universities put together, with Oxford, LSE, Birkbeck, Bristol and UCL all in the 10 to 15 range. There is one stray signature from the National Institute of Economic and Social Research (NIESR), closely associated with and dependent on the government; and none at all from Liverpool, Minford's base and the monetarist bastion. Identifiable monetarists are also noticeably absent including from the LSE, London Business School (LBS) and City University Business School (CUBS)—all seeking government funds and with monetarist leanings.[17]

Philip Booth, of the Thatcherite think tank Institute of Economic Affairs (IEA), edited a collation of reflections on the '364 Letter' in 2006—25 years down the line—and offers "two cheers" to Hahn "because he did at least try to defend the 1981 letter" (2006b, p. 35, n12) in the face of some contemporary criticism (which incidentally Hahn duly demolished with scathing sarcasm, essentially likening the defenders of the Thatcher-Walters monetarist budget to quacks),[18] and observes that in contrast to Hahn "most of the 364 have clammed up ... [he] knows a few of them—with later careers of great public prominence who would prefer not to be reminded that they signed it" (ibid., p. 35n12). Not in this volume, but independently, there is a thoughtful reflection and robust defence of the letter and its critique by the other principal author, Robert Neild (Neild, 2012). Nickell (also elsewhere) alludes to some of his close friends who were signatories, implying most probably Mervyn King, not standing up to be counted later—it seems not to have harmed either's subsequent career; if anything, *not* having signed a letter put out by Frank Hahn could well have done so at that stage of their unfolding careers; Nickell (2006, p. xx) stated later that he signed the letter "because it was the only game in town" (quoted in Booth, 2006a).

Actually, it wasn't; the Statement of 364 drew a strong letter in defence of Thatcherite monetarism from Patrick Minford:

> The biggest political fight was over the 1981 Budget. This cut the budget deficit at what seemed to be the deepest point of the recession. The knives were out, and 364 economists famously joined in the attack on her. My view—which I shared with my mentor Alan Walters, her personal economic adviser whom I helped— was that budgetary toughness was vital to creating confidence in sustained

---

[17] The Statement, List of Signatories and the Official Government response can be found in Booth (2006b, Appendix, pp. 121–133).

[18] "Suppose 364 doctors stated that there is 'no basis in medical theory or supporting evidence' that a man with an infection will be cured by the administration of toad's liver. Suppose, none the less, that the man is given toad's liver and shows signs of recovery. Mr Congdon wants us to conclude that the doctors were wrong. This is slightly unfair since Mr Congdon provides a 'theory' of how toad's liver may do good to the patient." The quotation is from Hahn's letter in *The Times*, 29 July 1981, in response to Tim Congdon's letter of July criticising the contents of the '364 Letter'; quoted in Booth (2006b, p. 35, n13). Needless to say, disagreements over the Letter remain rife.

monetary tightness: a large deficit is most cheaply financed by printing money. I therefore defended the Thatcher policies against my fellow economists vigorously in a Times article, though I was a sadly lone voice; typically, she wrote me a personal letter with reassuring words. Fortunately, attempts to get rid of her and reverse the policies failed; the economy recovered well from around that time and by 1983 it was growing robustly. (Minford, 2013)

From Booth again:

> The whole of the academic establishment—including some luminaries of today—stood against the government. The 364 included Third-Way guru Anthony Giddens; the current Governor of the Bank of England; Monetary Policy Committee member Stephen Nickell; and former and future Nobel Prize winners. Only a brave few stood out against them. Indeed, it is said that Mrs Thatcher was asked in heated debate in the Commons whether she could even name two economists who agreed with her. She replied that she could: Patrick Minford and Alan Walters. As the story goes on, her civil servant said when she returned to Downing Street: 'It is a good job he did not ask you to name three'. (Booth, 2006a)

The ramming through of the Thatcherite monetarist agenda occurred against the unequivocally expressed misgivings of an overwhelming majority of professional economists drawn from diverse schools of thought. Writing in 1976, David Laidler, another diehard monetarist Friedmanite,[19] observes:

> The view that the quantity of money is unimportant is an article of faith in British Keynesian economics, receiving its most famous statement in the Radcliffe Report. It is still influential. ... There has, however, always existed a minority of economists in Britain who have taken the opposite position on this matter ... for instance, Lionel Robbins, Frank Paish, Alan Walters, and Harry Johnson. So-called 'monetarist' views however have never, as far as one can tell, had any influence on policy. (Laidler, 1976, p. 485, n1)

That was David Laidler writing ruefully in 1976; he would only have to hold his breath for another three years before David prevailed over Goliath, when in 1979 Thatcher turned the tables on Keynesian received wisdom in government policy: the protest by the 364 economists was flatly rejected. In its aggressive response the government scribe stated that

> the Government has read with interest the four points to which these 364 economists subscribe. The Government, however, agree with the substantial school of economists which do believe that there is a strong connection between monetary growth and the rate of inflation, and has itself set out its thinking on this in evidence to the Treasury Select Committee. So far as output and employment are

---

[19] David Laidler obtained his PhD from Chicago in 1964 and had apprenticed with Milton Friedman and Anna J. Schwarz as a research assistant in their *Monetary History of the United States, 1867–1960*, published in 1963.

concerned, the Government's supply side policies have been designed with the objective of raising both output and employment specifically in mind. Such policies are directed in particular to fostering the more effective working of market forces and the restoration of incentive. But experience has shown that injections of monetary demand can at best have limited effect, and are ultimately counter-productive. For these reasons, the Government totally disagrees with the assertion that present policies will deepen the depression and weaken the UK's industrial base. Countries pursuing policies broadly of the kind being implemented here are those with the strongest industrial base. It is conspicuous that although the 364 economists assert that there are alternative policies, they are unable to specify any such agreed alternatives. (Booth, 2006b, pp. 132–133)

6.1.8 *Thatcher in the Garage of the Federal Reserve*

The 'substantial school of economists' to which the government response alludes was to be found, of course, not (as was plain from the letter) in the UK, but in the USA, where Friedmanite monetarism was taking hold of government policy under the supervision of Paul Volcker. And further, the reference to the application of monetarism in "countries ... with the strongest industrial base" surely refers again to the USA (unless Thatcher and Walters had in mind the case of Chile, where Walters was closely involved in the Friedman-Pinochet extreme monetarism implemented by the Chicago boys, who proudly boasted that the origins of Thatcherism lay in their pre-dating monetarist exercise in Chile from the early years of the Pinochet regime).

The Hayek-Friedman school regarded inflation as socially immoral and argued that restraining money supply was the cure. Says Volcker (2000, p. 12):

> Inflation is related to monetary policy. It's related to the issue of money. The issue of money is a governmental responsibility predominantly, and to use that authority in a way that leads to inflation is a system that fools a lot of people, and to keep fooling them you have to do it more and more; [that] is a moral issue. I put myself in that camp. ... It corrodes trust, particularly trust in government. It is a governmental responsibility to maintain the value of the currency that they issue. And when they fail to do that, it is something that undermines an essential trust in government.

Here, Volcker's position is virtually identical to Hayek and Friedman, as well as Thatcher and Joseph.

There were parallel tracks with distinct points of comparison between Reagan's USA and Thatcher's UK; these are best picked up in the words of Volcker himself. One of these was the relationship between labour and government in the time of inflation. Volker says:

> One of the major factors turning the tide on the inflationary situation was the [air traffic] controllers strike [of 1981] about wages [and] working conditions. But the controllers were government employees, and the government didn't back

down. And he [Reagan] stood there and said, 'If you're going to go on strike, you're going to lose your job, and we'll make out without you'. That had a profound effect on the aggressiveness of labor at the time, in the midst of this inflationary problem and other economic problems. That was something of a watershed. (ibid., p. 14)

Reagan fired 11,345 striking air traffic controllers and banned them for life from federal employment and decertified their union. The comparison with the miners' strike in the UK, and Thatcher's direct assault on trade unions, is immediate.

There was a Reagan revolution in terms of the cutting edge of this moving back from this feeling that [if] you've got a problem, the government would answer it. Here's a big brother here to help you, as Mr. Reagan used to mock ... He did it with some vigor ... in a way that helped restore the confidence of America in America, which had been lost, or at least greatly eroded, during the 1970s. (ibid.)

America had been humiliated in Vietnam; Reagan's bellicose stance and his Star Wars dramatics reinjected American nationalism into the political bloodstream. Thatcher did the same with the Falklands war. Volcker says: "In some ways what we were doing was paralleling what she was trying to do, and even in some ways on the inflation side it was very close. She admired tough monetary policies. We got along pretty well" (ibid.). "I was a great admirer of hers. She was taking a tough stand, trying to change the direction of Britain. They had had a lot of problems that we had in the 1970s, so I had enormous respect for what she was trying to do. I thought she was much tougher, ... much more driven that I was" (ibid., p. 15). Thatcher would drop in to see Volcker when she was in the USA, and he would reciprocate when in London. "She always came to see me, which was always slightly embarrassing that the prime minister of the UK was driving into the Federal Reserve garage instead of the other way around" (ibid., p. 14).

Volcker regards the parallel movements in the USA and UK against inflation, alongside the privatisations in the UK and the deregulation drive in the USA, as marking the beginning of a world movement with the so-called retreat of government from the economy: "what happened in the United States, similar to what happened in Britain, had a big influence on others" (ibid., p. 16). One might add, with respect to the developing economies, that this influence was often exerted through the structural coercion by multilateral agencies which were under the control primarily of the OECD group, as demonstrated in the global roll out of the Washington Agenda of structural adjustment and stabilisation in the developing economies after the debt crisis following the oil price hikes of the 1970s.

Of course, an alternative narrative is possible, and Tony Benn, speaking in 2000, leaves little unsaid about the contributions of Margaret Thatcher:

The voting machine and the ballot box do give you a chance to sack the people who govern you, and that means they have to listen. But there's no way you can sack the corporations or the gamblers. You can't sack them at all. They're there forever. What Mrs Thatcher did was to take the huge power of the state and transfer it from looking after people to looking after big corporations. And now people are being driven back to where they were before the Industrial Revolution when they were serfs in the presence of the great barons of the private corporations, most of which were international in character.

She destroyed our manufacturing industry. She brought unemployment to the highest rate we've had since the pre-war years. She began to dismantle the welfare state. She deprived the health service of the resources that it needed. She deprived education, schools, and so on, and she did enormous damage to the fabric of society. In the end, her own party threw her out. They didn't want her anymore. They introduced the poll tax, and that finished her off. So I think Mrs. Thatcher will not be remembered as a great figure, but she was a passionate advocate of money running the world instead of the people running their own society. That was her great contribution to a debate that I think she has lost.[20]

The interviewer gently chides Tony Benn: "You say she has lost the debate, but on the whole, what appears to be more or less Thatcherite policies—privatization, deregulation, and so on—are sweeping the world. It's not re-nationalisation and collectivism." But Benn, citing the New Deal and the British Welfare State as illustrations of alternatives, disagrees. "This idea that market forces have won the day is a complete illusion, spread by academics adhering to this new religion of monetarist fundamentalism. Monetarism is much more dangerous than Islamic fundamentalism."[21] But the New Deal and the British Welfare State were precisely the projects that Reagan and Thatcher were dismantling at the time, with spite, speed and success.

6.1.9   1981: Brixton Riots, Toxteth Fires: "A Concentration of Hopelessness"

Andy Beckett (2015) excavates two contrasting Liverpool narratives about 1981 that set the stage. While the protesting economists were getting together setting pen to paper, youth in Toxteth were gathering on streets, setting fire to cars and buildings. Black youth unemployment here was recorded at over 80 per cent. Patrick Minford, of Liverpool and of the Liverpool Model, was a faithful and faith follower of his monetarist PhD supervisor Alan Walters—then the chief economic adviser to Thatcher—and of the grand guru of both, Milton

---

[20] This view of Thatcher and Thatcherism arguably bears more than passing affinity with the contemporary policy perspectives developed by the Godley-Cripps CEPG in Cambridge during the 1971–1981 decade. Francis Cripps is the grandson of Sir Stafford Cripps, the socialist Labour politician, co-founder of the left-wing Tribune group, and MP for Bristol, a constituency then passed on to the leftist Tony Benn, who served as the Secretary for Energy in the Callaghan government, and had Francis Cripps, then with the CEPG, as an economic advisor.

[21] Quotations from the Commanding Heights interview (Benn, 2000).

Friedman. Minford, with his Liverpool Macroeconomic Model, was primed to prove the viability of Thatcher's monetarism. "In the Liverpool Model, we were too optimistic about the speed with which the economy would ... come right; ... the bit we were way out on was unemployment" (Minford, quoted in Beckett, 2015). Beckett writes: "Minford conceded that the sheer scale of the shake-out in Britain's jobs market had surprised him. The initial versions of the Liverpool Model had assumed, as did many Thatcherites, that the country's 'natural' rate of unemployment was low, and therefore purging the economy of inefficiencies with monetarism would mean, at worst, hundreds of thousands of redundancies—rather than millions" (ibid.).

But the shake-out had not shaken Minford's belief in his guru and gospel. "Unemployment is ... unlikely to cause major unrest," Minford had written just weeks before Toxteth was burning. Did that matter? It would appear not: "The thing is, I think the behaviour in Liverpool really pointed up the sanity of Margaret Thatcher's policies—all she had to say was, 'Look, the policies are working, and there's nowhere more in need of them than Liverpool'" (ibid.). "I was regarded with a mixture of contempt and hatred by colleagues in the profession," says Minford, but "I just wrote them off. I thought, 'It's lucky I don't want a get a chair anywhere else. I've got my chair in Liverpool. No one can stop me!'" (ibid.).

Minford might have had cause for thinking otherwise when the 364 economists, of all persuasions and from the full spectrum of political colours—barring monetarists and Thatcher whateverists—signed their unprecedented collective protest. But he needn't really have worried, even if he had the support of just one man and one woman—the man was Alan Walters, and the woman happened to be Margaret Thatcher.

John Hoskyns,[22] whose maternal grandfather had once been the MP for Toxteth—the scene of the inner-city Liverpool Riots in July 1981 involving the local police and heavily unemployed black community—"saw little point in spending more money in Liverpool saying 'this money is likely to be money wasted'". Likewise, Geoffrey Howe, the Chancellor, equated spending money on Merseyside with trying to "pump water uphill" (Travis, 2011). "Thatcher's closest advisers told her that the 'concentration of hopelessness' on Merseyside was very largely self-inflicted with its record of industrial strife"; pushing this were Keith Joseph, John Hoskyns and Robin Ibbs. Heseltine had wanted £100 m for a regeneration but was met with hard opposition from Howe and Co: "Isn't this pumping water uphill? Should we go rather for a 'managed decline'? This is not a term for use, even privately. It is much too negative ..." (ibid.). Howe implied that Heseltine was inventing for himself "a godfather

---

[22] Sir John Hoskyns played a significant role in formulating the Thatcherite economic and political strategy through his 'Stepping Stones' Report in 1977. He was highly regarded by Thatcher: "He propagated the theory that a 'culture of decline' was the ultimate cause of many of Britain's economic problems" (Thatcher, 1993, p. 30); he also argued that the intransigence of the trade unions, in the face of inflation, had to be overcome as a precondition. For good advice and loyal support, Thatcher elevated Hoskyns to a knighthood in 1982.

role", as a "minister for Merseyside". In his argument, Heseltine had referred to the 30–50 per cent unemployment in several inner-city areas. When Thatcher went to Merseyside 'to listen' to 'them'; the black community complained bitterly about local police tactics; the Archbishop of Liverpool, Derek Worlock, told her that there was "a silent colour bar" and that the local community was imbued with a "hatred of the police" (ibid.). Travis reports that the meeting records the attitude of the Merseyside Chief Constable, Kenneth Oxford: "He believed in slapping people down and keeping them down[23] ... The police had attacked the very community leaders who had tried to bring the riot to an end. They said the Liverpool police regarded anyone who was black as a criminal and acted accordingly." The 'colour-blind' Thatcher condemned the rioters as criminals. Travis refers to "her well-documented reaction to the first televised pictures of rioting and looting in Toxteth—'Oh, those poor shopkeepers'; ... While she stood firm against Heseltine's attempt to create a traditional Tory drive to save Britain's inner cities, Whitelaw set about re-equipping the police with more modern helmets, shields and batons that would prove as important as building up coal stocks in Thatcher's showdown with the miners in 1984" (ibid.).

6.1.10 The CEPG: A Thorn in the Thatcher Hide

In the 40-month period between May 1979, when Thatcher assumed power, and October 1982, when the SSRC handed out its negative decision to CEPG, Wynne Godley wrote 33 letters to the press, all critiques of government policy; barely a week passed without a CEPG pigeon delivering the next irritating instalment to the government. Godley, CEPG and the Cambridge left-Keynesians were somehow always there to be seen and to be heard. And Nicky Kaldor could be trusted to be prominently audible and visible: notable in this

---

[23] An attitude that was shared, Amiya Bagchi reports, with Alan Walters, Thatcher's hardline monetarist adviser. "Changing the law was not, however, enough: examples had to be made. The government inflicted 'a series of defeats on unions in set-piece battles with the public sector, and encouraged private sector employers to take on the unions'. The first to face Margaret Thatcher's iron fist were the steelworkers in 1980, who lost a thirteen-week strike battle and would pay the price with thousands of jobs. She also privatised public utilities, the railways, electricity and gas. All of them were downsized and trade unions lost members. By the time Margaret Thatcher finished her eleven-year reign, trade unions had lost half their numbers. As Sir Alan Walters told me at an Asian Development Bank seminar in Manila: 'I told Mrs Thatcher to kick the trade unions, and go on kicking them when they were down'" (Bagchi, 2019). Bagchi's recall is entirely credible: In his personal diary for 1981, Walters (1981) has an entry for July 10 saying "More bloody riots ... usual excuses"; and another on July 27, "'Willie Whitelaw very much approves of my measures. He said Brixton is where 'Enoch is right. It is the only place'. Railton Road should be bulldozed." Not known are what other measures Walters might have suggested, apart perhaps from flattening Railton Road, the epicentre of the Brixton Riots (or Brixton Uprising as it was also called by others) during 10–12 April 1981.

context was his hard-hitting evidence to the Treasury and Civil Service Committee in July 1980.[24]

Sandwiched between these dates came the comprehensive version of the CEPG-Cambridge in the form of a detailed analysis, and warning to the nation of "The Economic Consequences of Mrs Thatcher", an article that appeared in the *Cambridge Journal of Economics* in 1981, jointly authored by four members of the CEPG team, Ken Coutts, Roger Tarling, Terry Ward and Frank Wilkinson (Coutts et al., 1981).

> The Thatcher Government has embraced a doctrinaire monetarist strategy for controlling inflation and a laissez-faire approach to the supply side of the economy without attempting to moderate the social impact of these policies ... Unemployment is at a level not experienced since the inter-war depression and increasing rapidly towards 3 million, or 13% of the labour force, which would mean rates of 20% and above in large areas of the country. ... It is not just a matter of the financial hardship suffered by those thrown out of work through no fault of their own, or of the strain imposed on the social welfare system, but also of the mental stress, disillusionment and sense of helplessness which come with not being able to find a job. This could well have a damaging long-term effect on attitudes to work, particularly among young people condemned to go straight from school on to the unemployment register and is almost bound to lead to widespread social unrest. (Coutts et al., 1981, p. 81)

Coutts et al. conclude with dire warnings:

> what is clear is that the longer attempts are made to keep down Government borrowing as output falls and the longer support for industry is withheld, the more the economy will be driven into recession and the more complete will be the destruction of the industrial base. There will be no self-generated recovery. Such is the deflationary impetus of present policies and such is the speed with which the situation is deteriorating, it will take a long time merely to get back to where we are now. (ibid., p. 92)

The Cambridge authors surmise that "the economy has behaved more or less precisely as a Keynesian analysis would have predicted: the response to deflationary measure has taken the form almost entirely of reduction in real output rather than lower inflation" (ibid., p. 87). Coutts et al. observe that "all the major forecasting models [including those from the two Cambridge macro-modelling teams] are predicting a further fall in output between 1980 and 1981, the size ranging from 1 to over 3%" (ibid., p. 84, n2); only Professor Patrick Minford, the Thatcher minion's predictions from Liverpool, supported the government's stance.

From the CEPG, Terry Ward adds alarming detail to the grim scenario. "In 1956 unemployment in the UK stood at 250,000 or 1 percent of the labour

---

[24] An anti-monetarism classic: see Kaldor (1980).

force. Ten years later it was 350,000. By 1976 it had risen to 1.25 million or 5 per cent. Toward the endo of 1981 it was just under 3 million, or over 12 percent of the workforce, and according to virtually all forecasters, it will go on rising. The figures, moreover, exclude unemployed school-leavers, elderly people forced into premature retirement, and the many married women discourage from trying to find work. They also exclude almost half a million people temporarily employed on official government schemes and an equally large amount of concealed unemployment in services." Ward, a Senior Research Officer at the DAE, pins the tail on Thatcherite monetarist austerity: "between 1979 and mid-1981 GDP has fallen by considerably more than over any equivalent period since the war. Manufacturing output has declines by 16 percent; this exceeds the fall in the worst years of the Great Depression, 1929 to 1931 (11 percent). Manufacturing production in 1981 is no higher than it was in the mid-1960s, and in some major industries it is back to the level of the 1950s" (Ward, 1982, pp. 516–517). "Rising exchange rates made British manufacturing even more uncompetitive; and North Sea oil was used to support consumption rather than a longer-term strategy of structural transformation of British manufacturing" (Ward, 1982).

Coutts et al. challenge the basis of the Government's monetarist approach: "The lack of any sound theoretical basis or empirical support for these assertions has not inhibited the Government from regarding them as fundamental truths, central to its policy approach" (ibid., p. 82); "The philosophy underlying this strategy is clear. It amounts to a rejection of the Keynesian principles on which economic policy in the post-war period has largely been based" (ibid., p. 83); "All this has the frightening ring of pre-Keynesian times, before the importance of effective demand was recognised, when insistence on wage cuts as a cure for endemic unemployment produced only bitter conflict between workers and employers" (ibid., p. 83). This indictment resonates with the words of Joan Robinson in her Tanner Lecture delivered the same year, 1981, in the USA:

> The Keynesian thesis is now (in 1981) being illustrated the reverse way round in the U.K. Cutting central and local government expenditure and keeping the sterling exchange rate high so as to encourage imports is increasing unemployment and inhibiting growth. ... I hope you are going to make a very thorough study of the consequences of Mrs. Thatcher's policies in the U.K. before you allow President Reagan to pursue them here. (Robinson, 1981, pp. 282–283)

She was a little late with her warning—which would have fallen on deaf ears anyway—as Paul Volcker, appointed by Jimmy Carter in 1979 and retained by Reagan as the Chairman of the Federal Reserve Board, had already set about dispensing monetarist medicine to cure American inflation with predictable effects on American workers and industry. Reagan and Thatcher were in sync, so to speak.[25]

6.1.11 The Bogey of Import Controls and the Spectre of Bennism

With its novel theoretical take on Keynesianism, its radical interventionist policy package and its associated political affinities, the generally 'left-wing' CEPG was attracting a full circle of antagonistic reaction in the national domain, but even within Cambridge itself. The neoclassicals were naturally antagonistic towards anything anti-'free market'; the econometricians, especially outside Cambridge, were annoyed with the CEPG's modelling methodologies; the traditional Keynesians were up in arms against the 'New Cambridge' interpretations that underlay the policy position of the CEPG group; for some, wartime memories of shortages were revived causing alarm; for political moderates and conservatives, the Bennite connection generated hostility if not panic. Locally, one opinion held that the CEPG was riding on the street-cred of the 'Cambridge' logo to push its own political agenda; for all rivals or opponents, it was open season for attacking the Kaldor-Godley-Cripps group.

Public opinion, lay and professional, was mobilised by a willing media against the 'left' wing policy options proposed by the CEPG by floating an exaggerated bogey of import controls and invoking the traumatic baggage of wartime memories of rationing. The tinder-box atmosphere of public debate prompted the *New Scientist* to organise a high-profile symposium around the issue of whether UK was, or could become, totally self-sufficient. The papers discussed at the conference—held on 19 March 1975 at the Café Royal, London, with Sir Michael Swann as Chair—were published as a symposium "Towards Self-sufficiency?" in *New Scientist* (1975, March 20) and included contributions on energy, food and agriculture, minerals, waste, and economic self-sufficiency.

---

[25] Following the Coutts et al. (1981) evaluation, Kevin Albertson and Paul Stepney (2020: 319) construct another elaborate report card on the consequences of Thatcher: "we judge Thatcher's policies by no standards other than her own. Utilising a holistic approach, we consider whether neoliberal policies facilitated or undermined the UK's achieving Thatcher's stated moral outcomes: the growth of democratic capitalism and the strengthening of the moral economy. We demonstrate, in contrast to contemporary narratives of her "saving the country", the neo-liberal economic experiment has failed to deliver, even on Thatcher's own terms." This begs the question: was there another prefabricated agenda in that handbag: she knew what she wanted to do, and she knew how to do it. Albertson and Stepney quote David Cameron saying "she made Britain great again"; and that she did for all those, arguably the majority, with imperial nostalgia and hangovers, when she went to war over the Falklands-Malvinas. She—had wanted to take left Keynesianism out of the policy corridors and replace it with a gross monetarism—and she managed that very well too; she wanted to sell off some of the national silver in the form of public sector enterprises, and she did so in a regressive manner adding to inequalities. She had wanted to reboot the game, shift goalposts of national discourse—and that was done too, as Albertson and Stepney observe, with the sustained support of the neoliberal media barons. Egged on by Hayek and Friedman from the outside and a raft her politicians and advisers within, she had the firm intention of smashing trade union power—and she was spectacularly successful in that. She set about trade unions and the miners; after increasing sharply in the 1970s, trade union membership fell from 13.2 million in 1979 to 9.3 million in 1991.

Specialists were asked by the moderator to respond to a very unlikely scenario resembling autarky: could UK survive? "It might be a silly question to ask. Short of a world war ... it is highly unlikely that Britain will ever have to think about national survival in these extreme terms. Nor do we suggest that any government should make self-sufficiency a matter of national policy to deal with our present trading difficulties. But we thought it was worth asking the question, after the unprecedented international activity of the past two years. ... Could we hold out? ... Could Britain, say, by 1980, stand an economic siege?" The responses to this extreme brief are understandably contingent and qualified, but they nevertheless allow the moderator, Peter Laurie, to reach a conclusion: "Well, the answer is, broadly, that we could. ... From a practical point of view, these papers sketch a road to whose end we hardly want to go. But it might be worth moving a little way along the road, for although in an ideal world, a high level of international trade may be efficient, amid the instabilities of the real world it can expose a country heavily reliant on such trade to unseasonable buffeting. A modest increase in our capacity to provide for ourselves would save us many blows. It is something we should think seriously about."[26]

William Peterson, then a Research Officer in the Cambridge Growth Project in the DAE, and who could not fairly be labelled as a fellow traveller of the left-wing Keynesian group of the CEPG, using the CGP model "shows that although self-sufficiency means large changes in employment, our standard of living, measured in money terms, would hardly be changed" (ibid., p. 706). Of course, the model is unable to catch all transitional difficulties; "the model has not been designed to consider the problems of transforming foreign exchange dealers into ploughmen." Peterson provides a bottom line to the debate: "it is difficult to resist the comment that all that this exercise shows is that the UK is still capable of fighting the Second World War, an experience which I would have thought most people would prefer not to repeat. It is clear from the estimates presented here that self-sufficiency would involve a loss of private consumption and of economic welfare, and although quantitatively this loss may be comparatively small, I can see no economic argument at all for recommending the voluntary adoption of a policy of maximal self-reliance. But I suppose it is comforting to know that the safety net is there if it is really needed" (ibid.).

---

[26] Focussing on energy, Dr Walter Marshall, FRS, Chief Scientist at the Department of Energy and Director of the Atomic Energy Authority's Harwell research establishment, opines, "the world is in a strange situation which I can best describe as a 'creeping crisis'", and after his analysis concludes that "Britain should soon be self-sufficient in energy; the aim of today's research and development policy must be to extend that independence for as long as possible" (New Scientist, 1975, p. 695). Dr Kenneth Blaxter, FRS, Director of the Rowett Research Institute and consultant director of the Commonwealth Bureau of Nutrition, concludes that "agricultural and nutritional calculations show that we could, if necessary, become self-sufficient in food", though there could be some difficulties in "the amount of fat", which would call for some policies of the adjustment of the sizes of the different herds of cattle. "It is reassuring to know that we could feed ourselves, given the original, curious premise that we cannot purchase food from abroad. ... Whatever the future holds, it would be prudent to take some steps in that direction now" (ibid., pp. 697, 702). With respect to minerals, there could be shortfalls in a range of expensive minerals.

In this context, Ron Smith, then very much a member of the Cambridge 'left' grouping, recollected "Reddaway telling [his] women's clothing story as an argument against our proposals of import controls" (personal communication). The reference is to Brian Reddaway's role in providing an algorithm for a scheme for the rationing of women's clothing during the war years.[27]

The brief given to the specialists was of a hypothetical scenario close to autarky and, comforting as it might be to confirm that Britain could carry on through another war, it would be fallacious to equate such an exercise with the CEPG's policy-mix which included the selective management of imports through tariffs and/or controls for a discrete time frame, with the objective of enhancing the competitiveness of British manufacturing to levels where open trading policies, with good growth rates and acceptable exchange rates, would not generate large foreign trade imbalances. For many, such high-octane media discourse could well have had the effect of intensifying, rather than allaying, their smoky fears about Bennism.[28]

Underlying this since the 1970s was a raging battle for the soul of the Labour Party, with the Bennite left constructing a radical challenge to the inherited, and now widely acknowledged to be failing, traditional Labour formulae around conservative Keynesianism. The Labour left offered its own Alternative Economic Strategy (AES) to this compromised Keynesianism and the slide into monetarism. "The AES, had it been implemented, would have preserved the Keynesian commitment to full employment but sought to underpin it with a regime of expanded public ownership, price and rent controls, economic planning, the expansion of social housing, a wealth tax, and an extensive programme of economic democracy, including democratisation of the nationalised industries—all in all, what Benn memorably termed 'a fundamental and irreversible shift in the balance of wealth and power in favour of working people and their families' (Medhurst, 2014, p. 11)" (Guinan, 2015, p. 28).

[27] For Richard Kahn's version of this story, see Chap. 4, p. 15, n.25.
[28] Away from the media glare, Cripps and Godley (1978) set out the considered rationale of the CEPG case for import controls for UK in a think-piece in the *Cambridge Journal of Economics*. "Fiscal expansion accompanied by direct control of imports (whether through tariffs or quotas) is the only practical means by which the UK, and probably several other industrial countries, can sustain expansion of national output sufficient to restore full employment in the next decade". Using alternative scenarios, they argue that "the use of import controls fiscal expansion to raise the level of activity need not be a 'beggar-my-neighbour' policy". They argue that "control of imports need not 'featherbed' inefficiency in domestic industries. On the contrary, expansion of demand made possible by import control is likely to assist innovation and productivity growth". And they caution that "creeping protectionism, adopted on an *ad hoc* basis, may reduce world trade … and may perpetuate inefficiency if it involves the subsidy of obsolete processes in conditions of stagnation" (Cripps & Godley, 1978, p. 327). This import-substitution strategy is paired with the imperative of the expansion of exports, and here they point out that "it is by now firmly established that the ability to see in world markets turns not only on relative prices but also on a host of other 'quality' factors"—developing international competitiveness in industrial exports was crucial for success, and a degree of contingent protection coupled with fiscal expansion stimulating demand were vital preconditions. The fundamental premise is that UK's longer-term economic prospects rested on reversing the process of deindustrialisation, then ongoing, into a dynamic revival a competitive export-oriented manufacturing sector, and that this could not be achieved simply by devaluation.

There was a fundamental contribution of the younger cohort of Cambridge left economists in the construction of this alternative platform involving also the Institute of Workers' Control (IWC) and Ken Coates, its Director. Joe Guinan (2015, pp. 29–30) writes: "The IWC played a critical role in the early formulation of these alternatives. In 1974 Ken Coates published, under the auspices of Spokesman Books, a pamphlet by Michael Ellman, Bob Rowthorn, Ron Smith, and Frank Wilkinson,[29] a group of left-wing economists at Cambridge, entitled *Britain's Economic Crisis*, which was 'offered as a discussion document in the hope that it will stimulate debate within the labour movement on alternative socialist strategies for the British economy' (Cambridge Political Economy Group, 1974, p. 2). In this it succeeded, becoming one of the precursors of the AES advanced by the left inside and outside the Labour Party in the seventies and eighties" (Guinan, 2015, pp. 29–30).[30]

"The work of the IWC unfolded against this dynamic background, both feeding into and drawing upon the greatest upsurge in working class industrial mobilisation and militancy in Britain in half a century. … As the crisis of long-term underinvestment in British industry grew increasingly apparent, the IWC understood something that continued to elude Labour's traditional social democrats: that the social and economic arrangements of the post-war settlement were simply unsustainable. Like the Thatcherites critiquing the status quo from the

---

[29] There was a long-standing connection between Ken Coates and Frank Wilkinson. Frank, the fourth of eleven children, left school at 15, became a farm labourer, then served as a cook in the Army Catering Corps, and upon returning from national service, became a steel worker at Stanton Iron Works; "from there in 1959 he started day release on a joint venture between the Workers' Educational Association and Nottingham University Extra-Mural Department." Deakin and Ewing (2021) write that Frank was "encouraged by one of his lecturers to apply for a trade union scholarship to attend Ruskin College, Oxford in 1961". Jill Rubery notes that "Ken Coates was Frank Wilkinson's tutor at the extramural department in Nottingham when Frank was still a steel worker and was instrumental in Frank going to Ruskin College and then on to Cambridge" where Frank won a place to read economics at King's College and later took up a research position at the Department of Applied Economics, his permanent institutional base in Cambridge. (Jill Rubery, personal communication, email dated 29 November 2021). Amongst everything else he achieved, Frank was also one of the enthusiastic founders of the Institute of Employment Rights established in 1989—in a meaningful way completing the honourable circle from tutor to student; Coates investment in his working-class student had paid high returns and would surely have taken satisfaction from publishing this important document jointly authored by Frank.

[30] "Another source was the 1973 *Programme for Britain*, described by Tony Benn as 'the most radical and comprehensive pro-gramme ever produced by the Labour Party' (Thompson, 2005, p. 216). The basic elements of the AES were an expansionary policy of full employment to be achieved via a planned reflation of the economy through increases in public spending; capital controls and managed trade; an industrial strategy and firm-level planning, expanding public ownership and industrial democracy; a national economic plan; and price controls to combat inflation (Conference of Socialist Economists, 1980, p. 6). Workers' control, as propagated by the IWC, was a central component of the strategy, but would be flanked by major new public institutions such as the proposed National Enterprise Board, a state holding company modelled after the Italian Instituto per la Ricostruzione Industriale (IRI), which would establish a significant public stake in manufacturing industry and exercise control over both public and private sectors through a system of planning agreements with the hundred largest companies (Thompson, 2005, p. 217)" (Guinan, 2015, pp. 29–30).

opposite direction, the Labour New Left viewed Keynesianism as having lost much of its explanatory power. Observing important structural changes in the economy, they were driven to the supply side to look for root causes of crisis and decline. In this vein, the IWC played an important role in the development of wider left economic alternatives to both moribund social democracy and emerging neo-liberalism. Their response to the collapse of the post-war settlement was to call for the socialisation of capital and the democratisation of both the economy and the state—and, for that matter, of the Labour Party" (Guinan, 2015, p. 27).

Guinan (2015, pp. 20–21) highlights the dire background against which the AES emerged:

> massive corporate rationalisation and increasingly acute balance of payments problems were beginning to force the trade unions to widen their scope beyond pay and working conditions to substantive engagement with issues related to corporate strategy, investment, and production itself. This raised questions about the wider social costs of plant closures and the need to broaden the basis of economic decision-making beyond a narrow commercial focus on balance sheets of profit and loss within a given company to 'the democratic expression of social needs' (Thompson, 2005, p. 199). The possibilities inherent in an increasingly skilled and educated workforce were beginning to come to the fore. Earlier debates over workers' control within the Labour Party in the 1930s and 1940s had been closed down by arguments about the impracticability of workers assuming management responsibilities, epitomised by Stafford Cripps' claim, during the 1946 debates over nationalisation, that it would be 'extremely difficult to get enough people who are qualified to do that sort of job, and, until there has been more experience by workers of the managerial side of industry, I think it would be almost impossible to have worker-controlled industry in Britain' (Coates, 1975, p. 50). By the onset of the 1970s it was no longer possible to make such excuses, as Britain had 'probably the most industrially experienced work-force in the world' (Scanlon, 1968). (Guinan, 2015, pp. 20–21)

Following his grandfather, two generations later, Francis Cripps, as part of the Cambridge left group, was able to argue the converse, viz., that under contemporary conditions, the strategy of workers' involvement and control at industrial level was viable and desirable.

In his doctoral dissertation at the LSE on "Thatcherism and the remaking of the Labour Party 1979–1997", Richard Heffernan (1997, p. 130) observes that "a recent history of Labour's stance on public ownership can usefully begin in the policy debates of the 1970–1974 period from which emerged Labour's Programme for Britain 1973 and, in turn, the 1974 February manifesto. Together with an interventionist industrial strategy and planning agreements (as well as redistributive taxation and welfare policies), Labour committed itself to setting up a state holding company (a National Enterprise Board) which would acquire a large stake in manufacturing industry. Although Harold Wilson successfully fought off attempts to commit the party to the specific nationalisation of some twenty five companies, Labour's February 1974 manifesto accepted that North Sea oil, the docks, aircraft manufacture, and shipbuilding would be taken into public ownership. Public ownership was an integral part of what became known as the Alternative Economic Strategy (the AES)."

"In the face of the Cabinet's dramatic shift to the right in office, the party remained steadfastly committed to the politics of the 1973 Programme, and as such the 1974 manifesto became a symbol of thwarted radicalism: Here, the ideas around the AES and the radical Keynesianism of the Cambridge School were enthusiastically taken up by a party wholly disillusioned by what most party figures considered a disappointing government (even one embroiled in difficult economic circumstances) and which many deemed to have been unredeemedly reactionary. After the defeat of the Labour government in May 1979 the party imploded into bitter recriminations as the Labour left seized the political agenda. Public ownership was less of an issue in the battles between left and right than many others, most notably the question of incomes policy, Europe, and defence (as well as the constitutional battle for power waged between the parliamentary leadership and the Bennite insurgents" (Heffernan, 1997, p. 134).

"The election of 1979 saw the electorate turn out a Labour government that had been in office (however precariously) since 1974. The 1979–1983 period was a dramatic reaction to the 1979 defeat and the governmental record that preceded it symbolised by a left-wing sponsored grassroots revolt assisted by trade union discontent with the Callaghan leadership. Headed by Tony Benn, a high profile Labour figure who had opposed the direction of the Wilson and Callaghan governments from within the Cabinet, the Labour left wanted to commit the party to radical pledges to dramatically take British politics to the left. Whatever else may be said about the so-called 'Bennite' left (as problematic a term as Thatcherism), it too was a 'modernising' movement, one keen to advance a programmatic agenda and put right past failings evidenced in Labour's record in office in 1964–1970 and 1974–1979. Here, Labour's policy stance was based upon a root and branch rejection of everything the Thatcher Cabinet stood for. In its own way, Benn's argument was as radical as that offered by Thatcher: Labour had failed because its tried and tested prescriptions were no longer up to the job: by itself the existing mixed economy and public expenditure had proved illusory at a time Labour widely believed that the capitalism was no longer capable of sustaining the welfare politics upon which post-war Britain depended: Actually existing moderate social democracy had proved far too cautious for Labour to deal with the political and economic crisis it faced. ... both the National Executive Committee (NEC) and the Labour Conference came to represent alternative powerbases to the Parliamentary leadership. Encouraged by the weakness of the Labour leadership and a demoralised right wing (the two being virtually synonymous), the Bennite left pursued policy changes hand in hand with far reaching constitutional amendments to secure the predominance of the extra-Parliamentary party by limiting the powers of the Parliamentary leadership. Faced with the perceived necessity to ensure its leaders would deliver on policy promises in the future, the left organised around a constitutional agenda embracing the mandatory reselection of MP's; the election of the leader and deputy leader under a wider electoral franchise comprising party members, trade union affiliates and Labour MP's; and granting control of the party manifesto to the Executive at the expense of the Cabinet or the Shadow Cabinet. These were all devices to bind the parliamentary leadership to the wider party and to ensure that Conference policy would be implemented by a future Labour government" (Heffernan, 1997, pp. 118–119).

Thatcher won in 1979, and Callaghan gave up his leadership of Labour, and Michael Foot defeated Denis Healey and became the new leader, drifting to the centre, reflecting his status as a 'unity' candidate. Heffernan (1997, p. 120) writes that "Callaghan timed his departure to forestall the election of any successor under the wider franchise to be agreed at a one-day Conference in January 1981; in particular he wanted to deny Tony Benn a successful run at the leadership. Aware he could not win any election confined to Labour MP's, Benn declined to stand and backed Foot against Healey but once the electoral college for leadership elections was established he sought the deputy leadership, the consolation prize gifted Healey the previous autumn. Widely portrayed as a battle for Labour's soul, the contest which ensued between Healey, bete noir of the left, and Benn brought about an extended period of vicious Labour infighting which greatly exacerbated internal party tensions. Despite his efforts and his command of the support of Labour activists, Benn lost very narrowly by a margin of less than one per cent. While Benn's challenge had been welcomed by the broad left coalition he had assembled, it did divide the Tribune Group and helped create a group of 'inside leftists' led by Neil Kinnock. Their abstention in the deputy leadership ballot paved the way for Healey's narrow victory." Carlton (2016) provides a blow-by-blow account from the anti-left camp of how the anti-Benn vote was organised.

Heffernan (1997, pp. 123–124) concludes that "In hindsight, Tony Benn's narrow defeat for the deputy leadership in 1981 was both the highpoint of the left's fortunes and the beginning of the Labour right's successful efforts to claw back authority stripped away in earlier years. Under Michael Foot's successor, Neil Kinnock (and, in time, Tony Blair), both the organisational structures of the party and its policy and doctrine were transformed. The left was gradually weakened and its power within the party gradually whittled away; denied a majority on the NEC, its Conference base was slowly eroded and it was completely marginalised within the Parliamentary Party. As the left retreated, the revitalised Labour right (its ranks ever swollen by 'realigning' former leftists) advanced. By the late 1980s, Labour had gradually altered the cast of its policy. As a result, in contrast to past appeals, the party acknowledged the role of the state in the economy should be confined to the provision of the fiscal and monetary conditions required to enable the market to facilitate economic activity."

And this set the stage for the Labour slide into neo-Thatcherite, neoliberal strategies. The transition from Benn to Kinnock in national Labour politics was paralleled—in terms of Cambridge economics—in a significant sense, from Francis Cripps to John Eatwell. What is relevant in terms of the fate of the

Godley-Cripps CEPG group is that the rise and decline and demise of the Bennite left challenge against the conservative labour leadership was occurring at precisely at the point where its application to SSRC for the renewal of its core grant. Given this conjuncture, it is not implausible to conjecture that the eventual negative decision meted out by the SSRC causing the closure of the CEPG might have been made in circumstances where the criteria used might have been tinged with subliminal political considerations of (members of) committees not generally known for sharing the leftist Bennite perspective on the future of the UK economy. And Francis Cripps, as the close adviser to Tony Benn, was perhaps the lightning conductor absorbing the strike.

6.2 SSRC and CEPG: Dispensing Instant Injustice

In the upcoming SSRC funding cycle for macroeconomic research, when Keynesian CEPG was chopped down in 1982, Patrick Minford's monetarist Liverpool Model was a surprising beneficiary. No one saw that coming, except perhaps the backroom choreographers of the move, and the spotlight must turn to the players at the SSRC to which Michael Posner had been appointed Chairman in the dying days of the Callaghan Labour government before Thatcher swept into power in 1979. Posner, whose term ran from 1979 till 1983, was an experienced hand, well versed in the ways of Cambridge economics (and Faculty politics)—where he was a Reader at the Faculty and a Fellow of Pembroke—as also of Whitehall bureaucracy—where he had served in various capacities at HM Treasury, culminating in 1975–1976 in the position of Deputy Chief Economic Advisor. And he seemed to carry an old grudge and a chip or two into his new assignment.

6.2.1 Posner's Parlour

The short- and medium-term macroeconomic forecasting and policy work of the CEPG was underwritten primarily and on a regular basis by the cycle of project grants from the SSRC. A fresh grant application was duly made to the SSRC now run by Michael Posner, a long-standing New Cambridge and CEPG sparring partner. His tenure marked a dramatic turnaround in the thus-far supportive relationship between the SSRC/ESRC (Economic and Social Research Council) and the Cambridge/DAE modelling units that it had funded—the Cambridge Growth Project (CGP) since 1967, and the CEPG since 1971. The previous round had been funded prior to Posner's assumption of the Chairmanship of SSRC when it was under the watch of the renowned Oxford labour economist Derek Robinson who was unlikely to have taken any particularly deep personal interest in the mechanics of the SSRC funding of research on macroeconomic modelling, not really a topic at the top of his list. With Michael Posner it was different—this was the cacophonous cockpit he had been sparring and quarrelling in for a decade, and his approach was a full-energy hands-on one. Shortly after taking over, he set about redesigning the space, rearranging the furniture to welcome the next round of applicants into his parlour. He was well prepared: he had set up a Sub-committee to report on the state of macroeconomic research in the UK and to make recommendations about what and how to fund; he was responsible for its composition and chaired it himself. In this process, he engaged with the main academic and institutional players, and then wrote a paper on "the organisation and finance of the modelling effort in the UK"; in this he shared his perspectives on his general approach and specific plans (Posner, 1981). This note is revelatory in several ways and helps to explain the SSRC process and outcomes that followed.

Posner (1981) starts by stating that "this is as near as is possible a personal paper—it does not represent the considered opinion of any body or Committee within the SSRC"; this was "the first paper being circulated outside the Ad Hoc Committee on Macro-economic Models" set up and being chaired by himself. Yet, personal or not—reading between the lines and beyond the economist's two-handedness—the paper presents a fairly explicit plan of action, and that is quite the way that future action unfolded. As such, it provides a fair summary of Posner's personal views, and this has much relevance in deciphering what later happened, how, and possibly on what motive power.

Posner highlights "four substantial teams in the academic world with long-standing interests in this area": NIESR, the two Cambridge teams, viz., the Stone-Barker CGP and the Godley-Cripps CEPG, and the London Business School; he notes that "a Liverpool model (Minford) is developing" and there were a variety of other smaller-scale enterprises at Birkbeck, LSE and Imperial College. He notes the existence of some private sector initiatives, especially the 'St James Club' and 'the Henley Centre'. The 'big four' account for about 1m GBP per year, a small fraction of the heavy resource absorption in such activities within the Her Majesty's Treasury (HMT) and the Bank of England (BoE). Posner identifies "the high degree of vertical integration: model specification, econometric technique, computer algorithms, the preparation of forecasts and the provision of policy commentary ... all these are typically conducted by one team under the control of one of two persons ... leading to the stamping of each with a 'personality' and a separate identity." He asks rhetorically: "Is the activity of systematic modelling really worthwhile?" and answers, "YES." "The present extent of the diversity of views available is not wildly excessive, and the dispute about 'how the system works' that the exercise gives rise to can be instructive." He asks again: "How much is it worth spending on this sort of work?"—and then offers a very marginalist answer: "The only way to find answers is to consider alternative ways of saving some money, or of spending a bit more, and to compare the losses or gains from those changes with alternative actions." It would have been interesting to see what method of cost-benefit analysis Posner would use to get any sensible answer to this question. Noticeably, there is nothing said about pushing against the very low budget line set by the government, especially in comparison with the vast amounts spent on the sciences, and in contrast to the experience of other countries. Then: "Could we do without one of [the big four] completely? Could we afford to add another one or two? Could their scale be diminished keeping roughly the same number?" Posner points to the possibility of marginal net cost savings. But on the big question of closure, he says, "Any reduction in the diversity of opinion and approaches available must be severely limited if it is to be acceptable to a wide spectrum of opinion." And, there must be room left for a "reversible" expansion in funding of new entrants—which brings him to his "deliberately radical question" about how far each team could "be weaned ... from its reliance on public funds, ... by cutting off the supply of taxpayers' milk ... and transferred to dependence on a gritty diet of market-tested private money obtained in competition with other outfits in both the academic and non-academic sectors" (ibid., pp. 3–4).

Citing the case of the CGP—already goaded towards commercialisation earlier—he expostulates in one direction, then the other, and finally: "My own opinion is that there may be insufficient weight in the argument for privatization to enable us to press through such a change now against the forceful case for preserving at least the present degree of diversity of commentary" (ibid., p. 4). But then, he muddies the water again: "It is important that public sector involvement in this activity does not lead to the perpetuation and ossification of those institutions which happen to have established themselves by the fact of history. But I hope we won't be starry-eyed about this." Then, in what seems to be a typical trait, he swings the other way, again: "While it might be fun for grant-giving authorities [i.e., himself at SSRC] to stir the pot from time to time it would be grossly irresponsible to do so in a way which disrupts the necessarily complex and delicate network of academic and administrative arrangements carefully nurtured through the years in specific institutions." He borrows from the Science Research Council (SRC): would it be possible for the SRC "to deny any continued privileged existence to, say, the Cavendish Laboratory at Cambridge or to the National Physics Laboratory. I cannot believe that the SRC would accept that remit." But this must not "inhibit or discourage the introduction of new academic teams into this work", and anyway, "discouragement must not amount to prohibition". The barrier for new entrants "must be jumpable, and a particular skill required to make the leap should be a clearly defined innovatory promise, either in methodology, or in theoretical apparatus, or conceivably in policy interest". That said, Posner proceeds to raise the bogey of closure of one of the big four: in contrast to the "innovation" criterion applied to aspiring new entrants, "the task of judging whether some of the existing teams should be retired from the fray is however to be judged not only on technical grounds, but on grounds of general policy: this is deliberately asymmetrical with the criterion proposed for entry to the trade, and I believe that such asymmetry can be justified. This is not to say that technical criteria are wholly irrelevant in the testing of the performance of existing teams, far from it." As is fairly obvious from this instrumental dithering, Posner could arguably be read as preparing the ground for all eventualities—though significantly, he develops the case more than once for the closure of one of the big teams.

Posner's paper raises some questions. First, it is dated February 1981, well before Keith Joseph took over as Education Secretary in September 1981. This paper was preceded by the setting up of the SSRC Sub-committee, chaired by Posner himself, on Macroeconomic Research in the UK in April 1980; their report is filed in June 1981. Thus, Posner's paper presented to the Panel of Advisers at the Bank of England, in the interim, is during the period that he was completing his investigation and report, and could be regarded as a dry testing run for his approach, findings and likely implementation. As such, the paper is sourced in Posner's mind and agenda, and has little to do, at this stage, with the ensuing imbroglios with Joseph or Rothschild. It could be said, of course, that Posner might have anticipated the future and that the steps he was contemplating vis-à-vis macroeconomic modelling might have been a preparation for warding off future attacks, since Mark Carlisle, Joseph's predecessor, had already instituted cuts on the SSRC budget; this cannot really explain Posner's studied steps with regard to the SSRC funding of macroeconomic research.

Second, it is arguably an 'insiders' conversation' between the members of a mandarin club. Virtually everyone sitting in on this was from some government department or other, the majority comprising economists from the Treasury and the Bank; there is virtually no presence or voice of the academic community, though no doubt these bureaucrat-economists would wish to dig up their academic credentials buried somewhere under multiple overlays of their official assignments and engagements. This bias leads to an asymmetry of orientation and agendas: these government bureaucrats become the decision makers, and downstream academics are reduced effectively to decision takers. The SSRC was itself a government-funded body; and Posner, though nominally a Cambridge don, was more likely to be spotted donning one of his official hats at the Treasury or the Bank or the SSRC or the National Economic Development Office (NEDO). This tendency shows up in the contents of the paper in question. Demands are placed on all academics to raise private monies through the commercialisation of their respective products, viz., models; yet, the official players—HMT[31] and BoE which together account for 2.2 m GBP of the cost of macroeconomic work, with the academic sector costs being less than one-third of this, at 0.8 m GBP—have no strictures placed on them for the content or orientation of their work or to make it more cost effective in terms of their vast absorption of labour time and funds.

Third, the composition of the various committees involved in this do not stand up well to scrutiny in the sense that there is a clear conflict of interest: HMT and BoE, and their related, dependent experts and consultants, could justifiably be expected not to be too keen to recommend the funding of academic units and models that could and did challenge official policy prescriptions and

---

[31] "About a year ago the Treasury was known to employ about 50 professional man-years of staff on all sorts of macro-economic work, of which modeling and forecasting in only a part" (Posner, 1981, p. 1).

the models and methodologies underlying them. And indeed, the composition of the different committees was skewed in this direction, whether it was the membership of the Council, the Economics committee, or Posner's own Sub-committee on macroeconomic research or, crucially, the membership of the Consortium of donors that was formed on the recommendation of Posner's Sub-committee to decide on the choice of applicants to be funded.

Fourth, there is the puzzle of why a huge chunk of the funds, thought to be so scarce as to cut down long-running and dynamic research units, should be diverted on an annually recurrent basis to a permanent new unit which would not be doing the research but comparing the different models produced by various research units—"a new Centre for Quality Control, Comparison, and Common Services" (ibid., p. 7). It is possible to argue that this was a redundant, expensive and self-indulgent step, and little more could really be expected from such a Centre than a string of occasional papers that could perhaps have been left to the academics and aspiring scholars who would see this as a prime possibility for publications and advancing their careers.[32] That said, it has also been argued that the Bureau played a valuable role in ensuring quality control and productive interactions between groups. The Bureau was duly inaugurated, with Ken Wallis as its head.

After due to-ing and fro-ing, Posner concludes his note with his "tentative" plan: "A package involving: the trimming of existing activity; a firm push towards private finance; a controlled inflow of competition; and the development of a new facility for comparative work and common services, seems to me an appropriate way forward" (ibid., p. 7). There was nothing tentative about it; that is how he saw the process through. And finally: "For the funding agencies themselves, there are important question of machinery—who makes what decisions?—but those are probably not of concern to the Panel as such" (ibid., p. 7). And he was wrong or dissembling in this regard since "the funding agencies", including the BoE, HMT and the SSRC itself, were acutely interested in this process. It is relevant to note that Posner was presenting his views and getting a nod from this Bank of England Panel that was formed and chaired by

---

[32] The questionable rationale for this project is indirectly acknowledged in Posner's text: "The deficiencies of the present system—inadequate dissemination of the four teams' output in a way which would facilitate some kind of comparative analysis, and the absence of a systematic evaluation of that output—seem to call for the development of a centre whose remit would be to remedy these deficiencies and also perhaps to function as a common service unit by constructing a common data bank and offering access to programmes, equations and models to interested parties. The successful operation of such a centre which would be supported by public funds would depend heavily on the caliber of its people, especially its director. It may be argued that to contrast and compare is in itself a rather intellectually boring job and to attract good people would mean allowing them to develop yet another new model. I tend to discount this view—perhaps through excessive naivete. However some of the critical evaluation would inevitably need to be done by way of development work not all that different from the work that goes into model building. The cooperation of the four existing teams and of any newcomers would be imperative for the unit's work, and this might require modest but significant increases in the resources used" (Posner, 1981, pp. 6–7).

his CLARE (Cambridge, London and the Rest of England) friend and colleague,[33] Robin Matthews who, along with Frank Hahn, was formulating the strategy to restructure Faculty and DAE economics and power politics in Cambridge, and who therefore had an instrumental interest in the outcome of this 'machinery' that would make decisions about funding macroeconomic models, including those of the DAE that were targets in the Hahn-Matthews anti-heterodox campaign in Cambridge; the handlers of Posner's decision-making 'machine' were well populated with experts with shared affinities. The bustling and busy Posner, it seems, had assembled his game plan and the 'machinery' to deliver preferred outcomes. He could now welcome all comers into his parlour.

6.2.2 Posner's Process

SSRC's trial of the CEPG case was quick, and its judgement quicker. The attack was surprisingly sharp and short with the judgement pronounced, the appeal rejected and the death sentence carried out in the space of a month; to the aggrieved it might have had the feel of a kangaroo court handing out a lynching. The rather speedy and shabby mode of conduct of the episode could give rise to an innocent impression that the managers were in a bit of an unseemly hurry or possibly on something of a premeditated mission.

All macro-modelling teams were summoned to London for a briefing (on 18 February 1982) on recommendations of the Posner Sub-committee's Review, announcing the new Consortium and the proposed Macroeconomic Modelling Bureau. Thirty economists were on the listening side, including the CGP and CEPG teams. In due course, the CEPG team were summoned, in a letter[34] dated Wednesday, 17 March, to the SSRC to be interviewed by the Consortium the next Monday, 22 March, on their funding submission. In preparation for this interview, the initial letter received by CEPG from the Secretary to the Consortium informs CEPG about the points raised by the Consortium about its application, and seems innocuous, even complimentary: "The referees have praised your team's contribution to macro-economic debate. The CEPG emphasis upon the necessity of embedding national analysis in the general trends of the European and world economy—something being

---

[33] For instance, John Flemming, a core member of Matthews's CLARE Group, had moved base from Oxford to the Bank of England by this time; and he was known to be a strong antagonist of what was labelled left-wing Cambridge Keynesianism in its theoretical versions or in its applied incarnations in the Cambridge macroeconomic modelling. There were other members also who served on the Panel during the 1980s who were not kindly inclined towards CGP and/or CEPG, including, for instance, David Hendry.

[34] All letters cited are from the Archives of the Cambridge Growth Project held at the Marshall Library, University of Cambridge, and are quoted with permission. The SSRC-CEPG correspondence is filed in Folder CGP/41/3: "Folder containing copy of SSRC grant application and related correspondence between Cambridge Economic Policy Group (CEPG) which ran alongside CGP in the DAE. This includes issues raised between SSRC Macroeconomic Modelling and Forecasting Consortium and CEGP response in 1982."

developed by Francis Cripps—has attracted favourable comments." On the critical side, questions were raised about "the absence of cheap labour" of MSc/PhD students, and there is a suggestion that CEPG should be more explicit about its methodology, linking the quantitative research to its theoretical framework and "presenting simple mathematical versions of the model". Then the letter lists seven extremely generic questions (e.g. "Do markets clear in the long run?"; "Are unions important?"; "What are the fundamental determinants of inflation?" etc.)—"fundamental questions" which apparently the Consortium feels none of the teams test seriously. And members and consultants who attend "might wish to ask more technical questions". In a subsequent phone call before the interview, the Secretary informed Francis Cripps that one of the consultants had filed "an extremely critical report", but the substance of this criticism was not divulged. In the event, the interview, chaired by Michael Posner, turned out to be more of a grilling, with David Hendry and David Laidler throwing specific technical econometric questions at Godley and Cripps. The very next day apparently, on Tuesday, 23 March, the Consortium made its decisions, and the outcome for CEPG was communicated to Godley in a letter, dated 26 March, from Michael Posner. The Consortium, and hence the SSRC, was unwilling to provide any funding for the CEPG's modelling work, since "the technical properties of the model have received very critical comments" and "concern has been expressed about the team's interaction with other academics"; but Posner says that the Consortium values the CEPG contributions to macroeconomic debate and can offer funds for two research staff for this. (At this point, there were a dozen researchers and related staff on the CEPG rolls.) In his note of response, dated 5 April 1982, Godley points out the impossibility of continuing meaningful policy work without the macroeconomic modelling framework from which it derives and makes it clear that it is meaningless to fund policy work without funding the model on which it rests. Thus, with a single stroke, the Consortium/SSRC decision effectively kills off the CEPG initiative.

There are two strong responses from a shaken Godley. The first is a lengthy, detailed and meticulously argued rejoinder, in a Note dated 5 April, that provides a convincing rebuttal of virtually all the "technical criticisms", and other peripheral and some ill-judged charges levelled by the Consortium. The technical issues are conveyed by Francis Cripps for a definitive adjudication by Hashem Pesaran who finds no econometric merit in the criticisms that clearly formed a significant part of the justification for rejection.[35] The issue of the employment of students also receives a flat response: Cambridge rules do not allow such employment, and so on. The substantive basis of the Consortium's decision is thus directly challenged.

---

[35] *Francis Cripps to Hashem Pesaran*, Letter dated 2 April 1982; *Hashem Pesaran to Francis Cripps*, Letter dated 5 April 1982; *Wynne Godley to Michael Posner*, Letter dated 6 April 1982; Appendix B. Cambridge Growth Project Archives, Marshall Library, Faculty of Economics, University of Cambridge.

More significant is Wynne Godley's second communication, a three-page covering letter to Michael Posner, dated 6 April, that takes up the serious governance issue of multiple procedural lapses in the Consortium and SSRC's decision-making in this case. For one, the SSRC's Sub-committee, chaired by Posner himself, had indicated that the Consortium would be deciding on the distribution of funds between the existing teams, new entrants and the new proposed small macroeconomic modelling bureau; then, the guidelines made it clear that a fully detailed description of the work was not necessary and that there would be scope for amplification later in interactions and exchanges with referees or consultants; then there was the letter sent to CEPG a few months earlier saying that "the Consortium wishes referees' and consultants' comments to be made available to applicants so that there would be an opportunity for them to answer any critical points made" (quoted by Godley in his covering letter of 6 April 1982); then, CEPG was told of one very critical consultant, but without being provided the promised details for any response; some written comments were communicated to CEPG earlier about what might be addressed in the interview, but the interrogation then focussed on very different issues—"we had been given no notice of these two questions and could not answer them satisfactorily off the cuff" (ibid., p. 2). These were fully addressed and shown to be invalid in the lengthy Note attached by Godley to his letter. So, overriding his frustration one imagines, Godley concludes: "It therefore seems to me that the Consortium is not in a position to be sure that its decision was entirely fair and correct," and on this basis, he is moved "formally to ask the Consortium to reassess its decision ... on the grounds that the provisional decision notified in your letter of March 26th may have been the result of certain misunderstandings due in part to the rather truncated procedures which the Consortium followed in assessing applications" (ibid., p. 1). Godley points out that even at this last stage, he has not been made aware of the detailed substantive issues that might have been raised by the referees or consultants, and as such is prevented from assessing and responding to these. Usually, it was standard SSRC practice to make a site visit during which many such matters would have been expected to be considered and dealt with; but then again, CEPG did not receive the courtesy of such a visit either. The procedure was all over the place; the quick negative decision seemed already to have been in place. But all this fell on deaf ears; the 'impartial' policeman had taken 'evidence', found this undesirable to be 'loitering with intent to cross the road', in possession of 'thick lips' and 'curly hair', and proceeded with the incarceration.

The list of grants made in this SSRC round does include a minor grant to CEPG for 'policy work', but as Wynne had categorically indicated earlier, this was meaningless without the foundation provided by the CEPG modelling, simulation and forecasting work. The decision dealt a devastating personal blow to Wynne Godley, but not just to him: Francis Cripps, who had given up a Faculty position to move to CEPG, decided to leave—he took a year's sabbatical (in 1986) to which he was entitled and then resigned to relaunch his career (on another parallel productive trajectory); Terry Ward took a similar track, resigning in 1987; and virtually all CEPG staff, other than Frank Wilkinson and Ken Coutts, left their positions and had to seek careers elsewhere; Ken had shifted earlier to the Faculty as Assistant Director of Research. Wynne was badly scarred.

The later obituary in *The Telegraph* (2010) notes that "the work of the group came to an abrupt end when the ESRC (sic) cut off its funding without any consultation, an act widely attributed to Thatcherite vindictiveness". As Tiago Mata in his excellent (2012) piece on Wynne Godley writes: "It was payback time"; and the time keeper was Michael Posner, perhaps nursing his old disagreements and grudges, who devised the procedures, without fully following them, and selected the committees and consultants who wielded the knife, consciously—and Pontiusly—delegating to himself the sole role of being merely the reluctant carrier of the bad message.

The Godley-Cripps duo, through the CEPG, and other senior Cambridge economists, such as Nicky Kaldor, had made themselves a thorn in the side of the Heath Government with their persistent critiques through their policy reviews and public statements; and then generally carried on in similar vein, not pulling their punches, when the Wilson-Callaghan Labour governments made their compromises with the IMF. It is worth recalling that the 1970s were a politically charged decade: the Heath Government was hit by the first OPEC oil price hike; the Callaghan Government by the second in 1979 following the Iran-Iraq war; the 'incomes policy' was a shambles and inflation was spiking; internationally, the USA was deep in its apocalyptic Vietnam misadventure, shortly to be defeated in 1975; nationally, there was a rash of strikes; and locally in Cambridge, the first half of the 1970s had witnessed the famous Economics Faculty student protests leading to the sit-in at the Old Schools prompting an Enquiry by Lord Devlin, as well as angry anti-Vietnam War protests including the hostile receptions to Harold Wilson, Enoch Powell and Dennis Healey who apparently had to beat a hasty retreat from Cambridge under police protection. Cambridge had earned the reputation in the national media as a hotbed of leftist politics.

> In January 1981, [Keith Joseph] returned to Cambridge to defend the government against a motion of no confidence. He arrived with egg spattered over the back of his head. The students rejected Joseph's case and passed the motion, which had been proposed by the hated John Kenneth Galbraith. One of the eggs had hit Galbraith; Joseph immediately apologised, assuring his rival that he had been the real target. (Denham & Garnett, 2001, p. 357, n78; based on personal letter from Galbraith to Denham and Garnett)

Joseph regarded Galbraith as "about the most dangerous intellectual opponent that we have" (ibid., p. 317).

Meanwhile, the Cambridge left-Keynesians kept up with their regular exercise of throwing darts at the Thatcher regime: in the 33 months between the time the CEPG made its last application to the SSRC, and the point where SSRC made its negative decision, Wynne Godley and his colleagues published 40 letters in the national newspapers and journals, with the critiques becoming sharper and louder as Thatcher imposed her monetarist cutbacks.

Godley had made too many enemies in high places, amongst ministers as well as mandarins. Said someone, somewhere, will no one rid me of this turbulent priest? And lo and behold, Wynne Godley's head, immortalised already by his famous father-in-law, the sculptor Jacob Epstein,[36] wound up on an SSRC platter, detached from its CEPG body. Howsoever this was accomplished, it is unlikely that Keith Joseph or Margaret Thatcher, or for that matter Frank Hahn and Robin Matthews in Cambridge, were particularly displeased.

6.3 Epilogue

6.3.1 *Vengeance*

Through its uncompromising forthrightness, but more through challenging established political and material power structures, the CEPG made a host of enemies in right-wing governmental and political circles. "The highly regarded and at times controversial Cambridge Economic Policy Group headed by Wynne Godley [was] known to some as 'the Treasury in exile'" (Keegan, 2015). One obituary of Wynne Godley noted that the closure of the CEPG was "an act widely attributed to Thatcherite vindictiveness" (The Telegraph, 2010). William Keegan (2010) in *The Guardian* expanded on the theme: "The Thatcher government of 1979 onwards benefited enormously from Godley's pioneering work on public expenditure control. This did not stop that government from allying with certain academic rivals of Godley's to cut off the research grant on which his Cambridge economic policy group depended. This was a vindictive act by lesser mortals, and Godley felt bitterly hurt by it to his dying day." Similar sentiments were expressed from within academe. Schlefer (2013) writes: "In the early 1980s, the British Tory government, allied with increasingly conventional economists at Cambridge, began 'sharpening its knives to stab Wynne', according to Kumaraswamy Velupillai, a close friend who now teaches [at the time taught] at the New School in New York. They killed the policy group he headed, and ultimately, the Department of Applied Economics." Payback time, it indeed was, as Mata had pithily remarked.

But, on one view, they were not making new or retaining old friends within Cambridge either. An unsympathetic Cambridge confidant privy to the on-goings there during those turbulent years might argue that the

---

[36] Jacob Epstein used Wynne Godley's head as the model for his sculpture of St Michael slaying the Devil at the rebuilt Coventry Cathedral. The devil obviously survived to settle scores.

Godley-Cripps team had managed to antagonise sections of potential local support: the Old Keynesians were angry with the way New Keynesians connected the current account with domestic fiscal policy; the neoclassicals and technically driven econometricians picked their own quarrels; mainstream orthodox economists were implacably hostile to the idea of an industrial policy picking and attempting to create winners; some launched attacks on the prescription of import controls reviving the wartime spectre of austerity and rationing; and on the bizarre side, some might have perceived and resented any indirect association of the Cripps-Bennite left-wing with their own precious identity of 'Cambridge' economics. Critiques came from an arc of personal, ideological and material interests: their central target was the left-wing radical policy package proposed as an alternative to Thatcherism that had entered the Labour mainstream.

All such references to Thatcherite 'vindictiveness' or 'payback', credible as they are, raise an intriguing question: How did such vengeance work its way from Thatcherite sources in government, politics or academics, into the ostensibly independent and officially impartial SSRC committee/s that made the hostile decision vis-à-vis the Cambridge Economic Policy Group? In what way, through which channels, could Thatcherite agency have influenced the outcome? Plausible, if unpleasant, answers to such questions are sought and conditionally identified in the following chapter; these tend to query if it was possible to sniff, proverbially speaking, something rotten in the state of SSRC decision-making where questionable substantive decisions could have been generated even through a managed system of 'good governance'.

6.3.2 The Team Scattered

Godley (2008) notes that "not one of the Consortium had ever built a model; there was no recourse and that was really a catastrophe as it meant that the group was broken up". Without a grant they didn't have a future in the DAE. Thus, the team scattered, all went their own ways, the collective work ended, reconstituted in bits and pieces for different purposes in different locations.

Terry Ward observes that "both Francis and I could have stayed on. It was made known to us that we would be helped to find funding, but on condition that we did not engage in policy relevant projects. So we chose to leave rather than being dismissed." They, and others, moved "mainly into the private sector, ironically to give ourselves more freedom to study policy-related issues". Terry emphasises "Francis's considerable skills as a computer programmer—a fact often forgotten but key to the development of the various models he constructed when in Cambridge and subsequently on projects for the European Commission, which was more concerned with the policy relevance of the work we carried out than with the niceties of the underlying theories."

Francis Cripps and Terry Ward set up Alphametrics,[37] with a US partner, Charles Renfro of Philadelphia, to support a PC database and modelling package, MODLER. In 1986 they won a contract to develop a front-office dealer support system for the Bank of Tokyo in London. Throughout the 1980s they had worked with European researchers and EU institutions on labour market, regional and social policy issues and in 1992 established Applica *sprl* in Brussels. Then in 1993 Francis set up a team in Thailand to maintain the dealer support system for the Japanese bank's branches in Asia. More recently, he developed a new global databank and policy simulation system for UN DESA (Department of Economic and Social Affairs) and latterly UNCTAD, and continues to work with Terry Ward and other international researchers on global and European issues. Terry points out that "these companies are still going strong to this day; Alphametrics between the UK and Thailand now has a work force of around 100." Looking back on that era from the great distance

---

[37] *A short history of Francis Cripps and Terry Ward since the DAE.*

1983: Alphametrics was set up in 1983, with the joint aim of developing software for PCs and modelling the European economies.

1984–1985: A deal was almost done to produce regular forecasts of the European economies for PCs with the Economist Intelligence Unit and distributed on floppy disk (remember those?). The EIU get cold feet and decide not to go ahead, preferring instead to continue with traditional paper publications. Francis makes contact with Charles Renfro with whom he helps to further develop MODLER for sale as a software modelling package.

1986: Alphametrics signs a contact with Bank of Tokyo (subsequently Tokyo-Mitsubishi) to produce a Forex and Money market software system to run on networked PCs in real-time for its London dealing-room (possibly the first anywhere). This has since been updated and is still in use in bank offices.

1988: A contract is signed with the European Commission to produce an Employment in Europe report using desk-top publishing methods (one of the first substantial reports to do so, if not the first). This turns into an annual publication and stimulates other parts of the Commission to do the same.

1986–1992: Alphametrics grows to employ over 50 people on back of dealer-room software and European Commission contracts.

1992: Applica set up by Terry and Francis in Brussels to be centre of European work.

1994: Alphametrics software business sold to Temenos, a Swiss company producing banking software. Alphametrics continues as an Economic consultancy with six people; Francis moves to Thailand (he had a Thai wife from the mid-1960s) and sets up Alphametrics Thailand there to produce software.

1996: Francis buys back Alphametrics software business.

1996–2021: Alphametrics Thailand under Francis expands to employ close to 100 people. Alphametrics and Applica economic consultancies under Terry to employing 20 people, producing some of the most prestigious reports and carrying out numerous studies on employment, social issues and regional development for the Commission along the way. Francis is lured back into economics over the past 10–15 years or so and develops the world model much further with support from the UN and from the EU Framework Programme (*Source: Terry Ward, personal communication, email dated 1 April 2021*).

of the present, Terry reflects: "so perhaps Posner & Co. did us a favour to help us get out of the Cambridge 'cesspool' (to use Partha Dasgupta's term) at the time, which was becoming nastier by the day and really soul-destroying" (personal communication).

Barry Moore went to the Department of Land Economy in September 1985, becoming Assistant Director of Research there; he and John Rhodes continued to work and publish jointly on regional economic policy and they, together with Roger Tarling, set up a private consultancy on both regional and employment issues. Moore "came to be regarded as a leading authority in the evaluation of innovation and science policy" (Keegan, 2015); in 1976, he had written one of the early papers on the relative decline of the British manufacturing sector. The Labour Studies Group continued to function as a group for a while after the CEPG lost its funding, as it won a series of ESRC grants including as part of the ESRC's leading Social Change and Economic Life Initiative, but Roger Tarling left for private consultancy in 1987, followed by Jill Rubery for a lectureship in Manchester in 1989. Frank Wilkinson continued in the DAE until retirement, mainly working with Alan Hughes in his ESRC centre on small businesses and then after retirement continuing to work with the Centre for Business Research (again run by Alan Hughes) in the Judge Business School. Ken Coutts moved to the Faculty as Assistant Director of Research and remained remarkably productive, producing a steady flow of research and publications, this time from the Faculty side of the building, working jointly with his old colleagues, prominently including several members of the erstwhile CEPG. Those who remained in Cambridge for the most part continued their close involvement, including editorial duties, with the *Cambridge Journal of Economics*, where Frank Wilkinson, in the later years till his demise in 2021, was one of the Patrons along with Luigi Pasinetti and Amartya Sen.

6.3.3 The Model Reincarnated

And what happened to their rubbished models: Did they wind up in a charity shop or in the weekly garbage? That should have been the expectation of anyone who took at face value the insults, slings and slurs cast at them by the SSRC Consortium's hatcheteers and Thatcheteers. As it happened, the original core model was also 'not for turning' and refused to die quietly in some corner. If anything, it evolved and developed with new researchers, new uses, with the original model serving as the progenitor of multiple reincarnations.

The evolution and use of later generations of the CEPG models is also illustrated in the joint work of Francis Cripps, Alex Izurieta and Ajit Singh on an analysis of global imbalances, under-consumption and over-borrowing, with special reference to China and India, in *Development and Change* (Cripps et al., 2011) where

> the simulations are constructed with the Cambridge-Alphametrics model (CAM), which is a derivative of a model originally developed at the Department of Applied

Economics of the University of Cambridge (UK) in the late 1970s to analyse the global implications of oil price increases. Since the 1970s the model has been modified various times in significant ways taking advantage of the improved availability of statistics and reflecting more recent historical experience. (ibid., p. 240).[38] The model has successfully integrated trade flows and financial flows and contains date for most of the economies of the world, which can then be combined, ingeniously through a variable geography facility, so that the model can be used to analyse in detail any individual part of the global economy.

Apart from this, the use of CEPG modelling continues to the present in the Centre for Economic Research on Finance (CERF) in the Judge Business School in Cambridge.

And finally, the focus must shift to Wynne Godley. He had become a professor in Cambridge in 1980, just a year prior to the SSRC shutting down his modelling unit at the DAE, effectively rendering him an intellectual nomad pursuing his own intellectual path, even while he held his professorship till retirement in 1993.

> In 1974 I started on a line in macroeconomic research; I had an insight about how the economy as a whole was put together and started to write about it in 1978; Francis joined me and we published the book in 1983 but only about six people thought it was the work of genius that I thought it was; but the point was that it was not completely thought out; I was not deterred in my belief in the fundamental model. (Godley, 2008)

He was first in Denmark, then in the USA:

> I continued writing about whatever economy I was in; ... simultaneously I was evolving a new version of the book and making all the models myself; I also started to understand the economics which most people teach; ... in the end I came to what I now believe to be a proper understanding of the system of ideas that I had been opposed to. (ibid.)

En route, he developed a fine partnership with Marc Lavoie who co-authored Godley's final and definitive work, *Monetary Economics: An Integrated Approach to Credit, Money, Income, Production, and Wealth* (Godley & Lavoie, 2007). Wynne Godley, with Marc Lavoie, took the original modelling initiative to another plane, developing a stock-flow methodology that has now become standard practice for such macro-modelling. Wynne Godley the intuitive,

---

[38] A variant of the model was used separately in Izurieta and Singh (2010). For the original DAE model, see Cripps et al. (1979). Terry Ward adds that the world model was constructed by Francis Cripps in 1978 to analyse the global implications of the oil price increases and was developed further under the aegis of the UN and still lives on till this day, when it is an impressive set of equations combining physical and financial flows between countries in an essentially closed Keynesian system (see for an example of its use: *Challenges for Europe in the World of 2030*, AUGUR Project, FP7, CORDIS, European Commission [Europa.eu]). (Personal communication)

nose-savvy short-term forecaster had reinvented himself as a model-conceptualising maestro, and as earlier with the CEPG team, there was now a group of accomplished theoreticians and modellers working as a team again.

From close quarters, Ken Coutts observes: "The wonderful collaboration between Marc Lavoie and Wynne, which began in 1999, culminated in the publication of their book *Monetary Economics, an Integrated Approach to Credit, Money, Income, Production and Wealth*. The title indicates the breadth and scope that this synthesis of monetary economics and macroeconomics aimed to achieve and in the past decade it has achieved that aim. ... Wynne lived long enough to appreciate that young researchers were beginning to take up his approach and to elaborate and develop the ideas in the book. In the ten years since his death, there has been an explosion in the number of research papers taking a SFC approach to Post-Keynesian macroeconomics" (Coutts, 2021, p. 31).

Unsurprisingly, in the era of financial crises and meltdowns, which has so spectacularly confirmed the helplessness and hopelessness of mainstream economics, there has been a growing return to Keynesian perspectives, including a steadily rising recognition of the stock-flow consistent approach to macroeconomic modelling that Godley had been developing. Various appreciations have endorsed his pioneering contributions. His collaborator of old at the CEPG, Francis Cripps, pointed out that "what they were doing was Keynesian monetary economics; it was not neoclassical let alone general equilibrium monetary economics" (Cripps, quoted in Lavoie, 2010, p. 7). His later research partner, Marc Lavoie, observed that "My view of Wynne's theoretical work is that his work is a quest for the Holy Grail of Keynesianism ... the need to integrate the real and the monetary sides of economics" (2010, p. 6). The journey which had started in 1983 with *Macroeconomics* by Godley and Cripps[39] had found a destination in 2007 in *Monetary Economics, An Integrated Approach* by Godley and Lavoie.

Mata (2012) provides a critical appreciation of Wynne's craft, observing that "Godley moves in mysterious ways"; and James Galbraith (2012), in like mode, declares: "Keynesliness is next to Godleyness", going on to laud his powers of prediction well before time—using his New Cambridge analytical apparatus and going against the grain of the contemporary mainstream consensus—of the collapse of the US boom. Further appreciative commentaries and insights come from John Maloney (2012) and from Graeme Smith (2016); Marc Lavoie and Gennaro Zezza (2012) have very usefully pulled together Godley's various writings on the stock-flow consistent approach; Papadimitriou and Zezza (2012) have supplemented this with their volume of essays in honour of

---

[39] The 1970s were a creative period in the hothouse intellectual environment of the Cambridge Economic Policy Group, with policy and political engagements on the one side, applied modelling and theoretical work on the other. See also Cripps and Godley (1976) for an early attempt at a formal statement of their model.

Wynne Godley; and most recently, Alan Shipman has added to this mounting pile with his biography of Wynne Godley (Shipman, 2019).

Smith (2016, p. 16) identifies three subsequent strands of macroeconomic modelling that have their roots in the New Cambridge theorising of the 1970s, and this includes the work of Godley, Lavoie, Cripps, Izurieta, Coutts, Gudgin, Gibson and Zezza, amongst others. First: Godley's work on the Levy Institute Model and from there to stock-flow consistent modelling (SFC) in the Godley and Lavoie tradition (Godley & Lavoie, 2007); second: Francis Cripps's work on the Cambridge Alphametrics Model (CAM) (Cripps & Izurieta, 2014);[40] and third: UKMOD, a model of the UK economy from the Centre for Business Research at the University of Cambridge (Gudgin et al., 2015).

Smith also identifies "five essential features of the SFC modelling approach that are traceable back to their New Cambridge origins" and notes that

> the SFC approach has been enthusiastically taken up mainly by heterodox economists and especially the post-Keynesians, so that many models are often labelled PK-SFC. Hopes have been expressed that SFC modelling can become a new *lingua franca* for heterodox economics, providing a common mode of communication that addresses the whole economy as a system, that integrates the monetary and the real sides of the economy and is empirically grounded. Godley (2004) offers the 'SFC approach as a reconstruction of macroeconomics and a radical alternative to the neoclassical approach'. Taylor (2004) uses it in his *Reconstructing Macroeconomics*. ... It has lately become quite routine for published post-Keynesian papers to include a stock-flow model in some form. (Smith, 2016, p. 17)

All these developments need to be read against the general backdrop of the revival of post-Keynesian thought, as for instance in Pasinetti (2007) and Eatwell and Milgate (2011).

There are two ironies here: first, that this expanding acknowledgement and appreciation of the salience of the New Cambridge approach as developed further by the old Cambridge hands led by Godley, and new collaborators elsewhere, has emerged mainly after 2010, the year that Wynne died; and second, that what these later developments establish is that the theoretical approach being developed by Kaldor, Godley, Cripps, Neild and other Cambridge colleagues in the 1970s had a viable and productive potential future—one which was abruptly and arbitrarily cut short prematurely in its formative phase by the firm of Hahn, Matthews, Posner and Co. in 1982. Meanwhile, the general equilibrium approach has lost salience and credibility in the face of its profound inability to engage the real-world crises confronting the global economy. Counterfactuals are often a distraction, but a case can be argued that Frank Hahn and Co. caused significant damage through their wanton intellectual vandalism in hacking down Cambridge heterodox, especially macroeconomic,

---

[40] See also Cripps et al. (2011) for an application.

traditions of theoretical and applied economics in the 1970s and 1980s as they were entering a phase of serious evolutionary development. As believers in the power of foresight, Hahn and Co. cannot take refuge in the excuse that this allegation is made with hindsight. The great Cambridge tradition of policy-relevant work was broken, and Cambridge economics has been made to shift direction into a desert of irrelevance.

6.3.4 The Rehabilitation of Wynne

A wounded Wynne Godley wandered off into the wilderness in 1982—but didn't yield. He stayed at the DAE till the mid-1980s, completing his 15-year term as Director; in the last five years, he tried, unsuccessfully, to ward off a sustained assault on the DAE itself; and in parallel, saw the same internal and external hostile forces, working with the SSRC and the ESRC, bring down the Cambridge Growth Project in 1987.

The year 1992 saw Godley in his mettle as he critiqued the UK's position in the ERM leading up to Black Wednesday:

> I believed very strongly when they tried at the last minute to defend [the pound] that it was unrealistic. It was so obviously a losing battle—they were making fools of themselves ... I wrote an article at the time which began, 'the crazy fools!' I was surprised when [the Conservative Chancellor] Norman Lamont later asked me to be one of his 'Wise Men'. (Stewart, 2002)

He stood vindicated and rehabilitated. Godley's return from "exile" was, he admitted, an "emotional experience" (The Telegraph, 2010). George Soros in/famously made his billion in a day; but Wynne Godley also put his money where his mouth was, even if not on the same scale: "The other thing I remember about Black Wednesday was that I made GBP 10,000 out of it, without putting anything up—by buying options" (Stewart, 2002). Sufficient, with change left over one would imagine, for a celebratory party, or for a swing or two of the roulette that he favoured.

Another strike came a month later in October 1992, when Godley was in full flow providing, before anyone else, a concise and incisive commentary on the fundamental design flaw, the Achilles' heel, of the Maastricht treaty.

> There has to be a quid pro quo for giving up the devaluation option in the form of fiscal redistribution. ... If a country or region has no power to devalue, and if it is not the beneficiary of a system of fiscal equalization, there is nothing to stop it suffering a process of cumulative and terminal decline leading, in the end, to emigration as the only alternative to poverty or starvation.
>
> Sovereignty should not be given up in the noble cause of European integration, but that if all these [fiscal, monetary, exchange rate, redistribution, borrowing etc.] functions are renounced by individual governments they simply have to

be taken on by some other authority. The incredible lacuna on the Maastricht programme is that, while it contains a blueprint for the establishment and modus operandi of an independent central bank, there is no blueprint whatever of the analogue, in Community terms, of a central government. There would simply have to be a system of institutions which fulfils all those functions at a Community level which are at present exercised by the central governments of individual member countries.

I sympathise with the position of those (like Margaret Thatcher) who, faced with the loss of sovereignty, wish to get off the EMU train altogether. I also sympathise with those who see integration under the jurisdiction of some kind of federal construction with a federal budget very much larger than that of the Community budget. What I find totally baffling is the position of those who are aiming for economic and monetary union without the creation of new political institutions (apart from a new central bank), and who raise their hands in horror at the words 'federal' or 'federalism'. This is the position currently adopted by the Government and by most of those who take part in the public discussion. (Godley, 1992)

The strategic policy warnings could not be clearer and would not have been lost, even if in the full glare of hindsight, on those responsible for causing and 'solving' the Greek sovereign debt crisis of 2010 following on from the financial crisis of 2007–2008, which mirrored the course described by Godley; or in the UK's struggle to seek sense, clarity or progress a decade later in 2018 in the confused throes of the Brexit stalemate. It is striking that the structural flaws identified two decades ago still prevail in the EU.

Shortly after, he shifted his modelling work to the Levy Institute in the USA, where he, aided now by Alex Izurieta, began to diagnose and pronounce on the inherent, though at the time latent, unsustainability of USA and global performance in money markets; and once again, he did rather well. "Keynesliness is next to Godleyness," exclaimed James Galbraith. "The Cambridge (UK) economist Wynne Godley and a team at the Levy Economics Institute have built a series of strategic analyses of the U.S. economy ... warning repeatedly of unsustainable trends in the current account and (most of all) in the deterioration of the private financial balance. They showed that the budget surpluses of the late 1990s (and relatively small deficits in the late 2000s) corresponded to debt accumulation ... in the private sector. They argued that the eventual cost of servicing those liabilities would force private households into financial retrenchment, which would in turn drive down activity, collapse the corresponding asset prices, and cut tax revenues. The result would drive the public budget deficits through the roof. And thus—so far as the economics are concerned—more or less precisely these events came to pass" (Galbraith, 2012, pp. 90–91). Wynne Godley had found his model and his mojo.

6.3.5 Wynne Godley:[41] 'My Credo' ...

In 1995, the DAE—then under its new and last Director, David Newbery—marked its 50th anniversary with a conference, pulling together contributions by some of the old hands into a memorial volume. Richard Stone had passed away; Brian Reddaway was noticeably missing from its pages. The ensuing commemorative volume carried a preface from the Director remarkably without a single mention of the CEPG or the CGP teams once the pride of Cambridge applied economics. But Wynne Godley was at hand, and had the last word, literally, in the book with a typically and brutally honest self-appraisal with reflections on "using figures to guide macroeconomic policy" (Godley, 1998, p. 258). He describes, in all of six pages, "what it is that I do and why"—a reduced form of a classic "I believe" reflection.[42]

---

[41] Wynne Godley was the descendent of some famous other Godleys—leaving aside the rather sad life of his father, recounted with painful plainness by Wynne in his remarkable personal piece on his brush with truth and healing (Godley, 2001). His great grandfather, John Robert Godley, had a distinguished career in New Zealand where he founded the Canterbury Settlement and the Province of Christchurch, and then in England where he was Permanent Undersecretary of State in the War Office; his wife Charlotte was the daughter of the well-known parliamentarian G.C. Wynne, so perhaps that is where Wynne's first name derives from. John Robert died early, and his son, Sir John Arthur Godley, took up the civil service mantle, becoming the fourth Permanent Undersecretary of State at the India Office in 1883 at the age of 35 and serving longer than all his predecessors combined (Kaminsky, 1986, p. 12), thought of generally as "the best man in the Civil Service" (ibid., p. 232), and at one point being shortlisted for the exalted position of Viceroy of India, but thought to be too bureaucratic for this task (ibid., p. 8). Kaminsky observes that "the Oxford connection also had a great influence on Arthur Godley's subsequent career at the India Office". At Balliol in Oxford, H.H. Asquith referred to him as "the most distinguished Balliol man of his time". Oxford "old school tie" connections were an important asset; Lord Rosebery, his lifelong friend, asked light-heartedly: "What would Godley have been had he gone to Cambridge instead of Oxford?" (ibid., p. 238). On his retirement from the India Office in 1909, Sir John Arthur Godley was raised to the peerage as Baron Kilbracken of Killegar. Both great grandfather and grandfather had distinguished careers. "Gladstone knew them both intimately, and once admitted candidly that he had great difficulty in saying 'which was the greater man, the father or the son', and the family today [in 1909] is equally divided as to which man was 'the Great Godley'" (ibid., p. 237). Wynne's own career made no use whatsoever of any school or college tie or ties, and showed no particular harm coming his way in moving from Oxford to Cambridge. But he would have added to the family conundrum by throwing a third candidate into the hat for being the Great, Greater or Greatest Godley of them all. Incidentally, Wynne at Cambridge was a protectionist; and on the authority of Francis Cripps, we have it that so was his grandfather at the India Office with regard to Indian textiles suffering in competition with Manchester (Francis Cripps, personal communication). "He was proud of his grandfather's support for the protection of Indian industries" (Cripps, 2021, p. 25). Wynne says he was very close to his grandfather: "He was good with children whom he could entertain endlessly; I loved him and think about him more and more" (Godley, 2008).

[42] Wynne is no carpet bagger: "The methodology described here is the same as that which has always been used by the Cambridge Economic Policy Group. But my present model is impoverished compared with the models which Francis Cripps made in the seventies" (Godley, 1998, p. 263, n1).

I think the idea of an econometric model which in any real sense thinks for one is anomalous. The purpose of the model is rather to enlarge the capacity of the mind to encompass a far more complex system of inter-relationships that would otherwise be possible. (ibid., p. 260).

Whilst there has to be an element of forecasting, my object is not to produce a forecast as such but to provide a navigational chart which lays down alternative courses to desirable destinations and which should make it possible to skirt hazards and be prepared for surprises. (ibid., p. 261)

The results of this kind of analysis cannot properly be summarised in a single table which shows unemployment, inflation, and GDP one year from now with no verbal commentary at all. Apart from the fact that forecasting in this sense is, as I believe, impossible (and there is no evidence that it has improved significantly over the years or that one method is better than another) it is never going to tell the policymaker what to do. I do not think that the more serious statistical evaluations of econometric forecasts, for instance by the Warwick Bureau, are much better. They are all trying to find something which will always elude them—a model which can predict, without fudging (or with it for that matter), the future with any acceptable degree of reliability. In my opinion the quest is a foolish one. (ibid., pp. 261–262)[43]

Pertinent here is a recent reflection by Francis Cripps on econometrics and macro-modelling: "In the late 1990s, Wynne sent me a paper with an econometric model of growth rates that Pesaran claimed was fully consistent with Wynne's macro-economics. Wynne was baffled. He could not see any relationship between the reduced-form econometric model in the paper and the structured, behavioral analysis that we believed to be the best or only way to get a handle on real-life macro-economic problems. But I don't think we lost the war on this front. Policy institutions today still use national accounting identities and stock-flow relationships as a framework for measuring and understanding the behavior of aggregates. They still need institutional explanations informed by more detailed evidence and studies and have to be ready to learn and change their analysis from place to place and time to time. And their research does inform what van der Pijl calls the cadres (I think he means us) if not so much the leaders or the wider public. Let's not give up" (Cripps, 2021, p. 24).

With regard to this "econometrics—macroeconomic modelling" binary, Matias Vernengo provides a comparative commentary on the approaches of Lawrence Klein and Wynne Godley. In the course of his criticism of Paul Krugman for wrongly equating Wynne Godley's approach to "the old hydraulic Keynesianism, i.e., Neoclassical Synthesis", Vernengo (2013) draws a comparison between the modelling approaches of Klein and Godley: "Conventional hydraulic models, including the sort of Cowles models like the Klein-Goldberger

---

[43] This is much in consonance with the position of Kaldor as expressed to the Treasury and also to the Rothschild Enquiry into the SSRC in 1982.

model of the US economy, put great emphasis on the estimation of parameters based on certain simplistic macro behavior. Wynne took a very different approach to modeling than Klein-Goldberger. He was more concerned with what he referred to as 'model architecture' than with parameter estimation. The architecture, which was careful about stock-flow consistency, showing that everything came from somewhere and went somewhere so to speak, also imposed a clear causality structure, which determined most of the results. In fact, Wynne believed that significant variations of the parameters might not greatly influence the end result of the model, which was used for simulations and scenarios that helped to understand how the economy functioned, rather than for strictly forecasting purposes."[44]

In the early years, while Wynne Godley was famous as a zen master for his cannily accurate forecasting, he moved steadily from this towards methodologies that were based on comprehensive macroeconomic models as first with Francis Cripps at the CEPG in the DAE and later with Marc Lavoie and Alex Izurieta. You had to be right for the right reasons, Godley had observed; if you are only interested in forecasting you wouldn't care if you got something right for the wrong reasons—but then this was unlikely to be repeated again and again; he was not a Chicago man. But a model still remained a device to use, not some magical soothsaying black box that ran the show.

> Any power I have to persuade others resides not in the model 'runs', let alone in single point forecasts, but in the verbal argument deployed. Although I work with a computer model, I aspire to the tradition of the great quantitative political economists such as Keynes, Kaldor or, for that matter, Samuel Brittan, who argue their case with reason and rhetoric [which Godley reads, using Chambers Dictionary, as 'the whole art of using language so as to persuade others']—supported with whatever evidence they think appropriate for the particular purpose in mind. (ibid., p. 261)

Then follows a brutally honest self-evaluation: "How well did we do, my Cambridge colleagues and I? I think our strategic evaluation in 1989 and in the period up to September 1992 served the public discussion very well" (ibid., p. 262); Godley et al. had made the right calls, leading to a long-overdue recognition of earlier injustices and a public vindication when he was invited to join the Treasury's panel of independent forecasters, the six soothsayers, in autumn 1992—a decade after CEPG modelling had been closed down by the SSRC.

---

[44] This paragraph is shared with the discussion of Lawrence Klein's *The Keynesian Revolution* in Chap. 4, p. 74. Marc Lavoie offers a qualifying observation, pointing out that Klein later wrote his piece on the potential linkages for input-output analysis and flow of funds; "so in a way, he was suggesting to put together the research programmes of Godley and Stone". (Personal communication, email dated 22 December 2021).

I hesitate to say, at this stage, more than a word about the seventies and early eighties. I believe that during that time we made an important contribution to the public discussion—even if had no influence over the course of events—... which was well served by the CEPG between 1979 and 1982, when we correctly foresaw that the attempt to subordinate all macroeconomic policy to controlling the stock of M3 would cause an extremely large rise in unemployment from which no recovery would occur without a dramatic change in policy. (ibid., pp. 262–263)

He admits,

there was much that was wrong with what we wrote in the mid-seventies, partly because, like everyone else, we did not understand inflation accounting properly. And I now think we were probably wrong to back protection in such a (relatively) unqualified way. At least we tried, with integrity and without fear, to think through the consequences of Britain's progressive failure to compete successfully in international trade at that time and subsequently. And we doggedly resisted the abandonment of full employment as a valid target of macroeconomic policy, by a Labour government, in 1976. (ibid., p. 263)

He forgets to mention that in the years that followed, the CEPG arguably formed the epicentre of opposition to Thatcherite monetarism that swept all and everything ahead of it, with the consequences, both in the short and longer terms, that he and his CEPG colleagues had well predicted; they had been the vanguard of Cambridge left-Keynesianism till they were silenced.

6.3.6   The Pacification of the CEPG

At the end, Wynne came out of it with his reputation restored, indeed lifted to far higher and rising levels—but there had been a heavy and unnecessary price to pay in terms of losses of time and peace of mind for an unusually sensitive soul; and these personal losses also had wider externalities with social costs spread through a negative multiplier. But there was no similar public restitution for the other members of the team who had to build and rebuild their work and reputations from fresh starts elsewhere, having to negotiate broken career paths with the burden of the opprobrium heaped upon them by the SSRC as unwanted baggage.[45]

And of course, there were very considerable implications for the DAE and Cambridge itself—as subsequent events made obvious. Radical voices from the DAE were effectively silenced in the charged global and national debates on economic issues of prime significance. It had lost its faculty with regard to

---

[45] Terry Ward provides a qualification, observing that he and some others "chose to leave academia rather than being thrown out"; he feels that the writing was on the wall—"I don't believe if we had survived Posner we would have been able to resist the rise of neoclassical thinking"; "we were killed off not so much by Thatcherism but rather economic orthodoxy" (Personal communication).

contributing to the analyses of the dramatically changing role of global finance; it was notably absent when the Asian crisis of 1997 struck on when the big crash of 2007 hit;[46] there was no one to answer the Queen's Question; no Cambridge institutional capacity to investigate and interrogate economic issues relating to the European Union—harking back here to Godley's sharp insights of 1992 when Godley and CEPG were well ahead of the game on the ERM, on Maastricht and related issues; and at the moment of writing, no Cambridge team to stand up to provide independent alternative analyses that could inform a nation caught in the Brexit morass within a post-truth political environment. Separate and distinct they might have been, but the DAE siblings, the CGP and the CEPG, had complementary curiosities and capabilities that were potentially invaluable for informing public debate and discourse in economics and politics. The DAE teams were well into, if not also well ahead of, the game; regrettably, mainstream Cambridge economics is arguably a no-show, not even on the playing field, having converted itself to a spectator sitting knitting its myriad mathematical patterns on the sidelines.

A couple of qualifications could be considered. First, it could rightly be pointed out that DAE research shifted its focus towards other policy issues: towards the transition of central Europe and towards providing theoretical and quantified analyses supporting the tidal wave of privatisation unleased by post-socialist regimes, global capital and Bretton-Woods institutions, in that region; towards setting up a capacity for applied consultancy work on the energy sector, specifically electricity, again in the era of the privatisation of everything. As with the earlier Directorships of Stone, Reddaway and Godley, the takeover by Newbery shifted the vision towards research areas that he might have prioritised; this was not unusual or unexpected. But it cannot be gainsaid that this change constituted a sharp shift, if not a reversal, in direction in the ideological and substantive orientation of erstwhile policy perspectives and constituted a break from the cumulative body of DAE macroeconomic policy engagement which it replaced. Second, it could, in principle, be claimed, as indeed it questionably was, that the DAE was intended to support research projects by faculty members with facilities and research assistants, the research agenda would reflect the activated interests of Faculty staff (apart from initiatives from the Director's desk). This was indeed one of the objectives of the DAE, one which

---

[46] It is striking that though the DAE 50th anniversary volume appeared in 1998, there is no mention of the Asian Crisis. Of course, individual staff of the Faculty were deeply involved in the analysis of the Asian Crisis, but this was not within the framework of any DAE research programme. The extensive research and publications of Ajit Singh bear testimony to this. Additionally, with the abdication of this crucial field by the 'new' DAE and the closure of the macroeconomic teams, such work was relocated to CERF (Cambridge Endowment for Research on Finance) launched with external funding, at the Judge Institute. Responding to the exploding demand for research in this field, and building on the earlier reputation of Cambridge, CERF expanded rapidly with active involvement of several Faculty and DAE economists, including Ajit Singh, John Eatwell, Ha-Joon Chang and Jose Gabriel Palma, amongst others; CERF also hosted, in difficult times, the modelling work of Wynne Godley and Alex Izurieta.

received consistent and strong support from all earlier Directors;[47] as such, it cannot account for the virtual disappearance of the ongoing macroeconomic research of DAE; there was no sudden loss of interest from staff—the reality was, rather, that their funding got cut off. Additionally, there were still staff with a deep interest in global finance, but, as noted, this capacity shifted and relocated in the Judge Institute of Management in the form of CERF, the new Cambridge Endowment for Research on Finance. This explanation also begs the question whether the DAE could have built up its phenomenal capacities and reputation had it been simply a disparate collection of the research projects of individual Faculty staff; to say that the Stone-Brown, Stone-Barker or the Godley-Cripps edifices emerged from such individual research preoccupations would be patently disingenuous. The DAE had long gone past the idea that it was 'primarily' for providing desks for research assistants on a scatter of mostly small-time individual research projects; it had recognised, as was patently obvious elsewhere, not least in the USA, that serious macroeconomic modelling work could only be done with heavy and sustained investment in the construction of specialised teams. These were the collective capacities that were dismantled in the 1980s. Indeed, if anything, the premium on teamwork collective institutional and infrastructural capacity was again demonstrated in the case of CERF at the Judge Institute. Additionally, it is worth noting that with the closures of the CGP and the CEPG, and takeover of DAE by the new Director, the 1980s also effected a transformation in the public policy stance widely identified with the DAE: from a structural and (left-) Keynesian approach to state policy resisting the predations of neoliberalism and unbound global finance, to a stance which saw and professionally supported this transition and privatisation not just as a reality but also as a solution. Whichever side of the barricades any onlooker stood on, not to acknowledge such an ideological reorientation would be to deny the obvious.

It is also ironical that the SSRC and the ESRC, public bodies spending public monies for the public weal, acted as aggressive agents for the privatisation of macroeconomic modelling. Richard Stone had raised a warning about this in the early years when the SSRC was jostling the CGP in this direction, cautioning that this would influence the kinds of questions researched, and also the ownership of the data and results generated; it fell on the deaf ears of public servants and tax-financed academics in the committees. The models of the CGP and the CEPG have both evolved subsequently under the leadership of Terry Barker and Francis Cripps, respectively. But these developments have per force occurred mostly within the private companies that were formed consequent to the closure of their teams at the hands of the SSRC and the ESRC.

There can be little doubt that in the torrid decade of the 1970s, Wynne Godley, Francis Cripps and the CEPG team and their models were innovating and developing rapidly; the SSRC dead-ended that evolution. Wynne

---

[47] This argument, used by Hahn, Matthews and others as a stick with which to beat the DAE, is discussed (and dismissed) in the chapter dealing with the University Review of the DAE.

eventually earned his professional reinstatement and the recovery of his reputation, but not within the CEPG and the DAE. If the CEPG's life had not been cut short by the SSRC, all these innovations and recognition would have taken place within the Cambridge and DAE base reinforcing the public role that Cambridge economics, especially in its Keynesian incarnation, had traditionally performed.

Looking back on those times from the distance of the present, Terry Ward, then in the thick of CEPG modelling analysis and policy campaigns, and subsequently Francis Cripps's partner in setting up their private modelling and policy consultancy, reflects on what might have been, had Francis been appointed to the Faculty professorship in 1985 or to the Directorship of the DAE (and attached professorship in applied economics) a couple of years later.[48] "Things may well have been different if we had succeeded. Francis has the intellectual power to have attracted a new generation of economists to Cambridge and to have opened up new avenues of policy research with a European and global perspective. and if he had become the Director of the DAE even more so. But whether he would have had the patience and diplomatic nous to fight the inevitable political battles is questionable. The American neoclassical invasion was probably unstoppable. But who knows?" (Terry Ward, personal email, dated 3 April 2021). The counterfactual can be extended: with the benefit of hindsight, with regard to the progressive evolution of the CEPG models in different locations, the dismal failure of the general equilibrium agenda and repeated economic crises at global levels which left the orthodox neoclassical camp generally witless and speechless, a null hypothesis that the DAE, as was, could have evolved to make critical, even profound, contributions to creatively reorienting national and global economic policy towards humane, egalitarian, stable and sustainable pathways, cannot be easily rejected. That said, with even less certainty might it be possible to reject another null hypothesis, viz., that such a reincarnated CEPG might have remained a thorn in the side of right-wing Labour and Tory governments, and thus induced a hostile response.

Subsequent developments give the lie to the peremptory disparaging treatment and reputational assassination at the hands of SSRC committees comprising an unholy alliance of hostile rivals and antagonists, all with their own axes

---

[48] When asked, Francis recalled: "It is quite possible that I was being considered as a candidate. What I do recall clearly is FH telling me that there was no way I could get a chair as what I had been doing (policy-orientated applied macro-economics) has no academic value. The really big shift for me was what happened regarding the post of the DAE Director which I and many others had assumed would be passed on from Wynne to me. ... Kaldor assure me that the university statutes required the post to be advertised and an election held—and there was no way the statutory requirement could be blocked. The shock came when Wynne learned that the statues had been suspended which was a more or less unprecedented event. This was the main event that convinced me to leave rather than hanging on in a mood of regret. ... So to be honest I might not have taken candidature for a chair as anything more than a gesture" (Personal communication, email dated 19 May 2021).

to grind; the SSRC's stoppage of funding causing the closure of the Cambridge Economic Policy Group can be regarded, with much justification, as an act of political vengeance and intellectual vandalism—abrupt, arbitrary and arrogant.

APPENDIX 6.1: OLD CAMBRIDGE, NEW CAMBRIDGE, 1974: AND ALL THE KING'S MEN

A string of stinging exchanges, during May–June 1974, between representatives of 'old' and 'new' Cambridge are in evidence in the King's College Archives, 'Old' versus 'New' Cambridge; the extracts from unpublished letters cited below are variously written or copied to Richard Kahn (RFK), Michael Posner (MP), Nicky Kaldor (NK), Wynne Godley (WG), Robert Neild (RN), Francis Cripps (FC), Martin Fetherston, Adrian Wood, Douglas Wass, Kenneth Berrill, and Luigi Pasinetti; the letters were sent on to Joan Robinson by Richard Kahn (JVR/vii/228/3; Joan Robinson Papers, King's College Archives, University of Cambridge).

1. Letter WG to RFK 23 May 1974. JVR/vii/228/3/3
Wynne Godley had presented a paper at an LSE seminar on 17 May 1974; Kenneth Berrill was present and wrote a Note on Wynne's exposition and sent it to Richard Kahn, who sent on a copy to Joan Robinson. WG sends RFK his LSE seminar paper, with a letter:
  "My Dear Richard, ... perhaps we could discuss. I am really very sorry that we should be in the position of having a confused debate in public without trying harder to make contact between ourselves and reach agreement—even may be little difference between us in reality".

2. Letter NK to RFK 20 May 1974. JVR/vii/228/3/14-16
Richard Kahn and Michael Posner, evidently, had sent a Note [not on file] to Nicky Kaldor, who expresses annoyance in his response.
  "I am not sure that I could fully decipher or appreciate your note, but here are some comments ... where you and Michael went haywire is in thinking ..."
  "Stripped of its unnecessarily argumentative and rather tortuous manner of exposition, what you and Michael are contending ..."

3. Letter from RFK and MP to NK 24 May 1974. JVR/vii/228/3/17-20
  "Your suggestion that we do not understand the New School's exposition of the effect on the level of activity and the balance of payments of lowering taxation I [find?] entirely unwarranted. If you have really read our articles, how can you maintain that we fail to realise that the level of activity would be raised? Do you really seriously believe that the great contribution of the New School is to demonstrate, in the face of Keynesian orthodoxy, that a lowering of taxation would raise the level of activity, while we, loyal to the Keynes tradition, believe that the level of activity would be unaffected but that the balance of payments would be

improved—for some mysterious reason we fail to explain (presumably the reason would be that we have heard attributed to Nicky Kaldor the view that the current balance of payments deficit is the mirror image of the public sector deficit)?"

"But your presentation was precisely the opposite to that of Robert, who in his letter to The Times of the 26th February last wrote:—'The Budget should be used to determine the foreign balance and the exchange rate to determine the level of activity'."

"Leaving aside the mild abuse which you mete out to us ...."

4. *Letter from RFK and MP to NK 28 May 1974. JVR/vii/228/3/24*
On the content of NK's *New Statesman* articles (that NK had sent to them):

"We agree with a lot of what you were saying of course, and our disagreement for the most part is only tangential and arises only here and there. We did not—and do not now—seek to make a great fuss about passing comments made by you or other of our friends; we were driven to write our articles only because Robert, Wynne and Francis seemed to be collecting together these passing comments into a theoretical structure that seemed to us unacceptable. We hope very much that these theoretical differences can be resolved and in that spirit do not want to pick at niggling points in your New Statesman articles."

5. *Letter from FC to RFK 29 May 1974. JVR/7/228/3/25*
"I fear that little is to be gained by a 'theological' debate with attendant dangers of misrepresentation and misunderstanding."

6. *Reply from RFK to FC 6 June 1974. JVR/7/228/3/24*
"Michael and I much appreciated the terms and tone of your letter of 29th May. We are delighted if we can agree that the only difference between us is over ...."

7. *In the interim, NK replied to RFK and MP. JVR/7/228/3/26*
"On reading your letter of 24th May, I realized that I had started something with which it is beyond my power to cope. I feel that every time I try to explain my position you raise numerous other points, the answers to which would involve me in giving an account of the development of growth theories in the last ten years—something on which I should have written a book, but unfortunately have not. But with my present pre-occupations I am just not able to carry on the correspondence in the normal way by answering each point raised on its merits. ... The key question in your present letter is, 'Why does not each price-leader try to earn a profit higher than needed to finance its desired investment?' I suggest that this would be a very good subject for an undergraduate dissertation. It is probably too difficult to answer in an examination question or an essay."

"I am glad to know that when it comes to economic policy there seem to be no differences between us—these are confined to a purely theoretical (or theological) level."

8. Letter from NK to RFK. RFK/12/2/132/3
"*Dear Richard, This is to acknowledge your letter of 23 January. I cannot really enter into controversies on my 1939 article on Speculation which I don't think you have quite understood either at that time or now. I only wish to say that I am sorry if I didn't make it sufficiently clear ...*"[49]

References

Albertson, K., & Stepney, P. (2020). 1979 and all that: A 40-year reassessment of Margaret Thatcher's legacy on her own terms. *Cambridge Journal of Economics*, 44(2), 319–342.

Allan, L. (2008). *Thatcher's economists: Ideas and opposition in 1980s Britain*. Doctoral dissertation, Trinity College, Oxford.

Bagchi, A. K. (2004). *Keynes, Kaldor and development economics*. Occasional Paper No. 1. Institute of Development Studies.

Bagchi, A. K. (2019, September 13). The practical economist. *Frontline*.

BBC. (1997, June 11). http://www.bbc.co.uk/news/special/politics97/background/pastelec/ge87.shtml

Beckett, A. (2015, September 14). Toxteth, 1981: The summer Liverpool burned – By the rioter and economist on opposite sides. *The Guardian*. https://www.theguardian.com/cities/2015/sep/14/toxteth-riots-1981-summer-liverpool-burned-patrick-minford-jimi-jagne

Benn, T. (2000). Interview. Commanding Heights, Public Broadcasting Service, Interviewed on 26 October 2000. https://www.pbs.org/wl7h/commanding-heights/hi/people/pe_name.html

Booth, P. (2006a, March 15). How 364 economists got it totally wrong. *The Telegraph*. https://www.telegraph.co.uk/comment/personal-view/3623669/How-364-economists-got-it-totally-wrong.html

Booth, P. (Ed.). (2006b). *Were 364 economists all wrong?* Institute of Economic Affairs.

Cambridge Political Economy Group. (1974). Britain's economic crisis. Spokesman pamphlet No. 44. Bertrand Russell Peace Foundation, for *The Spokesman*.

Carlton, A. (2016, August 10). How Tony Benn's deputy leadership campaign was defeated. *New Statesman*. https://www.newstatesman.com/politics/elections/2016/08/how-tony-benn-s-deputy-leadership-campaign-was-defeated

Chakravarty, S. (1987). *Post-Keynesian theorists and the theory of economic development*. Working Paper No. 23. WIDER-UNU.

Conference of Socialist Economists London Working Group. (1980). *The alternative economic strategy: A labour movement response to the economic crisis*. CSE Books.

Coutts, K. (2021). The legacy of Wynne Godley: Notes for a talk on the legacy of Wynne Godley, Wednesday 12 May 2020. *Journal of Post Keynesian Economics*, 44(1), 27–31.

Coutts, K., Tarling, R., Ward, T., & Wilkinson, F. (1981). The economic consequences of Mrs Thatcher. *Cambridge Journal of Economics*, 5(1), 81–93.

---

[49] Amiya Bagchi provides an exposition of Keynes's and Kaldor's analysis of speculation and stock markets, also with reference to Kaldor's differences with Kahn, in his treatment of Keynes, Kaldor and development economics (Bagchi, 2004, pp. 7–13). See also Sukhamoy Chakravarty's insightful discussion of the post-Keynesians theorists and development economics (Chakravarty, 1987).

Cripps, F. (2021). The legacy of Wynne Godley: Godley and the world today. *Journal of Post Keynesian Economics, 44*(1), 24–26.

Cripps, F., & Godley, W. (1976). A formal analysis of the Cambridge Economic Policy Group model. *Economica (New Series), 43*(172), 335–348.

Cripps, F., & Godley, W. (1978). Control of imports as a means to full employment and the expansion of world trade. *Cambridge Journal of Economics, 2*(3), 327–334.

Cripps, F., & Izurieta, A. (2014). *The UN global policy model: Technical description.* Technical manual. https://unctad.org/en/PublicationsLibrary/tdr2014_GPM_TechnicalDescription.pdf

Cripps, F., Gudgin, G., & Rhodes, J. (1979). Technical manual of the CEPG model of world trade. *Cambridge Economic Policy Review, 3*(June).

Cripps, F., Izurieta, A., & Singh, A. (2011). Global imbalances, under-consumption and over-borrowing: The state of the world economy and future policies. *Development and Change, 42*(1), 228–261.

Cunningham, C. (2006, March 17). Michael Posner: Applied economist and champion of the social sciences. *The Guardian.*

Daedalus. (1975). The oil crisis: In perspective. *Daedalus, 104*(4, Theme issue).

Davis, J. (2007). *Prime ministers and Whitehall 1960–74.* Hambledon Continuum.

Deakin, S. F., & Ewing, K. D. (2021, April 13). *Frank Wilkinson 1934–2021.* Institute of Employment Rights. https://www.ier.org.uk/news/frank-wilkinson-1934-2021/

Deane, P. (1988b). Review of: *The rise and fall of monetarism: The theory and politics of an economic experiment* by David Smith, and Why Reaganomics and Keynesian economics failed by James E. Sawyer. *International Affairs, 64*(3), 486–487.

Denham, A., & Garnett, M. (2001). *Keith Joseph.* Routledge.

Dow, J. C., with Hacche, G., & Taylor, C. (2013). *Inside the Bank of England: Memoirs of Christopher Dow, Chief Economist 1973–84.* Palgrave Macmillan.

Eatwell, J., & Milgate, M. (2011). *The fall and rise of Keynesian economics.* Oxford University Press.

Edmunds, J. (1997). *The Left's views on Israel: From the establishment of the Jewish State to the Intifada.* PhD Thesis, London School of Economics and Politics. http://etheses.lse.ac.uk/2847/1/U615796.pdf

Feinstein, C., & Reddaway, W. B. (1978). OPEC surpluses, the world recession and the U.K. economy. *Midland Bank Review*, Spring; reprinted in Matthews and Sargent (1983).

Galbraith, J. K. (2012). Who are these economists anyway? In D. B. Papadimitriou & G. Zezza (Eds.), *Contributions to stock-flow modelling: Essays in honour of Wynne Godley* (Chapter 4). Palgrave Macmillan.

Girvan, N. (1975). Economic nationalism. *Daedalus, 104*(4), 145–158.

Glyn, A., Hughes, A., Lipietz, A., & Singh, A. (1988). *The rise and fall of the golden age.* UNU-WIDER Working Paper No. 43. UNU-WIDER.

Godley, W. (1992). Maastricht and all that. *London Review of Books, 14*(19), 3–4.

Godley, W. (1998). Using figures to guide macroeconomic policy. In I. Begg & S. G. B. Henry (Eds.), *Applied economics and public policy* (pp. 258–263). Cambridge University Press.

Godley, W. (2001). Saving Masud Khan. *London Review of Books, 23*(4), 3–7.

Godley, W. (2004). *Towards a reconstruction of macroeconomics using a Stock Flow Consistent (SFC) model.* CFAP Working Paper No. 16. Judge Business School, University of Cambridge.

Godley, W. (2008, May 16). Interview with Wynne Godley. In S. Harrison & A. Macfarlane, *Encounter with economics.* Interviews filmed by A. Macfarlane and edited by S. Harrison. University of Cambridge. http://sms.cam.ac.uk/collection/1092396

Godley, W., & Cripps, F. (1973, January 8). GBP 1,000m payments deficit this year if economy grows at 5 per cent. *The Times.*

Godley, W., & Lavoie, M. (2007). *Monetary economics: An integrated approach to credit, money, income, production and wealth.* Palgrave Macmillan.

Gudgin, G., Coutts, K., & Gibson, N. (2015). *The CBR macroeconomic model of the UK economy (UKMOD).* Working Paper No. 472. Centre for Business Research, University of Cambridge.

Guinan, J. (2015). Ownership and control: Bring back the Institute for Workers' Control. *Renewal: A Journal of Social Democracy, 23*(4), 11–36. https://www.academia.edu/20411866/Bring_back_the_Institute_for_Workers_Control

Harcourt, G. C. (2012b). *The making of a post-Keynesian economist: Cambridge harvest. Selected essays of G. C. Harcourt.* Palgrave Macmillan.

Hattersley, R. (2009, March 22). The party's over. *The Observer.*

Heffernan, R. (1997). *Exploring political change: Thatcherism and the remaking of the Labour Party 1979–1997.* Ph.D. thesis, London School of Economics and Political Science, University of London. http://etheses.lse.ac.uk/2133/1/U613365.pdf

ITV News. (2014, March 14). Funeral for former Chesterfield MP Tony Benn. https://www.itv.com/news/calendar/update/2014-03-14/scargill-benn-was-an-outstanding-trade-unionist-and-friend/

Izurieta, A., & Singh, A. (2010). Does fast growth in India and China help or harm US workers? *Journal of Human Development and Capabilities, 11*(1), 115–140.

Jackson, D., Turner, H. A., & Wilkinson, F. (1972). *Do trade unions cause inflation?* Occasional Paper No. 36. Cambridge University Department of Applied Economics.

Johnson, H. G. (1973). National styles in economic research: The United States, United Kingdom, Canada, and various European countries. *Daedalus, 102*(2), 65–74.

Kahn, R., & Marcuzzo, M. C. (2020). Richard Kahn: A disciple of Keynes. *History of Economics Review,* 57p. https://doi.org/10.1080/10370196.2020.1767930

Kaldor, N. (1980, July). Evidence to the Treasury and Civil Service Committee. Reproduced in N. Kaldor, *The scourge of monetarism* (pp. 45–48). Oxford University Press, 1986.

Kaminsky, A. P. (1986). *The India Office, 1880–1910.* Contributions in comparative colonial studies 20. Greenwood Press.

Keegan, W. (2010, May 20). Wynne Godley obituary: Economist with a flair for anticipating and responding to crises. *The Guardian.* https://www.theguardian.com/politics/2010/may/20/wynne-godley-obituary

Keegan, W. (2015, September 16). Barry Moore obituary: Economist who became a noted authority on the business of scientific innovation and the revival of ailing regions. *The Guardian.* https://www.theguardian.com/business/2015/sep/16/barry-moore

King, J. E. (2009). *Nicholas Kaldor.* Palgrave Macmillan.

Kuiken, J. R. (2013). *Empires of energy: Britain, British petroleum, Shell and the remaking of the international oil industry, 1957–1979.* Doctoral dissertation, Department of History, Boston College. https://dlib.bc.edu/islandora/object/bc-ir:104079/datastream/PDF/view

Kuiken, J. R. (2014). Caught in transition: Britain's oil policy in the face of impending crisis, 1967–1973. *Historical Social Research / Historische Sozialforschung, 39*(4), 272–290.

Laidler, D. (1976). Inflation in Britain: A monetarist perspective. *American Economic Review, 66*(4), 485–500.

Lavoie, M. (2010). *From macroeconomics to monetary economics: Some persistent themes in the theory work of Wynne Godley.* Department of Economics, University of Ottawa. http://www.levyinstitute.org/conferences/godley2011/Lavoie.pdf

Lavoie, M., & Zezza, G. (Eds.). (2012). *The stock-flow consistent approach: Selected writings of Wynne Godley.* Palgrave Macmillan.

Layard, R. (1982). *More jobs, less inflation: The case for a counterinflation tax.* McIntyre.

Lee, F. S. (2007, November 1–3). *Making history by making identity and institutions: The emergence of Post-Keynesian–heterodox economics in Britain, 1974–1996.* Paper presented at the EAPE Conference, Universidade Porto, Porto.

Levy, D. (1999, March 1). Interview with Arnold Harberger: An interview with the dean of the "Chicago Boys". *The Region.* Federal Reserve Bank of Minneapolis.

Levy, W. J. (1971). Oil power. *Foreign Affairs, 49,* 652–668.

Levy, W. J. (1982). *Oil strategy and politics, 1941–1981.* Westview Press.

Maloney, J. (2012). The Treasury and the New Cambridge School in the 1970s. *Cambridge Journal of Economics, 36*(4), 997–1017. https://academic.oup.com/cje/article/36/4/997/1710182

Marcuzzo, M. C., & Rosselli, A. (2019). The Cambridge Keynesians: Kahn, J. Robinson and Kaldor: A perspective from the archives. In M. C. Marcuzzo (Ed.), *Essays in Keynesian persuasion* (Chapter 5, pp. 76–102). Cambridge Scholars Publishing.

Mata, T. (2012). Godley moves in mysterious ways: The craft of economic judgment in post-war Britain. In D. B. Papadimitriou & G. Zezza (Eds.), *Contributions to stock-flow modelling: Essays in honour of Wynne Godley* (pp. 12–35). Palgrave Macmillan.

Matthews, R. C. O. (1989). Joan Robinson and Cambridge – A theorist and her milieu: An interview. In G. R. Feiwel (Ed.), *Joan Robinson and modern economic theory* (pp. 911–915). Palgrave Macmillan.

Medhurst, J. (2014). *That option no longer exists: Britain 1974–76.* Zero Books.

Minford, P. (2013, April 9). We should treasure Margaret Thatcher for saving us from economic disaster. *WalesOnline.* https://www.walesonline.co.uk/news/wales-news/margaret-thatcher-saved-britain-economic-2569217

Neild, R. (2012). The '1981 statement by 364 economists' revisited. *Royal Economic Society Newsletter, 159,* 11–14.

New Scientist. (1975, March 20). Towards a self-sufficient Britain? *65*(941).

Newbery, D. (2017). Frank Horace Hahn 1925–2013. *Biographical Memoirs of Fellows of the British Academy, XVI,* 485–525. https://www.britac.ac.uk/sites/default/files/23 Hahn 1837 9_11_17.pdf

Nickell, S. (2006). The budget in 1981 was over the top. In P. Booth (Ed.), *Were 364 economists all wrong?* (pp. 54–61). Institute of Economic Affairs.

Papadimitriou, D. B., & Zezza, G. (Eds.). (2012). *Contributions to stock-flow modelling: Essays in honour of Wynne Godley.* Palgrave Macmillan.

Pasinetti, L. L. (1991). Richard Ferdinand Kahn, 1905–1989. *Proceedings of the British Academy, 76,* 423–443.

Pasinetti, L. L. (2007). *Keynes and the Cambridge Keynesians. A 'revolution in economics' to be accomplished.* Cambridge University Press.

Penrose, E. (1975). The development of crisis. *Daedalus, 104*(4), 39–57.

Philpot, R. (2017). *Margaret Thatcher: The honorary Jew. How Britain's Jews helped shape the Iron Lady and her beliefs.* Biteback Publishing.

Posner, M. V. (1981). *The organisation and finance of the modelling effort in the UK* (Unpublished). Paper for The Bank of England Panel of Economic Advisors.

Robinson, J. (1981, April 14 and 16). *The arms race. The Tanner lectures on human values delivered at the University of Utah.* https://tannerlectures.utah.edu/_documents/a-to-z/r/robinson82.pdf

Scanlon, H. (1968). *The way forward for workers' control.* Pamphlet Series No. 1. Institute for Workers' Control.

Schiffman, D. (2013). *Richard Kahn and Israeli economic policy, 1957 and 1962.* Ariel University. https://ssrn.com/abstract=2373517

Schlefer, J. (2013, September 10). Embracing Wynne Godley, an economist who modeled the crisis. *The New York Times.*

Shipman, A. (2019). *Wynne Godley: A biography.* Palgrave Macmillan.

Smith, R. P. (1976). Demand management and the 'New School'. *Journal of Applied Economics, 8*(3), 193–205.

Smith, D. (1987). *The rise and fall of monetarism: The theory and politics of an economic experiment.* Penguin.

Smith, G. (2016). *The New Cambridge School: Contribution and legacy.* http://www.cpes.org.uk/dev/wp-content/uploads/2016/07/Graeme_Smith.pdf

Stewart, H. (2002, September 16). View from the terraces. *The Guardian.*

Tarling, R., & Wilkinson, F. (1977). The social contract: Post-war incomes policies and their inflationary impact. *Cambridge Journal of Economics, 1*(4), 395–414.

Taylor, L. (2004). *Reconstructing macroeconomics: Structuralist proposals and critiques of the mainstream.* Harvard University Press.

Thatcher, M. (1993). *The Downing Street years.* Harper-Collins.

The Telegraph. (2010, May 21). Professor Wynne Godley. *The Telegraph.* https://www.telegraph.co.uk/news/obituaries/finance-obituaries/7750835/Professor-Wynne-Godley.html

Thirlwall, A. (1987a). *Nicholas Kaldor.* New York University Press.

Thompson, J. B. (2005). The new visibility. *Theory, Culture and Society, 6,* 31–51.

Travis, A. (2011, December 30). Thatcher government toyed with evacuating Liverpool after 1981 riots. *The Guardian.*

Tribe, K. (Ed.). (1997). *Economic careers: Economics and economists in Britain 1930–1970.* Routledge.

Vernengo, M. (2013, September 14). Hydraulic Krugman on Wynne Godley. *Naked Keynesianism: Hemlock for Economics Students.* http://nakedkeynesianism.blogspot.com/2013/09/hydraulic-krugman-on-wynne-godley.html

Vernon, R. (1975). An interpretation. *Daedalus, 104*(4), 1–14.

Volcker, P. (2000). *Interview. Commanding heights, public broadcasting service.* Interviewed on 26 September, 2000. https://www.pbs.org/wgbh/commandingheights/hi/people/pe_name.html

Walters, A. (1981). *Alan Walter's diary 1981.* Transcribed from the original at Churchill Archive Centre (WTRS 3/1/1). https://www.margaretthatcher.org/document/137536

Ward, T. (1982). Mrs. Thatcher's economic strategy in practice. *Cambridge Journal of Economics, 4*(4), 516–530.

CHAPTER 7

'Unintended' Collateral Damage? The Cambridge Economic Policy Group and the Joseph-Rothschild-Posner SSRC Enquiry, 1982

Abstract Two independent processes, first, the periodic CEPG funding application to the SSRC being dealt with by the Consortium set up by the SSRC Chairman Michael Posner to adjudge the competition for macroeconomic modelling grants and second, the Rothschild Enquiry launched by Keith Joseph in 1981, run in close parallel, and are co-terminus in reaching their final decisions. It is known that Posner had form and history in opposition to the Cambridge group with which he had (jointly with Richard Kahn) engaged in running policy, theoretical and doctrinal skirmishes, often ill-tempered, through the 1970s; that his politics had come to be well to the right of the some of the left-leaning leading members of the CEPG and related Cambridge Keynesians, and that he was a key member of Robin Matthews' CLARE Group of like-minded, and like-acting, economists who were prominently of SDP loyalty and affiliation—with Matthews, at the time, along with Frank Hahn, leading an assault on the Cambridge heterodox economists within the Cambridge Faculty and the DAE, the home of CEPG. Belying all apocalyptic predictions based on the known Thatcher-Joseph hostility towards radical social science, the SSRC emerged from the Rothschild Review only lightly, not mortally, wounded; in sharp contrast, the outcome was negative and fatal outcome for the CEPG, with the tidings, both the happy and the sad, coming almost simultaneously from Posner in the SSRC. Strikingly, while the Godley-Cripps team—a vanguard of opposition to Thatcherite monetarism—was axed out of existence, a couple of other units of monetarist persuasion that were prominent for their support for the Thatcher policy regime, received financial support in the same application round from Posner's SSRC Consortium.

© The Author(s), under exclusive license to Springer Nature Switzerland AG 2022
A. Saith, *Cambridge Economics in the Post-Keynesian Era*, Palgrave Studies in the History of Economic Thought,
https://doi.org/10.1007/978-3-030-93019-6_7

At a formal institutional level, the two processes were entirely distinct, and ran their separate courses. However, their curious inter-weaving and final confluence raises intriguing questions over the possibility that the imperatives released by the process underlying the Rothschild SSRC Enquiry might directly or indirectly have influenced some outcomes with regard to SSRC's choices pertaining to the funding of macroeconomic modelling. The circumstantial evidence could credibly suggest such a hypothesis—but in the unsurprising absence of conventional forensic evidence, all that can be adduced is a corpse and a conjecture with no visible sign of a hand holding that smoking gun. This hypothesis is sketched out, partly because the case of the Rothschild Enquiry also highlights aspects of the deep ideological schism in this tumultuous period when neoliberalism, in its various manifestations, took hold in the UK, and globally, and systematically began to assert its hegemonic authority to discipline the inherently unruly, that is, left-oriented, social sciences. Cambridge post-Keynesian economics led by left-leaning economists were in the forefront of the firing line. This saga also reveals how the downfall of Cambridge heterodox traditions in economics was not just a local affair, a coup that started and ended within Sidgwick Site, but how the Cambridge episode was an expression of the wider ideological, political and material forces of global capitalism in the 1975–85 decade that was arguably the period of inflexion—where extreme free-market and libertarian agendas began to challenge and roll back the post-War social contract involving the welfare state and Keynesian macroeconomic management. In this charged ideological environment with the SSRC ostensibly under existential threat, did the CEPG come to be a bargaining counter quietly traded down the river out of the public eye? Was the closure of the CEPG a convenient case of collateral damage that conceivably served multiple interests? The truth lies dead and buried with the principals involved in the key transactions.

7.1 Joseph—Rothschild—Posner—Godley

The saga of the Rothschild Enquiry into the Social Science Research Council (SSRC) in 1982 and its fallout has four main characters: Keith Joseph, who commissioned the Enquiry with a hostile agenda and an axe to grind and wield against the SSRC, a proxy for the social sciences, sociologists, socialists, Cambridge Keynesians and their leftist ilk; the seasoned Lord Rothschild, to whom Joseph mistakenly delegated the task of undertaking the full-scale Enquiry that he expected to provide the ammunition, even the direct recommendation, for dismantling the SSRC as an organisation; the polymath Michael Posner, conflicted Keynesian, many things to many people, who had assumed the chair of SSRC months before Thatcher came into power in May 1979, and who was confronted by the challenge of damage limitation in the face of the Thatcherite assault; and the almost-other-worldly Wynne Godley, whose high-profile Cambridge macroeconomic modelling team, the Cambridge Economic Policy Group (CEPG), powerfully opposed to Thatcherite policies, was mid-stream with SSRC in the processing of its periodic application for SSRC funding on which it depended—funding that Posner and his appointed committees abruptly and arbitrarily terminated during the period when Posner was horse-trading with Joseph over the recommendations of the Rothschild Report which supported SSRC continuation, and when Joseph was seeking ways to further his original agenda via deals and understandings with SSRC, via Posner. Godley could also be posted as Wynne the Silent, since his role in the drama seems really to be to wait in the side-lines till it is time for the CEPG to come on to stage to be stabbed by the Consortium, at which point he is scripted to complain from beyond the grave.

The two processes, vis-à-vis the CEPG application to the SSRC being dealt with by the SSRC Consortium set up by Posner to adjudge the competition for macroeconomic modelling grants, and the Rothschild Enquiry, run in close parallel, and are co-terminus in coming to their final decisions. It is known that Posner had form and history in opposition to the Cambridge group with which he had (jointly with Richard Kahn) engaged in running policy, theoretical and doctrinal skirmishes, often ill-tempered, through the 1970s; that his politics were well to the right of the some of the leading members of the CEPG and related Cambridge Keynesians, and that he was a leading member of Robin Matthews' CLARE Group[1] of like-minded, and like-acting, economists who were prominently of SDP loyalty and affiliation—with Matthews, at the time, along with Frank Hahn, leading an assault on the Cambridge heterodox economists within the Cambridge Faculty and the DAE, the home of CEPG. Remarkably, the positive outcome for the SSRC which emerged from the Rothschild Enquiry, leaving SSRC wounded though not mortally, and the negative, fatal outcome for the CEPG, were announced on the same day, virtually in the same communication from Posner in the SSRC. While the Godley-Cripps CEPG team—a vanguard of opposition to Thatcherite monetarism—was axed out of existence, a couple of others of monetarist persuasion, that were prominent for their support for the Thatcher policy regime, received SSRC support in the same application round.

At a formal institutional level, the two processes are entirely distinct, and run their separate courses. However, their curious inter-weaving and final confluence raises intriguing questions over the possibility that the imperatives released by the SSRC Enquiry process might directly or indirectly have influenced some outcomes with regard to SSRC's choices pertaining to the funding of macroeconomic modelling. The circumstantial evidence supports such a hypothesis—but in the absence of conventional forensic evidence, all that can be adduced is a smoking gun and a conjecture. This hypothesis is sketched out partly because the case of the SSRC Enquiry also highlights aspects of the deep ideological schism in this tumultuous period when neoliberalism, in its various manifestations, took hold in the UK and globally and also systematically began to assert its hegemonic authority to discipline the inherently unruly social

---

[1] CLARE stands for Cambridge, London and the Rest of England.

sciences. Cambridge post-Keynesian economics and left-leaning economists were in the forefront of the firing line. This saga also reveals how the downfall of Cambridge heterodox traditions in economics was not just a local affair, a coup that started and ended within Sidgwick Site, but how the Cambridge episode was an expression of, and embedded in the wider ideological, political and material forces of global capitalism in the 1975–85 decade that was arguably the period of inflexion—where extreme free-market and libertarian agendas began to challenge and roll back the post-War social contract involving the welfare state and Keynesian macroeconomic management (Table 7.1).

7.2 The Posner-the-Saviour Narrative

"The future of social science rests on two old gentlemen eating lox together", said Posner about himself and Lord Rothschild (Cunningham, 2006). Posner might have had a point if he had claimed to be saving the organisation rather than the discipline. A narrative has been constructed that ordains Posner as the saviour of the social sciences. It originates in the rightful recognition of his tremendous lobbying efforts to influence the outcome of the Enquiry; but the burnishing of this image has come mostly from internal quarters, from a glossy Economic and Social Research Council (ESRC) write up about its past, from Posner himself in his own retrospective piece written in 2002 from the safe distance of Paris and retirement, and then from correctly appreciative obituaries in 2006 from his friends and colleagues in SSRC or Cambridge. They tell a tale of heroism; is it perhaps just a bit too tall?

> Described today as 'the unsung hero of the SSRC/ESRC' and 'the man who saved the Council', Posner possessed charisma and vision. He also possessed an absolute determination to succeed and the relentless energy to network with establishment figures. All of this would be crucial to ensure the survival of the Council through the Rothschild Inquiry. (ESRC, n.d., pp. 16–17)

> Michael fought hard and skillfully for this conclusion. He realised, as did his fellow heads of research councils, that he was defending not only the social sciences but the independence of all publicly funded research from political pressure. His acquiescence to a change of name to the Economic and Social Research Council (ESRC) drew much criticism from the social science community. Michael's view was that he had lost one battle but won the war. (Cunningham, 2006)

> [The SSRC's] survival could be considered Michael's greatest achievement. (Cunningham, 2006)

Another obituary[2] says that Michael Posner played "a pivotal role safeguarding social science research in the UK" and that "his most salient achievement took place at the Social Science Research Council (SSRC) where he had in

---

[2] See also Bagchi (2010) for a biographical brief which cites the SSRC episode in similar vein.

Table 7.1 Timelines of actions and decisions leading up to the closure of the Cambridge Economic Policy Group, DAE Cambridge

	Date/period	Events or actions at different level involving various stakeholders							
		Government House of Lords	SSRC Enquiry 1982			At SSRC	SSRC–DAE	At Cambridge	
		Thatcher, Joseph	Joseph, Rothschild	Rothschild, Posner	Joseph, Posner	Posner	Posner, Godley	Various	
	C1	C2	C3	C4	C5	C6	C7	C8	
R1	January 1979					Posner appointed SSRC Chair by Callaghan Govt.			
R2	28 March 1979	Vote of No Confidence against Callaghan Labour Govt.; carried 311-310							
R3	May 1979	General Election Conservative Party wins, led by Margaret Thatcher.						In the 40-month period between May 1979 and October 1982, Wynne Godley wrote thirty three letters to the press, all critiques of government policy.	

(*continued*)

Table 7.1 (continued)

	Date/period	Events or actions at different level involving various stakeholders							
		Government House of Lords		SSRC Enquiry 1982			At SSRC	SSRC–DAE	At Cambridge
		Thatcher, Joseph	Joseph, Rothschild	Joseph, Rothschild	Rothschild, Posner	Joseph, Posner	Posner	Posner, Godley	Various
C1		C2	C3		C4	C5	C6	C7	C8
R4	June 1979	Margaret Thatcher becomes Prime Minister							
R5	1979–80	Mark Carlisle as Education Secretary					Two years of cuts Posner restructuring of SSRC priorities into themes		
R6		House of Lords concern over SSRC restructuring							
R7	April 1980						Posner forms and chairs SSRC Subcommittee on Review of Macro-econ Research in UK		
R8	July 1980	Kaldor gives Evidence to HMT & Civil Service Co; powerful attack on monetarism espoused by Govt. and its advisers							Kaldor gives Evidence to HMT & Civil Service Co; powerful attack on monetarism espoused by Govt. and its advisers

R9	29 July 1980	SSRC Sub-Co (Posner & Secretary) meet with CGP (Barker et al)	
R10	1980		Hahn & Neild letter to *The Times* attacking Thatcherite monetarism
R11	January 1981		Joseph debates with Galbraith in Cambridge. Joseph is pelted with eggs
R12	February 1981	Posner presents his paper on Financing Modelling etc. to BoE Panel of Econ Advisors; indicates new approach	
R13	13 March 1981		Hahn & Neild letter, attacking Thatcherite monetarism, circulated to UK universities
R14	28 March 1981		Hahn & Neild letter signed by 364 economists published in *The Times*

(*continued*)

Table 7.1 (continued)

	Date/period	Events or actions at different level involving various stakeholders						
		Government House of Lords	SSRC Enquiry 1982			At SSRC	SSRC–DAE	At Cambridge
		Thatcher, Joseph	Joseph, Rothschild	Rothschild, Posner	Joseph, Posner	Posner	Posner, Godley	Various
C1		C2	C3	C4	C5	C6	C7	C8
R15	7 April 1981	Patrick Minford Letter in *The Times* defending the Government and rebutting Hahn & Neild						Patrick Minford Letter in *The Times* defending the Government and rebutting Hahn & Neild
R16	April 1981	Brixton "disturbances"						
R17	29 April 1981	Thatcher writes personal letter of thanks to Patrick Minford						
R18	June 1981					SSRC accepts recommendations of Posner Sub-Co "in full"; formation of Consortium for grants, and new Macro-econ Modelling Bureau		

R19	14 July 1981	Tim Congdon Letter to *The Times* "how 364 economists can be wrong"	Tim Congdon Letter to *The Times* "how 364 economists can be wrong"
R20	July 1981	Liverpool Toxteth "disturbances" in Patrick Minford's backyard	
R21	29 July 1981	Frank Hahn Letter to *The Times*, scathing response to Congdon	Frank Hahn Letter to *The Times*, scathing response to Congdon
			Ken Coutts et al CJE article; strong attack on Thatcherite policies
R22	July 1981		
R23	September 1981	Keith Joseph succeeds Mark Carlisle as Secretary, Education & Science	
R24	1 October 1981		SSRC Sub Co Review of Macro-economic Research in UK published

(continued)

526 A. SAITH

Table 7.1 (continued)

Date/period	Events or actions at different level involving various stakeholders							
	Government House of Lords	SSRC Enquiry 1982				At SSRC	SSRC–DAE	At Cambridge
	Thatcher, Joseph	Joseph, Rothschild	Rothschild, Posner	Joseph, Posner		Posner	Posner, Godley	Various
C1	C2	C3	C4	C5		C6	C7	C8
R25 November 1981						Consortium (HMT, BoE, SSRC) on Macroeconomic Modelling established		
R26 10 December 1981	Joseph writes to Howe indicating further cuts to SSRC budget; and selection of Rothschild for SSRC Enquiry	Joseph mentions selection of Lord Rothschild for conducting an Enquiry into the SSRC						
R27 15 December 1981	Attack on SSRC by Lord Beloff in House of Lords							
R28 22 December 1981		Announcement of the SSRC Rothschild Enquiry						
R29 7 January 1982	Leak of Joseph letter of (10 Dec 1981 to Howe) in *New Society* causing a stir							

R30	February 1982	Lord Rothschild's Enquiry into SSRC opens; to report back in three months. No further contact between Joseph and Rothschild till submission of Draft Report
R31	18 February 1982	SSRC general orientation meeting on formation of MEM Bureau and related matters; DAE teams attend.
R32	February–April 1982	Rothschild takes evidence from over 600 sources; SSRC/Posner network and lobby; SSRC supplies materials (requested by Rothschild, and others) to Rothschild.
R33	18 February–17 March 1982	Decision-making period at SSRC for grants for projects on Macroeconomic modelling, including CGP and CEGP

(*continued*)

Table 7.1 (continued)

Date/period	Events or actions at different level involving various stakeholders							
	Government House of Lords	SSRC Enquiry 1982			At SSRC	SSRC–DAE	At Cambridge	
	Thatcher, Joseph	Joseph, Rothschild	Rothschild, Posner	Joseph, Posner	Posner	Posner, Godley	Various	
C1	C2	C3	C4	C5	C6	C7	C8	
R34 22 February 1982							Kaldor letter to Rothschild on SSRC including negative comments on Sociology and esp. Macro-econ forecasting models	
R35 17 March 1982						CEPG at DAE receives SSRC letter of invitation for application interview in London		

R36	22 March 1982		Hostile interview of CEPG by SSRC Consortium experts
R37	23 March 1982	Consortium makes decisions on funding of MEM projects	
R38	26 March 1982		Negative decision letter from Posner to Godley/CEPG application Godley Response-1 to Posner Godley Response-2 to Posner
R39	5 April 1982		
R40	6 April 1982		
R41	1 May 1982	Lord Rothschild delivers (draft) report to Keith Joseph	
R42	2 May 1982	Margaret Thatcher orders the sinking of the Argentinian ship Admiral Belgrano.	

(continued)

Table 7.1 (continued)

Date/period	Events or actions at different level involving various stakeholders							
	Government House of Lords	SSRC Enquiry 1982			At SSRC	SSRC–DAE	At Cambridge
	Thatcher, Joseph	Joseph, Rothschild	Rothschild, Posner	Joseph, Posner	Posner	Posner, Godley	Various
C1	C2	C3	C4	C5	C6	C7	C8
R43 12 May 1982	Keith Joseph has a half-hour meeting with Margaret Thatcher on the SSRC; it may be speculated that KJ was informing and getting approval of possible informal agreements reached and to be put into the public domain in Rothschild's formal report submission to KJ, which happens a week later						
R44 19 May 1982		Rothschild reports to Keith Joseph with twenty five recommendations. SSRC distributes Report with covering letter from Posner saying the first round of awards by the new Macro-economic Modelling Consortium were being announced the same day.			On behalf of Consortium, SSRC announces 7 awards, incl. savage cut to CEPG rejecting all funding for its macroeconomic modelling activity. CEPG effectively terminated; CGP survives with conditions; Liverpool/ Minford, and LBS win grants.		

R45	May–October 1982	• Keith Joseph "sitting on the Report"; declared a two-month period for public consideration of report and its recommendations; then government assessment for response and action; • Joseph sends Oliver Letwin to SSRC for deep investigations to ferret out problems and issues; • Setting up of Berrill Committee to investigate allegations of research biased in favour of trade unions by IRRU/Warwick of SSRC; Committee reported on 5 May 1983 rejecting the charge of bias. • Negotiations between Posner and Joseph, and between Joseph and Rothschild on details of final report and its recommendations, and other steps to be taken by SSRC as part of the deal between Joseph and Posner.	In the forty-month period between May 1979 and October 1982, Wynne Godley wrote thirty three letters to the press, all critiques of government policy.
R46	30 June 1982	House of Lords: Debate on Report of Rothschild SSRC Enquiry	
R47	14 October 1982		Joseph decision letter to SSRC
R48	14 October 1982		Posner's letter of response to Joseph's decision letter.
R49	October 1982	Emergence of the narrative of Posner as the saviour of the social sciences; SSRC survives thanks to Posner's efforts; with just the nominal condition of a name change from SSRC to ESRC as the price to pay.	

1979 been appointed chairman by Labour ministers about to depart office. The post plunged him into a fierce battle to save the council's existence once its future role, if any, had been questioned by the incoming Thatcher team" (The Times, 2006).

Posner himself refers to "negotiations" with Joseph (Posner, 2002, #76). "I played a poor hand as best as I could", said Posner (Kuczynski, 2006). Kuczynski observes that in the end, "Joseph's aversion to 'social science' allowed Posner to outmanoeuvre him into accepting Rothschild *in toto* in return for replacing the offending term by 'economic and social' in the council's title." Posner said, "I told him [Joseph] that I could persuade scores of academics to accept a name change if he would promise, on the record, the continuing independence of the SSRC. He agreed" (2002, #74) Posner told the press, "Sir Keith can call it the White Fish Authority if he likes" (Kuczynski, 2006). But had Posner really pulled a large rabbit out of a small hat? Was this the only price to pay?

One popular narrative tends to suggest that this was almost all there was to it, a name change; Posner was declared "the saviour of the social sciences". There was a fair bit of jocularity directed towards Keith Joseph. Thus, "The new name provoked an outburst of sarcasm from Lord Rothschild, who described Joseph's initiative as 'timely, creative, logical, apposite, epistemologically unassailable and psychologically desirable'" (Denham & Garnett, 2001, p. 380). "Lord Rothschild also allowed himself one final word, congratulating the 'originality and intellectual penetration of the Secretary of State's proposal to substitute the old English word *Wissenshaft* for Science in the name of the SSRC'" (Flather, 1987, p. 365).

Posner (2002, #25) recalls Joseph suddenly throwing him the ball in a conversation on cuts, "Tell me, Mr. Posner, do you think the social sciences observe the Popperian paradigm?". At the business end of the Enquiry, the significance of the question was obvious. Posner points out that he "recognised that despite the fact that he could not now dissolve the SSRC, he could not fail to demonstrate his power and displeasure. Joseph opted for a public, but very light punishment: a change of name", with SSRC becoming ESRC, with the word "science", that offended Popperian sensibilities, being dropped. Posner accepted "with little compunction". In doing so:

> I often reminded academics of how the (Protestant) King of Navarre became King Henri IV of France by changing his religion, saying '*Paris vaut bien une messe*'. Alas, nobody ever laughed at this joke—I used to think it was because social scientists lack a sense of humour, but in retrospect it may be that they took their 'religion' a bit more seriously than I did. (ibid., #74, #75)

In this constructive popular narrative, Keith Joseph comes across as The Hapless Buffoon, left holding nothing at the end, his hubris and pride punctured; Rothschild comes across, statesmanlike, The Pronouncer of Wisdom standing up to raw power and meting out justice, standing bravely in the way of 'intellectual vandalism'; and Michael Posner as The Eventual Saviour. SSRC gets away with just a notional change of name, Rothschild and Posner each, separately, poke fun at Joseph about the outcome, and Joseph, in keeping with his destiny as loser, is left fuming in high dudgeon. Such bouts of smug self-congratulation were perhaps stimulated by the immediate sense of relief of survival; however, darker realities lurked in the shadows.

7.3   Setting Up the Enquiry

"Following two years of major cuts in the council's budget, Sir Keith Joseph, newly appointed secretary of state for education, questioned the need for a research council for the social sciences. To him the disciplines were not scientific, and social scientists in general had leanings towards socialism" (Cunningham, 2006). Keith Joseph's views were strongly held, and well known. He, as Margaret Thatcher, believed that university social science research was rife with left-wing bias that needed to be rooted out. Indeed, Thatcher, in her earlier stint as Secretary of State for Education in the Heath Government, had had a go at the SSRC—then defended effectively by Robin Matthews who was Chairman of the Council at the time. So Joseph was picking up the hatchet where Thatcher had left it in the Tory closet. In this, he was aided by fellow fundamentalist liberals who took up cudgels against social science research in general, and the SSRC in particular, including especially Lord Max Beloff, and Lord Ralph Harris. Beloff raised the spectre, bogey as it turned out, of SSRC consciously funding left-wing research units biased in favour of trade union positions, citing the case of the Industrial Relations Research Unit at Warwick University. "Sir Keith Joseph authorized an investigation into alleged 'left-wing bias' in courses run by the Open University (Times Higher Education Supplement, 15 October 1982)". Margaret Thatcher had rejected the validity of any notion of "society"; and her guru Keith Joseph following his guru Karl Popper, raised an existential threat against the SSRC: "believing that the term 'social science' was philosophically a contradiction in terms, Joseph would have summarily abolished the Social Science Research Council late in 1981" (Brown, 1998, p. 274). Fortuitously, or by design, or by caution, Keith Joseph agreed to advice to avoid precipitate action against the SSRC as this would draw extensive criticism across a broad swathe of informed opinion; it would be wiser to lay a paper trail, to base his actions on the outcome of an enquiry, which it was presumed would confirm the Thatcher-Joseph charges and claims of biased research.

The ostensible reasoning was that Lord Victor Rothschild had earlier conducted a similar review of the Natural Sciences, that Social Sciences had not then been included in the remit of that enquiry, and hence a fresh, similar, enquiry was justified, even essential for good order, perhaps also in view of the ongoing fiscal cuts that would demand sharper interrogation of research priorities. There are well-known dangers in believing your own propaganda, and Keith Joseph might well have imagined that the case against social science research funded by the SSRC would surely be as obvious to Rothschild as to himself. That, of course, was not to be. Rothschild was a powerful, independent minded and vastly experienced and networked scientist, intellectual and mandarin; he was his own man.

> On 10 December 1982 [this should almost definitely be 1981] Joseph wrote to Sir Geoffrey Howe, suggesting a further cut of around GBP 2 million in the Council's budget and informing the Chancellor that he had set up an inquiry under Lord Victor Rothschild to decide whether projects might be funded by the private sector in future. If so, Rothschild was asked to consider whether 'there would be any continuing justification of the Council's existence'. Evidently, Joseph was confident that Rothschild would reach the right conclusions, and he pointed out to Howe the benefits 'of proceeding with a tried and respected operator' (*New Society* 7 January 1982, cited in Denham & Garnett, 2001, pp. 379–380.) Five days later an attempt was made to soften up public opinion, when Lord Beloff launched a stinging attack on the Council in the House of Lords. Perhaps the co-ordinated attempt to give the SSRC a bad name before hanging it persuaded a civil servant to be 'careless'; Joseph's confidential letter found its way to *New Society*, along with Howe's encouraging reply. Rothschild had been an eccentric choice for a hatchet-job in any case; his high standing arose from his reputation for objectivity as well as his formidable intellect. But even if he had been persuaded about the need for action by stories of some of the SSRC's more outlandish acts of generosity, the leak compromised his position. His report, published on 19 May 1982, was typical of the man; the polished prose of an experienced public servant betrays Rothschild's real feelings about the task Joseph had invited him to perform. (Denham & Garnett, 2001, pp. 379–380)

7.4 Who Proposed Rothschild?

"He [Keith Joseph] was persuaded to invite Rothschild to conduct a one-man inquiry into the SSRC before taking action" (Cunningham, 2006). Who did the 'persuading'? Again, in the popular narrative, the appointment of Rothschild for conducting the SSRC enquiry is painted as a stroke of inspired genius—it is as if there was a quiet conspiracy amongst some to subvert the process, as if they all knew that Rothschild would reject Joseph's poorly disguised agenda to shut down the SSRC. Such claims to clairvoyance on the part of the proposers of the name, and presumption of naiveté on the part of Joseph in accepting the proposal, also go further than they really should. The idea that Posner, and/or Ralf Dahrendorf, might have 'saved' the SSRC through manoeuvring the appointment of Rothschild can be laid to rest. "Although Posner had seen Joseph more often in three months than Carlisle (the previous Secretary of State for Education) in two years, he was not told of the Rothschild Enquiry till the evening before the announcement to Parliament. He briefly considered resigning" (Kuczynski, 2006). Posner, then, had no hand in manipulating the suggestion to, or the persuasion of Joseph, to appoint Rothschild to the job.

That the suggestion of Victor Rothschild's name came really from William Waldegrave is entirely credible; he was then the Under Secretary of State for Education working under Keith Joseph, and a rising Tory star. Peter Hennessy (2015) writes, "William Waldegrave adored Victor Rothschild". He quotes Waldegrave's words:

> he was a very good scientist and had been every Boy's Own hero—a first class cricketer, George Medal for bomb disposal, taught to play jazz by Teddy Wilson ... A Renaissance Man. And he was a tremendous believer in what, at its worst, can become a sort of scientism—that there is a scientific explanation for everything ... The thing he taught me ... is the absolute commitment to the application of intelligence to the solution of problems. [And he was] a tremendous operator.[3]

The expectant Joseph, however, had reasons to be quietly satisfied with his appointment. For one, Rothschild—the ex-research coordinator of Shell and head of the Central Policy Review Staff the government think tank liaising with the Prime Minister's office—was not Labour or a labour DNA carrier; he had links with the Conservative party.[4] So there could be no presumption of predetermined animosity. Then, we know from Waldegrave, that Mrs Thatcher quite liked Victor Rothschild. He had been the head of the CPRS, the think tank created to directly support the Prime Minister, in his case, Ted Heath. As David Walker notes: "Joseph felt he needed the cover of an inquiry and Victor Rothschild was an obvious candidate: biologist, sufficiently Tory friendly and eminent" (Walker, 2016, p. 45).

However, the notion that Waldegrave, in suggesting Rothschild as the person to undertake the SSRC Enquiry, was acting with cunning to subvert the Thatcher-Joseph agenda with regard to the social sciences and the SSRC hardly bears scrutiny. If anything, Joseph might have been quite comfortable about the person recommending the name. As Hennessy (2015) says, "Lord Waldegrave got on well with Mrs Thatcher which is perhaps surprising given his being the son of an earl (who was a minister in the Macmillan government), Eton, All Souls, Toffdom incarnate". And Joseph was equally comfortable also with the name recommended, that is, Rothschild, as was confirmed by his

---

[3] "Victor used to give lunches on Wednesday after the permanent secretaries' meeting with sandwiches from the Mirabelle and what was called cider cup made by his butler Rifleman Sweeney, which was mostly brandy and the purpose of which was to get the permanent secretaries drunk"; and Hennessy adds that "it tended to work" (Hennessy, 2015). Waldegrave is referring here to his time with Rothschild when he was a junior in the Central Policy Review Staff, the Prime Minister's think-tank headed by Rothschild. Adding further spice to the exotic Rothschild cocktail, there were intriguing rumours where his name got metioned in speculations over the identity of the "fifth man" (Leitch, 1994).

[4] For instance, Keith Brito, a member of the Conservative Research Department reported, "In 1980 Lord Rothschild wanted to finance a major research project for the Conservative Party. He was not prepared to give money directly to the Party and he did not want his involvement to be known. At the suggestion of the Policy Unit at No. 10, we suggested a research project on the level of economic literacy in the electorate. The research was commissioned with Marplan and paid for by Lord Rothschild via a third party" (Brito, 1982). The Economic Literacy Project was completed in April 1981 and the final report made in July 1981. It was subsequently due to be published.

endorsement in his leaked correspondence with Geoffrey Howe, the Chancellor, regarding the SSRC issue.

The polymath Baron Rothschild's reputation for intellectual ability and fearless independence and unwavering impartiality were well known. The weight and power of his persona were such that, according to Flather (1987, p. 358), "one colleague confessed: 'When I go to see him, I can only speak the truth'". Posner knew both Rothschild (with whom he had worked in the CPRS on energy policy in the early 1970s) and William Waldegrave; but the idea that Rothschild was some kind of puppet responsive to the tugs and pulls on the strings in the hand of Posner the puppeteer is a non-starter (and not attributable in any way to Posner himself).

Second, Rothschild, in his earlier, similar, commission in 1971 to review the natural sciences, had espoused the "customer-contractor principle", and this could well have induced Joseph to believe—wrongly as it actually turned out but might have been impossible to predict at the point of appointment—that he would apply the same model to the social sciences, in line with what Joseph would have liked in order to discipline the social sciences into dancing to the tune of the pay masters, the government, or the private sector that he wanted to push as potential alternative sources of public research funding. Clearly, with hindsight, Joseph read this incorrectly, and there were apparently indications in Rothschild's earlier report that pointed in this direction.

Third, while it might have been a good bet—though far from being odds-on—that Rothschild would not suggest an outright closure of the SSRC, there were a good many areas of serious vulnerability that remained for the SSRC, and Rothschild with his vast experience and skills, would have fished all these out and placed them on the table; and to a considerable extent, that is arguably what happened. Posner himself stated after the report was done that it was far from the "hatchet-job" that might have been feared but it was also as far from being a "white-wash". Apparently, "he revealed that almost to the last minute he had felt the Council might be closed, and he 'banished to a Siberian salt mine'" (Flather, 1987, p. 364).

Fourth, the 'clean chit' narrative overlooks some strongly critical aspects of the report, some of which were arguably damaging even if not that well informed. This applied clearly to Rothschild's dismissive treatment of and strictures against the rising discipline of Sociology—and in this regard, Rothschild was widely thought to have been off the mark. Several other heavy criticisms of the structure and function of the SSRC could also have served as instruments for Joseph to carry his battle against the SSRC, and to a considerable extent, it did.

In David Walker's assessment,

> Rothschild's report reeks of intellectual condescension but, amid the jibes, sarcasm and world-weary self-regard, he stuck with the view that some mechanism was needed to support a distinct body of work and the research council was it. The science establishment, with which he shared views critical of the intellectual

quality of much social science, was willing to rely on the judgement of an FRS. Rothschild threw one-lines to the gallery on sociology and the SSRC's administrative costs and opened the way for the Tories to flog a hobbyhorse in the shape of allegedly marxisant SSRC research on industrial relations. (Walker, 2016, p. 46)

Council folklore sees the reprieve as a watershed, but Walker is less convinced. The ESRC, rechristened, became more professional, relocated to a business park in Swindon and—allegedly, became more attuned to government and business. Administratively, the council became more cautious, more civil service like. Its capacity to think for itself, rather than function as an intermediary between Whitehall and universities, diminished. (ibid., 47)

And ultimately, it would be useful to remember that the final authority still rested with the Secretary of State; Rothschild's powerfully expressed and unambiguous opposition to a total shut-down of the SSRC might have thwarted this extreme part of Joseph's political agenda, but there were several strictures and punishments that he could mete out, even if not the guillotine. And so he did.

7.5 Rothschild Report Writing Process

Here again, we have accounts of how Rothschild, a known commodity, worked; and a hazy parallel suggestion that in his writing and recommendations, Posner and the SSRC managed to shift him towards a more favourable stance vis-à-vis the SSRC; and this adds to the 'saviour' narrative.

> In May 1982, the survival of the SSRC was still being decided. Together with Dr. Cyril Smith, the Secretary of the SSRC, and with Cathy Cunningham, the Deputy Secretary, I worked very hard to defend the SSRC. We had supplied Rothschild with a plethora of well-ordered reports ... The summer months had been difficult with Joseph re-considering even further financial cuts. (Posner, 2002, #71)

Rothschild was extremely active in asking for feedback and relied on over 300 submissions, both solicited and unsolicited, both before and after the deadline for submissions of comments, and held interviews with a wide range of members of the intellectual elite, many of them drawn from his vast personal network within academe and government, including a dense smattering of the great and the good. So the idea that SSRC bombarded Rothschild and thus influenced his thinking needs qualification—the collection of evidence was as much demand-driven by Rothschild himself, as supply-driven from the SSRC side.

Flather (1987, p. 359) writes about Rothschild's mode of work:

> he proceeded in his usual thorough fashion—the scientist at work. He wanted the facts about the SSRC's spending, definitions of what social science was, and alter-

native options for funding social research. He asked SSRC staff for endless detail about their operation, pursuing them relentlessly until they delivered. Many useful statistics thus emerged, some for the first time. Above all he consulted a select group of experts plus a number of trusted colleagues. Without doubt this group had a decisive impact on Lord Rothschild's thinking on the subject.

And most of these were from his own network of close contacts from academe.

Posner himself notes:

to find the answers to his inquiries, [Rothschild] canvassed the opinions of the 'leading experts' in any given field—he called them simply 'the best people'. If he could not find the experts, he would seek help from a specialist he knew to be 'best' in a related field. When he found his experts, he listened, argued, cross-referenced and searched for hidden flaws. If all the advice seemed to lead to a particular conclusion, he would try to find a contrary opinion and see if it could stand up to his rigorous examination. Evidently, much depends on what is meant by leading experts on (sic) the 'best people'. They will not necessarily be individuals from a chosen social class or with certain political opinions. Only those recognised by the scientific community as embodying the highest levels of excellence in their field would be considered. To find such individuals, Rothschild searched his list of acquaintances working in the social sciences, selecting them based on integrity, intelligence and achievement. The report is therefore full of the opinions of these experts. (Posner, 2002, #64–#67).

The final report carries an Appendix covering the testimonies provided by a selection of experts. But significantly, beyond this, there is reason to believe that other views were sought from unnamed experts that Rothschild approached directly for an opinion as, for instance, Lord Kaldor, whose comments were far from what Posner might have scripted if he held the pen. And according to David Walker (2016, pp. 46–47, citing Flather, 1987) "pressure from social science as an organised interest group was a negligible factor in the reprieve". Thus, the element of the narrative that Rothschild was influenced and 'guided', pointed in the desired direction, through a bombardment of materials from Posner and his colleagues at the SSRC is arguably another exaggeration.

Once commissioned, Rothschild never saw Joseph at all while doing his report (Flather, 1987); and in the eventual debate in the House of Lords, Lord Annan approvingly observes that "Sir Keith has given a completely clear run to Lord Rothschild". But Posner's reference to the joint eating of lox suggests that Rothschild did interact with Michael Posner during the writing of the draft and the period till its release, at least over one meal.

Jeff McMahan accidentally had a brief peep through the keyhole and recollects what he saw. Reminiscing about his time with his illustrious teacher Bernard Williams, McMahan (2012) winds up saying something about Rothschild instead:

I will mention one final recollection and then be done. Williams moved in exalted circles. When his friend, Lord Victor Rothschild, was commissioned by the Thatcher government to report on the future of the Social Science Research Council, he consulted Williams for a recommendation of someone who could check the logic of the arguments and the soundness of the grammar in his report. Williams's recommendation of me for the job led to a number of meetings with Rothschild in his magnificent house in Cambridge, to which I was invariably summoned by a handwritten note delivered to my door by his liveried chauffeur. There I was served fine wine and treated to conversation almost as exhilarating as Williams's own. While I was helping Rothschild to revise his report, there was much speculation in the British press about what his recommendations would be, which added a touch of *frisson* to the otherwise insular life of a graduate student, since I possessed that knowledge. I recall Rothschild's telling me that, although the Thatcher government both wanted and expected him to recommend the abolition of the SSRC, he was of course going to do nothing of the sort. For this the Tories never forgave him.

7.6 The Judgement of Rothschild

Rothschild made twenty-five recommendations, some brilliant, some fair and some fairly ugly.

For the SSRC, there were three huge positives up front: first, "the SSRC should not be dismembered nor liquidated" (R.2); second, that the SSRC's budget "should not be reduced in real terms below its 1982–83 level for a minimum period of three years" (R.4); and third, that "there should be no further enquiries into the SSRC apart from the recommended extensions to this enquiry and those required by Parliament, for a minimum period of three years from June 1, 1982" (R.5).

Rothschild borrows his incisive phrase from Barry Supple's one-paragraph comment to the Enquiry which would have provided the clearest possible statement on how a large part of the academic community viewed the exercise.

> To cut the amount of academic social-science research below the already exiguous figure for any reason would be an extraordinary act of intellectual vandalism; to do so because of any political resentment at the possible outcome of that research would be not merely an expression of ignorance about the nature, purposes and result of such research but would be a bitterly shameful step, quite contrary to this country's best traditions. (Rothschild, 1982, #9.141)

Given Joseph's transparent agenda, these three recommendations were easily the most powerful, and were unequivocal enough to have made Keith Joseph squirm, leaving him little room to dissemble and dismantle. Rothschild pronounced that "the dismemberment of liquidation" of the SSRC "would not only be an act of intellectual vandalism, but would also have damaging consequences for the whole country—and ones from which it would take a long time to recover." "Michael fought hard and skilfully for this conclusion", says Cathy Cunningham (2006), who was the Deputy Secretary at SSRC, and sticks this feather in Posner's hat. Of course, Posner had fought long and hard for such an outcome, but as Popper would no doubt have pointed out, this did not establish causality.

7.7 Between Draft and Release and Response: Handshakes and Cigars

Rothschild had let SSRC off the hook, at least in terms of its survival, and Joseph was seriously "riled", as the headline (on 28 May) of the THES announced. Beloff opened the debate in the House of Lords asking if it is so that Joseph "is very annoyed about the report"; it was indeed so. "It was known that his first reaction on receiving the Rothschild report was to pen a memorandum to the Prime Minister that was utterly dismissive of the finding. It had to be toned down by the civil servants" (Flather, 1987, p. 364). This is not quite what he had expected of the "tried and tested operator", who had obviously run rogue. But irate as Joseph might have been, he was not about to give up and walk away.

According to Cunningham (2006), Rothschild submitted his report to Joseph on 1 May—this would have to be the draft report to which some amendments were apparently made before the final report was released with its twenty-five recommendations on 19 May. The report was debated in the House of Lords on 30 June, where Lord Sandys informed the House that Keith Joseph had declared a two-month period for the public consideration of the report and its recommendations before any government response and action. In reality, Joseph sent his letter of decision to the SSRC on 14 October. Kuczynski (2006) states, "by sitting on the report from May to October, he gave the SSRC the advantage of getting briskly to work on its 25 recommendations. Posner, discreetly briefed from inside the DES on the mutilation to expect and prevent, had plenty of ammunition; and he had support among junior ministers". This 'waiting period' in this cat-and-mouse game gave Posner some room to manoeuvre, thus making it more difficult for Joseph to take summary hostile steps against the SSRC.[5] Posner wrote, later in 2002, "In May 1982, the survival of the SSRC was still being decided. ... Together with Dr Cyril Smith, the Secretary of the SSRC, and with Cathy Cunningham, the Deputy Secretary, I worked very hard to defend the SSRC. We had supplied Rothschild with a plethora of well-ordered reports and were now eager to receive the letter

---

[5] Joseph, possibly, was waiting for the outcome of the Kenneth Berrill Inquiry—initiated by Posner on 29 May, ten days after the Rothschild Report was sent to Joseph, and just a day before the scheduled debate on the Report in the House of Lords—into the allegations of pro-trade union bias in the work of the SSRC-funded Industrial Relations Research Unit (IRRU) at Warwick University. Joseph could have been keeping his powder dry, to use in a second-round assault on the SSRC should the Berrill Inquiry provide sufficient grounds for supporting the charge against IRRU. As it happened, the Berrill report was taking its own time, and it was not received till 1983, well after the dust had settled on the immediate aftermath of the Rothschild report.

from the Secretary of State Joseph announcing his intentions" (Posner, 2002, #71).

According to the well-informed Flather,[6] after the "Rothschild report was submitted in May 1982, there followed a series of meetings between Posner and Joseph. By late September it was clear the Council would be saved—but at a cost. After much re-drafting and various amendments Joseph wrote officially to the Council on 14 October outlining his decision on the SSRC, and Posner replied the same day" [This immediate response is remarkable in itself, and suggests that the contents of the communication from Joseph were known to him and held no surprises, being the statement of a mutual position already agreed]. "When the details were officially revealed four days later there was some dismay in the social science community—but overall the feeling remained one of relief. It transpired that Posner had been forced to 'buy off' Joseph with a series of promised reforms—a gentleman's agreement—that he was duty bound to stick with, whatever the ensuing reaction" (Flather, 1987, p. 363). What might these have been?

Though Rothschild placed various strictures on the SSRC, he had denied Joseph the justification and opportunity to close down the SSRC or to overly interfere with it in the immediate future. But Joseph was not done and mounted a rear-guard action. Having set up a full-scale enquiry in full view, he was not just going to walk away empty handed. He promptly opened a second potential line of attack.

> Joseph dispatched his new young political adviser, Oliver Letwin, a young right-wing Cambridge philosopher, the son of William Letwin, professor of govern-

---

[6] "Victor Rothschild I always admired; I got to know him when I was a journalist because he was appointed as the chairman of the inquiry into the future of the Social Science Research Council; Keith Joseph had decided that sociology, particularly, but maybe humanities more generally, was too left-wing. He admired economists particularly, but found economists here at Cambridge were generally too Keynesian. He liked Patrick Minford up in Liverpool who was a bit more monetarist and different, and there is something to be said for a degree of diversity in ideas; anyway he was convinced it was all a big Marxist plot, and he set up this inquiry, ostensibly to abolish the Social Science Research Council, and he appointed Victor Rothschild to chair it. Michael Posner was the Chairman of the SSRC, and I got to know him quite well; I went to interview Victor Rothschild, and apparently, he didn't like journalists but somehow we got on. I did a profile of him, and in the profile I happened to mention that he felt his greatest achievement was hitting 54 not out in a school match, and he was so thrilled that somebody had actually mentioned this in print that he and I became quite good friends and he was able to give me the inside track. I wrote a series of five very long articles about this inquiry, the biases and so on, and eventually Victor Rothschild came out with the conclusion that the SSRC should be saved, but maybe the name should be changed! What happened in the end was that it was called the Economic and Social Research Council. He was an amazing man; anything he wrote would be as sparse as possible. He had this excellent secretary and he used to write his letters and notes on thirds of a foolscap sheet, so you couldn't write more than a paragraph, and he would edit and edit, removing words until it was as sparse as possible and then he would send it" (Flather, 2019).

ment at the LSE and Shirley Robin Letwin,[7] the author, friends of Sir Keith, to re-examine the Council and presumably come up with the 'right answer'. The issue was far from dead in spite of Rothschild's tight stitching. Gloom once again descended on the council's Temple Avenue headquarters as staff were forced to ferret away, answering the young Letwin's questions. (ibid.)

It is not known what dirt Letwin dug up to aid Joseph in his subsequent negotiations and "gentlemen's agreements" with Posner, but at the time, "senior staff feared the worst, and Posner dropped public hints to that effect". Young Oliver had been sent "to ferret through SSRC documents to find the smoking gun" (ibid.).

What did Letwin and Joseph dig up from these excavations, and how was any such 'dirt' deployed in the subsequent 'negotiations' between Joseph and Posner, and up to a point almost certainly insofar as the content of the report was concerned, also Rothschild?[8] There were clearly two negotiating periods: first, between 1 May, when Rothschild submitted his draft to Joseph, and 19 May, when the finalised report was sent to Joseph, and it is not known how far Rothschild might have divulged the substance of these exchanges and changes to Posner. It is highly significant that Keith Joseph went to see Margaret Thatcher on 12 May and had a half-hour meeting with her explicitly on the topic of "SSRC", as recorded in her official diary for the day;[9] it can be fairly presumed that he was filling her in on the outcomes of the Rothschild draft, taking her mind on what might be their wish list for amendments to the draft, and agreeing to what final outcomes to achieve at the SSRC. And the second negotiating window would be between 19 May and sometime in the months of September/October, involving Joseph and Posner, before Joseph firmed up his mind and dispatched the letter of decision to Posner on 14 October. Some changes can be ascribed to one period or the other: for instance, Willy Brown (1998) confirms that the negative comment and hostile recommendation on IRRU was absent in the draft but there in the final report; and neither the draft nor the final report had any reference to a change of name—if anything,

---

[7] Oliver Letwin's parents were thoroughbred Hayekian libertarians, with close connections from LSE, and Chicago, where Shirley had been one of "a number of very able students" that Hayek attracted when he went there in 1950 (Doherty, 1995); and Charles Moore notes that Margaret Thatcher, assiduous at researching her speeches, had Shirley Letwin, alongside Bauer, Friedman, Hayek, Walkers, Skidelsky, Brittan and Johnson, on her reading (and heavy underlining) list. (Moore, 2013). Oliver grew up in the regular presence of the senior Hayekians in the libertarian salon that his parents ran at their home, was well-groomed in that tradition and was closely linked with its British luminaries, including Anthony Fisher, who started the Institute of Economic Affairs.

[8] Rothschild would most likely have to be part of the horse-trading since his draft report sent to Joseph apparently differed sharply from the final version with regard to the Beloff-Joseph issue of left-bias in the research of IRRU at Warwick.

[9] "MT Engagement Diary, 1982 May 12 Wed—1600 S/S Education [Sir Keith Joseph] re SSRC". The following appointment was for 1630 hrs. The digitalised archive for the Diary includes attachments of "all documents relating to this day", but there are none included for the KJ—MT appointment. https://www.margaretthatcher.org/document/124828.

Rothschild went to town on the question of the definition of social science and made provocative remarks about Popper etc.—but the name change appeared on the table in the second period between Joseph and Posner. While changes between the draft and the final reports are subject to direct comparison—for those with access—the smoke-room agreements between Joseph and Posner remain just there and can only be subjects of informed speculation.

7.8 Did Posner Get Away with Just a Change of Name?

In the Posner-as-Saviour narrative, he managed the stage and pulled the strings to get SSRC off the hook with little more than a change of name, kowtowing to Joseph's intellectual Popperian foibles, simply dropping the offending word, 'science' from the name of the organisation. Was it so simple? Was it just a change of name? The relief and hilarity that generally ensued in SSRC-related circles at this outcome distracted attention from several damaging underlying realities; this narrative simply slurps the sugar-coating without getting to the bitter pill.

The name-change demand was indeed a superficial and nominal one, though it did run into a good deal of hostile reaction from the social science academics as being intrinsically wrong. It went unremarked that this call for a name change—which did not figure at all in the Rothschild Report—was set off by two peers, Lord Annan and Lord Sefton, in the debate in the House of Lords on 30 June; and these were two strong *defenders* of the SSRC and virulently hostile to the Joseph agenda; the demand did not emanate from the Joseph-Popper camp represented in the debate by Beloff, Harris and Robbins. So Keith Joseph was not breaking any fresh ground anyway. What was afoot; were the two sympathetic peers throwing the growling wolves a bone to take them off the scent? If they were, whether individually or in tandem, the ruse might well have worked; Joseph conveniently picked on the change of name as a requirement in this period of 'public discussion' on the report. Joseph, however, spotted the red herring, and pushed hard on his other demands. Four other areas of impact need acknowledgment.

First, apart from the three positives, there were another twenty-two recommendations on the list, many of them negative, and some questionable. Even for the positive strictures, there were qualifications of concern. For instance, the stricture on the funding came perhaps too late: Rothschild himself noted in the Report that the budget of the SSRC had already been cut by 24 per cent in real terms in the previous five years with the result that only the top echelons of social scientists could now be supported. Rothschild fulsomely challenged the miniscule share of public funds going into social science research when compared with the natural sciences, and at an existential level, the Report provides full protection and relief to the SSRC. But, as noted by many (e.g. Halsey, David Walker), the damage had been done already by serious cuts in the previous three years. And the cuts continued apace, regardless of the stern recommendation.[10] Joseph squeezed the SSRC budget further to the tune of 6 million GBP over the following three years, the equivalent of approximately 8 per cent (Flather, 1987, p. 364).

Second, there was a paradox: on the one side, Rothschild, the proponent of the customer-contractor principle in his 1971 Review of the Science Research Council, had turned away from applying this in the case of the social sciences review, following extensive feedback arguing that this principle was unworkable as the 'customer' was not identifiable in any meaningful manner; there were simultaneously calls for a reversal of the ongoing 'Rothschildisation' of social science research (referring no doubt to Rothschild-SRC and not Rothschild-SSRC). Again, in reality, "during the 1980s ... the Council was also urged to direct its activities to problems of the national interest as understood in Whitehall and Westminster" (Halsey, 2004, p. 137). The person who had set off this trend was none other than Posner himself. He had been active in vigorously pushing both 'policy relevance' and 'commercial funding by customers', as for instance in the case of SSRC funding of macroeconomic modelling research—ignoring repeated concerns that such a compromise, systematically applied, would lead to a serious attrition, if not destruction, of the 'public good' dimension of much social science research. Kuczynski (2006) puts this in a positive light, citing it as an example of his skill and dynamism: "By the time Joseph arrived at the DES, Posner had dismantled the SSRC's subject-by-subject baronies, skillfully using interdisciplinary committees to shift limited funds (with some personal misgivings) from support for postgraduate training to collaborative 'managed' research initiatives". But it could equally be argued that this was a step in an undesirable direction, and this process was subsequently taken up and further as an explicit funding criterion by the ESRC chaired by Posner's successor, Douglas Hague, one of Thatcher's mentors.

Third, there was the dismal IRRU affair, presumably regarded, and largely ignored, as part of the butcher's bill, a marginal cost on the side for winning the main battle. Yet, it has been pointed out that these costs were not inconsiderable or incidental. Posner (2002) cites Willy Brown's (1998) paper to say that while the review of the Warwick Industrial Relations Research Unit carried out by Kenneth Berrill[11]—appointed for the task by Posner following the recommendation of the Rothschild enquiry—exonerated the research from the Beloff accusation of being biased in favour of trade unions, Beloff's

---

[10] The SSRC "was subjected to a sharp reduction in the flow of cash. The real resources of the Council both for research projects and for postgraduate studentships were cut step by step. In 1979 (at 1980 survey prices), the SSRC received just over GBP 20 million; by 1982 it was down by a quarter to GBP 15.2 million. In that year the number of postgraduate student awards for the main social science disciplines was less than one half of what it had been in the mid-1970s. During the 1980s, the SSRC (later ESRC) research budget was halved and the number of doctoral students supported by it fell by 75 per cent. The Council was also urged to direct its activities to problems of the national interest as understood in Whitehall and Westminster" (Halsey, 2004, p. 137).

[11] For the report, see Berrill et al. (1983).

intervention and Rothschild's recommendation were not without cost to the researchers as well as to the research initiative itself. Brown injects a note of sobriety: "Victories are never total, and the fact that both the SSRC and the IRRU had avoided abolition did not mean they were unharmed" (Brown, 1998, p. 278). The positive result was a close-run thing; he writes, "had there been a few more 'injudicious' words in the, perhaps, three million words in the [IRR] unit's publications, the verdict could have been disastrously different".

In Brown's assessment, Posner "was acutely aware of the unpredictability of the outcome of any such inquiry, especially one into such vague charges. An adverse or uncertain verdict could, in the hands of the SSRC's detractor, have broad repercussions". Posner deftly pre-empted such extreme outcomes by appointing one of his old Cambridge colleagues and friends, the hugely experienced and Whitehall-seasoned Sir Kenneth Berrill, to the task.

Brown rightly draws attention to the quiet, indirect, negative side effects that are overlooked in the narrative of acquittal. "Despite the unit's exoneration, it is likely that industrial relations research in Britain suffered lasting damage. The year-long period of uncertainty during the investigation, and continuing official hostility to industrial relations research, branded the subject politically risky in the thinking of both funding bodies and universities long after the episode had, for all but the few people immediately involved, been completely forgotten" (ibid., 279).

And Paul Flather, writing in the *Times Higher Education Supplement*, pertinently observed:

> Uneasy questions remain. Why were the charges taken so seriously in the first place and why was the trial not called off once the charge sheet was found to be empty? The probable answer is that Lord Rothschild needed some palliative to help the Government to swallow his whole report reprieving the SSRC, and that the air can only be cleared if 'serious charges' are 'investigated away'. The assumption [presumably on the side of Rothschild and SSRC] was that the unit could stand up well to scrutiny. (Paul Flather, *THES* 27 May 1983; quoted in Brown, 1998, p. 278)

Tellingly, Brown points out that there was little in the draft Rothschild report about the matter of left-wing biased research at IRRU, Warwick; if anything, "the main text contained two sympathetic references to the IRRU". Brown asserts, "there is authoritative evidence that this recommendation [that the IRRU's 'biased' research be investigated] was added after Rothschild sent his draft report to Keith Joseph" (Brown, 1998, p. 275). Likewise, there is no suggestion in the draft report that the name of the SSRC be amended to accommodate the belligerent Thatcher-Joseph stance on 'social science' being an oxymoron.

The investigation concerned allegations of unfair bias—emanating primarily from Lord Beloff—against the SSRC's Industrial Relations Research Unit (IRRU) at Warwick University, but somehow also included the SSRC's six-person Panel on Monitoring Industrial Relations. In explaining the delay in filing his Report, Berrill mentions "the task of reducing the allegations from the level of generalisations to specific charges was a lengthy one but produced only the relatively meagre list of instances" dealt with by the Report. Further, Berrill observes, "in reporting the accusations against the IRRU, Lord Rothschild associated them also with the SSRC Panel for the Monitoring of Labour Legislation (*sic*). The Berrill investigation discovered no complaints of bias against this Panel, and Lord Rothschild has agreed that 'he was under a misapprehension in linking the Panel and the IRRU'".[12]

Fourth, there was a remarkable assault on sociology as a discipline including highly restrictive and damaging recommendations that the community of sociologists regarded as being biased and misguided. "The SSRC [was] not to help establish new departments or sub-departments of sociology, nor finance those which specialists consider to be sub-standard".[13] In this, there seemed to be a streak of intellectual vandalism after all, pandering to popular philistine prejudice, pleasing the politicians. But the critique was too extensive and aggressive not to be read as a reflection of the personal perspective of Rothschild-the-natural-scientist. In contrast to other social science disciplines, including social anthropology, sociology got a separate chapter and, in it and elsewhere in the report, a battering. Halsey (2004, pp. 139–140) questions Rothschild's treatment of his discipline: "the lay reader would gain the impression that sociology was a pretentious mistake now discredited and replaced by more sensible [and in Rothschild's words] 'less ambitious and better established disciplines which are the heirs to the grander claims of sociology—for example, human geography, social psychology and social anthropology'". Halsey rightly protests, "this was a highly tendentious and ill-informed judgement" (ibid., 140). David Walker (2016, p. 46) adds, "Rothschild threw one-liners to the gallery on sociology and the SSRC's administrative costs and opened the way for the Tories to flog a hobbyhorse in the shape of allegedly marxisant SSRC research on industrial relations". The rising discipline of sociology could justifiably then

---

[12] "Lord Rothschild's Report itself offers no reasons for joining the Panel in his recommendation for an investigation into complaints of bias. Lord Beloff's evidence, which contains the accusation of bias on the part of the IRRU, makes no mention of the Panel. We asked those we interviewed to comment on the references to the Panel in Recommendation 21: no one was able to throw any light on the matter. When later we discussed the matter with Lord Rothschild, he told us that he had included the Panel in the recommendation because he had believed that the Panel and the IRRU were closely connected. He explained that the time limit set by the Secretary of State for Education and Science for his enquiry into the SSRC had precluded him from carrying out a full investigation into the affairs of either the IRRU or the Panel. Pressure of time had also prevented him from giving the members of the IRRU and the Panel opportunity to comment on the accusations made against them before submitting his Report to the Secretary of State. None of our witnesses made any complaints of bias against the Panel or could offer any explanation for its inclusion in our terms of reference. Lord Rothschild agrees that he was under a misapprehension in linking the Panel and the IRRU and that there was no ground for including the Panel in our terms of reference" (Berrill et al., 1983, pp. 4–5).

[13] Recommendation R.25, Report of the Rothschild Enquiry into the SSRC, May 1982.

not have endorsed the epithet of 'saviour of the social sciences' bestowed upon Posner.

A paradox calls for a detour picking on the sturdy defence of the SSRC and its mandate by Lord Sefton of Garston, speaking on behalf of Liverpool and Merseyside, in the debate on the SSRC Enquiry Report in the House of Lords in June 1982.

> I speak as an ultimate customer of the Social Science Research Council, not a representative of it. By 'ultimate customer' I mean somebody who has been elected to be responsible for looking at, and trying to solve, some of the problems which concern the Social Science Research Council: crime, poverty, race riots, drug addiction, urban deprivation, unemployment, and the state of the economy. If anyone wants a lesson in trying to gauge the necessary amount of resources to meet those problems, I recommend him to go and live in and try to manage a local authority such as Merseyside. The universities of this land have known about the social problems that I have mentioned, and have lived alongside them—and in Liverpool we have one of the best universities in the land, I am told—but they have made no contribution that I know of (they have certainly made none in my hearing) to the solution of those problems. The fundamental political principle behind the setting up of the Social Science Research Council was a general feeling that following the war, and beginning with the decline in our economic affairs ... the social problems that were becoming manifest needed an organisation to look into the subject and to propose solutions ... Evidently the problems are still there. ... I believe the reason lies inside Parliament. We talk about dismembering the Social Science Research Council, or we talk about putting their responses out to the market forces, or carrying out research where somebody finds a need for research and is willing to pay for it. What happens to the young kid in Liverpool who is now glue sniffing? Who pays for the research into that social problem? That can be applied to every social problem that exists. Nobody in the debate tonight has mentioned the ultimate consumer. I should not have spoken if the academics had bothered themselves about the fundamental requirements of the social services and the problems to be resolved by research. ... But I had to do so because I know what it is like and I know the kind of social problems that there are in Merseyside and the North East and in North East Wales and I know that they will come out of this depression, when the rest of the country is going to boom again, considerably worse off than when they went in. And what are the politicians doing about it? They are having a debate on whether or not we should keep an organisation like the SSRC whose responsibility is to research these problems and to come up with the answers. It will be a crime against the Humanities, against the academic life of this nation, if the academic world in this nation cannot come up with a solution perhaps to reorganise the SSRC into another body, perhaps to rename it, perhaps to give it more resources. But to dismember it will be disloyal to the nation's academic profession and, worse still, disloyal to the nation itself. (Lord Sefton of Garston, Debate on the Report of the SSRC Enquiry by Lord Rothschild, June 1982. *Hansard*)

The irony will be not be lost on the reader that it was in Sefton's Liverpool that Patrick Minford had been defending Thatcherite monetarism as the solution to the Merseyside's "concentration of hopelessness" (see Chap. 6); and that while Sefton was stoutly defending the SSRC citing Liverpool to underscore its relevance, Rothschild, who protected the SSRC as a whole, apparently liked Patrick Minford and his Thatcherite monetarism; and it was under the authority of Michael Posner, the "saviour" of the social sciences, that Minford's monetarist model received its SSRC funding, while that for the Godley-Cripps model (which had been sounding the alarm bells on rising unemployment as in Liverpool) was axed.

Rothschild's slate of twenty-five recommendations contained other insults and injuries which went largely unnoticed in the euphoria released by the narrative of 'survival'. The size and location of SSRC were challenged; the Chairperson need not be full-time, and need not be a social scientist; SSRC should "encourage social science departments to initiate American style PhD programmes with a rigorous first year of taught courses followed by an examination, and two further years devoted to a thesis in which competence is to be as important as originality"; delayed PhD submissions to be sanctioned; SSRC "to improve its links with industry, both in the public and private sectors"; SSRC to improve its communication skills, substance and style, with the supercilious observation added that "copies of *Plain Words* by Sir Ernest Gowers would help".

7.9 CEPG—Collateral Damage? Or, Traded Down the River?

At the end, this brings the SSRC episode to a zone of conjecture: its interface with the parallel, ongoing SSRC decision-making process on the allocation of its funding for alternative macroeconomic modelling applicants, including the two Cambridge teams, the Cambridge Growth Project (CGP) and the Cambridge Economic Policy Group. Sociology generally, and the IRRU Warwick, were bloodied in full public view by the Rothschild Enquiry and its aftermath, being high on the Thatcher-Joseph-Harris culling list of undesirables; but perhaps at the top of the hit-list were the leftist Cambridge Keynesians, most prominently the high-profile and highly vocal Godley-Cripps CEPG that was a constant presence in the media challenging Thatcherism and its monetarist agenda. Several questions and coincidences arise, even if without ready answers and explanations. The SSRC's Consortium, set up by Posner, remarkably, refuses funding for the CEPG, but finds resources for monetarist models, enough to attract press comment on the government exercising vengeance against its critics; this grant procedure and decisions come precisely in the months when Joseph is negotiating with Rothschild and Posner to extract outcomes that meet his political agenda; and he succeeds in the case of the IRRU; Joseph could not be unaware of the ongoing grant process at SSRC for macroeconomic modelling. It is a remarkable coincidence that SSRC outcomes emerge that would clearly match Joseph's wish list: the monetarist camp given voice, and the CEPG silenced. And it turns out that these SSRC grant decisions were announced at the same time as Joseph sent his decision about the Rothschild Enquiry to Posner at the SSRC. And through those months, Posner was engaged in meetings with Joseph reaching various deals, including that of the name change—these deals remaining a secret gentlemen's agreement that Posner was bound to implement, come what may. That the pacification of Cambridge Keynesian left—with which Posner had himself had a running battle—might have been a gentleman's request or requirement would hardly seem unexpected, prima facie. And would Rothschild, Posner and Joseph have been aided and emboldened in this by the swingeing critique of such modelling made from the heart of Cambridge by none other than by Nicky Kaldor himself? If radical sociology was bludgeoned in broad daylight, the left Keynesians were perhaps mugged 'independently' in a dark alley, out of sight.

There was no call on Rothschild to devote any special attention to the funding and supporting role of the SSRC with regard to the field of macroeconomic modelling of the UK economy, though this was an area that was a very substantial part of the SSRC economics portfolio—and also very much in the public eye at the time. There were several practitioners of this dark art of extracting prophecies each from their own crafted black-box: there was modelling within the government at the Treasury and the Bank of England; then there was the National Institute of Economic and Social Research (NIESR) that was a de-facto government out-sourced enterprise which soaked up the larger fraction of all SSRC funding in this field; prominently, there were the two top Cambridge teams, the 'old' CGP and the 'new' CEPG; and then there were various other initiatives in London, Liverpool and wider afield, including some new entrants of monetarist persuasion which appeared first as a flavour of the month but quickly became a taste of the future. The SSRC funding round was ongoing at the time that Joseph commissioned the Rothschild Enquiry, and the hostility of Thatcher, Joseph and Co. to Keynesian macroeconomic approaches was no secret, in particular their frequently aired distaste of left-wing Keynesianism of which Cambridge—both at the Faculty and at the DAE—was the epicentre. Was there an interface between the Enquiry and macroeconomic forecasting models, in particular, any fallout that could have some bearing on the SSRC's active decision making in this field? A trawl through some of the exchanges identifies three sets of comments, each drawn from a different source: first, feedback provided to Rothschild in the writing of the report; second, the specific commentary from Lord Kaldor, all the more significant in view of its provenance and timing, not to mention its typical bluntness; and third, allusions that arise when the Report is debated in the House of Lords.

7.10 THE ROTHSCHILD REPORT: GLEANINGS ON MACROECONOMIC MODELLING

The submission from The Royal Society makes a pertinent observation with direct relevance to the SSRC funding of macroeconomic modelling.

> A primary point which we all regarded as being of great importance is that the body making grants for research in the social sciences must be politically independent. This is especially important for the SSRC since most of the topics within it are to some extent political. In this area there are special difficulties if, for example, research is conducted on behalf of a Government department acting as 'customer'. To give one important example: because there were no completely objective laws of economics, it is possible, and perhaps tempting, to formulate and bias economic models to support the policy of the government of the day. The development of several different models lessens this danger. The fact that they may give different answers may be inconvenient, but at least highlights the uncertainties and may illuminate the nature of the problem even if the forecasts themselves are of limited or doubtful value. (Cited in Rothschild, 1982, #9.131)

Indeed, this also stands as a criticism of the SSRC's use of the newly created Consortium—created by Posner—to assess applications and award funding to competing macroeconomic models when most members of the Consortium, drawn largely from the Treasury and the Bank of England, were interested parties themselves, if not often the objects of criticism from some of the models they were assessing as 'independent', 'impartial' adjudicators. This problem was fully on display in the case of the denial of funding to the CEPG, and indeed later to the CGP. The irony is that the SSRC is presumed to be a bulwark against government bias, ignoring the possibility that the SSRC is itself a client of the government at a higher level of funding, and therefore not free from the pressures of manipulation.

The idea that research funded by the SSRC should be oriented to government policy needs is queried by Amartya Sen. He cautions against making social science research shift its funding dependence on to government departments in order to make it "practical". This could make the research ignore longer-term issues, become more susceptible to political pressure, and there would be "a real danger that research that could be potentially embarrassing to the government in power would not receive support. This will be, in fact, a giant step backward". He warns that "the confusing anxiety to make things look immediately practical—and not traditional 'academic'—would be then replaced by the real tyranny of excluding anything that would not fit into the narrow priorities of the then government policy or vision". And he follows up by dismissing Keith Joseph's idea of 'the ultimate customer', pointing out that "research findings in the social sciences are used by journalists, academics, policy makers, businessmen, administrators, politicians, social workers, lawyers, writers, and the public at large"; virtually, "the nation as whole is the customer". As such, linking specific research to specific paying ultimate customers is not a viable idea for the social sciences (Sen cited in Rothschild, 1982, #9.137–140).

Sir Donald MacDougall (Rothschild, 1982, p. 64, #9.98–100) highlights the conflict between public interest and private funding with reference to the NIESR's macroeconomic model.

> I have found the response of trade and industry most encouraging in showing growing confidence in, and support for, the NIESR's work, particularly in these difficult times. But it has become increasingly clear to me that industry and commerce are most unlikely ever to provide enough money to finance research at the NIESR which is in the general public interest rather than specifically geared to their own individual needs. The other main sources of non-public money are the charitable Foundations, and we continue to raise as much as we can from them; they cannot provide more that a limited amount. This means that adequate public finance for economic research is vital to the future of the NIESR. Now that the Treasury is withdrawing its support for the macro-economic programme, the SSRC has become the major source. Cutbacks in SSRC funds have already affected us and any further reduction in the volume of support from that source would be very damaging indeed to the work of the NIESR.

This reads virtually like a funding application to the SSRC, and it is striking that Rothschild includes this in his limited selection of feedback responses included in his report. MacDougall queries the popular argument from the Thatcherite group that 'public interest' research should find private money or perish.

7.11 Lord Kaldor—Off the Record, Off the Cuff, Off the Mark?

Rothschild also sought and received feedback from persons whose names were kept off the list of submissions in the Report. One such was from his friend Lord Kaldor,[14] who sent in a wide-ranging and hard-hitting letter (Kaldor, 1982). "I think there is a strong case for the continued existence of some such body as the SSRC in order to discover more than we know at present of how the British economy works and thus make it possible to pursue more appropriate policies and a better use of available instruments". But on these criteria, "much of the research financed by the SSRC up to now has not been justified ... the money spent was largely wasted".

Three types of research ventures receive a dismissive Kaldorian lashing. The first is thoughtless empirical research involving "endless fact-gathering with no clear purpose", a charge he levels mainly at sociology, for worrying about "the

---

[14] Keynes had also been a friend; Skidelsky (1992, p. 704) writes, "in the 1930s JMK used to dine frequently with Victor [Rothschild] and his first wife Barbara ...at their house in Newmarket"; this, notwithstanding the wide age gap: Keynes would have been between 50–57 years old, and Rothschild, 23–30 years in age.

number of times a week people take a bath or go to the cinema etc." But economics does not escape, excoriated for

> finding the 'realistic' values of hypothetical constructs which may have no real existence and whose only purpose is to enable a purely a-aprioristic model based on abstract and arbitrary assumptions (not supported by any empirical evidence as such) to take on a more scientific appearance ... a good example is the elaborate economic techniques that have been developed to measure marginal productivities of 'factors of production' when the thing of which measurement is sought (marginal productivity or the 'factor of production' to which it refers) may have no actual existence. ...In most research of this kind, the empirical results serve to 'decorate' a model rather than to 'verify' it.[15]

Kaldor (ibid.) points out that

> in the pre-war period there was very little research done on the Social Sciences on a collective or co-operative basis ... But during the great economic expansion of the post-war era it became almost a status symbol for a University Faculty in the Social Sciences (and particularly in Economics) to have its own research outfit attached to it; ... these research outfits of varying sizes have fully paid research workers and research assistants attached to them on short-term appointments. The continuation of their jobs depends on the receipt of grants from charitable foundations (like the Leverhulme Trust or the Nuffield Foundation) and later, from the SSRC. Naturally, they prefer to apply for a 'programme grant' comprising a large number of projects (which need not be closely related to one another) to a 'project grant' where each project is judged separately on its own merits.

Anyone could be forgiven for imagining that for some reason, Kaldor had the Cambridge DAE in his sights—but Kaldor clarifies that "the conspicuous example is the Economics Department of the University of York, though there are numerous others".[16] Kaldor's use of a twelve-bore, bird-shot cartridge

---

[15] Knowing Kaldor's penchant for unfiltered forthright expression, one might speculate which economists and which projects might have stirred his ire: could it be Hahn's Risk Project across the foyer in Cambridge? Or, the book by his Cambridge colleagues (and adversaries in faculty politics) Matthews, Feinstein (and Odling-Smee), just completed at the time Kaldor was writing his letter to Rothschild, on British national income using Solow's neoclassical model and methodology, attempting to empirically estimate the contributions of "factors of production" to output growth, measuring "total factor productivity", with the "unexplained residual" being attributed to "any contribution that may arise from increasing returns to scale and from the effects of technical progress and advances in knowledge, of shifts in resources between sectors, and of changes in the extent of obstacles to more efficient use of resources (e.g. restrictive practices on the part of management or trade unions). It will also reflect many errors in the measurement of inputs and outputs, and in the specification of the relationship between them" (Matthews et al., 1982, p. 15, quoted in Offer, 2008, p. 11). All this would be anathema to the Cambridge Keynesian economists like Joan Robinson, and Kaldor himself.

[16] Kaldor (ibid.) volunteers that he "was asked to pronounce on a large 'programme grant' for the University of York research outfit for five years on which I commented most adversely ... [but] the whole of the sum requested was granted by the SSRC". Coincidentally, the chairman of the

could well have risked wider collateral damage beyond his immediate target, including indeed the DAE at his Cambridge home base.

He goes on to his preferred mode of organisation of research: "I think teaching and research in the Social Sciences are best done together and not in isolation from each other and such research is best financed as academic research—i.e. by the Universities, and directed by the relevant faculties, the work being undertaken by people who are appointed mainly as teachers but who are given sufficient free time to do their own research". Again, legitimate as this position was, and much as it reflected Kaldor's personal style of research and teaching, he was attacking the emerging mode of collective research in teams, not least in his own discipline, and his own patch in Cambridge. This individualist, teacher- and teaching-driven approach, the standard template of which would be the term-off-teaching and the sabbatical after 'n' years, was indeed used a few years later by the Hahn-Matthews group to attack the DAE on precisely the same grounds. This is not to imply Kaldor supported that gang; but Kaldor was a self-starting, self-contained maverick one-off who did not depend on external finance, or on teamwork. As he says a little later in his letter to Rothschild where he refers to a project proposal, "this is the first time in my life that I have applied for a research grant either to the SSRC or to any other grant giving foundation". But there were other modes of research, and one can wonder where the Stone-Barker CGP and the Godley-Cripps CEPG teams at DAE would have fitted in Kaldor's preferred organisational framework for conducting economic research. Once again, there is the possibility of a negative fallout, even if implicitly, which could be perceived as being critical of team projects such as at the DAE.

Kaldor's third critical observation perhaps carries even greater salience, especially when read from a Cambridge, DAE vantage point—which was, of course, not the position from which Kaldor was responding to Rothschild's enquiry. But regardless of whichever hat Kaldor was wearing when writing, his words might not have made comfortable reading in the two macro-modelling teams of the DAE, both financially dependent on, and then with pending grant applications with the SSRC. Kaldor's critique of macroeconomic forecasting models, and their financing by SSRC, carries very considerable weight, given the breadth of his exposure to all functioning players, and the depth of his knowledge about the policy purposes that the models were supposed to address.

His first objection is to the charge to public funds: "my feeling is that to finance through the SSRC forecasting work on a running basis is not really an appropriate use of the funds as this is a case in which the work undertaken should be financed by the customers who benefit from them". It is worth noting that in this view, Kaldor is following the 'contractor pays' principle that

SSRC during 1979–83 was Michael Posner, and Charles Feinstein had moved to a chair in York in 1981; both had had run-ins with Kaldor in various academic and faculty interactions. "After that, I refused to act as referee".

Rothschild had promulgated in his earlier review of the SRC, and which now was one of the apparent objectives of Keith Joseph. It was a view that had already been put to the Cambridge DAE CGP team by the Treasury and also by SSRC and it had led to the creating of a separate DAE consultancy company—Cambridge Econometrics. But there were problems with this type of sub-contracting arrangement. For one, the paymaster who paid the piper called the tune, so there could be no independence in the research agenda; then, such an arrangement could induce biases of various kinds; also, those who paid for the modelling might also want to own the data and versions of the models they had financed, thereby converting a public resource into a private commodity. Richard Stone was to point this out to the ESRC a few years later down the line; and then, when it came to such national models, there was an imperative to protect the public interest from being manipulated by the political preferences and predilections of which group or party happened to be in power—indeed, Kaldor had himself emphasised this danger in no uncertain terms.

Kaldor singles out the large NIESR unit for special comment: "In the case of the NIESR, finance through the SSRC also served cosmetic purposes. The Treasury has its own forecasting outfit, but it thought it valuable to have an independent check on its own forecasting methods which required the existence of another large, independently run forecasting body, which, in appearance at least, was independently financed".

The Kaldor broadside against macroeconomic forecasting models continues apace:

> my own feeling is that ... with all the forecasting efforts since the war ... the return was a meagre one and did not justify the large outlays incurred both inside and outside the Government as a result of an endless process of elaboration of the 'models' on which forecasting was based. The early 'models' contained 60–70 equations; this rose in a few years to 700, then to 1700, without any commensurate gain in the reliability of the results. When I was at the Treasury we made a comparative analysis of the national income forecasts over a ten year period by five different bodies (one of which was the Treasury and one was the OECD in Paris) and found that in general, forecasting did not yield any valuable results for periods longer than six or, at most, nine months, and that no single agency consistently 'outperformed' the others.[17]

---

[17] This has since been confirmed by various investigations; in particular, Professor Theiss, the famous Dutch econometrician, has shown that the forecasts of the Dutch Economic Bureau had a "negative bias—they were worse than would have been obtained by pure chance". Incidentally, a few years later, SSRC/ESRC created a special Macroeconomic Modelling Bureau to monitor and compare the various models of the UK economy, and their findings replicated those reported for the comparative exercise reported by Kaldor. With regard to the issue of 'negative' bias, Kaldor, had he lived to tell the tale, would surely have chuckled in citing the outcome of a forecasting competition organised by *The Economist*. "In December 1984, the editors asked four ex-finance ministers in developed economies, four chairmen of multinational firms, four students at Oxford University and four London garbage collectors to predict a variety of economic variables (growth, inflation, and exchange rate) for the next ten years. ... In its June 3, 1995 issue, *The Economist*

True to form, Nicky cannot resist the temptation to let loose a parting shot aimed at the Thatcher government: "when the present Government came in, Treasury Ministers made the most ludicrous claims on the effects of changes in money supply on the movement of prices—all of which have since been falsified by events. I cannot help feeling that this would not have been possible if more serious research had been undertaken on the causes of inflationary processes or on the role of changes in the money supply or of the effects of Government borrowing on the rate of interest". Then for good measure, just in case Rothschild had missed the point: "The ignorance of Ministers and high officials both of the Bank of England and the Treasury was little short of scandalous. As the individuals in question—many of whom were known to me—had intellectual qualities of a high order, I can only conclude that the very fact that they were working for an institution seriously biased their vision, and the setting in which the questions were examined made it impossible to conduct an impartial inquiry".

Kaldor's bottom line is clearly stated:

> Apart from these two fields [viz., endless data gathering with no clear purpose, mostly by sociologists; and medium- to long-term macroeconomic forecasting modelling, by teams of economists] which, in my opinion do not justify the continued existence of the SSRC, there is ... a third one which does, and that consists of the verification of particular hypotheses concerning the manner in which market impulses operate and the efficacy or otherwise of various policy measures ... [these] are subjects which are highly political but which are nevertheless of a nature that the main facts can be investigated objectively and the truth or falsehood (or rather, the probability) of certain propositions established independently of the personal views of the policy-maker ... [this is] a large potential field in which on cannot expect that Government Departments can do their own research with sufficient impartiality and attention.

7.12 Lord Harris' Vitriol

In the House of Lords Debate on the Rothschild Report, Lord Harris, a battering ram of Thatcherism, locks horns against the SSRC.

> In my opinion ... research and dissemination of ideas in social studies is best conducted by competing organisations supported from widely dispersed private sources of finance. By all means let the Government encourage charity by tax concessions, although I would personally favour fewer concessions and much lower rates of tax. But why, for example, should the National Institute of Economic and Social Research draw over 60 per cent of its income from the SSRC and the Treasury when many economists would join me in holding its resulting influence to blame for a great deal of our inflationary troubles? Having at one time put all their money on the NIESR as the chief source of macro-reported the results ... and compared the forecasts with the facts of what actually happened ... the dustmen's predictions fared as well as those of the so-called experts" (Sarvary, 2012, p. 61).

economic forecasting, it is true that the Government and the SSRC now support a half-a-dozen such oracles. I believe that it is an improvement. I think that if you are going to gamble on the economic Grand National, it is better to hedge your bets. But I think that it would be better still to turn academics away from what I regard as the contaminated public feeding trough. They believe that their macro-forecasts are of great value. Very well, let them tap the many sources of pure spring water to fertilise their researches Where they claim their work will yield fruit, let them appeal for support to the voracious fruit-eaters in business, the trade unions and Government departments. If they have more far-fetched projects, there is always the Rowntree Trust. On the other hand, where research promises little prospect of fruit or of early fruit, it should take its chance in appealing to the large universe of charities, trusts and private benefactors. An incidental advantage of this market approach would be that more economists might come to see the merits of lower taxation so that money could fructify in the pockets of potential donors. One of the troubles is that the very existence of the SSRC has encouraged the art of grantsmanship which diverts attention into fashionable, often highly mathematical, research known to be favoured by the grant-giving establishment.[18]

7.13   Catholicity and Independence

On 28 May, in the period between the filing of Rothschild's report and the despatch of Joseph's decision letter, the editorial of the *Times Higher Education Supplement*—which had generally kept up a running commentary on affairs—stated:

> Two battles remain to be fought by the SSRC, both in an important sense more crucial to the council's future that Sir Keith's kamikaze attack or Lord Beloff's partisan gripes against the Warwick unit. The first is to put right the imbalance between academic inquiry and 'customer demand' that has grown up under intense political pressure which the SSRC has suffered in recent years. This creeping Rothschildization should be reversed. The second is to adopt a successful strategy to reverse the equally damaging decline in funding for social science research. (Times Higher Education Supplement, 1982)

The editorial hits the mark with regard to funding, but misses the crucial point, one which is unambiguously highlighted by Rothschild himself:

> The need for independence from government departments is particularly important because so much social science research is the stuff of political debate. All such research might prove subversive of government policies because it attempts to submit such policies to empirical trial, with the risk that the judgement may be adverse. It would be too much to expect Ministers to show enthusiasm for research designed to show that their policies were misconceived. But it seems

---

[18] House of Lords Debate on the Report of the Enquiry into the SSRC, June 30, 1982, Hansard, Vol. 432.

obvious that in many cases the public interest will be served by such research being undertaken. (Rothschild, 1982, #3.12)

Thus, Rothschild is seen to argue the case for the reversal of "creeping Rothschildization" in government policies.

The mandate, or least the proclivity, of social science to interrogate the policies of the government of the day is highlighted by Rothschild in his defence of social science in a manner diametrically opposite to the Joseph-Thatcher doctrine (as unequivocally pronounced by Lord Harris in the SSRC debate), and later the position of the next ESRC Chairman, D.C. Hague[19] (another of Thatcher's gurus) who would have liked social science projects to be assessed on their practical support for government policies and interventions, something that would reduce social science to a dependent out-sourced shop for government ministries that doled out the research consultancies on questions and issues of their choosing. Indeed, it is arguable that it was Michael Posner who had set the ball rolling in this direction in his tenure, including the insistence that the modelling units raise funds from commercialisation of their models to the private sector. Thus, in the context of the social sciences, Rothschild could justifiably be regarded as having reversed his earlier stance in favour of the customer-client contract that he had espoused in the different context of the sciences. The contractor-customer relationship becomes even tighter in the context of private sector funding. Seen thus, the key issue was whether there was to be an autonomous 'public' space for social science to independently raise issues for research and pursue them at will, regardless of the wishes of the government or private sectors. This was a concern that was forcefully and explicitly expressed by Richard Stone (later, in 1986) when the CGP at DAE was being pushed to go with its funding bowl and knock on the doors of commercial clients. Stone said he was "still convinced that work like that of the Cambridge Growth Project needs, as it has had in the past, a good measure of disinterested support which will enable it to fulfil its scientific purpose and be of some use to the country at large". He points out that "if customers are to put a lot of money into research they usually want the results to be their property, so that one ends up building a black box for Messrs A, B, and C the contents of which are not available to the general public or even to one's colleagues for discussion". Stone argued that research such as that of the CGP should be regarded essentially as a public good (Stone to Hadjimatheou, 3 July 1986).[20]

---

[19] "He is credited in *New Society* (11 August 1983) as being 'a long-standing friend of Mrs Thatcher', was her economic adviser in the 1979 election campaign and has been Adviser to the PM's Policy Unit since 1979—a post which he resigned upon his designation to the SSRC/ESRC. He was awarded the CBE in 1978 and was knighted in 1982". https://www.britsoc.co.uk/files/NETWORK%20No27%20OCT1983.pdf.

[20] Archives of the Cambridge Growth Project, held at the Marshall Library, University of Cambridge.

Shortly after Posner's Sub-committee on Macroeconomic Research started its work, Posner embarked on a series of meetings, including one held (on 29 July 1980) with the DAE-CGP team.[21] The DAE version of the Notes of the meeting, due to Terry Barker, ends with the following sentence, clearly recording the view of the DAE members: "The SSRC should continue to provide money for licenced opposition to Government activities of this kind". Such licence may well have been generally tolerated, though not always without governmental annoyance or irritation, under the protective political umbrella of the previous Labour Government, or with the passive indifference of the earlier Conservative Government. But such opposition, and there was a lot of it from Cambridge left Keynesian quarters, was unlikely to pass without reaction and retaliation under the vindictive and aggressive stance of the viscerally hostile Thatcher regime.

At the end of the day, these distinctions and exhortations become of, what can ironically be termed, 'academic' interest, since it always remains possible for the government or its designated contractors (such as the SSRC) to maintain nominal 'diversity', or as Posner called it, 'catholicity', while squeezing out those research units that do not conform to dominant government ideology and thinking. And that is roughly what happened. The SSRC survived with its questioning role underscored by Rothschild; the SSRC advertised and collected brownie points for having a catholic approach in ensuring diversity in supporting various macroeconomic modelling units; but, nevertheless, the two Cambridge units that were the most independent and critical of government thinking were starved out by funding cuts. Not all blame could be left at the door of the government, however: the SSRC committees that made the decisions would obviously have been mindful of the identity and orientation of the holder of the purse, but there were also rivalries, animosities and histories which explained the outcomes. This draws attention to the composition of the relevant decision-making committees of the SSRC, what Posner called the 'machinery'; Michael Posner was the engineer working the levers on the shop floor during 1979–83, when CEPG was crunched to a halt, and the first spanner thrown into the CGP works; and Douglas Hague, Margaret Thatcher's economics 'tutor', picked up where Posner had left off and finished the job with the CGP in the next funding cycle; incidentally, Posner stayed the full course and put in some tellingly undermining feedback against the DAE when it was under hostile review by the General Board of the University of Cambridge.

In the final sentence in his 2002 retrospective piece on this saga, Posner concludes with his "impression that with the careful assistance of my successors at the Economic and Social Research Council, those active in social science research have made good use of the time" (Posner, 2002, #78). This perception might not have been shared at the DAE in Cambridge, where, under the

---

[21] The meeting was between Michael Posner and Christina Hadjimatheou for the SSRC, and Terry Barker and William Peterson of the CGP. The resulting two-sheet document is clearly a draft with various amendments and corrections, but none in the final sentence quoted here.

supervision of Douglas Hague (Michael Posner's successor to the chair) and many of Posner's committee appointees, the remaining Cambridge macroeconomic modelling project, the Cambridge Growth Project, was terminated—just as the Cambridge Economic Policy Group under the watch of Michael Posner. It was far from obvious that the crucial third battle, of protecting social science research from political pressure from government departments, had been won.

7.14 Rothschild's Last Word

Rothschild closes his Report with a single paragraph "Epilogue" which is simultaneously open ended, but also pointed and potentially damaging.

> The time allowed for this enquiry made it impossible to examine adequately the large number of social science issues raised in the Evidence. Is it the case, for example that the number of equations, 1700 it is said, put into some models of the economy, has not become so large as to make these models ridiculous? Was the expansion of the Universities in the 1960s so great as to make it impossible to fill all the Departments of Sociology then created with academics of high enough calibre?[22]

It is striking to note that both concerns have direct resonance with the main criticisms raised by Nicky Kaldor in his direct communication to his friend Victor Rothschild.

The Rothschild recommendations had a mixed outcome: some were ignored; some followed, such as the shift in location, and the setting up of an enquiry into the IRRU project and Panel; there was no further enquiry into SSRC for three years, but there were further financial cuts; sociology and macroeconomic modelling were given a bad name, with negative ramifications and consequences for those disciplines and their practitioners, including especially the vilified IRRU and the Panel of Advisers on Industrial Relations.

For present purposes, some significance could be attached to the dismissive attack on large macroeconomic models by Kaldor, picked up by Rothschild; something that chimed with the frontal assault on this branch of economic research by Lord Harris in debate in the House of Lords. It is arguable that between the throwaway remarks of Kaldor, Rothschild and the pointed assault by Harris, the door, or window, had been opened to pitch such models out; Posner and his SSRC macroeconomic committees could not have missed the allusion, and its implications; did it provide the SSRC the cover of an alibi to take the decision to terminate the CEPG grant?

---

[22] Another sentence follows that asks why the UK spends so little on social science research compared to France and Germany.

7.15 Joseph's Last Laugh

Was the fate of the CEPG a trading counter in the 'gentlemen's pact' between Keith Joseph and Michael Posner when the latter was trying to save as much as possible of and for the SSRC? If so, it would have been a useful bargaining chip to have: Joseph might have attached a lot more value to a CEPG closure than Posner might have attached to saving it. As it is, Posner and his various SSRC Committees had expressed themselves fairly unequivocally against the Cambridge teams. And Matthews and his CLARE Group (prominently including Posner) were no particular friends of the DAE teams (with a couple of exceptions). Now, Kaldor with his swingeing broadside against macroeconomic forecasting models, with Rothschild in tow on this, might have pushed the Cambridge teams further into no-man's land. Noticeably, when CEPG got chopped down, Liverpool and CUBS were funded; a Thatcherite poster boy economist was welcomed in, as her bête noir was shown the door; and the award announcements were made more or less simultaneously with the SSRC receipt of Joseph's letter of "reprieve". There are no tape-recorders under the table, no drones overhead or flies on the wall; so much depends on how long a string of coincidences one is willing to accept before contemplating pathologies of causality.

To the Posner-as-Saviour narrative, then, a hypothetical alternative is possible. Joseph got what he wanted: corralling and punishing sociology, destroying the persistently annoying Cambridge left Keynesian Godley-Cripps CEPG, reorganising student research grants to his agenda, imposing further financial cuts (Rothschild's exhortation notwithstanding), introducing the criterion of official policy orientation in research (started autonomously, prior to the Thatcher government by Posner, completed later by Douglas Hague, as Thatcher-Joseph took direct control over the ESRC apex), and taming and humiliating the SSRC, not least by banishing it from its salubrious London environs to a concrete hinterland. Cynically, or realistically, the game could be summarised as yielding an interactively managed win-win-win outcome: Posner, crowned saviour of the social sciences, enveloped in the fragrance of laurel leaves; Rothschild, with his reputation further burnished as the wise, independent judge, now becoming the new poster boy of social sciences (except for sociologists); while Joseph, having squeezed what he wanted out of the exercise, might well have had the last laugh.

References

Bagchi, A. K. (2010). Posner, Michael (1931–2006), economist. In *Oxford dictionary of national biography*. Oxford University Press. https://doi.org/10.1093/ref:odnb/97802

Berrill, K., Phelps Brown, E. H., & Williams, D. G. T. (1983, May). *The Berrill Report: Report of an investigation into certain matters arising from the Rothschild Report on the Social Science Research Council.* Social Sciences Research Council, RFK/14/6/1, Richard Kahn Papers, King's College Archives.

Brito, K. (1982). Memorandum to Party Chairman Cecil Parkinson, dated 12/01/1982. Correspondence and memoranda concerning a project to increase public understanding of the workings of the economic system at Lord Rothschild's behest, and funded by him. Conservative Party Archive, Chairman's Office, Economic Policy, 1957–1982; CCO 20/9/7; catalogued at the Bodleian Library, University of Oxford by Emily Tarrant, 2003. http://www.bodley.ox.ac.uk/dept/scwmss/wmss/online/modern/cpa/cco/cco20.html

Brown, W. (1998). Funders and research: The vulnerability of the subject. In K. Whitfield & G. Strauss (Eds.), *Researching the world of work: Strategies and methods in studying industrial relations* (pp. 267–285). ILR Press.

Cunningham, C. (2006, March 17). Michael Posner: Applied economist and champion of the social sciences. *The Guardian.*

Denham, A., & Garnett, M. (2001). *Keith Joseph.* Routledge.

Doherty, B. (1995, June). Best of both worlds: An interview with Milton Friedman. *Reason.* https://reason.com/1995/06/01/best-of-both-worlds/

ESRC. (n.d.). *SSRC/ESRC: The first forty years.* ESRC. https://esrc.ukri.org/files/news-events-and-publications/publications/ssrc-and-esrc-the-first-forty-years/

Flather, P. (1987). 'Pulling through': Conspiracies, counterplots, and how the SSRC escaped the axe in 1982. In M. Bulmer (Ed.), *Social science research and government: Comparative essays on Britain and the United States* (pp. 353–372). Cambridge University Press.

Flather, P. (2019, January 9). *Paul Flather interviewed by Alan Macfarlane.* https://www.sms.cam.ac.uk/media/3058954

Halsey, A. H. (2004). *A history of sociology in Britain: Science, literature and society.* Oxford University Press.

Hennessy, P. (2015, August 5). A feeble minister blames the civil service for not delivering his policies: William Waldegrave interviewed by Peter Hennessy. *Civil Service World.* https://www.civilserviceworld.com/articles/interview/feeble-minister-blames-civil-service-not-delivering-his-policies-william

Kaldor, N. (1982). *Letter to Lord Rothschild concerning the Enquiry into the SSRC.* NK/3/98/2-4; 22 February. King's College Archives, University of Cambridge.

Kuczynski, M. (2006, March 9). Michael Posner: Versatile applied economist. *The Independent.*

Leitch, D. (1994, October 23). Rothschild 'spied as the Fifth Man'. *The Independent.* https://www.independent.co.uk/news/uk/home-news/rothschild-spied-as-the-fifth-man-1444440.html

Matthews, R. C. O., Feinstein, C. F., & Odling-Smee, J. (1982). *British economic growth 1856–1973: The post-war period in historical perspective.* Oxford University Press.

McMahan, J. (2012). *Bernard Williams: A reminiscence.* http://jeffersonmcmahan.com/wp-content/uploads/2012/11/Williams-A-Reminiscence-FINAL.pdf

Moore, C. (2013). *Margaret Thatcher: The authorized biography. Volume one: Not for turning.* Penguin Books.

Offer, A. (2008). *Charles Feinstein (1932–2004), and British Historical National Accounts.* Discussion papers in Economic and Social History No. 70. University of Oxford.

Posner, M. V. (2002). Social sciences under attack in the UK (1981–1983). *La revue pour l'histoire du CNRS, 7*. https://doi.org/10.4000/histoire-cnrs.547

Rothschild, N. M. V. (1982). *An enquiry into the Social Science Research Council*. Her Majesty's Stationery Office.

Sarvary, M. (2012). *Gurus and oracles: The marketing of information*. MIT Press.

Skidelsky, R. (1992). *John Maynard Keynes: The economist as saviour, 1920–1937*. Macmillan.

The Times. (2006, March 20). Michael Posner: Cambridge economics lecturer turned government adviser who later worked to safeguard social science research in the UK. *The Times*.

Times Higher Education Supplement. (1982, May 28). Lord Rothschild's truce. *Times Higher Education Supplement*.

Walker, D. (2016). *Exaggerated claims? The ESRC, 50 years on*. Sage Publications.

CHAPTER 8

Cambridge Growth Project: Running the Gauntlet

Abstract This chapter deals with the second episode of The DAE Trilogy and narrates the sorry tale of the prolonged demise of an iconic unit of Cambridge applied economics, the Cambridge Growth Project (CGP), launched by Richard Stone and Alan Brown in 1960, and wilfully terminated in 1987 by a hostile Economic and Social Research Council (ESRC). CGP had received substantial funding support from the Social Science Research Council (SSRC) from 1967 onwards under various chairmen and had become the flagship project of the DAE, with an enviable reputation, nationally and internationally. A good many names and reputations were fashioned here, and three "Nobel" economics awards were linked to Stone, including his own. This refusal led to the closure of the Stone-Barker CGP in 1987 with the dispersal of most of its research team; a cumulative stock of intellectual capital and research capacity was summarily lost to the DAE. When Stone retired in 1980, work continued on the development of the disaggregated, dynamic model that analysed the process of structural change in the UK economy—both zooming in on the regional level and also zooming out to take account of the articulation of the UK economy with the European and world economies. Contemporary documentation reveals the wide range of criticisms made by the SSRC/ESRC decision-making Consortium but also records the precise rejections, including an outraged response from Richard Stone, of each of these objections; the defense fell on deaf ears at ESRC. *Inter alia*, the CGP response challenged and rebutted charges pertaining to methodology and technique, in particular about the value of its approach of disaggregation; substantive issues especially concerning aspects of innovation; treatment of policy issues, especially employment. The CGP reply also raised unsettling issues of procedural probity; of goal posts being continually shifted by the Consortium; of questionable selections of unsuitable and predictably biased experts; of the uneven application of

© The Author(s), under exclusive license to Springer Nature
Switzerland AG 2022
A. Saith, *Cambridge Economics in the Post-Keynesian Era*, Palgrave
Studies in the History of Economic Thought,
https://doi.org/10.1007/978-3-030-93019-6_8

evaluative criteria across competing applicants; and about egregious, gratuitous reputational attacks on the CGP team. It made no difference; notwithstanding the outrage and the clamour, the deed was done and, with the Godley-Cripps Cambridge Economic Policy Group having also been shut down by a similarly hostile denial of SSRC funds a few years earlier, the era of applied macroeconomics at the DAE came to a sad and savage end. A contemporary report in *The Economist* observed that the ESRC allocation had "revived talk of conspiracy theory" denying funding to units, mentioning both the CEPG and the CGP, to units that "have been critical of government policies".

8.1 Background and Conjuncture

What follows is the second episode of The DAE Trilogy, a short story of the prolonged demise of an iconic unit of Cambridge applied economics, the Cambridge Growth Project (CGP), launched by Richard Stone and Alan Brown in 1960, and wilfully terminated in 1987 by a hostile Economic and Social Research Council (ESRC). CGP had received substantial funding support from the Social Science Research Council (SSRC) from 1967 onwards under various chairmen and had become the flagship project of the DAE, with an enviable reputation, nationally and internationally. A good many names and reputations were fashioned here, and it was in this powerful base that Richard Stone nurtured the research that, in 1984, was honoured with the 'Nobel' award for Economic Science citing his work on the System of National Accounts on which the CGP estimated its models. The CGP members worked extensively on the development and application of the Social Accounting Matrix to the UK economy. Both Angus Deaton, who went on to win the same prize later, and Mervyn King, who later became the Governor of the Bank of England, had been part of the CGP unit; and Richard Stone had also supervised the doctoral dissertation of Jim Mirrlees, who went on to win the 'Nobel' prize in 1996. A string of econometricians had also earned their fame on the basis of technical work they developed working earlier with Richard Stone in the DAE, including Durbin, Watson, Cochrane and Orcutt; and another eminent applied econometrician, in the person of Hashem Pesaran, stepped into the limelight later and worked with the Cambridge Economic Policy Group (CEPG), the DAE's macroeconomic modelling team. When Stone retired in 1980, work continued on the development of the disaggregated, dynamic model that analysed the process of structural change in the UK economy— both zooming in on the regional level, and also zooming out to take account of the articulation of the UK economy with the European and world economies.

Though CGP had been a pioneer in the field in the UK, other rival units and competing models had emerged,[1] some within the government, some others closely linked with it, and some independent—though all non-government modelling was substantially dependent on funding from the SSRC and later the ESRC. However, CGP retained its ranking position, and also distinct structural modelling features that made its work stand apart, and arguably above, its rivals; the CGP model was an order-of-magnitude more detailed than the other models; and, at the least, it could address questions using paired methodologies in a manner that the other models could not. But money, as always, was short, and there was competition for accessing SSRC and ESRC funds. The overall size and nature of effort devoted to industrial forecasting in the project had already been questioned by the SSRC, following a report it commissioned in 1973 to assess the commercialisation of the research (Cunningham, 1973); in 1977 the SSRC made the provision of a commercial service a condition of future funding of the project. This led to the formation in 1978 of Cambridge Econometrics, a company limited by guarantee focussed on structural macroeconomic analysis and forecasting. This was one of the earliest British university spinoffs of economic research.[2]

In 1981, a regular funding application was made by the CGP to SSRC, where Michael Posner had taken over as Chairman, appointed in the dying days of the Callaghan Labour government in late 1979. Early on, Posner initiated some significant changes to the orientation of the SSRC's grant-giving parameters. Then, the incoming Thatcher Government had straightaway imposed a 20 per cent cut on the SSRC budget. With regard to SSRC's funding of macroeconomic modelling, Posner, with typical bustling energy and alacrity, proposed and himself chaired a Sub-committee to review the state of macroeconomic research in the UK. This Sub-committee submitted its report—presumably to Posner himself, this time as Chair SSRC—in mid-1981, making two key recommendations: first, that a unit be set up which could monitor and evaluate various macroeconomic modelling research—and a macroeconomic modelling bureau was duly set up and located at Warwick and began to report from 1984, feeding into subsequent decision-making; and second, that a Consortium be set up comprising, amongst others, experts from

---

[1] These include the modelling work at the National Institute of Economic and Social Research (NIESR), London Business School (LBS), the City University Business School, and Liverpool University, though CGP was not in direct competition with NIESR and LBS in the modelling field till later in the 1970s. It is worth noting that there had been strong ties between the NIESR and Cambridge economists from the early days of the DAE involving Austin Robinson, Dick Stone and many others; for illustration, NIESR was also the base from which a young Phyllis Deane set out to her illustrious Cambridge career in the DAE and the Faculty. Cambridge economists, though not from the Keynesian-left, served in the governance structures of the NIESR.

[2] Oxford Economic Forecasting and London Economics followed in 1981 and 1986 respectively; the latter unit, run by John Kay, focussed on microeconomic analysis of competition and regulation issues, amongst others.

the Bank of England (BoE), Her Majesty's Treasury (HMT) and the SSRC itself, to assess and decide upon macroeconomic modelling applications for grants from the SSRC—and this Consortium was put in place with impressive alacrity, became operational almost immediately and was functioning in 1981 itself.

The Consortium held an orientation meeting in 1981 to make the various applicants, actual and potential, aware of the new framework for decision-making. Various applications already made were reviewed and decided upon in 1981/1982 by the Consortium, including those by the Cambridge Economic Policy Group (CEPG), by the Cambridge Growth Project, and all their rivals and competitors. However, unlike the CEPG, which received an immediate life-ending rejection for its modelling research work, the CGP was grudgingly given a two-year conditional grant running to 1983. A fresh four-year grant application was made by CGP in 1983; in turn, this also ran into hostile Consortium opposition which made funds initially available only for the first two years (1983–1985), making the latter two years (1985–1987) again conditional on desired progress and responses to criticisms of the application—these to be assessed and monitored by the Consortium via an evaluation in 1984. In the end, the two-year extension was granted, again reluctantly, and with conditions set yet again for continued support. A fresh CGP application was made for the four-year research round starting in 1987, and this was flatly declined by the ESRC[3] on 19 June 1986, effectively bringing closure to the Cambridge Growth Project when the ongoing grant ended in 1987. A major, high-profile, long-running project, involving researchers with fine skills and reputations, was thereby terminated, with serious implications within a national framework, and profound consequences within Cambridge economics. What really happened?

8.1.1 The Decision

On 19 June 1986, the ESRC communicated its decision to terminate its funding for the Cambridge Growth Project.[4] Responding on 1 July 1986, Terry Barker, with justifiable pride, describes the CGP

> as one of the oldest established model-building teams in the UK with a history going back to 1960 when it was founded by Richard Stone and Alan Brown. The first ESRC funding dates from 1967. The project has made significant contributions to theory, methods, data and policy analysis and has an unrivalled international reputation as the main UK disaggregated modelling group. Many former

---

[3] In the interim, the SSRC was reinvented, much the same, but with a name change to ESRC. This followed the Rothschild Review initiated by Keith Joseph, Education Secretary in the Thatcher Government.

[4] Letter from Christina Hadjimatheou, Secretary, Economic Affairs Committee, ESRC, dated 19 June 1986, to Dr Terry Barker.

members of the project (for example Mervyn King, Angus Deaton and Graham Pyatt) have gone on to distinguished careers in the economics profession.

We were therefore shocked to learn that the Consortium is proposing to close down the project on the basis of three sentences of unsupported assertions in your letter of 19 June. After 26 years of existence, and after the ESRC has spent large sums of public money, we expect a reasoned case supported by expert opinion. Instead we find that the only referee's report on our proposed research you sent us gives very strong support to our work. (Barker to Christina Hadjimatheou, Secretary, Economic Affairs Committee, ESRC, Letter, 1 July 1986: #1)

In classic understatement mode, Terry Barker observes: "the history of the CGP relationship with the Consortium has been a difficult one", but then he rises to the challenge of rebuttal. Barker's response is understandably emotive, even scathing,[5] but these expressions are attached to pertinent and precise rebuttals of every specific criticism or argument advanced by the Consortium as an ostensible justification for its decision to terminate the funding for the CGP, in full knowledge that this would imply the closure of the enterprise altogether.

Sensing existential risk, Richard Stone enters the fray. Elected as President of the Royal Economic Society (1978–1980) and knighted in 1978, he had handed over the reins of the CGP to Terry Barker when he retired in 1980; in 1984, his work was acknowledged and honoured with the Nobel Prize in Economics[6] bringing plaudits also for the DAE where the work had been done over the decades. Subsequently, he was rarely sighted at the DAE or the Faculty, having "always preferred to work at home" (Stone, 1984)—or as Angus Deaton described it, "Aladdin's cave, surrounded by the gems of a good life" (Deaton, 2014). But the peace of the genial bow-tied Homburg-hatted genius was shattered by the peremptory decision of the ESRC. Stone writes to Christina Hadjimatheou at the ESRC. "I have just read the letter [Terry Barker] has sent to you two days ago in reply to the bad news contained in your letter to him of 19 June. This one of mine may sound like a voice from beyond the tomb … but I would not like this critical stage in the affairs of the Growth Project to pass without my letting you know how I feel about it although I am no longer one of the investigators." Taking umbrage at the specious criticisms of the ESRC, and rejecting these point by point, he growled his outrage: "Britain should not become a scientific banana republic, or rather I should say monarchy" (Richard Stone to Christina Hadjimatheou, Letter, 3 July 1986). Separately, Sir Richard Stone—the same person who had been, just one round

---

[5] He employs a range of emotive terms such as: "shocked", "unsupported assertions" (#2); "unfair" (#3); "dismayed" (#5); "unfair procedure" (#7); "difficult to understand" (#8); "antipathetic" (#10); "misapprehension" (#12); "prejudiced" (#13); "difficult to justify" (#20); "deluding themselves and the Consortium", "disservice to the profession" (#23); "not true" (#24); "not being treated equitably" (#28).

[6] Sveriges Riksbank Prize in Economic Sciences in Memory of Alfred Nobel.

earlier, the winner of the Nobel Prize in economics for his work based in the CGP and DAE—penned a note to Stephen Nickell in Oxford, one of the antagonists on the ESRC committees. Of course, it made not a lot of difference; forced since 1981 by the SSRC/ESRC to run the gauntlet, the Cambridge Growth Project had staggered as far as 1987, when the ESRC terminated its funding, and with it the life of the CGP within the DAE.

Matthews, then Acting Chair of the Committee of Management of the DAE, had written to Christina Hadjimatheou on 2 July; he speaks of being "very distressed" at the decision, and of the significance of the CGP's disaggregated models, and says, rather weakly, that "a smaller grant of the order of half of that originally requested, would allow the project to support the core research needed to keep the model alive, to develop it, and to use it as the basis for fundamental research".[7] He goes on to make a significant point: "I understand that the Consortium is contemplating running a competition for disaggregated models. We should welcome such an initiative and should likewise welcome the existence of more than one team working in the field. However, it appears to us that if such an initiative is undertaken it will make it all the more important not to bring about the destruction of the intellectual capital that the Growth project has accumulated—capital that a new team would have to build up from scratch." This scenario requests higher authorities to grant the CGP half a life after its pronounced death.[8]

The enforced shutdown of the CGP raises two categories of issues: first, those pertaining to the validity of the substantive judgements made by the Consortium in coming to its decision to terminate funding; and second, concerns regarding shortfall in the procedural probity of the Consortium's decision-making.

---

[7] Letter from Robin Matthews to Christina Hadjimatheou, dated 2 July 1986 (CGP/42/4.22).

[8] It is a trifle difficult to accept this belated expression of support from Matthews for the CGP at face value. The two substantive points he makes are not without merit. On the other hand, there is a credible evidential basis for arguing that the Hahn-Matthews camp had been systematically acting to undermine the reputation and the viability of the DAE and its big modelling teams over the previous years; so this sudden *volte face* gives at least the partial impression of being double-faced. The Consortium that dealt out the negative decision was stacked with a heavy majority of members aligned in one manner or other with the Hahn-Matthews axis: this prominently included the two hostile consultant experts—and also three other important members, Charles Feinstein, Michael Artis and John Flemming, who were strongly embedded in Matthews's CLARE group. Matthews and Hahn were the uncles to this nest of nephews; so in principle, if Matthews really had wanted to save the CGP, the nephews could have been expected to behave differently at the earlier stages of the decision-making process. As it happens, there is reason to believe that there was just one member of the Consortium that argued in favour of the CGP when the negative decision was being made. Matthews's belated support needs not to be ignored, but it cannot really be taken too seriously; more credibly it can be ascribed to Matthews following through on his formal obligation, given that, temporarily at the time, he was wearing the hat of Acting Chairman of the Committee of Management of the DAE. If requested to write such a letter of support, he could hardly have declined. And compared to the scathing rebuttal by Terry Barker, or the pointed and full-blooded objections and rebuttal by Richard Stone, the yielding letter of Robin Matthews is notably anaemic; it virtually throws the towel in, accepting the outcome but pleading for just half the original grant.

8.2 Substantive Issues

8.2.1 No Innovation?

Much weight is placed on "the Consortium's view [that] not enough innovative ideas are stemming from this model, while most of the staff efforts are devoted to updating and maintaining it. Consequently, they saw no grounds for confidence that there was an adequate research element in your proposal to warrant further support" (Letter from Christina Hadjimatheou to Terry Barker, dated 19 June 1986). However, a careful reading of the correspondence on the transactions between the CGP and the SSRC/ESRC provides firm support for Terry Barker's conclusion that "the Consortium has given us no evidence that our model is in any way inferior to the other groups in respect of the three critical areas of model properties, forecasting performance or usefulness for policy formulation" (Letter, 1 July 1986, p. 1). Richard Stone goes further and highlights the dimension of innovation: "it seems to me that the improvements that have taken place in the last ten years have made the model an altogether more practical and scientific tool than our [Richard Stone and Alan Brown's] original creation was. The large number of innovations that have been introduced under Terry's leadership in developing the dynamic version are apparent from the Project's forthcoming book. In view of the work there described I am surprised that there can be any doubt about the innovative character of the Project at the present time" (Letter, 3 July 1986, p. 1).[9]

8.2.2 Catholicity, Turnover and the Value of Disaggregation

Terry Barker's letter of response to Christina Hadjimatheou begins by pointing out that the very first recommendation of the Report of the SSRC Subcommittee of 1981, initiated and chaired himself by Michael Posner, then Chair of SSRC (1981) was that "care should be taken to encourage a suitable catholicity of style, methodology and approach"; but, Barker says, "in practice, the Consortium is reducing the variety of approaches to model-building in the UK forcing most of the approved models into being similar aggregate quarterly models adhering to the structures of the 'rational expectations hypothesis'" (Barker, Letter, 1 July 1986: #6). In similar vein, Barker (ibid.: #5, #6) cites Sargent (then Chairman of the Economics Committee of the ESRC) as declaring, in November 1984: "we will be paying closer attention to the extent to which macro-economic modelling can provide an adequate framework for the analysis and treatment of structural problems which call for change in contemporary Britain. A more disaggregated approach now seems desirable, designed to fill gaps in recent work on the dynamics of resource allocation." Barker is clearly puzzled and "dismayed" that in contrast, "the Consortium are

---

[9] Stone's letter is incorrectly dated 3 July 1983; corrected to 1986, with an explanation in a File Note attached to the letter by Terry Barker.

prepared to eliminate the one team expressly concerned with long-term issues of structural change", with "arguably the most distinctive approach of the UK models in methodology, disaggregation". The ESRC decision to withdraw funding therefore clearly "seems to go against ESRC policy". It also makes nonsense of its pontification on 'catholicity', but perhaps that call for generous pluralism might have been beyond the reach of the anointed members of the committee who, one might say, were more crusaders than catholic.[10]

Barker notes that earlier, the Consortium "was not convinced of the value of disaggregation" and had repeated its criticism in January 1986; but he points out the CGP's substantial development and progress in this regard in publications, in technical conference presentations, in a forthcoming book, supported by additional independent justification from other independent research, including the Brookings Model that found that disaggregation performed better. "No mention of this appears in your letter and we assume that we have been able to satisfy the Consortium on the value of disaggregation. However, this makes the rejection of our application even more difficult to understand" (ibid., p. 2).

A couple of days later, Richard Stone addresses this issue in his letter: "I have also been puzzled ... by the objections that have been raised to the fact that that model is a disaggregated one. These objections are made on the assumption that all one wants are aggregate results, but is this sound, I wonder. It seems to me that many of the problems with which we are faced call for a good deal of detailed analysis. Unemployment, for example, or taxation cannot be properly studied in an aggregated model, since they impinge differently on different bits of the system and each individual impact may have repercussions which alter the functioning of the system as a whole. I believe that disaggregation pays off even if one is interested only in aggregate results" (Stone to Hadjimatheou, Letter, 3 July 1986, pp. 1–2).

Barker directly challenges the credentials of the two experts on this matter. Professor Helliwell felt basically that disaggregated modelling "is difficult and not likely to work"; but Barker replies that while it is indeed difficult, "we have shown that it does work—witness the many applications of the model over the past few years including the provision of regular forecasts"—which incidentally performed better than others (Barker, Letter, 1 July 1986).

Turning his attention to the second expert, Barker writes: "Professor Gordon in particular had clearly not read our application properly. He starts out under the misapprehension that we were asking for funds to cover over 12 economists [which Gordon ridicules in his report] when in fact the application is intended to fund only about 6 economists. He then says that no concrete

---

[10] The Consortium response acknowledges Barker's point to be "a fair one"; it could hardly say otherwise. Then it enters, once again, its zone of obfuscation: "However, policymakers disagree on their approaches to structural problems and one wonders whether these coincide with the industrial/regional structure of the model". Was the Consortium constituted to generally 'wonder' or to precisely specify?

examples of issues which have been uniquely elucidated by the CGP model were given in the application. In fact, two issues were mentioned under the heading 'The Contribution of the CGP Model to Modelling the British Economy'; ...and before the interview we added two more issues" Barker (ibid., p. 3).

The problems arose perhaps from the fact that Gordon was not up to speed on disaggregated modelling work of this kind, he was essentially a one-equation man; and Helliwell was known for his aggregated model of the Canadian economy and had been in competition against disaggregated models. The choice of unmatched experts led inevitably, and predictably, to inappropriate if not incompetent advice, which the ESRC principals who had appointed the experts seemed to be accept uncritically as the justification for wielding the axe. Was bias introduced through the choice of consultants?[11] It would be very difficult to reject this hypothesis.

And, it is little short of bizarre that, having repeatedly, and unjustifiably, beaten the CGP application with the 'disaggregation' stick, and having implicitly accepted the inappropriateness of their selection of anti-disaggregation consultants, the Consortium response blithely does a U-turn and states: "the Consortium recognises that disaggregated input-output work is different from the other models and is preparing a separate competition for contracts on it"— and the Secretary brazenly concludes the ESRC letter by stressing that "the Consortium considers you to be one of the serious contenders to the forthcoming competition for disaggregated models" (Letter from Christina Hadjimatheou to Terry Barker, dated 21 July 1986, p. 2).

The issue of disaggregation rumbles on and there is a sequel to this exchange on the ESRC's prevarication on this account. In a later letter, Terry Barker returns to the fray: "it is now clear that the CGP is the only model which is no longer to be supported in the round of applications just completed. Surely this represents a continuing 'reduction in the variety of approaches' since the principal new group being supported at Oxford and Southampton is concerned with evaluation techniques, not with a distinctive approach to modelling. I emphasise once again a fact which is not disputed: the CGP model represents an approach to macroeconometric modelling *completely distinct in its disaggregation* from that in all the models supported."[12] However, in line with Barker's earlier complaint that the ESRC kept shifting the goal posts of its evaluations, Hadjimatheou had recently communicated another instance of this; Barker continues: "You say 'health requires turnover as well as catholicity', but this

---

[11] Though both experts were drawn from North America, they can be located within the 'Uncles-and-Nephews' networks: Gordon's doctoral supervisor was Hahn's pal, Bob Solow; and Helliwell had Hahn's other partner, Terry Gorman, as his teacher and mentor in Oxford, where he was part of a nexus that included Martin Feldstein and John Flemming, the latter being one of the drivers of the SSRC/ESRC committees dealing with the macroeconomic modelling grants; in short, both had form.

[12] Terry Barker to Christina Hadjimatheou, Secretary, Economic Affairs Committee, ESRC, Letter dated 11 September 1986 (CGP/42/4.35); emphasis in original.

implies that you are supporting a replacement to the CGP approach, which you are not. And where is the turnover of the quarterly short-term aggregate models?"—these being the stock in trade of the methodologically similar, rival applications that were continuing to receive support. ESRC had touted catholicity as an important selection criterion; CGP had used this to point out ESRC's inconsistency in decision-making; so post-facto, ESRC introduced another criterion, turnover, to legitimise its selections and exclude CGP. Then to square the circle on this chaos, it remarkably announced a separate funding competition on disaggregation—the very approach it had rejected in turning down its main practitioner, CGP—and brazenly asked CGP to apply. Barker, however, smelt something foul and was apprehensive that, going on the ESRC's demonstrated pattern of behaviour and its revealed preferences, this would be another frustrating cycle of injury and insult, and so held back.

Barker shares his worries about walking into another ambush:

> I had understood from your letter that we still stand a chance of being supported under the new initiative on disaggregated modelling. However in the Press Release I was very disturbed to read that 'The Consortium wished to support *a* project on disaggregated modelling of the UK economy' [emphasis placed by Barker, not in ESRC Press Release]. This seems to go completely against a previous assurance from you that more than one project could be supported. If seen in relation to the earlier statement in the Release that 'The Consortium has not extended support for the Cambridge Growth Project', it would seem to imply that the CGP has no hope of support in the separate competition. Will you confirm that the Cambridge Growth Project is encouraged to apply in the new competition and will be given an equal standing with any other applicants? (Barker to Hadjimatheou, Letter, 11 September 1986, p. 1)

So much for catholicity, turnover, the worth of disaggregated modelling, and the worthlessness of ESRC consistency.

8.2.3 Use of Input-Output Tables

Consortium members were "unhappy with the use of the input-output tables in the disaggregated modelling as a matter of principle" (as conveyed by telephone by Hadjimatheou to Barker); Barker (Letter 1 July 1986, p. 8) responds: "nearly every disaggregated macro model uses such tables as part of their accounting framework, at the very least", including static and dynamic Leontief input-output models, combined I-O and time-series econometric models such as CGP, CGE models, as well as systems-dynamics models—was the Consortium going to exclude all applications using any of these? This comment and other similar ones conveyed in communications by the Consortium go to indicate the fact that the reviewers had not grasped that the CGP methods had gone far beyond a static input-output model. The CGP had developed a dynamic structural model of the UK economy, which was revolutionary at the time in that it allowed the effects of macroeconomic policies to be explored at a detailed industrial level, for example, the effects of fiscal policy on employment for forty industrial sectors.

8.2.4 CGP Presence in Policy Debates

Another curiosity in the Consortium letter of 21 July 1986 (Hadjimatheou to Barker) is its treatment of the issue of the CGP's usefulness in the policy domain. It admits that it has not provided any evidence in this regard; nevertheless, it asserts: "it is, however, true that in general macroeconomic policy debate, the CGP voice is not heard clearly". Pertinent here is Barker's earlier rejection of such a claim (when the Consortium raised doubts about the ability of the CGP model to offer fresh insights into important contemporary policy issues): "It may be the case that the model does not provide the 'insights' some would find acceptable" (Barker, Letter, 1 July: #22). The Consortium letter of 21 July then explains itself: "It is a pity if the prize goes to the shrill but official policymakers do not often *use* other models" (emphasis in the original). Being itself populated by senior policy makers, was the Consortium making an admission of being audibly challenged in intellectual discourse when conversations were within a normal civilised decibel band? Should CGP have used dog whistles to attract attention?[13] And then: "it should also be mentioned that the CGP is not active on the Treasury's academic panel"; which makes one wonder if memberships were open on request to all comers year round, and if not, who might make the invitations if not a panel like the Consortium itself. It is of interest, and some relevance, to note here that at this time, Professor R. C. O. Matthews—who, along with Frank Hahn was making a heavy attack on the DAE within the framework of a University Review which was widely believed to have been instigated by them—was the Chairman of the Panel of Academic Consultants of the Bank of England.

In his later letter, Terry Barker returns to the question of the CGP's interface with policy making more explicitly:

> As regards the remark you report that official policymakers do not often use models other than those of 'the shrill', has the Consortium received evidence of the

---

[13] There is resonance here to the earlier episode of the effective shutting down of the Godley-Cripps CEPG in 1982, as narrated earlier. It was clear that in that case, decision makers and the powers-that-be, upfront or behind the scenes, had found the CEPG too 'shrill', too high profile, too much and too often stirring things up at the centre of the policy debates and storms of the 1970s, and that (recalling that those were years of a Labour government) CEPG and Cambridge had a good representation on government academic panels. But the result for CEPG was no different—it was shut down. It is also worth noting that CGP modelling used a different time frame dealing as it did with medium- and longer-term structural issues, compared to the here-and-now, cut-and-thrust of the CEPG short/er-term forecasting models; hence the demand that CGP shout its wares like a street peddler is a touch puerile.

official use of the different models being supported? I know that many policy studies using the CGP model have been commissioned by H.M. Treasury and the Department of Trade and Industry and one at least of these has been published. ... Several Government departments have also subscribed to a comparatively expensive forecasting service based on the CGP model. I would not be surprised if the CGP model was the most officially-used of the models although this might not be apparent to most members of the Consortium. (Barker to Hadjimatheou, Letter, 11 September 1986)

But Barker seemed to be speaking into deaf ears.

8.2.5 Insularity

The Consortium levies a charge that the CGP is too much of a closed shop, too insular and removed room from peer groups in the same field. A similar criticism had been made years earlier when the SSRC shut down the CEPG, and the same refrain also came up in the University Review of the DAE, running in parallel to the CGP's funding application to the ESRC. The criticism had been only partially accepted by Godley in the context of the CEPG, but is rejected by Barker for the CGP. It was pointed out that CGP might not have been overly interactive in relation to other units in the country, but that it had very significant participation in international forums. When defending CGP staff quality and performance against arbitrary attack from the Consortium, Barker pointed out that "the proportion of publications that came out abroad increased substantially from 22 per cent in the first period [1970–75] to 32 per cent in the second [1980–85], as the Project's international reputation developed" (Barker to Hadjimatheou, Letter, 11 September 1986). In any case, Cambridge self-preoccupation was generally taken to mean insularity, which in turn was read by, and rankled, outsiders who read it as arrogance. Be it as it may, this was hardly a serious consideration for judging quality; on this criterion, the entire Faculty, if not the University, would be guilty and in need of being shut down.

8.2.6 On Exploiting the Cheap Labour of Graduate Students

The CGP is criticised for not making cost savings by using the cheap labour of research students.[14] This practice, widely followed in many research units, is not without potential problems. For one, in the Cambridge context where the graduate students select their own research topics on admission, there is the issue of finding or forcing a match between the interest of the student and that of the project. The intrinsic merits of the practice are also questionable, as

---

[14] Noticeably, this criticism also shows up 'independently' in the parallel Review of the DAE being carried out by the General Board of the University, providing a clue that these two separate committees—one of the ESRC, and the other of the General Board of the University of Cambridge—were in some form of communication with each other in the conduct of the ostensibly independent enquiries.

good training for students does not automatically convert into good value for the research project and the Consortium appears to betray a fundamental lack of appreciation of the intricacies of the processes of data search and identification, of mining, cleaning, preparing and processing statistics before they enter any modelling exercise or software. The act of research cannot often be separated from this process dealing with the data, and the Consortium might have received short shrift had it demanded this of any of the DAE stalwarts, Richard Stone or Angus Deaton[15] or Brian Reddaway[16] or Ajit Singh, all highly accomplished and equally fastidious about their data. Apart from these pragmatic and intrinsic issues, there is also the question of research ethics. When the same question, viz., the exploitation of the cheap labour of graduate students in order to reduce data processing costs of the project, had been posed by the University Review Committee to the DAE, a full response had been returned by Geoff Meeks in his capacity of Assistant Director Research, and this is equally applicable in the present exchange between the ESRC and the CGP. Then, Meeks had informed the relevant critics that such use of 'cheap labour' violated the rules of the university and the terms on which the graduate students were enrolled; and also that it went against the intellectual and career interests of the students themselves. He went on to reel off an impressive list of independent PhDs produced by research officers of the DAE based on their own work[17]: Deaton, Ellman, Peterson, Vines, Whittington and Winters, "all

---

[15] "I was told to get a research assistant, which was sensible advice, but I have never really figured out how to use research assistance: for me, the process of data gathering—at first with paper and pencil from books and abstracts—programming, and calculation has always been part of the creative process, and without doing it all, I am unlikely to have the flash of insight that tells me that something doesn't fit, that not only this model doesn't work, but that all such models cannot work. Of course, this process has become much easier over time. Not only are data and computing power constantly and easily at one's fingertips, but it is easy to explore data graphically. The delights and possibilities can only be fully appreciated by someone who spent his or her youth with graph paper, pencils, and erasers" (Deaton, 2014, p. 6).

[16] In a different vein but equally pertinent is an exchange between Tony Atkinson and Nick Stern on Brian Reddaway:

Atkinson: The other person I should mention in terms of my sort-of apprentice years was Brian Reddaway, who is someone people probably don't remember much now, but he was, I think, a masterful applied economist. From him, I learned about taking data seriously and asking, 'Where'd that number come from?' and 'Who actually wrote that number on a piece of paper?'. This sort of thing. But he was also willing to use theory and would argue about issues such as the selective employment tax and so on. He did mathematics as a student.

Stern: Was it Brian that said, 'Unless you've plotted the points on the graph paper yourselves, you don't really understand the data'?

Atkinson: It could well have been, actually. But he was very good at teaching applied statistics, and he used to set this wonderful examination paper. It was one question for three hours, and you had to answer the question with any sources you wanted. (Atkinson & Stern, 2017, p. 8)

[17] Here it is pertinent to cite the nostalgic recollections of Angus Deaton about his time in the DAE in the 1960s and 1970s: "Not long after I joined the Department of Applied Economics,

of whom now hold senior positions; and a strong further crop is currently coming to the exam stage". Then he shifted the response to the ethical plane (obviously quite lost on the reviewers and donors): "there would be objections to moving far in the direction favoured by some universities and weakening significantly the role of independent research by our Economics students; and that the more generous supervising tradition of the DAE makes a significant contribution to the subject which appears in the graduates' names whereas in some institutions it would appear in the publications list of the staff members".[18]

8.3 Issues of Procedural Probity

Were the Consortium's procedures robust and unbiased? Barker thinks not, and complains, with justifications attached, that the procedures repeatedly fell well short of basic thresholds of probity, in that these were predisposed towards negativity towards the CGP approach and application. Several grounds for this frustration can be elicited from archived correspondence.

8.3.1 Shifting Goalposts Across Evaluations

A fundamental concern is with the lack of stability of the criteria on which the Cambridge proposal was judged over successive evaluation rounds. Barker complains that the Consortium keeps relocating the goal posts arbitrarily with every round. "Since our first application to the Consortium of December 1981 our work has been subject to shifting lines of criticism so that when we apparently satisfied the Consortium on one question, a new one immediately appeared" (Barker to Hadjimatheou, Letter, 1 July 1986: #3; cf. also #9). Barker provides a sequence of specific illustrations of this devious device to underscore his charge; CGP is specified one set of requirements, and then judged on another: first there was the criticism over the issue of 'disaggregation'; by the time this was resolved, a new criticism emerged concerning 'expectations'; this issue was tackled through "an ambitious programme for a more general treatment of expectations"; and "we are then faced with the new criticism in your letter that our research is not sufficiently innovative" (Barker, Letter 1 July 1986, p. 3).[19]

Cambridge University changed its rules so that researchers in the Department could obtain a PhD by submitting the research that they were paid to do, a terrific arrangement that suited me perfectly. By the mid-1970s I had a published book on demand systems and a paper on how to run horse races between various then popular demand systems (published in *Econometrica*, and which was later to win the Econometric Society's first Frisch medal), and my PhD was duly awarded, but not until I had passed a terrifying oral exam" Angus Deaton (2014, p. 4).

[18] In the context of the then-ongoing University Review of the DAE, this point may not have been received well by three University heavyweights who had high-level roles in the Review, Jack Lewis, John Butterfield or Ken Edwards, all from science departments where the 'tradition' of supervisors co-authoring the work of their supervisees is widely the norm; a similar question was raised 'independently' by the committee members of that Review.

[19] The Consortium's response to this, in its final letter of 21 July 1987 is odd: "concerning the procedure for criticising the CGP research, it is true that once a model drops behind a lot of deriva-

8.3.2 Unequal Application of Criterion of Commercial Funding

Another issue pertains to ensuring comparability in the application of the same criterion to competing submissions—does the ESRC meet this condition? One requirement laid down by the ESRC pertains to generating commercial funding independently to self-finance part of the activities of the proposal. Midway, when conditionally extending CGP monies for a two-year period, the Consortium stipulates that "we expect you to expand the Cambridge Econometrics clientele so that our contribution ... would be limited to about 60 per cent of your expected total costs" (Letter from Christina Hadjimatheou to Terry Barker, 30 March 1983). CGP achieved this, funding 62 per cent of its work through non-Consortium sources, but "the business of raising so much money with a commercial service has been demanding" (Barker, Letter 1 July 1986, p. 7); it calls for much project work which carries a significant opportunity cost in terms of CGP's independent research agenda. "The other team most similar to ours in its commercial arrangements is the Liverpool one, which also has an associated commercial company. Has a similar requirement for commercial funding been placed on other teams?". The Barker rebuttal shows two major rivals, LBS and NIESR,[20] with private financing at the distinctly lower levels of 41 per cent and 21 per cent, respectively. The implication is obvious. In its response to the CGP letter of objection on this particular point, the Consortium takes an indeterminate dissembling position: "it is not true that other groups are not expected to raise commercial funds". This wasn't the CGP assertion anyway. "The proportion varies with the academic/commercial balance of interest in the product." This is again tantamount to dodging the issue; were the others required to raise 40 per cent as well from commercial sources? Or did they get an easier ride since their product was actually less saleable? The Consortium's answer prevaricates.

8.3.3 Public Good or Private Resource?

With regard to commercial funding, three observations are relevant. First: even while acknowledging the need for some commercial involvement, Stone remains "still convinced that work like that of the Cambridge Growth Project needs, as it has had in the past, a good measure of disinterested support which will enable it to fulfil its scientific purpose and be of some use to the country at large", and also to "maintain a leadership in scientific endeavour" (Stone to Hadjimatheou, Letter, 3 July 1986).

---

tive work is required to get to the point at which innovation is possible. A group that has dropped behind is thus at a real, but proper, disadvantage." This seems to have little to do with the complaint about perennially shifting goal posts in each exchange between CGP and the Consortium; there is no substantive evidence cited to justify its negative assertion of CGP having 'dropped behind'.

[20] London Business School and National Institute of Economic and Social Research.

Second: Stone rightly points out that "if customers are to put a lot of money into research they usually want the results to be their property, so that one ends up building a black box for Messrs A, B, and C the contents of which are not available to the general public or even to one's colleagues for discussion" (ibid.). Stone argues that research such as that of the CGP should be regarded essentially as a public good.[21] But the 1970s commercialisation and the 1980s ESRC protracted withdrawal effectively forced the CGP to reinvent itself as a private company if it was to maintain its particular Keynesian structural approach to economic analysis. Cambridge Econometrics (CE) had thus emerged earlier—required to be formally outside the University—in response to the direct insistence on the CGP generating commercial funding underwriting its own research; the pressure came from HM Treasury, the Department of Industry and the SSRC were brought into the discussion about the commercialisation of the industrial forecasting capability of the CGP model. This pressure on the company contributed to its bankruptcy in 1985. In a management buyout, led by Terry Barker, it continued to provide an unbroken forecasting service but with the closure of the CGP the public good became fully privatised. Now, it must respond to the beck and call of its clients without the basic research driven by public interest. CE's response was (and is) to emphasise its independence and unique approach to economic analysis, contributing to the public good by providing governments and academics with data and conditional forecasts. Its analysis is deeply rooted in the Keynesian tradition, but without making the neoclassical assumptions such as equilibrium or representative agent.

Third: it also means that the Bank of England, or Her Majesty's Treasury, or the Department of Industry, or any other comer, could just pay and buy individual pieces of tailored research; they do not have to pay to maintain CGP as a whole, pay for its data collection, rent, paper and pencils, staff salaries and pensions, all year round. The closure can also be viewed as an illustration of privatisation: having first encouraged, then required the CGP to engage heavily in commercial work, the principal clients would be the financial beneficiaries of the CGP's reinvention, from being a flagship university research project, to a private company. This was consonant with the Thatcher-Joseph vision of useful research: "you pays your pennies and you buys your research", or "you sells your works and you makes your living".

---

[21] In the same year, 1986, as the rejection of the CGP's funding application to the ESRC, Richard Stone delivered the prestigious Raffaele Mattioli Lectures on British empiricists in the social sciences starting from 1650; significantly, Phyllis Deane, was a discussant of her mentor's exposition, and some of her words resonate volubly: "It is worth noting that Richard Stone has never had any inclination to 'privatise' his own contributions to the advancement of knowledge. In this he has more in common with the seventeenth- and eighteenth-century political arithmeticians than with many of their twentieth-century descendants, who seem often to be more concerned to copyright their academic achievements than to share them with the rest of the world" (Deane, in Stone, 1997, p. 389).

8.3.4 ESRC Ignored CGP Model Performance: Why?

Barker levels a further charge that in its decision-making the Consortium has wilfully ignored or misread independent evidence on the quality of CGP modelling. The same Posner-chaired SSRC Sub-committee that had recommended the creation of the Consortium had also suggested the setting up of the Macroeconomic Modelling Bureau at Warwick with the mandate to compare and evaluate the performance of the various UK macroeconomic models. This it had done in several exercises—under the direction of the Bureau chief Kenneth Wallis—including the issues of disaggregation and the treatment of the labour market. "In these studies, the properties of the CGP model emerge as at least as sensible as those of the others." So, rightly, Barker demands: "What evidence has the Consortium taken from the work of the Bureau to justify the decision to stop funding? What is the purpose of putting resources and public money into model evaluation if the research of the Bureau is to be ignored in these 4-yearly competitions?" (Barker to Hadjimatheou, Letter, 1 July 1986, p. 4).

Going on, Barker cites several up to date studies which demonstrate that "in virtually every case the forecast from the CGP model outperforms *all* the other forecasts" (emphasis in the original), and that "the forecast made in September 1985 for this year is turning out to be considerably better than those from the three other models supported by the Consortium". Barker asks: "So why is the Consortium proposing to cease supporting the one model which has done better than the others in forecasting unemployment? The proposed cut becomes even more difficult to justify when unemployment is acknowledged as *the* major problem facing the British economy. The CGP application puts the study of the causes of unemployment and of policies to reduce unemployment at the centre of the group's programme" (emphasis in the original); significantly, "the CGP/CE's annual 1, 2, and 3 year-ahead forecasts for unemployment and GDP were consistently better than those of the LBS, the National Institute and Liverpool, and the comparable inflation forecasts were much the same as those of the National Institute". Given the size and composition of the Consortium, it is not credible to ascribe this incongruity to ignorance or to carelessness; this opens the window to less favourable hypotheses explaining the Consortium's decision. Prima facie, the CGP's complaints clearly have more than just a semblance of justification.[22]

---

[22] The same cannot be said for the Consortium's final response to this CGP criticism: "The points you make on Evaluation of Models and Forecasts are taken, though members expressed some doubts about the insights achieved into the unemployment problem" (Letter from Christina Hadjimatheou to Terry Barker, dated 21 July 1986, p. 2). This reaction, again, is little short of wilful obfuscation or prevarication. It is worth quoting the relevant section from Barker's letter of objection (1 July):

> You say that the Consortium is concerned about the ability of the model to provide new insights into crucial aspects of the British Economy. It may be the case that the model does not provide the 'insights' some would find acceptable. However, as we have shown, besides

8.3.5 Compromised 'Independent' Evidence

A fourth problem pertains not to the reading of independent evidence, but to the prior question of the sources from which 'independent' evidence or 'expert' opinion is sought by the Consortium. These comprise one (unnamed) referee and two external consultants, Professors John Helliwell and Robert Gordon, selected by the Consortium. The CGP response notes: "as far as we are aware none of the members, referees or consultants of the Consortium belong to the mainstream of the input-output tradition in macroeconomic model-building. Indeed, the position is worse in that the external consultants have may be regarded as antipathetic to that tradition" (Barker, Letter 1 July: #10). Helliwell was responsible for the Bank of Canada's primarily aggregated, monetary and financial model of the Canadian economy, "and was in competition" with a rival disaggregated model. Gordon was known from his published work to be hostile to industrially disaggregated macro-modelling, and appreciative of new one-equation models—a far cry from CGP methodology. Expect as you select: and both consultants duly gave a thumbs-down to CGP; Helliwell predictably took issue with disaggregation; and Gordon cut loose across a swathe of swingeing attacks, concluding that the proposal did not "warrant the support of two or three economists, much less 12.5" (Robert Gordon on "The Barker Proposal")[23] though the application is in fact for six economists. Terry Barker's response systematically takes up and rejects each of the unfounded criticisms of the consultants and fairly comprehensively dismantles Gordon's imprecise and wayward critique of the CGP's research.

"Professor Gordon is clearly prejudiced against disaggregated modelling and appears to be unfamiliar with recent developments in the use of input-output techniques. At the interview he asked us whether it was not sufficient to look up input-output tables for disaggregated results rather than work within a model framework; this is like asking whether it was not sufficient to look up the Blue Book for the behaviour of consumers' expenditure rather than estimate a consumption or private expenditure function and embed it in a

> producing more accurate forecasts of unemployment, the CGP model has provided an understanding of the phenomenon and not just at the aggregate level, but also at the industrial and regional level. Thus, what the project provides is not just a single number for the numbers employed, but also an analysis of how total employment is distributed across different industries with attendant implications for regions. ... In using the model, the CGP has not put forward any simple solution to the unemployment problem. Any policies put forward to 'solve' the unemployment problem have been a complex package of initiatives at the industrial level, measures to improve competitiveness and measures to improve productivity. The Project has repeatedly emphasised the magnitude, the complexity and stubbornness of the problem. Those who claim that easy solutions exist are deluding themselves and Consortium, as well as doing a disservice to the profession.

---

[23] Comments by Professor Robert Gordon on The Barker Proposal, ESRC Report, pp. 11–12; sent by ESRC to Terry Barker; Archives of the Cambridge Growth Project, The Marshall Library, Cambridge; CGP/42/4.12.

macroeconomic model" (Barker, Letter 1 July: #13). Servaas Storm provides a striking assessment confirming that the subsequent course of this part of applied economics strongly validates the Stone-Barker position and, if anything, confirms the inappropriateness of the wayward critiques submitted by the pair of experts no doubt carefully chosen the Consortium[24] (Personal communication).

It only remains to ask why the Consortium chose two consultants who were known, through their work and publications, for their antipathy, even hostility, to the CGP's approach and disaggregation methodology. The Consortium response is once again defensive and obfuscating; it does not refer at all to its choice of Gordon—who had duly carried out the expected hatchet job that was accepted by the Consortium—but now faced with the challenge over its choice and procedure that it cannot easily answer, it obliquely says, "we will try to employ different consultants" next time. This could be construed as constituting more an admission of guilt than a valid defence.

---

[24] "Both reviewers were no experts on multi-sector IO modelling, but openly hostile to it. They gave the ESRC the 'stick' to beat the CGP to a premature and unjustified death. Subsequent history has proved Messrs. Gordon and Helliwell's negative view of IO modelling completely wrong (and by implication, Terry Barker has been proven to be completely, and sadly, right). Look at what happened:

- The European Commission funded a large research project called EU KLEMS as part of the 6th Framework Programme, Priority 8, 'Policy Support and Anticipating Scientific and Technological Needs'. In the project large multisector (IO) open-access databases were constructed for 40 economies during 1960/70–now—to facilitate and support empirical research multisector (productivity) growth. See http://www.euklems.net/ and http://www.worldklems.net/ These databases have been used in many publications, including Jorgenson, Fukao and Timmer (eds). 2016, The World Economy: Growth or Stagnation (Cambridge University Press).
- The European Commission funded a large research project called World Input-Output Database (WIOD), see http://wiod.org/project. The world input-output table is a consistent IO table including 35–40 industries and 40 countries/regions and is available for the years 1995-2017. The WIOD has been used widely in papers on the world economy and global value chains, published in the AER, QJE, PNAS, Economic Journal, JEP etc. WIOD tables are used for global environmental analyses including analyses of global carbon footprints, emissions exports and imports, and global energy studies.
- Some of the most influential studies on the employment impact of globalisation are detailed multi-industry analyses of how imports into and outsourcing of production out of the USA and the European Union have impacted jobs and incomes; see, for example, https://economics.mit.edu/files/12751. One can add many other studies.

It turns out that only a decade or so after the CGP was discontinued, IO modelling became a major method in (mainstream) economic research. How myopic were the supposed experts Gordon and Helliwell! 'The only function of economic forecasting is to make astrology look respectable', wrote John Kenneth Galbraith—which holds true for the Gordon-Helliwell episode" (Servaas Storm, personal communication).

8.4 Other Concerns

8.4.1 'Reds'?

By no stretch could CGP staff be labelled 'reds under the bed', leftists or Marxists; as a group, they formed a lineage of Cambridge economics distinct from the Sraffian, or the Robinsonian family trees. They were pragmatic practitioners in the best traditions—in fact, prime movers—of the famed Cambridge empirical macroeconomics within a neo-Keynesian frame. But significantly, they were inherently hostile to market fundamentalisms; when the barricades were up in the Cambridge Faculty, the majority would have been found in the heterodox camps in opposition to neoclassical orthodoxy; and as a group they constituted a sizeable bloc of votes in the crucial arena of elections to the Faculty Board. Only two of the CGP team shifted to lectureships in the Faculty, William Peterson and Tony Lawson, one on each side of this divide.

8.4.2 Crowding Out Competitors?

Another ESRC concern which registers obliquely is that the old incumbents, prominently including Cambridge, take up most of the funding available and thereby crowd out newer smaller entrants and rivals. Prima facie, this would not stand up well to scrutiny: when the collective demands of the various applicants exceed the available funding budget of the ESRC, some form of rejection, exclusion, or 'crowding out'—call it what you will—is inevitable. As such, this is an outcome of the application of independent quality criteria, and not a judgement of quality in itself. If the ESRC so wished, it could have included an explicit reservation of some funds for one or more fresh initiatives, but this was not the case. And further, when some applicant was rejected for lack of funding, the charge of crowding out, untenable as it was, could hardly be directed against any specific project of the slate that had received funding. There is also the empirical dimension: in the cycle in which CGP was rejected, the City University Business School was awarded 30,000 GBP; the London Business School, 125,000 GBP; Liverpool University, 80,000 GBP; the Cambridge Growth Project, 0 GBP; and the National Institute for Economic and Social Research (closely linked to the government) a whopping 250,000. So if anyone was crowded out, it was CGP itself; if anybody did the elbowing out, it was the NIESR. As *The Economist* reported at the time, "thanks to strong academic support it escaped" (The Economist, 1986); in contrast, the composition of the ESRC and Consortium committees was stacked full of members and experts hostile to CGP, the DAE, and to Cambridge heterodox economics.

8.4.3 Deadweight Loss of Built-up Intellectual Capital

The Consortium's letter (of 21 July 1986, p. 2) rejecting the CGP objection/appeal is of course right when it says: "the fact that the Project has been supported for 19 years isn't a good enough reason to justify continuation". But nor could that constitute sufficient, or even pertinent, grounds for rejection.

It does raise some relevant and difficult policy issues with regard to the criteria to be applied in making selections and grants across applications from units with widely divergent past profiles. A thoughtful reflection was provided early in 1981 by Michael Posner as Chair, SSRC (Posner, 1981). Posner's position, as expressed in his Note, is rather typically ambivalent, but there is a clear recognition of reputation, and weight of the cumulative body of work—keeping in view the cost of continuation—which seems to tip the scale in favour of the incumbents, as against newcomers. Posner makes a case for differential criteria for the old heavies and the new aspirants. New entrants should be obliged to demonstrate clear potential and innovation, that is, their value-addition, while these criteria are not equivalently applicable to old groups. Posner also speaks of protecting a public good but does refer to the opportunity costs of such consideration. However, Posner left the SSRC in 1983; Sir Douglas Hague took over as Chairman of the renamed ESRC, ushering in a change of stance with the new Consortium chaired by him. Now, the Consortium seemed to dismiss the notion of public good and was not inclined to attach value to historical built-up capital, suggesting there would be no concession favouring the old incumbents on these grounds. Further, Posner had referred to the need for research to be socially useful and relevant for government policy; now Hague took this much further, arguably too far, and generally expected publicly funded research to serve government policy needs. There is no recognition that such modelling teams tended generally to be small, and that as internal compositions change (in response to career moves or personal circumstances), team balance could be affected in the short term. Teams have life cycles, and these can be brittle and influenced by such individual-level changes. A longer view might therefore be appropriate, except for large institutional applications, perhaps such as the NIESR where continuity could and should be expected.

Posner argued for catholicity of approach, and it would appear that he might wish to build diversity and turnover around some gravity provided by some of the four heavyweights. Hague, in contrast, seemed not to attach any special value to history. When challenged by CGP, Posner's idea of catholicity received lip service from Hague, but then this was not meant to stand in the way of diversity through 'turnover'—clearly militating against any premium to be attached to the continuity of the old heavyweights.

So ESRC-86 rejigged the criteria: built-up capital was devalued; the notion of turnover overtook diversity; the idea of a public good had already been tempered by commercial self-financing by applicants but autonomy was further compromised by the requirement of being useful to government needs; so the Consortium under Douglas Hague gave itself the freedom of manoeuvre to bestow its munificence or wield its axe in any direction it chose, as CGP discovered.

On reflection, there are two issues here. First, there could be a substantial downside to the discontinuation of a long-standing big team because that could imply the atrophy and destruction of a historical cumulative asset—an outcome which would clearly not apply to an independent new team starting out fresh. Second, the problem also lies in how 'catholicity', 'diversity', 'turnover', 'historical value' are defined, interpreted and valued in the process of decision-making. Inevitably, this brings into play the predilections, preferences, prejudices, aka 'judgement', of the decision makers. What the discussion of the CGP episode reveals fairly clearly is that there are serious deficits in the manner in which official criteria are applied to different teams—rendering superficial, cosmetic or even hypocritical, the use of these generic words and phrases in exploiting them to provide a cloak of propriety to decision or procedures—even to cloak naked bias.

8.4.4 Gratuitously Offensive: Up Close and Out of Order

Finally, the Consortium rather gives the game away and reveals its visceral hostility not just to the CGP application but also to the applicants. In its response (Letter of 21 July 1986) to Terry Barker's letter of objection, the Consortium opens with a gratuitously insulting remark, pronouncing that "the last distinguished economist who was nursed there [in the CGP] left the Project about ten years ago.[25] There is no evidence that the flow is continuing. In fact, … some members wondered whether the flow is going to the other way."

This bizarre reaction from the Consortium also induces curiosity about the criteria it employed: was the Consortium comparing quality and skills across teams? Or was it, in the case of CGP, comparing the present team with past CGP groups? 'You're not as good as the best in the past, therefore you're no good, you're fired'?

Terry Barker's response is composed and objective: "the remarks about members of the project since Angus Deaton and Mervyn King left in 1976 are unwarranted". He points out that "of the nine people who left the project in the 10 years after 1976, two of them now hold Chairs in economics at British Universities, four of them hold Lectureships and two are in important positions in industry.[26] It is too much to expect many members of the project to

---

[25] The 'last distinguished economist' referred to could be Angus Deaton or his friend Mervyn King, both having left in 1976, well prepared by the experience with the CGP at the DAE for their fine careers ahead.

[26] Barker provides a list of the status as in 1986: Vivian Woodward was the UK Director of DRI (Data Resources Incorporated) a big US company in the 1980s; David Vines became the Adam Smith Professor at Glasgow University; John Beath took up a lectureship at the University of Bristol; Alan Winters went to a Chair at the University of Wales, Bangor; Roger Witcomb took up a post in British Petroleum; Tony Lawson shifted to a lectureship in the Faculty at Cambridge; Frederick van der Ploeg got a lectureship at the LSE; Martin Weale became the Houblon Norman Fellow at the Bank of England; William Peterson took up a lectureship in the Faculty at Cambridge. Of course, it was true that none of them went on to win the Nobel Prize in economics.

become editors of *Econometrica* after they leave" (Barker CGP Note 86/9 "Letter from the ESRC Consortium", 24.7.86). The pattern is almost identical to that for the nine persons who left the project in the previous ten years, 1966–1976. "The picture is very similar to the two 10-year periods"; "the record is very creditable".[27] This gratuitous and unjustifiable insult is quite out of order and unbecoming of a formal senior committee—it serves no purpose, but it is indicative of the extra-rational animosity of the Consortium team towards the CGP and its application.

8.4.5 The Consortium: 'Revived Talk of Conspiracy Theory'

With all these idiosyncrasies and aberrations in their transactions, the Consortium unavoidably invites the spotlight upon itself. The official criteria and the recorded process do not stand sufficient scrutiny to constitute good governance. Inevitably, there appears to be more underlying the decisions than meets the eye. Could there have been other wheels whirring away quietly, submerged agendas at work, hidden axes to grind? Such unworthy considerations suggest themselves as viable null hypotheses. Howsoever viewed, the Consortium position is arguably coloured with prejudice and an apparent predisposition towards hostility against the Cambridge group. It was a mistrial—for justice to have prevailed, probably a majority of the Consortium, perhaps most of its powerful members, would have needed to recuse themselves.

There was sufficient interest in the results of the funding competition to merit a report in *The Economist*.

> After months of nail-biting, Britain's five non-government economic forecasting teams now know how much public money they will get during the four years from October 1987. ... The allocation has revived talk of conspiracy theory. At the time of the previous allocation in 1982, the Social Science Research Council, the ESRC's predecessor, withdrew all its support from the Cambridge Economic Policy Group (CEPG)—no connection with the Cambridge Growth Project—which was headed by Professor Wynne Godley. But it handed more money to Liverpool University's forecasting team, headed by Professor Patrick Minford, and to CUBS. The CEPG was staunchly Keynesian and had been highly critical of the Thatcher government's policies, producing endless doom-laden forecasts. Both Liverpool University and CUBS are faithful proponent of the favoured Tory creed of monetarism and supply side economics. This time, two of the losers, the NIESR and the Cambridge Growth Project—have been critical of the govern-

---

[27] In a later letter dated 11 September 1986, Barker cites publication data to rebut the Consortium's assault on the academic reputation of CGP staff. He compares the period 1970–1975 (taken by the Consortium to be the 'good' years) with the period 1980–1985 (alleged by the Consortium to be the years of low quality). In both periods, the team size was eight. The number of articles or books published rose from 78 to 107; those published in refereed journals rose from 36 to 49; publications by Richard Stone dropped from 19 to 15, so the improved performance could not be attributed to a Stone effect.

ment's policies and, as usual, they are forecasting the slowest rates of growth for pre-election 1987. (The Economist, 1986, p. 27)

The report mentions the two principles that apparently underlay the decisions: money was to be given only for modelling, while forecasting was to be financed by paying clients; and 'value for money': "the consortium was unconvinced about the value of the Cambridge Growth Project's highly disaggregated model which contains no less than 8,000 variables covering 39 industries". The author notes: "The NIESR also came under strong attack on value-for-money grounds. … Thanks to strong academic support, it escaped … but NIESR's Keynesians are still by far the largest recipients of government money" (ibid.). The plausibility of such interpretations was widely acknowledged: after the arrival of Thatcher and Thatcherism in 1979, the DAE macroeconomic modelling teams were especially in jeopardy; in contrast, their rivals were far more secure—the NIESR was too closely linked with the Treasury to be suppressed, and the London Business School enjoyed political protection through its intimate links, through Terry Burns, with the Conservative government.

8.4.6 *In Defence, a Lone Voice, Overruled*

Immediately after the Consortium rejected the CGP application, essentially ringing its death knell, Chris Taylor wrote to Terry Barker: "Since I attended the meeting in John Flemming's place it might be fairly supposed that I share responsibility for the decisions. I should, however, like you and your colleagues to know that I think that the decision to discontinue the support is wrong, and I did my best at the meeting to persuade others to reconsider. I regret very much that I could make little headway" (Chris Taylor to Terry Barker, Letter, 10 July 1986; CGP/42/4.25, Marshall Library Archives). Others on the Consortium panel then included: Douglas Hague (Margaret Thatcher's economics guru) as Chair, also Chair ESRC; Charles Feinstein, Mike Artis and Stephen Nickell, all marked critics of Cambridge macroeconomic modelling approaches; Peter Sloane, a serial SSRC/ESRC/Consortium panel member and an ex-student of Douglas Hague when in Sheffield; David Laidler, arch Friedmanite and vehement opponent of the Cambridge take on monetarism; and a few others, most with connections and/or sympathies with the Hahn-Matthews group, or with antipathy towards the Cambridge heterodox positions. Then there were the 'experts' appointed by the Consortium, and (as suggested above) these choices were revelatory as well. Both John Helliwell and Robert Gordon were close to the Hahn-Matthews camp. Gordon's doctorate had been supervised by Bob Solow, Hahn's old and close friend; John Helliwell had been a contemporary and close buddy of John Flemming when they, and Martin Feldstein, had all been brought up in Oxford by Hahn's other close collaborator and pal, Terry Gorman; and the connection had continued over the years.[28] There seemed to be three strains of opposition in the Consortium: those from rivals, even if some variety of Keynesians, and their dedicated supporters who might take hostile positions against Cambridge, seeing it as a zero-sum game; those in intellectual/theoretical and doctrinal/ideological opposition to Cambridge macroeconomics; and these could be both from the neoclassicals (including those led by Hahn) but also the monetarists with whom there could be an expedient tactical alliance. And the gavel was in the hands of a Thatcherite chairman not kindly inclined towards the Cambridge critics of his clan, then in full control and power.

In contrast, Chris Taylor, "by training and instinct a Keynesian, sceptical of the claims of monetary control as a panacea", "a firm believer in state action" and that "fiscal policy was the key to achieving an optimal balance of inflation and output" (Broadbent, 2018) was perhaps the sole member of the panel with affinity to the DAE, having worked there (also as Deputy Director) in the mid-1960s, lectured on macroeconomics at the Judge Business School, and published joint papers with Wynne Godley in the 1970s. It could not have been a comfortable meeting for Chris Taylor, and he obviously came away carrying a conscience weighed down by the burden of having to accept responsibility, howsoever 'collective', for a deeply questionable judgement—enough for him to feel obliged to break with conventional protocol and write a letter of exculpation.

With nods and winks, whispers and handshakes, the cumulative Cambridge Faculty-cum-DAE's capacity on macroeconomic modelling, both for tracking and analysing structural long-run change, as well as for short- and medium-term policy forecasts and simulations, was demolished by what, with fair justification, can be called a sustained campaign of intellectual vandalism. The internal political and theoretical balance within the Faculty was thereby shifted drastically in favour of the neoclassical wing, which then launched its next stage, the steady systematic purge of all effective vestiges of theoretical heterodoxy, whether neo- or post- or new Keynesianism, Marxists or development structuralists, from the corridors of the Faculty. The DAE continued of course, but the replacement director, staff and projects were not from the earlier macro streams, but essentially microeconomics oriented; and fresh appointments to the Faculty could now roll on the mainstream, US-gauge tramlines laid down by neoclassical orthodoxy.

8.5   Epilogue: CGP—Life After Death?

What came of the famous Stone-Barker CGP model embodying the brain labour of over a hundred man-years? What happened to their boys' toys, their rubbished models: did they wind up in a charity shop, or did they trash the CGP model and dump it in the garbage bin as they left the Austin Robinson Building?

---

[28] See, for instance, the special issue of the *European Economic Review* jointly co-edited by Robert J. Gordon in 1985 including papers by John Flemming and John Helliwell (de Ménil & Gordon, 1985).

Here is what a quick tracking exercise finds. The CGP macroeconomic model, so freely denigrated by the Consortium, survived, indeed thrived in fresh locations: some of the people involved continued to work on projects using the methods and model of the CGP funded by the ESRC after 1987; and Cambridge Econometrics Ltd. had been reinvented as a fully private company and continued to use and develop the model as the basis of an industrial, then energy-economy and then regional model of the UK, EU and global economies. The company now has a total staff of economists comparable in size with those of the Faculty of Economics and with a comparable, if not greater, international reputation for macroeconomic modelling. The CGP tree, rooted in the DAE, was chopped down, but there was fresh growth from the old roots, though not in the original location, and a commercial offshoot steadily gaining in strength with widespread intellectual development and use in many universities and government bodies. Terry Barker stayed on in DAE, led a succession of projects after the CGP was closed, and played a leading role in the Intergovernmental Panel on Climate Change as an economist from his base in the DAE till it merged with the Faculty in 2004; then, facing a discouraging environment for multidisciplinary research, he left altogether and relocated to the more intellectually accommodating and congenial institutional environment of the Department of Land Economy. The successor models to those developed by the CGP are centred in CE.

One can turn to Terry Barker's role and experience: "In 1977 and 1978, at the instigation of the official sponsors of the CGP (the SSRC, H.M. Treasury and the Department of Industry), members of the project founded a company, Cambridge Econometrics, to provide a commercial service using the model of the British economy developed by the project (MDM). I was Chairman of the company 1978–83 and editor of the forecasts 1981–83. The company was re-launched as Cambridge Econometrics (1985) Ltd. in 1985 under my Chairmanship. The company has published 2 to 4 long-term UK industrial forecasts a year since 1978. Following the closure of the CGP, the company took over responsibility for maintaining and updating the CGP model. I have also acted as Joint Editor of some reports. The company is highly successful with a staff of some 30 people and has become one of the leading consultancies in its field in Europe."[29]

Remarkably, the ESRC committee that shut CGP down had gratuitously disparaged not just the research but the quality of the researchers of the team. With spectacular superciliousness, the Consortium and the ESRC had conveyed its judgement to the CGP that its team was no good and going nowhere, likely to get worse, and so it gave CGP the boot. Then, Terry Barker had stood up to respond and robustly defend the team. But as the sustained opposition of the Consortium was progressively revealed, CGP staff would have been set thinking understandably about their futures, and as events turned out, they were proven right. Several left before the CGP was closed down in 1987, others stayed to the end.

---

[29] See www.camecon.com Terry Barker (2016), "Curriculum Vitae", April, pp. 12–13.

What then happened to these rejects? To add to Barker's analysis of the career tracks of past cohorts in the two decades prior to the closure, it is pertinent to follow their post-closure trajectories. Having received their termination notices, did these CGP emigrants wind up on social benefits; if they were as hopeless as ESRC declared them to be, did they need to retrain as gardeners, brick layers or shop assistants, or bus drivers, travel agents, or door-to-door insurance salesmen, venture into fast-food start-ups, as schoolteachers, or perhaps, given their comparative advantage become Cambridge college porters? Endless career possibilities beckoned.

Significantly, in the context of the inordinately prolonged University Review of the DAE that started in 1984 and ran alongside in parallel for over three years—almost identical to the period of the CGP's application to the ESRC and its final negative decision—Wynne Godley had written to complain directly to the Vice Chancellor, referring to the damaging effect that this delay had had on the research staff: "a quite unusually large number of academic staff (most of whom have College fellowships) have left the Department (or have informed me of their intention to leave) since the beginning of the academic year 1985/86. Of the thirteen regular academic staff who have left (or will leave) five have obtained Chairs or roughly equivalent senior posts, three have gone into private consultancy, three have obtained tenured teaching posts (two in Cambridge), one has gone to the IMF and one to an assistant lectureship in Cambridge" (Wynne Godley to Vice Chancellor, Letter dated 23 January 1987).

And so, what of the other going-nowhere CGP researchers? Terry Barker, still sensitive on the issue, observes: "It is quite astonishing how distinguished the CGP members over the period 1984–1987 became after they left the CGP. They took chairs at other universities or other top positions in the profession" (personal communication, email). CGP was not a large team, and at the time the Consortium's rejection game started in the 1980s, included many who went on to distinguish themselves in the profession, including: Vani Borooah, Senior Research Officer, DAE 1979–1987, went to a Chair in Applied Economics at the University of Ulster, was elected Member of the Royal Irish Academy, President of the Irish Economic Association, President of the European Public Choice Society, and has been a prolific and widely published scholar applying rigorous quantitative methodologies to vital social policy concerns; Michael Landesmann, Senior Research Officer DAE, went to a Chair in Austria, and for twenty years was the President of a major Austrian think tank on international economic affairs that was ranked fourth of eighty-five think tanks globally; Martin Weale CBE went on to become head of the rival NIESR, and was a distinguished, free-thinking member of the Monetary Policy Committee of the Bank of England; Frederic van der Ploeg went on to hold Chairs in the European University Institute in Florence, University of Amsterdam, the Amsterdam School of Economics, and then to a Chair at the University of Oxford, having held Cabinet rank for Culture and Media in a Labour government in the Netherlands; Tony Lawson, who switched to the Faculty of Economics where he became a Professor in Economics and

Philosophy with major contributions in ontology and social theorising, works that lobotomised neoclassical economists could read with benefit; Andrew Snell and Richard Pierse, both then young econometricians, went on to fine careers, the former as Professor at the Edinburgh School of Economics and the latter as a Reader in Econometrics at the University of Surrey; William Peterson, econometrician, was admitted into the Faculty at Cambridge in 1985, was joint signatory along with Hahn, Newbery, Dasgupta and a few others to letters to the General Board during the DAE Review, and eventually retired there in 2011, still a lecturer; and Terry Barker himself, who continued to develop the disaggregated modelling approach in the DAE and Cambridge Econometrics and converted it into a highly successful research enterprise, personally making a range of significant contributions to the economics of climate-change mitigation.[30] This was clearly an intellectually accomplished cohort with an impressive diversity of roots and backgrounds and curiosities which took each of them into related aspects of policy that collectively could only have added massive value to the CGP domain had it been allowed to evolve and grow along its trajectory responding to new policy contexts and challenges. No, neither in the case of the CEPG nor in the case of the CGP did the research staff retrain to become chefs or gardeners or truck drivers or call-centre telephone operators. The team dispersed, with most members going on to remarkably productive and distinguished careers elsewhere, giving the lie to the insults and aspersions gratuitously cast upon them by an arrogant Consortium.

Michael Posner had quietly set the ball rolling with his memorandum for discussion at the Bank of England in February 1981, where—while paying lip service to the big four macroeconomic modelling units in the country, including the Cambridge duo—he had laid the ground for making them run the gauntlet of survival on his terms as the new Chair of SSRC. Almost within a year, one of the duo, CEPG, was unceremoniously killed off, and the wheels were set in motion leading inexorably, in the next major cycle, to the termination of CGP, the surviving Cambridge team. In the short space of five years, the DAE (and the Faculty) had lost two of its most famous and active research teams; quantitative macroeconomic research, which had been at the heart of the DAE since its inception, was summarily eliminated. Were they really getting everything so terribly wrong in Cambridge, or was there possibly some other more credible explanation, it makes one wonder. ... Some other justifications have been proposed as possible explanations of the Consortium's decision, and these generally tend to cast the Consortium in a better professional light.

First, it is argued that the CGP model did not incorporate the exchange rate as a free forward-looking market-determined variable; rather, it was used as a parameterised policy variable. It is then argued that neither the CGP nor Cambridge Econometrics, the commercial arm of CGP, could have made the changes which have proved computationally difficult, given the computational

---

[30] See Terry Barker's contribution in the DAE 50th anniversary volume (1998); see also: https://en.wikipedia.org/wiki/Terry_Barker

technologies then available, and too expensive to be profitably sold by CE to commercial clients. This was, indeed, a new policy frame then emerging; but this would apply surely to all modelling, not selectively to CGP, since most other UK models shared the same practice with the CGP (and the CEPG). If anything, the Consortium should have been supporting all the UK models to make such a transition. This 'justification' does not stand scrutiny.

Second, switching to market-determined exchange rates might have had a disproportional impact on the costs of disaggregated modelling. This is in the realm of speculation. But if such unverified assumption was a factor, why was it so absent from the extensive correspondence where the Consortium did not seem to hold back on listing its reasons for rejection? This was hardly a consideration to hide. More likely, it is invisible because it was not actually a factor.

A third speculation perhaps could have more purchase: the disaggregation approach of the CGP ran against the framework of Thatcherite neoliberalism where, by definition, disaggregated industrial outcomes were left to be determined downstream by free-market processes, so that the need for disaggregated modelling was negated for policy purposes. This was indeed a general trend. Again, this is not the reasoning cited by the Consortium, and it would be denial of its independence, and integrity, if this was indeed the real unstated reason underlying the rejection, rather than the feeble and off-key critiques of the selected experts. It would also imply that the Consortium was sensitive and yielding to real or perceived political pressures on matters that should have been dealt with strictly on professional academic grounds.

A fourth 'justification' points pertinently in the direction of the perceived agenda and role of the HM Treasury in influencing the Consortium's decision towards the termination of the CGP in 1987. Someone from the Treasury corner could interpret it as a case of successful commercialisation; even after the closure, CE carried on engaging in commercial consultancies for external clients, providing forecasts and other tasked work, using the CGP model; the revenues generated supported the maintenance, updating and even some innovation of the model incorporating fresh data as appropriate. In this view, CE would become a reduced form, specialised avatar of the deceased parent CGP. Such an outcome, when viewed from the narrow window of the Treasury as a regular CGP client, would suit it admirably—it would pay only for what it wanted it, and junk the rest of the enterprise and its other accumulated assets. The appropriate word for such a strategy is 'asset stripping'—and this explanation, which has indeed been considered in this chapter, casts a public institution such as the Treasury squarely in the role of a privatiser of a public good in the academic field, and this no less an entity than this iconic DAE enterprise. Here again, the criterion of self-financing through commercial means was indeed brought into play, without any supporting evidence that the application of this criterion worked against, rather than in favour of, the CGP.

There are side currents to this particular argument which highlight the awkward and often contentious equations that the formation of the CE—through external Treasury pressure, as noted—set up both within the DAE research staff, and also with University authorities who were the main funding source of the DAE. A potential problem could have been a sub-optimal institutional profit-sharing contract between the University and CE. It is known that when Cambridge Econometrics was created in 1978, it was virtually a unique institutional innovation since at that time the University had little experience and no standardised template for the establishment of such commercially oriented companies within University departments. CE was based on research assets that were effectively created and owned by the University (part-) funded the DAE and the CGP, so it was established as a spin-out company, limited by guarantee and overseen by a board of directors drawn from the CGP and the University, with the idea that some of the profits should accrue to the University. So, hypothetically, focussing on CE tasks, could negatively impact on CGP productivity; while expanding CE staff could reduce the profits going to the University and cause other sorts of trouble. At this time, Robin Matthews served as a University-appointment director of CE and he would have been fully cognisant of such embedded trade-offs and conflicts of interest; as such, he and the University authorities might well have preferred to condone the ESRC's termination of the CGP's funding, thereby leaving the CE as a purely consultancy-oriented commercial unit bringing in money for the University, with no obligation to plough its profits into supporting CGP or DAE research activities. If this were the case, it would suggest that, just like the Treasury in an earlier 'explanation', the University was also willy-nilly party to a process of asset stripping which undermined a major public asset, the CGP, in favour of a commercial company CE, from which it stood to gain financially. Indeed, one commentator wryly opines that "this conflict is exactly what Cambridge-developed theories of managerial capitalism would predict". It is also noteworthy that Matthews seems to have been in management positions on both sides of the equation: his role in the ongoing DAE Review is well acknowledged and confirmed; and here he was also acting as an appointee of the University authorities, as a director of CE, and also as Acting Chair of the Committee of Management of the DAE, while he also held considerable clout in high circles of government bodies. Given the Hahn-Matthews campaign in relation to the DAE, there were strategic spaces here for the pursuit of such an agenda.

Finally, the buck of explanation could be passed on to external forces beyond Cambridge, SSRC/ESRC and the Consortium. CGP, as pointed out earlier, was indeed not overtly political as the CEPG had been, and its methodologies were to some extent eclectic, in that the mainstream Keynesian approach also used specific elements, as in the modelling of consumer demand, that could be classified as being neoclassical in nature.

This leads a reviewer to conclude that "I do not think, therefore, that there was significant internal opposition from the Cambridge neoclassicals to the CGP research programme"—and this deduction could hold some validity. Then: "however, I do think that by the mid-1980s the programme was seriously at odds with the vision of macroeconomics which was taking over at a national and international level". This suggests that CGP more or less fell on its sword in the face of this rising tide of opposition presumably from the Chicago schools of theory and policy. There can be little doubt that this ideological reconfiguration of 'economics' powered by the US neoliberalism and monetarism was a major factor in transforming the environment in which economics was conducted in the UK. But these new forces needed to be translated into action on the ground, and in the UK, it was the neoclassicals—led by Frank Hahn in Cambridge—and the soft middle Keynesians—of the kind that Robin Matthews had is his CLARE Group, that were the carriers of this force into the Cambridge environment. And as Thatcherism and neoliberalism won the day, civil servants, research council bosses, government advisors, BoE and HM Treasury consultants changed their hymn sheet with alacrity, and those that wouldn't melt away. Indeed, the external environment turned hostile; it was not a meta process but a hands-on exercise that harnessed and used this new ideological and institutional power to complete its agenda of establishing control over Cambridge economics. Here, it is essential to view the collapse of the CEPG, and then the CGP, not as isolated episodes that just happened somehow without the exercise of direct agency and campaign at the local level. As such, significant as the external factors were, they fed into, and catalysed the success of the Hahn-Matthews campaign which showed itself to be adept at instrumentally harnessing these powers both within and beyond Cambridge, to their ends. In this, it was crucial that the power of the left-oriented staff body of the DAE as a voting bloc in elections to the Faculty Board be broken. The closure first of the CEPG and then of the CGP ensured that. All caveats and qualifications considered, it remains arguable with a high degree of confidence that, in the time and manner executed, these were ideologically inspired acts of intellectual and institutional vandalism.

APPENDIX 8.1: CGP STAFF MEMBERS, TIMELINE 1960–1987

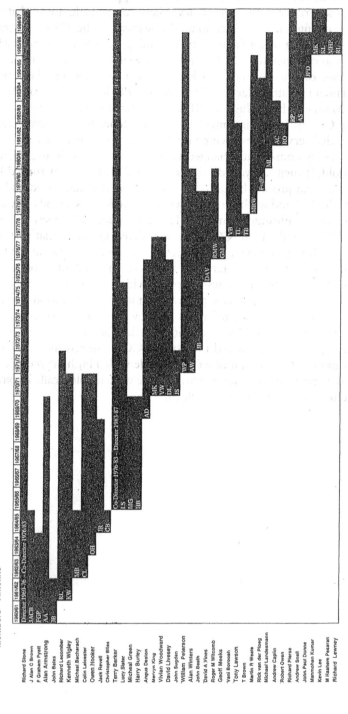

APPENDIX 8.2: PUBLICATIONS OF CGP STAFF

CGP publications/papers statistics (.960-87)

	Books	Journal Articles	Book Sections	Conference papers	Unpublished papers	Totals
Richard Stone	32	45	40	31	44	192
Alan Brown	1	2			45	48
F Graham Pyatt	1				14	15
Alan Armstrong	1	1	1		20	23
John Bates					36	36
Richard Lecomber	3	1	1	1	34	40
Kenneth Wigley	1	2	2	1	18	24
Michael Bacharach	1				12	13
Colin Leicester	2				13	15
Owen Hooker					47	47
Jack Revell	1	1			3	5
Christopher Bliss					3	3
Terry Barker	3	61	29	50	102	245
Lucy Slater	7				26	33
Michael Green					18	18
Harry Burley					1	1
Angus Deaton	3	11	4	5		23
Mervyn King	3	7	3	7	9	29
Vivian Woodward		1	1		36	38
David Livesey	1	7	3	5	15	31
John Sugden					4	4
William Peterson	1	4	10	19	70	104
Alan Winters		3	9	7	21	40
John Beath			1	5	23	29
David A Vines		1		1	7	9
Roger M Witcomb				1	3	4
Geoff Meeks		2	2			4
Vani Borooah	1	11	9	15	23	59
Tony Lawson		7	2	6	10	25
Martin R Weale		9	7	9	34	59
Rick van der Ploeg	1	14	4	6	21	46
Michael Landesmann				6	8	14
Andrew Caplin					3	3
Robert Owen		1		1		2
Richard Pierse		2	1	4	2	9
Andrew Snell			1	2	8	11
John Paul Dunne		2	1	1	2	6
Manmohan Kumar		3		2		5
Kevin Lee		1	1			2
M Hashem Pesaran	2	5	3		2	12
Totals	65	204	135	185	737	1326

References

Atkinson, A. B., & Stern, N. (2017). Tony Atkinson on poverty, inequality, and public policy: The work and life of a great economist. *Annual Review of Economics, 9*, 1–20. https://doi.org/10.1146/annurev-economics-110216-100949

Barker, T. (1998). Large-scale energy-environment-economy modelling of the European economy. In I. Begg & S. G. B. Henry (Eds.), *Applied economics and public policy* (pp. 15–40). Cambridge University Press.

Broadbent, S. (2018, April 5). Christopher Taylor obituary. *The Guardian.* https://www.theguardian.com/business/2018/apr/05/christopher-taylor-obituary

Cunningham, C. (1973). *A survey of economic forecasting.* Report submitted to the SSRC. SSRC.

Deaton, A. (2014). Puzzles and paradoxes: A life in applied economics. In M. Szenberg & L. Ramrattan (Eds.), *Eminent economists II: Their life and work philosophies* (pp. 84–101). Cambridge University Press. https://wws.princeton.edu/system/files/research/documents/deaton_puzzles_and_paradoxes.pdf

The Economist. (1986, September 6). The price of prediction. *The Economist.*

de Ménil, G., & Gordon, R. J. (Eds.), (1985). Special issue. *European Economic Review, 28*(1–2).

Posner, M. V. (1981). *The organisation and finance of the modelling effort in the UK* (Unpublished). Paper for The Bank of England Panel of Economic Advisors.

SSRC. (1981). *A review of macroeconomic research in the UK. The report of a Social Science Research Council Sub-committee.* SSRC.

Stone, J. R. N. (1984). Richard Stone: Biographical. *The Nobel Prize.* https://www.nobelprize.org/prizes/economics/1984/stone/auto-biography/

Stone, J. R. N. (1997). Some British empiricists in the social sciences, 1650–1900. In A. M. Cardani & G. Stone (Eds.), *Raffaele Mattioli lectures 1986.* Cambridge University Press.

CHAPTER 9

The DAE Review 1984–1987: A Four-Year Inquisition

Abstract In 1984, the General Board of the University of Cambridge unusually and unexpectedly launched a formal Review of the Department of Applied Economics. This protracted and unorthodox Review, allegedly instigated by the orthodox camp in the Faculty and running across four years, forms the final element of The DAE Trilogy, following the first, which involved the closure of the outspoken Godley-Cripps Cambridge Economic Policy Group, and the second episode, which saw the termination of the iconic Stone-Barker Cambridge Growth Project—both through hostile funding decisions by the SSRC/ESRC. Using archival materials and interviews with contemporary actors, this third part which, in time, ran parallel to the second offers a revealing keyhole to peep into covert and submerged aspects of the relationship between the warring orthodox and heterodox groups, and through this between the DAE and its parent body, the Faculty of Economics. For three attritional years, DAE and its staff lived under the Damoclean sword, uncertain about its future, its leadership, its organisational structure and its constituents, indeed of its very survival. Insecurity was rife, demoralisation mounted, the departures lounge filled up. When it ended in 1987, the Review achieved the outcome of transferring authority and power over the DAE from the heterodox to the orthodox camp in the Faculty. The year 1984, when this hostile review was launched, is ironically also especially remembered for the award of the 'Nobel' Prize in economic science to the DAE pioneer Richard Stone—though, given the way the Review went—it was perhaps also apposite in an Orwellian sense. The trilogy of DAE episodes marked the termination of macroeconomic modelling, whether analysing structural change as in the Cambridge Growth Project, or engaging with current macroeconomic policy issues as in the Cambridge Economic Policy Group; it also signposted the

© The Author(s), under exclusive license to Springer Nature
Switzerland AG 2022
A. Saith, *Cambridge Economics in the Post-Keynesian Era*, Palgrave
Studies in the History of Economic Thought,
https://doi.org/10.1007/978-3-030-93019-6_9

change of direction towards applied microeconomic research within the mainstream, neoclassical theoretical frame; it constituted a sea change in the intellectual orientation of the Department of Applied Economics.

9.1 The Campaign of Attrition

The DAE Review of 1984–1987 forms the third element of The DAE Trilogy and offers a remarkably revealing keyhole to peep into covert and occluded aspects of the relationship between the warring groups, and through this between the DAE and the parent body, the Faculty of Economics. The first part of the serial involved the abrupt closure of the DAE's high-profile Godley-Cripps Cambridge Economic Policy Group (CEPG) at the hands of the Social Science Research Council (SSRC) under Michael Posner. It dealt a bitter blow personally and professionally to Wynne Godley, but no less to the other members of the team who were abruptly stopped dead in their nationally significant macroeconomic policy engagement, and forced to leave to look for alternative employment, for a few in Cambridge and for most, elsewhere. But barely had that shabby episode ended when the next attack was mounted, this time on the DAE's Stone-Barker Cambridge Growth Project (CGP), which had received a reluctant, conditional reprieve by Posner's hostile SSRC panel in the same funding round in which the CEPG had been chopped down. Perhaps simultaneously ending two of the four major national players in the macro-modelling field, both Cambridge flagships, would have attracted too much media attention and academic opprobrium, and induced questions about the very bona fides of the SSRC process and committees involved; so, by discretion or default, CGP lived to die another day. That CGP story, running in parallel to the DAE Review, formed the second episode of the trilogy, ending in mid-1987, when the Growth Project was itself terminated.

Even as members of the CEPG teams booked their tickets to leave, and their colleagues on the CGP breathed a sigh of relief, the next stage of the attack on the parent DAE was already being operationalised. It took the form of a completely unexpected Review of the DAE by the General Board of the Faculties of the University. The Review was launched in 1984 and its first stage ended in 1985, at which point the baton, or stick, was passed on to a second stage which attritionally dragged on its work between 1985 and mid-1987; for three years, the DAE and its staff lived under the Damoclean sword, uncertain about its future, its leadership, its organisational structure and its constituents, indeed its very survival. Insecurity was rife, demoralisation mounted, the departures lounge filled up. Marshall had some nuggets on how insecurity and investment do not partner well; so it was with intellectual creativity and external funding, both suffered under this existential threat. The year 1984, when this hostile review was launched, is ironically also especially remembered for the award of the Nobel Prize to the DAE pioneer Richard Stone—though, given the way the Review went—it was perhaps also apposite in the Orwellian sense.

9.1.1 Occluded Origins

The mysterious origins of the internal University Review are shrouded in smoke—pipes and cigars in club lounges and college lodges. Who thought it up, suggested it to whom and why? As in Akira Kurosawa's *Rashomon*, or in Lawrence Durrell's *The Alexandria Quartet*, multiple readings are possible. A benign baseline take would run thus: Wynne Godley was approaching the mandatory end of his fifteen-year term as Director of the DAE, so it was a good time to undertake a stock-taking in the form of a University review. But then a reasonable and normal expectation would be that this exercise would have been done in an open, cooperative manner within a mutually discussed and designed framework, especially where the unit concerned had an unparalleled historical record and distinguished reputation as an exemplar of achievement in applied economics. In reality, there was little advance notice or knowledge of the review for those being reviewed, including Godley himself. One justification offered by the General Board (GB) by way of explanation to allay misgivings was that other units, and three are mentioned, had also been reviewed in the past, though apparently these three units might have been rather specialist enterprises,[1] none quite in the Premier League academically, and therefore would not provide a credible basis for passing off the sudden review of a unit such as the DAE as a routine exercise. Then, it hardly made sense to review DAE in isolation—any meaningful exercise would surely need to be done jointly for the DAE *and* the Faculty of Economics as a pair, since the two units were proverbially joined at the hip. And further, long-serving staff with deep institutional memories could not recall a similar review having been done at the end of Reddaway's fifteen-year term in 1970. And surely, for any stock-taking exercise to be meaningful and productive, it would need to be planned carefully along with the incumbent leader as well as the staff of the reviewed group; a review is inherently a cooperative exercise, not an adversarial one. Godley still had about three years to do, but the smoke and whispers were already swirling around. Clearly there was something afoot.

No one within the DAE had a clue. Francis Cripps was in the thick of things at DAE, and well connected, but equally in the dark:

> Regarding the DAE and the replacement of Wynne Godley when his term of office was up: Kaldor told me that the appointment had to be advertised and made as stated in the Statutes meaning that the left would control the outcome as usual. One day Wynne came to work and told me he had met Nichols, [Ian Nicol] Secretary of the General Board, in the street by chance and Nichols told

---

[1] However, suspicions would have been intensified, rather than eased by considering the likely identities of these three: one was the quaint unit of Oriental Studies; another was the estimable, rather niche, Scott Polar Research Institute and the third was the curious case of Aerial Photography which had a good arrangement with the RAF for taking its photographs; when that broke down, it hired a plane, employed a pilot, and in 1965 acquired its own Cessna 337 which flew for the next 40 years taking its wonderful collection of photographs. See: Wikipedia, "Kenneth St Joseph", accessed 3 September 2018. https://en.wikipedia.org/wiki/Kenneth_St_Joseph.

him the Statutes would be suspended and the usual election would not take place. Then we (DAE staff) heard there would be an inquiry but we couldn't be represented or give evidence. That was it really. No one knew what to do as the General Board is a somewhat mysterious ruling body. Barry Moore [a fellow senior research officer in the DAE] told me the Master of his College, who was on the General Board, [this would be John Butterfield, then Master of Downing College, where Moore was a Fellow, and then the Vice Chancellor of the University] thought there were reds in the DAE or Economics Faculty and something had to be done about it.[2]

But then, who whispered what, why and to whom? And who had the Vice Chancellor's ear on this in the first place—another Master, appropriately motivated? Or was it some interested senior economist at a College High Table? Or a combination of the two, or a chat in some secret society or lodge? The answer remains unknown.

Later, peering back into those murky times, Godley, in his remarkable letter to the Vice Chancellor, shares his recollections. (Godley to Vice Chancellor, Letter dated 23 January 1987: 2) "In mid-1983, about two years before the end of my appointment it came to my attention, by rumour, that some kind of review of the DAE was in prospect, and some of my staff expressed a very lively interest about their future and that of the Department", Godley writes. He subsequently addressed Secretary General Nicol that there were "rumours abound that some kind of enquiry is taking place of a fundamental kind into the constitutional function and activities of this Department. ... May I just suggest to you that any inquisitors might find it helpful to consult me, perhaps at a relatively early stage?". His telephonic response "although guarded ... carried the clear meaning that if there was an enquiry nothing more than small changes were likely to be considered".

In contrast, Godley notes, Dr Nicol wrote (on 11 July 1984) to the Faculty Board, without prior consultation or notification to him, that the General Board had decided, on 6 June 1984, not to proceed with the urgent need to advertise for a new Director but, instead, to institute a Review Committee, with what Godley rightly describes as "rather vague, and therefore very wide, terms of reference to review the future of the Department. This Review Committee was set up on the basis of a secret memorandum"—presumably to the previous Vice Chancellor—by the General Board which was chaired by the then Vice Chancellor John Butterfield in 1984, the last year of A. D. I. Nicol's tenure as the Secretary General (SG) of the Faculties. It is apparent from the records that Nicol had produced a Note that framed the rationale and strategy of the entire enquiry, including some results that might be expected from it. In view of this, he was invited by his successor K. J. R. Edwards, a Cambridge geneticist, who took over from Nicol as SG in 1984, soon after the DAE Review began, to the opening meeting of the Review Committee in order to

---

[2] Francis Cripps, personal communication, email dated 11 February 2018.

transfer his knowledge and guidance to the members and orient them in the desired direction. There is no information about the contents of this meeting, or of Nicol's note circulated to the Review Committee. There are scattered references to the 'Nicol Note' in the records, but it is shared neither with Wynne Godley, nor with Alan Hughes (then Chair of the Faculty Board), despite several enquiries from the latter. A forceful letter, dated 16 October 1984, from the Faculty Board to the Secretary General, says pointedly: "It has come to the Faculty Board's attention that the former Secretary General supplied to the Committee an extended memorandum giving guidance on how the review should proceed and suggesting points to be examined, *inter alia* in relation to the organisation of research in the Department and Faculty. The Faculty Board requests that this memorandum be provided to its Chairman and to the Director of the DAE in order to assist them to prepare as full a response as possible to the Committee's request for evidence in the limited time available." Nevertheless, there is no evidence that this crucial document, which seemingly lays out the driving intentions, suggested strategies and desired outcomes for the Review, is ever circulated, and repeated requests from Alan Hughes are also parried.

It would appear that the 'Note on the DAE' by Ian Nicol had been circulated to the members of the Review Committee earlier, certainly by August 1984. Barry Supple acknowledges receipt on 7 September, apologising for "the inordinate delay in my response. We moved into the Lodge here in the middle of August and have been overwhelmed for the last three weeks." Supple conveniently summarises the comprehensive scope of this Note: "your memorandum touches on the principal points at issue which relate [to] the economic standing of the Department and the quality of its research work; its internal organisation and its relationships with the Faculty; and the role, status and authority of its Director. These issues in their turn, are related to the problems of financial support and the definition of the scope of the Department's research." Then, strikingly, Supple adds a new, potentially sinister, dimension which clearly resonates with the Hahn-Matthews agenda: "In structural terms I feel that we should devote a fair amount of attention to the effects of the existence of the Department and the roles of its members on the Faculty—as well as to the consequences of organisational arrangements for the Department itself. I am, or course, entirely prepared to be persuaded otherwise, but my initial impression is that the size and personnel have had a disproportionate influence on the character and academic policy of the Faculty." One can wonder what the source and evidential basis for Supple's 'initial impression' might have been, but an informed guess would probably pin the tail on the correct donkey. And then Supple closes by adding: "I assume that at our initial meeting we shall discuss the taking of evidence not simply from members of the Faculty and the Department but also from distinguished economists outside

Cambridge".[3] That such external opinion should be taken is entirely appropriate; however, the slate of names suggested by Supple had an uncanny and almost total overlap with a list of experts who had expressed strong negative views against DAE when, as SSRC committee members or experts, they had reviewed the funding applications made by the DAE's macroeconomic modelling teams to the SSRC under Michael Posner. Supple's suggestions appear to be clearly aimed at orienting and widening the remit of the Review Committee to focus explicitly on the implied negative impact of DAE staff on the functioning of the Faculty of Economics, precisely the point of the Hahn-Matthews campaign.

However, it gets curiouser and curiouser: while neither the Faculty Board (or even its Chair) nor the Director of DAE, are privy to this mysterious 'guiding' note, Professor R. C. O. Matthews, who has no formal *locus standi* per se in the enquiry, other than as a senior member of the Faculty, refers—in his letter dated 2 November 1984 to the Secretary General, Ken Edwards—to the detailed contents of 'the Nicol Note' in terms which clearly suggest that he is privy to its contents.

K. J. R. Edwards has a note in his file (dated 11 October 1984):[4] "Wynne Godley came to see me, obviously somewhat agitated, about the activities of the General Board's Committee on the DAE"; the note ends: "He went away I think a little happier than he came, although I don't suppose this will be the last time that he visits me before this matter is over". Four days later Godley returns with a letter to Edwards (dated 15 October 1984): "I have realised that you revealed to me something further in the 'Nicol memorandum', the implication of which I did not immediately realise. This was that the Department had been set up as the 'laboratory' of the Faculty and the question should be asked whether it had outlived this function. This query seems to call into question the very existence of the Department in anything at all like its present form." Edwards appears to be playing games with Wynne.

Smoke found its way into the offices of the *Cambridge Evening News* which ran a story on the DAE on 10 November (Fitzsimons, 1984, November 10). The report notes that the investigation of the DAE, which is to happen in the last year of Wynne Godley's tenure and prior to the appointment of his successor, "had already caused disquiet among university members" and "alarmed dons and fellows", something acknowledged by the Secretary General of the Faculties, Kenneth Edwards who said, rather disingenuously as it turns out, that "we have had a few phone calls from worried members of the department but there is no need for concern; this is simply a look at the nuts and bolts running of the department to see if some of the procedures have become a little

---

[3] Letter from Barry Supple, Master, St Catherine's College, to Dr A. D. I. Nicol, Secretary General of the Faculties, dated 7 September 1984.

[4] In all probability, this was his first day in office as Secretary General. Elsewhere, Edwards recollects that Wynne Godley came to see him on his first day of work (Ken Edwards, interviewed by Alan Macfarlane, 2009).

outdated." The department, he said, had been running for more than 30 years with the same organisational arrangements; given the DAE's diverse funding sources, the University might wish to consider its relative contribution and the committee would also review the appointments procedures "to ensure that the right range of interests were being represented and would discuss whether having a 15-year limit on the director's tenure was still appropriate" (Fitzsimons, 1984, November 10). Edwards declared that "there is absolutely no hint of negligence or malpractice. We simply feel that this is the right time to re-examine the running of the department." Fitzsimons notes that Godley found it inappropriate to comment on the matter. Edwards had just about walked into his job, and the seed of the idea of an investigation had obviously been sown well in advance of his arrival, though it fell into his lap and indeed would become his mission to manage the enquiry.

The assistant staff of the DAE are also clearly perturbed about the Review about which they too know little. The DAE Administrative Secretary is sufficiently moved to write to Wynne Godley (dated 15 November 1984) to convey these anxieties: "Several members of the Assistant Staff feel very strongly that they should be informed about the situation regarding the Enquiry, especially following the article which appeared in the *Cambridge Evening News*. I do know that quite a number are very worried about it and would like to ask you some questions. (JH) also told me that even members of the cleaning staff have been phoning to ask if they will lose their jobs. Could we possibly have a short meeting with you sometime soon, to put everybody's mind at rest?" So Godley writes to Edwards, and receives a response the same day (16 November 1984): "Thank you for your letter of today's date. ... No one can, in fact, give any absolute guarantee about the long-term future of any Department, but I suggest that you try to evade this topic and stress the immediate tasks of the Committee" (KJRE to WG GB.8411.460 of 16.11.84). The early indications of dissembling and manipulation are a touch ominous and threatening.

In keeping with the standard issue of any generic bureaucrats' manual of *How to Obfuscate Agendas and Procedure and Keep Them Guessing*, the precise origin of the institution of the University's Review of DAE is not traceable in the files of the DAE or in (accessible sections of the) University Archives, and different views can be taken on it. Maybe it was time for a stock-taking review anyway; but there was also talk in corridors and colleges of concerns that the DAE and Faculty had become a hotbed of Marxists and leftists who needed to be flushed out; that these DAE radicals were overly represented in the decision-making structures of the Faculty of Economics, and were thereby interfering with appointments, with the design and implementation of the curriculum and the teaching of economics, diverting it from its ordained path, as scripted by the staff bearers of disciplinary orthodoxy. The smoke, thick and toxic, was hiding the fire.

Later, John Wells, lecturer in the Faculty, in the opening paragraphs of his remarkable six-page letter in response to the Secretary General's circular invitation, sums it up:

At first sight I found it rather curious that you, the General Board and the Committee of Enquiry should be devoting valuable time to the matters referred to in your letter. ... After long reflection, I have been forced to conclude that beneath the apparent obscurity of the Terms of Reference, there is something much more sinister to which I must draw attention in my response. I started by wondering who could be persuading the General Board that there was anything in this area that could conceivably warrant the attention of a Committee of Enquiry. I do not believe it could have been the present Director of the DAE, nor any of the Department's research officers. However, there are persistent rumours in the Faculty to the effect that the General Board's efforts in this direction have been prompted by one or more of the Professors in this Faculty. I do not have hard and fast evidence as to whether this is true. But, if it is, the Committee of Enquiry ought first to consider what might be the motives of the Professors in this instance. (J. R. Wells to K. J. R. Edwards, Letter dated 16 November 1984 [date not fully legible]: 1)

The question of motives appears independently in the response of John Rhodes to Edwards: "One is forced to the conclusion that the motive for such criticisms has not got very much to do with the outcome of any comprehensive evaluation of the DAE's performance. It would be extremely unfortunate, both for the Faculty of Economics and the University, if the DAE were to become the battleground for those who want control of the Faculty and for those who want to dictate the future direction of the subject of economics within excessively narrow confines" (GB.8411.784 dated 20 Nov 1984).

9.1.2 Two Stages, Two Committees

The Review Committee constituted was to operate in two stages: in the first, it was to deal "as rapidly as possible ... hopefully during the course of Michaelmas Term 1984 ... to review some constitutional questions—of the kind to which Godley had drawn the General Board's attention shortly after taking over as Director in 1970"—though with no response. The second, wider stage could "take considerably longer to complete" and Nicol writes explicitly to the Faculty Board that this stage would be undertaken "when the views of a new Director could be taken into account" (quotations refer to extracts from Nicol's Letter to the Faculty Board of 27 July 1984; cited by Godley in his letter to the Vice Chancellor, dated 23 January 1987).

Review-I was instituted in June 1984, and this Review Committee-I, comprising three members, was set its terms of reference. The report of this first-stage committee was late coming in, received by the General Board in 1985. In reporting, this committee declared itself unqualified to adjudge on a couple of specialised items in its terms of reference directly relating to the conduct of the academic disciplines involved, or to issues concerning the relations between the DAE and the Faculty of Economics, and for this purpose it recommended that a separate committee be formed to deal with these left-over items subsequently. So, the process became: two stages, two committees. This posed a question about the composition of the second committee. Eventually, a new Chair was appointed in the person of Sir Jack Lewis, another Master, also on the General Board alongside John Butterfield, and someone K. J. R. Edwards describes as one of the "movers and shakers ... and opinion makers" (Edwards, 2009). Jack Lewis, incidentally, was an organic chemistry man.

Thus, a second-stage Review-II was conducted by a seven-person Review Committee-II of the General Board, which concluded its business well into 1987. The affairs of the two reviews were managed in the General Board by the Secretary General of the Faculties. When mooted and given shape and direction in 1983, the matter was in the hands of Alexander Nicol, and when he retired in 1984, the reins were taken over by K. J. R. (Ken) Edwards, who saw it through to the end. The Vice Chancellor, who as Chair of the General Board both initiated the reviews, and received their reports, was (later Sir) John Butterfield, Master of Downing College.

Crucial to such committees sitting in judgement is the identity of the experts whose privileged views provide the basis, and the legitimacy, of the pronouncements and decisions that follow. That mythical *Manual of Devious Procedures* would probably advise: select the expert you need; get the decision you want—that is an old time-tested formula when a hatchet job has to be dressed as a fair hearing. But equally, the experts and procedures, in principle, could be ethical and balanced in approach and method.

The first Review Committee (RC-I) comprised D. E. C. (David) Yale (an English Legal History expert, and Fellow of Christ's College as Chair), with Professor Barry Supple (Professor of Economic History at the Faculty of History and Professorial Fellow at Christ's College, and just appointed Master of St Catherine's College), and Dr George A. Reid (St John's, former senior bursar, former head of inter-collegiate services and former lecturer in mathematics). K. J. R. Edwards, a geneticist by former academic training, was the Secretary to the Committee. John Butterfield, the VC, was a medical specialist, with a knighthood awarded in the Callaghan years, and an elevation to the House of Lords in the Thatcher era. Thus, apart from Supple (to a limited extent as a historian of business), there was really no expertise whatsoever in relation to the substantive academic affairs of the DAE and the Faculty of Economics, and as such, the VC, the SG and the members of RC-I would per force have had to seek informal counsel in these regards from sources and resources of their choosing. This would hold all the more, since this Review Committee was initially charged with reporting on terms of reference which included specialist advice on substantive and organisational dimensions directly impinging on the doing of economics and sociology as disciplines.[5] This mismatch between terms of reference and the expertise of the committee members arguably was the cause of considerable suspicion and distrust—leaving aside

---

[5] The Terms of Reference and the List of Members of the two Review Committees are reproduced in the Appendix to this chapter. In both cases, the questions are sufficiently broad and vague to allow the Review to be pursued in any direction.

possibilities of inefficiency and dithering. What is apparent from a trawl through the records, however, is that there was clearly a strong role for opinion-forming 'guidance' and 'advice' from the senior orthodox economists within the Faculty, notably Matthews, Hahn, Newbery and Dasgupta (first, as an external expert from the LSE, then as a professor within the Faculty) who seem to constitute what can be fairly described as a powerful, coordinated and vociferous pressure group bringing its considerable weight to bear on the Review Committee in both its stages; indeed, sometimes the missives, and there are many, from Matthews to Edwards could be perceived by an unsuspecting lay reader as careful orientation rather than take-it-or-leave-it suggestion. The degree of receptivity of the review committees to such inputs must ultimately, of course, be a matter of conjecture and careful assessment. It is perhaps worth noting here that R. C. O. Matthews, apart from being Master of Clare College, was also Professor of Political Economy at the Faculty, Chair of the Panel of Academic Consultants at the Bank of England, and President of the Royal Economic Society. In contrast, Yale, Reid and Edwards could fairly be regarded as being innocents in substantive matters pertaining to the academic disciplines involved, and would probably need to recuse themselves, or be generally reduced to silence when such matters came up, which would, or should, have been frequently; the only person with any brush with the pertinent academic side was Barry Supple, and he was a fellow Master of a friendly college, and a fellow researcher in their shared field of economic history with academic interactions before, and jointly authored research (Matthews & Supple, n.d.) after, they became heads of Cambridge colleges. Supple had sought Matthews's counsel in connection with competing for the professorship in economic history in Cambridge.[6] To boot, Matthews occupied multiple powerful positions at the top of the profession, so his words could easily have appeared to come across loud and clear as His Master's Voice. Incidentally, when near the end of RC-I's task Yale and Edwards are mulling over the composition of the new, second-stage committee and whether some of the members of the first stage should carry over into the second committee, Yale writes that "probably we ought not to consider the Master of St Cath [viz., Barry Supple] because of the evident feeling about him"; "might be wise to let all three of us go" (David Yale to Ken Edwards, Letter of 8 March 1985). In the end, Yale and Reid carry over as members of the second committee, but not Supple, and one must wonder what the substance of "the evident feeling about him" might have been.[7]

---

[6] In a later interview, Supple (2011) recollects: "the Cambridge chair [of economic history in the Faculty of History] became vacant again when Donald Coleman retired early; I talked to Chelly Halsey at Nuffield and with Robin Matthews at Cambridge; I conducted a thought experiment: supposing I was on my deathbed and being asked why I had refused to take the Chair at Cambridge; I knew then that I had to apply, and I got it."

[7] Could attitudes to 'leftist' politics have possibly been a subliminal factor? Supple (2011) observes:

9.2 The Orthodox Gambit

The neoclassical campaign against Cambridge heterodox traditions in economics was a long-drawn one and was prosecuted at multiple levels, in multiple locations, and variously on different constituents of the loose heterodox formation. Most often, the campaign was executed by proxies for the Cambridge neoclassical axis. The charge against the CEPG and the CGP, both flagship units of the DAE, was at the hands of the members, and especially the experts, of the relevant decision-making committees of the SSRC and its successor ESRC (Economic and Social Research Council); and these had extensive links to the hostile Hahn-Matthew group and its followers within and outside Cambridge. And now in Cambridge itself, the next step of the campaign was under the direction of the General Board of the Faculties of the University, and the attack on the DAE was made, ostensibly, not by the neoclassicals themselves, and not on the grounds of substantive disciplinary issues, but by the University, persuaded that it had to intervene as guardians of good governance to protect the reputational assets of the University, in this case of its famous Economics tradition that was now allegedly being jeopardised by the heterodox groups in the Faculty and the DAE. However, underlying and propelling this formal University action on governance grounds was the hidden motivation of the gang of neoclassical economists whose own agenda—to control

> In 1964 I had got a contingent immigrant visa even though I was only going for three months; my wife had one, and two of the children were already American citizens; I was offered a job at Berkeley, and hosted there by Henry Rosovsky ... who subsequently became Dean at Harvard. I was on the point of accepting when Henry phoned me to say that he could no longer advise me to go to Berkeley as he was leaving and so was ... David Landes, and that there was turmoil and anarchy on campus. It was the beginning of the student rebellion, and Henry described it as becoming like the University of Saigon. That put me off, and ... I came back to Britain thinking I would have a quiet life. But neither Henry at Harvard nor I, a little later at Sussex, could enjoy tranquillity: student unrest saw to that. (Supple, 2011)

Had Supple actually gone to Berkeley, he could possibly have run into Ajit Singh who was very much part of that unrest in Berkeley. As it happens, they would have made their acquaintance in Cambridge, when Supple was made a member of the DAE Review Committee appointed by the General Board of the University, and Ajit, now part of the leftist vanguard at the Faculty and the DAE, was defending the DAE against the move by the orthodox economists of the Faculty, led by Hahn and his friend Matthews, and backed by the University authorities, to possibly suppress the DAE, and clean out that stable of alleged red influence; Supple's was apparently viewed by the left and heterodox groups as an unsympathetic, if not hostile, presence on the Review Committee. Ajit had been hyperactive on Vietnam and was also involved in Faculty roles in the Student Sit-in of 1972. The first Review Committee, which included Supple, recommended that some of the terms of reference it had not dealt be taken up by a second Review Committee; in discussions over its composition, it was suggested that Barry Supple be ruled out from chairing this second review committee on account of the animosity that his earlier participation in the first committee had apparently aroused; and, as it happened, he was not included even as a member in this follow-up review committee; Barry Supple had done his job reviewing the DAE. He progressed to becoming Master of St. Catherine's College in 1984, just as the first Review Committee reported.

Faculty decision-making—was intended to be advanced indirectly through the instruments of the Review initiated by the University.

The hidden heart, or differently the bone of contention, lay buried deep in some institutional practices of Cambridge economics—practices that had long been codified and followed. The DAE Report for the 1958–1964 period, when Brian Reddaway was the Director, states:

> Although the Department has a separate identity it is closely associated with the rest of the Faculty of Economics and Politics. Holders of University posts on the research staff of the Department are automatically made members of the Faculty, and are eligible for election as members of the Faculty Board. They may also be appointed by the Faculty to serve as members of the Department's Committee of Management. Teaching officers of the Faculty who are not members of the Department's research staff take an active part in the research activities of the Department. The majority of the research projects being undertaken by the Department in 1964–1965 were initiated by teaching officers of the Faculty and were under their immediate direction.[8]

This was the key part of the long-standing Faculty-DAE constitution that the Hahn-Matthews group wanted overturned, viz., the codified right of the DAE research staff to vote in the Faculty Board elections, and also to be elected on to the Faculty Board, as well as on to the Committee of Management of the DAE. If they could break this numerical hold of the combined heterodox groups, they could wrest control of the Faculty Board, and through that of the DAE, and effectively be in complete command of almost all decision-making in the production, delivery and diffusion of Cambridge economics, starting with the definition of what constituted the subject itself.

Thus, there are two forms of the narrative: one runs in terms of bureaucratese and the institutional lexicon of university administrators and guardians of good governance; the other narrative breaks through this veil of dissembling and tells the story in terms which reflect the real motivations and ambitions of the antagonists and players involved. Multiple and alternative renditions are possible, depending on the motives and methods of the storyteller.

9.2.1 The Agenda Revealed

It is best to let the G4 team make its case for the prosecution in its own words. Frank Hahn's views as expressed in his interview with the Committee,[9] and summarised by Edwards, offer a crisp opening:

---

[8] DAE 1965, *Fifth Report of the DAE covering the period January 1958–December 1964*, p. 5, para 4.

[9] K. J. R. Edwards, "Notes on Meeting of the General Board's Committee to Review the Department of Applied Economics—29 November 1984", 4 December 1984, 3p. The Review Committee conducted three interviews: with Frank Hahn, Bob Rowthorn and Ajit Singh.

He believed that the reputation of the Department has suffered a 'catastrophic decline' since the days of Professor Stone. It is far too inward looking and is not at all highly regarded outside Cambridge. It does not put on joint seminars and it has not in recent years attracted any distinguished visitors.

He would like to see it [DAE] treated as a separate sub-Faculty because this would help to protect the Faculty and, more specifically, elections to the Faculty Board from the DAE.

R. C. O. Matthews then states his reasons for changing the composition of the Committee of Management of the DAE.

> Dear Ken,
> On the composition of the committee of management: This needs alteration, for two reasons. First, the staff of the Dept are represented not only through their own members on the Committee but also indirectly through their membership of the Faculty Board and through the influence of their votes on the composition of the Faculty Board (total DAE staff are about as numerous as teaching officers). Given their lack of tenure, the staff are naturally much preoccupied with the question of reappointment; the dangers do not require to be spelled out. Secondly, although this is an argument that the General Board can scarcely deploy publicly, the politicisation of the Faculty Board of Economics makes it a profoundly unsatisfactory body. This is a serious matter, which has brought about a major fall in the national and international standing of the Cambridge Economics Faculty. However I cannot realistically see it changing in the near future, so the best that the University can do is probably to minimise its ill effects.

How is this to be done? And here Matthews offers his concurrence with the position laid out in the mysterious Nicol memorandum which he somehow has seen, but not Wynne Godley, the head of the DAE, nor Alan Hughes, Chairman of the Faculty Board of Economics.

> I support the kind of change that Ian Nicol had in mind, with the Committee consisting of say (a) Director and Dy Dir (b) 4 profs ex officio (c) 2 members elected by the Faculty Board (including its Chairman if not already a member) (d) 2 appointed by the GB (e) 3 co-opted (normally members of DAE staff). The numbers can be amended, but for the reason already given those in classes (c) and (e) should not form a majority. The Chairman of the Committee should be elected by the Committee from among its own number.

It is worth noting that with very minor variations, this is the final construction that eventually goes into the recommendations in the final Report of the Review Committee.

And then he offers further recommendations, while egging the Committee on:

> I can understand that your committee may naturally wish to contemplate more radical changes than any I have suggested. Thus in most Faculties and Depts.

most of the officers at the DAE would be research assistants, without officer status, ... I do feel ... that it is wrong for DAE staff to serve on the Faculty's Appointments Co, as has happened and currently happens. Your committee may also ask itself why it is necessary to have a DAE at all and whether the University could not save money by abolishing it. ... Change is urgently needed in the Economics Faculty and that change in the DAE is much the easiest way of bringing it about, given that teaching officers have tenure and that, even when vacancies occur, the process of filling them is subject to the difficulties I mentioned earlier about the Economics Faculty Board. These difficulties spill over into its Appointments Committee. Indeed, this where they are worst. (Matthews to Edwards, Letter dated 2 November 84. GB.8410.408)

And then David Newbery is moved to type up a lengthy, self-explanatory individual note elaborating the case being argued by the orthodox group. His views carry special interest, since he later emerges as the new Director of DAE and simultaneously as Professor of Applied Economics in the Faculty. Newbery provides an admirably clear statement of what he sees as the core problem, of the diagnostics, and of his prescription.

The DAE [has] researchers on limited tenure, who might be expected to find a job in a University teaching department here or elsewhere after a relatively short period. However, there is nothing to force such people to leave, and, if they are successful in finding grant money, they can continue indefinitely. But, they are insecure. They lack tenure (for good reasons), but do not necessarily have the confidence that they could find some equally attractive alternative employment at short notice (as in a Faculty, or at the World Bank). They naturally respond by trying to reduce the uncertainty in which they live, and to gain greater control over their environment. They are necessarily, therefore, political animals, who will support those who promise them greater security. In the DAE, their main fear is that the Faculty, which has in principle considerable powers over the DAE, will not support their own objectives of security. Hence their need to control elections to the Faculty Board, on which should sit those well disposed towards, or actually representing, the DAE. Any one in the Faculty shrewd enough to see the advantages of a potential alliance with the DAE to achieve the gradual transformation of the Faculty in directions they desire (via selective appointments and promotions) and willing to pay the price of this support—namely the preservation of the status quo in the DAE—is clearly in a position of power. It is unlikely that such people will be genuinely concerned with the quality of research in either the Faculty or the DAE, since such an undertaking requires adopting different criteria, namely solidarity, not academic excellence. It is important to realise how powerful this power base can be, for the Faculty Board determines its electorate. At a special annual meeting of the Economics Faculty at which elections to the Faculty Board are made, the number present and voting is typically 80–90, when the Faculty boasts 35 UTOs and the DAE 34 Research Officers. Of the elected members of the Faculty Board, 4 out of 10 are from the DAE, and it has been many years since a member of what outside Cambridge would be regarded as mainstream economics has been elected. The Faculty Board in turn selects the appointments committee, which in turn selects future UTOs and advises on promotions. In the past the Faculty Board's choice has on at least one occasion been so outrageous that the university members blocked the appointment of any UTOs.

The behaviour of the appointments committee is widely perceived outside the university as scandalously biased, and the reputation of the Faculty suffers in consequence. Several notable cases in which high class candidates were passed over and went on to achieve international recognition have done much to spread this scandal abroad, whilst the difficulty faced by the university representatives in upgrading or appointing outstanding candidates is that they have to accept unsatisfactory candidates as part of a quid pro quo, since blocking is viewed as a desperate measure of last resort.

It is difficult to know how to change this structural weakness of the Faculty—the DAE is discussed below. In principle, what is needed is that the Faculty Board is selected by those economists committed to the academic excellence of research and teaching in the Faculty. If appointments to the Faculty have been proper, then the Faculty itself is the natural electorate. There is a case for NUTO's engaged primarily in college teaching and research being included, again on the assumption that the colleges appoint those they anticipate will be successful in appointment to the Faculty (here or elsewhere). It is clearly undesirable on the above analysis to include members of the DAE, whose interests may conflict—perhaps only subconsciously—with those objectives for a successful Faculty. Of course, it would be argued that members of the DAE hold college teaching fellowships, and also lecture. But this is a spurious analogy, since they are not appointed by the same stringent criteria as UTOs and college teaching Fellows all of whose salaries are to be paid by the colleges. It is very difficult to see why visitors to Cambridge should be eligible to vote, since again they are invited by a wide range of sponsors, and whilst some are of high academic prestige, this is not true of a significant fraction at the moment.

It is also unclear why stray colleagues in vaguely cognate disciplines should be members of the electorate. There is a powerful case for excluding sociologists who are members of SPS [Social and Political Studies], for reasons not dissimilar to that for excluding the DAE.

How might this rearrangement of the electorate be achieved? One possibility is to have two sub-faculties of mutually exclusive members, who are naturally allocated either to the Faculty or to the DAE. For cases where it is not obvious to which the member should be assigned, there is a case for allowing choice to one or the other, once made irrevocable except by change of status. I don't know if this is feasible or politic within the archaic power structure of the university, and it may in any case be too late to save the Faculty since it has pursued such an unsatisfactory strategy of appointments over the past two decades. (Letter from Newbery to Edwards; pp. 2–4)[10]

Views were sought from selected external experts, and one of those asked was Partha Dasgupta, a rising star in Frank Hahn's 'academy' of long-standing from earlier rounds both in Cambridge, and then at the LSE when Hahn was a professor there, and where Dasgupta now held a chair. Dasgupta's lengthy

---

[10] Letter listed in "Corrected List of Papers received by the Committee; DAE Paper-15: Letters from Individuals".

response is unequivocally negative: to wit, DAE is sliding down the tubes, and drastic external intervention is critical for saving it. "Ultimately, your committee will have to decide by what means the DAE could be made to contribute to the intellectual capital that is Cambridge—as it did in the past—rather than live off it" (Partha Dasgupta to K. J. R. Edwards, Letter dated 13 November 1984; p. 4).[11] Of course, Dasgupta has suggestions to make, having "spoken with a number of bright young economists who have been associated with the DAE in recent years and who now have teaching posts elsewhere and who have a great deal of affection for Cambridge. ... I shall then speculate on what the source of the problems may be on the basis of a perusal of the DAE's annual reports of the past few years" (ibid.: 1). In terms both the content and strength of opinion expressed, his feedback coincidentally appears to mirror the positions communicated, independently of course, by other members of the Hahn-Matthews group.

First, the bottom line: "the DAE is no longer in the top league. Its high point as a centre of excellence was undoubtedly the decade of the 1950s" (ibid.: 1–2). Dasgupta says DAE's prestige has slipped below that of the NBER in the USA "and even the newly established ICERD at LSE". Then, he hones the focus on his real targets: "I am for the most part talking of what has in recent years been the central thrust of the DAE, as exemplified by, say, the Growth Project, the Economic Policy Group, and the Labour Studies Group, in which many Senior Research Officers are involved". These constituted the three large teams within the DAE. Their work, Dasgupta writes, is "highly routinized ... profoundly insular ... they have reinvented concepts which have been around in the subject for over a decade, with no recognition of the fact that they are reinventions" (*emphasis in the original*). More generally, he complains that DAE is not keeping up with trends, witness there is no project within the DAE on panel data, a new-fangled methodological technique then arousing the passions of econometricians; further, there is no high-level international exchange; "deep rooted insularity" gets another mention, and then the damning verdict: "DAE work does not, in its major research concerns, rise above the average and in some instances does not reach even that".

The letter deftly diverts the diagnosis away from issues of disciplinary and related ideological orientation. "The problem is not at all that its [the DAE's] concerns are unorthodox: they are for the most part supremely orthodox. The problem is quality ... the number of publications by DAE Senior Research Officers in major academic journals (possessing as they do a strong anonymous refereeing system) is well below what one would expect from a research institution of eminence. I don't think it would do to infer that is due to doctrinal strife within the profession" (ibid.: 2).

This view is tendentious and inherently misleading in that it suggests there is some unique objective measure of quality, and this conflates with publishing

---

[11] Dasgupta's letter, dated 13 November 1984, is in response to Edwards's Letter of 9 October 1984 (GB.8410.185).

in what he regards as top economics journals. This familiar one-eyed view passes only amongst the similarly one-eyed. With its limited field of vision, it fails, or refuses, to acknowledge the breadth and diversity of 'economics', especially as had evolved and been practised in Cambridge over decades. It fails to accept that the DAE was fundamentally concerned with policy issues, and that by their very nature, the research groups and their output pursued different questions, methodologies and addressed different audiences through different channels. Dasgupta had just his one measuring rod that he was using as a stick to beat all those deviants who did not conform to this one-eyed view of 'economics'.

Dasgupta need not have included the CEPG, the policy-oriented macro-modelling team, in his disparagement of DAE quality; that team had effectively already been terminated by the SSRC under Posner. The case of the CGP is interesting, in that this was Stone's long-standing project, taken over by his deputy Terry Barker in 1980 when Stone retired. One thrust of the Hahn-Matthews group, also prominently including Dasgupta and Newbery, was to hark back on the DAE of the 1950s, Stone's heyday, and then to argue that the current DAE did not stand up to comparison with the original article. As it happens, just a week before he received the letter of advice from Dasgupta, Edwards had actually interviewed Richard Stone about the DAE; tellingly, or puzzlingly, there is nothing in the notes (made by Edwards) of that meeting where Stone is asked about the quality or value addition of the CGP's research. But Stone did have views on how it was all going with the CGP after him, and his views are recorded elsewhere in full,[12] and also in a later letter he sent to the ESRC (in 1986), complaining bitterly about the poor judgement exercised by the ESRC Consortium in turning down the grant of CGP, thereby bringing

[12] Significantly, Stone mentions the CGP at some length in his 1984 Autobiographical Note linked to his 'Nobel' Economics prize: "Towards the end of the 1950s, stimulated by Alan Brown who had been working with me at the Department since 1952, I thought it would be a good idea to bring together various studies that were in progress at the Department and build an econometric model of the British economy. This was the start of the Cambridge Growth Project. In 1962, Alan and I published our ideas in A Computable Model of Economic Growth, the opening volume in our series, A Programme for Growth. The beginnings were comparatively modest, though the principal characteristics of the model were present from the outset: it was a disaggregated model in which several branches of production, types of commodity, consumers' goods and services and government purposes were distinguished, and it was based on a social accounting matrix. At first, it was a static model which provided projections for a period about five years ahead, without considering the path that would be followed in reaching the projected situation. Now it is one of the largest existing models of a national economy, and under the influence of T.S. Barker, who succeeded me as director of the project, it has assumed a dynamic form: given an initial state of the economy and future values of the exogenous variables such as tax rates and the level of world trade which we do not try to model, we can solve the several thousand equations of the system iteratively year by year so as to trace the course of each of the endogenous variables into the future. The model can also be used for purposes other than forecasting. Just for the record, I should add that the team engaged on the project, though changing in composition through the years, has never numbered more than ten people." https://www.nobelprize.org/prizes/economic-sciences/1984/stone/biographical/

the entire project to a close. Though this is reported earlier (in Chap. 8), some of Stone's response is relevant here, in particular concerning the charge that the CGP is not innovative any more. "It seems to me that the improvements that have taken place in the last ten years have made the model an altogether more practical and scientific tool than our [Richard Stone and Alan Brown's] original creation was. The large number of innovations that have been introduced under Terry's leadership in developing the dynamic version are apparent from the Project's forthcoming book. In view of the work there described I am surprised that there can be any doubt about the innovative character of the Project at the present time" (Richard Stone to Christina Hadjimatheou, Letter dated 3 July 1986: 1).

The third group, the Labour Studies team, was clearly engaged in very different kinds of multidisciplinary, heterodox research issues that might have been distant from those of mainstream economists, but perhaps for those very reasons, the relevance and the quality of their work could be judged on the basis of the criterion offered by Dasgupta; it is worth noting that this generally left-oriented team's research generally enjoyed a fine reputation within Cambridge and beyond; it also had an interdisciplinary approach where it relied on sociological methods as well, as appropriate for the research questions being pursued. Frank Wilkinson, the lead person in the group, was interviewed by members of the DAE Review Committee and followed it up with further views in a letter, mainly emphasising the multidisciplinary nature of the group's research. Citing especially the ESRC's Social Change and Economic Life initiative, he points out that the research in "each of the [regional] sub-groups [of this Project in the DAE] was interdisciplinary so that the collaboration between sociology, social psychology and economics is a feature of research at each level. It is also worth saying that the Cambridge team is by far the most integrated of any of the six teams of the Initiative. This I attribute in large measure to past co-operation fostered by the important part played by sociology in the teaching and research of the Faculty. I was also asked about the research links between the Labour Studies Group and other economists in the Faculty and Department. I talked about the joint work with the macro-economists on inflation and wage determination and input made to macro-economic modelling. But I failed to mention the work on labour supply by Roger Tarling in which he collaborated with Dr Hashem Pesaran or that on family income and labour supply undertaken jointly by Jill Rubery and Dr Jane Humphries of the Faculty (which extends to a joint undergraduate lecture course). Furthermore, we see developments in these areas as important parts of our future research effort. I would conclude by re-emphasising how important to the work of the Labour Studies Group are the close research links with economists in the Faculty and the Department and with social scientists in other disciplines. These relationships are not always, or even usually, a formal part of joint research projects; but they are on-going and very fruitful."[13]

---

[13] Frank Wilkinson 1986, Letter to K. J. R. Edwards dated 26 March 1986.

Even more pertinent here, coming from an impartial source, is the feedback on the standing of the Labour Studies Group (LSG) in the DAE, sent to Edwards by William Brown, then the newly appointed Montague Burton Professor of Industrial Relations in the Faculty of Economics; coincidentally, both his and Dasgupta's appointments were made in 1985. Brown writes: "My specific observation is that a major attraction drawing me to Cambridge has been the fairly recent emergence of an outstanding group of researchers in labour economics at the D.A.E. Their distinctive, multi-disciplinary, and policy-oriented approach made Cambridge the most stimulating place in Britain for me to move to from Warwick. Their work has had a substantial impact upon the way the labour market is viewed and upon public policy. Within the past few months, for example, by adding empirical and analytic substance to an otherwise ill-informed debate about the consequence of low pay, their work has been the major influence tempering the present Government's plans to reform Wage Councils. It would be a serious loss to Cambridge economics if this team were obliged to break up" (W. Brown to K. J. R. Edwards, Letter dated 2 October 1985, pp. 1–2). The divergence between the feedback provided by Brown and Dasgupta in their respective characterisations of the same Labour Studies Group is little short of spectacular. Orthodoxy prevailed and the LSG was dealt a dire blow: the team dispersed—but it was undefeated, as its members sustained their productive research collaborations and publications, interacting from their scattered locations (see Appendix 2).

Anyway, having thus established that the DAE was in catastrophic decline, Dasgupta moves on: "Why has the decline occurred?", he asks (p. 3). "I can only speculate." "A potential source of strength that the DAE has not sufficiently tapped are PhD students at the Faculty of Economics as PhD students. It is remarkable to an outsider why research officers and senior research officers at the DAE continue to do work of the kind that research students could be employed to do. It would be a great deal cheaper, it would benefit research students enormously in terms of finance and research experience towards their PhDs. Moreover, and this is only my guess, it would probably improve the quality of research because very often students are more motivated as regards details and techniques" (ibid.: 3). This argument, pertaining to the role of research students as a resource, crops up repeatedly in feedback from some others from the orthodox side; but repetition does not render it any more valid, and there is comprehensive rebuttal of this charge by Geoff Meeks as the Assistant Director of Research, on institutional, substantive and ethical grounds which ultimately, though somewhat belatedly, had to be accepted by the Committee.[14]

Another complaint from Dasgupta was that the SROs were hanging about for too long. "The semi-permanent research officers limit the number of fresh people who can be accommodated within the DAE, and this in turn limits the number of new ideas that are pursued and developed there" (ibid.: 3). "I

---

[14] Geoff Meeks to Sir Jack Lewis, Letter dated 15 September 1986.

suspect strongly that the academic deficiencies of the DAE have a great deal to do with the procedures by which the Management Committee is elected. There must be strong internal pressures to renew the five-year limit more of less indefinitely. While this offers security to the research officers themselves, it at the same time bars outstanding young economists from undertaking research and teaching at Cambridge for a period in their lives. From the point of view of college teaching as well, this is a great loss." So apart from exceptional cases, SROs should not be allowed to stay for more than five years. And "colleges would benefit greatly by being able to elect able and lively teaching Fellows" (ibid.: 4–5). Dasgupta here is dispensing unproveable hypotheses and, as it happens, Dasgupta's analysis is comprehensively negated by the evidence provided to the Review Committee by the Faculty Board, as well as by various other Faculty members providing feedback to the Committee with regard to the range and quality of teaching contributions of DAE research officers.

"The DAE is potentially an outstanding centre. It has the resources of a great university behind it. In principle it can pick from the very best applied economists in the country. I have little doubt that when Cambridge appoints the new Director it can choose, should it wish to, from among the most able of persons. But I don't think the centre can be improved unless the Management Committee contains a number of senior members of the university not deeply connected to the DAE. There is in fact a case for having in the Committee distinguished economists from outside Cambridge, to give the institution a much-needed airing. For the moment it is rather like a closed shop" (ibid.: 4). Dasgupta would have the Review Committee and the University grasp this nettle. Dasgupta's letter in effect pillories the SROs who are deemed to be not good enough and who stay on for too long, extending their presence through control of the Committee of Management; the opportunity cost of which is the crowding out of new young staff who could bring the research up to speed; the evidence is in the lack of publications in what he regards as top economics journals; and the three groups that are 'named-and-shamed' are the CEPG, the CGP and the Labour Studies Group; he calls for a new broom to sweep away all this; and this new broom would be the new Director.

Partha Dasgupta would have had an additional legitimate motivation for providing his feedback on how to improve, from his perspective, the state of Cambridge economics in the DAE and the Faculty—around the same time, he was in transition from his professorship in LSE, returning as Professor Economics[15] to Cambridge. His letter of advice written to the Review Committee—1 is dated November 1984; in 1985, he re-entered Cambridge, and his letter was carried over as advice to the Review Committee—2 which

---

[15] The relevant University authorities were persuaded to elevate the nominal status of his new position from being just another professorship to a higher *Brahmanical* level through converting it into a named chair; after interactions, the University eventually agreed in April 1994 to rename his position as the Frank Ramsey Professor of Economics, the change of nomenclature to be coterminous with Dasgupta's tenure, though later, in January 2011 after Dasgupta retired, the change of name was made permanent (Table 2.1).

carried on through 1986. Even before 1984, the Godley-Cripps Cambridge Economic Policy Group had disbanded courtesy the negative funding decision by the SSRC; and even as he moved, the ESRC had begun its hostile interrogation of the CGP which was wound up in parallel with the working and reporting of Review Committee-2, and process in which Dasgupta now participated as a professor in the Faculty of Economics; the end result of these imbricated episodes was the eventual appointment of the new Director of the DAE, a position for which, in due course, the appointments committee selected David Newbery, a colleague of old who had stayed the course in the Faculty even as many others of what Dasgupta labelled Frank Hahn's 'academy' took up professorships or senior positions outside Cambridge. With this appointment, the orthodox group was in complete control of the DAE, and greatly strengthen its grip on Faculty decision-making processes. However, in real time in 1984, the Hahn-Matthews axis had several, overlapping strategic options.

9.2.2 The Game Plan: Four Options

The core objective covertly yet clearly and repeatedly stated, was to find a way to get rid of the influence of DAE staff on Faculty policy through its participation in the elections to the Faculty Board. The Hahn-Matthews axis could push its campaign on several salients.

Closure
One option would be to seek the closure of the DAE altogether; this was clearly in the air at the outset, an option most likely put on the table in the Nicol Memorandum that set the ball rolling; it surfaces clearly in the early Edwards papers, as is clearly twigged by Godley. Edwards puts it on record.

Early on, Matthews writes to Edwards: "I can understand that your committee may naturally wish to contemplate more radical changes than any I have suggested. ... Your committee may also ask itself why it is necessary to have a DAE at all and whether the University could not save money by abolishing it" (Matthews to Edwards, Letter dated 2 November 1984, GB.8410.408).

But, in the end, this balloon does not fly far: even those linked to the Hahn-Matthews axis cannot entertain the thought, given the massive stature of the DAE in the discipline and profession within Cambridge, nationally and internationally, to close the place down. Even directors of units in direct competition with the DAE express due respect and appreciation. Alec Cairncross ends his handwritten response thus: "What I do hold very strongly is that Cambridge should retain and reinforce the Department since a University of Cambridge's standing and history is bound to have a major contribution to make to our thinking about economic problems and much of this contribution should come from the DAE".[16] Given Cairncross's stature, that would have let all the air out of the 'closure' balloon. It is notable though, that the issue of closure was on

---

[16] Letter from Alec Cairncross to K. J. R. Edwards, dated 26 November 1985, GB 8511.592.

the table and the Review Committee felt the need, as late as July 1986, to say "that the Committee are minded to recommend to the General Board that the Department should continue" (Minutes of the Meeting on 25 July 1986, 39(iii)). It is reasonable to argue, though, that the 'closure' gun was being kept oiled and loaded, to be held against the heads of DAE or Faculty opponents in order to render them more amenable to the 'organisational' changes that the Review Committee wished to push through.

Separation
A second option is mooted by Hahn, based on his assertion that the DAE only does research and no teaching, and hence should be kept out of participation in decision-making on Faculty policy; he supports this with his statistic that DAE research officers gave only sixty-five lectures per year, clearly a very insignificant contribution. Hence, "He would like to see it [DAE] treated as a separate sub-Faculty because this would help to protect the Faculty and, more specifically, elections to the Faculty Board from the DAE" (Edwards' summary of Hahn's comments made in interview; 15 October 1984).

But Hahn was a neoclassical theory supremo, and he rather dismally fails the numbers test, as his empirical evidence is shown to be entirely invalid. There is a barrage of responses from a large number of Faculty staff who emphasise the absolutely critical role played by the DAE research staff in underpinning the entire collegiate teaching of economics on the one side, and their extensive and vital role in supporting MPhil and PhD supervisions on the other. Peter Nolan leaves the matter in no doubt: "People researching in the DAE are a key element in the supervision system for economics. A reduction in numbers in the DAE, if substantial would cause enormous difficulties in supervising and might lead to the collapse of an already over-stretched structure" (Nolan to Edwards, 2 October 1985); Geoff Harcourt emphasises the quantitative necessity of their role, but then widens it into a qualitative appreciation, pointing out "that many of the most vital topics covered in the supervisions related to original research done by the DAE officers" (Harcourt to Edwards 6 October 1985); Jill Rubery pertinently points out that DAE staff, unlike Faculty staff, are available on a year-round basis: "in the Easter vacation, DAE staff supervises both undergraduates and DPhil students writing dissertations while many UTO supervisors are unavailable to help with the final stages of preparing the dissertations"; and a comprehensive denunciatory response, condensed later on, comes from Jane Humphries.

So, Hahn the theoretician is found well short on empirics, in his claim that DAE staff are minor contributors to Faculty teaching. A statistical collation ("Teaching Carried out by the Officers of the DAE")[17] is produced for the Faculty Board, inventorising DAE inputs for 1984–1985: it shows, indeed, that DAE research officers gave only sixty-nine lectures out of a total of approximately 1300 for the Economics Tripos as a whole, or just 5.3 per cent. But

---

[17] September 1985, 2p. DAE Paper 10, in List of Papers received by the Committee.

that is not the whole truth, since they also delivered 110 hours of the 280 hours, that is, 39 per cent of lectures and classes in MPhil courses; they supervised 17 of 24 MPhil students; and 18 students in the PhD programme. For college supervisions, taking the average number of hours per supervisor per week, the figure for the Faculty (1981–1982, the year for which some centralised data were available) was 6.2, and that for DAE was 3.7, which is proportionally very high, given that the prime task of the DAE officers is research, and that there was a maximum limit of four hours of teaching per week officially in place for JROs, with a higher limit of six hours for ROs and SROs. It is noted that it is the smaller- and the medium-sized colleges that make use of the valuable services of the DAE since they cannot afford their own teaching fellows in all subjects, and hence any damage to the DAE would be transmitted quickly to these colleges, their students and to the performance of the Economics Tripos as a whole. The Note also informs the Review Committee that "of the 29 officers at present in the DAE, 18 are Fellows of Colleges. Of these 6 are Directors of Studies in Economics and one is a Director of Studies in Social and Political Sciences".

This evidence goes to show the cavalier disregard for ground realities in the swingeing attacks made by the Hahn-Matthews group who are thus seen to be willing to pick up any weapon to hand. In fact, many DAE staff wind up teaching more hours than the officially decreed limits. The Faculty Board collates the relevant data that incontrovertibly confirm that the DAE staff is indeed highly active in the teaching of economics. As Iain Begg put it in his response: "[the] ample evidence of the teaching role of the DAE ... is more than sufficient to justify continuing full membership of the Faculty for DAE staff" (GB 8411.653, dated 19 November 1984). So, the arguments of the autonomy and separation of the DAE are demonstrably invalid. As such, there is no empirical or institutional basis for excluding them from participating as equal members on the Faculty Board, including its elections. Thus, this tendentious and rather disgraceful assault denigrating the sterling teaching contributions of DAE staff is rightly and effectively neutralised, and the key empirical legitimation for a separation of the DAE from the Faculty is nullified.

In his extensive memorandum submitted to the Review Committee (Stage II), Wynne Godley had detailed the very substantial contributions of DAE staff to the teaching of economics in the Faculty and the Colleges, and also for undergraduate, MPhil and PhD students. "The Department receives just over 20% of the University's total subvention to the Faculty, but according to Dr Meeks [evidence to the Review Committee, dated 15 October 1986] it undertakes approximately one-third of all graduate teaching, including teaching for the M.Phil., nearly one-third of all undergraduate supervision (providing 20 Fellow of Colleges of whom 14 are Directors of Studies); in 1984–1985 ... 69 hours of lectures for undergraduates, in addition to lectures for the M.Phil. course." He further points out that "neither the Department nor individual members of its staff receive payment for any teaching or lecturing done for the University. The contribution of the DAE to graduate teaching is not just a matter of filling in the slots in terms of hours: there are certain types of skill which DAE staff deploy which are essential for graduate teaching and which at present are in very short supply among the teaching members of the Faculty. Graduate students are also able to exploit data and software developed in the course of DAE research." He cautions: "if the external income at present earned by the DAE (and therefore its establishment) were substantially reduced, a large new cost would fall on the University and many Colleges would be in a very awkward position unless the teaching of economics were substantially reduced". This was a comprehensive confirmation of the critical contributions made by DAE staff to the teaching of economics. There would not have been much need for this but for the attack from Hahn on the DAE which was dismissive of its teaching role; and there should have been no need for it given that "the contribution of the Department to University and College teaching was thoroughly investigated by a Joint Committee on University and College teaching set up by the Council of the Senate in 1982 and chaired by Dr G.A. Reid. Their report recognised the DAE contribution as 'an important and valuable one'." Notwithstanding this, at a later stage of the process when responding to the contents of the Draft Report of the Review Committee, Godley had to write to its Chairman, Sir Jack Lewis, with a complaint, to say that "the Committee of Management [of the DAE] is surprised by the lack of recognition accorded by the Draft Report to the contribution by the DAE to University and College teaching"; and he reminds the Review Committee again about the Reid Committee Report; and it is odd that such a reminder was necessary at all in view of the fact that Dr G. A. Reid was one of the three members of the First Stage DAE Review Committee (Wynne Godley to Sir Jack Lewis, Letter dated 29 October 1986).

Absorption
One line of attack, initiated by James Meade (an old-school senior in the Hahn-Matthews camp), in his three-page handwritten submission (Letter to David Yale dated/ack 8/11/84) harks back to the original mandate of the DAE to serve as the research wing of the Faculty; DAE should support Faculty research initiatives. "I, as a general Political Economist (in the old-fashioned sense of that term!) have ideas—hunches if you like—about the best principles on which to apply these various financial instruments. ... But the economic system is a very complicated network of dynamic relationships etc. ... I am not a technically qualified econometrician or control theorist or dynamic model builder or operator. My project with the DAE has thus involved the services of highly qualified persons in these three spheres"; "It would be a sad day for Cambridge economics if this sort of interest of a teaching officer could not be met"; the implicit critique is that the DAE does not adequately cater to these research interests of the University Teaching Officers (UTOs, i.e., teaching staff of the Faculty) and that DAE has become an overly autonomous research unit employing a lot of independent staff (who then influence Faculty policy and

elections). The DAE should return to its original mandate and restrict itself to supporting the research of Faculty members as and when sought.

Matthews[18] attempts to build on this, without evidence, by simple force of assertion: "Problems have led some UTOs to feel that carrying out a project through the DAE is a lot of trouble without corresponding benefit, and if an alternative centre is available, such as some of the independent research institutes in London offer to University staff, that is simpler and preferable". And here comes the 'hard' evidence: "These complaints are not to be overstated. Some of those who expressed them do in fact have projects in the DAE. Complaints, moreover, have not been made by the more senior UTOs who have or have considered having projects in the DAE, like Professor Hahn—they have been felt more by people lower down the scale." One has to make of this charge, and the evidence, whatever one can. But clearly, even such rubbishy criticisms find room right till the end of the Review process.

An independent comment from the knowledgeable and respected Brian Reddaway, the ex-Director of the DAE (1955–1970), cannily speaks directly to, and rejects, this argument. He emphasises that DAE has always supported research projects of Faculty: "I regarded it as an important part of the Director's duties to help Faculty members to produce workable schemes of research out of what might be no more than broad ideas"; he refers to the 1956 "constitution" of DAE which "provided that a minimum number of research workers must be made available in this way if suitable projects were brought forward. ... I readily embraced this rule—as my successor [Wynne Godley] also did. I always regretted that the number of schemes arising in this was not big enough to have very much impact on the DAE's size" (Reddaway comment dated 9 September 1985: 1–2). Reddaway thus makes it clear that there is no constraint or lack of welcome from the DAE side; it is more a matter of individual Faculty not coming up with their "hunches", à la Meade, or "no more than broad ideas", à la Reddaway; it is a demand side issue. It is typical of the partial style of the Review that this particular criticism still persists and is listed a year later in the Committee's *Summary of Adverse Views* which is sent to Wynne Godley for a comment; and Godley "rejects very vehemently the charge that the DAE does not allow sufficient opportunities for UTOs", citing various projects established and run in the DAE by Kaldor, Savin and Ajit Singh, amongst many others; and remarkably, also by James Meade and Frank Hahn, two of the DAE's antagonists. Godley is emphatic: "I have gone out of my way to make life easy for the UTOs in question. I have also from time to time positively encouraged UTOs to use the DAE though with very little success" (Godley to Edwards, Letter dated 9 September 1986). Frank Hahn's much-vaunted fifteen-year 'Risk Project' with its extensive external links ran, as it

---

[18] R. C. O. Matthews to K. J. R. Edwards, Letter dated [6] June 1986, signed 'Robin'; p. 2. The date on the image of the letter appears to be '6', though it could conceivably be another single digit date.

happens, from the DAE;[19] but, paradoxically, this does not seem to deserve even a mention when he and his group castigate the DAE for becoming insular. In conversation, Alan Hughes informed the author that it was Ajit Singh, presciently, who spoke with Wynne Godley to facilitate the location of Hahn's project within the DAE.

Godley's Memorandum, given to the Review Committee–II close to the start of its deliberations, begins with some extracts that he excises from the original pre-War Pigou Report of 1939 that state the key objectives motivating the formation of the DAE:[20]

> It is clear from the first sentence of [the first paragraph of this report] that what the Pigou Committee had in mind as the primary purpose of the DAE was applied research, in the sense of the advancement of knowledge by empirical enquiry, undertaken with the use of outside funds. The second paragraph ... suggests, apparently as a subsidiary function of the Department, that it would aid teaching by helping Teaching officers of the Faculty to obtain "first-hand information about current economic conditions".

The significance of this archival reminder becomes evident in the arguments during the DAE Review, when Hahn, Matthews and others highlight the *second* objective to the exclusion of the *first*: this would undermine the DAE's justification for its large teams, and ostensibly support the Hahn-Matthews-Meade-Newbery argument that the DAE should limit itself essentially to supporting the individual research projects of Faculty staff. In this vein, Newbery has recently observed: "it is also worth pointing out that the DAE was primarily set up to support research project by faculty members needing desks and support for RAs". Resuming Godley's quotation from Pigou's Report: "The final clause of the foregoing sentence, pointing out the provision of this service was desirable because 'Cambridge is at some disadvantage as compared with Universities in industrial centres' implies that the provision of such a service was not just a matter of looking up figures in books, but of obtaining new data e.g. by making survey of business behaviour like the famous enquiry by Hall and Hitch which asked businessmen whether prices were really determined in the way contemporary textbooks postulated."[21]

---

[19] For descriptions, see Dasgupta (2013); Newbery (2017: 502, 518–520). Hahn's 'Risk' Project is discussed in Chap. 4 as the 'Quaker' seminar, the name attached to it.

[20] The existence of the DAE was originally notified in the University in a Report of the General Board dated 1/11/39 (*Reporter* 1939/1940, p. 241); this Report contained a report from the Faculty, chaired by Pigou.

[21] A little later in his Memorandum, Godley shares a reflection: "Our motto might be taken from [the] opening words of Chapter 3 of Edmond Malinvaud's new book *Mass Unemployment*. He writes 'The ultimate aim of economics is to provide guidance for action'." It is difficult to guess whether, in view of Malinvaud's status as a high priest in the general equilibrium faith, this was said tongue-in-cheek or meant to be taken seriously; a few years earlier, Kahn, in his review of Malinvaud's book on Keynes, *The Theory of Unemployment Reconsidered* in the CJE wrote similarly: "there is something in it to please everyone: Walrasian equilibrium, unemployment that can

Another line argues that research support for Faculty could be provided by research assistants within the Faculty itself, thereby obviating the need for a separate DAE. Matthews would find this "logical" since "in most Faculties and Departments most of the officers at the DAE would be research assistants, without officer status, apart from a few ADRs and SARs for particular purposes" (Matthews to Edwards, Letter dated 2 November 1984). And Stephen Nickell, a selected external from the Hahn-Gorman "academy", widens the wedge, arguing that "the separation of researchers in a separate category is not very satisfactory"; "the best applied research tends to be done by active faculty members, not by specialist researchers" (Nickell to Edwards, 21 January 1985).

Capture
Another option, which feeds into some of the others, is to denounce the DAE staff for being of poor academic quality, not matching up to the standards of the teaching staff of the Faculty. They are alleged to produce low-quality work of little consequence.

Part of this option involves a sustained reputational attack on DAE research and researchers, and this is done systematically in response after response from the Hahn-Matthews camp. Strikingly, the specific criticisms, and often even the phraseology, matches that of the earlier attacks on the CEPG and the CGP teams by the SSRC-ESRC panels—which were themselves heavily dominated by the Hahn-Matthews group. Since the Review is in hands that are sympathetic to the Hahn-Matthews agenda, much of the external opinion is sought from like-minded experts who generally have a good outing further chipping away or tarnishing the DAE reputation through various devices: faint praise, particular criticisms, outright assault are all in evidence—and these go unchallenged since there is no person or mechanism to assess them fairly. It is worth noting that DAE staff, whether individually or collectively, are not invited to respond to such criticisms at the points where these are made. So, the main unopposed critiques, established essentially through assertion and repetition in concert by various Hahn-Matthews followers, are that the Department isn't as good as it used to be; that it is insular; that it does not have high-quality academic visitors; that its work is no longer the best in the UK. Hahn's comments, summarised by Edwards, say it all: "he stated that it is possible to get money for low-level descriptive work such as 'donkey work' for Government Ministries". Hahn had also alleged, amongst other charges, that the DAE's international reputation had plummeted, that it was too introverted, that it did not attract economists of distinction as in the days of Richard Stone.

The draft version of the Report[22] states:

be reduced by cutting real wages, unemployment that can be reduced by raising real wages, workers who prefer leisure to earnings, savings equal to investment and prices equal to marginal cost—all presented in an ostensibly precise and elegant model. But the reader needs to keep his wits about him to follow the intricacies of the argument" (Kahn, 1977: 375)

[22] "The Department of Applied Economics" (General Board Office, The Old Schools, Cambridge, dated 11 September 1984, 5p. typescript, paragraph 7, p. 4).

> On such important matters as the appointment of staff, choice of research programme and use of Departmental facilities the Director can be, and in recent times has been, out-voted from time to time on the Committee. This obviously leads to a situation where decisions can be unduly influenced by the career interests of relatively junior staff rather than by the quality and balance of the research programme taken as a whole. There is some evidence that the Department is no longer regarded by outside bodies as a dominant centre for applied economic research it undoubtedly once was.

This text, which should be treated only as being indicative of the train of discussion and thinking within the Committee, offers a few pointers. First, that the Director can be out-voted seems to be taken as an inherently negative outcome, which it might not be—and in any case the idea of a voting committee is to settle matters where appropriate by the use of the vote; second, there is a presumption that in this vote, the 'career interests' of the relatively junior staff override the DAE's research interests; it is clearly implied that this is associated with the fall in the DAE's standing in the field, but this link is extremely questionable; and finally, that there is 'some evidence' from 'outside bodies' of this decline in standing, and this arguably is based on opinions, assertions and hearsay, including some from invited external experts selected by the Committee. It should also be noted that an earlier page of the same draft (ibid.: 2) provides details of the establishment of the DAE as on 1 October 1984, which comprised a total of forty research staff, of which four were Junior Research Officers, and nine were Research Officers—not a profile that could sustain the charge that 'relatively junior officers' could hijack the Departmental agenda for their 'career interests'. (There were also eight unfilled posts, an unusually high number, reflecting in all probability the staff attrition referred to elsewhere by Wynne Godley, arising possibly from the closure of the CEPG a couple of years earlier, and the premonitions about the fate of the CGP which was then critically under review by its major donor, the ESRC.)

Of course, if the quality premise failed to stick, the rest of the Hahn-Matthews construction would collapse. But in the smoke room, those in authority had bought into the proposition being purveyed by the Matthews-Hahn combine that Cambridge economics was teetering at the edge of the cliff, if not already over it: quality and reputation were said to have experienced a 'catastrophic decline' at home and abroad; appointments made, or not made, were seen as 'scandalous'; the 'politicisation' of the Faculty was disastrous. A litany of repetitions helped make the message stick. And the case was reinforced by seeking external advice—a lot of it from known antagonists of Cambridge heterodox economics and/or the macroeconomic work at the DAE. Quality and reputation assassination was first established, almost as a self-evident truth. And it worked, since the Review Committee accepted and collated these critiques at face value, without verification or validation or response from other independently appointed referees suggested by the DAE itself, or even responses in defence from the DAE researchers being criticised and vilified. Having thus established bad quality, the finger changed direction and now pointed at poor appointments under the control of junior staff, appointments which were perennially renewed and so on. How then was this to be set right? How was DAE to be pulled back from the brink? Hahn and Matthews had 'a cunning plan'.

All this justifies the option of preventing sub-standard DAE staff from easily getting reappointments and extensions through appointment committees they can influence through the collective participation of the DAE in these procedures and decisions. And to lift the allegedly declining quality of DAE work, this option demands the appointment of a top-quality Director[23] with wider powers free from the control of a management committee that DAE and the Faculty Board can control. The 'quality', 'reputation' and 'politicisation' allegations are used to bombard and sway the non-economists on the University and General Board committees; and this is not a difficult task when you are the only voice in the room. In the end, partly by a process of elimination of more extreme options, this was the route followed by the Review Committees.

9.2.3 External Critiques: Collusion as Consultation?

A couple of features of this process are striking. While the Review consults widely, there are some telling testimonies from invited external experts whose views invariably carry disproportional weight, on the unscrutinised presumption that being external conflates with being impartial. This must remain questionable. One of the experts who put in a comprehensibly hostile report, in 1984, was Partha Dasgupta, then a professor at LSE. Fortuitously at that point, a professorial vacancy emerged with the early retirement of Robert Neild and in 1985, following the usual competitive appointment procedure, the Faculty appointed Partha Dasgupta to the professorship. The appointment also had the effect of completing a triumvirate with Dasgupta now joining his seniors Hahn and Matthews and maintaining consistency, continuing with his critiques of the DAE now as a senior member of the Faculty. Several, though not all, of the others asked could be associated with negative views vis-à-vis the DAE, some of its staff, or some of its research programmes.

The available evidence offers various examples of interconnections between the Reviews of the DAE mounted by the General Board of the University, and the SSRC's earlier transactions with the two main DAE teams. The CEPG, led by Wynne Godley himself, had its funding so severely truncated by the SSRC (under Michael Posner), its financial underwriter for years past, that it was terminated in 1982; and the CGP (where Terry Barker had taken over from Richard Stone) also funded by the SSRC since 1967, had barely survived in the same round with the same panels. The CGP was effectively forced by SSRC to run their gauntlet, and perished in it in 1987, with ESRC funding refused.

Ostensibly, the two processes, viz., the University reviews in Cambridge, and the SSRC/ESRC funding evaluations in London, were entirely

---

[23] This can be read, of course, as an implicit gratuitous attack on the quality of the incumbent Director, Wynne Godley.

independent. However, gleaning through the records, there are enough straws in the wind to make a fair-sized bundle. Some examples provide corroborative illustrations. The first concerns the choice of members, advisers and experts engaged by the Review Committees. In the first Review, it quickly becomes clear that there is a division of opinion within the Faculty—though not within the DAE. In an early letter to the members of RC-I, Edwards asks, "is there indeed a justification for a separate Department to run the research programme of the Faculty?" and continues: "it seems to me that in order to resolve this question whether we want to consider the possibility of some such major structural changes, we ought to consider the implications of the very diverse views which we have received of the quality of the work of the Department, and in this context to ask the question of whether we have gathered as much opinion from outside as we need". This could be innocuous or ominous, depending on who is to be asked, and how. George Reid chips in: "the recipients will have to be expected to do some reading between the lines and we must just hope for the best. ... Recipients might wonder who this committee was. What we want are frank opinions, in whatever sense, and I suppose that a person might choose his words in writing to a committee containing, say, Wynne Godley, than to a committee from outside (or almost outside) the Faculty. Would it be worth giving the names of the members of the committee?" (George Reid to Ken Edwards, Letter dated 11 December 1984; handwritten). The Committee gives the suggestion of fishing for 'frank' opinions they would not give directly to Godley; one can fairly assume these to be negative ones.

Edwards drafts the letter to be sent to carefully selected 'outsiders' to solicit their 'frank' opinion; Supple writes back to say "it seems to be admirable", and then suggests a list of eight recipients: A. B. Atkinson, S. Nickell, J. Flemming, M. Feldstein, R. Gordon, E. Malinvaud, J. Pechman, M. Miller. Since none of the other members of RC-I have a clue about anything substantive to do with economics, Supple the economic historian becomes the driver of this process. The outstanding feature of his selection is that it seems rather a listing of the usual suspects. Leaving aside Malinvaud—who could have been expected not to take up the out-of-the-blue request to write about a unit he did not have dealings with—and Pechman, all the other six members could be said to have some form; they were all well known to each other and formed a sort of kindred group of shared disciplinary orientations; and several of them were already known, in differing capacities, to have taken positions hostile to DAE macro-modelling teams, leading to the negative funding decisions meted out earlier by SSRC panels to the DAE teams. Supple, of course, had nothing to do with the SSRC processes where most of these names figure, and the credible connection for this remarkable coincidence would appear to be R. C. O. Matthews who was well connected with the SSRC, had been involved directly in some of the relevant panels where these experts had figured. Many of these worthy academics also figure, in one way or another, in the earlier 'Uncles and Nephews' account where they would qualify as 'nephews' to one or other of the 'uncles', Hahn, Gorman or Matthews. Some of them also figure in the

CLARE Group run by Matthews at Clare College. Duly, views come in and predictably are not particularly favourable to the DAE. This incident is strongly suggestive of the behind-the-scenes influence of string-pulling by Matthews to point the committee in the right direction. Incidentally, of this group, Atkinson became a member of the second-stage RC-II the following year.

Further down the line, additional feedback is sought by RC-II, this time explicitly about the quality of DAE work—though this was not, as Wynne Godley is at pains to point out, part of the terms of reference of the Review Committee—from SSRC and ESRC personages.

There are two responses: one from Michael Posner, who chaired and oversaw the CEPG fiasco and termination at SSRC; and the second from Charles Feinstein, as Chair of the Economic Affairs Committee under Douglas Hague, who had taken over as Chair of the ESRC (the erstwhile SSRC with a name change), following Posner, in 1984. Posner's prose is poetic, nostalgic—and noxious: "I am afraid the Cambridge DAE has become somewhat of a backwater. To the outsider there is no apparent relationship between the different strands of work. It's like a garden, rather overrun with weeds in some places, pretty barren in others, where only a careful and affectionate eye can identify and cherish once flourishing and striking specimens. Occasionally, surprisingly tight little plots can be found, producing good, sound products which are read fairly widely outside; but the ordinary applied economist would not reach first for the DAE phone number if he wanted to find the leading mainstream worker in any field" (Michael Posner to Ken Edwards; Letter dated 2 October 1985: 4).

He harks back to the good old days. As examples of prime high quality, Posner says, "it means writing about industrial economics, and the economics of company finance following the tradition that Singh and Whittington established twenty years ago, but taking full note of the modern developments in the subject" (ibid.: 4–5). Posner overlooks the fact that Singh and Whittington were both extremely productive, and that Ajit had stimulated and catalysed the work of the next generation of researchers in Alan Hughes and Andy Cosh, along with others in contiguous fields. Or that Alan Hughes and Andy Cosh, like Ajit, had the DAE as a base for their research, and that the research that the trio had accomplished in the tenure of Wynne Godley's directorship was distinguished enough to win peer reviewed open competition ESRC grants and that their track record, established with earlier DAE Directors subsequently continued with strong support from David Newbery as Director.[24] Yet, there was no room for Alan, or Ajit, for appropriate promotions in the Faculty; and they both progressively shifted their research base to the new Judge Business School, where Alan had won an open competition for the prestigious Margaret Thatcher Professorship—while hitherto he had been a lecturer in the Faculty. And Alan, like Ajit, was fully abreast of the latest in applied econometrics relevant for their research.

---

[24] Grants were won for a three-year ESRC-funded Small Business Research Centre, followed by a ten-year ESRC award to set up the Centre for Business Research with parallel projects funded, amongst others, by the Leverhulme Trust.

Posner has several stabs at the DAE body,[25] just in case his six pages of single-spaced typescript in two letters[26] have missed the heart of the matter: DAE problems are "partly because the DAE has been starved of outside funds" [yes, by the SSRC on Posner's watch]; "partly because it has been beset by internal management problems" [which, while partly so, was still subject to widely different interpretations]; "partly because the ideological fashion of the times is against both the CGP and the CEPG" [with the SSRC and the ESRC panels providing the proof of this]. "If this were all, it would be right for your review committee to ignore the problems of the present and to back the present approach well into the next century. I think, however, this would be a mistake." Posner would like the DAE to shift mainly into mainstream work that he emphasised was "footnoteable" by those hundreds of eager and well-organised professional economists who one meets at conferences anywhere in Europe or North America. Maybe, he opines, "one" or "maybe even two" strands of work could be of the "Cambridge" type. So: there was room for Cambridge heterodoxy, so long as it occupied one little corner of the global mainstream orthodox church to which Posner seems to owe allegiance and be in awe of. In a real sense, this gratuitous criticism goes to the heart of the matter, substantively speaking, and confirms the chasmic gap between Posner's intellectual stance, where he wants Cambridge economists to work with the objective of producing footnotes in the mainstream literature, and the Cambridge heterodox positions that have as their shared objective the dislodging of neoclassical mainstream discourse, or at the very least, the production of alternative intellectual and disciplinary platforms for addressing real world problems.

"The DAE should cease being exclusively attached to playing its own game, with its own ball, and its own rules"—they should "come to terms with conventional econometrics, with mainstream economic theory" as in the USA and Europe; to express "humility, and willingness to imitate outside success, to follow hares started by others". "Unless some fairly dramatic changes are made, the Cambridge DAE will sink to the bottom of the league of the first half dozen research institutes in the country, and therefore into the third or fourth division internationally." Michael Posner clearly wants the English garden dug up and replanted as a Versailles showpiece with clean mathematical shapes and lines.

And further opinion is received from Charles Feinstein on behalf of the ESRC based on the DAE's interaction with the SSRC and ESRC. Feinstein

---

[25] In familiar double-handed style, he argues in support of multidisciplinarity before coming down strongly in favour of sociologists leaving the DAE. And significantly, in a second letter, Posner declares himself—though "I have blown hot and cold on this matter over the years"—in favour of "the traditional role of the DAE in providing a home for the research activity of the University teaching officers [viz., the Faculty]", thereby supporting the line of attack opened by James Meade, questioning the independent research projects started by and implemented within the DAE by its own staff.

[26] The two letters are dated 2 October 1985 and 16 October 1985.

goes through the files and discovers "a general theme running through most of the comments: either initially promising projects had failed to live up to expectations, or the standard of performance had declined after a very successful start"; the Stone-Barker Growth Project is cited as an example in the former category, the Godley-Cripps Macroeconomic Policy Project for the latter. As justification, Feinstein repeats all the old criticisms of the CGP and CEPG made—and thoroughly challenged and in most cases repudiated by the two teams earlier—without reference to these rebuttals, and so for the unknowing or unsuspecting, the unfair one-sided critiques become a truth again through repetition.[27] The Northern Ireland project is mentioned as an exception, but "other research has been less favourably regarded". There is no mention of the work of the sociologists, or of the vibrant interdisciplinary collaborative work of economists and sociologists funded by the ESRC itself. The drift and the conclusions are damning (Charles Feinstein to K. J. R. Edwards, Letter dated 4 March 1986).

A draft version of the Report of the second-stage Review Committee has a section of text which says: "There has also from time to time been criticisms of the work of the Department not only within the University but from outside authorities such as the Chairman of the then SSRC, now the ESRC. In addition, over the last three years there has been growing difficulty in attracting outside support for the research programmes at present undertaken in the Department."[28] This comment has an ink line running across it, but it nevertheless confirms the links between the Review Committee and the SSRC through its Chairman, Michael Posner, who had obviously communicated criticism of the DAE's work. This implies that the critiques against the CGP and the CEPG made by the SSRC committees and experts in the context of their grant applications are being taken over by the Review Committee— though it is known that the two units had very robust critiques of these critiques. There is also an implicit negative multiplier effect at work, which runs thus: the SSRC Chairman makes a determination of the members and experts of the committee, who then write opinions against the DAE units; the units reject the criticism on very credible grounds, but this rejection is ignored or not responded to by the SSRC, which in turn has negative consequences for the award of the grants; this rejection of the grant is then recycled as evidence to criticise the quality of the research work of the DAE units and sent on to the University Review Committee; and the Cambridge Review Committee is pleased to accept this external feedback as truth without independent validation. Naturally, this multiplier works more easily when there are clear overlaps between the memberships of the SSRC and the Review Committees, but these

---

[27] An example of this is Feinstein's regurgitation of an external reviewer's critique of the CGP methodology with regard to 'disaggregation', without adding the robust rebuttal of these criticisms by the CGP in its response to the SSRC. As noted, Feinstein was very closely associated with Matthews, personally, academically and institutionally.

[28] "The Department of Applied Economics" (General Board Office, The Old Schools, Cambridge, dated 11 September 1984, 5p. typescript, paragraph 6, p. 2, 3)

are not essential if significant members of both Committees—at the SSRC and the University—have strong associations with the same network of economists generally known to be hostile to Cambridge heterodox economics, and to DAE macroeconomic modelling; this hypothetical chain is clearly illustrated, though hard 'proof' is elusive, by the multiple hats worn by at least three experts: Michael Posner, Charles Feinstein and Tony Atkinson.

Another aspect of the use made by the University's Review Committees of the prior materials from the SSRC/ESRC is apparent from the kinds of questions that are posed by the second Review Committee (which now prominently includes Tony Atkinson[29] and Kenneth Berrill[30] as economics experts) to the surviving Cambridge Growth Project. Terry Barker, having just received a rejection from the ESRC—the fairness and propriety of which had been seriously challenged, though to no avail, by the CGP—now finds on his desk a letter from the University Review Committee asking him, as the leader of the CGP, many of the same questions, wanting responses to many of the now familiar critiques of the CGP and the DAE that were made in the context of the CEPG and the CGP applications to the SSRC and the ESRC, and then curiously repeated almost exactly by the neoclassical group in the Faculty, led by Frank Hahn—and repeated separately by Matthews in his individual letters to the Review Committee. Coincidences flourish; or could it not just be a case of many different minds thinking alike.

---

[29] Tony Atkinson was one of 'uncle' Hahn's 'nephews' and, though his social values as abundantly expressed in his applied work placed him in the middle ground, remained continuously a close member of the neoclassical camp concentrated in the LSE with significant presence in Oxford and Cambridge. He had served as an external respondent, from the LSE where he was a professor, to RC-I, and then became a full member (though still from the LSE) of RC-II during 1985–1987.

[30] Berrill's views on finance and development ran counter to those held by leading members of the Cambridge left economists. Ajit Singh wrote directly against positions adopted by the influential report of the WIDER Study Group chaired by Sir Kenneth Berrill with respect to the role of stock markets and equity finance in the wake of the debt crisis. Berrill's report argued in favour of foreign portfolio investment from advanced economies into the developing economies, and "urged stock market development as well as removal of capital controls, including a withdrawal of Article VI, Section 3 of the IMF Articles of Agreement, which have traditionally allowed developing countries to exercise exchange controls" (Singh, 1996a: 12). Ajit Singh later amplifies on his critique, observing: "It is unsurprising that the IFIs and economic orthodoxy should promote stock markets in DCs. However, unexpectedly such an evolution is also being recommended by many practitioners who have traditionally not been regarded as orthodox. Thus, Sir Kenneth Berrill's distinguished Study Group for the UNU/WIDER,—a generally heterodox think-tank for DCs—recommended that DCs should encourage stock markets, partly to attract non-debt-creating foreign portfolio capital" (Singh, 1999: 4) Ajit Singh, as would be well known, and consistently and resolutely argued against these mainstream positions associated with finance capital (Saith, 2018, 2019). On the other hand, though Berrill was long associated with King's, Kahn and 'old' Keynesianism, he had also the head of the Central Policy Review Staff under Edward Heath; and from 1980 he had become Chairman of Vickers da Costa, London (and global) stockbroking firm which counted Churchill among its clients.

9.3 The Heterodox Defence

Even a cursory scan of the General Board's records of the DAE Review brought to notice something rather unusual. Very many letters of response received from DAE or Faculty staff, or from the selected external respondents, carried highlighter markings—but strikingly, virtually all the sentences and bits picked out for highlighting expressed negative opinions—and this applied even in cases where much of the substance of the letter was positive. Later, these highlighted bits get selectively distilled and find expression in the *Summary of Adverse Views* (SAV). This conveys the impression of being a rather one-sided approach being employed to bolster prejudged positions. Relatedly, when such negative views are expressed, they are recorded as if they are valid and verified truths which then form the basis for seeking corrective actions from the University; no thought or space is given to the possibility that many of these negative views need qualification or contextualisation, let alone correction or outright rejection as being incorrect or prejudiced.

This draws attention to another procedural issue, viz., that when these comments are sought, received and interpreted by the Review Committee, there is no presence there that can contest or correct or qualify them from the vantage point of the DAE; there is no assessment of the worth of such 'evidence'.

What also becomes fairly obvious in this exercise is that the views of one camp, and within that, of a few individuals have greater presence and visibility at least in a numerical sense. This small group has multiple submissions: Hahn, Dasgupta and Newbery each have a few, individually or collectively; and Matthews, on his own account, seems to be able to fire off heavy letters and notes almost at will; nothing like this is visible on the other side; of course, there is a regular exchange between the heads of the DAE and the Faculty Board, but none of the antagonists of the neoclassical camp are acting in these formal capacities. The contents of the various submissions from this pressure group also repeatedly highlight the same points—which eventually are reflected in the final reports. This might not be a matter of great surprise, since some key expert committee members were generally known to be their allies.

The attacks on the DAE and on the heterodox groups—aka 'reds', 'communists', 'radicals', 'the left', 'Marxists'—served, if anything, to consolidate their ranks in the face of existential threats. Latent passive solidarity is not enough: it needs to be mobilised and organised, and then to express itself through all channels available to it within the rulebook. This task fell on the small group of like-minded radical heterodox economists of the younger cohort, both from the Faculty and the DAE, prominently and usually led by Ajit Singh and Bob Rowthorn, with a varying group of no less than a dozen other colleagues at any time—strengthened by the support of several 'seniors' even if on a case-by-case basis.[31] The loss of the *Economic Journal*, and the

---

[31] For a detailed account of these radical mobilisations of the Cambridge heterodox groups in the 1970s and 1980s, see Saith (2019).

abrupt closure of the Godley-Cripps CEPG were clear manifestations of the rising power of the orthodox ranks in the Faculty. These losses had been inflicted in or from spaces external to Cambridge economics, and generally beyond the reach and persuasion of the radical group. Additionally, the national and global political climate had changed decisively with the onset of the Reagan-Thatcher era, and this had strongly influenced national discourse and attitudes; the right felt enabled and empowered; the Cambridge left in economics, with a few economists prominently singled out, were marked as being subversive. New alliances, explicitly hostile to Cambridge heterodox economics and economists, had been fashioned in external institutional domains. And with the University Review of the DAE, this force had now come to Cambridge town, to Sidgwick Site. Heterodox solidarity was imperative as never before on home turf.

The DAE would surely have received support and protection from its two eminent past Directors, Richard Stone and then Brian Reddaway; the latter knew the university system backwards, and was always logical, procedurally sound and usually successful in his exchanges with various university committees and boards; Stone was not of this mentality or mettle. Despite his status, he had been informed about the formation of the Review on 1 November 1984, a full five months after the event, thus confirming that he was in no way part of its subsequent mechanics and machinations, though he fully acknowledged the formal right of the General Board to hold the Review. As it was, both Stone and Reddaway were born in 1913, both reached the Cambridge mandatory retirement age of 67 in 1980 and were thus no longer part of the fray. So on the day, and at the crucial professorial level, the triumvirate of Hahn, Matthews and Dasgupta, with the recently appointed Willy Brown[32] generally in support and seldom in effective opposition, were virtually unchallenged, with Robert Neild having taken early retirement in 1984 with the golden handshake proffered in the Thatcherite cuts. Thus the lone professor on the defending side was Wynne Godley himself, and he was the one standing in the dock.

At the time of the Review, the Faculty Board was still left-majority and chaired by the amiable Alan Hughes, a young stalwart who, like his senior co-researcher, friend and mentor Ajit Singh, was an accomplished applied economist. And like Ajit, the acknowledged political commissar of the radical groups, Alan was shrewd as a Faculty strategist, known to be fair-minded, and again like Ajit, always impeccably within the rulebook. The Economics Faculty was part of a Group of Faculties that included several smaller ones, and as had been the democratic protocol, there was a consensual agreement that the Faculties would take it in turns to send up one of its Faculty Chairs to represent the Group on the General Board of the Faculties. 1984 saw the turn of Economics to wear this hat. Alan picks up the story: "It so happened that in 1984 I was Chair of Economics when it was Economics' turn. Hahn and Matthews knew

---

[32] Both Dasgupta and Brown joined the Faculty as professors in 1985.

that my membership of the General Board would undermine persistent attempts to paint the Faculty as a pile of mediocre reds under the bed. The upshot was: in November 1984 the only ever contested General Board election, with me proposed by Bob Rowthorn, and Robin Matthews proposed by Professor Barry Supple (both Masters of Colleges). I won by a canter with around 70 per cent of the votes" (personal communication, email 13 August 2018). Of course, the Review had been mooted almost definitely some time in 1983, launched in June 1984, and strikingly, Barry Supple was one of the three members of RC-I; Supple and Matthews had also been joint authors earlier. For Hahn, Matthews & Co., it would have been most felicitous to have Barry Supple in the Review Committee and Matthews on the General Board. There can be little doubt that the presence of Alan Hughes in the General Board preempted the attempts of the Hahn-Matthews axis to influence the outcome of the two-stage Review. There was significant injury done to the DAE body, but things might have been rather worse but for this factor, though the Review Committee did attempt to manipulate matters behind Alan's, and Wynne's, back.

9.3.1 Solidarity, Testimonies, Rebuttals

The broad-spectrum disparagement of the heterodox economists, especially of the DAE—with some individual exceptions made for mathematicians or econometricians—was met by a solid wall of individual testimonies rebutting the various charges and pinpointing and critiquing their latent agendas. The archives include scores of letters of response to the Secretary General, involving a large majority of DAE and Faculty staff whether individually or collectively; it is striking that of this large number, only about eight, or about 10 per cent, explicitly sign up to what can be identified as support for the H-M-D-N position, and that includes those four themselves. There are some remarkable pieces of writing here that provide deep insights into the state and functioning of the Faculty at the time; and put together, these add up to a comprehensive heterodox rebuttal of the charges laid by the orthodox prosecution. Expectedly, there are very many communications from and with Wynne Godley as the Director of the unit under Review, and several involving Alan Hughes, then Chair of the Faculty Board of Economics, the partner to which the DAE was welded, if not wedded.

Ajit Singh has a significant, if finite, role in this process. In the course of the Review process, the Committee had decided to interview some senior members of the Faculty Board. In this regard, Ken Edwards, the Secretary General, notes: "Perusal of the Faculty Board membership over the last 10 years or so shows that if we were to decide to interview (a) the Professors in the Faculty and (b) teaching officers who have had continuous membership of the FB for the past 10 years, we would come up with the following list: Hahn, Matthews, Rowthorn, Singh" (Note dated 15 Oct 84; UA 770 DAE 983A). All four are duly interviewed, and there are brief notes made by Edwards from these interviews: Hahn predictably, and Rowthorn surprisingly, register negative views that subsequently enter the Committee's language; Ajit is recorded as defending the external reputation of the DAE, and arguing against heavy Faculty professorial presence on the Management Committee; no cracks there. Separately from this interview, Ajit's individual testimony in defence of the DAE takes the form of a solid, detailed six-page Note sent to the Secretary General of the General Board; the document is typical of Ajit's style: it is formal, it is balanced, it offers his views clearly expressed, and it provides evidence in support; and it is tactically sound; there is no chink in the argument that can be exploited, no ambivalence or loose prose that might provide the basis for being appropriated or misinterpreted.

Ajit Singh was the political commissar, the Chief Whip, the first among equals, of the loose formation of the heterodox and radical left-oriented groups of younger economists in Cambridge, and his mobilisation, organisation and strategisation of these political energies into an effective electoral force came into full play especially in relation to the elections to the all-important Faculty Board. He had started his Cambridge career as a research officer in the DAE and then moved over to the Faculty, while remaining active with his DAE-based projects; he was also an exemplary Director of Studies at Queens' College where he had lifted the standard of undergraduate teaching to pull the college up into the upper ranks of economics teaching in Cambridge. His response to the Committee of Enquiry selectively highlights key issues.[33]

First, he deals with the shopkeeper's question of 'value for money'. "It is worth emphasizing that for every pound contributed to the DAE by the University, the DAE itself raises two pounds in research grants from outside, thereby substantially increasing the number of economists employed in the University and available for University and College teaching." At the end, he returns to this point with a caution: "the University, despite financial stringencies, should continue its present level of financial contribution to the Department from University funds. Although the Department has been very successful in raising outside funds, without the guaranteed University income it will have to respond to ad hoc research demands and will not be able to plan its research effort. The University funds give it the necessary independence to pursue a longer-term academic research strategy."[34]

Second, he argues that the existing structure serves DAE best, and that it has in-built flexibility and efficiency: DAE researchers must have their projects approved by the Committee of Management; their positions approved by the

---

[33] Ajit Singh's response to the General Board's Committee to Review the Department of Applied Economics is reproduced in full as Appendix B in Saith (2019: 347–354). In this, he cites the exceptional record of the DAE in the earlier periods under the Stone, and then the Reddaway, directorships; he refers to the continuity of the progressive eclectic research themes and methods, and lauds the work in the current Godley phase as being highly innovative and significant.

[34] This is much the same point as made by the CEPG and especially the CGP in their exchanges with the SSRC/ESRC; Richard Stone underscored the importance of public funds for public goods, such as their model; raising funds from commercial clients would tie down the research, and restrict to those paying the piper.

Faculty or Department Appointments Committee for continuation for another round; and, "above all, they regularly face the 'market' test of raising research funds for their projects. This structure has evolved historically and served the Department and the University well."

Third, Ajit reminds the Committee of the very substantial teaching contributions made by DAE members: "any marked diminution in this contribution would result in a collapse of the Faculty's teaching programme". He refers the Committee to the available statistics that confirm the DAE inputs for the Tripos, for MPhil and PhD supervisions, for College teaching, pointing out that "there are 10 or more Colleges where DAE economists are Director of Studies. I am sure that the Committee will not need to be reminded of the importance of College teaching for the Tripos, as well as the Collegiate nature of this University. In principle, the University could take a legalistic view and say that college teaching is not its concern, and that the University's responsibility is only for University teaching. This in my opinion would be misguided, since if there were fewer DAE economists available for College teaching, the Colleges would have to appoint more NUTOs (non-University Teaching Officers), which the poorer Colleges certainly could not afford. Consequently, the teaching of Economics in the University as a whole would suffer."

Finally, he makes some shrewd and acute comments with regard to DAE research. While extolling its merits over the years down to the present, he mentions the fact that work of Wynne Godley and his team has attracted controversy and disagreement in some quarters (while being equally appreciated by other respected economists). "In the present state of economic science, I think it would be unwise to attempt to arrive at a definitive answer to the question as to which view is correct." "Nevertheless, compared with other leading research institutes in this country, the DAE continues to have a high reputation. ... I do not think any reputable economists (including Oxford economists themselves) would deny that the DAE's work has been far superior to that of the Oxford Institute of Economics and Statistics. I also think that most economists would accept that in its range, quality and innovativeness in research, as well as in the standing of the research staff, the DAE is at least as good as, if not better than, the National Institute of Economic and Social Research."

He cautions the Committee from jumping to superficial conclusions, citing "the great difficulties involved in assessing the quality of research in a social science subject such as Economics, where there is no accepted paradigm and there is profound disagreement on the working of the economic system as well as regarding the methodological approaches to studying the subject", and for good measure, he offers to provide "some suitable names" to sound out "a very wide range of international economic opinion" in this regard.[35] Ajit amplifies on the difficulty of making unique evaluative judgements, and advises that

---

[35] It is worth noting here, though, that the SSRC, using its own sample of experts, had already cut short the life of the Godley-Cripps macroeconomic modelling team in 1982.

the Committee not be swayed by views emanating from a particular camp located at one extreme end of, potentially, a wide spectrum.

Ajit Singh to K. J. R. Edwards, Letter dated 17 October 1985.

Incidentally, Richard Stone was also interviewed—not by the Review Committee but separately by Ken Edwards alone—and in the records there is a brief one-page, six-point, summary, written up by Edwards, which provides Stone's responses; the summary is not signed by Stone.[36] The interview occurred on 7 November 1984 (three weeks after the announcement of the award of the 'Nobel' Prize to Stone), when he was in the fifth year of his retirement. The six answers are collapsed into seven sentences; no elaboration is provided. Points 3–5, prima facie, provide clear support for the positions that appeared already to have been adopted internally by the Review Committee, in particular, those indicated by Edwards—following the orientation offered in his predecessor's note framing the intentions and expectations related to the Review. Point 3 states: "He sees the role of the Committee of Management as being a supportive one to the Director"; Point 4 states: "He acknowledges that the role of the Committee of Management in making junior appointments is anomalous and would approve of the setting up of a standing sub-committee for such appointments"; Point 5 says: "He thinks it undesirable to have too high a representation of members of the Department on the Management Committee, and is in favour of a substantial senior Faculty representation". It is fairly obvious that such specific observations from Stone could only have been offered in response to precisely targeted questions; and the issues raised by Edwards, in so far as these are thought to be worthy of recording, are remarkably in keeping with the Hahn-Matthews recommendations; indeed, these are very early indications of the eventual direction taken by the Review, in its own meandering time two years later.

This begs the question whether, Edwards—the self-professed, self-confessed, follower of Machiavelli—might have corralled Stone, talking him into walking into these bare bottom-line conclusions noted by Edwards. That this concern is not unreasonable is suggested by the fact that, going on this record, the interview did not touch upon any aspects of the substantive work of the DAE, of the quality of its research and its researchers, on its international standing. After all these were all points on which the extended Hahn-Matthews axis had, almost in unison, vehemently voiced virtually identical criticisms—and these had been filed in sufficient detail to generated a lengthy document 'Summary of Adverse Views' expressed against the DAE; indeed, these critiques were systematically used in supporting the organisational reforms recommended by the Review Committee, which, as mentioned, were almost entirely in line with the detailed suggestions coming from Matthews et al. Would it not have been worthwhile to hear and record Stone's views as expressed by Stone on these matters? For instance, running in parallel with the University Review of the

---

[36] K. J. R. Edwards, "Note of Meeting between the Secretary General and Professor Sir Richard Stone—7 November 1984".

DAE were the SSRC/ESRC decision-making procedures pertaining to the funding application by the Cambridge Growth Project, the long-term home of Stone till he retired in 1980. That funding request was eventually rejected leading to the closure of the CGP—and from the archives, there is clear evidence that Richard Stone was extremely upset by the decision, enough to make him refer to the process using the term "banana republic"; he wrote extensively and powerfully in support of the CGP, the significance, merit and innovative nature of the work of the team. And this was one of the two major teams of the DAE. It would seem incredible that Stone would have just gone along with the Hahn-Matthews-Dasgupta critiques of the DAE's work and reputation. And surely if he had, it could be readily expected that Edwards would have made an explicit note to this effect, as this would have greatly legitimised the orientation adopted by the Review Committee. But this dog did not bark. Was the topic not discussed? Or if it was, was it that Stone's views in this regard were not convenient to place on record? There is no way to tell. It is noteworthy, though, that the first point states: "Professor Stone thinks that communication and cooperation between the Department of Applied Economics and the Faculty presents no problems", which *prima facie*, runs counter to the key claim asserted repeatedly by the Hahn-Matthews group.

A handful of extracts from the submissions made by Faculty staff is illustrative of the high-quality and charged sentiment expressed virtually across the board by the large majority of DAE and Faculty staff, and also gives examples of rebuttals of specific Hahn-Matthews-Newbery charges. The selection is not at all intended to provide a comprehensive picture of the nature and intensity of contestations that were rife at the Economics home at Sidgwick Site.

Jane Humphries makes a thoughtful and passionate response with respect to the claim by Hahn et al. that the DAE's contribution to Faculty teaching was insignificant.

> The Faculty could not hope to maintain its current teaching standards without the enormous direct and indirect teaching contribution of the DAE. I myself give a series of lecture jointly with two members of DAE, scholars with whom I also do research. Without their contributions these lectures would not simply be weaker—they would be impossible. The DAE contribution to the lectures and seminars for both graduates and undergraduates is huge. Plus, they provide the distinctive Cambridge edge to our pedagogy: a relentless demand for the applications, for the usefulness of the principles, for the impact on the real world. Without the major donations of time and effort from DAE members, not only would the lectures be severely reduced in number (and more significantly in range) but the MPhil seminars would also be very adversely affected. Our range of specialist offerings would have to be cut. Also ... without DAE input, the supervision system in Economics would grind to a halt. ... Finally, I want to emphasise that DAE officers are invaluable also to the PhD programme both directly as supervisors and indirectly as resource people for Faculty supervisors. I have often sent my own students 'upstairs', to particular colleagues, for advice or references that I know will be forthcoming. Just because it is unrecorded, this

kind of contribution should not go unrecognized. ... One very unfortunate repercussion of the recent review procedure has been the undermining of the generosity of the DAE members who were suddenly made to feel that this work was for nothing in the University's accounting. I sincerely hope that the next stage of the review will disavow this most unfortunate impression. (Jane Humphries to K. J. R. Edwards, Letter dated 20 November 1985)

The dense six-page submission by John Wells,[37] running to over 3000 words, is more a prize essay than a letter (J. W. Wells to K. J. R. Edwards, Letter dated 14 November 1985, UA GB DAE Review 983–985). It is remarkable in its field and depth of vision of a murky ongoing process. At the outset, Wells politely chides the Committee for working to the hidden agenda of a couple of Faculty professors of orthodox faith (and the name of Frank Hahn appears later in the text); it supplies the Committee members a tutorial in the significance of distinctions between the orthodox and the heterodox approaches to economic problems, with an illustrative application to the labour market, showing how the orthodox tradition, "enthusiastically espoused by the Chancellor of the Exchequer, who has recently been exhorting the unemployed to price themselves back into low-paid, low-tech jobs. What is proposed, in essence, is that as many as 15% or 20% of the working population should become low-paid cleaners, gardeners and handymen, that we should re-create a vast servant class ... re-creating a degree of relative income inequality that we have not witnessed in Britain since the Victorian era; it is a proposal which stems quite directly from the orthodox economists' belief in the optimal properties of an unregulated, market economy" Wells (ibid.: 2). In contrast, Wells asserts that the heterodox approach seeks to restrict absolute poverty and relative income inequality to low levels, and to create high-tech, high-wage jobs, utilising the important potential role of the State in economic life. "These divergences", John Wells points out, "go to the very essence of the view we take about how society should be organized". Such words might have appeared as a preacher's sermon to the two economists on the Committee, but there were five others, several of them fairly innocent and untroubled with any sig-

---

[37] John Wells got a first in Economics Part II, and was in one of the early batches of undergraduates that came under Ajit's supervision at Queens' College; he joined the Faculty in 1975, became lecturer in 1978. "Because of his mood swings, he would sense slights and take great offence", mentions Geoff Harcourt (1999b); the hostility of the orthodox regime at the Faculty proved too much to bear, and he took early retirement in 1999 at the age of 52, and committed suicide later the same year. Geoff recalls him as a "genuine democratic socialist who lived his principles" till his sadly premature death. He left the Labour Party when Tony Blair came into power; wrote regularly in the national and the radical fringe press on contemporary issues; his formal contributions were on the development of the Brazilian economy, and with Bob Rowthorn on deindustrialisation in Britain—a theme opened up by Ajit Singh's prior research. John's comments on Sociology are an extract from a six-page individual polemical and discursive submission to the Review Committee in which he lambasts the orthodox camp, especially its two unnamed professorial leaders, across the board; it makes remarkable reading and could serve as an introduction to the subject for undergraduates, as it probably did for his supervisees.

nificant knowledge of the intrinsic salience of what the real hidden agenda camouflaged in the general and broad terms of reference of the Committee. Invoking Keynes, Joan Robinson and Kaldor, Wells observes that "the Faculty of Economics and Politics is one of the few institutions in which heterodox economists have managed to create a space where they are free to pursue their particular lines of enquiry and teach students from their perspective; ... beneath the obscurity of the terms of reference set out in your letter, there lies a determined attempt to curtail the space currently occupied by heterodox economics here in Cambridge" (ibid.: 3).

Wells cannily sniffs out the reference in the Committee's letter (seeking feedback) to 'the development of the DAE within the Faculty of Economics and Politics', and explains that "for a number of years, Professor Hahn has made little attempt to disguise his criticisms of the fact that the research officers of the DAE are included on the list of Faculty member, who are entitled to vote for the elected members of the Faculty Board of Economics and Politics. He seems to believe that the DAE votes are responsible for ensuring that heterodox economists frequently though not invariably, win these elections." He rightly points out that the DAE research officers and the Faculty teaching officers both engage in both teaching and research, publish widely, act as Director of Studies in many colleges, undertake Faculty and college supervisions—and as such they are a full-fledged equal part of Cambridge economics. "Thus, to follow Professor Hahn's suggestion and disenfranchise DAE research officers from the elections to the Faculty Board would be to treat them as second class citizens in our Faculty and would be utterly unjustified. I personally consider this suggestion utterly repugnant and I believe it demonstrates a lack of regard, bordering on contempt, for our DAE colleagues."

These two professors have their own reasons "to curtail the space occupied by heterodox economics in the life of our Faculty; in many other University departments ... they could expect to be at the apex of the Faculty's power structure"—unlike Cambridge, where "at the present time, there is no doubt that the unilateral exercise of professorial power in the Faculty is definitely blocked, but on the other hand, the heterodox wing does not exercise hegemony either. There is, in effect, a power stalemate between the two sides." As a result, the two professors cannot have their way with appointments, and find "this situation quite frustrating". "This power balance is potentially rather unstable. From time to time, the temptation arises for either side to try to exercise their hegemony and obliterate the other. This gives rise to a great deal of paranoia."

"Flushed by their successes in influencing public and governmental opinion and not content with their domination of economics departments in the rest of the country, orthodox economists would dearly love to see Cambridge brought into line. In a recent conversation with Lord Kaldor, he used the word *Gleischschaltung*[38] to refer to this process—along the lines of 'the strategy employed by the Nazis during the 1930s, for bringing all social and political

---

[38] 'Equalising', 'levelling'; the standardisation of political, economic and social institutions as carried out in authoritarian states.

institutions under their hegemony'. The parallel drawn by Professor Lord Kaldor is not entirely fanciful. I believe that a deliberate attempt is being made to curtail the current pluralism in our Faculty. Cambridge University's claim to intellectual eminence down through the decades has, in large measure, been based on the contributions which its academics have made to overturning orthodoxy in their respective fields. I firmly believe that, at this moment of acute international crisis, every attempt should be made to preserve the position which heterodox economics has succeeded in creating for itself here in Cambridge. This is simply because, like Keynes in the 1930s, heterodox economists have some useful things to say about the problems which currently confront us." This passionate exposition leads John Wells to his main response "that the Committee should do nothing to disturb the present balance of power in the Faculty. Both sides, it is true, still have a lot to learn in terms of mutual tolerance. But changing the current situation ... would certainly not contribute to that goal."

Wells is not done, still. He turns his penetrating eye on the second aspect of *Gleischschaltung*, the Committee's focus on the relationship between the DAE's Director and its Committee of Management, which "can best be described a *primus inter pares*. This arrangement seems to be perfectly satisfactory and it is exactly the sort of arrangement we should be encouraging in an advanced democratic society in the last fifteen years of the twentieth century." He cites the current patterns of healthy plurality in the research projects of the DAE, both in terms of the questions researched and the methodologies employed. "This seems to me to be an eminently satisfactory outcome." This is the kind of applied economics work, Wells rightly points out, "for which the DAE is justly famous"; this should not be interfered with; "the only suggestion I would make is that more effort should be devoted to encouraging cross-fertilization between projects".

Then, following up as the representative of the Faculty of Economics on the SPS Committee, John Wells first castigates the General Board: "I presume that raising this issue corresponds to the frequently heard wish amongst orthodox economists to 'get rid of the sociologists', in the hope that this might also have a favourable effect for them for the distribution of power". He goes on: "most orthodox economists feel that sociological issues are extraneous to the study of economic issues. This is clearly absurd. ... If economists and others had a better appreciation of the peculiar character of the British class structure and of the particular social and political institutions to which it gave rise, then Britain's post-war economic performance may well have been stronger." He argues for increasing the role of sociologists and sociology in the Faculty, "by getting economists to spell out the implications of most of their policy prescriptions for specific groups in society. Perhaps, in this way, we might avoid the present climate of confrontation in our country, which must surely be damaging to its long-run development."

He proceeds with his suspicion, soon to be proven accurate: "However, the thought has occurred to me that certain persons, anxiously coveting the shortly-to-be vacated Directorship, might wish for a more dictatorial set of arrangements, either for themselves or for a like-minded economist. What is the point of an orthodox economist, with a mission to transform the DAE's research programme, being appointed to the Directorship, if his plans are likely to be held in check by the Committee of Management? My own answer to this question is that it would be quite wrong for the Department to be run in such a way that research programmes with which the Director disagreed were ruthlessly suppressed."

Summing up his case, Wells observes that

> the Committee of Enquiry's terms of reference suggest that it is being invited to alter the very delicate power equilibrium that currently obtains in the Faculty. Members of the Committee may dismiss this view as being unduly paranoid. Their task, they might reply, is merely to undertake a minor tidying-up of the regulations. If so, nobody would be more pleased than myself. Whatever the Committee does recommend, I do hope it will do nothing to diminish the space which heterodox economists have managed to establish for themselves in our Faculty. At this time, when the world is facing its most acute economic, political and military crisis since the end of World War II, nothing should be done to diminish the range of informed opinion in our society which can be brought to bear on these issues. The University has a duty to maintain pluralism in its departments—nowhere more so than in the Faculty of Economic and Politics. The committee should not allow itself to be used as an instrument of petty ambition or of intellectual conformism. However, if the Committee can suggest anything which might improve relations in the Faculty, promote tolerance and goodwill and sustain the present diversity of opinions, I, for one, would take the Committee's suggestions extremely seriously. (ibid.: 4)

John's concluding summation might have given sensitive souls on the Committee a guilty conscience about the judgements they were about to deliver; but that would apply only if committee members felt they had anything at all to feel guilty about in the first place.

Another submission came from Tony Lawson who, by 1985, was well embarked on the course where he has subsequently made major contributions, dealing with methodological and interdisciplinary dimensions of economics and social science.

> I am writing as someone whose research interests include the methodology of applied economics and social analysis. ... A vital form of research based on case-study methods and an interdisciplinary approach is, unfortunately, far too thin on the ground in the UK. And one of the very few places where excellent work of this kind has been and continues to be, carried out is in the Cambridge DAE. The reason for the neglect of this sort of research, in general, appears to be the prevalence amongst professional economists of a rather naïve view that the exclusive use of formal methods of analysis borrowed from nineteenth century physics (but methods which do not lend themselves easily to case-study work) constitutes something called 'proper science' and as such are desirable. Consequently such

'scientific work' tends to be rewarded with relative job security, faster promotion, and an easy route to publication in 'prestigious' journals. ... This unfortunate state of affairs does nothing to further our understanding of the 'real world', to facilitate informed economic and social policy, nor to alleviate the negative image that the public at large appears to hold of economists and economics. Such criticism, however, cannot be levelled at the work produced over the years in the DAE, which has consistently fostered work employing a variety of methodologies, whilst maintaining high standards. (Tony Lawson to K. J. R. Edwards, Letter dated 14 October 1985)

In the assessment of John Eatwell, who was engaged primarily in teaching theoretical economics, and not directly involved with DAE, the research work of the DAE is "of outstanding quality", and has made "major contributions to theoretical economics", especially in two fields: macroeconomic policy and labour markets. "This work has been the product of groups of research workers who have been able to develop their ideas in concert over an extended period of time. Such work would not be possible in the case of individual short-term appointments associated with faculty members' projects"; "it is vitally important that the current framework whereby the department both pursues research in conjunction with faculty members on short and long term bases *and* develops major long term projects of its own, must be preserved. To do otherwise would be to damage those positive and constructive aspects of the work of the Department to which I have referred above" (John Eatwell to K. J. R. Edwards, Letter dated 30 November 1984; GB 8410.185; emphasis in the original).

John Rhodes challenges the criticisms of the DAE regarding the flow and quality of the research output of the DAE research officers. The Hahn camp had been pushing for short, fixed-term contracts linked to projects, leading to a high turnover, as against what they claimed as the observed low turnover, of DAE staff. Rhodes attacks the Hahn position thus:

In organisations generally a high rate of staff turnover is usually associated with high costs and low productivity and it has always been a puzzle to me why teaching officers with tenure should assert that, in the case of contract research staff, a high turnover rate should lead to low costs and high productivity—certainly no hard evidence on the matter has ever come to light. In my experience there is nothing uniquely productive or efficient about young inexperienced academic researchers or about one- and two-year employment contracts. The validity of these criticisms is asserted without any supporting documented evidence and the logic behind them is not even coherently and consistently argued for the whole of university activities including teaching and administration. One is forced to the conclusion that the motive for such criticisms has not got very much to do with the outcome of any comprehensive evaluation of the DAE's performance. It would be extremely unfortunate, both for the Faculty of Economics and the University, if the DAE were to become the battleground for those who want control of the Faculty and for those who want to dictate the future direction of the subject of economics within excessively narrow confines. (John Rhodes to K. J. R. Edwards, Letter dated 20 November 1984; GB.8411.784)

Geoff Meeks speaks of the brilliant internal financing device introduced by Brian Reddaway in the form of the Research Fund that provided a tiding-over bridging function to overcome uncertainty or breaks in short-term funding between project cycles. This crucially allowed long-term research framing—otherwise there would a high turnover, good high-quality staff wouldn't stay, and meaningful research projects could not be guaranteed. This strengthens the argument made by Rhodes and challenges the criticism that conflates low turnover of staff with low quality of research[39] (Geoff Meeks to K. J. R. Edwards, Letter dated 16 November 1984; GB.8410.185).

On a different, highly important issue, Geoff Meeks provides a comprehensive rebuttal of the charge that much of the Department's research work could be carried out by doctoral students. Incidentally, this charge seems to have been taken over almost *verbatim* from the separate critiques of the CEPG and the CGP funding applications to the SSRC-ESRC—and this provides one of several such instances of 'the transfer of knowledge', or simply collusion, linking the different attacks on the DAE and its constituent elements. Then, as now, these criticisms were robustly rejected, including by the Assistant Director of Research, Geoff Meeks, who makes three significant observations in doing so: first, that hiring graduate students would be in violation of the formal conditions of their status; second, that several very impressive PhDs had been produced within the DAE by its own research officers, including Angus Deaton, Michael Ellman, William Peterson, David Vines and Geoff Whittington; and third that using graduate students to support DAE research and publications could constitute an unethical practice in that much of the research in which they would engage could appear in the names of the senior staff as authors.[40]

9.3.2   Chinks in the DAE Armour?

In contrast to the solidarity expressed to the Committee, often in impassioned communications by virtually every member of the DAE and a majority of the respondents from the Faculty, there are a couple of outliers that draw attention by their unexpectedness: Wynne Godley and Bob Rowthorn.

Wynne clearly put up a vigorous defence of the DAE over the entire process, but paradoxically, some of his communications and testimonies at various

---

[39] For instance, the joint letter to the Review Committee by Frank Hahn, Partha Dasgupta, David Newbery and four others (being Margaret Bray, J. S. S. Edwards, A. W. A. Peterson and Timothy J. Kehoe), all seven being from the teaching Faculty, concludes thus: "The general implication of our view of the appropriate organisation of the DAE ... is that the presumption of permanence which seems to apply at present for a large proportion of the DAE staff must be rejected". Their argument appears to reflect an ill-informed prejudice: in fact, apart from the Director, *all* DAE staff was on project-cycle contracts without tenure. (Frank Hahn and six others, "Submission to the General Board's committee to review the Department of Economics", undated, DAE Paper 28, 3p.)

[40] This matter, including Geoff Meeks's response, has been dealt with at greater length in Chap. 8.

points also offered more than just straws to the opposition to build and legitimise its case *against* the DAE. The exchanges between Godley and Edwards are quite frequent, as might be expected; they are often initiated by Godley; and several of these contain elements that are, or could be easily construed as criticisms of aspects of the DAE, of the behaviour of its staff, of its decision-making processes, of restraints placed on his directorial remit; and these are complemented by other comments which seem quite self-critical not just of himself in almost personal terms, but also of the DAE in various other aspects, such as 'insularity', 'econometric capabilities' and so on—aspects on which his DAE colleagues elsewhere put up a vigorous defence, which then is undermined by such commentaries and casual reflections in letters which sometimes ricochet between the professional and personal planes. Those at all aware of the personal trials and tribulations in Wynne's life—as publicly and uncompromisingly shared with painful, naked honesty, by Wynne himself (Godley, 2001)—might not be overly surprised and take them as a case of Wynne being classically Wynne. Others might generally be inclined to read these at face value; and then, those ranged against him in the DAE Review, could easily use all this as invaluable ammunition to support the case for the prosecution, even while being aware of their unusual provenance.

Some examples convey the nature of the phenomenon, and also its inherent dangers. Wynne Godley attends his first DAE meeting on 6 December 1969, when it is announced that he will be the new Director. He takes over in 1970, and relatively soon tables a paper *Notes on the Role, Organization and Orientation of the DAE*. "The Director wanted a clearer research direction for the Department as a whole and to reduce the size of the department slightly."[41] One can surmise a sense of dissatisfaction and, a year later, there is a record of Godley's unhappiness over the obstacles arising from DAE governance procedures and practices on the use of his powers as Director to shape the Department. "Godley calls into question some of the appointments by the Board by restating his powers as set down in the statutes and ordinances saying ultimate responsibility lies with him."[42] These frustrations had been expressed long years ago; Godley, in the interim had apparently reassessed some of his earlier dissatisfaction, things (or he himself) had changed, and improved. But now, within the process of the Review, the old wounds are scratched and reopened again by him—not it should be noted with his own staff, but with the ongoing Review in the form of recollections of his apparently difficult early period as DAE Director and his dealings then with staff on the one side, and the Committee of Management on the other. So after a lapse of twelve years, Godley's past grumbles were now being heard, absorbed and reoriented into an existential critique of the DAE by the Review Committee—which could conveniently use his shoulder to fire their volley against DAE; unwittingly or naively, Godley had provided rounds of heavy ammunition for the firing squad.

[41] Minute 137 of the Meeting of the DAE Management Committee, January 1971.
[42] Minute 144, Meeting of the DAE Management Committee, February 1972.

This is confirmed by an exchange which Edwards conveys to the Committee: "I explained to him that we found his statements about the difficulties he had encountered in giving an overall direction to the work of the Department extremely interesting ... [and] the committee would find it extremely helpful if, in their Report, they could refer to the problems he had encountered. ... He agreed that he should stand up on this issue and he reminded me that he had said at his interview with the committee that he had not been allowed to run the Department in the way that he had hoped when he arrived" (Edwards to Review Committee, 22 September 1986). Wynne subsequently approves the exact wording of the statement to be included in the Report.[43]

In another intriguing short letter to Edwards following a meeting between them, Godley writes: "Forgive this bombardment: I am sending you three letters simultaneously. This one is to explain that by removing any reference of the possible interviewing of Messrs. Singh and Rowthorn from my account of my meeting with you, that letter can, I believe, stand as an 'on the record' account of that meeting. I am extremely grateful to you for listening to me and

---

[43] Edwards has a note on file:

> I explained to him that we found his statements about the difficulties he had encountered in giving an overall direction to the work of the Department extremely interesting. I also told him, in confidence, that the Committee had concluded that the powers of the Committee of Management produced undesirable constraints on the freedom of a Director to mould a Department and to provide effective management as well as intellectual leadership, and I explained that the Committee would find it extremely helpful if, in their Report, they could refer to the problems he had encountered and which were, in part, on record in the Minutes of the Committee of Management. He agreed that he ought to stand up on this issue and he reminded me that he had said at his interview with the Committee that he had not been allowed to run the Department in the way that he had hoped when he arrived. He also said that he would not have accepted the Directorship had he realised that he would have so little freedom. We agreed that I would draft a possible statement of the history of his difficulties for inclusion in the Report of the Committee, but I would consult him before it was finally incorporated into the Report.

This Edwards does, conveying the text in a telephone call to Godley, who then agrees to the following final wording:

> The Committee have been told by Professor Godley of his disappointment at his discovery, on assuming the Directorship, that the constitutional relationship between the Director and the Committee of Management was such as *could be used and was being used* to prevent the Director creating a general policy for the Department or any coherence in the research programme. He raised his concern with the Committee of Management in February 1972, both on the general grounds of the constitutional relationship between the Director and the Committee of Management, and on the specific grounds of the provision of facilities for his own research activities. Professor Godley has told the Committee that while an agreement was subsequently reached on the provision of facilities for his own research, he continued to regard the constitutional position as unsatisfactory, and in 1973 reported his view to the Secretary General.

for letting me have these assurances. As you will see, none of the accompanying letter is copied to anyone and I shall keep their contents to myself for the time being" (Godley to Edwards, Letter dated 12 October 1984). It seems reasonable to deduce that Godley has expressed unfavourable views to Edwards about 'Messrs Singh and Rowthorn' that he did not wish to be circulated; the impact of the words, and this follow-up letter, could only have deleterious consequences not just for Ajit Singh and Bob Rowthorn, but also for the overall defence of the DAE's position.

And yet again, in a three-page letter to Edwards (dated 9 September 1986; DAE Paper 64), Godley responds to the *Summary of Adverse Views* (SAV) sent to him. The contents and the form of the letter are equally remarkable. It is written as if addressing a confidante, a person of trust with empathy and appreciation for one's own experience and point of view; but Godley is actually writing to a person who he has had reason to bitterly criticise, amongst other things, for the adversarial conduct of the Review. In terms of content, Godley gives away a lot very quickly: he complains explicitly about staff—again when he arrived at DAE—"they made it extremely and offensively clear that my participation in their work was the last thing they needed"; "the constitution of the department ... was actively exploited by people who were determined to pursue their own interests"; "maybe I should have resigned rather than abdicate responsibility". He then changes tense: "another factor which has tended to make the research effort to some extent disparate and diluted is that the system of tenure and funding has sometimes led people to undertake work simply because money was available to do it. It has, for instance, turned out to be difficult to turn down any projects which had a good chance of raising money partly for the very reason that if the person concerned could not get money, he would not have his appointment renewed. I have no doubt that the lack of overall direction and the frantic search for money have partly been responsible for the output of the department having been less distinguished than it might have been and also, directly and indirectly, for the lack of interaction with individuals and institution in other universities." Later, he concedes "that we have been parochial"; he also "concedes immediately that the theoretical part of [my own work] has not been successful"; and he shares his "conclusion that a major improvement might be achieved by setting a maximum tenure—say five years—to all new DAE appointments". And then he closes: "I wonder whether there is any way in which I can help your Committee further!" (exclamation mark in original). One would have thought Edwards might reply, "thank you Wynne, that is pretty much enough!" His motivations and agenda might have been different, but on many key points, Godley's position is at one with that of the Hahn-Matthews group in terms of diagnostics as well as solutions. One must wonder what Godley might have thought the utility and impact of such an approach might have been. But clearly nothing sufficiently positive came from it, apart from piling up further ennui for Godley himself—who was clearly doing no favours to himself or the DAE through what conveys the impression of being a forlorn tactic of appeasement. It might be safe to surmise that the somewhat naïve and gullible Wynne Godley was no match for the wiles and guiles of well-practised university bureaucrats.[44]

Incidentally, much earlier, in his interview, Ajit Singh had informed the Review Committee that "the presence of Research Officers [in the Management Committee of the DAE] can be traced to the changeover of Directorships from Reddaway to Godley, at which time many Research Officers felt that they had been exploited as research assistants by some members of the Faculty" (as summarised by K. J. R. Edwards in his record of the interview).

Interspersed between all these contributions by Godley which strengthen the case against the DAE are also robust defences on specific issues: he thinks various research officers are doing excellent research and he frontally challenges the Committee's attempts to denigrate the quality of their work, sharply pointing out that this falls outside its terms of reference, and in any event cannot be done without the staff having a fair chance to respond to the criticisms; he strongly rejects, with conclusive evidence, the charge that the DAE is UTO-unfriendly; apropos the old chestnut of 'insularity', he says the DAE is positively reorienting itself looking outwards. And with an incisive flourish, he points out "that there is a grave danger in trying to track the rapidly changing configuration of fashionable activities that eddy in the U.S. and now Europe [this has resonance with Posner's commercial for mainstream economics]. I also continue to believe that econometrics has only a subsidiary role to play in the understanding of how real economic systems work; and that the work of Messrs Layard and Nickell is fundamentally and dangerously mistaken (for reasons which I hope shortly to publish)"—but they had done their damage already, cf. the CEPG experience with SSRC under Posner, where Nickell had been a key hostile expert.

Godley had plans to be away from Cambridge from later in 1987, but to his (and not just his) great frustration the Review was still not done, and there was no prospect of a new Director being appointed by then. At the end of his tether, Godley pens a remarkable no-holds barred, unrestrained letter of complaint to the Vice Chancellor with a freedom which comes from an awareness of an unjust defeat, when niceties are of little matter and true feelings, kept bottled up for the greater good, can be unleashed. He spectacularly switches tack from helping to attacking the functioning of the Review Committee, but by then, matters were done and dusted.

Apart from Wynne Godley, a second odd outlier is provided by the opinions attributed to Bob Rowthorn, then a Marxist mathematician and, with Ajit Singh, a lead member of the local radical left within the Faculty and outside. Ajit and he had served for long periods on the Faculty Board, and he was interviewed in that capacity by K. J. R. Edwards, the Secretary General running the Review. Edwards took notes on the views expressed by Rowthorn in his

---

[44] Cripps and Lavoie (2017: 950) observe in their concentrated yet comprehensive appreciation of his contributions, Wynne "approached intellectual and political issues in a more open way than the more combative academics".

interview, and these need to speak for themselves. Two comments find their way into Edwards' record, and both are highly critical of the DAE. The first reads like an attack on the DAE, and its two main team projects, the CEPG and the CGP: "He accepted that the DAE has drifted in the last few years. The economic policy group has lost focus and coherence, and the growth project has become an empire which has lost its way and has become too dominant within the Department." This is curious in one respect, in that the CEPG had already folded up a couple of years earlier. Rowthorn's outspoken criticism of what was presumably his own side could only be music to the ears of Hahn and Matthews. The second, even more damaging comment clearly gives tactical support to the Hahn-Matthews allegations with regard to Faculty elections: Edwards' notes continue: "He argued that Faculty membership is bestowed too freely on casual visitors, part-time supervisors, etc., and that this unduly influences the outcome of elections to the Faculty Board"; again, unexpected support, surely much appreciated by the Hahn-Matthews group. These comments, such as are on record,[45] are strong enough to raise uncomfortable questions, though it has to be said that Rowthorn's words might have been taken out of context, misunderstood or misinterpreted by Edwards; believable if you believe it. Famously unguarded and unpredictable, Bob could well have changed his mind the next day or in the next meeting. But what is recorded is what it is, and you believe what you like. Bob's unpredictability and changes of direction have spawned a genre of humour on Sidgwick Site—but nothing in these recorded comments is funny or to be trivialised as just a joke.

9.4 On the Rack: Bleeding the DAE

The DAE was on the rack for an excruciating period of four years—or five if one includes the unsettling year of rumour and premonition prior to the announcement of the Review. This raises two first-order questions: why the review of a small department of thirty-plus staff should really be stretched out to such extreme limits; and then, about its exceedingly untimely timing, continuing as it did till the last few months of Godley's fifteen-year term of office. It prompts Godley, in his final letter written directly to the Vice Chancellor: "there is no reason whatever why a review should not have been instituted three years—or for that matter eleven or twelve years—before the end of my term"; he has a point, since there was no 'automatic' review triggered by the General Board at the end of Reddaway's fifteen-year term as Director. From the start of the Review, Godley had repeatedly emphasised "that there should be *continuity* between Directors" [emphasis in the original]; that "it is highly desirable that as the period of office of one Director draws to a close, it is already decided and known who the next Director will be"; "this is how things

---

[45] Apart from these couple of short paragraphs of summary notes made by Edwards in the course of the interview with Bob Rowthorn, there is no other response made by him to the Committee; his name does not appear in the long list of responders to the Secretary General.

happened when I myself was first appointed" (Godley to Vice Chancellor, Letter dated 23 January 1987: 1). This was deemed essential to ensure the sustainability of external funding and the work programmes dependent on it. But contrary to the declared timetable, the second-stage review had gone ahead without any prospect of a new Director in place till October 1988. Godley points out: "The prolonged, delayed, confused and still incomplete review process has had extremely undesirable consequences, most particularly because it has generated a long interregnum".

On 3 July 1986, a letter signed by as many as 41 persons—virtually the entire complement of DAE staff—was sent to the Vice Chancellor[46] exhorting him not to delay the appointment of the new Director and emphasising the massive negative impact that the delay was having on DAE finances and sustainability. And being aware of the collations of negative comments put together by the Committee, the signatories convey their view "that fairness requires that an early opportunity be given to individuals ... to respond to criticism of their work". In fact, in this regard, the Committee was operating in the convenient grey zone provided by the vagueness of the terms of reference, since there was no explicit call for evaluation of the quality of the research work. Godley made this point forcefully in his own letter to the Vice Chancellor six months later, but this was a lost cause. The SAV (Summary of Adverse Views) document makes depressing reading, with a series of six paragraphs each bristling with hostility and dismissive criticism, much of it without substance, including a lot repeated from earlier airings without any acknowledgement of the fact that most of the criticisms had been shown to be invalid. The premise of 'poor quality' and 'declining reputation' was critical, since it provided the basis and legitimacy for corrective intervention based on the Hahn-Matthews solution. A similar strategy had been utilised at the SSRC and the ESRC for terminating the DAE's two macroeconomic modelling projects, and a distinct sense of déjà vu hung over the DAE Review; it was a well-practiced technique and guaranteed to work if the carefully composed committees could be relied upon to do the needful. And there is multiplier effect in reputation assassination, as rumour begins to substitute any independent impartial assessment or reassessment; so if the SSRC makes the first determination of bad quality with its committees; then this is taken as currency and used again in another round elsewhere where it is taken as recorded confirmation of bad quality. The usual suspects move from committee to committee circulating, recirculating and regurgitating the same reports between themselves treating them as fresh independent evidence. Kafkaesque, perhaps; or, bearing in mind the year when the University Review was announced, Orwellian.

"The morale of the Department's staff and the vitality and coherence of the research effort have been very adversely affected. The reputation of the

---

[46] Letter to Sir Jack Lewis dated 3 July 1986, copied to the Chairman of the Faculty of Economics and Politics, and of the Committee of Management of the DAE; Director of the DAE; Secretary General of the Faculties; 2p.

Department and its members has been, to no good purpose whatever, damaged by a great deal of diffused and ill-concealed calumny—people talk very freely in Common Rooms in Cambridge and elsewhere."[47] Godley points out that the DAE "has already been under review for *over two and a half years* [emphasis in the original] during most of which time there has not been a Director proper and no new Director has been in prospect"; this has been partly the reason why "the very recent research of the department has been disparate" (ibid.).

Godley reminds the Vice Chancellor that "the University has a duty to protect and promote the academic standing and achievement of those whom it employs, as well, more generally as their wellbeing in a much wider sense". In contrast to this, though: "a quite unusually large number of academic staff (most of whom have College fellowships) have left the Department (or have informed me of their intention to leave) since the beginning of the academic year 1985/1986. Of the thirteen regular academic staff who have left (or will leave) five have obtained Chairs or roughly equivalent senior posts, three have gone into private consultancy, three have obtained tenured teaching posts (two in Cambridge), one has gone to the IMF and one to an assistant lectureship in Cambridge" (ibid.). This, incidentally, gives the lie to the allegation, levelled by the neoclassical Faculty camp, concerning the low quality of DAE staff (Table 9.1). Godley closes his unrestrained, though entirely justified, tirade thus: "the record I have set down is, in my view, one of very damaging and needless incompetence. The fact that the University has a complex constitution and that there is a considerable amount of change in the composition, say of the General Board or in the person of the Secretary General, cannot be held in any degree to excuse the long drawn out, inconsistent and apparently adversarial way in which this whole affair has been conducted" (ibid.).

Early in 1987, on the realistic expectation that the report of the review committee was imminent and likely to include derogatory observations on the quality of DAE research and researchers, Jill Rubery led a group of ten DAE researchers, as members of the Association of University Teachers (AUT), in approaching their trade union seeking advice and exhorting it to intervene, citing the likelihood of the report "potentially causing serious and unwarranted damage to the professional reputations of academic staff at DAE"; and also setting an unacceptable precedent for how university reviews of departments might be conducted in the future. Rubery (1987, 26 January) communicates their "disquiet", "main complaints and worries", and their anxiety that "because of the inordinate delay in completing this review, it is probable that the General Board will be urged to come to a decision very quickly on the report and it is therefore essential that the AUT consider this issue with all possible haste" (Rubery, J., 1987, 26 January).[48] In a second letter to Joan

---

[47] Letter from Wynne Godley to the Vice Chancellor, dated 23 January 1987, 5p.

[48] Jill Rubery to Joan Whitehead, letter dated 26 January. Attached to their letter was a four-page note "DAE Review Procedure": "the enclosed document lists the main complaints and worries

Table 9.1 Research staff who have left the DAE since July 1984 or who will be leaving by the end of 1986–1987 academic year

Name	Date of departure	Destination
N. Christodoulakis	30.09.86	Professor, Athens School of Economics
F. Cripps	30.09.86	Private enterprise
A. Goudie	31.07.85	World Bank—On special leave
G. Gudgin	30.09.85	Director, Northern Ireland Economic Research Centre
R. Lewney	31.01.85	Henley Centre for Forecasting
D. Lovatt	31.01.85	Information not available
B. Moore	30.09.85	Assistant Director of Research, Department of Land Economy, Cambridge
W. Peterson	01.07.85	Lectureship, Faculty of Economics & Politics, Cambridge
A. Snell	30.09.86	University of Edinburgh
A. Stewart	30.08.85	Chair of Sociology, University of Edinburgh
D. Vines	30.08.85	Chair of Economics, University of Glasgow
T. Worrall	30.09.85	Information not available
V. Borooah	28.02.87	Chair of Applied Economics, University of Ulster
M. Kumar	31.03.87	IMF—On special leave
J. Rhodes	30.09.87	Private enterprise
R. Tarling	31.03.87	Private enterprise
M. Weale	30.09.87	Assistant Lectureship, Faculty of Economics & Politics, Cambridge

Other staff that had left earlier included a.o., Rick van der Ploeg, Martin Fetherston, Ken Coutts; Terry Ward left in 1987 to join Francis Cripps in Alphametrics; those who left a little later included the sociologists Bob Blackburn, Ken Prandy and Brendan Burchell; Jill Rubery of the Labour Studies Group; Michael Landesmann of the CGP, though he stayed on as SRO at the DAE till 1993; Paul Dunne left CGP in 1986

Whitehead at AUT a month later, Rubery re-emphasises the potential jeopardy for the body of DAE research staff: "As was always predictable, the report [by the General Board to the University] is unlikely to say anything about existing research staff and protection of their interests. There is still therefore the real possibility that the review of the DAE could be used by an incoming Director to oppose the reappointment of staff. It is still crucial, both to protect the research staff's position, and to ensure that similar 'reviews' do not take place in future, for the AUT to object to the procedures that were used in the review process and to insist that the review should have no bearing in future employment prospects of research staff." Rubery cites the review procedures used by the ESRC, "sent to us by Sarah from AUT Headquarters, and the MRC/ESRC procedure which William Brown has passed on to you"; the Note attached to the earlier letter of January 26 draws uncomplimentary comparisons with the procedures followed by the General Board. "The Faculty Board is also committed to sending a letter concerning its objection to procedure."

that the DAE staff have over the way the assessment of their research has been carried out"; the letter lists ten names: John Rhodes, Ken Coutts, Bob Blackburn, Iain Begg, Paul Dunne, Jill Rubery, Michael Kitson, Brendan Burchell, Ken Prandy and Michael Landesmann (the last name handwritten in ink).

And indeed, a forceful letter is duly sent by Alan Hughes, the Chairman of the Faculty Board expressing its deep concerns and listing the many shortcomings in the University's procedures. This letter refers to an earlier communication (dated 6 February 1987) where the Faculty Board had pointed out that "some aspects of the procedures followed by the ad hoc committee to be less than completely satisfactory. The Board consider them to have fallen considerably short of the review procedures used in establishments elsewhere. We are writing now to detail these shortcomings." The shoddy procedure had already done its damage and work, the Faculty Board was writing now, rather forlornly, "in the hope that such observations may be useful to the General Board in any exercise of a similar nature in the future". Based on the formal procedures in use by the Medical Research Council and the ESRC, Hughes lists ten salient features of a proper review, and then proceeds to point out that apart from only a couple of these having been followed, and that too only after forceful requests sent earlier by the Faculty Board, all the other procedures, followed as standard practice in the two major research councils, had been flouted by the General Board in the work of the second-stage DAE Review Committee.

Hughes observes: "The Faculty Board would particularly like to draw the General Board's attention to:

- The inappropriateness of the timing of the review coming so close to the expected end of Professor Godley's Directorship and the complete lack of consultation on the first stage terms of reference, and review committee membership;
- The continuing uncertainty over the length of time to be take in carrying it out;
- The relative concentration in practice of the Review Committee on assessing the quality of research and the relationship between the Director and the Committee of Management compared with those elements in the terms of reference which were singled out for particular attention;
- Given the focus on assessing research quality the failure to consult with the Director or staff on appropriate referees for assessing the quality of research, or to provide any information which would satisfy those concerned that these assessments were made on the basis of detailed knowledge of published work and research in progress;
- And the absence of any indication of the names or affiliations of the outside experts consulted."[49]

Whether reading above, between or below the lines, the letter from Hughes constitutes a blistering critique of the shoddy almost procedure-less process run by the General Board, which could conceivably have formed grounds potentially for being formally challenged.

---

[49] Alan Hughes, Chair Faculty Board, draft letter to K. J. R. Edwards concerning DAE Review Procedure, in relation to agenda item 566/6; FB.87.24.

Alan Hughes, then Chairman of the Faculty Board and a member of the General Board, was copied in Godley's letter to Sir Jack Lewis. In conversation, Alan shared his feeling that by the end of this shabby long-drawn out episode, various members of the General Board had come to see through the machinations and manipulations of the orthodox mainstream protagonists and had become somewhat inured and unresponsive to their tugging and shoving; Alan's personal observation would carry reliability.[50] But by then, much of the damage had already been done, and the key objectives of the neoclassical group had been achieved; the DAE shop was in disarray, and the new proprietor, now firmly in control, could in due course restock many of the shelves left bare by the closure of the CEPG and CGP macroeconomic modelling teams, with wares more of his preference, now favouring applied microeconomic research and research on transitions in Eastern European economies, replacing the erstwhile concentration on policy-engaged macroeconomic modelling.

With regard to the installation of a new DAE Director, there seemed to be problems virtually till the last post, even to the point apparently when final choices were being inked by the Advisory Body set up by the General Board, as is indicated in a letter from one member of this Advisory Body to another—both being professors located in the Faculty of Economics—shortly prior to the deciding meeting of this Board.[51] It would hardly be surprising that members might hold different preferences, and little doubt is left in this regard in the letter from Willy Brown to Robin Matthews where the former expresses serious objections to the latter's choice of candidate to anoint (Willie Brown to Robin Matthews; Letter dated 29 December 1987; 3p).

Brown is quite forthright: "If you remain unpersuaded, we are likely to hand a dead-lock to the General Board. This would not be disastrous—a rather different form of negotiation would take over. But it would hardly be a satisfactory way for our Advisory Body to conclude its work. I am certainly unimpressed by the view that the General Board may recommend the withdrawal of all support from the DAE. For one thing, they will by now be well aware of the inadequate procedures they followed in their review, and of the difficulties of closing departments even where proper procedures are followed. Furthermore, to abolish a multi-disciplinary, applied economics department in a university which will always attract outstanding economists would show a bizarre lack of long-term political judgement. Something very like the Department would have to be re-invented soon and its library, support staff, and expertise reassembled at great cost. Colleges would have to fund substantial numbers of supervisors for one of the most prosperous of undergraduate subjects. My short time on Council has made me optimistic that the University would

---

[50] Personal communication; interview on 13 August 2018, Sidney Sussex College, Cambridge.

[51] The Advisory Body was to meet on Tuesday, 5 January 1988, to come to its recommendation to the GB. The full composition of the AB is not available, but Professor Willy Brown is known to have been "one of the University's representatives" on the Advisory Body; and R. C. O. Matthews was also on the Advisory Body, in all likelihood from a different constituency of members selected by the General Board.

discount supposed intra-Faculty disagreement in its evaluation of the long-term interests of the University. Perhaps I should make clear at this stage that if there were a successful campaign to abolish the DAE, I am afraid that my own research interests would oblige me [to] look elsewhere, if not outside Cambridge then probably towards whatever happens in Management Studies" (p. 2). Willy Brown, Professor of Industrial Relations, had built up quite a reputation as a specialist in complex arbitrations, but he lost this round; when the music stopped, Matthews's preferred candidate was in the chair. And Brown stayed on at the Faculty as it reinvented itself, adapting well to the changing environment.

Each from its distinct vantage point, the three missives—Rubery et al to AUT; Alan Hughes, Chairman of the Faculty Board to the Secretary General of the Faculties; and Professor Brown to Professor Matthews, both members of the Advisory Board—share their baleful view of the improprieties in the procedures followed by the DAE Review process and Committee; it must remain an open question whether these were witless or wilful.

In the end, the vacancy of Director was filled after inordinate and inexcusable delay which inflicted severe costs on the work, viability and reputation of the Department as a whole. Their mounting frustration and desperation had been repeatedly brought to the attention of the Review Committee, with little effect or response. There was also an arrogant and unconscionable disregard shown by the University authorities to the negative implications of this prolonged three-year period of uncertainty for the professional morale and domestic well-being of all staff in the DAE, academic but also non-academic.

9.4.1 The Secretary General, The Prince and the Chess Master

A brief meditation on the presence of Ken Edwards might be in order, particularly in view of the marshalling, if not court martialling, role that he had through the first and the second stages of the DAE Review—having taken over as Secretary General of the General Board of the Faculties just at the point of the very first meeting of the first-stage Review Committee, and staying just long enough to sign off the final outcome of the second-stage Review Committee three years later.

Edwards was a geneticist by training, drawn to the field for its affinity with his background; his father was a farmer, his grandfather a farm labourer who became a farmer. Edwards (2009): "I did not focus enough on research as I should have and now describe myself as having somewhat of a butterfly mind; ... those impulses were most fully satisfied when I was a Vice-Chancellor because I had a good reason for going round departments and asking what they were doing; my greatest joy was doing this."

Ken Edwards was interviewed by Alan Macfarlane in February 2009, twenty-three years after he left Cambridge, and he recalled with precision how he started: "on my first day in the job three people had made appointments to see me ...; the second[52] visitor was Wynn *(sic)* Godley who was then Director of the Department of Applied Economics into which a University review was taking place; he wanted to talk to me about how the department was run and how one did research in economics; there was either his way of measuring patterns and associations, and the other was to have a theoretical idea about how the economy might work which allowed you to make predictions which is what Frank Hahn did." Edwards confesses that he didn't have much of an idea about economics, and so can be forgiven for thinking that "what Frank Hahn did" had anything all to do with predictions about any economy, but there are two intriguing aspects: first, that Wynne Godley had made an appointment to present himself, the DAE, and his case on the very day Edwards had started; that he had introduced a binary between the way he and DAE did things with the other, Frank Hahn's, way; and second, that twenty-three years later, Edwards recalled this incident, including the reference to Frank Hahn, with precision and without hesitation. Edwards observes that the Review had been started under his predecessor Ian Nicol. It could be surmised that Wynne might have wished to bring Edwards in on the lie of land and the opposing camps in the Faculty of Economics; and equally that Edwards would have been briefed about the occluded background and the General Board's strategic agenda and orientation as put down in Nicol's secretive Note. So Edwards was primed and came in running from the start. As Secretary General, he was akin to the traffic cop, directing and routing all academic transactions between the Faculties and the University administration, and his name figures more prominently in the case of the DAE Review than almost any other. As such, his perspectives on university governance could provide a clue to decipher some of the puzzles and curiosities of the DAE Review episode.

> I sometimes think that here there is a fairly small group of unrepresentative people who decide they want to have a say in the running of the University but don't represent anyone in particular but themselves; Cornford's *Microcosmographia Academica* is to a certain extent a caricature, but there is a lot of truth there; I used to reread that every summer while I was at Leicester along with Machiavelli's *The Prince*, as guides on how to deal with my job. (Edwards, 2009)

At Cambridge, the hat of Vice Chancellor was worn three years at a time, in rotation between the various heads of Colleges, and most VCs were far too busy with other matters: so usually the 'Registrary' looked after administrative affairs, and the Secretary General ran the academic side of things, being the SG of the General Board of the Faculties of the University; effectively, the SG exercised, by proxy or default, the powers and authority of the Vice Chancellor to whom he reported; the University world was his oyster. These are general

---

[52] Edwards remembers that the first was John Taylor, Professor of Theoretical Physics and Applied Mathematics, worrying that Britain might withdraw out of CERN; and the third was Don Cupitt who was then Chairman of the Faculty Board of Divinity, anxious about pre-empting a personnel scandal-in-the-making (Edwards, 2009).

terms in which Edwards refers to his equation with Butterfield, who was the VC when Edwards took over the position of SG from Ian Nicol; the VC effectively left the SG to make the running; matters reverted to him in general only towards the end when he chaired the General Board of the Faculties.

"As Secretary General, the fact that Cambridge is a collegiate university did not really impinge a great deal; there was quite a heavy weighting of heads of colleges in the Council of the Senate but I found them really pretty constructive and I got to know many of them quite well; they were useful people to talk to about what was going on in the University and what their ideas were; got to know 'H', Master of 'J', very well; 'B' at 'E' was also very good to talk to; it was important to know the movers and shakers, the opinion makers, and 'G' was one, Jack Lewis was another; certainly, when I went to Leicester, one of the first things that I tried to work out was who were the people who were regarded as framers of opinion in the University; I would try to get to know them and to gain their trust; in both jobs there is the challenge of providing leadership but also getting people to the position where they feel they have had their say, and recognise in the end somebody has to take the decision." Does this enter the operational manual as: "slow things down, wear them out, then confront with them with the decision as fait accompli"—'them' here being the academic plebs—while on the other side, look out and do the deals with the movers and shakers—these being the Masters of Colleges and other opinion makers. Edwards names several such luminaries, and one wonders how much port might have been had with the well-established Master of Clare and his friend the newly appointed Master of St Catherine's; one can only imagine animated meetings of the puppet masters, one a devotee of Machiavelli, the other an acknowledged international master in composing three-move chess problems, as they picked over strategic algorithms for channelling college and university governance problems to desired solutions. On the other side, one wonders what common ground or conversation topics might have been shared between Edwards the aspiring, Machiavellian son of a farmer, grandson of a farm labourer, and Vice Chancellor to be; and Godley, the flighty, multi-talented son of an Irish peer rooted in the landed gentry, both a performing oboist and a professional economist—butterflies, estate management, evolutionary economics? Wynne, as far as it might be possible to be from Machiavelli, or Lady Macbeth; the face of the thane was indeed that open book where men could read strange matters; no prospect here of being that serpent underneath the innocent flower.

As it happens, Secretary General K. J. R. Edwards would have been two years old in 1936 when Eric Hobsbawm enrolled in Cambridge, soon to join the Communist Party, to be elected to the Apostles, and to be on his way to becoming the scourge of the right and the icon of the left that he became. In his free-ranging retro autobiographical script, he makes a wry reference to what was to become later a go-to guide for Edwards:

The main contribution of Cambridge to political theory and practice, as described brilliantly by the classicist F.M. Cornford in his little squib *Microcosmographia Academica* (1908), was 'the principle of unripe time'. Whatever anyone proposed, the time for doing it was not yet ripe. It was powerfully reinforced by the principle of 'the entering wedge'. Of course, our undergraduate lives were lived at a level far below that of the master-operators of these principles, but those of us who became dons soon discovered their force. (Hobsbawm, 2002: 103). Wynne Godley, as besieged don, was seriously mismatched, he never stood a chance

Ken Edwards occupied the post of Secretary General for just one three-year stint, timed, as it happens, almost exactly to begin and end with the DAE Review. "Others can judge how well I performed in these roles", he remarked perhaps too modestly. For the DAE itself, it had indeed been an ill wind that buffeted it throughout his tenure—but it blew no harm for the bureaucrat. Shortly after the Review ended in 1987, the administrative talents of Ken Edwards were rewarded: he became Vice Chancellor of Leicester University, not for three, but for a run of thirteen years from 1987 to 1999, on some accounts becoming something of a 'legend', and had buildings and lecture halls named after him; clearly those regular refresher readings of Machiavelli and Cornford's *Microcosmographia* each summer had served him well. At the end of the 'thick-as-thieves' partnership in the Review process, one of Edwards' co-members on the Review Committee conveyed his congratulations, and commiserations, to Edwards for his move from "one bed of nails to another".[53]

9.4.2 The Capture

A final question remains to be confronted: why the appointment of the new Director of the DAE was so inordinately and blatantly delayed, despite it being patently obvious, despite regular exhortations, that such a delay would impose an extremely heavy cost on the department, its researchers and its other staff. The Review, with all its opening shenanigans, was formally started in June 1984, and the new Director took over at the DAE more than four years later in October 1988, and over three years beyond the long-known endpoint of Wynne Godley's tenure. It is not possible to walk away from a review of the Review without exploring this open question.

The most immediate, and for many perhaps the most credible explanation might simply be the complacent and arrogant inefficiency of a self-regarding university administration; and this conduct of the Review would appear to offer ample support for such a view. However, it would be too easy and lazy, if not disingenuous, to ascribe this simply to the slow-turning wheels of university

---

[53] Edwards was also, later, President of the Association of European Universities. (https://www2.le.ac.uk/staff/community/people/visits/ken-edwards-former-vice-chancellor-of-the-university-of-leicester) And a little later he became Chairman of the Observatory of the Magna Charta Universitatum based in Bologna (King, Roger (2003) *The University in the Global Age*. London: Macmillan International Higher Education).

bureaucracy, with inefficiency slowing the rotations even further. Looking at the process in reverse, three speculations are possible, all based on the hypothesis that the various delays, adding up to nearly four years in total, were at least in part intentional and instrumental.

First, delays would inevitably lead to attrition in staff morale and hence staff numbers in the DAE, where everyone but the Director was on short-term contracts. Given the acute uncertainties, and in-your-face hostilities in the Austin Robinson Building, many could have been expected to leave, and many so did, thereby demoralising and weakening the DAE and softening its opposition to the 'reforms' being pushed by the neoclassicals. This could be seen as unfortunate collateral damage but, on another reading, also as the attrition of the target itself. This sounds cynical, but cynicism was perhaps the softest emotion on display on either side at the time.

Second, the General Board uses its powers not to move on the appointment of the new Director even in the face of strong exhortations from the DAE Director to the Chair of the Faculty Board pointing to the critical costs of such delay on the prospects of funding for project sustainability; instead, quite tellingly, the Committee consciously decides to use this delay instrumentally as a leveraging tool, as a bargaining counter in effectively forcing the DAE and the Faculty to accept unpalatable organisational changes the Review Committee has already decided upon on its side.

For one, if the directorship was dealt with quickly as originally announced—by the end of Michaelmas Term 1984—moves to impose such changes might have met with much greater internal DAE and Faculty resistance, and on top of that, the unknown position of a new Director would make the outcome all the more unpredictable. Given the state of play in the early 1980s prior to the scheduled retirement of Wynne Godley in 1985, there was a fair expectation, speculative as that would have been, that the mantle of the leadership of the DAE would most likely fall on the shoulders Francis Cripps, the dynamic force behind the CEPG's high-profile macroeconomic modelling and national policy engagement; another possibility could have been Terry Barker, who had taken over the running of the CGP from Richard Stone. Though the two had distinct profiles and styles, and though the two units worked at a collegial but discrete distance, either unit could have expected to remain institutionally secure in the event of the new Director being from the sister modelling team. Given the dominance of the heterodox and radical groups over the Faculty Board at that point in time, these might have appeared, with good reason, to be the most likely scenarios to emerge, though clearly neither of these outcomes might have appealed to those, in the Faculty and their fellow travellers in University decision-making bodies, who wished to shift the intellectual, institutional and ideological profiles of the DAE into a distinctly different direction altogether.

However, there was an alternative possible course of action, which as it happens actually came to transpire—the Review Committee could always subtly offer a quid pro quo: you quickly accept the proposed changes, and we will quickly announce the directorship. But this real reason for the delay is kept secret, while some other specious constructions are used to justify this behaviour of the Committee. This was clearly unethical and fell well short of expected standards of university governance, but the records offer support that, to some extent, this factor was definitely at play.

Consider the following. As early as February 1985, a good three and a half years before the new DAE Director eventually takes charge, Alan Hughes, as Chair of the Faculty Board, earnestly writes to Secretary General Edwards re-emphasising Godley's exhortation for a quick appointment of the new Director, since any delay would be extremely damaging for funding, for morale and sustainability: "The increasing uncertainty surrounding the appointment of a new Director is already undermining morale and threatens the continued efficient operation of the Department" (Letter from A. Hughes to K. J. R. Edwards).

But Edwards is not listening, and seems to have a cunning plan up his sleeve: he writes to David Yale, Chair of the Review Committee: "Dear David, I have been giving some thought to the question of how best to present the DAE Sub-committee case to the GB and to deal with the likely response that the procedure for the appointment of a Director should start without waiting for the approval of any changes in regulations. Our main reason, namely, that we would give away our leverage on the Department and Faculty to accept these changes, is one which we cannot deploy with Alan Hughes present, but it does seem that there are two other good reasons which we can use and these are: …. If, when you have considered these suggestions, you would like to talk about them before the GB meeting, I would be happy to do so" (K. J. R. Edwards to D. Yale, note in file). It is reasonable to surmise that the Secretary General is here trying to dissemble and obfuscate, and to go behind Alan Hughes' unbendable back and sell him a dummy. And to prove the point, there follows a letter from him to Alan Hughes along the conspiratorial line he has communicated to Yale (Edwards to Hughes, Letter dated 18 February 1984; GB.852.395, cc to Godley). It is an open question whether this qualifies just as skilful management technique, dissembling or deception.

The Review Committee does not wish to do this, it seems, because they want to drag it out and hold this, that is, prompt action to appoint the new Director, as a bargaining counter to sell or force the changes to governance that they have quietly been working out (without discussing them with the DAE or with the Faculty Board) before yielding to this genuinely urgent plea from the DAE and the Faculty Board.

The third speculative explanation, equally brazen, is that the Hahn-Matthews duo might have wished the appointment of the new Director to be held back till such time as they had readied the candidate/s they might have been grooming for the job.[54] It would be a poor outcome for them if the appointment

---

[54] If so, this might not have been the first time that Hahn might have resorted to such a practice. Dasgupta (2013) in his obituary of Hahn, recalls that when at the LSE in the late 1960s, "Hahn persuaded the other professors to call a moratorium on appointments to Lectureships until a suitable cohort had been trained. David Hendry and Stephen Nickell were among the first of the new

occurred as planned in 1984 itself and, say, installed a new Director not amenable to their continuous and generous avuncular advice. And hypothetically, continuing the speculation, their candidate at that point might well still have been a few steps short of the necessary threshold for this 'top quality' appointment. Machiavelli might have advised that lengthening the fractious process would also discourage serious external contenders; after all, which 'top quality economist with an international reputation' might wish to volunteer to enter such a snake pit, aka cesspool? That might make it easier to shoe-horn in a candidate of their preference. So might have counselled The Prince to whom apparently the Secretary General frequently turned for inspiration.

All along, the neoclassical group from the Faculty (prominently Hahn, Matthews, Dasgupta and their followers and co-signatories) keeps exerting pressure for the need for a top-quality academic of the highest reputation to take over the directorship—and the terms of the appointment are to be adjusted to make it more attractive to an international field. In fact, the Review Committee holds out an explicit possibility that if this is not done, it would consider a recommendation that the DAE be closed down altogether. Then comes an extensive exchange on whether the directorship (for a maximum of fifteen years) should be automatically linked to a professorship at the Faculty in order to make the position more attractive and to give it status, and that the person should automatically switch to a permanent professorship at the Faculty at the end of the fifteen-year directorship. Hahn, along with six other signatories including David Newbery, argue that "these proposals simply codify the arrangements that have been made for the present Director of the DAE", and this recommendation is duly accepted by the Review Committee (Joint Letter to K. J. R. Edwards, November 1984). Then Matthews, in another of his volleys, also emphasises this point and goes as far as to say that he would oppose the appointment of anyone who he thought did not meet the criteria (one supposes as interpreted and assessed by himself) and that, should the right person not be found, he would prefer to settle for a period with just a stand-in Acting Director of DAE—the potential negative implications of this, as spelled out by Godley, notwithstanding. It is difficult to comprehend Matthews's formal locus standi in this regard and therefore what significance to attach to this messaging; it is safest to read the words and their import at face value.

9.4.3 *How it Transpired, Perhaps Not Just by Chance*

As it happens, that is the way it goes. The main, ostensible justification for the Review itself was the completion of Godley's fifteen-year term as Director,

---

batch of lecturers there." From David Newbery (2017: 498), there is a description of his entry into the Faculty: "Although Hahn had recruited me to replace him as the economics teaching fellow at Churchill College starting in 1966, I spent my first year after graduation (1965–1966) as an Overseas Development Institute Nuffield Fellow in the Treasury of the Tanzanian Government. I was invited while there to apply for an assistant lectureship in the faculty, and was appointed without even an interview, so powerful was Hahn's influence at that time."

known forever to be in 1985; yet on one pretext or another, the procedure is dragged on and on; Wynne Godley stays on as Acting Director till September 1987; then another Acting Director is indeed appointed for 1987–1988, in the person of Alan Hughes; overseen by none other than R. C. O. Matthews as the Acting Chair of the controlling Committee of Management of the DAE. Eventually, the post is announced and filled. And it turns out that the candidate who best met the criteria as visualised by the advisory committee set up for the task was actually David Newbery—perhaps the last of the symbolic 'nephews' of 'Uncle' Frank who had not till then been seated in a chair. When the Review process was announced in June 1984, David Newbery was a lecturer in the Faculty; so, then, were Ajit Singh, Alan Hughes and (incredibly) Geoff Harcourt (who did not get promoted to a readership till 1990); Francis Cripps, widely regarded as the deserving heir apparent to Wynne Godley, was still a Senior Research Fellow at the DAE; Bob Rowthorn had somehow jumped the queue and was made an *ad hominem* reader in 1982 in the midst of all the fracas. While the Review unfolded at its grinding attritional pace, Newbery (who was spending much of his time on various assignments in the USA) was promoted to reader in October 1986. Hashem Pesaran, the econometrician with indeed a worldwide reputation, had become reader in 1985, and would have been a strong and worthy contender as the new Director of the DAE which had been his spiritual home. But as circumstances unfolded, the unfilled vacancy had been held back in abeyance for a full three years from the start of the Review—and in the interim, Newbery was successful in a promotion to a readership; and in 1988 anointed the new Director with the attached position of Professor of Applied Economics—a position (of Director) that he holds for its full fifteen years till 2003, after which in October 2004 the Faculty pulls the shutters down, locks the door and bring to a close the life of the DAE as an independent unit; Newbery keeps his chair, as per the new 'codification', till he retires in 2010. The DAE, especially its flagship team projects, the CEPG and the CGP, had both been purposefully attacked by allegations of weakness in econometrics, so, hypothetically, Pesaran's appointment to Director of DAE would have responded directly to this and filled the perceived skill gap; but even while the DAE Director's post was kept vacant, the ESRC had terminated the DAE's surviving macroeconomic team, the CGP in 1987; so perhaps macroeconomic econometric skills were no longer deemed essential and so Newbery, the neoclassical applied microeconomist, and academic disciple of Frank Hahn, was the winner, and Hashem Pesaran, who was widely known to have also sought the post, was apparently the runner-up; but surely no harm done, since Hashem was almost immediately accommodated and promoted to an *ad hominem* professorship the same year.

The stakes were high, and the game could have gone wrong for the orthodox camp; what if the selection committee preferred some other candidate?

What if this 'some other' was, say, someone like Terry Barker[55] who had applied for the post (and had been Richard Stone's understudy and then successor as Director of the CGP); or Francis Cripps (who was the co-team leader with Wynne Godley of the then disbanded CEPG), should he have been induced to

---

[55] There were 'good' reasons why Frank Hahn & Co. might not have shared Richard Stone's enthusiasm for Terry Barker, his understudy at the CGP, to succeed him as the Director of the DAE, and these are perhaps best comprehended through the words of Barker himself in his book *Space-Time Economics*, where he writes thus:

> It will also be seen that the supply-demand curves used extensively to describe the determination of prices do not appear in this book. The reason is that the well-known chart of intersecting curves completely misrepresents the fundamental features of economic behaviour. The curves are not usually dated, they show an equilibrium outcome, they are continuous, and they are certain. In economic life all actions take place in time, all markets are more or less in disequilibrium, indivisibilities and discontinuities are pervasive in production, distribution and consumption (and essential to the explanation of economic behaviour and uncertainty rules. ... The curves are pure speculation invented for their mathematical properties. Even the value to the consumer at the point of sale is uncertain, since only in the act of consumption, normally carried out after the contract is concluded, can consumers be sure that they have what they wanted. Learning-by-consuming is how we grow up in our economic behaviour. The equilibrium price may be at some indefinite point in the future, or it may not exist at all. Each of these features on its own should be sufficient to disqualify the chart as an accurate representation of an economic market. However, there are two further features that are equally problematic and have even further-reaching consequences for economics as a discipline. The first is the fact that the supply and demand curves are usually treated almost as if they were independent entities, meeting only at the point of intersection. This has led to the assumption that supply can be treated independently of demand. Courses are taught and books are written on demand theory; other courses and other books on the production function. Some economists specialize in demand theory; others in production theory. In fact, consumption and production are intimately and continuously linked; there should be no separation. ... The second, further, problem with the chart is that it shows only one solution—one price, one quantity—in the market. In the theory of this book there is an infinity of long-run, price-quantity solutions in any market, or no solution at all, although admittedly some solutions are more likely than others. My conclusion from this assessment of supply-demand curves is that they are so misleading as to be not only worthless in describing a market outcome, but inimical to understanding and progress. The curves are representative of General Equilibrium theory, which is a special case of the determination of prices and quantities in a market economic in which a long-run equilibrium solution of the supply and demand equations *may* exist, but in which the assumptions necessary are so peculiar as to make the theory irrelevant to applied economics. In order to move forward in understanding the economy, General Equilibrium theory with all its implications and assumptions is best abandoned as a particular case, worthy at most of a footnote (except in textbooks on the history of economic thought). (Barker, 1996: xxi, xxii)

Terry Barker was stating a judgement as formed and held over a career dedicated to applied macroeconomics, though these views are expressed in the Preface to his book *Space-Time Economics* published later in 1996. But these opinions—widely characteristic of the heterodox schools—were long-standing and no secret then or later, and the uncompromising honesty with which they are conveyed could not have endeared his candidature to Frank Hahn, then the field marshal conducting the Battle of General Equilibrium.

apply to return; or the free-thinking[56] Hashem Pesaran, the top-notch econometrician who did apply; or (heaven forbid) Ajit Singh, the leader of the Faculty left and the bête noir of the orthodox camp, but also an excellent applied economist with intimate knowledge and association with the DAE; or some serious and senior macro-modeller from another respected research organisation, say, the NIESR? After all, Wynne Godley had explicitly said that he could even contemplate someone from a rival unit appointed to the position if the appointment could be made quickly to avoid further erosion of DAE capacity due to further delays. Even before the DAE Review had been launched, Francis Cripps had reported on disturbing rumours afloat in university circles: "Regarding the DAE and the replacement of Wynne Godley when his term of office was up: Kaldor told me that the appointment had to be advertised and made as stated in the Statutes meaning that the left would control the outcome as usual. One day Wynne came to work and told me he had met Nichols [Ian Nicol], Secretary of the General Board, in the street by chance and Nichols told him the Statutes would be suspended and the usual election would not take place. Then we (DAE staff) heard there would be an inquiry, but we couldn't be represented or give evidence. That was it really. No one knew what to do as the General Board is a somewhat mysterious ruling body" (personal communication). And indeed, that is about the way it had unfolded.

The University Archives (of the transactions of the General Board) hold a Note that provides details of the approach of the General Board to the DAE directorship. Apropos the appointment of the new Director for a fixed term of fifteen years, but to hold a professorship till retirement after the end of the term, the Note records a procedural conundrum. "It would be unusual to have a Professorship with a limited tenure of a fixed number of years and all the other cases of this kind are one-year Professorships." Then, the bureaucrats dig deeper: "Nevertheless, the Statutes do allow for such an appointment and indeed Statute D, XIV,1(d)(iii) provides that in the case of 'any Professorship the tenure of which is ... [sic] limited to a specified number of years' the election shall be made by the General Board". Thus, a provision that ostensibly was generally used for one-year appointments is extended to a fifteen-year appointment; and this with the added bonus that the 'advisory committee' would be set up by the General Board, and not be a hostage to fortune as the outcome

---

[56] Andrew Harvey (2012: 3) writes about Hashem Pesaran: "Of his works, my personal favourite is *The Limits to Rational Expectations*, [Pesaran, 1987] which appeared in the 1980s and challenged the current orthodoxy. This was a brave move: he was actually warned that it might stop him ever getting a job in America. But of course he was right: although rational expectations provides important insights into economic behaviours, it can, when taken to extremes, become intellectually indefensible if not plain silly. Unfortunately, despite Hashem's efforts, far too much of modern macroeconomics still takes rational expectations too seriously and the folly of assuming that financial markets are efficient and self-regulating has been exposed by the events of recent years." Hashem Pesaran had published several critical articles previously in the 1980s on the theme of rational expectations, building up to this book which appeared around the time when he was turned down for the appointment for the Director of DAE.

of processes at the Faculty level, over which the General Board could not have control, and where, if Francis Cripps's reading was right, the left could be expected to hold sway. The Note then proceeds: "In such a case the Board would set up an advisory committee the size and compositions of which would be determined by the Board itself, although it would, no doubt, wish to consult the Faculty Board in deciding the membership". Further: "Such a procedure would replace the current standing Board of Electors, which at present consists of:

> Sir Kenneth Berrill
> Professor P.M. Deane
> Professor F.H. Hahn
> Professor R.C.O. Matthews
> Professor D.K. Stout
> Professor D.E.C. Wedderburn
> Mr K.J. Coutts
> Mr A. Hughes."[57]

With this composition, Hahn and Matthews might have found it quite an uphill, if not impossible, task to persuade the majority of the Committee to come down in favour of their preferred candidate, especially if the opposing applicant had just the credentials that they had been promoting, a card-carrying member of the top club of econometricians, say, like Hashem Pesaran. Of the externals, Berrill was indeed close to Kahn and Posner; but Stout was a solid applied economist, much in line with the interests and expertise of Alan Hughes, with little time for 'mathism' à la Hahn. And the redoubtable sociologist Dorothy Wedderburn would certainly not be for turning. Eric Hobsbawm tells us about her in the obituary he penned. "She was also a socialist, university principal, enemy of all self-advertisement and an untypical member of the community of 'the great and the good'." Her father was "a class-conscious trade unionist carpenter and joiner, and the grandfathers of both her parents were blacksmiths"; she rose from this background, did economics at Girton College, Cambridge, joined the Communist party, remaining there till the 1950s, and "remained steadily, if sometimes sceptically, loyal to the labour movement and the left"; she was a senior/research officer of the DAE for 15 years; she did not take a PhD, but was awarded honorary doctorates by Cambridge and six other

---

[57] General Board, 'Possible Restructuring of D.A.E.', DAE Paper 59, 2 June 1986; 5p; DAE Review Boxes. It is perhaps worth noting that while this Note is contained in the set of submissions to the Review Committee, this might not guarantee that it was circulated to all members of the General Board at that, or even a later, point of time. The members of the GB would of course have received the Final (or even some interim) Report of the Review Committee, but not necessarily all the paperwork behind it. For instance, it would be unlikely that this Note, 'Possible Restructuring of the D.A.E.', might have been seen by Alan Hughes, then Chair of the Faculty Board of Economics and Politics, and also the representative on the General Board itself; Alan Hughes was very much a leading figure on the heterodox side of the Faculty divide, and therefore generally in opposition, rather than allied, to the Hahn-Matthews campaign against the DAE.

universities; she rose to become Professor of Industrial Sociology at Imperial College; she served on various significant national committees and commissions, "quietly refusing the title offered in such cases". Hobsbawm asks: "Why Labour governments made so little use of a social policy expert so deeply committed to the labour movement puzzled many. In the 1960s she may have been considered too radical. In the era of Tony Blair, Downing Street had no enthusiasm for politically unreliable academic intellectuals" (Hobsbawm, 2012).[58] And in the 1980s, she would have been at the top of her game; no pushover then for Hahn and/or Matthews whether at their best or their worst. The closing score line could probably be expected to read 5–3, or more likely 6–2.

The final section of this strategic Note of the General Board is remarkable for its clarity of purpose, and for the explicit confirmation that the game was being played along the moves prescribed by Matthews the chess master:

> The requirement that a guarantee that sufficient funding is available before an appointment or reappointment can be made could, if combined with a change in the regulations for the Committee of Management (on the lines suggested in paragraphs 7 and 8) leave the control of applications for external grants clearly in the hands of the Director, give him greater power to determine the membership of the Department. The exercise of such powers in relation to officers who had been in the Department for, say, ten years or more would require considerable toughness on the part of the Director and would be likely to generate a great deal of unpleasantness and controversy, because the status of being a University officer creates a feeling of some independence and certain expectations of continuity. These problems would be eased if the research workers employed on short term contracts dependent entirely upon external funding held unestablished posts rather than University offices. There seems to be no reason under the present regulations why a new Director should not make such appointments if he wished, gradually reducing the number of officers in the Department. The *maximum* [emphasis in the original] number of officers in the Department is determined by the University but this need not be changed until such time as practice had led to a situation where there were very few officers, except perhaps for two or three SRO's (who might be converted into ADR's) who might be team leaders. Thus the Department could evolve towards the model favoured by Professor Matthews without it being necessary to change the regulations, other than the change of the Committee of Management into an advisory committee. (General Board, 'Possible Restructuring of D.A.E.', DAE Paper 59: 4–5)

A reminder might be appropriate that neither Professor Matthews, nor Professor Hahn, were members of this Review Committee (RC-II); but it

---

[58] Elsewhere, Hobsbawm wrote, Dorothy Wedderburn "whom I got to know after the war was to become and remain an intimate friend of Marlene and myself" was the younger sister of George Barnard of St. John's, who was "the student Party's chief local commissar at the time ... a lean-and-hungry-looking mathematician from a working-class family ... who ended his career as President of the Royal Statistical Society and in a chair at Essex University" (Hobsbawm, 2002: 116). For another sensitive and affectionate contemporary recollection, see Sen (2021, pp. 310–311).

might appear that, with their generous external advice and suggestions, they did not need to be in order to orient the outcomes of the committee in their desired direction.

All this, with the proviso, of course, that the Director on whose part "considerable toughness would be required" was in agreement with "the model favoured by Professor Matthews"; no pressure, then, to ensure that 'the right person' was appointed Director! This clear statement of intent and rationale, or the endgame plan for evolving towards the Hahn-Matthews 'model', is dated June 1986, and surely would have taken some time to evolve itself, indicating that the RC-II had been working towards this design more or less from the time it took up its assignment in Easter term, 1985, that is, the plan appears to have been pre-meditated.

Of course, the status of this Note is that of an internal document of the DAE RC-II, and its title refers to 'possible restructuring'—is this how things came to pass? This Review Committee would submit its report to the General Board, which in turn would again carefully consider matters before making its own final report and recommendations to the University, the final port of call. The answer is to be found in the Final Report of the General Board, processed by the University draughtsman and sent to press on 1 April 1987. The General Board's report clearly confirms the plan and fills in some operational detail. Conclusion #8 of the General Board reads:

> The Board believes that the most appropriate way to proceed to making an appointment to the proposed Professorship is for them to establish an advisory committee consisting of three members nominated by the Faculty Board of Economics and Politics and five nominated by the General Board. The advisory committee would consider applications and would advise the Board on the choice of a suitable person for appointment. The Board would then report again to the University recommending the establishment of a Professorship for a named person, and its assignment in the Department of Applied Economics.

And as agreed, this professor would concurrently also hold the position of Director of the DAE for a fixed tenure of fifteen years. Thus, the General Board confirmed its effective control over the outcome of the process, since its five nominees could override the three from the then recalcitrant Faculty Board.[59]

With the assiduous efforts of Robin Matthews and Frank Hahn, the script, stage and set were in place, but the performance was apparently not without a sense of suspense, though perhaps not surprise. The vacancy induced a strong response from within and beyond Cambridge. At this point, the storyline turns

---

[59] More likely, the Faculty Board's nominations would almost definitely include one name that could be expected to side with the Hahn-Matthews camp. Thus, for the Hahn-Matthews plan to be adopted, just three other persons from the slate of five nominated by the General Board would need to agree to take the matter to a casting vote by the Chair of the advisory committee appointed by the General Board itself; given the General Board's clarity of purpose, its nominations would more likely ensure a 6–2, or 5–3, rather than a 4–4, result.

away from the formal pronouncements of the Review Committee, the General Board and the University, and enters the talkative ambience of the Faculty corridors and tearoom where diverse narratives get passed down adding to the rich genre of folklore. Widely shared local knowledge had Hashem Pesaran and David Newbery as leading and competing contenders. One rendition[60] speaks of the alarm supposedly felt by Hahn, then away from Cambridge, on learning of internal rivalries within 'the family' leading to some notable exclusions from what was thought to be the short list[61]—a discovery that seemingly drew him back to get everything back to the script.

Information about the appointment process for the DAE Director-Professor position is understandably unavailable, though it is possible to reconstruct a timeline that is 'interesting'. The procedure to be followed was laid down by the General Board which had unusually taken up the authority to make the selection and recommendation to the University; the announcement of the post was delayed till 1987 and applications were being received in August; references taken up shortly thereafter in September; and the appointment made in 1988. The GB Note that announces the procedure is dated 2 June 1986. At this point, Hashem Pesaran, supposedly one of the main contenders and on multiple sources the runner-up, was a reader, appointed in 1985.

In 1985, David Newbery was a lecturer. Prima facie, it would seem improbable to the lay person that Newbery as a lecturer could have jumped over Pesaran, a reader, to the winning line. But that presumption could easily be overturned, depending on the profiles of the candidates, particular attributes being sought by the selectors and the criteria used for assessing quality. Then the wheel of fortune turns and Newbery is promoted to reader in October 1986, just as university business resumes after the summer break, the promotion coming just four months after the GB Note of June 1986; Newbery and Pesaran are now at par in terms of rank, both readers. Finally, the professorship goes to Newbery in early 1988; but as it happens, Pesaran also winds up with a professorship, an ad hominem chair announced in quick time on 5 May 1988.

Pesaran, on the assumption that he was indeed a candidate as was widely understood in local circles, and Newbery were both highly qualified and competent economists, but their orientation, bag of skills, institutional embedding and research agendas were widely different. Some speculative simulations could

---

[60] This story does not breach the usual confidentiality that attaches to the inner workings of an Appointments Committee—it merely refers to things happening outside it in open space. How seriously this should be taken depends much on how 'folklore' is assessed as a source of knowledge. That said, the broad story does meet the usual journalists' test requiring two converging sources.

[61] Of course, the standard stratagem for pre-empting an 'undesired' but strong candidate from being appointed is to keep that name altogether off the shortlist; on this speculative account, Hahn is said to have intervened to counter such a move in the case of his favoured candidate. Incidentally, Terry Barker was another very credible internal candidate: he had taken over as Director of the Cambridge Growth Project and enjoyed the strong support of his eminent predecessor, Sir Richard Stone who had won the 'Nobel' Economics Prize in 1984, and whose strong support he enjoyed. (Personal communication)

tease out what might have been at stake. Hypothetically, what if Pesaran had got the DAE position? While his stature as a top-flight econometrician and credibility for the post were widely acknowledged, he would most likely have broadly sustained the extant DAE research portfolio, and not been predictably responsive to, or hold shared theoretical affinities with, the research agendas or methodological approaches of the orthodox mainstream; Pesaran was in the Stone mould; it could be hypothesised that under him there would have been a change of guard, but no discernible change of regime. Pesaran had also been a close collaborator in the macroeconomic modelling teams of the DAE and perhaps not readily amenable to jettisoning that cumulative intellectual capital and research capacity. Of course, it is impossible to learn what criteria the selection committee, howsoever composed, used. Given Hashem Pesaran's unquestionable academic strength, it could be a reasonable hypothesis that the selectors might have placed some premium on the aspect of the disciplinary orientation of the candidates. Be it as it may, it was David Newbery, the neoclassical applied microeconomist, who was appointed. But some kind of a saddle point seems to have been discovered by the powers that made these decisions: Newbery got the post of DAE Director-cum-Professor, and the well-respected Hashem Pesaran was rewarded with an ad hominem chair announced very soon thereafter.[62] Viewed from the vantage point of the orthodox group, the imperative perhaps was to establish control over the future structure and direction of the DAE; in the end, all was well, Newbery was ensconced in his chair as the new Director, and the Hahn-Matthews orthodox group could not really have hoped for a more congenial outcome than the one that emerged after the long drawn-out, much-contested process.

It is striking that of the eight specific items in its Terms of Reference to which RC-II 'are asked to pay special attention', the issue of directorship and the Management Committee of the DAE do not get a mention. In contrast, the Review Committee and the General Board turn out to be focussed almost exclusively on these two dimensions—answering presumably to the general direction concerning 'a flexible and efficient framework for future research in Economics and related fields'. The related field of Sociology is listed as Item 7 in the ToR, and this item is explicitly addressed, leading to the recommendation that the DAE sociologists should find another home—something the Hahn-Matthews group had vehemently demanded, and which virtually the entire body of heterodox economists both in the Faculty and in the DAE had passionately opposed.

The orthodox group got the three key results they wanted: a Director of their choice; far greater powers for the Director, through the replacement of

---

[62] It is worth noting that the procedure for ad hominem chairs is heavily dependent on the support of the professoriate of the Department/Faculty. In Economics at the time, the professoriate comprised Frank Hahn, Robin Matthews, Partha Dasgupta, Willy Brown, Wynne Godley, Barry Supple (Professor Economic History) and Tony Giddens (Professor of Sociology). If Giddens, as a sociologist, kept out of such economists' frays, Godley could have been generally expected to be outvoted 5 or 6 to 1 on such matters if he disagreed.

the Committee of Management by a toothless Advisory Body; and the expulsion of the group of sociologists, who tended to vote with the heterodox group in the Faculty Board elections, much to their frustration. The Review Committee's report, and subsequently also that of the General Board, largely washes its hands of the other items of the Terms of Reference, leaving those matters to be resolved by the new Director as he saw fit.

As decided through the Review, the Committee of Management of the DAE was abolished with the appointment of the new Director who now held executive authority, aided by an Advisory Committee that comprised nominees and appointees from close to a dozen constituencies. Included in this list are some of 'the usual suspects', Frank Hahn, Robin Matthews, Tony Atkinson and John Flemming, each of whom had recently been members of committees that had led to the demise of various elements of the DAE. Sociologists were not represented since they had emigrated, as desired, to SPS. Under the new institutional arrangement of DAE governance, the incoming Director would only be obliged, metaphorically speaking, to offer a cup of tea to the Advisory Board and hear them out, and then would be formally free, if he so wished, to do more or less as he pleased. So in the end, as in a folk tale replete with happy coincidences, everything fits and falls conveniently into place—quite by chance, no doubt—and everybody who remains alive lives happily ever after. The orthodox mainstream group could now set about fashioning the future of the DAE in its new incarnation as visualised through neoclassical microeconomics spectacles—rubbed clean of heterodox macroeconomics and associated modelling; still applied economics, yes, but incrementally predominantly within a micro and a neoclassical frame.[63] For Hahn, Matthews, Dasgupta & Co., the battle against heterodox applied macroeconomics had been won, and they came out of the transitional decade of the 1980s far stronger than they had been before; they had effectively wrested control of the bastion of DAE.

---

[63] Some qualification is essential here: for one, some of the microeconomic applied economics research in corporate and industrial economics, as exemplified by the oeuvre of Ajit Singh, Alan Hughes and Andy Cosh was far from being neoclassical—thus the micro-neoclassical binary breaks down, as also in so many other instances of other research on industrial economics, including Sraffa (1926) for instance. Likewise, 'macro' takes different, often oppositional forms, for example, Cambridge (post-)Keynesians as against the American synthetic versions. It is also inappropriate to classify economists as being exclusively 'micro' or 'macro', and again the cases of Ajit Singh and Alan Hughes, amongst others, serve as good examples; in 1987, the final year of the DAE before Newbery took over as Director, they were working on a WiDER project on Global Macroeconomics. This also qualifies Leijonhufvud's (1973: 331) reductionist binary conflating micro with 'right' and macro with 'left' is his engaging allegory on the tribe of Econ: "It is reported that the Macro belittle the prospecting of the Micro among themselves saying that the Micro 'can't keep from gazing right'. The Micro, on their side, claim the Macro 'gaze left'. No one has offered a sensible hypothesis to account for this particular piece of liturgical controversy. Chances are that far-fetched explanations are out of place and that this should simply be accepted as just another hum-drum example of the continual bickering among the Econ."

9.4.4 Checkmate: A Constitutional Coup

What then were the outcomes? Who were the victors, who the vanquished; what was gained, what lost? Some answers are fairly clear to see; others lie in the eye of the beholder.

Alan Hughes was in the thick of things: he was simultaneously the Chair of the Faculty Board, and the representative of the Faculty Group (that included Economics) on the General Board of the Faculties which had set up the Review Committee and which would receive its Final Report. He was also much present and liked in both the DAE and Faculty Common Rooms as he had projects on the DAE side of the building while holding a Lectureship on the Faculty side. He was also part of the left group, and hence privy to its perspectives, information and strategies. His assessment of the balance sheet of outcomes therefore carries weight.

In his reading, the Hahn-Matthews-Dasgupta group got far less out of the Review than they would have wished or might have strongly expected at the start of the process. He identifies three objectives of "the agenda of the mainstream critics". First: "to remove DAE staff from voting in Faculty Board Elections"; second: "to discredit the research reputation of the DAE with a view to moving it back towards more mainstream research and publication in so called core journals"; and third: "to gain control over DAE reserves to increase the number of Faculty posts and to gain control over top floor rooms allocated to DAE and its specialist Library".[64]

He does not comment on the second, but firmly feels that the first and third objectives were not met; that the changes made to the DAE organisational and management structure were "entirely sensible", and it was a "perfectly reasonable outcome"; and that "the DAE critics failed in their core objective of removing DAE staff from Faculty membership and Board voting". Relatedly, the procedures for the appointment and reappointment of ROs and JROs in the DAE were amended along 'perfectly reasonable' lines, and the actual outcome of the Review made virtually no difference on the ground.

Thus, his bottom-line verdict is that the structural changes effected were good and sensible; and that the mainstream group's strategy to remove DAE staff from the Faculty voting lists did not materialise. And with regard to the third, money-and-space objective, Alan notes that David Newbery fought off this attempt, and it only happened fifteen years later when Newbery's term ended and the DAE as an independent entity was closed down. It can be added to this, that Newbery himself was apparently not in favour of the disappearance of the DAE through its absorption into the Faculty when he retired in 2003, and there is little reason, or evidence, to question this point.

Prima facie, then, in Alan Hughes's reading, nothing much really changed significantly, except the Director, and the Committee of Management being replaced by a differently constituted Advisory Committee. And of course, a

---

[64] Personal communication from Alan Hughes; email dated 13 August 2021.

formal Review was not out of order and well within the power of the General Board to institute, especially at the end of Godley's term.

Was it, then, not the perfect storm, but really just a four-year storm in a teacup? It depends. Alan is quite justified in taking satisfaction from a job, his job, well done. One paradox which arises is that if all these sensible and reasonable changes were all that was intended by the mainstream, why should it have taken four years, with the Review Committees contorting and tying themselves in all sorts of knots, generating extreme anxiety, insecurity and hostility between university bodies and the academic staff under review? Why could the motivation, objectives and terms of references of the Review not have been laid out and discussed in an open manner expediting a timely and quick process of cooperative implementation of the University with the Director and staff of the DAE on the one side, and the Faculty Board and staff on the other?

As might be viewed within Alan's broad assessment,[65] that it all ended much more satisfactorily than perhaps was intended by the antagonists might then be due to the sustained resistance that the more extreme (not so) hidden agendas encountered from DAE and Faculty staff, and the growing realisation within the university decision-making bodies that the mainstream antagonists had their own axes to grind and were manipulating these bodies into outcomes outside the stated formal objectives of the review. The university authorities might well have been panicked by all the reds-under-the-bed talk and overreacted. In this scenario, a perfect storm might well have been averted, and the resistance of the DAE and the Faculty heterodox, radical groups, effectively mobilised in the Faculty and DAE by harnessing the 'left' leadership, prevented the worst outcomes; in this resistance, Alan Hughes, in his formal capacity first as Chairman of the Faculty Board and then as representing its position in the General Board, might have been a highly significant factor. So there would be all the more reason for him, along with the band of Faculty radicals to which he then belonged, to take a bow.

However, even very largely accepting Alan's assessment, there remain other perspectives to consider, and the DAE Review episode might be viewed in different colours when hypothesised as part of a larger frame of an unfolding campaign by what Alan refers to as "the mainstream critics", that is, the Hahn-Matthews-Dasgupta triumvirate, itself seen in articulation with its wide circuits of well-embedded peers and followers. Yes, the DAE survived and was not shut down, as was the bizarre talk at some stage of the Review; but it was effectively taken over, captured by the mainstream by the end of the Review process, culminating in the appointment—through the necessary selection procedures—of one of its prime members as the new Director. Yes, the DAE research officers could carry on voting in the Faculty Elections; but very many had left when the CEPG had been shut down earlier through the attentions of the same mainstream formation in Cambridge and beyond; and the CGP team was also

---

[65] The description of Alan's assessment is based on an interview and email communications with him in August.

simultaneously under attack through a parallel process, a déjà vu rerun of the earlier CEPG-SSRC episode, this time at the hands of the ESRC. The departure of the majority of the members of these two teams would already meet the objective of cutting out DAE research staff from voting in Faculty elections, so there wasn't too much remaining to fight for in this regard. And yes, the DAE kept its money and rooms; but that would be quite the right thing if the unit as a whole was captured. And yes, indeed, the new Director was extremely supportive of Alan Hughes in setting up an interdisciplinary research unit within the DAE with external funding, and in making large grant applications to the ESRC (where he (David Newbery) had been an Economics Committee member in the last round till he became Director DAE); but which incoming Director in his right mind would have wished to expel Alan's well regarded research outfit, all the more since it focussed primarily on microeconomic themes not smacking of any overt leftist Keynesian agenda? That said, it is right to record the consistent backup that David Newbery, as Director of DAE, extended, and Alan Hughes points out that "I was only able to secure funding because David Newbery was willing to commit DAE rooms and support for the grant applications that ultimately were successful" (Personal communication).

But over the 1980s leading up to the appointment of the new Director of the DAE, in the coordinated internal and/or external assaults on the DAE and its component units, two of its flagship projects were shut down, and these together involved more than half the research staff; the group of sociologists and some of the labour economists also wound up leaving; with it, the multidisciplinary orientation of the DAE, while not obliterated, was weakened and reoriented. The erstwhile practice of applied macroeconomics with its close engagement with national policy issues was effectively was killed off. Emphasising these very significant losses of cumulative intellectual and academic assets does not really amount to 'totemisation'—the macroeconomic tradition of the DAE was unquestionably a profound one, and its destruction—at least in its long-running Stone-Barker and Godley-Cripps incarnations—was arguably a first-order loss. That era of radical, structural engagement with macroeconomic transformation and policy was effectively at an end.

This in no way diminishes the value of the applied microeconomic research that Robin Marris, Ajit Singh and Geoff Whittington had variously pioneered in the DAE, and which had been carried to a stage of high maturity by Alan's remarkably productive initiative in the form of the Centre of Business Research that he located in the DAE with Newbery's support. The loss of CEPG and CGP could not but have left gaping holes in the DAE research and staff profile. These spaces needed to be filled, and urgently. Any new Director would have been delighted to recognise the worth of Alan's offerings, supported them and drawn institutional benefit and kudos, especially in such a difficult transition; and all the more so when the new Director was widely known to be under sustained pressure even from other sections of the orthodox branch of the Faculty, from a rival section that would have wished the Faculty to claim the material resources of the DAE in the form of its space, rooms and money.[66] Alan Hughes recalled that "David Newbery was under pressure to stop supporting the CBR and kick it out", and it goes much to his credit that "he consistently resisted that pressure" (Personal communication). But the CBR unit did leave for the JBS, perhaps because it had reached the limits of infrastructural or institutional possibilities within the DAE. At the Judge Business School, the CBR is described as "an interdisciplinary research centre linking Economics, Law, Geography, Engineering, Social and Political Sciences, and Land Economy, with Management Studies";[67] this hub of multidisciplinarity came to be located in the JBS, not within the Faculty of Economics or the DAE.

Newbery was a neoclassical applied microeconomist, and over time, the composition of DAE research and staff would shift inexorably in that direction as the new Director stamped his own research vision and agenda on the unit—this had always been so at DAE as part of the reorientation of the research and staff profile subsequent to the arrival of a new Director. And indeed, as it did, the identity and orientation of the teams of DAE researchers would steadily be transformed; and the new cohorts of micro, neoclassically oriented researchers would vote with the orthodox side in Faculty elections; and so, the objectives of the orthodox camp would be achieved anyway even if through a somewhat different route. To a large extent, the key was to obtain control over the DAE resources and its direction, and the Hahn-Matthews group was eminently successful in this regard.

This would become plain by considering a counterfactual: how might things have gone if another left-wing applied economist, say such as the accomplished Ajit Singh, or another eminent econometrician such as Hashem Pesaran, or (as Wynne Godley has alluded to) a leader of one of the DAE macro-modelling competitors such as the NIESR or LBS, or one of the two accomplished seniors of the high-profile macro teams, viz., Francis Cripps of the CEPG or Terry Barker of the CGP, had taken over as the next Director? The story of Cambridge heterodox economics might then have evolved significantly differently.

The neoclassical squad would have become aware very early on in the game that outright closure of the DAE was the worst option, as the DAE resources would almost definitely have reverted to the University; and the option of a separate sub-Faculty might have meant, analogously with the precedent of the

---

[66] Confirmation of this aspect comes later: at the point of the end of David Newbery's tenure as Director, the General Board conducted another Review of the DAE where it stated its decision to close it down. The General Board's Report then states that "the separate offices of Senior Research Officer, Research Officer, and Junior Research Officer in the Department would be abolished; the remaining research, administrative, and assistant staff of the DAE will be assimilated into the Faculty on terms equivalent to those of their current posts. ... *The Department's substantial accumulated reserves would also be available for deployment at the discretion of the Faculty Board*, subject to meeting any outstanding commitments entered into by the Department" (Cambridge University General Board 2004; emphasis added). Such predatory motives were also alluded to by Alan Hughes, as mentioned earlier, as one element of the objectives of the mainstream group.

[67] https://www.jbs.cam.ac.uk/faculty-research/centres/business-research/.

SPS sub-Faculty, that Faculty bosses might not have been able to control it, especially if the idea was to exclude these new sub-Faculty members from the Faculty elections. The only real options were full-scale absorption as equals, which would have made for a very messy transition at the time, and led to an extreme counterproductive outcome by ensconcing the DAE vote bank within the Faculty; or of capture, through selecting their own Director, and with some organisational changes that nudged the control over various appointments procedures in the direction of the Faculty increasingly controlled, at the senior levels, by the orthodox mainstream group—and this indeed is what did happen to a large extent.

Another outcome that cannot be overlooked is that the appointment of David Newbery expanded the triumvirate running Cambridge economics into a G4—a group of four in the lexicon of international politics, or a 'gang-of-four' for those deploying the more colourful Chinese political parlance—albeit not without some internal dissensions between its junior members; and since promotions to *ad hominem* readerships and professorships were heavily influenced by the professoriate, this change would clearly give greater leverage to the mainstream critics in their drive to clean out what Dasgupta had called the 'cesspool' of 'mediocrity' in the Faculty[68]—and that was their next line of attack. Indeed, promotions of heterodox economists, macro or micro, theory or applied, were systematically and wilfully blocked on grounds of quality as perceived and measured by the orthodox mainstream tradition. Alan, as the Director of the CBR which was set up as a new University Department physically located in the DAE, received a professorial salary and fully bought out his Lectureship; his full professorship came when he won the open competition for the Margaret Thatcher chair *outside* the Faculty. That his research units had been shoring up the DAE, and holding up the Faculty from exercising the option of absorption, became evident after he emigrated, with his well-resourced Centre and his big-sized team, to the Judge Business School after further funding, to the tune of around GBP 1 million was secured to refurbish space in the JBS building to house the CBR staff.[69] Reportedly, this departure, incidentally, was generally perceived by the residual heterodox economists of the Faculty as a turning point after which the orthodox school had a virtually unrestrained control over all decision-making matters without any pressing constraint for making any concessions or compromises. None of this reduces the institution-protecting, and building, contributions of Alan Hughes within and outside the DAE, but these successes, howsoever viewed, do not conflate with success for heterodox economics at Sidgwick Site, where the loss of control of the DAE and the decimation of its macroeconomic units constituted a

---

[68] The provenance of the term is the interview of Partha Dasgupta by Alan Macfarlane; for the original context of its usage in this interview, see Dasgupta (2010).

[69] Alan Hughes points out that "this amount of funding is an indication in itself of the degree of support and accommodation that David Newbery had been providing up to that point" (Personal communication).

point of inflexion, another bend in the road leading to the domination of neoclassical orthodoxy in the Faculty, the epicentre of Cambridge economics. Attention could now turn to the two residual strains of undisciplined impurities: the heterodox, and the radical development economists within the Faculty. Their demise or departure is what happened next, in different ways but not entirely by accident, and not always by volition. These stories follow.

9.5 Epilogue

The 50th Anniversary of the founding of the DAE was marked in 1995 with a conference leading to an eclectic volume involving persons and papers spanning the work of the DAE over the years (Begg & Henry, 1998). David Newbery, halfway through his tenure as Director, shared his views on the future of Enterprise DAE, and on its past as viewed from the present (Newbery, 1998: xix–xxii). The value of the prominence comes from its provenance.

With regard to the origins, Newbery says that "the idea of setting up a Department of Applied Economics, originally floated in 1939, was to provide the empirical research support for the theoretical advances in macroeconomics pioneered in Cambridge by Keynes" (ibid.: xix–xx). This reconstruction of the *raison d'etre* and subsequent life of the DAE returns the narrative to the beginning, both of the DAE and of this trilogy. While applied Keynesian macroeconomics was indeed a central concern, the DAE's research objectives were far wider, as is readily confirmed from the early years of its evolution. But having ascribed this identity to early DAE, Newbery says, times have changed: "the old Keynesian macro certainties may have faded as barriers to trade, communications and financial arbitrage have been eroded, but these same changes have increased the prominence of research into microeconomics, which flourishes with better data, better theory, and fewer impediments to market behaviour" (ibid.: xxi). So we can read from this that the old macroeconomics agenda is passé, has passed and has been buried; thus, post-Keynesian applied macroeconomics stands dismissed. In its place come two agendas that define the modern DAE's research agenda.

The first of these harks back to years even prior to the DAE; having walked away from Keynes, paternity is sought in the early econometrics work of and under Stone (ibid.: xx, emphasis added):

> The early report of the Department set out the objectives very clearly and they remain valid today. They were:
>
> (i) to restate economic theories and principles in a form which will allow them to be **tested** empirically
> (ii) to collect together such relevant observations as have been made and to make others which are required in order that empirical **tests** may be applied
> (iii) to develop the necessary statistical and other tools for the **testing** of economic hypotheses

(iv) actually, to make the **test**, using either the new tools and data already mentioned or those proved by others working in the same field.

Thus, the spotlight is shifted from Keynesian macroeconomics to the econometrics of inference testing as Newbery highlights econometric theory and techniques—an area in which the DAE indeed excelled, but from which even Stone himself progressively moved away, increasingly towards applied econometrics engaging directly with contemporary policy issues and longer-term structural change. In this, the Stone agenda remained very much within the broad rubric of Keynesian macroeconomics, and this remained in the forefront all the way through till Stone retired. It is worth recalling that the citation of Stone's Nobel award highlights his work in the development of the concept and methodology of national income accounts. In his appreciation for his former Director, one of the original cohort of the DAE, Graham Pyatt reflects on the hallmarks of his former Director's intellectual orientation and contributions.

> Among the pioneers of econometrics (he was elected a Fellow of the Econometric Society in 1938 and President in 1955) Stone was first and foremost an empiricist. In a little-known paper, *The a priori and the empirical in economics,* Stone argues that there is more than one way of approaching most problems in economics. His personal preference for an empirical approach may be even less fashionable to-day than it was twenty years ago. Yet it did not prevent Stone from making important contributions to econometrics, to multi-sector modelling and to socio-demographic analysis. The essential point is that Richard Stone believed in a methodology that started with the facts, that recognised the need for conceptual frameworks to organise the collection and presentation of those facts, and for the formal analysis of the facts in order to draw inferences from them. His contributions to the second phase of this approach constitute his outstanding achievements. But they need to be appreciated in the context of the whole. The fact that others have not had to reinvent the architecture of the national accounts in particular is perhaps the most telling measure of the importance of Richard Stone's contributions and their enduring significance. (Pyatt, 2005)

"I am not an economic theorist", he said; Stone's deep and sustained affinity with the empiricist tradition is apparent in the sketches he did of the lives and works of a dozen eminent British empiricists in the social sciences starting from William Petty in 1650, running through till 1900, including Charles Booth, and Florence Nightingale—"twelve people whom for one reason or another I find particularly sympathetic"—portraits that formed the substance of his Raffaele Mattioli Lectures in 1986, and published posthumously in 1997.[70]

---

[70] The year 1997 also happened to be the bicentenary of the publication of *The State of the Poor* by Sir Frederick Morton Eden, a person and work included in Stone's dozen empiricists. Coincidentally, on the occasion of the landmark, an appreciation of Eden's work was independently produced by Graham Pyatt and Michael Ward, who refer to it as "a happy circumstance" (Pyatt & Ward, 1999: 19).

"The chief protagonists of my story came from all walks in life and had very different careers, but they had one thing in common: none of them had any formal training in the fields to which they contributed so much. Few of them went to university, and those who did studied subjects, such as medicine, astronomy and divinity, which had nothing to do either with economics or demography. As far as their contributions to these two disciplines are concerned, they are all twelve outstanding examples of the English amateur tradition" (Stone, 1997: xxi). It would be futile, if not puerile, to reduce Richard Stone's, and by proxy the early DAE's, professional imagination, orientation and objectives simply to theoretical econometrics and the development of tests of inference; it would then be quite disingenuous to justify the shift in the DAE's research direction after 1988 by harking back to the 'good old days' of Dick Stone when allegedly theoretical econometrics was king (mis)using Stone as a body shield for objectives and agendas that he might not have shared.

The second element of the new, post-1988, research agenda of the DAE understandably reflects the preferences of the new Director, though here it needs to be remembered that Reddaway had no such dominating personal research agenda that he imposed on the department, and that Stone was enjoined, and guided, by the Committee of Management to run a broad research shop embracing much more than his own preferred specialised fields of interest.

Newbery (ibid.: xxi): "My personal taste in economics is to start where theory and evidence sit most comfortably, at the level of the firm and consumer behaviour, and build up from there to model and understand the interactions of these players with each other and their economic environment, conditioned as that is by institutions and policy interventions. Whether it is privatisation in Britain, or the transition of Eastern Europe, macroeconomic behaviour is profoundly influenced by microeconomic performance, and a proper study of these large questions requires that these interactions be modelled and informed by evidence. ... Good examples of this would include the application of microeconometrics to tax reform and the study of transition." This is entirely valid and unquestionable as a personal statement of the research perspective of the new Director. However, Newbery goes on to claim that "In this I am following the spirit of the Stone Growth Project agenda of moving between micro and macro, both based on quantification and estimation". This seems to be a questionable reinvention of the Stone Growth Project, whose agenda, incidentally, had been systematically brought down through the chain of orthodox campaigns during the 1980s leading up to the University Review of the DAE, creating the circumstances for the selection and appointment of David Newbery himself as the new Director after Godley. No single theoretical tradition dominated the DAE or the Cambridge Growth Project, and it would be inappropriate to club it together with the core neoclassical vision of the macro as not much more than what emerges from the behaviour of microagents that constitute the economy. Having rejected old Keynesianism and having linked descent directly to the original theoretical econometrics of Stone, Newbery's words carry the implication that the Cambridge Growth Project could be read as a macro-aggregation based on microeconomic behavioural elements. However, the development of disaggregated macroeconomic models, under Stone and Barker, cannot be equated with the neoclassical vision of micro-to-macroeconomic theorising.

This vision is further elaborated: "Improved data and techniques together with advances in theory allow us to probe the previously obscure links between micro and macro and give greater coherence to the subject. An increased awareness of the importance of institutions, laws and customs of society, informed by game theory and the recognition that agents interact over time under incomplete information, has made us more receptive to the other social sciences, leading to increased collaboration across subject boundaries" (ibid.: xxi). It is indeed heartening to see that over time a rising awareness of the surrounding world as is might have opened the eyes and made the neoclassical mind "more receptive to other social sciences, leading to increased collaboration across subject boundaries". Such maturity, however belated, is all the more welcome when expressed from quarters that had vehemently argued the case for the expulsion of their sociology colleagues of the DAE and those from the Social and Political Sciences group in their drive for the purification of economics, referring to them as stray colleagues from what Newbery had referred to as "vaguely cognate disciplines".[71]

The massive inheritance of the accumulated intellectual capital of diverse applied Keynesian and other heterodox traditions of the DAE, and especially its CGP and CEPG teams, deserved to be acknowledged with a more inclusive and respectful requiem on such a landmark occasion.

Symbolically, 2004 was especially notable for Cambridge economics on several counts.

First, it was the final year of the once-iconic Department of Applied Economics, put down in its 60th year through squabbles within the now-orthodox Faculty. University authorities, after a review, were "concerned that ... the existence of a Department with a focus on research in applied economics, and operating separately from the main Faculty, does not facilitate the development of an integrated research programme, encompassing the full range of a modern economics department, and aspiring to the highest standards of excellence".[72] And so, the General Board recommended "that, with

---

[71] The phrase alludes to the term used by David Newbery is his comments to the General Board in the course of the DAE Review; for the context in which the term is originally used, see Chap. 9, p. 13.

[72] Unlike the procedurally disastrous Review of the DAE instituted by the University at the time of Godley's end of term as Director of the DAE, this time, "in anticipation of the end of Professor Newbery's tenure as Director and as part of their normal programme of Faculty and Departmental Review in 2001, the General Board constituted a Review Committee ... which received written submissions from the Faculty Board of Economics and Politics, and the Director of the Department. They also visited the Faculty and interviewed a wide range of the senior members of the Faculty, staff of the Department, and students. ... the Review Committee reported to the General Board in

effect from 1 October 2004, ... the Department of Applied Economics be suppressed, and that the existing functions of the Department be integrated with the Faculty of Economics" (Cambridge University General Board, 2004). Says Michael Kitson, a long-term standard bearer of the heterodox clans: "the death sentence to the DAE is a first-rate example of the vapid and disingenuous language deployed by some of the *apparatchiks* at Cambridge" (Kitson, 2005: 834).

Second, the Faculty formally recast its identity, from then on to be known purely as a Faculty of Economics having excised 'and Politics' from its long-standing title—a standard renaming sanskritising ritual followed by lower order castes looking to seek a rank promotion in the hierarchy by shedding a part of its name that revealed its original status; or as Michael Kitson (2005: 834) puts it, "with 'Politics' discarded as unwanted cumbersome appendage". The Report of the General Board to the University formally proposed the name change "in order to reflect more accurately the breadth [for breadth, read narrowness?] of the teaching and research interests that would be represented in the integrated Faculty". A century earlier, in 1903, Marshall had fought successfully to detach economics from its original moral sciences home and create the Economics Tripos, though the institutional context and academic motivations then were very different.

Third, to mark the centenary of the Economics Tripos, from the scattered heterodox constituency of Cambridge economics, the Cambridge Political Economy Society (CPES), also the publisher of the CJE, organised a landmark conference fittingly titled 'Economics for the Future', with a selection of papers then published in the CJE. In his introduction to the special issue, Michael Kitson (2005: 829) notes: "Cambridge Economics was originally grounded in moral philosophy, its *raison d'etre* was traditionally to understand why societies malfunction, and the devising of policies to offset the impact of malfunctioning and, especially, to protect those most vulnerable to their impact. The purpose of the conference was to build on this tradition by encouraging open dialogue amongst social scientists concerned about the future prospects for economics."

Fourth, the year 2004, most unusually, saw two eminent female historians break through that ceiling and take up chairs in economic history: Jane Humphries in Oxford, and Sheilagh Ogilvie in Cambridge. Jane had entered the Faculty as a Marxist, feminist economist and chose to leave when undervalued and blocked; Sheilagh, in contrast, was a Postanian historian and flourished in the same Faculty; arguably, their contrasting trajectories indirectly mirrored the change of regimes in the Faculty.

---

the Easter Term of 2003" (Cambridge University General Board, 2004). The Review Committee comprised an archaeologist, also head of a college, as Chair; a geographer, a lawyer and one mainstream economist with close career links to several senior members of the Faculty; in coming to academic judgements, say on research quality, the Review Committee would inevitably have to rely heavily on its economist member.

Fifth, in 2004, the sociologists—denigrated in the 1980s as those "stray colleagues from a vaguely cognate discipline"[73] and bade farewell from the DAE and the Faculty by the orthodox economists—finally established their identity as a regular Department of Sociology. Put together, these symbolic events serve as markers of the continued vibrancy of persons, units and lineages that were purged from the DAE and the Faculty by the mainstream orthodox group.

In more ways than one, the orthodox campaign was reaping the bitter harvest.

APPENDIX 9.1: DAE REVIEW COMMITTEES: COMPOSITION AND TERMS OF REFERENCE

First Advisory Committee. Constituted: Easter Term 1984; Reported: May 1985

> With the impending completion on 30 September 1985 by Professor Godley of fifteen years as Director of the Department, the Board decided in the Easter Term 1984 to conduct a further review of the arrangement for, and the role of, the Department. The Board accordingly agreed to set up an advisory Committee with the following terms of reference: to review the regulations for the Committee of Management of the Department of Applied Economics and for the Director, with a view to clarifying the relationship between the roles of both authorities; and to review the development of the Department within the Faculty of Economics and Politics and its relationship to work falling within the scope of the Social and Political Sciences Committee.
>
> The members of the Committee were Dr G.A. Reid, Professor B.E. Supple, and Mr D.E.C. Yale.
>
> At their first meeting the Committee agreed to consider the first part of the terms of reference with a view to making an interim report to the General Board with recommendations on these matters and to making proposals for a further review to consider the second part of the terms of reference.

[Extract; page 1, paragraph 2 from *Report of the General Board on the regulations for the Department of Applied Economics*, dated 3 June 1985. Signed by John Butterfield, Vice Chancellor on 29 May 1985.]

Second Advisory Committee: Constituted: Easter Term 1985; Reported April 1987

> The [1st] review Committee advised the Board that they were not themselves appropriately constituted to conduct a review of the development of the Department, and recommended that a larger Committee, including persons with

---

[73] The phrase alludes to the term used by David Newbery is his comments to the General Board in the course of the DAE Review; for the context in which the term is originally used, see Chap. 9, p. 13.

appropriate special knowledge who were not resident members of the University, should be constituted to carry out this more general review.

In the Easter Term 1985, the Board set up an *ad hoc* Committee with the following terms of reference:

To review the structure of the Department of Applied Economics within the Faculty of Economics and Politics and to make recommendations to ensure a flexible and efficient framework for future research in Economics and related fields. The Committee are asked to pay particular attention to the following:

(i) the size of the establishment of the Department in relation to the size and the establishment of the Faculty;

(ii) the financial contribution to the Department from University funds;

(iii) the ratio of senior to junior posts in the Department;

(iv) bearing in mind the various sources of funding likely to be available in the Department, the relative merits of the current system of established posts and those of a system including unestablished posts as in other Departments;

(v) the possible advantages and disadvantages of providing for short-term Visiting Fellowships;

(vi) the possible advantages and disadvantages of a situation whereby, as for the Director, there is a limit on the maximum number of years for which any individual is permitted to hold office in the Department;

(vii) the role of sociological research in the Department in the context of teaching and research in sociology in the University in general and of the Social and Political Sciences Committee in particular;

(viii) the contribution of the Department to the undergraduate and graduate teaching programmes of the Faculty.

The members of the Committee are:

Professor Sir Jack Lewis (Chairman), Professor A.B. Atkinson, Sir Kenneth Berrill, Professor D. Lockwood, Dr G.A. Reid, Professor D.K. Stout, and Mr D.E.C. Yale.

Appendix 9.2: Labour Studies Group: Dispersed, Not Defeated

The DAE in the 1970s and 1980s was the institutional home to a variety of research entities, most formed in the eclectic Reddaway tenure, but some emerging subsequently, a prime case being that of the Labour Studies Group. The dominant presence, undoubtedly, was that of the two formal macroeconomic teams, the Stone-Brown-Barker Cambridge Growth Project, and the Godley-Cripps Cambridge Economic Policy Group. Another group, especially in the early years, was Economic History, though once the national accounting data bases were done, the economic historians involved tended to shift to the Faculty or relocate outside Cambridge. Apart from this, there was a good deal of research in industrial economics mainly at this point done by Alan Hughes and Andy Cost, continuing the work in the 1960s with the large-scale work of Robin Marris, Ajit Singh and Geoff Whittington, and which led to the establishment of a distinct applied economics research unit on the industrial and corporate sector, led by Alan Hughes; this was the Centre for Business Research which later moved to the Judge Business School. Also, from the 1960s, there was the small Sociology group which had its own space and budget within the DAE, but which also drew in Cambridge sociologists who had college fellowships and who ran major research projects from within the DAE, with the focus here on David Lockwood, John Goldthorpe, Frank Bechhofer and Jennifer Platt for their celebrated research on The Affluent Worker. The Sociology group, headed by Bob Blackburn, had some affinity with the Industrial Relations lines of research led by Bert Turner, though they usually had distinct research projects. The youngest research team to emerge, in the Godley tenure, was the Labour Studies Group (LSG), a team name that is first visible in the 1979–1980 Annual Report of the DAE.

The Annual Reports of the DAE list its research projects under groups. The Stone tenure (ending 1955) is covered in the first four reports and the research portfolio comprises projects on quantitative economic research, including national, regional and social accounts, on the one side, and econometric testing methods, on the other side; there is virtually no mention of non-economics themes. Change is visible in the fifth report (1958–1964) with the arrival of Reddaway in 1955: while the primary focus remains on the economics group, three new clusters are listed separately—Studies in Economic History, Studies in Industrial Economics and Sociological Studies. The 1965–1966 Annual Report includes a group labelled as Industrial Relations, Sociology and Politics; and from 1966 to 1967 till 1975 to 1976, there is a stable label, Industrial Relations (IR) and Sociology. The following three years till 1978–1979 place the industrial relations projects under the umbrella label of economics, with a separate group entry for Sociology. In the IR area, Professor Bert Turner went on leave in 1976; Dudley Jackson and another IR researcher, L. J. Handy left the unit; and Frank had joined Godley's CEPG—thus creating a gap that partly induced the emergence of the LSG. For the first time, the title of Labour Studies Group is encountered in the Annual Report for 1979–1980. By the end of the 1980s, following the controversial and bruising DAE Review, key members of the LSG had moved away from the DAE or from Cambridge altogether. As such, the period of the formal operational existence of the LSG in the DAE can be bookended as the decade of the 1980s when the group was in full flow and establishing a reputation for itself in the academic, activist and policy circles.

The LSG was not formed at a stroke; rather, its distinctive identity emerged organically through funded research projects, initially from the Department of Employment, and other interactions and activities involving staff across DAE. From the 1976 till the mid-1980s, there was a core group of four: the earlies to join the DAE, as Research Officer;[74] 1970–1971 saw the arrival of

---

[74] She joined the DAE in the 1958–1964 period to work on a project on nutrition, but later worked with Dorothy Wedderburn, the notable DAE sociologist, followed by research with Bert Turner.

Frank Wilkinson and Roger Tarling, both as Research Officers; and Jill Rubery joined as a Research Associate in 1976–1977, the year that both Frank and Roger were promoted to Senior Research Officer. She became JRO in 1978–1979 and was then promoted to RO in 1979–1980 and to SRO in 1986–1987.[75] Meanwhile from 1985 to 1986, Brendan Burchell joined the group working in the ESRC-funded Social Change and Economic Life Initiative (SCELI) project along with the others. In March 1985 a Cambridge team was selected to participate in the ESRC's interdisciplinary Social Change and Economic Life initiative which involved the study of six local labour market areas in England and Scotland, each under the responsibility of a separate team, with the Cambridge team researching Northampton. The aim of the initiative was to study social change and economic life from an interdisciplinary perspective and through a range of different methods: from the perspective of employers, individuals and households, involving research by economists, sociologists, social psychologists and statisticians; and the research would have both a historical and a contemporary dimension, apart from cross-regional comparative analysis. The project involved several rounds of heavy data generation on the basis of a range of surveys. The team assembled at DAE included: Frank Wilkinson, Jill Rubery, together with Ray Jobling, Colin Fraser, Cathie Marsh, lecturers from Social and Political Sciences, while Brendan Burchell joined the DAE group as the main research officer in 1986.[76] Two linked research students, John Devereux and Sara Horrell, were also associated with the project.[77] This was a major research initiative which yielded long-term dividends in different forms going beyond the considerable list of project publications.

In their tribute to Frank Wilkinson, his erstwhile LSG colleagues emphasise a key epistemological and methodological contribution through the deployment of new forms of survey work. "Perhaps the most distinctive of these surveys were those in which employers, trade union officials and employees within the same organisation were interviewed, revealing their different perceptions of the reality in and beyond their places of work; this method was pioneered by the Cambridge team in the SCELI initiative in the 1980s ... and repeated in the 1990s Rowntree project on job insecurity and work intensity ... which were followed with other more modest surveys on professions ... and on trust. The fieldwork typically involved travelling to workplaces around the UK

---

[75] All four participated in the Department of Employment projects from 1976 to 1982 (joined also by a Cambridge sociologist, Elizabeth Garnsey, who moved to a lectureship at the management school, later the JBS, in 1984).

[76] Roger Tarling's name appears on the list of project staff, and that of Elizabeth Garnsey in the authors of publications attached to the project entry in the DAE Annual Report of 1985–1986.

[77] The entry for the project in the DAE Annual Report (1985–1986: 22) names Bob Blackburn and Ken Prandy as 'Associate Members'; however, there is no mention of their names in the details of the tasks and publications of this project. The relationship between the Sociology and the Labour Studies Groups, while collegial, was apparently not one displaying natural intellectual synergy.

to interview both bosses and employees on their attitudes to and experiences of topics such as job insecurity, pay, training, bargaining, trust, and the intensification of work" (Rubery et al., 2022); also for details of researchers and publications arising from the work).[78]

Belying its small size, LSG was also institutionally well embedded. During the period, Frank and Jill were members of the DAE Committee of Management representing the DAE staff constituency, Frank from as early as 1972–1973 till 1981–1982, a period when all was relatively calm, and Jill from 1984 to 1985 when DAE had entered a zone of buffeting turbulence.[79] In the mid-1970s, Frank joined Wynne Godley's CEPG, with contributions to its CEPR, alongside Roger Tarling who had come with Wynne Godley from the Treasury (where the two had worked together) when the CEPG was set up and worked on LSG projects (alongside his work in the CEPG) from 1976 onwards. Frank was also one of the founding group of young turks who set up the CJE in 1977, eventually becoming a Patron of the journal till his demise in 2021; Roger Tarling was also a member of the Editorial Board from the start in 1977; Jill Rubery joined soon after in 1980, with Brendan Burchell and Simon Deakin, an outstanding Cambridge lawyer with interests in both labour and corporate law, and a close associate of the LSG also joining as CJE editors from 1993. Simon continued to be a key collaborator with Frank both on labour rights issues and in the Centre for Business Research that he now leads after Alan's retirement.

Outside Cambridge, Frank was also a founder of the Institute of Employment Rights (IER), also a passionate and lasting commitment resonating with the early trajectory of his own life;[80] and from the 1980s, he had a welcome space in Alan Hughes's CBR where he was an Assistant Director for a number of years after it was founded, a position he held alongside his Readership in the DAE; even after retirement, he maintained his active research relationship with CBR by when it had institutionally relocated to the Judge Business School.[81] From the mid-1980s, Frank developed a close research network in USA at Notre Dame, Indiana, manifest in much joint work into his post-retirement years with Suzanne Konzelmann (who moved to Cambridge around 2000) and Chuck Craypo.[82] Rubery et al. (2022 CJE) provide a

---

[78] Worthy of mention here is the earlier work, also based on intensive surveys, on the working class by Lockwood, Goldthorpe, Bechhofer and Platt focussing on Luton in the 1960s which carried a similar depth and sensitivity in its exploration of working-class lives, though with a different set of research questions to pursue; their field methodology was also pioneering in its time and was part of their iconic series on *The Affluent Worker*.

[79] Both Frank and Jill also served for terms on the Faculty Board.

[80] On this, see Deakin and Ewing (2021).

[81] Personal communication: email dated 3 December 2021.

[82] The connection with Notre Dame was made under the department leadership there of Chuck Craypo with whom also Frank had a research collaboration (Craypo & Wilkinson, 2011). Jill Rubery notes that the link was forged in part because Frank's Ph.D. student Ned Lorenz took a job there; she also spent one semester as a visiting professor there in 1989. The link between Notre

detailed and sensitive appreciation of Frank Wilkinson's approach, involvements and contributions.

The oeuvre of the LSG is a rich and rare amalgam of academic work, policy-oriented research and labour activism. Its research work kept consistently to high academic standards; some of its policy interventions were of profound significance; and around this core, there was deep commitment to activism in support of the rights and aspirations of working people. These were features which, in differentiated forms, characterise the various groups of applied heterodox economics being vigorously practised at the time in the DAE and in the Faculty. Jill Rubery highlights her pick of two important legacies of the research by the Cambridge Labour Studies Group.[83]

The first is the body of work analysing labour market segmentation. "In 1979, we set up the International Working Party on Labour Market Segmentation (IWPLMS))—this has since held 40 conferences," writes Jill who is still the core organiser. "We have an international network across Europe, the U.S., Australia ... and links to the ILO, ETUI etc. This international networking and comparative institutional research across Europe was extremely rare when we started." This also came to be the direct focus of her own research as she became Professor of Comparative Employment Systems in Manchester. Jill observes that this internationalism clearly belies the accusation of insularity, casually and frequently, levied by the orthodox group against DAE research and researchers.

"The second legacy relates to work on the national minimum wage and low wage labour markets. Our 1982 book (Craig et al., 1982), calling for a national minimum wage, was an early contributor to the debate and was part of the process of persuading trade unions in particular to support a national minimum wage." Both Frank and Jill, with her colleague Damian Grimshaw and other members of the International Working Party on Labour Market Segmentation (IWPLMS), continued to build on this work on this important theme.

It is possible to briefly elicit four facets of LSG research and researchers that adduce to the inherent interdisciplinarity of their oeuvre. First, the gendering of the research on work, employment, labour markets and labour rights. The gender dimension pervades much of the work of the group and is highlighted by the contributions of Jill Rubery in partnership with Jane Humphries (Humphries & Rubery, 1984),[84] Roger Tarling, Sara Horrell and Brendan Burchell; notably, this also involved a significant teaching course by Jill and Jane on women and the labour market. Second, the embedding of contemporary work within historical and comparative perspectives as evidenced in the book on *Women and Recession* (Rubery, 1988) which was followed up later by

---

Dame and Cambridge was wider: Ajit Singh was the William M. Scholl Visiting Professor of International Economics for four weeks annually during 1987–1995 (Saith, 2019: 365).

[83] Personal communication, email dated 29 November 2021.

[84] For a more detailed reference to this joint work, and to the wider range of research and publication encompassing the historical and comparative dimensions, also involving Sara Horrell and Roger Tarling, see Chap. 12 dealing with Economic History. See also Burchell et al. (1989, 1990).

Women and Austerity (Karamessini & Rubery, 2013). Third, the focus on research methods, as is displayed in the work of Brendan Burchell and Cathie Marsh, with their incisive investigations into survey methods[85]—with a resonance to the survey-based research in the early years of the DAE. And fourth, through Frank Wilkinson (1983, 2003), the ambitious search for an overarching analytical labourist "productive systems" framework that eschewed all reductionist ideological templates but was theoretically and methodologically flexible and reflexive enough to accommodate the challenges of interrogating the performance of different economic formations and contexts from the vantage point of labour and working people.[86]

Jill trains the LSG spotlight on the charged years of the DAE Review of the 1980s. Rather ruefully, she points out that "at that time we were probably the most successful group by far in raising new research income but at no point was our research given any consideration by the Review Committee—they were concerned with groups that were already closed down. During the 11 years I was in the DAE we secured two large grants from the Department of Employment—one to look at the abolition of wages councils that led to an influential book [cited earlier] calling for a national minimum wage, one on equal pay issues in small firms that continued the work on low wages and labour market segmentation; and that was followed by two major ESRC grants: one associated with Frank's work on 'productive systems' that was more a combined industrial and labour economics approach, and then the ESRC Social Change and Economic Life Initiative that was the main new project during the period of the Review to my knowledge. Other projects such as the CGP were winding down and moving off into private enterprise[87] but we were the group

---

[85] See, for instance, Burchell and Marsh (1992); Marsh (1982); Marsh and Elliot (2008); Marsh (1985) and Marsh et al. (1991).

[86] Any 'de-ideologised' analytical framework would still need to thread a fine line between Alfred Marshall (whose work on industrial districts influenced Frank) and Joan. In his appreciation of Alfred Marshall, Maynard Keynes (1924) quotes from his Inaugural Lecture: "That part of economic doctrine which alone can claim universality, the principles to wit, has no dogmas. It is not a body of concrete truth but an engine for the discovery of concrete truth." Diametrically on the other side of the line stands Joan, one of Frank's mentors: "There is no such thing as a 'purely economic' problem that can be settled by purely economic logic ... the participants in every controversy divide into schools—conservative or radical—and ideology is apt to seep into logic" (Robinson, 1977: 1318). Frank stood very much on Joan's side of the line; he wished more to 'de-theologise'. For a condensation of the key features of this approach, see the tribute to Frank Wilkinson (Rubery et al., 2022); see also Burchell et al. (2002), and Konzelmann and Wilkinson (2016).

[87] This assessment needs some clarification and qualification. It was true that the CEPG had been terminated following the cessation of SSRC funding and also that CGP was beginning to wind down leading up to its closure on account of the stoppage of ESRC funding, by the end of the Review process; but both had been highly productive projects till these arbitrary closures. Also, while the CGP was indeed raising funds from its commercial spin-off 'Cambridge Econometrics', this 'privatisation' was willy-nilly juxtaposed upon it by the suggestion, 'encouragement', and requirement by the Consortium, led by the Treasury—the entire process being handed by the ESRC. Richard Stone had vehemently opposed the idea of going commercial, citing the DAE-

that was keeping doing well until the Review which was instrumental in Roger [Tarling] leaving, and then myself ... Frank was the person most at risk as he refused to contemplate leaving, but fortunately Alan's ESRC Centre came in to the DAE and he was able to work under that umbrella till retirement. Somehow, the division between the main economics groups, sociology and economic history leaves those of us doing interdisciplinary work a bit invisible ... LSG was a group that was doing well but who were still dragged down by the Review ..." (Personal communication; email dated 29 November 2021). Roger Tarling left to start private consultancy work; in 1988, Brendan Burchell left for a lectureship in the Faculty of Human, Social and Political Science following Cathie Marsh's move to Manchester, later becoming a professor and head of the department; and Jill Rubery relocated to launch a remarkably productive career at the University of Manchester, duly becoming Professor of Comparative Employment Systems, and Director of the Work and Equalities Institute at Alliance Manchester Business School. While the sharp end of the critiques by the orthodox group during the DAE Review were directed mainly at the macroeconomic modelling teams, LSG was casually, indirectly or by default, included in the disparaging commentary, including that from some of the external experts selected by the committee instituted by the General Board. The attacks induced a strong defence and rebuttal from several DAE and Faculty staff, and tellingly also from Willy Brown, the Montague-Burton Professor of Industrial Relations (successor to Bert Turner) who had close research interactions with the Labour Studies Group and could appreciate the salience of its work in the contemporary policy context but also as a valuable interdisciplinary project in its own right. All this, though, to little avail, since the LSG was effectively disbanded at the end of the Review with just one member, Frank Wilkinson, remaining in the DAE, till on retirement he shifted base to Alan Hughes's ESRC-funded Centre for Business Studies. Orthodoxy prevailed and the LSG was dealt a dire blow: the team dispersed—but it was undefeated, as its members sustained their productive research collaborations and publications, interacting from their new scattered locations.[88]

REFERENCES

Barker, T. (1996). *Space-time economics*. Cambridge Econometrics.
Begg, I., & Henry, S. G. B. (Eds.). (1998). *Applied economics and public policy*. Cambridge University Press.
Burchell, B., & Marsh, C. (1992). The effect of questionnaire length on survey response. *Quality and Quantity, 26*, 233–244.

CGP research as a public good. For a detailed discussion, see Chap. 8 on the demise of the Cambridge Growth Project. With regard to the Sociology group, Wynne Godley's reports do provide some evidence of a net budgetary deficit.

[88] This is evidenced in the *References* by the spate of joint research publications, in various permutations and combinations, authored by Brendan Burchell, Simon Deakin, Jill Rubery, Roger Tarling, Frank Wilkinson, along with the economic historians Sara Horrell and Jane Humphries.

Burchell, B., Horrell, S., & Rubery, J. (1989). Unequal jobs or unequal pay? *Industrial Relations Journal, 20*(3), 176–191.

Burchell, B., Horrell, S., & Rubery, J. (1990). Gender and skills. *Work, Employment and Society, 4*(2) Reprinted in *Gender and Economics*, J. Humphries (ed.), Edward Elgar, 1994.

Burchell, B., Deakin, S., Michie, J., & Rubery, J. (Eds.). (2002). *Systems of production: Markets organisation and performance*. Routledge.

Cambridge University General Board. (2004, July 21). Report of the General Board on the Faculty of Economics and Politics and the Department of Applied Economics. *Cambridge Reporter*.

Craig, C., Rubery, J., Tarling, R., & Wilkinson, F. (1982). *Labour market structure, industrial organisation and low pay*. Cambridge University Press.

Craypo, C., & Wilkinson, F. (2011). The low road to competitive failure: Immigrant labour and emigrant jobs in the US. *The Handbook of Globalization* (2nd ed., pp. 356–380). Edward Elgar.

Cripps, F., & Lavoie, M. (2017). Wynne Godley (1926–2010). In R. A. Cord (Ed.), *The Palgrave companion to Cambridge economics* (pp. 929–953). Palgrave Macmillan.

Dasgupta, P. (2010). Interview with Partha Dasgupta 6th April 2010. In S. Harrison & A. Macfarlane, *Encounter with economics*. Interviews filmed by A. Macfarlane and edited by S. Harrison. University of Cambridge. http://sms.cam.ac.uk/collection/1092396

Dasgupta, P. (2013). Obituary: Frank Hahn. *Royal Economic Society Newsletter, 161*(April).

Deakin, S. F., & Ewing, K. D. (2021, April 13). *Frank Wilkinson 1934–2021*. Institute of Employment Rights. https://www.ier.org.uk/news/frank-wilkinson-1934-2021/

Department of Applied Economics (various years). *DAE Annual Reports, 1946–48 to 1986–87*. Cambridge: Department of Applied Economics, Marshall Library Archives, digitalized.

Edwards, K. J. R. (2009, February 5). *Ken Edwards, interviewed by Alan Macfarlane*. Film interview with leading thinkers, University of Cambridge. http://www.alan-macfarlane.com/DO/filmshow/edwardstx.htm

Fitzsimons, C. (1984, November 10). University to investigate department. *Cambridge Evening News*.

Godley, W. (2001). Saving Masud Khan. *London Review of Books, 23*(4), 3–7.

Harcourt, G. C. (1999b, November 18). Obituary: John Wells. *The Independent*. https://www.independent.co.uk/arts-entertainment/obituary-john-wells-1126818.html

Harvey, A. (2012). Hashem Pesaran. *Cambridge Economics: News from the Cambridge Faculty of Economics, 5*(Autumn).

Hobsbawm, E. (2002). *Interesting times: A twentieth-century life*. Knopf Doubleday Publishing Group.

Hobsbawm, E. (2012, September 21). Dorothy Wedderburn obituary. *The Guardian*.

Humphries, J., & Rubery, J. (1984). The reconstitution of the supply side of the labour market: The relative autonomy of social reproduction. *Cambridge Journal of Economics, 8*(4), 331–346.

Kahn, R. (1977). Malinvaud on Keynes. Reviewing: Edmond Malinvaud, *The theory of unemployment reconsidered*, Basil Blackwell, Oxford, 1977; Three lectures delivered for the Yrjo Jahnsson Foundation, Helsinki. *Cambridge Journal of Economics, 1*(4), 375–388.

Karamessini, M., & Rubery, J. (Eds.). (2013). *Women and austerity: The economic crisis and the future for gender equality*. Routledge.

Keynes, J. M. (1924). Alfred Marshall, 1842–1924. *The Economic Journal*, *34*(135), 311–372.

Kitson, M. (2005). Economics for the future. *Cambridge Journal of Economics*, *29*, 827–835.

Konzelmann, S., & Wilkinson, F. (2016). Cooperation in production, the organization of industry and productive systems: A critical survey of the 'district form of industrial organisation and development'. *CBR Working Paper No. 481*. Centre for Business Research.

Leijonhufvud, A. (1973). Life among the econ. *Economic Inquiry*, *11*(3), 327–337.

Marsh, C. (1982). *The survey method: The contribution of surveys to sociological explanation*. Allen & Unwin.

Marsh, C. (1985). Back on the bandwagon: The effect of opinion polls on public opinion. *British Journal of Political Science*, *15*(1), 51–74.

Marsh, C., & Elliot, J. (2008). *Exploring data: An introduction to data analysis for social scientists* (2nd ed.). Polity Press.

Marsh, C., et al. (1991). The case for samples of anonymized records from the 1991 Census. *Journal of the Royal Statistical Society: Series A (Statistics in Society)*, *4*(2), 305–340.

Matthews, R. C. O., & Supple, B. (n.d.). *The ordeal of economic freedom: Marshall on economic history*. Typescript in E.A.G. Robinson Papers, Marshall Library Archives, University of Cambridge, EAGR 6/4/16, 23p. Also published as Matthews, R. C. O., & Supple, B. (1991). The ordeal of economic freedom: Marshall on economic history. *Quaderni di Storia dell'Economia Politica*, *9*(2–3), 189–213.

Newbery, D. (1998). Foreword. In I. Begg & S. G. B. Henry (Eds.), *Applied economics and public policy* (pp. xix–xxii). Cambridge University Press.

Newbery, D. (2017). Frank Horace Hahn 1925–2013. *Biographical Memoirs of Fellows of the British Academy*, *XVI*, 485–525. https://www.britac.ac.uk/sites/default/files/23 Hahn 1837 9_11_17.pdf

Pesaran, M. H. (1987). *The limits to rational expectations*. Basil Blackwell.

Pyatt, G. (2005). *Sir Richard Stone: An appreciation*. https://www.copsmodels.com/webhelp/viewhar/index.html?hc_stone2.htm

Pyatt, G., & Ward, M. (1999). An appreciation of Eden's contribution to the study of poverty. In G. Pyatt & M. Ward (Eds.), *Identifying the poor: Papers on measuring poverty to celebrate the bicentenary of the publication in 1797 of 'The State of the Poor' by Sir Frederick Morton Eden* (pp. 17–34). IOS Press.

Robinson, J. (1977). What are the questions? *Journal of Economic Literature*, *15*(4), 1318–1339.

Rubery, J. (Ed.). (1988). *Women and recession*. Routledge and Kegan Paul.

Rubery, J., Burchell, B., Deakin, S., & Konzelmann, S. J. (2022). A tribute to Frank Wilkinson. *Cambridge Journal of Economics*, *46*(3), 429–445.

Saith, A. (2018). Ajit Singh (1940–2015), the radical Cambridge economist: Anti-imperialist advocate of third world industrialization. *Development and Change*, *49*(2), 561–628.

Saith, A. (2019). *Ajit Singh of Cambridge and Chandigarh: An intellectual biography of the radical Sikh economist*. Palgrave Macmillan.

Sen, A. (2021). *Home in the world: A memoir*. Allen Lane and Penguin Random House.
Singh, A. (1996a). The world economy under the market supremacy model and third world industrialisation. *Indian Economic Journal, 44*(1), 1–16.
Singh, A. (1999). Should Africa promote stock market capitalism? *Journal of International Development, 11*(3), 343–367.
Sraffa, P. (1926). The laws of returns under competitive conditions. *Economic Journal, 36*(144), 535–550.
Stone, J. R. N. (1997). Some British empiricists in the social sciences, 1650–1900. In A. M. Cardani & G. Stone (Eds.), *Raffaele Mattioli lectures 1986*. Cambridge University Press.
Supple, B. (2011). *An interview of the economic historian and former Master of St. Catharine's College, Cambridge, Professor Barry Supple, talking about his life and work*. Filmed by Alan Macfarlane on 3rd July 2010 and edited by Sarah Harrison. https://www.sms.cam.ac.uk/media/1130704
Wilkinson, F. (1983). Productive systems. *Cambridge Journal of Economics, 7*(3–4), 413–429.
Wilkinson, F. (2003). Productive systems and the structuring role of Economic and social theories. In B. Burchell, S. Deakin, J. Michie, & J. Rubery (Eds.), *Systems of production: Markets, organisations and performance* (pp. 10–39). Routledge.